DATAPEDIA
of the United States
1790-2000
America Year by Year

George Thomas Kurian

BERNAN PRESS
Lanham, MD

Published 1994
Printed in the United States of America

99 98 97 96 95 94   4 3 2 1

≋BERNAN PRESS™
Bernan Press
An Imprint of Bernan Associates
4611-F Assembly Drive
Lanham, MD 20706-4391
(301) 459-7666

ISBN: 0-89059-012-5

Table of Contents

Introduction

Datapedia of the United States presents the most significant historical statistics of the United States in 23 selected areas from 1776 to 1990. In some areas, such as demography, where projections are possible, the data are extended to 2010.

For the period up to 1970 *Datapedia of the United States* is based entirely on *Historical Statistics of the United States from Colonial Times*. For the two decades from 1970 to 1990 it is based on the annual *Statistical Abstract of the United States* as well as data scattered in numerous other publications. However, *Datapedia* is not merely a supplement to *Historical Statistics*. It selects the most important of the time series contained in *Historical Statistics* and present them in a reader-friendly format with Highlights for each section and over 30 charts. In doing so, it brings together in one source the best available data on the United States from 1770 to 1990. Except in cases where a reader is seeking highly specialized data, *Datapedia* will serve as a convenient and complete statistical profile of the United States covering all its vital sectors.

All chapter divisions in *Historical Statistics* have been maintained in *Datapedia* in the same sequence. The table numbers also have been kept in an effort to make cross references and comparisons easier. Generally, only national data are shown. Some exceptions are made where regional or state statistics are useful for the correct interpretation of data, or where national data in the subject field cannot be summarized effectively. Of course, in the early part of many series, the data are limited to the Atlantic seaboard.

Historical Statistics of the United States, on which *Datapedia* is based, has an interesting history. The first edition which covered the years from 1770 to 1945 was initiated by the Social Research Council following a proposal by the Bureau of Census to prepare a historical supplement to the *Statistical Abstract*. It was published in 1949. The second edition brought the coverage to 1957, again with the participation of the Social Research Council. Work on the third edition began in 1969 and was completed in 1976, bringing the coverage to 1970. This time the Bureau of Census undertook the project alone. It included

over 12,500 time series, a 50% increase over the last edition. There were also substantial changes in the scope and density of the data.

Statistics have become essential tools for historians, social scientists, political scientists, journalists, demographers and marketers. Historical statistics, now named cliometrics, serve an even more important function. Contrary to popular notion, statistical data never become outdated or useless. True, data are perishable, like fruits, and have an active shelf life of only a few months, but when preserved or pickled, help to illuminate historical trends and explain cyclical phenomena that otherwise remain obscure. Some of the most interesting data in *Historical Statistics* are derived from little-known 19th century documents and publications, but without them historians will be at a loss to understand why, for example, farm prices rose or fell, and why certain types of industrial changes took place the way they did. Historical statistical data also serve as touchstones on which political, economic, and social theories and assumptions can be tested.

The quality of the statistical tables spanning over two centuries is remarkably even. The collection of statistics was not considered as a primary function of the government in the early years of the republic and much of the data have been gathered from occasional and fugitive publications and documents. Much data also have been lost. But, because the catchment area was so small, the degree of accuracy was much higher. As the complexity of statistical operations grew, so did the techniques of collection and analysis. Finally, with the introduction of computers in the 20th century, number crunching became extremely sophisticated, providing us with raw and refined data of exceptionally high quality. Data collection also is beginning to be focused on a number of areas in which few statistics were collected before. Still, not all subjects are equally well-endowed with numbers. In some there is an embarrassment of riches, while in others one has to scrape the bottom of the barrel to obtain a few crumbs.

As in *Historical Statistics*, data are arranged for macro subjects in lettered chapters and micro subjects in numbered series within the chapter. Each series or column is assigned a unique letter and number. Most of the data are annual, but certain series are presented only for years in which a national census was held. In general, only absolute rather than derived data are included because one-dimensional aggregates at gross levels offer somewhat greater flexibility to the user. Criteria for inclusion vary, but in most cases are based on the quantity and quality of data available and the extent to which they enhance our understanding of historic trends.

Datapedia owes its genesis to the strong commitment of Bernan Press and its director, Don Hagen, to the publication of innovative statistical reference books. My thanks also are due to Celina Bednar and Carolyn Cocca for their dedicated and professional editorial work.

April 14, 1994   — George Thomas Kurian

SECTION **A**

POPULATION

POPULATION
Highlights

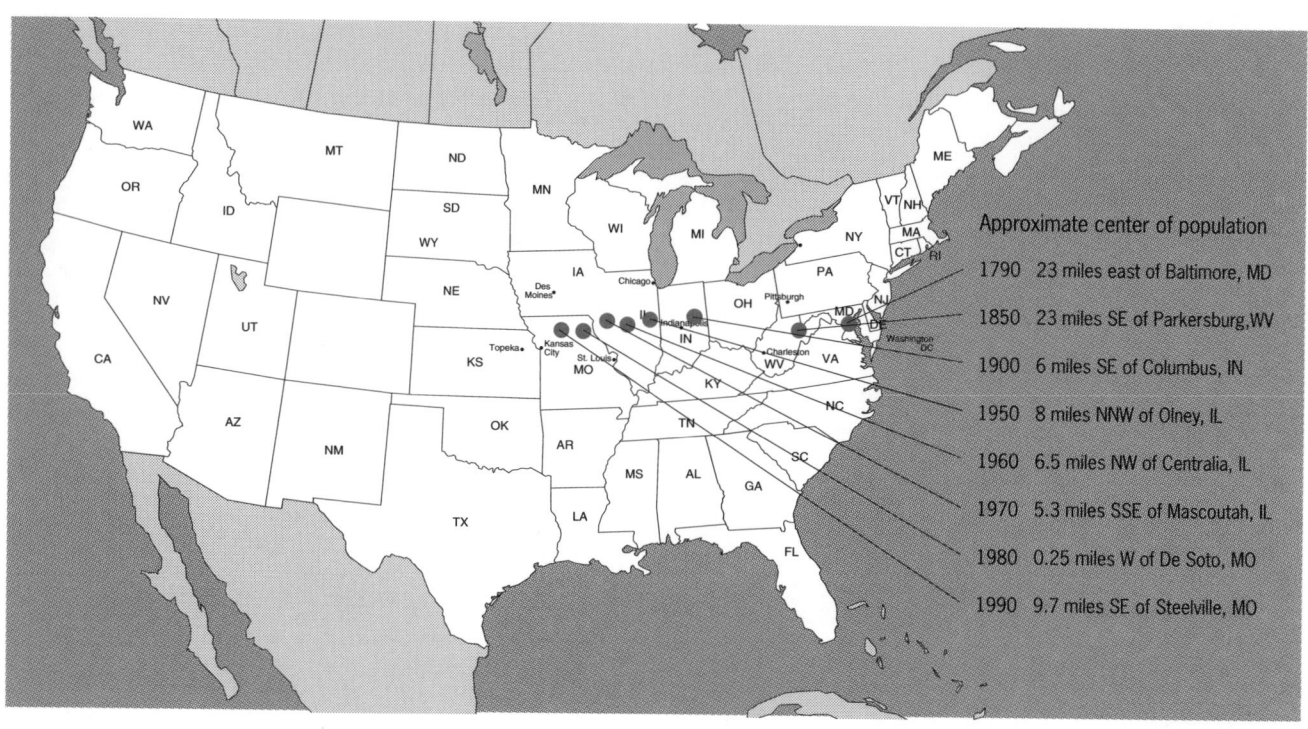

Approximate center of population

1790 23 miles east of Baltimore, MD

1850 23 miles SE of Parkersburg, WV

1900 6 miles SE of Columbus, IN

1950 8 miles NNW of Olney, IL

1960 6.5 miles NW of Centralia, IL

1970 5.3 miles SSE of Mascoutah, IL

1980 0.25 miles W of De Soto, MO

1990 9.7 miles SE of Steelville, MO

1 Between 1790 and 1990, the Center of Population moved from Maryland to Missouri.

Year	North Latitude	West Latitude	Approximate Location
1790	39 16 30	76 11 12	23 miles east of Baltimore, MD
1850	38 59 0	81 19 0	23 miles SE of Parkersburg, WV
1900	38 9 36	85 48 54	6 miles SE of Columbus, IN
1950	38 50 21	89 9 33	8 miles NNW of Olney, IL
1960	38 55 58	89 12 35	6.5 miles NW of Centralia, IL
1970	38 27 47	89 42 22	5.3 miles SSE of Mascoutah, IL
1980	38 8 13	90 34 26	0.25 miles W of De Soto, MO
1990	37 52 20	91 12 55	9.7 miles SE of Steelville, MO

2 Americans resident outside the United States numbered 6.269 million in 1990. The countries with the largest number of resident U.S. civilians were Mexico (495,000), Canada (278,000), the United Kingdom (213,000), France (126,000), Israel (124,000), Germany (107,000), the Philippines (109,000), Italy (102,000), the Dominican Republic (87,000), and Australia (65,000).

3 The population of the United States doubled five times between the first decennial census of 1790 and the 17th census in 1950. The first three doublings took 25 years each through 1865. The fourth required 35 years from 1865 to 1900. The fifth doubling took a half century, to 1950. A sixth doubling appears improbable.

4 Between 1790 and 1850, the annual increase of population exceeded 3%, with the highest being 3.6% during 1800-1810. In the remaining four decades of the 19th century and the first decade of this century, the rate of growth ranged from 2.7% to 2.1%. The growth rate slumped to 1.5% between 1910 and 1920, rose to 1.6% in the following decade, and then plummeted to 0.7% during the Depression in the 1930s. It rebounded to 1.9% during the 1950s (known as the Baby Boom), and was followed by a rate of 1.3% in the 1970s (the Baby Bust). After the 1970s, the growth rate declined to an average of 1%.

5 The Census of the United States was authorized by Act of Congress, March 1, 1790, providing for "the enumeration of the inhabitants of the United States." The first census cost $44,377 and utilized the services of 17 marshals and 650 assistants. It counted a population of 3,939,326 in 16 states and the Ohio Territory. Virginia was the most populous state with 747,610 inhabitants and Rhode Island the least with 68,825 inhabitants. New York City had a population of 33,131, Philadelphia 28,522, and Boston 18,320.

6 Until 1830 the deaf, mute, and blind were excluded from the census.

7 The fifth census (1830) was the first in which the population of the United States exceeded 10 million; the first census in which the count exceeded 100 million was that of 1920; the first in which the count exceeded 200 million was that of 1970.

8 The 1890 census was the first to utilize enumerating machines.

9 The first states to exceed 1 million in population were New York, Virginia, and Pennsylvania in 1820. The first state to exceed 5 million in population was New York in 1880.

10 New York City was the first city to exceed 1 million in population (excluding Brooklyn, which was then an independent city) in 1880.

11 Census counts are subject to a margin of error, estimated between 1.4% and 3.3%. Based on post-enumeration surveys, the figures were subject to an error of 2.5% in 1990 and 3.3% in 1950.

12 Data on urban population were first published in 1870. Urban centers were defined as having a population of 8,000 or more. In 1880, 1890, and 1900, that figure was reduced to 4,000. In 1900, a population of 2,500 or more was designated as constituting an urban area. This definition, with minor modifications, was accepted in later censuses up to and including 1940. In 1950, the Bureau of the Census adopted the concept of the urbanized area and delineated boundaries for unincorporated places. The urban population was defined as all persons living in urbanized areas and, outside these areas, in all places, incorporated or unincorporated, which had 2,500 inhabitants or more. This definition has remained substantially unchanged in the following censuses. Minor modifications of this definition are employed in some states, such as Alaska, New York, the New England states, and Wisconsin.

13 Rural population is subdivided into two categories: rural farm and rural nonfarm. The definition of farm population is based on the size of the farm and the cash value of farm produce.

14 The first attempt to define metropolitan population was made in the 1910 census. Metropolitan districts were defined for cities of 200,000 or more. Each metropolitan district included contiguous minor civil divisions which met certain rules of proximity and population density. In 1950, metropolitan districts were replaced by Standard Metropolitan Areas (SMAs), Consolidated Metropolitan Statistical Areas (CMSAs), and Primary Metropolitan Statistical Areas (PMSAs). These are defined in terms of entire counties, except in New England where the definitions are in terms of cities or towns. In general, an urbanized area is defined as a city (or twin cities) of 50,000 or more and the surrounding closely settled areas. From time to time new metropolitan areas are created and boundaries of others change. As a result, data over time may not be comparable.

15 The classification by race in censuses reflects common usage rather than strict biological stock. The data are obtained primarily through self-classification. The standard racial categories are White, Black, American Indian, Asian and Pacific Islander, and Hispanic (although Hispanics may be Black or White). The 1990 census included an "Other Race" category with provisions for a write-in entry. The census of 1860 was the first in which American Indians were distinguished from other ethnic groups; however, it excluded those American Indians living on Indian reservations.

16 Area measurements of the United States are undoubtedly the most precise of all data in this book. They have been refined over the years with the use of greatly improved measurement techniques (such as better geodetic instruments and other more advanced technology). The first measurement was made for the 1880 census by Henry Gannett, the second for the 1940 census by Batschelet and Proudfoot, and the third for the 1960 census by a team of specialists. Water is classified as either inland water or water other than inland water. The former consists of ponds and lakes, 40 acres or more, and streams and canals 1/8th of a mile or more in width. Water other than inland water consists of bays, Great Lakes, coastal waters, etc.

17 The highest decennial jump in population was the 36.4% reported in the third census (1810), followed by 35.9% in 1850, 35.6% in 1860 and 35.1% in 1800. The lowest was 7.2% reported in 1940, followed by 9.8% in 1990, and 11.4% in 1980.

18 The United States had a surplus of males over females until the end of World War II in 1945. Since then, the sex ratio has been in favor of females. However, more male than female children are born so that the sex ratio is 104.9 in favor of males in the under-14 category and 104.7 in favor of males in the 14-24 category.

19 Urbanized areas accounted for 75.2% of the population and 74.5% of housing units but only 2.5% of the land area in 1990. The West was the most urbanized with 86.3% of the total state population, followed by the Northeast

(78.9%), the Midwest (71.7%), and the South (68.6%). The most urbanized state was California with 92.6% followed by New Jersey (89.4%), Hawaii (89%), Nevada (88.3%), Arizona (87.5%), Utah (87.0%), Rhode Island (86%), Florida (84.8%), Illinois (84.6%), Massachusetts (84.3%), New York (84.3%), Colorado (82.4%), Maryland (81.3%), and Texas (80.3%). The least urbanized state was Vermont with 32.2%, followed by West Virginia (36.1%) and Mississippi (47.1%).

20 In 1790, the percentage of urban population was 5.4%.

21 In 1990, 53% of the U.S. population lived within 50 miles of a coast, compared to 52% in 1960; 23% lived on the Atlantic coast, 13% on the Pacific coast, 12% near the Great Lakes, and 6% on the Gulf of Mexico.

22 The percentage of foreign-born population has been declining steadily. It was 6.2% in 1980, compared to 13.2% in 1920, and 49.3% in 1890. In 1990, the largest group of the foreign-born was Asian (25%), followed by European (22.2%).

23 The median age of the population in 1991 was 33.1 compared to 16.7 in 1820. The median age passed the 20 year-mark in 1870, and the 30 year-mark in 1950.

24 There were 18,088 cities of all sizes in the United States in 1990 compared to 1,348 in 1890, 1,737 in 1900, 2,262 in 1910, 2,722 in 1920, 3,165 in 1930, 3,464 in 1940, 4,741 in 1950, 6,041 in 1960, and 7,062 in 1970. Of the 18,088 cities in 1990, eight had populations of over 1 million, 15 between 500,000 and 999,999, 40 between 250,000 and 499,999, 131 between 100,000 and 249,999, 309 between 50,000 and 99,999, 567 between 25,000 and 49,999, 978 between 10,000 and 24,999, and 16,434 below 10,000. Cities with the highest population growth were those with populations between 25,000 and 499,999.

25 Blacks comprised 12.3% of the population in 1990 compared to 13.1% in 1880. Whites made up 83.9% in 1990 compared to 84.3% in 1880. In 1990, 52.8% of Blacks lived in the South, 19.1% in the Midwest, 18.7% in the Northeast, and 9.4% in the West.

26 The average size of the American family declined from 5.79 in 1790 to 3.18 in 1990. Hispanic families numbered 3.82 members, Black families 3.51, and White families 3.12. The average first fell below 4 in 1940, and is expected to fall below 3 by the first decade of the 21st century.

27 Annually, 17% of the U.S. population change residence. Of these, 11% move to the same county, 3% to the same state, and 3% to a different state.

28 Immigrants tend to settle on the coasts. Asians from the Far East and Hispanics from Mexico are concentrated on the West Coast, while Asians from the Indian subcontinent and Puerto Ricans prefer the East Coast. American Indians are most numerous on the West Coast and, to a lesser extent, in the South.

29 Three states had negative growth rates in the 1990 census: Iowa, Wyoming, and West Virginia. Twenty states had double-digit growth rates compared to 30 in 1970-80. Of these, only two were in the Northeast—New Hampshire and Vermont—and none in the Midwest. The fastest growing state remained Nevada with a growth rate of 50.1%, down from 63.8% in 1970-80. The second was Alaska (36.9%) and the third, Arizona (34.8%).

30 In 1990, there were 3.16 million Americans over 85 years of age. Of these, 2.22 million were women. Of the 29.6 million people 65 years and over, 11.4 % were living below the poverty level, 31% were living alone, and 11.5% were employed.

31 The largest group of people of Caucasian ancestry in 1990 was German (23.3%), followed by Irish (16.6%), and English (13.1%).

32 Cities with the largest population gains in 1990 were either in the West or South. The city with the largest gain was Plano, TX, with a 77.9% increase while that with the largest loss was Newark, NJ, with a 16.4% decrease.

33 The population of the United States is expected to reach 276,241,000 in 2000 and 300,431,000 in 2010, with a growth rate of 0.5% until 2000 and 0.7% from 2000-2010.

34 Future Data: Population (2010)

Age 18-24	27,155,000	Males	138,333,000
25-34	37,572,000	Females	144,241,000
35-44	37,202,000	Whites	278,978,000
45-54	43,207,000	Blacks	38,833,000
55-6	35,430,000	Other Races	14,764,000
65-74	21,039,000		
75—	18,323,000		

Median Age (2000): 36

Fertility Rate (2000):

Total: 1,846	White: 1,780
Black: 2,095	Other: 2,110

Distribution of Births (2000):

Age	All Races	White	Black	Other
Under 20	13.0	11.4	20.8	9.8
Age 35—	9.8	9.7	8.9	13.6

Composition of Family (2000):
Married Couples: 53%
Nonfamily: 32%
Single Parent: 15%

Dependency Ratio (2000):
Elderly Dependency
Ratio: 20
Youth Dependency
Ratio: 31

Series A 1-5.   Area and Population of the United States: 1790 to 1990

Year	Land area[1] (square miles)	Number	Population — Increase from preceding census — Number	Percent[2]	Per square mile of land area	Year	Land area[1] (square miles)	Number	Population — Increase from preceding census — Number	Percent[2]	Per square mile of land area
	1	2	3	4	5		1	2	3	4	5
1990 (Apr. 1)	3,787,425	248,709,873	22,164,068	9.8	70.3	1880 (June 1)	2,969,640	50,155,783	10,337,334	26.0	16.9
1980 (Apr. 1)	3,618,770	226,545,805	23,243,774	11.4	64.0	1870 (June 1)	2,969,640	[5] 39,818,449	8,375,128	26.6	13.4
						1860 (June 1)	2,969.640	31,443,321	8,251,445	35.6	10.6
1970 (Apr. 1)[3]	3,536,855	203,235,298	23,912,123	13.3	57.5	1850 (June 1)	2,940.042	23,191,876	6,122,423	35.9	7.9
1960 (Apr. 1) *	3,540,911	179,323,175	28,625,814	19.0	50.6	1840 (June 1)	1,749,462	17,069,453	4,203,433	32.7	9.8
1960 (Apr. 1)[4]	2,968,054	178,464,236	27,766,875	18.4	60.1						
1950 (Apr. 1)	2,974,726	150,697,361	19,028,086	14.5	50.7	1830 (June 1)	1,749,462	12,866,020	3,227,567	33.5	7.4
1940 (Apr. 1)	2,977,128	131,669,275	8,894,229	7.2	44.2	1820 (Aug. 17)	1,749,462	9,638,453	2,398,572	33.1	5.5
						1810 (Aug. 6)	1,681,828	7,239,881	1,931,398	36.4	4.3
1930 (Apr. 1)	2,977,128	122,775,046	17,064,426	16.1	41.2	1800 (Aug. 4)	864,746	5,308,483	1,379,269	35.1	6.1
1920 (Jan. 1)	2,969,451	105,710,620	13,738,354	14.9	35.6	1790 (Aug. 2)	864,746	3,929,214	(X)	(X)	4.5
1910 (Apr. 15)	2,969,565	91,972,266	15,977,691	21.0	31.0						
1900 (June 1)	2,969,834	75,994,575	13,046,861	20.7	25.6						
1890 (June 1)	2,969,640	62,947,714	12,791,931	25.5	21.2						

* Denotes first year for which figures include Alaska and Hawaii.
X Not applicable.
[1] Gross area (including inland water) in square miles: 1790-1800=888,811; 1810=1,716,003; 1820-1840=1,788,006; 1850=2,992,747; 1860-1950=3,033,387; 1960 conterminous=3,022,261; 1960 including Alaska and Hawaii=3,615,123; 1970=3,615,122.

[2] Based on interval since preceding census which is not always exactly 10 years.
[3] Official resident population. 1970 census tables show a population of 203,211,926. The net difference of 23,372 reflects errors found after the tabulations were completed.
[4] Conterminous United States (excludes Alaska and Hawaii).
[5] Revised to include adjustment of 1,260,078 for under enumeration in the southern states. Unrevised census count is 38,558,371.

Series A 6-8.   Annual Population Estimates for the United States: 1790 to 1991

(In thousands, As of July 1. 1960–1970)

Year	Total including Armed Forces overseas (6)	Total resident population (7)	Civilian resident population (8)
1991	253,688	252,177	250,566
1990	249,924	249,415	247,775
1989	247,343	246,820	245,132
1988	245,057	244,534	242,852
1987	242,836	242,321	240,582
1986	240,680	240,162	238,441
1985	238,492	237,950	236,245
1984	236,370	235,847	234,131
1983	234,321	233,806	232,111
1982	232,191	231,669	229,999
1981	229,958	229,457	227,809
1980	227,722	227,220	225,616
1979	225,055	224,567	222,969
1978	222,585	222,095	220,467
1977	220,239	219,760	218,106
1976	218,035	217,563	215,894
1975	215,973	215,465	213,789
1974	213,854	213,342	211,636
1973	211,909	211,357	209,600
1972	209,896	209,284	207,511
1971	207,661	206,827	204,866
1970	204,879	203,810	201,722
1969	202,677	201,385	199,145
1968	200,706	199,399	197,113
1967	198,712	197,457	195,264
1966	196,560	195,576	193,420
1965	194,303	193,526	191,605
1964	191,889	191,141	189,141
1963	189,242	188,483	186,493
1962	186,538	185,771	183,677
1961	183,691	182,992	181,143
1960	180,671	179,979	178,140
1959 *	177,830	177,135	175,277
1959	177,073	176,289	174,521
1958	174,141	173,320	171,485
1957	171,274	170,371	168,400
1956	168,221	167,306	165,373
1955	165,275	164,308	162,311
1954	162,391	161,164	159,059
1953	159,565	158,242	155,975
1952	156,954	155,687	153,292
1951	154,287	153,310	151,009
1950	151,684	151,235	150,203
1949	149,188	148,665	147,578
1948	146,631	146,093	145,168
1947	144,126	143,446	142,566
1946	141,389	140,054	138,385
1945	139,928	132,481	127,573
1944	138,397	132,885	126,708
1943	136,739	134,245	127,499
1942	134,860	133,920	130,942
1941	133,402	133,121	131,595
1940	132,122	131,954	131,658

Year	Total resident population (7)
1939	130,880
1938	129,825
1937	128,825
1936	128,053
1935	127,250
1934	126,374
1933	125,579
1932	124,840
1931	124,040
1930	123,077
1929	121,767
1928	120,509
1927	119,035
1926	117,397
1925	115,829
1924	114,109
1923	111,947
1922	110,049
1921	108,538
1920	106,461
1919	[1]104,514
1918	[1]103,208
1917	[1]103,268
1916	101,961
1915	100,546
1914	99,111
1913	97,225
1912	95,335
1911	93,863
1910	92,407
1909	90,490
1908	88,710
1907	87,008
1906	85,450
1905	83,822
1904	82,166
1903	80,632
1902	79,163
1901	77,584
1900	76,094
1899	74,799
1898	73,493
1897	72,189
1896	70,885
1895	69,580
1894	68,275
1893	66,970
1892	65,666
1891	64,361
1890	63,056

Year	Total resident population (7)
1889	61,775
1888	60,496
1887	59,217
1886	57,938
1885	56,658
1884	55,379
1883	54,100
1882	52,821
1881	51,542
1880	50,262
1879	49,208
1878	48,174
1877	47,141
1876	46,107
1875	45,073
1874	44,040
1873	43,006
1872	41,972
1871	40,938
1870	39,905
1869	39,051
1868	38,213
1867	37,376
1866	36,538
1865	35,701
1864	34,863
1863	34,026
1862	33,188
1861	32,351
1860	31,513
1859	30,687
1858	29,862
1857	29,037
1856	28,212
1855	27,386
1854	26,561
1853	25,736
1852	24,911
1851	24,086
1850	23,261
1849	22,631
1848	22,018
1847	21,406
1846	20,794
1845	20,182
1844	19,569
1843	18,957
1842	18,345
1841	17,733
1840	17,120

Year	Total resident population (7)
1839	16,684
1838	16,264
1837	15,843
1836	15,423
1835	15,003
1834	14,582
1833	14,162
1832	13,742
1831	13,321
1830	12,901
1829	12,565
1828	12,237
1827	11,909
1826	11,580
1825	11,252
1824	10,924
1823	10,596
1822	10,268
1821	9,939
1820	9,618
1819	9,379
1818	9,139
1817	8,899
1816	8,659
1815	8,419
1814	8,179
1813	7,939
1812	7,700
1811	7,460
1810	7,224
1809	7,031
1808	6,838
1807	6,644
1806	6,451
1805	6,258
1804	6,065
1803	5,872
1802	5,679
1801	5,486
1800	5,297
1799	5,159
1798	5,021
1797	4,883
1796	4,745
1795	4,607
1794	4,469
1793	4,332
1792	4,194
1791	4,056
1790	3,929

* Denotes first year for which figures include Alaska and Hawaii.

[1] Total population, including Armed Forces overseas (in thousands): 1917=103,414; 1918=104,550; 1919=105,063; civilian population (in thousands): 1917=102,796; 1918=101,488; 1919=104,158.

Series A 23-25.   Annual Estimates of the Population by Sex: 1900 to 1991

(In thousands. As of July 1. 1900–1939, resident population: 1940–1991, total population,
including Armed Forces overseas. 1960–1991, preliminary)

Year	Total	Sex Male	Sex Female	Year	Total	Sex Male	Sex Female
	23	24	25		23	24	25
1991	252,688	123,431	129,257	1946	141,389	70,631	70,757
1990	249,924	122,049	127,875	1945	139,928	70,035	69,893
1989	248,240	120,982	127,258	1944	138,397	69,378	69,020
1988	257,807	119,738	126,069	1943	136,739	68,546	68,194
1987	243,419	118,539	124,880	1942	134,860	67,597	67,263
1986	241,078	117,360	123,718	1941	133,402	66,920	66,482
1985	238,740	116,161	122,579	1940	132,122	66,352	65,770
1984	236,158	114,765	121,393	1939	130,880	65,713	65,166
1983	234,023	113,721	120,302	1938	129,825	65,235	64,590
1982	231,821	112,644	119,177	1937	128,825	64,790	64,035
1981	229,307	111,423	117,884	1936	128,053	64,460	63,594
1980	227,061	110,528	116,533	1935	127,250	64,110	63,140
1979	220,099	107,006	113,093	1934	126,374	63,726	62,648
1978	218,228	106,120	112,108	1933	125,579	63,384	62,195
1977	216,432	105,240	111,092	1932	124,840	63,070	61,770
1976	214,669	104,477	110,192	1931	124,040	62,726	61,314
1975	213,051	103,723	109,328	1930	123,077	62,297	60,780
1974	211,391	102,945	108,446	1929	121,767	61,680	60,087
1973	209,851	102,229	107,622	1928	120,509	61,101	59,408
1972	208,232	101,450	106,782	1927	119,035	60,397	58,638
1971	206,230	100,439	105,791	1926	117,397	59,588	57,809
1970	204,879	100,266	104,613	1925	115,829	58,813	57,016
1969	202,677	99,287	103,390	1924	114,109	57,985	56,124
1968	200,706	98,426	102,280	1923	111,947	56,861	55,086
1967	198,712	97,564	101,148	1922	110,049	55,886	54,163
1966	196,560	96,620	99,941	1921	108,538	55,292	53,246
1965	194,303	95,609	98,694	1920	106,461	54,291	52,170
1964	191,889	94,518	97,371	1919	[1] 104,514	[2] 53,103	51,411
1963	189,242	93,303	95,939	1918	[1] 103,208	[2] 51,974	51,234
1962	186,538	92,066	94,472	1917	[1] 103,268	[2] 52,788	50,480
1961	183,691	90,740	92,952	1916	101,961	52,234	49,727
1960	180,671	89,320	91,352	1915	100,546	51,573	48,973
1959 *	177,830	87,995	89,834				
				1914	99,111	50,883	48,228
1959	177,073	87,621	89,453	1913	97,225	49,957	47,268
1958	174,141	86,236	87,905	1912	95,335	49,025	46,310
1957	171,274	84,892	86,382	1911	93,863	48,290	45,573
1956	168,221	83,434	84,786	1910	92,407	47,554	44,853
1955	165,275	82,030	83,246				
				1909	90,490	46,545	43,945
1954	162,391	80,647	81,744	1908	88,710	45,594	43,116
1953	159,565	79,295	80,270	1907	87,008	44,682	42,326
1952	156,954	78,061	78,893	1906	85,450	43,841	41,609
1951	154,287	76,792	77,496	1905	83,822	42,965	40,857
1950	151,684	75,539	76,146				
				1904	82,166	42,089	40,077
1949	149,188	74,335	74,853	1903	80,632	41,262	39,370
1948	146,631	73,130	73,502	1902	79,163	40,483	38,680
1947	144,126	71,946	72,180	1901	77,584	39,649	37,935
				1900	76,094	38,867	37,227

*Denotes first year for which figures include Alaska and Hawaii..
[1] Estimates including Armed Forces overseas, in thousands: 1917=103,414; 1918=104,550; 1919=105,063

[2] Estimates including Armed Forces overseas, in thousands: 1917=52,934; 1918=53,316; 1919=53,658.

Series A 29-37. Annual Estimates of the Population, by Age: 1900 to 1990

(As of July 1. 1900-1939, resident population; 1940-1970, total population, including Armed Forces overseas.)

Year	Total	Under 5	5-14	15-24	25-34	35-44	45-54	55-64	65 and over
	29	30	31	32	33	34	35	36	37
1990	248,710,000	18,354,000	35,213,000	37,774,000	43,176,000	37,579,000	25,224,000	21,148,000	31,242,000
1980	226,109,000	16,348,000	34,942,000	42,487,000	37,082,000	25,634,000	22,799,000	21,148,000	25,669,000
1970	204,879,000	17,156,000	40,733,000	36,496,000	25,293,000	23,142,000	23,310,000	18,664,000	20,085,000
1969	202,677,000	17,376,000	40,884,000	35,236,000	24,681,000	23,383,000	23,047,000	18,390,000	19,680,000
1968	200,706,000	17,913,000	40,772,000	34,090,000	23,990,000	23,731,000	22,758,000	18,088,000	19,365,000
1967	198,712,000	18,563,000	40,496,000	33,196,000	23,156,000	24,038,000	22,440,000	17,752,000	19,071,000
1966	196,560,000	19,208,000	40,051,000	32,012,000	22,725,000	24,276,000	22,125,000	17,408,000	18,755,000
1965	194,303,000	19,824,000	39,426,000	30,773,000	22,465,000	24,447,000	21,839,000	17,077,000	18,541,000
1964	191,889,000	20,165,000	38,783,000	29,519,000	22,396,000	24,562,000	21,580,000	16,758,000	18,127,000
1963	189,242,000	20,342,000	38,124,000	28,223,000	22,410,000	24,584,000	21,346,000	16,436,000	17,778,000
1962	186,538,000	20,469,000	37,435,000	26,909,000	22,494,000	24,519,000	21,124,000	16,131,000	17,457,000
1961	183,691,000	20,522,000	37,031,000	25,242,000	22,692,000	24,392,000	20,875,000	15,847,000	17,089,000
1960	180,671,000	20,341,000	35.735,000	24,576,000	22,919,000	24,221,000	20,578,000	15,625,000	16,675,000
1959*	177,830,000	20,175,000	34,564,000	23,988,000	23,169,000	24,023,000	20,262,000	15,401,000	16,248,000
1959	177,073,000	20,055,000	34,390,000	23,890,000	23,062,000	23,917,000	20,189,000	15,357,000	16,213,000
1958	174,141,000	19,768,000	33,322,000	23,162,000	23,430,000	23,693,000	19,857,000	15,139,000	15,771,000
1957	171,274,000	19,379,000	32,515,000	22,311,000	23,737,000	23,496,000	19,513,000	14,973,000	15,353,000
1956	168,221,000	18,895,000	31,423,000	21,869,000	24,015,000	23,160,000	19,143,000	14,815,000	14,902,000
1955	165,275,000	18,467,000	30,248,000	21,667,000	24,175,000	22,818,000	18,824,000	14,586,000	14,489,000
1954	162,391,000	17,962,000	29,092,000	21,641,000	24,233,000	22,571,000	18,501,000	14,350,000	14,040,000
1953	159,565,000	17,548,000	27,880,000	21,658,000	24,233,000	22,359,000	18,171,000	14,135,000	13,582,000
1952	156,954,000	17,228,000	26,656,000	21,796,000	24,197,000	22,109,000	17,881,000	13,918,000	13,169,000
1951	154,287,000	17,252,000	25,055,000	22,018,000	24,085,000	21,833,000	17,623,000	13,654,000	12,768,000
1950	151,684,000	16,331,000	24,477,000	22,260,000	23,932,000	21,557,000	17,400,000	13,364,000	12,362,000
1949	149,188,000	15,607,000	23,770,000	22,570,000	23,729,000	21,187,000	17,260,000	13,145,000	11,921,000
1948	146,631,000	14,919,000	23,089,000	22,866,000	23,494,000	20,794,000	17,107,000	12,824,000	11,538,000
1947	144,126,000	14,406,000	22,257,000	23,122,000	23,236,000	20,421,000	16,970,000	12,528,000	11,185,000
1946	141,389,000	13,244,000	21,844,000	23,382,000	22,954,000	20,073,000	16,820,000	12,244,000	10,828,000
1945	139,928,000	12,979,000	21,599,000	23,705,000	22,734,000	19,787,000	16,642,000	11,988,000	10,494,000
1944	138,397,000	12,524,000	21,573,000	23,999,000	22,511,000	19,505,000	16,419,000	11,719,000	10,147,000
1943	136,739,000	12,016,000	21,699,000	24,065,000	22,194,000	19,226,000	16,199,000	11,472,000	9,867,000
1942	134,860,000	11,301,000	21,823,000	24,093,000	21,911,000	18,950,000	15,976,000	11,220,000	9,584,000
1941	133,402,000	10,850,000	22,089,000	24,074,000	21,691,000	18,692,000	15,759,000	10,959,000	9,288,000
1940	132,122,000	10,579,000	22,363,000	24,033,000	21,446,000	18,422,000	15,555,000	10,694,000	9,031,000
1939	130,880,000	10,148,000	22,701,000	23,819,000	21,176,000	18,178,000	15,336,000	10,487,000	8,764,000
1938	129,825,000	10,176,000	23,146,000	23,655,000	20,953,000	18,001,000	15,077,000	10,310,000	8,508,000
1937	128,825,000	10,009,000	23,564,000	23,487,000	20,723,000	17,866,000	14,785,000	10,132,000	8,258,000
1936	128,053,000	10,044,000	23,942,000	23,309,000	20,505,000	17,783,000	14,495,000	9,949,000	8,027,000
1935	127,250,000	10,170,000	24,213,000	23,130,000	20,275,000	17,712,000	14,208,000	9,739,000	7,804,000
1934	126,374,000	10,331,000	24,402,000	22,963,000	20,022,000	17,640,000	13,933,000	9,502,000	7,582,000
1933	125,579,000	10,612,000	24,531,000	22,820,000	19,750,000	17,569,000	13,684,000	9,249,000	7,363,000
1932	124,840,000	10,903,000	24,614,000	22,716,000	19,484,000	17,504,000	13,481,000	8,992,000	7,147,000
1931	124,040,000	11,179,000	24,629,000	22,617,000	19,242,000	17,412,000	13,296,000	8,735,000	6,928,000
1930	123,077,000	11,372,000	24,631,000	22,487,000	19,039,000	17,270,000	13,096,000	8,477,000	6,705,000
1929	121,767,000	11,734,000	24,470,000	22,151,000	18,941,000	16,921,000	12,761,000	8,315,000	6,474,000
1928	120,509,000	11,978,000	24,320,000	21,811,000	18,953,000	16,540,000	12,430,000	8,178,000	6,299,000
1927	119,035,000	12,111,000	24,152,000	21,430,000	18,948,000	16,172,000	12,092,000	8,003,000	6,127,000
1926	117,397,000	12,189,000	23,906,000	21,037,000	18,867,000	15,847,000	11,786,000	7,805,000	5,960,000
1925	115,829,000	12,316,000	23,614,000	20,691,000	18,720,000	15,576,000	11,521,000	7,605,000	5,786,000
1924	114,109,000	12,269,000	23,358,000	20,314,000	18,557,000	15,337,000	11,278,000	7,387,000	5,609,000
1923	111,947,000	12,119,000	23,089,000	19,798,000	18,231,000	15,066,000	11,068,000	7,165,000	5,411,000
1922	110,049,000	12,031,000	22,788,000	19,402,000	17,924,000	14,823,000	10,899,000	6,951,000	5,231,000
1921	108,538,000	11,879,000	22,515,000	19,140,000	17,747,000	14,665,000	10,721,000	6,791,000	5,080,000
1920	106,461,000	11,631,000	22,158,000	18,821,000	17,416,000	14,382,000	10,505,000	6,619,000	4,929,000

See footnotes at end of table.

Series A 29-37. Annual Estimates of the Population, by Age: 1900 to 1990—Cont'd.

(As of July 1. 1900-1939, resident population; 1940-1970, total population, including Armed Forces overseas.)

				Age group (in years)					
Year	Total	Under 5	5-14	15-24	25-34	35-44	45-54	55-64	65 and over
	29	**30**	**31**	**32**	**33**	**34**	**35**	**36**	**37**
1919	104,514,000	11,536,000	21,849,000	18,465,000	16,912,000	14,008,000	10,402,000	6,456,000	4,886,000
1918	103,208,000	11,606,000	21,732,000	18,071,000	16,445,000	13,879,000	10,293,000	6,356,000	4,826,000
1917	103,268,000	11,527,000	21,369,000	18,836,000	16,913,000	13,647,000	10,068,000	6,194,000	4,714,000
1916	101,961,000	11,442,000	21,008,000	18,872,000	16,776,000	13,388,000	9,846,000	6,026,000	4,603,000
1915	100,546,000	11,347,000	20,660,000	18,844,000	16,580,000	13,130,000	9,613,000	5,866,000	4,501,000
1914	99,111,000	11,244,000	20,816,000	18,796,000	16,370,000	12,875,000	9,398,000	5,711,000	4,401,000
1913	97,225,000	11,082,000	19,904,000	18,649,000	16,070,000	12,562,000	9,135,000	5,542,000	4,281,000
1912	95,335,000	10,915,000	19,503,000	18,477,000	15,772,000	12,252,000	8,875,000	5,372,000	4,169,000
1911	93,863,000	10,796,000	19,214,000	18,355,000	15,530,000	12,003,000	8,657,000	5,234,000	4,074,000
1910	92,407,000	10,671,000	18,950,000	18,212,000	15,274,000	11,759,000	8,454,000	5,101,000	3,986,000
1909	90,490,000	10,509,000	18,670,000	17,871,000	14,923,000	11,471,000	8,204,000	4,964,000	3,878,000
1908	88,710,000	10,364,000	18,440,000	17,526,000	14,585,000	11,202,000	7,974,000	4,840,000	3,779,000
1907	87,008,000	10,220,000	18,240,000	17,184,000	14,257,000	10,945,000	7,755,000	4,724,000	3,684,000
1906	85,450,000	10,092,000	18,067,000	16,864,000	13,952,000	10,705,000	7,554,000	4,621,000	3,595,000
1905	83,822,000	9,944,000	17,888,000	16,526,000	13,631,000	10,461,000	7,350,000	4,517,000	3,505,000
1904	82,166,000	9,791,000	17,697,000	16,178,000	13,315,000	10,211,000	7,150,000	4,410,000	3,414,000
1903	80,632,000	9,645,000	17,524,000	15,858,000	13,019,000	9,974,000	6,964,000	4,313,000	3,335,000
1902	79,163,000	9,502,000	17,360,000	15,555,000	12,737,000	9,745,000	6,788,000	4,220,000	3,256,000
1901	77,584,000	9,336,000	17,158,000	15,242,000	12,442,000	9,504,000	6,606,000	4,122,000	3,174,000
1900	76,094,000	9,181,000	16,966,000	14,951,000	12,161,000	9,273,000	6,,437,000	4,026,000	3,099,000

* Denotes first year for which figures include Alaska and Hawaii.

Series A 91-104. Population, by Sex and Race: 1790 to 1990

| Year | All races | | Year | All races | | Year | All races | |
| | Male | Female | | Male | Female | | Male | Female |
	91	98		91	98		91	98
1991	123,431,000	129,257,000	1977	105,278,000	111,122,000	1910	47,332,277	44,639,989
			1976	104,484,000	110,196,000	1900	38,816,448	37,178,127
1990	122,049,000	127,875,000				1890	32,237,101	30,710,613
1989	121,445,000	127,317,000	1975	103,723,000	109,328,000			
1988	119,724,000	126,060,000	1974	102,954,000	108,435,000	1880	25,518,820	24,636,963
1987	118,541,000	124,886,000	1973	102,240,000	107,619,000	1870	19,493,565	19,064,806
1986	117,370,000	127,737,000	1972	101,477,000	106,757,000	1860	16,085,204	15,358,117
			1971	100,445,000	105,775,000	1850	11,837,660	11,354,216
1985	116,160,000	122,576,000				1840	8,688,532	8,380,921
1984	115,022,000	121,455,000	1970	98,912,192	104,299,734			
1983	113,919,000	120,365,000	1960*	88,331,494	90,991,681	1830	6,532,489	6,333,531
1982	112,772,000	119,224,000	1960	87,864,510	90,599,726	1820	4,896,605	4,741,848
1981	111,611,000	118,027,000	1950	74,833,239	75,864,122	1810	(1)	(1)
			1940	66,061,592	65,607,683	1800	(1)	(1)
1980	110,528,000	116,533,000				1790	(1)	(1)
1979	107,006,000	113,093,000	1930	62,137,080	60,637,966			
1978	106,120,000	112,108,000	1920	53,900,431	51,810,189			

* Denotes first year for which figures include Alaska and Hawaii.

[1] Data by sex not available. See Series A 1-5 for total population.

Series A 143-151.   Median Age of the Population, by Race and Sex: 1790 to 1991

Year	All Races			White			Black		
	Total	Male	Female	Total	Male	Female	Total	Male	Female
	143	144	145	146	147	148	149	150	151
1991	33.1	31.9	34.3	—	—	—	—	—	—
1990	32.6	31.5	33.8						
1989	32.6	31.6	33.8	33.6	32.5	34.7	27.7	26.3	29.1
1988	32.0	31.2	33.5	33.3	32.1	34.4	27.5	26.1	28.8
1987	31.7	30.9	33.3	33.0	31.9	34.2	27.2	25.8	28.5
1986	31.6	30.6	33.0	32.7	31.5	33.9	26.9	25.5	28.2
1985	31.5	30.3	32.7	32.4	31.2	33.6	26.6	25.2	27.8
1984	31.2	30.0	32.8	32.2	31.0	33.4	26.3	24.9	27.6
1983	30.9	29.6	32.2	31.8	30.5	33.1	25.8	24.4	27.2
1982	30.6	29.4	31.9	31.5	30.2	32.8	25.5	24.1	26.8
1981	30.3	29.1	31.6	31.2	29.9	32.5	25.2	23.9	26.5
1980	30.0	28.8	31.3	30.9	29.6	32.2	24.9	23.6	26.2
1979	29.8	38.9	31.3	30.9	29.7	32.2	24.6	23.5	25.9
1978	29.5	28.6	31.0	30.6	29.4	32.0	24.3	23.2	25.5
1977	29.2	28.2	30.6	30.3	29.0	31.6	24.1	22.9	25.2
1976	28.9	—	—	—	—	—	—	—	—
1975	28.8	27.6	30.3	29.6	28.4	31.0	23.4	22.2	24.6
1974	28.7	27.4	29.8	29.5	28.2	30.8	23.2	21.9	24.3
1973	28.4	—	—	—	—	—	—	—	—
1972	28.2	26.8	29.4	29.2	—	—	23.0	—	—
1971	28.0	—	—	—	—	—	—	—	—
1970	28.1	26.8	29.3	28.9	27.6	30.2	22.4	21.0	23.6
1960*	29.5	28.7	30.3	30.3	29.4	31.1	23.5	22.3	24.5
1960	29.6	28.7	30.4	30.3	29.5	31.2	23.5	22.3	24.5
1950	30.2	29.9	30.5	30.8	30.4	31.1	26.1	25.8	26.4
1940	29.0	29.1	29.0	29.5	29.5	29.5	25.3	25.3	25.3
1930	26.5	26.7	26.2	26.9	27.1	26.6	23.5	23.7	23.3
1920	25.3	25.8	24.7	25.6	26.1	25.1	22.3	22.8	22.0
1910	24.1	24.6	23.5	24.5	24.9	23.9	20.8	21.0	20.7
1900	22.9	23.3	22.4	23.4	23.8	22.9	19.5	19.5	19.5
1890	22.0	22.3	21.6	22.5	22.9	22.1	18.1	17.9	18.3
1880	20.9	21.2	20.7	21.4	21.6	21.1	(NA)	(NA)	(NA)
1870	20.2	20.2	20.1	20.4	20.6	20.3	18.3	17.8	18.8
1860	19.4	19.8	19.1	19.7	20.1	19.3	17.5	17.5	17.5
1850	18.9	19.2	18.6	19.2	19.5	18.8	17.4	17.3	17.4
1840	17.8	17.9	17.8	17.9	18.0	17.8	17.6	17.5	17.6
1830	17.2	17.2	17.3	17.3	17.2	17.3	17.2	17.1	17.3
1820	16.7	16.6	16.8	16.6	16.5	16.6	17.2	17.1	17.4
1810	—	—	—	16.0	15.9	16.1	—	—	—
1800	—	—	—	16.0	15.7	16.3	—	—	—
1790	—	—	—	—	(¹)	—	—	—	—

* Denotes first year for which figures include Alaska and Hawaii.
NA Not available.

¹ Median falls in the open-ended age group, 16 years and over, which includes 50.3 percent of the white male population.

Series A 160-171. Marital Status of the Population, by Age and Sex: 1890 to 1991

(For 1940-1970, marital status not reported was allocated on basis of other characteristics)

| Year and age | Males, 14 years old and over | | | | | | Females, 14 years old and over | | | | | |
	Total	Single	Married	Widowed	Divorced	Status not reported	Total	Single	Married	Widowed	Divorced	Status not reported
	160	161	162	163	164	165	166	167	168	169	170	171
1991 Total 14 years and over	87,800,000	22,900,000	55,900,000	2,400,000	6,600,000		95,800,000	18,500,000	56,800,000	11,300,000	9,200,000	
1990 Total 14 years and over	86,900,000	22,400,000	55,800,000	2,300,000	6,300,000		95,000,000	17,900,000	56,700,000	11,500,000	8,800,000	
1989 Total 14 years and over	85,800,000	22,200,000	55,300,000	2,300,000	6,000,000		94,000,000	17,800,000	56,200,000	11,500,000	8,500,000	
1988 Total 14 years and over	84,800,000	21,500,000	55,200,000	2,300,000	6,700,000		92,900,000	17,400,000	56,100,000	11,200,000	8,200,000	
1987 Total 14 years and over	83,700,000	21,100,000	54,900,000	2,100,000	5,600,000		91,900,000	17,100,000	55,600,000	11,100,000	8,000,000	
1986 Total 14 years and over	82,800,000	20,900,000	54,300,000	2,200,000	5,500,000		90,900,000	16,600,000	54,900,000	11,300,000	8,100,000	
1985 Total 14 years and over	81,500,000	20,500,000	53,500,000	2,100,000	5,300,000		89,900,0000	16,400,000	54,400,000	11,400,000	7,800,000	
1984 Total 14 years and over	80,500,000	20,500,000	53,000,000	2,100,000	4,900,000		88,900,000	16,400,000	54,100,000	11,100,000	7,400,000	
1983 Total 14 years and over	79,300,000	19,900,000	52,900,000	1,900,000	4,600,000		87,700,000	16,000,000	53,800,000	10,900,000	7,000,000	
1982 Total 14 years and over	78,100,000	19,100,000	52,500,000	1,900,000	4,600,000		85,600,000	15,300,000	53,600,000	10,800,000	6,900,000	
1981 Total 14 years and over	76,900,000	18,400,000	52,100,000	1,900,000	4,400,000		85,200,000	14,800,000	53,200,000	10,800,000	6,400,000	
1980 Total 14 years and over	75,700,000	18,000,000	51,800,000	2,000,000	3,900,000		83,800,000	14,300,000	52,800,000	10,800,000	6,000,000	
1979 Total 14 years and over	72,700,000	17,000,000	50,300,000	1,900,000	3,500,000		80,600,000	13,600,000	51,200,000	10,400,000	5,400,000	
1978 Total 14 years and over	71,500,000	16,100,000	50,100,000	1,900,000	3,400,000		79,300,000	13,000,000	50,900,000	10,100,000	5,300,000	
1977 Total 14 years and over	70,300,000	15,400,000	49,900,000	1,900,000	3,200,000		77,900,000	12,200,000	50,900,000	10,000,000	4,900,000	
1976 Total 14 years and over	69,100,000	14,700,000	49,800,000	1,800,000	2,800,000		76,700,000	11,500,000	50,800,000	10,000,000	4,400,000	
1975 Total 14 years and over	67,900,000	14,100,000	49,400,000	1,800,000	2,500,000		75,300,000	11,000,000	50,300,000	10,100,000	4,000,000	
1974 Total 14 years and over	66,500,000	13,300,000	49,000,000	1,800,000	2,300,000		74,000,000	10,500,000	50,000,000	9,800,000	3,600,000	
1973 Total 14 years and over	65,200,000	12,700,000	48,600,000	1,900,000	1,900,000		72,800,000	10,100,000	49,500,000	9,800,000	3,200,000	
1972 Total 14 years and over	64,200,000	12,500,000	48,000,000	1,800,000	1,700,000		71,500,000	9,800,000	49,000,000	9,600,000	3,000,000	
1971 Total 14 years and over	63,700,000	12,600,000	47,200,000	1,900,000	1,800,000		70,700,000	9,900,000	48,100,000	9,700,000	2,800,000	

See footnotes at end of table.

Series A 160-171. Marital Status of the Population, by Age and Sex: 1890 to 1991—Cont'd.

(For 1940-1970, marital status not reported was allocated on basis of other characteristics)

| Year and age | Males, 14 years old and over | | | | | | Females, 14 years old and over | | | | | |
	Total	Single	Married	Widowed	Divorced	Status not reported	Total	Single	Married	Widowed	Divorced	Status not reported
	160	161	162	163	164	165	166	167	168	169	170	171
1970[1] Total 14 years and over	71,485,878	20,426,937	47,001,412	2,130,932	1,926,597		77,910,094	17,624,105	47,666,431	9,615,280	3,004,278	
14 years	2,136,818	2,111,778	20,768	2,451	1,821		2,049,056	2,019,680	22,010	5,421	1,945	
15-19 years	9,718,189	9,315,441	381,500	8,529	12,719		9,485,229	8,358,248	1,073,147	23,038	30,796	
15-17 years	6,071,485	5,986,895	74,740	5,057	4,793		5,825,133	5,553,582	250,529	12,382	8,640	
18 and 19 years	3,646,704	3,328,546	306,760	3,472	7,926		3,660,096	2,804,666	822,618	10,656	22,156	
20-24 years	7,761,209	4,207,592	3,329,772	12,878	110,967		8,354,509	3,030,876	5,054,321	56,508	212,804	
25-29 years	6,569,924	1,288,594	5,066,314	19,196	195,830		6,810,076	827,906	5,616,300	71,530	294,340	
30-34 years	5,607,593	601,868	4,803,203	19,574	182,948		5,868,858	435,897	5,055,678	86,494	290,789	
35-44 years	11,261,731	884,372	9,895,931	75,546	405,882		11,860,315	672,255	10,187,753	353,760	646,547	
45-54 years	11,138,181	711,099	9,813,513	186,144	427,425		11,996,408	662,506	9,728,095	942,796	663,011	
55-64 years	8,858,893	574,425	7,587,085	364,665	332,718		9,827,148	669,051	6,677,855	1,988,096	492,146	
65 years and over	8,433,330	631,768	6,103,326	1,441,949	256,287		11,658,495	947,686	4,251,272	6,087,637	371,900	
1960[2] * Total 14 years and over	61,315,358	15,313,822	42,630,422	2,071,910	1,299,204		64,961,189	12,320,199	42,905,285	7,880,607	1,855,098	
14 years	1,402,724	1,394,426	7,756	163	379		1,345,136	1,330,089	14,250	391	406	
15-19 years	6,698,837	6,437,186	254,377	1,784	5,490		6,588,597	5,528,745	1,033,804	4,751	21,297	
15-17 years	4,341,635	4,290,310	48,850	897	1,578		4,174,262	3,886,610	277,151	1,874	5,627	
18 and 19 years	2,357,202	2,146,876	205,527	887	3,912		2,417,335	1,642,135	756,653	2,877	15,670	
20-24 years	5,283,228	2,807,784	2,417,552	4,780	53,112		5,519,937	1,567,622	3,833,956	17,252	101,107	
25-29 years	5,333,282	1,111,768	4,117,072	9,548	94,894		5,537,104	582,114	4,772,006	37,047	145,937	
30-34 years	5,840,287	694,924	5,000,763	17,246	127,354		6,111,422	422,915	5,423,228	74,109	191,170	
35-44 years	11,739,191	948,784	10,410,091	76,436	303,880		12,336,341	748,766	10,741,606	374,216	471,753	
45-54 years	10,139,671	749,390	8,896,768	182,260	311,253		10,485,709	738,266	8,379,825	921,258	446,360	
55-64 years	7,569,153	605,187	6,351,408	380,508	232,050		8,138,691	648,264	5,375,362	1,819,043	296,022	
65 years and over	7,308,985	564,373	5,174,635	1,399,185	170,792		8,898,252	753,418	3,331,248	4,632,540	181,046	
1950[3] Total 14 years and over	54,601,105	14,399,840	36,866,055	2,263,850	1,071,360		57,102,295	11,418,335	37,576,800	6,734,275	1,372,885	
14 years	1,090,929	1,080,370	6,660	1,670	1,320		1,047,370	1,039,610	6,980	565	215	
15-19 years	5,323,470	5,146,610	166,955	4,995	4,910		5,321,755	4,412,565	887,615	5,260	16,315	
15-17 years	3,187,510	3,151,360	30,410	3,460	2,280		3,116,230	2,893,350	217,325	2,055	3,500	
18 and 19 years	2,135,960	1,995,250	136,545	1,535	2,630		2,205,525	1,519,215	670,290	3,205	12,815	
20-24 years	5,559,265	3,281,540	2,217,810	9,060	50,855		5,878,040	1,898,910	3,856,760	25,280	97,090	
25-29 years	5,904,975	1,404,860	4,381,375	15,485	103,255		6,277,480	833,040	5,227,960	57,490	158,990	
30-34 years	5,562,315	734,195	4,690,995	20,945	116,180		5,896,625	546,245	5,082,260	91,945	176,175	
35-44 years	10,402,195	996,570	9,046,675	94,865	264,085		10,837,650	900,480	9,140,055	409,250	387,865	
45-54 years	8,484,515	725,355	7,267,615	240,755	250,790		8,687,605	680,150	6,737,675	967,595	302,185	
55-64 years	6,540,100	551,185	5,320,670	495,140	173,105		6,633,170	525,405	4,310,160	1,636,660	160,945	
65 years and over	5,734,250	479,155	3,767,300	1,380,935	106,860		6,522,600	581,930	2,327,335	3,540,230	73,105	
1940 Total 14 years and over	50,553,748	17,593,379	30,192,334	2,143,612	624,423		50,549,176	13,935,866	30,090,488	5,700,202	822,620	
14 years	1,218,116	1,216,784	1,247	60	25		1,187,614	1,184,094	3,353	110	57	
15-19 years	6,180,153	6,073,165	104,935	1,031	1,022		6,153,370	5,425,023	713,940	6,423	8,984	
15-17 years	3,684,780	3,670,287	14,002	311	180		3,629,909	3,461,246	165,131	1,729	1,803	
18 and 19 years	2,495,373	2,402,878	90,933	720	842		2,523,461	1,962,777	548,809	4,694	7,181	
20-24 years	5,692,392	4,109,304	1,557,104	8,394	17,590		5,895,443	2,781,001	3,025,923	32,751	55,768	
25-29 years	5,450,662	1,964,118	3,417,046	20,973	48,525		5,645,976	1,288,092	4,185,325	71,878	100,681	
30-34 years	5,070,312	1,050,199	3,912,820	36,714	70,579		5,172,076	761,698	4,155,872	128,256	126,250	
35-44 years	9,164,794	1,283,994	7,551,974	155,405	173,421		9,168,426	950,876	7,430,791	537,584	249,175	

See footnotes at end of table.

Series A 160-171. Marital Status of the Population, by Age and Sex: 1890 to 1991—Cont'd.

(For 1940-1970, marital status not reported was allocated on basis of other characteristics)

Year and age	Males, 14 years old and over						Females, 14 years old and over					
	Total	Single	Married	Widowed	Divorced	Status not reported	Total	Single	Married	Widowed	Divorced	Status not reported
	160	161	162	163	164	165	166	167	168	169	170	171
45-54 years	7,962,019	885,004	6,590,954	328,130	157,931		7,550,052	654,312	5,736,614	991,448	167,678	
55-64 years	5,409,180	577,170	4,245,427	488,620	97,963		5,163,025	462,407	3,254,768	1,365,044	80,806	
65 years and over	4,406,120	433,641	2,810,827	1,104,285	57,367		4,613,194	429,363	1,583,902	2,566,708	33,221	
1930 Total 14 years and over	45,035,691	16,143,512	26,311,682	2,022,588	488,688	69,221	43,970,842	12,465,795	26,159,771	4,728,565	572,574	44,137
14 years	1,206,486	1,205,662	761	42	21	X	1,175,899	1,171,393	4,241	167	98	X
15-19 years	5,757,825	5,645,359	100,362	1,513	1,348	9,243	5,794,290	5,032,174	731,967	12,337	12,371	5,441
15-17 years	3,493,718	3,482,706	10,553	281	178	X	3,465,118	3,279,560	179,404	3,284	2,870	X
18 and 19 years	2,264,107	2,162,653	89,809	1,232	1,170	9,243	2,329,172	1,752,614	552,563	9,053	9,501	5,441
20-24 years	5,336,815	3,779,443	1,500,493	17,657	221,900	17,322	5,533,563	2,547,057	2,857,665	56,375	62,464	10,002
25-29 years	4,860,180	1,785,413	2,977,004	39,013	50,229	8,521	4,973,428	1,079,923	3,697,645	102,041	89,124	4,695
30-34 years	4,561,786	965,945	3,468,176	59,493	62,669	5,503	4,558,635	603,048	3,715,648	148,571	88,219	3,149
35-44 years	8,816,319	1,261,705	7,189,452	218,881	137,180	9,101	8,382,521	839,130	6,832,581	547,562	157,650	5,598
45-54 years	6,803,569	776,863	5,551,146	357,047	111,471	7,042	6,214,514	564,466	4,673,539	872,676	98,874	4,959
55-64 years	4,367,500	442,505	3,407,751	445,262	66,499	5,483	4,029,398	360,188	2,499,285	1,119,802	45,881	4,242
65 years and over	3,325,211	280,617	2,116,537	883,680	37,371	7,006	3,308,594	268,416	1,147,200	1,869,034	17,893	6,051
1920 Total 14 years and over	37,861,085	13,969,763	21,823,326	1,754,302	234,519	79,175	36,134,659	10,608,384	21,301,014	3,909,736	272,736	42,789
14 years	1,033,297	1,029,971	3,173	118	35	X	1,012,968	1,007,088	5,554	269	57	X
15-19 years	4,673,792	4,567,770	96,374	1,830	759	7,059	4,756,764	4,137,650	596,542	12,239	6,017	4,316
15-17 years	2,828,546	2,815,533	12,521	384	108	X	2,861,030	2,711,081	145,390	3,091	1,468	X
18 and 19 years	1,845,246	1,752,237	83,853	1,446	651	7,059	1,895,734	1,426,569	451,152	9,148	4,549	4,316
20-24 years	4,527,045	3,200,623	1,280,318	20,511	10,280	15,313	4,749,976	2,164,051	2,483,697	65,414	28,582	8,232
25-29 years	4,538,233	1,789,721	2,662,124	51,470	22,856	12,062	4,548,258	1,048,285	3,336,501	117,389	41,243	4,842
30-34 years	4,130,783	995,869	3,023,357	74,454	28,080	9,023	3,940,410	588,119	3,155,854	152,893	40,188	3,356
35-44 years	7,359,904	1,188,586	5,873,308	220,700	63,592	13,718	6,730,934	767,882	5,426,434	485,493	75,027	6,098
45-54 years	5,653,095	677,420	4,580,056	329,976	56,162	9,481	4,845,398	464,838	3,587,794	739,058	48,562	5,146
55-64 years	3,461,865	337,592	2,697,429	386,587	34,249	6,008	3,069,807	257,029	1,878,478	906,362	23,451	4,487
65 years and over	2,483,071	182,211	1,607,187	668,656	18,506	6,511	2,450,144	173,442	830,160	1,430,621	9,609	6,312
1910 Total 14 years and over	33,247,336	13,455,690	18,066,188	1,466,839	155,604	103,015	30,904,861	9,826,911	17,667,119	3,167,432	184,621	58,778
14 years	935,974	934,980	898	82	14	X	912,148	908,435	3,482	198	33	X
15-19 years	4,527,282	4,448,067	51,877	1,110	347	25,881	4,536,321	3,985,764	513,239	10,261	3,650	23,407
15-17 years	2,688,370	2,667,874	4,990	252	70	15,184	2,683,806	2,543,264	121,803	2,697	867	15,175
18 and 19 years	1,838,912	1,780,193	46,887	858	277	10,697	1,852,515	1,442,500	391,436	7,564	2,783	8,232
20-24 years	4,580,290	3,432,161	1,100,093	18,815	6,732	22,489	4,476,694	2,163,683	2,225,362	55,354	20,370	11,925
25-29 years	4,244,348	1,816,137	2,353,525	45,092	15,503	14,091	3,935,655	981,556	2,823,935	95,385	29,153	5,626
30-34 years	3,656,768	951,820	2,611,244	65,339	19,068	9,297	3,315,417	535,170	2,619,959	128,942	28,109	3,237
35-44 years	6,153,366	1,026,502	4,873,153	198,701	42,688	12,322	5,504,321	628,516	4,410,310	411,896	49,269	4,330
45-54 years	4,488,929	499,751	3,658,931	286,222	36,502	7,523	3,881,059	331,573	2,904,043	610,386	31,934	3,123
55-64 years	2,674,403	222,950	2,112,699	312,420	21,675	4,659	2,379,698	167,991	1,479,454	714,452	15,200	2,601
65 years and over	1,985,976	123,322	1,303,768	539,058	13,075	6,753	1,963,548	124,223	687,335	1,140,558	6,903	4,529
1900 Total 14 years and over	26,286,316	11,053,813	13,920,057	1,173,509	83,828	55,109	24,951,254	8,319,285	13,784,538	2,706,332	114,476	26,923
14 years	793,340	792,267	667	33	7	366	775,224	770,742	3,783	126	30	543
15-19 years	3,750,451	3,706,382	37,781	871	194	5,223	3,805,638	3,374,814	415,682	9,336	2,418	3,388

See footnotes at end of table.

Series A 160-171. Marital Status of the Population, by Age and Sex: 1890 to 1991—Cont'd.

(For 1940-1970, marital status not reported was allocated on basis of other characteristics)

Year and age	Males, 14 years old and over						Females, 14 years old and over					
	Total	Single	Married	Widowed	Divorced	Status not reported	Total	Single	Married	Widowed	Divorced	Status not reported
	160	161	162	163	164	165	166	167	168	169	170	171
20-24 years	3,624,580	2,812,113	782,907	14,332	3,322	11,906	3,710,436	1,913,552	1,726,296	52,545	13,124	4,919
25-29 years	3,323,543	1,520,782	1,746,620	38,781	8,218	9,142	3,205,898	882,875	2,209,357	91,847	18,461	3,358
30-34 years	2,901,321	800,664	2,025,729	58,312	10,307	6,309	2,654,718	441,409	2,071,698	121,944	17,384	2,283
35-44 years	4,872,781	826,201	3,840,575	174,535	22,630	8,840	4,339,166	481,668	3,451,375	372,677	29,953	3,493
45-54 years	3,402,458	349,429	2,797,354	230,656	19,498	5,521	2,994,983	234,413	2,212,223	526,456	19,111	2,780
55-64 years	2,062,424	156,823	1,644,373	245,424	12,297	3,507	1,940,111	128,954	1,172,904	626,271	9,566	2,416
65 years and over	1,555,418	89,152	1,044,051	410,565	7,355	4,295	1,525,080	90,858	521,220	905,130	4,129	3,743
1890 Total 14 years and over	21,397,501	9,331,617	11,176,124	811,110	48,708	29,942	20,239,343	6,906,714	11,101,645	2,144,496	71,584	14,904
14 years	723,158	723,015	23	X	1	119	695,801	694,281	1,411	17	12	80
15-19 years	3,248,711	3,230,935	16,746	137	28	965	3,308,852	2,987,949	313,983	4,845	1,101	974
20-24 years	3,104,893	2,505,460	585,748	7,610	1,468	4,607	3,091,783	1,601,266	1,444,712	36,456	6,931	2,418
25-29 years	2,698,311	1,240,797	1,421,407	26,601	4,340	5,166	2,529,466	641,988	1,805,064	69,965	10,588	1,861
30-34 years	2,425,664	642,827	1,728,930	43,777	5,832	4,298	2,152,966	326,306	1,717,204	96,797	11,161	1,498
35-44 years	3,705,648	568,511	2,997,030	120,796	12,837	6,474	3,346,031	330,139	2,698,266	296,302	18,899	2,425
45-54 years	2,627,024	239,928	2,213,901	157,920	11,393	3,882	2,430,878	171,454	1,796,979	447,370	13,080	1,995
55-64 years	1,630,373	111,144	1,342,414	166,686	7,835	2,294	1,499,997	86,573	905,627	499,420	6,721	1,656
65 years and over	1,233,719	69,100	869,925	287,583	4,974	2,137	1,183,569	66,758	418,399	693,324	3,091	1,997

*Denotes first year for which figures include Alaska and Hawaii.
X Represents zero.
[1] 5-percent sample.
[2] 25-percent sample.
[3] 20-percent sample.

Series A 172-194.   Population of Regions, by Race and Residence: 1790 to 1990

(In thousands)

Region and Year	Total population	White	Black	Other races	Urban	Rural
			Race		Residence	
	172	175	176	177	178	179
Northeast						
1990	50,809	42,069	5,613	5,214	40,092	10,717
1980	49,137	42,328	4,849	1,950	38,904	10,232
1970	49,041	44,311	4,344	386	39,450	9,591
1960	44,678	41,522	3,028	127	35,840	8,838
1950	39,478	37,399	2,018	61	31,373	8,105
1940	35,977	34,567	1,370	40	27,568	8,409
1930	34,427	33,237	1,147	43	26,707	7,720
1920	29,662	28,958	679	25	22,404	7,258
1910	25,869	25,361	484	23	18,563	7,305
1900	21,047	20,638	385	24	13,911	7,136
1890	17,407	17,122	270	15	10,266	7,141
1880	14,507	14,274	229	4	7,370	7,137
1870	12,299	12,117	180	2	5,448	6,851
1860	10,594	10,438	156	(Z)	3,787	6,807
1850	8,627	8,447	150	X	2,289	6,338
1840	6,761	6,619	142	X	1,253	5,508
1830	5,542	5,417	125	X	785	4,758
1820	4,360	4,246	114	X	480	3,880
1810	3,487	3,384	102	X	380	3,107
1800	2,636	2,553	83	X	245	2,391
1790	1,968	1,901	67	X	160	1,809
Midwest						
1990	59,669	52,018	5,716	2,833	42,774	16,894
1980	58,666	52,195	5,337	1,334	41,466	17,388
1970	56,572	51,641	4,572	359	40,481	16,091
1960	51,619	48,003	3,446	170	35,481	16,138
1950	44,461	42,119	2,228	114	28,491	15,970
1940	40,143	38,640	1,420	83	23,437	16,706
1930	38,594	37,151	1,262	181	22,351	16,243
1920	34,020	33,164	793	62	17,776	16,244
1910	29,889	29,279	543	66	13,487	16,401
1900	26,333	25,776	496	61	10,165	16,168
1890	22,410	21,914	431	65	7,418	14,992
1880	17,364	16,961	386	17	4,198	13,166
1870	12,981	12,699	273	10	2,702	10,279
1860	9,097	8,900	184	13	1,263	7,833
1850	5,404	5,268	136	X	499	4,904
1840	3,352	3,262	89	X	129	3,222
1830	1,610	1,569	42	X	42	1,569
1820	859	841	18	X	10	850
1810	292	286	7	X	3	290
1800	51	50	1	X	X	51
South						
1990	85,446	65,582	15,829	8,452	58,656	26,790
1980	73,572	58,949	14,048	2,364	50,414	24,958
1970	62,795	50,420	11,970	405	40,540	22,255
1960	54,973	43,477	11,312	185	32,160	22,813
1950	47,197	36,850	10,225	122	22,956	24,241
1940	41,666	31,659	9,905	103	15,290	26,375
1930	37,858	27,674	9,362	882	12,904	24,953
1920	33,126	24,132	8,912	81	9,300	23,826
1910	29,389	20,547	8,749	92	6,623	22,767
1900	24,524	16,522	7,923	79	4,421	20,103

See footnote at end of chart.

Series A 172-194.   Population of Regions, by Race and Residence: 1790 to 1990—Cont'd.

(In thousands)

Region and Year	Total population	White	Black	Other races	Urban	Rural
	172	175	176	177	178	179
1890	20,028	13,193	6,761	74	3,261	16,767
1880	16,517	10,555	5,954	7	2,017	14,500
1870	12,288	7,863	4,421	4	1,497	10,791
1860	11,133	7,034	4,097	2	1,067	10,067
1850	8,983	5,630	3,352	X	744	8,239
1840	6,951	4,309	2,642	X	463	6,488
1830	5,708	3,546	2,162	X	301	5,407
1820	4,419	2,776	1,644	X	204	4,216
1810	3,461	2,191	1,268	X	143	3,318
1800	2,622	1,704	918	X	78	2,544
1790	1,961	1,271	690	X	42	1,919
West						
1990	52,786	40,017	2,828	15,087	45,531	7,255
1980	43,172	34,890	2,262	6,020	36,211	6,961
1970	34,804	31,377	1,695	1,732	28,854	5,950
1960	28,053	25,830	1,086	1,137	21,787	6,266
1950	20,190	18,574	571	416	14,027	6,163
1940	14,379	13,350	171	363	8,409	5,969
1930	12,324	10,802	120	974	7,199	5,125
1920	9,214	8,567	79	258	4,773	4,440
1910	7,082	6,544	51	231	3,391	3,691
1900	4,309	3,873	30	188	1,718	2,591
1890	3,134	2,872	27	203	1,161	1,974
1880	1,801	1,612	12	144	544	1,257
1870	991	910	6	74	256	735
1860	619	551	4	64	99	520
1850	179	178	1	X	11	167

Z represents less than .5.
X represents 0

Series A 195-209.   Population of States, by Race: 1790 to 1990

(In thousands, except series A 196)

State and year	Resident population Total	Resident population Per square mile of land area	Race White	Race Black	State and year	Resident population Total	Resident population Per square mile of land area	Race White	Race Black
	195	196	199	200		195	196	199	200
Alabama					**Arkansas**				
1990	4,041	79.6	2,976	1,021	1990	2,351	45.1	1,945	374
1980	3,890	76.7	2,873	996	1980	2,286	43.9	1,890	374
1970	3,444	67.9	2,534	903	1970	1,923	37.0	1,566	352
1960	3,267	64.2	2,284	980	1960	1,786	34.2	1,396	389
1950 [1]	3,062	59.9	2,080	980	1950 [1]	1,910	36.3	1,482	427
1950 [2]	—	—	—	—	1950 [2]	—	—	—	—
1940	2,833	55.5	1,849	983	1940	1,949	37.0	1,466	483
1930	2,646	51.8	1,701	945	1930	1,854	35.2	1,375	478
1920	2,348	45.8	1,447	901	1920	1,752	33.4	1,280	472
1910	2,138	41.7	1,229	908	1910	1,574	30.0	1,131	443
1900	1,829	35.7	1,001	827	1900	1,312	25.0	945	367
1890	1,513	29.5	834	678	1890	1,128	21.5	819	309
1880	1,263	24.6	662	600	1880	803	15.3	592	211
1870	997	19.4	521	476	1870	484	9.2	362	122
1860	964	18.8	526	438	1860	435	8.3	324	111
1850	772	15.0	427	345	1850	210	4.0	162	48
1840	591	11.5	335	256	1840	98	1.9	77	20
1830	310	6.0	190	119	1830	30	.6	26	5
1820	128	2.5	85	42	1820	14	.1	13	2
1810 [3]	9	—	—	—	1810	1		—	
1800 [3]	1	—	—	—					
Alaska					**California**				
					1990	29,760	190.8	20,524	2,209
1990	550	1.0	415	22	1980	23,668	151.7	18,031	1,819
1980	400	.7	310	14					
					1970	19,953	127.6	17,761	1,400
1970	300	.5	237	9	1960	15,717	100.4	14,455	884
1960	226	.4	179	7	1950 [1]	10,586	67.5	9,915	462
1950	129	.2	93	X	1950 [2]	—	—	—	—
1940 [4]	73	.1	39	(Z)	1940	6,907	44.1	6,597	124
1930 [5]	59	.1	29	(Z)					
					1930	5,677	36.2	5,408	81
1920	55	.1	28	(Z)	1920	3,427	22.0	3,265	39
1910	64	.1	36	(Z)	1910	2,378	15.3	2,260	22
1900	64	.1	30	(Z)	1900	1,485	9.5	1,403	11
1890	32	—	4	—	1890	1,213	7.8	1,112	11
1880	33	—	(Z)	—	1880	865	5.5	767	6
Arizona					1870	560	3.6	499	4
1990	3,665	32.3	2,963	111	1860	380	2.4	323	4
1980	2,718	23.9	2,241	75	1850	93	.6	92	1
1970	1,771	15.6	1,605	53	**Colorado**				
1960	1,302	11.5	1,170	43	1990	3,294	31.8	2,905	133
1950 [1]	750	6.6	655	26	1980	2,890	27.9	2,571	102
1950 [2]	—	—	—	—					
1940	499	4.4	427	15	1970	2,207	21.3	2,112	66
					1960	1,754	16.9	1,701	40
1930	436	3.8	379	11	1950 [1]	1,325	12.8	1,297	20
1920	334	2.9	291	8	1950 [2]	—	—	—	—
1910	204	1.8	171	2	1940	1,123	10.8	1,107	12
1900	123	1.1	93	2					
1890	88	.8	56	1	1930	1,036	10.0	1,019	12
					1920	940	9.1	924	11
1880	40	.4	35	(Z)	1910	799	7.7	783	11
1870	10	.1	10	(Z)	1900	540	5.2	529	9
					1890	413	4.0	405	6

See footnotes at end of table.

Series A 195-209. Population of States, by Race: 1790 to 1990—Cont'd.

(In thousands, except series A 196)

State and year	Resident population		Race		State and year	Resident population		Race	
	Total	Per square mile of land area	White	Black		Total	Per square mile of land area	White	Black
	195	196	199	200		195	196	199	200
1880	194	1.9	191	2	1970	757	12,401.8	209	538
1870	40	.4	39	(Z)	1960	764	12,523.9	345	412
1860	34	.3	34	(Z)	1950	802	13,150.5	518	281
					1940	663	10,870.3	474	187
Connecticut					1930	487	7,981.5	354	132
1990	3,287	678.4	2,859	274					
1980	3,108	641.3	2,799	217	1920	483	7,292.9	327	110
					1910	331	5,517.8	236	94
1970	3,032	623.6	2,835	181	1900	279	4,645.3	192	87
1960	2,535	520.6	2,424	107	1890	230	3,972.3	155	76
1950 [1]	2,007	409.7	1,952	53	1880	178	3,062.5	118	60
1950 [2]	—	—	—	—					
1940	1,709	348.9	1,675	33	1870	132	2,270.7	88	43
					1860	75	1,294.5	61	14
1930	1,607	328.0	1,577	29	1850	52	891.2	38	14
1920	1,381	286.4	1,359	21	1840	34	485.7	24	10
1910	1,115	231.3	1,099	15	1830	30	442.6	21	9
1900	908	188.5	892	15					
1890	746	154.8	733	12	1820	23	367.1	16	7
					1810	15	266.9	10	5
1880	623	129.2	611	12	1800	8	156.6	6	2
1870	537	111.5	528	10					
1860	460	95.5	452	9	**Florida**				
1850	371	76.9	363	8	1990	12,938	239.6	10,749	1,760
1840	310	64.3	302	8	1980	9,746	180.5	8,185	1,343
1830	298	61.8	290	8	1970	6,789	125.5	5,719	1,042
1820	275	57.1	267	8	1960	4,952	91.5	4,064	880
1810	262	54.3	255	7	1950 [1]	2,771	51.1	2,166	603
1800	251	52.1	245	6	1950 [2]	—	—	—	—
1790	238	49.4	233	6	1940	1,897	35.0	1,382	514
Delaware					1930	1,468	27.1	1,035	432
1990	666	340.8	535	112	1920	968	17.7	638	329
1980	594	304.1	488	96	1910	753	13.7	444	309
					1900	529	9.6	297	231
1970	548	276.5	466	78	1890	391	7.1	225	166
1960	446	225.2	384	61					
1950 [1]	318	160.8	274	44	1880	269	4.9	143	127
1950 [2]	—	—	—	—	1870	188	3.4	96	92
1940	267	134.7	231	36	1860	140	2.6	78	63
					1850	87	1.6	47	40
1930	238	120.5	206	33	1840	54	1.0	28	27
1920	223	113.5	193	30	1830	35	.6	18	16
1910	202	103.0	171	31					
1900	185	94.0	154	31	**Georgia**				
1890	168	85.7	140	28	1990	6,478	111.9	4,600	1,747
					1980	5,463	94.3	3,947	1,465
1880	147	74.6	120	26					
1870	125	63.6	102	23	1970	4,590	79.0	3,391	1,187
1860	112	57.1	91	22	1960	3,943	67.8	2,817	1,123
1850	92	46.6	71	20	1950 [1]	3,445	58.9	2,381	1,063
1840	78	39.7	59	20	1950 [2]	—	—	—	—
					1940	3,124	53.4	2,038	1,085
1830	77	39.1	58	19					
1820	73	37.0	55	17	1930	2,909	49.7	1,837	1,071
1810	73	37.0	55	17	1920	2,896	49.3	1,689	1,206
1800	64	32.7	50	14	1910	2,609	44.4	1,432	1,177
1790	59	30.1	46	13	1900	2,216	37.7	1,181	1,035
					1890	1,837	31.3	978	859
Dist. of Columbia									
1990	607	9,882.8	180	400	1880	1,542	26.3	817	725
1980	638	10,394.6	172	449	1870	1,184	20.2	639	545

See footnotes at end of table.

Series A 195-209.   Population of States, by Race: 1790 to 1990—Cont'd.

(In thousands, except series A 196)

State and year	Resident population		Race		State and year	Resident population		Race	
	Total	Per square mile of land area	White	Black		Total	Per square mile of land area	White	Black
	195	196	199	200		195	196	199	200
1860	1,057	18.0	592	466	1850	851	15.2	846	5
1850	906	15.4	522	285	1840	476	8.5	472	4
1840	691	11.8	408	284					
					1830	157	2.8	155	2
1830	517	8.8	297	220	1820	55	1.0	54	1
1820	341	5.8	190	151	1810	12	.1	12	1
1810	252	4.3	145	107					
1800	163	1.5	102	60	**Indiana**				
1790	83	.6	53	30	1990	5,544	154.6	5,021	432
					1980	5,490	153.1	5,004	415
Hawaii									
1990	1,108	172.5	370	27	1970	5,194	143.9	4,820	357
1980	965	150.2	319	17	1960	4,662	128.8	4,389	269
					1950 [1]	3,934	108.7	3,759	174
1970	769	119.6	298	8	1950 [2]	—			
1960	633	98.5	202	5	1940	3,428	94.7	3,305	122
1950	500	78.0	115	3					
1940	423	66.0	104	(Z)	1930	3,239	89.4	3,126	112
1930	368	57.5	80	1	1920	2,930	81.3	2,849	81
					1910	2,701	74.9	2,640	60
1920	256	39.9	55	(Z)	1900	2,516	70.1	2,459	58
1910	192	30.0	44	1	1890	2,192	61.1	2,147	45
1900	154	24.0	29	(Z)					
					1880	1,978	55.1	1,939	39
Idaho					1870	1,681	46.8	1,656	25
1990	1,007	12.2	950	3	1860	1,350	37.6	1,339	11
1980	944	11.4	902	3	1850	988	27.5	977	11
					1840	686	19.1	679	7
1970	713	8.6	699	2					
1960	667	8.1	657	2	1830	343	9.6	338	4
1950 [1]	589	7.1	581	1	1820	147	4.1	146	1
1950 [2]	—	—	—	—	1810	25	.6	24	1
1940	525	6.3	519	1	1800	6	(6)	5	(Z)
1930	445	5.4	439	1	**Iowa**				
1920	432	5.2	426	1	1990	2,777	49.7	2,683	48
1910	326	3.9	319	1	1980	2,914	52.1	2,839	42
1900	162	1.9	154	(Z)					
1890	89	1.1	82	(Z)	1970	2,824	50.5	2,783	33
					1960	2,758	49.2	2,729	25
1880	33	.4	29	(Z)	1950 [1]	2,621	46.8	2,600	20
1870	15	.2	11	(Z)	1950 [2]	—	—	—	—
					1940	2,538	45.3	2,521	17
Illinois									
1990	11,431	205.6	8,953	1,694	1930	2,471	44.1	2,453	17
1980	11,427	205.5	9,233	1,675	1920	2,404	43.2	2,384	19
					1910	2,225	40.0	2,209	15
1970	11,114	199.4	9,600	1,426	1900	2,232	40.2	2,219	13
1960	10,081	180.4	9,010	1,037	1890	1,912	34.4	1,901	11
1950 [1]	8,712	155.8	8,046	646					
1950 [2]	—	—	—	—	1880	1,625	29.2	1,615	10
1940	7,897	141.2	7,504	387	1870	1,194	21.5	1,188	6
					1860	675	12.1	674	1
1930	7,631	136.4	7,295	329	1850	192	3.5	192	(Z)
1920	6,485	115.7	6,299	182	1840	43	.2	43	(Z)
1910	5,639	100.6	5,527	109					
1900	4,822	86.1	4,735	85	**Kansas**				
1890	3,826	68.3	3,768	57	1990	2,478	30.3	2,232	143
					1980	2,364	28.9	2,168	126
1880	3,078	55.0	3,031	46					
1870	2,540	45.4	2,511	29	1970	2,247	27.5	2,122	107
1860	1,712	30.6	1,704	8	1960	2,179	26.6	2,079	91
					1950 [1]	1,905	23.2	1,829	73

See footnotes at end of table.

Series A 195-209. Population of States, by Race: 1790 to 1990—Cont'd.

(In thousands, except series A 196)

State and year	Resident population		Race		State and year	Resident population		Race	
	Total	Per square mile of land area	White	Black		Total	Per square mile of land area	White	Black
	195	196	199	200		195	196	199	200
1950²	—	—	—	—	1830	216	4.8	89	126
1940	1,801	21.9	1,734	65	1820	153	3.4	74	80
					1810	77	2.2	34	42
1930	1,881	22.9	1,812	66					
1920	1,769	21.6	1,709	58	**Maine**				
1910	1,691	20.7	1,634	54	1990	1,228	39.8	1,208	5
1900	1,470	18.0	1,416	52	1980	1,125	36.4	1,110	3
1890	1,428	17.5	1,377	50					
					1970	992	32.1	985	3
1880	996	12.2	952	43	1960	969	31.3	963	3
1870	364	4.5	346	17	1950¹	914	29.4	911	1
1860	107	1.3	106	1	1950²	—	—	—	—
					1940	847	27.3	845	1
Kentucky									
1990	3,685	92.8	3,392	263	1930	797	25.7	795	1
1980	3,661	92.1	3,379	259	1920	768	25.7	766	1
					1910	742	24.8	740	1
1970	3,219	81.2	2,982	231	1900	694	23.2	682	1
1960	3,038	76.2	2,820	216	1890	661	22.1	659	1
1950¹	2,945	73.9	2,742	202					
1950²	—	—	—	—	1880	649	21.7	647	1
1940	2,846	70.9	2,631	214	1870	627	21.0	625	2
					1860	628	21.0	627	1
1930	2,615	65.2	2,388	226	1850	583	19.5	582	1
1920	2,417	60.2	2,181	236	1840	502	16.8	500	1
1910	2,290	57.0	2,028	262					
1900	2,147	53.4	1,862	285	1830	399	13.4	398	1
1890	1,859	46.3	1,590	268	1820	298	10.0	297	1
					1810	229	7.7	228	1
1880	1,649	41.0	1,377	271	1800	152	5.1	151	1
1870	1,321	32.9	1,099	222	1790	97	3.2	96	1
1860	1,156	28.8	919	236					
1850	982	24.4	761	221	**Maryland**				
1840	780	19.4	590	190	1990	4,781	489.2	3,394	1,190
					1980	4,217	431.4	3,159	958
1830	688	17.1	519	170					
1820	564	14.0	435	129	1970	3,922	396.6	3,195	699
1810	407	10.1	324	82	1960	3,101	313.5	2,574	518
1800	221	5.5	180	41	1950¹	2,343	237.1	1,955	386
1790	74	1.8	61	13	1950²	—	—	—	—
					1940	1,821	184.2	1,518	302
Louisiana									
1990	4,220	96.9	2,839	1,299	1930	1,632	165.0	1,354	276
1980	4,206	96.5	2,912	1,238	1920	1,450	145.8	1,205	244
					1910	1,295	130.3	1,063	232
1970	3,641	81.0	2,541	1,087	1900	1,188	119.5	952	235
1960	3,257	72.2	2,212	1,039	1890	1,042	104.9	826	216
1950¹	2,684	59.4	1,797	882					
1950²	—	—	—	—	1880	935	94.0	725	210
1940	2,364	52.3	1,512	849	1870	781	78.6	605	175
					1860	687	69.1	516	171
1930	2,102	46.5	1,323	776	1850	583	58.6	418	165
1920	1,799	39.6	1,097	700	1840	470	47.3	318	152
1910	1,656	36.5	941	714					
1900	1,382	30.4	730	651	1830	447	45.0	291	156
1890	1,119	24.6	558	559	1820	407	41.0	260	147
					1810	381	38.3	235	145
1880	940	20.7	455	484	1800	342	34.4	216	125
1870	727	16.0	362	364	1790	320	32.0	209	111
1860	708	15.6	357	350					
1850	518	11.4	255	262	**Massachusetts**				
1840	352	7.8	158	194	1990	6,016	767.6	5,405	300
					1980	5,737	732.0	5,363	221

See footnotes at end of table.

Series A 195-209. Population of States, by Race: 1790 to 1990—Cont'd.

(In thousands, except series A 196)

State and year	Resident population			Race		State and year	Resident population			Race	
	Total	Per square mile of land area	White	Black			Total	Per square mile of land area	White	Black	
	195	196	199	200			195	196	199	200	
1970	5,689	727.0	5,478	176		1900	1,751	21.7	1,737	5
1960	5,149	657.3	5,023	112		1890	1,310	16.2	1,296	4
1950 [1]	4,691	596.2	4,612	73						
1950 [2]	—	—	—	—		1880	781	9.7	777	2
1940	4,317	545.9	4,258	55		1870	440	5.4	438	1
						1860	172	2.1	169	(Z)
1930	4,250	537.4	4,193	52		1850	6	(6)	6	(Z)
1920	3,852	479.2	3,804	45						
1910	3,366	418.8	3,325	38		**Mississippi**				
1900	2,805	349.0	2,770	32		1990	2,573	54.9	1,633	915
1890	2,239	278.5	2,215	22		1980	2,521	53.7	1,615	887
1880	1,783	221.9	1,764	19		1970	2,217	46.9	1,633	816
1870	1,457	181.3	1,443	14		1960	2,178	46.0	1,258	916
1860	1,231	153.1	1,221	10		1950 [1]	2,179	46.1	1,189	986
1850	995	123.7	985	9		1950 [2]	—	—	—	—
1840	738	91.7	729	9		1940	2,184	46.1	1,106	1,075
1830	610	75.9	603	7		1930	2,010	42.4	998	1,010
1820	523	65.1	516	7		1920	1,791	38.6	854	935
1810	472	58.7	465	7		1910	1,797	38.8	786	1,009
1800	423	52.6	417	6		1900	1,551	33.5	641	908
1790	379	47.1	373	5		1890	1,290	27.8	545	743
Michigan						1880	1,132	24.4	479	650
1990	9,295	163.6	7,756	1,292		1870	828	17.9	383	444
1980	9,262	163.0	7,872	1,199		1860	791	17.1	354	437
						1850	607	13.1	296	311
1970	8,875	156.2	7,833	991		1840	376	8.1	179	197
1960	7,823	137.7	7,086	718						
1950 [1]	6,372	111.7	5,918	442		1830	137	2.9	70	66
1950 [2]	—	—	—	—		1820	75	1.6	42	33
1940	5,256	92.2	5,040	208		1810 [3]	31	.4	23	17
						1800 [3]	8	.3	5	4
1930	4,842	84.9	4,664	169						
1920	3,668	63.8	3,602	60		**Missouri**				
1910	2,810	48.9	2,785	17		1990	5,117	74.3	4,486	548
1900	2,421	42.1	2,399	16		1980	4,917	71.4	4,346	514
1890	2,094	36.4	2,073	15						
						1970	4,677	67.8	4,177	480
1880	1,637	28.5	1,615	15		1960	4,320	62.6	3,923	391
1870	1,184	20.6	1,167	12		1950 [1]	3,955	57.1	3,656	297
1860	749	13.0	736	7		1950 [2]	—	—	—	—
1850	398	6.9	395	3		1940	3,785	54.6	3,539	244
1840	212	3.7	212	1						
						1930	3,629	52.4	3,404	224
1830	32	.2	31	(Z)		1920	3,404	49.5	3,225	178
1820	9	(6)	9	(Z)		1910	3,293	47.9	3,135	157
1810	5	.1	5	(Z)		1900	3,107	45.2	2,945	161
						1890	2,679	39.0	2,528	150
Minnesota						1880	2,168	31.6	2,023	145
1990	4,375	55.0	4,130	95		1870	1,721	25.0	1,603	118
1980	4,076	51.2	3,936	53		1860	1,182	17.2	1,063	119
						1850	682	9.9	592	90
1970	3,805	48.0	3,736	35		1840	384	5.6	324	60
1960	3,414	43.1	3,372	22						
1950 [1]	2,982	37.3	2,954	14		1830	140	2.1	115	26
1950 [2]	—	—	—	—		1820	67	1.0	56	11
1940	2,792	34.9	2,769	10		1810	20	(NA)	17	4
1930	2,564	32.0	2,543	9						
1920	2,387	29.5	2,369	9						
1910	2,076	25.7	2,059	7						

See footnotes at end of table.

Series A 195-209.   Population of States, by Race: 1790 to 1990—Cont'd.

(In thousands, except series A 196)

State and year	Resident population		Race		State and year	Resident population		Race	
	Total	Per square mile of land area	White	Black		Total	Per square mile of land area	White	Black
	195	196	199	200		195	196	199	200
Montana					1970	738	81.7	733	3
1990	799	5.5	741	2	1960	607	67.2	604	2
1980	787	5.4	740	2	1950 [1]	533	59.1	532	1
					1950 [2]	—	—	—	
1970	694	4.8	663	2	1940	492	54.5	491	(Z)
1960	675	4.6	651	1					
1950 [1]	591	4.1	572	1	1930	465	51.6	464	1
1950 [2]	—	—	—	—	1920	443	49.1	442	1
1940	559	3.8	540	1	1910	431	47.7	430	1
					1900	412	45.6	411	1
1930	538	3.7	520	1	1890	377	41.7	376	1
1920	549	3.8	534	2					
1910	376	2.6	361	2	1880	347	38.4	346	1
1900	243	1.7	226	2	1870	318	35.2	318	1
1890	143	1.0	128	1	1860	326	36.1	326	(Z)
					1850	318	35.2	317	1
1880	39	.3	35	(Z)	1840	285	31.5	284	1
1870	21	.1	18	(Z)					
					1830	269	29.8	269	1
Nebraska					1820	244	27.0	243	1
1990	1,578	20.5	1,487	57	1810	214	23.7	214	1
1980	1,570	20.4	1,490	48	1800	184	20.4	184	1
					1790	142	15.7	142	1
1970	1,483	19.4	1,433	40					
1960	1,411	18.4	1,375	29	**New Jersey**				
1950 [1]	1,326	17.3	1,301	19	1990	7,730	1,042.0	6,130	1,037
1950 [2]	—	—	—	—	1980	7,365	992.7	6,127	925
1940	1,316	17.2	1,298	14					
					1970	7,168	953.1	6,350	770
1930	1,378	18.0	1,360	14	1960	6,067	805.5	5,539	515
1920	1,296	16.9	1,279	13	1950 [1]	4,835	642.8	4,512	319
1910	1,192	15.5	1,180	8	1950 [2]	—	—	—	—
1900	1,066	13.9	1,057	6	1940	4,160	553.1	3,931	227
1890	1,063	13.8	1,047	9					
					1930	4,041	537.3	3,830	209
1880	452	5.9	450	2	1920	3,156	420.0	3,037	117
1870	123	1.6	122	1	1910	2,537	337.7	2,446	90
1860	29	.2	29	(Z)	1900	1,884	250.7	1,812	70
					1890	1,445	192.3	1,397	48
Nevada									
1990	1,202	10.9	1,013	79	1880	1,131	150.5	1,092	39
1980	800	7.3	700	51	1870	906	120.6	875	31
					1860	672	89.4	647	25
1970	489	4.4	448	28	1850	490	65.2	466	24
1960	285	2.6	263	13	1840	373	49.7	352	22
1950 [1]	160	1.5	150	4					
1950 [2]	—	—	—	—	1830	321	42.7	300	21
1940	110	1.0	104	1	1820	278	36.9	258	20
					1810	246	32.7	227	19
1930	91	.8	85	1	1800	211	28.1	194	17
1920	77	.7	71	(Z)	1790	184	24.5	170	14
1910	82	.7	74	1					
1900	42	.4	35	(Z)	**New Mexico**				
1890	47	.4	39	(Z)	1990	1,515	12.5	1,146	30
					1980	1,303	10.7	978	24
1880	62	.6	54	(Z)					
1870	42	.4	39	(Z)	1970	1,016	8.4	916	20
1860	7	.1	7	(Z)	1960	951	7.8	876	17
					1950 [1]	681	5.6	630	8
New Hampshire					1950 [2]	—	—	—	—
1990	1,109	123.7	1,087	7	1940	532	4.4	492	5
1980	921	102.6	910	4					

See footnotes at end of table.

Series A 195-209. Population of States, by Race: 1790 to 1990—Cont'd.

(In thousands, except series A 196)

State and year	Resident population Total	Per square mile of land area	White	Black	State and year	Resident population Total	Per square mile of land area	White	Black
	195	196	199	200		195	196	199	200
1930	423	3.5	391	3	1810	556	11.4	376	179
1920	360	2.9	335	6	1800	478	9.8	338	140
1910	327	2.7	305	2	1790	394	8.1	288	106
1900	195	1.6	180	2					
1890	160	1.3	143	2	**North Dakota**				
					1990	639	9.3	604	4
1880	120	1.0	109	1	1980	653	9.5	626	3
1870	92	.7	90	(Z)	1970	618	8.9	599	2
1860 [7]	94	.4	83	(Z)	1960	632	9.1	620	1
1850 [8]	62	.3	62	(Z)	1950	620	8.8	608	(Z)
New York					1940	642	9.2	631	(Z)
1990	17,990	381.0	13,385	2,859	1930	681	9.7	672	(Z)
1980	17,558	371.8	13,961	2,402	1920	647	9.2	640	(Z)
					1910	577	8.2	570	1
1970	18,237	381.3	15,834	2,169	1900	319	4.5	312	(Z)
1960	16,782	350.6	15,287	1,418					
1950 [1]	14,830	309.3	13,872	918	1890	191	2.7	182	(Z)
1950 [2]	—	—	—	—	1880 [10]	37	.9	133	(Z)
1940	13,479	281.2	12,880	571	1870 [10]	2	.1	13	(Z)
					1860 [10]	5	(6)	3	X
1930	12,588	262.6	12,153	413					
1920	10,385	217.9	10,172	198	**Ohio**				
1910	9,114	191.2	8,967	134	1990	10,847	264.9	9,522	1,155
1900	7,269	152.5	7,157	99	1980	10,798	263.7	9,597	1,077
1890	6,003	126.0	5,924	70					
					1970	10,652	260.0	9,647	970
1880	5,083	106.7	5,016	65	1960	9,706	236.6	8,910	786
1870	4,383	92.0	4,330	52	1950 [1]	7,947	193.8	7,428	513
1860	3,881	81.4	3,832	49	1950 [2]	—	—	—	—
1850	3,097	65.0	3,048	49	1940	6,908	168.0	6,567	339
1840	2,429	51.0	2,379	50					
					1930	6,647	161.6	6,335	309
1830 [9]	1,919	40.3	1,868	45	1920	5,759	141.4	5,572	186
1820	1,373	28.8	1,333	39	1910	4,767	117.0	4,655	111
1810	959	20.1	919	40	1900	4,158	102.1	4,060	97
1800	589	12.4	556	31	1890	3,672	90.1	3,585	87
1790	340	7.1	314	26					
					1880	3,198	78.5	3,118	80
North Carolina					1870	2,665	65.4	2,602	63
1990	6,629	136.1	5,008	1,456	1860	2,340	57.4	2,303	37
1980	5,882	120.7	4,458	1,319	1850	1,980	48.6	1,955	25
					1840	1,519	37.3	1,502	17
1970	5,082	104.1	3,902	1,126					
1960	4,556	93.2	3,399	1,116	1830	938	23.3	928	10
1950 [1]	4,062	82.7	2,983	1,047	1820	581	14.5	577	5
1950 [2]	—	—	—	—	1810	231	5.7	229	2
1940	3,572	72.7	2,568	981	1800	45	1.1	45	(Z)
1930	3,170	64.5	2,235	919	**Oklahoma**				
1920	2,559	52.5	1,784	763	1990	3,146	45.8	2,584	234
1910	2,206	45.3	1,501	698	1980	3,025	44.0	2,598	205
1900	1,894	38.9	1,264	624					
1890	1,618	33.2	1,055	561	1970	2,559	37.2	2,280	172
					1960	2,328	33.8	2,108	153
1880	1,400	28.7	867	531	1950 [1]	2,233	32.4	2,033	146
1870	1,071	22.0	678	392	1950 [2]	—	—	—	—
1860	993	20.4	630	362	1940	2,336	33.7	2,104	169
1850	869	17.8	553	316					
1840	753	15.5	485	269	1930	2,396	34.6	2,131	172
					1920	2,028	29.2	1,821	149
1830	738	15.1	473	265	1910	1,657	23.9	1,445	138
1820	639	13.1	419	220					

See footnotes at end of table.

Series A 195-209. Population of States, by Race: 1790 to 1990—Cont'd.

(In thousands, except series A 196)

State and year	Resident population		Race	
	Total	Per square mile of land area	White	Black
	195	196	199	200
1900	790	11.4	670	56
1890	259	3.7	173	22
Oregon				
1990	2,842	29.6	2,637	46
1980	2,633	27.4	2,491	37
1970	2,091	21.7	2,032	26
1960	1,769	18.4	1,732	18
1950[1]	1,521	15.8	1,497	12
1950[2]	—	—	—	—
1940	1,090	11.3	1,076	3
1930	954	9.9	939	2
1920	783	8.2	769	2
1910	673	7.0	655	1
1900	414	4.3	395	1
1890	318	3.3	302	1
1880	175	1.8	163	(Z)
1870	91	1.0	87	(Z)
1860	52	.5	52	(Z)
1850	12	(6)	13	(Z)
Pennsylvania				
1990	11,882	265.1	10,520	1,090
1980	11,864	264.7	10,652	1,047
1970	11,794	262.3	10,738	1,017
1960	11,319	251.4	10,454	853
1950[1]	10,498	233.1	9,854	638
1950[2]	—	—	—	—
1940	9,900	219.8	9,427	470
1930	9,631	213.8	9,196	431
1920	8,720	194.5	8,433	285
1910	7,665	171.0	7,468	194
1900	6,302	140.6	6,142	157
1890	5,258	117.3	5,148	108
1880	4,283	95.5	4,197	86
1870	3,522	78.6	3,457	65
1860	2,906	64.8	2,849	57
1850	2,312	51.6	2,258	54
1840	1,724	38.5	1,676	48
1830	1,348	30.1	1,310	38
1820	1,049	23.4	1,017	30
1810	810	18.1	787	23
1800	602	13.4	586	16
1790	434	9.7	424	10
Rhode Island				
1990	1,003	960.3	917	39
1980	947	906.4	897	28
1970	947	902.5	915	25
1960	859	819.3	839	18
1950[1]	792	748.5	777	14
1950[2]	—	—	—	—
1940	713	674.2	702	11

State and year	Resident population		Race	
	Total	Per square mile of land area	White	Black
	195	196	199	200
1930	687	649.8	677	10
1920	604	566.4	594	10
1910	543	508.5	532	10
1900	429	401.6	419	9
1890	346	323.8	338	7
1880	277	259.2	270	6
1870	217	203.7	212	5
1860	175	163.7	171	4
1850	148	138.3	144	4
1840	109	102.0	106	3
1830	97	91.1	94	4
1820	83	77.8	79	4
1810	77	72.1	73	4
1800	69	64.8	65	4
1790	69	64.5	65	4
South Carolina				
1990	3,487	115.8	2,407	1,040
1980	3,122	103.7	2,147	949
1970	2,591	85.7	1,794	789
1960	2,383	78.7	1,551	829
1950[1]	2,117	69.9	1,293	822
1950[2]	—	—	—	—
1940	1,900	62.1	1,084	814
1930	1,739	56.8	944	794
1920	1,684	55.2	819	865
1910	1,515	49.7	679	836
1900	1,340	44.0	558	782
1890	1,151	37.7	462	689
1880	996	32.6	391	604
1870	706	23.1	290	416
1860	704	23.1	291	412
1850	669	21.9	275	394
1840	594	19.5	259	335
1830	581	19.1	258	323
1820	503	16.5	237	265
1810	415	13.6	214	201
1800	346	11.3	196	149
1790	249	8.2	140	109
South Dakota				
1990	696	9.2	638	3
1980	691	9.1	640	2
1970	666	8.8	630	2
1960	681	9.0	653	1
1950[1]	653	8.5	629	1
1950[2]	—	—	—	—
1940	643	8.4	619	(Z)
1930	693	9.1	670	1
1920	637	8.3	619	1
1910	584	7.6	564	1
1900	402	5.2	381	(Z)
1890	349	4.5	328	1

See footnotes at end of table.

Series A 195-209. Population of States, by Race: 1790 to 1990—Cont'd.

(In thousands, except series A 196)

State and year	Resident population Total	Per square mile of land area	White	Black
	195	196	199	200
1880 [10]	98	—	97	(Z)
1870 [10]	12	—	11	(Z)
1860 [10]	—	—	—	—
Tennessee				
1990	4,877	118.3	4,048	778
1980	4,591	111.4	3,835	726
1970	3,924	94.9	3,294	621
1960	3,567	86.2	2,978	587
1950 [1]	3,292	78.8	2,760	531
1950 [2]	—	—	—	—
1940	2,916	69.5	2,407	509
1930	2,617	62.4	2,139	478
1920	2,338	56.1	1,886	452
1910	2,185	52.4	1,711	473
1900	2,021	48.5	1,540	480
1890	1,768	42.4	1,337	431
1880	1,542	37.0	1,139	403
1870	1,259	30.2	936	322
1860	1,110	26.6	827	283
1850	1,003	24.1	757	246
1840	829	19.9	641	189
1830	682	16.4	536	146
1820	423	10.1	340	83
1810	262	6.3	216	46
1800	106	2.5	92	14
1790	36	.8	32	4
Texas				
1990	16,987	64.9	12,775	2,022
1980	14,229	54.3	11,198	1,710
1970	11,197	42.7	9,717	1,399
1960	9,580	36.4	8,375	1,187
1950 [1]	7,711	29.3	6,727	977
1950 [2]	—	—	—	—
1940	6,415	24.3	5,488	924
1930	5,825	22.1	4,967	855
1920	4,663	17.8	3,918	742
1910	3,897	14.8	3,205	690
1900	3,049	11.6	2,427	621
1890	2,236	8.5	1,746	488
1880	1,592	6.1	1,197	393
1870	819	3.1	565	253
1860	604	2.3	421	183
1850	213	.8	154	59
Utah				
1990	1,723	21.0	1,616	12
1980	1,461	17.8	1,383	9
1970	1,059	12.9	1,032	7
1960	891	10.8	874	4
1950 [1]	689	8.4	677	3
1950 [2]	—	—	—	—
1940	550	6.7	543	1

State and year	Resident population Total	Per square mile of land area	White	Black
	195	196	199	200
1930	508	6.2	500	1
1920	449	5.5	442	1
1910	373	4.5	367	1
1900	277	3.4	272	1
1890	211	2.6	206	1
1880	144	1.8	142	(Z)
1870	87	1.1	86	(Z)
1860	40	.3	40	(Z)
1850	11	(6)	11	(Z)
Vermont				
1990	563	60.8	555	2
1980	511	55.3	507	1
1970	444	47.9	443	1
1960	390	42.0	389	1
1950	378	40.7	377	(Z)
1940	359	38.7	359	(Z)
1930	360	38.8	359	1
1920	352	38.6	352	1
1910	356	39.0	354	2
1900	344	37.7	343	1
1890	332	36.4	331	1
1880	332	36.4	331	1
1870	331	36.2	330	1
1860	315	34.5	314	1
1850	314	34.4	313	1
1840	292	32.0	291	1
1830	281	30.8	280	1
1820	236	25.9	235	1
1810	218	23.9	217	1
1800	154	16.9	154	1
1790	85	9.4	85	(Z)
Virginia				
1990	6,187	156.3	4,792	1,163
1980	5,347	135.0	4,230	1,009
1970	4,648	116.9	3,762	861
1960	3,967	99.6	3,142	816
1950 [1]	3,319	83.2	2,582	734
1950 [2]	—	—	—	—
1940	2,678	67.1	2,016	661
1930	2,422	60.7	1,770	650
1920	2,309	57.4	1,618	690
1910	2,062	51.2	1,390	671
1900	1,854	46.1	1,193	661
1890	1,656	41.1	1,020	635
1880	1,513	37.6	881	632
1870	1,225	30.4	712	513
1860 [12]	1,220	24.8	1,047	549
1850 [12]	1,119	22.1	895	527
1840 [12]	1,025	19.3	748	502
1830 [12]	1,044	18.9	701	520
1820 [12]	938	16.6	610	465

See footnotes at end of table.

Series A 195-209. Population of States, by Race: 1790 to 1990—Cont'd.

(In thousands, except series A 196)

State and year	Resident population — Total (195)	Per square mile of land area (196)	Race — White (199)	Race — Black (200)
1810 [12]	878	15.2	557	426
1800 [12]	808	13.7	518	367
1790 [12]	692	11.6	442	306
Washington				
1990	4,867	73.1	4,309	150
1980	4,132	62.1	3,779	106
1970	3,409	51.2	3,251	71
1960	2,853	42.8	2,752	49
1950 [1]	2,379	35.6	2,316	31
1950 [2]	—	—	—	—
1940	1,736	25.9	1,698	7
1930	1,563	23.3	1,522	7
1920	1,357	20.3	1,320	7
1910	1,142	17.1	1,109	6
1900	518	7.8	496	3
1890	357	5.3	341	2
1880	75	1.1	67	(Z)
1870	24	.4	22	(Z)
1860 [13]	12	.1	11	(Z)
1850 [11]	1	—	—	—
West Virginia				
1990	1,793	74.5	1,726	56
1980	1,950	80.9	1,875	65
1970	1,744	72.5	1,673	67
1960	1,860	77.2	1,770	89
1950 [1]	2,006	83.3	1,890	115
1950 [2]	—	—	—	—
1940	1,902	79.0	1,784	118
1930	1,729	71.8	1,614	115
1920	1,464	60.9	1,377	86
1910	1,221	50.8	1,157	64
1900	959	39.9	915	43
1890	763	31.8	730	33
1880	618	25.7	593	26
1870	442	18.4	424	18
1860 [12]	377	—	—	—
1850 [12]	302	—	—	—
1840 [12]	225	—	—	—

State and year	Resident population — Total (195)	Per square mile of land area (196)	Race — White (199)	Race — Black (200)
1830 [12]	177	—	—	—
1820 [12]	137	—	—	—
1810 [12]	105	—	—	—
1800 [12]	79	—	—	—
1790 [12]	56	—	—	—
Wisconsin				
1990	4,892	90.1	4,513	245
1980	4,706	86.6	4,443	183
1970	4,418	81.1	4,259	128
1960	3,952	72.6	3,859	75
1950 [1]	3,435	62.8	3,393	28
1950 [2]	—	—	—	—
1940	3,138	57.3	3,113	12
1930	2,939	53.7	2,916	11
1920	2,632	47.6	2,617	5
1910	2,334	42.2	2,321	3
1900	2,069	37.4	2,058	3
1890	1,693	30.6	1,681	2
1880	1,315	23.8	1,310	3
1870	1,055	19.1	1,051	2
1860	776	14.0	774	1
1850	305	5.5	305	1
1840	31	.4	31	(Z)
Wyoming				
1990	454	4.7	427	4
1980	470	4.8	446	3
1970	332	3.4	323	3
1960	330	3.4	323	2
1950	291	3.0	284	3
1940	251	2.6	247	1
1930	226	2.3	221	1
1920	194	2.0	190	1
1910	146	1.5	140	2
1900	93	.9	89	1
1890	63	.6	59	1
1880	21	.2	19	(Z)
1870	9	.1	9	(Z)

X Represents zero.

Z Less than 500

[1] Urban definition comparable with later data.

[2] Urban definition comparable with earlier data.

[3] Population of those parts of Mississippi Territory now in present State. Population per square mile, sex, race and age detail for Alabama included with Mississippi.

[4] Census taken October 1, 1939.

[5] Census taken October 1, 1929.

[6] Less than 1/10 of a person.

[7] Includes population of area taken to form part of Arizona Territory in 1863.

[8] Data for Territory of New Mexico which included parts of present States of Arizona and New Mexico, and smaller parts of Colorado and Nevada.

[9] Includes 5,602 persons for whom sex, race and age detail are not available.

[10] North and South Dakota comprised Dakota Territory. Population per square mile, sex and age detail for South Dakota included with North Dakota.

[11] Population total of those parts of Oregon Territory taken to form part of Washington Territory in 1853 and 1859 excluded from Oregon included under Washington. Population per square mile, sex and age detail for Washington included with Oregon.

[12] Sex, race and age detail for West Virginia, 1790-1860, included with Virginia.

[13] Includes population of Idaho and parts of Montana and Wyoming.

Series A 210-262. Land Area of the United States, by States and Territories: 1790 to 1990

(In square miles)

Series No.	State or territory	Year of admission to statehood	1990	1980	1970	1960	1950	1940	1930	1920	1910	1900	1890
210	United States	(X)	3,536,342	3,539,289	3,536,855	3,540,911	2,974,726	2,977,128	2,973,776	2,973,774	2,973,890	2,974,159	2,973,965
211	Alabama	1819	50,750	50,767	50,078	50,851	51,078	51,078	51,279	51,279	51,279	51,279	51,279
212	Alaska	1959	570,374	570,833	566,432	566,432	(X)	(X)	(X)	(X)	(X)	(X)	(X)
213	Arizona	1912	113,642	113,508	113,417	113,563	113,575	113,580	113,810	113,810	113,810	113,840	113,840
214	Arkansas	1836	52,075	52,078	51,945	52,175	52,675	52,725	52,525	52,525	52,525	52,525	52,525
215	California	1850	155,973	156,299	156,361	156,537	156,740	156,803	155,652	155,652	155,652	156,092	155,900
216	Colorado	1876	103,730	103,595	103,766	103,794	103,922	103,967	103,658	103,658	103,658	103,658	103,658
217	Connecticut	[1] 1788	4,845	4,872	4,862	4,870	4,899	4,899	4,820	4,820	4,820	4,820	4,820
218	Delaware	[1] 1787	1,955	1,932	1,982	1,982	1,978	1,978	1,965	1,965	1,965	1,965	1,965
219	District of Columbia	(X)	61	63	61	61	61	61	62	60	60	60	58
220	Florida	1845	53,997	54,153	54,090	54,136	54,262	54,262	54,861	54,861	54,861	54,861	54,861
221	Georgia	[1] 1788	57,919	58,056	58,073	58,197	58,483	58,518	58,725	58,725	58,725	58,725	58,725
222	Hawaii	1959	6,423	6,425	6,425	6,425	(X)	(X)	(X)	(X)	(X)	(X)	(X)
223	Idaho	1890	82,751	82,412	82,677	82,677	82,769	82,808	83,354	83,354	83,354	83,354	83,354
224	Illinois	1818	55,593	55,645	55,748	55,875	55,935	55,947	56,043	56,043	56,043	56,002	56,002
225	Indiana	1816	35,870	35,932	36,097	36,189	36,205	36,205	36,045	36,045	36,045	35,885	35,885
226	Iowa	1846	55,875	55,965	55,941	56,043	56,045	55,986	55,586	55,586	55,586	55,586	55,586
227	Kansas	1861	81,823	81,778	81,787	82,056	82,108	82,113	81,774	81,774	81,774	81,774	81,774
228	Kentucky	1792	39,732	39,669	39,650	39,851	39,864	40,109	40,181	40,181	40,181	40,181	40,181
229	Louisiana	1812	43,566	44,521	44,930	45,131	45,162	45,177	45,409	45,409	45,409	45,409	45,409
230	Maine	1820	30,865	30,995	30,920	30,933	31,040	31,040	29,895	29,895	29,895	29,895	29,895
231	Maryland	[1] 1788	9,775	9,837	9,891	9,891	9,881	9,887	9,941	9,941	9,941	9,941	9,941
232	Massachusetts	[1] 1788	7,838	7,824	7,826	7,833	7,867	7,907	8,039	8,039	8,039	8,039	8,039
233	Michigan	1837	56,809	56,954	56,817	56,817	57,022	57,022	57,480	57,480	57,480	57,480	57,480
234	Minnesota	1858	79,617	79,548	79,289	79,289	80,009	80,009	80,858	80,858	80,858	80,858	80,858
235	Mississippi	1817	46,914	47,233	47,296	47,358	47,248	47,420	46,362	46,362	46,362	46,362	46,362
236	Missouri	1821	68,898	68,945	68,995	69,046	69,226	69,270	68,727	68,727	68,727	68,727	68,727
237	Montana	1889	145,556	145,388	145,587	145,603	145,878	146,316	146,131	146,131	146,201	146,201	146,201
238	Nebraska	1867	76,878	76,644	76,483	76,522	76,663	76,653	76,808	76,808	76,808	76,808	76,808
239	Nevada	1864	109,806	109,894	109,889	109,889	109,789	109,802	109,802	109,821	109,821	109,821	109,821
240	New Hampshire	[1] 1788	8,969	8,993	9,027	9,033	9,017	9,024	9,031	9,031	9,031	9,031	9,031
241	New Jersey	[1] 1787	7,419	7,468	7,521	7,532	7,522	7,522	7,514	7,514	7,514	7,514	7,514
242	New Mexico	1912	121,365	121,335	121,412	121,445	121,511	121,511	122,503	122,503	122,503	122,503	122,503
243	New York	[1] 1788	47,224	47,377	47,831	47,869	47,944	47,929	47,654	47,654	47,654	47,654	47,654
244	North Carolina	[1] 1789	48,718	48,843	48,798	48,880	49,097	49,142	48,740	48,740	48,740	48,740	48,740
245	North Dakota	1889	68,994	69,300	69,273	69,280	70,057	70,054	70,183	70,183	70,183	70,183	70,183
246	Ohio	1803	40,953	41,004	40,975	41,048	41,000	41,122	40,740	40,740	40,740	40,740	40,740
247	Oklahoma	1907	68,679	68,655	68,782	68,983	69,031	69,283	69,414	69,414	69,414	38,624	38,624
248	Oregon	1859	96,003	96,184	96,184	96,209	96,315	96,350	95,607	95,607	95,607	95,607	95,607
249	Pennsylvania	[1] 1787	44,820	44,888	44,966	45,025	45,045	45,045	44,832	44,832	44,832	44,832	44,832
250	Rhode Island	[1] 1790	1,045	1,055	1,049	1,049	1,058	1,058	1,067	1,067	1,067	1,067	1,067
251	South Carolina	[1] 1788	30,111	30,203	30,225	30,280	30,305	30,594	30,495	30,495	30,495	30,495	30,495
252	South Dakota	1889	75,898	75,952	75,955	75,956	76,536	76,536	76,868	76,868	76,868	76,868	70,868
253	Tennessee	1796	41,220	41,155	41,328	41,366	41,797	41,961	41,687	41,687	41,687	41,687	41,687
254	Texas	1845	261,914	262,017	262,134	262,970	263,513	263,644	262,398	262,398	262,398	262,398	262,398
255	Utah	1896	82,168	82,073	82,096	82,381	82,346	82,346	82,184	82,184	82,184	82,184	82,184
256	Vermont	1791	9,249	9,273	9,267	9,274	9,278	9,278	9,124	9,124	9,124	9,124	9,124
257	Virginia	[1] 1788	39,598	39,704	39,780	39,841	39,893	39,899	40,262	40,262	40,262	40,262	40,292
258	Washington	1889	66,582	66,511	66,570	66,663	66,786	66,977	66,836	66,836	66,836	66,836	66,836
259	West Virginia	1863	24,087	24,119	24,070	24,084	24,080	24,090	24,022	24,022	24,022	24,022	25,022
260	Wisconsin	1848	54,314	54,426	54,464	54,466	54,705	54,715	55,256	55,256	55,256	55,256	55,256
261	Wyoming	1890	97,105	96,989	97,203	97,281	97,506	97,506	97,548	97,548	97,594	97,594	97,594
262	Indian Territory and unorganized territory	(X)	(X)	(X)	(X)	(X)	(X)	(X)	(X)	(X)	(X)	30,790	30,790

See footnotes at end of table.

Series A 210-262. Land Area of the United States, by States and Territories: 1790 to 1990—Cont'd.

(In square miles)

Series No.	State or territory	1880	1870	1860	1850	1840	1830	1820	1810	1800	1790
210	United States	2,973,965	2,973,965	2,973,965	2,944,337	1,753,588	1,753,588	1,753,588	1,685,865	867,980	867,980
211	Alabama	51,279	51,279	51,279	51,279	51,279	51,279	51,279	(X)	(X)	(X)
212	Alaska	(X)	(X)	(X)	(X)	(X)	(X)	(X)	(X)	(X)	(X)
213	Arizona	113,840	113,840	(X)	(X)	(X)	(X)	(X)	(X)	(X)	(X)
214	Arkansas	52,525	52,525	52,525	52,525	52,525	52,525	105,275	(X)	(X)	(X)
215	California	155,900	155,900	155,900	155,900	(X)	(X)	(X)	(X)	(X)	(X)
216	Colorado	103,658	103,658	103,658	(X)	(X)	(X)	(X)	(X)	(X)	(X)
217	Connecticut	4,820	4,820	4,820	4,820	4,820	4,820	4,820	4,820	4,820	4,820
218	Delaware	1,965	1,965	1,965	1,965	1,965	1,965	1,965	1,965	1,965	1,965
219	District of Columbia	58	58	58	58	90	90	90	90	90	(X)
220	Florida	54,861	54,861	54,861	54,861	54,861	54,861	54,861	(X)	(X)	(X)
221	Georgia	58,725	58,725	58,725	58,725	58,725	58,725	58,725	58,725	111,877	145,196
222	Hawaii	(X)	(X)	(X)	(X)	(X)	(X)	(X)	(X)	(X)	(X)
223	Idaho	83,354	83,360	(X)	(X)	(X)	(X)	(X)	(X)	(X)	(X)
224	Illinois	56,002	56,002	56,002	56,002	56,002	56,002	56,002	192,381	(X)	(X)
225	Indiana	35,885	35,885	35,885	35,885	35,885	35,885	35,885	42,933	252,084	(X)
226	Iowa	55,586	55,586	55,586	55,586	191,656	(X)	(X)	(X)	(X)	(X)
227	Kansas	81,774	81,774	81,774	(X)	(X)	(X)	(X)	(X)	(X)	(X)
228	Kentucky	40,181	40,181	40,181	40,181	40,181	40,181	40,181	40,181	40,181	40,181
229	Louisiana	45,409	45,409	45,409	45,409	45,409	45,409	45,409	34,065	(X)	(X)
230	Maine	29,895	29,895	29,895	29,895	29,895	29,895	29,895	29,895	29,895	29,895
231	Maryland	9,941	9,941	9,941	9,941	9,941	9,941	9,941	9,941	9,941	9,999
232	Massachusetts	8,039	8,039	8,039	8,041	8,041	8,041	8,041	8,041	8,041	8,041
233	Michigan	57,480	57,480	57,480	57,480	57,480	186,052	186,052	42,625	(X)	(X)
234	Minnesota	80,858	80,858	80,858	163,457	(X)	(X)	(X)	(X)	(X)	(X)
235	Mississippi	46,362	46,362	46,362	46,362	46,362	46,362	46,362	97,641	33,319	(X)
236	Missouri	68,727	68,727	68,727	68,727	68,727	65,618	65,618	(X)	(X)	(X)
237	Montana	146,201	146,195	(X)	(X)	(X)	(X)	(X)	(X)	(X)	(X)
238	Nebraska	76,172	76,172	118,915	(X)	(X)	(X)	(X)	(X)	(X)	(X)
239	Nevada	109,821	109,821	61,260	(X)	(X)	(X)	(X)	(X)	(X)	(X)
240	New Hampshire	9,031	9,031	9,031	9,031	9,031	9,031	9,031	9,031	9,031	9,031
241	New Jersey	7,514	7,514	7,514	7,514	7,514	7,514	7,514	7,514	7,514	7,514
242	New Mexico	122,503	122,503	247,782	236,548	(X)	(X)	(X)	(X)	(X)	(X)
243	New York	47,654	47,654	47,654	47,652	47,652	47,652	47,652	47,652	47,652	47,652
244	North Carolina	48,740	48,740	48,740	48,740	48,740	48,740	48,740	48,740	48,740	48,740
245	North Dakota	(X)	(X)	(X)	(X)	(X)	(X)	(X)	(X)	(X)	(X)
246	Ohio	40,740	40,740	40,740	40,740	40,740	40,228	40,228	40,228	40,228	(X)
247	Oklahoma	(X)	(X)	(X)	(X)	(X)	(X)	(X)	(X)	(X)	(X)
248	Oregon	95,607	95,607	95,607	282,257	(X)	(X)	(X)	(X)	(X)	(X)
249	Pennsylvania	44,832	44,832	44,832	44,832	44,832	44,832	44,832	44,832	44,832	44,832
250	Rhode Island	1,067	1,067	1,067	1,067	1,067	1,067	1,067	1,067	1,067	1,067
251	South Carolina	30,495	30,495	30,495	30,495	30,495	30,495	30,495	30,495	30,495	30,495
252	South Dakota	(X)	(X)	(X)	(X)	(X)	(X)	(X)	(X)	(X)	(X)
253	Tennessee	41,687	41,687	41,687	41,687	41,687	41,687	41,687	41,687	41,687	46,977
254	Texas	262,398	262,398	262,398	262,398	(X)	(X)	(X)	(X)	(X)	(X)
255	Utah	82,184	82,184	122,887	230,610	(X)	(X)	(X)	(X)	(X)	(X)
256	Vermont	9,124	9,124	9,124	9,124	9,124	9,124	9,124	9,124	9,124	9,124
257	Virginia	40,262	40,262	64,284	64,284	64,252	64,252	64,252	64,252	64,252	64,284
258	Washington	66,836	66,836	183,254	(X)	(X)	(X)	(X)	(X)	(X)	(X)
259	West Virginia	24,022	24,002	(X)	(X)	(X)	(X)	(X)	(X)	(X)	(X)
260	Wisconsin	55,256	55,256	55,256	55,256	82,643	(X)	(X)	(X)	(X)	(X)
261	Wyoming	97,594	97,594	(X)	(X)	(X)	(X)	(X)	(X)	(X)	(X)
262	Indian Territory and unorganized territory	69,414	69,414	69,414	535,003	511,967	52,750	(X)	(X)	(X)	(X)

X Not applicable

[1] Year of ratification of Constitution; one of the original 13 States.

Series A 335-349. Households, by Number of Persons: 1790 to 1991

(Number in thousands. As of March, except as noted)

Year	Number of households	Size of household							Percent distribution of number of households						
		1 person	2 persons	3 persons	4 persons	5 persons	6 persons	7 or more persons	1 person	2 persons	3 persons	4 persons	5 persons	6 persons	7 or more persons
	335	336	337	338	339	340	341	342	343	344	345	346	347	348	349
1991	94,300	23,600	30,200	16,100	14,600	6,200	2,200	1,500	25.0	32.0	17.0	15.0	7.0	2.0	2.0
1990	93,300	23,000	30,100	16,100	14,500	6,200	2,100	1,300	24.5	32.3	17.5	15.7	6.7	2.2	1.2
1985	86,800	20,600	27,400	15,500	13,600	6,100	2,300	1,300	23.7	31.6	17.8	15.7	7.0	2.6	1.5
1980	80,800	18,300	25,300	14,100	12,700	6,100	2,500	1,800	22.5	31.3	17.5	15.8	7.6	3.2	2.2
1975	71,100	13,900	21,800	12,400	11,100	6,400	3,100	2,500	19.6	30.6	17.4	15.6	9.0	4.3	3.5
1970	62,874	10,692	18,129	10,903	9,935	6,532	3,505	3,178	17.0	28.8	17.3	15.8	10.4	5.6	5.1
1969	61,806	10,333	17,916	10,698	9,714	6,345	3,534	3,266	16.7	29.0	17.3	15.7	10.3	5.7	5.3
1968	60,446	9,743	17,272	10,513	9,565	6,281	3,605	3,467	16.1	28.6	17.4	15.8	10.4	6.0	5.7
1967	58,845	9,139	16,659	10,334	9,496	6,235	3,468	3,527	15.5	28.3	17.6	16.1	10.6	5.9	6.0
1966	58,092	9,044	16,589	9,939	9,414	6,223	3,446	3,446	15.6	28.6	17.1	16.2	10.7	5.9	5.9
1965	57,251	8,603	16,067	10,230	9,239	6,293	3,316	3,503	15.0	28.1	17.9	16.1	11.0	5.8	6.1
1964	55,996	7,800	15,579	10,007	9,539	6,311	3,364	3,396	13.9	27.8	17.9	17.0	11.3	6.0	6.1
1963	55,189	7,490	15,257	9,974	9,431	6,231	3,468	3,337	13.6	27.6	18.1	17.1	11.3	6.3	6.0
1962	54,652	7,458	15,429	10,056	9,328	6,004	3,361	3,016	13.6	28.2	18.4	17.1	11.0	6.1	5.5
1961	53,291	7,077	15,110	9,731	9,343	6,022	3,070	2,938	13.3	28.4	18.3	17.5	11.3	5.8	5.5
1960*	52,610	6,871	14,616	9,941	9,277	6,064	2,976	2,865	13.1	27.8	18.9	17.6	11.5	5.7	5.4
1959	51,302	6,317	14,538	9,788	9,123	5,793	2,948	2,795	12.3	28.4	19.1	17.8	11.3	5.7	5.4
1958	50,402	6,078	14,303	9,715	8,933	5,609	3,002	2,762	12.1	28.4	19.3	17.7	11.1	6.0	5.5
1957	49,543	5,451	14,274	9,743	9,096	5,487	2,848	2,644	11.0	28.8	19.7	18.4	11.1	5.7	5.3
1956	48,785	5,396	13,827	9,936	9,152	5,287	2,624	2,563	11.1	28.3	20.4	18.8	10.8	5.4	5.3
1955	47,788	5,212	13,612	9,725	9,052	5,291	2,568	2,328	10.9	28.5	20.4	18.9	11.1	5.4	4.9
1954	46,893	5,032	13,249	9,776	8,820	5,170	2,521	2,325	10.7	28.3	20.8	18.8	11.0	5.4	5.0
1953 [1]	46,828	6,148	13,530	9,868	8,300	4,658	2,332	1,992	13.1	28.9	21.1	17.7	9.9	5.0	4.3
1952 [2]	45,464	5,388	13,460	9,908	8,106	4,378	2,142	2,082	11.9	29.6	21.8	17.8	9.6	4.7	4.6
1951 [2]	44,564	(NA)	(NA)	(NA)	(NA)	(NA)	(NA)	(NA)	(NA)	(NA)	(NA)	(NA)	(NA)	(NA)	(NA)
1950 [1]	43,468	4,737	12,529	9,808	7,729	4,357	2,196	2,113	10.9	28.8	22.6	17.8	10.0	5.1	4.9
1940 [2]	34,949	2,481	8,667	7,829	6,326	4,019	2,377	3,250	7.1	24.8	22.4	18.1	11.5	6.8	9.3
1930 [2]	29,905	2,357	6,983	6,227	5,235	3,574	2,273	3,255	7.9	23.4	20.8	17.5	12.0	7.6	10.9
1900	15,964	814	2,395	2,810	2,698	2,267	1,740	3,257	5.1	15.0	17.6	16.9	14.2	10.9	20.4
1890 [3]	12,690	457	1,675	2,119	2,132	1,916	1,472	2,919	3.6	13.2	16.7	16.8	15.1	11.6	23.0
1790	558	21	44	65	77	78	74	200	3.7	7.8	11.7	13.8	13.9	13.2	35.8

* Denotes first year for which figures incude Alaska and Hawaii.
NA Not available.
[1] Covers related persons only; therefore, not strictly comparable with other years.
[2] As of April.
[3] As of June; includes a small number of quasi-households.

SECTION B

VITAL STATISTICS AND HEALTH

SECTION B

VITAL STATISTICS AND HEALTH

Highlights

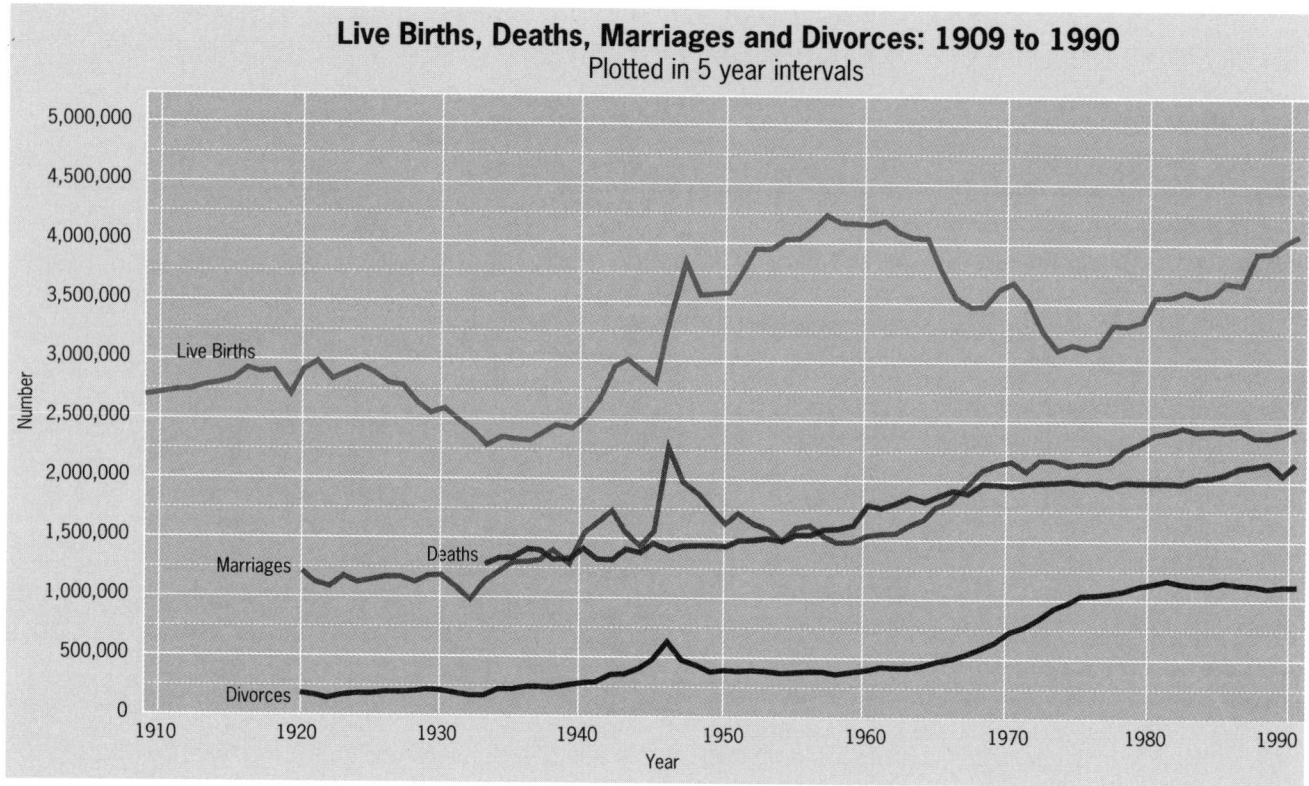

Live Births, Deaths, Marriages and Divorces: 1909 to 1990
Plotted in 5 year intervals

1 Vital statistics—births, deaths, marriages and divorces—are compiled by the National Center for Health Statistics, successor to the Office of Vital Statistics. From 1900 to 1946, the collection of these data was the responsibility of the Census Bureau.

2 Vital statistics are compiled on the basis of records received from the registration offices of all states, certain cities, and the District of Columbia. Reporting of these events is mandatory in many localities. The annual *Vital Statistics of the United States* summarizes these data, presenting final figures and an annual life table. The life table (also known as a mortality table) is an actuarial table, and contains data on life expectancy and deaths.

3 The annual collection of mortality statistics began in 1900 and the collection of birth statistics in 1915. Since 1933, the entire United States has been included in birth-

and death-registration areas. Alaska was added in 1959 and Hawaii in 1960. National statistics on fetal deaths have been compiled since 1922.

4 Birth statistics are based either on complete counts for states participating in the Vital Statistics Cooperative Program or on 50% samples. Mortality statistics are compiled in accordance with World Health Organization (WHO) regulations based on the *International Statistical Classification of Diseases, Injuries and Causes of Death.* The degree of accuracy of birth data is believed to be over 99.1%. While death data may be nearly as complete as birth data, underreporting may be a problem in isolated places. The reporting of fetal deaths is likely to be even less complete.

5 Since 1944, marriage and divorce statistics have been available on the uniform basis (i.e., the data are tabulated under standardized headings for all units). A census block for the collection of data on marriage-registration was established in 1957, and for divorce-registration in 1958.

6 Data on illegitimate births are based on estimates. In the 1930s, all states had a query concerning legitimacy or illegitimacy on their birth certificates. This query was removed during the 1940s on grounds of confidentiality. As a result, the data suffer from potential misreporting. The term illegitimate was discarded and replaced by Births to Unmarried Women in the 1990 Census.

7 In 1990, the leading causes of death in the United States were heart disease (725,000), cancer (506,000), stroke (145,340), accidents (93,550), and chronic lung disease (88,989).

8 The difference between the birth rates per 1,000 of White and Black women declined from 31.3 in 1970 (84.1 for Whites and 115.4 for Blacks) to 25.7 in 1989 (64.7 for Whites and 90.4 for Blacks).

9 In 1990, the national birth rate per 1000 of 16.7 was exceeded in three regions: Pacific (19.7), Mountain (17.7), and West-South Central (17.8). Six regions had below average birth rates: South Atlantic (16.1), New England (15.5), Middle Atlantic (15.7), East North Central (15.8), West North Central (15.3), and East-South Central (15.8). In 1970, only three regions had below average birth rates per 1000: New England, Middle Atlantic, and West North Central. The states with the highest birth rates in 1990 were Alaska (21.8), Utah (21.6), and California (20.7), and those with the lowest birth rates were West Virginia (12.6), New Hampshire (13.1), and Iowa and Wyoming (13.9).

10 The total fertility rate declined from an average of 3,449 (3,326 for Whites and 4,326 for Blacks) in 1960-64 to 2,014 (1,885 for Whites and 2,583 for Blacks) in 1989. The total rate bottomed out in 1976 at 1,738 but has since rebounded. The intrinsic rate of natural increase has always been negative for Whites since 1972, and positive for Blacks, with a high of 14.4 in 1970.

11 The number of Caesarean deliveries rose continuously from 195,000 in 1970 to 938,000 in 1989. These deliveries are most common among women 35 years of age and older and are less prevalent among younger women.

12 The percentage of children born with low birth weight, defined as anything below 5 lbs. 8 oz., increased from 6.8% in 1980 to 7.0% in 1990. By racial origin, Blacks and Puerto Ricans have the greatest percentage of such births with 13.2% and 9.5% respectively while Whites have children with an average birthweight of 7lbs. 8 oz.

13 The percentage of births to teenage mothers rose from 12.7% in 1985 to 12.8% in 1989. Blacks, American Indians, and Hispanics have above average percentages of teenage pregnancies: The rate was 23.1% for Blacks, 18.8% for American Indians, 21.9% for Puerto Ricans, and 17.4% for Mexicans. Asians generally have very low rates: 1.2% for Chinese and 2.9% for Japanese. The rates of teenage pregnancies dropped in all regions between 1980 and 1990. Among states, New Hampshire has the lowest rate (7.5%) and Mississippi the highest (20.7%).

14 In 1990, among women of all races who have ever married, 19% were childless. The percentage was slightly higher for White women (20%) and lower for Black women (13%).

15 In 1988, 57.9 million women used contraceptives. Of these, 36.7% used nonsurgical contraceptives, such as the pill, IUD, condom, and other methods.

16 The number of abortions in the United States rose from 586,800 in 1972 (around the time of Roe v Wade) to 1,590,800 in 1988. During the same period, the rate for 1,000 women increased from 13.2 to 27.3 and the ratio per 1,000 live births from 184 to 401. The relative figures were 21.2 and 333 for White women and 57.3 and 638 for Black women. Of the total abortions in 1988, 14,000 were performed on girls under 15 years of age, and 393,000 on girls between 15 and 19; 83% of the abortions were performed on unmarried women and 11% after the lapse of the legally permitted trimester. The states with the highest abortion rates per 1,000 women were California (45.9) and New York (43.3), and the lowest, Wyoming (5.1), South Dakota (5.7), West Virginia (7.5), and Idaho (8.2).

17 Although Americans can expect to live 28.1 years longer than their foreparents in 1900, the United States at 75.4 years still trails a number of countries in life expectancy. Japan (79 years), Sweden and Switzerland (78 years), and Norway, Canada, France, the Netherlands, Australia, Italy, and Greece (77 years) are all ahead of the United States in this key indicator of the quality of life.

18 In the United States, 250 Americans die every hour. This averages to four Americans every minute. The death rate in 1990 was fairly uniform in all regions and states and was lowest in Hawaii (5.8 per 1,000) and Florida (10.5 per 1000).

19 Major cardiovascular diseases and malignancies (cancers) are the leading killers in the United States. On the basis of crude death rate per 100,000, the former leads with 295.6 and the latter follows with 183.0. The other leading causes of death (with the relative rates in parens) are: stroke (69.3), pneumonia (32.1), chronic obstructive pulmonary disease (28.4), accidents (24.5), diabetes (21.3), chronic liver disease (7.4), suicide (4.8), and homicide and legal intervention (4.1). Accidents are the leading cause of death for two age groups (1-14, 15-24), cancer for people 45-64 years old, and heart disease for those over 65.

20 AIDS was first included as a cause of death in 1982. Since then, the number of deaths from AIDS grew from 3,266 in 1984 to 19,718 in 1991. The total number of deaths from AIDS was estimated at 126,827, 68% of those between 30 to 49 years of age. Males made up 90% of the victims, Whites 56%, Blacks 30%, and Hispanics 13%. The total number of reported AIDS cases from 1981 to 1989 was 199,516. New York accounted for 45.1% and California for 20.2%, males for 92.6%, Whites for 56.4%, and Blacks for 28.3%.

21 The number of deaths from accidents has declined steadily since 1970. In 1989, there were 95,028 accidental deaths compared to 114,638 in 1970. The largest category, motor vehicle fatalities, declined from 54,633 in 1970 to 47,575 in 1989. Other categories also registered steep declines:

	1970	1989
Air accidents	1,612	1,123
Railway accidents	852	652
Accidental falls	16,926	12,151
Fire	6,718	4,716
Complications from medical procedures	3,581	2,992

22 The national suicide rate per 100,000 grew from 11.6 in 1970 to 12.2 in 1989. Whites and males have higher suicide rates than Blacks and females. The White male rate was 21.4 compared to 12.2 for Black males, 7.1 for White females and 2.4 for Black females.

23 The median age at first marriage rose for females from 20.6 in 1970 to 23.7 in 1988, and from 22.5 in 1970 to 25.5 in 1988 for males.

24 More divorced men and widowers remarry than divorced women and widows. On a rate per 1,000 persons 15 years and older, 5.3 widows and 78.6 divorced women remarried in 1988 compared to 25.1 widowers and 109.7 divorced men.

25 Health expenditures are the fastest growing component of the Gross National Product (GNP), rising from 3.5% in 1929 to 12.2% in 1990 and from $24.29 per capita in 1929 to $2,566 per capita in 1990. Insurance premiums grew from $5.9 billion in 1960 to $216.8 billion in 1990 while Medicare payments increased from $7.6 billion in 1970 to $111.2 billion in 1990.

26 The Federal government has directly provided hospital and medical care for specified groups of beneficiaries since 1798, when President John Adams signed into law the Act for the Relief of Sick and Disabled Seamen. Since that time, federally sponsored and financed medical care has been expanded to include such groups as Native Americans, Alaskan natives, veterans, narcotics addicts, and owners of commercial fishing boats, in addition to Federal employees. State, local, and county governments also provide hospital and medical care for their residents.

27 Beginning in 1966, the Medicaid Program, enacted as Title XIX of the Social Security Act in 1965, enabled states to provide a single health program for the indigent, with Federal financial participation. Medicaid offers five basic services: inpatient hospital care; outpatient hospital services; laboratory and X-ray services; nursing home services; and physician's services. In addition, states may offer other services, such as drugs or dental care, for which they receive Federal matching funds.

28 Federal health insurance for the aged (Medicare) became effective July 1, 1966, providing hospital and medical protection to an enrolled population aged 65 and over. It includes Part A (hospital program) and Part B (a supplementary program covering physicians' services, outpatient hospital services, therapy, tests, ambulance services, and certain medical supplies). The Part A program is financed on a self-supporting basis through a Federal tax, the proceeds of which are placed in a trust fund. Part B is financed through monthly premium payments paid by enrollees and matched by the Federal government.

29 The first medical school in the United States, the College of Philadelphia, Department of Medicine (now the University of Pennsylvania School of Medicine), was founded in 1765. The number of medical schools increased to three by 1800, 52 in 1850, and 162 in 1906. From 1906 to 1929, the number declined sharply because of tougher accreditation procedures by the American Medical Association's Council on Medical Education.

30 The first dental school, Baltimore College of Dental Surgery, was founded in 1840. Before that date, physicians also practiced dentistry. From 1840 to 1880, dental practitioners learned their trade as apprentices, and it was not until 1880 that most states enacted laws requiring graduation from an accredited dental school.

31 Nursing education began in 1873 with the opening of three schools, and by 1893 there were 70 in operation. By 1923, all states had licensing bodies for the nursing profession.

32 The first physician in the American Colonies was Dr. Lawrence Bohune, physician of the London Company, who arrived in Virginia in 1610. The first physician in New England was Dr. Samuel Fuller, one of the signers of the Compact on board the *Mayflower* on November 21, 1620. The first American medical graduate was Dr. John Archer, who graduated with nine others from the University of Pennsylvania in 1768.

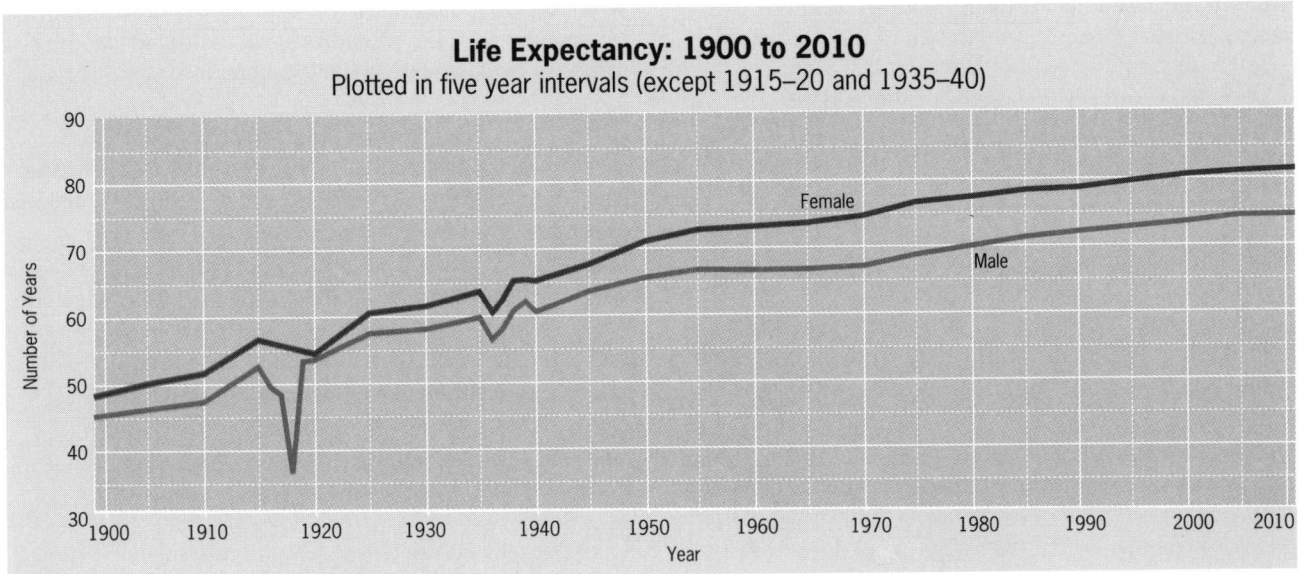

Life Expectancy: 1900 to 2010
Plotted in five year intervals (except 1915–20 and 1935–40)

33 The first American dentist was Josiah Flagg, who, at the age of 18, began practicing dentistry in Boston in 1782.

34 The first trained nurse in the United States was Linda Ann Judson Richards, who graduated from the Training School of the New England Hospital for Women and Children in 1873.

35 Disease notification began in the Colonial period on a local basis, particularly in the port cities. It was limited to epidemics of pestilential diseases. Statewide notification was not required until 1883 when Michigan passed a law under which physicians were asked to report certain diseases to health officers or boards of health. Over the next three decades all states made similar requirements. In 1871, the Federal government passed a law providing for the collection of such statistics. By 1912, data were supplied by 19 states and the District of Columbia on diphtheria, measles, poliomyelitis, scarlet fever, tuberculosis, typhoid, and small pox. None of these are now considered important threats to public health. General statistics on health are collected and published by the National Center for Health Statistics in its *National Health Interview Survey* and the *National Health and Nutrition Examination Surveys*. Data on diseases are compiled by the Public Health Service through its Centers for Disease Control in Atlanta and published in *Morbidity and Mortality Report*.

36 Expenditures on medical research grew from $2 billion in 1970 to $12.4 billion in 1990 and expenditures on new medical construction from $3.4 billion in 1970 to $10.4 billion in 1990.

37 In 1990, private insurance met 57.8% of all private health expenditures, 87% of hospital care expenses, and 71.2% of physicians' services. Insurance premiums grew from $16.743 billion in 1970 to $216.828 billion in 1990.

Health insurance companies paid out $139.090 billion in 1987 compared to $15.320 billion in 1970. Of the 1987 total, Blue Cross-Blue Shield accounted for $44.525 billion, insurance companies $51.549 billion, and independent plans $43.016 billion.

38 In 1990, 34 million Americans carried no health insurance. Of these, 38.3% were unemployed.

39 In 1990, Medicare enrolled 34.203 million and paid out $108.707 billion. Medicaid enrolled 25.255 million and paid out $64.859 billion.

40 Based on 1967=100, the Index of Medical Care Prices (a part of the Consumer Price Index) grew from 36.1 in 1935 to 433.5 in 1986. Based on 1982-84=100, the Index grew from 34 in 1970 to 177 in 1991.

41 There were 556 Health Maintenance Organizations (HMOs) in 1991, compared to 175 in 1976. Their total enrollment was 34.072 million.

42 Of the 645,000 active physicians in the United States in 1989, 116,000 held foreign medical degrees.

43 The average American male visits his doctor 4.7 times a year and his dentist 1.9 times. The average American female, however, visits her doctor 6.1 times and her dentist 2.2 times.

44 The mean annual income of physicians grew from $5,224 in 1929 to $12,324 in 1950, $97,700 in 1982 and $155,800 in 1989. In 1992, the highest income was reported by cardiovascular surgeons who earned an average of $574,769 annually, and the lowest by family practitioners who received an average of $119,186. The highest mean malpractice insurance premium in 1989 was carried by obstetricians and gynecologists who paid $37,000 annually.

45 Outpatient visits to hospitals numbered 368.2 million in 1990 compared to 219.2 million in 1972. Emergencies numbered 92.8 million in 1990 compared to 60.1 million in 1972.

46 The average cost per day of a hospital stay rose from $5.21 in 1946 to $10.67 in 1954, $21.00 in 1963, $45.01 in 1969, $53.95 in 1970, $134 in 1975, $245 in 1980, $460 in 1985, and $687 in 1990. The states with the highest per day hospital costs were Alaska ($1,070), California ($939), Nevada ($854), Utah ($832), Connecticut ($825), Washington ($817), and Oregon ($800). The states with the lowest relative costs were South Dakota ($391), Montana ($405), North Dakota ($427), Mississippi ($439), Wyoming ($462), Nebraska ($490), Iowa ($495), and Kansas ($532).

47 The average stay in hospitals declined from 15.3 days in 1931 to 10.1 days in 1953, 9.5 days in 1970, 8 days in 1980, and 6.5 days in 1990.

48 In 1990, 21.9 million surgeries were performed in hospitals compared to 14.8 million in 1972. Of the surgeries in 1990, 11.678 million were outpatient surgeries.

49 In 1990, 14,204 organ transplants were performed in 148 centers compared to 4,976 organ transplants in 1981. The 1990 figure included 1,998 heart transplants, 2,534 liver transplants, and 9,433 kidney transplants.

50 In 1988, there were 4,941 mental health facilities, including 1,172 mental hospitals. Inpatients numbered 228,000 compared to 150,000 in 1904, 634,000 in 1955 (the peak year), and 391,000 in 1970.

51 In 1989, 59.2 million personal injuries required medical attention. Personal injuries per capita have declined from 28 in 1970 to 24.6. More males than females receive personal injuries; the rate per 100 is 27.7 for men and 21.6 for women. The largest number of injuries were sustained as a result of falling down stairs and ramps. Other major causes of injury were home maintenance chemicals, home workshop equipment, yard and garden equipment, bicycles, playground equipment, and toys.

52 In 1990, the cost of accidents was estimated at $173.8 billion, including wage loss of $48.2 billion and medical expenses of $28.4 billion.

53 In 1989, there were 6,374 alcoholism treatment centers with 374,437 patients and 6,170 drug abuse treatment centers with 344,529 patients.

54 The consumption of drugs of all kinds has been steadily declining since 1974. The percentage of marijuana users dropped from 12.0% in 1974 to 4.3% in 1991 and that of cocaine users from 1.0% in 1974 to 0.4% in 1991.

55 Between 1965 and 1988, the percentage of cigarette smokers declined from 47.8% to 27.6% for the 20-24 age group, 49.5% to 32.9% for the 25-44 age group, 39.9% to 29.4% for the 45-64 age group, and from 17.1% to 14.9% for the over 65 age group. Only 25.3% of women and 30.9% of men smoked cigarettes in 1988 in contrast to 31.9% and 50.2% respectively in 1965.

56 Despite access to better health information, personal health practices have not shown much improvement. In 1990, thirteen percent of Americans were overweight, 30.1% smoked, 37.5% had five or more drinks on any given day, 22% slept less than six hours a day, and 39% snacked every day.

57 The consumption of red meat per capita dropped from 132 pounds in 1970 to 112.3 pounds in 1990. Over that same period, the consumption of poultry products per capita grew from 34.1 pounds to 63.6 pounds.

58 The per capita consumption of alcoholic products grew from 35.7 gallons in 1970 to 39.5 gallons in 1990. Much of this increase came from beer; the wine consumption increased only slightly while the consumption of distilled spirits dipped. Coffee became less popular—its per capita consumption over the same period dropped from 33.4 gallons to 26.7 gallons. Soft drinks replaced coffee as the leading drink. Their per capita consumption grew from 20.6 gallons in 1970 to 42.5 gallons in 1990.

59 Future Data, 2000:
Number of Physicians: 656,100
Number of Dentists: 161,200
Number of Nurses: 1,980,000
Healthcare Expenditures $1.6 trillion
Healthcare Expenditures as % of GNP: 17% (37% in 2030)
Nursing Home Population: 1.8 million (4.8 million in 2050)
Real Healthcare Expenditures per capita: $3,021

Series B 1-4.   Live Births, Deaths, Marriages and Divorces: 1909 to 1990

(In thousands. Birth, marriage and divorce figures represent estimates of all such events; death figures, the number of registered events)

Year	Live births [1,2]	Deaths [3]	Marriages	Divorces [4]	Year	Live births [1,2]	Deaths [3]	Marriages	Divorces [4]
	1	2	3	4		1	2	3	4
1990	4,179	2,162	2,448	1,175	1948	3,637	1,444	1,811	408
1989	4,041	2,050	2,404	1,163	1947	3,817	1,445	1,992	483
1988	3,910	2,168	2,396	1,167	1946	3,411	1,396	2,291	610
1987	3,809	2,123	2,403	1,166					
1986	3,757	2,105	2,407	1,178	1945	2,858	1,402	1,613	485
					1944	2,939	1,411	1,452	400
1985	3,761	2,086	2,413	1,190	1943	3,104	1,460	1,577	359
1984	3,669	2,039	2,477	1,169	1942	2,989	1,385	1,772	321
1983	3,639	2,019	2,446	1,158	1941	2,703	1,398	1,696	293
1982	3,681	1,975	2,456	1,170					
1981	3,629	1,978	2,422	1,213	1940	2,559	1,417	1,596	264
					1939	2,466	1,388	1,404	251
1980	3,612	1,990	2,390	1,189	1938	2,496	1,381	1,331	244
1979	3,494	1,914	2,331	1,181	1937	2,413	1,450	1,451	249
1978	3,333	1,928	2,282	1,130	1936	2,355	1,479	1,369	236
1977	3,327	1,900	2,178	1,091					
1976	3,168	1,909	2,155	1,083	1935	2,377	1,393	1,327	218
					1934	2,396	1,397	1,302	204
1975	3,144	1,893	2,153	1,036	1933	2,307	1,342	1,098	165
1974	3,160	1,934	2,230	977	1932	2,440	—	982	164
1973	3,137	1,973	2,284	915	1931	2,506	—	1,061	188
1972	3,258	1,964	2,282	845					
1971	3,556	1,928	2,190	773	1930	2,618	—	1,127	196
					1929	2,582	—	1,233	206
1970	3,731	1,921	2,163	708	1928	2,674	—	1,182	200
1969	3,600	1,922	2,145	639	1927	2,802	—	1,201	196
1968	3,502	1,930	2,069	584	1926	2,839	—	1,203	185
1967	[5] 3,521	1,851	1,927	523					
1966	3,606	1,863	1,857	499	1925	2,909	—	1,188	175
					1924	2,979	—	1,185	171
1965	3,760	1,828	1,800	479	1923	2,910	—	1,230	165
1964	4,027	1,798	1,725	450	1922	2,882	—	1,134	149
1963	4,098	1,814	1,654	428	1921	3,055	—	1,164	160
1962	4,167	1,757	1,577	413					
1961	4,268	1,702	1,548	414	1920	2,950	—	1,274	171
					1919	2,740	—	—	—
1960 *	4,258	1,712	1,523	393	1918	2,948	—	—	—
1959 [6]	4,245	1,657	1,494	395	1917	2,944	—	—	—
1958	4,255	1,648	1,451	368	1916	2,964	—	—	—
1957	4,308	1,633	1,518	381					
1956	4,218	1,564	1,585	382	1915	2,965	—	—	—
					1914	2,966	—	—	—
1955	4,104	1,529	1,531	377	1913	2,869	—	—	—
1954	4,078	1,481	1,490	379	1912	2,840	—	—	—
1953	3,965	1,518	1,546	390	1911	2,809	—	—	—
1952	3,913	1,497	1,539	392					
1951	3,823	1,482	1,595	381	1910	2,777	—	—	—
					1909	2,718	—	—	—
1950	3,632	1,452	1,667	385					
1949	3,649	1,444	1,580	397					

* Denotes first year for which figures include Alaska and Hawaii.
[1] 1959-1970, registered live births; 1909-1958, adjusted for under-registration.
[2] Based on 50 percent sample for 1951-1954, 1956-1966 and 1968-1970.
[3] Excludes fetal deaths.

[4] Includes reported annulments.
[5] Based on 20- to 50-percent sample.
[6] Includes Alaska.

Series B 5-10. Birth Rate—Total and for Women 15–44 Years Old, by Race: 1800 to 1989

(Based on estimated total live births per 1,000 population for specified group. Based on a 50-percent sample of births for 1951-1954, 1956-1966 and 1968-1970; on 20- to 50-percent sample for 1967. Prior to 1959, births adjusted for under-registration; thereafter, registered live births)

| Year | Rate, total population | | | Rate, women 15–44 years [1] | | | Year | Rate, total population | | | Rate, women 15–44 years [1] | | |
| | Total | White | Black | Total | White | Black | | Total | White | Black | Total | White | Black |
	5	6	7	8	9	10		5	6	7	8	9	10
1989	16.3	15.0	23.1	69.2	64.7	90.4	1943	22.7	22.1	28.3	94.3	92.3	111.0
1988	15.9	14.7	22.2	67.2	63.0	86.6	1942	22.2	21.5	27.7	91.5	89.5	107.6
1987	15.7	14.5	21.6	65.7	62.0	83.8	1941	20.3	19.5	27.3	83.4	80.7	105.4
1986	15.6	14.5	21.2	65.4	61.9	82.4							
							1940	19.4	18.6	26.7	79.9	77.1	102.4
1985	15.8	14.8	21.1	66.2	63.0	82.2	1939	18.8	18.0	26.1	77.6	74.8	100.1
1984	15.5	14.5	20.8	65.4	62.2	81.4	1938	19.2	18.4	26.3	79.1	76.5	100.5
1983	15.5	14.6	20.9	65.8	62.4	81.7	1937	18.7	17.9	26.0	77.1	74.4	99.4
1982	15.9	14.9	21.4	67.3	63.9	84.1	1936	18.4	17.6	25.1	75.8	73.3	95.9
1981	15.8	14.8	21.6	67.4	63.9	85.4							
							1935	18.7	17.9	25.8	77.2	74.5	98.4
1980	15.9	14.9	22.1	68.4	64.7	88.1	1934	19.0	18.1	26.3	78.5	75.8	100.4
1979	15.9	14.8	22.3	68.5	64.5	90.5	1933	18.4	17.6	25.5	76.3	73.7	97.3
1978	15.3	14.2	21.6	66.6	62.7	88.6	1932	19.5	18.7	26.9	81.7	79.0	103.0
1977	15.4	14.4	21.7	67.8	64.0	89.8	1931	20.2	19.5	26.6	84.6	82.4	102.1
1976	14.8	13.8	20.8	65.8	62.2	87.2							
							1930	21.3	20.6	27.5	89.2	87.1	105.9
1975	14.8	13.8	20.9	66.7	63.0	89.2	1929	21.2	20.5	27.3	89.3	87.3	106.1
1974	14.9	14.0	21.0	68.4	64.7	90.8	1928	22.2	21.5	28.5	93.8	91.7	111.0
1973	14.9	13.9	21.5	69.2	65.3	94.3	1927	23.5	22.7	31.1	99.8	97.1	121.7
1972	15.6	14.6	22.9	73.4	69.2	100.3	1926	24.2	23.1	33.4	102.6	99.2	130.3
1971	17.2	16.2	24.7	81.8	77.5	109.5							
							1925	25.1	24.1	34.2	106.6	103.3	134.0
1970	18.4	17.4	25.1	87.9	84.1	113.0	1924	26.1	25.1	34.6	110.9	107.8	135.6
1969	17.8	16.9	24.4	86.5	82.4	114.8	1923	26.0	25.2	33.2	110.5	108.0	130.5
1968	17.5	16.6	24.2	85.7	81.5	114.9	1922	26.2	25.4	33.2	111.2	108.8	130.8
1967 [2]	17.8	16.8	25.0	87.6	83.1	119.8	1921	28.1	27.3	35.8	119.8	117.2	140.8
1966	18.4	17.4	26.1	91.3	86.4	125.9							
							1920	27.7	26.9	35.0	117.9	115.4	137.5
1965	19.4	18.3	27.6	96.6	91.4	133.9	1919	26.1	25.3	32.4	111.2	(NA)	—
1964	21.0	20.0	29.1	105.0	99.9	141.7	1918	28.2	27.6	33.0	119.8	(NA)	—
1963 [3]	21.7	20.7	29.7	108.5	103.7	144.9	1917	28.5	27.9	32.9	121.0	(NA)	—
1962 [3]	22.4	21.4	30.5	112.2	107.5	148.8	1916	29.1	28.5	—	123.4	121.8	—
1961	23.3	22.2	34.6	117.2	112.2	153.5							
							1915	29.5	28.9	—	125.0	123.2	—
1960 *	23.7	22.7	32.1	118.0	113.2	153.6	1914	29.9	29.3	—	126.6	124.6	—
1959 [4]	24.0	22.9	32.9	118.8	113.9	156.0	1913	29.5	28.8	—	124.7	122.4	—
1958	24.5	23.3	34.3	120.2	114.9	160.5	1912	29.8	29.0	—	125.8	123.3	—
1957	25.3	24.0	35.3	122.9	117.7	163.0	1911	29.9	29.1	—	126.3	123.6	—
1956	25.2	24.0	35.4	121.2	116.0	160.9							
							1910	30.1	29.2	—	126.8	123.8	—
1955	25.0	23.8	34.7	118.5	113.8	155.3	1909	30.0	29.2	—	126.8	123.6	—
1954	25.3	24.2	34.9	118.1	113.6	153.2	1900	32.3	30.1	—	—	130	—
1953	25.0	24.0	34.1	115.2	111.0	147.3	1890	(NA)	31.5	—	—	137	—
1952	25.1	24.1	33.6	113.9	110.1	143.3	1880	39.8	35.2	—	—	155	—
1951	24.9	23.9	33.8	111.5	107.7	142.1							
							1870	(NA)	38.3	—	—	167	—
1950	24.1	23.0	33.3	106.2	102.3	137.3	1860	44.3	41.4	—	—	184	—
1949	24.5	23.6	33.0	107.1	103.6	135.1	1850	(NA)	43.3	—	—	194	—
1948	24.9	24.0	32.4	107.3	104.3	131.6	1840	51.8	48.3	—	—	222	—
1947	26.6	26.1	31.2	113.3	111.8	125.9	1830	(NA)	51.4	—	—	240	—
1946	24.1	23.6	38.4	101.9	100.4	113.9							
							1820	55.2	52.8	—	—	260	—
1945	20.4	19.7	26.5	85.9	83.4	106.0	1810	—	54.3	—	—	274	—
1944	21.2	20.5	27.4	88.8	86.3	108.5	1800	—	55.0	—	—	278	—

* Denotes first year for which figures include Alaska and Hawaii.
NA Not available.
[1] Computed by relating total births, regardless of age of mother, to women aged 15-44 years.

[2] Based on 20- to 50-percent sample of births.
[3] Figures by race exclude New Jersey; state did not want required reporting of race.
[4] Includes Alaska.

Series B 11-19.   Fertility Rate by Age of Mother, by Race: 1940 to 1989

(Total fertility rates are the sums of birth rates, by age of mother, multiplied by 5. Prior to 1959, births adjusted for under registration; thereafter, registered live births. Based on 50-percent sample of births for 1951-1954, 1956-1966 and 1968-1970; on 20- to 50-percent sample for 1967)

| Year | Fertility rate | | | Year | Fertility rate | | | Year | Fertility rate | | |
| | Total | White | Black | | Total | White | Black | | Total | White | Black |
	11	11	11		11	11	11		11	11	11
1989	2,014	1,885	2,583	1972	2,022	1,919	2,651	1955	3,580	3,446	4,550
1988	1,932	1,814	2,463	1971	2,275	2,169	2,933	1954	3,543	3,415	4,474
1987	1,871	1,767	2,349					1953	3,424	3,306	4,283
1986	1,836	1,742	2,282	1970	2,480	2,385	3,067	1952	3,358	3,250	4,147
				1969	2,465	2,360	3,148	1951	3,269	3,157	4,091
1985	1,843	1,754	2,263	1968	2,477	2,368	3,197				
1984	1,806	1,719	2,224	1967	2,573	2,453	3,385	1950	3,091	2,977	3,928
1983	1,803	1,718	2,225	1966	2,736	2,609	3,615	1949	3,110	3,009	3,855
1982	1,829	1,742	2,265					1948	3,109	3,022	3,742
1981	1,815	1,726	2,275	1965	2,928	2,790	3,891	1947	3,274	3,230	3,575
				1964	3,208	3,074	4,153	1946	2,943	2,901	3,238
1980	1,840	1,749	2,323	1963 [1]	3,333	3,201	4,269				
1979	1,808	1,716	2,310	1962 [1]	3,474	3,348	4,396	1945	2,491	2,421	3,017
1978	1,760	1,668	2,265	1961	3,629	3,502	4,533	1944	2,568	2,501	3,075
1977	1,790	1,703	2,279					1943	2,718	2,664	3,128
1976	1,738	1,652	2,223	1960	3,654	3,533	4,522	1942	2,628	2,577	3,022
				1959	3,670	3,544	4,595	1941	2,399	2,328	2,956
1975	1,774	1,686	2,276	1958	3,701	3,560	4,727	1940	2,301	2,229	2,870
1974	1,835	1,749	2,339	1957	3,767	3,625	4,798				
1973	1,896	1,798	2,474	1956	3,689	3,546	4,730				

[1] Race figures exclude New Jersey; state did not require reporting of race.

Series B 28-35. Illegitimate Live Births and Birth Rates, by Age and Race of Mother: 1940 to 1989

(Refers only to illegitimate births occurring within the United States. Rates are illegitimate live births per 1,000 unmarried females in specified group. Figures for age of mother not stated are distributed. Based on 5-percent sample of births for 1951-1954, 1956-1966 and 1968-1970; on 20- to 50-percent sample for 1967)

| | Total | | Rate, by age of mother [2] | | | | | | | | White | | | Black | |
| Year | Births (1,000) | Rate, all ages [1] | 15-19 years | 20-24 years | 25-29 years | 30-34 years | 35-39 years | 40-44 years | Year | Births (1,000) | Rate, all ages [1] | Year | Births (1,000) | Rate, all ages [1] |
	28	29	30	31	32	33	34	35		28	29		28	29
1989	1,094.2	41.8	337.3	378.1	215.5	106.3	46.3		1989	593.9	29.2	1989	457.5	93.1
1988	1,005.3	38.6	312.5	350.9	196.4	94.9	40.7		1988	539.7	26.6	1988	426.7	88.9
1987	933.0	36.1	293.0	331.3	179.3	84.2	35.8		1987	498.6	24.6	1987	399.1	84.7
1986	878.5	34.3	280.7	316.2	165.7	74.9	31.6		1986	466.8	23.2	1986	380.3	80.9
1985	828.2	32.8	270.9	300.4	152.0	67.3	28.2		1985	433.0	21.8	1985	365.5	78.8
1984	770.4	31.0	261.1	279.2	137.0	59.3	24.8		1984	391.9	20.1	1984	378.4	71.4
1983	737.9	30.4	261.3	265.6	126.5	53.9	21.8		1983	370.9	19.3	1983	367.0	72.3
1982	715.2	30.0	260.6	257.5	119.0	49.6	19.9		1982	355.2	18.8	1982	360.0	73.9
1981	686.6	29.6	259.2	246.9	109.2	45.3	17.4		1981	337.1	18.2	1981	349.6	75.4
1980	665.7	29.4	262.8	237.3	99.6	41.0	16.1		1980	320.1	17.6	1980	345.7	77.2
1979	597.8	27.2	253.2	210.1	80.6	31.3	13.1		1979	263.0	14.9	1979	334.8	78.2
1978	543.9	26.2	239.7	186.5	70.0	26.5	11.7		1978	233.6	13.7	1978	310.2	76.5
1977	515.7	26.6	239.7	168.6	62.4	23.7	11.1		1977	220.1	13.5	1977	295.5	77.4
1976	488.1	24.7	225.0	145.4	55.4	21.0	10.9		1976	197.1	12.6	1976	271.0	76.4
1975	447.9	24.8	222.5	134.0	50.2	19.8	10.4		1975	186.4	12.4	1975	261.6	79.0
1974	418.1	24.1	210.8	122.7	44.9	18.6	10.5		1974	168.5	11.8	1974	249.6	81.5
1973	407.3	24.5	204.9	119.1	43.1	18.5	10.8		1973	163.0	11.9	1973	244.3	84.2
1972	403.2	24.9	202.3	119.6	41.2	19.0	11.3		1972	160.5	12.0	1972	242.7	86.9
1971	401.4	25.6	194.1	125.2	40.9	19.3	12.4		1971	163.8	12.5	1971	237.5	90.6
1970	399	26.4	22.4	38.4	37.1	27.0	13.3	3.6	1970	175	13.8	1970	224	89.9
1969	361	25.0	20.6	37.4	38.1	27.4	13.6	3.6	1969	164	13.5	1969	197	86.6
1968	339	24.4	19.8	37.3	38.6	28.2	14.9	3.8	1968	155	13.2	1968	184	86.6
1967	318	23.9	18.6	38.3	41.4	29.2	15.4	4.0	1967	142	12.5	1967	176	89.5
1966	302	23.4	17.5	39.1	45.6	33.0	16.4	4.1	1966	133	12.0	1966	170	92.8
1965	291	23.5	16.7	39.9	49.3	37.5	17.4	4.5	1965	124	11.6	1965	168	97.6
1964	276	23.0	15.8	39.9	50.2	37.2	16.3	4.4	1964	114	11.0	1964	161	97.2
1963	259	22.5	15.2	40.3	49.0	33.2	16.1	4.3	1963 [4]	102	10.5	1963	151	97.1
1962	245	21.9	14.8	40.9	46.7	29.7	15.6	4.0	1962 [4]	93	9.8	1962	147	97.5
1961	240	22.7	15.9	41.7	46.5	28.3	15.4	3.9	1961	91	10.0	1961	149	100.8
1960	224	21.6	15.3	39.7	45.1	27.8	14.1	3.6	1960 *	83	9.2	1960	142	98.3
1959	221	21.9	15.5	40.2	44.1	28.1	14.1	3.3	1959 [3]	80	9.2	1959	141	100.8
1958	209	21.2	15.3	38.2	40.5	27.5	13.3	3.2	1958	75	8.8	1958	134	97.8
1957	202	21.0	15.8	37.3	36.8	26.8	12.1	3.1	1957	71	8.6	1957	131	95.3
1956	194	20.4	15.6	36.4	35.6	24.6	11.1	2.8	1956	68	8.3	1956	126	92.1
1955	183	19.3	15.1	33.5	33.5	22.0	10.5	2.7	1955	64	7.9	1955	119	87.2
1954	177	18.7	14.9	31.4	31.0	20.4	10.3	2.5	1950	54	6.1	1950	88	71.2
1953	161	16.9	13.9	28.0	27.6	17.3	9.0	2.4	1940	40	3.6	1940	49	35.6
1952	150	15.8	13.5	25.4	24.8	15.7	8.2	1.9						
1951	147	15.1	13.2	23.2	22.8	14.6	7.6	2.2						
1950	142	14.1	12.6	21.3	19.9	13.3	7.2	2.0						
1949	133	13.3	12.0	21.0	18.0	11.4	6.8	1.9						
1948	130	12.5	11.4	19.8	16.4	10.0	5.8	1.6						
1947	132	12.1	11.0	18.9	15.7	9.2	5.6	1.8						
1946	125	10.9	9.5	17.3	15.6	7.3	4.4	1.8						
1945	117	10.1	9.5	15.3	12.1	7.1	4.1	1.6						
1944	105	9.0	8.8	13.1	10.1	7.0	4.0	1.3						
1943	98	8.3	8.4	11.4	8.8	6.7	3.8	1.3						
1942	97	8.0	8.2	11.0	8.4	6.3	3.8	1.2						
1941	96	7.8	8.0	10.5	7.8	6.0	3.7	1.4						
1940	90	7.1	7.4	9.5	7.2	5.1	3.4	1.2						

* Denotes first year for which figures include Alaska and Hawaii.

[1] Rates computed by relating total illegitimate births regardless of age of mother to women aged 15-44 years.

[2] Rates for total computed by relating illegitimate births to mothers aged 40 and over to unmarried women aged 40-44 years. Rates for race detail computed by relating births to mothers aged 35 and over to women aged 35-44 years.

[3] Includes Alaska.

[4] Excludes New Jersey; state did not require reporting of race.

Series B 107-115. Expectation of Life (in years) at Birth, by Race and Sex: 1900 to 2010
(Prior to 1929, for death-registration area only)

Year	Total			White			Black and other		
	Both sexes	Male	Female	Both sexes	Male	Female	Both sexes	Male	Female
	107	108	109	110	111	112	113	114	115
2010	77.9	74.4	81.3	78.3	74.9	81.7	—	—	—
2005	77.6	74.2	81.0	78.1	74.6	81.5	—	—	—
2000	77.0	73.5	80.4	77.5	74.0	80.9	—	—	—
1995	76.3	72.8	79.7	76.8	73.4	80.2	—	—	—
1990	75.4	72.0	78.8	76.0	72.6	79.3	72.4	68.4	76.3
1989	75.3	71.8	78.6	76.0	72.7	79.2	71.2	67.1	75.2
1988	74.9	71.5	78.3	75.6	72.3	78.9	71.2	67.1	75.1
1987	75.0	71.5	78.4	75.6	72.2	78.9	71.3	67.3	75.2
1986	74.8	71.3	78.3	75.4	72.0	78.8	71.2	67.2	75.1
1985	74.7	71.2	78.2	75.3	71.9	78.7	71.2	67.2	75.0
1984	74.7	71.2	78.2	75.3	71.8	78.7	71.3	67.4	75.0
1983	74.6	71.0	78.1	75.2	71.7	78.7	71.3	67.4	74.9
1982	74.5	70.9	78.1	75.1	71.5	78.7	71.0	66.8	75.0
1981	74.2	70.4	77.8	74.8	71.1	78.4	70.3	66.1	74.4
1980	73.7	70.0	77.4	74.4	70.7	78.1	69.5	65.3	73.6
1979	73.9	70.0	77.8	74.6	70.8	78.4	69.8	65.4	74.1
1978	73.5	69.6	77.3	74.1	70.4	78.0	69.3	65.0	73.5
1977	73.3	69.5	77.2	74.0	70.2	77.9	68.9	64.7	73.2
1976	72.9	69.1	76.8	73.6	69.9	77.5	68.4	64.2	72.7
1975	72.6	68.8	76.6	73.4	69.5	77.3	68.0	63.7	72.4
1974	71.9	68.1	75.8	72.7	68.9	76.6	67.6	62.9	71.3
1973	71.3	67.6	75.3	72.2	68.4	76.1	65.9	61.9	70.1
1972	71.1	67.4	75.1	72.0	68.3	75.9	65.6	61.5	69.9
1971	71.1	67.4	75.0	72.0	68.3	75.8	65.6	61.6	69.7
1970	70.9	67.1	74.8	71.7	68.0	75.6	65.3	61.3	69.4
1969	70.5	66.8	74.3	71.3	67.8	75.1	64.3	60.5	68.4
1968	70.2	66.6	74.0	71.1	67.5	74.9	63.7	60.1	67.5
1967	70.5	67.0	74.2	71.3	67.8	75.1	64.6	61.1	68.2
1966	70.1	66.7	73.8	71.0	67.6	74.7	64.0	60.7	67.4
1965	70.2	66.8	73.7	71.0	67.6	74.7	64.1	61.1	67.4
1964	70.2	66.9	73.7	71.0	67.7	74.6	64.1	61.1	67.2
1963 [1]	69.9	66.6	73.4	70.8	67.5	74.4	63.6	60.9	66.5
1962 [1]	70.0	66.8	73.4	70.9	67.6	74.4	64.1	61.5	66.8
1961	70.2	67.0	73.6	71.0	67.8	74.5	64.4	61.9	67.0
1960 *	69.7	66.6	73.1	70.6	67.4	74.1	63.6	61.1	66.3
1959 [2]	69.9	66.8	73.2	70.7	67.5	74.2	63.9	61.3	66.5
1958	69.6	66.6	72.9	70.5	67.4	73.9	63.4	61.0	65.8
1957	69.5	66.4	72.7	70.3	67.7	73.7	63.0	60.7	65.5
1956	69.7	66.7	72.9	70.5	67.5	73.9	63.6	61.3	66.1
1955	69.6	66.7	72.8	70.5	67.4	73.7	63.7	61.4	66.1
1954	69.6	66.7	72.8	70.5	67.5	73.7	63.4	61.1	65.9
1953	68.8	66.0	72.0	69.7	66.8	73.0	62.0	59.7	64.5
1952	68.6	65.8	71.6	69.5	66.6	72.6	61.4	59.1	63.8
1951	68.4	65.6	71.4	69.3	66.5	72.4	61.2	59.2	63.4
1950	68.2	65.6	71.1	69.1	66.5	72.2	60.8	59.1	62.9
1949	68.0	65.2	70.7	68.8	66.2	71.9	60.6	58.9	62.7
1948	67.2	64.6	69.9	68.0	65.5	71.0	60.0	58.1	62.5
1947	66.8	64.4	69.7	67.6	65.2	70.5	59.7	57.9	61.9
1946	66.7	64.4	69.4	67.5	65.1	70.3	59.1	57.5	61.0
1945	65.9	63.6	67.9	66.8	64.4	69.5	57.7	56.1	59.6
1944	65.2	63.6	66.8	66.2	64.5	68.4	56.6	55.8	57.7
1943	63.3	62.4	64.4	64.2	63.2	65.7	55.6	55.4	56.1
1942	66.2	64.7	67.9	67.3	65.9	69.4	56.6	55.4	58.2
1941	64.8	63.1	66.8	66.2	64.4	68.5	53.8	52.5	55.3

See footnotes at end of chart.

Series B 107-115. Expectation of Life (in years) at Birth, by Race and Sex: 1900 to 2010—Cont'd.

(Prior to 1929, for death-registration area only)

Year	Total			White			Black and other		
	Both sexes	Male	Female	Both sexes	Male	Female	Both sexes	Male	Female
	107	108	109	110	111	112	113	114	115
1940	62.9	60.8	65.2	64.2	62.1	66.6	53.1	51.5	54.9
1939	63.7	62.1	65.4	64.9	63.3	66.6	54.5	53.2	56.0
1938	63.5	61.9	65.3	65.0	63.2	66.8	52.9	51.7	54.3
1937	60.0	58.0	62.4	61.4	59.3	63.8	50.3	48.3	52.5
1936	58.5	56.6	60.6	59.8	58.0	61.9	49.0	47.0	51.4
1935	61.7	59.9	63.9	62.9	61.0	65.0	53.1	51.3	55.2
1934	61.1	59.3	63.3	62.4	50.6	64.6	51.8	50.2	53.7
1933	63.3	61.7	65.1	64.3	62.7	66.3	54.7	53.5	56.0
1932	62.1	61.0	63.5	63.2	62.0	64.5	53.7	52.8	54.6
1931	61.1	59.4	63.1	62.6	60.8	64.7	50.4	49.5	51.5
1930	59.7	58.1	61.6	61.4	59.7	63.5	48.1	47.3	49.2
1929	57.1	55.8	58.7	58.6	57.2	60.3	46.7	45.7	47.8
1928	56.8	55.6	58.3	58.4	57.0	60.0	46.3	45.6	47.0
1927	60.4	59.0	62.1	62.0	60.5	63.9	48.2	47.6	48.9
1926	56.7	55.5	58.0	58.2	57.0	59.6	44.6	43.7	45.6
1925	59.0	57.6	60.6	60.7	59.3	62.4	45.7	44.9	46.7
1924	59.7	58.1	61.5	61.4	59.8	63.4	46.6	45.5	47.8
1923	57.2	56.1	58.5	58.3	57.1	59.6	48.3	47.7	48.9
1922	59.6	58.4	61.0	60.4	59.1	61.9	52.4	51.8	53.0
1921	60.8	60.0	61.8	61.8	60.8	62.9	51.5	51.6	51.3
1920	54.1	53.6	54.6	54.9	54.4	55.6	45.3	45.5	45.2
1919	54.7	53.5	56.0	55.8	54.5	57.4	44.5	44.5	44.4
1918	39.1	36.6	42.2	39.8	37.1	43.2	31.1	29.9	32.5
1917	50.9	48.4	54.0	52.0	49.3	55.3	38.8	37.0	40.8
1916	51.7	49.6	54.3	52.5	50.2	55.2	41.3	39.6	43.1
1915	54.5	52.5	56.8	55.1	53.1	57.5	38.9	37.5	40.5
1914	54.2	52.0	56.8	54.9	52.7	57.5	38.9	37.1	40.8
1913	52.5	50.3	55.0	53.0	50.8	55.7	38.4	36.7	40.3
1912	53.5	51.5	55.9	53.9	51.9	56.2	37.9	35.9	40.0
1911	52.6	50.9	54.4	53.0	51.3	54.9	36.4	34.6	38.2
1910	50.0	48.4	51.8	50.3	48.6	52.0	35.6	33.8	37.5
1909	52.1	50.5	53.8	52.5	50.9	54.2	35.7	34.2	37.3
1908	51.1	49.5	52.8	51.5	49.9	53.3	34.9	33.8	36.0
1907	47.6	45.6	49.9	48.1	46.0	50.4	32.5	31.1	34.0
1906	48.7	46.9	50.8	49.3	47.3	51.4	32.9	31.8	33.9
1905	48.7	47.3	50.2	49.1	47.6	50.6	31.3	29.6	33.1
1904	47.6	46.2	49.1	48.0	46.6	49.5	30.8	29.1	32.7
1903	50.5	49.1	52.0	50.9	49.5	52.5	33.1	31.7	34.6
1902	51.5	49.8	53.4	51.9	50.2	53.8	34.6	32.9	36.4
1901	49.1	47.6	50.6	49.4	48.0	51.0	33.7	32.2	35.3
1900	47.3	46.3	48.3	47.6	46.6	48.7	33.0	32.5	33.5

* Denotes first year for which figures include Alaska and Hawaii.
[1] Excludes New Jersey; state did not require reporting of race.

[2] Includes Alaska.

Series B 136-147. Fetal Death Ratio; Neonatal, Infant and Maternal Mortality Rates, by Race: 1915 to 1989

(Prior to 1933, for registration area only)

Year	Fetal death ratio per 1,000 live births [1]			Neonatal mortality rate per 1,000 live births			Infant mortality rate per 1,000 live births			Maternal mortality rate per 10,000 live births		
	Total	White	Black	Total	White	Black	Total	White	Black	Total	White	Black
	136	137	138	139	140	141	142	143	144	145	146	147
1989	7.5	6.4	11.4	6.2	5.2	9.6	9.8	8.2	15.2	7.9	5.6	16.5
1988	7.5	6.4	11.4	6.3	5.4	9.7	10.0	8.5	15.0	8.6	5.9	17.4
1987	7.7	6.7	11.5	6.5	5.5	10.0	10.1	8.6	15.4	6.6	5.1	12.0
1986	7.7	6.8	11.2	6.7	5.8	10.1	10.4	8.9	15.7	7.2	4.9	16.0
1985	7.9	7.0	11.3	7.0	6.1	10.3	10.6	9.3	15.8	7.8	5.2	18.1
1984	8.2	7.4	11.5	7.0	6.2	10.2	10.8	9.4	16.1	7.8	5.4	16.9
1983	8.5	7.5	12.4	7.3	6.4	10.8	11.2	9.7	16.8	8.0	5.9	16.3
1982	8.9	7.9	12.7	7.7	6.8	11.3	11.5	10.1	17.3	7.9	5.8	16.4
1981	9.0	8.0	12.8	8.0	7.1	11.8	11.9	10.5	17.8	8.5	6.3	17.3
1980	9.2	8.2	13.4	8.5	7.5	12.5	12.6	11.0	19.1	9.2	6.7	19.8
1979	9.4	8.4	13.8	8.9	7.9	12.9	13.1	11.4	19.8	9.6	6.4	22.7
1978	9.7	8.5	14.7	9.5	8.4	14.0	13.8	12.0	21.1	9.6	6.4	23.0
1977	9.9	8.7	14.6	9.9	9.7	14.7	14.1	12.3	21.7	11.2	7.7	26.0
1976	10.5	9.3	15.2	10.9	9.7	16.3	15.2	13.3	23.5	12.3	9.0	26.5
1975	10.7	9.5	16.0	11.6	10.4	16.8	16.1	14.2	24.2	12.8	9.1	29.0
1974	11.5	10.2	17.0	12.3	11.1	17.2	16.7	14.8	24.9	14.6	10.0	35.1
1973	12.2	10.8	18.6	13.0	11.8	17.9	17.7	15.8	26.2	15.2	10.7	34.6
1972	12.7	11.2	19.5	13.6	12.4	19.2	18.5	16.4	27.7	18.8	14.3	38.5
1971	13.4	11.8	21.2	14.2	13.0	19.6	19.1	17.1	28.5	18.8	13.0	45.3
1970	14.2	12.4	22.6	15.1	13.8	21.4	20.0	17.8	30.9	2.2	1.4	5.6
1969	14.1	12.4	22.5	15.6	14.2	22.5	20.9	18.4	32.9	2.2	1.5	5.6
1968	15.8	13.8	25.6	16.1	14.7	23.0	21.8	19.2	34.5	2.5	1.7	6.4
1967	15.6	13.5	25.8	16.5	15.0	23.8	22.4	19.7	35.9	2.8	2.0	7.0
1966	15.7	13.6	26.1	17.2	15.6	24.8	23.7	20.6	38.8	2.9	2.0	7.2
1965	16.2	13.9	27.2	17.7	16.1	25.4	24.7	21.5	40.3	3.2	2.1	8.4
1964	16.4	14.1	28.2	17.9	16.2	26.5	24.8	21.6	41.1	3.3	2.2	9.0
1963 [2]	15.8	13.7	26.7	18.2	16.7	26.1	25.2	22.2	41.5	3.6	2.4	9.7
1962 [2]	15.9	13.9	26.7	18.3	16.9	26.1	25.3	22.3	41.4	3.5	2.4	9.6
1961	16.1	14.1	27.0	18.4	16.9	26.2	25.3	22.4	40.7	3.7	2.5	10.1
1960 *	16.1	14.1	26.8	18.7	17.2	26.9	26.0	22.9	43.2	3.7	2.6	9.8
1959 [3]	16.2	14.2	27.3	19.0	17.5	27.7	26.4	23.2	44.0	3.7	2.6	10.2
1958	16.5	14.5	27.5	19.5	17.8	29.0	27.1	23.8	45.7	3.8	2.6	10.2
1957	16.3	14.5	26.8	19.1	17.5	27.8	26.3	23.3	43.7	4.1	2.8	11.8
1956	16.5	14.6	27.2	18.9	17.5	27.0	26.0	23.2	42.1	4.1	2.9	11.1
1955	17.1	15.2	28.4	19.1	17.7	27.2	26.4	23.6	42.8	4.7	3.3	13.0
1954	17.5	15.5	28.9	19.1	17.8	27.0	26.6	23.9	42.9	5.2	3.7	14.4
1953	17.8	15.9	29.6	19.6	18.3	27.4	27.8	25.0	44.7	6.1	4.4	16.6
1952	18.3	16.1	32.2	19.8	18.5	28.0	28.4	25.5	47.0	6.8	4.9	18.8
1951	18.8	16.7	32.1	20.0	18.9	27.3	28.4	25.8	44.8	7.5	5.5	20.1
1950	19.2	17.1	32.5	20.5	19.4	27.5	29.2	26.8	44.5	8.3	6.1	22.2
1949	19.8	17.5	34.6	21.4	20.3	28.6	31.3	28.9	47.3	9.0	6.8	23.5
1948	20.6	18.3	36.5	22.2	21.2	29.1	32.0	29.9	46.5	11.7	8.9	30.1
1947	21.1	18.7	39.6	22.8	21.7	31.0	32.2	30.1	48.5	13.5	10.9	33.5
1946	22.8	20.4	40.9	24.0	23.1	31.5	33.8	31.8	49.5	15.7	13.1	35.9
1945	23.9	21.4	42.0	24.3	23.3	32.0	38.3	35.6	57.0	20.7	17.2	45.5
1944	27.0	24.5	45.4	24.7	23.6	32.5	39.8	36.9	60.3	22.8	18.9	50.6
1943	26.7	24.2	46.2	24.7	23.7	32.9	40.4	37.5	62.5	24.5	21.1	51.0
1942	28.2	25.5	49.3	25.7	24.5	34.6	40.4	37.3	64.6	25.9	22.2	54.4
1941	29.9	26.5	54.0	27.7	26.1	39.0	45.3	41.2	74.8	31.7	26.6	67.8
1940	31.3	27.7	56.7	28.8	27.2	39.7	47.0	43.2	73.8	37.6	32.0	77.4
1939	32.0	28.2	59.0	29.3	27.8	39.6	48.0	44.3	74.2	40.4	35.3	76.2
1938	32.1	28.1	61.1	29.6	28.3	39.1	51.0	47.1	79.1	43.5	37.7	84.9
1937	33.4	29.2	63.2	31.3	29.7	42.1	54.4	50.3	83.2	48.9	43.6	85.8
1936	34.4	29.8	66.9	32.6	31.0	43.9	57.1	52.9	87.6	56.8	51.2	97.2

See footnotes at end of table.

Series B 136-147. Fetal Death Ratio; Neonatal, Infant and Maternal Mortality Rates, by Race: 1915 to 1989—Cont'd.

(Prior to 1933, for registration area only)

Year	Fetal death ratio per 1,000 live births [1]			Neonatal mortality rate per 1,000 live births			Infant mortality rate per 1,000 live births			Maternal mortality rate per 10,000 live births		
	Total	White	Black	Total	White	Black	Total	White	Black	Total	White	Black
	136	137	138	139	140	141	142	143	144	145	146	147
1935	35.8	31.1	68.7	32.4	31.0	42.7	55.7	51.9	83.2	58.2	53.1	94.6
1934	36.2	31.4	70.1	34.1	[4] 32.3	[4] 45.3	60.1	[4] 54.5	[4] 94.4	59.3	[4] 54.4	[4] 89.7
1933	37.0	32.2	71.1	34.0	[4] 32.1	[4] 45.8	58.1	[4] 52.8	[4] 91.3	61.9	[4] 56.4	[4] 96.7
1932	37.8	32.7	74.4	33.5	[4] 32.0	[4] 43.7	57.6	[4] 53.3	[4] 86.2	63.3	[4] 58.1	[4] 97.6
1931	38.2	33.4	74.1	34.6	33.2	45.2	61.6	57.4	93.1	66.1	60.1	111.4
1930	39.2	34.0	79.9	35.7	34.2	47.4	64.6	60.1	99.9	67.3	60.9	117.4
1929	39.5	34.4	79.7	36.9	35.6	47.3	67.6	63.2	102.2	69.5	63.1	119.9
1928	40.2	35.0	81.5	37.2	35.7	48.8	68.7	64.0	106.2	69.2	62.7	121.0
1927	38.8	34.8	74.8	36.1	35.0	46.1	64.6	60.6	100.1	64.7	59.4	113.3
1926	38.1	35.1	73.0	37.9	37.1	48.0	73.3	70.0	111.8	65.6	61.9	107.1
1925	38.1	35.1	73.1	37.8	36.8	49.5	71.7	68.3	110.8	64.7	60.3	116.2
1924	39.3	35.8	76.2	38.6	37.4	51.2	70.8	66.8	112.9	65.6	60.7	117.9
1923	38.9	35.9	71.8	39.5	38.6	49.9	77.1	73.5	117.4	66.5	62.6	109.5
1922	39.4	36.4	73.4	39.7	38.8	49.9	76.2	73.2	110.0	66.4	62.8	106.8
1921	—	—	—	39.7	38.7	50.3	75.6	72.5	108.5	68.2	64.4	107.7
1920	—	—	—	41.5	40.4	55.0	85.8	82.1	131.7	79.9	76.0	128.1
1919	—	—	—	41.5	40.3	55.2	86.6	83.0	130.5	73.7	69.6	124.4
1918	—	—	—	44.2	43.3	60.5	100.9	97.4	161.2	91.6	88.9	139.3
1917	—	—	—	43.4	42.6	58.0	93.8	90.5	150.7	66.2	63.2	117.7
1916	—	—	—	44.1	43.5	68.9	101.0	99.0	184.9	62.2	60.8	117.9
1915	—	—	—	44.4	—	—	99.9	98.6	181.2	60.8	60.1	105.6

* Denotes first year for which figures include Alaska and Hawaii.
[1] For 1945-1970,, includes only deaths for which the period of gestation was given as 20 weeks or more or not stated. For earlier years, includes all fetal deaths, regardless of gestation. In 1945, ratios based on all fetal deaths, regardless of gestation, were: Total, 26.6, white, 24.1 black and other, 44.6.

[2] Figures by race exclude New Jersey; state did not require reporting of race.
[3] Includes Alaska.
[4] Mexicans included with Black and other.

Series B 167-180.   Death Rate, by Race and Sex: 1900 to 1990
(Number of deaths, excluding fetal deaths, per 1,000 population. Prior to 1933 for death-registration area only)

Year	Total	Both sexes	White Male	White Female	Black and other Both sexes	Black and other Male	Black and other Female	Year	Total	Both sexes	White Male	White Female	Black and other Both sexes	Black and other Male	Black and other Female
	167	168	169	170	171	172	173		167	168	169	170	171	172	173
1990	8.6	8.9	9.4	8.5	8.2	9.4	7.1	1945	10.6	10.4	12.5	8.6	11.9	13.5	10.5
1989	8.7	8.9	9.3	8.5	8.7	10.1	7.5	1944	10.6	10.4	12.2	8.8	12.4	13.8	11.1
1988	8.8	9.1	9.5	8.6	8.7	10.1	7.5	1943	10.9	10.7	12.2	9.2	12.8	14.0	11.6
1987	8.7	9.0	9.5	8.5	8.6	9.9	7.4	1942	10.3	10.1	11.4	8.7	12.7	14.0	11.4
1986	8.7	9.0	9.5	8.4	8.5	9.9	7.3	1941	10.5	10.2	11.4	8.9	13.5	14.8	12.2
1985	8.7	9.0	9.6	8.4	8.5	9.8	7.3	1940	10.8	10.4	11.6	9.2	13.8	15.1	12.6
1984	8.6	8.9	9.5	8.2	8.3	9.6	7.1	1939	10.6	10.3	11.3	9.2	13.5	14.7	12.4
1983	8.6	8.8	9.6	8.2	8.3	9.6	7.1	1938	10.6	10.3	11.3	9.2	14.0	15.2	12.9
1982	8.5	8.7	9.5	8.0	8.2	9.6	6.9	1937	11.3	10.8	12.0	9.6	14.9	16.4	13.4
1981	8.6	8.8	9.7	8.0	8.4	9.9	7.1	1936	11.6	11.1	12.3	9.9	15.4	16.9	13.9
1980	8.8	8.9	9.8	8.1	8.8	10.3	7.3	1935	10.9	10.6	11.6	9.5	14.3	15.6	13.0
1979	8.5	8.7	9.8	7.7	8.4	10.0	7.0	1934	11.1	10.6	11.7	9.6	14.8	16.0	13.5
1978	8.7	8.8	9.8	7.8	8.6	10.2	7.1	1933	10.7	10.3	11.2	9.3	14.1	15.1	13.1
1977	8.6	8.7	9.8	7.7	8.6	10.3	7.2	1932	10.9	10.5	11.3	9.6	14.5	15.4	13.5
1976	8.9	9.0	10.1	7.9	8.2	9.8	6.8	1931	11.1	10.6	11.5	9.6	15.5	16.5	14.5
1975	8.5	8.7	10.0	7.8	8.8	10.6	7.3	1930	11.3	10.8	11.7	9.8	16.3	17.4	15.3
1974	9.2	9.2	10.4	8.1	8.7	10.4	7.2	1929	11.9	11.3	12.2	10.4	16.9	18.0	15.8
1973	9.4	9.4	10.7	8.2	9.1	10.8	7.6	1928	12.0	11.4	12.3	10.5	17.1	18.0	16.2
1972	9.4	9.5	10.8	8.2	9.2	11.0	7.6	1927	11.3	10.8	11.6	10.0	16.4	17.2	15.6
1971	9.3	9.3	10.7	8.1	9.2	10.8	7.7	1926	12.1	11.6	12.3	10.8	17.8	18.7	16.9
1970	9.5	9.5	10.9	8.1	9.4	11.2	7.8	1925	11.7	11.1	11.8	10.4	17.4	18.2	16.6
1969	9.5	9.5	10.9	8.2	9.6	11.3	8.0	1924	11.6	11.0	11.8	10.3	17.1	17.9	16.3
1968	9.7	9.6	11.1	8.2	9.9	11.6	8.3	1923	12.1	11.7	12.3	11.0	16.5	17.0	16.0
1967	9.4	9.4	10.8	8.0	9.4	10.9	7.9	1922	11.7	11.3	11.9	10.7	15.2	15.7	14.8
1966	9.5	9.5	10.9	8.1	9.7	11.3	8.3	1921	11.5	11.1	11.6	10.6	15.5	15.7	15.4
1965	9.4	9.4	10.8	8.0	9.6	11.1	8.2	1920	13.0	12.6	13.0	12.1	17.7	17.8	17.5
1964	9.4	9.4	10.8	8.0	9.7	11.1	8.3	1919	12.9	12.4	13.0	11.8	17.9	18.1	17.8
1963 ¹	9.6	9.5	11.0	8.1	10.1	11.5	8.7	1918	18.1	17.5	19.3	15.8	25.6	26.7	24.4
1962 ¹	9.5	9.4	10.8	8.0	9.8	11.2	8.5	1917	14.0	13.5	14.6	12.4	20.4	21.4	19.4
1961	9.3	9.3	10.7	7.8	9.6	10.9	8.4	1916	13.8	13.4	14.4	12.4	19.1	19.9	18.4
1960 *	9.5	9.5	11.0	8.0	10.1	11.5	8.7	1915	13.2	12.9	13.7	12.0	20.2	20.8	19.5
1959 ²	9.4	9.3	10.8	7.9	9.9	11.3	8.6	1914	13.3	13.0	13.9	12.1	20.2	20.9	19.4
1958	9.5	9.4	10.9	8.0	10.3	11.6	9.0	1913	13.8	13.5	14.5	12.5	20.3	21.0	19.6
1957	9.6	9.5	11.0	8.0	10.5	11.9	9.1	1912	13.6	13.4	14.3	12.4	20.6	21.3	19.7
1956	9.4	9.3	10.8	7.8	10.1	11.4	8.8	1911	13.9	13.7	14.5	12.8	21.3	21.9	20.6
1955	9.3	9.2	10.7	7.8	10.0	11.3	8.8	1910	14.7	14.5	15.4	13.6	21.7	22.3	21.0
1954	9.2	9.1	10.6	7.6	10.1	11.4	8.8	1909	14.2	14.0	14.9	13.2	21.8	22.3	21.2
1953	9.6	9.4	11.0	8.0	10.8	12.3	9.4	1908	14.7	14.5	15.3	13.6	22.4	22.8	22.0
1952	9.6	9.4	11.0	8.0	11.0	12.5	9.6	1907	15.9	15.7	16.8	14.5	24.3	25.0	23.5
1951	9.7	9.5	11.0	8.0	11.0	12.5	9.8	1906	15.7	15.5	16.5	14.4	24.2	24.7	23.6
1950	9.6	9.5	10.9	8.0	11.2	12.5	9.9	1905	15.9	15.7	16.5	14.8	25.5	26.8	24.3
1949	9.7	9.5	11.0	8.1	11.2	12.5	10.0	1904	16.4	16.2	17.1	15.3	26.1	27.6	24.7
1948	9.9	9.7	11.2	8.3	11.4	12.7	10.1	1903	15.6	15.4	16.2	14.6	24.5	25.5	23.4
1947	10.1	9.9	11.4	8.5	11.4	12.5	10.3	1902	15.5	15.3	16.2	14.4	23.6	24.8	22.3
1946	10.0	9.8	11.2	8.5	11.1	12.2	10.0								
								1901	16.4	16.2	17.1	15.4	24.3	25.6	23.1
								1900	17.2	17.0	17.7	16.3	25.0	25.7	24.4

* Denotes first year for which figures include Alaska and Hawaii.
¹ Excludes New Jersey; state did not require reporting of race.
² Includes Alaska.

Series B 214-215.   Marriage Rate: 1920 to 1988

Year	Per 1,000 population 214	Per 1,000 unmarried females[1] 215	Year	Per 1,000 population 214	Per 1,000 unmarried females[1] 215	Year	Per 1,000 population 214	Per 1,000 unmarried females[1] 215	Year	Per 1,000 population 214	Per 1,000 unmarried females[1] 215
1988	9.7	54.6	1970	10.6	76.7	1953	9.8	83.7	1936	10.7	74.0
1987	9.9	55.7	1969	10.6	80.0	1952	9.9	83.2	1935	10.4	72.5
1986	10.0	56.2	1968	10.4	79.1	1951	10.4	86.6	1934	10.3	71.8
1985	10.1	57.0	1967	9.7	76.4	1950	11.1	90.2	1933	8.7	61.3
1984	10.5	59.5	1966	9.5	75.6	1949	10.6	86.7	1932	7.9	56.0
1983	10.5	59.9	1965	9.3	75.0	1948	12.4	98.5	1931	8.6	61.9
1982	10.6	61.4	1964	9.0	74.6	1947	13.9	106.2	1930	9.2	67.6
1981	10.6	61.7	1963	8.8	73.4	1946	16.4	118.1	1929	10.1	75.5
1980	10.6	61.4	1962	8.5	71.2	1945	12.2	83.6	1928	9.8	74.1
1979	10.4	63.6	1961	8.5	72.2	1944	10.9	76.5	1927	10.1	77.0
1978	10.3	64.1	1960 *	8.5	73.5	1943	11.7	83.0	1926	10.2	78.7
1977	9.9	63.6	1959 [2]	8.5	73.6	1942	13.2	93.0	1925	10.3	79.2
1976	9.9	65.2	1958	8.4	72.0	1941	12.7	88.5	1924	10.4	80.3
1975	10.0	66.9	1957	8.9	78.0	1940	12.1	82.8	1923	11.0	85.2
1974	10.5	72.0	1956	9.5	82.4	1939	10.7	73.0	1922	10.3	79.7
1973	10.9	76.0	1955	9.3	80.9	1938	10.3	69.9	1921	10.7	83.0
1972	10.9	77.5	1954	9.2	79.8	1937	11.3	78.0	1920	12.0	92.0
1971	10.6	76.3									

* Denotes first year for which figures include Alaska and Hawaii.
[1] 15 years old and over.
[2] Includes Alaska.

Series B 216-220.   Divorce: 1920 to 1988
(Includes reported annulments)

Year	Divorce rate Per 1,000 population 216	Per 1,000 married females[1] 217	Median duration of marriage (years) 218	Year	Divorce rate Per 1,000 population 216	Per 1,000 married females[1] 217	Median duration of marriage (years) 218	Year	Divorce rate Per 1,000 population 216	Per 1,000 married females[1] 217	Median duration of marriage (years) 218
1988	4.7	20.7	—	1965	2.5	10.6	7.2	1942	2.4	10.1	—
1987	4.8	20.8	—	1964	2.4	10.0	7.4	1941	2.2	9.4	—
1986	4.9	21.2	—	1963	2.3	9.6	7.5				
				1962	2.2	9.4	7.3	1940	2.0	8.8	—
1985	5.0	21.7	—	1961	2.3	9.6	7.1	1939	1.9	8.5	—
1984	5.0	21.5	6.9					1938	1.9	8.4	—
1983	4.9	21.3	7.0	1960 *	2.2	9.2	7.2	1937	1.9	8.7	—
1982	5.0	21.7	7.0	1959 [2]	2.2	9.3	7.0	1936	1.8	8.3	—
1981	5.3	22.6	7.0	1958	2.1	8.9	6.4				
				1957	2.2	9.2	6.7	1935	1.7	7.8	—
1980	5.2	22.6	6.8	1956	2.3	9.4	6.5	1934	1.6	7.5	—
1979	5.3	22.8	6.8					1933	1.3	6.1	—
1978	5.1	21.9	6.6	1955	2.3	9.3	6.4	1932	1.3	6.1	—
1977	5.0	21.1	6.6	1954	2.4	9.5	6.4	1931	1.5	7.1	—
1976	5.0	21.1	6.5	1953	2.5	9.9	6.1				
				1952	2.5	10.1	6.1	1930	1.6	7.5	—
1975	4.9	20.3	6.5	1951	2.5	9.9	6.0	1929	1.7	8.0	—
1974	4.6	19.3	6.5					1928	1.7	7.8	—
1973	4.4	18.2	6.6	1950	2.6	10.3	5.8	1927	1.6	7.8	—
1972	4.1	17.0	6.7	1949	2.7	10.6	—	1926	1.6	7.5	—
1971	3.7	15.7	—	1948	2.8	11.2	—				
				1947	3.4	13.6	—	1925	1.5	7.2	—
1970	3.5	14.9	6.7	1946	4.3	17.9	—	1924	1.5	7.2	—
1969	3.2	13.4	6.9					1923	1.5	7.1	—
1968	2.9	12.4	7.0	1945	3.5	14.4	—	1922	1.4	6.6	—
1967	2.6	11.2	7.1	1944	2.9	12.0	—	1921	1.5	7.2	—
1966	2.5	10.9	7.1	1943	2.6	11.0	—	1920	1.6	8.0	—

* Denotes first year for which figures include Alaska and Hawaii.
[1] 15 years old and over. Population enumerated as of April 1 for 1940, 1950 and 1960 and estimated as of July 1 for all other years; includes Armed Forces abroad for 1941-1946.
[2] Includes Alaska.

Series B 221-235. Total and Per Capita National Health Expenditures, by Type of Service: 1929 to 1990

(Calendar year data. Totals in million dollars.)

| Year | Total | Health services and supplies | | | | | | | | | | | Research and medical-facilities construction | |
| | | Total | Hospital care | Physicians' services | Dentists' services | Other professional services[1] | Drugs and drug sundries[2] | Eyeglasses and appliances[2] | Nursing home care | Government public health activities | Other health services | Research[2] | Construction |
	221	222	223	224	225	226	227	228	229	231	232	234	235
1990	666,200	643,400	256,000	125,700	34,000	31,600	54,600	12,100	53,100	19,300	11,300	12,400	10,400
1989	602,800	582,100	232,600	113,600	31,600	27,100	50,600	11,400	47,700	18,300	9,700	11,000	9,600
1988	546,000	526,200	212,000	105,100	29,400	23,800	46,300	10,100	42,800	16,600	8,700	10,300	9,500
1987	494,100	476,800	194,200	93,000	27,100	21,100	43,200	9,100	39,700	14,600	7,800	9,000	8,200
1986	458,200	442,000	179,600	92,000	29,600	14,100	30,600	8,200	38,100	13,400	11,900	8,200	8,000
1985	422,600	407,200	168,300	74,000	23,300	16,600	36,200	7,100	34,100	12,300	6,400	7,800	7,600
1984	391,100	375,400	156,300	75,400	24,600	10,900	26,500	7,000	31,700	11,000	9,400	6,800	8,900
1983	357,200	341,800	146,800	64,800	21,700	9,300	24,500	6,200	29,400	9,900	8,300	6,200	9,200
1982	322,400	308,300	135,500	61,800	19,500	7,100	22,400	5,700	27,300	8,600	7,600	5,900	8,200
1981	286,600	273,500	118,000	54,800	17,300	6,400	21,300	5,700	24,200	7,700	6,900	5,700	7,500
1980	250,100	238,900	102,400	41,900	14,400	8,700	21,600	4,600	20,000	7,200	4,600	5,400	5,800
1979	215,000	204,500	86,100	40,200	13,300	4,700	17,200	4,600	17,600	6,200	5,100	4,800	5,700
1978	189,300	179,500	75,700	35,800	11,800	4,100	15,400	4,100	15,200	5,300	4,500	4,400	5,300
1977	162,600	153,900	65,600	32,200	10,000	3,200	12,500	2,100	12,600	3,700	4,300	3,700	5,100
1976	141,000	132,400	55,600	27,500	8,700	2,400	11,300	1,900	10,700	3,500	4,000	3,600	5,000
1975	132,700	124,300	52,100	24,900	8,200	2,600	11,900	3,200	10,100	3,200	3,700	3,300	5,100
1974	106,300	99,300	41,000	19,700	6,900	1,900	9,400	1,700	7,500	2,500	3,200	2,500	4,500
1973	99,069	—	38,270	18,200	5,970	1,900	9,300	2,091	7,050	1,905	3,643	2,484	4,258
1972	90,391	—	34,219	16,916	5,581	1,717	8,628	1,896	6,274	1,804	3,306	2,173	4,180
1971	81,294	—	30,552	15,835	5,068	1,547	7,821	1,839	5,446	1,811	2,897	1,954	3,845
1970	71,573	66,365	27,597	14,294	4,419	1,466	7,297	1,866	3,070	1,568	2,690	1,842	3,366
1969	64,142	59,351	24,093	12,654	4,047	1,313	6,812	1,765	2,650	1,316	2,592	1,818	2,973
1968	56,587	52,532	20,926	11,099	3,623	1,271	6,165	1,731	2,280	1,098	2,332	1,795	2,260
1967	50,696	46,987	18,145	10,287	3,360	1,158	5,652	1,609	1,858	942	2,099	1,703	2,006
1966	44,974	41,440	15,583	9,156	2,964	1,123	5,309	1,413	1,526	885	1,800	1,574	1,960
1965	40,468	37,087	13,605	8,745	2,808	1,038	4,850	1,230	1,328	698	1,492	1,469	1,912
1964	37,461	34,375	12,697	8,056	2,648	940	4,446	1,072	1,214	610	1,511	1,324	1,762
1963	33,530	30,890	11,709	6,891	2,277	921	4,235	952	891	540	1,380	1,184	1,456
1962	31,295	28,857	10,658	6,498	2,234	902	4,095	908	695	505	1,277	1,032	1,406
1961	28,783	26,766	9,921	5,895	2,067	882	3,824	804	606	452	1,320	844	1,174
1960	26,895	25,185	9,092	5,684	1,977	862	3,657	776	526	414	1,336	662	1,048
1959	24,878	23,354	8,177	5,481	1,894	801	3,525	722	434	428	1,138	526	998
1958	22,848	21,442	7,548	4,910	1,850	729	3,242	678	383	424	1,045	416	990
1957	21,108	19,885	6,892	4,419	1,737	673	3,010	678	368	415	1,011	344	879
1956	19,246	18,348	6,347	4,067	1,625	610	2,686	668	358	402	965	270	628
1955	17,745	16,884	5,900	3,689	1,508	562	2,384	604	312	377	924	210	651
1954	16,799	15,946	5,502	3,574	1,406	541	2,181	606	270	374	904	183	670
1953	15,745	14,895	5,085	3,278	1,234	499	2,152	612	248	378	911	164	686
1952	14,988	13,949	4,685	3,042	1,098	459	2,071	586	228	427	952	150	889
1951	13,992	12,912	4,254	2,868	997	426	1,989	551	207	416	883	134	946
1950	12,662	11,702	3,851	2,747	961	396	1,726	491	187	361	666	117	843
1949	11,576	10,811	3,557	2,633	920	371	1,557	458	168	338	539	105	660
1948	10,612	10,184	3,203	2,611	900	354	1,466	436	150	306	470	89	339
1940	3,987	3,868	1,011	973	419	174	637	189	33	153	112	3	116
1935	2,936	2,875	763	773	302	153	475	133	—	117	64	—	61
1929	3,649	3,436	663	1,004	482	252	606	133	—	96	91	—	213

See footnotes at end of chart.

Series B 221-235. Total and Per Capita National Health Expenditures, by Type of Service: 1929 to 1990—Cont'd.

(Calendar year data. Totals in million dollars.)

			Health services and supplies									Research and medical-facilities construction	
Year	Total	Total	Hospital care	Physicians' services	Dentists' services	Other professional services[1]	Drugs and drug sundries[2]	Eyeglasses and appliances	Nursing home care	Government public health activities	Other health services	Research[2]	Construction
	221	222	223	224	225	226	227	228	229	231	232	234	235
1990	2,479	—	986	484	131	122	210	47	205	74	44	—	—
1989	2,265	—	905	442	123	105	197	45	186	71	38	—	—
1988	2,068	—	833	413	116	93	182	40	168	65	34	—	—
1987	1,892	—	771	369	108	84	171	36	157	58	31	—	—
1986	1,772	—	720	369	119	56	122	33	153	54	48	—	—
1985	1,647	—	676	335	110	50	116	30	141	50	44	—	—
1984	1,533	—	638	308	101	45	108	28	130	45	39	—	—
1983	1,410	—	605	282	90	38	101	26	121	41	34	—	—
1982	1,288	—	563	257	81	33	92	24	111	39	31	—	—
1981	1,152	—	501	230	73	29	87	22	100	36	28	—	—
1980	1,004	—	432	199	66	24	80	22	87	31	25	—	—
1979	876	—	373	173	57	20	74	20	75	25	22	—	—
1978	792	—	334	158	52	18	68	18	67	24	20	—	—
1977	697.32	—	297.38	145.84	45.41	14.56	56.72	9.45	57.18	16.90	19.59	—	—
1976	606.19	—	254.49	125.87	39.99	12.59	51.63	8.90	48.82	15.96	18.48	—	—
1975	536.09	—	223.36	110.07	36.34	10.98	47.82	8.08	43.13	13.66	16.02	—	—
1974	484.73	—	202.00	96.09	32.99	9.49	47.13	10.46	38.16	14.11	13.05	—	—
1973	431.55	—	178.88	85.07	27.90	8.88	43.47	9.77	32.95	8.90	17.03	—	—
1972	395.77	—	161.15	70.66	26.28	8.09	40.63	8.93	29.55	8.50	15.57	—	—
1971	358.57	—	145.11	75.21	24.07	7.35	37.14	8.73	25.87	8.60	13.76	—	—
1970	343.44	318.45	132.42	68.59	21.20	7.03	35.01	8.95	14.73	7.52	12.91	8.83	16.15
1969	311.06	287.83	116.84	61.37	19.63	6.37	33.04	8.56	12.85	6.38	12.57	8.81	14.41
1968	277.14	257.28	102.49	54.36	17.74	6.22	30.19	8.48	11.17	5.38	11.42	8.79	11.07
1967	250.77	232.42	89.76	50.89	16.62	5.73	27.96	7.96	9.19	4.66	10.38	8.42	9.92
1966	224.89	207.22	77.92	45.78	14.82	5.62	26.55	7.07	7.63	4.43	9.00	7.87	9.80
1965	204.68	187.58	68.81	44.23	14.20	5.25	24.53	6.22	6.72	3.53	7.55	7.43	9.67
1964	191.88	176.07	65.04	41.31	13.56	4.81	22.77	5.49	6.22	3.12	7.74	6.78	9.03
1963	174.15	160.44	60.81	35.79	11.83	4.78	22.00	4.94	4.63	2.80	7.17	6.15	7.56
1962	164.89	152.05	56.16	34.24	11.77	4.75	21.58	4.78	3.66	2.66	6.73	5.44	7.41
1961	154.02	143.23	53.09	31.55	11.06	4.72	20.46	4.30	3.24	2.42	7.06	4.52	6.28
1960	146.30	137.00	49.46	30.92	10.75	4.69	19.89	4.22	2.86	2.25	7.27	3.60	5.70
1959	137.94	129.49	45.34	30.39	10.50	4.44	19.54	4.00	2.41	2.37	6.31	2.92	5.53
1958	128.81	120.88	42.55	27.68	10.43	4.11	18.28	3.82	2.16	2.39	5.89	2.35	5.58
1957	121.00	113.99	39.51	25.33	9.96	3.86	17.25	3.89	2.11	2.38	5.80	1.97	5.04
1956	112.32	107.07	37.04	23.73	9.48	3.56	15.67	3.90	2.09	2.35	5.63	1.58	3.66
1955	105.38	100.27	35.04	21.91	8.96	3.34	14.16	3.59	1.85	2.24	5.49	1.25	3.87
1954	101.54	96.37	33.26	21.60	8.50	3.27	13.18	3.66	1.63	2.26	5.46	1.11	4.05
1953	96.84	91.61	31.27	20.16	7.59	3.07	13.24	3.76	1.53	2.32	5.60	1.01	4.22
1952	93.69	87.19	29.29	19.02	6.86	2.87	12.95	3.66	1.43	2.67	5.95	.94	5.56
1951	88.95	82.08	27.04	18.23	6.34	2.71	12.64	3.50	1.32	2.64	5.61	.85	6.01
1950	81.86	75.66	24.90	17.76	6.21	2.56	11.06	3.17	1.21	2.33	4.31	.76	5.45
1949	76.11	71.08	23.39	17.31	6.05	2.44	10.24	3.01	1.10	2.22	3.54	.69	4.34
1948	70.97	68.11	21.42	17.46	6.02	2.37	9.80	2.92	1.00	2.05	3.14	.60	2.27
1940	29.62	28.74	7.51	7.23	3.11	1.29	4.73	1.40	.25	1.14	.83	.02	.86
1935	22.65	22.18	5.89	5.96	2.33	1.18	3.67	1.03	—	.90	.49	—	.47
1929	29.49	27.77	5.36	8.11	3.90	2.04	4.90	1.07	—	.78	.74	—	1.72

[1] Services of registered and practical nurses in private duty, visits of nurses, podiatrists, physical therapists, clinical psychologists, chiropractors, naturopaths and Christian Science practitioners.

[2] Research expenditures of drug companies included in expenditures for drugs and drug sundries and excluded from research expenditures.

[3] Includes fees of optometrists and expenditures for hearing aids, orthopedic appliances, artifical limbs, crutches, wheelchairs, etc.

[4] Based on July 1 data from the Bureau of the Census for total U.S. population, including Armed Forces and federal civilian employees overseas and the civilian population of outlying areas.

Series B 236-247. National and Personal Health Care Expenditures, by Source of Funds: 1929 to 1990

(In billions of dollars, except percent. Calendar year data.)

| Year | National health expenditures | | Personal health care expenditures | | Year | National health expenditures | | Personal health care expenditures | | Year | National health expenditures | | Personal health care expenditures | |
| | Amount | Percent of gross national product | Private insurance benefits | Public expenditures | | Amount | Percent of gross national product | Private insurance benefits | Public expenditures | | Amount | Percent of gross national product | Private insurance benefits | Public expenditures |
	236	237	245	247		236	237	245	247		236	237	245	247
1990	666.2	12.2	216.8	268.6	1975	132.9	8.3	32.9	50.2	1960	26.9	5.3	5.0	5.2
1989	602.8	11.6	196.4	240.0	1974	116.1	7.9	27.8	42.8	1959	24.9	5.1	4.4	4.8
1988	546.0	11.2	174.4	215.1	1973	102.5	7.5	24.6	35.9	1958	22.8	5.1	3.9	4.5
1987	494.1	10.9	154.8	197.7	1972	92.3	7.6	21.9	31.8	1957	21.1	4.8	3.5	4.2
1986	454.8	10.7	143.2	180.3	1971	82.3	7.5	19.1	28.2	1956	19.2	4.6	3.0	3.9
1985	422.6	10.5	134.1	165.4	1970	71.6	7.3	15.7	21.9	1955	17.7	4.4	2.5	3.6
1984	389.6	10.3	123.7	150.8	1969	64.1	6.9	13.1	19.7	1954	16.8	4.6	2.2	3.4
1983	358.6	10.5	111.4	139.5	1968	56.6	6.5	11.3	17.5	1953	15.7	4.3	1.9	3.3
1982	326.1	10.3	100.5	127.0	1967	50.7	6.4	9.5	14.6	1952	15.0	4.3	1.6	3.3
1981	290.2	9.5	86.9	114.2	1966	44.9	6.0	9.1	9.5	1951	14.0	4.3	1.3	3.0
1980	250.1	9.2	73.4	98.1	1965	40.5	5.9	8.7	7.3	1950	12.7	4.5	1.0	2.4
1979	217.2	8.7	63.2	84.1	1964	37.5	5.9	7.8	6.9	1949	11.6	4.5	.8	2.0
1978	193.7	8.6	55.0	73.6	1963	33.5	5.7	7.0	6.4	1948	10.6	4.1	.6	1.8
1977	172.0	8.6	47.8	64.6	1962	31.3	5.6	6.3	6.0	1940	4.0	4.0	—	.6
1976	152.2	8.5	39.7	56.9	1961	28.8	5.5	5.7	5.6	1935	3.0	4.0	—	.4
										1929	3.6	3.5	—	.3

Series B 275-290.   Physicians, Dentists and Nurses; and Medical, Dental and Nursing Schools: 1810 to 1989

(Census figures in italics. Figures for schools and students are for academic session ending in the specified year)

Year	Physicians[1]		Medical schools[2]			Dentists[4]		Dental schools			Active professional graduate nurses		Professional nursing schools[6]		
	Number	Rate per 100,000 population	Number[3]	Students	Graduates	Number	Rate per 100,000 population	Number[5]	Students	Graduates	Number	Rate per 100,000 population	Number	Students	Graduates
	275	276	278	279	280	281	282	283	284	285	286	287	288	289	290
1989	645,000	261	142	71,600	17,200	168,000	59	58	16,200	4,300	1,666,000	675	1,457	201,000	62,000
1988	629,000	257	142	71,900	17,500	164,000	58	58	17,100	4,600	1,648,000	674	1,442	185,000	65,000
1987	612,000	253	142	72,300	17,400	161,000	58	58	17,900	4,700	1,627,000	671	1,465	183,000	71,000
1986	595,000	248	142	72,800	17,700	158,000	58	59	18,700	5,000	1,589,000	662	1,469	194,000	77,000
1985	577,000	243	142	73,200	17,800	156,000	58	60	19,600	5,400	1,544,000	649	1,473	218,000	82,000
1984	(NA)	(NA)	142	73,600	17,600	153,000	57	60	20,600	5,300	1,486,000	630	1,477	237,000	80,000
1983	542,000	232	142	73,500	17,100	150,000	56	60	21,400	5,800	1,439,000	616	1,466	251,000	77,000
1982	523,000	222	142	72,600	17,000	147,000	55	60	22,200	5,400	1,380,111	595	1,432	242,000	74,000
1981	505,000	217	142	71,600	16,800	144,000	54	60	22,600	5,600	1,327,000	578	1,401	235,000	74,000
1980	487,000	214	141	70,100	16,200	141,000	54	60	22,800	5,300	1,273,000	560	1,385	231,000	76,000
1979	472,000	207	138	66,500	16,000	138,000	53	60	22,200	5,400	1,200,000	534	1,374	235,000	77,000
1978	454,000	201	124	64,300	15,400	136,000	52	59	21,500	5,300	(NA)	(NA)	1,340	239,000	78,000
1977	438,000	196	126	61,900	14,500	133,000	52	59	21,000	5,200	1,028,000	468	1,339	245,000	78,000
1976	426,000	194	123	59,600	14,300	(NA)	52	59	20,800	5,300	961,000	449	1,349	250,000	78,000
1975	409,000	190	123	59,300	13,900	127,000	50	59	20,800	5,000	961,000	446	1,360	250,000	75,000
1974	394,000	182	121	53,700	12,200	(NA)	—	58	19,400	4,500	857,000	404	1,359	233,000	68,000
1973	382,000	178	114	50,100	11,000	122,000	48	56	18,400	4,200	815,000	390	1,363	213,000	59,000
1972	371,000	174	115	46,000	10,000	120,000	47	52	17,300	4,000	780,000	376	1,350	188,000	52,000
1971	359,000	174	110	42,600	9,400	118,000	47	53	16,600	3,800	723,000	353	1,343	165,000	47,000
1970	348,328	166	107	39,666	8,799	118,175	58	53	16,008	3,700	700,000	345	1,328	150,795	43,639
1969	338,942	163	104	37,712	8,486	115,610	57	52	15,408	3,433	680,000	338	1,287	145,588	42,196
1968	330,732	161	100	36,368	8,400	113,636	57	50	14,955	3,457	659,000	331	2,262	141,948	41,555
1967	322,045	158	95	35,212	8,148	112,152	56	49	14,421	3,360	640,000	325	1,219	139,070	38,237
1966	313,559	156	93	34,516	7,934	111,130	56	49	14,020	3,198	621,000	319	1,191	135,702	35,125
1965	305,115	153	93	34,089	7,803	109,301	56	49	13,876	3,181	613,188	319	1,153	129,629	24,686
1964	297,089	159	92	33,595	7,691	107,820	56	48	13,691	3,213	582,000	306	1,142	124,744	35,259
1963	289,188	149	92	33,072	7,631	106,230	56	48	13,576	3,233	—	—	1,128	123,861	32,398
1962	270,136	145	92	32,633	7,530	105,252	56	47	13,513	3,207	550,000	297	1,118	123,012	31,186
1961	—	—	92	32,232	7,500	103,596	56	47	13,580	3,290	—	—	1,123	118,849	30,267
1960	274,833	148	*91	*31,999	*7,508	101,947	56	*47	*13,581	*3,253	*504,000	*282	*1,119	*115,057	*30,113
1959	*236,818	*133	85	29,614	6,860	*100,615	*57	47	13,509	3,156	—	—	1,126	113,518	30,312
1958	—	—	85	29,473	6,861	98,540	57	47	13,279	3,083	460,000	268	1,118	112,989	30,410
1957	226,625	132	85	29,130	6,796	100,534	59	45	13,004	3,050	—	—	1,115	114,674	29,933
1956	—	—	82	28,639	6,845	99,227	59	43	12,730	3,038	430,000	262	1,125	114,423	30,236
1955	218,061	132	81	28,583	6,977	97,529	59	43	12,601	3,081	7 430,000	259	1,139	107,572	28,729
1954	214,200	132	80	28,227	6,861	95,883	59	43	12,516	3,084	7 389,600	244	1,141	103,019	28,539
1953	210,900	132	79	27,688	6,668	93,726	59	42	12,370	2,945	—	—	1,148	102,019	29,308
1952	207,900	132	79	27,076	6,080	91,638	58	42	12,169	2,975	—	—	1,167	102,550	29,016
1951	205,500	133	79	26,186	6,135	—	—	42	11,891	2,830	—	—	1,183	103,433	28,794
1950	203,400	134	79	25,103	5,553	89,441	59	41	11,460	2,565	7 375,000	249	1,203	98,712	25,790
1950	*191,947*	*128*	—	—	—	*74,855*	*50*	—	—	—	—	—	—	—	—
1949	201,277	135	78	23,670	5,094	—	—	41	10,132	1,574	—	—	1,215	88,817	21,379
1948	—	—	77	22,739	5,543	—	—	40	8,996	1,755	—	—	1,245	91,643	34,268
1947	—	—	77	23,900	6,389	82,990	58	40	8,287	2,225	—	—	1,253	106,900	40,744
1946	—	—	77	23,216	5,826	—	—	39	7,274	2,666	—	—	1,271	128,828	36,195
1945	—	—	77	24,028	5,136	—	—	39	*8,590	3,212	—	—	1,295	126,576	31,721
1944	—	—	77	*48,195	*10,303	—	—	39	*9,014	2,470	—	—	1,307	112,249	28,276
1943	—	—	76	22,631	5,223	—	—	39	*8,847	1,926	—	—	1,297	100,486	26,816
1942	180,496	134	77	22,031	5,163	—	—	39	*8,355	1,784	—	—	1,299	91,457	25,613
1941	—	—	77	21,379	5,275	—	—	39	7,720	1,568	—	—	1,303	87,588	24,899
1940	175,163	133	77	21,271	5,097	—	—	39	7,407	1,757	7 284,200	216	1,311	85,156	23,600
1940	*165,989*	*126*	—	—	—	*69,921*	*53*	—	—	—	—	—	—	—	—
1939	—	—	77	21,302	5,089	—	—	39	7,331	1,794	—	—	1,328	82,095	22,485
1938	169,628	131	77	21,587	5,194	—	—	39	7,184	1,704	—	—	1,349	74,305	20,655

See footnotes at end of chart

Series B 275-290.   Physicians, Dentists and Nurses; and Medical, Dental and Nursing Schools: 1810 to 1989—Cont'd.

(Census figures in italics. Figures for schools and students are for academic session ending in the specified year)

Year	Physicians [1] Number	Rate per 100,000 population	Medical schools [2] Number [3]	Students	Graduates	Dentists [4] Number	Rate per 100,000 population	Number [5]	Dental schools Students	Graduates	Active professional graduate nurses Number	Rate per 100,000 population	Professional nursing schools [6] Number	Students	Graduates
	275	276	278	279	280	281	282	283	284	285	286	287	288	289	290
1937	—	—	77	22,095	5,377	—	—	39	7,397	1,739	—	—	1,389	73,286	20,400
1936	165,163	129	77	22,564	5,183	—	—	39	7,306	1,736	—	—	1,417	69,589	18,600
1935	—	—	77	22,888	5,101	—	—	39	7,175	1,840	—	—	1,472	67,533	19,600
1934	161,359	128	77	22,799	5,035	—	—	39	7,160	1,864	—	—	—	—	—
1933	—	—	77	22,466	4,895	—	—	39	7,508	1,986	—	—	—	—	—
1932	—	—	76	22,135	4,936	—	—	38	8,031	1,840	—	—	1,781	84,290	25,312
1931	156,406	126	76	21,982	4,735	—	—	38	8,129	1,842	—	—	1,844	100,419	25,971
1930	—	—	76	21,597	4,565	—	—	38	7,813	1,561	7214,300	174	—	—	—
1930	*153,803*	*125*	—	—	—	*71,055*	*58*	—	—	—	—	—	—	—	—
1929	152,503	125	76	20,878	4,446	—	—	40	8,200	2,442	—	—	1,885	78,771	23,810
1928	—	—	80	20,545	4,262	67,334	56	40	—	2,563	—	—	—	—	—
1927	149,521	126	80	19,662	4,035	—	—	40	10,333	2,642	—	—	1,797	77,768	18,623
1926	—	—	79	18,840	3,962	—	—	44	—	2,610	—	—	—	—	—
1925	147,010	127	80	18,200	3,974	64,481	56	43	11,863	2,590	—	—	—	—	—
1924	—	—	79	17,728	3,562	—	—	43	—	3,422	—	—	—	—	—
1923	145,966	130	80	16,960	3,120	—	—	45	13,099	3,271	—	—	—	—	—
1922	—	—	81	15,635	2,520	—	—	45	—	1,765	—	—	—	—	—
1921	145,404	134	83	14,466	3,186	—	—	45	11,745	1,795	—	—	—	—	—
1920	—	—	85	13,798	3,047	—	—	46	—	906	7103,900	98	1,755	54,953	14,980
1920	*144,977*	*137*	—	—	—	*56,152*	*53*	—	—	—	—	—	—	—	—
1919	—	—	85	13,052	2,656	—	—	46	—	3,587	—	—	—	—	—
1918	147,812	141	90	13,630	2,670	—	—	46	—	3,345	—	—	—	—	—
1917	—	—	96	13,764	3,379	45,988	44	46	—	3,010	—	—	—	—	—
1916	145,241	142	95	14,012	3,518	—	—	49	—	2,835	—	—	—	—	—
1915	—	—	96	14,891	3,536	—	—	49	—	2,388	—	—	1,509	46,141	11,118
1914	142,332	144	102	16,502	3,594	42,606	43	48	—	2,254	—	—	—	—	—
1913	—	—	107	17,015	3,981	—	—	51	—	2,022	—	—	—	—	—
1912	137,199	144	118	18,412	4,483	38,866	41	52	—	1,940	—	—	—	—	—
1911	—	—	122	19,786	4,273	—	—	54	—	1,742	—	—	—	—	—
1910	135,000	146	131	21,526	4,440	37,684	41	54	—	1,646	750,500	55	1,129	32,636	8,140
1910	*151,132*	*164*	—	—	—	*39,997*	*43*	—	—	—	—	—	—	—	—
1909	134,402	149	140	22,145	4,515	—	—	56	—	1,761	—	—	—	—	—
1908	—	—	151	22,602	4,741	36,670	41	55	—	2,005	—	—	—	—	—
1907	—	—	159	24,276	4,980	—	—	55	—	1,724	—	—	—	—	—
1906	134,688	158	162	25,204	5,364	35,238	41	55	—	1,519	—	—	—	—	—
1905	—	—	158	26,147	5,600	—	—	55	—	2,621	—	—	862	19,824	5,795
1904	128,950	157	160	28,142	5,747	32,204	39	56	—	2,168	—	—	—	—	—
1903	—	—	160	27,615	5,698	—	—	55	—	2,198	—	—	—	—	—
1902	123,196	156	160	27,501	5,009	28,109	36	56	—	2,294	—	—	—	—	—
1901	—	—	160	26,417	5,444	—	—	57	—	2,304	—	—	—	—	—
1900	119,749	157	160	25,171	5,214	25,189	33	57	—	2,091	—	—	432	11,164	3,456
1900	*132,002*	*173*	—	—	—	*29,665*	*39*	—	—	—	—	—	—	—	—
1898	115,524	157	—	—	—	23,911	33	54	—	1,894	—	—	—	—	—
1896	104,554	147	—	—	—	20,063	28	48	—	1,432	—	—	—	—	—
1893	103,090	154	—	—	—	—	—	37	—	—	—	—	—	—	—
1890	100,180	159	133	15,404	4,454	—	—	31	—	960	—	—	35	1,552	471
1890	*104,805*	*166*	—	—	—	*17,498*	*28*	—	—	—	—	—	—	—	—
1886	87,521	151	—	—	—	—	—	23	—	473	—	—	—	—	—
1880	82,000	163	100	11,826	3,241	—	—	14	—	315	—	—	15	323	157
1880	*85,671*	*171*	—	—	—	*12,314*	*25*	—	—	—	—	—	—	—	—
1870	60,000	150	75	—	—	—	—	10	—	147	—	—	—	—	—
1870	*64,414*	*162*	—	—	—	*7,988*	*20*	—	—	—	—	—	—	—	—
1860	*55,055*	*175*	*65*	—	—	*5,606*	*18*	*3*	—	*64*	—	—	—	—	—

See footnotes at end of chart

Series B 275-290. Physicians, Dentists and Nurses; and Medical, Dental and Nursing Schools: 1810 to 1989—Cont'd.

(Census figures in italics. Figures for schools and students are for academic session ending in the specified year)

Year	Physicians [1]		Medical schools [2]			Dentists [4]		Dental schools			Active professional graduate nurses		Professional nursing schools [6]		
	Number	Rate per 100,000 population	Number [3]	Students	Graduates	Number	Rate per 100,000 population	Number [5]	Students	Graduates	Number	Rate per 100,000 population	Number	Students	Graduates
	275	276	278	279	280	281	282	283	284	285	286	287	288	289	290
1850	*40,755*	*176*	52	—	—	2,923	13	2	—	17	—	—	—	—	—
1840	—	—	35	—	—	1,000	6	1	—	—	—	—	—	—	—
1830	—	—	20	—	—	300	2	—	—	—	—	—	—	—	—
1820	—	—	10	—	—	100	1	—	—	—	—	—	—	—	—
1810	—	—	5	—	—	50	1	—	—	—	—	—	—	—	—

* Denotes first year for which figures include Alaska and Hawaii.

NA Not available.

[1] Beginning 1960, includes osteopaths.

[2] Beginning 1954, includes Puerto Rico; beginning 1960, includes osteopaths and their schools.

[3] Approved medical and basic science schools.

[4] Beginning 1958, excludes graduates of year stated.

[5] For 1840 and 1926-1931, schools offering courses in dentistry; for 1850-1925, schools conferring degrees; for other years, schools in operation. Includes Puerto Rico.

[6] Includes Hawaii and Puerto Rico beginning 1950 for number and students and 1952 for graduates.

[7] Census estimate adjusted to exclude student nurses enumerated as graduates.

Series B 305-318. Hospitals and Beds, by Type of Service and Ownership (AHA): 1946 to 1990

| | Total | | Non-Federal | | | | Federal, all types | | |
| | | | Long-term general and special | | Psychiatric | | | | |
Year	Hospitals	Beds	Hospitals	Beds	Hospitals	Beds	Hospitals	Beds	Total beds per 1,000 population
	305	306	309	310	311	312	315	316	317
1990	6,649	1,211,000	131	25,000	757	158,000	337	98,000	5.1
1989	6,720	1,224,000	138	27,000	741	160,000	340	100,000	5.1
1988	6,780	1,241,000	129	27,000	726	163,000	342	104,000	5.0
1987	6,821	1,261,000	131	28,000	684	165,000	342	109,000	5.3
1986	6,841	1,283,000	133	30,000	634	165,000	342	111,000	5.4
1985	6,872	1,309,000	128	31,000	610	169,000	343	112,000	5.5
1984	6,872	1,339,000	131	30,000	579	175,000	341	112,000	5.7
1983	6,888	1,350,000	131	30,000	564	185,000	342	113,000	5.8
1982	6,915	1,360,000	138	34,000	558	195,000	346	114,000	5.9
1981	6,933	1,362,000	146	35,000	549	202,000	348	116,000	6.0
1980	6,965	1,365,000	157	39,000	534	215,000	359	117,000	6.0
1979	6,988	1,372,000	165	40,000	527	224,000	361	117,000	6.1
1978	7,015	1,381,000	169	41,000	526	235,000	370	122,000	6.2
1977	7,099	1,407,000	189	45,000	541	261,000	377	124,000	6.4
1976	7,082	1,434,000	197	49,000	528	291,000	380	129,000	6.6
1975	7,156	1,466,000	215	51,000	544	330,000	382	132,000	6.8
1974	7,174	1,513,000	221	54,000	543	383,000	387	136,000	7.2
1973	7,123	1,535,000	229	57,000	543	422,000	397	142,000	7.3
1972	7,061	1,550,000	216	54,000	529	457,000	401	143,000	7.6
1971	7,097	1,556,000	218	54,000	513	469,000	407	148,000	7.5
1970	7,123	1,615,771	236	59,961	519	526,889	408	160,969	8.0
1969	7,144	1,649,663	260	63,075	509	570,550	415	169,681	8.3
1968	7,137	1,663,203	280	66,517	505	593,916	416	174,645	8.4
1967	7,172	1,671,125	331	80,311	470	609,075	416	175,065	8.5
1966	7,160	1,678,658	291	67,337	476	639,041	425	173,005	8.7
1965	7,123	1,703,522	283	65,897	483	685,175	443	173,962	8.9
1964	7,127	1,696,039	300	68,783	487	691,367	441	175,490	9.0
1963	7,138	1,701,839	323	73,525	499	714,661	446	176,318	9.1
1962	7,028	1,689,414	323	73,474	491	716,781	447	177,677	9.2
1961	6,923	1,669,789	321	70,536	483	714,622	437	177,554	9.2
1960	6,876	1,657,970	308	67,214	488	722,493	435	177,105	9.3
1959*	6,845	1,612,822	330	68,323	459	688,410	438	178,820	9.2
1958	6,786	1,572,036	321	78,383	475	646,270	439	180,574	9.1
1957	6,818	1,588,691	340	77,608	452	641,455	437	183,002	9.2
1956	6,966	1,607,692	395	75,646	525	695,331	432	184,121	9.6
1955	6,956	1,604,408	402	76,278	542	707,162	428	183,162	9.8
1954	6,970	1,577,961	406	70,926	554	691,176	430	189,233	9.8
1953	6,978	1,580,654	406	68,039	541	691,855	435	202,604	10.0
1952	6,903	1,561,809	405	69,731	546	675,749	439	213,018	10.0
1951	6,832	1,521,959	394	62,768	551	655,932	422	214,597	9.9
1950	6,788	1,455,825	412	70,136	533	619,530	414	189,477	9.6
1949	6,277	1,435,288	395	79,145	507	614,465	376	186,764	9.7
1948	6,160	1,411,150	362	77,040	504	601,103	386	185,846	9.7
1947	6,173	1,400,318	385	84,758	499	580,273	403	199,771	9.8
1946	6,125	1,435,778	389	83,415	476	568,473	404	235,964	10.3

* Denotes first year for which figures include Alaska and Hawaii.

Series B 359-370.   Average Daily Census and Admissions to Hospitals, by Type of Service and Ownership (AHA): 1946 to 1990

(In thousands)

Year	Average daily census	Admissions during year	Year	Average daily census	Admissions during year	Year	Average daily census	Admissions during year	Year	Average daily census	Admissions during year
	359	360		359	360		359	360		359	360
1990	843.7	36,820	1978	1,041.9	37,200	1967	1,380	29,361	1956	1,356	22,090
1989	—	—	1977	1,065.9	37,100	1966	1,398	29,151			
1988	863.4	34,100	1976	1,089.7	36,800				1955	1,363	21,073
1987	872.6	34,400				1965	1,403	28,812	1954	1,343	20,345
1986	882.6	35,200	1975	1,124.9	36,200	1964	1,421	28,266	1953	1,342	20,184
			1974	1,187.4	35,500	1963	1,430	27,502	1952	1,336	19,624
1985	909.8	36,300	1973	1,189.0	34,400	1962	1,407	26,531	1951	1,298	18,783
1984	970.3	37,900	1972	1,208.9	33,300	1961	1,393	25,474			
1983	1,027.9	38,900	1971	1,236.8	32,700				1950	1,253	18,483
1982	1,052.7	39,100				1960	1,402	25,027	1949	1,240	17,224
1981	1,060.9	39,200	1970	1,298	31,759	1959*	1,363	23,605	1948	1,241	16,821
			1969	1,346	30,729	1958	1,323	23,697	1947	1,190	17,689
1980	1,059.7	38,900	1968	1,378	29,766	1957	1,320	22,993	1946	1,142	15,675
1979	1,043.4	37,800									

* Denotes first year for which figures include Alaska and Hawaii.

Series B 389-400.   Hospital Expense Per Patient Day: 1946 to 1990

(In dollars. Covers hospitals accepted for registration by the American Hospital Association)

Year	Amount	Year	Amount	Year	Amount	Year	Amount
	389		389		389		389
1990	687	1978	194	1967	32.54	1955	11.24
1989	637	1977	174	1966	27.94	1954	10.67
1988	586	1976	153			1953	9.73
1987	539			1965	25.29	1952	9.14
1986	501	1975	134	1964	23.20	1951	8.26
		1974	114	1963	21.00		
1985	460	1973	84	1962	19.73	1950	7.98
1984	411	1972	74	1961	18.46	1949	7.70
1983	369	1971	64			1948	6.35
1982	327			1960	16.46	1947	5.42
1981	284	1970	53.95	1959 *	15.65	1946	5.21
		1969	45.01	1958 [1]	14.74		
1980	245	1968	37.78	1957	13.48		
1979	217			1956	12.16		

* Denotes first year for which figures include Alaska and Hawaii.
[1] Includes Alaska.

Series B 413-422. Hospitals—Assets, Expenses and Personnel, by Type of Control and Service: 1946 to 1990

Year	Total	Federal	Year	Total	Federal	Year	Total	Federal	Year	Total	Federal
	413	414		413	414		413	414		413	414
EXPENSES (mil. dol.)											
1990	234,900	15,200	1978	70,900	6,700	1967	16,395	1,795	1955	5,594	837
1989	214,900	15,100	1977	63,600	6,200	1966	14,198	1,633	1954	5,229	927
1988	196,700	14,600	1976	56,000	5,300				1953	4,765	853
1987	178,700	13,700				1965	12,948	1,568	1952	4,456	925
1986	165,200	13,100	1975	48,700	4,500	1964	12,031	1,503	1951	3,913	743
			1974	41,406	3,971	1963	10,956	1,458			
1985	153,300	12,300	1973	36,290	3,524	1962	10,129	1,408	1950	3,651	712
1984	144,100	11,200	1972	32,700	3,100	1961	9,387	1,308	1949	3,486	764
1983	136,300	10,700	1971	28,812	2,821				1948	2,875	480
1982	123,200	9,500				1960	8,421	1,134	1947	2,354	405
1981	107,100	8,600	1970	25,556	2,483	1959 *	7,789	1,119	1946	1,963	373
			1969	22,103	2,350	1958	7,133	1,051			
1980	91,900	7,900	1968	19,061	2,032	1957	6,496	1,013			
1979	79,800	7,300				1956	6,017	968			
PERSONNEL (1,000)											
1990	4,063	303	1978	3,280	277	1967	2,203	214	1955	1,301	192
1989	3,937	288	1977	3,213	278	1966	2,106	206	1954	1,246	195
1988	3,840	295	1976	3,108	269				1953	1,169	198
1987	3,742	297				1965	1,952	199	1952	1,119	206
1986	3,647	296	1975	3,023	256	1964	1,887	193	1951	1,075	197
			1974	2,919	244	1963	1,840	206			
1985	3,625	299	1973	2,769	238	1962	1,763	207	1950	1,058	169
1984	3,630	290	1972	2,671	232	1961	1,696	202	1949	963	161
1983	3,707	286	1971	2,589	225				1948	939	154
1982	3,959	302				1960	1,598	186	1947	883	161
1981	3,661	283	1970	2,537	216	1959	1,520	179	1946	830	162
			1969	2,426	213	1958	1,465	181			
1980	3,492	279	1968	2,309	210	1957	1,401	186			
1979	3,382	273				1956	1,375	198			

* Denotes first year for which figures include Alaska and Hawaii.

Series B 448-452. Index Per Capita Consumption of Selected Nutrients: 1909 to 1985

(1967 = 100. Beginning 1941, civilian only)

Year	Protein 448	Fat 449	Carbohydrate 450	Year	Protein 448	Fat 449	Carbohydrate 450	Year	Protein 448	Fat 449	Carbohydrate 450
1985	106	112	110	1958	96	95	101	1933	92	89	117
1984	105	106	107	1957	97	94	100	1932	93	89	120
1983	104	107	106	1956	98	97	101	1931	94	90	123
1982	103	105	106					1930	95	89	127
1981	102	106	105	1955	97	97	101	1929	96	91	126
				1954	96	95	102	1928	96	90	129
1980	102	105	104	1953	97	95	103	1927	97	89	128
1979	104	109	108	1952	96	95	104	1926	96	89	128
1978	104	106	105	1951	95	93	105				
1977	104	105	105					1925	97	89	127
1976	105	107	105	1950	96	97	108	1924	98	90	127
				1949	96	93	107	1923	98	90	125
1975	100	98	101	1948	96	93	106	1922	96	86	129
1974	100	102	101	1947	99	95	110	1921	93	81	118
1973	100	103	103	1946	104	95	110	1920	95	82	123
1972	106	102	102					1919	99	87	128
1971	103	105	102	1945	104	92	112	1918	99	86	124
				1944	101	95	114	1917	98	81	126
1970	102	105	102	1943	102	95	115	1916	98	84	126
1969	102	103	102	1942	99	93	114	1915	99	84	129
1968	101	103	101	1941	96	96	119	1914	100	85	129
1967	100	100	100					1913	102	83	131
1966	99	98	99	1940	95	95	115	1912	104	83	131
				1939	94	93	118	1911	103	84	131
1965	98	97	99	1938	92	89	116				
1964	99	99	100	1937	92	89	116	1910	104	83	133
1963	98	97	99	1936	93	89	117	1909	106	85	133
1962	96	95	100								
1961	97	95	100	1935	90	85	117				
				1934	93	89	115				
1960	97	95	101								
1959	97	98	101								

SECTION C

MIGRATION

MIGRATION
Highlights

1 The continuous record of immigration into the United States began with the Act of 1819. This required the captain or master of a vessel arriving at an American port to deliver a list or manifest of all passengers taken on board to the local collector of customs which designated the age, sex, nationality, and occupation as well as the number of passengers that had died during the voyage. Copies of the manifests were transmitted to the Secretary of State, who reported the information periodically to Congress. Although the reporting of alien arrivals had also been required by the Act of 1798 (which expired in 1817), the number of arrivals prior to 1819 is not known. William J. Bromwell, author of *History of Immigration to the United States*, estimates the number of foreign arrivals between the close of the Revolutionary War and 1819 at 250,000. Immigration statistics were compiled by the Department of State from 1820 to 1870, by the Treasury Department's Bureau of Statistics from 1867 to 1895, and since 1892 by the Office or Bureau of Immigration (later the Immigration and Naturalization Service). Annual reports have presented the data on immigration statistics since 1892 with the exception of 1942 when no report was issued because of wartime conditions. Since 1820, reporting of immigration data has undergone many changes. Only arrivals by vessels at Atlantic and Gulf ports were included until 1850 when Pacific ports were added. During the Civil War, Southern ports under Confederate control were excluded. Later, the reporting area was expanded to include outlying possessions: Alaska from 1871 (although irregularly until 1904), Hawaii from 1901, Puerto Rico from 1902, and the Virgin Islands from 1942. The government did not require arrivals at land borders to be counted until 1904 when land border stations were established. By 1908, such arrivals were fully incorporated into the annual totals. In any case, until the first decade of this century, there were few Canadian or Mexican immigrants into the United States.

2 Since 1933, aliens arriving in the United States have been classified as immigrants or nonimmigrants. Immigrants are nonresident aliens admitted to the United States for permanent residence. Until July 1, 1968, they were further classified into quota and nonquota immigrants. The former were subject to the established quotas of Eastern Hemisphere countries while nonquota immigrants included natives of the Western Hemisphere and certain groups of special immigrants (classes of immigrants admitted to the U.S. for political reasons). Since July 1, 1968, this distinction was abolished in favor of numerical ceilings for regions and countries, but the category of special immigrants has been retained. The collection of data on emigrants has been suspended since 1957. Net immigration data suffer from the lack of reliable emigration figures as well as conflicts in enumeration of nonimmigrant arrivals.

3 From 1925 to 1929, the annual immigration quota of 164,667 was based on 2% of foreign-born residents of the United States as determined by the 1890 census. The national origin formula provided that the annual quota equal one-sixth of 1% of the number of White inhabitants of the continental United States in 1920, less Western Hemisphere immigrants and their descendants. The annual quota for each nationality was then determined by the same ratio to 150,000 as the number of inhabitants of each nationality living in the continental United States in 1920 to the total inhabitants (with a minimum of 100). The Act of 1965 replaced the quota system with an annual numerical limitation of 170,000 on the Eastern Hemisphere and 120,000 on the Western Hemisphere, with a ceiling of 20,000 for each country.

4 Prior to 1882, various states' laws excluded undesirable aliens from admission, such as paupers, felons, and the diseased. The first Chinese Exclusion Law was passed in 1882, which also excluded lunatics, idiots, and those likely to become public charges. Nine years later, Congress passed a much broader exclusion law in the Act of 1891. Statistics on excluded aliens were first compiled in 1892. Subsequent acts, principally those of 1917 and 1952, extended the excluded categories to anarchists, criminals, drug traffickers, subversives, and mental and physical defectives. However, landed immigrants enjoy all the judicial protection of citizens, and may appeal deportation or expulsion orders.

5 Since the first naturalization statute of 1790, there have been 3 requirements for immigrants seeking U.S. citizenship: (1) residence in the United States for five years, (2) a good moral character, and (3) an oath to support the Constitution. The residence requirement is only three years for a spouse of a U.S. citizen. Prior to

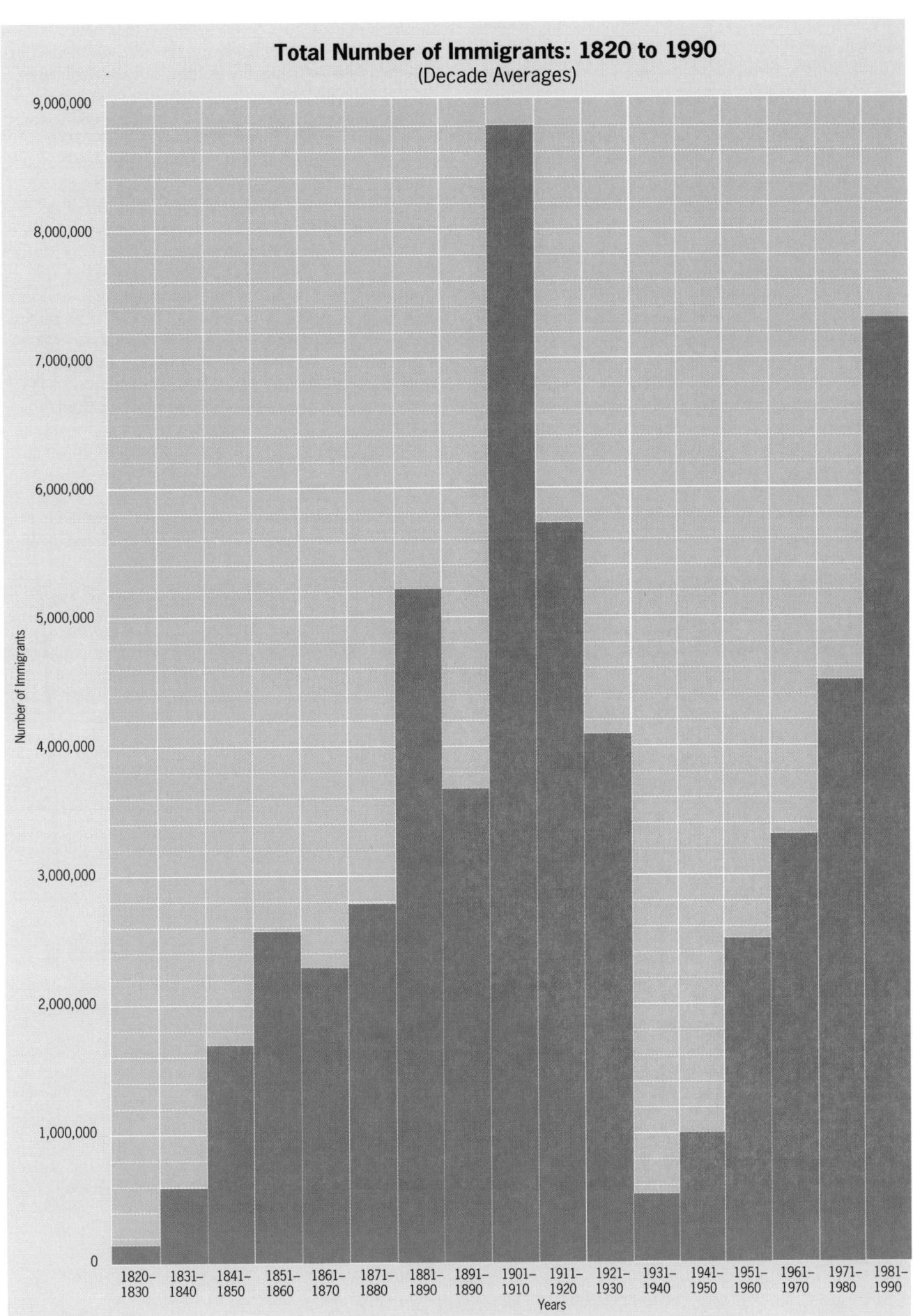

Total Number of Immigrants: 1820 to 1990
(Decade Averages)

1906, individual courts kept naturalization records but no national data were compiled. Since 1906, all courts have been required to file petitions and certificates of naturalization with the Bureau of Immigration and Naturalization.

6 Most European countries were represented in the immigration totals in the early 19th century; however, the first immigrant from Korea arrived in 1948, from the Philippines in 1936, from Japan in 1861, and from Australia in 1870.

7 The annual number of legal immigrants exceeded 1 million in eight years: 1905, 1906, 1907, 1910, 1913, 1914, 1989, and 1990. There is no official count of illegal immigrants.

8 The Refugee Act of 1980 provides for the admission of refugees and asylees based on United Nations guidelines. Authorized admission ceilings are set annually by the President of the United States in consultation with Congress. After one year of residence, refugees are eligible for immigrant status. Beginning in 1966, Cubans admitted or paroled (admitted without an immigration visa) into the United States after 1959 and present in the United States for at least two years could obtain permanent resident status. The Refugee Act of 1980 reduced the residency requirement to one year. In addition, the 125,000 Cuban immigrants admitted to the United States as part of the Mariel boat lift are eligible to become immigrants. Since 1977, refugees from Vietnam, Laos, and Cambodia have been eligible to apply for permanent resident status after living for at least two years (later reduced to one year) in the United States. Other refugee streams have been permitted into the United States under the Refugee Relief Act of 1953, the Hungarian Parolees Act of 1958, and the Refugees-Escapees-Parolees Act of 1960. A total of 212,843 refugees-asylees were admitted in the 1960s, 539,447 in the 1970s, and 1,013,620 in the 1980s.

C. Immigration: 1820-1990

(In thousands, except rate. For fiscal years ending in year shown, except as noted. For 1820-1867, alien passengers arriving; 1868-1891 and 1895-1897, immigrants arriving; 1892-1894 and 1898 to the present, immigrants admitted. Rates based on Bureau of the Census estimates as of July 1 for resident population through 1929, and for total population thereafter (excluding Alaska and Hawaii prior to 1959). Population estimates for 1980 through 1989 reflect revisions based on the 1990 Census of Population. See also *Historical Statistics, Colonial Times to 1970*, series C 89)

Period	Number	Rate[1]	Period or year	Number	Rate[1]	Year	Number	Rate[1]
1820 to 1990	56,994	3.4	1911 to 1920	5,736	5.7	1981	597	2.6
1820 to 1830 [2]	152	1.2	1921 to 1930	4,107	3.5	1982	594	2.6
1831 to 1840 [3]	599	3.9	1931 to 1940	528	0.4	1983	560	2.4
1841 to 1850 [4]	1,713	8.4	1941 to 1950	1,035	0.7	1984	544	2.3
1851 to 1860 [4]	2,598	9.3	1951 to 1960	2,515	1.5	1985	570	2.4
1861 to 1870 [5]	2,315	6.4	1961 to 1970	3,322	1.7	1986	602	2.5
1871 to 1880	2,812	6.2	1971 to 1980	4,493	2.1	1987	602	2.5
1881 to 1890	5,247	9.2	1981 to 1990	7,338	3.1	1988	643	2.6
1891 to 1900	3,688	5.3	1970	373	1.8	1989 [6]	1,091	4.4
1901 to 1910	8,795	10.4	1980	531	2.3	1990 [6]	1,536	6.1

[1] Annual rate per 1,000 U.S. population. Rate computed by dividing sum of annual immigration totals by sum of annual U.S. population totals for same number of years.
[2] Oct. 1, 1819, to Sept. 30, 1830.
[3] Oct. 1, 1830 to Dec. 31, 1840.
[4] Calendar years.
[5] Jan. 1, 1861, to June 30, 1870.
[6] Includes persons who were granted permanent residence under the legalization program of the Immigration Reform and Control Act of 1986.

Series C 89-119. Immigrants, by Country: 1820 to 1990

(For years ending June 30, except: 1820-1831 and 1844-1849, years ending Sept. 30; 1833-1842 and 1851-1867, years ending Dec. 31; 1832 covers 15 months ending Dec. 31; 1843, 9 months ending Sept. 30; 1850, 15 months ending Dec. 31; 1868, 6 months ending June 30)

			Europe					
			Northwestern Europe		Central Europe			
Year	All Countries [1]	Total	Great Britain	Ireland [2]	Germany [3]	Poland	Commonwealth of Independent States [4]	Italy
	89	90	91	92	95	96	98	100
1990	1,536,500	112,400	15,900	10,300	7,500	20,500	25,500	3,300
1981-1989	5,801,600	593,200	126,200	22,500	62,600	76,900	58,500	29,600
1971-1980	4,493,300	801,300	123,500	14,100	66,000	43,600	43,200	130,100
1970	373,326	110,653	14,089	1,583	10,632	2,013	836	27,369
1969	358,579	114,052	15,072	1,981	10,380	2,115	574	27,033
1968	454,448	129,022	26,025	2,995	16,590	3,676	974	25,882
1967	361,972	128,775	23,004	2,765	16,595	4,356	876	28,487
1966	323,040	115,898	18,777	3,267	17,654	8,490	768	26,447
1965	296,697	101,468	24,135	5,187	22,432	7,093	632	10,874
1964	292,248	108,215	25,758	6,055	24,494	7,097	763	12,769
1963	306,260	109,066	22,708	5,746	24,727	6,785	591	16,175
1962	283,763	103,989	18,066	5,118	21,477	5,660	753	20,119
1961	271,344	108,532	18,719	5,738	25,815	6,254	996	18,956
1960	265,398	120,178	19,967	6,918	29,452	4,216	856	13,369
1959	260,686	138,191	18,325	6,595	32,039	2,800	775	16,804
1958	253,265	115,198	24,147	9,134	29,498	1,470	641	23,115
1957	326,867	169,625	24,020	8,227	60,353	571	663	19,624
1956	321,625	156,866	19,008	5,607	44,409	263	643	40,430
1955	237,790	110,591	15,761	5,222	29,596	129	523	30,272
1954	208,177	92,121	16,672	4,655	33,098	67	475	13,145
1953	170,434	82,352	16,639	4,304	27,329	136	609	8,432
1952	265,520	193,626	22,177	3,526	104,236	235	548	11,342
1951	205,717	149,545	14,898	3,144	87,755	98	555	8,958
1950	249,187	199,115	12,755	5,842	128,592	696	526	12,454
1949	188,317	129,592	21,149	8,678	55,284	1,673	694	11,695
1998	170,570	103,544	26,403	7,534	19,368	2,447	897	16,075
1947	147,292	83,535	23,788	2,574	13,900	745	761	13,866
1946	108,721	52,852	33,552	1,816	2,598	335	153	2,636
1945	38,119	5,943	3,029	427	172	195	98	213
1944	28,551	4,509	1,321	112	238	292	157	120
1943	23,725	4,920	974	165	248	394	159	49
1942	28,781	11,153	907	83	2,150	343	197	103
1941	51,776	26,541	7,714	272	4,028	451	665	450
1940	70,756	50,454	6,158	839	21,520	702	898	5,302
1939	82,998	63,138	3,058	1,189	33,515	3,072	1,021	6,570
1938	67,895	44,495	2,262	1,085	17,199	2,403	960	7,712
1937	50,244	31,863	1,726	531	10,895	1,212	629	7,192
1936	36,329	23,480	1,310	444	6,346	869	378	6,774
1935	34,956	22,778	1,413	454	5,201	1,504	418	6,566
1934	29,470	17,210	1,305	443	4,392	1,032	607	4,374
1933	23,068	12,383	979	338	1,919	1,332	458	3,477
1932	35,576	20,579	2,057	539	2,670	1,296	636	6,662
1931	97,139	61,909	9,110	7,305	10,401	3,604	1,396	13,399
1930	241,700	147,438	31,015	23,445	25,569	9,231	2,772	22,327
1929	279,678	158,598	21,327	19,921	46,751	9,002	2,450	18,008
1928	307,255	158,513	19,958	25,268	45,778	8,755	2,652	17,728
1927	335,175	168,368	23,669	28,545	48,513	9,211	2,933	17,297
1926	304,488	155,562	25,528	24,897	50,421	7,126	3,323	8,253
1925	294,314	148,366	27,172	26,650	46,068	5,341	3,121	6,203
1924	706,896	364,339	59,490	17,111	75,091	28,806	20,918	56,246
1923	522,919	307,920	45,759	15,740	48,277	26,538	21,151	46,674
1922	309,556	216,385	25,153	10,579	17,931	28,635	19,910	40,319
1921	805,228	652,364	51,142	28,435	6,803	95,089	10,193	222,260

See footnotes on next page

Series C 89-119. Immigrants, by Country: 1820 to 1990—Cont'd.

(For years ending June 30, except: 1820-1831 and 1844-1849, years ending Sept. 30; 1833-1842 and 1851-1867, years ending Dec. 31; 1832 covers 15 months ending Dec. 31; 1843, 9 months ending Sept. 30; 1850, 15 months ending Dec. 31; 1868, 6 months ending June 30)

| | | | Europe | | | | | |
| | | | Northwestern Europe | | | Central Europe | | |
Year	All Countries [1]	Total	Great Britain	Ireland [2]	Germany [3]	Poland	Commonwealth of Independent States [4]	Italy
89	**90**	**91**	**92**	**95**	**96**	**98**	**100**	
1920	430,001	246,295	38,471	9,591	1,001	4,813	1,751	95,145
1919	141,132	24,627	6,797	474	52	(5)	1,403	1,884
1918	110,618	31,063	2,516	331	447	(5)	4,242	5,250
1917	295,403	133,083	10,735	5,406	1,857	(5)	12,716	34,596
1916	298,826	145,699	16,063	8,639	2,877	(5)	7,842	33,665
1915	326,700	197,919	27,237	14,185	7,799	(5)	26,187	49,688
1914	1,218,480	1,058,391	48,729	24,688	35,734	(5)	255,660	283,738
1913	1,197,892	1,055,855	60,328	27,876	34,329	(5)	291,040	265,542
1912	838,172	718,875	57,148	25,879	27,788	(5)	162,395	157,134
1911	878,587	764,757	73,384	29,112	32,061	(5)	158,721	182,882
1910	1,041,570	926,291	68,941	29,855	31,283	(5)	186,792	215,537
1909	751,786	654,875	46,793	25,033	25,540	(5)	120,460	183,218
1908	782,870	691,901	62,824	30,556	32,309	(5)	156,711	128,503
1907	1,285,349	1,199,566	79,037	34,530	37,807	(5)	258,943	285,731
1906	1,100,735	1,018,365	67,198	34,995	37,564	(5)	215,665	273,120
1905	1,026,499	974,273	84,189	52,945	40,574	(5)	184,897	221,479
1904	812,870	767,933	51,448	36,142	46,380	(5)	145,141	193,296
1903	857,046	814,507	33,637	35,310	40,086	(5)	136,093	230,622
1902	648,743	619,068	16,898	29,138	28,304	(5)	107,347	178,375
1901	487,918	469,237	14,985	30,561	21,651	(5)	85,257	135,996
1900	448,572	424,700	12,509	35,730	18,507	(5)	90,787	100,135
1899	311,715	297,349	13,456	31,673	17,476	(5)	60,982	77,419
1898	229,299	217,786	12,894	25,128	17,111	4,726	29,828	58,613
1897	230,832	216,397	12,752	28,421	22,533	4,165	25,816	59,431
1896	343,267	329,067	24,656	40,262	31,885	691	51,445	68,060
1895	258,536	250,342	28,833	46,304	32,173	790	35,907	35,427
1894	285,631	277,052	22,520	30,231	53,989	1,941	39,278	42,977
1893	439,730	429,324	35,189	43,578	78,756	16,374	42,310	72,145
1892	579,663	570,876	42,215	51,383	119,168	40,536	81,511	61,631
1891	560,319	546,085	66,605	55,706	113,554	27,497	47,426	76,055
1890	455,302	445,680	69,730	53,024	92,427	11,073	35,598	52,003
1889	444,427	434,790	87,992	65,557	99,538	4,922	33,916	25,307
1888	546,889	538,131	108,692	73,513	109,717	5,826	33,487	51,558
1887	490,109	482,829	93,378	68,370	106,865	6,128	30,766	47,622
1886	334,203	329,529	62,929	49,619	84,403	3,939	17,800	21,315
1885	395,346	353,083	57,713	51,795	124,443	3,085	17,158	13,642
1884	518,592	453,686	65,950	63,344	179,676	4,536	12,689	16,510
1883	603,322	522,587	76,606	81,486	194,786	2,011	9,909	31,792
1882	788,992	648,186	102,991	76,432	250,630	4,672	16,918	32,159
1881	669,431	528,545	81,376	72,342	210,485	5,614	5,041	15,401
1880	457,257	348,691	73,273	71,603	84,638	2,177	5,014	12,354
1879	177,826	134,259	29,955	20,013	34,602	489	4,453	5,791
1878	138,469	101,612	22,150	15,932	29,313	547	3,048	4,344
1877	141,857	106,195	23,581	14,569	29,298	533	6,599	3,195
1876	169,986	120,920	29,291	19,575	31,937	925	4,775	3,015
1875	227,498	182,961	47,905	37,957	47,769	984	7,997	3,631
1874	313,339	262,783	62,021	53,707	87,291	1,795	4,073	7,666
1873	459,803	397,541	89,500	77,344	149,671	3,338	1,634	8,757
1872	404,806	352,155	84,912	68,732	141,109	1,647	1,018	4,190
1871	321,350	265,145	85,455	57,439	82,554	535	673	2,816
1870	387,203	328,626	103,677	56,996	118,225	223	907	2,891
1869	352,768	315,963	84,438	40,786	131,042	184	343	1,489

See footnotes on next page

Series C 89-119. Immigrants, by Country: 1820 to 1990—Cont'd.

(For years ending June 30, except: 1820-1831 and 1844-1849; years ending Sept. 30; 1833-1842 and 1851-1867, years ending Dec. 31; 1832 covers 15 months ending Dec. 31; 1843, 9 months ending Sept. 30; 1850, 15 months ending Dec. 31; 1868, 6 months ending June 30)

| | | | Europe | | | | | |
| | | | Northwestern Europe | | Central Europe | | | |
Year	All Countries[1]	Total	Great Britain	Ireland[2]	Germany[3]	Poland	Commonwealth of Independent States[4]	Italy
	89	90	91	92	95	96	98	100
1868	138,840	130,090	24,127	32,068	55,831	X	141	891
1867	315,722	283,751	52,641	72,879	133,426	310	205	1,624
1866	318,568	278,916	94,924	36,690	115,892	412	287	1,382
1865	248,120	214,048	82,465	29,772	83,424	528	183	924
1864	193,418	185,233	53,428	63,523	57,276	165	256	600
1863	176,282	163,733	66,882	55,916	33,162	94	77	547
1862	91,985	83,710	24,639	23,351	27,529	63	79	566
1861	91,918	81,200	19,675	23,797	31,661	48	34	811
1860	153,640	141,209	29,737	48,637	54,491	82	65	1,019
1859	121,282	110,949	26,163	35,216	41,784	106	91	932
1858	123,126	111,354	28,956	26,873	45,310	9	246	1,240
1857	251,306	216,224	58,479	54,361	91,781	124	25	1,007
1856	200,436	186,083	44,658	54,349	71,028	20	9	1,365
1855	200,877	187,729	47,572	49,627	71,918	462	13	1,052
1854	427,833	405,542	58,647	101,606	215,009	208	2	1,263
1853	368,645	361,576	37,576	162,649	141,946	33	3	555
1852	371,603	362,484	40,699	159,548	145,918	110	2	351
1851	379,466	369,510	51,487	221,253	72,482	10	1	447
1850	369,980	308,323	51,085	164,004	78,896	5	31	431
1849	297,024	286,501	55,132	159,398	60,235	4	44	209
1848	226,527	218,025	35,159	112,934	58,465	X	1	241
1847	234,968	229,117	23,302	105,536	74,281	8	5	164
1846	154,416	146,315	22,180	51,752	57,561	4	248	151
1845	114,371	109,301	19,210	44,821	34,355	6	1	137
1844	78,615	74,745	14,353	33,490	20,731	36	13	141
1843	52,496	49,013	8,430	19,670	14,441	17	6	117
1842	104,565	99,945	22,005	51,342	20,370	10	28	100
1841	80,289	76,216	16,188	37,772	15,291	15	174	179
1840	84,066	80,126	2,613	39,430	29,704	5	X	37
1839	68,069	64,148	10,271	23,963	21,028	46	7	84
1838	38,914	34,070	5,420	12,645	11,683	41	13	86
1837	79,340	71,039	12,218	28,508	23,740	81	19	36
1836	76,242	70,465	13,106	30,578	20,707	53	2	115
1835	45,374	41,987	8,970	20,927	8,311	54	9	60
1834	65,365	57,510	10,490	24,474	17,686	54	15	105
1833	58,640	29,111	4,916	8,648	6,988	1	159	1,699
1832	60,482	34,193	5,331	12,436	10,194	34	52	3
1831	22,633	13,039	2,475	5,772	2,413	X	1	28
1830	23,322	7,217	1,153	2,721	1,976	2	3	9
1829	22,520	12,523	3,179	7,415	597	X	1	23
1828	27,382	24,729	5,352	12,488	1,851	1	7	34
1827	18,875	16,719	4,186	9,766	432	1	19	35
1826	10,837	9,751	2,319	5,408	511	X	4	57
1825	10,199	8,543	2,095	4,888	450	1	10	75
1824	7,912	4,965	1,264	2,345	230	4	7	45
1823	6,354	4,016	1,100	1,908	183	3	7	33
1822	6,911	4,418	1,221	2,267	148	3	10	35
1821	9,127	5,936	3,210	1,518	383	1	7	63
1820	8,385	7,691	2,410	3,614	968	5	14	30

X Represents zero.
[1] For 1820-1867 excludes returning citizens.
[2] Comprises Eire and Northern Ireland.
[3] Includes Austria, 1938 to 1945.
[4] Comprises former Soviet Union.
[5] Between 1899 and 1919, included with Austria-Hungary, Germany, and Russia.

Series C 89-119. Immigrants, by Country: 1820 to 1990—Cont'd.

(For years ending June 30, except: 1820-1831 and 1844-1849, years ending Sept. 30; 1833-1842 and 1851-1867, years ending Dec. 31; 1832 covers 15 months ending Dec. 31; 1843, 9 months ending Sept. 30; 1850, 15 months ending Dec. 31; 1868, 6 months ending June 30)

		Asia							America		
Year	Total	Turkey in Asia [1]	China [2]	India	Japan [3]	Korea [4]	Philippines	Total	Canada and Newfoundland [5]	Mexico	
	102	103	104	105	106	107	108	110	111	112	
1990	338,600	2,500	31,800	30,700	5,700	32,300	63,800	1,043,400	16,800	679,100	
1980-1989	2,478,800	18,400	341,800	231,200	37,500	306,500	431,500	2,537,500	102,400	974,200	
1971-1979	1,633,800	18,600	202,500	176,800	47,900	272,000	360,200	1,929,400	114,800	637,200	
1970	90,215	495	6,427	8,795	4,731	8,888	30,507	161,727	26,850	44,821	
1969	72,959	556	5,264	5,205	4,095	5,854	20,263	164,045	29,303	45,748	
1968	56,298	325	4,851	4,165	3,810	3,592	16,086	262,736	41,716	44,716	
1967	57,574	491	7,118	4,129	4,125	3,845	10,336	170,235	34,768	43,034	
1966	40,113	365	2,948	2,293	3,468	2,414	5,894	162,551	37,273	47,217	
1965	20,040	365	1,611	467	3,294	2,139	2,963	171,019	50,035	40,686	
1964	21,279	331	2,684	488	3,774	2,329	2,862	158,644	51,114	34,448	
1963	23,242	307	1,605	965	4,147	2,560	3,483	169,966	50,509	55,986	
1962	20,249	304	1,356	390	4,054	1,463	3,354	155,871	44,272	55,805	
1961	19,495	296	900	292	4,490	1,442	2,628	139,580	47,470	41,476	
1960	21,604	200	1,380	244	5,699	1,410	2,791	119,525	46,668	32,708	
1959	25,259	229	1,702	351	6,248	1,614	2,503	93,061	34,599	22,909	
1958	20,870	197	1,143	323	6,847	1,470	2,034	113,132	45,143	26,791	
1957	20,008	77	2,098	196	6,829	577	1,874	134,160	46,354	49,321	
1956	17,327	48	1,386	185	5,967	579	1,792	144,713	42,363	61,320	
1955	10,935	54	568	194	4,150	263	1,598	110,436	32,435	43,702	
1954	9,970	33	254	144	3,846	175	1,234	95,587	34,873	30,645	
1953	8,231	13	528	104	2,579	75	1,074	77,650	36,283	17,183	
1952	9,328	12	263	123	3,814	47	1,179	61,049	33,354	9,079	
1951	7,149	3	335	109	271	21	3,228	47,631	25,880	6,153	
1950	4,508	13	1,280	121	100	24	729	44,191	21,885	6,744	
1949	7,595	40	3,415	175	529	39	1,157	49,334	25,156	8,083	
1948	11,907	16	7,203	263	423	44	1,168	52,746	25,485	8,384	
1947	6,733	22	3,191	432	131	—	910	52,753	24,342	7,558	
1946	2,108	16	252	425	14	—	475	46,066	21,344	7,146	
1945	461	13	71	103	1	—	19	29,646	11,530	6,702	
1944	231	15	50	41	4	—	4	23,084	10,143	6,598	
1943	342	36	65	71	20	—	8	18,162	9,761	4,172	
1942	615	31	179	36	44	—	51	16,377	10,599	2,378	
1941	1,971	16	1,003	94	289	—	170	22,445	11,473	2,824	
1940	2,050	7	643	52	102	—	137	17,822	11,078	2,313	
1939	2,281	15	642	36	102	—	119	17,139	10,813	2,640	
1938	2,492	11	613	34	93	—	116	20,486	14,404	2,502	
1937	1,149	13	293	47	132	—	84	16,903	12,011	2,347	
1936	793	20	273	13	91	—	72	11,786	8,121	1,716	
1935	682	31	229	32	88	—	(6)	11,174	7,782	1,560	
1934	597	22	187	28	86	—	—	11,409	7,945	1,801	
1933	552	27	148	44	75	—	—	9,925	6,187	1,936	
1932	1,931	43	750	87	526	—	—	12,577	8,003	2,171	
1931	3,345	139	1,150	123	653	—	—	30,816	22,183	3,333	
1930	4,535	118	1,589	110	837	—	—	88,104	65,254	12,703	
1929	3,758	70	1,446	103	771	—	—	116,177	66,451	40,154	
1928	3,880	80	1,320	102	550	—	—	144,281	75,281	59,016	
1927	3,669	73	1,471	102	723	—	—	161,872	84,580	67,721	
1926	3,413	37	1,751	93	654	—	—	144,393	93,368	43,316	
1925	3,578	51	1,937	65	723	—	—	141,496	102,753	32,964	
1924	22,065	2,820	6,992	183	8,801	—	—	318,855	200,690	89,336	
1923	13,705	2,183	4,986	257	5,809	—	—	199,972	117,011	63,768	

See footnotes at end of chart.

Series C 89-119. Immigrants, by Country: 1820 to 1990—Cont'd.

(For years ending June 30, except: 1820-1831 and 1844-1849, years ending Sept. 30; 1833-1842 and 1851-1867, years ending Dec. 31; 1832 covers 15 months ending Dec. 31; 1843, 9 months ending Sept. 30; 1850, 15 months ending Dec. 31; 1868, 6 months ending June 30)

		Asia							America		
Year	Total	Turkey in Asia [1]	China [2]	India	Japan [3]	Korea [4]	Philippines	Total	Canada and Newfoundland [5]	Mexico
	102	103	104	105	106	107	108	110	111	112
1922	14,263	1,998	4,406	360	6,716	—	—	77,448	46,810	19,551
1921	25,034	11,735	4,009	511	7,878	—	—	124,118	72,317	30,758
1920	17,505	5,033	2,330	300	9,432	—	—	162,666	90,025	52,361
1919	12,674	19	1,964	171	10,064	—	—	102,286	57,782	29,818
1918	12,701	43	1,795	130	10,213	—	—	65,418	32,452	18,524
1917	12,756	393	2,237	109	8,991	—	—	147,779	105,399	17,869
1916	13,204	1,670	2,460	112	8,680	—	—	137,424	101,551	18,425
1915	15,211	3,543	2,660	161	8,613	—	—	111,206	82,215	12,340
1914	34,273	21,716	2,502	221	8,929	—	—	122,695	86,139	14,614
1913	35,358	23,955	2,105	179	8,281	—	—	103,907	73,802	11,926
1912	21,449	12,788	1,765	175	6,114	—	—	95,926	55,990	23,238
1911	17,428	10,229	1,460	524	4,520	—	—	94,364	56,830	19,889
1910	23,533	15,212	1,968	1,696	2,720	—	—	89,534	56,555	18,691
1909	12,904	7506	1,943	203	3,111	—	—	82,208	51,941	16,251
1908	28,365	9,753	1,397	1,040	15,803	—	—	59,997	38,510	6,067
1907	40,524	8,053	961	898	30,226	—	—	41,762	19,918	1,406
1906	22,300	6,354	1,544	216	13,835	—	—	24,613	5,063	1,997
1905	23,925	6,157	2,166	190	10,331	—	—	25,217	2,168	2,637
1904	26,186	5,235	4,309	261	14,264	—	—	16,420	2,837	1,009
1903	29,966	7,118	2,209	94	19,968	—	—	11,023	1,058	528
1902	22,271	6,223	1,649	93	14,270	—	—	6,698	636	709
1901	13,593	5,782	2,459	22	5,269	—	—	4,416	540	347
1900	17,946	3,962	1,247	9	12,635	—	—	5,455	396	237
1899	8,972	4,436	1,660	17	2,844	—	—	4,316	1,322	161
1898	8,637	4,275	2,071	X	2,230	—	—	2,627	352	107
1897	9,662	4,732	3,363	X	1,526	—	—	4,537	291	91
1896	6,764	4,139	1,441	X	1,110	—	—	7,303	278	150
1895	4,495	2,767	539	X	1,150	—	—	3,508	244	116
1894	4,690	X	1,170	X	1,931	—	—	3,551	194	109
1893	2,392	X	472	X	1,380	—	—	2,593	(7)	(8)
1892	(7)	—	—	—	—	—	—	(7)	(7)	(8)
1891	7,678	2,488	2,836	42	1,136	—	—	5,082	234	(8)
1890	4,448	1,126	1,716	43	691	—	—	3,833	183	(8)
1889	1,725	593	118	59	640	—	—	5,459	28	(8)
1888	843	273	26	20	404	—	—	5,402	15	(8)
1887	615	208	10	32	229	—	—	5,270	9	(8)
1886	317	15	40	17	194	—	—	3,026	17	(8)
1885	198	—	22	34	49	—	—	41,203	38,336	323
1884	510	—	279	12	20	—	—	63,339	60,626	430
1883	8,113	—	8,031	9	27	—	—	71,729	70,274	469
1882	39,629	—	39,579	10	5	—	—	100,129	98,366	366
1881	11,982	5	11,890	33	11	—	—	127,577	125,450	325
1880	5,839	4	5,802	21	4	—	—	101,692	99,744	492
1879	9,660	31	9,604	15	4	—	—	33,043	31,286	556
1878	9,014	7	8,992	8	2	—	—	27,204	25,592	465
1877	10,640	3	10,594	17	7	—	—	24,065	22,137	445
1876	22,943	8	22,781	25	4	—	—	24,686	22,505	631
1875	16,499	1	16,437	19	3	—	—	26,640	24,097	610
1874	13,838	6	13,776	17	21	—	—	35,339	33,020	386
1873	20,325	3	20,292	15	9	—	—	40,335	37,891	606
1872	7,825	X	7,788	12	17	—	—	42,205	40,204	569

See footnotes at end of chart.

Series C 89-119. Immigrants, by Country: 1820 to 1990—Cont'd.

(For years ending June 30, except: 1820-1831 and 1844-1849, years ending Sept. 30; 1833-1842 and 1851-1867, years ending Dec. 31; 1832 covers 15 months ending Dec. 31; 1843, 9 months ending Sept. 30; 1850, 15 months ending Dec. 31; 1868, 6 months ending June 30)

		Asia				America		
Year	Total	Turkey in Asia [1]	China [2]	India	Japan [3]	Total	Canada and Newfoundland [5]	Mexico
	102	103	104	105	106	110	111	112
1871	7,240	4	7,135	14	78	48,835	47,164	402
1870	15,825	X	15,740	24	48	42,658	40,414	463
1869	12,949	2	12,874	3	63	23,767	21,120	320
1868	5,171	—	5,157	X	X	3,415	2,785	129
1867	3,961	—	3,863	2	67	24,715	23,379	292
1866	2,411	—	2,385	17	7	33,582	32,180	239
1865	2,947	—	2,942	5	X	22,778	21,586	193
1864	2,982	—	2,975	6	X	4,607	3,636	99
1863	7,216	—	7,214	1	X	4,147	3,464	96
1862	3,640	—	3,633	5	X	4,175	3,275	142
1861	7,528	—	7,518	6	1	2,763	2,069	218
1860	5,476	—	5,467	5	—	6,343	4,514	229
1859	3,461	—	3,457	2	—	5,466	4,163	265
1858	5,133	—	5,128	5	—	5,821	4,603	429
1857	5,945	—	5,944	1	—	6,811	5,670	133
1856	4,747	—	4,733	13	—	9,058	6,493	741
1855	3,540	—	3,526	6	—	9,260	7,761	420
1854	13,100	—	13,100	X	—	8,533	6,891	446
1853	47	—	42	5	—	6,030	5,424	162
1852	4	—	X	4	—	7,695	6,352	72
1851	2	—	X	2	—	9,703	7,438	181
1850	7	—	3	4	—	15,768	9,376	597
1849	11	—	3	8	—	8,904	6,890	518
1848	8	—	X	6	—	7,989	6,473	24
1847	12	—	4	8	—	5,231	3,827	62
1846	11	—	7	4	—	5,525	3,855	222
1845	6	—	6	X	—	5,035	3,195	498
1844	6	—	3	1	—	3,740	2,711	197
1843	11	—	3	2	—	2,854	1,502	398
1842	7	—	4	2	—	3,994	2,078	403
1841	3	—	2	1	—	3,429	1,816	352
1840	1	—	X	1	—	3,815	1,938	395
1839	—	—	X	X	—	3,617	1,926	353
1838	1	—	X	1	—	2,990	1,476	211
1837	11	—	X	11	—	3,628	1,279	627
1836	4	—	X	4	—	4,936	2,814	798
1835	17	—	8	8	—	3,312	1,193	1,032
1834	6	—	X	6	—	2,779	1,020	885
1833	3	—	X	3	—	3,282	1,194	779
1832	4	—	X	4	—	2,871	608	827
1831	1	—	X	1	—	2,194	176	692
1830	—	—	X	X	—	2,296	189	983
1829	2	—	1	1	—	3,299	409	2,290
1828	3	—	X	3	—	2,090	267	1,089
1827	1	—	X	1	—	580	165	127
1826	1	—	X	1	—	831	223	106
1825	1	—	1	X	—	846	314	68
1824	1	—	X	1	—	559	155	110
1823	—	—	X	X	—	382	167	35
1822	1	—	X	1	—	378	204	5
1821	—	—	X	X	—	303	184	4
1820	5	—	1	1	—	387	209	1

See footnotes at end of chart.

Series C 89-119. Immigrants, by Country: 1820 to 1970—Cont'd.

(For years ending June 30, except: 1820-1831 and 1844-1849, years ending Sept. 30; 1833-1842 and 1851-1867, years ending Dec. 31; 1832 covers 15 months ending Dec. 31; 1843, 9 months ending Sept. 30; 1850, 15 months ending Dec. 31; 1868, 6 months ending June 30)

Year	Africa, total	Year	Africa, total	Year	Africa, total	Year	Africa, total
	115		115		115		115
1990	35,900	1931	417	1890	112	1849	3
1981-1989	156,400			1889	187	1848	10
1971-1980	91,500	1930	572	1888	65	1847	——
		1929	509	1887	40	1846	1
1970	7,099	1928	475	1886	122		
1969	4,460	1927	520			1845	4
1968	3,220	1926	529	1885	112	1844	14
1967	2,577			1884	59	1843	6
1966	1,967	1925	412	1883	67	1842	3
		1924	900	1882	60	1841	14
1965	1,949	1923	548	1881	33		
1964	2,015	1922	520			1840	6
1963	1,982	1921	1,301	1880	18	1839	10
1962	1,834			1879	12	1838	10
1961	1,851	1920	648	1878	18	1837	2
		1919	189	1877	16	1836	6
1960	1,925	1918	299	1876	89		
1959	1,992	1917	566			1835	14
1958	2,008	1916	894	1875	54	1834	1
1957	1,600			1874	58	1833	1
1956	1,351	1915	934	1873	28	1832	2
		1914	1,539	1872	41	1831	2
1955	1,203	1913	1,409	1871	24		
1954	1,248	1912	1,009			1830	2
1953	989	1911	956	1870	31	1829	1
1952	931			1869	72	1828	6
1951	845	1910	1,072	1868	3	1827	4
		1909	858	1867	25	1826	——
1950	849	1908	1,411	1866	33		
1949	995	1907	1,486			1825	1
1948	1,027	1906	712	1865	49	1824	——
1947	1,284			1864	37	1823	——
1946	1,516	1905	757	1863	3	1822	——
		1904	686	1862	12	1821	2
1945	406	1903	176	1861	47		
1944	112	1902	37			1820	1
1943	141	1901	173	1860	126		
1942	473			1859	11		
1941	564	1900	30	1858	17		
		1899	51	1857	25		
1940	202	1898	48	1856	6		
1939	218	1897	37				
1938	174	1896	21	1855	14		
1937	155			1854	——		
1936	105	1895	36	1853	8		
		1894	24	1852	——		
1935	118	1893	(7)	1851	3		
1934	104	1892	(7)				
1933	71	1891	103	1850	——		
1932	186						

X Represents zero.
[1] No record of immigration from Turkey in Asia until 1869.
[2] Beginning 1957, includes Taiwan.
[3] No record of immigration from Japan until 1861.
[4] No record of immigration from Korea prior to 1948.
[5] Prior to 1920, Canada and Newfoundland were recorded as British North America.
[6] Philippines included in "All other countries" prior to 1936.
[7] Included in "All other countries."
[8] No record of immigration from Mexico for 1886 to 1893.

Series C 158-161. Aliens Deported, Required to Depart and Excluded: 1892 to 1990

(For years ending June 30)

Year	Aliens expelled			Year	Aliens expelled			Year	Aliens deported
	Total	Deported	Required to depart		Total	Deported	Required to depart		
	158	159	160		158	159	160		159
1990	1,045,000	26,000	1,019,000	1953	905,236	19,845	885,391	1917	1,853
1989	860,000	30,000	830,000	1952	723,959	20,181	703,778	1916	2,781
1988	934,000	23,000	911,000	1951	686,713	13,544	673,169	1915	2,564
1987	1,113,000	22,000	1,091,000	1950	579,105	6,628	572,477	1914	4,610
1986	1,608,000	22,000	1,586,000	1949	296,337	20,040	276,297	1913	3,461
1985	1,062,000	21,000	1,041,000	1948	217,555	20,371	197,184	1912	2,456
1984	931,000	18,000	913,000	1947	214,543	18,663	195,880	1911	2,788
1983	944,000	17,000	927,000	1946	116,320	14,375	101,945	1910	2,695
1982	824,000	14,000	810,000	1945	80,760	11,270	69,490	1909	2,124
1981	837,000	17,000	820,000	1944	39,449	7,179	32,270	1908	2,069
1980	737,000	17,000	719,000	1943	16,154	4,207	11,947	1907	995
1979	992,000	26,000	966,000	1942	10,613	3,709	6,904	1906	676
1978	1,004,000	28,000	976,000	1941	10,938	4,407	6,531	1905	845
1977	897,000	30,000	867,000	1940	15,548	6,954	8,594	1904	779
1976	793,000	28,000	765,000	1939	17,792	8,202	9,590	1903	547
1975	679,000	23,000	656,000	1938	18,553	9,275	9,278	1902	465
1974	738,000	19,000	719,000	1937	17,617	8,829	8,788	1901	363
1973	585,000	17,000	568,000	1936	17,446	9,195	8,251	1900	356
1972	467,000	16,000	451,000	1935	16,297	8,319	7,978	1899	263
1971	388,000	18,000	370,000	1934	16,889	8,879	8,010	1898	199
1970	320,241	16,893	303,348	1933	30,212	19,865	10,347	1897	263
1969	251,463	10,505	240,958	1932	30,201	19,426	10,775	1896	238
1968	189,082	9,130	179,952	1931	29,861	18,142	11,719	1895	177
1967	151,603	9,260	142,343	1930	28,018	16,631	11,387	1894	417
1966	132,851	9,168	123,683	1929	38,796	12,908	25,888	1893	577
1965	105,406	10,143	95,263	1928	31,571	11,625	19,946	1892	637
1964	81,788	8,746	73,042	1927	26,674	11,662	15,012		
1963	76,846	7,454	69,392	1926	10,904	10,904	—		
1962	61,801	7,637	54,164	1925	9,495	9,495	—		
1961	59,821	7,428	52,383	1924	6,409	6,409	—		
1960	59,625	6,829	52,796	1923	3,661	3,661	—		
1959	64,598	7,988	56,610	1922	4,345	4,345	—		
1958	67,742	7,142	60,600	1921	4,517	4,517	—		
1957	68,461	5,082	63,379	1920	2,762	2,762	—		
1956	88,188	7,297	80,891	1919	3,068	3,068	—		
1955	247,797	15,028	232,769	1918	1,569	1,569	—		
1954	1,101,228	26,951	1,074,277						

SECTION D

LABOR

Highlights

Average Weekly Earnings and Hours Worked: 1909 to 1991
Manufacturing Production Workers

1 Techniques for measuring labor force (or work force) data were developed during the late 1930s by the Work Projects Administration (WPA). For every week containing the 12th of each month, the Bureau of the Census collects data for the Bureau of Labor Statistics; this is part of the former's Current Population Survey and is based on a scientifically designed sample of households. The survey includes all employed and unemployed persons as well as self-employed persons, unpaid family workers and domestic servants, and others who do not ordinarily appear on the payrolls of any establishment. Labor force data are also collected in the decennial censuses.

2 The concepts of employment, unemployment, and labor have changed over the years. By current definitions,

employed persons are those who work as paid employees or in their own business or profession, or on their farm, or who work 15 hours or more as unpaid workers in a family enterprise. It also includes those who are temporarily absent from work or business because of illness, vacation, bad weather, labor-management dispute, or personal reasons. Volunteer workers are excluded. Unemployed persons are those who do not work during the survey week, but who make efforts to secure a job, and are available for work. The civilian labor force (persons 14 years and over until 1966 and over 16 years thereafter) is the sum of the employed and unemployed. Data on the size of the armed forces is obtained from the Department of Defense and added to the civilian labor force to obtain the Total Labor Force. For years prior to 1940 (when detailed labor force data became available for the whole nation), the data are based on Stanley Legerbott's *Manpower in Economic Growth: The American Record Since 1800.* Legerbott obtained his data by interpolating between detailed worker rates in the census years and applying the resultant series to unpublished census estimates of population. The gainful worker concept differs from other concepts in that its primary purpose is a count of occupations and occupational status rather than employment. It excludes students as well as women doing housework, but includes retired people who report their former line of work.

3 Unemployment figures are politically the most sensitive. Because they are based on reports of unemployment insurance claims, they may be generally lower than actual unemployment. They exclude those long-term unemployed who have become discouraged and opted out of the employment market. In earlier years, unemployment estimates were calculated as a residual; that is, the total number of employed persons was deducted from the total civilian labor force. The unemployment rate presents the data on unemployed persons as a percentage of the civilian labor force. The lowest unemployment rate (that is, the closest United States ever came to the concept of full employment) was achieved in 1944 during wartime (1.2%); the highest rates were in 1894 (18.3%) and 1939 (17.2%).

4 Economically Active Population is a concept developed by David L. Caplan and M. Claire Casey. Before 1940, it referred to both employed and unemployed workers in the civilian labor force 10 years old and over; after 1940, 14 years old and over. It is similar to the gainful workers concept, which is also based on occupation and marketable skills rather than on employment. The occupational classification system is generally comparable with the system used in the *Dictionary of Occupational Titles.*

5 The most common range of wages for agricultural laborers in the United States in the 19th century was from $8 to $12 per month, the same range that prevails in many Third World countries today. Data on wages after the Civil War and before 1900 comes from a number of published reports, such as Joseph D. Weeks's *Report on the Statistics of Wages in the Manufacturing Industries,* 1886 and the Aldrich Reports on *Wholesale Prices, on Wages and on Transportation,* 1893. Since 1939, private industry employment and payrolls are based principally upon records of the Social Security programs.

6 The average weekly hours worked and paid for differ from average hours worked per week, both during times of substantial unemployment as well as times of relative full employment because of the overtime element. The widespread adoption of paid vacations of increasing length and the increasing number of paid holidays have raised average weekly hours paid for while keeping the average weekly hours worked low.

7 The Bureau of Labor Statistics monitors and publishes biennial data on labor unions, their membership, dues, collective agreements, and voting rights. Union membership figures are available since 1951, and include both the AFL-CIO, the principal labor federation, and independent unions. The decline in union membership reflects the decline in the influence of labor on U.S. industry and politics.

8 Data on work stoppages, including strikes and lockouts, were first published in 1881 and at five-year intervals thereafter with the exception of the period from 1906-13. This seven-year lapse occurred while the charge of collecting labor statistics was moved from the Bureau of Labor (which collected these data from 1881 to 1905) to the Department of Labor, which was officially founded in 1913. During the transition period, there was no government agency for the collection of labor statistics. Until 1927, these data were quite fragmentary and based on press reports and other secondary sources.

9 Compilation of work injury statistics began in 1910 for the iron and steel industry, and by 1925 covered 24 industries. Since 1920, reports have been standardized with the injury-frequency rate defined as the average number of disabling injuries per million man-hours worked.

10 The total civilian labor force participation rate will increase from 60.4% in 1990 to appoximately 69.0% in 2005. The increase will come primarily from the growth in labor force participation of White women from 57.5% in 1990 to 63.5% in 2005, of Black women from 57.8% in 1990 to 61.7% in 2005, and of Hispanic women from 53.0% in 1990 to 59.0% in 2005. The rates for men, both White and Black, will decrease.

11 The Hispanic labor force of 14.770 million in 1990 included estimates of undocumented and illegal workers, most of whom are of Hispanic origin.

12 The percentage of workers who have not completed high school declined from 36.1% in 1970 to 12.8% in 1991. During the same time, the percentage of college graduates grew from 14.1% to 26.7%.

13 The states with the highest unemployment rate in 1991 were West Virginia (10.5%), Michigan (9.2%), Massachusetts (9%), Mississippi (8.6%), and Alaska (8.5%). The states with the lowest unemployment rates were Nebraska (2.7%), Hawaii (2.8%), and South Dakota (3.4%).

14 The labor force participation of married women with children under 6 years old grew from 18.8% in 1960 to 59.9% in 1991. The relative rate for married women with children less than a year old was 55.8%.

15 In 1990, the unemployment rate was highest for Black males and Black females 16 to 19 years old (36.5% and 36.1%, respectively). It was lowest for White males 55 to 64 years old (3.3%).

16 A total of 10.341 million persons were self-employed in 1991 compared to 7.031 million in 1970. By industry, the largest self-employed group was in services, and by occupation, the largest group was managers.

17 In 1991, a total of 118,000 workers failed to show up at work because of bad weather, compared to 128,000 in 1970.

18 More women than men are employed in part-time work. In 1991, of a total 20.302 million part-time workers, 13.645 million were women and 6.657 million were men.

19 In 1991, 7.183 million workers, constituting 6.2% of the total employed, held multiple jobs. More men than women tended to hold down two or more jobs. Technical professionals formed the largest group of multiple jobholders.

20 The jobs with the fastest potential growth rate from 1990 to 2005 are: home health aids, systems analysts and computer scientists, personal and home care aides, medical assistants, human services workers, radiologic technologists and technicians, medical secretaries, psychologists, travel agents, correction officers, flight attendants, computer programmers, management analysts, and child care workers. The jobs with the fastest potential decline during the same period are: electrical and electronic equipment assemblers, textile machine operators, telephone and cable TV line installers and repairers, machine tool cutting operators, private household cleaners and servants, machine forming operators, switchboard operators, farmers and farm workers, garment sewing machine operators, and typists and word processors.

21 Of the total 10,012,500 workers employed by high-tech industries in 1990, 312,600 were employed in research and development.

22 In 1991, 3.015 million males and 1.503 million females were fired from their jobs; 35% of the males and 31.6% of the females were unemployed for 15 weeks or more after losing their jobs.

23 The Index of Help Wanted Advertising in Newspapers, based on 1967=100, grew from 93 in 1970 to 128 in 1989.

24 The numbers of hours worked declined nationally from 38.6 in 1960 to 34.3 in 1991. Weekly hours worked were highest in mining (44.4) and manufacturing (40.7) and lowest in retail trade (28.6) and services (32.5).

25 Weekly earnings grew nationally from $81 in 1960 to $355 in 1991. These earnings are highest in mining ($631) and construction ($534) and lowest in retail trade ($200) and services ($333).

26 Based on 1982=100, the index of business sector output grew from 52.3 in 1960 to 131.0 in 1991, business compensation per hour from 21.1 in 1960 to 145.1 in 1991, and unit labor costs from 32.1 in 1960 to 131.9 in 1991.

27 In 1989, 38.3% of all workers used computers at work. More than 59.9% of four-year college graduates did so compared to 29.8% of high school graduates. There was no significant difference in computer use between men and women.

28 The states with the highest average annual pay in 1990 were Alaska ($29,704), Connecticut ($28,995), New York ($28,873), and New Jersey ($28,449). The states with the lowest annual pay were South Dakota ($16,430), North Dakota ($17,626), Mississippi ($17,718), Montana ($17,895), and Arkansas ($18,204). Nationally, the annual pay grew from $363 in 1860 to $483 in 1900, $1,236 in 1920, $1,368 in 1930, $1,299 in 1940, $2,992 in 1950, $4,743 in 1960, $7,564 in 1970, $15,757 in 1980, and $25,889 in 1990.

29 The wage disparity between men and women is reflected in their respective median wages. In 1990, men received median earnings of $21,522 and women $12,250. Most men work in higher-paying jobs, such as management, machine operations, and transportation.

30 The minimum hourly wage was 75 cents in 1950. It was increased to $1 in 1956, $1.15 in 1961, $1.25 in 1963, $1.40 in 1967, $1.60 in 1968, $2.00 in 1974, $2.10 in 1975, $2.30 in 1976, $2.65 in 1978, $2.90 in 1979, $3.10 in 1980, $3.35 in 1981, $3.80 in 1990, and $4.25 in 1991.

31 In 1991, supplementary benefits added $4.27 to the payroll for every hour worked. Of these benefits, paid leave accounted for $1.05, insurance $1.01, Social Security $0.92, pensions and savings $0.44, supplemental pay for $0.36, workers' compensation $0.33, Federal and state unemployment $0.12.

32 The death rate in industrial accidents declined from 21 per 100,000 workers in 1960 to 9 in 1990. The rate was lower in manufacturing than in nonmanufacturing industries. The industry with the highest occupational illness and injury rate was shipbuilding, and the lowest, nonferrous diecasting.

33 As measured by the number of work stoppages, strikes, lockouts, etc., the 1980s were marked by relative industrial peace. In 1991, there were only 40 work stoppages involving 392,000 workers and 4,584,000 lost days. From 1980 through 1989, there were 831 work stoppages, involving 5.066 million workers, and 119.542 million lost workdays compared to 2,888 work stoppages, involving 14.878 million workers and 260.098 million lost workdays from 1970 through 1979.

34 Nationally, union membership declined from 17.717 million in 1983 to 16.568 million in 1991, or from 20.1% of the employed to 16.1%. Union members received higher weekly earnings of $526 compared to $404 received by non-union workers.

35 Future Data:

A) Industrial Employment (2005):

Manufacturing	18.5%
Construction	6.1%
Agriculture	1.9%
Mining	0.7%
Services	50.5%
Retail Trade	24.8%
Government	10.8%
FIRE (Finance, Insurance, Real Estate)	8.1%
Wholesale Trade	7.2%
Transportation	6.7%

B) Civilian Labor Force Participation Rate (2000):

Total	69%
White	69.5%
Black	66.5%
Male	75.9%
Female	62.6%
White women	62.9%
Black women	62.5%
Hispanic women	59.4%
Asian women	57.5%

C) Age Distribution of Labor (2005):

16-24:	24 million
25-34:	32 million
35-44:	37 million
45-54:	36 million
Over 55:	22 million

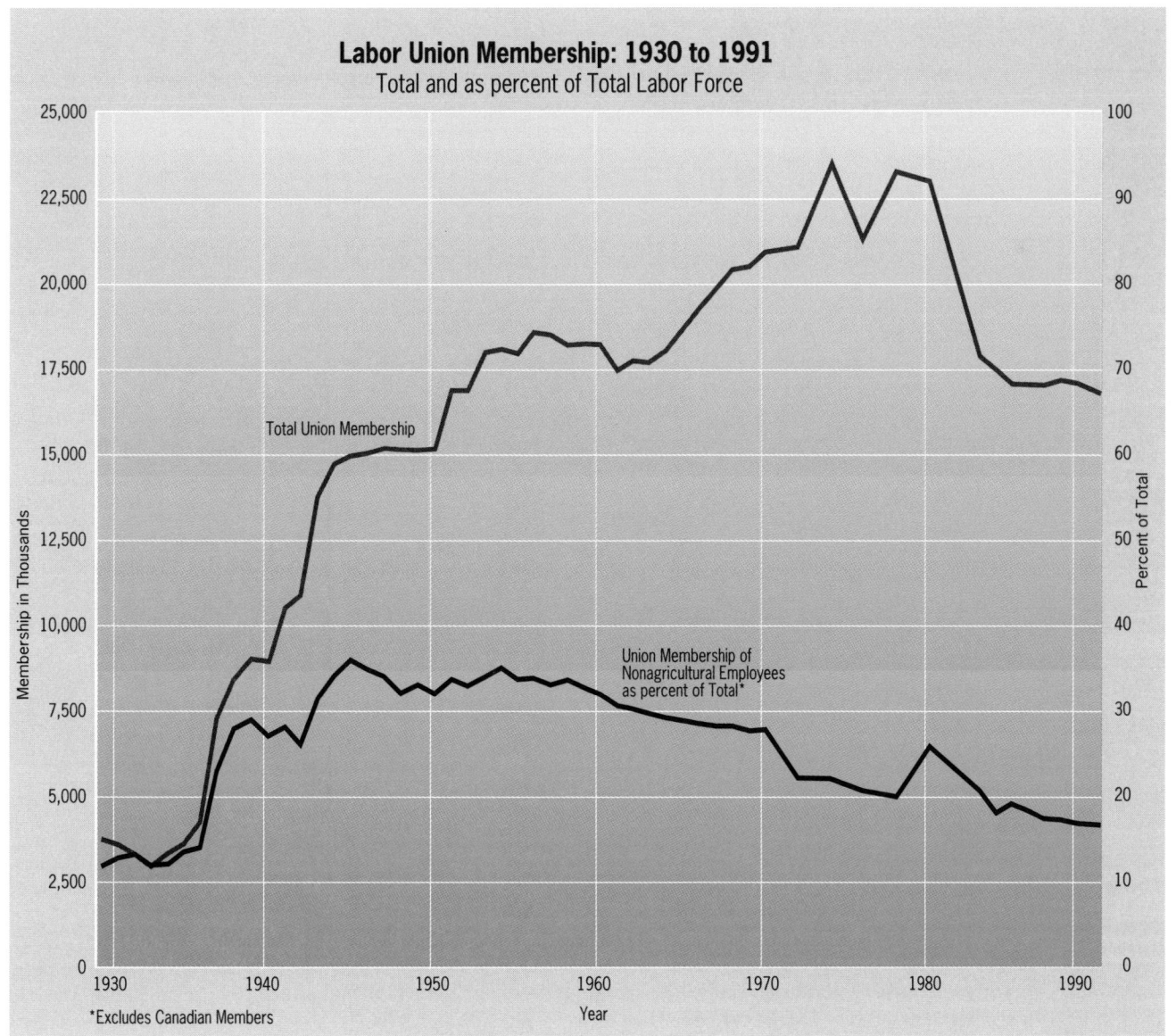

Labor Union Membership: 1930 to 1991
Total and as percent of Total Labor Force

Total Union Membership

Union Membership of Nonagricultural Employees as percent of Total*

Membership in Thousands

Percent of Total

*Excludes Canadian Members

Year

Series D 11-25. Labor Force Status of the Population by Sex: 1870 to 1991

(In thousands of persons 16 years and older, except as noted. Annual estimates are averages of monthly figures. The introduction of data from the decennial censuses into the estimation procedure in 1953 and 1962 and the inclusion of Alaska and Hawaii beginning in 1960 have resulted in three periods of noncomparability.)

Year	Non-institutional population [1]	Total labor force [2]	Total civilian labor force	Agriculture —Employed	Nonagriculture —Employed	Unemployed	Total not in labor force
	11	12	14	16	17	18	19
1991	191,329	126,867	116,877	3,233	113,644	8,426	64,462
1990	189,686	126,424	117,914	3,186	114,728	6,874	63,262
1989	188,081	125,557	117,342	3,199	114,142	6,528	62,523
1988	186,322	123,378	114,968	3,169	110,800	6,701	62,944
1987	184,490	121,602	112,440	3,208	109,232	7,425	62,888
1986	182,293	119,540	109,597	3,163	106,434	8,237	62,752
1985	179,912	117,167	107,150	3,179	103,971	8,312	62,744
1984	178,080	115,241	105,005	3,321	101,685	8,539	62,839
1983	175,891	113,226	100,834	3,383	97,450	10,717	62,665
1982	173,939	111,872	99,526	3,401	96,125	10,678	62,067
1981	171,775	110,315	100,397	3,368	97,030	8,273	61,460
1980	169,349	108,544	99,303	3,364	95,938	7,637	60,806
1979	166,460	106,559	98,824	3,347	95,477	6,137	59,900
1978	163,541	103,882	96,048	3,387	92,661	6,202	59,659
1977	160,689	100,665	92,017	3,283	88,734	6,991	60,025
1976	157,818	97,826	88,752	3,331	85,421	7,406	59,991
1975	154,831	95,453	85,846	3,408	82,438	7,929	59,377
1974	150,800	93,200	91,000	3,500	83,300	5,100	57,600
1973	148,300	91,000	88,700	3,500	81,600	4,300	57,200
1972	145,800	89,000	86,500	3,500	78,700	4,800	56,800
1971	142,600	86,900	84,100	3,400	76,000	5,000	55,700
1970	140,182	85,903	82,715	3,462	75,165	4,088	54,280
1969	137,841	84,240	80,734	3,606	74,296	2,832	53,602
1968	135,562	82,272	78,737	3,817	72,103	2,817	53,291
1967	133,319	80,793	77,347	3,844	70,527	2,975	52,527
1966	131,180	78,893	75,770	3,979	68,915	2,875	52,288
1965	129,236	77,178	74,455	4,361	66,726	3,366	52,058
1964	127,224	75,830	73,091	4,523	64,782	3,786	51,394
1963	125,154	74,571	71,833	4,687	63,076	4,070	50,583
1962	122,981	73,442	70,614	4,944	61,759	3,911	49,539
1961	121,343	73,031	70,459	5,200	60,546	4,714	48,312
1960*	119,759	72,142	69,628	5,458	60,318	3,852	47,617
1959	117,881	70,921	68,369	5,565	59,065	3,740	46,960
1958	116,363	70,275	67,639	5,586	57,450	4,602	46,088
1957	115,065	69,729	66,929	5,947	58,123	2,859	45,336
1956	113,811	69,409	66,552	6,283	57,517	2,750	44,402
1955	112,732	68,072	65,023	6,449	55,724	2,852	44,660
1954	111,671	66,993	63,643	6,206	53,903	3,532	44,678
1953	110,601	66,560	63,015	6,261	54,922	1,834	44,041
1952	108,823	65,720	62,138	6,501	53,753	1,883	43,093
1951	107,721	65,117	62,017	6,726	53,239	2,055	42,604
1950	106,645	63,858	62,208	7,160	51,760	3,288	42,787
1949	105,611	62,903	61,286	7,656	49,990	3,637	42,708
1948	104,527	62,080	60,621	7,629	50,713	2,276	42,447
1947	103,418	60,941	59,350	7,891	49,148	2,311	42,477
Decennial census:							
1970 (April) [3]	139,130	82,049	80,051	2,750	73,804	3,497	57,082
1960 (April)* [3]	124,517	69,877	68,144	4,257	60,383	3,505	54,639
1950 (April) [3]	110,267	59,643	58,646	[4] 6,876	[4] 48,912	2,858	50,624
1940 (April) [3]	[4] 100,147	53,011	52,705	8,449	36,621	7,635	[4] 47,136
1930 (April) [5]	98,723	48,830	——	10,472	38,358	——	49,893
1920 (Jan.) [5]	82,739	41,614	——	10,666	30,948	——	41,125
1910 (April) [5]	71,580	38,167	——	12,388	25,779	——	33,413
1900 (June) [5]	57,950	29,073	——	10,382	18,691	——	28,877
1890 (June) [5]	47,414	23,318	——	9,148	14,170	——	24,095
1880 (June) [5]	36,762	17,392	——	7,714	9,678	——	19,370
1870 (June) [5]	28,229	12,506	——	5,949	6,557	——	15,723

* Denotes first year for which figures include Alaska and Hawaii.
[1] 1870–1930, total population includes institutional.
[2] 1940–1970, includes Armed Forces.
[3] Data for persons 14 years old and older.
[4] Estimated from data based on different sample.
[5] Data for persons 10 years old and over reporting a gainful occupation.

Series D 85-86. Unemployment: 1890 to 1991

(In thousands of persons 16 years old and over except, prior to 1947, 14 years and over. Annual averages)

Year	Percent of civilian labor force 86	Year	Percent of civilian labor force 86	Year	Percent of civilian labor force 86	Year	Percent of civilian labor force 86	Year	Percent of civilian labor force 86
1991	5.5	1970	4.9	1950	5.3	1930	8.7	1910	5.9
1990	4.4	1969	3.5	1949	5.9	1929	3.2	1909	5.1
1989	4.4	1968	3.6	1948	3.8	1928	4.2	1908	8.0
1988	4.7	1967	3.8	1947	3.9	1927	3.3	1907	2.8
1987	5.7	1966	3.8	1946	3.9	1926	1.8	1906	1.7
1986	6.1								
		1965	4.5	1945	1.9	1925	3.2	1905	4.3
1985	6.1	1964	5.2	1944	1.2	1924	5.0	1904	5.4
1984	6.6	1963	5.7	1943	1.9	1923	2.4	1903	3.9
1983	9.0	1962 [1]	5.5	1942	4.7	1922	6.7	1902	3.7
1982	7.6	1961	6.7	1941	9.9	1921	11.7	1901	4.0
1981	7.6								
		1960 [1] *	5.5	1940	14.6	1920	5.2	1900	5.0
1980	5.0	1959	5.5	1939	17.2	1919	1.4	1899	6.5
1979	5.8	1958	6.8	1938	19.0	1918	1.4	1898	12.4
1978	6.1	1957	4.3	1937	14.3	1917	4.6	1897	14.5
1977	7.0	1956	4.1	1936	16.9	1916	5.1	1896	14.4
1976	7.7								
		1955	4.4	1935	20.1	1915	8.5	1895	13.7
1975	6.9	1954	5.5	1934	21.7	1914	7.9	1894	18.4
1974	5.6	1953 [1]	2.9	1933	24.9	1913	4.3	1893	11.7
1973	4.9	1952	3.0	1932	23.6	1912	4.6	1892	3.0
1972	5.6	1951	3.3	1931	15.9	1911	6.7	1891	5.4
1971	5.9							1890	4.0

* Denotes first year for which figures include Alaska and Hawaii.

[1] See headnote for series D 11-25.

Series D 87-101.   Unemployment Rates for Selected Groups in the Labor Force: 1947 to 1991

(Percent of each group specified of persons 16 years and over in the civilian labor force)

| Year | All civilian workers | | | White | Black | Year | All civilian workers | | | White | Black |
	Total	Male	Female	Total	Total		Total	Male	Female	Total	Total
	87	88	89	90	93		87	88	89	90	93
1991	6.7	7.0	6.3	6.0	12.4	1968	3.6	2.9	4.8	3.2	6.7
1990	5.5	5.6	5.4	4.7	11.3	1967	3.8	3.1	5.2	3.4	7.4
1989	5.3	5.2	5.4	4.5	11.4	1966	3.8	3.2	4.8	3.3	7.3
1988	5.5	5.5	5.6	4.7	11.7						
1987	6.2	6.2	6.2	5.3	13.0	1965	4.5	4.0	5.5	4.1	8.1
1986	7.0	6.9	7.1	6.0	14.5	1964	5.2	4.6	6.2	4.6	9.6
						1963	5.7	5.2	6.5	5.0	10.8
1985	7.2	7.0	7.4	6.2	15.1	1962	5.5	5.2	6.2	4.9	10.9
1984	7.5	7.4	7.6	6.5	15.9	1961	6.7	6.4	7.2	6.0	12.4
1983	9.8	9.9	9.2	6.4	19.5						
1982	9.7	9.9	9.4	8.6	16.9	1960	5.5	5.4	5.9	4.9	10.2
1981	7.6	7.4	7.9	6.7	15.6	1959	5.5	5.3	5.9	4.8	10.7
						1958	6.8	6.8	6.8	6.1	12.6
1980	7.1	6.9	7.4	6.3	14.3	1957	4.3	4.1	4.7	3.8	7.9
1979	5.8	5.1	6.8	5.1	12.3	1956	4.1	3.8	4.8	3.6	8.3
1978	6.1	5.2	7.2	5.2	12.8						
1977	7.1	6.2	8.1	6.2	14.0	1955	4.4	4.2	4.9	6.9	8.7
1976	7.7	—	—	7.0	14.0	1954	5.5	5.3	6.0	5.0	9.9
						1953	2.9	2.8	3.3	2.7	4.5
1975	8.5	7.9	9.3	7.8	14.8	1952	3.0	2.8	3.6	2.8	5.4
1974	5.6	—	—	5.0	9.9	1951	3.3	2.8	4.4	3.1	5.3
1973	4.9	—	—	4.3	8.9						
1972	5.6	5.0	6.6	5.1	10.4	1950	5.3	5.1	5.7	4.9	9.0
1971	5.9	—	—	5.4	9.9	1949	5.9	5.9	6.0	5.6	8.9
						1948	3.8	3.6	4.1	3.5	5.9
1970	4.9	4.4	5.9	4.5	8.2	1947	3.9	4.0	3.7	—	—
1969	3.5	2.8	4.7	3.1	6.4						

Series D 102-115.   Unemployment Rates, by Industry: 1948 to 1991

(Percent of each industry specified of persons 16 years and over in the civilian labor force)

Year	Total unemployed[1]	Agriculture	Mining	Construction	Manufacturing	Transportation and public utilities	Wholesale and retail trade	Finance, insurance, real estate	Service industries	Government
	102	104	106	107	108	111	112	113	114	115
1991	6.7	11.6	7.7	15.4	7.2	5.3	7.6	4.0	5.7	3.2
1990	5.5	9.7	4.8	11.1	5.8	3.8	6.4	3.0	5.0	2.6
1989	5.3	9.6	5.8	10.0	5.1	3.9	6.0	3.1	4.8	2.7
1988	5.5	10.6	7.9	10.6	5.3	3.9	6.2	3.0	4.9	2.8
1987	6.2	10.5	10.0	11.6	6.0	4.5	6.9	3.1	5.4	3.5
1986	7.0	12.5	13.5	13.1	7.1	5.1	7.6	3.5	6.1	3.6
1985	7.2	13.2	9.5	13.1	7.7	5.1	7.6	3.5	6.2	3.9
1984	7.5	13.5	10.0	14.3	7.5	5.5	8.0	3.7	6.6	4.5
1983	9.6	16.0	17.0	18.4	11.2	7.4	10.0	4.5	7.9	5.3
1982	9.7	14.7	13.4	20.0	12.3	6.8	10.0	4.7	7.6	4.9
1981	7.6	12.2	6.3	15.6	8.3	5.2	8.1	3.5	6.6	4.7
1980	7.1	11.0	6.4	14.1	8.5	4.9	7.4	3.4	5.9	4.1
1979	5.8	9.1	4.9	10.3	5.6	3.7	6.5	3.0	5.5	3.7
1978	6.0	8.8	4.1	10.6	5.5	3.7	6.9	3.1	5.7	3.9
1977	7.0	11.1	3.8	12.7	6.7	4.7	8.0	3.9	6.6	4.2
1976	7.7	11.7	4.7	15.6	7.9	5.0	8.6	4.4	7.2	4.4
1975	8.5	10.4	4.1	18.0	10..9	5.6	8.7	4.9	7.1	4.1
1974	5.6	7.3	2.9	10.6	5.7	3.2	6.4	3.1	5.1	3.0
1973	4.9	6.9	2.9	8.8	4.3	3.0	5.6	2.7	4.8	2.7
1972	5.6	7.6	3.2	10.3	5.6	3.5	6.4	3.4	5.3	2.9
1971	5.9	7.9	4.0	10.4	6.8	3.8	8.4	3.3	5.6	2.0
1970	4.9	7.5	3.1	9.7	5.6	3.2	5.3	2.8	4.7	2.2
1969	3.5	6.0	2.8	5.4	3.3	2.1	4.1	2.1	3.5	1.9
1968	3.6	6.3	3.1	6.2	3.3	1.9	4.0	2.2	3.6	1.8
1967	3.8	6.9	3.4	6.6	3.6	2.3	4.2	2.5	3.9	1.8
1966	3.8	6.6	3.5	7.1	3.2	2.0	4.4	2.1	3.9	1.8
1965	4.5	7.5	5.3	10.1	4.0	2.9	5.0	2.3	4.6	1.9
1964	5.2	9.7	6.7	11.2	5.0	3.5	5.7	2.6	5.3	2.1
1963	5.7	9.2	7.3	13.3	5.7	4.2	6.2	2.7	5.7	2.2
1962	5.5	7.5	7.7	13.5	5.8	4.1	6.3	3.0	5.5	2.1
1961	6.7	9.6	11.1	15.7	7.8	5.3	7.3	3.3	6.2	2.5
1960	5.5	8.3	9.5	13.5	6.2	4.6	5.9	2.4	5.1	2.4
1959	5.5	9.0	9.7	13.4	6.1	4.4	5.8	2.5	5.3	2.2
1958	6.8	10.3	10.9	15.3	9.3	6.1	6.8	2.8	5.7	2.5
1957	4.3	6.9	5.8	10.9	5.1	3.3	4.5	1.8	4.2	1.9
1956	4.1	7.3	6.8	10.0	4.7	3.0	4.5	1.7	4.6	1.7
1955	4.4	7.2	9.0	10.9	4.7	4.0	4.7	2.3	5.2	2.0
1954	5.5	8.9	14.4	12.9	7.1	5.6	5.7	2.3	5.5	2.2
1953	2.9	5.6	4.6	7.2	3.1	2.2	3.4	1.7	3.4	1.5
1952	3.0	4.8	3.8	6.7	3.5	2.3	3.5	1.7	3.6	1.6
1951	3.3	4.3	4.0	7.2	3.8	2.3	3.9	1.5	4.2	1.8
1950	5.3	9.0	6.7	12.2	6.2	4.7	6.0	2.2	6.4	3.0
1949	5.9	7.1	8.9	13.9	8.0	5.9	6.2	2.1	6.7	3.1
1948	3.8	5.5	3.0	8.7	4.2	3.5	4.7	1.8	4.8	2.2

[1] Also includes the self-employed, unpaid family workers and those with no previous work experience, not shown separately.

Series D 167-181.   Labor Force and Employment, by Industry: 1800 to 1991

(In thousands of persons 10 years old and over)

Year	Labor force	Agriculture	Mining	Construction	Manufacturing	Trade
				Employment		
	167	170	172	173	174	177
1991	116,877	3,233	733	7,087	20,434	24,055
1990	117,914	3,186	730	7,696	21,284	24,269
1989	117,342	3,199	719	7,680	21,652	24,230
1988	114,968	3,169	753	7,603	21,320	23,663
1987	112,440	3,208	818	7,456	20,935	23,392
1986	109,597	3,163	880	7,288	20,962	22,813
1985	107,150	3,179	939	6,987	20,879	22,296
1984	105,005	3,321	957	6,665	20,995	21,979
1983	100,634	3,541	921	6,149	19,946	21,145
1982	99,526	3,571	1,028	5,756	20,286	20,758
1981	100,397	3,518	1,118	6,060	21,817	20,524
1980	99,303	3,364	979	6,215	21,942	20,191
1979	96,945	3,455	865	6,299	22,137	19,672
1978	94,373	3,501	828	6,043	21,497	19,253
1977	90,546	3,383	814	5,504	20,637	18,706
1976	87,485	3,417	770	5,162	20,044	18,025
1975	84,783	3,476	732	5,015	19,275	17,470
1974	85,936	3,588	655	5,454	20,879	17,253
1973	80,285	3,452	638	4,028	20,054	16,665
1972	81,702	3,585	597	5,246	19,866	16,470
1970	78,678	3,463	516	4,818	20,746	15,008
1960	74,060	5,970	709	3,640	17,145	14,051
1950	65,470	7,870	901	3,029	15,648	12,152
1940	56,290	9,575	925	1,876	11,309	9,328
1930	48,830	10,560	1,009	1,988	9,884	8,122
1920	41,610	10,790	1,180	1,233	11,190	5,845
1910	37,480	11,770	1,068	1,949	8,332	5,320
1900	29,070	11,680	637	1,665	5,895	3,970
1890	23,320	9,960	440	1,510	4,390	2,960
1880	17,390	8,920	280	900	3,290	1,930
1870	12,930	6,790	180	780	2,470	1,310
1860	11,110	5,880	176	520	1,530	890
1850	8,250	4,520	102	410	1,200	530
1840	5,660	3,570	32	290	500	350
1830	4,200	2,965	22	—	(NA)	—
1820	3,135	2,470	13	—	(NA)	—
1810	2,330	1,950	11	—	75	—
1800	1,900	1,400	10	—	—	—

NA Not available

Series D 722-727. Average Annual Earnings of Employees: 1929 to 1990

Year	Full-time employees (OBE-BEA)[1] 722	Year	Full-time employees (OBE-BEA)[1] 722	Year	Full-time employees (OBE-BEA)[1] 722	Year	Full-time employees (OBE-BEA)[1] 722	Year	Full-time employees (OBE-BEA)[1] 722
1990	$25,889	1977	12,379	1965	5,710	1952	3,402	1940	1,299
1989	24,766	1976	11,620	1964	5,503	1951	3,217	1939	1,264
1988	24,032			1963	5,243			1938	1,230
1987	22,913	1975	10,836	1962	5,065	1950	2,992	1937	1,258
1986	21,935	1974	9,994	1961	4,884	1949	2,844	1936	1,184
		1973	9,298			1948	2,786		
1985	21,079	1972	8,610	1960	4,743	1947	5,589	1935	1,137
1984	20,168	1971	—	1959	4,594	1946	2,359	1934	1,091
1983	19,330			1958	4,375			1933	1,048
1982	18,488	1970	7,564	1957	4,230	1945	2,190	1932	1,120
1981	17,218	1969	7,095	1956	4,055	1944	2,109	1931	1,275
		1968	6,657			1943	1,951		
1980	15,757	1967	6,230	1955	3,851	1942	1,709	1930	1,368
1979	14,376	1966	5,967	1954	3,667	1941	1,443	1929	1,405
1978	13,287			1953	3,581				

[1] OBE = Office of Business Economics (1929-1967);
BEA = Bureau of Economic Analysis (1928-1970).

Series D 802-810.   Earnings and Hours of Production Workers in Manufacturing: 1909 to 1991

Year	All manufacturing			Year	All manufacturing			Year	All manufacturing		
	Average hourly earnings 802	Average weekly hours 803	Average weekly earnings 804		Average hourly earnings 802	Average weekly hours 803	Average weekly earnings 804		Average hourly earnings 802	Average weekly hours 803	Average weekly earnings 804
1991	$10.34	34.3	$355	1965	2.61	41.2	107.53	1938	.62	35.6	22.07
1990	10.02	34.5	346	1964	2.53	40.7	102.97	1937	.62	38.6	23.82
1989	9.66	34.6	334	1963	2.46	40.5	99.63	1936	.55	39.2	21.56
1988	9.28	34.7	322	1962	2.39	40.4	96.56				
1987	8.98	34.8	313	1961	2.32	39.8	92.34	1935	.54	36.6	19.91
1986	8.76	34.8	305					1934	.53	34.6	18.20
				1960	2.26	39.7	89.72	1933	.44	38.1	16.65
1985	8.57	34.9	299	1959*	2.19	40.3	88.26	1932	.44	38.3	16.89
1984	8.32	35.2	293	1958	2.11	39.2	82.71	1931	.51	40.5	20.64
1983	8.02	35.0	281	1957	2.05	39.8	81.59				
1982	7.68	34.8	267	1956	1.95	40.4	78.78	1930	.55	42.1	23.00
1981	7.25	35.2	255					1929	.56	44.2	24.76
				1955	1.86	40.7	75.70	1928	.56	44.4	24.70
1980	6.66	35.3	235	1954	1.78	39.6	70.49	1927	.54	45.0	24.47
1979	6.16	35.7	220	1953	1.74	40.5	70.47	1926	.54	45.0	24.38
1978	5.69	35.8	204	1952	1.65	40.7	67.16				
1977	5.25	37.0	189	1951	1.56	40.6	63.34	1925	.54	44.5	24.11
1976	4.86	36.1	175					1924	.54	43.7	23.67
				1950	1.44	40.5	58.32	1923	.52	45.6	23.56
1975	4.53	36.1	164	1949	1.38	39.1	53.88	1922	.48	44.2	21.28
1974	4.22	36.5	154	1948	1.33	40.0	53.12	1921	.51	43.1	21.94
1973	3.92	37.1	145	1947	1.22	40.4	49.17				
1972	3.67	37.1	136	1946	1.08	40.3	43.32	1920	.55	47.4	26.02
1971	3.44	39.9	127					1919	.47	46.3	21.84
				1945	1.02	43.5	44.20	1918	—	—	19.12
1970	3.36	39.8	133.73	1944	1.01	45.2	45.70	1917	—	—	14.97
1969	3.19	40.6	129.51	1943	.96	45.0	43.07	1916	—	—	12.63
1968	3.01	40.7	122.51	1942	.85	43.1	36.68				
1967	2.83	40.6	114.90	1941	.73	40.6	29.48	1915	—	—	11.22
1966	2.72	41.3	112.34					1914	.22	49.4	10.92
				1940	.66	38.1	24.96	1909	.19	51.0	9.74
				1939	.63	37.7	23.64				

*Denotes first year for which figures include Alaska and Hawaii.

Series D 946-951. Labor Union Membership and Membership as Percent of Total Labor Force and of Nonagricultural Employment: 1930 to 1991

(In thousands, except percent)

Year	Total union membership	Non-agricultural employment as percent of total [1]	Year	Total union membership	Non-agricultural employment as percent of total [1]	Year	Total union membership	Non-agricultural employment as percent of total [1]	Year	Total union membership	Non-agricultural employment as percent of total [1]
	946	951		946	951		946	951		946	951
1991	16,568	16.1	1975	—	—	1960	18,117	* 31.4	1945	14,796	35.5
1990	—	—	1974	23,408	21.7	1959	18,169	32.1	1944	14,621	33.8
1989	16,960	16.4	1973	—	—	1958	18,081	33.2	1943	13,642	31.1
1988	17,002	16.8	1972	20,893	21.8	1957	18,431	32.8	1942	10,762	25.9
1987	16,913	17.0	1971	—	—	1956	18,477	33.4	1941	10,489	27.9
1986	16,975	18.0									
			1970	20,752	27.4	1955	17,749	33.2	1940	8,944	26.9
1985	16,996	18.8	1969	20,382	27.1	1954	17,955	34.7	1939	8,980	28.6
1984	17,340	17.9	1968	20,258	27.9	1953	17,860	33.7	1938	8,265	27.5
1983	17,717	20.1	1967	19,712	27.9	1952	16,750	32.5	1937	7,218	22.6
1982	—	—	1966	19,181	28.1	1951	16,750	33.3	1936	4,164	13.7
1981	—	—									
			1965	18,519	28.4	1950	15,000	31.5	1935	3,728	13.2
1980	22,811	25.2	1964	17,976	28.9	1949	15,000	32.6	1934	3,249	11.9
1979	—	—	1963	17,586	29.2	1948	15,000	31.9	1933	2,857	11.3
1978	23,306	19.7	1962	17,630	29.8	1947	15,414	33.7	1932	3,226	12.9
1977	—	—	1961	17,328	30.2	1946	14,974	34.5	1931	3,526	12.4
1976	21,171	20.3							1930	3,632	11.6

* Denotes first year for which figures include Alaska and Hawaii.
[1] Excludes Canadian members.

Series D 970-985. Work Stoppages, Workers Involved, Man-Days Idle, Major Issues, and Average Duration: 1927 to 1991

(From 1971, excludes work stoppages involving fewer than 1,000 workers and lasting less than one day)

	Work stoppages and man-days idle					Work stoppages and man-days idle			
	Stoppage beginning in year		Man-days idle			Stoppage beginning in year		Man-days idle	
Year	Total	Workers involved, number (1,000)	Number (1,000)	% of estimated total working time	Year	Total	Workers involved, number (1,000)	Number (1,000)	% of estimated total working time
	970	971	973	974		970	971	973	974
1991	40	392	4,584	0.02	1958	3,694	2,060	23,900	0.18
1990	44	185	5,926	0.02	1957	3,673	1,390	16,500	0.12
1989	51	452	16,996	0.07	1956	3,825	1,900	33,100	0.24
1988	40	118	4,364	0.02					
1987	46	174	4,469	0.02	1955	4,320	2,650	28,200	0.22
1986	69	533	11,861	0.05	1954	3,468	1,530	22,600	0.18
					1953	5,091	2,400	28,300	0.22
1985	54	324	7,079	0.03	1952	5,117	3,540	59,100	0.48
1984	62	376	8,499	0.04	1951	4,737	2,220	22,900	0.18
1983	81	909	17,461	0.08					
1982	96	656	9,061	0.04	1950	4,843	2,410	38,800	0.33
1981	145	729	16,908	0.07	1949	3,606	3,030	50,500	0.44
					1948	3,419	1,960	34,100	0.28
1980	187	795	20,844	0.09	1947	3,693	2,170	34,600	0.30
1979	295	1,021	20,409	0.09	1946	4,985	4,600	116,000	1.04
1978	219	1,006	23,774	0.11					
1977	298	1,212	21,258	0.10	1945	4,750	3,470	38,000	0.31
1976	231	1,519	23,962	0.12	1944	4,956	2,120	8,720	0.07
					1943	3,752	1,980	13,500	0.10
1975	235	965	17,563	0.09	1942	2,968	840	4,180	0.04
1974	424	1,796	31,809	0.16	1941	4,288	2,360	23,000	0.23
1973	317	1,400	16,260	0.08					
1972	250	975	16,764	0.09	1940	2,508	577	6,700	0.08
1971	298	2,516	35,538	0.19	1939	2,613	1,170	17,800	0.21
					1938	2,772	688	9,150	—
1970	5,716	3,305	66,414	0.37	1937	4,740	1,860	28,400	—
1969	5,700	2,481	42,869	0.24	1936	2,172	789	13,900	—
1968	5,045	2,649	49,018	0.28					
1967	4,595	2,870	42,100	0.25	1935	2,014	1,120	15,500	—
1966	4,405	1,960	25,400	0.15	1934	1,856	1,470	19,600	—
					1933	1,695	1,170	16,900	—
1965	3,963	1,550	23,300	0.15	1932	841	324	10,500	—
1964	3,655	1,640	22,900	0.15	1931	810	342	6,890	—
1963	3,362	941	16,100	0.11					
1962	3,614	1,230	18,600	0.13	1930	637	183	3,320	—
1961	3,367	1,450	16,300	0.11	1929	921	289	5,350	—
					1928	604	314	12,600	—
1960	3,333	1,320	19,100	0.14	1927	707	330	26,200	—
1959 *	3,708	1,880	69,000	0.50					

* Denotes first year for which figures include Alaska and Hawaii.

Series D 1029-1036.   Work Injury Frequency Rates in Manufacturing, Mining and Class I Railroads: 1922 to 1990

(Rate is average number of disabling injuries per million man-hours worked)

Year	Manufacturing [1]	Mining	Year	Manufacturing [1]	Mining	Year	Manufacturing [1]	Mining	Year	Manufacturing [1]	Mining
	1029	1030		1029	1030		1029	1030		1029	1030
1990	13.2	8.3	1972	15.6	—	1955	12.1	38.3	1938	15.1	67.5
1989	13.1	8.5	1971	—	—	1954	11.9	37.7	1937	17.8	70.5
1988	13.1	8.8				1953	13.4	40.3	1936	16.6	70.2
1987	11.9	8.5	1970	15.2	28.9	1952	14.3	43.6			
1986	10.6	7.4	1969	14.8	28.0	1951	15.5	45.1	1935	17.9	72.7
			1968	14.0	27.8				1934	20.2	73.8
1985	10.4	8.4	1967	14.0	28.0	1950	14.7	46.3	1933	19.3	71.7
1984	10.6	9.7	1966	13.6	28.4	1949	14.5	48.3	1932	19.6	74.8
1983	10.0	8.4				1948	17.2	53.2	1931	18.9	79.9
1982	10.2	10.5	1965	12.8	28.3	1947	18.8	55.8			
1981	11.5	11.8	1964	12.3	28.8	1946	19.9	58.0	1930	23.1	—
			1963	11.9	28.8				1929	24.0	—
1980	12.2	11.2	1962	11.9	28.6	1945	18.6	55.5	1928	22.5	—
1979	13.3	11.4	1961	11.8	29.5	1944	18.4	57.2	1927	22.6	—
1978	13.2	11.5				1943	20.0	59.4	1926	24.2	—
1977	13.1	10.9	1960	12.0	29.8	1942	19.9	61.2			
1976	13.3	11.0	1959	12.4	29.2	1941	18.1	63.2	1925	—	—
			1958	[2] 11.4	[3] 31.9				1924	—	—
1975	13.0	11.0	1957	11.4	35.8	1940	15.3	65.2	1923	—	—
1974	14.6	10.2	1956	12.0	37.1	1939	14.9	64.8	1922	—	—
1973	15.3	12.5									

[1] Excludes petroleum refining, smelting and refining of nonferrous metals, cement and lime manufacturing and coke production.
[2] Industry definition revised to conform to the 1957 edition of the *Standard Industrial Classification*
Manual. Comparisons to prior years should be made with caution.
[3] Beginning 1958, includes data on sand and gravel operations.

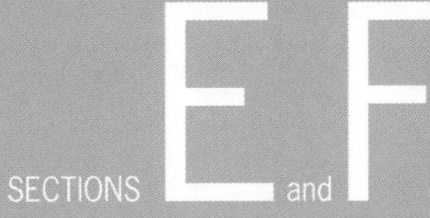

SECTIONS E and F

NATIONAL INCOME
AND WEALTH

NATIONAL INCOME AND WEALTH

Highlights

1 The earliest statistics of prices were compiled by Samuel Blodgett, Jr. in *Economica: A Statistical Manual of the United States of America*, published in 1806. It included a collection of prices for 16 important commodities in five markets for the years 1785-1805. The first serious attempt to summarize price data in the form of index numbers was made by Horatio C. Burchard, Director of the Mint, in his report to the Secretary of the Treasury in 1881. In 1886, a special report containing retail prices for about 60 "necessaries of life" was included in volume 20 of the Tenth Census. In 1891, a Senate Resolution led Roland P. Falkner to collect a voluminous body of data covering wholesale prices, 1840-1891, and retail prices for the 28-month period ending September 1891. This information was published in the Aldrich Reports. In 1900, Falkner extended his indexes to 1899 with quotations for 142 articles collected by the Department of Labor.

In 1902, the Department of Labor began publishing its Index of Wholesale Prices, which it has published continuously to the present day. In addition to this series, John R. Commons published an Index of Wholesale Prices for 1878-1900 in the *Quarterly Bulletin of the Bureau of Economic Research*. Bradstreet's Index of Wholesale Prices for about 96 commodities was established in 1897 and included data beginning from 1890. Dun's index numbers of wholesale prices for about 350 commodities were published in *Dun's Review* beginning in 1901 and extending back to 1860. Walter B. Smith and Arthur H. Cole computed wholesale commodity price indexes covering 1792-1862 for *Fluctuations in American Business, 1790-1860,* published by Harvard University Press in 1935. It covered Boston, New York, and Philadelphia.

The most extensive historical price investigations, however, were undertaken under the auspices of the International Scientific Committee on Price History. They were summarized by *Wholesale Commodity Prices in the United States, 1700-1861*, published by Harvard University Press in 1938. Wholesale Price Indexes were compiled by Frederick C. Mills for economically significant commodities. Part of this series was first published by the National Bureau of Economic Research for 1830-1931 in *Economic Tendencies in the United States*. (Wholesale prices are compiled from prices in primary markets and pertain to the first major commercial transaction for each commodity. The

quotations are generally selling prices of manufacturers or producers.) The current price index was begun in 1952 and spliced to the former series. While the 1952 revision did not alter the conceptual definition of the index, it did adopt major changes in coverage and methods. The list of priced commodities was expanded from 947 to 1,800 in 1952, 2,450 in 1970 and 3,100 today. The index is currently known as the Producer Price Index. The base years have changed from 1890-99 to 1913, 1926, 1967, and 1982. The weighting factors for each commodity represent the value of shipments for the specific commodity priced and for all others in the same group known to have similar price movements. The indexes are calculated as averages of relatives weighted by value of shipments. Changes in quality are factored into the index.

2 The volume of information available for wholesale prices is not matched at the retail level, especially for the early years. The official Consumer Price Index (CPI) was initiated by the Bureau of Labor Statistics (BLS) in 1904 with a food index covering the years 1890-1903. The food index was continued until the end of World War I when it became one component group of a comprehensive Cost of Living Index. Since then, the index has been expanded in scope, resulting in an improvement in the quality of data. At present the index is issued monthly. From 1918 to 1958, the National Industrial Conference Board also compiled a consumer price index. Consumer price data prior to 1913 are extremely patchy. The only cost of living indexes computed from retail price data prior to 1913 are Wesley C. Mitchell's *Relative Cost of Living for 1860 to 1880*, Ethel Hoover's *Consumer Price Index for 1851 to 1880* and Rees' *Cost of Living Index, 1890-1914.* They were compiled from newspapers and other sources, and their reliability is affected by changes in quality, incomplete files, nominal prices, changes in consumer tastes, and demographic and other changes. In 1919, the BLS began the publication of complete indexes at semiannual intervals. The first major revision of the Consumer Price Index occurred in 1940, with subsequent revisions in 1953, 1964, 1978, and 1987. The last revision changed the base year to 1982-84. The BLS publishes CPI's for two population groups: CPI-W covering Urban Wage-Earners and Clerical Workers, who comprise about 32% of the population; and CPI-U for all urban

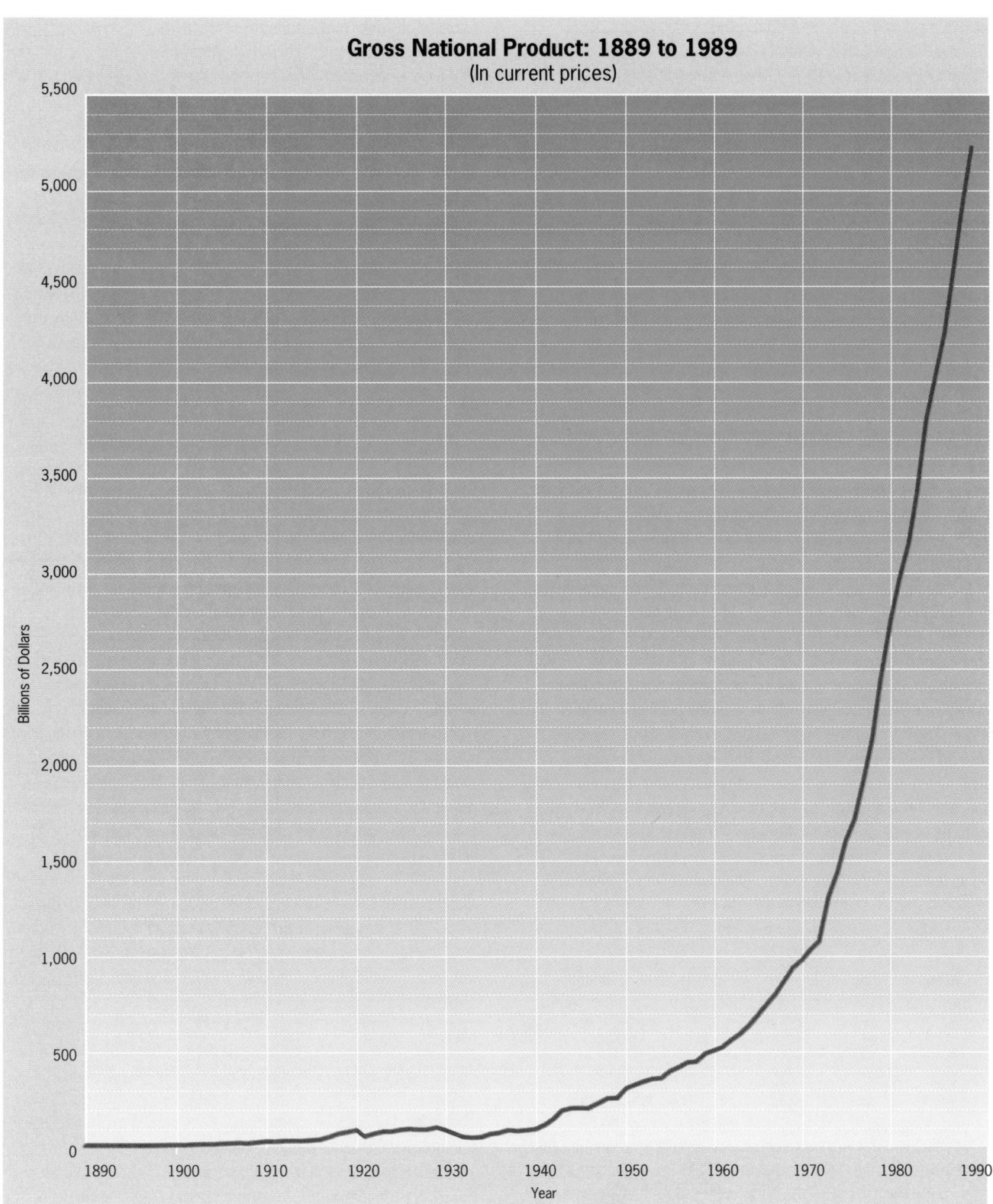

Gross National Product: 1889 to 1989
(In current prices)

consumers, including groups excluded from CPI-W, such as the unemployed, self-employed, retirees, professionals, and managers. The current CPI is based on a market basket of goods and services, including food, clothing, shelter, fuels, transportation, healthcare, etc. It is based on data collected from 85 areas across the country (up from 40 in 1952, 46 in 1953, 50 in 1964, and 56 in 1966), and from over 57,000 housing units and 19,000 establishments. The BLS publishes a national index as well as separate indexes for regions, area-size classes, and 29 local areas.

3 Income and expenditures represent two facets of an economy. They are commonly measured by the Gross National Product (GNP) or Gross Domestic Product (GDP). In 1991, the Bureau of Economic Analysis began featuring GDP rather than GNP as the measure of national production because it is the more appropriate measure for short-term monitoring of the economy, and also because it facilitates international comparisons. GDP is the primary measure of production in the System of National Accounts and is the total national output of goods and services valued at market prices. It includes purchases of goods and services by consumers and government, gross private domestic investment, and net exports of goods and services. GNP measures the output attributable to all labor and property supplied by U.S. residents. It differs from national income mainly in that GNP includes allowances for depreciation and for indirect business taxes. The dollar levels of GDP and GNP differ little but percentage changes may differ more significantly. The annual rates of growth of real GNP have been slightly less than the annual rates of growth of real GDP for most of the 1980s. The short-term differences are greater and tend to fluctuate more. National income is the aggregate of labor and property earnings which arise in the current production of goods and services. It is the sum of employee compensation, proprietors' income, rental income of persons, corporate profits, and net interest. It measures the total factor cost of the goods and services produced by the economy. Capital consumption adjustment for corporations, sole proprietorships, and partnerships is the difference between capital consumption claimed on income tax returns and capital consumption allowances measured at straightline depreciation, consistent service lives, and replacement cost. Personal income is the current income received by persons from all sources minus their contributions for social insurance, (including transfers from government, such as Social Security, but excluding interpersonal transfers.) Disposable personal income (income available for spending or saving) is personal income less personal tax and nontax payments.

4 In recent years, discussion has focused on the limitations of the standard measurements of national income and wealth. First, national product is primarily a measure of the output of the market economy. No account is taken of the value of homemakers' services, home repairs or noncommercial recreation. Second, there is no agreement on what goods should be properly considered as end products of the economy. As ordinarily constituted, national product includes all items of consumer expenditure, including expenditures on commuting and labor union dues, which are not end products in themselves. It also overstates the growth of the economy because it includes defense expenditures, as well as police and fire protection. Third, because of the techniques used in adjusting for price changes, national product fails to reflect fully the changes in the quality of goods. This limitation tends to understate economic growth. Fourth, aggregate figures on national product mask changes in the distribution of income between rich and poor, the age-composition of the population, and man-hours spent in economic activity.

5 The primary source of national income and product data is the *Survey of Current Business*, published monthly by the Department of Commerce. Detailed historical data appear in the two-volume *National Income and Product Accounts of the United States*. For earlier years, the classic sources are Simon Kuznets' *National Income and its Composition, 1919-1938, Capital in the American Economy: Its Formation and Financing, National Product Since 1869*, and *Enterprise and Social Progress*, Willford I. King's *The Wealth and Income of the People of the United States*, and Robert F. Martin's *National Income in the United States, 1799-1938*.

6 Generally speaking, national saving equals national income minus national consumption and is identical to net national investment. Although data on saving are imperfect for statistical and conceptual reasons, they throw important light on the nature of the different groups of savers and the various forms of savings.

7 The Poverty Index was devised by the Social Security Administration in 1964 and revised by the Federal Inter-agency Committee in 1969 and 1980. It is based solely on money income and does not include noncash benefits, such as food stamps, Medicaid, and public housing (which many poor people receive.) The Poverty Threshold is updated every year to reflect changes in the Consumer Price Index. In 1980, it was $4,290 for one person under 65, $3,949 for one person over 65, and $11,269 for six persons. In 1983, the matrix was expanded to nine persons. In 1990, the threshold was $6,800 for one person under 65 and $6,268 for one person over 65, rising incrementally to $26,848 for a unit of 9 persons.

8 The 1980s were the healthiest years in terms of growth of the GDP. Every year in that decade the GDP grew by over 5%, the highest growth rate being 7.9% during 1987-88. In contrast, the GDP grew by only 2.9% in the recession-bound 1990-91.

9 Until 1989, industry contributed more to the GDP than services. Since then the ratio of services to goods has grown to 3:2.

10 Wages and salaries of employees grew from $551.5 billion in 1970 to $2.808 trillion in 1991. During the same period, supplements to wages and salaries (such as health benefits, subsidized food or travel, tuition, etc.) grew from $66.8 billion to $580 billion.

11 Between 1970 and 1991, farm income of proprietors grew by 2.5 times from $14.6 billion to $35.1 billion. Over the same period, nonfarm income of proprietors grew 5.2 times from $65.3 billion to $344.5 billion.

Per Capita Income and Product for Selected Items in Current Prices: 1929 to 1991
Includes armed forces abroad. Plotted in five year intervals (except 1985–1991)

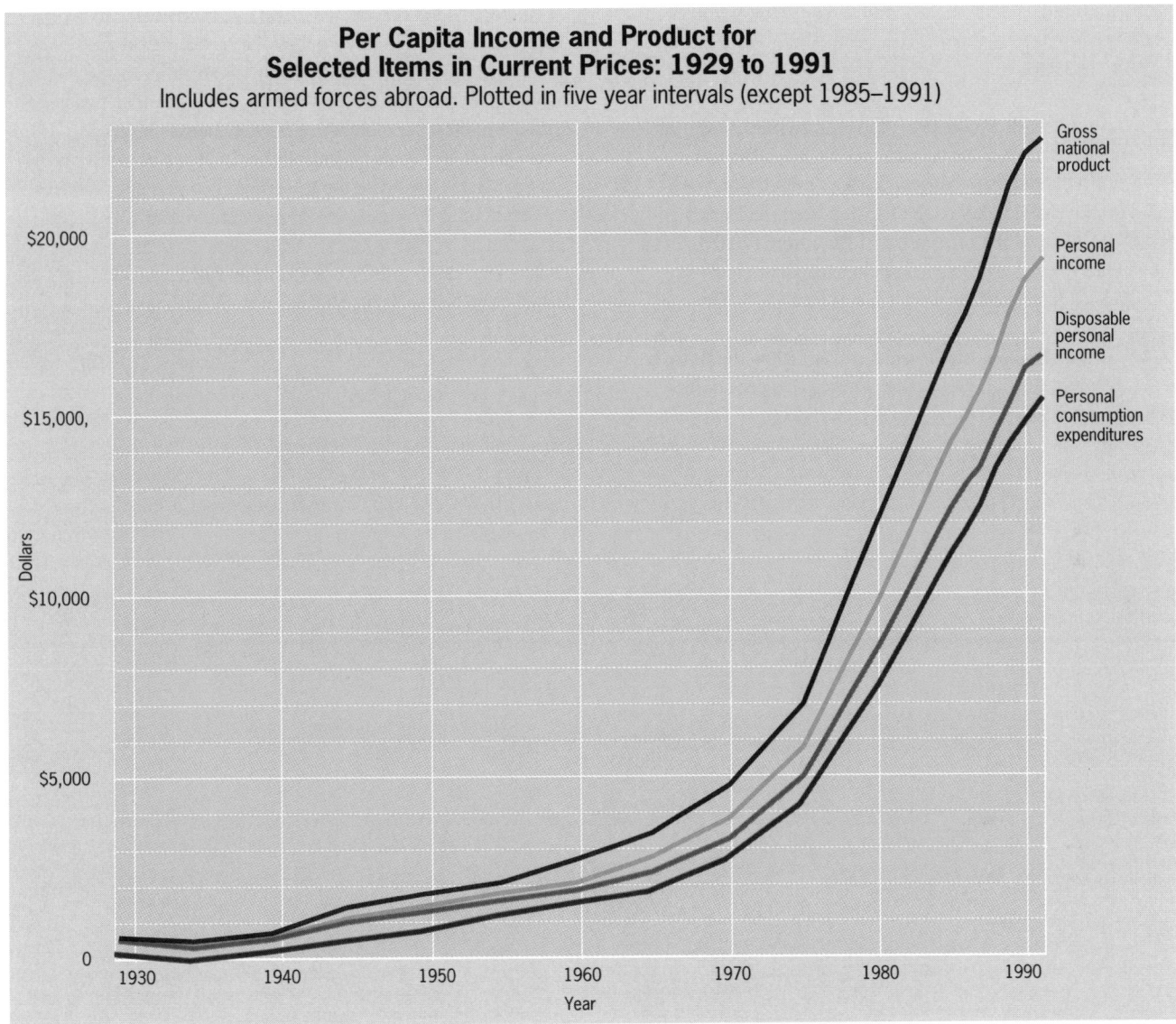

12 Of personal consumption expenditures, the fastest growing categories between 1970 and 1990 were: legal services from $4.9 billion to $49.2 billion (a 1,004% increase), medical care from $60 billion to $593 billion (988%), religious and welfare activities from $12.1 billion to $103.8 billion (857%), household utilities from $22.7 billion to $135.9 billion (598%), and housing from $94 billion to $547.1 billion (582%).

13 The share of wages and salaries in personal income declined from 66.4% in 1970 to 58.1% in 1991. During the same period, the share of personal interest income grew from 8.3% to 14.9%.

14 The Boston-Washington Corridor Consolidated Metropolitan Statistical Areas led the nation in per capita personal income in 1990. The top CMSAs in this corridor are New York-Northern New Jersey-Long Island ($25,405), Washington DC-Maryland-Virginia ($25,363), Hartford-New

Britain-Middletown-Bristol ($24,444), and Boston-Lawrence-Salem-Lowell-Brockton ($24,315). The San Francisco-Oakland-San Jose CMSA ranks second overall with $25,037.

15 In 1990, the average U.S. consumer spent $8,886 on housing, including $1,890 on fuel and utilities; $5,122 on transportation; $2,952 on taxes, $2,485 on food at home; $1,811 at restaurants; $1,617 on apparel; $1,480 on health care; and $293 on alcoholic beverages.

16 The percentage of households earning below $10,000 declined for Whites from 14.3% in 1970 to 12.8% in 1990, while it increased for Blacks from 28.0% to 30.8%, and for Hispanics from 20.3% to 21.1% over the same period. The percentage of households earning over $75,000 grew for all races: for Whites from 6.1% to 10.4%, for Blacks from 1.5% to 3.8% and for Hispanics from 2.0% to 4.3%. Between 1970 and 1990, the median family income rose from $10,326 to $36,915 for Whites, and from $6,279 to $21,423 for Blacks.

Hispanic families earn slightly more than Black families. Their median family income rose from $8,715 in 1973 to $23,431 in 1990.

17 Between 1979 and 1987, the cities with the highest percentage changes in per capita income were Boston (98.1%), Atlanta (78.8%), New York (77.8%), Charlotte (75.4%), Nashville-Davidson (72.9%), Virginia Beach (70.6%), Jacksonville (70.1%), and Baltimore (70.0%). The cities with the lowest percentage changes were Houston (36.0%), Oklahoma City (44.4%), and Tulsa (45.1%).

18 In 1990, 13.5% of Americans lived below the poverty level, compared to 22.4% in 1959. During this period, the percentage of Whites below poverty level declined from 18.1% to 10.7%, and the percentage of Blacks from 55.1% to 31.9%. The percentage of children below the poverty level grew from 14.9% to 19.9%. In 1990, 15.1% of White children and 44.1% of Black children lived below the poverty level. The two states with the highest percentages of persons below the poverty level were both in the South: Mississippi (25.7%) and Louisiana (23.6%). The states with the lowest relative percentages were Connecticut (6.0%) and New Hampshire (6.3%).

19 The mean family net worth in 1989 was $203,800 for Whites and $45,900 for Blacks, non-Whites, and Hispanics.

Series F 1-5. Gross National Product, Total and Per Capita, in Current and 1958 Prices: 1869 to 1989

(In billions of dollars)

Year	Current prices 1	Year	Current prices 1	Year	Current prices 1	Year	Current prices 1	Year	Current prices 1	Year	Current prices 1
1989	5,201.0	1970	977.1	1952	345.5	1935	72.2	1917	60.4	1900	18.7
1988	4,880.6	1969	930.3	1951	328.4	1934	65.1	1916	48.3	1899	17.4
1987	4,524.3	1968	864.2			1933	55.6			1898	15.4
1986	4,231.6	1967	793.9	1950	284.8	1932	58.0	1915	40.0	1897	14.6
		1966	749.9	1949	256.5	1931	75.8	1914	38.6	1896	13.3
1985	4,014.9			1948	257.6			1913	39.6		
1984	3,772.2	1965	684.9	1947	231.3	1930	90.4	1912	39.4	1895	13.9
1983	3,405.7	1964	632.4	1946	208.5	1929	103.1	1911	35.8	1894	12.6
1982	3,166.0	1963	590.5			1928	97.0			1893	13.8
1981	2,957.8	1962	560.3	1945	211.9	1927	94.9	1910	35.3	1892	14.3
		1961	520.1	1944	210.1	1926	97.0	1909	33.4	1891	13.5
1980	2,732.0			1943	191.6			1908	27.7		
1979	2,417.8	1960 *	503.7	1942	157.9	1925	93.1	1907	30.4	1890	13.1
1978	2,163.9	1959	483.7	1941	124.5	1924	84.7	1906	28.7	1889	12.5
1977	1,899.5	1958	447.3			1923	85.1			1879-1888 [1]	11.2
1976	1,702.2	1957	441.1	1940	99.7	1922	74.1	1905	25.1	1869-1878 [1]	7.4
		1956	419.2	1939	90.5	1921	69.6	1904	22.9		
1975	1,598.4			1938	84.7			1903	22.9		
1974	1,434.0	1955	398.0	1937	90.4	1920	91.5	1902	21.6		
1973	1,306.6	1954	364.8	1936	82.5	1919	84.0	1901	20.7		
1972	1,171.1	1953	364.6			1918	76.4				
1971	1,063.4										

* Denotes first year for which figures include Alaska and Hawaii.

[1] Decade average.

Series F 17-30. Per Capita Income and Product for Selected Items in Current Prices: 1929 to 1991

(In dollars. Based on Bureau of the Census estimated population as of July 1, including Armed Forces abroad)

| Year | Current prices | | | | Year | Current prices | | | |
| | Gross national product | Personal income | Disposable personal income | Personal consumption expenditures | | Gross national product | Personal income | Disposable personal income | Personal consumption expenditures |
	17	18	19	20		17	18	19	20
1991	22,502	19,133	16,695	15,392	1959	2,731	2,166	1,905	1,758
1990	22,099	18,720	16,236	14,971	1958	2,569	2,074	1,831	1,666
1989	21,213	17,705	15,313	14,219	1957	2,576	2,050	1,801	1,643
1988	20,026	16,630	14,477	13,448	1956	2,492	1,980	1,743	1,585
1987	18,712	15,655	13,545	12,568					
1986	17,773	14,917	13,010	11,843	1955	2,408	1,881	1,666	1,539
					1954	2,247	1,787	1,585	1,456
1985	16,995	14,170	12,339	11,184	1953	2,285	1,806	1,583	1,441
1984	16,081	13,345	11,673	10,048	1952	2,201	1,736	1,518	1,381
1983	14,657	12,216	10,642	9,634	1951	2,129	1,657	1,469	1,337
1982	13,694	11,589	9,989	8,868					
1981	13,321	11,021	9,455	8,375	1950	1,877	1,501	1,364	1,259
					1949	1,719	1,389	1,264	1,185
1980	12,042	9,948	8,576	7,677	1948	1,757	1,434	1,290	1,184
1979	10,745	8,728	7,367	6,848	1947	1,605	1,327	1,178	1,115
1978	9,733	7,857	6,672	6,179	1946	1,475	1,264	1,132	1,014
1977	8,578	7,061	6,017	5,579					
1976	7,910	6,420	5,504	5,064	1945	1,515	1,223	1,074	855
					1944	1,518	1,194	1,057	782
1975	7,159	5,879	5,088	4,584	1943	1,401	1,106	976	726
1974	6,666	5,449	4,646	4,197	1942	1,171	911	867	656
1973	6,210	5,002	4,385	3,849	1941	934	719	695	604
1972	5,608	4,513	3,837	3,510					
1971	5,320	4,302	3,779	3,372	1940	754	593	573	536
					1939	691	555	537	510
1970	4,769	3,945	3,376	3,015	1938	651	526	504	492
1969	4,590	3,705	3,130	2,859	1937	701	575	552	516
1968	4,306	3,433	2,945	2,671	1936	643	535	518	483
1967	3,995	3,167	2,749	2,476					
1966	3,815	2,987	2,604	2,372	1935	567	474	459	437
					1934	514	427	414	406
1965	3,525	2,773	2,436	2,228	1933	442	374	362	364
1964	3,296	2,592	2,283	2,091	1932	465	401	390	389
1963	3,120	2,460	2,138	1,981	1931	611	531	516	487
1962	3,004	2,373	2,065	1,903					
1961	2,831	2,269	1,984	1,825	1930	734	625	605	567
					1929	846	705	683	634
1960 *	2,788	2,219	1,937	1,800					

* Denotes first year for which figures include Alaska and Hawaii.

Series F 192-209. National Income, by Sector and Legal Form of Organization: 1929 to 1990

(In billions of dollars)

Year	192 National income	193 Total	Corporate business, including mutual financial institutions				Originating in business				Other private business				206 Government and commercial enterprise	207 Originating in general government	208 Originating in private households and nonprofit institutions	209 Originating in the rest of the world
			194 Total	195 Compensation of employees	196 Corporate profits and inventory valuation adj.	197 Net interest	198 Total	199 Compensation of employees	200 Income of unincorporated enterprises and inventory valuation adj.	201 Net interest	202 Total	203 Compensation of employees and proprietors	204 Rental income	205 Net interest				
1990	4,459.6	3,634.5	2,608.3	2,186.8	258.8	162.7	678.4	199.5	374.1	104.7	279.2	21.2	-12.9	271.8	68.7	589.2	225.1	10.8
1989	4,244.7	3,487.2	2,532.1	2,078.5	297.8	155.8	630.1	186.0	345.0	99.1	261.2	19.9	-7.9	247.2	63.7	548.3	205.0	4.2
1988	4,002.6	3,295.4	2,399.6	1,965.8	315.9	118.0	584.4	177.3	322.5	84.6	250.8	18.6	4.3	226.2	60.4	511.7	187.6	7.9
1987	3,692.3	3,038.5	2,210.2	1,817.7	280.3	112.2	540.0	159.3	308.6	72.1	232.7	17.1	3.2	210.8	55.6	478.7	170.5	4.6
1986	3,437.9	2,825.9	2,057.1	1,777.0	238.7	101.5	497.8	136.2	282.2	79.4	218.9	15.8	8.7	192.8	52.0	449.6	153.3	9.1
1985	3,268.4	2,688.3	1,963.8	1,621.3	250.0	92.6	464.6	133.1	258.2	73.3	210.3	13.9	18.7	176.0	49.6	423.6	141.7	14.8
1984	3,058.3	2,507.9	1,838.0	1,516.5	233.0	88.5	428.6	126.7	234.1	67.8	195.5	12.1	23.3	158.2	45.7	394.1	132.0	24.3
1983	2,719.5	2,180.4	1,609.4	1,360.6	183.6	65.2	361.0	118.5	189.3	53.4	167.2	9.8	13.2	142.7	42.6	366.4	122.9	49.9
1982	2,518.4	2,010.6	1,478.0	1,287.8	121.9	68.2	340.6	114.0	174.0	52.7	152.4	9.0	13.6	128.2	39.6	343.9	112.7	51.2
1981	2,443.5	1,973.7	1,457.3	1,235.0	159.4	62.9	342.2	108.7	185.4	48.1	136.5	8.4	13.3	113.4	37.6	316.7	101.0	52.1
1980	2,198.2	1,785.0	1,320.8	1,121.4	142.7	56.7	308.9	102.9	170.5	35.4	122.1	7.8	13.2	99.8	33.2	289.8	89.3	34.1
1979	1,963.3	1,595.7	1,199.8	1,011.5	166.5	21.9	245.2	88.9	130.1	26.3	121.0	7.2	30.5	81.7	29.7	248.1	75.7	43.8
1978	1,745.4	1,418.7	1,073.1	891.8	165.8	15.5	214.7	78.0	115.7	20.9	104.1	6.3	27.4	69.0	26.9	229.2	67.5	29.9
1977	1,546.5	1,251.6	948.8	782.6	149.2	17.0	187.9	68.2	102.2	17.6	90.2	5.6	25.1	58.3	24.6	210.4	61.0	23.5
1976	1,379.2	1,108.5	833.8	694.4	123.8	15.5	171.9	63.6	92.9	15.4	79.7	5.0	23.5	50.1	23.1	194.6	55.6	20.5
1975	1,289.1	1,031.8	740.6	617.0	103.2	20.4	205.8	65.8	124.5	15.5	63.9	4.7	13.5	44.8	21.5	187.7	52.0	17.5
1974	1,160.7	933.0	687.8	589.5	78.6	19.7	157.0	56.6	87.8	12.6	69.1	4.3	23.5	40.3	19.1	162.2	45.8	19.8
1973	1,082.2	878.4	642.9	535.9	94.5	12.5	156.3	52.7	93.1	10.5	62.3	4.0	22.6	35.0	16.9	149.6	42.1	16.0
1972	941.8	762.0	517.6	428.9	84.9	3.8	170.1	88.2	73.7	8.2	60.2	3.5	24.1	32.0	14.1	135.4	41.1	9.6
1971	859.4	693.9	468.6	389.2	74.4	5.0	155.5	79.9	68.2	7.3	56.7	3.2	24.5	28.5	13.1	125.1	33.5	7.0
1970	800.5	650.3	438.7	369.0	64.5	5.1	147.1	74.2	66.4	6.5	52.4	3.4	23.9	25.0	12.1	114.7	30.8	4.6
1969	766.0	629.8	428.4	351.5	75.3	1.7	141.6	69.4	66.7	5.5	49.3	3.1	22.6	23.6	10.5	103.8	28.1	4.3
1968	711.1	586.0	400.1	319.5	80.3	.2	130.8	62.4	63.8	4.5	45.4	2.9	21.2	21.4	9.8	94.9	25.5	4.7
1967	653.6	541.2	366.7	291.8	75.1	-.2	122.5	56.6	61.7	4.2	43.3	2.7	21.1	19.5	8.7	85.1	22.8	4.5
1966	620.6	519.7	353.7	275.5	79.2	-1.2	117.5	52.9	60.9	3.7	40.3	2.5	20.0	17.9	8.1	76.6	20.2	4.1
1965	564.3	473.9	320.5	249.8	72.8	-2.0	108.4	48.4	56.9	3.1	37.6	2.4	19.0	16.3	7.4	67.8	18.5	4.2
1964	518.1	433.8	292.2	231.6	63.2	-2.5	99.7	45.0	51.9	2.8	34.9	2.2	18.0	14.7	7.0	63.0	17.3	4.0
1963	481.9	404.4	270.4	216.3	56.4	-2.4	95.0	42.2	50.6	2.2	32.5	2.2	17.1	13.2	6.6	58.1	16.0	3.4
1962	457.7	384.8	256.4	205.9	53.1	-2.6	92.0	40.4	49.7	1.9	30.4	2.1	16.7	11.7	6.0	54.7	15.0	3.3
1961	427.3	359.5	237.3	191.8	48.0	-2.5	88.3	38.6	48.0	1.6	28.3	2.0	16.0	10.4	5.7	50.9	14.0	2.9
1960 *	414.5	351.4	234.1	188.8	48.0	-2.8	85.0	37.7	45.8	1.5	26.9	1.9	15.8	9.2	5.4	47.5	13.2	2.4
1959	400.0	341.3	226.8	179.6	49.9	-2.6	84.0	36.5	46.2	1.3	25.5	1.8	15.6	8.1	5.0	44.3	12.2	2.2
1958	367.8	312.2	201.5	163.9	39.4	-1.8	81.5	34.2	46.2	1.2	24.4	1.8	15.4	7.2	4.8	42.1	11.4	2.0

See footnote at end of chart.

Series F 192-209. National Income, by Sector and Legal Form of Organization: 1929 to 1990—Cont'd.

(In billions of dollars)

Year	National income 192	Total 193	Originating in business — Total 194	Corporate business, including mutual financial institutions — Compensation of employees 195	Corporate profits and inventory valuation adj. 196	Net interest 197	Sole proprietorships and partnerships — Total 198	Compensation of employees 199	Income of unincorporated enterprises and inventory valuation adj. 200	Net interest 201	Other private business — Total 202	Compensation of employees 203	Rental income 204	Net interest 205	Government and commercial enterprise 206	Originating in general government 207	Originating in private households and nonprofit institutions 208	Originating in the rest of the world 209
1957	366.1	314.3	208.8	166.4	43.8	-2.1	79.0	34.3	43.7	1.0	22.9	1.7	14.8	6.4	4.3	39.1	10.5	2.2
1956	350.8	302.3	200.2	158.1	44.3	-2.2	76.4	33.1	42.4	.9	21.6	1.7	14.3	5.6	4.1	36.6	9.8	2.1
1955	331.0	286.0	188.0	144.6	45.3	-1.9	73.6	31.5	41.4	.8	20.4	1.6	13.9	4.9	3.9	34.2	9.1	1.8
1954	303.1	261.0	167.1	132.1	36.5	-1.5	70.9	30.5	39.7	.7	19.4	1.5	13.6	4.2	3.6	32.5	8.1	1.6
1953	304.7	263.7	170.7	133.9	38.5	-1.7	71.6	30.7	40.2	.7	17.9	1.5	12.7	3.7	3.6	31.9	7.8	1.3
1952	291.4	251.7	160.2	123.0	38.8	-1.6	71.8	29.3	41.8	.7	16.2	1.4	11.5	3.3	3.5	31.2	7.2	1.3
1951	278.0	242.4	154.6	114.5	41.6	-1.5	70.1	27.7	41.7	.7	14.6	1.3	10.3	3.0	3.0	27.4	6.9	1.3
1950	241.1	212.6	134.0	98.6	36.7	-1.3	62.7	24.9	37.2	.5	13.1	1.2	9.4	2.5	2.7	20.9	6.4	1.2
1949	217.5	191.1	117.8	88.8	30.0	-.9	59.0	23.4	35.1	.5	11.7	1.1	8.4	2.2	2.6	19.4	5.9	1.0
1948	224.2	200.2	122.5	91.0	32.2	-.8	64.3	23.9	40.0	.4	11.0	1.0	8.0	2.0	2.3	17.4	5.6	1.0
1947	199.0	176.3	106.6	82.0	24.9	-.3	58.0	22.3	35.3	.3	9.8	.9	7.1	1.8	2.0	16.7	5.1	.8
1946	181.9	156.0	88.1	69.7	18.9	-.5	56.9	20.3	36.3	.3	9.0	.8	6.6	1.6	1.9	20.8	4.5	.6
1945	181.5	141.8	83.3	64.1	18.9	.2	49.1	17.6	31.3	.3	7.8	.7	5.6	1.5	1.6	35.2	4.1	.4
1944	182.6	146.3	91.0	67.1	23.5	.3	46.1	16.1	29.7	.3	7.7	.7	5.4	1.5	1.5	32.2	3.7	.4
1943	170.3	141.2	88.8	64.2	24.1	.5	43.5	14.6	28.5	.4	7.4	.6	5.1	1.7	1.5	25.6	3.2	.4
1942	137.1	118.7	73.7	52.9	20.1	.7	36.9	12.7	23.7	.5	6.9	.5	4.5	1.8	1.2	15.1	2.9	.4
1941	104.2	91.9	57.4	41.6	15.0	.8	27.7	9.8	17.4	.5	5.7	.4	3.5	1.8	1.1	9.4	2.5	.4
1940	81.1	70.6	43.3	32.9	9.6	.9	21.3	7.8	13.0	.5	5.0	.3	2.9	1.8	1.0	7.8	2.4	.4
1939	72.6	62.4	37.1	29.8	6.1	1.1	19.5	7.2	11.8	.5	4.9	.3	2.7	1.8	.9	7.6	2.3	.3
1938	67.4	57.2	33.1	27.3	4.7	1.2	18.5	6.8	11.3	.5	4.7	.3	2.6	1.8	.9	7.6	2.2	.3
1937	73.7	64.2	38.4	30.6	6.6	1.2	20.7	7.1	13.2	.5	4.2	.3	2.1	1.8	.9	6.9	2.3	.4
1936	65.0	55.4	33.0	26.3	5.5	1.3	17.6	6.2	10.9	.5	3.9	.3	1.8	1.8	.8	7.3	2.0	.3
1935	57.2	49.0	27.8	23.1	3.2	1.5	16.7	5.5	10.7	.5	3.8	.2	1.7	1.9	.8	5.9	1.9	.4
1934	49.5	41.8	24.2	21.1	1.7	1.5	13.2	5.0	7.7	.6	3.8	.2	1.7	1.9	.7	5.6	1.8	.3
1933	40.3	33.6	18.0	18.0	-1.2	1.2	10.9	4.4	5.9	.6	4.1	.2	2.0	1.9	.6	4.7	1.7	.3
1932	42.8	36.1	19.2	19.0	-1.2	1.5	11.2	4.8	5.6	.7	4.9	.2	2.7	2.0	.7	4.4	1.9	.4
1931	59.7	52.2	29.0	25.4	2.0	1.6	16.4	6.4	9.1	.8	6.1	.3	3.8	2.1	.8	4.7	2.3	.5
1930	75.4	67.4	39.2	30.8	6.8	1.5	20.4	7.8	11.8	.8	7.1	.3	4.8	2.0	.8	4.5	2.7	.7
1929	86.8	78.8	45.9	34.3	10.2	1.4	24.3	8.6	15.1	.6	7.8	.3	5.4	2.1	.8	4.3	2.9	.8

* Denotes first year for which figures include Alaska and Hawaii

Series F 226-237. National Income, by Industrial Origin, in Current Prices: 1929 to 1989

(In billions of dollars)

Year	Total	Agriculture, forestry and fisheries	Mining	Contract construction	Manufacturing	Wholesale and retail trade	Finance, insurance and real estate	Transportation	Communications and public utilities	Services	Government and government enterprises	Rest of the world
	226	227	228	229	230	231	232	233	234	235	236	237
1989	5,201.0	113.0	80.0	248.0	966.0	825.0	897.0	172.0	290.0	971.0	619.0	38.0
1988	4,874.0	104.0	80.0	237.0	941.0	777.0	827.0	165.0	279.0	885.0	573.0	33.0
1987	4,526.7	94.9	85.4	218.5	853.6	740.4	775.4	150.8	257.4	793.5	535.3	29.5
1986	3,713.3	100.4	118.1	168.3	812.2	644.6	551.3	129.2	199.2	564.9	405.4	29.8
1985	3,607.5	93.6	78.9	130.6	790.3	612.2	523.6	125.0	200.1	541.3	399.0	36.0
1984	3,501.4	82.2	68.5	133.0	757.9	578.9	506.6	123.7	196.7	514.6	392.1	43.9
1983	3,279.1	74.5	61.3	125.4	675.5	529.0	489.0	113.7	178.2	486.6	387.4	47.9
1982	3,073.0	84.3	116.1	122.4	630.9	490.2	507.1	106.0	173.8	431.1	363.4	47.3
1981	2,954.1	90.6	126.5	124.6	644.4	474.2	461.6	106.1	156.2	387.6	337.5	49.6
1980	3,187.1	76.2	135.6	161.6	665.4	500.4	464.3	129.5	163.9	442.6	382.7	55.5
1979	2,413.9	78.4	69.4	113.1	569.5	392.0	350.8	90.7	121.1	302.5	280.7	46.0
1978	2,156.1	65.2	53.6	99.9	519.0	355.3	310.0	81.7	111.1	264.7	256.1	36.3
1977	1,918.0	53.8	48.6	86.7	462.4	322.5	274.0	71.2	99.3	234.3	235.0	27.9
1976	1,718.0	51.2	43.0	76.6	410.4	291.4	238.6	63.2	89.4	208.2	217.7	25.6
1975	1,549.2	53.3	38.8	69.9	358.2	266.2	216.2	55.6	80.1	186.2	201.0	22.8
1974	1,057.5	43.8	13.6	61.1	294.2	178.5	130.3	45.1	43.8	152.7	180.6	14.4
1973	1,075.7	47.8	10.4	58.3	281.6	162.6	121.2	41.6	40.6	136.9	165.8	9.0
1972	956.8	30.6	8.7	52.3	251.8	144.6	112.5	36.5	37.9	122.3	152.5	7.0
1971	866.0	25.7	7.4	47.8	224.7	132.9	103.1	33.0	34.6	111.2	139.0	6.6
1970	800.5	25.6	7.7	42.8	217.5	121.3	89.9	29.8	31.5	102.9	126.9	4.6
1969	766.0	24.8	6.8	40.9	222.3	114.8	84.5	28.7	30.0	94.7	114.3	4.3
1968	711.1	22.1	6.7	36.3	212.7	106.1	77.8	26.9	27.5	85.7	104.7	4.7
1967	653.6	21.6	6.3	33.2	195.2	97.5	71.9	25.2	25.7	78.5	93.8	4.5
1966	620.6	22.7	6.3	32.0	191.5	91.4	67.4	24.9	24.6	71.1	84.7	4.1
1965	564.3	21.0	6.1	29.1	172.6	84.3	61.9	23.2	22.7	64.1	75.2	4.2
1964	518.1	18.0	5.9	26.5	155.6	79.3	57.1	21.2	21.5	59.1	70.0	4.0
1963	481.9	18.6	6.0	24.2	143.8	73.4	53.6	20.0	20.2	54.1	64.7	3.4
1962	457.7	18.5	5.7	22.8	137.0	70.3	50.7	19.1	19.0	50.7	60.7	3.3
1961	427.3	17.9	5.7	21.5	125.1	66.2	48.0	18.3	18.0	47.2	56.6	2.9
1960 *	414.5	16.9	5.7	20.8	125.8	64.2	45.8	18.2	17.2	44.5	52.9	2.4
1959	400.0	16.0	5.5	20.5	124.0	63.3	43.7	17.9	15.8	41.8	49.3	2.2
1958	367.8	17.9	5.7	19.0	107.7	58.2	40.9	16.6	14.4	38.4	46.9	2.0
1957	366.1	15.5	6.5	19.3	116.3	57.2	38.2	17.4	13.6	36.5	43.4	2.2
1956	350.8	15.5	6.6	18.5	113.1	54.8	35.9	17.0	12.8	33.9	40.7	2.1
1955	331.0	15.4	5.9	16.6	107.9	52.3	34.1	15.9	11.9	31.1	38.1	1.8
1954	303.1	16.4	5.3	15.6	94.6	48.3	32.0	14.6	11.0	27.8	36.1	1.6
1953	304.7	17.2	5.4	15.6	100.4	47.3	29.3	15.8	10.2	26.8	35.5	1.3
1952	291.4	19.2	5.5	15.2	92.5	46.7	26.5	15.5	9.3	25.1	34.7	1.3
1951	278.0	20.1	5.7	14.1	90.0	45.1	24.1	14.9	8.4	23.5	30.4	1.3
1950	241.1	17.6	5.2	11.9	76.2	40.9	22.0	13.4	7.3	21.8	23.6	1.2
1949	217.5	16.6	4.5	10.5	64.8	39.0	19.8	12.1	6.7	20.5	22.0	1.0
1948 [1]	224.2	21.6	5.4	10.6	68.7	39.9	18.4	12.8	6.0	20.0	19.8	1.0
1948 [2]	224.2	21.5	5.4	10.6	67.6	41.7	18.3	12.8	6.0	19.5	19.8	1.0
1947	199.0	18.9	4.2	8.4	59.5	37.6	16.1	11.6	5.1	18.1	18.7	.8
1946	181.9	18.2	3.0	6.5	49.1	34.6	15.3	10.3	4.8	16.7	22.7	.6
1945	181.5	15.2	2.8	4.3	52.2	28.0	13.0	10.5	4.2	14.1	36.8	.4
1944	182.6	14.5	3.0	4.1	60.3	25.8	12.3	11.2	4.0	13.2	33.7	.4
1943	170.3	14.4	2.8	5.5	58.3	23.9	11.6	10.8	3.9	11.8	27.0	.4
1942	137.1	12.2	2.6	6.5	45.4	20.4	10.7	8.6	3.7	10.3	16.3	.4
1941	104.2	8.4	2.4	4.2	33.2	17.4	9.3	6.3	3.3	8.9	10.5	.4
1940	81.1	6.1	1.9	2.6	22.5	14.5	8.3	5.0	3.0	8.0	8.8	.4
1939	72.6	6.0	1.6	2.3	18.1	12.6	8.0	4.6	2.8	7.6	8.5	.3
1938	67.4	5.9	1.5	2.0	15.2	12.1	7.7	4.1	2.7	7.2	8.5	.4

See footnotes at end of chart.

Series F 226-237. National Income, by Industrial Origin, in Current Prices: 1929 to 1989—Cont'd.

(In billions of dollars)

Year	Total	Agriculture, forestry and fisheries	Mining	Contract construction	Manufacturing	Wholesale and retail trade	Finance, insurance and real estate	Transportation	Communications and public utilities	Services	Government and government enterprises	Rest of the world
	226	227	228	229	230	231	232	233	234	235	236	237
1937	73.7	7.6	2.0	2.1	19.5	12.4	7.3	4.6	2.7	7.5	7.8	.3
1936	65.0	5.7	1.5	2.0	16.3	10.8	6.7	4.3	2.4	6.8	8.1	.3
1935	57.2	6.7	1.2	1.3	13.4	9.4	6.0	3.7	2.2	6.2	6.7	.4
1934	49.5	4.2	1.1	1.1	11.1	8.3	5.6	3.4	2.2	5.8	6.3	.3
1933	40.3	3.9	.6	.8	7.7	5.6	5.9	3.0	2.0	5.1	5.3	.3
1932	42.8	3.5	.7	1.1	7.3	6.5	7.0	3.2	2.3	5.7	5.2	.4
1931	59.7	5.2	1.0	2.2	12.5	9.9	8.8	4.4	2.6	7.2	5.4	.5
1930	75.4	6.4	1.7	3.2	18.3	12.4	10.7	5.6	2.7	8.4	5.3	.7
1929	86.8	8.5	2.1	3.8	21.9	13.5	12.8	6.6	2.8	8.8	5.1	.8

* Denotes first year for which figures include Alaska and Hawaii.
[1] Based on 1957 Standard Industrial Classification System; comparable with later years.

[2] Based on 1942 Standard Industrial Classification System; comparable with earlier years.

Series F 297-348.   Personal Income by States: 1929 to 1991

Year	Alabama	Alaska	Arizona	Arkansas	California	Colorado	Connecticut	Delaware	Florida	Georgia	Hawaii	Idaho	Illinois	Indiana
	298	299	300	301	302	303	304	305	307	308	309	310	311	312
	TOTAL INCOME (millions of dollars)													
1991	63,700	12,500	61,500	35,000	636,500	65,600	85,200	13,800	250,700	115,000	24,200	16,000	240,400	96,600
1990	60,700	11,900	58,900	33,400	619,800	62,300	83,500	13,400	241,800	110,900	22,700	15,400	233,800	94,000
1989	56,100	11,400	56,200	31,000	579,200	58,200	79,900	12,400	223,600	103,300	20,500	13,900	219,400	88,300
1988	52,600	10,100	52,200	29,100	535,700	54,400	75,000	11,500	203,800	96,900	18,500	12,700	204,000	81,800
1987	48,800	9,600	48,500	27,500	493,000	51,400	68,300	10,800	187,400	89,000	17,000	11,800	190,400	77,000
1986	45,700	9,800	44,900	26,100	453,400	49,400	62,400	9,800	171,000	82,100	15,600	11,200	179,100	72,200
1985	43,000	9,800	41,000	24,800	422,600	47,500	57,900	9,100	158,400	75,400	14,600	10,900	170,000	68,300
1984	39,800	8,600	35,500	22,800	367,500	43,700	51,600	8,300	137,800	66,800	13,300	10,200	158,000	64,900
1983	36,500	8,200	31,600	20,800	333,700	40,100	46,900	7,600	123,800	59,600	12,400	9,400	142,400	57,900
1982	34,100	7,400	29,100	19,400	310,700	37,400	43,400	7,100	114,400	54,000	11,600	8,700	138,500	54,800
1981	32,500	6,200	27,500	18,700	292,100	33,900	40,300	6,600	105,900	50,200	10,900	8,500	132,900	53,500
1980	29,200	5,100	24,000	16,700	259,600	29,000	36,500	6,200	88,700	44,200	9,800	7,600	120,400	49,200
1979	26,300	4,600	20,300	14,800	225,000	24,800	31,000	5,600	75,600	38,500	8,500	6,700	110,300	46,900
1978	23,400	4,400	17,400	13,500	197,300	21,400	27,600	5,000	64,500	34,100	7,400	6,000	98,300	41,400
1977	20,700	4,300	14,900	11,900	173,200	18,800	25,100	4,500	56,500	30,400	6,800	5,100	87,300	36,900
1976	—	—	—	—	—	—	—	—	—	—	—	—	—	—
1975	16,800	3,800	11,900	9,500	139,500	15,200	21,100	3,800	46,600	24,800	5,700	4,200	75,400	29,800
1974	15,100	2,300	11,100	8,700	126,100	13,800	19,900	3,600	43,800	23,200	5,100	3,900	69,800	27,700
1973	13,700	2,000	9,700	8,100	113,700	12,300	18,300	3,300	37,800	20,900	4,600	3,400	64,800	26,500
1972	11,700	1,700	8,400	6,600	102,400	10,500	16,500	2,800	30,400	18,200	4,000	2,700	57,700	23,200
1971	10,800	1,500	7,300	6,000	94,100	9,500	15,300	2,600	27,600	16,800	3,700	2,500	53,400	21,100
1970	10,053	1,404	6,507	5,527	89,312	8,541	14,803	2,466	25,275	15,269	3,476	2,352	50,023	19,539
1969	9,163	1,250	5,765	5,004	83,067	7,623	13,819	2,271	22,542	14,347	3,044	2,148	47,233	19,110
1968	8,369	1,111	5,062	4,597	76,720	6,855	12,674	2,070	19,791	12,784	2,700	1,885	43,653	17,413
1967	7,659	1,022	4,516	4,236	69,807	6,122	11,703	1,882	17,451	11,541	2,414	1,790	40,627	16,002
1966	7,245	916	4,110	3,999	65,002	5,697	10,657	1,790	15,683	10,568	2,220	1,681	38,266	15,278
1965	6,713	855	3,773	3,577	60,104	5,295	9,765	1,704	14,182	9,531	2,014	1,668	35,070	14,067
1964	6,108	788	3,529	3,387	56,471	4,984	9,004	1,561	12,976	8,635	1,907	1,459	32,188	12,640
1963	5,666	702	3,362	3,104	52,522	4,745	8,449	1,453	11,859	7,895	1,772	1,409	30,174	11,869
1962	5,274	664	3,177	2,899	48,948	4,559	7,999	1,350	11,050	7,280	1,676	1,410	28,948	11,214
1961	5,025	633	2,905	2,704	45,601	4,294	7,447	1,275	10,248	6,746	1,595	1,310	27,486	10,542
1960	4,887	647	2,681	2,461	42,913	4,018	7,122	1,244	9,739	6,477	1,476	1,238	26,689	10,271
1959	4,699	562	2,455	2,421	40,955	3,752	6,785	1,202	9,303	6,211	1,315	1,227	25,751	9,817
1958	4,442	528	2,220	2,210	37,321	3,524	6,446	1,135	8,453	5,767	1,178	1,161	24,353	9,192
1957	4,261	537	2,028	2,091	35,497	3,365	6,398	1,125	7,730	5,531	1,114	1,104	24,056	9,187
1956	4,005	548	1,861	2,035	33,177	3,066	6,029	1,124	6,972	5,350	1,041	1,047	23,024	8,875
1955	3,761	505	1,655	1,970	30,378	2,804	5,552	980	6,070	5,000	972	951	21,167	8,265
1954	3,314	495	1,514	1,810	27,682	2,566	5,160	857	5,328	4,536	908	902	19,933	7,653
1953	3,432	511	1,478	1,842	27,002	2,528	5,087	835	5,050	4,581	896	899	19,812	8,073
1952	3,287	494	1,399	1,823	25,214	2,498	4,710	782	4,554	4,447	865	932	18,608	7,326
1951	3,077	448	1,230	1,763	22,756	2,313	4,335	731	4,048	4,122	793	850	17,711	6,938
1950	2,691	322	1,006	1,575	19,774	1,970	3,779	684	3,599	3,574	692	764	15,948	5,998
1949	2,446	—	906	1,474	17,878	1,820	3,374	586	3,177	3,150	685	712	14,607	5,388
1948	2,571	—	879	1,597	17,633	1,810	3,450	537	3,043	3,154	723	725	15,521	5,624
1940	792	—	251	496	5,802	615	1,511	275	971	1,047	—	235	5,958	1,889
1929	852	—	255	567	5,505	649	1,585	245	758	1,014	—	235	7,291	1,983

Series F 297-348. Personal Income by States: 1929 to 1991—Cont'd.

Year	Alabama	Alaska	Arizona	Arkansas	California	Colorado	Connecticut	Delaware	Florida	Georgia	Hawaii	Idaho	Illinois	Indiana
	298	299	300	301	302	303	304	305	307	308	309	310	311	312
PER CAPITA INCOME (dollars)														
1991	15,567	21,932	16,401	14,753	20,952	19,440	25,881	20,349	18,880	17,364	21,306	15,401	20,824	17,217
1990	14,998	21,646	16,006	14,176	20,689	18,860	25,395	20,095	18,539	17,045	20,361	15,250	20,433	16,921
1989	13,625	21,656	15,802	12,901	19,929	17,553	24,683	18,483	17,647	16,053	18,472	13,707	18,824	15,779
1988	12,814	19,237	14,995	12,141	18,915	16,471	23,190	17,347	16,515	15,280	16,840	12,652	17,567	14,721
1987	11,982	18,282	14,355	11,385	17,749	15,624	21,288	16,319	15,538	14,316	15,540	11,838	16,366	13,894
1986	11,293	18,378	13,679	11,025	16,792	15,114	19,547	15,498	14,622	13,454	14,683	11,172	15,503	13,124
1985	10,698	18,785	12,957	10,525	16,035	14,699	18,227	14,547	13,935	12,616	13,900	10,817	14,730	12,424
1984	9,981	17,155	11,629	9,724	14,344	13,742	16,369	14,111	12,553	11,441	12,761	10,174	13,728	11,799
1983	9,229	17,225	10,653	8,936	13,256	12,771	14,945	12,615	11,593	10,389	12,115	9,534	12,401	10,570
1982	8,683	16,854	10,050	8,432	12,617	12,242	13,963	11,828	10,927	9,654	11,590	9,008	12,012	10,057
1981	8,284	14,904	9,871	8,178	12,064	11,389	12,844	11,033	10,438	9,012	11,068	8,875	11,616	9,748
1980	7,704	13,835	9,172	7,465	11,603	10,598	12,112	10,249	9,764	8,348	10,617	8,569	10,837	9,245
1979	6,976	11,252	8,305	6,785	9,913	8,945	9,959	9,557	8,532	7,515	9,353	7,446	9,823	8,686
1978	6,247	10,851	7,374	6,183	8,850	8,001	8,914	8,604	7,505	6,700	8,380	6,813	8,745	7,696
1977	5,622	10,586	6,509	5,540	7,911	7,160	8,061	7,697	6,684	6,014	7,677	5,980	7,768	6,921
1976	—	—	—	—	—	—	—	—	—	—	—	—	—	—
1975	4,634	9,673	5,364	4,527	6,580	6,006	6,795	6,573	5,634	5,029	6,711	5,205	6,734	5,612
1974	4,198	7,023	4,989	4,280	5,997	5,343	6,471	6,227	5,235	4,662	5,882	4,934	6,337	5,263
1973	3,864	5,926	4,687	3,956	5,508	4,966	5,931	5,813	4,820	4,343	5,525	4,381	5,801	4,998
1972	3,333	5,162	4,300	3,357	5,002	4,449	5,342	4,983	4,188	3,846	4,995	3,635	5,126	4,391
1971	3,087	4,875	3,913	3,078	4,640	4,153	4,995	4,673	3,930	3,599	4,738	3,409	4,775	4,027
1970	2,913	4,603	3,631	2,869	4,467	3,839	4,871	4,483	3,692	3,318	4,562	3,280	4,492	3,752
1969	2,664	4,223	3,319	2,616	4,214	3,519	4,606	4,205	3,394	3,153	4,097	3,038	4,279	3,716
1968	2,429	3,899	3,010	2,417	3,956	3,233	4,276	3,876	3,077	2,852	3,755	2,712	3,970	3,419
1967	2,215	3,675	2,743	2,228	3,640	2,982	3,987	3,585	2,796	2,618	3,409	2,602	3,711	3,167
1966	2,092	3,380	2,547	2,106	3,447	2,839	3,671	3,469	2,569	2,413	3,185	2,440	3,531	3,056
1965	1,950	3,154	2,382	1,888	3,234	2,668	3,418	3,362	2,382	2,200	2,885	2,431	3,280	2,858
1964	1,799	2,997	2,268	1,785	3,111	2,530	3,218	3,141	2,245	2,028	2,813	2,145	3,042	2,603
1963	1,687	2,744	2,210	1,655	2,973	2,451	3,098	3,009	2,107	1,892	2,641	2,062	2,901	2,473
1962	1,587	2,699	2,180	1,564	2,867	2,401	3,022	2,879	2,025	1,782	2,567	2,038	2,816	2,368
1961	1,515	2,659	2,065	1,497	2,764	2,329	2,880	2,765	1,955	1,680	2,481	1,916	2,713	2,229
1960	1,493	2,824	2,030	1,376	2,704	2,271	2,800	2,772	1,946	1,637	2,366	1,846	2,646	2,198
1959	1,467	2,507	1,947	1,378	2,648	2,194	2,689	2,725	1,935	1,606	2,156	1,867	2,579	2,128
1958	1,405	2,357	1,861	1,280	2,508	2,114	2,635	2,621	1,826	1,516	1,981	1,797	2,463	2,006
1957	1,371	2,323	1,802	1,207	2,489	2,023	2,712	2,641	1,768	1,469	1,944	1,720	2,488	2,028
1956	1,304	2,446	1,767	1,194	2,419	1,887	2,603	2,754	1,723	1,445	1,900	1,667	2,416	1,991
1955	1,233	2,273	1,677	1,142	2,313	1,814	2,414	2,519	1,620	1,375	1,838	1,539	2,243	1,894
1954	1,099	2,300	1,623	1,044	2,172	1,718	2,294	2,328	1,520	1,259	1,802	1,503	2,154	1,795
1953	1,124	2,492	1,654	1,035	2,204	1,767	2,346	2,379	1,526	1,288	1,795	1,509	2,186	1,930
1952	1,071	2,612	1,662	992	2,167	1,830	2,263	2,293	1,442	1,241	1,748	1,588	2,078	1,766
1951	1,006	2,836	1,566	927	2,044	1,745	2,137	2,209	1,359	1,167	1,580	1,443	2,015	1,694
1950	880	2,384	1,330	825	1,852	1,487	1,875	2,132	1,281	1,034	1,386	1,295	1,825	1,512
1949	815	—	1,270	800	1,730	1,406	1,660	1,853	1,191	947	1,354	1,249	1,685	1,361
1948	866	—	1,274	875	1,752	1,433	1,713	1,720	1,180	968	1,407	1,315	1,815	1,451
1940	278	—	502	254	835	544	885	1,023	507	336	—	450	754	550
1929	322	—	593	306	995	644	994	1,037	525	349	—	502	959	615

Series F 297-348.   Personal Income by States: 1929 to 1991—Cont'd.

Year	Iowa	Kansas	Kentucky	Louisiana	Maine	Maryland	Massachusetts	Michigan	Minnesota	Mississippi	Missouri	Montana	Nebraska	Nevada
	313	314	315	316	317	318	319	320	321	322	323	324	325	326
	TOTAL INCOME (millions of dollars)													
1991	48,900	46,200	57,700	64,400	21,400	107,300	137,300	175,000	84,700	34,600	92,000	13,000	28,400	24,600
1990	48,100	44,900	55,300	61,200	21,200	105,000	135,800	171,200	82,200	33,000	89,600	12,200	27,600	23,300
1989	44,000	41,500	51,200	56,600	19,900	98,600	131,100	161,800	76,900	30,700	84,100	11,300	24,900	21,400
1988	40,500	39,200	47,700	53,900	18,100	90,800	123,100	151,400	71,000	29,000	78,800	10,400	23,400	18,800
1987	40,300	37,400	44,900	51,200	16,600	82,200	112,100	141,600	67,600	27,000	74,900	10,000	22,800	18,500
1986	38,000	35,700	42,000	50,500	15,100	75,600	102,900	135,300	63,200	25,400	70,600	9,600	21,700	14,900
1985	36,200	33,800	40,100	50,700	13,900	70,200	95,000	127,200	59,300	24,200	66,700	9,100	20,800	13,800
1984	35,200	32,500	38,600	48,400	12,300	61,400	84,500	113,600	55,000	23,000	60,700	8,400	19,700	12,000
1983	31,100	29,400	34,900	45,500	11,300	56,200	76,500	104,100	49,300	21,100	54,800	8,100	17,800	11,100
1982	31,300	28,300	32,800	44,700	10,300	52,200	69,900	99,700	46,200	19,800	50,400	7,700	16,900	10,600
1981	31,300	26,800	31,400	42,000	9,600	49,100	64,900	97,900	43,900	18,800	48,200	7,400	16,300	10,000
1980	27,300	23,600	27,900	35,600	8,900	44,200	58,200	92,300	39,700	16,600	44,300	6,700	14,700	8,600
1979	24,900	21,500	25,900	30,000	7,700	38,000	51,000	85,300	35,600	15,000	39,600	5,800	13,100	7,200
1978	22,800	18,800	23,100	26,300	6,900	34,400	46,600	77,600	31,500	13,800	35,700	5,500	11,600	6,000
1977	19,800	16,600	20,600	23,200	6,200	31,300	42,000	69,600	28,300	12,000	31,900	4,700	10,500	5,100
1976	—	—	—	—	—	—	—	—	—	—	—	—	—	—
1975	16,900	13,600	16,600	18,300	5,000	26,400	35,300	54,600	22,700	9,500	26,100	4,000	9,100	3,900
1974	15,100	12,500	14,900	16,500	4,800	24,300	33,400	53,500	21,200	8,800	24,100	3,600	8,100	3,500
1973	15,300	12,100	13,500	14,800	4,200	22,200	30,600	50,200	20,000	8,200	23,000	3,400	8,100	3,100
1972	12,400	10,400	11,900	13,100	3,700	19,900	28,200	43,700	16,900	6,900	20,000	2,800	6,600	2,700
1971	11,100	9,500	10,800	12,000	3,400	18,100	26,300	29,900	15,600	6,300	18,600	2,600	6,100	2,500
1970	10,609	8,635	10,008	11,180	3,255	16,856	24,731	36,993	14,709	5,753	17,682	2,438	5,653	2,195
1969	9,907	8,138	9,214	10,364	2,986	15,437	22,926	35,782	13,509	5,262	16,140	2,200	5,297	2,047
1968	9,132	7,528	8,518	9,887	2,762	14,020	21,049	32,831	12,205	4,848	15,074	2,029	4,653	1,792
1967	8,509	6,902	7,772	9,052	2,544	12,590	19,286	29,667	11,150	4,425	13,832	1,915	4,413	1,581
1966	8,315	6,599	7,202	8,247	2,431	11,668	17,715	28,206	10,366	4,122	12,874	1,875	4,242	1,510
1965	7,559	6,030	6,553	7,412	2,262	10,681	16,421	25,860	9,523	3,743	11,975	1,722	3,851	1,434
1964	6,643	5,581	5,996	6,799	2,090	9,749	15,392	23,005	8,604	3,420	11,028	1,592	3,481	1,353
1963	6,347	5,327	5,751	6,298	1,923	8,959	14,514	21,039	8,303	3,289	10,407	1,587	3,340	1,265
1962	6,001	5,183	5,444	5,908	1,876	8,342	13,878	19,568	7,858	2,976	9,896	1,581	3,274	1,122
1961	5,742	4,945	5,139	5,589	1,808	7,800	13,220	18,243	7,570	2,819	9,415	1,371	3,046	911
1960	5,473	4,714	4,807	5,417	1,788	7,285	12,657	18,318	7,227	2,630	9,142	1,383	2,988	829
1959	5,317	4,484	4,667	5,361	1,686	6,952	12,123	17,588	6,787	2,569	8,936	1,344	2,757	770
1958	5,200	4,443	4,441	5,105	1,637	6,567	11,438	16,603	6,585	2,349	8,461	1,370	2,713	711
1957	5,077	4,006	4,291	5,028	1,583	6,314	11,074	16,870	6,135	2,172	8,053	1,297	2,615	673
1956	4,580	3,804	4,107	4,547	1,534	5,976	10,497	16,529	5,778	2,141	7,844	1,241	2,274	625
1955	4,307	3,626	3,866	4,114	1,449	5,467	9,891	15,900	5,483	2,102	7,450	1,178	2,191	604
1954	4,525	3,597	3,692	3,881	1,314	5,069	9,293	14,354	5,202	1,875	6,974	1,079	2,253	519
1953	4,200	3,434	3,752	3,858	1,298	5,041	9,179	14,741	5,079	1,943	6,948	1,096	2,125	480
1952	4,338	3,524	3,587	3,636	1,291	4,721	8,675	13,050	4,823	1,907	6,576	1,075	2,187	440
1951	4,127	3,077	3,361	3,336	1,188	4,318	8,344	12,176	4,660	1,796	6,245	1,049	2,067	378
1950	3,897	2,765	2,881	3,021	1,087	3,772	7,654	10,895	4,227	1,643	5,672	962	1,978	327
1949	3,392	2,477	2,659	2,857	1,060	3,392	6,971	9,627	3,846	1,441	5,196	788	1,697	286
1948	4,042	2,523	2,788	2,679	1,084	3,331	7,012	9,691	4,106	1,639	5,338	876	1,909	283
1940	1,274	756	908	852	437	1,304	3,367	3,595	1,475	470	1,974	316	573	101
1929	1,449	1,013	1,026	863	476	1,265	3,855	3,809	1,548	573	2,287	315	827	81

Series F 297-348. Personal Income by States: 1929 to 1991—Cont'd.

Year	Iowa	Kansas	Kentucky	Louisiana	Maine	Maryland	Massachusetts	Michigan	Minnesota	Mississippi	Missouri	Montana	Nebraska	Nevada
	313	314	315	316	317	318	319	320	321	322	323	324	325	326
PER CAPITA INCOME (dollars)														
1991	17,505	18,511	15,539	15,143	17,306	22,080	22,897	18,679	19,107	13,343	17,842	16,043	17,852	19,175
1990	17,301	18,104	14,992	14,528	17,183	21,857	22,555	18,378	18,731	12,830	17,479	15,304	17,490	19,049
1989	15,487	16,498	13,743	12,921	16,248	21,013	22,174	17,444	17,657	11,724	16,292	14,078	15,446	19,269
1988	14,316	15,688	12,792	12,238	15,045	19,639	20,898	16,391	16,472	11,055	15,331	12,870	14,569	17,849
1987	13,859	14,962	11,963	11,439	13,985	18,231	19,140	15,473	15,716	10,250	14,582	12,331	13,976	16,381
1986	13,335	14,503	11,268	11,233	12,846	16,934	17,635	14,807	14,995	9,663	13,946	11,726	13,572	15,453
1985	12,619	13,812	10,768	11,302	11,903	15,970	16,305	14,001	14,144	9,249	13,250	11,015	12,967	14,693
1984	12,090	13,319	10,374	10,850	10,678	14,111	14,574	12,518	13,219	8,857	12,129	10,216	12,280	13,216
1983	10,697	12,102	9,396	10,262	9,861	13,047	13,260	11,476	11,901	8,155	11,029	9,945	11,175	12,441
1982	10,638	11,743	9,097	10,048	9,278	12,261	12,285	10,748	11,277	7,775	10,469	9,618	10,885	11,902
1981	10,749	11,237	8,567	9,778	8,494	11,522	11,248	10,620	10,684	7,414	10,911	9,252	10,331	11,816
1980	9,537	9,941	8,022	8,682	8,218	10,790	10,612	10,165	10,062	6,926	9,298	8,924	9,274	11,421
1979	8,589	9,055	7,342	7,477	7,057	9,150	8,844	9,269	8,760	6,167	8,132	7,412	8,341	10,204
1978	7,873	8,001	6,615	6,640	6,333	8,306	8,063	8,442	7,847	5,736	7,342	7,051	7,391	9,032
1977	6,878	7,134	5,945	5,913	5,734	7,572	7,258	7,619	7,129	5,030	6,654	6,125	6,720	7,988
1976	—	—	—	—	—	—	—	—	—	—	—	—	—	—
1975	5,907	5,955	4,882	4,808	4,762	6,401	6,071	6,008	5,785	4,042	5,475	5,387	5,887	6,636
1974	5,302	5,406	4,470	4,310	4,439	5,881	5,731	5,928	5,450	3,764	5,056	4,776	4,877	6,073
1973	5,347	5,338	4,050	3,950	4,040	5,446	5,268	5,540	5,144	3,546	4,831	4,626	5,299	5,712
1972	4,318	4,593	3,601	3,528	3,571	4,897	4,870	4,817	4,332	3,063	4,206	3,897	4,341	5,215
1971	3,877	4,192	3,306	3,252	3,375	4,522	4,562	4,430	4,032	2,788	3,940	3,629	4,030	4,822
1970	3,749	3,841	3,104	3,068	3,272	4,281	4,340	4,156	3,848	2,596	3,768	3,498	3,794	4,452
1969	3,532	3,639	2,881	2,864	3,010	3,991	4,058	4,075	3,595	2,370	3,478	3,170	3,594	4,264
1968	3,258	3,397	2,666	2,744	2,779	3,675	3,747	3,775	3,296	2,185	3,300	2,899	3,172	3,862
1967	3,047	3,141	2,450	2,528	2,534	3,351	3,448	3,438	3,047	1,986	3,047	2,731	3,029	3,521
1966	3,011	3,000	2,288	2,323	2,433	3,158	3,200	3,314	2,866	1,836	2,846	2,652	2,914	3,385
1965	2,757	2,733	2,087	2,120	2,269	2,967	2,985	3,094	2,651	1,667	2,681	2,439	2,618	3,229
1964	2,419	2,527	1,916	1,973	2,105	2,792	2,825	2,810	2,418	1,526	2,483	2,255	2,349	3,177
1963	2,310	2,403	1,857	1,865	1,937	2,646	2,716	2,611	2,351	1,466	2,370	2,258	2,263	3,185
1962	2,182	2,323	1,768	1,766	1,887	2,556	2,637	2,467	2,237	1,327	2,271	2,264	2,236	3,188
1961	2,083	2,232	1,683	1,700	1,817	2,456	2,533	2,311	2,182	1,278	2,165	1,969	2,107	2,893
1960	1,986	2,159	1,581	1,662	1,834	2,340	2,453	2,338	2,110	1,205	2,113	2,036	2,108	2,848
1959	1,948	2,076	1,556	1,671	1,772	2,268	2,369	2,264	2,016	1,202	2,099	2,009	1,974	2,760
1958	1,920	2,074	1,500	1,618	1,734	2,202	2,283	2,165	1,988	1,126	2,021	2,057	1,962	2,645
1957	1,869	1,882	1,465	1,614	1,679	2,198	2,247	2,229	1,874	1,040	1,922	1,944	1,876	2,588
1956	1,694	1,795	1,417	1,500	1,635	2,126	2,146	2,214	1,783	1,026	1,884	1,891	1,628	2,502
1955	1,608	1,732	1,328	1,396	1,552	1,994	2,026	2,183	1,729	1,020	1,802	1,852	1,594	2,549
1954	1,723	1,762	1,272	1,346	1,417	1,888	1,893	2,031	1,671	908	1,715	1,729	1,681	2,437
1953	1,598	1,722	1,293	1,346	1,421	1,964	1,910	2,161	1,665	923	1,728	1,779	1,612	2,462
1952	1,652	1,783	1,229	1,279	1,411	1,888	1,866	1,962	1,592	886	1,656	1,786	1,668	2,429
1951	1,577	1,578	1,143	1,205	1,297	1,769	1,793	1,874	1,548	830	1,556	1,761	1,571	2,249
1950	1,485	1,443	981	1,120	1,186	1,602	1,633	1,701	1,410	755	1,431	1,622	1,490	2,018
1949	1,316	1,287	933	1,084	1,174	1,456	1,470	1,520	1,310	691	1,339	1,385	1,304	1,823
1948	1,590	1,333	990	1,032	1,235	1,467	1,500	1,560	1,431	790	1,389	1,616	1,509	1,814
1940	502	423	317	360	515	709	780	676	529	216	521	566	436	890
1929	589	543	394	414	597	780	912	794	602	287	631	801	602	896

Series F 297-348. Personal Income by States: 1929 to 1991—Cont'd.

Year	New Hampshire	New Jersey	New Mexico	New York	North Carolina	North Dakota	Ohio	Oklahoma	Oregon	Pennsylvania	Rhode Island	South Carolina	South Dakota	Tennessee
	327	328	329	330	331	332	333	334	335	336	337	338	339	340
						TOTAL INCOME (millions of dollars)								
1991	23,100	196,900	23,000	405,500	112,100	10,200	196,000	50,200	51,400	228,800	18,900	54,900	11,500	80,900
1990	23,100	192,500	21,700	398,400	108,200	9,800	190,800	48,600	49,200	222,100	18,900	53,000	11,100	77,500
1989	22,400	183,900	20,100	378,300	99,900	9,000	178,600	45,600	44,900	207,900	17,900	47,900	9,800	72,600
1988	21,100	171,800	18,700	352,100	92,400	8,200	167,600	43,000	41,000	193,600	16,800	44,700	9,000	68,100
1987	18,500	156,100	17,800	320,900	85,400	8,700	157,600	41,100	38,200	181,600	15,300	41,100	8,900	62,500
1986	16,800	143,300	16,900	299,300	78,700	8,400	148,900	40,500	35,800	169,900	14,200	38,200	8,400	57,500
1985	15,300	133,300	16,200	280,300	73,000	8,200	142,000	40,200	34,000	160,800	13,300	35,800	7,800	53,600
1984	12,800	114,800	14,700	250,400	66,300	8,600	132,400	38,700	31,000	146,900	12,200	33,200	7,800	49,100
1983	11,600	104,500	13,500	229,900	59,600	7,900	125,000	36,200	28,700	136,400	11,200	29,900	6,900	44,600
1982	10,200	97,600	12,500	217,200	54,400	7,300	115,100	36,100	27,400	130,000	10,300	27,200	6,700	41,400
1981	9,400	90,800	11,600	201,900	51,500	7,200	110,900	32,900	26,700	123,800	9,700	25,800	6,400	39,400
1980	8,400	80,700	10,200	180,600	46,000	5,700	102,400	27,600	24,600	112,200	9,000	22,700	5,400	35,500
1979	7,300	71,100	9,100	160,600	41,300	5,100	94,200	23,800	22,300	100,400	7,700	20,600	5,100	32,000
1978	6,300	64,600	7,900	146,700	36,800	4,900	84,000	20,000	19,200	90,900	7,000	18,200	4,700	28,300
1977	5,500	58,600	7,000	135,100	32,800	4,000	75,800	17,800	16,700	82,600	6,300	16,200	4,100	24,900
1976	—	—	—	—	—	—	—	—	—	—	—	—	—	—
1975	4,400	49,800	5,500	117,800	26,900	3,800	62,000	14,300	13,200	69,300	5,300	13,100	3,400	20,000
1974	4,000	45,800	4,600	111,500	24,800	3,600	59,200	12,400	12,000	64,500	5,000	12,000	3,200	18,800
1973	3,700	43,000	4,300	104,200	22,600	3,600	54,500	11,600	10,800	59,400	4,700	10,600	3,300	16,900
1972	3,200	37,800	3,900	97,700	19,400	2,400	48,700	10,000	9,400	53,000	4,300	9,200	2,500	14,700
1971	2,900	35,100	3,400	91,700	17,700	2,200	44,800	9,100	8,500	49,300	4,000	8,300	2,300	13,200
1970	2,779	33,347	3,173	86,070	16,383	1,928	42,665	8,617	7,765	46,593	3,748	7,691	2,080	12,118
1969	2,475	30,423	2,908	80,923	15,036	1,867	40,424	7,827	7,276	43,301	3,453	6,985	1,995	11,231
1968	2,286	27,987	2,656	75,041	13,566	1,656	37,098	7,224	6,631	39,938	3,270	6,353	1,886	10,214
1967	2,079	25,638	2,463	68,657	12,288	1,596	33,788	6,675	6,096	37,062	2,988	5,728	1,731	9,280
1966	1,905	23,862	2,380	63,717	11,341	1,568	32,201	6,154	5,760	34,783	2,740	5,303	1,681	8,663
1965	1,728	22,105	2,269	59,487	10,092	1,505	29,383	5,668	5,333	31,943	2,504	4,702	1,528	7,850
1964	1,601	20,515	2,115	55,987	9,292	1,288	26,878	5,231	4,892	29,936	2,346	4,253	1,320	7,138
1963	1,510	19,372	2,031	52,559	8,606	1,292	25,189	4,889	4,553	27,876	2,193	3,928	1,350	6,640
1962	1,442	18,430	1,969	50,535	8,154	1,370	24,208	4,698	4,287	26,918	2,110	3,733	1,407	6,255
1961	1,356	17,333	1,871	47,821	7,596	964	23,008	4,561	4,046	25,747	1,964	3,450	1,227	5,881
1960	1,300	16,526	1,799	46,178	7,123	1,087	22,762	4,358	3,939	25,451	1,895	3,283	1,218	5,521
1959	1,237	15,849	1,759	44,301	6,712	949	22,035	4,137	3,804	24,719	1,844	3,119	981	5,394
1958	1,132	14,823	1,618	41,715	6,263	1,030	20,637	4,000	3,556	23,594	1,748	2,885	1,094	5,025
1957	1,102	14,550	1,442	40,818	5,980	905	20,959	3,744	3,416	23,414	1,701	2,810	1,068	4,872
1956	1,035	13,719	1,284	38,608	5,935	881	19,992	3,591	3,422	22,295	1,674	2,697	914	4,671
1955	983	12,688	1,181	36,453	5,571	848	18,762	3,390	3,198	20,669	1,614	2,599	857	4,374
1954	915	11,957	1,077	34,275	5,120	766	17,397	3,193	2,961	19,515	1,523	2,434	916	4,105
1953	884	11,750	1,048	33,206	5,040	757	17,423	3,201	2,990	19,938	1,531	2,615	892	4,080
1952	833	10,934	1,004	31,396	4,851	740	15,942	3,087	2,966	18,617	1,446	2,527	828	3,810
1951	792	10,151	936	30,009	4,691	794	14,894	2,837	2,784	17,752	1,384	2,321	942	3,645
1950	704	8,934	811	27,841	4,219	782	12,930	2,547	2,482	16,189	1,262	1,886	814	3,295
1949	671	8,131	719	26,046	3,675	674	11,749	2,460	2,251	14,553	1,151	1,724	689	3,001
1948	668	8,063	655	26,051	3,732	813	12,269	2,390	2,278	14,716	1,175	1,779	916	3,037
1940	281	3,406	198	11,724	1,155	218	4,575	851	671	6,408	531	572	231	982
1929	320	3,705	160	14,171	1,044	246	5,179	1,076	652	7,546	596	467	288	976

Series F 297-348. Personal Income by States: 1929 to 1991—Cont'd.

Year	New Hampshire	New Jersey	New Mexico	New York	North Carolina	North Dakota	Ohio	Oklahoma	Oregon	Pennsylvania	Rhode Island	South Carolina	South Dakota	Tennessee
	327	328	329	330	331	332	333	334	335	336	337	338	339	340
	PER CAPITA INCOME (dollars)													
1991	20,951	25,372	14,844	22,456	16,642	16,088	17,916	15,827	17,592	19,128	18,840	15,420	16,392	16,325
1990	20,773	24,881	14,254	22,129	16,266	15,355	17,568	15,451	17,182	18,679	18,809	15,141	15,890	15,868
1989	20,267	23,778	13,140	21,073	15,198	13,563	16,373	14,154	15,919	17,269	17,950	13,634	13,685	14,694
1988	19,410	22,265	12,401	19,663	14,243	12,342	15,427	13,306	14,811	16,135	16,870	12,907	12,599	13,895
1987	18,032	20,303	11,872	17,906	13,284	12,641	14,529	12,481	13,850	15,103	15,644	12,070	12,370	12,913
1986	16,396	18,793	11,459	16,821	12,423	12,440	13,857	12,249	13,239	14,281	14,589	11,286	11,803	11,984
1985	15,367	17,618	11,197	15,773	11,662	11,951	13,176	12,139	12,628	13,554	13,779	10,729	11,029	11,252
1984	13,148	15,282	10,330	14,121	10,758	12,461	12,314	11,745	11,582	12,343	12,730	10,075	11,049	10,400
1983	12,109	14,000	9,656	13,014	9,805	11,664	11,218	10,988	10,768	11,468	11,694	9,168	9,851	9,515
1982	11,189	13,089	9,301	12,222	9,148	10,877	10,664	11,084	10,168	10,939	10,937	8,605	9,366	9,013
1981	10,051	12,230	8,707	11,473	8,648	10,911	10,274	10,606	10,017	10,423	10,129	8,128	9,245	8,516
1980	9,788	11,573	8,169	10,721	7,999	8,538	9,723	9,393	9,866	9,891	9,518	7,589	8,217	8,030
1979	8,231	9,702	7,294	9,098	7,359	7,774	8,775	8,226	8,842	8,559	8,266	7,027	7,334	7,299
1978	7,277	8,818	6,505	8,267	6,607	7,478	7,812	6,951	7,839	7,733	7,526	6,242	6,841	6,489
1977	6,536	7,994	5,857	7,537	5,935	6,190	7,084	6,346	7,007	7,011	6,775	5,628	5,957	5,785
1976	—	—	—	—	—	—	—	—	—	—	—	—	—	—
1975	5,431	6,786	4,836	6,523	4,943	5,896	5,771	5,233	5,764	5,832	5,705	4,665	4,995	4,823
1974	5,143	6,384	4,137	6,244	4,612	5,547	5,549	4,566	5,270	5,490	5,376	4,258	4,218	4,484
1973	4,615	5,874	3,877	5,720	4,258	5,730	5,070	4,331	4,845	5,010	4,869	3,885	4,771	4,124
1972	4,092	5,126	3,656	5,319	3,721	3,718	4,512	3,802	4,296	4,447	4,399	3,448	3,716	3,640
1971	3,796	4,811	3,298	5,000	3,424	3,538	4,175	3,515	3,959	4,147	4,126	3,142	3,441	3,300
1970	3,745	4,635	3,117	4,714	3,218	3,120	3,992	3,350	3,694	3,943	3,941	2,963	3,124	3,082
1969	3,418	4,288	2,877	4,470	2,989	3,006	3,827	3,088	3,528	3,688	3,705	2,718	2,987	2,882
1968	3,224	3,995	2,672	4,157	2,711	2,667	3,528	2,886	3,309	3,402	3,546	2,483	2,819	2,634
1967	2,982	3,701	2,463	3,828	2,481	2,549	3,245	2,682	3,081	3,173	3,287	2,261	2,580	2,405
1966	2,797	3,483	2,364	3,571	2,316	2,424	3,117	2,508	2,925	2,982	3,048	2,104	2,461	2,267
1965	2,556	3,267	2,242	3,354	2,075	2,319	2,880	2,323	2,753	2,749	2,804	1,885	2,208	2,067
1964	2,414	3,089	2,102	3,183	1,935	1,985	2,666	2,138	2,591	2,599	2,650	1,719	1,883	1,893
1963	2,326	2,966	2,053	3,010	1,815	2,006	2,522	2,004	2,457	2,440	2,504	1,597	1,906	1,786
1962	2,282	2,890	2,011	2,921	1,732	2,151	2,438	1,936	2,358	2,371	2,422	1,541	1,996	1,703
1961	2,193	2,767	1,939	2,803	1,629	1,504	2,335	1,917	2,264	2,260	2,289	1,432	1,770	1,624
1960	2,135	2,708	1,886	2,742	1,558	1,714	2,338	1,865	2,223	2,247	2,216	1,372	1,783	1,544
1959	2,076	2,635	1,914	2,655	1,506	1,536	2,278	1,807	2,179	2,200	2,152	1,329	1,471	1,532
1958	1,948	2,517	1,826	2,513	1,431	1,699	2,150	1,764	2,070	2,134	2,038	1,252	1,668	1,448
1957	1,927	2,536	1,702	2,493	1,369	1,479	2,227	1,641	1,996	2,137	1,998	1,236	1,603	1,419
1956	1,829	2,443	1,593	2,396	1,377	1,437	2,171	1,580	2,016	2,032	1,993	1,210	1,365	1,368
1955	1,765	2,306	1,504	2,283	1,313	1,378	2,081	1,507	1,927	1,889	1,962	1,181	1,293	1,281
1954	1,651	2,231	1,412	2,167	1,239	1,254	1,961	1,445	1,821	1,804	1,866	1,119	1,398	1,222
1953	1,616	2,247	1,386	2,139	1,223	1,244	2,028	1,467	1,867	1,870	1,878	1,199	1,376	1,229
1952	1,557	2,134	1,367	2,067	1,181	1,217	1,926	1,391	1,875	1,773	1,804	1,160	1,282	1,137
1951	1,497	2,028	1,306	2,015	1,139	1,314	1,848	1,284	1,789	1,697	1,765	1,071	1,438	1,081
1950	1,323	1,834	1,177	1,873	1,037	1,263	1,620	1,143	1,620	1,541	1,605	893	1,242	994
1949	1,259	1,663	1,117	1,749	940	1,130	1,474	1,169	1,573	1,401	1,437	850	1,091	927
1948	1,284	1,689	1,084	1,797	973	1,401	1,558	1,144	1,621	1,431	1,493	891	1,497	944
1940	571	816	373	871	323	340	660	366	618	648	739	301	360	334
1929	685	929	381	1,164	333	365	782	454	689	776	871	269	417	375

Series F 297-348.   Personal Income by States: 1929 to 1991—Cont'd.

Year	Texas	Utah	Vermont	Virginia	Washington	West Virginia	Wisconsin	Wyoming
	341	342	343	344	345	346	347	348
	TOTAL INCOME (millions of dollars)							
1991	300,200	25,700	10,100	125,600	97,600	25,500	89,400	7,900
1990	285,100	24,200	9,900	122,400	92,200	24,600	86,300	7,400
1989	266,800	22,300	9,300	115,400	84,000	22,900	80,100	6,900
1988	248,300	20,700	8,500	106,500	76,100	21,700	74,300	6,600
1987	232,800	19,100	7,800	97,500	70,800	20,900	—	—
1986	225,200	18,300	7,200	89,400	66,300	20,300	—	—
1985	220,700	17,500	6,600	82,500	62,000	19,500	62,900	6,500
1984	202,000	16,100	5,700	73,600	55,400	19,200	58,700	6,400
1983	183,800	14,600	5,200	67,900	52,300	18,000	53,700	6,100
1982	174,500	13,800	4,900	60,600	49,100	17,100	51,000	6,200
1981	161,300	12,900	4,600	56,700	47,100	16,200	48,800	6,000
1980	136,100	11,200	4,000	50,300	42,700	15,200	44,100	5,200
1979	115,700	9,800	3,600	44,700	37,000	14,000	39,700	4,300
1978	100,200	8,700	3,200	39,200	31,900	12,000	35,500	3,900
1977	87,300	7,500	2,800	35,200	27,500	11,100	32,000	3,100
1976	—	—	—	—	—	—	—	—
1975	68,300	5,900	2,300	28,700	22,400	8,900	25,500	2,300
1974	59,700	5,200	2,100	26,200	19,900	7,800	24,000	1,900
1973	53,900	4,700	1,900	23,600	17,700	7,100	21,700	1,700
1972	47,100	4,200	1,800	20,300	15,400	6,400	19,000	1,500
1971	42,600	3,800	1,700	18,400	14,200	5,800	17,500	1,300
1970	40,240	3,451	1,480	17,000	13,730	5,320	16,818	1,268
1969	36,678	3,116	1,426	15,461	13,118	4,780	15,299	1,112
1968	33,309	2,892	1,305	14,123	12,067	4,487	14,208	997
1967	30,019	2,672	1,178	12,741	10,890	4,251	13,094	932
1966	27,676	2,517	1,089	11,684	9,876	3,994	12,442	893
1965	24,956	2,356	956	10,718	8,627	3,728	11,345	854
1964	23,116	2,220	856	9,905	8,058	3,492	10,449	825
1963	21,646	2,156	798	8,983	7,736	3,266	9,665	813
1962	20,576	2,071	777	8,443	7,599	3,124	9,396	795
1961	19,615	1,910	731	7,777	7,051	3,031	8,885	776
1960	18,588	1,774	715	7,340	6,680	2,987	8,619	750
1959	18,047	1,678	672	6,995	6,514	2,968	8,376	717
1958	17,175	1,549	626	6,591	6,114	2,887	7,755	677
1957	16,538	1,482	619	6,349	5,912	2,967	7,547	645
1956	15,472	1,381	598	6,084	5,583	2,768	7,211	605
1955	14,438	1,272	549	5,638	5,306	2,492	6,682	570
1954	13,504	1,165	526	5,338	5,035	2,347	6,212	533
1953	13,196	1,166	521	5,292	4,934	2,473	6,265	549
1952	12,837	1,116	496	5,150	4,697	2,462	6,093	547
1951	11,914	1,053	482	4,763	4,414	2,365	5,837	556
1950	10,486	911	425	4,070	3,995	2,146	6,078	484
1949	9,839	835	396	3,648	3,600	1,994	4,633	445
1948	9,142	810	407	6,624	3,608	2,126	4,701	429
1940	2,762	266	183	1,245	1,140	767	1,734	151
1929	2,764	283	224	1,053	1,165	790	2,007	152

Series F 297-348.   Personal Income by States: 1929 to 1991—Cont'd.

Year	Texas	Utah	Vermont	Virginia	Washington	West Virginia	Wisconsin	Wyoming
	341	342	343	344	345	346	347	348
	PER CAPITA INCOME (dollars)							
1991	17,305	14,529	17,747	19,976	19,442	14,174	18,046	17,118
1990	16,717	13,985	17,506	19,701	18,777	13,744	17,590	16,283
1989	15,702	13,079	16,371	18,927	17,647	12,345	16,449	14,508
1988	14,753	12,225	15,268	17,712	16,364	11,578	15,378	13,720
1987	13,734	11,532	14,256	16,531	15,535	10,959	14,652	12,819
1986	13,494	10,968	13,320	15,423	14,866	10,587	13,923	12,723
1985	13,476	10,653	12,376	14,468	14,076	10,073	13,234	12,834
1984	12,636	9,719	10,692	13,067	12,728	9,846	12,309	12,586
1983	11,686	9,005	9,957	12,122	12,162	9,160	11,311	11,920
1982	11,378	8,714	9,516	11,386	11,682	8,970	10,777	12,157
1981	10,954	8,478	8,877	10,450	11,163	8,336	10,227	12,217
1980	9,798	7,952	8,577	9,827	10,725	7,915	9,845	11,339
1979	8,649	7,185	7,280	8,605	9,435	7,470	8,419	9,657
1978	7,697	6,622	6,541	7,624	8,450	6,456	9,597	9,096
1977	6,803	5,923	5,823	6,865	7,528	5,986	6,890	7,562
1976	—	—	—	—	—	—	—	—
1975	5,583	4,903	4,923	5,770	6,300	4,968	5,616	6,127
1974	4,790	4,452	4,588	5,265	5,651	4,390	5,210	5,156
1973	4,558	4,096	4,185	4,868	5,151	3,974	4,781	4,696
1972	4,045	3,745	3,865	4,258	4,476	3,574	4,207	4,345
1971	3,726	3,442	3,638	3,899	4,132	3,275	3,912	3,929
1970	3,576	3,228	3,311	3,653	4,022	3,047	3,794	3,796
1969	3,321	2,976	3,262	3,351	3,924	2,738	3,495	3,380
1968	3,079	2,810	3,035	3,098	3,690	2,545	3,270	3,077
1967	2,832	2,622	2,785	2,826	3,431	2,403	3,043	2,895
1966	2,638	2,495	2,638	2,622	3,231	2,250	2,911	2,765
1965	2,405	2,377	2,365	2,430	2,908	2,087	2,681	2,571
1964	2,251	2,270	2,146	2,273	2,721	1,943	2,509	2,435
1963	2,131	2,213	2,010	2,101	2,618	1,819	2,350	2,419
1962	2,047	2,162	1,976	2,020	2,583	1,727	2,321	2,386
1961	1,997	2,041	1,875	1,899	2,447	1,658	2,216	2,304
1960	1,931	1,971	1,839	1,842	2,340	1,612	2,175	2,267
1959	1,919	1,929	1,736	1,770	2,309	1,600	2,153	2,239
1958	1,856	1,833	1,648	1,684	2,205	1,565	2,018	2,148
1957	1,823	1,794	1,647	1,652	2,170	1,610	1,991	2,054
1956	1,752	1,707	1,586	1,634	2,092	1,491	1,927	1,938
1955	1,667	1,625	1,463	1,571	2,038	1,326	1,816	1,857
1954	1,611	1,554	1,395	1,501	2,001	1,232	1,722	1,818
1953	1,583	1,578	1,374	1,488	2,001	1,282	1,787	1,892
1952	1,544	1,542	1,324	1,470	1,919	1,258	1,757	1,866
1951	1,469	1,491	1,275	1,387	1,821	1,192	1,697	1,911
1950	1,349	1,309	1,121	1,228	1,674	1,065	1,477	1,668
1949	1,291	1,244	1,074	1,108	1,569	1,033	1,366	1,605
1948	1,199	1,241	1,133	1,130	1,600	1,120	1,418	1,595
1940	430	482	505	458	655	402	552	606
1929	480	558	625	434	749	460	684	683

Series F 552-565.   Sources and Uses of Gross Savings: 1929 to 1991
(In billions of dollars)

Year	Total	Personal saving	Undistributed corporate funds	Corporate inventory valuation adjustment	Capital consumption allowances	Gross saving and statistical discrepancy — Government surplus or deficit (-) Total	Federal	State and local	Capital grants received by the U.S.	Statistical discrepancy	Gross investment Total	Gross private domestic investment	Net foreign investment
	552	553	555	556	557	558	559	560	561	562	563	564	565
1991	887.0	219.3	44.7	3.1	-8.7	-171.5	-201.5	30.0	—	18.8	734.3	726.7	7.6
1990	850.4	205.8	49.9	-14.2	.8	-139.5	-165.3	25.7	—	8.1	719.0	802.6	-83.6
1989	826.5	166.1	85.8	-17.5	24.7	-83.0	-124.2	41.1	—	-2.7	740.7	837.6	-96.8
1988	802.3	155.7	112.6	-27.3	44.7	-98.3	-136.6	38.4	—	-28.4	675.6	793.6	-118.0
1987	730.7	142.0	86.5	-14.5	46.4	-111.7	-151.8	40.1	—	-24.8	594.2	749.3	-155.1
1986	721.4	187.5	55.4	9.7	44.1	-146.8	-201.0	54.3	—	1.2	575.9	717.6	-141.7
1985	735.7	189.3	91.9	.2	55.5	-125.3	-181.4	56.1	—	-13.9	596.5	714.5	-118.1
1984	742.7	222.0	87.5	-4.1	27.8	-108.8	-166.9	58.1	—	-9.0	624.9	718.9	-94.0
1983	592.2	130.6	65.0	-10.9	17.0	-128.6	-176.0	47.5	—	5.2	468.8	502.3	-33.5
1982	557.1	153.9	20.0	-10.4	-9.2	-110.8	-145.9	35.1	—	-.1	446.3	447.3	-1.0
1981	550.5	159.4	43.2	-24.2	-14.4	-29.7	-63.8	34.1	1.1	4.1	526.1	515.5	10.6
1980	499.6	153.8	33.9	-43.0	-20.2	-35.3	-60.1	24.8	1.2	13.6	479.1	467.6	11.5
1979	445.8	118.1	62.0	-43.2	-14.0	11.5	-16.1	27.6	1.1	-1.0	457.4	454.8	2.6
1978	409.8	110.2	69.0	-25.3	-10.9	-.4	-29.3	28.9	—	-1.9	406.7	416.8	-10.1
1977	295.6	65.0	35.2	-15.2	-12.0	-19.5	-46.3	26.8	—	7.5	283.6	303.3	-19.6
1976	271.9	68.6	25.5	-44.6	-14.5	-35.7	-53.6	17.9	—	6.1	242.3	243.0	-.7
1975	303.6	104.6	37.1	-11.0	-6.2	-64.9	-69.4	4.5	—	2.5	241.2	219.6	21.6
1974	215.7	74.0	7.6	-38.5	-2.3	-3.6	-11.7	8.1	—	.6	209.5	212.2	-2.8
1973	213.8	72.7	24.1	-18.4	1.6	6.0	-6.9	12.9	.7	.4	220.2	220.5	-.3
1972	180.4	49.4	25.9	-6.6	2.5	-3.5	-17.3	13.7	.7	1.7	179.2	188.3	-9.0
1971	171.9	60.2	22.5	-4.9	60.4	-18.1	-22.2	4.0	.7	-3.4	151.1	153.2	-2.1
1970	153.2	56.2	14.6	-4.8	87.3	-10.1	-11.9	1.8	.9	-6.4	137.6	136.3	1.3
1969	135.2	38.2	20.5	-5.1	81.6	8.8	8.1	.7	—	-6.1	137.9	139.0	-1.0
1968	135.2	39.8	24.2	-3.3	74.5	-6.8	-6.5	-.3	—	-2.7	125.6	126.0	-.4
1967	133.4	40.4	25.3	-1.1	68.9	-13.9	-12.4	-1.6	—	-.7	118.8	116.6	2.2
1966	123.8	32.5	29.1	-1.8	63.9	1.1	-.2	1.3	—	-1.0	123.9	121.4	2.4
1965	113.1	28.4	26.7	-1.7	59.8	2.2	1.2	1.0	—	-3.1	112.2	108.1	4.1
1964	102.4	26.2	20.6	-.5	56.1	-1.4	-3.0	1.7	—	-1.3	99.7	94.0	5.7
1963	88.7	19.9	16.6	-.5	52.6	1.8	.7	1.2	—	-.3	90.3	87.1	3.1
1962	87.9	21.6	16.0	.3	50.0	-2.9	-3.8	.9	—	.5	85.5	83.0	2.5
1961	79.8	21.2	13.5	-.1	45.2	-4.3	-3.8	-.5	—	-.8	74.7	71.7	3.0
1960	73.9	17.0	13.2	.2	43.4	3.7	3.5	.2	—	-1.0	76.5	74.8	1.7
1959	75.9	19.1	15.9	-.5	41.4	-2.1	-1.2	-.8	—	-.8	73.0	75.3	-2.3
1958	71.7	22.3	10.8	-.3	38.9	-12.5	-10.2	-2.3	—	1.6	60.7	60.9	-.2
1957	70.5	20.7	14.2	-1.5	37.1	.7	2.1	-1.4	—	(Z)	71.2	67.9	3.4
1956	67.8	20.6	15.9	-2.7	34.1	4.9	5.7	-.9	—	-1.1	71.6	70.0	1.5
1955	62.1	15.8	16.5	-1.7	31.5	2.7	4.0	-1.3	—	2.1	66.9	67.4	-.5
1954	55.6	16.4	11.3	-.3	28.2	-7.0	-5.9	-1.1	—	2.7	51.3	51.7	-.5
1953	54.4	18.3	11.5	-1.0	25.7	-6.9	-7.0	.1	—	3.0	50.5	52.6	-2.1
1952	53.3	18.1	11.0	1.0	23.2	-3.8	-3.8	(Z)	—	2.2	51.6	51.9	-.3
1951	50.3	17.3	13.0	-1.2	21.2	5.8	6.2	-.4	—	3.3	59.5	59.3	.2
1950	42.5	13.1	16.0	-5.0	18.3	7.9	9.1	-1.2	—	1.5	51.8	54.1	-2.2
1949	39.0	9.4	11.3	1.9	16.6	-3.2	-2.4	-.7	—	.3	36.2	35.7	.5
1948	41.4	13.4	15.6	-2.2	14.5	8.5	8.4	.1	—	-2.0	47.9	46.0	1.9
1947	27.5	7.3	13.9	-5.9	12.2	14.4	13.4	1.0	—	.9	42.9	34.0	8.9
1946	29.7	15.2	9.9	-5.3	9.9	5.4	3.5	1.9	—	.1	35.2	30.6	4.6
1945	44.7	29.6	4.4	-.6	11.3	-39.5	-42.1	2.6	—	3.9	9.1	10.6	-1.4
1944	54.3	37.3	6.5	-.3	11.0	-51.8	-54.5	2.7	—	2.5	5.0	7.1	-2.1
1943	49.7	33.4	6.6	-.8	10.3	-44.1	-46.6	2.5	—	-2.0	3.5	5.7	-2.2
1942	42.0	27.6	5.9	-1.2	9.8	-31.4	-33.1	1.8	—	-1.1	9.6	9.8	-.2
1941	22.4	11.0	5.7	-2.5	8.2	-3.8	-5.1	1.3	—	.4	19.0	17.9	1.1

See footnote at end of chart

Series F 552-565. Sources and Uses of Gross Savings: 1929 to 1991—Cont'd.

(In billions of dollars)

			Private saving			Gross saving and statistical discrepancy						Gross investment		
			Gross business saving				Government surplus or deficit (-)							
Year	Total	Personal saving	Undistributed corporate funds	Corporate inventory valuation adjustment	Capital consumption allowances	Total	Federal	State and local	Capital grants received by the U.S.	Statistical discrepancy	Total	Gross private domestic investment	Net foreign investment
	552	**553**	**555**	**556**	**557**	**558**	**559**	**560**	**561**	**562**	**563**	**564**	**565**
1940	14.3	3.8	3.2	-.2	7.5	-.7	-1.3	.6	—	1.0	14.6	13.1	1.5
1939	11.0	2.6	1.8	-.7	7.3	-2.2	-2.2	(Z)	—	1.3	10.2	9.3	.9
1938	8.7	.7	-.2	1.0	7.3	-1.8	-2.1	.4	—	.6	7.6	6.5	1.1
1937	11.5	3.8	.6	(Z)	7.2	.3	-.4	.7	—	(Z)	11.8	11.8	.1
1936	10.3	3.6	.4	-.7	7.0	-3.1	-3.6	.5	—	1.2	8.4	8.5	-.1
1935	8.6	2.1	-.2	-.2	6.9	-2.0	-2.6	.6	—	-.2	6.4	6.4	-.1
1934	5.6	.4	-1.0	-.6	6.8	-2.4	-2.9	.5	—	.5	3.8	3.3	.4
1933	2.3	-.9	-1.6	-2.1	7.0	-1.4	-1.3	-.1	—	.6	1.6	1.4	.2
1932	2.5	-.6	-5.2	1.0	7.4	-1.8	-1.5	-.3	—	.3	1.1	1.0	.2
1931	8.0	2.6	-4.9	2.4	7.9	-2.9	-2.1	-.8	—	.7	5.8	5.6	.2
1930	12.1	3.4	-2.6	3.3	8.0	-.3	.3	-.6	—	-.8	11.0	10.3	.7
1929	15.3	4.2	2.8	.5	7.9	1.0	1.2	-.2	—	.7	17.0	16.2	.8

Z Less than $50 million or less than – $50 million.

SECTION G

CONSUMER INCOME AND EXPENDITURES

CONSUMER INCOME AND EXPENDITURES
Highlights

1 Reasonably reliable nationwide estimates of income distribution are available only from the 1940s when the minimum income requirement for filing income tax returns was substantially lowered to cover the vast majority of the population. Annual tabulations of tax-return data began during World War I but initially covered only a small fraction of the upper-income population. Sample field surveys of family incomes covering all income and occupation groups were introduced in the 1930s. Estimates of income distribution before the 1940s were pieced together from sample surveys in *American Studies of the Distribution of Wealth and Income by Size* (1939) by C. L. Merwin, *The Present Distribution of Wealth in the United States* (1896) by Charles B. Spahr, *Wealth and Income of the People of the United States* (1915) by Willford I. King, *Income in the United States* (1921/22) by W. C. Mitchell, W. I. King, F. R. Macaulay, and O. W. Knauth, and *America's Capacity to Consume* (1934) by Maurice Leven, H. H. Moulton, and Clark Warburton. The Consumer Purchase Study of 1935-36 conducted by the National Resources Committee under Hildegarde Kneeland was the first sample field survey in which income data were collected from all types of families. Based largely on 300,000 family income schedules, it represented a marked improvement over earlier estimates by providing data for numerous subgroups classified by occupation, community, region, color and family size. The Survey of Spending and Saving in Wartime is the only other pre-World War II source on the distribution of family income nationwide. The 1940 decennial census was the first to include income questions, making it possible to compare pre-war and post-war income levels. For the post-World War II years, income data are available from two sources: the annual Current Population Surveys of the Census Bureau and the annual surveys of consumer finances conducted by the Survey Research Center of the University of Michigan. In addition, all censuses from 1950 provide detailed information on the level of total money income as well as wage and salary income, classified by demographic and socio-economic characteristics, and cross classified by sex, race and occupation and industry groups. Complementing these sources are income and expenditure surveys conducted by the Bureau of Labor Statistics for selected population groups, studies of farm family income by the Department of Agriculture, and, since 1937, surveys of income

distributions of workers covered under the Old Age, Survivors, Disability and Health Insurance (OASDHI) program. The much broader coverage of Federal individual income tax returns since World War II has made it possible to measure changes in relative income distribution over time. As part of its national income work, the Bureau of Economic Analysis, formerly the Office of Business Economics, publishes a personal income series by combining census and income tax data. In order to derive meaningful comparisons over time, the data for the prewar period have been adjusted to make them compatible with the postwar data. Direct compatibility among income distribution series has not been fully achieved because of variations in definitions and coverage. Definitional differences apply to the basic unit of classification, the income measure, the time period, and the family unit.

2 Collection of data on consumer expenditures began in the United States in the 1870s. The most substantial of these studies was made for Massachusetts by Carroll D. Wright in 1875. The usefulness of the data gathered in this study led Congress to request that further studies of this type on a broader base be conducted by the newly formed U.S. Bureau of Labor (of which Wright was made commissioner). The data on food expenditures obtained in the 1901 survey were used to devise an index of food prices purchased by workers. During that period, the need for a more inclusive index of retail prices became clearer because food prices rose much faster than those of many other commodities and rent. A nationwide study of the expenditures of wage earners and clerical workers was undertaken in 1918. The survey was first undertaken in seacoast cities (because of the number of wage disputes in shipbuilding centers) but later was expanded to other industrial centers. The first study of overall consumer expenditures of farm families was made in Livingstone County in New York State in 1909. Dramatic increases in industrial and agricultural productivity and the collapse of the economy in 1929 led a number of economists to study the factors affecting consumer expenditures and to estimate changes in consumption patterns over time. The pioneer investigation in this field was presented in Simon Kuznets' *Commodity Flow and Capital Formation* (1938). It showed national aggregates for four types of consumer goods and services. The Brookings Institution published

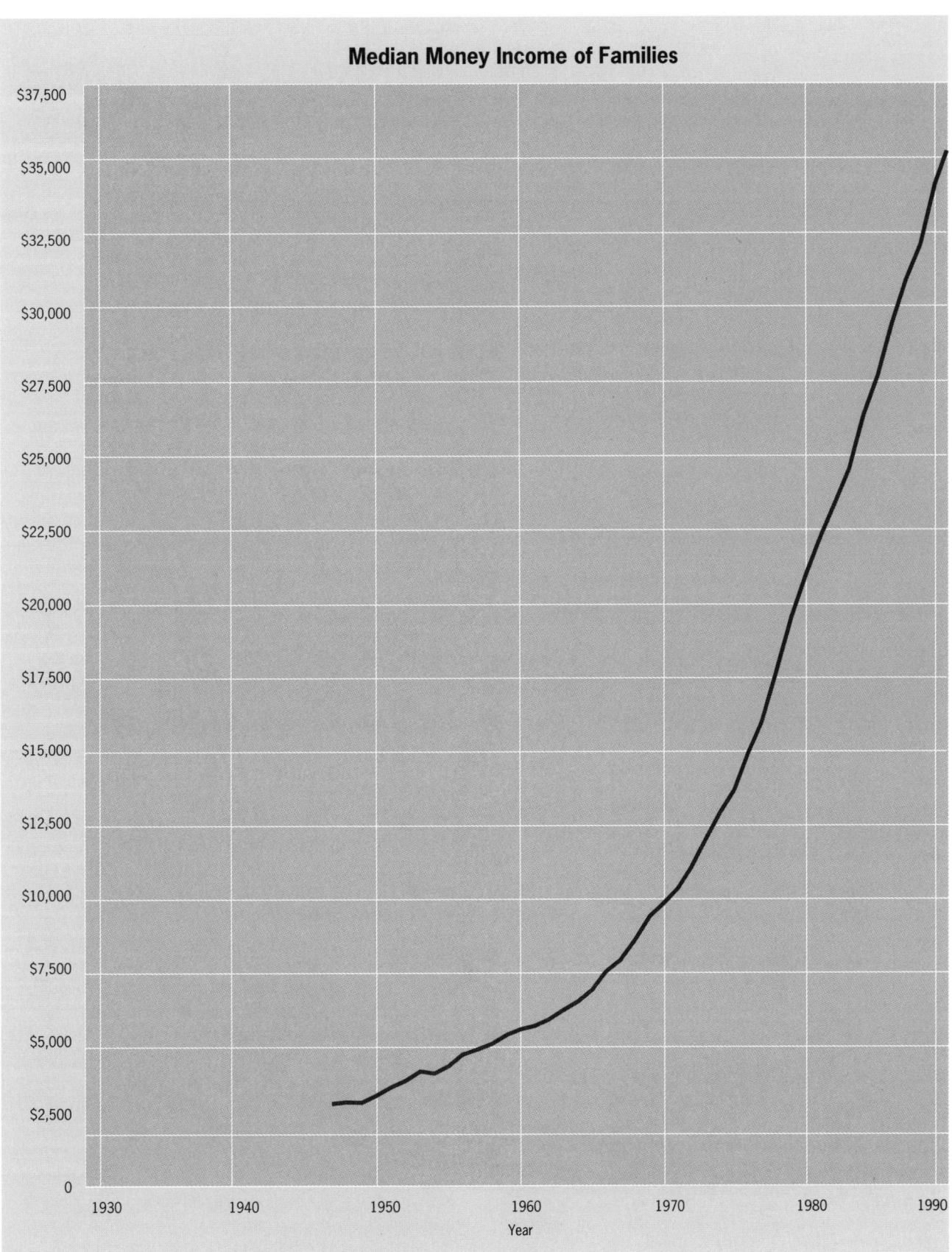

Median Money Income of Families

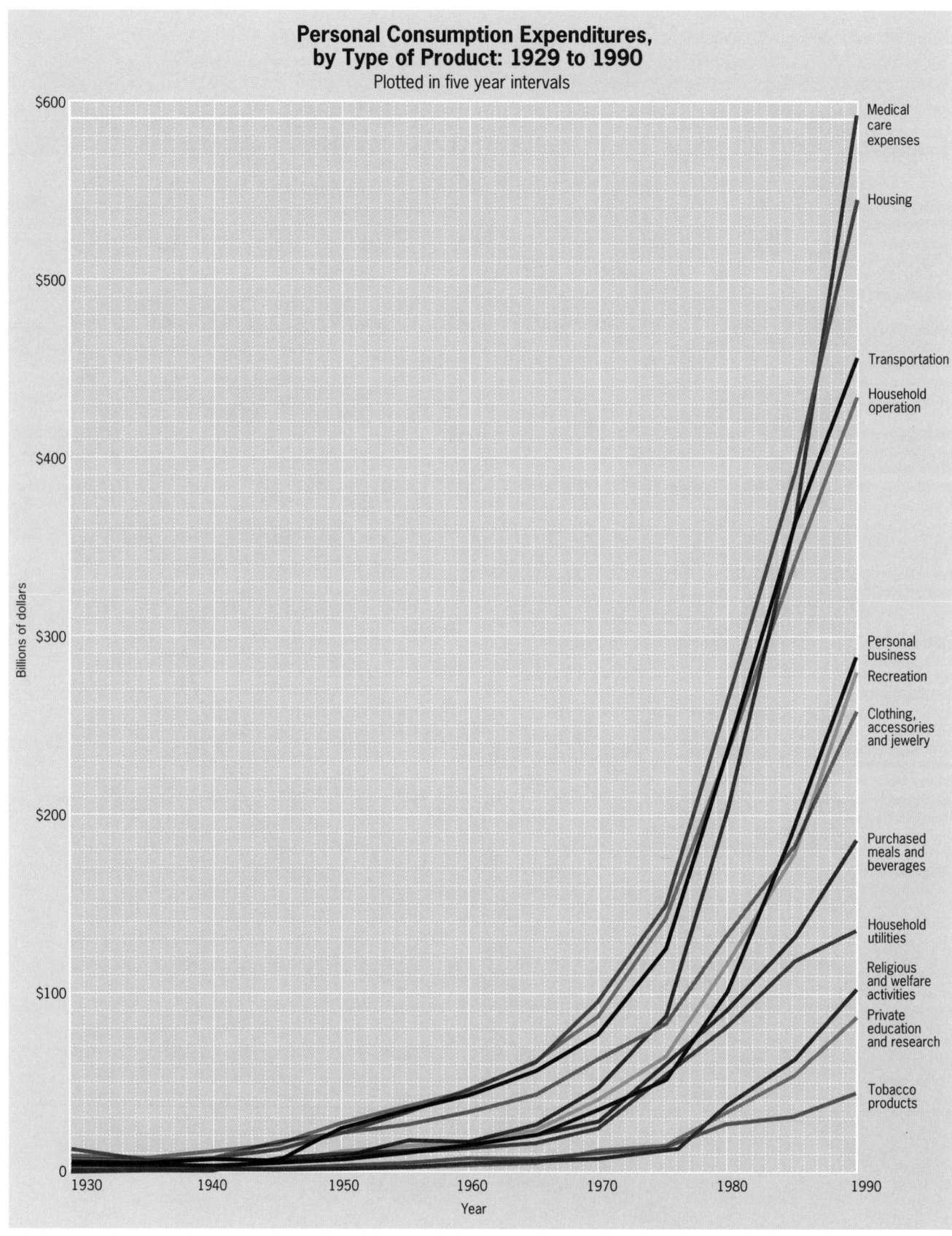

Personal Consumption Expenditures, by Type of Product: 1929 to 1990

Plotted in five year intervals

Billions of dollars

Year

Medical care expenses

Housing

Transportation

Household operation

Personal business

Recreation

Clothing, accessories and jewelry

Purchased meals and beverages

Household utilities

Religious and welfare activities

Private education and research

Tobacco products

$600

$500

$400

$300

$200

$100

0

1930 1940 1950 1960 1970 1980 1990

estimates of expenditure patterns at different income levels for farm and nonfarm families in 1934, and for single individuals in 1929. In the middle 1930s, two national cross section studies of consumer expenditure patterns were undertaken. The first, conducted by the Bureau of Labor Statistics, covered employed city wage and clerical workers and was initiated to provide a new list of items and weights for the Consumer Price Index. The second, the Study of Consumer Purchases, was conducted jointly by the Bureau of Labor Statistics and the Bureau of Home Economics of the Department of Agriculture. The results of the second study were used by the National Resources Planning Board as the basis for a national estimate of consumer expenditures. The first detailed estimates of aggregate consumer expenditures in goods and services appeared in *High-Level Consumption* by William H. Lough in 1935 and covered the period from 1909 to 1931. Data for later years were revised and extended in *Outlay and Income in the United States, 1921-1938* by Harold Barger, and in *America's Needs and Resources* (1947) by J. Frederic Dewhurst. The first detailed estimates by the Department of Commerce of consumer expenditures for commodities and services were published in the *Survey of Current Business* in June 1944. As defined by the Department of Commerce, consumer expenditures represent the market value of purchases of goods and services by individuals and nonprofit institutions as well as the value of food, clothing, housing, and financial services received by them as income in kind. Rental value of owner-occupied houses is included, but purchases of dwellings, which are classified as capital goods, are not. Other national sample surveys include the Surveys of Consumer Finances, conducted for the Board of Governors of the Federal Reserve System by the Consumer Research Center of the University of Michigan, and the Household Food Consumption Surveys of the Department of Agriculture.

3 Based on 1982-1984=100, the Consumer Price Index in 1991 was 136.2. By major groups and items, the rise in consumer prices was highest in oranges and tangerines (249.4), tobacco (202.7), prescription drugs (199.7), elementary and high school tuition (198.0), hospital and related services (196.1), college tuition (192.8), automobile

insurance (191.5), refuse collection (189.2), medical care (177.0), apples (172.8), and fresh and frozen fish (163.8). The slowest rising consumer prices were apparel and upkeep (128.7), ground beef (119.9), telephone services (119.87), sporting goods and equipment (118.5), household furnishing and operations (116.0), housefurnishing (107.5), fuel oil (92.4), automobile finance charges (98.0), appliances and electronic equipment (86.0), and interstate toll charges (67.6).

4 Based on 1982-84=100, the purchasing power of the dollar in 1991 declined to 73 cents according to the Consumer Price Index and 82 cents according to the Producer Price Index.

5 Based on 1982-84=100, the CMSA's with the highest consumer price indexes in 1990 were Honolulu (148.0), Boston-Lawrence-Salem (145.0), New York-Northern New Jersey-Long Island (144.8), San Diego (143,4), Philadelphia-Wilmington-Trenton (142.2), Los Angeles-Anaheim-Riverside (141.4), and Washington D.C. (141.2). The CMSA's with the lowest consumer price indexes were New Orleans (116.0), Tampa-St.Petersburg-Clearwater (116.4), and Anchorage (124.0).

6 Based on 1982-84=100, housing in 1990 was most expensive in Honolulu and least expensive in Houston, medical care was most expensive in Boston and least expensive in New Orleans, and fuel and other utilities were most expensive in Atlanta and least expensive in Seattle-Tacoma.

7 Although the annual percentage rise in consumer prices declined in the United States from a high of 13.5% in 1980 to 5.4% in 1990, 11 other developed countries had a lower inflation rate: Canada (4.8%), Norway (4.1%), Luxembourg (3.7%), Belgium (3.4%), France (3.4%), Ireland (3.3%), Austria (3.3%), Japan (3.1%), Germany (2.7%), Denmark (2.7%), and the Netherlands (2.5%).

8 The weekly food costs for an average family with two children aged 12 to 19 years old was $138.60 in May 1991 compared to $67.20 in 1975.

Series G 31-138. Distribution of Money Income of Families and Unrelated Individuals Ranked by Fifths According to Income Received: 1947 to 1990

(Families: all races)

Year	Lowest fifth	Second fifth	Third fifth	Fourth fifth	Highest fifth	Top 5 percent
	Percent distribution of aggregate income					
	85	86	87	88	89	90
1990	4.6	10.8	16.6	23.8	44.3	17.4
1989	4.6	10.6	16.5	23.7	44.6	17.9
1988	—	—	—	—	—	—
1987	4.6	10.8	16.9	24.1	43.7	16.9
1986	4.6	10.8	16.8	24.0	43.7	17.0
1985	5.0	11.2	16.9	23.9	42.9	16.5
1984	4.7	11.0	17.0	24.4	42.9	16.0
1983	4.7	11.1	17.1	24.4	42.7	15.8
1982	4.7	11.2	17.1	24.3	42.7	16.0
1981	5.0	11.3	17.4	24.4	41.9	15.4
1980	5.2	11.5	17.5	24.3	41.5	15.3
1979	5.3	11.6	17.5	24.1	41.6	15.7
1978	5.2	11.6	17.5	24.1	41.5	15.6
1977	5.2	11.6	17.5	24.2	41.5	15.7
1976	5.4	11.8	17.6	24.1	41.1	15.6
1975	5.4	11.8	17.6	24.1	41.1	15.5
1974	5.5	12.0	17.5	24.0	41.0	15.5
1973	5.5	11.9	17.5	24.0	41.1	15.5
1972	5.4	11.9	17.5	23.9	41.4	15.9
1971	5.5	12.0	17.6	23.8	41.1	15.7
1970	5.4	12.2	17.6	23.8	40.9	15.6
1969	5.6	12.4	17.7	23.7	40.6	15.6
1968	5.6	12.4	17.7	23.7	40.5	15.6
1967	5.5	12.4	17.9	23.9	40.4	15.2
1966	5.6	12.4	17.8	23.8	40.5	15.6
1965	5.2	12.2	17.8	23.9	40.9	15.5
1964	5.1	12.0	17.7	24.0	41.2	15.9
1963	5.0	12.1	17.7	24.0	41.2	15.8
1962	5.0	12.1	17.6	24.0	41.3	15.7
1961	4.7	11.9	17.5	23.8	42.2	16.6
1960	4.8	12.2	17.8	24.0	41.3	15.9
1955	4.9	12.3	17.9	23.8	41.1	15.9
1959	4.8	12.2	17.7	23.4	41.8	16.8
1950	4.5	11.9	17.4	23.4	42.8	17.3
1947	5.0	11.8	17.0	23.1	43.2	17.5

Series G 179-188. Number and Median Money Income of Families and Unrelated Individuals: 1947 to 1990

(Income for calendar year shown)

Year	Total median income	Year	Total median income	Year	Total median income	Year	Total median income	Year	Total median income	Year	Total median income
	179		179		179		179		179		179
1990	$35,353	1980	21,023	1970	9,867	1960	5,620	1950	3,319		
1989	34,213	1979	19,587	1969	9,433	1959	5,417	1949	3,107		
1988	32,191	1978	17,640	1968	8,633	1958	5,087	1948	3,187		
1987	30,970	1977	16,009	1967	7,933	1957	4,971	1947	3,031		
1986	29,458	1976	14,958	1966	7,532	1956	4,783				
1985	27,735	1975	13,719	1965	6,957	1955	4,421				
1984	26,433	1974	12,902	1964	6,569	1954	4,173				
1983	24,580	1973	12,051	1963	6,249	1953	4,233				
1982	23,433	1972	11,116	1962	5,956	1952	3,890				
1981	22,388	1971	10,285	1961	5,737	1951	3,709				

Series G 416-469. Personal Consumption Expenditures by Type of Product: 1929 to 1990

(In billions of dollars)

Year	Purchased meals and beverages	Tobacco products	Clothing, accessories and jewelry	Housing	Household operation	Household utilities	Medical care expenses	Personal business	Transpor-tation	Recreation	Private education and research	Religious and welfare activities
	420	423	424	429	433	435	440	445	446	452	457	458
1990	187.5	43.9	259.7	547.1	434.2	135.9	593.0	289.2	458.1	280.2	86.7	103.8
1989	188.8	41.7	257.8	533.9	404.9	139.3	483.5	243.1	425.7	264.4	64.3	82.9
1988	179.9	36.9	240.0	502.3	386.1	132.6	444.0	227.1	407.5	245.1	57.7	75.9
1987	167.1	35.6	222.3	468.9	363.3	125.8	399.0	215.4	379.7	223.2	50.9	68.1
1986	151.6	33.6	207.2	434.2	347.5	122.4	357.6	192.5	366.3	201.2	46.6	62.9
1985	132.9	31.7	185.9	392.5	342.3	119.3	364.7	184.9	363.3	187.9	54.5	63.3
1984	134.1	30.5	181.8	371.3	316.9	117.5	298.4	145.8	329.5	168.3	39.1	52.6
1983	123.5	28.2	167.2	344.1	294.1	110.8	268.7	136.7	295.4	152.1	35.8	47.8
1982	112.9	24.7	153.3	321.1	272.4	103.2	245.4	116.3	267.6	138.8	32.6	44.4
1981	106.7	22.7	148.2	295.6	255.2	93.4	219.3	103.5	261.5	128.6	30.6	41.0
1980	93.4	20.9	131.8	255.2	233.6	81.1	207.2	101.6	235.7	117.6	33.6	38.6
1979	76.0	19.2	117.5	241.5	219.5	—	146.8	82.2	212.2	101.0	23.5	19.2
1978	69.3	17.9	107.6	212.2	195.0	—	131.0	71.1	191.3	91.2	20.8	17.2
1977	62.8	16.5	96.7	187.3	176.5	—	116.6	61.1	171.9	81.0	18.4	15.4
1976	56.3	16.2	89.0	166.2	158.5	—	101.2	56.5	150.8	73.3	17.1	14.3
1975	50.2	14.7	82.0	150.2	142.3	—	89.2	51.6	125.5	66.5	15.5	13.0
1974	44.4	13.8	76.3	136.5	130.6	—	76.9	46.5	115.1	60.9	13.8	11.6
1973	39.9	13.1	71.8	123.2	117.7	—	68.3	40.6	110.9	55.2	12.6	10.6
1972	35.5	12.2	64.8	112.3	105.2	—	61.2	37.4	101.4	49.1	11.6	10.1
1971	32.7	11.3	59.6	102.7	94.4	—	54.7	34.3	90.9	43.7	10.6	9.1
1970	29.3	11.1	62.8	90.9	87.4	24.3	47.4	35.3	77.8	40.7	10.4	8.6
1969	26.7	10.1	59.9	84.1	82.3	22.4	42.8	33.3	77.8	36.9	9.5	8.1
1968	25.0	9.8	55.4	77.3	76.2	20.9	37.8	29.5	72.0	33.6	8.7	7.6
1967	23.2	9.3	51.0	71.8	70.5	19.8	34.5	26.2	62.6	30.8	7.6	7.0
1966	22.0	8.9	48.4	67.6	66.8	18.9	31.1	24.3	60.5	28.9	6.6	6.4
1965	20.1	8.4	43.3	63.6	61.8	17.8	28.1	21.9	58.2	26.3	6.0	6.0
1964	18.8	7.9	40.4	59.3	58.0	16.9	25.8	20.1	51.4	24.6	5.2	5.7
1963	17.6	7.8	37.0	55.4	54.1	16.1	23.3	18.4	49.1	22.2	4.7	5.3
1962	17.0	7.4	35.7	52.0	51.1	15.2	22.0	16.5	46.0	20.5	4.4	5.1
1961	16.4	7.2	33.8	48.7	48.3	14.4	20.3	16.0	41.5	19.5	4.0	4.9
1960 *	16.2	7.0	33.0	46.3	46.9	13.7	19.1	15.0	43.1	18.3	3.7	4.7
1959	15.9	6.5	31.9	43.7	45.2	13.0	17.9	13.9	41.2	17.4	3.4	4.4

See footnote at end of chart.

Series G 416-469. Personal Consumption Expenditures by Type of Product: 1929 to 1990—Cont'd.

(In billions of dollars)

Year	Purchased meals and beverages	Tobacco products	Clothing, accessories and jewelry	Housing	Household operation	Household utilities	Medical care expenses	Personal business	Transportation	Recreation	Private education and research	Religious and welfare activities
	420	423	424	429	433	435	440	445	446	452	457	458
1958	15.3	6.0	29.9	41.1	42.3	12.3	16.5	12.8	35.6	15.8	3.1	4.2
1957	15.2	5.7	29.5	38.5	41.2	11.6	15.2	11.9	38.0	15.3	2.9	3.9
1956	14.5	5.3	29.2	36.0	39.8	10.9	13.9	11.0	34.8	15.0	2.6	3.7
1955	13.8	5.0	28.0	33.7	37.3	10.2	12.8	10.0	35.6	14.1	2.3	3.3
1954	13.4	4.9	26.8	31.7	33.7	9.3	12.0	9.2	29.7	13.1	2.1	3.2
1953	13.4	5.1	26.7	29.3	33.1	8.7	11.2	8.4	29.7	12.7	2.0	2.9
1952	13.1	4.9	26.4	26.5	31.7	8.3	10.2	7.8	25.1	12.1	1.9	2.8
1951	12.5	4.5	25.5	23.9	31.4	7.9	9.5	7.4	24.5	11.6	1.7	2.4
1950	11.1	4.3	23.7	21.3	29.4	7.3	8.8	6.9	24.7	11.1	1.6	2.3
1949	10.8	4.1	23.3	19.3	25.9	6.5	8.1	6.2	20.8	10.0	1.5	2.2
1948	11.0	4.0	24.2	17.5	26.4	6.6	7.8	6.0	17.7	9.7	1.4	2.2
1947	10.9	3.7	22.8	15.7	24.0	5.8	6.9	5.4	15.2	9.2	1.2	2.0
1946	10.9	3.4	22.0	13.9	20.1	5.0	6.2	5.1	12.0	8.6	1.0	1.9
1945	9.5	2.9	19.6	12.5	15.5	4.5	5.0	4.7	6.9	6.1	.9	1.7
1944	8.1	2.6	17.4	12.0	14.0	4.2	4.7	4.3	5.8	5.4	.9	1.7
1943	7.1	2.6	16.0	11.5	13.1	4.1	4.2	4.0	5.6	5.0	.9	1.4
1942	5.7	2.3	13.1	11.0	12.7	3.9	3.7	3.6	5.5	4.7	.8	1.2
1941	4.6	2.1	10.5	10.2	12.0	3.6	3.3	3.5	8.4	4.2	.7	1.1
1940	3.9	1.9	8.9	9.4	10.5	3.4	3.0	3.3	7.1	3.8	.6	1.0
1939	3.6	1.8	8.4	9.1	9.6	3.1	2.8	3.3	6.4	3.4	.6	.9
1938	3.4	1.7	8.0	8.9	8.9	3.0	2.7	3.3	5.6	3.2	.6	.9
1937	3.5	1.7	8.1	8.5	9.5	3.0	2.7	3.4	6.5	3.4	.6	.9
1936	3.0	1.5	7.7	8.0	8.8	3.0	2.5	3.2	6.1	3.0	.5	.9
1935	2.6	1.4	7.0	7.7	7.7	2.8	2.3	3.0	5.3	2.6	.5	.9
1934	2.2	1.4	6.6	7.6	7.2	2.7	2.2	2.9	4.6	2.4	.5	.9
1933	1.8	1.2	5.4	7.9	6.5	2.6	2.0	2.8	4.0	2.2	.5	.9
1932	2.1	1.3	6.0	9.0	6.8	2.6	2.1	2.9	4.0	2.4	.6	1.0
1931	2.5	1.5	8.2	10.3	8.4	2.8	2.6	3.3	5.0	3.3	.7	1.1
1930	2.8	1.5	9.7	11.1	9.6	3.1	2.8	3.7	6.1	4.0	.7	1.2
1929	2.9	1.7	11.2	11.5	10.7	3.0	2.9	4.2	7.6	4.3	.7	1.2

* Denotes first year for which figures include Alaska and Hawaii.

Series G 881-915.   Apparent Civilian Per Capita Consumption of Foods: 1849 to 1990
(In pounds, except eggs. Calendar years, except as noted)

Year	Meats (carcass weight)				Edible fats and oils			Fruits Fresh (farm weight)		
	Total	Beef and veal	Pork, excluding lard	Fish (edible weight)	Total[1] (fat content)	Margarine[2] (actual weight)	Butter, farm and factory (actual weight)	Total[3]	Citrus[4]	Apples
	881	882	883	885	886	888	889	890	891	892
1990	112.3	64.9	46.3	15.5	62.7	10.9	4.4	92.3	22.6	19.8
1989	115.9	66.4	48.4	15.6	61.1	10.2	4.4	99.2	24.9	21.6
1988	119.5	69.7	48.8	15.2	63.0	10.3	4.5	99.2	26.4	20.0
1987	117.4	70.8	45.6	16.2	62.9	10.5	4.7	101.1	25.8	21.3
1986	122.2	76.0	45.2	15.5	64.3	11.4	4.6	95.9	26.1	18.2
1985	124.9	76.1	47.7	15.1	64.3	10.8	4.9	89.3	22.6	17.5
1984	151.9	79.9	61.5	13.7	58.6	10.4	4.9	91.7	24.0	18.6
1983	152.3	79.8	61.9	13.1	60.0	10.4	4.9	93.2	29.5	18.5
1982	147.0	78.5	58.5	12.3	58.2	11.0	4.3	87.6	24.8	17.7
1981	154.4	78.7	64.9	12.9	57.7	11.1	4.2	83.1	24.1	16.1
1980	126.4	73.4	52.1	12.5	57.2	11.3	4.5	90.0	28.9	19.2
1979	177.8	107.5	68.8	13.0	55.8	11.2	4.5	83.3	24.5	17.0
1978	182.7	120.8	60.3	13.4	54.6	11.2	4.4	81.5	26.5	15.8
1977	190.0	127.8	60.5	12.7	53.0	11.4	4.3	82.0	26.2	17.0
1976	192.1	131.6	58.7	12.9	54.8	11.9	4.3	85.5	29.0	18.7
1975	180.5	123.7	54.8	12.2	52.6	11.0	4.7	85.0	29.4	19.5
1974	188.0	119.1	66.6	12.0	53.5	11.3	4.6	78.3	27.3	15.8
1973	175.7	111.4	61.6	12.7	54.4	11.3	4.8	75.6	27.3	14.5
1972	189.0	118.3	67.4	12.5	54.2	11.3	4.9	77.0	27.2	17.4
1971	191.8	115.7	73.0	11.5	52.2	11.1	5.1	79.8	29.2	16.2
1970	186.3	116.6	66.4	14.8	53.2	11.0	5.3	81.0	28.6	18.3
1969	182.5	114.1	65.0	14.2	51.9	10.8	5.4	79.0	28.3	14.9
1968	183.2	113.3	66.2	14.0	51.2	10.8	5.7	78.3	26.3	15.7
1967	178.3	110.3	64.1	13.6	49.4	10.5	5.5	80.9	31.6	16.2
1966	170.9	108.8	58.1	13.9	49.7	10.5	5.7	81.4	29.1	16.1
1965	167.1	104.7	58.7	13.9	47.8	9.9	6.4	81.1	29.1	16.3
1964	174.7	105.1	65.4	13.5	47.6	9.7	6.9	78.7	26.2	17.9
1963	169.7	99.4	65.4	13.7	46.3	9.6	6.9	74.5	22.1	16.7
1962	163.1	94.4	63.5	13.6	45.7	9.3	7.3	83.4	29.5	17.4
1961	160.5	93.4	62.0	13.7	45.1	9.4	7.4	88.6	30.8	16.4
1960 *	160.9	91.2	64.9	13.2	45.3	9.4	7.5	93.4	33.7	18.3
1959	159.5	87.1	67.6	13.7	46.2	9.2	7.9	95.7	34.0	21.1
1958	151.6	87.2	60.2	13.3	45.3	9.0	8.3	94.0	31.0	22.5
1957	158.7	93.4	61.1	12.8	44.4	8.6	8.3	96.7	37.1	19.3
1956	166.7	94.9	67.3	12.9	45.2	8.2	8.7	98.9	39.1	18.9
1955	162.8	91.4	66.8	12.9	45.9	8.2	9.0	99.4	41.8	19.6
1954	154.7	90.1	60.0	13.5	45.5	8.5	8.9	105.1	42.0	20.0
1953	155.3	87.1	63.5	13.6	44.1	8.1	8.5	109.4	44.1	20.9
1952	146.0	69.4	72.4	13.3	44.1	7.9	8.6	114.4	45.1	21.6
1951	138.0	62.7	71.9	13.2	42.1	6.6	9.6	118.0	45.8	25.7
1950	144.6	71.4	69.2	13.8	45.9	6.1	10.7	108.8	41.7	22.7
1949	144.6	72.8	67.7	12.9	42.5	5.8	10.5	122.9	47.9	24.7
1948	145.5	72.6	67.8	13.1	42.6	6.1	10.0	131.6	54.4	26.3
1947	155.3	80.4	69.6	12.3	42.0	5.0	11.2	143.7	62.2	25.4
1946	154.1	71.6	75.8	12.8	40.0	3.9	10.5	133.9	59.1	23.0
1945	145.2	71.3	66.6	11.9	39.1	4.1	10.9	139.9	66.6	22.9
1944	154.2	68.0	79.5	10.7	40.9	3.9	11.9	140.1	68.2	25.5
1943	146.8	61.5	78.9	9.9	41.5	3.9	11.8	118.4	60.3	24.9
1942	140.3	69.4	63.7	10.7	44.9	2.8	15.9	130.0	57.7	28.1
1941	143.7	68.5	68.4	13.2	47.6	2.8	16.1	146.0	57.7	31.7
1940	142.4	62.3	73.5	13.0	46.4	2.4	17.0	139.1	56.7	29.7
1939	133.6	62.3	64.7	12.7	46.4	2.3	17.4	148.2	61.4	30.7
1938	127.1	62.0	58.2	12.8	45.3	3.0	16.6	131.7	49.1	28.2
1937	126.2	63.8	55.8	13.8	45.5	3.1	16.8	138.6	44.5	33.6
1936	130.6	68.9	55.1	13.7	45.7	3.1	16.8	125.6	46.2	27.6

See footnotes at end of chart.

Series G 881-915. Apparent Civilian Per Capita Consumption of Foods: 1849 to 1990—Cont'd.

(In pounds, except eggs. Calendar years, except as noted)

| Year | Meats (carcass weight) | | | | Edible fats and oils | | | Fruits Fresh (farm weight) | | |
| | Total | Beef and veal | Pork, excluding lard | Fish (edible weight) | Total [1] (fat content) | Margarine [2] (actual weight) | Butter, farm and factory (actual weight) | Total [3] | Citrus [4] | Apples |
	881	882	883	885	886	888	889	890	891	892
1935	117.4	61.7	48.4	12.5	44.1	3.0	17.6	133.2	44.6	32.9
1934	143.9	73.2	64.4	11.2	44.5	2.1	18.6	116.3	39.8	25.3
1933	136.1	58.6	70.7	10.7	43.0	1.9	18.2	124.8	39.4	40.0
1932	131.1	53.3	70.7	10.4	42.9	1.6	18.5	125.9	36.7	39.2
1931	130.7	55.2	68.4	10.8	44.4	1.9	18.3	160.3	42.3	51.7
1930	129.0	55.3	67.0	12.2	—	2.6	17.6	129.9	31.2	42.1
1929	131.2	56.0	69.6	13.9	—	2.9	17.6	139.2	39.8	39.7
1928	131.6	55.2	70.9	14.1	—	2.6	17.6	146.1	29.5	48.9
1927	134.9	61.9	67.7	14.2	—	2.3	18.3	126.0	32.2	37.4
1926	138.0	68.5	64.1	13.4	—	2.0	18.3	160.8	31.4	62.3
1925	140.1	68.1	66.8	13.1	—	2.0	18.1	132.2	28.9	46.3
1924	147.3	68.1	74.0	13.0	—	2.0	17.8	148.0	33.9	54.1
1923	147.6	67.8	74.2	12.7	—	2.0	17.8	144.5	32.5	54.7
1922	137.7	66.9	65.7	13.3	—	1.7	17.1	144.8	24.6	57.5
1921	134.0	63.1	64.8	12.5	—	2.0	16.3	112.8	30.5	36.1
1920	136.0	67.1	63.5	13.8	—	3.4	14.9	142.6	26.0	63.0
1919	138.9	69.3	63.9	13.6	—	3.4	15.2	122.3	23.5	45.2
1918	141.6	75.8	61.0	12.9	—	3.3	14.1	119.6	16.5	56.9
1917	135.3	71.9	58.9	12.9	—	2.7	15.7	129.8	22.0	56.1
1916	140.1	65.3	69.0	13.0	—	1.8	17.3	133.7	22.0	63.9
1915	134.9	62.3	66.5	13.2	—	1.4	17.2	154.5	23.1	69.0
1914	140.0	67.8	65.1	13.7	—	1.4	17.0	160.4	24.1	71.8
1913	143.7	69.6	66.9	13.5	—	1.5	16.5	130.2	16.6	59.3
1912	145.9	71.5	66.7	13.3	—	1.5	16.6	156.5	18.5	74.6
1911	151.9	75.6	69.0	13.3	—	1.1	18.6	152.6	19.8	73.5
1910	146.4	77.6	62.3	13.2	—	1.6	18.3	134.7	17.8	59.4
1909	155.2	81.5	67.0	13.0	—	1.2	17.8	135.0	16.2	62.2
1908	163.3	79.3	77.7	—	—	1.0	19.7	—	—	—
1907	158.2	77.8	74.1	—	—	.9	17.6	—	—	—
1906	155.6	78.3	71.0	—	—	.8	17.8	—	—	—
1905	155.2	77.9	71.0	—	—	.6	19.9	—	—	—
1904	152.7	75.6	70.6	—	—	.6	18.5	—	—	—
1913	152.1	77.0	68.2	—	—	.6	18.3	—	—	—
1902	144.8	71.0	66.7	—	—	.9	17.6	—	—	—
1901	151.1	73.3	70.8	—	—	1.6	20.0	—	—	—
1900	150.7	72.3	71.9	—	—	1.3	20.1	—	—	—
1899	150.7	72.4	71.8	—	—	1.4	19.6	—	—	—

| Year | Butter (actual weight) | Year | Butter (actual weight) | Year | Butter (actual weight) | Year | Butter (actual weight) | Year | Butter (actual weight) | Year | Butter (actual weight) |
	889		889		889		889		889		889
1898	19.8	1892	15.9	1887	16.3	1882	13.9	1877	14.4	1872	10.6
1897	20.8	1891	16.7	1886	16.8	1881	15.2	1876	14.5	1871	11.7
1896	22.2										
		1890	18.2	1885	16.1	1880	15.5	1875	12.4	1870	10.7
1895	18.4	1889	20.5	1884	15.3	1879	15.6	1874	13.4	1869	13.6
1894	15.4	1888	16.0	1883	15.2	1878	14.6	1873	13.4	1859	14.8
1893	15.5									1849	13.7

* Denotes first year for which figures include Alaska and Hawaii.
[1] Computed from unrounded numbers.
[2] Prior to 1909, data are for year beginning July.

[3] Beginning in 1934, excludes apples from non-commercial areas. Citrus fruits on crop year basis, 1941 to date.
[4] Beginning 1941, year begins October or November prior to year indicated.

Series G 881-915. Apparent Civilian Per Capita Consumption of Foods: 1849 to 1990—Cont'd.

(In pounds, except eggs. Calendar years, except as noted)

Year	Potatoes (farm weight)	Fresh vegetables (farm weight)	Dairy products Fluid milk and cream [1]	Cheese	Ice cream (product weight)	Eggs (number)	Chicken and turkey [2] (ready-to-cook)	Wheat flour	Peanuts (shelled) [3]	Coffee (green-bean basis)
	897	899	905	907	908	909	910	912	914	915
1990	127.2	111.0	233.2	24.7	15.7	233	63.6	137.8	6.0	10.2
1989	126.7	112.9	236.4	23.9	16.1	236	60.8	129.2	7.0	10.3
1988	122.2	109.6	234.6	23.7	17.3	246	57.4	130.0	6.9	9.8
1987	125.7	105.7	238.5	24.1	18.4	254	55.5	129.9	6.4	10.2
1986	125.7	99.3	240.5	23.1	18.4	254	51.3	125.7	6.4	10.5
1985	122.4	100.2	241.0	22.5	18.1	255	49.4	124.7	6.3	10.5
1984	121.9	100.3	236.0	21.4	18.1	259	66.5	118.1	6.0	10.1
1983	118.4	92.6	236.1	20.5	18.0	260	64.6	117.4	5.9	10.2
1982	114.8	95.9	235.7	19.9	17.6	264	63.5	116.7	5.9	10.2
1981	69.6	71.5	240.6	18.2	17.4	264	62.0	115.8	5.5	10.3
1980	114.3	92.7	245.6	17.5	17.5	271	42.6	116.9	4.8	10.3
1979	116.0	105.9	254.0	17.2	17.1	278	60.5	117.0	6.8	11.3
1978	119.0	103.6	257.0	17.0	17.4	273	55.8	115.0	6.8	10.5
1977	120.0	101.6	260.0	16.1	17.5	268	53.2	115.0	6.3	9.4
1976	114.0	100.9	264.0	15.7	17.9	270	51.8	119.0	6.2	12.5
1975	122.2	89.9	261.4	14.3	18.6	276	48.9	114.5	6.0	12.2
1974	116.0	105.0	244.0	14.6	17.5	287	49.9	106.0	6.4	12.8
1973	116.0	100.0	257.0	13.7	17.5	294	49.2	109.0	6.6	13.7
1972	119.0	98.3	263.0	13.2	17.4	307	51.0	109.0	6.2	13.9
1971	119.0	99.2	259.0	12.2	17.5	314	49.8	110.0	5.9	13.3
1970	91.0	98.9	264.0	11.5	17.7	319	49.5	110	5.9	13.8
1969	92.0	98.9	272.0	11.0	18.0	318	47.4	112	5.9	14.2
1968	94.0	98.7	280.0	10.6	18.4	321	45.4	112	5.8	14.9
1967	92.0	98.1	285.0	10.1	17.8	324	45.8	112	5.7	14.8
1966	96.0	96.0	297.0	9.8	18.2	314	43.9	112	5.5	14.5
1965	93.0	98.6	302.0	9.6	18.5	314	40.9	113	5.6	14.8
1964	96.0	98.6	304.0	9.4	18.3	318	38.5	114	5.3	15.3
1963	100.0	101.4	307.0	9.2	18.0	318	37.5	114	5.0	15.7
1962	98.0	101.4	308.0	9.2	17.9	327	37.0	115	4.9	15.9
1961	102.0	103.8	312.0	8.6	18.0	329	37.4	118	4.9	15.8
1960 *	101.0	105.9	322.0	8.3	18.3	335	34.2	118	4.9	15.8
1959	101.0	102.3	330.0	8.0	18.7	352	35.2	120	4.7	15.9
1958	101.0	103.7	337.0	8.1	17.8	354	34.0	121	4.5	15.5
1957	106.0	106.4	344.0	7.7	18.0	362	31.4	119	4.5	15.7
1956	99.0	107.0	348.0	8.0	18.0	369	29.6	121	4.4	15.8
1955	106.0	105.2	348.0	7.9	18.0	371	26.3	123	4.1	15.3
1954	106.0	107.2	346.0	7.9	17.4	376	28.1	126	4.2	14.7
1953	106.0	109.1	346.0	7.5	18.0	379	26.7	128	4.4	16.9
1952	101.0	111.6	350.0	7.6	17.9	390	26.8	131	4.4	16.9
1951	113.0	111.9	350.0	7.2	17.4	393	26.1	133	4.6	16.6
1950	106	115.2	348.0	7.7	17.2	389	24.7	135	4.5	16.1
1949	110	116.2	352.0	7.3	17.6	383	22.9	136	4.1	18.7
1948	105	123.0	355.0	6.9	18.5	389	21.4	137	4.6	18.4
1947	125	122.4	369.0	6.9	20.1	383	21.7	139	4.5	17.4
1946	123	129.9	389.0	6.7	23.1	379	23.1	156	5.3	20.1
1945	122	134.3	399.0	6.7	15.7	403	25.1	161	6.6	16.4
1944	136	123.9	381.0	4.9	14.3	354	23.1	149	6.0	15.8
1943	125	116.7	371.0	4.9	13.1	347	25.7	163	5.7	12.9
1942	127	119.0	354.0	6.4	15.8	318	20.7	157	6.2	13.6
1941	128	113.8	334.0	5.9	13.6	311	18.3	156	4.8	15.9
1940	123	116.9	331.0	6.0	11.4	319	17.0	155	5.0	15.5
1939	122	116.6	332.0	6.0	11.0	313	16.6	158	4.4	14.9
1938	129	114.5	329.0	5.9	10.4	310	15.0	160	4.3	14.9
1937	126	111.0	331.0	5.5	10.6	308	15.9	159	4.4	13.3
1936	130	112.5	330.0	5.4	9.5	289	15.9	163	4.6	13.7

See footnotes at end of chart.

Series G 881-915. Apparent Civilian Per Capita Consumption of Foods: 1849 to 1990—Cont'd.

(In pounds, except eggs. Calendar years, except as noted)

Year	Potatoes (farm weight)	Fresh vegetables (farm weight)	Fluid milk and cream [1]	Cheese	Ice cream (product weight)	Eggs (number)	Chicken and turkey [2] (ready-to-cook)	Wheat flour	Peanuts (shelled) [3]	Coffee (green-bean basis)
	897	899	905	907	908	909	910	912	914	915
1935	142	111.2	326.0	5.3	8.1	280	14.8	158	4.0	13.4
1934	135	115.2	322.0	4.9	7.1	289	15.3	157	3.3	12.3
1933	132	104.5	337.0	4.6	6.1	296	16.7	162	3.6	12.8
1932	134	108.8	339.0	4.4	6.3	313	16.0	170	4.1	12.4
1931	136	108.3	335.0	4.5	8.6	333	15.5	169	4.4	13.0
1930	132	111.9	337.0	4.7	9.8	331	17.2	171	3.2	12.5
1929	159	112.6	340.0	4.7	10.7	334	15.7	177	4.1	12.2
1928	147	104.2	337.0	4.4	9.9	338	14.6	179	3.8	11.9
1927	141	106.0	336.0	4.6	9.9	342	15.2	181	3.9	12.2
1926	128	100.6	338.0	4.6	9.5	339	14.2	182	3.4	12.4
1925	157	101.3	337.0	4.7	9.7	318	14.3	180	3.6	10.6
1924	154	100.9	336.0	4.6	8.8	324	13.7	180	3.5	12.2
1923	174	90.1	328.0	4.5	9.0	326	14.6	180	3.2	12.6
1922	143	92.8	342.0	4.3	8.2	316	14.2	180	2.7	11.8
1921	156	82.2	346.0	4.2	7.6	300	13.4	167	2.7	12.0
1920	140	95.0	348.0	4.0	7.6	299	13.7	179	3.0	11.7
1919	152	76.6	335.0	4.2	6.8	303	14.2	192	4.6	11.8
1918	174	—	361.0	3.9	6.4	284	13.3	179	2.8	10.0
1917	146	—	328.0	3.7	4.8	281	13.3	191	4.2	12.1
1916	143	—	315.0	3.8	4.3	299	13.8	204	2.8	11.5
1915	185	—	318.0	4.1	3.9	313	14.4	205	2.8	10.6
1914	157	—	321.0	4.2	3.4	295	14.5	207	2.5	9.2
1913	189	—	342.0	4.2	3.0	303	14.5	209	2.5	9.0
1912	179	—	355.0	3.9	2.7	312	14.9	211	2.3	10.8
1911	157	—	301.0	4.0	2.3	329	15.6	213	2.3	8.3
1910	198	—	315.0	4.3	1.9	306	15.5	214	2.5	9.2
1909	187	—	343.0	3.8	1.6	293	14.7	217	2.4	—

Year	Cheese	Year	Cheese	Year	Cheese	Year	Cheese	Year	Cheese	Year	Cheese
	907		907		907		907		907		907
1908	3.8	1900	3.7	1893	2.9	1885	3.0	1878	3.5	1870	3.2
1907	3.5	1899	3.7	1892	3.7	1884	3.1	1877	2.7	1869	3.0
1906	3.5	1898	3.4	1891	3.5	1883	3.3	1876	2.6	1859	2.9
		1897	3.6			1882	3.1			1849	4.1
1905	4.1	1896	2.9	1890	3.8	1881	3.2	1875	3.1		
1904	4.1			1889	3.5			1874	2.6		
1903	4.0	1895	2.9	1888	3.5	1880	2.7	1873	2.9		
1902	4.0	1894	2.9	1887	3.2	1879	2.2	1872	3.0		
1901	4.5			1886	2.8			1871	2.4		

[1] Cream included on whole-milk equivalent basis.
[2] Chicken only, 1909-1928, but turkey consumption very small during that time.
[3] September- August year through 1939; August-July year, thereafter.

SOCIAL STATISTICS

SECTION H

SOCIAL STATISTICS
Highlights

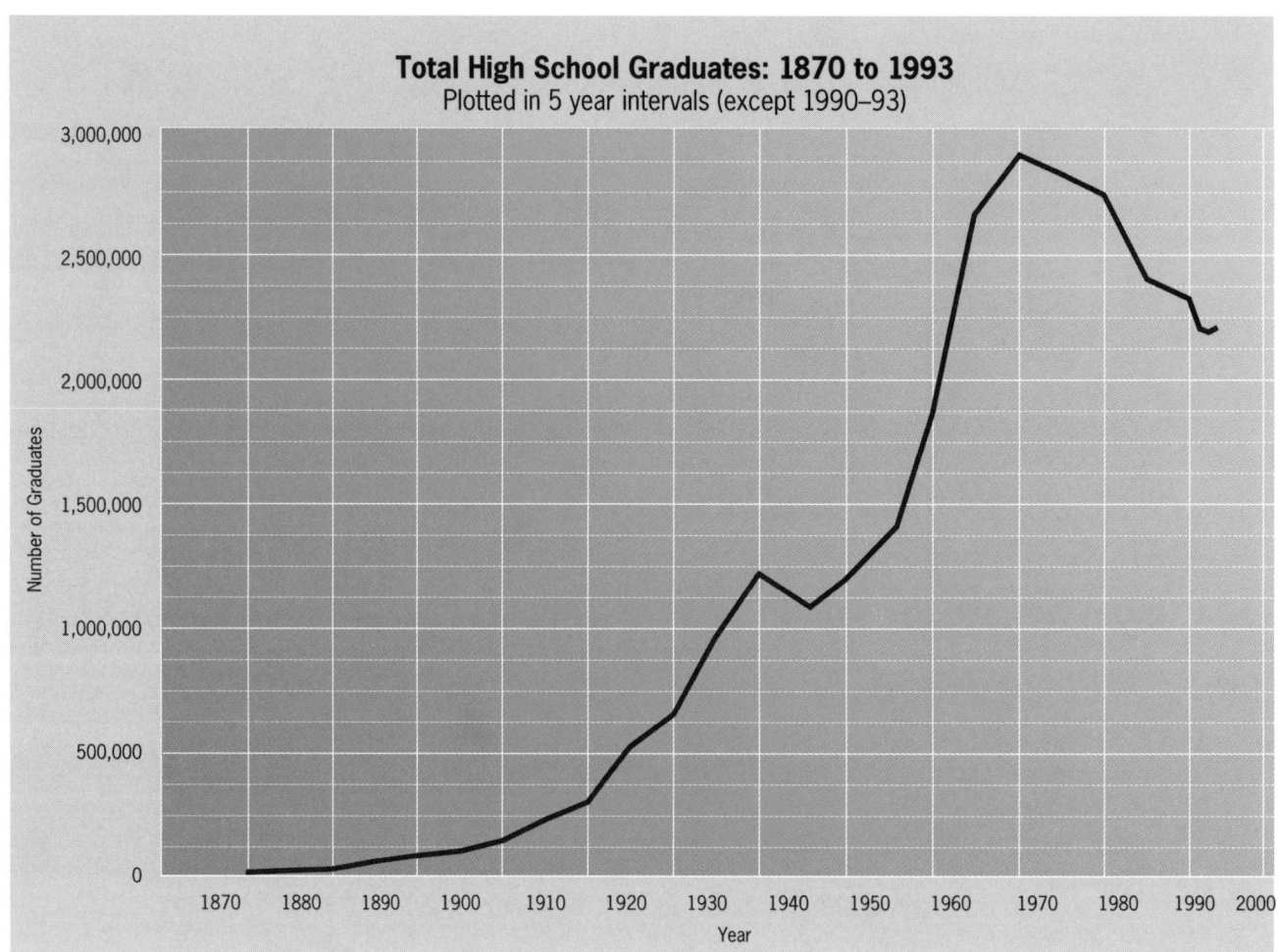

Total High School Graduates: 1870 to 1993
Plotted in 5 year intervals (except 1990–93)

Number of Graduates

Year

1 The United States adopted the concepts of Social Security and Welfare much later than other Western democracies. Throughout the 19th century, social welfare activities remained a local responsibility. Following public support of education in Massachusetts and other states, state intervention was extended to health programs, care of the blind and the orphaned, workman's compensation, and retirement pensions. It was not until the Social Security Act of 1935 that the Federal government participated in any major way in permanent welfare programs for the general population. The Act established a national system of old age insurance and unemployment insurance, and provided Federal grants-in-aid to the states for public assistance, maternal and child health and welfare services, general public health services, and vocational rehabilitation services. The Social Security Administration administers many of these programs and its annual and monthly reports carry an enormous volume of statistical data.

2 As a percentage of GNP, social welfare expenditures grew from 2.4% in 1890 to 18.6% in 1989 and as percentage of total government outlays from 38% in 1890 to 53% in 1989.

3 Of the total 94.312 million households in the United States, 16.098 million receive at least one means-tested non-cash benefit, such as food stamps, free school lunch, public housing, or Medicaid.

4 The minimum Social Security tax grew from $374 on maximum taxable earnings of $7,800 in 1970 to $3,924 on maximum taxable earnings of $51,300 in 1990.

5 The number of beneficiaries under Social Security programs in 1989 was 39.151 million, who received a total of $230.85 billion in benefits.

6 In 1990, there were 729,900 active pension plans under the Employee Retirement Income Security Act (ERISA) with a total of 77.7 million participants. The assets of public and private pension plans in 1991 were $3.473 trillion. In 1990, the value of Individual Retirement Accounts Plans was $529 billion.

7 In 1990, a total of 14.164 million persons, or 8.9% of the total population, had a work disability.

8 In 1990, Mississippi was the state with the highest percentage of public aid recipients (11.4% of the state population), while New Hampshire had the lowest relative percentage (2.2%).

9 Of the total of 9.955 million women legally awarded child support in 1990, 3.206 million were below the poverty level. Of the 4.953 million entitled to receive payments, 28% did not receive any payments from the delinquent fathers.

10 Of the 3.189 million women awarded alimony payments, only 922,000 actually receive payments from their former spouses.

11 The number of adoptions declined from a high of 175,000 in 1970 to 104,088 in 1986, and the number of foreign adoptions from 10,097 in 1987 to 9,088 in 1991. The five foreign countries from which the most children were adopted were: Romania (2,552), Korea (1,817), Peru (722), Colombia (527), and India (448).

12 In 1988, primary child care arrangements for the 9.483 million under-five children of employed mothers included: care in the child's own home (28.2%), in another home by a grandparent or relative (13.2%), in another home by a nonrelative (23.6%), and in organized child-care facilities (25.8%). In 7.6% of cases, the mother cared for the child at work.

13 In 1988, 38.042 million Americans (20.4% of the population) did volunteer work. Of these, 37.4% did volunteer work for churches and religious organizations, 15.1% for schools, 13.2% for civic and political organizations, 10.4% for hospitals, 9.9% for social or welfare organizations, and 7.8% for sports or recreational groups.

14 In 1989, the average amount of donations to charity of all contributing households was $978, or 2.5% of household income. Those with income below $10,000 contributed 5.5% of their incomes while those with incomes between $50,000 and $75,000 contributed only 1.7%. Total private philanthropy grew from $21 billion in 1970 to $122.6 billion in 1990. Of the total amount of the contributions, 53.2% went to religious activities. (The Census does not distinguish between religious organizations and religion-affiliated charities. Religion itself is considered a charity, even if it does not engage in what is generally considered charitable work.) Of the total number of households, 24.9% did not contribute anything to charity.

15 In 1990, charitable foundations in the United States numbered 31,996 with total assets of $137.553 billion and grants of $7.912 billion. By dollar value, 25.7% of the grants went to education, 16.8% to health, 14.4% to human services, 14.3% to arts and culture, 5.0% to science and technology, 4.7% to environment, and 1.9% to religion. The same pattern dominated corporate philanthropy where health and human services, education, culture and art, and civic and community activities were the largest recipients.

16 Educational statistics have been collected and issued since 1870—by the Office of Education from 1870 to 1953; by the Department of Health, Education, and Welfare from 1953 to 1979; and by the Department of Education from 1979 to the present. From 1870 to 1917, these statistics were included in the *Annual Report of the United States Commissioner of Education*, and from 1918 to 1958 in the *Biennial Survey of Education*. Since 1962, the National Center for Education Statistics has published summary data on U.S. education in two annual publications: *Digest of Educational Statistics* and *Condition of Education*. Two problems that arise in the study of educational statistics are inconsistencies in the definitions of terms and procedures, and a lack of timeliness. School authorities are not compelled by law to report to the Office of Education, but the vast majority of them do so voluntarily. Nonpublic schools under the operational control of private individuals and groups have reported their data in a slightly different format over the years, making them incomparable with public school data. Enrollment information is collected on a state-by-state basis and represents a cumulative count of the total number of pupils registered at any time during the school year in each state. Pupils enrolled in more than one state in a school year are counted more than once, which results in inflated total counts.

17 The first school in America was established by the Dutch West India Company on Manhattan Island in 1633, with Adam Roelantsen appointed its first master. In 1783, the school's name was changed to Collegiate School. The first school committee or board was elected in Dorchester, Massachusetts, in 1645. The first school to operate on a one class to one room basis was set up in Quincy,

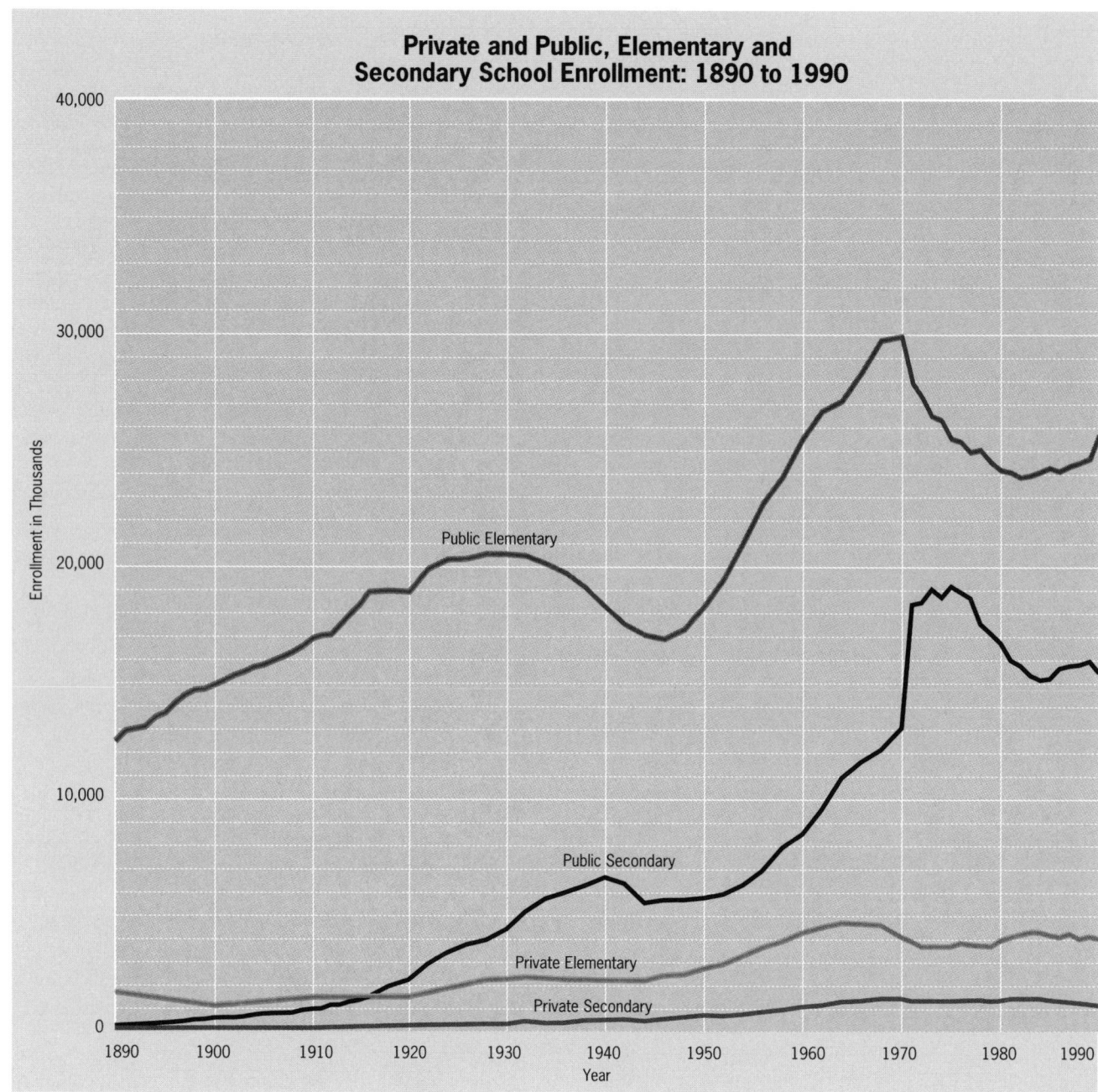

Private and Public, Elementary and Secondary School Enrollment: 1890 to 1990

Enrollment in Thousands

Public Elementary

Public Secondary

Private Elementary

Private Secondary

Year

Massachusetts in 1846. The first school superintendent, Roswell William Haskins, was appointed in 1836 by Buffalo, New York. The Compulsory School Law, the first piece of educational legislation, was passed on June 14, 1642 by Massachusetts. According to the Records of the Governor and Company of Massachusetts Bay, it stated that "This Court, taking into consideration the great neglect of many parents and masters in training up their children in learning and labor and other employments which may be profitable to the Commonwealth, so hereupon order and decree that in every town the chosen men appointed for managing the prudential affairs of the same shall henceforth stand charged with the care of the redress of this evil." On November 11, 1647, Massachusetts ordered that "every town in this jurisdiction, after the

Lord hath increased them to the number of 50 households, shall then forthwith appoint one within their town to teach all such children as shall resort to him to write and read, whose wages shall be paid either by the parents or masters of such children, or by the inhabitants in general." In 1852 the governor of Massachusetts ordered that children between the ages of 8 and 14 must attend school for 12 weeks in the year, six of which must be consecutive.

The first public school tax was an act providing "for the establishment of free schools," enacted January 15, 1825 by the State of Illinois. The tax was levied at the rate of 2%. The first schoolbook was the *New England Primer* of 1689-90 printed by R. Pierce, and sold by Benjamin Harris, at the London Coffee House in Boston. Middlesex County Association for the Improvement of Common

Schools was the first local education association, organized in Middlesex, Connecticut in May 1799. The first national education association, the American Institute of Instruction, was founded in Boston in 1830. The oldest educational magazine, the *Juvenile Mirror,* first appeared in New York City in 1811.

18 The Department of Education was founded by Act of Congress on March 2, 1867 as an agency for the "purpose of collecting such statistics and facts as shall show the condition and progress of education in the several states and territories, and of diffusing such information respecting the organization and management of school systems and methods of teaching as shall aid the people of the United States in the establishment and maintenance of efficient school systems and otherwise promote the cause of education." The first commissioner was Henry Barnard. The Act of July 28, 1868 abolished the Department of Education and created in its stead the Office of Education in the Department of Interior.

19 The first college in the United States was Harvard College, founded in 1636. It received £400 from the General Court of Massachusetts Bay and £800 and 300 books from the estate of John Harvard. The first commencement was held in 1642 and presided by Henry Dunster, the college's first president, who served from 1640 to 1654. Georgetown College, the first Catholic college, was established in Washington, D.C. in 1791. The first city college, the College of Charleston in Charleston, South Carolina, was founded in 1770, chartered in 1785, and opened in 1790. Oberlin Collegiate Institute, the first coeducational college, which opened in 1833. The first college to receive a royal charter was the Royal College of William and Mary in 1693. The first college for women was Mount Holyoke Seminary in South Hadley, Massachusetts, founded in 1837. The Cooper Union in New York City was the first college to prohibit discrimination on account of race, religion, or color, in 1851. The first state university was the University of Georgia in Athens, Georgia, chartered in 1785 and opened in 1801. Lincoln University, the first Black university, was chartered in 1854 as Ashmun Institute in Chester County, Pennsylvania. The first educational institution legally designated as a university was the University of the State of Pennsylvania in 1791, known since 1791 as the University of Pennsylvania. The first university founded by a federal land grant was Ohio University in Athens, Ohio, chartered in 1804 and opened in 1808. The first college alumni association was the Society of Alumni of Williams College, Williamstown, Massachusetts, founded in 1821. Yale University awarded the first doctorates in 1861 to Eugene Schuyler, James Morris Whiton, and Arthur Williams Wright.

20 Education ranks among the largest expenditure items in the national budget. It grew from $103.1 billion in 1960 to $371.9 billion in 1991. Of this amount, $224.4 billion was for elementary and secondary schools and $147.3

billion for colleges and universities; $302.1 billion was for the public sector and $69.7 billion for the private sector.

21 Reflecting the decline in birth rates in the baby bust years (1968-1978), the number of high school graduates will decline to approximately 2.464 million in 1993 but will rise again to 2.943 million in 2000.

22 College and university enrollments have grown continuously since the end of World War II and will reach approximately 15.692 million by 2000. Of these students, 55.8% will be females, 22.1% will be enrolled in private colleges, and 37.4% will be in two-year colleges. The total faculty strength will reach 955,000, of whom 30% will be in private colleges. This reflects a higher faculty/student ratio in private institutions.

23 In 1990, state governments bore the largest share of elementary and secondary school expenditures (45.4%), while nongovernmental sources bore the largest share of higher educational expenditures (56.2%).

24 Between 1970 and 1988, the share of the private sector in education rose only slightly (2.1%), from 17.1% to 19.2%.

25 The percentage of Whites is greater in private than in public schools. In 1991, White enrollment was 79.3% in public schools compared to 86.7% in private schools.

26 Until 1980, more males enrolled in college than females. In 1960, male enrollment was 2.3 million compared to a female enrollment of 1.2 million. In 1991, the relative numbers were 6.4 million and 7.6 million.

27 Blacks have made dramatic gains in the area of education since the end of World War II. In 1950, only 12.9% of Blacks over 25 were high school graduates and 2.1% held college degrees, whereas in 1991, 66.7% graduated high school and 11.5% graduated college. Median school years completed rose from 6.8 to 12.4 during the same period, to only 0.3 years less than the national average. The Black-White gap, however, is more prominent at the college level where Blacks trail the national average by 9.9%.

28 In 1991, 6.334 million of the total population of 11.370 million children between three and five were enrolled in nursery and kindergarten programs. Of the 2.824 million enrolled in nurseries, about two-thirds were enrolled in private nurseries. On the other hand, six out of seven children were enrolled in public kindergartens.

29 Of the 83,425 schools (not including colleges or universities) in the United States in 1990, there were 7,442 schools with fewer than 100 pupils, and 83 schools with more than 3,000 pupils.

30 Of all teachers, 12.2% moonlight all year and 8.4% moonlight during their summer break. The average starting salary of teachers of $21,542 in 1991 was lower than that of all other comparable professions.

31 Of all schools, 97.2% used computers as part of their curricula in 1990. The total number of microcomputers in elementary and secondary schools was 2.028 million, or one per 20.9 students.

32 In 1990, the number of children with disabilities in educational programs for the disabled was 4.261 million, of whom 48.5% were learning disabled, 22.9% speech impaired, and 13.3% mentally retarded.

33 The average tuition in 1988 was $3,382 in Catholic schools, $2,052 in other denominational schools, and $3,941 in non-sectarian schools.

34 Average Scholastic Aptitude Test (SAT) scores have been steadily declining in the United States from 466 for Verbal and 492 for Math in 1967 to 422 for Verbal and 474 for Math in 1991. In 1961, females (with an average of 468) did better in Verbal than males (who averaged 463), but their scores decreased in 1991 (418 for Verbal and 453 in Math) compared to relative scores for males (426 and 497). Only 7.2% of the participants scored above 600 in Verbal whereas 42.4% scored less than 400. The relative percentages in Math were 17.8% and 29.1%.

35 American College Testing (ACT) scores inched higher, from 19.9% in 1967 to 20.6% in 1991.

36 On proficiency tests in 1990, females scored higher than males in reading, lower than males in science, and about equally with males in mathematics. Blacks trailed Whites in all three areas by substantial margins.

37 The percentage of dropouts 16 to 24 years of age declined for all races between 1973 and 1990: from 11.6% to 9.0% for Whites, from 22.2% to 13.2% for Blacks, and from 33.5% to 32.4% for Hispanics.

38 With 1983=100, the Higher Education Price Index grew from 29.8 in 1965 to 133.1 in 1989. The two largest components of growth were fringe benefits, which grew from 13 to 159, and library acquisitions, which grew from 19.3 to 149.9.

39 In 1990, higher education institutions received $7.781 billion in gifts and grants. This was in addition to endowment earnings of $3.144 billion.

40 Charges (including tuition, room, and board) at private 4-year institutions grew from $4,076 in 1975 to $15,165 in 1990. Rates at public institutions also grew, although at a slower rate, from $1,760 in 1975 to $5,289 in 1990.

41 In 1991, 24% of college freshmen were A students, 57% B students, and 19% C students. The percentage of liberals among freshmen declined from 34% in 1970 to 23% in 1990, while during the same period moderates increased from 45% to 55% and conservatives increased from 17% to 20%.

42 In 1991, 408,000 foreign students were enrolled in U.S. institutions of higher education, compared to 179,000 in 1976. The largest contingent, by region, was from Asia which accounted for 263,000, and, by country, from Japan (37,000), China/Taiwan (34,000), and India (29,000). The flow of students from Iran declined from 51,000 in 1980 to 6,000 in 1990. For economic reasons, fewer African students are attending U.S. universities. In 1985, Nigeria had 18,000 students in the United States, but only 4,000 in 1991.

43 In 1990, 1.183 million students were enrolled in foreign language courses. The highest number of students enrolled in Spanish (533,600), followed by French (272,600) and German (33,400). Students still enroll in classical languages courses as well. Latin was chosen by 28,200 and Ancient Greek by 16,400. The number of students of Japanese grew from 1,700 in 1960 to 45,700, which made it the fifth most chosen language.

44 While women receiving bachelor's and master's degrees outnumbered men in 1990, men still received more doctoral degrees. Out of every 10 doctorates awarded, men received six and women four. From 1960 to 1989, women increased their share of professional degrees—from 5.5% to 33.2% in medicine, 0.8% to 26.1% in dentistry, 2.5% to 40.8% in law, and 2.3% (in 1970) to 22.7% in theology.

45 In 1990, nonresident aliens accounted for 10.3% of the graduate population but received 11% of the master's degrees and 21.5% of the doctorates. Their doctoral share was highest in fields such as engineering (48.2%), mathematics (47.6%), and computer and information science (38.1%).

46 In 1990, there were 34,613 libraries in the United States, including 9,060 public libraries and 4,593 academic libraries. College and university libraries have a combined holding of 718.5 million volumes to which 21.907 million volumes are added annually at a cost of $891.281 million. Harvard University, with 10.93 million volumes, has the largest university library.

47 National statistics on religious bodies were compiled and published between 1850 and 1936 by the Bureau of Census and since then by the magazine *Christian Herald*, the *Yearbook of American and Canadian Churches* (published by Abingdon Press), as well as decennially in *Churches and Church Membership* (by the Glenmary Research Center in Atlanta). Practically all national religious bodies compile reports or estimates from time to time based on records kept by local churches. Many of the larger denominations also publish these figures periodically. The data gathered by the denominations are designed primarily for their own use and thus vary in scope and nature. Further, local church records are kept by people untrained in statistical methods and thus may suffer in consistency. Denominations also differ in their definitions of membership; accordingly there are variations also in the bases of compilation. Thus, the Eastern Orthodox churches report estimates of the total number of persons within their cultural and nationality groups; Jews, the number of ethnic Jews in the community; Roman Catholics, Lutherans, and Episcopals the total number of baptized persons (including infants); and Protestants, those who have attained full membership and are active members. One denomination, the Church of Christ, Scientist, forbids the enumeration of its members as contrary to Scripture, and ceased reporting its membership figures from after 1936. The total of unreported membership is estimated at less than 1%. Another point to bear in mind is that these figures relate to membership and not to belief. Orthodoxy cannot be measured by numbers. The number of those who subscribe to some valid religious beliefs could conceivably be higher than membership numbers.

48 Religious statistics were included in nine censuses from 1850 to 1936. The early ones included the number of members as well as the number and value of edifices, but the 1880 data were not published. In 1906, the Census of Religious Bodies was published in two parts and was the first to be compiled by means of a questionnaire, to which 99% of those asked mailed returns. The compilation of 1926 is regarded by students of church statistics as the most adequate ever made. It reported a total membership of 50,495,104 (43% of total resident population) compared to 42,954,512 in 1916. The total reported religious membership was 147,607,000 in 1989 (59% of total resident population). This data appears to contradict the popular perception that institutional religion is in decline.

49 In 1990, church-affiliated Christians made up slightly less than one-half of the national population at 49.3%. By regions, the highest proportion of Christians was found in the Northeast (55%) followed by the Midwest (53%), the South (49.8%), and the West (37%). The states with the highest number of professing Christians were Utah (75.1%), Rhode Island (75%), North Dakota (73.8%), South Dakota (66.9%), Minnesota (64.9%), Wisconsin (64.4%), Massachusetts (64%), and Nebraska (63.1%). Christians formed more than half the population in Iowa (61.1%), Connecticut (60.8%), Pennsylvania (60.5%), New Mexico (58.9%), Oklahoma (57.9%), Alabama (57.3%), Louisiana (57.2%), Arkansas (56.1%), Mississippi (54.9%), Illinois (54.7%), Texas (54.5%), Kentucky (54.1%), Tennessee (54.1%), North Carolina (53.9%), Kansas (53.4%), New Jersey (53.3%), Missouri

(53.1%), South Carolina (51.3%), Idaho (50%). Generally, Western states had very low church membership. The states with the lowest percentages of Christians were in Nevada (29.1%), Alaska (30.6%), Washington (30.9%), Hawaii (33.1%), California (34.1%), Oregon (35.9%), and Colorado (36.4%). Jews comprised 2.4% of the national population, with the highest concentration in New York (10.3%). Other states with large Jewish communities were Florida, Massachusetts, and Maryland. In 31 states, Jews made up less than 1% of the population. The Jewish share of the population has consistently dropped from the early decades of the century when they formed over 5%. The main reasons for this decline are the rise in the immigration of non-Jews and growing intermarriage with gentiles.

50 Roman Catholics made up the largest single denomination in the United States in 1990, with a membership roll of 57 million. Other large denominations were Southern Baptist (14.9 million), Methodists (8.9 million), Presbyterians (2.8 million), Lutherans (2.6 million), Evangelical Lutherans (5.2 million), Episcopals (2.4 million), Mormons (4.1 million), Church of God in Christ (3.7 million), and Assemblies of God (2.1 million).

51 In 1990, the total number of pastors, priests, and other religious leaders was estimated at 340,094, serving 350,337 churches. The number of church edifices reported in the 1936 Census was 142,487.

52 The percentage of persons holding no religious beliefs grew from 3% in 1957 to 11% in 1990. Such disaffiliation was most severe among Protestants (56% in 1990 compared to 66% in 1957) but only slight among Catholics (25% in 1990 compared to 26% in 1957).

53 Statistics on recreation have not generally been compiled and published systematically. One major difficulty is in defining the term "recreation"; another is that even the compiled data remain in the files of the collecting agency. The National Park Service is the most dependable source. Since 1850, it has administered the large areas set aside for recreational purposes by Congress or by Executive Order. These include National Parks, National Seashores, National Monuments, National Historical and Military areas, and National Parkways. Data on Municipal Parks and State Parks come from the National Recreation and Park Association and data on National Forests from the Forest Service.

54 Information on travel is compiled annually by the Bureau of Economic Analysis and published periodically in the *Survey of Current Business*. Statistics on arrivals in the United States are reported by the U.S. Travel and Tourism Administration, and those on departures are reported in *International Air Travel Statistics*. Data on domestic travel are published by the Travel Data Center.

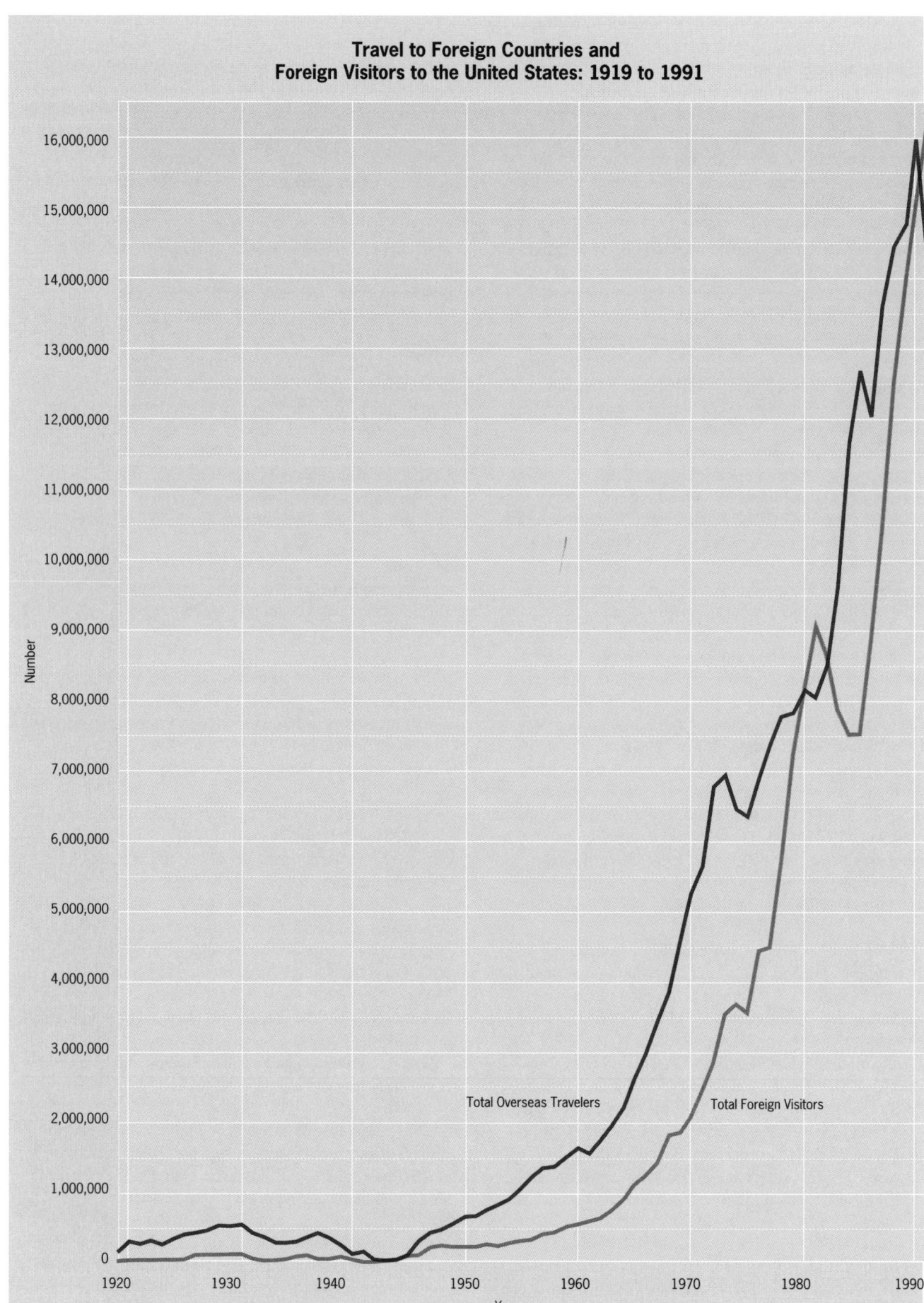

**Travel to Foreign Countries and
Foreign Visitors to the United States: 1919 to 1991**

Number

Total Overseas Travelers

Total Foreign Visitors

Year

55 In 1990, the highest number of tourists to the United States came from Japan, followed by the United Kingdom, Mexico, Germany, France, Australia, the Bahamas, Italy, Brazil and Switzerland.

56 The 10 most popular sports activities in 1990 were: exercise walking, swimming, bicycle riding, camping, fishing, bowling, exercising with equipment, basketball, jogging, and aerobic exercising. More women than men exercised by walking, swimming, and aerobic exercising. Among men, the most popular sports were swimming, bicycle riding, and fishing.

57 In 1990, horseracing was the most popular spectator sport, with an annual attendance of 63.8 million. It was followed by baseball (55.5 million), football (36.6 million), basketball (33 million), and greyhound racing (28.6 million). Hockey (12.5 million) and jai alai (5.3 million) were also popular.

58 Among selected recreational activities, the most popular in 1990 was tenpin bowling with 71 million participants, followed by softball (41 million), golf (27.8 million), and tennis (18.4 million). The number of boats in the United States was 16 million, of which 7.9 million were outboard boats, 2.1 million inboard boats, 1.3 million sailboats, and 2.2 million rowboats.

59 The number of drive-in motion picture theaters declined from 4,000 in 1970 to 1,000 in 1990. They may soon disappear. On the other hand, four-wall theaters grew in number during the same period from 10,000 to 23,000. The average admission price grew from $1.55 in 1970 to $4.75 in 1990. As a result, although the attendance remained relatively steady (growing from 921 million in 1970 to 1.058 billion in 1990), box office receipts quadrupled from $1.225 billion in 1970 to $5.022 billion in 1990.

60 The growth in leisure time for Americans is reflected in the growth of sporting goods sales from $16.691 billion in 1980 to $45.056 billion in 1991, or from 1.7% of all retail sales to 2.4%. In 1988 alone, sales grew by 24%. The largest items were pleasure boats ($7.524 billion), recreational vehicles ($3.486 billion), bicycles ($2.544 billion), firearms and hunting equipment ($2.364 billion), golf equipment ($1.252 billion), and gym shoes and sneakers ($1.212 billion).

61 Legitimate theater (Broadway) lost ground in the 1980s. The number of new productions dropped from 62 in 1970 to 29 in 1989 and the number of tickets sold from $9.380 million in 1980 to 7.968 million in 1990. However, as a result of sharply higher ticket prices, gross box office receipts grew from $53.3 million to $262 million during the same period. The number of nonprofit professional theaters grew from 39 in 1975 to 192 in 1990. Although their gross income grew to $349 million, it fell short of their expenses by $200,000, and as a result they have been barely able to survive. Total attendance at these theaters in 1989 was 18.7 million compared to 5.4 million in 1975.

62 The number of opera companies doubled from 648 in 1970 to 1,285 in 1989. Of these, 209 were considered major (with budgets over $100,000) in 1989. They performed 731 operas and 279 musicals of which 169 were world premieres. Total attendance was 21.4 million. Symphony orchestras have grown more slowly, from 1,441 in 1970 to 1,866 in 1989. Their 17,774 concerts in 1989 were attended by 23.6 million but earned a total profit of only $9.5 million.

63 In 1990, total support for the arts was $1.173 billion, of which $242.842 million represented state appropriations for arts, $171.1 million the National Endowment for the Arts (NEA) appropriations, $125.2 million the National Endowment for the Humanities (NEH) appropriations, and $634 million grants from private business corporations. Grants from the NEA and the NEH rose dramatically over the past two decades, from $15.7 million and $13 million respectively in 1970 to $170.8 million and $141 million respectively in 1990.

64 Americans took 422.3 million vacation trips and 280 million weekend trips in 1990. On pleasure trips, the average mileage per trip was 867, but the number of nights spent on a trip declined from 5.6 in 1980 to 4.4 in 1990. Of the travelers, 77% went by car (7% by rental cars) and 18% by plane, and 37% stayed in a hotel.

65 California leads all states in domestic travel expenditures with $38.241 billion, followed by Florida ($24.437 billion), New York ($18.301 billion), Texas ($15.543 billion), Illinois ($10.865 billion), Nevada ($9.753 billion), New Jersey ($8.974 billion), Pennsylvania ($8.664 billion), Virginia ($7.827 billion), and Ohio ($7.253 billion). South Dakota ($6.79 billion) is the state least favored as a tourist destination.

66 In 1990, more than half of all U.S. tourists visited Europe, which also accounted for over half of all tourist expenditures. Of the 15.990 million U.S. tourists abroad, 8.043 million visited Europe and spent $14.403 billion.

67 In 1991, the number of foreign tourists in the United States was almost equal to the number of U.S. tourists abroad, at 42.114 million and 42.320 million respectively. However, foreign tourists spent more money in the United States than U.S. tourists abroad. As a result, foreign tourist expenditures in the United States ($59.387 billion) exceeds by $10.680 billion U.S. expenditures abroad ($48.707 billion).

68 The travel industry has become one of the largest sectors of the U.S. economy, with total receipts in 1990 of $334.881 billion. Eating and drinking places accounted for over one-half at $182.44 billion, followed by motels and hotels ($60.490 billion), air fares ($45.324 billion), and amusement and recreation ($44.135 billion).

69 The pet population has remained fairly steady in recent years: 54.6 million cats, 52.4 million dogs, 12.9 million pet birds and 6.6 million horses. While the number of horses has remained steady, that of cats and birds rose slightly, and that of dogs declined. However, dogs remain the most popular of pets, with 38.2% of all households owning at least one, followed by 28.4% of all households owning a cat. Total veterinary care expenditures were $3.012 billion for dogs, $1.573 billion for cats, and $330 million for horses.

70 Technology has dramatically changed the music recording industry. In 1975, 421 million phonograph records were sold for $1.695 billion, and 110.8 million prerecorded cassettes for $681.8 million. Compact discs had not yet been invented. In 1991, the sales of phonograph records were down to 26.8 million units for $93.3 million, and prerecorded cassette sales rose to 429.1 million units for $3.250 billion. But the sales of both were overshadowed by CDs, which sold 333.3 million units for $4.337 billion.

71 Like telephones, cameras have become virtually universal items, with 91.9% of all households owning at least one. Between 1985 and 1988, the percentage of households owning videocassette recorders and video camera/camcorders grew from 20.9% to 66.5% and from 2.2% to 7.2% respectively.

72 In 1990, 2 billion books were sold in the United States at a cost of $19.043 billion. Although more paperback books than hardbound ones were sold (1.181 billion against 824 million), the latter brought in more revenues ($11.789 billion) than the former ($7.254 billion). General retailers sold almost half the units, with college stores, schools, direct mail, and libraries accounting for the balance. One-third of the units sold was trade, and about one-fourth, mass market paperbacks. The number of titles issued annually peaked in 1989 at 53,446, declined to 41,223 in 1991, and then rebounded slightly in 1992 and 1993. The percentage share of subject categories has remained virtually unchanged over the years, with sociology and economics leading and followed by juveniles, fiction, medicine, science, technology, religion, history, literature, biography, philosophy and psychology, and business. The average price of a hardbound book rose from $24.64 in 1980 to $39.91 in 1990, of a mass market book from $3.36 (in 1985) to $4.47 in 1990, and of a trade paperback from $8.60 in 1980 to $16.62 in 1990. The annual subscription rates of journals rose across the board even more sharply, from $34.54 in 1980 to $104.36 in 1990. The rise was most marked in science and technology; the average subscription price of journals in chemistry and physics in 1990 was $472.84.

73 Under the U.S. Constitution, law enforcement is a function of state and municipal governments. Under federal jurisdiction are offenses against the U.S. government and against or by its employees while engaged on official duties, and offenses which involve the crossing of state lines or interfere with interstate commerce. Excluding the military and the federal jurisdictions, there are 51 separate criminal law jurisdictions: one in each of the 50 states and one in the District of Columbia. Each of these has its own criminal law and procedure and its own law enforcement agencies with substantial differences in penalties for like offenses. While almost all of them follow the Anglo-Saxon Common Law, Louisiana's legal heritage, for example, is largely French and Continental.

74 The major sources of law enforcement and criminal justice data are the Federal Bureau of Investigation and the Bureau of Justice Statistics. The latter has emerged in recent years as an incomparable data provider, publishing such reports as *Sourcebook of Criminal Justice Statistics, Criminal Victimization in the United States, Prisoners in State and Federal Institutions, Children in Custody, National Surveys of Courts, Census of State Correctional Facilities, Survey of Prison Inmates, Parole in the United States, Capital Punishment,* and *Expenditure and Employment Data for the Criminal Justice System.* The FBI's major publication is *Crime in the United States.* It grew out of the Uniform Crime Reporting Program initiated in 1930 by the International Association of Chiefs of Police. In 1958, a special committee was appointed to study the program. The 22 recommendations in their report were incorporated in the *Uniform Crime Reports,* beginning with the 1958 issue. Its major innovations were the Crime Index and the Crime Rates per 100,000. Offenses are divided into two groups designated Part I and Part II. Part I offenses make up the Crime Index. The original seven FBI Index offenses are: murder and nonnegligent manslaughter, forcible rape, robbery, aggravated assault, burglary, larceny, and motor vehicle theft. Arson was added as the eighth Index offense in 1979. The FBI reports are complemented by the National Crime Survey (NCS) of the Bureau of Justice Statistics. NCS data come directly from the victims and include offenses reported to the police as well as those not reported. When an offense involves more than one criminal act, it is counted only once under the more serious category.

75 The earliest statistics on the courts were collected and published by the Bureau of Census from 1932 to 1945. There are several types of courts with varying degrees of jurisdiction: Original, Appellate, General, and Limited or Special. The 94 federal courts of original jurisdiction are known as District Courts.

76 Statistics on prisoners were collected by the Bureau of Census in connection with each decennial Census of Population from 1850 to 1890. Independent enumerations of prisoners were made in 1904, 1910, 1923, and 1933. The first nationwide collection of data was made in 1926 by the Bureau of Census which published an annual summary until 1950. From 1950 to 1971, the data were published by the FBI, from 1971 to 1979 by the Law Enforcement Assistance Administration, and since 1979 by the Bureau of Justice Statistics.

77 Between 1980 and 1990, the number of criminal offenses grew by 8% but the crime rate per 100,000 declined by 2.2%. This decline in the crime rate resulted from a 4.9% drop in property crime rate, whereas the violent crime rate during the same period rose by 22.6%. The highest growth in the number of offenses took place between 1985 and 1990 when violent crime grew by 36.9%. Aggravated assault grew the most; by 45.9% in number and 39.9% in rate per 100,000.

78 In 1990, the 10 states with the highest crime rates per 100,000 were Florida (8,811), Arizona (7,889), Texas (7,827), Georgia (6,764), New Mexico (6,684), California (6,604), Louisiana (6,487), New York (6,364), Washington (6,223), and Hawaii (6,107). The states with the lowest crime rates were West Virginia (2,503), South Dakota (2,909), North Dakota (2,922), Kentucky (3,299) and Mississippi (3,869).

79 In 1990, the 15 cities with the highest crime rates per 100,000 were Atlanta (19,236), Miami (19,024), Tampa (17,125), Newark, NJ (16,256), Dallas (15,520), Fort Worth (14,977), St. Louis (14,671), Kansas City, MO (12,953), Seattle (12,601), Charlotte, NC (12,594), San Antonio (12,477), New Orleans (12,436), Baton Rouge (12,384), St. Petersburg (12,289), and Detroit (12,192). The cities with the lowest crime rates were San Jose (4,869), Anchorage (5,747), Virginia Beach (5.779), Honolulu (6,102) and Louisville (6,424).

80 Although Blacks form only 12.3% of the total population, they make up nearly one half of all homicide victims. Of the 22,909 homicide victims in 1989, 10,962 were Black. The Black homicide rate per 100,000 was 61.1 for males and 12.9 for females, compared to the White homicide rate of 8.2 for males and 2.8 for females.

81 The forcible rape rate for 100,000 females over 12 grew from 46.3 in 1970 to 96.6 in 1990. The rate fluctuates widely over the years. In some years, there is a sharp drop as in 1982 when it was -5.6, but in 1990 it grew by 8.1.

82 In 1990, one in 13 Americans was a victim of a violent crime, according to the National Crime Survey; 23.7% of all households were touched by at least one criminal incident. Blacks were more often victimized than Whites; the relative rates were 40 per 1,000 for Blacks and 28 per 1,000 for Whites. Most crimes, including 41.2% of robberies and 20% of assaults, took place on a street; except for rape—35% of which took place within the home of the victim. Of all criminal incidents, 31.7% involved firearms and 26.6% involved handguns; therefore, 5.1% of all criminal incidents were due to non-handgun firearms.

83 In 1987, the number of neglected and abused children reached 2.025 million, up from 765,000 in 1980. Of the total, 15.7% were involved in sexual abuse cases.

84 Of the 11.25 million persons arrested in 1990; 81.6% were males, 5.3% under 15 years, 15.6% under 18 years, and 30.1% between 18 to 24 years. The rates drop sharply after the age of 45; only 0.7% were over 65, and 1.8% between 55 and 64. The largest number of arrests was for driving while intoxicated (1.391 million), larceny-theft (1.241 million) and drunkenness (717,000). In 1991, 1.152 million people (including 1.095 million Mexicans) were arrested by the Immigration Border Patrol.

85 The arrest rates for drug abuse violations per 100,000 grew from 256 in 1980 to 437.5 in 1990. Heroin or cocaine (the Drug Enforcement Agency does not distinguish between the two) remains the most popular drug, with arrest rates for its sale, manufacture, and possession accounting for more than half the total arrests. In 1990, 222,518 kg. of heroin, cocaine, and marijuana were seized. In 1991, narcotics worth $910 million were seized by the Immigration Border Patrol.

86 In 1987, there were 15,118 law enforcement agencies in the United States, with 757,508 employees and $28.071 billion in expenditures. Local police accounted for 79.3% of the agencies, 65.2% of the employees, and 64.2% of the expenditures.

87 In 1990, the states with the most police personnel per 10,000 population were Nevada (39.9), New Jersey (39.5), New York (37.0), Wyoming (34.1), Illinois (33.2), Florida (31.3), and Maryland (30.4). The states with the fewest police personnel per 10,000 were West Virginia (17.0), North Dakota (19.5), Kentucky (19.7), and Minnesota (19.9).

88 The number of lawyers in the United States rose from 285,933 in 1960 to 723,189 in 1988, a 252% growth. The percentage of female lawyers rose from 2.6% to 19.1% during the same period.

89 In 1990, the median time between the commencement and disposition of appeals in the U.S. Courts of Appeals was 10.1 months. About 79% of the appeals were successful.

90 Of the 217,879 civil suits in 1990, 46,039 were contract actions, 43,759 were tort actions, 118,465 were actions under statutes (such as civil rights), 13,841 were labor disputes, 908 were environmental matters, and 407 were suits under the Freedom of Information Act.

91 In 1990, 1,176 public officials were indicted and 1,084 convicted for corruption, compared to 255 indicted and 179 convicted in 1975. Of the total indicted in 1990, more than half were Federal officials (615).

92 In 1989, 1.189 million juveniles were convicted of violent, property, and delinquency offenses. Of these, 77,000 were violent offenses, 514,000 property offenses, and 599,000 delinquency offenses. During that year, 96,148 juveniles were in custody, 58,303 in public institutions, and 37,845 in private institutions.

93 The prisoner population in 1990 was 738,894, up from 212,953 in 1960. Blacks formed 43% of the jail population, but comprised only 12.3% of the total population.

94 The campaign against the death penalty was successful enough in the early 1970s to bring all executions to a halt. From 1968 to 1976 no one was executed in the United States. The steep rise in homicides in that decade led to a clamor for the restoration of the death penalty in most states. Between 1977 and 1980, three people were executed. From 1980 to 1990, 140 people were executed; of these, 56 were Black.

95 In 1990, there were 2.019 million fires in the United States, resulting in total property damage of $8.609 billion. Of these, 624,000 structure fires were of incendiary or suspicious origin.

Series H 1-31. Social Welfare Expenditures Under Public Programs: 1890 to 1989

(In millions of dollars. Years ending June 30 for Federal government, most states and some localities)

Year	Total	Total expenditures Percent of gross national product	Percent of all government expenditures [1]	Total social insurance	Total public aid	Total education	Total veterans' programs	Total other social welfare
	1	2	3	5	14	17	21	28
1989	956,000	18.6	53.0	468,055	127,475	238,631	30,104	16,609
1988	886,000	18.5	52.8	434,048	118,495	219,382	29,254	15,480
1987	833,000	18.8	53.4	415,023	110,695	201,540	28,051	15,278
1986	782,786	18.5	52.2	390,769	104,602	189,276	27,445	14,161
1985	731,000	18.5	52.2	372,529	98,086	172,103	27,042	13,552
1984	678,116	18.2	52.8	341,120	91,661	157,189	26,275	13,295
1983	643,437	19.3	54.5	331,161	86,644	141,815	25,802	12,466
1982	595,869	19.4	55.7	302,615	80,852	133,874	24,708	11,654
1981	550,841	18.6	56.9	267,395	82,424	128,145	23,441	11,983
1980	492,000	18.4	57.1	229,754	71,799	121,050	21,446	13,599
1979	430,280	17.5	58.4	194,288	64,622	109,262	20,602	11,076
1978	394,377	19.3	57.8	175,090	59,394	101,519	19,744	10,563
1977	360,602	19.6	59.4	160,883	53,266	93,878	19,015	9,071
1976	331,955	20.4	60.3	145,703	48,693	87,730	18,958	8,472
1975	289,000	19.0	56.6	123,013	41,308	80,834	17,019	6,947
1974	239,397	17.6	58.5	99,002	31,520	70,534	14,112	6,722
1973	213,942	17.3	55.5	86,166	28,691	64,734	13,026	5,698
1972	191,357	17.2	53.2	74,809	26,078	59,385	11,522	5,364
1971	171,908	16.9	51.7	66,369	21,262	56,705	10,456	4,983
1970	145,893	15.3	47.8	54,676	16,488	50,848	9,018	4,409
1969	127,149	14.1	44.7	48,772	13,439	43,673	7,934	3,792
1968	113,840	13.8	43.2	42,740	11,092	40,590	7,247	3,285
1967	99,710	12.9	42.4	37,339	8,811	35,808	6,898	2,848
1966	88,000	12.2	43.4	31,934	7,301	32,825	6,358	2,309
1965	77,175	11.8	42.4	28,123	6,283	28,108	6,031	2,066
1964	71,491	11.7	40.0	26,971	5,642	24,989	5,862	1,746
1963	66,766	11.6	39.5	26,614	5,296	22,671	5,751	1,593
1962	62,659	11.6	39.4	24,194	4,945	21,005	5,654	1,415
1961	58,236	11.5	39.3	22,365	4,444	19,337	5,624	1,343
1960	52,293	10.6	38.0	19,307	4,101	17,626	5,479	1,139
1959	49,821	10.6	(2)	18,287	3,998	16,498	5,472	1,010
1958	45,457	10.3	(2)	15,957	3,615	15,313	5,427	920
1957	39,350	9.1	(2)	12,472	3,309	13,732	5,119	823
1956	35,131	8.6	(2)	10,646	3,115	12,154	5,061	735
1955	32,640	8.6	32.7	9,835	3,003	11,157	4,834	619
1954	29,547	8.2	(2)	8,265	2,788	10,084	4,631	612
1953	27,045	7.5	(2)	6,607	2,728	9,231	4,735	503
1952	25,576	7.6	(2)	5,671	2,585	8,246	5,256	451
1951	24,055	7.7	(2)	4,772	2,592	7,415	5,996	462
1950	23,508	8.9	37.6	4,947	2,496	6,674	6,866	448
1949	21,165	8.1	(2)	4,186	2,089	5,807	6,927	396
1948	18,652	7.6	(2)	3,603	1,702	4,897	6,638	369
1947	17,337	7.8	(2)	4,160	1,442	4,089	5,683	316
1946	12,798	6.1	(2)	3,652	1,151	3,297	2,403	233
1945	9,205	4.4	8.4	1,409	1,031	3,076	1,126	198
1944	8,228	4.1	(2)	1,256	1,032	2,800	720	182
1943	8,283	4.7	(2)	1,259	1,550	2,793	623	159
1942	8,609	6.1	(2)	1,376	2,777	2,694	645	154
1941	8,953	8.0	(2)	1,330	3,524	2,617	613	136

See footnotes at end of chart.

Series H 1-31. Social Welfare Expenditures Under Public Programs: 1890 to 1989—Cont'd.

(In millions of dollars. Years ending June 30 for Federal government, most states and some localities)

	Total expenditures							
Year	Total	Percent of gross national product	Percent of all government expenditures [1]	Total social insurance	Total public aid	Total education	Total veterans' programs	Total other social welfare
	1	2	3	5	14	17	21	28
1940	8,795	9.2	49.0	1,272	3,597	2,561	629	116
1939	9,213	10.5	(2)	1,181	4,230	2,504	606	114
1938	7,924	9.0	(2)	849	3,233	2,563	627	108
1937	7,858	9.1	(2)	545	3,436	2,376	893	105
1936	10,184	13.2	(2)	456	3,079	2,228	3,826	101
1935	6,548	9.5	48.6	406	2,998	2,008	597	99
1934	5,832	9.7	(2)	362	2,531	1,914	530	96
1933	4,462	7.9	(2)	344	689	2,104	819	89
1932	4,303	6.4	(2)	355	256	2,352	825	81
1931	4,201	5.1	(2)	368	164	2,440	744	79
1930	4,085	4.2	(2)	361	78	2,523	668	78
1929	3,921	3.9	36.3	342	60	2,434	658	76
1913	1,000	2.5	34.0	15	(3)	525	196	3 114
1890	318	2.4	38.0	—	(3)	146	113	3 41

Z Less than $500,000.

[1] Government expenditures exclude workmen's compensation and temporary disability insurance payments made through private insurance carriers and self-insurers, although these (payable under statutory provisions) are included as social welfare expenditures, series H 1.

[2] Not computed.

[3] "Public aid" included with "Other social welfare."

Series H 48-56. Civilian Labor Force and Workers Covered Under Government Social Insurance Programs: 1934 to 1990

(In millions. As of December except as indicated. OASDHI=Old Age, Survivors, Disability and Health Insurance)

| | Civilian labor force | | | Retirement systems | | | | |
Year	Total [1]	Paid employees	OASDHI [2]	Railroad retirement	Public employee [3]	Workman's compensation	Unemployment insurance [4]	Temporary disability insurance [5]
	48	**49**	**51**	**52**	**53**	**54**	**55**	**56**
1990	126.2	117.0	109.8	0.3	5.9	96.7	110.8	—
1989	125.7	117.4	110.1	0.3	5.9	95.3	109.1	22.2
1988	123.8	115.6	108.4	0.3	5.8	92.8	106.9	21.8
1987	122.0	113.3	106.0	0.3	5.9	90.0	103.7	21.6
1986	119.8	110.2	102.9	0.3	5.9	87.2	100.2	20.3
1985	117.5	107.7	100.3	0.3	6.0	85.1	98.2	19.8
1984	115.7	105.5	98.0	0.4	6.0	83.4	95.8	19.3
1983	113.5	102.2	92.7	0.4	6.4	80.5	91.3	18.7
1982	112.7	98.4	88.9	0.4	6.4	78.1	87.9	18.1
1981	110.7	99.0	89.5	0.5	6.4	79.8	89.9	18.4
1980	106.9	98.9	89.3	0.5	6.6	79.1	87.2	18.4
1979	106.0	98.6	(NA)	(NA)	(NA)	(NA)	(NA)	(NA)
1978	103.7	93.9	(NA)	0.6	5.5	78.1	82.9	18.0
1977	100.6	92.2	83.5	0.5	5.5	74.2	75.8	16.7
1976	98.1	89.0	79.7	0.5	5.5	70.9	72.1	16.2
1975	94.9	86.2	75.7	0.5	5.5	68.6	69.7	16.7
1974	—	87.1	75.2	0.6	5.5	67.8	69.5	15.7
1973	—	85.9	75.6	0.6	5.3	68.6	69.0	16.0
1972	—	83.5	72.6	0.6	5.2	63.4	66.0	16.0
1971	—	81.5	69.8	0.6	5.2	60.5	57.1	14.8
1970	83.2	70.8	69.2	0.6	4.8	58.7	55.8	14.6
1969	81.4	71.0	68.6	0.7	4.6	60.0	57.0	14.8
1968	79.1	68.8	67.1	0.7	4.5	58.3	55.5	14.2
1967	78.1	67.3	65.7	0.7	4.6	56.3	53.8	14.0
1966	77.3	65.7	64.9	0.7	4.6	55.1	52.8	13.7
1965	75.6	63.6	62.8	0.8	4.1	52.5	50.3	13.3
1964	73.8	60.8	60.1	0.8	3.9	50.0	47.9	12.7
1963	72.5	59.1	58.5	0.8	3.7	48.2	46.3	12.5
1962	71.4	58.0	57.3	0.8	4.0	46.8	45.4	12.3
1961	70.6	56.3	56.1	0.8	4.0	46.0	44.6	11.8
1960 *	70.5	55.3	55.7	0.9	3.9	44.6	43.7	11.3
1959	69.3	55.1	55.4	0.9	3.8	45.1	44.1	11.4
1958	68.1	53.7	53.4	1.0	3.9	42.7	42.6	11.0
1957	67.8	53.9	53.7	1.1	3.9	43.1	43.2	11.2
1956	67.0	54.1	53.2	1.2	4.5	44.1	43.8	11.5
1955	66.6	53.4	51.8	1.3	4.7	42.9	41.7	11.2
1954	63.5	50.0	45.3	1.2	4.6	40.4	37.2	10.7
1954 (monthly average)	64.5	49.8	45.3	1.2	4.5	39.7	36.6	10.6
1949 (monthly average)	62.1	45.9	34.3	1.4	4.4	35.3	33.1	5.3
1944 (monthly average)	54.6	41.9	30.8	1.7	4.7	33.0	31.6	.2
1939 (monthly average)	55.2	33.2	24.0	1.2	2.0	22.0	22.4	—
1934 (monthly average)	52.2	28.9	—	—	1.4	17.0	—	—

* Denotes first year for which figures include Alaska and Hawaii.
[1] Bureau of the Census total of persons 14 years old and over (16 and over, beginning December 1967) in the civilian labor force; includes unpaid family members and the unemployed, not shown separately.
[2] Beginning 1955, includes persons covered under both a government retirement system and OASDHI (about 5.3 million in December 1970); excludes persons whose coverage was authorized on an elective or optional basis but not in effect (about 3.5 million in December 1970); also excludes railroad employees jointly covered by OASDHI and their own retirement program.
[3] Excludes persons covered under both a government retirement system and OASDHI; see footnote 2.
[4] State, railroad and federal employee programs.
[5] State and railroad programs. Excludes government employees covered by sick-leave provisions.

Series H 346-367. Public Assistance—Payments, Recipients and Average Monthly Payments: 1936 to 1990

(As of December. Through 1942, conterminous U.S. only; thereafter, data include Alaska and Hawaii; beginning 1950, Puerto Rico and Virgin Islands; beginning 1959, Guam)

Year	Payments for year [1] (mil. dollars)				Number of recipients (1,000)				Average monthly payment per recipient (dollars)			
	Old age assistance	Aid to the blind	Aid to the permanently and totally disabled	Aid to families with dependent children	Old-age assistance	Aid to the blind	Aid to the permanently and totally disabled	Aid to families with dependent children	Old-age assistance	Aid to the blind	Aid to the permanently and totally disabled	Aid to families with dependent children
	350	351	352	353	355	356	357	358	362	363	364	365
1990	3,736	334	12,521	19,067	1,454	84	3,279	4,218	213	342	337	392
1989	3,476	316	11,180	17,466	1,439	83	3,071	3,875	199	320	309	383
1988	3,299	302	10,177	16,827	1,433	83	2,948	3,752	188	306	294	379
1987	3,194	291	9,458	16,373	1,455	83	2,486	3,734	181	297	287	365
1986	3,096	277	8,700	16,033	1,473	83	2,713	3,777	174	287	282	358
1985	3,035	264	7,755	15,196	1,504	82	2,551	3,721	164	274	261	341
1984	2,973	249	7,143	14,505	1,530	81	2,419	3,674	158	265	256	335
1983	2,814	229	6,357	13,838	1,515	79	2,307	3,721	158	256	245	321
1982	2,824	217	5,909	12,878	1,549	77	2,231	3,596	146	242	229	310
1981	2,818	206	5,566	12,981	1,678	79	2,262	3,833	138	228	214	302
1980	2,734	190	5,014	12,475	1,808	78	2,256	3,843	128	213	198	288
1979	2,526	166	4,381	11,069	1,872	77	2,201	3,560	123	212	182	271
1978	2,433	152	3,966	10,730	1,968	77	2,172	3,488	100	164	155	256
1977	2,448	146	3,709	10,604	2,051	77	2,109	3,547	97	159	150	250
1976	2,508	138	3,422	10,141	2,148	76	2,012	3,585	94	153	146	242
1975	2,605	131	3,142	9,211	2,307	74	1,933	3,568	91	147	141	229
1974	2,503	130	2,602	7,917	2,286	75	1,636	3,323	92	143	144	216
1973	1,743	104	1,610	7,212	1,852	78	1,217	3,156	78	111	110	195
1972	1,894	105	1,393	7,020	2,933	80	1,169	3,123	80	113	106	192
1971	1,923	100	1,085	5,653	2,024	80	1,068	2,918	78	106	102	191
1970	1,866	98	1,000	4,853	2,082	81	935	2,552	77.65	104.35	97.65	187.95
1969	1,850	94	827	3,565	2,074	81	803	1,875	73.90	98.75	90.15	176.05
1968	1,779	91	692	2,851	2,027	81	702	1,522	69.55	92.15	82.65	168.15
1967	1,859	90	612	2,280	2,073	83	646	1,297	70.15	90.45	80.60	161.70
1966	1,908	90	566	1,924	2,073	84	588	1,127	68.05	86.85	74.75	150.10
1965	2,046	90	561	1,809	2,087	85	557	1,054	63.10	81.35	66.50	136.95
1964	2,039	98	473	1,634	2,120	95	509	1,012	63.65	76.15	62.25	131.30
1963	2,023	96	415	1,466	2,152	97	464	954	62.80	73.95	59.85	122.40
1962	1,955	94	359	1,386	2,183	99	428	932	61.55	71.95	58.50	119.10
1961	1,886	93	316	1,228	2,229	103	389	916	57.60	68.05	57.05	114.65
1960	1,922	94	287	1,056	2,305	107	369	803	58.90	67.45	56.15	108.35
1959	1,875	90	259	995	2,370	108	346	776	56.70	65.60	54.15	103.70
1958	1,824	87	228	891	2,438	110	325	755	56.95	63.55	53.80	100.40
1957	1,768	83	200	750	2,480	108	290	667	55.50	62.20	52.35	95.15
1956	1,671	77	176	660	2,499	107	266	615	53.25	60.00	50.70	91.50
1955	1,606	71	156	633	2,538	104	241	602	50.05	55.55	48.75	85.50
1954	1,590	68	137	590	2,553	102	222	604	48.70	54.35	48.35	83.70
1953	1,597	66	116	559	2,582	100	192	547	48.90	54.05	47.90	82.30
1952	1,527	61	91	551	2,635	98	161	596	48.80	53.50	48.40	82.10
1951	1,469	56	58	559	2,701	97	124	592	44.55	48.05	46.45	75.80
1950	1,485	53	8	556	2,786	97	69	651	43.05	46.00	44.10	71.45
1949	1,373	48	—	472	2,736	93	X	599	44.75	46.10	X	74.20
1948	1,128	41	—	363	2,498	86	X	475	42.00	43.55	X	71.90
1947	986	36	—	294	2,332	81	X	416	37.40	39.60	X	63.00
1946	820	31	—	208	2,196	77	X	346	35.30	36.65	X	62.25

See footnotes at end of chart.

Series H 346-367.   Public Assistance—Payments, Recipients and Average Monthly Payments: 1936 to 1990—Cont'd.

(As of December. Through 1942, conterminous U.S. only; thereafter, data include Alaska and Hawaii; beginning 1950, Puerto Rico and Virgin Islands; beginning 1959, Guam)

Year	Payments for year [1] (mil. dollars)				Number of recipients (1,000)				Average monthly payment per recipient (dollars)			
	Old-age assistance	Aid to the blind	Aid to the permanently and totally	Aid to families with dependent children	Old-age assistance	Aid to the blind	Aid to the permanently and totally disabled	Aid to families with dependent children	Old-age assistance	Aid to the blind	Aid to the permanently and totally disabled	Aid to families with dependent children
	350	351	352	353	355	356	357	358	362	363	364	365
1945	726	27	—	150	2,056	71	X	274	30.90	33.50	X	52.05
1944	691	25	—	135	2,066	72	X	254	28.45	29.30	X	45.60
1943	650	25	—	140	2,149	76	X	272	26.65	27.95	X	41.55
1942	593	25	—	158	2,230	79	X	349	23.35	26.55	X	36.25
1941	540	23	—	153	2,238	77	X	391	21.25	25.80	X	33.65
1940	473	22	—	133	2,070	73	X	372	20.25	25.35	X	32.40
1939	434	20	—	115	1,912	70	X	316	19.30	25.45	X	31.75
1938	395	19	—	98	1,779	67	X	281	19.55	25.20	X	31.95
1937	310	16	—	71	1,579	56	X	229	19.45	27.20	X	31.50
1936	156	13	—	50	1,108	45	X	162	18.80	26.10	X	29.85

X Represents zero.   [1] Beginning 1950, includes vendor payments for medical care.

Series H 398-411. Private Philanthropy—Estimated Fund Flows by Donors and Recipients: 1929 to 1990

(In billions of dollars)

| | Philanthropy payments by donors | | | | | Philanthropy revenues of recipients | | |
Year	Living donors	Charitable bequests	Corporation contributions	Foundation grants	Total	Religious organizations	Higher education	Hospitals and health
	399	400	401	402	405	406	408	409
1990	101.8	7.8	5.9	5.9	122.6	65.8	12.4	9.9
1989	96.8	7.0	5.6	5.6	115.9	62.5	11.0	9.9
1988	86.5	6.6	5.4	5.4	104.6	55.6	10.2	9.6
1987	75.9	6.6	5.0	5.0	93.4	48.7	9.8	9.2
1986	74.6	5.7	5.2	5.2	90.9	41.7	9.4	8.4
1985	65.9	4.8	4.5	4.5	80.1	38.2	8.2	7.7
1984	58.6	4.0	4.1	4.1	70.7	35.6	7.3	6.8
1983	53.5	3.9	3.6	3.6	64.7	31.8	6.7	6.7
1982	48.5	5.2	2.9	3.2	59.8	28.1	6.0	6.2
1981	46.4	3.6	2.5	3.1	55.6	25.1	5.8	5.8
1980	40.7	2.9	2.4	2.8	48.7	22.2	5.0	5.3
1979	36.5	2.2	2.3	2.2	43.3	20.1	6.0	6.0
1978	32.8	2.6	2.1	2.6	40.1	18.5	5.6	5.5
1977	29.3	3.0	1.7	2.0	36.0	16.9	4.8	4.9
1976	26.6	2.4	1.5	2.1	32.5	14.2	4.5	4.9
1975	23.5	2.2	1.2	2.0	28.6	12.8	4.0	4.4
1974	22.3	2.1	1.2	2.1	27.7	11.9	4.1	4.3
1973	20.4	2.0	1.2	2.0	25.6	10.5	4.1	4.2
1972	16.9	2.7	.8	2.2	22.6	9.7	3.5	3.6
1971	15.0	3.0	1.0	2.1	21.0	8.5	3.4	3.5
1970	14.0	2.1	.8	1.5	18.1	6.9	2.5	2.4
1969	13.3	2.1	1.1	1.2	17.0	6.5	2.4	2.3
1968	12.5	1.9	1.0	1.2	16.0	6.3	2.3	2.1
1967	11.3	1.7	.8	1.2	15.3	6.4	2.0	1.9
1966	10.6	1.5	.8	1.1	14.0	5.9	2.0	1.7
1965	10.0	1.3	.8	1.1	13.5	5.9	2.0	1.6
1964	9.5	1.2	.7	1.0	12.5	5.3	1.8	1.5
1963	8.9	1.0	.7	.8	12.0	5.0	1.6	1.3
1962	8.6	.9	.6	.8	11.3	4.8	1.5	1.2
1961	8.1	.9	.5	.7	10.7	4.7	1.3	1.1
1960	7.9	1.0	.5	.7	10.0	4.5	1.2	.9
1959	7.3	.8	.5	.6	(NA)	(NA)	(NA)	(NA)
1958	7.2	.7	.4	.6	8.6	4.0	1.1	.8
1957	6.7	.6	.4	.7	(NA)	(NA)	(NA)	(NA)
1956	6.3	.5	.4	.6	7.5	3.5	.9	.9
1955	5.8	.5	.4	.3	6.8	3.2	.8	.6
1954	5.3	.4	.3	.2	(NA)	(NA)	(NA)	(NA)
1953	5.2	.4	.5	.2	(NA)	(NA)	(NA)	(NA)
1952	4.8	.3	.4	.1	(NA)	(NA)	(NA)	(NA)
1951	4.3	.3	.3	.1	(NA)	(NA)	(NA)	(NA)
1950	3.8	.3	.3	.1	4.4	2.0	.4	.5
1949	3.5	.2	.2	.1	(NA)	(NA)	(NA)	(NA)
1948	3.4	.3	.2	.1	(NA)	(NA)	(NA)	(NA)
1947	3.1	.2	.2	.1	(NA)	(NA)	(NA)	(NA)
1946	2.7	.2	.2	.1	(NA)	(NA)	(NA)	(NA)
1945	2.4	.2	.3	.1	2.6	1.0	.2	.3
1944	2.2	.2	.2	.1	(NA)	(NA)	(NA)	(NA)
1943	2.1	.2	.2	.1	(NA)	(NA)	(NA)	(NA)
1942	1.7	.2	.1	.1	(NA)	(NA)	(NA)	(NA)
1941	1.3	.2	.1	.1	(NA)	(NA)	(NA)	(NA)

See footnotes at end of chart.

Series H 398-411.   Private Philanthropy—Estimated Fund Flows by Donors and Recipients: 1929 to 1990—Cont'd.

(In billions of dollars)

	Philanthropy payments by donors					Philanthropy revenues of recipients		
Year	Living donors	Charitable bequests	Corporation contributions	Foundation grants	Total	Religious organizations	Higher education	Hospitals and health
	399	**400**	**401**	**402**	**405**	**406**	**408**	**409**
1940	1.1	.1	X	.1	1.2	.6	.2	.1
1939	1.0	.2	X	.1	(NA)	(NA)	(NA)	(NA)
1938	.9	.2	X	.1	(NA)	(NA)	(NA)	(NA)
1937	.9	.1	X	.1	(NA)	(NA)	(NA)	(NA)
1936	.8	.1	X	.1	(NA)	(NA)	(NA)	(NA)
1935	.7	.1	X	.1	1.0	.5	.1	X
1934	.7	.1	X	.1	(NA)	(NA)	(NA)	(NA)
1933	.6	.1	X	.1	(NA)	(NA)	(NA)	(NA)
1932	.6	.2	X	.1	(NA)	(NA)	(NA)	(NA)
1931	.7	.2	X	.1	(NA)	(NA)	(NA)	(NA)
1930	.8	.2	X	.1	1.4	.8	.2	.1
1929	.9	.2	X	.1	(NA)	(NA)	(NA)	(NA)

X Less than .05 billion.   NA Not available.

Series H 412-432. Kindergarten, Elementary and Secondary Schools and Enrollment: 1870 to 2000

| | | Schools [1] | | Enrollment | | | |
| | | | | Public day schools | | Nonpublic school [1] | |
School year ending x	School districts [2]	Elementary public	Secondary public	Elementary pupils	Secondary pupils	Elementary pupils	Secondary pupils
	412	414	416	422	424	427	429
				1,000	1,000	1,000	1,000
2000	—	—	—	28,175	18,364	4,516	1,351
1991	15,344	—	—	—	—	—	—
1990	15,449	—	—	25,614	15,412	4,066	1,129
1989	15,513	—	—	24,620	15,906	4,162	1,193
1988	15,571	61,500	22,800	24,415	15,774	4,036	1,206
1987	15,684	61,500	22,900	24,304	15,703	4,232	1,247
1986	15,739	60,800	23,400	24,150	15,603	4,116	1,336
1985	15,812	—	—	24,229	15,193	4,195	1,362
1984	15,857	58,800	23,900	24,095	15,193	4,300	1,400
1983	15,909	—	—	23,949	15,303	4,315	1,400
1982	15,959	—	—	23,823	15,742	4,200	1,400
1981	16,001	—	—	24,087	15,957	4,100	1,400
1980	16,044	61,100	24,400	24,196	16,681	3,992	1,339
1979	—	64,400	24,200	24,547	17,104	3,700	1,300
1978	—	62,000	24,500	25,018	17,534	3,732	1,353
1977	—	62,600	25,400	24,954	18,623	3,797	1,343
1976	—	62,600	25,400	25,427	18,884	3,825	1,342
1975	—	63,600	25,700	25,656	19,164	3,700	1,300
1974	—	65,100	25,900	26,394	18,679	3,700	1,300
1973	—	64,900	25,900	26,443	19,001	3,700	1,300
1972	—	—	—	27,312	18,414	3,700	1,300
1971	—	65,800	25,400	27,882	18,389	3,900	1,300
1970 [3]	17,995	65,800	25,352	29,996	13,022	4,100	1,400
1968	22,010	70,879	27,011	29,775	12,488	4,600	1,400
1966	26,983	73,216	26,597	28,315	11,597	4,763	1,329
1964	31,705	77,584	26,431	27,172	10,883	4,796	1,287
1962	35,676	81,910	25,350	26,622	9,566	4,521	1,120
1960 *	40,520	91,853	25,784	25,679	8,485	4,286	1,035
1958	47,594	95,446	25,507	23,897	7,860	3,944	931
1956	54,859	104,427	26,046	22,726	6,873	3,623	823
1954	63,057	110,875	25,637	21,072	6,290	3,275	747
1952	71,094	123,763	23,746	19,409	5,882	2,922	656
1950	83,718	128,225	24,542	18,353	5,725	2,575	672
1948	94,926	146,760	25,484	17,302	5,653	2,269	602
1946	101,382	160,227	24,314	16,905	5,622	2,213	565
1944	111,383	169,905	28,973	17,016	5,554	2,022	421
1942	115,493	183,112	25,123	17,549	6,388	2,085	483
1940	117,108	(NA)	(NA)	18,237	6,601	2,096	458
1938	119,001	221,660	25,467	19,141	6,227	2,252	437
1936	(NA)	232,174	25,652	19,786	5,975	2,253	387
1934	(NA)	236,236	24,714	20,163	5,669	2,371	360
1932	127,531	232,750	26,409	20,434	5,140	2,384	403
1930	—	238,306	23,930	20,556	4,399	2,255	341
1928	—	—	—	20,573	3,911	2,235	341
1926	—	—	—	20,311	3,757	—	—
1924	—	—	—	20,289	3,390	—	—
1922	—	—	—	19,837	2,873	—	—
1920	—	—	—	18,897	2,200	1,456	214
1918	—	—	—	18,920	1,934	—	—
1916	—	—	—	18,896	1,456	—	—

See footnotes at end of chart.

Series H 412-432. Kindergarten, Elementary and Secondary Schools and Enrollment: 1870 to 2000—Cont'd.

School year ending x	Schools [1]			Enrollment			
				Public day schools		Nonpublic school [1]	
	School districts [2]	Elementary public	Secondary public	Elementary pupils	Secondary pupils	Elementary pupils	Secondary pupils
	412	414	416	422	424	427	429
1915	—	—	—	18,375	1,329	—	—
1914	—	—	—	17,935	1,219	—	—
1913	—	—	—	17,474	1,135	—	—
1912	—	—	—	17,078	1,105	—	—
1911	—	—	—	17,050	985	—	—
1910	—	—	—	16,899	915	1,440	117
1909	—	—	—	16,665	841	—	—
1908	—	—	—	16,292	770	—	—
1907	—	—	—	16,140	751	—	—
1906	—	—	—	15,919	723	—	—
1905	—	—	—	15,789	680	—	—
1904	—	—	—	15,620	636	—	—
1903	—	—	—	15,417	592	—	—
1902	—	—	—	15,367	551	—	—
1901	—	—	—	15,161	542	—	—
1900	—	—	—	14,984	519	1,147	111
1899	—	—	—	14,700	476	—	—
1898	—	—	—	14,654	450	—	—
1897	—	—	—	14,414	409	—	—
1896	—	—	—	14,118	380	—	—
1895	—	—	—	13,894	350	—	—
1894	—	—	—	13,706	289	—	—
1893	—	—	—	13,229	254	—	—
1892	—	—	—	13,016	240	—	—
1891	—	—	—	12,839	212	—	—
1890	—	—	—	12,520	203	1,662	95
1889	—	—	—	—	—	—	—
1888	—	—	—	—	—	—	—
1887	—	—	—	—	—	—	—
1886	—	—	—	—	—	—	—
1885	—	—	—	—	—	—	—
1884	—	—	—	—	—	—	—
1883	—	—	—	—	—	—	—
1882	—	—	—	—	—	—	—
1881	—	—	—	—	—	—	—
1880	—	—	—	9,757	110	—	—
1879	—	—	—	—	—	—	—
1878	—	—	—	—	—	—	—
1877	—	—	—	—	—	—	—
1876	—	—	—	—	—	—	—
1875	—	—	—	—	—	—	—
1874	—	—	—	—	—	—	—
1873	—	—	—	—	—	—	—
1872	—	—	—	—	—	—	—
1871	—	—	—	7,481	80	—	—
1870	—	—	—	—	—	—	—

* Denotes first year for which figures include Alaska and Hawaii.
NA Not available.
[1] Data for nonpublic schools for most years are partly estimated.
[2] Includes operating and nonoperating districts.
[3] Statistics are for 1970-71.

Series H 492-507.   Public Elementary and Secondary School Expenditures: 1870 to 1989
(In millions of dollars)

School year ending x	Total expenditures, all schools	School year ending x	Total expenditures, all schools	School year ending x	Total expenditures, all schools	School year ending x	Total expenditures, all schools	School year ending x	Total expenditures, all schools	School year ending x	Total expenditures, all schools
	492		492		492		492		492		492
1989	183,400	1973	55,100	1944	2,453	1915	605	1900	215	1885	110
1988	172,000	1972	51,400	1942	2,323	1914	555	1899	200	1884	103
1987	160,900	1971	47,600			1913	522	1898	194	1883	97
1986	148,600			1940	2,344	1912	483	1997	188	1882	89
		1970	40,683	1938	2,233	1911	447	1896	183	1881	84
1985	137,000	1968	32,977	1936	1,969						
1984	127,500	1966	26,248	1934	1,720	1910	426	1895	176	1880	78
1983	118,425	1964	21,325	1932	2,175	1909	401	1894	173	1879	76
1982	111,186	1962	18,373			1908	371	1893	164	1878	79
1981	104,125			1930	2,317	1907	337	1892	156	1877	79
		1960 *	15,613	1928	2,184	1906	308	1891	147	1876	83
1980	95,962	1958	13,569	1926	2,026						
1979	88,712	1956	10,955	1924	1,821	1905	292	1890	141	1875	84
1978	80,444	1954	9,092	1922	1,581	1904	273	1889	133	1874	80
1977	74,194	1952	7,344			1903	251	1888	124	1873	76
1976	70,601			1920	1,036	1902	238	1887	116	1872	74
		1950	5,838	1918	764	1901	228	1886	113	1871	69
1975	64,846	1948	4,311	1916	641					1870	63
1974	59,800	1946	2,907								

* Denotes first year for which figures include Alaska and Hawaii.

Series H 520-530.   Public Elementary and Secondary Day Schools— Attendance and Instructional Staff: 1870 to 1991

School year ending x	Average daily attendance	Average annual salary in current dollars [1]	Instructional staff — Total classroom teachers and other nonsupervisory staff [2]	School year ending x	Average daily attendance	Average annual salary in current dollars [1]	Instructional staff — Total classroom teachers and other nonsupervisory staff [2]	School year ending x	Average daily attendance	Average annual salary in current dollars [1]	Instructional staff — Total classroom teachers and other nonsupervisory staff [2]
	520	524	526		520	524	526		520	524	526
	1,000		1,000		1,000		1,000		1,000		1,000
1991	38,215	33,021	2,400	1950	22,284	3,010	914	1900	10,633	325	423
1990	37,534	31,361	2,365	1948	20,910	2,639	861	1899	10,389	—	414
1989	37,174	29,568	2,324	1946	19,849	1,995	831	1898	10,356	—	411
1988	37,066	28,023	2,284	1944	19,603	1,728	828	1997	10,053	—	405
1987	36,905	26,569	2,249	1942	21,031	1,507	859	1896	9,781	—	400
1986	36,681	25,199	2,215								
				1940	22,042	1,441	875	1895	9,549	286	398
1985	36,530	23,600	2,175	1938	22,298	1,374	877	1894	9,188	—	389
1984	36,508	21,900	2,144	1936	22,299	1,283	871	1893	8,856	—	383
1983	36,752	20,700	2,134	1934	22,458	1,227	847	1892	8,561	—	374
1982	37,072	19,300	2,158	1932	22,245	1,417	872	1891	8,329	—	368
1981	37,857	17,600	2,192								
				1930	21,265	1,420	854	1890	8,154	252	364
1980	38,411	15,970	2,211	1928	20,608	1,364	832	1889	8,006	—	357
1979	39,100	15,000	2,199	1926	19,856	1,277	814	1888	7,907	—	347
1978	40,200	14,200	2,208	1924	19,132	1,227	761	1887	7,682	—	339
1977	—	13,400	2,186	1922	18,432	1,166	723	1886	7,526	—	331
1976	41,300	12,600	2,196								
				1920	16,150	871	680	1885	7,298	224	326
1975	41,476	11,700	2,171	1918	15,549	635	651	1884	7,056	—	314
1974	41,400	10,800	2,155	1916	15,359	563	622	1883	6,652	—	304
1973	—	10,200	2,109	1915	14,986	543	604	1882	6,331	—	299
1972	42,300	9,700	2,070	1914	14,216	525	580	1881	6,146	—	294
1971	—	9,300	2,063								
				1913	13,614	512	565	1880	6,144	195	287
1970	41,934	8,840	2,131	1912	13,302	492	547	1879	5,876	—	280
1968	40,828	7,885	1,957	1911	12,872	466	534	1878	5,783	—	277
1966	39,154	6,935	1,786					1877	5,427	—	267
1964	37,405	6,240	1,625	1910	12,827	485	523	1876	5,291	—	260
1962	34,682	5,700	1,504	1909	12,685	—	506				
				1908	12,154	—	495	1875	5,248	—	258
1960*	32,477	5,174	1,387	1907	11,926	—	481	1874	5,051	—	248
1958	29,722	4,702	1,261	1906	11,712	—	466	1873	4,745	—	238
1956	27,740	4,156	1,149					1872	4,659	—	230
1954	25,644	3,825	1,042	1905	11,482	386	460	1871	4,545	—	220
1952	23,257	3,450	963	1904	11,318	—	455	1870	4,077	189	201
				1903	11,055	—	449				
				1902	11,064	—	442				
				1901	10,716	—	432				

* Denotes first year for which figures include Alaska and Hawaii.
[1] Prior to 1920, computed for teaching positions only; beginning 1920, also includes supervisors and principals.

[2] Prior to 1938, number of different persons employed rather than number of positions. Includes librarians and guidance and psychological personnel.

Series H 535-544.   Catholic Elementary and Secondary Schools: 1920 to 1990

(In thousands, except number of schools)

Year [1]	Elementary schools		Teachers			Secondary schools		Teachers		
	Number	Pupils enrolled	Total	Religious	Lay	Number	Pupils enrolled	Total	Religious	Lay
	535	536	537	538	539	540	541	542	543	544
1990	7,291	1,884	91	11	80	1,296	592	40	6	34
1989	7,395	1,893	94	12	82	1,324	606	43	8	35
1988	7,501	1,912	94	14	80	1,362	639	44	8	36
1987	7,601	1,942	93	15	78	1,391	681	47	10	37
1986	7,693	1,998	94	17	77	1,409	728	48	10	38
1985	7,806	2,057	97	18	79	1,430	762	50	11	39
1984	7,891	2,120	100	20	80	1,449	782	50	12	38
1983	7,937	2,180	99	21	78	1,464	788	48	12	36
1982	7,950	2,225	97	22	75	1,482	801	49	13	36
1981	7,996	2,266	97	24	73	1,498	828	49	14	35
1980	8,043	2,269	97	25	72	1,516	837	49	14	35
1979	8,100	2,293	98	27	70	1,540	846	50	15	35
1978	8,159	2,365	99	29	70	1,564	853	49	16	33
1977	8,204	2,421	100	32	68	1,593	867	51	18	33
1976	8,281	2,483	100	34	66	1,623	882	51	19	32
1975	8,340	2,525	99	35	64	1,653	890	50	20	30
1974	8,437	2,602	100	38	62	1,690	902	50	21	29
1973	8,569	2,714	103	41	62	1,728	907	51	23	29
1972	8,766	2,874	105	44	61	1,790	927	51	23	27
1971	8,982	3,076	106	47	59	1,857	959	53	26	27
1970	9,362	3,355	112	52	60	1,981	1,008	54	27	26
1969	9,695	3,607	110	56	54	2,076	1,051	53	29	23
1968	10,113	3,860	[2] 126	68	58	2,192	1,081	[2] 57	33	23
1967	10,350	4,106	[2] 124	70	53	2,277	1,093	[2] 55	34	21
1966	10,769	4,375	120	74	46	2,463	1,110	56	36	20
1965	10,879	4,492	120	76	44	2,413	1,082	57	38	19
1964	10,832	4,534	118	76	42	2,417	1,067	53	36	18
1963	10,775	4,546	115	77	38	2,430	1,044	51	35	16
1962	10,676	4,485	112	77	36	2,502	1,009	47	34	13
1961	10,631	4,445	111	78	33	2,376	938	47	34	14
1960	10,501	4,373	108	79	29	2,392	880	44	33	11
1956	9,615	3,571	85	71	14	2,311	705	35	28	7
1954	9,279	3,235	77	67	9	2,296	624	32	26	6
1952	8,880	2,842	72	66	6	2,180	549	29	24	5
1950	8,589	2,561	67	62	5	2,189	506	28	23	5
1948	8,285	2,305	62	59	3	2,150	483	27	23	4
1947	(NA)	(NA)	(NA)	(NA)	(NA)	2,111	467	27	23	4
1940	7,944	2,035	60	(NA)	(NA)	2,105	361	21	(NA)	(NA)
1936	7,929	2,103	59	55	3	1,946	285	17	14	3
1930	7,923	2,223	58	53	5	(NA)	(NA)	(NA)	—	—
1920	6,551	1,796	42	—	—	1,552	130	8	—	—

NA Not available.
[1] Prior to 1958, data for school year ending; thereafter, for October of year shown.
[2] Includes part-time teachers.

Series H 598-601. High School Graduates: 1870 to 1993

(In thousands)

Year of graduation	Total number 598	Year of graduation	Total number 598	Year of graduation	Total number 598	Year of graduation	Total number 598	Year of graduation	Total number 598	Year of graduation	Total number 598
1993	2,215	1973	2,737	1952	1,197	1925	528	1905	119	1885	32
1992	2,193	1972	2,706	1950	1,200	1924	494	1904	112	1884	31
1991	2,210	1971	2,643			1923	426	1903	105	1883	28
				1948	1,190	1922	357	1902	99	1882	27
1990	2,324	1970	2,906	1946	1,080	1921	334	1901	97	1881	25
1989	2,456.2	1969	2,839	1944	1,019						
1988	2,500.2	1968	2,702	1942	1,242	1920	311	1900	95	1880	24
1987	2,428.8	1967	2,680	1940	1,221	1919	298	1899	90	1879	23
1986	2,382.6	1966	2,672			1918	285	1898	84	1878	22
				1938	1,120	1917	272	1897	80	1877	21
1985	2,414.6	1965	2,665	1937	1,068	1916	259	1896	76	1876	20
1984	2,495	1964	2,290	1936	1,015						
1983	2,600	1963	1,950			1915	240	1895	72	1875	20
1982	2,711	1962	1,925	1935	965	1914	219	1894	65	1874	19
1981	2,725	1961	1,971	1934	915	1913	200	1893	59	1873	18
				1933	871	1912	181	1892	53	1872	17
1980	2,748	1960	1,864	1932	827	1911	168	1891	48	1871	17
1979	2,801	1959	1,639	1931	747					1870	16
1978	2,825	1958	1,506			1910	156	1890	44		
1977	2,840	1957	1,446	1930	667	1909	142	1889	39		
1976	2,844	1956	1,415	1929	632	1908	129	1888	33		
		1954	1,276	1928	597	1907	127	1887	32		
1975	2,823			1927	579	1906	126	1886	33		
1974	2,771			1926	561						

Series H 689-699.   Institutions of Higher Education—Number and Faculty: 1870 to 1989

School year ending x	Total	Junior colleges [1]	4-year colleges	Faculty	School year ending x	Total	Junior colleges [1]	4-year colleges	Faculty
	689	690	693	696		689	690	693	696
1989	3,535	1,408	2,127	824,000	1956	1,850	467	1,383	298,910
1988	3,565	1,436	2,129	804,000	1954	1,862	518	1,344	265,911
1987	3,587	1,452	2,135	793,000	1952	1,891	511	1,380	244,488
1986	3,406	1,336	2,070	722,000					
					1950	1,863	518	1,345	246,722
1985	3,340	1,311	2,029	715,000	1948	1,788	472	1,316	223,660
1984	3,331	1,306	2,205	717,000	1946	1,768	464	1,304	165,324
1983	3,284	1,271	2,013	724,000	1944	1,650	413	1,237	150,980
1982	3,280	1,296	1,984	865,000	1942	1,769	461	1,308	151,066
1981	3,253	1,274	1,979	865,000					
					1940	1,708	456	1,252	146,929
1980	3,231	1,274	1,957	686,000	1938	1,690	453	1,237	135,989
1979	3,152	1,195	1,957	823,000	1936	1,628	415	1,213	121,036
1978	3,134	1,193	1,941	809,000	1934	1,418	322	1,096	108,873
1977	2,826	1,018	1,808	812,000	1932	1,478	342	1,136	[4] 100,789
1976	2,785	1,002	1,783	793,000					
					1930	1,409	277	1,132	82,386
1975	3,026	1,128	1,898	781,000	1928	1,410	248	1,162	(NA)
1974	2,747	1,003	1,744	695,000	1926	1,377	153	1,224	(NA)
1973	2,720	1,003	1,717	634,000	1924	1,295	132	1,163	(NA)
1972	2,665	964	1,701	590,000	1922	1,162	80	1,082	(NA)
1971	2,606	931	1,695	596,000					
					1920	1,041	52	989	48,615
1970	2,525	[2] 886	1,689	[3] 729,000	1918	980	46	934	(NA)
1968	2,374	[2] 786	1,588	[3] 674,000	1916	(NA)	—	—	(NA)
1966	2,230	[2] 622	1,608	596,400	1910	951	—	—	36,480
1964	2,139	[2] 644	1,495	494,514					
1962	2,003	524	1,479	424,862	1900	977	—	—	23,868
					1890	998	—	—	15,809
1960 *	1,959	508	1,451	380,554	1880	811	—	—	11,552
1958	1,894	490	1,404	344,525	1870	563	—	—	5,553

* Denotes first year for which figures include Alaska and Hawaii.
NA Not available.
[1] Beginning 1950, includes 2-year normal schools.
[2] Includes institutions which do not offer courses creditable toward a bachelor's degree.
[3] Estimated.
[4] Full-time equivalent; total number of different persons not tabulated.

Series H 700-715.   Institutions of Higher Education—Degree-Credit Enrollment: 1946 to 1989

(In thousands, except percent)

Year	Number	Male	Female	4-year institution	2-year institution	Year	Number	Male	Female	4-year institution	2-year institution
	700	702	703	704	705		700	702	703	704	705
1989	13,458	6,115	7,302	8,374	5,083	1973	9,602	4,771	3,747	6,597	1,921
1988	13,055	6,002	7,053	8,180	4,875	1972	9,215	4,701	3,564	6,473	1,792
1987	12,767	5,932	6,835	7,990	4,776	1971	8,949	4,717	3,399	6,391	1,725
1986	12,504	5,885	6,619	7,824	4,680						
						1970	7,920	4,637	3,284	6,290	1,630
1985	12,247	5,818	6,429	7,716	4,531	1968	6,928	4,119	2,809	5,639	1,289
1984	12,242	5,864	6,378	7,711	4,531	1966	5,928	3,577	2,351	4,984	945
1983	12,465	6,024	6,441	7,741	4,723	1964	4,950	3,033	1,917	4,239	711
1982	12,426	6,031	6,394	7,654	4,772	1962	4,175	2,587	1,588	3,585	590
1981	12,372	5,975	6,397	7,655	4,716						
						1960 *	3,583	2,257	1,326	3,131	451
1980	12,097	5,874	6,223	7,571	4,526	1958	3,226	2,092	1,134	2,840	386
1979	11,570	5,683	5,887	7,353	4,217	1956	2,918	1,911	1,007	2,571	347
1978	11,260	5,641	5,619	7,232	4,028	1954	2,446	1,563	883	2,164	282
1977	11,286	5,789	5,497	7,243	4,043	1952	2,134	1,380	754	1,896	238
1976	11,012	5,811	5,201	7,129	3,883						
						1950	2,281	1,560	721	2,064	217
1975	11,185	5,321	4,410	7,143	2,588	1948	2,403	1,709	694	2,192	211
1974	10,224	4,969	4,055	6,825	2,198	1946	2,078	1,418	661	—	—

* Denotes first year for which figures include Alaska and Hawaii.
[1] Data for fall of year shown.

Series H 728-738. Institutions of Higher Education—Current Expenditures: 1930 to 1990

(In millions of dollars)

| School year ending x | Total expenditures | Educational and general expenditures | | | | | | | | Auxiliary enterprises and activities | Student aid and other expenditures |
| | | Total | Administration and general expense | Instruction and departmental research | Organized research | Libraries | Plant operation and maintenance | Organized activities related to instructional departments | Extension and public services | | |
	728	729	730	731	732	733	734	735	736	737	738
1990	134,656	105,585	42,146	12,674	12,506	3,254	9,458	9,438	4,690	13,204	6,656
1989	123,867	96,803	38,813	11,529	11,432	3,010	8,740	8,904	4,227	12,280	5,919
1988	113,786	89,157	35,834	10,774	10,351	2,836	8,231	8,142	3,786	11,400	5,325
1987	105,764	82,958	33,711	10,085	9,352	2,441	7,819	7,575	3,448	11,037	4,776
1986	97,536	76,128	31,032	9,351	8,437	2,551	7,605	6,667	3,120	10,528	4,160
1985	89,951	70,061	28,777	8,588	7,552	2,362	7,345	6,075	2,861	10,012	3,670
1984	81,993	63,741	26,436	7,763	6,724	2,231	6,730	5,531	2,499	9,250	3,302
1983	75,936	58,929	24,673	6,951	6,265	2,040	6,392	5,087	2,320	8,614	2,923
1982	70,339	54,849	22,963	6471	5,930	1,922	5,979	4,656	2,204	7,998	2,685
1981	64,053	50,074	20,733	5,773	5,658	1,759	5,350	4,273	2,058	7,288	2,505
1980	56,914	44,543	18,497	5,054	5,099	1,624	4,700	3,876	1,817	6,486	2,200
1979	50,721	39,833	16,663	4,557	4,448	1,427	4,179	3,471	1,593	5,750	1,945
1978	45,971	36,257	15,336	4,142	3,920	1,349	3,795	3,136	1,425	5,261	1,839
1977	42,600	33,152	14,031	3,762	3,600	1,250	3,437	2,795	1,343	4,858	1,770
1976	38,903	30,958	13,095	3,615	3,287	1,224	3,083	2,472	1,239	4,477	1,636
1975	34,735	27,250	11,720	2,964	3,126	998	2,738	2,240	1,088	4,059	1,429
1974	30,713	23,257	4,201	11,574	2,480	—	2,494	838	—	6,060	1,396
1973	27,956	21,078	3,713	10,528	2,394	—	2,141	791	—	5,555	1,322
1972	25,560	19,201	3,344	9,503	2,265	—	1,928	780	—	5,118	1,241
1971	23,375	17,616	2,984	8,695	2,209	—	1,730	693	—	1,305	1,098
1970	21,043	15,789	2,628	7,653	2,144	653	1,542	648	521	2,769	[1] 2,485
1969	18,482	13,835	2,278	6,610	2,034	572	1,338	535	468	2,539	[1] 2,107
1968	16,481	13,190	1,739	5,653	2,699	493	1,127	881	598	2,302	988
1966	12,509	9,951	1,251	3,911	2,448	346	845	711	438	1,888	671
1964	9,178	7,425	958	2,802	1,973	237	686	472	297	1,452	300
1962	7,155	5,768	730	2,202	1,474	177	564	375	244	1,158	229
1960 *	5,601	4,513	583	1,793	1,022	135	470	303	206	916	172
1958	4,510	3,604	474	1,466	728	110	406	246	175	775	130
1956	3,499	2,766	355	1,141	501	86	324	222	138	638	95
1954	2,883	2,271	288	961	373	73	278	187	112	538	74
1952	2,471	1,921	234	823	318	61	240	148	97	478	72
1950	2,246	1,706	213	781	225	56	225	119	87	476	63
1948	1,883	1,392	172	658	159	44	202	85	71	439	53
1946	1,088	820	105	375	87	27	111	61	55	242	26
1944	974	657	70	334	59	20	81	48	44	199	[2] 118
1942	738	572	67	299	34	20	73	38	43	137	28
1940	675	522	63	280	27	19	70	27	35	124	29
1938	614	473	56	253	25	18	63	24	34	116	[3] 26
1936	541	417	48	225	22	16	57	20	29	95	[3] 29
1934	469	362	43	203	17	13	51	14	20	79	[3] 28
1932	537	415	47	233	22	11	57	21	24	91	[3] 30
1930	507	378	43	221	18	10	61	(4)	25	3	126

* Denotes first year for which figures include Alaska and Hawaii.

[1] Includes "Major public service," previously included in "Educational and general expenditures" items, series H 729-736.

[2] Includes $97 million for federal contract courses.

[3] Includes unitemized educational and general expenditures as follows, in thousands of dollars: 2,020 in 1938; 2,580 in 1936; 7,502 in 1934; and 5,239 in 1932.

[4] Not tabulated separately; probably included in series H 738.

Series H 751-765.   Institutions of Higher Education—Degrees Conferred, by Sex: 1870 to 1995

| School year ending x | Total, all degrees | Bachelor's or first professional | | Master's or second professional | | Doctor's or equivalent | |
		Male	Female	Male	Female	Male	Female
	751	753	754	758	759	762	763
1995	2,062,000	510,000	590,000	165,000	189,000	24,000	16,000
1990	1,916,000	485,000	558,000	149,000	170,000	24,000	14,000
1989	1,870,000	483,000	535,000	149,000	161,000	23,000	13,000
1988	1,834,000	477,000	518,000	145,000	154,000	23,000	12,000
1987	1,825,000	481,000	510,000	141,000	148,000	22,000	12,000
1986	1,830,000	486,000	502,000	144,000	145,000	22,000	12,000
1985	1,828,000	483,000	497,000	143,000	143,000	22,000	11,000
1984	1,819,000	482,000	492,000	144,000	141,000	22,000	11,000
1983	1,822,000	479,000	490,000	145,000	145,000	22,000	11,000
1982	1,788,000	473,000	480,000	146,000	150,000	22,000	10,000
1981	1,752,000	470,000	465,000	147,000	149,000	23,000	10,000
1980	1,731,000	474,000	456,000	151,000	147,000	23,000	10,000
1979	1,727,000	477,000	444,000	153,000	148,000	24,000	9,000
1978	1,744,000	487,000	434,000	161,000	150,000	24,000	8,000
1977	1,741,000	496,000	424,000	168,000	149,000	25,000	8,000
1976	1,726,000	505,000	421,000	167,000	145,000	26,000	8,000
1975	1,666,000	505,000	418,000	162,000	131,000	27,000	7,000
1974	1,653,000	527,000	418,000	158,000	119,000	27,000	6,000
1973	1,586,000	518,000	404,000	109,000	120,000	29,000	6,000
1972	1,509,000	501,000	387,000	150,000	102,000	28,000	5,000
1971	1,393,000	476,000	364,000	138,000	92,000	28,000	5,000
1970	1,065,391	484,174	343,060	125,624	82,667	25,890	3,976
1969	984,129	444,380	319,805	121,531	72,225	22,752	3,436
1968	866,548	390,507	276,203	113,519	63,230	20,183	2,906
1967	768,871	353,349	237,198	103,092	54,615	18,163	2,454
1966	709,832	328,853	222,194	93,063	47,485	16,121	2,116
1965	663,622	316,286	213,717	77,544	39,608	14,692	1,775
1964	614,194	296,676	197,477	70,339	35,212	12,955	1,535
1963	551,810	271,882	171,636	64,198	31,272	11,448	1,374
1962	514,323	259,507	154,780	59,710	28,704	10,377	1,245
1961	487,513	253,077	142,171	55,267	26,423	9,463	1,112
1960 *	476,704	252,996	136,187	51,965	25,727	8,801	1,028
1959	461,823	252,517	127,414	48,360	24,172	8,371	989
1958	438,030	241,560	121,942	44,229	21,357	7,978	964
1957	409,132	221,650	116,786	41,329	20,611	7,817	939
1956	377,698	198,615	110,899	39,393	19,888	8,018	885
1955	352,881	182,839	103,002	38,739	19,461	8,014	826
1954	357,327	186,884	104,624	38,147	18,676	8,181	815
1953	372,315	199,793	103,256	40,946	20,213	7,515	792
1952	401,203	225,981	104,005	43,557	19,977	6,969	714
1951	454,960	278,240	104,306	46,196	18,881	6,663	674
1950	496,874	328,841	103,217	41,220	16,963	5,990	643
1949	421,282	263,608	101,884	35,212	15,529	4,527	522
1948	317,607	175,615	95,571	28,931	13,501	3,496	493
1946	157,349	58,664	77,510	9,484	9,725	1,580	386
1944	141,582	55,865	69,998	5,711	7,703	1,880	425
1942	213,491	103,889	81,457	14,179	10,469	3,036	461
1940	216,521	109,546	76,954	16,508	10,233	2,861	429
1938	189,503	97,678	67,265	13,400	8,228	2,502	430
1936	164,197	86,067	57,058	11,503	6,799	2,370	400
1934	157,279	82,341	53,815	11,516	6,777	2,456	374
1932	160,084	83,271	54,792	12,210	7,157	2,247	407
1930	139,752	73,615	48,869	8,925	6,044	1,946	353
1928	124,995	67,659	43,502	7,727	4,660	1,249	198
1926	108,407	62,218	35,045	6,202	3,533	1,216	193

See footnotes at end of table.

Series H 751-765. Institutions of Higher Education—Degrees Conferred, by Sex: 1870 to 1995—Cont'd.

School year ending x	Total, all degrees	Bachelor's or first professional		Master's or second professional		Doctor's or equivalent	
		Male	Female	Male	Female	Male	Female
	751	753	754	758	759	762	763
1924	92,097	54,908	27,875	5,515	2,701	939	159
1922	68,488	41,306	20,362	4,304	1,680	708	128
1920	53,516	31,980	16,642	2,985	1,294	522	93
1918	42,041	26,269	12,316	1,806	1,094	491	65
1916	49,823	31,852	13,398	2,934	972	586	81
1915	48,100	31,417	12,495	2,638	939	549	62
1914	48,097	32,183	12,085	2,256	1,014	486	73
1913	45,959	31,312	11,084	2,021	1,004	481	57
1912	42,943	29,560	9,848	2,215	820	436	64
1911	40,434	28,547	8,934	1,821	635	449	48
1910	39,755	28,762	8,437	1,555	558	399	44
1909	40,531	29,433	8,459	1,713	475	397	54
1908	36,162	26,376	7,424	1,511	460	339	52
1907	34,202	25,269	6,965	1,215	404	320	29
1906	34,189	25,215	6,804	1,366	421	358	25
1905	33,813	24,934	6,585	1,538	387	341	28
1904	32,514	24,237	6,264	1,340	339	302	32
1903	31,962	23,872	6,035	1,385	333	302	35
1902	31,117	23,225	5,741	1,464	394	264	29
1901	30,790	23,099	5,582	1,405	339	334	31
1900	29,375	22,173	5,237	1,280	303	359	23
1899	27,867	21,064	4,916	1,275	267	327	18
1898	26,816	20,358	4,694	1,188	252	285	39
1897	26,963	20,550	4,681	1,163	250	299	20
1896	26,342	20,076	4,517	1,213	265	236	35
1895	25,712	19,723	4,383	1,124	210	247	25
1894	23,352	17,917	3,933	1,013	210	261	18
1893	19,989	15,342	3,325	—	—	—	—
1892	17,722	13,840	2,962	—	—	—	—
1891	17,803	13,902	2,938	—	—	—	—
1890	16,703	12,857	2,682	—	—	147	2
1889	16,305	12,397	2,623	—	—	—	—
1888	16,383	12,562	2,694	—	—	—	—
1887	14,402	11,008	2,394	—	—	—	—
1886	14,040	10,731	2,366	—	—	—	—
1885	15,882	12,043	2,691	—	—	—	—
1884	13,732	10,408	2,357	—	—	—	—
1883	16,029	12,294	2,822	—	—	—	—
1882	15,928	12,168	2,830	—	—	—	—
1881	15,830	12,035	2,836	—	—	—	—
1880	13,829	10,411	2,485	—	—	51	3
1879	13,036	9,808	2,273	—	—	—	—
1878	12,381	9,416	2,117	—	—	—	—
1877	10,915	8,329	1,816	—	—	—	—
1876	12,871	9,911	2,094	—	—	—	—
1875	12,616	9,905	2,027	—	—	—	—
1874	12,366	9,593	1,900	—	—	—	—
1873	11,723	9,070	1,737	—	—	—	—
1872	8,660	6,626	1,226	—	—	—	—
1871	12,370	10,484	1,873	—	—	—	—
1870	9,372	7,993	1,378	—	—	1	—

* Denotes first year for which figures include Alaska and Hawaii.

Series H 793-799. Membership of Religious Bodies, 1890 to 1989 and by Major Groups: 1951 to 1989

(In thousands)

Year	Total membership	Buddhist	Old Catholic and Polish National Catholic [1]	Eastern churches	Jewish	Roman Catholic	Protestant [2]	Year	Total membership
	793	794	795	796	797	798	799		793
1989	147,607	19	980	4,057	5,944	57,020	79,387	1950	86,830
1988	145,384	100	827	4,077	5,935	54,919	79,329	1949	81,862
1987	143,831	100	829	3,973	5,944	53,497	79,296	1948	79,436
1986	142,800	100	829	3,980	5,814	52,893	78,991	1947	77,386
								1946 [5]	73,673
1985	142,926	100	1,024	4,026	5,835	52,655	79,096		
1984	142,172	100	1,024	4,053	5,817	52,286	78,702	1945 [5]	71,700
1983	140,816	70	1,150	4,034	5,728	52,293	77,254	1944	72,493
1982	139,603	100	925	3,860	5,725	52,089	76,754	1942	68,501
1981	138,453	60	921	3,853	5,921	51,208	76,339	1940	64,502
								1938	64,157
1980	134,817	60	924	3,823	5,920	50,450	73,479	1937	63,848
1979	133,469	60	937	3,822	5,861	49,812	72,815	1936	55,807 [6]
1978	133,749	60	809	3,633	5,781	49,602	73,704		
1977	132,812	60	801	3,753	5,776	49,836	72,383	1935	62,678
1976	131,898	60	846	3,755	6,115	49,326	71,587	1934	62,007
								1933	60,813
1975	130,013	60	846	3,696	6,115	48,882	71,043	1932	60,157
1974	132,287	60	849	3,696	6,115	48,702	72,485	1931	59,798
1973	131,245	60	848	3,706	6,115	48,465	71,667		
1972	131,424	100	913	3,740	6,115	48,460	71,649	1926	54,576
1971	131,390	100	867	3,848	5,870	48,391	71,865	1916	41,927
								1906	35,068
1970	131,046	100	848	3,850	5,870	48,215	72,162	1890	21,699
1969	128,505	100	818	3,745	5,780	47,872	70,189		
1968	128,470	100	599	2,660	5,725	47,873	71,513		
1967	126,445	(3)	580	2,651	5,725	47,468	70,021		
1966	123,826	(3)	(3)	(3)	5,725	46,865	71,236		
1965	124,682	92	484	3,172	5,600	46,246	69,088		
1964	123,307	110	491	3,167	5,600	45,641	68,299		
1963	120,965	60	498	3,094	5,585	44,874	66,854		
1962	117,946	60	597	3,002	5,509	43,848	64,930		
1961	116,110	60	573	2,800	5,365	42,877	64,435		
1960	114,449	20	590	2,699	5,367	42,105	63,669		
1959 *	112,227	20	484	2,808	5,500	40,871	62,544		
1958 [4]	109,558	10	488	2,545	5,500	39,510	61,505		
1957	104,190	10	469	2,540	5,500	35,847	59,824		
1956	103,225	63	351	2,598	5,500	34,564	60,149		
1955	100,163	63	368	2,387	5,500	33,397	58,449		
1954	97,483	63	368	2,024	5,500	32,403	57,124		
1953	94,843	63	366	2,100	5,500	31,476	55,837		
1952	92,277	73	367	2,354	5,500	30,253	54,230		
1951	88,673	73	337	1,859	5,500	29,242	52,162		

Major groups

* Denotes first year for which figures include Alaska and Hawaii.
[1] Beginning 1957, includes Armenian Church of North America.
[2] Includes non-Protestant bodies such as "Latter Day Saints" and "Jehovah's Witness"; non-Christian bodies such as "Spirtualists," "Ethical Culture Movement," and "Unitarian-Univeralists"; in 1966 and 1967, "Buddhists"; and in 1966, "Old Catholic and Polish National Catholic," and "Eastern churches."

[3] Included in "Protestant" category; not available separately.
[4] Includes Alaska.
[5] Includes only bodies with memberships over 50,000.
[6] The Christian Herald reported 1936 membership as 63,222,000.

Series H 806-828. National Parks, Monuments and Allied Areas—
Number, Area and Visits: 1850 to 1990

(For years ending Sept. 30 prior to 1941; thereafter, for years ending Dec. 31, or as of Jan. 1 of the following year. Includes areas in Alaska, Hawaii, Virgin Islands and Puerto Rico.)

Year	Total, enumerated areas [1]		National parks		National monuments visits	National historical and military areas [3] visits	National parkways visits
	Area	Visits [2]	Area	Visits [2]			
	807	808	810	811	814	817	820
	1,000 acres	1,000	1,000 acres	1,000	1,000	1,000	1,000
1990	76,362	258,700	46,089	57,700	23,900	57,500	29,100
1989	76,331	269,400	46,081	57,400	23,700	63,900	31,200
1988	76,176	282,500	45,985	56,400	23,200	61,200	42,000
1987	75,970	287,200	45,875	56,600	23,500	68,600	39,300
1986	75,863	281,100	45,791	53,500	21,200	65,500	41,600
1985	75,749	263,400	45,739	50,000	15,900	61,900	40,000
1984	74,913	248,600	45,454	49,700	15,800	63,600	37,900
1983	74,846	243,600	45,427	50,000	16,200	57,300	37,700
1982	74,800	244,100	45,414	49,600	16,200	62,300	36,100
1981	73,665	329,700	44,470	63,300	17,100	95,000	43,800
1980	70,936	300,300	15,801	60,200	16,300	88,500	40,200
1979	70,797	282,400	15,684	57,500	16,800	83,900	35,000
1978	70,541	283,100	15,679	62,900	19,100	88,400	37,700
1977	29,571	262,600	15,374	62,000	18,500	85,500	36,200
1976	29,389	267,700	15,365	60,600	19,300	82,800	30,900
1975	29,091	238,800	15,344	58,800	17,300	75,700	36,000
1974	29,031	217,400	14,777	53,100	15,200	72,900	18,100
1973	29,117	215,600	14,740	54,700	16,300	71,600	13,000
1972	28,878	211,600	14,730	54,400	16,300	72,600	30,900
1971	28,731	200,543	14,470	49,115	15,913	75,182	27,671
1970	28,543	172,005	14,307	[4]45,879	17,304	46,593	27,818
1969	28,460	163,990	14,275	42,519	14,610	47,052	26,678
1968	27,971	150,836	14,212	42,515	14,206	43,838	23,919
1967	27,187	139,676	13,664	39,641	13,741	40,403	21,130
1966	26,551	133,081	13,628	38,556	13,144	43,030	15,925
1965	26,549	121,312	13,619	36,566	12,286	39,022	12,977
1964	26,102	111,386	13,566	34,047	12,164	34,847	11,478
1963	25,869	102,711	13,338	33,438	11,676	30,786	12,523
1962	26,003	97,045	13,333	32,191	11,752	27,958	11,835
1961	25,958	86,663	13,211	27,906	10,922	26,356	9,733
1960	25,704	79,229	13,208	26,630	10,738	21,820	8,983
1959	24,497	68,901	13,205	22,392	10,696	15,437	8,952
1958	24,398	65,461	13,106	21,672	9,734	14,076	8,131
1957	24,410	68,016	13,136	20,903	9,351	15,582	7,890
1956	24,398	61,602	13,131	20,055	8,769	13,543	7,438
1955	23,924	56,573	12,670	18,830	7,953	12,605	6,700
1954	23,908	54,210	12,641	17,969	7,805	12,587	6,067
1953	23,902	52,268	12,640	17,372	7,540	12,593	5,693
1952	23,840	47,379	12,589	17,143	6,807	11,979	3,558
1951	23,702	37,106	12,557	15,079	6,187	10,590	2,449
1950	23,836	33,253	12,222	13,919	5,310	9,476	1,996
1949	22,976	31,736	11,420	12,968	4,923	8,778	1,422
1948	22,955	29,859	11,347	11,293	4,438	7,849	1,510
1947	22,824	25,534	11,347	10,674	4,027	7,575	1,247
1946	22,424	21,752	11,062	8,991	3,603	6,734	1,262
1945	22,126	11,714	11,061	4,538	2,512	3,694	383
1944	22,107	8,340	11,055	2,646	1,851	3,310	268
1943	21,061	6,828	10,303	2,054	1,578	2,851	131
1942	20,886	9,371	10,300	3,815	1,832	3,130	256
1941	20,817	21,237	10,285	8,459	3,745	7,292	896

See footnotes at end of chart.

Series H 806-828. National Parks, Monuments and Allied Areas—Number, Area and Visits: 1850 to 1990—Cont'd.

(For years ending Sept. 30 prior to 1941; thereafter, for years ending Dec. 31, or as of Jan. 1 of the following year. Includes areas in Alaska, Hawaii, Virgin Islands and Puerto Rico.)

Year	Total, enumerated areas [1]		National parks		National monuments visits	National historical and military areas [3] visits	National parkways visits
	Area	Visits [2]	Area	Visits [2]			
	807	808	810	811	814	817	820
1940	20,762	16,755	10,258	7,358	2,817	5,924	—
1939	19,892	15,531	9,459	6,854	2,592	5,472	—
1938	18,647	16,331	9,409	6,619	2,364	6,784	—
1937	16,537	15,133	8,750	6,705	1,966	6,073	—
1936	15,433	11,990	8,692	5,791	1,681	4,518	—
1935	15,115	7,676	8,486	4,056	1,332	2,288	—
1934	15,244	6,337	8,532	3,517	1,386	1,434	—
1933	15,140	3,482	8,435	2,867	523	91	—
1932	12,968	3,755	8,417	2,949	406	400	—
1931	12,523	3,545	8,027	3,153	392	—	—
1930	10,581	3,247	7,797	2,775	472	—	—
1929	10,538	3,248	7,755	2,757	491	—	—
1928	10,359	3,025	7,581	2,569	456	—	—
1927	10,320	2,798	7,570	2,381	417	—	—
1926	10,249	2,315	7,501	1,942	373	—	—
1925	9,987	2,055	7,286	1,762	292	—	—
1924	8,813	1,671	7,278	1,424	247	—	—
1923	8,790	1,494	7,278	1,281	213	—	—
1922	8,781	1,216	7,278	1,045	172	—	—
1921	8,452	1,172	6,950	1,007	164	—	—
1920	8,452	1,058	6,950	920	139	—	—
1919	8,372	811	6,873	757	54	—	—
1918	7,554	455	6,255	452	3	—	—
1917	7,491	491	6,254	488	2	—	—
1916	5,984	358	4,742	356	2	—	—
1915	5,880	335	4,666	335	1	—	—
1914	5,986	240	4,437	240	1	—	—
1913	5,984	252	4,437	252	(Z)	—	—
1912	5,977	230	4,431	229	(Z)	—	—
1911	5,978	224	4,431	224	(Z)	—	—
1910	5,998	199	4,431	199	—	—	—
1909	5,013	86	3,449	86	—	—	—
1908	4,363	69	3,449	69	—	—	—
1907	3,547	61	3,444	61	—	—	—
1906	3,265	31	3,251	31	—	—	—
1905	3,471	141	3,457	141	—	—	—
1904	3,471	121	3,457	121	—	—	—
1903	3,470	—	3,456	—	—	—	—
1902	3,459	—	3,445	—	—	—	—
1901	3,300	—	3,286	—	—	—	—
1900	3,300	—	3,286	—	—	—	—
1899	3,300	—	3,286	—	—	—	—
1898	3,287	—	3,274	—	—	—	—
1897	3,287	—	3,274	—	—	—	—
1896	3,287	—	3,274	—	—	—	—

See footnotes at end of chart.

Series H 806-828.   National Parks, Monuments and Allied Areas—
Number, Area and Visits: 1850 to 1990—Cont'd.

(For years ending Sept. 30 prior to 1941; thereafter, for years ending Dec. 31, or as of Jan. 1 of the following year. Includes areas in Alaska, Hawaii, Virgin Islands and Puerto Rico.)

	Total, enumerated areas [1]			National parks		National monuments visits	National historical and military areas [3] visits	National parkways visits
Year	Area	Visits [2]		Area	Visits [2]			
	807	808		810	811	814	817	820
1895	3,287	—		3,274	—	—	—	—
1894	3,058	—		3,052	—	—	—	—
1893	3,058	—		3,052	—	—	—	—
1892	3,058	—		3,052	—	—	—	—
1891	3,058	—		3,051	—	—	—	—
1890	2,889	—		2,889	—	—	—	—
1872-1889 [5]	1,921	—		1,921	—	—	—	—
1850-1871 [6]	1	—		1	—	—	—	—

Z Less than 500.
[1] Not the same as the "national park system." Definition of the latter has changed from time to time. For 1850-1962, series H 806-808 are merely totals of the other items listed; thereafter, totals include other national parks and allied areas not shown separately, as follows (as of year end or Jan. 1 of the following year): 1970, 16 areas, 100 thousand acres and 4,742 visits; 1969, 13 areas, 94 thousand acres, and 2,415 thousand visits; 1968, 14 areas, 128 thousand acres and 1,790 thousand visits; 1967, 10 areas, 48 thousand acres and 2,393 thousand visits; 1966, 10 areas, 23 thousand acres and 2,296 thousand visits; 1965, 1 area, 18 acres and 1,673 thousand visits; 1964, 1 area, 18 acres and 1,840 thousand visits; 1963, 1 area, 18 acres and no reported visits.
[2] Beginning 1964, includes visits to the White House.

[3] Includes national historical parks, national military parks, national battlefields, national battlefield parks, national battlefield sites, national cemeteries, national historic sties, national memorials, and one national memorial park. Does not include historical areas established under the Antiquities Act of 1906 and designated national monuments, nor the White House.
[4] Includes visits to two National Recreation Areas adjacent to North Cascades National Park.
[5] Yellowstone National Park, the first national park, established 1872.
[6] Hot Springs Reservation set aside by the federal government in 1832 and established as a national park in 1921. Initial federal acreage was much greater than indicated, but over a period of years was subdivided into tracts and sold, some 900-odd acres being permanently reserved to the federal government. These series begin with 1850, the first year following the establishment of the Department of the Interior.

Series H 836-848.   State Parks—Acreage, Expenditures, Funds, Revenue, Employees and
Attendance: 1939 to 1990

		Total				Total				Total	
Year	Acreage [1]	Expenditures [2]	Attendance [2]	Year	Acreage [1]	Expenditures [2]	Attendance [2]	Year	Acreage [1]	Expenditures [2]	Attendance [2]
	836	839	846		836	839	846		836	839	846
	1,000 acres	$1,000	1,000		1,000 acres	$1,000	1,000		1,000 acres	$1,000	1,000
1990	11,238	1,060,158	722,819	1975	9,838	649,000	566,000	1955	5,086	55,093	183,188
1989	11,061	981,760	762,842	1974	—	—	—	1954	5,005	49,134	166,427
1988	10,820	903,426	710,342	1973	—	—	—	1953	4,876	49,565	159,116
1987	13,752	848,290	694,432	1972	—	—	—	1952	4,928	40,469	149,255
1986	13,726	799,851	675,465	1971	—	—	—	1951	4,877	38,545	120,722
1985	10,128	101,500	661,916	1970	8,555	386,752	482,536	1950	4,657	36,399	114,291
1984	10,148	892,000	665,524	1967	7,352	279,520	391,063	1949	(NA)	31,921	106,792
1983	9,936	838,000	644,843	1962	5,763	108,881	284,795	1948	(NA)	32,059	105,248
1982	9,912	888,000	631,031	1961	5,799	110,101	273,484	1947	(NA)	25,991	109,995
1981	9,326	968,000	618,080					1946	4,634	15,445	92,507
				1960	5,602	87,373	259,001				
1980	9,468	993,000	548,912	1959 *	5,681	88,268	255,310	1945	(NA)	10,564	57,649
1979	9,411	1,078,000	609,010	1958	5,406	73,222	237,329	1944	(NA)	6,466	39,668
1978	—	—	—	1957	5,248	74,008	216,780	1943	(NA)	6,570	38,306
1977	—	—	—	1956	5,165	65,844	200,705	1942	(NA)	9,373	70,359
1976	—	—	—					1941	4,260	10,022	97,489
								1940	—	9,443	—
								1939	—	7,429	—

* Denotes first year for which figures include Alaska and Hawaii.
NA Not available.

[1] Excludes state forests, wildlife refuges and waysides not administered by state park agencies.
[2] Detail may not add to total because some states did not report detail.

Series H 862-877.   Participation in Selected Recreational Activities: 1901 to 1990

Year	Horseracing			Major league baseball attendance [1]			Motion pictures [1]	Paid hunting and fishing license holders	
	Racing days	Attendance [1]	Parimutuel turnover	American League	National League	World Series	Average weekly attendance	Hunting	Fishing
	865	866	867	868	869	870	873	875	876
		1,000	Mil dol.	1,000	1,000	1,000	Millions	Millions	Millions
1990	13,841	63,803	7,162	30,332	24,492	209	5,022	29.7	36.9
1989	14,240	69,551	13,867	29,849	25,324	223	5,033	29.3	36.6
1988	14,285	69,949	13,616	28,500	24,499	260	4,458	30.0	36.8
1987	14,208	70,015	13,122	27,277	24,734	387	4,253	28.8	36.5
1986	13,853	70,580	12,421	25,173	22,333	322	3,778	27.9	35.9
1985	13,745	73,346	12,222	24,532	22,292	327	3,749	27.7	35.7
1984	13,683	74,076	12,032	23,961	20,781	272	2,749	28.5	36.1
1983	13,545	75,693	11,733	23,991	21,549	304	2,115	28.9	37.8
1982	13,523	76,858	11,888	23,080	21,507	385	3,453	28.3	37.2
1981	13,464	75,463	11,677	14,066	12,478	338	2,966	27.9	37.9
1980	13,133	74,690	11,218	21,890	21,124	325	1,225	27.0	35.2
1979	13,160	72,783	10,728	22,372	21,178	368	2,821	26.4	35.4
1978	13,147	75,324	10,029	20,530	20,107	337	2,643	25.8	32.8
1977	13,300	75,987	9,698	19,640	19,070	338	2,672	25.4	34.0
1976	13,570	79,307	9,421	14,658	16,661	223	2,036	25.2	34.9
1975	13,110	78,662	7,862	13,189	16,600	308	2,115	25.9	34.7
1974	12,211	74,948	7,513	13,016	16,978	308	1,908	25.1	34.3
1973	11,805	75,016	7,027	13,434	16,675	260	1,500	23.3	33.5
1972	11,478	70,807	6,401	11,438	15,530	363	1,375	22.2	33.0
1971	10,792	73,619	6,350	11,869	17,325	351	1,214	22.9	32.4
1970	9,962	69,704	5,977	12,085	16,662	253	—	22.2	31.3
1969	9,539	68,099	5,723	12,135	15,095	272	—	21.6	29.9
1968	9,051	65,460	5,310	11,317	11,785	380	—	20.9	28.8
1967	8,621	63,373	4,922	11,337	12,971	304	—	20.2	27.1
1966	8,384	63,577	4,784	10,167	15,015	221	—	19.6	26.3
1965	8,051	62,887	4,615	8,861	13,581	364	44	19.4	25.0
1964	7,561	60,595	4,402	9,235	12,045	322	44	19.1	24.5
1963	7,136	55,754	3,975	9,095	11,382	247	42	18.7	24.0
1962	6,532	50,582	3,669	10,015	11,360	377	43	18.2	23.1
1961	6,280	49,560	3,467	10,163	8,732	223	42	[3] 18.2	23.1
1960	6,099	46,879	3,358	9,227	10,685	350	40	* [3] 18.4	* 23.3
1959	5,963	45,451	3,246	9,149	9,995	421	42	[3] 11.9	19.9
1958	5,348	43,373	3,039	7,296	10,165	394	40	14.8	20.2
1957	5,187	41,365	2,937	8,196	8,820	395	45	14.9	19.3
1956	5,052	39,871	2,791	7,894	8,650	346	47	14.5	18.7
1955	4,899	38,503	2,592	8,943	7,674	362	46	14.2	18.9
1954	4,734	38,637	2,515	7,922	8,014	252	49	14.1	18.6
1953	4,656	38,249	2,556	6,964	7,420	307	46	14.8	17.7
1952	4,397	35,065	2,326	8,294	6,339	341	51	13.9	17.1
1951	4,114	31,865	1,934	8,883	7,244	342	54	12.6	16.0
1950	4,018	29,251	1,638	9,142	8,321	196	60	12.6	15.3
1949	3,702	—	1,599	10,731	9,485	237	70	12.8	15.5
1948	—	—	—	11,150	9,771	358	90	11.4	14.1
1947	—	—	—	9,486	10,388	390	90	12.1	12.6
1946	—	—	—	9,621	8,902	250	90	9.9	11.1
1945	—	—	—	5,580	5,261	333	85	8.2	8.3
1944	—	—	—	4,798	3,975	207	85	7.5	7.8
1943	—	—	—	3,697	3,769	277	85	8.1	8.0
1942	—	—	—	4,200	4,353	277	85	8.5	8.4
1941	—	—	—	4,912	4,778	236	85	7.9	8.0
1940	—	—	—	5,434	4,390	282	80	7.6	7.9
1939	—	—	—	4,271	4,707	184	85	7.5	7.9
1938	—	—	—	4,446	4,561	201	85	6.9	7.4

See footnotes at end of chart.

Series H 862-877. Participation in Selected Recreational Activities: 1901 to 1990—Cont'd.

Year	Horseracing			Major league baseball attendance [1]			Motion pictures [1]	Paid hunting and fishing license holders [2]	
	Racing days	Attendance [1]	Parimutuel turnover	American League	National League	World Series	Average weekly attendance	Hunting	Fishing
	865	866	867	868	869	870	873	875	876
		1,000	Mil. Dol.	1,000	1,000	1,000	Millions	Millions	Millions
1935	—	—	—	3,688	3,657	287	80	6.0	5.1
1934	—	—	—	3,764	3,200	282	70	5.9	4.9
1933	—	—	—	2,926	3,163	163	60	5.7	4.9
1932	—	—	—	3,133	3,841	192	60	5.8	—
1931	—	—	—	3,883	4,584	232	75	6.4	—
1930	—	—	—	4,686	5,447	213	90	6.9	—
1929	—	—	—	4,662	4,926	190	80	6.4	—
1928	—	—	—	4,221	4,881	199	65	6.5	—
1927	—	—	—	4,613	5,310	202	57	6.0	—
1926	—	—	—	4,913	4,920	328	50	5.3	—
1925	—	—	—	5,187	4,354	283	46	4.9	—
1924	—	—	—	5,255	4,341	284	46	4.4	—
1923	—	—	—	4,603	4,070	301	43	4.3	—
1922	—	—	—	4,874	3,942	186	40	—	—
1921	—	—	—	4,620	3,987	270	—	—	—
1920	—	—	—	5,084	4,037	174	—	—	—
1919	—	—	—	3,654	2,878	237	—	—	—
1918	—	—	—	1,708	1,372	186	—	—	—
1917	—	—	—	2,859	2,361	129	—	—	—
1916	—	—	—	3,452	3,052	163	—	—	—
1915	—	—	—	2,435	2,430	143	—	—	—
1914	—	—	—	2,748	1,707	111	—	—	—
1913	—	—	—	3,527	2,832	151	—	—	—
1912	—	—	—	3,264	2,736	252	—	—	—
1911	—	—	—	3,340	3,232	180	—	—	—
1910	—	—	—	3,271	3,495	124	—	—	—
1909	—	—	—	3,740	3,496	145	—	—	—
1908	—	—	—	3,611	3,512	62	—	—	—
1907	—	—	—	3,399	2,640	78	—	—	—
1906	—	—	—	2,938	2,781	100	—	—	—
1905	—	—	—	3,121	2,734	92	—	—	—
1904	—	—	—	3,024	2,664	(NA)	—	—	—
1903	—	—	—	2,345	2,390	100	—	—	—
1902	—	—	—	2,206	1,683	—	—	—	—
1901	—	—	—	1,684	1,920	—	—	—	—

* Denotes first year for which figures include Alaska and Hawaii.
NA Not available.
[1] Excludes Alaska and Hawaii for all years.

[2] Beginning 1960, includes multiple counting of license holders who bought one or more non-resident licenses as well as a license for their own home state.
[3] Excludes Colorado, Michigan, Minnesota and Wisconsin.

Series H 878-893. Personal Consumption Expenditures for Recreation: 1909 to 1989

(In millions of dollars)

| Year | Total | Nondurable toys and sport supplies | Wheel goods, durable toys, sport equipment, boats and pleasure aircraft | Radio and television receivers, records, musical instruments | Radio and television repair | Admissions to specified spectator amusements | | | Clubs and fraternal organizations, except insurance | Commercial participant amusements | Parimutuel net receipts | Books and maps | Magazines, newspapers and sheet music | Flowers, seeds, potted plants |
| | | | | | | Total | Motion picture theaters | Theater entertainment (plays, operas, etc.) or non-profit institutions, except athletics | Spectator sports | | | | | | |
	878	879	880	881	882	883	884	885	886	887	888	889	890	891	892
1989	264,400	30,200	36,200	51,100	4,200	13,400	5,000	4,900	3,500	6,300	20,200	2,800	11,400	18,500	8,100
1988	245,100	28,000	35,400	47,100	3,900	12,100	4,400	4,500	3,200	5,900	18,700	2,800	10,500	17,000	7,500
1987	223,200	26,200	33,200	41,600	3,700	11,300	4,200	4,000	3,000	5,500	17,100	2,700	9,500	15,400	7,000
1986	201,200	23,100	29,700	38,800	3,300	10,200	3,900	3,300	2,900	5,000	16,000	2,600	8,600	13,900	5,800
1985	185,700	21,100	26,700	37,000	3,200	9,500	3,600	3,000	2,900	4,800	15,100	2,600	8,100	13,200	5,500
1984	168,300	19,700	24,800	31,500	2,800	9,500	3,900	2,700	2,900	4,500	14,100	2,600	7,800	12,700	5,200
1983	152,100	18,000	20,400	28,200	2,800	8,600	3,600	2,400	2,600	4,200	13,600	2,300	7,200	12,000	4,800
1982	138,300	16,800	19,300	24,500	2,800	7,800	3,300	2,100	2,300	3,800	12,500	2,200	6,600	11,400	4,500
1981	128,600	16,000	18,700	22,000	2,700	6,900	2,900	2,000	2,000	3,400	11,700	2,200	6,200	11,000	4,400
1980	115,000	14,600	17,200	19,900	2,600	6,500	2,700	1,800	2,000	3,000	9,700	2,100	5,600	10,400	4,000
1979	106,200	13,400	17,300	18,800	2,500	6,300	2,900	1,500	1,900	2,700	8,400	2,000	5,200	9,500	3,800
1978	89,313	11,304	13,905	18,654	2,925	5,450	2,442	1,064	1,944	1,922	4,898	1,722	5,505	7,427	4,156
1977	79,782	10,063	12,171	16,960	2,668	4,997	2,376	868	1,753	1,811	4,414	1,712	4,586	6,653	3,543
1976	72,587	9,437	10,530	16,065	1,474	5,598	2,987	907	1,704	1,654	3,901	1,876	3,590	8,092	3,860
1975	70,200	9,000	10,500	13,500	2,200	4,300	2,200	800	1,300	1,900	4,900	1,700	3,600	6,400	2,700
1974	60,892	8,005	8,644	13,266	1,240	4,621	2,495	733	1,393	1,434	3,227	1,614	3,034	7,045	3,250
1973	55,199	7,302	8,167	12,288	1,334	3,870	1,965	670	1,235	1,331	2,931	1,502	2,769	5,845	2,871
1972	49,100	6,542	7,315	10,964	1,222	3,487	1,644	632	1,211	1,266	2,650	1,389	2,530	4,685	2,655
1971	42,652	6,141	5,230	9,776	1,392	2,451	1,170	736	545	1,174	1,934	1,067	3,722	4,556	1,605
1970	39,049	5,726	4,873	8,328	1,322	2,413	1,162	735	516	1,158	1,819	1,018	3,441	4,097	1,436
1969	36,284	5,250	4,434	7,838	1,266	2,260	1,099	674	487	1,112	1,733	952	3,172	3,798	1,368
1968	33,623	4,701	3,937	7,715	1,227	2,130	1,045	632	453	1,047	1,662	861	2,825	3,508	1,251
1967	30,758	3,975	3,422	7,328	1,143	2,030	989	605	436	988	1,600	795	2,689	3,207	1,107
1966	28,850	3,743	3,248	6,905	1,072	1,923	964	545	414	934	1,555	765	2,365	3,059	1,078
1965	26,298	3,436	2,933	6,013	1,032	1,811	927	495	389	879	1,509	734	2,061	2,868	983
1964	24,571	3,174	2,805	5,409	954	1,762	913	484	365	854	1,486	694	1,969	2,735	870
1963	22,213	2,986	2,538	4,539	906	1,692	904	446	342	808	1,443	626	1,620	2,521	842
1962	20,474	2,792	2,269	3,935	882	1,646	903	417	326	773	1,366	564	1,523	2,415	739
1961	19,506	2,702	2,129	3,668	839	1,625	921	398	306	763	1,299	536	1,396	2,348	702
1960 *	18,295	2,417	2,106	3,412	801	1,606	951	365	290	733	1,161	517	1,304	2,193	641
1959	17,381	2,306	2,038	3,330	735	1,571	958	344	269	721	991	493	1,159	2,110	599
1958	15,817	2,115	1,845	2,836	681	1,538	992	297	249	692	848	454	1,022	2,061	544
1957	15,333	2,047	1,720	2,825	628	1,655	1,126	287	242	653	738	438	983	1,973	587
1956	14,979	1,951	1,573	2,938	573	1,899	1,394	268	237	611	654	414	951	1,880	554
1955	14,078	1,803	1,386	2,869	516	1,801	1,326	245	230	569	584	381	867	1,869	546
1954	13,077	1,624	1,174	2,726	482	1,672	1,228	220	224	539	528	368	806	1,825	540
1953	12,720	1,694	1,090	2,588	434	1,605	1,187	197	221	517	514	372	830	1,776	545
1952	12,102	1,708	989	2,349	393	1,655	1,246	189	220	498	489	327	788	1,689	526
1951	11,564	1,662	897	2,236	353	1,716	1,310	186	220	477	472	255	776	1,573	495
1950	11,147	1,394	869	2,421	283	1,781	1,376	183	222	462	448	239	674	1,495	457
1949	10,010	1,170	836	1,675	202	1,872	1,451	182	239	454	428	247	627	1,454	451
1948	9,692	1,076	965	1,450	174	1,918	1,506	180	232	435	425	257	584	1,374	440
1947	9,249	907	955	1,398	140	2,003	1,594	187	222	397	404	255	531	1,243	442
1946	8,539	840	793	1,116	115	2,066	1,692	174	200	359	379	241	589	1,099	416
1945	6,139	553	400	344	88	1,714	1,450	148	116	281	284	153	520	965	378
1944	5,422	459	323	311	72	1,563	1,341	142	80	236	241	131	450	880	327
1943	4,961	393	271	403	60	1,455	1,275	118	62	217	215	79	366	838	274
1942	4,677	404	306	634	46	1,204	1,022	92	90	205	213	69	291	703	241
1941	4,239	362	314	607	36	995	809	79	107	203	210	65	255	636	229

See footnotes at end of chart.

Series H 878-893. Personal Consumption Expenditures for Recreation: 1909 to 1989—Cont'd.

(In millions of dollars)

| Year | Total | Nondurable toys and sport supplies | Wheel goods, durable toys, sport equipment, boats and pleasure aircraft | Radio and television receivers, records, musical instruments | Radio and television repair | Admissions to specified spectator amusements | | | | | Clubs and fraternal organizations, except insurance | Commercial participant amusements | Parimutuel net receipts | Books and maps | Magazines, newspapers and sheet music | Flowers, seeds and potted plants |
| | | | | | | Total | Motion picture theaters | Theater entertainment (plays, operas, etc.) of non-profit institutions, except athletics | Spectator sports | | | | | | |
	878	879	880	881	882	883	884	885	886	887	888	889	890	891	892
1940	3,761	306	254	494	32	904	735	71	98	203	197	55	234	589	201
1939	3,452	285	228	420	28	821	659	64	98	199	183	41	226	554	191
1938	3,241	268	210	339	25	816	663	58	95	200	164	44	221	514	176
1937	3,381	269	210	385	23	818	676	53	89	203	194	38	243	518	186
1936	3,020	242	171	333	21	759	626	50	83	198	165	29	208	490	159
1935	2,630	216	136	248	21	672	556	44	72	197	141	26	183	456	130
1934	2,441	200	118	229	17	625	518	42	65	199	135	19	165	441	116
1933	2,202	181	93	195	14	573	482	41	50	208	121	6	152	419	90
1932	2,442	207	110	268	19	631	527	57	47	242	132	4	153	428	89
1931	3,302	266	159	478	24	854	719	78	57	277	175	6	253	479	134
1930	3,990	281	172	921	27	892	732	95	65	294	203	7	264	512	190
1929	4,331	336	219	1,012	26	913	720	127	66	302	207	8	309	538	221
1927	1 3,120	470		713		769	526	195	48	283	159		2 349		183
1925	1 2,835	411		739		588	367	174	47	275	145		2 318		182
1923	1 2,620	455		637		528	336	146	46	242	148		2 370		176
1921	1 2,055	338		439		412	301	81	30	242	128		2 239		128
1919	1 2,189	377		667		—	336		—	242	55		2 204		135
1914	1 1,000	186		193		—	191		—	140	25		2 131		56
1909	1 860	143		166		—	167		—	121	22		2 104		70

* Denotes first year for which figures include Alaska and Hawaii.
1 Includes estimates "Other" recreational expenditures.
2 Represents only 42 percent of the national estimated expenditures for books and maps, magazines, newspapers and sheet music; the remaining 58 percent was classified as educational rather than recreational outlay.

Series H 921-940.   Travel to Foreign Countries—Travelers and Expenditures: 1919 to 1991

(Travelers in thousands; expenditures in millions of dollars)

Year	Total overseas travelers [1]	Total expenditures abroad [2]	Year	Total overseas travelers [1]	Total expenditures abroad [2]	Year	Total overseas travelers [1]	Total expenditures abroad [2]	Year	Total overseas travelers [1]	Total expenditures abroad [2]
	921	931		921	931		921	931		921	931
1991	14,415	39,416	1972	6,790	4,944	1955	1,075	1,153	1937	435	348
1990	15,990	38,671	1971	5,667	4,311	1954	912	1,009	1936	381	297
1989	14,791	34,548				1953	827	929			
1988	14,443	33,098	1970	5,260	3,973	1952	772	840	1935	314	245
1987	13,616	30,022	1969	4,623	3,407	1951	684	757	1934	302	218
1986	12,038	26,746	1968	3,885	3,030				1933	300	199
			1967	3,425	3,207	1950	676	754	1932	393	259
1985	12,696	25,155	1966	2,975	2,657	1949	573	700	1931	438	341
1984	11,690	23,305				1948	495	631			
1983	9,628	13,149	1965	2,623	2,438	1947	435	573	1930	538	463
1982	8,510	12,394	1964	2,220	2,211	1946	329	457	1929	517	483
1981	8,040	11,479	1963	1,990	2,114				1928	518	448
			1962	1,767	1,939	1945	117	298	1927	471	400
1980	8,163	10,397	1961	1,575	1,785	1944	75	225	1926	433	372
1979	7,835	9,413				1943	57	173			
1978	7,790	8,475	1960	1,634	1,750	1942	71	155	1925	408	347
1977	7,390	7,451	1959	1,516	1,610	1941	170	212	1924	351	303
1976	6,897	6,856	1958	1,398	1,460				1923	291	260
			1957	1,369	1,372	1940	156	190	1922	320	243
1975	6,354	6,417	1956	1,239	1,275	1939	282	290	1921	294	200
1974	6,467	5,980				1938	370	303			
1973	6,933	5,371							1920	302	190
									1919	152	123

[1] Excludes the following: travel to Canada and Mexico; travel between conterminous United States and Alaska, Hawaii, Puerto Rico and Virgin Islands; cruise travelers; military personnel and other government employees and their dependents stationed abraoad and U.S. citizens residing abroad.

[2] Includes shore expenditures of cruise travelers; excludes travel expenditures of military personnel and other government employees and their dependents stationed abroad and U.S. citizens residing abroad.

Series H 941-951.   Foreign Visitors to the United States—Number and Receipts: 1919 to 1991

(Visitors' data are for years ending June and, except for 1933 and 1934, exclude Canada and Mexico. Receipts data excludes transocean fares)

Year	Total visitors (1,000)	Total receipts (million dollars)	Year	Total visitors (1,000)	Total receipts (million dollars)	Year	Total visitors (1,000)	Total receipts (million dollars)	Year	Total visitors (1,000)	Total receipts (million doll.)
	941	945		941	945		941	945		941	945
1991	16,155	34,407	1973	3,554	1,510	1955	328	654	1937	96	135
1990	15,059	30,885	1972	2,861	1,169	1954	307	595	1936	81	117
1989	13,999	26,923	1971	2,490	965	1953	287	574			
1988	12,512	22,297				1952	296	550	1935	69	101
1987	10,434	18,032	1970	2,193	2,330	1951	255	473	1934	75	81
1986	8,860	15,642	1969	1,894	2,058				1933	60	66
			1968	1,825	1,775	1950	242	419	1932	49	65
1985	7,537	13,079	1967	1,431	1,646	1949	258	392	1931	66	94
1984	7,528	12,533	1966	1,274	1,590	1948	282	334			
1983	7,873	6,289				1947	229	342	1930	83	129
1982	8,761	6,671	1965	1,130	1,380	1946	117	257	1929	78	139
1981	9,069	6,466	1964	937	1,207				1928	78	121
			1963	780	1,015	1945	102	162	1927	73	114
1980	8,200	5,566	1962	671	957	1944	70	117	1926	70	110
1979	7,230	6,051	1961	602	885	1943	50	84			
1978	5,764	4,717				1942	42	82	1925	65	83
1977	4,509	3,709	1960	572	919	1941	46	70	1924	79	77
1976	4,456	3,332	1959	520	902				1923	65	71
			1958	447	825	1940	81	95	1922	53	61
1975	3,674	2,592	1957	419	785	1939	100	135	1921	75	76
1974	3,700	2,478	1956	345	705	1938	98	130			
									1920	81	67
									1919	47	56

Series H 952-961.   Crimes and Crime Rates, by Type: 1957 to 1990

(In thousands, except rate. Data refer to offenses known to the police. Rates are based on Bureau of the Census population data, excluding Armed Forces abroad)

Year	Total	Violent crime Total	Murder and non-negligent manslaughter	Forcible rape	Robbery	Aggravated assault	Property crime Total	Burglary	Larceny, $50 and over	Auto theft
	952	953	954	955	956	957	958	959	960	961
				NUMBER OF OFFENSES						
1990	14,476	1,820	23.4	102.6	639	1,055	12,656	3,074	7,946	1,636
1989	14,251	1,646	21.5	94.5	578	952	12,605	3,168	7,872	1,565
1988	13,923	1,566	20.7	92.5	543	910	12,357	3,218	7,706	1,433
1987	13,509	1,484	20.1	91.1	518	855	12,025	3,236	7,500	1,289
1986	13,212	1,489	20.6	91.5	543	834	11,723	3,241	7,257	1,224
1985	12,431	1,329	19.0	88.7	498	723	11,103	3,073	6,926	1,103
1984	11,882	1,273	18.7	84.2	485	685	10,609	2,984	6,592	1,032
1983	12,109	1,258	19.3	78.9	507	653	10,851	3,130	6,713	1,008
1982	12,974	1,322	21.0	78.8	553	669	11,652	3,447	7,143	1,062
1981	13,424	1,362	22.5	82.5	593	664	12,062	3,780	7,194	1,088
1980	13,408	1,345	23.0	83.0	566	673	12,064	3,795	7,137	1,132
1979	12,153	1,179	21.5	76.0	467	614	10,974	3,299	6,578	1,097
1978	11,141	1,062	19.6	67.1	417	558	10,080	3,104	5,983	992
1977	10,936	1,010	19.1	63.0	405	523	9,926	3,052	5,906	968
1976	11,305	987	18.8	56.7	420	491	10,318	3,090	6,271	958
1975	11,257	1,026	20.5	56.1	465	485	10,230	3,252	5,978	1,001
1974	10,253	975	20.7	55.4	442	456	9,279	3,039	5,263	977
1973	8,718	875	19.6	51.4	384	421	7,842	2,566	4,348	929
1972	8,249	835	18.7	46.9	376	393	7,414	2,376	4,151	887
1971	8,588	817	17.8	42.3	388	369	7,772	2,399	4,424	948
1970	5,581	733	16	38	348	331	4,848	2,177	1,750	922
1969	5,013	657	15	37	297	308	4,357	1,956	1,528	872
1968	4,477	590	14	31	262	283	3,887	1,835	1,274	778
1967	3,811	496	12	27	202	254	3,316	1,611	1,049	655
1966	3,272	426	11	26	157	233	2,846	1,392	897	557
1965	2,937	384	10	23	138	213	2,553	1,266	794	493
1964	2,762	361	9	21	130	201	2,401	1,198	734	470
1963	2,442	314	9	17	116	172	2,128	1,072	650	405
1962	2,219	299	8	17	110	163	1,920	982	574	364
1961	2,088	287	9	17	106	155	1,801	937	530	334
1960 *	2,020	286	9	17	107	153	1,734	900	507	326
1959	1,630	223	9	15	75	124	1,408	698	416	294
1958	1,573	212	8	15	75	114	1,362	685	394	283
1957	1,422	199	8	¹ 13	67	111	1,224	604	355	265
				RATE PER 100,000 INHABITANTS						
1990	5,820	732	9.4	41.2	257	424	5,089	1,236	3,195	658
1989	5,741	663	8.7	38.1	233	383	5,078	1,276	3,171	630
1988	5,664	637	8.4	37.6	221	370	5,027	1,309	3,135	583
1987	5,550	610	8.3	37.4	213	351	4,940	1,330	3,081	529
1986	5,480	618	8.6	37.9	225	346	4,863	1,345	3,010	508
1985	5,207	557	7.9	37.1	209	303	4,651	1,287	2,901	462
1984	5,031	539	7.9	35.7	205	290	4,492	1,264	2,791	437
1983	5,175	538	8.3	33.7	217	279	4,637	1,338	2,869	431
1982	5,604	571	9.1	34.0	239	289	5,033	1,489	3,085	459
1981	5,858	594	9.8	36.0	259	290	5,264	1,650	3,140	475
1980	5,950	597	10.2	36.8	251	299	5,353	1,684	3,167	502
1979	5,521	535	9.7	34.5	212	279	4,986	1,499	2,988	499
1978	5,109	487	9.0	30.8	191	256	4,622	1,424	2,744	455
1977	5,055	467	8.8	29.1	187	242	4,588	1,411	2,730	448
1976	5,266	460	8.8	26.4	196	229	4,807	1,439	2,921	446

See footnotes at end of chart.

Series H 952-961.   Crimes and Crime Rates, by Type: 1957 to 1990—Cont'd.

(In thousands, except rate. Data refer to offenses known to the police. Rates are based on Bureau of the Census population data, excluding Armed Forces abroad)

Year	Total	Total	Violent crime Murder and non-negligent manslaughter	Forcible rape	Robbery	Aggravated assault	Property crime Total	Burglary	Larceny, $50 and over	Auto theft
	952	953	954	955	956	957	958	959	960	961
	RATE PER 100,000 INHABITANTS—Cont'd.									
1975	5,282	482	9.6	26.3	218	227	4,806	1,526	2,805	469
1974	4,850	461	9.8	26.2	209	216	4,389	1,438	2,490	462
1973	4,154	417	9.4	24.5	183	201	3,737	1,223	2,072	443
1972	3,961	401	9.0	22.5	181	189	3,560	1,141	1,994	426
1971	4,165	396	8.6	20.5	188	179	3,769	1,164	2,146	460
1970	2,747	361	8	19	171	163	2,836	1,071	861	454
1969	2,483	325	7	18	147	152	2,158	969	757	432
1968	2,240	295	7	16	131	142	1,945	918	637	389
1967	1,926	251	6	14	102	129	1,676	814	530	331
1966	1,671	218	6	13	80	119	1,453	711	458	285
1965	1,516	198	5	12	71	110	1,317	653	410	255
1964	1,443	189	5	11	68	105	1,255	626	383	245
1963	1,295	167	5	9	62	91	1,129	569	345	215
1962	1,194	161	5	9	59	88	1,033	528	309	196
1961	1,141	157	5	9	58	85	984	512	290	182
1960 *	1,126	160	5	10	60	85	967	502	283	182
1959	918	126	5	9	42	70	792	393	234	165
1958	904	121	5	8	43	65	781	393	226	162
1957	835	117	5	[1] 8	39	65	719	355	208	156

* Denotes first year for which figures include Alaska and Hawaii.
[1] Includes statutory cases.

Series H 971-986. Suicides: 1900 to 1990

(Refers only to deaths occurring within the United States. Rates per 100,000 resident population; for population bases used in computing rates, see series A 7)

Year	Suicides Number 979	Rate 980	Year	Suicides Number 979	Rate 980	Year	Suicides Number 979	Rate 980`	Year	Suicides Number 979	Rate 980
1990	30,800	12.3	1967	21,325	10.8	1945	14,782	11.2	1922	10,876	11.7
1989	30,200	12.2	1966	21,281	10.9	1944	13,231	10.0	1921	10,906	12.4
1988	30,407	12.4				1943	13,725	10.2			
1987	30,796	12.7	1965	21,507	11.1	1942	16,117	12.0	1920	8,790	10.2
1986	30,904	12.8	1964	20,588	10.8	1941	17,102	12.8	1919	9,543	11.5
			1963	20,825	11.0				1918	9,685	12.3
1985	29,500	12.3	1962	20,207	10.9	1940	18,907	14.4	1917	9,157	13.0
1984	29,286	11.9	1961	18,999	10.4	1939	18,511	14.1	1916	9,181	13.7
1983	28,295	12.1				1938	19,802	15.3			
1982	28,242	12.2	1960 *	19,041	10.6	1937	19,294	15.0	1915	10,011	16.2
1981	27,596	12.0	1959 [1]	18,633	10.6	1936	18,294	14.3	1914	9,802	16.1
			1958	18,519	10.7				1913	8,932	15.4
1980	26,900	11.9	1957	16,632	9.8	1935	18,214	14.3	1912	8,549	15.6
1979	27,206	12.1	1956	16,727	10.0	1934	18,828	14.9	1911	8,612	16.0
1978	27,300	12.5				1933	19,993	15.9			
1977	28,681	13.3	1955	16,760	10.2	1932	20,646	17.4	1910	7,283	15.3
1976	26,934	12.5	1954	16,356	10.1	1931	19,807	16.8	1909	7,061	16.0
			1953	15,947	10.1				1908	6,506	16.8
1975	27,100	12.7	1952	15,567	10.0	1930	18,323	15.6	1907	5,027	14.5
1974	25,683	12.1	1951	15,909	10.4	1929	16,045	13.9	1906	4,323	12.8
1973	25,118	12.0				1928	15,390	13.5			
1972	25,004	12.6	1950	17,145	11.4	1927	14,096	13.2	1905	2,940	13.5
1971	24,092	11.7	1949	16,993	11.4	1926	13,082	12.6	1904	2,611	12.2
			1948	16,354	11.2				1903	2,371	11.3
1970	23,480	11.6	1947	16,538	11.5	1925	12,209	12.0	1902	2,124	10.3
1969	22,364	11.1	1946	16,152	11.5	1924	11,846	11.9	1901	2,105	10.4
1968	21,372	10.7				1923	11,096	11.5	1900	2,036	10.2

* Denotes first year for which figures include Alaska and Hawaii.

[1] Includes Alaska.

Series H 987-998.   Police Officers Killed: 1945 to 1990
(Covers law enforcement officers killed in line of duty.)

Year	Total killed 987	Year	Total killed 987	Year	Total killed 987	Year	Total killed 987
1990	132	1978	146	1967	123	1955	55
1989	145	1977	123	1966	99	1954	61
1988	155	1976	140			1953	63
1987	148			1965	83	1952	63
1986	133	1975	185	1964	88	1951	64
		1974	179	1963	88		
1985	148	1973	176	1962	78	1950	36
1984	147	1972	157	1961	71	1949	55
1983	152	1971	181			1948	64
1982	164			1960	48	1947	67
1981	157	1970	146	1959	49	1946	82
		1969	125	1958	49	1945	59
1980	165	1968	123	1957	45		
1979	165			1956	46		

Series H 999-1011.   Persons Arrested, by Sex and Age: 1932 to 1990
(In thousands)

Year	Persons arrested [1] 999	Male 1004	Under 18 years 1006	Year	Persons arrested [1] 999	Male 1004	Under 18 years 1006	Year	Persons arrested [1] 999	Male 1004	Under 18 years 1006
1990	11,250	9,180	1,755	1970	6,257	5,624	1,661	1950	794	717	35
1989	11,261	9,234	1,745	1969	5,577	5,058	1,500	1949	792	713	33
1988	10,150	8,749	1,634	1968	5,349	4,891	1,457	1948	760	683	32
1987	10,796	8,882	1,781	1967	5,265	4,830	1,340	1947	734	659	34
1986	10,392	8,586	1,748	1966	4,798	4,407	1,149	1946	645	577	38
1985	10,290	8,499	1,763	1965	4,743	4,432	1,074	1945	544	460	50
1984	8,922	7,433	1,538	1964	4,381	4,138	961	1944	489	405	47
1983	10,287	8,582	1,726	1963	4,259	3,997	789	1943	491	412	48
1982	10,062	8,425	1,805	1962 [2]	3,923	3,645	653	1942	586	516	38
1981	10,296	8,633	2,036	1961 [2]	3,608	3,418	567	1941	631	573	37
1980	9,703	8,170	2,026	1960 [2]	3,499	3,272	527	1940	609	557	35
1979	9,506	8,011	2,143	1959 [2]	2,613	2,334	321	1939	577	533	36
1978	9,775	8,227	2,279	1958 [2]	2,340	2,092	284	1938	554	517	36
1977	9,029	7,581	2,170	1957 [2]	2,069	1,849	254	1937	520	484	33
1976	7,912	6,672	1,973	1956 [2]	2,071	1,845	234	1936	462	428	26
1975	8,014	6,752	2,078	1955 [2]	1,862	1,657	196	1935	392	365	23
1974	6,179	5,185	1,683	1954 [2]	1,689	1,503	164	1934	344	320	19
1973	6,500	5,502	1,717	1953 [2]	1,791	1,597	150	1933	320	297	18
1972	7,013	5,956	1,794	1952 [2]	1,111	991	86	1932 [3]	—	257	15
1971	6,967	5,923	1,797	1951	831	746	37				

[1] Each person arrested is counted rather than the number of charges filed against one person. Includes persons for whom age was not known. Prior to 1952, arrest data determined by examination of fingerprint cards.

[2] City arrest data.

[3] February 1 through December 31.

Series H 1012-1027.   Criminal Justice System—Public Expenditures, by Level of Government: 1902 to 1988

(In millions of dollars)

Year	All governments				Federal government			
	Total [1]	Police protection	Judicial activities	Correction	Total [1]	Police protection	Judicial activities	Correction
	1012	1013	1014	1015	1016	1017	1018	1019
1988	60,980	27,956	7,618	19,119	7,794	3,555	1,158	1,226
1987	51,428	24,684	—	16,638	—	—	—	—
1986	46,947	22,685	—	14,957	—	—	—	—
1985	45,607	22,014	5,780	13,034	5,819	2,768	852	779
1984	—						—	
1983	39,680	20,648	8,621	10,411	4,844	2,745	1,523	576
1982	35,839	19,022	7,771	9,047	4,269	2,366	1,390	513
1981	24,691	16,822	—	7,869	2,317	1,904	—	413
1980	22,064	15,163	—	6,901	2,126	1,739	—	387
1979	26,028	13,917	5,628	6,040	3,379	2,053	876	354
1978	24,132	13,120	5,051	5,523	3,122	1,952	746	337
1977	21,574	11,865	4,267	4,934	2,779	1,765	616	299
1976	19,681	11,028	3,807	4,386	2,450	1,612	472	256
1975	17,249	9,786	3,281	3,843	2,189	1,461	429	217
1974	14,954	8,512	1,708	3,240	1,961	1,222	136	215
1973	12,985	7,624	1,579	2,740	1,629	1,089	118	171
1972	11,721	6,903	1,491	2,422	1,492	962	179	133
1971	10,517	6,165	1,358	2,291	1,448	805	134	121
1970	8,571	5,081	1,190	1,706	978	589	129	83
1969	7,340	4,430	1,002	1,462	800	492	106	71
1968	6,070	3,725	976	1,369	445	290	90	65
1967	5,424	3,331	894	1,199	429	282	87	60
1966	4,903	3,033	793	1,077	393	257	79	57
1965	4,574	2,792	748	1,034	377	243	75	59
1964	4,222	2,586	697	939	342	220	66	56
1963	4,009	2,440	693	876	358	209	94	55
1962	3,795	2,326	628	841	304	196	57	51
1961	3,613	2,210	593	810	298	193	58	47
1960	3,349	2,030	597	722	291	173	74	44
1959	3,149	1,880	561	708	275	170	68	37
1958	2,861	1,769	519	573	261	159	63	39
1957	2,655	1,624	481	550	252	155	62	35
1956	2,434	1,487	447	500	250	156	61	33
1955	2,231	1,359	409	463	206	129	49	28
1954	2,080	1,254	399	427	210	124	56	30
1953	—	1,160	—	(NA)	—	122	—	(NA)
1952	—	1,080	—	365	—	141	—	28
1951	—	(NA)	—	—	—	104	—	—
1950	—	864	—	—	—	88	—	—
1948	—	724	—	—	—	80	—	—
1947	—	—	—	—	—	—	—	—
1946	—	549	—	—	—	70	—	—
1945	—	—	—	—	—	—	—	—
1944	—	497	—	—	—	83	—	—
1942	—	444	—	—	—	50	—	—
1940	—	386	—	—	—	21	—	—
1938	—	378	—	—	—	19	—	—
1936	—	331	—	—	—	17	—	—
1932	—	349	—	—	—	31	—	—
1927	—	290	—	—	—	20	—	—
1922	—	204	—	—	—	14	—	—
1913	—	92	—	—	—	3	—	—
1902	—	50	—	—	—	X	—	—

See footnotes at end of chart

Series H 1012-1027. Criminal Justice System—Public Expenditures, by Level of Government: 1902 to 1988—Cont'd.

(In millions of dollars)

Year	State government				Local government			
	Total [1]	Police protection	Judicial activities	Correction	Total [1]	Police protection	Judicial activities	Correction
	1020	1021	1022	1023	1024	1025	1026	1027
1988	22,120	4,513	3,071	12,671	33,535	20,333	3,688	6,530
1987	—	—	—	—	—	—	—	—
1986	—	—	—	—	—	—	—	—
1985	16,013	3,511	2,262	8,884	25,373	16,026	2,841	4,316
1984	—	—	—	—	—	—	—	—
1983	11,709	2,630	2,756	6,323	23,127	15,273	4,342	3,512
1982	10,649	2,486	2,606	5,557	20,922	14,170	3,775	2,976
1981	7,085	2,241	—	4,844	15,289	12,677	—	2,612
1980	6,285	2,027	—	4,258	13,653	11,397	—	2,256
1979	8,463	2,150	1,318	3,824	15,401	9,882	1,903	2,197
1978	6,888	1,892	1,497	3,177	14,322	9,276	2,809	2,009
1977	5,812	1,800	1,026	2,847	12,983	8,300	2,626	1,788
1976	5,204	1,696	903	2,475	12,027	7,720	2,432	1,654
1975	4,612	1,512	779	2,193	10,449	6,813	2,073	1,434
1974	3,906	1,308	439	1,813	9,092	5,982	1,223	1,213
1973	3,304	1,132	386	1,534	8,052	5,403	1,075	1,035
1972	2,948	903	346	1,378	7,281	4,948	965	911
1971	2,291	932	327	1,387	6,663	4,489	912	895
1970	2,134	689	282	1,051	5,454	3,803	779	572
1969	1,849	621	236	914	4,691	3,317	660	477
1968	1,622	541	209	872	4,003	2,894	677	432
1967	1,381	441	193	747	3,615	2,609	614	392
1966	1,224	385	175	664	3,286	2,391	539	356
1965	1,135	348	155	632	3,062	2,201	518	343
1964	1,042	315	141	586	2,838	2,051	490	297
1963	960	297	127	536	2,691	1,934	472	285
1962	902	276	118	508	2,589	1,854	453	282
1961	849	261	109	479	2,466	1,756	426	284
1960	769	245	99	425	2,289	1,612	424	253
1959	733	228	92	413	2,141	1,482	401	258
1958	671	214	87	370	1,929	1,396	369	164
1957	584	179	77	328	1,819	1,290	342	187
1956	526	159	72	295	1,658	1,172	314	172
1955	475	139	68	268	1,550	1,091	292	167
1954	446	130	66	250	1,424	1,000	277	147
1953	418	119	61	238	—	919	—	(NA)
1952	386	106	57	223	—	833	—	114
1951	365	97	53	215	—	(NA)	—	—
1950	332	85	49	198	—	691	—	—
1948	—	65	—	153	—	579	—	—
1947	—	—	—	107	—	—	—	—
1946	—	45	—	97	—	434	—	—
1945	—	—	—	82	—	—	—	—
1944	159	41	35	83	—	373	—	—
1942	—	40	—	80	—	354	—	—
1940	—	34	—	86	—	331	—	—
1938	—	30	—	85	—	329	—	—
1936	—	19	—	73	—	295	—	—
1932	—	15	—	87	—	303	—	—
1927	—	7	—	64	—	263	—	—
1922	—	4	—	64	—	186	—	—
1913	—	1	—	28	—	88	—	—
1902	—	X	—	14	—	50	—	—

X Represents zero.
NA Not available.

[1] Beginning 1969, legal services and prosecution and indigent defense included in totals.

Series H 1028-1062　Lawyers—Selected Characteristics: 1948 to 1989

(Data based on editions of *Martindale-Hubbell Law Directory*. Represents all persons who are members of the bar)

Series No.	Characteristic	1989	1985	1980	1970	1966	1963	1960	1957	1954	1951	1948
1028	All lawyers [1]	723,189	655,191	542,205	355,242	316,856	296,069	285,933	262,320	241,514	221,605	—
1033	Male	606,768	569,649	498,019	315,715	281,336	261,639	245,897	229,433	216,564	199,052	168,113
1034	Female	116,421	85,542	44,185	9,103	8,068	7,143	6,488	6,350	5,036	5,059	2,997
	Status in practice [2]											
1046	Government	57,742	53,035	50,490	35,803	31,280	29,314	25,621	24,245	21,279	19,910	14,143
1047	Federal	23,042	10,989	20,132	18,710	16,284	15,113	13,045	12,458	9,040	8,314	(NA)
1048	State	34,700	33,046	30,358	9,293	7,416	6,486	4,316	4,000	3,561	3,577	(NA)
1049	City or county	—	—	—	7,800	7,580	7,715	8,260	7,787	8,678	8,019	8,013
1050	Judicial	19,071	21,677	19,160	10,349	9,712	8,748	8,180	7,910	7,903	7,471	7,130
1051	Federal	2,551	3,003	2,611	878	800	707	599	769	621	675	(NA)
1052	State or county	16,520	18,674	16,549	7,548	6,823	5,712	5,301	5,056	5,041	4,561	(NA)
1053	City				1,923	2,089	2,329	2,280	2,085	2,241	2,235	(NA)
1054	Private practice	519,941	460,206	370,111	236,085	212,662	200,586	192,353	188,955	189,423	176,995	152,649
1058	Salaried	85,671	83,843	73,862	40,486	33,222	29,510	25,198	21,054	16,648	12,997	5,555
1059	Private industry	66,627	63,622	54,626	33,593	29,405	26,492	22,533	18,911	15,063	11,274	(NA)
1060	Educational institutions	7,575	7,254	6,606	3,732	2,717	2,100	1,798	1,504	1,351	1,213	(NA)
1061	Other private employment	11,469	12,967	12,630	3,161	1,100	918	867	639	234	510	(NA)

NA Not available.

[1] Includes lawyers not reporting and an adjustment (subtraction) for duplications.

[2] In some cases, if more than one subentry was applicable, the person was counted in each.

Series H 1063-1078.   U.S. Supreme Court—Cases Filed and Disposed of During October Terms: 1940 to 1990
(In thousands, except rate)

Year	Total cases Filed (1063)	Opinions disposed of (1065)	Year	Total cases Filed (1063)	Opinions disposed of (1065)	Year	Total cases Filed (1063)	Opinions disposed of (1065)	Year	Total cases Filed (1063)	Opinions disposed of (1065)
1990	6,316	237	1977	4,704	290	1964	2,288	275	1951	1,234	197
1989	5,746	275	1976	4,731	302	1963	2,294	393			
1988	5,657	301				1962	2,373	388	1950	1,181	191
1987	5,268	239	1975	4,761	314	1961	2,185	264	1949	1,270	202
1986	5,123	319	1974	4,688	287				1948	1,465	238
			1973	5,079	309	1960	1,940	282	1947	1,295	208
1985	5,158	317	1972	4,640	308	1959	1,862	249	1946	1,510	256
1984	5,006	309	1971	4,533	296	1958	1,819	275			
1983	5,100	331				1957	1,639	323	1945	1,316	215
1982	5,079	331	1969	3,405	347	1956	1,802	266	1944	1,237	274
1981	5,311	321	1968	3,271	346				1943	997	210
			1967	3,106	462	1955	1,644	246	1942	984	259
1980	5,144	275	1966	2,752	402	1954	1,397	196	1941	1,178	376
1979	4,781	285				1953	1,302	170	1940	977	281
1978	4,731	291	1965	2,774	338	1952	1,283	193			

Series H 1097-1111.   U.S. District Courts—Civil and Criminal Cases: 1941 to 1990
(For years ending June 30)

Year	Civil cases Total cases commenced (1097)	Total cases terminated (1098)	Cases commenced[1] (1099)	Criminal cases Defendants disposed of Not convicted (1101)	Convicted Total (1105)	Imprisonment (1108)	Probation[2] (1109)
1990	217,900	213,400	48,000	9,800	46,700	27,800	14,200
1989	233,500	234,600	44,900	10,100	44,500	24,900	15,000
1988	239,600	238,100	43,500	9,900	42,900	22,500	16,100
1987	239,000	237,500	42,200	10,200	43,900	23,300	16,000
1986	254,800	265,800	40,400	9,300	40,700	20,600	15,200
1985	273,700	268,600	38,500	8,800	38,500	18,700	14,400
1984	261,500	241,800	35,900	8,400	36,100	17,700	13,900
1983	241,800	213,600	34,900	7,700	35,600	17,900	14,100
1982	206,200	185,500	31,600	8,200	32,300	15,900	12,700
1981	180,600	172,900	30,400	8,300	29,900	13,700	12,200
1980	168,800	155,000	28,000	8,000	28,600	13,200	11,100
1979	154,700	140,000	31,500	8,300	32,900	14,600	13,500
1978	138,800	123,200	34,600	9,400	36,500	17,400	14,500
1977	130,600	115,500	39,800	11,700	41,500	19,600	16,100
1976	130,600	108,600	39,100	11,500	40,100	18,500	18,200
1975	117,300	103,800	41,100	11,800	37,400	17,300	17,900
1974	103,500	96,700	37,700	11,800	36,200	17,200	16,600
1973	98,560	97,402	40,367	11,741	34,983	17,540	15,026
1972	96,173	94,256	47,043	12,296	37,220	16,832	15,395
1971	93,396	85,368	41,290	12,512	32,103	14,378	13,243
1970	87,321	80,435	39,959	8,178	28,178	12,415	11,387
1969	77,193	73,354	35,413	5,993	26,803	12,847	9,991
1968	71,449	68,873	32,571	6,169	25,674	12,610	9,820
1967	70,961	70,172	32,207	5,191	26,344	13,085	9,435
1966	70,906	66,184	31,494	4,661	27,314	13,282	10,256
1965	67,678	65,478	33,334	4,961	28,757	13,668	10,779
1964	66,930	63,954	30,268	4,211	29,170	13,273	11,634
1963	63,630	62,379	39,920	5,042	29,803	13,639	12,047
1962	61,836	57,996	37,665	4,599	28,511	14,042	11,071
1961	58,293	55,416	28,460	4,046	28,625	14,162	10,714
1960	59,284	61,829	28,137	3,784	26,728	13,433	10,391
1959	57,800	62,172	28,729	3,696	27,033	13,648	10,726
1958	67,115	61,285	28,897	3,661	26,808	13,288	10,903
1957	62,380	63,568	28,120	3,471	26,254	12,986	10,760
1956	62,394	67,700	28,739	4,244	27,567	12,854	11,759
1955	59,375	58,974	35,310	5,135	33,855	16,889	14,021
1954	59,461	57,903	41,808	4,848	38,141	18,483	16,856
1953	64,001	57,490	37,291	4,289	33,473	15,637	15,118
1952	58,428	53,150	37,950	3,834	34,788	15,379	17,018
1951	51,600	52,119	38,670	4,066	37,000	14,963	19,271
1950	54,622	53,259	36,383	4,173	33,502	14,435	16,046
1949	53,421	48,396	34,432	4,190	32,074	14,204	14,690
1948	46,725	48,791	32,097	4,862	29,380	12,961	13,422
1947	58,956	54,515	33,652	5,527	31,108	14,375	12,612
1946	67,835	61,000	33,203	6,597	29,885	14,353	11,446
1945	60,965	52,300	39,429	7,536	34,117	16,311	13,153
1944	38,499	37,086	39,621	—	—	—	—
1943	36,789	36,044	36,588	—	—	—	—
1942	38,140	38,352	33,294	—	—	—	—
1941	38,477	38,561	31,823	—	—	—	—

[1] Excludes transfers.

[2] Includes probation and suspended sentence.

Series H 1112-1118.   U.S. District Courts—Trials: 1944 to 1990

(For years ending June 30. Through 1960, trials commenced; thereafter, trials completed)

Year	Total trials	Civil trials Total	Nonjury	Jury	Criminal trials Total	Nonjury	Jury	Year	Total trials	Civil trials Total	Nonjury	Jury	Criminal trials Total	Nonjury	Jury
	1112	1113	1114	1115	1116	1117	1118		1112	1113	1114	1115	1116	1117	1118
1990	20,433	11,502	6,737	4,765	8,931	3,870	5,061	1966	12,193	7,783	4,607	3,176	4,410	1,239	3,171
1989	20,102	12,085	6,878	5,207	8,017	3,553	4,464								
1988	19,901	12,536	7,088	5,448	7,365	3,215	4,150	1965	11,485	7,613	4,459	3,154	3,872	1,143	2,729
1987	19,985	13,162	7,597	5,565	6,823	2,912	3,911	1964	11,079	7,155	4,063	3,092	3,924	1,076	2,848
1986	20,242	13,276	8,054	5,222	6,966	3,066	3,900	1963	10,960	7,095	3,925	3,170	3,865	1,159	2,706
								1962	10,048	6,260	3,335	2,925	3,788	1,090	2,698
1985	20,729	14,254	8,817	5,437	6,475	2,778	3,697	1961	9,594	6,156	3,245	2,911	3,438	982	2,456
1984	20,830	14,374	9,037	5,337	6,456	2,823	3,633								
1983	21,345	14,689	9,712	4,977	6,856	3,003	3,653	1960	9,998	6,488	3,453	3,035	3,510	1,008	2,502
1982	21,397	14,753	10,074	4,679	6,644	3,076	3,568	1959	10,293	6,896	3,566	3,330	3,397	1,033	2,364
1981	21,239	14,697	10,047	4,650	6,542	2,962	3,580	1958	10,888	7,057	3,666	3,391	3,831	1,326	2,505
								1957	10,443	6,884	3,595	3,289	3,559	1,214	2,345
1980	19,825	13,191	9,254	3,937	6,634	3,216	3,418	1956	11,198	7,341	3,811	3,530	3,857	1,319	2,538
1979	18,563	11,764	8,348	3,416	6,799	3,132	3,667								
1978	18,851	11,515	8,326	3,189	7,336	3,344	3,992	1955	11,138	7,049	4,110	2,939	4,089	1,351	2,738
1977	18,827	11,605	7,792	3,813	7,222	2,661	4,561	1954	11,275	6,958	4,182	2,776	4,317	1,493	2,824
1976	19,580	11,656	8,098	3,558	7,924	2,773	5,151	1953	10,768	6,861	4,272	2,589	3,907	1,361	2,546
								1952	10,073	6,668	4,179	2,489	3,405	1,167	2,238
1975	19,236	11,603	7,903	3,700	7,633	2,726	4,907	1951	9,878	6,962	4,492	2,470	2,916	1,035	1,881
1974	18,572	10,972	7,403	3,569	7,600	2,753	4,847								
1973	19,467	10,896	7,289	3,607	8,571	2,927	5,644	1950	9,572	6,539	4,276	2,263	3,033	961	2,072
1972	18,780	10,962	7,285	3,677	7,818	2,968	4,850	1949	9,282	6,426	4,149	2,277	2,856	997	1,859
1971	17,549	10,093	6,600	3,493	7,456	2,923	4,533	1948	8,905	6,156	4,204	1,952	2,749	892	1,857
								1947	8,818	5,850	3,989	1,861	2,968	1,112	1,856
1970	16,032	9,449	6,078	3,371	6,583	2,357	4,226	1946	9,030	5,220	3,633	1,587	3,810	1,250	2,560
1969	14,397	8,834	5,619	3,215	5,563	1,883	3,680								
1968	14,221	8,688	5,478	3,210	5,533	1,800	3,733	1945	9,779	5,265	3,561	1,704	4,514	1,503	3,011
1967	12,500	8,095	4,742	3,353	4,405	1,345	3,060	1944	9,951	5,025	2,702	2,323	4,926	1,819	3,107

Series H 1119-1124.   Juvenile Court—Cases Handled: 1940 to 1989

(In thousands, except rate)

Year	Delinquency cases, 10 to 17 years old Total[1]	Rate per 1,000 population	Year	Delinquency cases, 10 to 17 years old Total[1]	Rate per 1,000 population	Year	Delinquency cases, 10 to 17 years old Total[1]	Rate per 1,000 population	Year	Delinquency cases, 10 to 17 years old Total[1]	Rate per 1,000 population
	1123	1124		1123	1124		1123	1124		1123	1124
1989	1,189	47.0	1976	1,077	35.1	1964	686	23.5	1951	298	16.8
1988	1,151	45.2				1963	601	21.4			
1987	1,145	44.5	1975	1,050	33.8	1962	555	20.6	1950	280	16.1
1986	1,150	44.2	1974	1,252	37.5	1961	503	19.3	1949	272	15.6
			1973	1,143	34.2				1948	254	14.9
1985	1,112	42.2	1972	1,112	33.6	1960	510	20.1	1947	262	15.1
1984	1,034	38.7	1971	1,125	34.1	1959	483	19.6	1946	295	16.9
1983	1,030	38.3				1958	470	20.0			
1982	1,073	39.1	1970	1,052	32.3	1957	440	19.8	1945	344	19.6
1981	1,100	39.1	1969	989	30.7	1956	520	25.2	1944	330	18.6
			1968	900	28.5				1943	344	18.7
1980	1,093	38.3	1967	811	26.3	1955	431	21.4	1942	250	13.4
1979	1,048	36.2	1966	745	24.7	1954	395	20.2	1941	224	11.8
1978	1,023	34.6				1953	374	19.7	1940	200	10.5
1977	1,076	35.8	1965	697	23.6	1952	332	18.2			

[1] For 1940-1956, includes traffic cases.

Series H 1135-1143. Federal and State Institutions—Prisoners: 1926 to 1990

(Prisoners in institutions for adult offenders only.)

Year	Prisoners present (at end of year)			Year	Prisoners present (at end of year)			Year	Prisoners present (at end of year)		
	Total	Federal institutions	State institutions		Total	Federal institutions	State institutions		Total	Federal institutions	State institutions
	1135	1136	1137		1135	1136	1137		1135	1136	1137
1990	738,894	50,810	688,084	1968	187,914	19,703	168,211	1946	140,079	17,622	122,457
1989	680,907	47,168	633,739	1967	194,896	19,579	175,317				
1988	603,732	42,738	560,994	1966	199,654	19,245	180,409	1945	133,649	18,638	115,011
1987	560,812	39,523	521,289					1944	132,456	18,139	114,317
1986	522,084	36,531	485,553	1965	210,895	21,040	189,855	1943	137,220	16,113	121,107
				1964	214,336	21,709	192,627	1942	150,384	16,623	133,761
1985	480,568	32,695	447,873	1963	217,283	23,128	194,155	1941	165,439	18,465	146,974
1984	443,398	27,602	415,796	1962	218,830	23,944	194,886				
1983	419,346	26,331	393,015	1961	220,149	23,696	196,453	1940	173,706	19,260	154,446
1982	395,516	23,652	371,864					1939	179,818	19,730	160,088
1981	353,674	22,169	331,505	1960	212,957	23,218	189,739	1938	159,382	17,083	142,299
				1959	207,446	22,492	184,954	1937	149,357	15,309	134,048
1980	315,974	20,611	295,363	1958	205,493	21,549	183,944	1936	143,573	15,373	128,200
1979	301,470	22,588	278,882	1957	195,256	20,420	174,836				
1978	294,396	26,391	268,005	1956	189,421	20,134	169,287	1935	144,665	14,777	129,888
1977	285,456	28,650	256,806					1934	138,220	12,080	126,140
1976	262,833	26,980	235,853	1955	185,780	20,088	165,692	1933	136,947	10,851	126,096
				1954	182,848	20,003	162,845	1932	137,183	12,282	124,901
1975	240,593	24,131	216,462	1953	173,547	19,363	154,184	1931	137,082	12,964	124,118
1974	218,466	22,361	196,105	1952	168,200	18,014	150,186				
1973	204,211	22,815	181,396	1951	165,640	17,395	148,245	1930	127,495	12,181	115,314
1972	196,183	21,713	174,470					1929	120,496	12,964	107,532
1971	198,061	20,948	177,113	1950	166,123	17,134	148,989	1928	116,626	8,204	108,422
				1949	163,749	16,868	146,881	1927	106,517	7,722	98,795
1970	196,429	20,038	176,391	1948	155,977	16,328	139,649	1926	96,125	6,803	89,322
1969	196,007	19,623	176,384	1947	151,304	17,146	134,158				

Series H 1155-1167. Prisoners Executed Under Civil Authority, by Race and Offense: 1930 to 1990

(Prior to 1960, excludes Alaska and Hawaii except for three federal executions in Alaska: 1939, 1948 and 1950)

Year	All offenses			Year	All offenses			Year	All offenses		
	Total	White	Black		Total	White	Black		Total	White	Black
	1155	1156	1157		1155	1156	1157		1155	1156	1157
1990	23	16	7	1963	21	13	8	1946	131	46	84
1989	16	8	8	1962	47	28	19				
1988	11	6	5	1961	42	20	22	1945	117	41	75
1987	25	13	12					1944	120	47	70
1986	18	11	7	1960	56	21	35	1943	131	54	74
				1959	49	16	33	1942	147	67	80
1985	18	11	7	1958	49	20	28	1941	123	59	63
1984	21	13	8	1957	65	34	31				
1983	5	4	1	1956	65	21	43	1940	124	49	75
1982	2	1	1					1939	160	80	77
1981	1	1	X	1955	76	44	32	1938	190	96	92
				1954	81	38	42	1937	147	69	74
1971-1980	3	3	X	1953	62	30	31	1936	195	92	101
1970	X	X	X	1952	83	36	47				
1969	X	X	X	1951	105	57	47	1935	199	119	77
1968	X	X	X					1934	168	65	102
1967	2	1	1	1950	82	40	42	1933	160	77	81
1966	1	1	X	1949	119	50	67	1932	140	62	75
				1948	119	35	82	1931	153	77	72
1965	7	6	1	1947	153	42	111	1930	155	90	65
1964	15	8	7								

X Represents zero.

LAND, WATER AND CLIMATE

LAND, WATER AND CLIMATE

Highlights

1 When the United States became a republic, no one was quite sure what its boundaries were. Its territorial claims were based on several treaties subject to interpretation. The boundaries themselves were illmarked and expanded or receded depending on the status of the Indian wars. Between 1781 and 1867, the Federal government acquired millions of acres of public domain. From 1781 to 1902, seven of the original 13 states relinquished their claims to the so-called "Western lands" to the Federal government. In 1788, the state of Maryland ceded the present area of the District of Columbia. Between 1803 and 1867, title to the remaining area west of the Mississippi River (except the state of Texas) and to Florida passed to the Federal government. The annual report to the General Land Office in 1850 contained the first reference to the areas of the states and territories, although there was no indication of the methods used in obtaining the measurements. In 1881, the Bureau of the Census initiated the first effort to obtain an accurate and detailed area measurement of the United States. This was revised in 1940 in *Areas of the United States*, and presented land and water areas as well as state, municipal, and county boundaries. Differences in land area figures over time reflect improvements in cartography which make possible a more accurate determination of the outer limits as well as inclusion or exclusion of certain bodies of water. For the 1990 Census, area measurements were calculated by computer and based on the information contained in a single data base, the TIGER (Topologically Integrated Geographic Encoding and Referencing) File. As a result, the number of inland water areas increased when coverage was extended to inland bodies of water of at least 40 acres, and streams with a width of at least one-eighth of a statute mile. An inventory of the nation's land resources by type of use/cover was conducted by the Soil Conservation Service in 1982 to 1987 and its results were published in the 1987 *National Inventory of Land Resources.*

2 The state with the largest land area and largest water area is Alaska. Alaska's water area of 85,051 sq. mi. is larger than the land area of all but 11 states.

3 In 1988, the Federal government owned 688.253 million acres, or 30.3% of the land area. This compares to 771.512 million acres or 33.9% of the total land area in 1960. Because of environmental considerations the divestiture of Federal land is likely to slow in the future.

4 The highest point in the United States is Mount McKinley in Alaska at 20,320 feet. The lowest point is Death Valley in California at -282 feet.

5 The Mississippi, the largest river, has a length of 2,340 miles, an average discharge at its mouth of 593,000 cubic feet per second, and a drainage area of 1,150,000 sq. miles. There are nine other rivers with a length of over 1,000 miles: Missouri (2,540 mi), Yukon (1,980 mi), St. Lawrence (1,900 mi), Arkansas (1,460 mi), Atchafalaya (1,420 mi), Ohio (1,310 mi), Red (1,290 mi), Columbia (1,240 mi), and Snake (1,040).

6 In 1990, total water withdrawal (all water withdrawn from natural reservoirs, lakes, rivers, etc., for human consumption and industrial use) per day in the United States was 399 billion gallons, or 144 gallons per capita. Of the total, 74 billion was ground water and 325 billion surface water. The largest amount of water used was for irrigation (137 billion gallons), followed by thermoelectric production (187 billion gallons). Public supply was third (39.9 billion gallons), and industrial use fourth (29.3 billion gallons). Per capita, the states that used the largest amounts of water per day were Idaho (22,200 gallons), Wyoming (12,200 gallons) and Montana (10,500 gallons). Among the lowest users were Rhode Island (152 gallons), Delaware (222 gallons), New Jersey (307 gallons), Maryland (321 gallons), Connecticut (365 gallons), and Oklahoma (386 gallons).

7 The principal agency for environmental monitoring in the United States is the Council on Environmental Quality (CEQ), and the principal agency for pollution abatement and control is Environmental Protection Agency (EPA). CEQ reports data on environmental conditions in its annual *Environmental Quality*. The National Ambient Air Quality Standards (NAAQS) are set by the EPA for particulate matter, sulfur dioxide, petrochemical oxidants (now called ozone), carbon monoxide and nitrogen dioxide. In 1990, there were 1,279 non-Federal sampling agencies for particulates, 741 for sulfur dioxide, 491 for

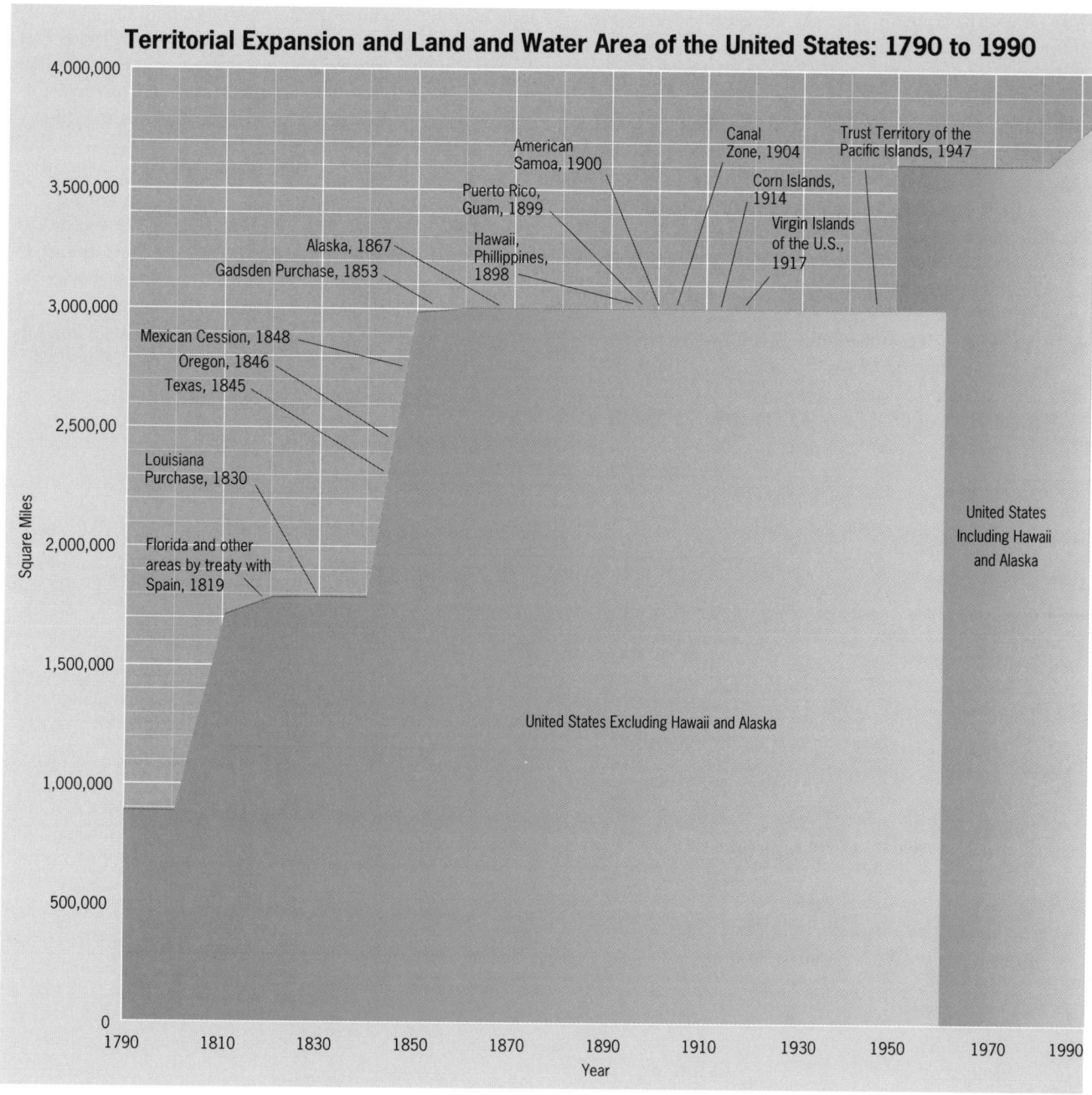

Territorial Expansion and Land and Water Area of the United States: 1790 to 1990

carbon monoxide, 812 for ozone, 330 for nitrogen dioxide, and 406 for lead. Data from these state networks are periodically submitted to the EPA's National Aerometric Data Bank for summarization in its annual reports.

8 Between 1983 and 1990, there were 217 violations nationwide of fecal coliform bacteria count in rivers and streams and 22 violations relating to dissolved oxygen below 5 mg. per liter. This number is indicative of the amount of sewage in the water.

9 Between 1973 and 1990, there were 172,181 oil polluting incidents in U.S. waters, with a total spillage of 201,972,146 gallons of oil. Both the number of incidents and the amount of spill have declined since 1987.

10 The National Ambient Air Pollutant Concentrations declined for all six major pollutants between 1982 and 1990: carbon monoxide from 7.95 ppm to 5.89; ozone from 0.125 ppm to 0.114; sulfur dioxide from 0.010 ppm to 0.008; suspended particulates from 48.7 ug/m to 47.3; nitrogen dioxide from 0.024 ppm to 0.022; and lead from 0.484 ug/m to 0.070.

11 In 1990, 29 metro areas failed to meet National Ambient Air Quality Standards for carbon monoxide. The metropolitan areas with the greatest number of days that exceeded standards were Los Angeles (72) and Las Vegas (26). In the same year, 60 metro areas failed the meet the standards for ozone. The worst area in this regard also was Los Angeles, which had 103 days that exceeded standards.

12 Nationwide, there were 1,211 hazardous waste sites on the National Priorities List for the Superfund Program. Of these, 118 were Federal and 1,082 non-Federal. New Jersey led the list with 109 sites followed by Pennsylvania (97), California (91), New York (84), Michigan (77), and Florida (52).

13 In 1989, pollution abatement expenditures totaled $91 billion. In 1990, state and local government expenditures for solid waste management and sewerage totaled $28,452,700,000, or $114 per capita.

14 In 1988, 179.6 million tons of solid waste were generated, as compared to 87.8 million tons in 1960. Per capita, the amount of waste generated per day was 4 lbs. in 1988 compared to 2.66 lbs. in 1960. In 1990, 23.5 million tons were recovered from solid waste or 0.52 lbs. per capita per day. Landfills claimed 130.5 million tons in 1988. The largest category of solid waste was paper and paperboard which accounted for 40% compared to 34.1% in 1960. Yard wastes accounted for 17.6%, but their share declined from 1960 when they made up 22.8%.

15 The number of endangered species found in the United States include 55 mammals, 73 birds, 16 reptiles, 6 amphibians, 53 fishes, 7 snails, 39 clams, 8 crustaceans, 13 insects, 3 arachnids, and 203 plants. Threatened species (or those likely to become endangered in the foreseeable future) include 8 mammals, 12 birds, 18 reptiles, 5 amphibians, 34 fishes, 6 snails, 2 clams, 2 crustaceans, 9 insects, and 52 plants.

Series J 1-2. Territorial Expansion and Land and Water Area of the United States: 1790 to 1990

(In square miles)

Accession	Date	Territorial expansion Gross area (land and water)	Year	Area Gross area	Land	Water
		1		2	2a	2b
Total	**1970**	**3,628,066**	United States			
United States	—	3,615,122	1990	3,787,425	3,536,342	251,083
Territory in 1790 [1]	—	888,685	1980	3,618,770	3,539,289	79,481
Louisiana Purchase	1830	827,192	1970 (April 1)	3,615,122	3,536,855	78,267
By treaty with Spain:			1960 (April 1)	3,615,123	3,540,911	74,212
Florida	1819	58,560	1950 (April 1)	3,615,211	3,552,206	63,005
Other areas	1819	13,443				
			Coterminous U.S. [6]			
Texas	1845	390,143				
Oregon	1846	285,580	1960 (April 1)	3,002,261	2,968,054	54,207
Mexican Cession	1848	529,017	1950 (April 1)	3,022,387	2,974,726	47,661
Gadsden Purchase	1853	29,640	1940 (April 1)	3,022,387	2,977,128	45,259
Alaska	1867	586,412	1930 (April 1)	3,022,387	2,977,128	45,259
Hawaii	1898	6,450	1920 (Jan. 1)	3,022,387	2,969,451	52,936
			1910 (April 15)	3,022,387	2,969,565	52,822
Other areas:						
The Philippines [2]	1898	115,600	1900 (June 1)	3,022,387	2,969,834	52,553
Puerto Rico	1899	3,435	1890 (June 1)	3,022,387	2,969,640	52,747
Guam	1899	212	1880 (June 1)	3,022,387	2,969,640	52,747
American Samoa	1900	76	1870 (June 1)	3,022,387	2,969,640	52,747
Canal Zone [3]	1904	553	1860 (June 1)	3,022,387	2,969,640	52,747
Corn Islands [4]	1914	4	1850 (June 1)	2,992,747	2,940,042	52,705
Virgin Islands of the U.S.	1917	133				
Trust Territory of the			1840 (June 1)	1,788,006	1,749,462	38,544
Pacific Islands [5]	1947	8,489	1830 (June 1)	1,788,006	1,749,462	38,544
All other	—	42	1820 (Aug. 7)	1,788,006	1,749,462	38,544
			1810 (Aug. 6)	1,716,003	1,681,828	34,175
			1800 (Aug. 4)	888,811	864,746	24,065
			1790 (Aug. 2)	888,811	864,746	24,065

[1] Includes that part of drainage basin of Red River of the North, south of 49th parallel, sometimes considered part of Louisiana Purchase.

[2] Not included in total. Ceded by Spain in 1898, the Philippines constituted a territorial possession of the United States until 1946. Granted independence July 4, 1946.

[3] Under jurisdiction of United States in accordance with treaty of Nov. 18, 1903, with Republic of Panama.

[4] Included in total for 1970. Leased (1914) from Republic of Nicaragua for 99 years, but returned April 25, 1971.

[5] Under trusteeship with the United States as administering authority. See *Trusteeship Agreement for the Former Japanese Mandated Islands (Documentary Supplement No.1)* of the Security Council of the United Nations which became effective on July 18, 1947.

[6] Excludes Alaska and Hawaii.

Series J 92-103. Estimated Water Use: 1900 to 2000
(In billions of gallons, daily average)

Year	Total water use	Total irrigation [1]	Total public water utilities	Total rural domestic [2]	Self-supplied use Total industrial and miscellaneous [3]	Total steam electric utilities
	92	94	96	98	100	102
2000	306	153	34	4.9	33	80
1985	400	140	38	7.8	30	190
1980	450	150	34	5.6	45	210
1975	420	140	29	4.9	45	200
1974	373	125	29	4.5	63	145
1973	361	124	29	4.5	61	142
1972	350	122	28	4.4	59	135
1971	338	120	27	4.4	57	128
1970	327.30	119.18	27.03	4.34	55.95	120.80
1969	403.30	156.82	26.60	6.82	83.44	129.62
1968	395.40	154.64	26.20	6.74	80.88	126.94
1967	387.50	152.46	25.80	6.66	78.32	124.26
1966	379.60	150.28	25.40	6.58	75.76	121.58
1965	269.62	110.85	23.74	4.08	46.41	84.54
1964	361.94	145.48	24.40	6.40	70.80	114.86
1963	352.18	142.86	23.80	6.30	68.40	110.82
1962	344.48	141.16	23.31	6.22	66.62	107.17
1961	334.72	138.54	22.71	6.12	64.22	103.13
1960 *	322.90	135.00	22.00	6.00	61.20	98.70
1958	299.26	127.52	19.72	5.76	56.40	89.86
1955	263.80	116.30	16.30	5.40	49.20	76.60
1950	202.70	100.00	14.10	4.60	38.10	45.90
1946	165.74	86.44	12.00	3.50	33.00	30.80
1945	170.46	83.06	12.00	3.20	41.00	31.20
1944	178.43	80.65	12.00	3.18	48.00	34.60
1940	136.43	71.03	10.10	3.10	29.00	23.20
1930	110.50	60.20	8.00	2.90	21.00	18.40
1920	91.54	55.94	6.00	2.40	18.00	9.20
1910	66.44	39.04	4.70	2.20	14.00	6.50
1900	40.19	20.19	3.00	2.00	10.00	5.00

* Denotes first year for which figures include Alaska and Hawaii.
[1] Total take, including delivery losses but not including reservoir evaporation.
[2] Rural farm and nonfarm household and garden use, and water for farm stock and dairies.

[3] For 1900-1960, includes manufacturing industries, mineral industries, rural commercial industries, air conditioning, resorts, hotels, motels, military and other state and federal agencies and other miscellaneous uses; thereafter, includes manufacturing, mining and mineral processing, ordnance and construction.

Series J 268-278. Tornadoes, Floods, and Tropical Cyclones: 1886 to 1990

Year	Number	Tornadoes Lives lost		Most in a single tornado	$500,000 and over in property loss	Floods Lives lost	Property loss ($1,000)	North Atlantic tropical cyclones (including hurricanes) Total reaching U.S. coast	Lives lost in United States
	268	270		271	273	274	275	276	278
1990	1,133	53		29	91	—	—	1	13
1989	856	50		21	60	81	415	4	56
1988	702	32		5	48	29	114	12	—
1987	656	59		30	38	82	1,490	7	—
1986	764	15		3	75	80	4,000	6	—
1985	684	94		18	69	304	3,000	11	9
1984	907	122		16	125	126	4,000	2	4
1983	931	34		3	95	200	4,100	2	22
1982	1,046	64		10	92	155	3,500	1	—
1981	783	24		5	55	90	1,000	2	—
1980	866	28		5	92	97	1,500	2	2
1979	852	84		42	73	100	4,000	5	11
1978	788	53		16	59	120	1,000	2	35
1977	852	43		22	46	212	1,393	1	—
1976	835	44		5	46	187	1,000	2	9
1975	920	60		9	42	114	1,051	1	21
1974	947	361		34	107	121	576	1	1
1973	1,102	87		7	76	105	859	1	5
1972	741	27		6	29	540	3,449	3	121
1971	888	156		58	35	74	258	5	8
1970	649	73		26	30	135	225,453	4	11
1969	604	66		32	19	297	902,654	3	256
1968	661	131		34	32	31	339,399	3	9
1967	912	116		33	41	34	375,218	2	18
1966	570	99		58	17	31	117,004	2	54
1965	899	298		44	41	119	788,046	2	75
1964	713	73		22	22	100	651,642	6	49
1963	461	31		5	16	39	177,946	1	11
1962	658	28		17	10	19	75,237	1	4
1961	682	51		16	22	52	154,033	3	46
1960	618	47		16	12	32	92,976	5	65
1959	589	58		21	5	25	141,255	7	24
1958	565	66		19	9	47	218,255	1	2
1957	864	191		44	29	82	360,303	5	395
1956	532	83		25	25	42	64,688	2	21
1955	593	125		80	14	302	995,491	5	218
1954	549	35		6	9	55	106,842	4	193
1953	437	516		116	25	40	122,204	6	2
1952	236	230		57	19	54	254,064	2	3
1951	272	34		6	13	51	1,028,741	1	—
1950	199	70		18	9	93	176,050	4	19
1949	249	212		58	13	48	93,931	3	4
1948	183	140		33	13	82	229,959	4	3
1947	165	313		169	8	55	272,328	7	53
1946	106	78		15	7	28	70,813	4	—
1945	121	210		69	11	91	165,798	5	7
1944	169	275		100	9	33	101,079	4	64
1943	152	58		5	8	107	199,732	4	16
1942	167	384		65	10	68	98,507	3	8
1941	118	53		25	1	47	39,524	4	10
1940	124	65		18	2	60	40,467	3	51
1939	152	87		27	3	83	13,834	3	3
1938	213	183		32	6	180	101,098	4	600

See footnote at end of chart.

Series J 268-278. Tornadoes, Floods, and Tropical Cyclones: 1886 to 1990—Cont'd.

Year	Tornadoes				Floods		North Atlantic tropical cyclones (including hurricanes)	
	Number	Lives lost		$500,000 and over in property loss	Lives lost	Property loss ($1,000)	Total reaching U.S. coast	Lives lost in United States
		Total	Most in a single tornado					
	268	270	271	273	274	275	276	278
1937	147	29	5	—	142	440,738	4	—
1936	151	552	216	6	142	282,549	7	9
1935	180	70	11	—	236	127,127	2	414
1934	147	47	6	3	88	10,362	5	17
1933	258	362	34	9	33	36,679	7	63
1932	151	394	37	2	11	10,295	5	—
1931	94	36	6	1	—	2,808	2	—
1930	192	179	41	6	14	15,850	1	—
1929	197	274	40	4	89	68,098	2	3
1928	203	92	14	7	15	44,611	3	1,836
1927	163	540	92	10	423	347,656	1	—
1926	111	144	23	—	16	23,468	4	269
1925	119	794	689	3	36	9,923	2	6
1924	130	376	85	12	—	—	3	2
1923	102	109	23	1	—	—	4	—
1922	108	135	16	5	—	—	1	—
1921	105	202	61	3	—	—	2	5
1920	87	498	87	10	—	—	3	2
1919	64	206	59	2	—	—	2	287
1918	81	135	36	5	—	—	2	34
1917	121	509	101	9	—	—	1	5
1916	90	150	30	1	—	—	8	107
1915	—	—	—	—	—	—	4	600
1914	—	—	—	—	—	—	1	(1)
1913	—	—	—	—	—	—	3	(1)
1912	—	—	—	—	—	—	4	12
1911	—	—	—	—	—	—	2	17
1910	—	—	—	—	—	—	2	13
1909	—	—	—	—	—	—	7	404
1908	—	—	—	—	—	—	2	(1)
1907	—	—	—	—	—	—	3	(1)
1906	—	—	—	—	—	—	6	285
1905	—	—	—	—	—	—	2	(1)
1904	—	—	—	—	—	—	3	(1)
1903	—	—	—	—	—	—	2	9
1902	—	—	—	—	—	—	3	(1)
1901	—	—	—	—	—	—	6	10
1900	—	—	—	—	—	—	3	—
1899	—	—	—	—	—	—	4	—
1898	—	—	—	—	—	—	6	—
1897	—	—	—	—	—	—	4	—
1896	—	—	—	—	—	—	4	—
1895	—	—	—	—	—	—	4	—
1894	—	—	—	—	—	—	3	—
1893	—	—	—	—	—	—	7	—
1892	—	—	—	—	—	—	3	—
1891	—	—	—	—	—	—	4	—
1890	—	—	—	—	—	—	—	—
1889	—	—	—	—	—	—	4	—
1888	—	—	—	—	—	—	6	—
1887	—	—	—	—	—	—	4	—
1886	—	—	—	—	—	—	7	—

[1] Not reported, believed to be small number.

SECTION K

AGRICULTURE

SECTION K

AGRICULTURE

Highlights

1 Annual agricultural statistics have been published by the Department of Agriculture since May 1, 1863. They are now compiled by the Statistical Reporting Service and the Economic Research Service. Beginning in 1840, a Census of Agriculture has been taken every 10 years and, beginning in 1925, a mid-decade Census of Agriculture has also been taken, based on mailed questionnaires. The first census was limited in scope to domestic animals, production of principal crops, and value of wool and dairy products. Number of farms, acreage, and value of farmland were first included in 1850, farm tenure in 1880, and classification of farmland by use in 1925.

2 The definition of a farm has varied from census to census. Before 1954, the cutoff was three acres with annual output valued at $150 or more, but farms smaller than three acres were included if the value of output reached the same level. Between 1925 and 1945, farms included places of three or more acres on which there were agricultural operations and places of less than three acres with an annual output of $250 or more. Between 1910 and 1920, the definition was even more liberal, including farms smaller than three acres with less than $250 in output, if they required the continuous services of one person. In 1860 and 1900 there were no acreage or value limits. In 1870, 1880, and 1890, farms smaller than three acres were included only if the value of output exceeded $500. In the first census of 1850 no acreage qualification was given, but there was a floor of $100 for value of products. In 1959 the acreage limit was raised to 10, and the value limit to $250 for smaller farms. For the 1974, 1978, 1982, and 1987 Censuses of Agriculture, a farm was defined as any place from which $1,000 or more of agricultural products were produced and/or sold.

3 Estimates of farm population are equally problematic. Since 1960, farm population has been defined as all persons living in rural territory on places of 10 or more acres producing at least $50 worth of agricultural produce. The principal characteristics of farm population are its higher age profile, higher outflow, and higher birth rates. The classification of Farm operator was first made in the Census of 1900. It designates a person who operates a farm as an owner, salaried employee, tenant, renter, or sharecropper. Because of the decreasing importance of the

cropper system in the South, croppers have not been classified since 1959. From 1880, farms have been classified by tenure, and since 1900, by race of the owner.

4 Estimates of farm income were started in 1924 on a crop-year basis. Only scattered data on farm income are available for the period before 1910. Willford I. King provides some data for census years from 1850 in *The Wealth and Income of the People of the United States;* the National Industrial Conference Board's *National Income in the United States, 1799 to 1938* provides decennial projections going back to 1800; and the Department of Agriculture's *Gross Farm Income and Indices of Farm Production and Prices in the United States, 1869-1937* extends back to 1869.

5 For many crops, estimates of acreage, production, and prices began in 1866 when the Department of Agriculture began making regular reports. These data are found in *Agricultural Statistics*, *Crop Production*, and *Crop Values*. Data on livestock have been published since 1867, based on the 10-year and five-year Censuses of Agriculture.

6 Early development of the dairy industry is indicated by the export statistics of 1890 which showed the New England States, New York, and Pennsylvania producing considerable amounts of butter and cheese in excess of their consumption requirements. By the middle of the 19th century, milk cows were distributed as far west as southern Wisconsin, eastern Iowa, western Missouri and Arkansas, and the eastern third of Texas. By 1860 they had spread to the Pacific Coast States. Prior to 1850, milk, butter, and cheese were produced mainly on farms. Factory cheese production began shortly after 1850, the first condensery was established in 1856 and the first commercial creamery in 1861. Unsweetened condensed milk was first produced in 1885.

7 The share of the farm sector has steadily declined as the United States moved into the post-industrial age. Between 1975 and 1990, it declined from 3.0% to 2.1% in employment. By value added (the value of output minus the value of input), the farm sector contributes only $76.2 billion in a five trillion dollar economy.

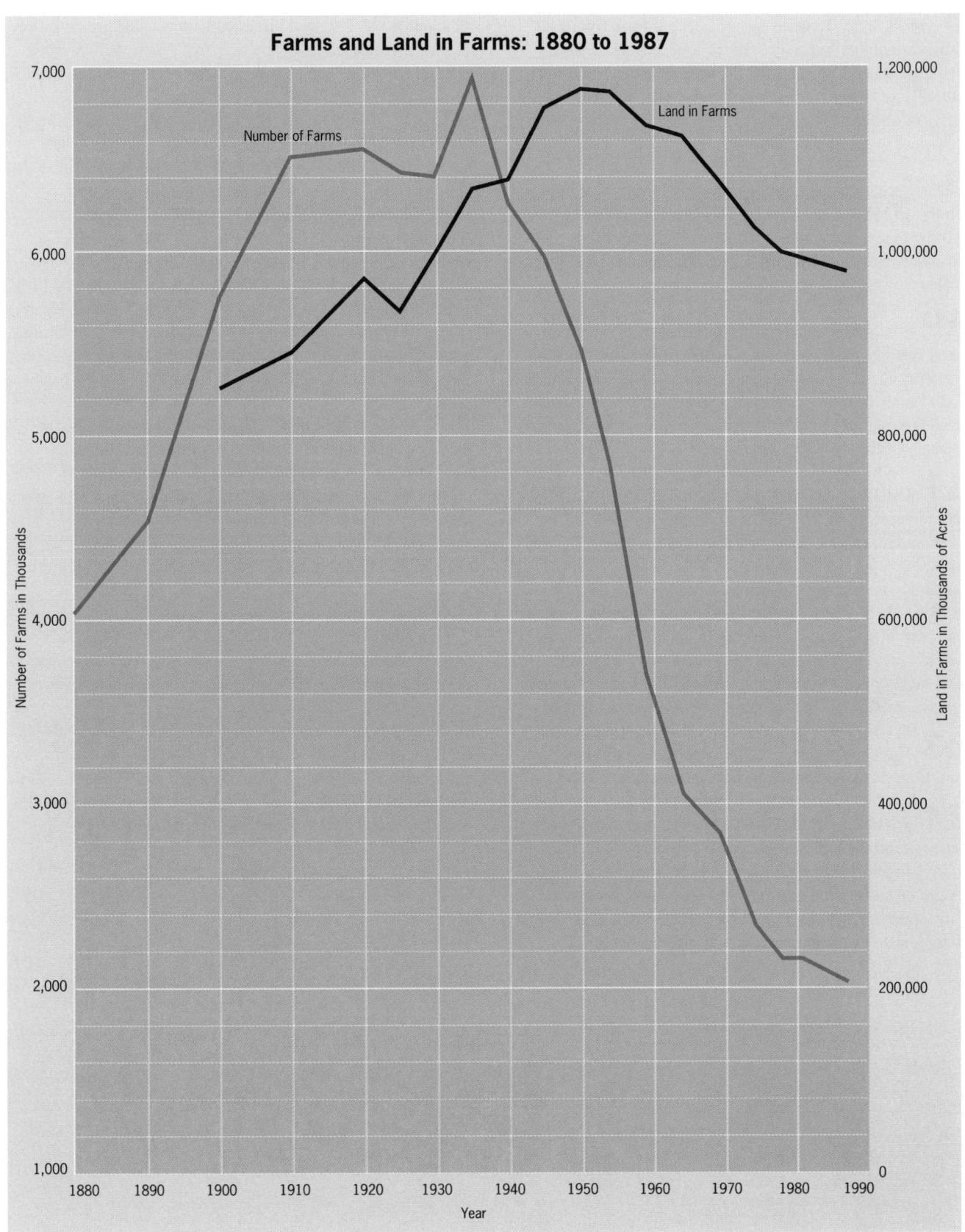

Farms and Land in Farms: 1880 to 1987

Number of Farms

Land in Farms

8 Farms under 10 acres in size account for 8.8% of all farms in number but only 0.1% of total acreage. Farms over 2,000 acres account for 3.2% of all farms in number but 48% of total acreage. Corporate farms account for 3.2% of all farms in number, 12.4% of total acreage, and 25.6% of value of products sold.

9 Irrigated lands are found primarily in the West and South. In 1990, California led all states in this respect with 7.596 million acres under irrigation, or 24.8% of all cropland, followed by Idaho (23.1%), Florida (14.5%), and Nebraska (12.5%).

10 Foreign ownership of U.S. agricultural land has been steadily increasing and reached 14.908 million acres in 1991; 91.3% of the foreign owned acreage is in farms of 1,000 acres or more. The largest shares of foreign agricultural holdings are held by Canada, the United Kingdom, France, Germany, and Switzerland.

11 The Balance Sheet of the Farming Sector was first attempted in 1944. In 1990, it showed assets of $757.5 billion, debt of $110.3 billion, and equity of $647.2 billion.

12 By cash receipts from farm marketings, the five principal U.S. crops are corn, soybean, vegetables, wheat and cotton, which together account for 60%. (Corn is a cereal, while only sweet corn is considered a vegetable.) The most popular vegetable is potato followed by tomato, and the most popular fruit is orange followed by grape.

13 The Commodity Credit Corporation had $1.858 billion in outstanding loans to the farm sector in 1991.

14 Based on 1977=100, the index of prices received by farmers and the index of prices paid by farmers in 1991 were 146 and 189 respectively. The disparity reflected that prices of farm outputs rose more slowly than prices of farm inputs. The fastest growing cost elements for farmers were feeder livestock, fuel and energy, and wages.

15 In 1990, 886,000 hired workers worked on the farm; 10% of them Black and 30% Hispanic. Their median weekly earnings were $200, which was below the poverty line.

16 The United States is the granary of the world, and agriculture is the only sector in which its leadership has not been challenged since the end of World War II. It accounts for 39.4% of world production of corn, and 50.8% of world production of soybeans. In exports, it accounts for 28.5% of wheat, 64.3% of corn, 66.3% of soybeans, and 33.5% of cotton. Agricultural exports have helped to bolster the trade balance consistently. In 1990, agricultural exports accounted for $39.3 billion, or 10% of all exports, with a surplus of $16.6 billion over agricultural imports; overall, 25.8% of total agricultural land was used for export crops.

17 New exotic styles of foods have created a demand for spices and herbs. In 1990, 590 million lbs. of spices were imported into the United States, including 160.3 million lbs. of mustard seed, 100.1 million lbs. of sesame seed, 92.6 million lbs. of pepper, 46 million lbs. of capsicum, 26.6 million lbs. of cinnamon and cassia, 18 million lbs. of ginger root, and 11.1 million lbs. of cumin.

18 California is the nation's principal fruit grower—it is the leading producer of 19 of the 31 major fruits and nuts. Florida, in second place, grows only six. California also grows 12 of the 20 leading commercial vegetables.

19 In 1991, Americans consumed 24.112 billion lbs. of beef, 16.395 billion lbs. of pork, 4.899 billion dozens of eggs, and 816 million gallons of ice cream. Per capita, this worked out to 95.42 lbs. of beef, 64.88 lbs. of pork, 19.39 dozens of eggs, and 3.23 gallons of ice cream.

Series K 1-16. Farm Population, Farms, Land in Farms and Value of Farm Property and Real Estate: 1850 to 1991

(Census figures in *italics*)

Year	Farm population Total (1,000)[3]	Percent of total population[3]	Number of farms (1,000)	Land in farms[1] Total (1,000 acres)	Average acreage per farm (acres)	Value of land and buildings (mil. dollars)[2]	Year	Farm population Total (1,000)	Percent of total population	Number of farms (1,000)	Land in farms[1] Total (1,000 acres)	Average acreage per farm (acres)	Value of land and buildings (mil. dollars)[2]
	1	2	4	5	7	11		1	2	4	5	7	11
1991	—	—	2,105	983,000	467	672,235	1947	25,829	18.0	5,871	1,148,394	196	68,463
1990	4,591	1.9	2,140	987,000	461	658,451	1946	25,403	18.0	5,926	1,145,003	193	61,046
1989	4,801	2.0	2,171	991,000	457	659,381							
1988	4,951	2.1	2,197	995,000	453	626,909	1945	24,420	17.5	*5,859*	*1,141,615*	*195*	*46,389*
1987	4,986	2.1	2,213	999,000	451	597,110	1944	24,815	18.0	6,003	1,125,461	187	46,200
1986	5,226	2.2	2,250	1,005,000	447	597,600	1943	26,186	19.2	6,089	1,109,308	182	41,604
							1942	28,914	21.5	6,202	1,093,155	176	37,547
1985	5,355	2.3	2,293	1,012,000	441	719,398	1941	30,118	22.6	6,293	1,077,002	171	34,400
1984	5,754	2.5	2,334	1,018,000	436	793,700							
1983	5,787	2.5	2,379	1,023,000	430	804,800	1940	30,547	23.2	[3]6,102	[3]1,065,114	[3]175	[3]33,758
1982	5,628	2.5	2,407	1,028,000	427	843,300	1939	30,840	23.6	6,441	1,059,582	165	34,074
1981	5,850	2.6	2,440	1,034,000	424	843,700	1938	30,980	23.9	6,527	1,058,315	162	35,170
							1937	31,266	24.3	6,636	1,057,047	159	35,213
1980	6,051	2.8	2,440	1,039,000	426	763,285	1936	31,737	24.8	6,739	1,055,780	157	34,260
1979	6,241	2.8	2,437	1,042,000	428	653,100							
1978	6,501	3.0	2,436	1,045,000	429	553,000	1935	32,161	25.3	*6,812*	*1,054,515*	*155*	*32,859*
1977	7,806	3.6	2,456	1,048,000	427	495,000	1934	32,305	25.6	6,776	1,040,963	154	32,201
1976	8,253	3.8	2,497	1,054,000	422	416,800	1933	32,393	25.8	6,741	1,027,415	152	30,802
							1932	31,388	25.2	6,687	1,013,865	152	37,180
1975	8,864	4.2	2,521	1,059,000	420	358,600	1931	30,845	24.9	6,608	1,000,317	151	43,730
1974	9,264	4.4	2,795	1,084,000	388	326,600							
1973	9,472	4.5	2,823	1,088,000	385	266,200	1930	30,529	24.9	[3]6,295	[3]991,112	[3]157	[3]47,994
1972	9,610	4.6	2,860	1,092,000	382	238,700	1929	30,580	25.2	6,512	974,277	150	47,985
1971	9,425	4.8	2,902	1,097,000	378	—	1928	30,548	25.4	6,470	961,787	149	47,532
							1927	30,530	25.7	6,458	949,297	147	47,680
1970	9,712	4.8	2,954	1,102,769	373	208,214	1926	30,979	26.5	6,462	936,806	145	49,000
1969	10,307	5.1	*2,730*	*1,063,346*	*390*	[3]206,751							
1968	10,454	5.3	3,071	1,115,231	363	193,703	1925	31,190	27.0	*6,372*	*924,319*	*145*	*49,468*
1967	10,875	5.5	3,162	1,123,456	355	182,456	1924	31,177	27.5	3,480	930,628	144	50,487
1966	11,595	5.9	3,257	1,131,844	348	172,532	1923	31,490	28.2	6,492	936,941	144	52,629
							1922	32,109	29.3	6,500	943,253	145	54,050
1965	12,363	6.4	3,356	1,139,597	340	160,942	1921	32,123	29.7	6,511	949,566	146	61,523
1964	12,954	6.8	*3,158*	*1,110,185*	*352*	[3]159,932							
1963	13,367	7.1	3,572	1,151,572	322	143,834	1920	31,974	30.1	[3]6,454	[3]958,677	[3]149	[3]66,446
1962	14,313	7.7	3,685	1,161,383	314	137,956	1919	31,200	29.7	6,506	948,169	146	54,533
1961	14,803	8.1	3,821	1,169,899	306	131,752	1918	31,950	30.6	6,488	940,461	145	49,980
							1917	32,430	31.5	6,478	932,752	144	45,524
1960	*15,635	*8.7	3,962	1,176,946	297	130,169	1916	32,530	32.0	6,463	925,044	143	42,264
1959	16,592	9.4	*3,711	*1,123,508	*303	[3]129,005							
1958	17,128	9.9	4,233	1,184,944	280	115,934	1915	32,440	32.4	6,458	917,335	142	39,590
1957	17,656	10.4	4,372	1,191,340	273	110,422	1914	32,320	32.8	6,447	909,627	141	39,579
1956	18,712	11.2	4,514	1,197,080	265	102,934	1913	32,270	33.4	6,437	901,918	140	38,456
							1912	32,210	33.9	6,430	894,209	139	37,298
1955	19,078	11.6	4,654	1,201,900	258	98,172	1911	32,110	34.3	6,425	886,501	138	36,042
1954	19,019	11.8	4,782	1,158,192	242	97,583							
1953	19,874	12.5	4,984	1,205,740	242	96,535	1910	32,077	34.9	[3]6,366	[3]881,431	[3]139	[3]34,885
1952	21,748	13.9	5,198	1,204,930	232	95,078	1900	29,875	41.9	[3]5,740	[3]841,202	[3]147	[3]16,614
1951	21,890	14.2	5,428	1,203,500	222	86,586	1890	24,771	42.3	4,565	623,219	137	13,279
							1880	21,973	43.8	4,009	536,082	134	10,197
1950	23,048	15.3	[3]5,388	[3]1,161,420	[3]216	[3]75,462	1870	—	—	2,660	407,735	153	7,444
1949	24,194	16.3	5,722	1,155,174	202	76,623	1860	—	—	2,044	407,213	199	6,645
1948	24,383	16.7	5,803	1,151,784	199	73,664	1850	—	—	1,449	293,561	203	3,272

* Except as indicated by footnote 3, denotes first year for which figures include Alaska and Hawaii.
[1] Intercensal estimates derived from straight-line interpolation. Excludes District of Columbia.
[2] Census years as of date of enumeration. All other years as of March 1. Excludes District of Columbia.
[3] Includes Alaska and Hawaii.

Series K 162-173. Farms and Land in Farms, by Size of Farm: 1880 to 1987

(Farms in thousands, land in farms in thousands of acres)

Year	Total	Under 10 acres	50-99 acres	1,000 acres and over	Year	Total	Under 10 acres	50-99 acres	1,000 acres and over
	162	163	168	173		162	163	168	173
Number of Farms					Land in Farms				
1987	2,088	183	311	169	1987	964,500	7,000	22,500	602,000
1982	2,241	188	344	163	1982	—	—	—	—
1978	2,258	151	356	161	1978	986,800	7,000	24,800	599,900
1974	2,314	128	385	155	1974	1,014,800	6,000	25,900	600,400
1969	2,730	162	460	151					
1964	3,158	183	542	145	1969	1,063,346	568	33,620	578,412
					1964	1,110,185	778	39,590	584,847
1959	3,711	244	658	136	1959	1,123,508	1,053	47,950	554,631
1954 [1]	4,782	484	864	130	1954 [1]	1,158,192	2,260	62,725	531,482
1950	5,388	489	1,048	121					
1945 [1]	5,859	595	1,157	113	1950	[3] 1,162,643	2,443	75,647	494,856
					1945 [1]	1,141,615	2,805	83,206	460,006
1940	6,102	509	1,291	101	1940	1,065,114	2,679	93,336	365,772
1935 [1]	6,812	571	1,444	89	1935 [1]	1,054,515	3,057	104,016	309,701
1930	6,295	362	1,375	81					
1925 [1]	6,372	379	1,421	63	1930	990,112	1,922	98,700	276,667
					1925 [1]	924,319	2,097	101,906	224,472
1920	6,454	[2] 292	1,475	67	1920	[4] 958,677	1,600	105,631	220,636
1910 [1]	6,362	335	1,438	50	1910 [1]	[4] 881,431	(NA)	103,121	167,082
1900	5,740	268	1,366	47	1900	841,202	1,482	98,600	200,324
1890	4,565	150	1,122	32					
1880	4,009	139	1,033	29					

NA Not available.
[1] Excludes Alaska and Hawaii.
[2] Excludes Alaska.

[3] Based on sample; therefore differs from series K 5.
[4] Total includes Alaska and Hawaii.

Series K 195-203. Farmers' Marketing and Purchasing Cooperatives—Number, Memberships and Business: 1913 to 1990

(Fiscal-year data)

Year	Cooperatives listed			Estimated memberships (1,000)			Estimated business [1] (mil. dollars)		
	Total	Marketing	Purchasing	Total	Marketing	Purchasing	Total	Marketing [2]	Purchasing
	195	196	197	198	199	200	201	202	203
1990	4,663	2,946	1,717	4,119	2,114	2,006	77,266	60,178	17,088
1989	4,799	2,996	1,803	4,134	2,099	2,035	72,129	55,222	16,907
1988	4,937	3,101	1,836	4,195	2,053	2,142	66,430	51,006	15,424
1987	5,109	3,168	1,941	4,440	2,158	2,282	60,318	46,047	14,271
1986	5,369	3,398	1,971	4,600	2,290	2,310	58,395	43,300	15,095
1985	5,625	3,589	2,036	4,781	2,383	2,398	65,601	48,961	16,641
1984	5,782	3,646	2,136	4,842	2,445	2,397	73,047	56,078	16,969
1983	5,989	3,781	2,208	4,955	2,402	2,553	66,755	50,812	15,943
1982	6,125	3,826	2,299	5,136	2,469	2,666	69,150	52,788	16,362
1981	6,211	3,855	2,356	5,335	2,479	2,856	71,534	54,475	17,059
1980	6,293	3,924	2,369	5,379	2,574	2,804	66,254	50,120	16,134
1979	6,445	3,938	2,507	5,627	2,567	3,060	56,268	42,747	13,521
1978	6,600	4,050	2,550	5,695	2,632	3,063	47,305	36,253	11,052
1977	6,736	4,143	2,593	5,758	2,692	3,066	43,584	33,027	10,557
1976	7,533	4,804	2,731	5,906	2,850	3,056	40,104	30,692	9,412
1975	7,645	4,916	2,729	6,123	3,151	2,972	41,342	32,682	8,660
1974	7,755	4,977	2,778	6,106	3,133	2,973	35,366	27,602	7,764
1973	7,854	5,053	2,801	6,128	3,140	2,988	25,991	20,076	5,915
1972	7,797	5,016	2,781	6,147	3,156	2,991	21,665	16,925	4,740
1971	7,995	5,264	2,731	6,158	3,130	3,028	20,556	16,210	4,340
1970	7,790	5,015	2,775	6,355	3,133	3,222	19,080	15,207	3,873
1969	7,747	4,954	2,793	6,364	3,175	3,189	17,396	13,796	3,600
1968	7,940	5,105	2,835	6,445	3,259	3,186	17,034	13,513	3,521
1967	8,125	5,254	2,871	6,502	3,333	3,169	16,557	13,218	3,339
1966	8,329	5,380	2,949	6,826	3,672	3,154	15,608	12,523	3,085
1965	8,583	5,498	3,085	7,082	3,831	3,251	14,742	11,832	2,910
1964	8,847	5,621	3,226	7,080	3,655	3,425	14,354	11,522	2,832
1963	8,907	5,696	3,211	7,219	3,623	3,596	13,842	11,138	2,704
1962	9,039	5,833	3,206	7,099	3,464	3,635	13,024	10,463	2,561
1961	9,163	5,941	3,222	7,203	3,523	3,680	12,409	9,937	2,472
1960	9,345	6,048	3,297	7,273	3,673	3,600	12,036	9,628	2,408
1959 *	9,658	6,271	3,387	7,559	3,915	3,644	11,747	9,376	2,371
1958	9,735	6,352	3,383	7,486	3,943	3,543	10,753	8,566	2,187
1957	9,891	6,518	3,373	7,673	4,184	3,489	10,379	8,233	2,146
1956	9,894	6,519	3,375	7,732	4,288	3,444	9,756	7,710	2,046
1955	9,903	6,557	3,346	7,604	4,281	3,323	9,642	7,620	2,022
1954	10,072	6,698	3,374	7,608	4,355	3,252	9,475	7,497	1,978
1953	10,128	6,750	3,378	7,475	4,336	3,139	9,521	7,508	2,013
1952	10,179	6,855	3,324	7,364	4,331	3,033	9,410	7,491	1,919
1951	10,064	6,781	3,283	7,091	4,212	2,879	8,147	6,462	1,685
1950	10,035	6,922	3,113	6,584	4,075	2,509	8,726	7,083	1,643
1949	10,075	6,993	3,082	6,384	3,973	2,411	9,320	7,700	1,620
1948	10,135	7,159	2,976	5,890	3,630	2,260	8,635	7,195	1,440
1947	10,125	7,268	2,857	5,436	3,378	2,058	7,116	6,005	1,111
1946	10,150	7,378	2,772	5,010	3,150	1,860	6,070	5,147	923
1945	10,150	7,400	2,750	4,505	2,895	1,610	5,645	4,835	810
1944	10,300	7,522	2,778	4,250	2,730	1,520	5,160	4,430	730
1943	10,450	7,708	2,742	3,850	2,580	1,270	3,780	3,180	600
1942	10,550	7,824	2,726	3,600	2,430	1,170	2,840	2,360	480
1941	10,600	7,943	2,657	3,400	2,420	980	2,280	1,911	369
1936	10,500	8,388	2,112	3,660	2,710	950	1,840	1,586	254
1931	11,950	10,362	1,588	3,000	2,608	392	2,400	2,185	215
1926	10,803	9,586	1,217	2,700	2,453	247	2,400	2,265	135
1921	7,374	6,476	898	(NA)	(NA)	(NA)	1,256	1,198	58
1915	5,424	5,149	275	651	592	59	636	624	12
1913	3,099	2,988	111	—	—	—	310	304	6

* Denotes first year for which figures include Alaska and Hawaii.
NA Not available.

[1] Data for years to 1951 are not entirely comparable due to revisions in statistical procedure.
[2] Includes services related to marketing or supply purchasing.

Series K 204-219. Balance Sheet of the Farming Sector: 1940 to 1990
(In billions of dollars. As of January 1. Excludes Alaska and Hawaii)

| | | | | Assets Physical Non-real estate | | | | Claims | | |
Year	Total	Real estate	Livestock and poultry [1]	Machinery and motor vehicles	Crops stored on and off farm [2]	Household equipment and furnishings	Investment in cooperatives	Total	Total liability	Proprietors' equities
	204	205	206	207	208	209	212	213	214	219
1990	996.2	702.6	69.1	91.7	22.4	46.3	27.6	996.2	145.1	851.1
1989	976.0	692.7	66.2	90.2	23.3	42.2	26.1	976.0	146.0	830.0
1988	956.8	687.0	62.2	86.7	22.7	37.0	25.1	956.8	148.5	808.3
1987	911.4	658.6	58.0	84.5	17.8	32.9	25.3	911.4	153.7	757.7
1986	848.0	613.0	47.8	86.1	16.6	28.7	24.4	848.0	166.6	681.3
1985	892.8	657.0	46.3	86.3	22.9	27.8	24.3	892.8	187.9	704.9
1984	975.9	735.0	49.5	91.1	26.3	24.3	24.3	975.9	204.3	771.5
1983	1,064.3	829.3	49.5	92.1	24.4	24.4	22.8	1,064.3	206.5	857.9
1982	1,056.8	819.1	53.0	92.6	26.4	23.0	21.9	1,056.8	203.1	853.7
1981	1,091.1	830.0	60.8	102.8	35.9	19.4	22.2	1,001.1	175.2	915.9
1980	1,089.2	850.1	60.6	86.9	32.8	19.4	19.3	1,089.2	178.7	910.5
1979	873.4	655.0	51.3	85.1	28.0	16.0	18.3	873.4	136.5	736.9
1978	736.3	554.7	31.9	76.9	24.4	13.8	15.2	736.3	119.3	617.0
1977	664.2	496.4	29.0	71.0	22.1	12.1	14.9	664.2	102.7	561.6
1976	576.3	418.1	29.4	64.0	21.3	11.7	13.4	576.3	90.8	485.5
1975	577.0	420.6	29.4	63.1	21.1	11.7	12.8	577.0	91.5	485.5
1974	478.5	327.7	42.4	44.2	22.0	12.3	10.8	478.5	74.1	404.4
1973	394.8	267.3	34.1	39.3	14.5	11.9	9.7	394.8	65.3	327.5
1972	351.8	239.6	27.3	35.6	11.8	10.8	8.8	351.8	59.1	292.7
1971	314.9	213.0	23.7	33.8	10.7	10.1	7.6	314.9	61.1	253.8
1970	305.8	207.1	23.5	31.8	10.9	9.7	7.2	305.8	58.1	247.7
1969	294.8	201.5	20.2	30.9	10.6	9.6	6.8	294.8	54.6	240.2
1968	280.1	192.0	18.8	29.5	9.6	9.0	6.5	280.1	50.4	229.7
1967	266.8	181.8	18.9	27.3	10.0	8.4	6.2	266.8	45.7	221.1
1966	253.8	172.2	17.6	25.8	9.7	8.6	5.9	253.8	41.6	212.2
1965	237.2	160.9	14.4	24.7	9.2	8.6	5.6	237.2	37.6	199.6
1964	229.2	152.1	15.8	23.9	9.8	8.8	5.4	229.2	34.9	194.3
1963	221.4	143.8	17.3	23.4	9.3	9.0	5.0	221.4	31.7	189.7
1962	212.8	138.0	16.4	22.5	8.8	9.1	4.8	212.8	28.7	184.1
1961	204.2	131.8	15.5	22.2	8.0	8.9	4.5	204.2	26.2	178.0
1960	203.5	130.2	15.2	22.7	7.7	9.6	4.2	203.5	24.8	178.7
1959	202.1	124.4	17.7	21.8	9.3	9.8	3.9	202.1	23.6	178.5
1958	185.8	115.9	13.9	20.2	7.6	9.9	3.7	185.8	20.4	165.4
1957	177.9	110.4	11.0	20.2	8.3	10.0	3.5	177.9	19.3	158.6
1956	169.6	102.9	10.6	19.3	8.4	10.5	3.2	169.6	18.8	150.8
1955	165.1	98.2	11.2	18.6	9.6	10.0	3.1	165.1	17.6	147.5
1954	161.2	95.0	11.7	18.4	9.2	9.9	2.9	161.2	16.9	144.3
1953	164.3	96.5	14.8	17.4	9.0	9.9	2.7	164.3	16.1	148.2
1952	167.0	95.1	19.5	16.7	8.8	10.3	2.5	167.0	14.7	152.3
1951	151.5	86.6	17.1	14.1	7.9	9.7	2.3	151.5	13.1	138.4
1950	132.5	75.3	12.9	12.2	7.6	8.6	2.1	132.5	12.4	120.1
1949	134.9	76.6	14.4	10.1	8.6	9.1	1.9	134.9	11.4	123.5
1948	127.9	73.7	13.3	7.4	9.0	8.5	1.7	127.9	9.3	118.6
1947	116.4	68.5	11.9	5.3	7.1	7.7	1.5	116.4	8.5	107.9
1946	103.5	61.0	9.7	5.4	6.3	6.1	1.4	103.5	8.0	95.5
1945	94.2	53.9	9.0	6.5	6.7	5.6	1.2	94.2	8.3	85.9
1944	84.6	48.2	9.7	5.4	6.1	5.3	1.1	84.6	8.9	75.7
1943	73.7	41.6	9.6	4.9	5.1	5.0	1.0	73.7	10.0	63.7
1942	62.9	37.5	7.1	4.0	3.8	4.9	.9	62.9	10.5	52.4
1941	55.0	34.4	5.3	3.3	3.0	4.2	.9	55.0	10.4	44.6
1940	52.9	33.6	5.1	3.1	2.7	4.2	.8	52.9	10.0	42.9

[1] Beginning 1961, excludes horses and mules.

[2] Includes crops held on farms and crops held off farms by farmers as security for CCC loans.

Series K 256-285. Farm Income and Expenses: 1910 to 1990

(In millions of dollars, except as indicated)

Year	Net income of farm operators from farming	Realized gross farm income	Realized gross income from farming			Government payments	Value of farm products consumed in farm households	Gross rental value of farm dwellings
			Cash receipts from marketings					
			Total	Crops	Livestock and livestock products			
	259	264	265	266	267	268	269	270
1990	50,800	195,100	186,000	80,400	89,600	9,300	700	5,600
1989	50,100	190,300	179,900	76,800	84,100	10,900	700	5,500
1988	40,600	174,500	171,900	71,600	79,400	14,500	700	5,400
1987	39,700	168,400	165,100	65,800	76,000	16,700	700	4,900
1986	31,000	156,100	152,800	63,700	71,600	11,800	900	4,600
1985	28,800	161,200	157,900	74,300	69,800	7,700	900	4,700
1984	26,100	168,000	156,100	69,900	72,900	8,400	1,000	4,900
1983	14,200	153,900	151,100	67,200	69,600	9,300	1,000	12,600
1982	23,800	164,100	151,300	72,300	70,300	3,500	1,100	13,100
1981	26,900	166,300	146,000	72,500	69,200	1,900	1,200	12,600
1980	16,100	149,300	143,300	71,700	68,000	1,300	1,200	11,000
1979	27,400	150,700	135,100	62,300	69,200	1,400	1,300	9,300
1978	25,200	128,400	117,300	53,200	59,200	3,000	1,200	8,100
1977	19,900	108,800	99,300	48,600	47,600	1,800	1,200	7,300
1976	18,682	101,812	94,780	48,668	46,112	734	1,334	5,973
1975	25,500	100,600	90,700	45,800	43,100	800	1,100	5,400
1974	26,130	98,340	92,449	51,090	41,359	531	1,295	4,687
1973	33,349	98,911	87,068	41,132	45,936	2,607	1,104	3,913
1972	18,171	70,119	61,190	25,520	35,670	3,961	831	3,474
1971	14,194	60,603	52,859	22,276	30,583	3,145	732	3,226
1970	16,825	57,925	50,522	20,907	29,615	3,717	773	2,913
1969	16,856	55,550	48,143	19,541	28,602	3,794	750	2,863
1968	14,825	50,897	44,117	18,620	25,497	3,462	732	2,586
1967	14,882	48,998	42,693	18,434	24,259	3,079	745	2,481
1966	16,253	49,740	43,294	18,373	24,921	3,277	817	2,352
1965	14,987	44,926	39,350	17,392	21,958	2,463	813	2,300
1964	12,266	42,567	37,233	17,377	19,856	2,181	930	2,223
1963	13,206	42,271	37,398	17,435	19,963	1,696	1,016	2,161
1962	13,215	41,258	36,356	16,294	20,062	1,747	1,076	2,079
1961	12,987	39,771	35,089	15,660	19,429	1,493	1,176	2,012
1960	12,079	38,088	34,154	15,208	18,946	702	1,250	1,981
1959	11,454	37,468	33,511	14,648	18,863	682	1,318	1,957
1958	13,500	37,911	33,456	14,229	19,227	1,089	1,505	1,861
1957	11,325	34,001	29,714	12,338	17,376	1,016	1,484	1,787
1956	11,444	34,274	30,401	14,038	16,363	554	1,585	1,734
1955	11,464	33,138	29,490	13,523	15,967	229	1,678	1,741
1954	12,503	33,589	29,832	13,556	16,276	257	1,789	1,711
1953	13,088	34,986	31,001	14,078	16,923	213	2,007	1,765
1952	15,051	36,759	32,528	14,290	18,238	275	2,220	1,736
1951	15,987	37,055	32,858	13,239	19,619	286	2,304	1,607
1950	13,673	32,271	28,461	12,356	16,105	283	2,063	1,464
1949	12,780	31,628	27,805	12,396	15,409	185	2,230	1,408
1948	17,664	34,722	30,227	13,098	17,129	257	2,733	1,505
1947	15,354	34,146	29,620	13,093	16,527	314	2,765	1,447
1946	15,068	29,539	24,802	11,016	13,786	772	2,662	1,303
1945	12,312	25,813	21,663	9,655	12,008	742	2,356	1,052
1944	11,705	24,448	20,536	9,185	11,351	776	2,181	955
1943	11,736	23,397	19,620	8,127	11,493	645	2,253	879
1942	9,853	18,794	15,565	6,526	9,039	650	1,758	821
1941	6,490	13,851	11,111	4,619	6,492	544	1,429	767

Series K 256-285. Farm Income and Expenses: 1910 to 1990—Cont'd.

(In millions of dollars, except as indicated)

Year	Net income of farm operators from farming	Realized gross farm income	Realized gross income from farming			Government payments	Value of farm products consumed in farm households	Gross rental value of farm dwellings
			Cash receipts from marketings					
			Total	Crops	Livestock and livestock products			
	259	264	265	266	267	268	269	270
1940	4,482	11,059	8,382	3,469	4,913	723	1,210	744
1939	4,414	10,585	7,872	3,336	4,536	763	1,209	741
1938	4,361	10,149	7,723	3,200	4,523	446	1,235	745
1937	6,005	11,367	8,864	3,924	4,940	336	1,434	733
1936	4,308	10,756	8,391	3,649	4,742	278	1,394	693
1935	5,278	9,696	7,120	2,977	4,143	573	1,320	683
1934	2,923	8,568	6,357	3,021	3,336	446	1,125	640
1933	2,555	7,107	5,332	2,486	2,846	131	1,030	614
1932	2,032	6,405	4,748	1,996	2,752	—	993	664
1931	3,344	8,421	6,381	2,540	3,841	—	1,265	775
1930	4,259	11,472	9,055	3,868	5,187	—	1,552	865
1929	6,152	13,938	11,312	5,130	6,182	—	1,713	913
1928	5,981	13,598	10,991	4,956	6,035	—	1,724	883
1927	5,699	13,336	10,733	5,125	5,608	—	1,725	878
1926	5,937	13,302	10,558	4,875	5,683	—	1,875	869
1925	6,734	13,716	11,021	5,545	5,476	—	1,827	868
1924	4,855	12,785	10,225	5,413	4,812	—	1,706	854
1923	5,068	12,167	9,545	4,865	4,680	—	1,772	850
1922	4,343	11,059	8,575	4,300	4,275	—	1,717	767
1921	3,370	10,573	8,058	4,106	3,952	—	1,746	769
1920	7,795	15,944	12,600	6,644	5,956	—	2,509	835
1919	9,078	17,918	14,538	7,603	6,935	—	2,556	824
1918	8,887	16,547	13,467	6,974	6,493	—	2,341	739
1917	8,304	13,410	10,736	5,642	5,094	—	2,003	671
1916	4,570	9,744	7,746	4,035	3,711	—	1,384	614
1915	4,307	8,147	6,392	3,263	3,129	—	1,192	563
1914	4,181	7,793	6,036	2,899	3,137	—	1,228	529
1913	3,728	7,978	6,238	3,077	3,161	—	1,222	518
1912	4,456	7,710	6,008	3,095	2,913	—	1,204	498
1911	3,371	7,213	5,584	2,905	2,679	—	1,165	464
1910	4,176	7,495	5,780	2,929	2,851	—	1,270	445

Series K 256-285. Farm Income and Expenses: 1910 to 1990—Cont'd.

(In millions of dollars, except as indicated)

| | | | Expenses of agricultural production | | | | | | | | |
| | | | Operating expenses (excluding hired labor) | | | | | | | | |
Year	Total	Feed purchased	Livestock purchased	Seed purchased [1]	Fertilizer and lime	Repairs	Miscellaneous [2]	Taxes on farm property	Wages paid hired farm labor [3]	Interest on farm mortgage debt	Net rent to nonfarm landlords
	271	273	274	275	276	277	278	280	281	282	283
1990	144,300	20,700	14,700	3,600	7,100	7,300	18,800	5,600	12,500	14,500	8,200
1989	140,200	21,000	13,100	3,600	7,200	7,300	19,200	5,100	11,100	14,700	7,900
1988	133,900	20,400	12,800	3,400	6,900	6,800	17,200	4,800	10,400	14,700	7,400
1987	128,700	17,500	11,800	3,300	6,500	6,800	17,500	4,900	10,000	15,000	7,300
1986	125,100	17,500	9,800	3,200	6,800	6,400	15,500	4,600	9,500	16,500	6,100
1985	132,400	16,900	9,200	3,100	7,500	6,400	16,500	4,500	10,000	18,600	7,700
1984	141,900	19,400	9,500	3,400	8,400	6,400	16,900	4,300	9,400	21,100	8,100
1983	139,600	20,600	8,800	2,700	7,100	6,500	17,100	4,500	8,900	21,400	5,200
1982	140,300	18,600	9,700	3,200	8,000	6,400	15,500	4,000	9,400	21,800	5,500
1981	139,400	20,900	9,000	3,400	9,400	7,000	12,400	4,200	8,900	19,900	6,200
1980	133,100	21,000	10,700	3,200	9,500	7,100	11,800	3,900	9,300	16,300	6,100
1979	123,300	19,300	13,000	2,900	7,400	7,300	11,500	3,900	9,000	13,100	6,200
1978	103,200	16,000	10,200	2,600	6,600	6,600	9,500	3,600	8,300	10,200	4,000
1977	89,000	14,000	7,100	2,500	6,500	5,800	6,700	3,700	8,000	8,500	3,400
1976	83,130	14,370	5,871	2,537	6,141	9,096	12,586	3,607	7,037	3,852	4,220
1975	75,100	12,900	5,000	2,100	6,700	4,500	5,600	3,200	6,600	6,400	4,000
1974	72,210	14,513	5,131	2,082	5,808	6,659	10,178	3,096	6,036	3,044	5,100
1973	65,562	13,224	8,065	1,617	3,354	5,229	8,836	2,888	5,232	2,495	5,679
1972	52,809	8,397	6,668	1,115	2,690	4,708	8,312	2,815	4,594	2,132	3,491
1971	47,806	8,049	5,123	1,072	2,633	4,707	7,650	2,704	4,367	1,905	2,246
1970	41,091	7,189	4,345	829	2,222	5,031	5,132	2,957	3,643	1,717	1,302
1969	38,759	6,602	4,219	737	2,084	4,896	4,732	2,732	3,299	1,599	1,297
1968	36,209	5,894	3,676	672	2,130	4,831	4,451	2,515	3,047	1,477	1,307
1967	34,775	6,472	3,391	678	2,124	4,495	4,068	2,275	2,878	1,343	1,305
1966	33,406	6,324	3,498	626	1,952	4,227	3,854	2,108	2,889	1,205	1,442
1965	30,933	5,749	2,913	637	1,754	4,073	3,628	1,943	2,849	1,077	1,328
1964	29,481	5,715	2,420	566	1,701	3,940	3,515	1,833	2,913	952	1,223
1963	29,688	6,128	2,917	553	1,570	3,942	3,315	1,763	2,990	846	1,193
1962	28,639	5,575	3,106	521	1,474	3,944	3,135	1,684	2,961	759	1,132
1961	27,125	5,121	2,730	521	1,373	3,858	2,936	1,597	2,977	686	1,109
1960	26,352	4,923	2,502	510	1,315	3,966	2,829	1,502	2,923	628	1,010
1959	26,106	4,744	2,693	491	1,291	4,069	2,724	1,401	2,882	572	1,011
1958	25,236	4,541	2,702	508	1,206	3,921	2,517	1,306	2,842	521	1,161
1957	23,294	4,035	1,934	510	1,166	3,917	2,332	1,242	2,734	482	1,029
1956	22,374	3,894	1,610	519	1,166	3,785	2,307	1,178	2,641	442	1,109
1955	21,889	3,880	1,539	566	1,185	3,600	2,204	1,141	2,615	402	1,057
1954	21,577	3,906	1,563	525	1,209	3,506	2,077	1,084	2,596	371	1,159
1953	21,275	3,770	1,320	551	1,178	3,541	2,106	1,060	2,736	345	1,214
1952	22,630	4,331	1,918	594	1,184	3,506	2,142	1,033	2,857	318	1,421
1951	22,252	4,144	2,437	551	1,064	3,282	2,064	983	2,921	291	1,368
1950	19,410	3,283	2,004	518	975	2,975	1,763	919	2,811	264	1,233
1949	17,982	3,024	1,529	543	895	2,896	1,702	872	2,806	243	1,107
1948	18,790	3,996	1,589	581	826	2,818	1,580	806	2,990	232	1,370
1947	17,032	3,746	1,379	514	755	2,468	1,421	733	2,783	225	1,455
1946	14,500	3,022	1,170	428	683	2,054	1,185	617	2,532	219	1,401
1945	13,062	2,738	1,011	435	657	1,689	1,081	557	2,299	221	1,064
1944	12,333	2,427	812	440	576	1,608	1,071	499	2,202	230	1,043
1943	11,608	2,135	908	406	505	1,465	1,026	477	2,027	246	1,044
1942	10,040	1,625	877	301	417	1,289	937	466	1,631	272	890
1941	7,781	1,089	635	203	334	1,132	875	463	1,249	284	647
1940	6,858	998	517	197	306	1,038	784	451	1,029	293	448
1939	6,266	732	465	169	273	959	759	456	988	305	379
1938	5,920	557	368	206	258	907	726	448	979	320	318

See footnotes at end of chart.

Series K 256-285.   Farm Income and Expenses: 1910 to 1990—Cont'd.

(In millions of dollars, except as indicated)

| | | | | | Expenses of agricultural production | | | | | | |
| | | | | Operating expenses (excluding hired labor) | | | | | | | |
Year	Total	Feed purchased	Livestock purchased	Seed purchased [1]	Fertilizer and lime	Repairs	Miscellaneous [2]	Taxes on farm property	Wages paid hired farm labor [3]	Interest on farm mortgage debt	Net rent to nonfarm landlords
	271	273	274	275	276	277	278	280	281	282	283
1937	6,178	805	332	194	279	879	732	452	988	341	380
1936	5,642	755	283	147	261	749	664	440	868	364	383
1935	5,116	528	312	108	188	717	647	434	775	396	347
1934	4,715	542	183	104	176	608	663	424	679	430	256
1933	4,358	422	199	65	120	554	669	438	617	472	158
1932	4,483	348	193	79	118	521	730	510	669	526	55
1931	5,537	448	253	117	202	635	834	589	914	553	136
1930	6,944	791	362	124	297	785	914	648	1,177	570	321
1929	7,664	919	504	122	300	886	998	651	1,300	582	486
1928	7,757	977	588	134	318	827	1,001	636	1,290	590	496
1927	7,462	892	465	140	267	787	986	620	1,302	593	520
1926	7,372	891	396	142	298	774	1,033	599	1,330	598	425
1925	7,347	988	382	136	299	711	1,021	589	1,267	612	470
1924	7,447	1,116	313	120	264	654	1,030	583	1,248	647	520
1923	7,054	819	304	111	263	637	1,027	590	1,251	679	430
1922	6,614	676	319	109	234	557	1,027	583	1,127	680	368
1921	6,638	710	202	123	249	550	1,052	586	1,170	653	304
1920	8,837	1,254	422	178	390	695	1,263	556	1,790	574	504
1919	8,331	1,097	567	138	358	615	1,143	454	1,515	476	928
1918	7,507	1,106	522	132	311	536	1,024	361	1,337	417	859
1917	6,092	614	414	122	232	464	863	339	1,127	379	825
1916	4,836	517	260	76	193	395	715	304	904	341	534
1915	4,167	411	207	62	165	343	639	284	815	314	403
1914	4,029	414	215	62	195	297	648	261	804	296	355
1913	3,974	406	250	62	175	289	634	257	804	276	340
1912	3,833	419	217	74	161	278	606	225	789	252	343
1911	3,582	350	188	65	168	251	588	215	758	225	331
1910	3,531	426	199	56	152	251	558	195	755	203	320

[1] Includes bulbs, plants and trees.
[2] Includes interest on non-real estate debt, marketing, charges, net insurance premiums (crop, fire, wind and hail) and miscellaneous supplies and services purchased.

[3] Includes value of perquisites.

Series K 358-360. Consumer Expenditures, Farm Value and Marketing Bill for All Farm Food Products Purchased by Domestic Civilian Consumer: 1913 to 1990

(In billions of dollars)

Year	Consumer expenditures [1]	Farm value	Marketing bill	Year	Consumer expenditures [1]	Farm value	Marketing bill	Year	Consumer expenditures [1]	Farm value	Marketing bill
	358	359	360		358	359	360		358	359	360
1990	440.8	106.6	334.2	1962	69.3	22.4	46.9	1937	14.2	6.0	8.2
1989	419.4	103.8	315.6	1961	67.1	22.0	45.1	1936	14.3	5.8	8.5
1988	398.8	96.8	301.9								
1987	375.5	90.4	285.1	1960	65.9	21.7	44.2	1935	13.8	5.2	8.6
1986	359.6	88.8	270.8	1959	63.1	20.9	42.2	1935 [4]	12.9	5.0	7.9
				1958	61.0	21.5	39.5	1934	12.5	4.3	8.2
1985	345.4	86.4	259.0	1957	58.3	21.4	37.9	1933	10.9	3.6	7.3
1984	332.0	89.8	242.2	1956	55.5	19.2	36.3	1932	10.6	3.4	7.2
1983	315.0	85.3	229.7					1931	13.1	4.7	8.4
1982	298.9	81.4	217.5	1955	53.1	18.7	34.4				
1981	287.7	83.2	204.5	1954	51.1	18.8	32.3	1930	16.2	6.3	9.9
				1953	51.0	19.5	31.5	1929 [4]	18.0	7.5	10.5
1980	264.4	81.7	182.7	1952	50.9	20.4	30.5	1929	17.1	7.2	9.9
1979	245.2	79.2	166.0	1951	49.2	20.5	28.7	1928	16.3	6.9	9.4
1978	216.9	69.5	147.4					1927	16.2	9.7	9.5
1977	189.3	57.3	132.0	1950	44.0	18.0	26.0	1926	16.4	7.0	9.4
1976	180.9	57.5	123.4	1949	43.4	17.4	26.0				
				1948	44.8	19.9	24.9	1925	15.7	6.8	8.9
1975	167.0	55.6	111.4	1947 [2]	41.9	19.3	22.6	1924	14.5	5.9	8.6
1974	152.3	55.8	96.5	1947 [3]	36.5	18.7	17.8	1923	14.0	5.6	8.4
1973	136.7	51.0	85.7	1946	30.8	15.7	15.6	1922	12.9	5.2	7.7
1972	120.3	39.3	81.0					1921	12.6	5.1	7.5
1971	—	—	—	1945	24.4	12.6	12.5				
				1944	22.5	11.6	11.4	1920	16.5	7.4	9.1
1970	101.6	33.1	68.5	1943	22.3	11.4	11.1	1919	15.2	7.6	7.6
1969	95.3	32.1	63.2	1942	19.8	9.3	10.5	1918	13.2	6.9	6.3
1968	90.1	29.0	61.1	1941	16.3	7.1	9.2	1917	12.4	6.1	6.3
1967	84.8	27.3	57.5					1916	9.5	4.4	5.1
1966	82.8	28.1	54.7	1940	14.1	5.6	8.5				
				1939	15.3	5.4	9.9	1915	8.0	3.6	4.4
1965	77.6	25.5	52.1	1939 [4]	13.4	5.2	8.2	1914	7.9	3.6	4.3
1964	47.6	23.4	51.2	1938	13.4	5.2	8.2	1913	7.4	3.6	3.9
1963	71.5	22.6	48.9								

[1] For 1913-1947, consumer expenditures for farm food eaten away from home are based on retail food store prices.
[2] Comparable with later years. Beginning 1947, a new series based on 1958 benchmark estimate.
[3] Comparable with earlier years.
[4] Revised figures according to the commodity flow method; comparable to 1947-1970 data based on 1958 benchmark estimate.

Series K 496-501. Acreages of Harvested Crops, by Use, and Indexes of Cropland Used for Crops and Crop Production Per Acre: 1910 to 1990

(Excludes Alaska and Hawaii)

Year	Acreages of harvested crops, by use (million acres)			Year	Acreages of harvested crops, by use (million acres)			Year	Acreages of harvested crops, by use (million acres)		
	Total	Export products	Products for domestic use		Total	Export products	Products for domestic use		Total	Export products	Products for domestic use
	496	497	499		496	497	499		496	497	499
1990	322	83	239	1963	300	77	223	1936	323	18	251
1989	318	103	215	1962	295	66	229				
1988	297	118	179	1961	303	67	¹ 232	1935	345	20	269
1987	302	106	196					1934	304	20	227
1986	325	96	229	1960	324	64	255	1933	340	28	253
				1959	324	61	257	1932	371	35	276
1985	342	81	263	1958	324	44	273	1931	365	36	267
1984	348	96	252	1957	324	48	268				
1983	306	124	182	1956	324	60	255	1930	369	39	265
1982	362	113	249					1929	365	44	254
1981	366	129	237	1955	340	47	283	1928	361	49	242
				1954	346	37	298	1927	358	49	236
1980	352	137	215	1953	348	31	304	1926	359	54	229
1979	348	115	232	1952	349	36	298				
1978	337	113	224	1951	344	59	267	1925	360	44	238
1977	344	112	232					1924	355	53	221
1976	337	97	240	1950	345	50	276	1923	354	47	223
				1949	360	45	293	1922	355	50	219
1975	336	100	236	1948	356	52	280	1921	359	66	206
1974	328	99	229	1947	355	42	287				
1973	321	96	225	1946	352	45	278	1920	360	60	210
1972	294	91	203					1919	364	56	217
1971	305	62	243	1945	354	42	280	1918	362	62	208
				1944	362	25	301	1917	349	44	213
1970	297	72	225	1943	357	21	299	1916	340	53	195
1969	294	61	233	1942	348	13	296				
1968	303	54	249	1941	344	12	292	1915	340	49	198
1967	308	69	239					1914	334	57	185
1966	295	69	226	1940	341	8	290	1913	333	43	198
				1939	331	23	263	1912	329	42	196
1965	298	76	222	1938	349	22	279	1911	330	40	200
1964	301	74	227	1937	347	29	266	1910	325	37	200

¹ 1961 and earlier, does not include feed for horses and mules.

Series K 502-516. Corn, Wheat, Oats and Barley—Acreage, Production, Price and Stocks: 1839 to 1991

(Census figures in *italics*)

Year	Corn for all purposes		All wheat for grain		Year	Corn for all purposes		All wheat for grain	
	Acreage harvested	Production	Acreage harvested	Production		Acreage harvested	Production	Acreage harvested	Production
	502	503	506	507		502	503	506	507
	1,000 acres	*Million bushels*	*1,000 acres*	*Million bushels*		*1,000 acres*	*Million bushels*	*1,000 acres*	*Million bushels*
1991	68,800	7,474	57,700	1,981	1945	87,625	2,869	65,167	1,108
1990	67,000	7,934	69,300	2,736	*1944*	*92,259*	*1 2,788*	*58,286*	*1,033*
1989	69,700	7,525	62,200	2,037	1944	94,014	3,088	59,749	1,060
1988	58,300	4,929	53,200	1,812	1943	92,060	2,966	51,355	844
1987	59,500	7,131	55,900	2,108	1942	87,367	3,069	49,773	969
1986	69,200	8,253	60,700	2,087	1941	85,357	2,652	55,935	942
1985	75,200	8,877	64,700	2,425	1940	86,429	2,457	53,273	815
1984	71,900	7,674	66,900	2,595	*1939*	*86,991*	*1 2,311*	*50,527*	*709*
1983	51,500	4,175	61,400	2,420	1939	88,279	2,581	52,669	741
1982	72,700	8,235	77,900	2,765	1938	92,160	2,549	69,197	920
1981	74,500	8,119	80,600	2,785	1937	93,930	2,643	64,169	874
					1936	93,154	1,506	49,125	630
1980	73,000	6,639	71,100	2,381					
1979	72,400	7,939	62,454	2,134	1935	95,974	2,299	51,305	628
1978	70,275	7,087	56,942	1,798	*1934*	*87,476*	*1 1,169*	*41,943*	*513*
1977	70,872	6,425	66,461	2,036	1934	92,193	1,449	43,347	526
1976	71,300	6,266	70,771	2,142	1933	105,918	2,398	49,424	552
					1932	110,577	2,930	57,851	756
1975	67,505	5,829	69,391	2,122	1931	106,866	2,576	57,704	942
1974	65,405	4,701	65,368	1,782					
1973	62,143	5,671	54,148	1,711	1930	101,465	2,080	62,637	887
1972	57,421	5,573	47,284	1,545	*1929*	*97,742*	*1 2,131*	*62,000*	*801*
1971	64,047	5,641	47,674	1,618	1929	97,805	2,516	63,392	824
					1928	100,336	2,666	59,226	914
1970	66,222	1 4,099	44,141	1,370	1927	98,357	2,616	59,628	875
1969 2	*60,402*	*1 4,357*	*45,373*	*1,328*	1926	99,452	2,547	56,616	832
1969	63,360	1 4,583	47,577	1,460					
1968	64,603	1 4,393	55,262	1,576	1925	101,331	2,798	52,443	669
1967	69,978	1 4,760	58,771	1,522	*1924*	*98,402*	*1 1,824*	*50,862*	*801*
1966	65,828	1 4,117	49,867	1,312	1924	100,420	2,223	52,463	842
					1923	101,123	2,875	56,920	759
1965	64,565	1 4,084	49,560	1,316	1922	100,345	2,707	61,397	847
1964	*63,515*	*1 3,361*	*47,958*	*1,218*	1921	103,155	2,928	64,566	819
1964	65,388	1 3,484	49,762	1,283					
1963	68,317	1 4,019	45,506	1,147	1920	101,359	3,071	62,358	843
1962	64,474	1 3,606	43,688	1,092	*1919*	*1 87,778*	*1 2,346*	*73,099*	*945*
1961	65,405	1 3,598	51,571	1,232	1919	98,145	2,679	73,700	952
					1918	102,195	2,441	61,068	904
1960	80,678	4,314	51,879	1,355	1917	110,893	2,908	46,787	620
1959 3	*79,616*	*1 3,697*	*49,567*	*1,056*	1916	100,561	2,425	53,510	635
1959	81,902	4,197	51,716	1,118					
1958	72,224	3,725	53,047	1,457	1915	100,623	2,829	60,303	1,009
1957	71,864	3,400	43,754	956	1914	97,796	2,524	55,613	897
1956	75,247	3,445	49,768	1,005	1913	100,206	2,273	52,012	751
					1912	101,451	2,948	48,413	720
1955	79,367	3,220	47,290	926	1911	101,393	2,475	49,894	618
1954	*78,123*	*1 2,613*	*51,362*	*909*					
1954	80,186	3,058	54,356	984	1910	102.267	2,853	45,793	625
1953	80,459	3,210	67,840	1,173	*1909*	*1 98,386*	*1 2,552*	*44,263*	*683*
1952	80,940	3,292	71,130	1,306	1909	100,200	2,611	44,262	684
1951	80,729	2,926	61,873	988	1908	95,285	2,567	45,102	643
					1907	96,094	2,614	44,139	629
1950	81,818	3,075	61,607	1,019	1906	95,624	3,033	46,230	741
1949	*83,337*	*1 2,778*	*71,163*	*1,007*					
1949	85,595	3,238	75,910	1,098	1905	95,746	2,954	46,306	706
1948	84,778	3,605	72,418	1,295	1904	95,228	2,687	43,155	556
1947	82,888	2,355	74,519	1,359	1903	93,555	2,515	48,456	663
1946	87,585	3,217	67,105	1,152	1902	97,177	2,774	46,244	687
					1901	94,422	1,716	50,847	763

See footnotes at end of chart.

Series K 502-516. Corn, Wheat, Oats and Barley—Acreage, Production, Price and Stocks: 1839 to 1991—Cont'd.

(Census figures in *italics*)

Year	Corn for all purposes		All wheat for grain		Year	Corn for all purposes		All wheat for grain	
	Acreage harvested	Production	Acreage harvested	Production		Acreage harvested	Production	Acreage harvested	Production
	502	503	506	507		502	503	506	507
	1,000 acres	Million bushels	1,000 acres	Million bushels		1,000 acres	Million bushels	1,000 acres	Million bushels
1900	94,852	2,662	49,203	599	1880	62,545	1,707	38,096	502
1899	¹ *94,917*	¹ *2,666*	*52,589*	*659*	*1879*	¹ *62,369*	¹ *1,755*	*35,430*	*459*
1899	94,591	2,646	52,342	655	1879	62,229	1,752	35,347	459
1898	87,784	2,351	50,506	768	1878	59,659	1,565	33,379	449
1897	89,965	2,288	43,413	606	1877	58,799	1,516	27,963	396
1896	89,074	2,671	40,828	523	1876	55,277	1,478	28,283	309
1895	90,479	2,535	38,998	542	1875	52,446	1,450	28,382	314
1894	80,069	1,615	40,167	542	1874	47,640	1,059	27,310	356
1893	79,832	1,900	40,790	506	1873	44,084	1,008	24,866	322
1892	76,914	1,897	42,979	612	1872	43,584	1,279	22,962	271
1891	78,855	2,336	41,090	678	1871	42,002	1,142	22,230	272
1890	74,785	1,650	36,686	449	1870	38,388	1,125	20,945	254
1889	¹ *72,088*	¹ *2,122*	*33,580*	*468*	*1869*	—	¹ *761*	—	*288*
1889	77,656	2,294	36,098	504	1869	35,833	782	21,194	290
1888	77,474	2,251	34,969	424	1868	35,116	920	19,140	246
1887	73,296	1,605	36,873	491	1867	32,116	794	16,738	211
1886	73,911	1,783	36,312	514					
					1866	30,017	731	15,408	170
1885	71,854	2,058	35,095	400	*1859*	—	¹ *839*	—	*173*
1884	68,834	1,948	38,485	571	*1849*	—	¹ *592*	—	*100*
1883	68,168	1,652	35,587	439	*1839*	—	¹ *378*	—	*85*
1882	66,157	1,755	36,496	552					
1881	63,026	1,245	36,795	406					

¹ Corn harvested for grain only.
² Not comparable with previous censuses; data for farms with farm product sales of $2,500 or more.

³ Beginning 1959, census data include Alaska and Hawaii.

Series K 517-531.   Flaxseed, Soybeans, Sorghum Grain, Rye and Buckwheat—Acreage, Production and Price: 1909 to 1991

(Census figures in *italics*)

Year	Soybeans for beans — Acreage harvested 520 (1,000 acres)	Soybeans for beans — Production 521 (Million bushels)	Sorghum grain — Acreage harvested 523 (1,000 acres)	Sorghum grain — Production 524 (Million bushels)	Year	Soybeans for beans — Acreage harvested 520 (1,000 acres)	Soybeans for beans — Production 521 (Million bushels)	Sorghum grain — Acreage harvested 523 (1,000 acres)	Sorghum grain — Production 524 (Million bushels)
1991	58,000	1,986	9,800	579	*1949*	*10,148*	*212.4*	*6,602*	*148*
1990	56,500	1,926	9,100	573	1949	10,482	234.2	6,325	141
1989	59,500	1,924	11,100	615	1948	10,682	227.2	7,317	131
1988	57,400	1,549	9,000	577	1947	11,411	186.5	5,480	93
1987	57,200	1,938	10,500	731	1946	9,932	203.4	6,669	106
1986	59,400	2,007	13,900	942					
					1945	10,740	193.2	6,324	96
1985	61,600	2,099	16,800	1,120	*1944*	—	*187.7*	*9,386*	*185*
1984	66,100	1,861	15,400	866	1944	10,245	192.1	9,061	178
1983	62,500	1,636	10,000	488	1943	10,397	190.1	6,889	110
1982	69,400	2,190	14,100	835	1942	9,894	187.5	5,991	110
1981	66,200	1,989	13,700	876	1941	5,889	107.2	6,015	114
1980	67,800	1,798	12,500	579	1940	4,807	78.0	6,374	86
1979	70,566	2,268	12,901	809	*1939*	*4,274*	*87.6*	*4,760*	*53*
1978	63,343	1,870	13,561	748	1939	4,315	90.1	4,693	52
1977	57,612	1,762	14,092	793	1938	3,035	61.9	4,699	67
1976	49,358	1,288	14,723	720	1937	2,586	46.2	4,915	70
					1936	2,359	33.7	2,793	30
1975	53,579	1,547	15,355	753					
1974	51,341	1,216	13,809	623	1935	2,915	48.9	4,597	58
1973	55,667	1,548	15,706	923	*1934*	—	*23.0*	*2,396*	*19*
1972	45,698	1,271	13,368	809	1934	1,556	23.2	2,370	19
1971	42,701	1,176	16,301	876	1933	1,044	13.5	4,354	54
					1932	1,001	15.2	4,400	66
1970	42,056	1,123.7	13,568	684	1931	1,141	17.3	4,443	72
1969[1]	*38,550*	*1,041.5*	*13,437*	*730*					
1969	40,982	1,126.3	—	—	1930	1,074	13.9	3,477	38
1968	41,104	1,103.1	13,890	731	*1929*	—	*8.7*	*3,522*	*49*
1967	39,767	976.1	14,988	755	1929	708	9.4	3,523	50
1966	36,546	928.5	12,813	715	1928	579	7.9	4,115	77
					1927	568	6.9	4,260	81
1965	34,449	845.6	13,029	673	1926	466	5.2	4,211	71
1964	*29,844*	*669.7*	*11,742*	*490*					
1964	30,793	700.9	11,168	463	1925	415	4.9	3,917	57
1963	28,615	699.2	13,326	585	*1924*	—	—	*3,519*	*61*
1962	27,608	669.2	11,571	510	1924	448	4.9	3,526	59
1961	27,003	678.6	10,985	480	1923	—	—	4,204	62
					1922	—	—	3,369	50
1960	23,655	555.1	15,601	620	1921	—	—	3,700	71
1959[2]	*22,080*	*515.6*	*15,406*	*555*					
1959	22,631	532.9	14,561	508	1920	—	—	4,027	88
1958	23,993	580.3	16,524	581	*1919*	*113*	*1.1*	*3,630*	*74*
1957	20,857	483.4	19,682	568	1919	—	—	3,619	72
1956	20,620	449.3	9,209	205	1918	—	—	—	—
					1917	—	—	—	—
1955	18,620	373.7	12,891	243	1916	—	—	—	—
1954	*16,444*	*324.1*	*11,718*	*236*					
1954	17,047	341.1	11,304	224	1915	—	—	—	—
1953	14,829	269.2	6,295	116	1914	—	—	—	—
1952	14,435	298.8	5,326	91	1913	—	—	—	—
1951	13,615	283.8	8,544	163	1912	—	—	—	—
					1911	—	—	—	—
1950	13,807	299.2	10,346	234					
					1910	—	—	—	—
					1909	*2*	*(Z)*	—	—

Z Less than 50,000.

[1] Not comparable with previous census; data for farms with farm products sales of $2,500 or more in 1969.

[2] Beginning 1959, census data include Alaska and Hawaii.

Series K 532-537. Irish Potatoes and Sweet Potatoes—Acreage, Production and Price: 1849 to 1991

(Census figures in *italics*. Prices are those received by growers)

Year	Irish potatoes — Acreage harvested 532 (1,000 acres)	Irish potatoes — Production 533 (1,000 cwt.)
1991	1,400	418,000
1990	1,400	402,000
1989	1,300	370,000
1988	1,300	356,000
1987	1,300	389,000
1986	1,200	362,000
1985	1,300	407,000
1984	—	—
1983	1,243	334,000
1982	1,267	355,000
1981	1,232	341,000
1980	1,155	301,000
1979	1,270	342,000
1978	1,371	365,000
1977	1,359	355,000
1976	1,375	358,000
1975	1,264	322,000
1974	1,392	342,000
1973	1,307	300,000
1972	1,254	296,000
1971	1,391	319,000
1970	1,420	325,588
1969[1]	*1,261*	*273,644*
1969	1,413	311,903
1968	1,376	293,984
1967	1,457	305,334
1966	1,464	306,902
1965	1,384	291,169
1964	*1,174*	*221,874*
1964	1,272	241,076
1963	1,323	271,158
1962	1,347	264,810
1961	1,480	293,166
1960	1,386	257,104
1959[3]	*1,200*	*224,140*
1959	1,331	245,272
1958	1,428	266,897
1957	1,359	242,522
1956	1,371	245,792
1955	1,405	224,696
1954	*1,211*	*204,113*
1954	1,413	219,547
1953	1,536	231,679
1952	1,397	211,095
1951	1,348	195,776
1950	1,698	259,112
1949	*1,515*	*219,917*

Year	Irish potatoes — Acreage harvested 532 (1,000 acres)	Irish potatoes — Production 533 (1,000 cwt.)
1949	1,755	240,950
1948	1,981	269,937
1947	2,001	233,391
1946	2,527	292,389
1945	2,664	251,639
1944	*2,537*	*213,928*
1944	2,780	230,356
1943	3,239	275,332
1942	2,671	221,339
1941	2,693	213,418
1940	2,832	226,152
1939	*2,645*	*190,999*
1939	2,813	205,423
1938	2,870	213,509
1937	3,055	225,869
1936	2,960	194,373
1935	3,469	227,337
1934	*3,582*	*242,052*
1934	3,599	243,889
1933	3,423	205,922
1932	3,568	224,815
1931	3,490	230,590
1930	3,139	206,290
1929	*3,945*	*193,480*
1929	3,030	200,035
1928	3,499	256,349
1927	3,182	221,786
1926	2,811	192,964
1925	2,810	177,880
1924	*2,911*	*211,477*
1924	3,106	230,500
1923	3,378	219,814
1922	3,901	249,224
1921	3,598	195,187
1920	3,301	221,342
1919	*3,253*	*174,293*
1919	3,300	178,405
1918	3,597	207,668
1917	3,801	239,192
1916	3,274	162,233
1915	3,433	202,056
1914	3,417	220,949
1913	3,477	199,468
1912	3,505	243,729
1911	3,532	181,628
1910	3,644	205,231
1909	*3,669*	*233,527*

Year	Irish potatoes — Acreage harvested 532 (1,000 acres)	Irish potatoes — Production 533 (1,000 cwt.)
1909	3,675	234,100
1908	3,417	183,148
1907	3,333	199,875
1906	3,254	204,876
1905	3,263	180,421
1904	3,208	209,695
1903	3,079	165,770
1902	3,077	177,941
1901	2,950	124,447
1900	2,997	155,813
1899	*2,939*	*163,997*
1899	2,939	163,541
1898	2,877	144,209
1897	2,809	118,904
1896	2,968	157,641
1895	3,090	181,269
1894	2,869	118,614
1893	2,614	122,534
1892	2,519	114,120
1891	2,633	158,170
1890	2,557	102,065
1889	*2,601*	*130,528*
1889	2,603	130,760
1888	2,604	143,785
1887	2,466	95,769
1886	2,393	117,045
1885	2,335	118,286
1884	2,307	124,789
1883	2,373	136,253
1882	2,216	118,390
1881	2,036	76,544
1880	1,968	99,095
1879	*(²)*	*101,675*
1879	1,961	101,663
1878	1,879	86,018
1877	1,878	104,221
1876	1,783	73,567
1875	1,789	107,887
1874	1,654	78,668
1873	1,543	77,698
1872	1,559	80,144
1871	1,496	80,833
1870	1,443	64,725
1869	*—*	*86,002*
1869	1,479	86,759
1868	1,400	72,175
1867	1,289	59,798
1866	1,225	66,969
1859	—	66,660
1849	—	39,479

[1] Not comparable with previous censuses; data for farms with farm products sales of $2,500 or more.

[2] Acreage reporting incomplete: 13 states reported 911,325 acres of Irish potatoes; 23 states 444,817 acres of sweet potatoes.

[3] Beginning 1959, census data include Alaska and Hawaii.

Series K 538-549. Rice, Sugarcane, Sugar Beets and Peanuts—Acreage, Production and Price: 1895 to 1991

(Census figures in *italics*)

Year	Rice — Acreage harvested (538)	Rice — Production (539)	Year	Rice — Acreage harvested (538)	Rice — Production (539)	Year	Rice — Acreage harvested (538)	Rice — Production (539)	Year	Rice — Acreage harvested (538)	Rice — Production (539)
	1,000 acres	1,000 cwt.		1,000 acres	1,000 cwt.		1,000 acres	1,000 cwt.		1,000 acres	1,000 cwt.
1991	2,800	155,000	1965	1,793	76,281	1942	1,457	29,082	1920	1,299	23,242
1990	2,800	156,000	*1964*	*1,815*	*74,824*	1941	1,214	23,095	*1919*	*917*	*16,195*
1989	2,700	155,000	1964	1,786	73,166				1919	1,083	19,310
1988	2,900	160,000	1963	1,771	70,269	1940	1,069	24,495	1918	1,101	17,999
1987	2,300	130,000	1962	1,773	66,045	*1939*	*852*	*19,732*	1917	953	15,621
1986	2,400	134,000	1961	1,589	54,198	1939	1,045	24,328	1916	843	17,795
						1938	1,076	23,628			
1985	2,500	135,000	1960	1,595	54,591	1937	1,099	24,040	1915	740	11,748
1984	2,800	139,000	*1959* [2]	*1,617*	*54,403*	1936	981	22,419	1914	646	10,565
1983	2,200	100,000	1959	1,586	53,647				1913	722	10,894
1982	3,300	154,000	1958	1,415	44,760	1935	817	17,753	1912	643	10,665
1981	3,800	183,000	1957	1,340	42,935	*1934*	*706*	*14,831*	1911	636	10,198
			1956	1,569	49,459	1934	812	17,571			
1980	3,300	146,000				1933	798	16,943	1910	666	11,129
1979	2,869	132,000	1955	1,826	55,902	1932	874	18,729	*1909*	*620*	*10,246*
1978	2,970	133,000	*1954*	*2,498*	*65,284*	1931	965	20,076	1909	662	10,614
1977	2,249	99,000	1954	2,550	64,193				1908	596	10,079
1976	2,480	116,000	1953	2,159	52,834	1930	966	20,218	1907	563	9,338
			1952	1,997	48,193	*1929*	*743*	*15,137*	1906	505	7,999
1975	2,818	128,000	1951	1,996	46,089	1929	860	17,790			
1974	2,531	112,000				1928	972	19,725	1905	457	7,217
1973	2,170	93,000	1950	1,637	38,820	1927	1,027	20,024	1904	574	8,647
1972	1,818	85,000	*1949*	*1,819*	*40,251*	1926	1,016	18,911	1903	547	8,590
1971	1,818	86,000	1949	1,858	40,769				1902	545	6,541
			1948	1,804	38,275	1925	853	14,866	1901	423	5,702
1970	1,815	83,754	1947	1,708	35,217	*1924*	*744*	*13,286*			
1969 [1]	2,131	91,544	1946	1,582	32,497	1924	838	14,689	1900	361	4,407
1969	2,128	90,838				1923	874	14,957	*1899*	*351*	*4,386*
1968	2,353	104,075	1945	1,499	30,668	1922	1,053	18,748	1899	338	4,029
1967	1,970	89,379	*1944*	*1,394*	*29,270*	1921	990	17,673	1898	314	3,737
1966	1,967	85,020	1944	1,480	30,974				1897	290	3,084
			1943	1,472	29,264				1896	270	2,340
									1895	292	3,341

[1] Not comparable with previous censuses; data for farms with farm products sales of $2,500 or more.

[2] Beginning 1959, census data include Alaska and Hawaii.

Series K 550-563. Hay, Cotton, Cottonseed, Shorn Wool and Tobacco—Acreage, Production and Price: 1790 to 1991

(Census figures in *italics*)

Year	Hay[1] Acreage harvested	Hay[1] Production	Cotton Acreage harvested	Cotton Production	Tobacco Acreage harvested	Tobacco Production
	550	**551**	**553**	**554**	**561**	**562**
	1,000 acres	*Million tons*	*1,000 acres*	*1,000 bales*	*1,000 acres*	*Million pounds*
1991	61,600	147	12,800	17,500	800	1,638
1990	63,300	146	11,700	15,500	700	1,625
1989	65,100	126	9,500	12,200	700	1,367
1988	60,100	148	11,900	15,400	600	1,370
1987	62,400	156	10,000	14,800	800	1,189
1986	62,300	155	8,500	9,700	600	1,166
1985	60,400	149	10,200	13,400	700	1,512
1984	61,400	151	10,400	13,000	800	1,728
1983	59,700	141	7,300	7,800	800	1,429
1982	59,800	149	9,700	12,000	900	1,994
1981	59,600	143	13,800	15,600	1,000	2,064
1980	58,900	131	13,200	11,100	900	1,786
1979	61,666	148	12,831	14,600	827	1,527
1978	61,515	142	12,370	10,900	948	2,024
1977	60,658	131	13,275	14,400	958	1,913
1976	60,311	120	10,914	10,600	1,045	2,136
1975	61,324	132	8,796	8,300	1,086	2,182
1974	60,195	126	12,547	11,500	963	1,990
1973	61,828	134	11,970	13,000	887	1,742
1972	59,821	129	12,984	14,000	842	1,749
1971	61,405	129	11,471	10,000	838	1,705
1970	62,911	127	11,160	10,166	899	1,908
1969[2]	*53,204*	*112*	*11,496*	*10,360*	*—*	*—*
1969	62,053	128	11,055	9,990	920	1,804
1968	62,693	126	10,160	10,925	880	1,710
1967	64,667	126	7,997	7,443	960	1,968
1966	65,140	121	9,552	9,555	974	1,887
1965	67,684	126	13,615	14,951	977	1,855
1964	*65,295*	*116*	*13,917*	*14,734*	*—*	*—*
1964	67,375	119	14,055	15,144	1,078	2,228
1963	66,428	118	14,212	15,294	1,176	2,344
1962	67,563	122	15,569	14,827	1,224	2,315
1961	67,376	117	15,634	14,318	1,174	2,061
1960	67,313	118	15,309	14,272	1,142	1,944
1959[3]	*63,549*	*107*	*14,649*	*13,914*	*—*	*—*
1959	66,266	111	15,117	14,558	1,153	1,796
1958	70,547	120	11,849	11,512	1,078	1,736
1957	71,912	120	13,558	10,964	1,122	1,668
1956	72,292	108	15,615	13,310	1,364	2,176
1955	74,956	113	16,928	14,721	1,495	2,193
1954	*69,940*	*104*	*18,858*	*12,921*	*—*	*—*
1954	73,721	108	19,251	13,697	1,668	2,244
1953	74,997	108	24,341	16,465	1,633	2,059
1952	75,147	106	25,921	15,139	1,772	2,256
1951	75,063	110	26,949	15,149	1,780	2,332
1950	75,150	104	17,843	10,014	1,599	2,030
1949	*67,470*	*89*	*26,599*	*15,419*	*—*	*—*
1949	72,821	97	27,439	16,128	1,623	1,969
1948	71,817	96	22,911	14,877	1,554	1,980
1947	74,666	101	21,330	11,860	1,852	2,107
1946	73,741	100	17,584	8,640	1,960	1,315
1945	76,697	107	17,029	9,015	1,821	1,991
1944	*73,402*	*95*	*18,962*	*11,838*	*—*	*—*
1944	77,639	103	19,617	12,230	1,750	1,951
1943	77,004	103	21,610	11,427	1,458	1,406

Year	Hay[1] Acreage harvested	Hay[1] Production	Cotton Acreage harvested	Cotton Production	Tobacco Acreage harvested	Tobacco Production
	550	**551**	**553**	**554**	**561**	**562**
	1,000 acres	*Million tons*	*1,000 acres*	*1,000 bales*	*1,000 acres*	*Million pounds*
1942	74,827	108	22,602	12,817	1,377	1,408
1941	73,136	96	22,236	10,744	1,307	1,262
1940	73,058	96	23,861	12,566	1,410	1,460
1939	*61,229*	*74*	*22,811*	*11,481*	*—*	*—*
1939	69,243	87	23,805	11,817	2,000	1,881
1938	68,175	91	24,248	11,943	1,601	1,386
1937	66,001	83	33,623	18,946	1,753	1,569
1936	67,732	70	29,755	12,399	1,441	1,163
1935	68,550	90	27,509	10,638	1,439	1,302
1934	*63,156*	*54*	*26,754*	*9,472*	*—*	*—*
1934	65,387	60	26,866	9,636	1,273	[3]1,085
1933	68,439	75	29,383	13,047	1,739	1,372
1932	70,412	84	35,891	13,003	1,405	1,018
1931	68,160	75	38,704	17,097	1,988	1,565
1930	67,947	75	42,444	13,932	2,124	1,648
1929	*67,823*	*82*	*43,228*	*14,574*	*—*	*—*
1929	69,531	87	43,232	14,825	1,980	1,533
1928	67,185	84	42,434	14,477	1,864	1,373
1927	72,131	98	38,342	12,956	1,556	1,211
1926	68,795	76	44,608	17,978	1,628	1,289
1925	70,105	79	44,386	16,105	1,751	1,376
1924	*71,692*	*88*	*39,204*	*13,683*	*—*	*—*
1924	74,459	91	39,501	13,630	1,702	1,245
1923	73,545	89	35,550	10,140	1,855	1,518
1922	75,432	95	31,361	9,755	1,616	1,254
1921	73,070	85	28,678	7,945	1,340	1,005
1920	73,033	92	34,408	13,429	1,935	1,509
1919	*70,936*	*89*	*33,740*	*11,376*	*—*	*—*
1919	73,156	92	32,906	11,141	1,959	1,444
1918	71,909	82	35,038	12,018	1,720	1,445
1917	71,017	85	32,245	11,284	1,616	1,326
1916	72,918	99	33,071	11,448	1,483	1,207
1915	69,518	91	29,951	11,172	1,419	1,157
1914	67,337	83	35,615	16,112	1,258	1,037
1913	66,873	77	35,206	14,153	1,284	992
1912	67,395	86	32,557	13,703	1,335	1,117
1911	65,885	65	34,916	15,694	1,133	941
1910	68,332	75	31,508	11,609	1,398	1,142
1909	*68,227*	*87*	*32,044*	*10,649*	*—*	*—*
1909	68,703	87	30,555	10,005	1,292	1,054
1908	51,487	72	31,091	13,241	1,009	836
1907	49,833	66	30,729	11,106	1,042	886
1906	48,650	60	31,404	13,274	1,123	973
1905	48,333	67	27,753	10,576	1,103	939
1904	47,480	66	30,377	13,438	1,026	857
1903	46,650	64	27,762	9,851	1,212	976
1902	44,716	59	27,561	10,630	1,189	960
1901	43,555	53	27,050	9,508	1,098	886
1900	42,488	50	24,886	10,124	1,086	852
1899	*61,691*	*79*	*24,275*	*9,535*	*—*	*—*
1899	43,395	54	24,163	9,346	1,102	870
1898	43,083	60	24,715	11,278	1,116	909
1897	42,396	56	25,131	10,899	978	703
1896	40,971	51	23,230	8,533	1,038	760

See footnotes at end of chart.

Series K 550-563. Hay, Cotton, Cottonseed, Shorn Wool and Tobacco—Acreage, Production and Price: 1790 to 1991—Cont'd.

(Census figures in *italics*)

Year	Hay [1] Acreage harvested	Hay Production	Cotton Acreage harvested	Cotton Production	Tobacco Acreage harvested	Tobacco Production
	550	**551**	**553**	**554**	**561**	**562**
	1,000 acres	*Million tons*	*1,000 acres*	*1,000 bales*	*1,000 acres*	*Million pounds*
1893	42,083	53	20,256	7,493	1,096	767
1892	41,328	53	18,869	6,700	1,039	757
1891	40,350	51	21,503	9,035	955	747
1890	39,613	51	20,937	8,653	851	648
1889	*52,949*	*67*	*20,175*	*7,473*	—	—
1889	38,867	50	20,191	7,473	758	525
1888	37,411	47	19,520	6,938	891	661
1887	36,480	42	18,793	7,047	722	469
1886	35,771	45	18,370	6,505	848	609
1885	34,507	43	17,922	6,576	815	611
1884	33,448	43	16,849	5,682	754	580
1883	32,077	44	16,295	5,713	750	509
1882	30,373	39	15,638	6,949	744	579
1881	28,619	35	16,483	5,456	698	426
1880	27,011	33	15,921	6,606	650	469
1879	*30,631*	*35*	*14,480*	*5,755*	—	—
1879	26,641	31	14,474	5,756	633	472
1878	25,627	33	13,539	5,074	651	455
1877	24,749	30	12,606	4,773	789	621
1876	23,986	29	11,747	4,474	625	466
1875	22,662	26	11,348	4,631	746	609
1874	21,861	25	10,753	3,836	378	217
1873	21,597	24	10,998	4,168	513	382
1872	21,081	24	9,580	3,933	492	385
1871	20,270	22	8,285	2,974	420	327
1870	19,719	21	9,238	4,352	424	345
1869	—	*27*	—	*3,012*	—	—
1869	19,310	25	7,751	3,011	395	264
1868	19,568	23	6,973	2,366	369	286
1867	18,641	23	7,864	2,520	370	260
1866	18,250	21	7,666	2,097	394	316

Year	Hay production [1]	Cotton production
	551	**554**
	Million tons	*1,000 bales*
1865	—	2,094
1864	—	299
1863	—	449
1862	—	1,597
1861	—	4,491
1860	—	3,841
1859	*19*	*5,387*
1859	—	4,508
1858	—	3,758
1857	—	3,012
1856	—	2,874
1855	—	3,221
1854	—	2,708
1853	—	2,766
1852	—	3,130
1851	—	2,799
1850	—	2,136
1849	*14*	*2,469*
1849	—	2,066
1848	—	2,615
1847	—	2,128
1846	—	1,604
1845	—	1,806
1844	—	2,079
1843	—	1,750
1842	—	2,035
1841	—	1,398
1840	—	1,348
1839	*10*	*1,976*
1839	—	1,654
1838	—	1,093
1837	—	1,428
1836	—	1,129

Year	Cotton production
	554
	1,000 bales
1835	1,062
1834	962
1833	931
1832	816
1831	805
1830	732
1829	764
1828	680
1827	565
1826	732
1825	533
1824	450
1823	387
1822	439
1821	377
1820	335
1819	349
1818	262
1817	272
1816	259
1815	209
1814	146
1813	157
1812	157
1811	167
1810	178
1809	172
1808	157
1807	167
1806	167
1805	146
1804	136

Year	Cotton production
	554
	1,000 bales
1803	126
1802	115
1801	100
1800	73
1799	42
1798	31
1797	23
1796	21
1795	17
1794	17
1793	10
1792	6
1791	4
1790	3

[1] All hay, 1909-1970; tame hay prior to 1909.
[2] Annual production estimates prior to 1962 are shown in 500-pound gross-weight bales; beginning 1962, 480-pound net-weight bales. Figures for census years are shown in running bales, and are not comparable with annual production estimates; the net weight per running bale was 383 pounds in 1839; 496.1 pounds in 1944; 482.0 pounds in 1954; 501.1 pounds in 1964; and 503.6 pounds in 1969.
[3] Includes 26.5 million pounds that were not utilized due to Agricultural Adjustment Act.

Series K 564-582. Livestock—Number, Value Per Head, Production and Price: 1867 to 1991

(Census figures in italics. All figures are as of January 1 except for 1870, 1880, 1890, 1900 (June 1); 1910 (April 15); 1930, 1940, 1950 (April 1); 1954, 1959 (October-November); 1964 (November-December); and 1969 (December 31))

	Number on farms and value per head					
	All cattle		Hogs		Stock sheep	
Year	Number	Value per head	Number	Value per head	Number	Value per head
	564	565	566	567	568	569
	1,000 head	Dollars	1,000 head	Dollars	1,000 head	Dollars
1991	99,400	653.0	54,500	85.40	11,200	65.60
1990	98,200	614.0	53,800	79.10	11,400	79.30
1989	98,100	580.0	55,500	66.30	10,900	82.40
1988	99,600	523.0	54,400	76.00	10,900	90.00
1987	102,100	407.0	51,000	91.90	10,600	75.70
1986	105,400	391.0	52,300	69.90	10,100	67.40
1985	109,600	402.0	54,100	75.00	10,700	61.10
1984	113,400	396.0	56,700	58.80	11,600	52.10
1983	115,000	406.0	54,500	89.90	12,100	51.80
1982	115,400	415.0	58,700	70.10	13,000	57.10
1981	114,400	473.0	64,500	74.70	12,900	69.90
1980	111,200	502.0	67,300	56.00	12,700	78.20
1979	110,900	403.0	60,400	83.20	12,400	72.10
1978	116,400	232.0	56,500	63.20	12,400	51.60
1977	122,800	206.0	54,900	47.00	12,700	42.50
1976	128,000	190.0	49,300	80.40	13,300	37.30
1975	132,000	159.0	54,700	44.90	14,500	30.50
1974	127,800	293.0	60,600	60.40	16,300	32.80
1973	121,500	252.0	59,000	42.00	17,600	26.70
1972	117,900	208.0	62,400	28.50	18,700	22.90
1971	114,600	184.0	67,300	23.50	19,700	23.60
1970	112,303	180.0	[1] 56,655	[1] 39.00	17,411	24.70
1969	*106,381*	—	*55,455*	—	*21,611*	—
1969	109,885	158.0	[1] 60,632	[1] 30.50	18,332	22.00
1968	109,152	149.0	58,777	28.30	19,105	19.20
1967	108,645	149.0	53,249	33.20	20,661	19.70
1966	108,862	133.0	47,414	45.20	21,456	19.70
1965	109,000	113.0	50,792	24.50	21,843	15.80
1964	*105,558*	—	*54,080*	—	*25,472*	—
1964	107,903	127.0	56,757	23.40	23,455	14.00
1963	104,488	142.0	57,993	27.50	25,122	14.40
1962	100,369	140.0	56,619	27.50	26,719	12.90
1961 *	97,700	134.0	55,560	27.20	28,320	14.60
1960	96,236	137.0	59,026	18.50	28,849	16.50
1959	*92,534*	—	*67,949*	—	*33,945*	—
1959	93,322	153.0	58,045	32.00	28,108	20.30
1958	91,176	120.0	51,517	30.20	27,167	19.40
1957	92,860	91.6	51,897	24.70	26,348	14.90
1956	95,900	88.1	55,354	17.70	26,890	14.30
1955	96,592	88.2	50,474	30.60	27,137	14.90
1954	*95,027*	—	*57,093*	—	*31,619*	—
1954	95,679	92.0	45,114	36.60	27,079	13.80
1953	94,241	128.0	51,755	26.10	27,593	15.70
1952	88,072	179.0	62,117	29.90	27,944	28.00
1951	82,083	160.0	62,269	33.30	27,251	26.50
1950	*76,762*	—	*55,722*	—	*31,387*	—
1950	77,963	124.0	58,937	27.10	26,182	17.80
1949	76,830	135.0	56,257	38.30	26,940	17.00
1948	77,171	117.0	54,590	42.90	29,486	15.00
1947	80,554	97.5	56,810	36.00	31,805	12.20
1946	82,235	76.2	61,306	24.00	35,525	9.57
1945	*82,654*	—	*46,735*	—	*41,224*	—
1945	85,573	66.9	59,373	20.60	39,609	8.45
1944	85,334	68.4	82,741	17.50	44,270	8.68
1943	81,204	69.3	73,881	22.50	48,196	9.68
1942	76,025	55.0	60,607	15.60	49,346	8.66
1941	71,755	43.2	54,353	8.34	47,441	6.77
1940 [2]	60,675	—	34,037	—	40,129	—
1940	68,309	40.6	61,165	7.78	46,266	6.35
1939	66,029	38.44	50,012	11.18	45,463	5.74
1938	65,249	36.58	44,525	11.26	44,972	6.13
1937	66,098	34.06	43,083	11.89	45,251	6.02
1936	67,847	34.06	42,975	12.71	45,435	6.35
1935	*68,284*	—	*37,213*	—	*48,358*	—
1935 [3]	68,846	20.20	39,066	6.31	46,139	4.33
1934 [3]	74,369	17.78	58,621	4.09	48,244	3.77
1933 [3]	70,280	19.74	62,127	4.21	47,303	2.91
1932	65,801	26.39	59,301	6.13	47,682	3.44
1931	63,030	38.99	54,835	11.35	47,720	5.40
1930 [2]	*63,896*	—	*56,288*	—	*56,975*	—
1930	61,003	56.36	55,705	13.45	45,577	9.00
1929	58,877	58.47	59,042	12.93	43,481	10.71
1928	57,322	50.63	61,873	13.17	40,689	10.36
1927	58,178	39.98	55,496	17.19	38,067	9.79
1926	60,576	36.80	52,105	15.66	35,719	10.53
1925	*60,760*	—	*50,854*	—	*35,590*	—
1925	63,373	31.72	55,770	13.15	34,469	9.63
1924	65,996	32.11	66,576	10.30	32,859	7.94
1923	67,546	31.66	69,304	12.29	32,597	7.50
1922	68,795	30.39	59,749	10.58	33,365	4.79
1921	68,714	39.07	58,942	13.63	35,426	6.34
1920	*66,640*	—	*59,346*	—	*35,034*	—
1920	70,400	52.64	60,159	20.00	37,328	10.59
1919	72,094	54.65	64,326	22.18	38,360	11.49
1918	73,040	50.01	62,931	19.69	36,704	11.76
1917	70,979	43.34	57,578	11.82	35,246	7.06
1916	67,438	40.10	60,596	8.48	36,260	5.10
1915	63,849	40.67	56,600	9.95	36,263	4.39
1914	59,461	38.97	52,853	10.51	38,059	3.91
1913	56,592	33.07	53,747	9.89	40,544	3.87
1912	55,675	27.68	55,394	7.99	42,972	3.42
1911	57,225	27.22	55,366	9.33	46,055	3.93
1910	*61,804*	—	*58,186*	—	*52,448*	—
1910	58,993	24.54	48,072	9.05	46,939	4.06
1909	60,774	21.99	52,508	6.45	47,098	3.42
1908	61,989	20.92	58,388	5.99	45,095	3.87
1907	63,754	20.91	56,543	7.54	43,460	3.81
1906	65,009	19.65	53,633	6.07	41,965	3.51
1905	66,111	18.39	53,176	5.89	40,410	2.77
1904	66,442	19.69	51,623	6.08	41,908	2.55
1903	66,004	21.55	48,100	7.69	44,436	2.62
1902	64,418	21.48	17,858	6.95	46,196	2.62
1901	62,576	22.68	50,681	6.08	46,126	2.96
1900	*67,719*	—	*62,868*	—	*61,504*	—
1900	59,739	26.50	51,055	5.36	45,065	2.97
1899	55,927	24.53	51,558	4.67	42,688	2.80
1898	52,868	22.79	53,282	4.70	40,097	2.51

See footnotes at end of chart.

Series K 564-582.   Livestock—Number, Value Per Head, Production and Price: 1867 to 1991—Cont'd.

(Census figures in italics. All figures are as of January 1 except for 1870, 1880, 1890, 1900 (June 1); 1910 (April 15); 1930, 1940, 1950 (April 1); 1954, 1959 (October-November); 1964 (November-December); and 1969 (December 31))

	Number on farms and value per head							Number on farms and value per head					
	All cattle		Hogs		Stock sheep			All cattle		Hogs		Stock sheep	
Year	Number	Value per head	Number	Value per head	Number	Value per head	Year	Number	Value per head	Number	Value per head	Number	Value per head
	564	565	566	567	568	569		564	565	566	567	568	569
	1,000 head	Dollars	1,000 head	Dollars	1,000 head	Dollars		1,000 head	Dollars	1,000 head	Dollars	1,000 head	Dollars
1897	50,447	18.62	51,232	4.36	38,891	1.84	1882	45,738	20.93	42,566	6.00	48,883	2.35
1896	49,205	17.86	49,154	4.50	39,609	1.71	1881	44,501	18.67	43,076	4.80	47,371	2.35
1895	49,510	16.56	47,628	5.09	41,827	1.57	*1880*	*39,676*	—	*49,773*	—	*42,192*	—
1894	51,713	16.84	46,522	6.06	43,414	1.97	1880	43,347	17.80	44,327	4.40	44,867	2.18
1893	55,119	17.00	43,652	6.37	44,567	2.64	1879	41,420	16.96	43,767	3.15	41,678	2.01
1892	58,126	16.81	45,165	4.65	44,628	2.60	1878	39,396	19.05	43,375	4.89	38,942	2.12
1891	59,968	16.49	47,435	4.24	43,882	2.51	1877	37,333	18.38	39,333	5.68	38,147	2.03
							1876	36,140	18.76	35,715	5.97	37,477	2.20
1890	*57,649*	—	*57,427*	—	*40,876*	—							
1890	60,104	16.95	48,130	4.80	42,693	2.29	1875	35,361	18.96	35,834	4.65	37,237	2.39
1889	59,178	18.77	44,508	5.81	42,365	2.14	1874	34,821	19.51	38,377	3.93	36,234	2.33
1888	58,599	19.39	42,134	5.12	43,011	2.06	1873	33,830	20.50	39,794	3.60	35,782	2.60
1887	56,602	21.18	42,563	4.60	44,217	2.05	1872	33,078	21.64	39,296	3.96	34,312	2.51
1886	54,868	22.20	45,457	4.30	46,654	1.95	1871	32,107	24.71	36,688	5.48	34,063	2.10
1885	52,463	24.40	47,330	5.06	49,620	2.19	*1870*	*23,821*	—	*25,135*	—	*28,478*	—
1884	49,804	25.26	45,961	5.64	51,101	2.40	1870	31,082	22.84	33,781	5.64	36,449	1.87
1883	47,387	23.87	43,440	6.74	50,935	2.53	1869	30,060	20.74	32,570	4.60	39,802	1.65
							1868	29,238	18.30	33,304	3.23	43,808	1.83
							1867	28,636	19.13	34,489	3.95	44,997	2.40

* Denotes first year for which figures include Alaska and Hawaii.
[1] December 1, preceding year.

[2] Excludes spring-born calves, pigs and lambs.
[3] Government purchases included in figures for all cattle, 1935 and 1934; for hogs, 1933.

Series K 583-594.   Meat Slaughtering, Production and Price: 1899 to 1991

(Prices are those at Chicago. Average price of all grades)

	Beef		Veal		Pork		Lamb and mutton	
Year	Cattle slaughtered [1]	Production, dressed weight	Calves slaughtered [1]	Production, dressed weight	Hogs slaughtered [1]	Production, dressed weight	Lambs and sheep slaughtered [1]	Production, dressed weight
	583	584	586	587	589	590	592	593
	1,000 head	Mil. lb.	1,000 head	Mil. lb.	1,000 head	Mil. lb.	1,000 head	Mil. lb.
1991	32,900	22,916	1,500	306	88,400	15,999	5,800	364
1990	33,400	22,743	1,800	327	85,400	15,354	5,700	363
1989	34,100	23,087	2,200	355	89,000	15,813	5,600	347
1988	35,300	20,589	2,600	396	88,100	15,684	5,400	335
1987	35,900	23,600	2,900	429	81,400	14,400	5,300	316
1986	37,600	24,400	3,500	524	80,000	14,100	5,800	337
1985	36,600	23,728	3,500	515	84,900	14,807	6,300	358
1984	37,900	23,600	3,400	495	85,600	14,800	6,900	380
1983	37,000	23,200	3,200	454	88,100	15,200	6,800	376
1982	36,200	22,500	3,100	448	82,800	14,200	6,600	365
1981	35,300	22,400	2,900	436	92,500	15,900	6,200	338
1980	34,100	21,643	2,700	400	97,200	16,617	5,700	318
1979	34,000	21,400	2,900	434	90,200	15,500	5,200	293
1978	40,000	24,200	4,300	632	78,400	13,400	5,500	309
1977	42,400	25,300	5,700	834	78,400	13,200	6,600	351
1976	43,200	26,000	5,500	853	74,900	12,400	6,900	371
1975	41,500	24,000	5,400	873	69,800	11,500	8,100	410
1974	37,300	23,100	3,200	486	83,100	13,800	9,000	465
1973	34,000	21,277	2,400	357	77,800	12,751	9,800	514
1972	36,100	22,387	3,200	459	85,700	13,631	10,500	543
1971	35,900	21,868	3,800	546	95,600	14,783	11,000	555
1970	35,354	21,651	4,204	588	86,962	13,427	10,802	551
1969	35,574	21,126	5,010	673	84,958	12,946	10,923	550
1968	35,414	20,846	5,613	734	86,401	13,055	12,119	602
1967	34,295	20,184	6,107	792	83,421	12,572	13,034	646
1966	34,171	19,694	6,861	910	75,325	11,328	13,003	650
1965	33,171	18,699	7,788	1,020	76,394	11,132	13,300	651
1964	31,678	18,429	7,632	1,013	86,284	12,503	14,895	715
1963	28,070	16,428	7,204	929	87,117	12,419	16,147	770
1962	26,911	15,298	7,857	1,015	83,424	11,819	17,168	808
1961	26,471	15,300	8,080	1,044	81,970	11,399	17,537	832
1960	26,029	14,728	8,615	1,109	84,150	11,598	16,240	768
1959	23,723	13,580	8,072	1,008	87,606	11,993	15,528	738
1958	24,368	13,330	9,738	1,086	76,822	10,454	14,495	688
1957	27,068	14,202	12,353	1,526	78,636	10,424	15,292	707
1956	27,755	14,462	12,999	1,632	85,064	11,200	16,328	741
1955	26,587	13,569	12,864	1,578	81,051	10,990	16,553	758
1954	25,889	12,963	13,270	1,647	71,495	9,870	16,255	734
1953	24,465	12,407	12,200	1,546	74,368	10,006	16,321	729
1952	18,625	9,650	9,388	1,169	86,572	11,527	14,304	648
1951	17,084	8,837	8,902	1,059	85,540	11,481	11,416	521
1950	18,614	9,534	10,501	1,230	79,263	10,714	13,244	597
1949	18,765	9,439	11,398	1,334	74,997	10,286	13,780	603
1948	19,177	9,075	12,378	1,423	70,869	10,055	17,371	747
1947	22,404	10,432	13,726	1,605	74,001	10,502	18,706	799
1946	19,824	9,373	12,176	1,443	76,115	11,136	22,788	968
1945	21,694	10,276	13,657	1,664	71,891	10,697	24,639	1,054
1944	19,844	9,112	14,242	1,738	98,068	13,304	25,355	1,024
1943	17,845	8,571	9,940	1,167	95,226	13,640	27,073	1,104
1942	18,033	8,843	9,718	1,151	78,547	10,876	25,585	1,042
1941	16,419	8,082	9,252	1,036	71,397	9,528	22,309	923
1940	14,958	7,175	9,089	981	77,610	10,044	21,571	876
1939	14,621	7,011	9,191	991	66,561	8,660	21,614	872
1938	14,822	6,908	9,306	994	58,927	7,680	22,423	897
1937	15,254	6,798	10,304	1,108	53,715	6,951	21,455	852
1936 [2]	15,897	7,358	10,008	1,075	58,730	7,474	21,555	854

See footnotes at end of chart.

Series K 583-594.   Meat Slaughtering, Production and Price: 1899 to 1991—Cont'd.

(Prices are those at Chicago. Average price of all grades)

| Year | Beef | | Veal | | Pork | | Lamb and mutton | |
	Cattle slaughtered [1]	Production, dressed weight	Calves slaughtered [1]	Production, dressed weight	Hogs slaughtered [1]	Production, dressed weight	Lambs and sheep slaughtered [1]	Production, dressed weight
	583	584	586	587	589	590	592	593
	1,000 head	*Mil. lb.*	*1,000 head*	*Mil. lb.*	*1,000 head*	*Mil. lb.*	*1,000 head*	*Mil. lb.*
1935 [2]	14,566	6,608	9,580	1,023	46,011	5,919	22,000	877
1934 [2]	15,071	[3] 8,343	10,106	1,246	68,760	8,397	20,444	851
1933 [4]	13,107	6,440	8,564	891	73,270	9,234	21,833	852
1932	11,980	5,789	7,970	822	71,425	8,923	23,043	884
1931	12,096	6,009	8,057	823	69,233	8,739	23,133	885
1930	12,056	5,917	7,761	792	67,272	8,482	21,125	825
1929	12,038	5,871	7,406	761	71,012	8,833	17,483	682
1928	12,028	5,771	7,651	773	72,889	9,041	17,076	663
1927	13,413	6,395	8,478	867	66,195	8,430	16,113	629
1926	14,781	7,089	9,354	955	62,585	7,966	16,444	639
1925	14,704	6,878	9,936	989	65,508	8,128	15,430	603
1924	14,750	6,877	9,804	972	76,809	9,149	15,578	597
1923	14,283	6,721	9,327	916	77,508	9,483	15,146	588
1922	13,706	6,588	8,832	852	66,201	8,145	14,373	553
1921	12,428	6,022	8,394	820	61,818	7,697	16,742	639
1920	13,470	6,306	8,481	842	61,502	7,648	13,984	538
1919	15,027	6,756	8,201	819	65,795	8,477	15,784	590
1918	17,093	7,726	7,485	760	65,100	8,349	13,220	506
1917	15,741	7,239	7,372	744	56,500	7,055	12,128	463
1916	13,793	6,460	6,628	655	67,000	8,207	15,160	585
1915	12,901	6,075	6,054	590	62,000	7,616	15,576	605
1914	12,676	6,017	5,927	569	55,000	6,824	18,035	693
1913	12,939	6,182	6,305	608	57,000	6,979	18,375	706
1912	13,386	6,234	6,828	662	55,500	6,822	19,131	735
1911	13,817	6,549	6,855	666	57,000	6,961	18,177	693
1910	14,140	6,647	6,917	667	48,215	6,087	15,332	597
1909	14,135	6,915	6,864	660	54,986	6,557	15,464	608
1908	13,569	6,662	6,546	637	63,463	7,535	14,200	559
1907	13,886	6,544	6,395	626	56,527	7,059	13,799	553
1906	13,456	6,537	6,187	598	54,698	6,793	13,800	543
1905	13,096	6,504	5,731	556	54,433	6,629	13,100	530
1904	12,257	6,176	5,076	491	52,072	6,387	13,100	538
1903	12,266	6,240	5,044	492	48,548	6,067	13,800	563
1902	11,751	5,649	4,854	476	48,306	5,936	13,700	534
1901	11,526	5,814	4,318	422	53,898	6,357	13,200	548
1900	10,792	5,628	4,105	397	51,885	6,329	12,000	493
1899	⎯	5,522	⎯	387		6,310	⎯	487

[1] Excludes inspected, noninspected, retail and farm slaughter.
[2] Excludes cattle and calves purchased for slaughter for Federal Surplus Relief Corporation from June 1934-Feb. 1935 and for Aug. 1936; excludes also cattle thus purchased for Sept. 1936.

[3] Includes slaughter under the Emergency Government Relief Purchase Program in 1934-1935.
[4] Excludes purchases on government account for the Emergency Hog Production Control Program from Aug. 22-Oct. 7, 1933.

Series K 595-608. Cows Kept for Milk on Farms, Milk Produced, Manufactured Dairy Products, Prices Received by Farmers, and Wholesale Prices of Cheese and Butter: 1849 to 1990

(Census figures in *italics*)

Year	Number of cows and heifers 2 years old and over kept for milk Jan. 1	Milk produced on farms during year	Butter [1]	Cheese [2]	Evaporated and condensed milk [3]	Ice cream
	595	597	598	599	600	601
	1,000 head	Millions pounds	Millions pounds	Millions pounds	Millions pounds	Millions gallons
1990	10,100	148,000	1,302	6,061	615	816
1989	10,100	144,000	1,295	5,615	545	831
1988	10,300	145,000	1,208	5,572	612	882
1987	10,300	143,000	1,104	5,344	597	928
1986	10,800	143,000	1,202	5,209	602	924
1985	11,000	143,000	1,248	5,081	656	901
1984	10,800	135,000	1,103	4,674	666	894
1983	11,000	140,000	1,299	4,819	710	882
1982	11,000	136,000	1,257	4,542	754	852
1981	10,800	133,000	1,228	4,278	758	832
1980	10,800	128,000	1,145	3,984	740	830
1979	10,800	123,000	985	3,717	810	811
1978	10,900	122,000	994	3,520	798	815
1977	11,000	123,000	1,086	3,359	827	810
1976	11,100	120,000	979	3,319	942	818
1975	11,100	115,000	984	2,811	938	837
1974	11,300	115,000	952	2,897	—	783
1973	11,600	115,000	919	2,685	—	774
1972	11,800	120,000	1,102	2,605	1,131	770
1971	11,900	119,000	1,144	2,374	1,187	766
1970	13,838	117,149	1,143	2,204	1,517	763
1969	*11,175*	—	—	—	—	
1969	14,152	116,345	1,129	1,990	1,776	766
1968	14,644	117,234	1,175	1,938	1,800	773
1967	15,198	118,769	1,238	1,919	1,886	745
1966	15,987	119,892	1,128	1,854	2,196	751
1965	16,981	124,173	1,346	1,755	2,178	757
1964	*14,623*	—	—	—	—	
1964	17,647	126,967	1,469	1,724	2,395	739
1963	18,379	125,202	1,454	1,632	2,369	718
1962	18,963	126,251	1,579	1,592	2,409	704
1961	*19,271	125,707	1,536	1,635	2,632	699
1960	19,527	*123,109	*1,436	*1,478	*2,666	*700
1959 [4]	*16,522*					
1959	20,132	121,989	1,411	1,383	2,743	699
1958	21,265	123,220	1,486	1,399	2,752	658
1957	22,325	124,628	1,533	1,407	2,872	651
1956	22,921	124,860	1,553	1,388	2,953	641
1955	23,462	122,945	1,545	1,367	2,922	629
1954	*20,183*	—	—	—	—	—
1954	23,896	122,094	1,628	1,383	2,845	597
1953	23,549	120,221	1,607	1,344	2,875	605
1952	23,060	114,671	1,402	1,170	3,165	593
1951	23,568	114,681	1,443	1,161	3,228	569
1950	*21,233*	—	—	—	—	—
1950	23,853	116,602	1,648	1,191	3,205	554
1949	23,862	116,103	1,688	1,199	3,106	558
1948	24,615	112,671	1,504	1,098	3,755	576
1947	25,842	116,814	1,640	1,183	3,630	631
1946	26,521	117,697	1,502	1,106	3,333	714
1945	*22,803*	—	—	—	—	—
1945	27,770	119,828	1,699	1,117	4,126	477

Year	Number of cows and heifers 2 years old and over kept for milk Jan. 1	Milk produced on farms during year	Butter [1]	Cheese [2]	Evaporated and condensed milk [3]	Ice cream
	595	597	598	599	600	601
	1,000 head	Millions pounds	Millions pounds	Millions pounds	Millions pounds	Millions gallons
1944	27,704	117,023	1,818	1,017	3,750	445
1943	27,138	117,017	2,015	993	3,344	412
1942	26,313	118,533	2,130	1,112	3,782	464
1941	25,453	115,088	2,268	956	3,555	390
1940	*21,937*					
1940	24,940	109,412	2,240	785	2,731	318
1939	24,600	106,792	2,210	710	2,367	306
1938	24,466	105,807	2,252	726	2,322	286
1937	24,649	101,908	2,135	653	2,131	291
1936	25,196	102,410	2,168	650	2,270	259
1935	*24,582*	—	—	—	—	—
1935	26,082	101,205	2,211	628	2,032	219
1934	26,931	101,621	2,286	587	1,908	192
1933	25,936	104,762	2,375	548	1,899	162
1932	24,896	103,810	2,307	491	1,780	168
1931	23,820	103,029	2,239	499	1,682	226
1930	*21,124*	—	—	—	—	—
1930	23,032	100,158	2,149	510	1,761	255
1929	22,440	98,988	2,184	499	1,849	277
1928	22,231	95,843	2,120	479	1,604	254
1927	22,251	95,172	2,188	462	1,576	251
1926	22,410	93,325	2,132	468	1,456	238
1925	*20,900*	—	—	—	—	—
1925	22,575	90,699	2,082	503	1,548	240
1924	22,331	89,240	2,066	474	1,507	213
1923	22,138	—	1,993	471	1,585	214
1922	21,851	—	1,870	432	1,281	191
1921	21,456	—	1,748	434	1,324	175
1920	*19,675*	—	—	—	—	—
1920	21,455	—	1,574	423	1,413	171
1919	21,545	67,124	1,647	486	1,883	153
1918	21,536	—	1,503	415	1,619	143
1917	21,212	—	1,644	472	1,391	106
1916	20,752	—	1,793	422	1,196	94
1915	20,270	—	1,751	440	1,028	—
1914	19,821	—	1,685	367	883	72
1913	19,580	—	1,608	359	787	—
1912	19,517	—	1,592	323	701	—
1911	19,422	—	1,762	345	624	—
1910	*20,625*	—	—	—	—	—
1910	19,450	—	1,706	355	556	—
1909	19,201	64,211	1,622	313	495	30
1908	18,992	—	1,763	313	450	—
1907	18,629	—	1,537	286	410	—
1906	18,230	—	1,545	292	373	—
1905	17,823	—	1,667	327	339	—
1904	17,485	—	1,540	331	308	12
1903	17,217	—	1,485	323	279	—
1902	16,992	—	1,401	318	252	—
1901	16,708	—	1,575	362	228	—
1900	*17,136*	—	—	—	—	—
1900	16,544	—	1,540	324	207	—

See footnotes at end of chart.

Series K 595-608. Cows Kept for Milk on Farms, Milk Produced, Manufactured Dairy Products, Prices Received by Farmers, and Wholesale Prices of Cheese and Butter: 1849 to 1990—Cont'd.

(Census figures in *italics*)

Year	Number of cows and heifers 2 years old and over kept for milk Jan. 1 (1,000 head) 595	Milk produced on farms during year (Millions pounds) 597	Butter [1] (Millions pounds) 598	Cheese [2] (Millions pounds) 599	Evaporated and condensed milk [3] (Millions pounds) 600	Ice cream (Millions gallons) 601
1897	15,382	—	1,533	311	—	—
1896	15,266	—	1,604	240	—	—
1895	15,230	—	1,297	234	—	—
1894	15,237	—	1,063	257	—	—
1893	15,164	—	1,047	254	—	—
1892	15,177	—	1,058	318	—	—
1891	15,133	—	1,091	293	—	—
1890	*16,512*	—	—	—	—	—
1890	15,000	—	1,171	318	—	—
1889	14,706	44,807	1,292	301	45	1
1888	14,350	—	978	286	—	—
1887	13,888	—	978	268	—	—
1886	13,478	—	989	244	—	—
1885	13,213	—	933	260	—	—
1884	12,883	—	869	275	—	—
1883	12,571	—	844	281	—	—
1882	12,234	—	743	261	—	—
1881	11,977	—	803	304	—	—
1880	*12,443*	—	—	—	—	—
1880	11,754	—	816	270	—	—
1879	11,486	—	807	243	13	(Z)
1878	11,222	—	726	303	—	—
1877	11,004	—	696	235	—	—
1876	10,821	—	677	214	—	—
1875	10,714	—	556	233	—	—
1874	10,562	—	585	206	—	—
1873	10,348	—	566	212	—	—
1872	10,191	—	434	187	—	—
1871	9,941	—	470	164	—	—
1870	*8,935*	—	—	—	—	—
1870	9,672	—	412	181	—	—
1869	9,205	—	514	163	4	(Z)
1868	8,705	—	—	—	—	—
1867	8,263	—	—	—	—	—
1866	—	—	—	—	—	—
1865	—	—	—	—	—	—
1864	—	—	—	—	—	—
1863	—	—	—	—	—	—
1862	—	—	—	—	—	—
1861	—	—	—	—	—	—
1860	*8,586*	—	—	—	—	—
1860	—	—	—	—	—	—
1859	—	—	460	104	—	(Z)
1858	—	—	—	—	—	—
1857	—	—	—	—	—	—
1856	—	—	—	—	—	—
1855	—	—	—	—	—	—
1854	—	—	—	—	—	—
1853	—	—	—	—	—	—
1852	—	—	—	—	—	—
1851	—	—	—	—	—	—
1850	*6,385*	—	—	—	—	—
1850	—	—	—	—	—	—
1849	—	—	313	106	—	—

* Denotes first year for which figures include Alaska and Hawaii.
Z Less than 500,000 gallons.
[1] Farm and factory production combined.
[2] Includes all types of cheese except cottage, pot and bakers' cheese; full-skim American cheese excluded since 1908. Farm output not estimated since 1926.
[3] For 1919-1970 includes all evaporated and condensed whole milk as compiled by the former Bureau of Agricultural Economics and Agricultural Marketing Service. Prior to 1919, includes total production of all condensed and evaporated milk as interpolated from census enumerations.
[4] Beginning 1959, census figures include Alaska and Hawaii.

Series K 609-623.   Poultry and Eggs—Number, Production and Price: 1909 to 1990

(Census figures in *italics* and as April 15, 1910; April 1, 1930, 1940, 1950 and 1954; January 1, 1920, 1925, 1935 and 1945; October-November, 1959; November-December, 1964; and December 31, 1969)

	Chickens			Broilers		Eggs		Turkeys
Year	Number, Jan. 1	Value per head, Jan. 1	Price per pound [1]	Number produced	Price per pound [1]	Number produced	Price per dozen [1]	Number, Jan. 1 [2]
	609	**610**	**613**	**614**	**616**	**617**	**618**	**619**
	Millions	Dollars	Cents	Millions	Cents	Millions	Cents	Millions
1990	351	2.29	9.6	5,865	32.6	67,800	71.6	283
1989	356	2.16	14.9	5,517	36.6	67,200	68.9	261
1988	356	2.04	9.2	5,238	33.1	69,700	52.8	242
1987	380	1.87	11.0	5,004	28.7	70,400	54.7	240
1986	373	1.87	12.5	4,649	34.5	68,400	61.6	207
1985	370	1.90	14.8	4,470	30.1	68,400	57.2	185
1984	374	2.02	15.9	4,283	33.7	68,232	72.3	171
1983	365	1.96	12.7	4,184	28.6	68,172	61.1	171
1982	379	1.85	10.3	4,149	26.9	69,720	59.5	165
1981	385	1.89	11.1	4,148	28.4	69,828	63.1	171
1980	392	1.88	11.0	3,963	27.7	69,700	56.3	165
1979	401	1.81	14.4	3,951	26.0	69,204	58.3	3,705
1978	397	1.75	12.4	3,613	26.3	67,152	52.2	3,370
1977	387	1.69	12.0	3,400	23.6	64,608	55.6	3,038
1976	378	1.70	12.9	3,283	23.6	64,512	58.3	3,069
1975	380	1.74	9.9	2,950	26.3	64,632	52.4	3,014
1974	384	1.70	9.7	2,993	21.5	65,616	53.2	2,970
1973	413	1.52	15.1	3,008	—	67,000	52.5	3,553
1972	406	1.28	9.0	—	—	70,000	30.9	3,303
1971	433	1.21	7.7	—	—	70,000	31.4	7,701
1970	434	1.35	8.8	2,987	13.6	70,312	37.6	6,769
1969	*371*	*1.31*	—	—	—	—	—	—
1969	420	1.21	9.7	2,789	15.2	69,086	40.0	6,604
1968	425	1.14	8.2	2,620	14.2	69,270	34.0	7,301
1967	429	1.20	7.9	2,592	13.3	70,031	31.2	7,817
1966	393	1.21	9.7	2,571	15.3	66,484	39.1	6,905
1965	394	1.17	8.9	2,334	15.0	65,692	33.7	6,105
1964	*343*	*1.17*	—	—	—	—	—	—
1964	382	1.16	9.2	2,161	14.2	65,215	33.8	5,996
1963	376	1.16	10.0	2,102	14.6	63,500	34.5	6,374
1962	377	1.15	10.2	2,023	15.2	63,569	33.8	6,423
1961	[3] 366	[3] 1.25	[3] 10.1	1,991	13.9	[3] 62,423	[3] 35.6	7,008
1960	369	1.06	12.2	1,795	16.9	61,602	36.1	5,633
1959 [4]	[4] *351*	[4] *1.06*	—	—	—	—	—	—
1959	387	1.26	11.0	1,737	16.1	63,335	31.4	6,105
1958	374	1.26	14.0	1,660	18.5	61,607	38.5	5,612
1957	391	1.17	13.7	1,448	18.9	61,026	35.9	5,828
1956	384	1.26	16.0	1,344	19.6	61,113	39.3	4,937
1955	391	1.05	18.6	1,092	25.2	59,526	39.5	4,917
1954	*376*	*1.04*	—	—	—	—	—	[5] *2,278*
1954	397	1.43	16.8	1,048	23.1	58,933	36.6	4,956
1953	398	1.41	22.1	947	27.1	57,891	47.7	5,086
1952	427	1.53	22.1	861	28.8	58,068	41.6	5,725
1951	431	1.46	25.0	789	28.5	58,063	47.7	5,037
1950	*343*	*1.09*	—	—	—	—	—	*2,849*
1950	457	1.36	22.2	631	27.4	58,954	36.3	5,124
1949	431	1.66	25.4	513	28.2	56,154	45.2	4,622
1948	500	1.44	30.1	371	36.0	54,899	47.2	3,959
1947	467	1.44	26.5	310	32.3	55,384	45.3	5,879
1946	523	1.27	27.6	293	32.7	55,962	37.6	7,862
1945	*433*	*1.23*	—	—	—	—	—	—
1945	516	1.21	25.9	366	29.5	56,221	37.7	7,082
1944	582	1.18	23.7	274	28.8	58,537	32.5	7,294
1943	542	1.04	24.3	285	28.6	54,547	37.1	6,584
1942	477	.83	18.7	228	22.9	48,610	30.0	7,447
1941	423	.65	15.6	192	18.4	41,894	23.5	7,150

See footnotes at end of chart.

Series K 609-623.   Poultry and Eggs—Number, Production and Price: 1909 to 1990—Cont'd.

(Census figures in *italics* and as April 15, 1910; April 1, 1930, 1940, 1950 and 1954; January 1, 1920, 1925, 1935 and 1945;
October-November, 1959; November-December, 1964; and December 31, 1969)

| Year | Chickens | | | Broilers | | Eggs | | Turkeys |
	Number, Jan. 1	Value per head, Jan. 1	Price per pound[1]	Number produced	Price per pound[1]	Number produced	Price per dozen[1]	Number, Jan. 1[1,2]
	609	610	613	614	616	617	618	619
	Millions	Dollars	Cents	Millions	Cents	Millions	Cents	Millions
1940	*338*	*.56*	—	—	—	—	—	*4,362*
1940	438	.60	13.0	143	17.3	39,707	18.0	8,569
1939	419	.70	13.2	106	17.0	38,843	17.4	6,489
1938	390	.76	14.8	82	19.0	37,356	20.3	6,096
1937	424	.66	16.0	68	21.4	37,564	21.3	6,358
1936	403	.75	15.0	53	20.6	34,534	21.8	5,731
1935	*372*	*.52*	—	—	—	—	—	*5,382*
1935	390	.54	14.9	43	20.0	33,609	23.4	5,499
1934	434	.42	11.1	34	19.3	34,429	17.0	6,309
1933	445	.45	9.5	—	—	35,514	13.8	6,852
1932	437	.62	11.7	—	—	36,298	14.2	5,946
1931	450	.70	15.8	—	—	38,532	17.6	5,318
1930	*379*	*.85*	—	—	—	—	—	—
1930	468	.93	18.4	—	—	39,067	23.7	5,969
1929	449	.91	22.8	—	—	37,921	29.8	5,541
1928	475	.86	21.4	—	—	38,659	28.1	—
1927	461	.91	20.2	—	—	38,627	25.1	—
1926	438	.89	22.1	—	—	37,248	28.9	—
1925	*409*	*.93*	—	—	—	—	—	—
1925	435	.79	20.5	—	—	34,969	30.4	—
1924	435	.76	19.4	—	—	34,592	26.7	—
1923	415	.75	—	—	—	35,000	26.5	—
1922	395	.81	—	—	—	33,000	25.0	—
1921	370	.89	—	—	—	30,800	28.3	—
1920	*360*	*1.04*	—	—	—	—	—	*3,627*
1920	381	.97	—	—	—	29,700	43.5	—
1919	391	.96	—	—	—	30,500	41.3	—
1918	363	.77	—	—	—	28,000	36.0	—
1917	359	.59	—	—	—	27,700	31.8	—
1916	369	.49	—	—	—	28,800	22.1	—
1915	379	.46	—	—	—	29,900	19.4	—
1914	367	.49	—	—	—	27,900	20.5	—
1913	365	.47	—	—	—	28,100	19.4	—
1912	367	.42	—	—	—	28,300	20.2	—
1911	382	.46	—	—	—	29,400	17.5	—
1910	*280*	*.50*	—	—	—	—	—	*3,689*
1910	356	.47	—	—	—	27,000	20.9	—
1909	340	.44	—	—	—	25,300	20.0	—

[1] Average annual price received by farmers.
[2] Beginning 1980, data are for breeder hens, and only 26 major producer states.
[3] Beginning 1961, Department of Agriculture data include Alaska and Hawaii.
[4] Beginning 1959, census data include Alaska and Hawaii.
[5] Data for October-November.

FORESTRY AND FISHERIES
Highlights

1 The National Forest Service is the largest landowner in the United States and oversees the National Forest System, which covered 231 million acres in 1991. A forest is defined as land which is at least 10% stocked by forest trees of any size. The states with the largest forest areas are California (24.434 million acres), Alaska (24.233 million acres), Idaho (21.694 million acres), Montana (19.101 million acres), and Oregon (17.496 million acres).

2 Data on lumber were first collected by the Census Office (later the Census Bureau) in 1810. Subsequent statistics were published by this agency for 1819 and decennially for 1839-1899, and annually from 1904 to 1954 except in 1905, 1906, 1913, 1915-18, 1920, and 1948. Current data are reported in *An Analysis of the Timber Situation of the United States, 1989-2040; Forest Statistics of the United States; U. S. Timber Production, Trade Consumption and Price Statistics, 1960-1988*; and the annual *Land Areas of the National Forest System.*

3 The total extent of forest land in the United States in 1987 was 731 million acres, of which 347 million acres (or 71.9%) was privately owned. About half of the total forest land, or 358 million acres, was in the West. The net volume of growing stock was 756 billion cubic feet, of which 451 billion cubic feet were soft wood.

4 Timber-based industries employed 1.469 million people in 1990. Total production was 41.204 billion board feet, of which 33.692 billion board feet were soft woods and 7.512 billion board feet hard woods. Total production of paper and paperboard in 1991 was 81 million short tons and the total production of newsprint 12.127 million metric tons. The recovery rate—the ratio of total recovered paper to new supply—was 36.7%.

5 The most popular hardwood is Douglas fir, and the most popular softwood is oak. However, stumpage prices for Southern pine are generally higher than those for Douglas fir because it is favored by carpenters and construction people.

6 The first comprehensive statistical study of fisheries and fishery industries was made for the year 1880 by the U.S. National Museum with the cooperation of the Commission of Fisheries and the Superintendent of the Tenth Census. The next general survey was made by the Bureau of the Census in 1908 followed by one in 1931 and another in 1950. Since then, annual data have been available for all coastal areas. Annual surveys are also made of the Mississippi River and its tributaries. Extended data are available for landing at the important fishing ports, for certain species, and for canned and industrial fishery products. Current fishery data are published in the *Current Fishery Statistics* and *Fisheries of the United States,* by the National Marine Fisheries Service. Statistics on commercial landed catches of fish are shown as round, salable weight of recoverable meat. Data do not include catches made for personal use by hobby fishermen, or landings by foreign fishing vessels.

7 The fish species most often caught are whiting, cod, flounder, haddock, herring, lobster, mackerel, and ocean perch in the New England states; menhaden, oysters, and crabs in Middle Atlantic and Chesapeake Bay states; shrimp, menhaden, and mullet in the South Atlantic and Gulf states; lake trout and whitefish in the Great Lakes states; tuna, salmon, sardine, halibut, and mackerel in the Pacific Coast states; tuna in Hawaii; and salmon, halibut, and herring in Alaska.

8 Total fish catch in 1990 was 9.708 billion lbs., valued at $3.572 billion. Of the total, Alaska accounted for over one-half at 5.404 billion lbs., Louisiana for 1.061 billion lbs., and Virginia for 787 million lbs. The fishing industry employed 364,000 persons in 1988, manning 111,000 fishing craft. The largest fishing ports (in terms of landed weight) are: Dutch Harbor in Alaska, Pascagoula-Moss Point in Mississippi, Kodiak in Alaska, and Empire-Venice in Louisiana. The largest fishing port (in terms of value of fish catch) is New Bedford, Massachusetts. By species, shellfish accounted for 1.312 billion lbs., pollock for 3.157 billion lbs., menhaden for 1.962 billion lbs., salmon for 733 million lbs., cod for 640 million lbs., and flounder for 502 million lbs. The most valuable catch, however, is salmon. Of total fish catch, 6.805 billion lbs. were sold fresh or frozen, 751 million lbs. were canned, and 126 million lbs. were cured.

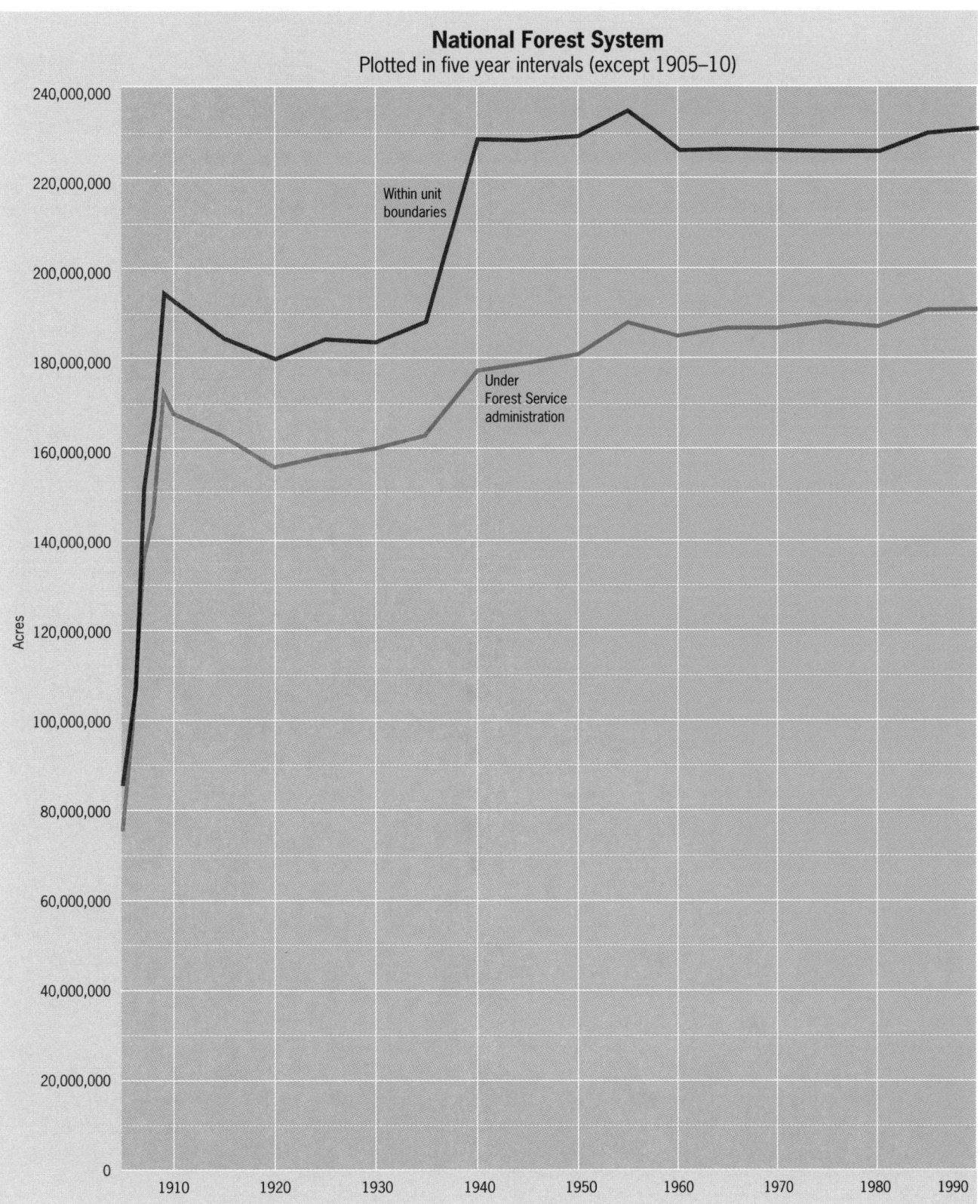

National Forest System
Plotted in five year intervals (except 1905–10)

Acres

Within unit
boundaries

Under
Forest Service
administration

9 Aquaculture is a growing industry which produced 721.089 million lbs. worth $613.653 million in 1987. The most popular species grown by aquaculturists are catfish and Pacific salmon, which together account for 69% of total production.

10 Tuna, which is the major fish caught by U.S. fishermen in international waters, remains the fish in most abundant supply. In 1990, 865 million lbs. of canned tuna were sold compared to 734 million lbs. of shrimp and 111 million lbs. of lobster.

Series L 10-14. National Forest System Areas and Purchases: 1905 to 1990

(Forest area data as of June 30; includes Alaska and Puerto Rico. Forest purchases for years ending June 30; includes Puerto Rico)

Year	Gross area of national forests and other lands [1]		Gross area approved for national forest purchase		Year	Gross area of national forests and other lands [1]		Gross area approved national forest purch	
	Within unit boundaries	Under Forest Service administration	Total area	Total price		Within unit boundaries	Under Forest Service administration	Total area	Total price
	10	**11**	**12**	**13**		**10**	**11**	**12**	**13**
	1,000 acres	1,000 acres	Acres	$1,000		1,000 acres	1,000 acres	Acres	$1,000
1990	231,000	191,000	51,000	24,000	1947	228,810	180,264	380,471	2,190
1989	231,000	191,000	99,000	34,000	1946	228,760	179,726	—	—
1988	230,000	191,000	42,000	235,000					
1987	230,000	191,000	87,000	38,000	1945	228,703	179,381	5	1
1986	230,000	191,000	23,000	7,000	1944	228,643	179,101	9	1
					1943	228,633	178,508	8,759	38
1985	230,000	191,000	16,000	6,900	1942	228,725	178,340	243,522	1,103
1984	230,000	191,000	8,000	4,200	1941	228,309	177,653	195,818	805
1983	230,000	191,000	7,000	2,400					
1982	230,000	191,000	2,000	1,500	1940	228,174	176,779	553,077	2,203
1981	230,000	191,000	111,000	50,400	1939	228,784	176,494	534,138	2,275
					1938	227,280	175,238	800,113	2,713
1980	226,000	187,000	42,000	27,900	1937	226,621	174,405	425,637	2,124
1979	226,000	187,000	58,000	30,200	1936	197,435	165,979	2,891,040	11,535
1978	226,000	188,000	51,000	22,500					
1977	226,000	188,000	45,000	16,600	1935	188,292	163,310	3,661,848	14,991
1976	226,000	188,000	43,000	12,300	1934	188,037	162,591	4,206,817	10,018
					1933	186,837	162,009	667,314	1,221
1975	226,000	188,000	12,000	3,300	1932	186,215	161,361	83,086	206
1974	226,000	187,000	25,000	6,000	1931	185,252	160,788	547,945	1,944
1973	226,000	187,000	117,000	17,500					
1972	225,000	187,000	79,000	14,752	1930	183,976	160,091	538,048	1,468
1971	225,000	187,000	32,000	4,467	1929	184,565	159,751	464,177	1,787
					1928	184,404	159,481	261,107	1,996
1970	226,064	186,900	92,437	11,539	1927	183,938	158,800	135,088	726
1969	226,045	186,632	126,341	12,353	1926	184,124	158,759	191,725	737
1968	226,502	186,921	112,767	9,413					
1967	227,721	186,799	104,507	7,037	1925	184,126	158,395	247,067	1,187
1966	226,519	186,497	171,947	13,307	1924	182,817	157,503	130,290	425
					1923	182,100	157,237	79,923	348
1965	226,434	186,577	28,507	1,364	1922	181,800	156,837	242,169	826
1964	225,743	186,476	40,873	1,600	1921	181,820	156,666	112,397	499
1963	225,584	186,316	24,698	1,795					
1962	225,613	186,324	22,556	964	1920	180,300	156,032	101,428	451
1961	226,110	186,385	10,355	236	1919	174,261	153,933	103,355	657
					1918	175,951	155,375	185,199	848
1960	226,623	185,772	7,845	114	1917	176,340	155,220	175,463	853
1959	227,359	185,805	8,716	224	1916	176,089	155,400	54,898	316
1958	231,080	188,042	10,463	722					
1957	231,293	188,013	17,519	416	1915	184,506	162,773	282,900	1,618
1956	232,118	188,117	21,376	372	1914	185,321	163,849	391,114	1,940
					1913	186,617	165,517	425,717	2,005
1955	235,728	188,120	18,665	192	1912	187,406	165,027	287,698	1,627
1954	235,694	188,138	7,761	109	1911	190,608	168,165	—	—
1953	229,112	181,568	7,969	99					
1952	229,165	181,293	10,181	106	1910	192,931	168,029	—	—
1951	229,258	181,255	25,317	265	1909	194,505	172,230	—	—
					1908	167,977	147,820	—	—
1950	229,341	181,205	61,078	532	1907	150,832	132,732	—	—
1949	229,175	180,895	60,719	464	1906	106,994	94,159	—	—
1948	228,936	180,528	103,490	739	1905	85,693	75,352	—	—

[1] On January 2, 1954, some 6,910,000 acres of land utilization project lands were transferred to the Forest Service for administration.

Series L 72-86. Production, Net Imports and Apparent Consumption of Industrial Timber Products in Roundwood Equivalent: 1900 to 1988

(In millions of cubic feet, rounded to the nearest 5 million. Excludes fuelwood)

| | Total | | | Industrial roundwood used for | | | | |
| Year | Domestic production | Net Imports | Apparent consumption | Domestic production of lumber | Domestic production of plywood and veneer | Domestic production of pulp products | Logs Imports | Logs Exports |
	72	73	74	75	78	81	85	86
1988	14,985	1,245	16,230	6,920	1,630	4,885	15	825
1987	14,670	1,925	16,595	6,990	1,650	4,670	15	705
1986	13,845	2,075	15,920	6,545	1,505	4,545	15	620
1985	12,515	2,270	14,785	5,665	1,420	4,165	20	655
1984	12,725	2,105	14,830	5,770	1,400	4,355	30	600
1983	12,065	1,600	13,665	5,370	1,365	4,165	30	565
1982	10,910	1,020	11,930	4,635	1,135	3,980	20	550
1981	10,710	1,665	11,775	4,395	1,180	4,125	20	435
1980	12,120	900	13,020	5,300	1,175	4,390	25	560
1979	12,510	1,520	14,030	5,680	1,370	4,110	25	665
1978	12,235	1,910	14,145	5,825	1,460	3,745	20	585
1977	11,965	1,515	13,480	5,730	1,425	3,645	30	525
1976	11,815	970	12,785	5,475	1,355	3,805	15	555
1975	10,575	530	11,105	4,890	1,165	3,485	15	455
1974	11,540	950	12,490	5,095	1,150	4,220	15	455
1973	11,925	1,395	13,325	5,670	1,320	3,755	5	575
1972	11,440	1,515	12,960	5,535	1,300	3,520	10	535
1971	11,310	1,565	12,875	5,715	1,225	3,560	15	360
1970	11,115	1,065	12,180	5,355	1,065	3,835	25	430
1969	11,000	1,375	12,370	5,535	1,050	3,585	15	375
1968	11,025	1,275	12,305	5,630	1,120	3,385	15	405
1967	10,410	1,205	11,615	5,360	1,030	3,190	15	310
1966	10,645	1,430	12,075	5,645	1,030	3,190	15	220
1965	10,540	1,385	11,930	5,670	1,030	3,095	10	190
1964	10,170	1,315	11,485	5,635	960	2,865	10	170
1963	9,560	1,360	10,920	5,355	870	2,670	15	150
1962	9,035	1,415	10,450	5,120	800	2,565	20	85
1961	8,745	1,250	9,995	4,945	765	2,475	20	75
1960	8,920	1,220	10,145	5,080	705	2,575	20	45
1959	9,390	1,345	10,735	5,745	720	2,355	20	35
1958	8,530	1,185	9,715	5,160	615	2,165	15	30
1957	8,615	1,155	9,770	5,100	560	2,350	25	25
1956	9,620	1,330	10,950	5,920	590	2,475	30	30
1955	9,225	1,270	10,495	5,785	575	2,200	35	25
1954	8,755	1,190	9,945	5,635	480	1,960	35	25
1953	8,790	1,230	10,020	5,710	475	1,910	40	20
1952	8,775	1,160	9,935	5,820	435	1,810	30	10
1951	8,740	1,205	9,950	5,780	390	1,825	35	15
1950	8,525	1,380	9,910	5,905	345	1,500	45	10
1949	7,355	935	8,290	5,000	320	1,275	30	10
1948	8,375	1,090	9,465	5,750	290	1,470	45	10
1947	8,090	815	8,905	5,500	275	1,370	30	10
1946	7,705	810	8,515	5,295	255	1,260	25	(Z)
1945	6,605	685	7,290	4,365	250	1,140	25	5
1944	7,455	555	8,010	5,115	270	1,160	25	5
1943	7,560	565	8,125	5,325	280	1,030	20	5
1942	8,085	705	8,790	5,645	305	1,130	30	5
1941	8,055	650	8,705	5,680	265	1,075	55	5
1940	6,990	420	7,410	4,845	235	930	35	10
1939	6,370	535	6,905	4,470	210	725	——	——
1938	5,570	470	6,040	3,860	195	595	——	——
1937	6,360	610	6,980	4,505	195	640	——	——
1936	5,990	560	6,540	4,295	165	555	——	——

See footnote at end of chart.

Series L 72-86. Production, Net Imports and Apparent Consumption of Industrial Timber Products in Roundwood Equivalent: 1900 to 1988—Cont'd.

(In millions of cubic feet, rounded to the nearest 5 million. Excludes fuelwood)

| Year | Total | | | Industrial roundwood used for | | |
| | Domestic production | Net Imports | Apparent consumption | Domestic production of lumber | Domestic production of plywood and veneer | Domestic production of pulp products |
	72	73	74	75	78	81
1935	5,090	420	5,515	3,565	145	485
1934	4,340	355	4,695	2,925	130	430
1933	4,040	345	4,385	2,665	125	415
1932	3,400	305	3,705	2,100	120	350
1931	4,600	335	4,945	3,105	125	400
1930	6,305	400	6,705	4,560	155	395
1929	8,045	330	8,375	6,020	200	445
1928	7,670	290	7,960	5,710	175	400
1927	7,780	340	8,115	5,790	175	380
1926	8,215	375	8,595	6,180	145	400
1925	8,350	360	8,710	6,375	135	345
1924	8,250	285	8,530	6,140	115	340
1923	8,535	345	8,880	6,375	115	340
1922	7,605	290	7,895	5,480	90	340
1921	6,560	165	6,730	4,505	75	260
1920	7,770	205	7,975	5,440	80	360
1919	7,725	125	7,850	5,370	105	330
1918	7,310	180	7,490	4,955	95	335
1917	7,940	170	8,110	5,570	90	245
1916	8,530	165	8,695	6,185	90	325
1915	8,020	135	8,150	5,750	85	300
1914	8,565	15	8,550	6,290	85	265
1913	9,170	165	9,005	6,835	80	260
1912	9,330	145	9,185	6,990	80	250
1911	9,020	150	8,870	6,680	80	240
1910	9,295	80	9,215	6,910	90	220
1909	9,275	50	9,225	6,910	80	230
1908	8,725	80	8,645	6,520	70	205
1907	9,555	115	9,440	7,145	65	235
1906	9,225	95	9,130	7,145	60	225
1905	8,625	90	8,535	6,755	35	195
1904	8,490	150	8,340	6,675	20	190
1903	8,215	140	8,075	6,445	15	175
1902	7,880	60	7,820	6,180	10	160
1901	7,580	110	7,470	5,930	5	150
1900	7,285	140	7,140	5,680	5	135

Z Less than 2.5 million cubic feet.

Series L 87-97. Per Capita Consumption of Timber Products, by Major Product: 1900 to 1988

Year	All products	Total	Lumber	Industrial roundwood used for Plywood and veneer	Pulp products	Miscellaneous products [1]	Fuelwood
	87	88	89	91	93	95	96
1988	79.5	65.9	34.2	6.9	22.7	2.1	13.6
1987	81.0	68.0	36.3	7.2	22.4	2.0	12.9
1986	78.8	65.9	35.0	6.7	22.2	2.0	12.9
1985	76.2	61.8	32.2	6.5	21.1	1.9	14.4
1984	77.9	62.6	31.9	6.3	22.3	1.9	15.3
1983	72.0	58.2	29.5	6.2	20.5	1.9	13.8
1982	65.7	51.3	24.9	5.2	19.3	1.9	14.4
1981	66.9	52.8	25.6	5.4	20.2	1.6	14.0
1980	70.8	57.2	28.3	5.5	21.4	1.8	13.6
1979	74.4	64.3	33.7	6.8	21.9	1.8	10.1
1978	67.7	64.6	34.1	7.5	21.2	1.8	3.1
1977	65.1	62.1	32.9	7.4	19.9	1.8	2.9
1976	62.2	59.4	30.1	7.0	20.5	1.8	2.8
1975	54.0	51.4	25.8	5.9	17.9	1.8	2.6
1974	61.5	58.9	28.0	5.9	23.1	1.9	2.5
1973	65.7	63.3	32.5	7.2	21.7	1.9	2.4
1972	64.3	62.1	32.3	7.4	20.4	1.9	2.3
1971	63.7	61.0	31.2	6.9	20.6	2.2	2.4
1970	62.1	59.5	29.8	6.0	21.5	2.1	2.6
1969	64.1	61.0	31.3	6.0	21.5	2.2	3.1
1968	64.8	61.3	31.9	6.4	20.2	2.4	3.5
1967	62.4	58.5	30.1	5.7	20.0	2.6	3.9
1966	65.8	61.5	32.0	5.8	20.7	2.9	4.3
1965	66.1	61.4	32.7	5.8	20.0	2.9	4.7
1964	65.0	59.9	32.9	5.5	18.7	2.8	5.1
1963	63.3	57.7	32.0	5.0	17.9	2.7	5.6
1962	62.0	56.0	30.9	4.7	17.8	2.5	6.0
1961	61.0	54.4	29.9	4.5	17.3	2.7	6.6
1960	63.3	56.1	30.8	4.2	18.2	2.8	7.2
1959	68.2	60.4	35.2	4.4	17.6	3.0	7.8
1958	64.0	55.5	31.9	3.8	16.5	3.2	8.5
1957	65.9	56.8	31.6	3.5	18.2	3.4	9.1
1956	74.6	64.8	37.5	3.7	19.9	3.6	9.8
1955	73.8	63.3	37.5	3.7	18.1	3.8	10.5
1954	72.3	61.0	36.8	3.1	16.8	4.0	11.3
1953	74.5	62.6	37.7	3.1	17.3	4.2	12.0
1952	75.8	63.0	38.7	2.8	16.9	4.4	12.7
1951	78.6	64.2	38.9	2.6	17.8	4.7	14.4
1950	80.0	65.1	41.8	2.3	15.6	5.1	14.9
1949	74.6	55.7	34.5	2.1	14.1	5.0	18.9
1948	81.9	63.7	40.5	2.0	15.3	5.8	18.2
1947	79.8	61.2	38.1	1.8	14.7	6.5	18.6
1946	78.4	59.4	38.1	1.8	13.3	6.3	18.9
1945	73.2	51.9	31.9	1.7	12.3	6.0	21.3
1944	78.6	57.6	37.7	1.9	11.5	6.5	21.1
1943	79.9	59.5	39.6	1.9	11.3	6.7	20.4
1942	86.3	65.1	43.1	2.2	12.3	7.4	21.2
1941	91.9	65.0	43.4	1.9	11.9	7.7	26.9
1940	85.3	55.8	36.4	1.7	10.4	7.3	29.4
1939	84.8	52.8	33.7	1.6	10.1	7.4	32.0
1938	79.8	46.5	29.2	1.5	8.7	7.1	33.3
1937	85.8	54.2	34.1	1.5	10.7	7.9	31.6
1936	84.3	51.1	32.7	1.2	9.4	7.6	33.3

See footnote at end of chart.

Series L 87-97.   Per Capita Consumption of Timber Products, by Major Product: 1900 to 1988—Cont'd

			Industrial roundwood used for				
Year	All products	Total	Lumber	Plywood and veneer	Pulp products	Miscellaneous products [1]	Fuelwood
	87	88	89	91	93	95	96
1935	78.8	43.4	27.0	1.1	8.3	7.0	35.5
1934	75.3	37.1	21.8	1.0	7.6	6.8	38.2
1933	74.8	34.9	20.1	1.0	7.2	6.6	39.8
1932	69.6	29.7	15.9	.9	6.3	6.7	39.9
1931	75.3	39.9	23.9	1.0	7.2	7.8	35.4
1930	85.3	54.5	35.6	1.2	7.9	9.7	30.8
1929	94.8	68.8	47.3	1.6	8.5	11.3	26.0
1928	92.8	66.1	45.1	1.5	8.0	11.5	26.8
1927	95.1	68.2	46.9	1.4	7.8	12.1	26.9
1926	99.3	73.2	51.4	1.2	7.9	12.7	26.1
1925	103.1	75.2	54.0	1.2	7.1	12.9	27.8
1924	104.4	74.7	52.4	1.0	6.8	14.5	29.6
1923	109.5	79.4	56.3	1.0	6.8	15.2	30.2
1922	105.9	71.7	49.2	.8	6.3	15.4	34.2
1921	101.4	62.0	40.8	.7	4.7	15.9	39.4
1920	113.1	74.9	50.5	.8	5.9	17.7	38.2
1919	113.5	74.7	50.6	1.0	4.9	18.2	38.8
1918	112.7	71.7	47.6	.9	4.8	18.4	41.1
1917	117.5	78.4	53.9	.9	5.0	18.7	39.1
1916	124.1	85.3	60.6	.9	4.9	18.9	38.8
1915	120.6	81.1	56.9	.8	4.6	18.8	39.6
1914	126.4	86.3	61.7	.9	4.4	19.4	40.1
1913	131.5	92.6	67.0	.8	4.3	20.5	38.9
1912	135.8	96.4	70.3	.8	4.1	21.1	39.5
1911	137.4	94.5	68.0	.9	4.0	22.5	43.0
1910	142.0	99.7	72.5	1.0	3.8	22.5	42.3
1909	144.2	101.9	74.7	.9	3.7	22.7	42.3
1908	142.3	97.5	71.7	.8	3.2	21.8	44.8
1907	152.5	108.5	79.7	.7	3.9	24.3	44.0
1906	152.6	106.9	81.7	.7	3.5	21.1	45.7
1905	150.2	101.8	78.8	.4	3.1	19.6	48.3
1904	152.6	101.5	78.7	.2	3.0	19.5	51.1
1903	154.2	100.2	77.6	.2	2.9	19.5	54.0
1902	155.6	98.7	76.6	.1	2.7	19.3	56.8
1901	156.2	96.3	74.5	.1	2.4	19.2	59.9
1900	156.9	93.8	72.3	.1	2.2	19.2	63.1

[1] Includes cooperage logs, poles and piling, fence posts, hewn ties, round mine timbers, box bolts, excelsior bolts, chemical wood, shingle bolts and miscellaneous items.

Series L 166-177. Pulpwood, Wood Pulp, Paper and Board, Turpentine and Rosin Production, Net Imports and Apparent Consumption: 1809 to 1991

(In thousands)

Year	Paper and board			Year	Paper and board			Year	Paper and board		
	Domestic production	Apparent consumption [1]	Waste paper consumption		Domestic production	Apparent consumption [1]	Waste paper consumption		Domestic production	Apparent consumption [1]	Waste paper consumption
	172	174	175		172	174	175		172	174	175
	Tons	Tons	Tons		Tons	Tons	Tons		Tons	Tons	Tons
1991	81,000	84,800	23,500	1957	30,666	35,268	8,493	1924	7,930	9,281	(NA)
1990	80,400	86,700	21,700	1956	31,441	36,496	8,836	1923	7,871	9,194	(NA)
1989	78,400	85,200	20,200					1922	6,875	7,865	(NA)
1988	78,100	85,600	19,700	1955	30,178	34,719	9,041	1921	5,333	6,027	(NA)
1987	78,000	83,600	18,700	1954	26,876	31,379	7,857				
1986	72,700	79,800	17,900	1953	26,605	31,360	8,531	1920	7,185	7,640	(NA)
				1952	24,418	29,017	7,881	1919	5,966	6,253	1,854
1985	68,700	76,100	16,400	1951	26,047	30,561	9,071	1918	5,938	6,275	(NA)
1984	70,600	77,300	16,700					1917	5,804	6,054	(NA)
1983	66,900	71,400	15,600	1950	24,375	29,011	7,956	1916	(NA)	(NA)	(NA)
1982	61,200	64,900	14,600	1949	20,315	24,694	6,600				
1981	64,400	64,100	15,000	1948	21,897	26,082	7,585	1915	(NA)	(NA)	(NA)
				1947	21,102	24,749	8,009	1914	5,153	5,395	1,510
1980	63,600	67,200	14,900	1946	19,278	22,510	7,278	1913	(NA)	(NA)	(NA)
1979	67,000	72,700	15,400					1912	(NA)	(NA)	(NA)
1978	64,300	70,400	14,800	1945	17,371	19,665	6,800	1911	(NA)	(NA)	(NA)
1977	62,100	66,500	14,100	1944	17,183	19,445	6,859				
1976	60,500	64,300	13,600	1943	17,036	19,437	6,368	1910	(NA)	(NA)	(NA)
				1942	17,084	19,780	5,495	1909	4,121	4,103	984
1975	52,800	56,000	11,700	1941	17,762	20,421	6,075	1908	(NA)	(NA)	(NA)
1974	61,100	65,500	14,000					1907	(NA)	(NA)	(NA)
1973	61,800	67,400	14,100	1940	14,484	16,757	4,668	1906	(NA)	(NA)	(NA)
1972	59,500	64,500	12,925	1939	13,510	15,949	4,366				
1971	55,100	59,700	12,100	1938	11,381	13,542	(NA)	1905	(NA)	(NA)	(NA)
				1937	12,837	16,028	(NA)	1904	3,107	3,029	589
1970	53,516	58,057	10,594	1936	11,976	14,651	(NA)	1903	(NA)	(NA)	—
1969	54,187	59,003	10,939					1902	(NA)	(NA)	—
1968	51,245	55,664	10,222	1935	10,479	12,758	3,587	1901	(NA)	(NA)	—
1967	46,926	51,945	9,888	1934	9,187	11,289	(NA)				
1966	47,113	52,680	10,564	1933	9,190	10,916	(NA)	1900	(NA)	(NA)	—
				1932	7,998	9,727	(NA)	1899	2,168	2,168	—
1965	44,080	49,102	10,231	1931	9,382	11,347	(NA)	1889	935	—	—
1964	41,703	46,384	9,843					1879	452	—	—
1963	39,230	43,715	9,613	1930	10,169	12,319	(NA)	1869	[2] 386	—	—
1962	37,541	42,216	9,075	1929	11,140	13,411	3,842				
1961	35,749	40,312	9,018	1928	10,403	12,451	(NA)	1859	127	—	—
				1927	10,002	11,925	(NA)	1849	[2] 78	—	—
1960	34,444	39,138	9,032	1926	9,794	11,584	(NA)	1839	[2] 38	—	—
1959	34,015	38,725	9,414					1819	[2] 12	—	—
1958	30,823	35,119	8,671	1925	9,002	10,417	(NA)	1809	[2] 3	—	—

NA Not available.
[1] Beginning 1929, includes changes in newsprint stocks.
[2] Estimated from values reported by the Bureau of the Census.

Series L 192-198. Newsprint Production, Shipments, Consumption, Stocks, Imports and Price: 1935 to 1990

(In thousands of short tons, except price)

Year	Production	Shipments from mills	Consumption by publishers	Imports	Year	Production	Shipments from mills	Consumption by publishers	Imports
	192	193	194	197		192	193	194	197
1990	5,997	6,007	12,127	—	1962	2,154	2,162	5,577	5,474
1989	5,523	5,515	12,241	8,765	1961	2,094	2,086	5,461	5,435
1988	5,427	5,415	12,244	8,592					
1987	5,300	5,310	12,303	8,976	1960	2,038	2,031	5,532	5,412
1986	5,107	5,115	11,873	8,589	1959	1,964	1,963	5,328	5,255
					1958	1,758	1,761	4,950	4,884
1985	4,924	4,927	11,507	8,472	1957	1,826	1,817	5,149	5,218
1984	5,025	5,065	11,349	7,899	1956	1,717	1,715	5,209	5,567
1983	4,688	4,674	10,529	6,919					
1982	4,574	4,525	10,107	5,925	1955	1,552	1,550	5,045	5,164
1981	4,753	4,735	10,165	6,329	1954	1,211	1,213	4,684	4,995
					1953	1,084	1,088	4,669	5,006
1980	4,239	4,234	10,088	7,280	1952	1,147	1,143	4,551	5,036
1979	4,096	4,100	11,240	7,223	1951	1,125	1,125	4,511	4,963
1978	3,768	3,779	10,874	7,484					
1977	3,870	3,866	10,230	6,559	1950	1,015	1,017	4,542	4,864
1976	3,736	3,728	9,611	6,569	1949	900	898	4,257	4,640
					1948	867	867	4,010	4,395
1975	3,348	3,347	8,395	5,847	1947	826	832	3,565	3,958
1974	3,561	3,560	10,284	7,399	1946	771	762	3,136	3,492
1973	3,738	3,742	10,784	7,410					
1972	3,422	3,437	7,569	7,101	1945	724	725	2,455	2,669
1971	3,296	3,288	7,057	6,835	1944	720	723	2,351	2,491
					1943	805	803	2,720	2,637
1970	3,310	3,303	7,130	6,635	1942	953	951	2,835	2,921
1969	3,232	3,233	7,344	6,790	1941	1,015	1,021	2,947	2,982
1968	2,935	2,946	7,025	6,463					
1967	2,620	2,602	6,907	6,599	1940	1,013	1,013	2,856	2,763
1966	2,408	2,405	6,898	6,991	1939	939	945	2,730	2,615
					1938	820	817	2,653	2,275
1965	2,180	2,183	6,387	6,323	1937	946	945	2,956	3,317
1964	2,261	2,273	6,031	5,954	1936	921	917	2,939	2,752
1963	2,218	2,208	5,585	5,413	1935	912	917	2,663	2,383

Series L 224-235. Yield and Value of Domestic Fisheries, Imports and Exports: 1880 to 1990

| | Yield (mil. lb.) Domestic | | | Value (mil. dol.) | | | Yield (mil. lb.) Domestic | | | Value (mil. dol.) | |
Year	Total	For human food	For industrial use	Domestic total	Total imports[1]	Total exports[1]	Year	Total	For human food	For industrial use	Domestic total	Total imports[1]	Total exports[1]
	224	225	226	229	230	233		224	225	226	229	230	233
1990	9,708	7,346	2,362	3,572	9,048	5,639	1950	4,901	3,307	1,594	347.4	198.3	27.5
1989	8,463	6,204	2,259	3,238	9,604	4,707	1949	4,804	3,305	1,499	342.7	151.6	35.1
1988	7,192	4,588	2,604	3,520	8,872	2,275	1948	4,513	3,146	1,367	371.1	156.6	24.4
1987	6,896	3,946	2,950	3,115	8,818	1,660	1947	4,349	3,020	1,329	312.0	110.0	52.8
1986	6,031	3,393	2,638	2,763	7,626	1,356	1946	4,467	3,049	1,418	313.0	129.7	40.0
1985	6,258	3,294	2,964	2,326	6,679	1,084	1945	4,598	3,167	1,431	269.9	101.3	38.5
1984	6,438	3,320	3,118	2,350	5,883	949	1944	4,533	2,865	1,668	213.0	78.4	35.9
1983	6,439	3,238	3,201	2,355	5,129	1,021	1943	4,162	2,737	1,425	204.0	67.2	48.5
1982	6,367	3,285	3,082	2,390	4,523	1,059	1942	3,875	2,683	1,192	170.3	39.6	31.9
1981	5,977	3,547	2,430	2,388	4,206	1,157	1941	4,900	3,062	1,838	129.0	41.0	22.0
1980	6,482	3,654	2,828	2,237	3,648	1,006	1940	4,060	2,675	1,385	96.1	41.8	17.8
1979	6,267	3,318	2,949	2,234	3,809	1,084	1939	4,445	2,713	1,732	97.6	46.0	14.2
1978	6,028	3,177	2,851	1,854	3,086	906	1938	4,254	2,639	1,615	94.2	39.3	14.4
1977	5,271	2,592	2,319	1,554	2,634	520	1937	4,353	2,703	1,650	101.4	50.6	14.6
1976	5,388	2,775	2,613	1,349	2,328	385	1936	4,826	2,854	1,972	94.8	41.9	13.2
1975	4,877	2,465	2,412	977	1,637	305	1935	4,135	2,583	1,552	82.8	36.2	14.4
1974	4,967	2,496	2,471	932	1,711	262	1934	4,104	2,434	1,670	76.8	30.8	13.8
1973	4,858	2,398	2,460	937	1,583	299	1933	2,997	2,087	911	61.1	30.5	8.3
1972	4,806	2,435	2,371	748	1,494	158	1932	2,612	1,864	748	56.0	29.6	7.8
1971	4,969	2,400	2,569	643	1,074	139	1931	2,630	2,129	501	77.0	43.0	11.6
1970	4,917	2,537	2,380	613.1	1,037.4	117.5	1930	3,224	2,478	746	109.0	50.8	17.3
1969	4,337	2,321	2,016	526.5	844.3	104.5	1929	3,491	2,601	890	125.8	66.6	23.8
1968	4,160	2,347	1,814	497.3	822.7	67.8	1928	3,061	2,370	691	114.3	58.9	21.2
1967	4,055	2,368	1,687	439.6	707.9	82.2	1927	2,806	2,172	634	111.5	55.6	18.7
1966	4,366	2,573	1,794	472.3	719.7	84.8	1926	2,871	2,198	673	106.7	50.1	20.3
1965	4,777	2,587	2,190	445.7	600.9	69.5	1925	2,891	2,029	862	105.1	49.0	21.3
1964	4,541	2,497	2,044	389.5	564.2	64.2	1924	2,461	1,874	587	—	46.3	20.9
1963	4,847	2,556	2,291	377.2	500.7	56.6	1923	2,726	1,807	919	—	—	—
1962	5,354	2,540	2,814	396.4	489.8	35.7	1922	2,619	1,677	942	—	—	—
1961	5,187	2,490	2,697	362.2	400.6	34.7	1921	2,255	1,451	804	—	—	—
1960	4,942	2,498	2,444	353.6	363.3	44.2	1917	2,676	—	—	71.1	—	—
1959	5,122	2,369	2,753	346.1	370.1	44.2	1908	2,053	—	—	62.7	—	—
1958	4,747	2,651	2,096	373.3	330.8	31.0	1907	1,930	—	—	60.9	—	—
1957	4,789	2,475	2,314	353.7	299.3	36.0	1906	2,046	—	—	59.3	—	—
1956	5,268	2,690	2,578	372.2	282.7	39.5	1905	2,002	—	—	57.3	—	—
1955	4,809	2,579	2,230	338.9	258.9	40.0	1892	1,652	—	—	40.7	—	—
1954	4,762	2,705	2,057	359.3	252.4	31.5	1891	1,709	—	—	42.3	—	—
1953	4,487	2,519	1,968	356.1	245.5	27.9	1890	1,758	—	—	41.3	—	—
1952	4,432	2,778	1,654	363.6	240.4	21.9	1889	1,685	—	—	39.0	—	—
1951	4,433	3,048	1,385	364.8	212.5	35.7	1880	1,706	—	—	39.1	—	—

[1] Includes Puerto Rico; beginning 1955, imports also include landings of tuna by foreign vessels in American Samoa, and imports of tuna into U.S. outlying areas.

Series L 254-261. Fisheries—Employment, Fishing Craft and Establishments: 1930 to 1989

Year	Persons employed (1,000)		Craft utilized				Fishery shore establishments
	Total	Fishermen	Total	Vessels [1]	Motorboats	Other boats	
	254	255	257	258	259	260	261
1989	—	—	111,000	36,000	75,000	—	4,500
1988	364	274	110,000	32,000	78,000	—	4,600
1987	359	256	93,000	23,000	68,000	2,000	4,200
1986	347	247	128,000	38,000	88,000	2,000	4,000
1985	351	239	130,000	24,000	104,000	2,000	4,000
1984	340	230	127,000	24,000	102,000	1,000	4,000
1983	333	223	127,000	21,000	105,000	1,000	3,900
1982	314	216	123,000	20,000	102,000	1,000	3,600
1981	303	198	115,000	20,000	93,000	2,000	3,600
1980	296	193	113,000	19,000	93,000	1,000	3,600
1979	267	184	103,000	18,000	84,000	1,000	3,400
1978	257	172	104,000	18,000	84,000	2,000	3,300
1977	269	173	104,000	11,000	84,000	2,000	3,600
1976	266	174	103,000	17,000	84,000	2,000	3,600
1975	260	168	103,000	16,000	85,000	2,000	3,600
1974	253	161	101,000	16,000	83,000	2,000	3,500
1973	243	149	90,000	15,000	72,000	2,000	3,600
1972	(NA)	(NA)	91,000	(NA)	(NA)	(NA)	3,700
1971	230	139	86,000	14,000	71,000	2,000	3,800
1970	227	140	88,400	13,300	73,100	2,000	3,735
1969	220	132	77,057	12,018	56,889	8,150	4,207
1968	217	128	81,614	13,150	66,654	1,810	3,967
1967	220	132	81,328	12,874	66,075	2,379	4,053
1966	224	136	82,122	12,677	66,941	2,504	4,187
1965	215	129	79,532	12,311	63,828	3,393	4,189
1964	212	128	76,412	11,808	60,945	3,659	4,121
1963	216	128	77,973	11,928	62,090	3,955	4,194
1962	217	126	70,733	11,511	54,406	4,816	4,135
1961	222	130	77,487	11,964	60,118	5,405	4,138
1960	224	130	77,057	12,018	56,889	8,150	4,207
1959	222	129	75,301	12,109	54,735	8,457	4,372
1958	227	129	75,291	11,496	54,821	8,974	4,402
1957	235	138	77,970	11,671	56,434	9,865	4,322
1956	248	145	82,300	11,300	52,000	19,000	4,000
1955	241	144	83,292	11,796	58,218	13,278	4,124
1954	246	145	82,090	11,179	51,814	19,097	4,012
1953	254	153	86,681	10,621	48,067	27,993	3,904
1952	254	152	88,136	11,065	46,291	30,780	3,843
1951	(NA)	155	89,791	11,242	45,749	32,800	(NA)
1950	263	161	92,310	11,496	46,067	34,747	3,883
1940	215	125	71,810	5,562	31,055	35,193	3,055
1930	199	120	77,772	4,374	35,437	37,961	2,995

NA Not available.

[1] 5 net tons and over.

MINERALS
Highlights

1 The principal source for minerals data is the *Minerals Yearbook* published annually since 1932-33 by the U.S. Bureau of Mines. For earlier years, the same data are provided by the *Mineral Resources of the United States* published from 1882 until 1932 by U.S. Geological Survey. Since 1977, mineral fuel data have been collected and published by the Energy Information Administration.

2 Censuses of mineral industries have been conducted by the Bureau of Census at various intervals since 1840. Since 1967, the census has been conducted every fifth year for years ending in 2 and 7.

3 Because of poor husbandry of natural resources and enormous consumption habits, the United States is losing its commanding position in production of major minerals. It now accounts for more than one-half of world production in only mica among nonmetals and molybdenum among metals. Its share of world production is over 40% in magnesium, over 30% in phosphate rock, over 20% in sulfur, natural gas, aluminum and lead, and over 10% in coal, crude oil, gypsum, feldspar, copper and gold. The United States is 100% dependent on foreign suppliers for columbium, strontium, and bauxite, 88% for the platinum group, 85% for tantalum, 82% for cobalt, 80% for chromium, 75% for tungsten, 74% for nickel, 73% for tin, 70% for barium, 67% for potassium, 57% for antimony, 54% for cadmium, and 52% for selenium.

4 U.S. dependence on foreign oil, which was significantly reduced in the late 1970s, is once again rising, passing the 2 billion barrel mark in 1989 and 1990. Such growing dependence has been accompanied by a decline in domestic production. The number of oil wells drilled, which peaked in 1985 at close to 70,000, dropped to less than 30,000 in 1990.

5 The share of mining in the GNP dropped from 4.2% in 1982 to 1.5% in 1989. In current dollars, it dropped from $132 billion in 1982 to $80.254 billion in 1987. Between 1958 and 1987, employment in mining declined from 734,000 to 698,000 and the number of mining establishments from 36,392 to 33,617. At the same time, payroll in the mining sector rose from $3.749 billion to $21.739 billion and the value added from $13.385 billion to $110.959 billion.

6 The Federal government maintains the world's largest stockpile of strategic minerals. In 1990, they included 169,000 metric tons of tin, 92 million troy oz. of silver, 53 million lbs. of cobalt, 18 million tons of bauxite, 4 million tons of manganese, 1.074 million tons of chromium, 82 million lbs. of tungsten, 379,000 tons of zinc, 37,000 tons of titanium, 453,000 troy oz. of platinum, and 7,777 carats of diamonds.

7 Proved U.S. reserves of petroleum will last for 10 years at current rates of production. The United States fares better in natural gas with reserves of 169 trillion cubic feet. U.S. production of natural gas accounts for 24% of world total.

8 The United States is the world's largest exporter of coal, with a share of 25%. In 1989, it exported 100.8 million tons. The largest coal mining states are Wyoming, Kentucky, and West Virginia. Because of technological improvements, the average per worker per day production grew from 18.84 short tons in 1970 to 31.75 short tons in 1989.

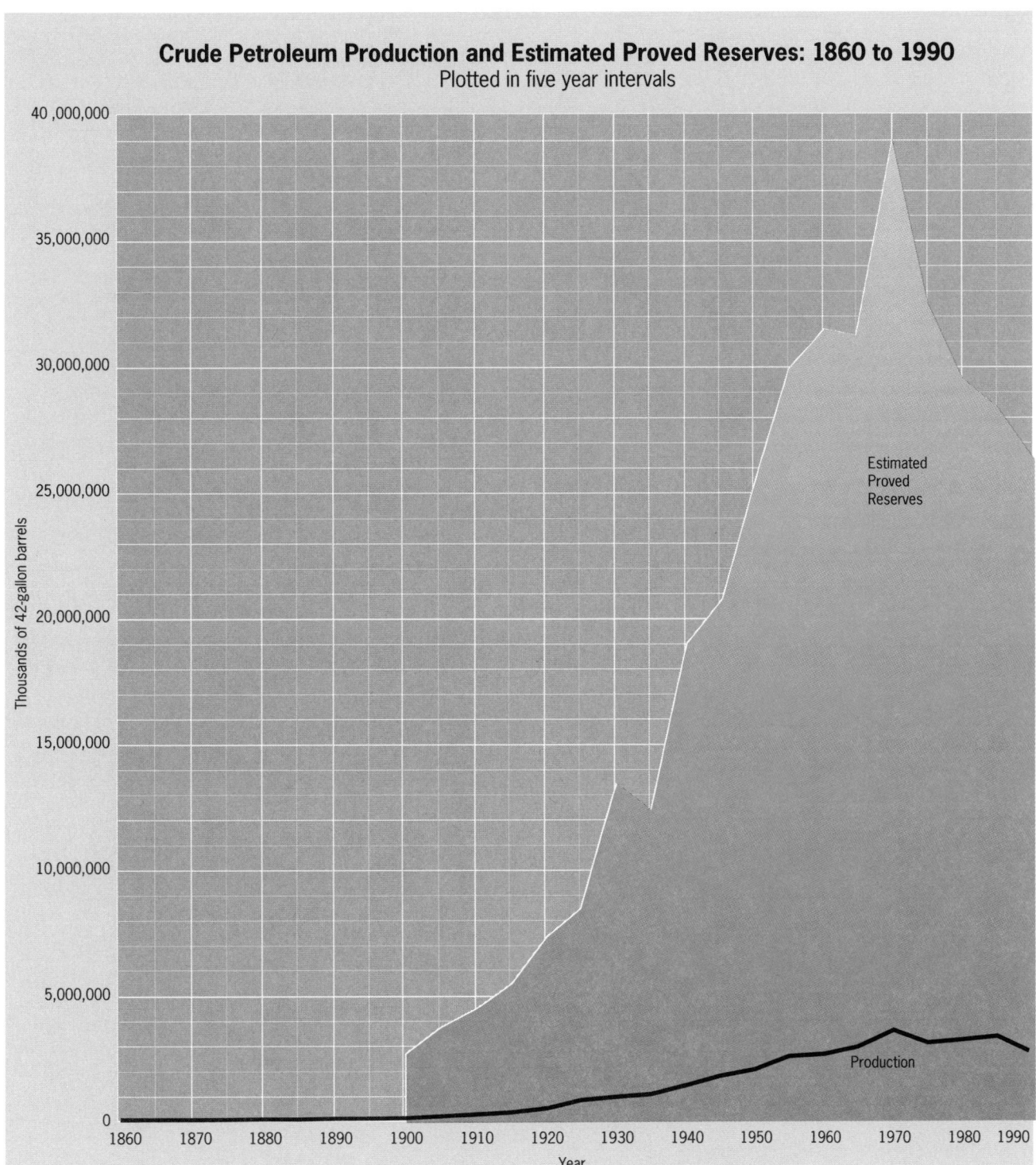

Crude Petroleum Production and Estimated Proved Reserves: 1860 to 1990
Plotted in five year intervals

Thousands of 42-gallon barrels

40,000,000
35,000,000
30,000,000
25,000,000
20,000,000
15,000,000
10,000,000
5,000,000
0

Estimated
Proved
Reserves

Production

1860 1870 1880 1890 1900 1910 1920 1930 1940 1950 1960 1970 1980 1990

Year

Series M 1-12. Summary of Mineral Operations: 1840 to 1987

(In general, includes data for mining operations at manufacturing establishments. For all years prior to 1935, excludes common clay, shale and peat (except as noted) and contract service operations; for years prior to 1929, excludes sand and gravel operations and crushed stone quarries at manufacturing plants, except as indicated)

Industry group and year	Number of establishments	Value added in mining (mil. dol.)	Production and development workers (1000)	Capital expenditures (mil. dol.)
	1	4	5	11
ALL MINERAL OPERATIONS				
1987	33,617	110,959	451.0	15,418
1982	42,241	188,056	—	—
1977	31,359	68,013	—	—
1967 [1]	29,688	19,621	447.6	4,062
1963	40,532	16,231	501.7	3,268
1958	37,958	13,685	585.2	2,807
1954	38,858	11,752	667.8	2,728
1939 [2]	24,703	2,680	774.1	—
1919	22,347	2,399	989.8	—
1909	25,698	928	961.1	—
1902 [3]	52,123	628	[4] 582.0	—
1889	—	336	[5] 529.6	—
1880	—	221	[5] 301.2	—
METAL MINING				
1987	1,027	4,610	34.0	899
1982	1,434	3,215	—	—
1977	1,206	3,504	—	—
1967 [1]	1,155	1,557	55.4	340
1963	1,614	1,418	62.2	231
1958	2,351	1,180	70.8	215
1954	3,668	[6] 1,084	82.7	222
1939 [2]	[7] 2,164	417	89.8	—
1929 [2][8]	1,799	496	115.8	—
1919 [9]	2,739	413	138.2	—
1909 [10]	7,834	267	164.9	—
1902 [3]	7,730	168	[4] 123.2	—
1889	(NA)	132	104.2	—
1880	4,048	104	62.6	—
1870	2,969	41	[5] 39.9	—
1860	7,462	37	[5] 53.6	—
COAL MINING				
1987	3,905	17,068	129.0	1,665
1982	5,087	18,631	—	—
1977	5,451	11,266	—	—
1967 [1]	4,484	2,091	115.1	341
1963	7,374	1,727	129.0	233
1958	8,188	1,780	183.8	205
1954	8,301	1,621	233.0	131
1939 [2]	[7] 6,468	765	454.1	—
1935 [2][11]	[12] 6,661	[12] 730	527.9	—
1929 [2]	5,193	1,141	601.6	—
1919	6,924	1,252	693.8	—
1909	4,765	462	657.8	—
1902 [2][3]	6,017	328	[4] 350.8	—
1889 [2]	[13] 12,552	138	291.5	—
1880 [2]	[14] 8,419	84	[5] 180.0	—
1870 [2]	1,566	68	[5] 94.8	—
1860 [2]	622	17	[5] 36.5	—
1850 [2]	510	7	[5] 15.1	—
1840 [2]	—	—	[5] 6.8	—

See footnotes at end of chart.

Series M 1-12.   Summary of Mineral Operations: 1840 to 1987—Cont'd.

(In general, includes data for mining operations at manufacturing establishments. For all years prior to 1935, excludes common clay, shale and peat (except as noted) and contract service operations; for years prior to 1929, excludes sand and gravel operations and crushed stone quarries at manufacturing plants, except as indicated)

Industry group and year	Number of establishments	Value added in mining (mil. dol.)	Production and development workers (1000)	Capital expenditures (mil. dol.)
	1	4	5	11
OIL AND GAS EXTRACTION				
1987	22,910	80,049	206.0	11,717
1982	29,974	159,937	—	—
1977	18,447	48,587	—	
1967 [1]	16,358	13,394	167.2	3,005
1963	21,242	11,020	192.0	2,552
1958	18,522	9,032	214.0	2,194
1954	17,591	[2][15] 7,674	235.5	2,228
1939 [2]	10,909	[15] 1,242	149.0	—
1919 [2]	9,970	614	93.7	—
1909	8,202	112	37.6	—
1902 [3]	[16] 31,736	59	[4] 22.4	—
1889	(NA)	15	26.9	—
1880 [17]	(NA)	18	[5] 11.5	—
1870	2,314	18	[5] 4.5	—
1860 [18]	64	2	[5] .9	—

NA Not available.

[1] First year that data for single unit establishments without paid employees were excluded from the census. For 1963, for mining as a whole, included 6,543 such establishments, accounting for approximately 3 percent of value added. The number of such establishments in 1963 for metal mining was 460; for coal mining, 1,347; for oil and gas extraction, 3,714; and for nonmetallic minerals (except fuels), 1,022.

[2] Excludes Alaska.

[3] Operators of mineral properties reported an average of 8,527 employees performing contract service operations for metal mines; 6,906 for coal mines; 12,143 for oil and gas field operations; and 592 for nonmetallic minerals (except fuels). These are not included in the employment series shown.

[4] Figures for average employment converted to a 300-day basis for establishments operating for a shorter period.

[5] "All other" employees included with production and exploration workers.

[6] Excludes uranium-radium-vanadium ores industry.

[7] Represents number of mining operations and service establishments.

[8] Except for number of establishments, includes 27 nonproducing establishments in the nonmetallic minerals mining industries.

[9] Except for number of establishments, excludes 1 chromite mine in Alaska.

[10] Except for number of establishments, includes 2 producting and 18 nonproducing establishments in the nonmetallic minerals mining industries.

[11] Represents producing operations only.

[12] Excludes anthracite stripping services.

[13] Includes 9,920 "Local mines and farmers' banks," producing about 2 percent of all bituminous coal and lignite, for which no data are available on labor and expenditures.

[14] Includes 5,148 bituminous coal and lignite mines, producing coal valued at $1.1 million, representing "irregular" operations for which no other data are available.

[15] For 1954 and 1939, no data obtained on value of gas received for processing at natural gas liquids plants or on value of residue gas sold or transferred. However, for 1954, estimated value (prior to processing) of natural gas liquids contained in such gas was included with value of natural gas liquids received for processing and used in computing value added. No figures for value of residue gas are included in the value of shipments and receipts shown for 1954. For 1939, cost of supplies, purchases for resale, and purchased fuels and electric energy for all oil and gas extraction industries include estimated cost of such items and subcontract work to oil and gas field services industries, for which such data were not requested in 1939. These estimates used in computing value added for such industries. For Alaska in 1958 and 1954, cost of supplies, purchased fuels and electric energy, contract work, and purchased machinery installed exceeded value of shipments and capital expenditures.

[16] Represents number of operating companies.

[17] Excludes natural gas operations.

[18] Reported as "oil, coal" and probably includes some refining as well as production of crude petroleum, or may represent primarily recovery of oil from coal.

Series M 13-37.   Value of Mineral Products, in Current Dollars: 1880 to 1990
[In millions of dollars]

Year	Mineral products	Total [1]	Fuels				Nonmetals (except fuels)			
			Bituminous coal and lignite	Pennsylvania anthracite	Petroleum	Natural gas	Total [1]	Cement	Raw clay	Lime
	13	**14**	**15**	**16**	**17**	**18**	**20**	**21**	**22**	**24**
1990	141,741	108,422	22,719	133	53,772	31,658	20,891	3,683	1,620	902
1989	123,603	96,378	21,268	142	44,071	30,627	20,357	3,592	1,515	852
1988	119,102	89,088	20,827	159	37,479	30,287	19,805	3,576	1,401	818
1987	123,840	97,499	21,050	157	46,930	29,008	18,894	3,647	1,202	786
1986	117,408	93,944	21,001	190	39,632	23,717	17,647	3,760	1,095	758
1985	168,154	144,847	22,063	215	78,871	43,343	17,678	3,817	1,011	809
1984	179,176	156,026	22,750	200	84,100	48,490	17,173	3,810.4	1,037.2	811.2
1983	168,848	147,748	20,110	210	83,050	43,570	15,263	3,315.7	931.1	757.6
1982	179,042	159,395	22,620	230	90,030	45,560	14,150	3,084.4	825.1	696.2
1981	187,187	161,899	21,510	240	99,400	39,510	16,446	3,515.6	988.8	884.2
1980	146,750	121,612	20,197	259	67,930	32,090	16,213	3,613	899	843
1979	106,856.7	82,888.6	18,243	183.7	39,453.4	24,115.1	15,449	3,650.4	846.1	862.5
1978	86,241.2	86,241	14,486.3	207.1	28,477.8	18,084.9	13,525.7	3,239.6	717.3	749.7
1977	77,112.0	60,182	13,705.2	184.8	25,790.7	15,825.0	11,702	2,727.6	579.2	666.5
1976	69,216.3	52,919	13,189.5	209.2	24,229.5	11,571.8	10,616	2,330.4	528.7	609.0
1975	62,190	47,781	12,472.5	198.5	23,116.1	8,945.1	9,494	2,015.6	424.6	523.8
1974	55,172	40,937	9,502	144.7	21,580.5	1,072.2	8,682	1,992.7	422.5	473.7
1973	36,788	25,012	5,050	90.0	13,057.9	668.8	7,413	1,810.3	354.1	365.8
1972	32,217	22,084	4,561.9	85.2	11,706.5	4,203.2	6,492	1,588.2	303	339.3
1971	30,732	21,258	3,901.4	103.4	11,692.9	4,096.5	6,068	1,421.3	274.4	308.1
1970	29,790	20,153	3,772	105	11,174	3,746	5,711	[2] 1,336	[3] 268	286
1969	26,921	17,965	2,797	94	10,427	3,456	5,624	[2] 1,354	[3] 264	281
1968	24,971	16,820	2,546	97	9,795	3,169	5,448	1,295	[3] 247	250
1967	23,729	16,195	2,555	96	9,376	2,899	5,206	1,211	[3] 224	240
1966	22,968	15,088	2,421	101	8,726	2,703	5,176	1,227	[3] 222	240
1965	21,524	14,047	2,276	122	8,158	2,495	4,933	1,221	[3] 205	233
1964	20,612	13,623	2,166	149	8,017	2,388	4,623	1,209	[3] 193	223
1963	19,635	13,317	2,013	154	7,966	2,328	4,316	1,157	[3] 181	199
1962	18,838	12,784	1,892	134	7,774	2,145	4,117	1,129	[3] 163	187
1961	18,230	12,357	1,845	140	7,566	1,996	3,946	1,106	[3] 157	177
1960	18,032	12,142	1,950	147	7,420	1,790	3,868	1,089	[3] 162	173
1959	17,381	11,950	1,966	172	7,473	1,557	3,861	1,145	[3] 160	164
1958	16,649	11,589	1,996	188	7,380	1,317	3,466	1,039	[3] 143	121
1957	18,233	12,709	2,504	228	8,079	1,202	3,387	961	[3] 156	135
1956	17,490	11,741	2,412	237	7,297	1,084	3,391	989	[3] 163	136
1955	15,911	10,780	2,092	206	6,870	978	3,076	884	[3] 140	127
1954	14,170	9,919	1,770	248	6,425	883	2,733	763	[3] 123	102
1953	14,418	10,257	2,248	299	6,327	775	2,350	698	[3] 125	112
1952	13,396	9,616	2,283	380	5,785	624	2,163	638	[3] 131	95
1951	13,529	9,779	2,622	406	5,690	543	2,079	612	[3] 129	97
1950	11,862	8,689	2,497	392	4,963	409	1,822	538	[3] 95	83
1949	10,580	7,920	2,134	358	4,675	344	1,559	475	79	69
1948	12,273	9,502	2,990	467	5,245	333	1,552	446	85	75
1947	9,610	7,188	2,620	413	3,578	275	1,338	357	74	63
1946	7,062	5,090	1,836	413	2,443	212	1,243	297	[3] 61	51
1945	6,231	4,569	1,768	324	2,094	191	888	175	[3] 43	46
1944	6,310	4,574	1,811	355	2,033	190	836	152	37	49
1943	5,931	4,028	1,585	307	1,809	177	916	202	40	49
1942	5,623	3,568	1,374	272	1,643	154	1,056	287	27	44
1941	5,107	3,228	1,125	240	1,602	139	989	251	27	43
1940	4,198	2,662	879	205	1,385	120	784	193	20	34
1939	3,808	2,423	728	187	1,294	120	754	184	17	30
1938	3,518	2,436	679	181	1,373	114	622	157	13	24
1937	4,265	2,798	864	198	1,513	123	711	171	18	30
1936	3,606	2,405	771	227	1,200	119	685	173	16	27

See footnotes at end of chart.

Series M 13-37. Value of Mineral Products, in Current Dollars: 1880 to 1990—Cont'd.

(In millions of dollars)

Year	Mineral products	Total [1]	Bituminous coal and lignite	Pennsylvania anthracite	Petroleum (Fuels)	Natural gas	Total [1] (Nonmetals except fuels)	Cement	Lime
	13	14	15	16	17	18	20	21	24
1935	2,942	2,013	658	210	961	110	564	115	22
1934	2,744	1,947	628	244	905	106	520	118	17
1933	2,050	1,413	446	207	608	97	432	86	14
1932	2,000	1,460	407	222	680	99	412	83	12
1931	2,578	1,620	589	296	551	108	671	143	19
1930	3,980	2,500	795	355	1,070	147	973	231	26
1929	4,908	2,940	953	386	1,280	158	1,166	255	33
1928	4,484	2,666	934	394	1,055	140	1,163	279	36
1927	4,698	2,875	1,030	421	1,173	127	1,201	282	39
1926	5,311	3,371	1,183	474	1,448	125	1,219	281	42
1925	4,812	2,910	1,060	328	1,285	112	1,187	281	43
1924	4,754	2,899	1,063	477	1,023	254	1,174	266	40
1923	5,252	3,317	1,515	507	978	240	1,157	260	40
1922	4,183	2,738	1,275	274	895	222	921	208	33
1921	3,828	2,703	1,200	452	815	175	780	182	25
1920	6,084	4,193	2,130	434	1,361	196	1,025	196	38
1919	4,007	2,511	1,161	365	760	161	752	147	29
1918	4,563	2,736	1,492	336	704	154	648	114	27
1917	4,131	2,238	1,249	284	523	142	666	123	24
1916	2,993	1,333	665	202	331	120	554	105	19
1915	2,078	973	502	185	179	101	429	75	14
1914	1,870	993	493	188	214	94	431	81	13
1913	2,092	1,088	565	195	237	88	467	90	15
1912	1,921	946	518	178	164	85	430	70	14
1911	1,675	836	451	175	134	75	407	67	14
1910	1,707	828	469	160	128	71	410	69	14
1909	1,571	746	405	149	128	63	386	54	14
1908	1,417	716	374	158	129	55	325	44	11
1907	1,667	789	451	164	120	54	376	56	13
1906	1,492	652	381	132	92	47	362	55	12
1905	1,313	602	335	142	84	42	319	36	11
1904	1,167	584	305	139	101	38	274	26	10
1903	1,215	634	352	152	95	36	272	32	9
1902	1,018	469	291	76	71	31	254	25	9
1901	960	442	236	113	66	27	219	16	8
1900	914	406	221	86	76	24	188	13	7
1899	798	341	168	88	65	20	185	13	7
1898	631	268	133	75	44	15	151	10	7
1897	574	254	120	79	41	14	128	8	6
1896	573	268	115	82	59	13	120	6	6
1895	555	268	116	82	58	13	126	5	7
1894	498	236	108	78	36	14	127	5	8
1893	480	252	123	86	29	14	70	4	(4)
1892	524	248	125	82	26	15	90	5	(4)
1891	504	237	117	74	31	16	83	5	(4)
1890	499	231	110	66	35	19	81	5	(4)
1889	456	208	95	66	27	21	83	5	8
1888	476	231	102	89	18	23	80	5	25
1887	448	217	98	85	19	16	77	6	23
1886	389	185	78	76	20	10	67	4	21
1885	374	183	82	77	19	5	62	3	20
1884	355	166	77	66	21	1	58	4	18
1883	383	186	82	77	26	(Z)	61	4	19
1882	378	170	76	71	24	(Z)	64	4	22
1881	340	150	60	64	25	—	61	3	20
1880	301	120	53	42	25	—	56	2	19

See footnotes at end of chart.

Series M 13-37.   Value of Mineral Products, in Current Dollars: 1880 to 1990—Cont'd.

(In millions of dollars)

| Year | Nonmetals (except fuels)—Cont'd. | | | | | | Metals | | | | | | |
| | Sand and gravel [5] | Stone (incl. slate) [5] | Phosphate rock | Salt | Sulphur | Total [1] | Iron ore | Copper | Lead | Zinc | Gold | Silver | Molybdenum |
	25	26	27	28	29	30	31	32	33	34	35	36	37
1990	3,686	5,591	1,075	827	395	12,428	1,741	4,310	481	847	3,610	336	346
1989	3,659	5,326	1,083	777	379	11,868	1,840	4,324	356	499	3,269	355	427
1988	3,514	5,558	888	680	431	10,209	1,717	3,764	315	324	2,831	349	271
1987	3,367	5,439	793	684	387	7,447	1,503	2,262	247	200	2,216	280	179
1986	3,107	4,228	897	665	509	5,817	1,473	1,671	165	170	1,377	189	241
1985	2,812	4,225	1,237	740	574	5,269	2,077	1,633	174	202	771	242	348
1984	2,621.2	3,910.5	1,182.2	675.1	546.1	5,977	(NA)	1,608.4	181.3	270.8	742.5	361.8	326.8
1983	2,270.2	3,474.8	1,021.1	597.1	414.2	5,837	1,938.5	1,751.5	214.7	251.2	829.5	496.7	166.6
1982	1,997.8	3,056.0	950.3	671.4	434.7	5,517	1,491.7	1,840.9	288.6	257.1	551.0	320.0	504.1
1981	2,260.3	3,275.4	1,438.0	637.6	715.7	8,842	2,914.7	2,886.4	350.8	306.9	633.9	427.9	945.5
1980	2,289.0	3,394.0	1,257.0	656.0	721.0	8,921.0	2,544	2,667	515	262	594	667	1,344
1979	2,427.0	3,399.0	1,045.7	538.4	449.4	8,519.1	2,814	2,955.7	609.9	219.8	298.3	422.0	871.1
1978	2,302.0	2,885.7	928.8	499.3	279.9	6,296.0	2,388	1,990.3	393.5	206.9	193.3	212.7	607.9
1977	2,028.0	2,456.9	821.7	451.6	294.7	5,228.0	1,417.4	2,009.3	363.8	309.3	163.2	176.3	450.4
1976	1,774.0	2,221.0	949.4	431.0	300.0	5,681.3	1,860.1	2,235.0	281.6	358.5	131.3	149.3	333.5
1975	1,340.3	2,120.3	1,122.2	368.1	304.8	4,914.9	1,620.6	1,814.8	267.2	366.1	169.9	154.4	259.3
1974	1,451.1	2,186.2	501.4	360.8	241.1	5,562.0	1,386.4	2,469.0	208.7	359.0	180.0	159.0	234.7
1973	1,359.4	1,990.5	238.7	306.1	138.6	4,362.0	1,163.7	2,044.3	196.5	197.0	115.0	96.8	217.7
1972	1,199.5	1,683.3	207.9	296.7	132.8	3,641.0	950.3	1,704.7	186.0	169.8	84.9	62.7	170.5
1971	1,148.9	1,601.3	203.8	303.6	118.2	3,406	891	1,583	159.6	161.8	61.6	64.2	164.9
1970	1,116	1,475	203	304	152	3,926	942	1,984	179	164	63	80	190
1969	1,070	1,425	209	288	177	3,332	929	1,468	152	162	72	75	174
1968	1,020	1,318	251	272	268	2,703	836	1,008	95	143	58	70	151
1967	981	1,240	266	251	252	2,333	818	729	89	152	55	50	134
1966	985	1,261	261	230	201	2,703	854	1,034	99	166	63	56	144
1965	957	1,204	193	216	165	2,544	801	957	94	178	60	51	121
1964	893	1,135	161	201	121	2,366	802	813	75	156	51	47	97
1963	847	1,068	140	185	99	2,002	678	747	55	123	51	45	91
1962	795	1,026	134	175	109	1,937	618	757	44	116	54	40	69
1961	751	947	131	160	120	1,927	651	699	54	107	54	32	88
1960	720	953	117	161	117	2,022	724	693	58	112	58	28	87
1959	729	912	99	156	123	1,570	514	506	59	98	56	28	65
1958	653	827	94	141	111	1,594	569	515	63	84	61	31	50
1957	600	825	88	149	124	2,137	866	654	97	123	63	35	68
1956	602	[6] 775	98	136	166	2,358	750	939	111	149	64	35	64
1955	536	[6] 715	75	123	177	2,055	749	745	101	127	66	34	67
1954	503	[6] 622	87	105	155	1,518	526	493	89	102	64	33	64
1953	374	489	77	78	150	1,811	790	532	90	125	69	34	52
1952	345	473	72	71	117	1,617	590	448	126	223	58	36	41
1951	330	448	65	70	112	1,671	630	449	134	249	61	36	36
1950	293	402	63	60	106	1,351	483	378	116	179	74	38	38
1949	246	352	51	54	86	1,101	378	297	130	149	62	31	19
1948	252	340	51	54	90	1,219	391	362	140	168	62	34	20
1947	213	298	47	52	85	1,084	318	356	111	153	64	32	15
1946	171	243	31	45	66	729	215	173	49	82	51	19	12
1945	129	185	24	44	61	774	244	185	46	80	33	21	24
1944	125	181	21	44	56	900	257	237	50	99	36	25	28
1943	153	189	19	42	47	987	269	258	52	102	49	29	38
1942	188	211	17	38	50	999	279	257	59	110	131	40	47
1941	147	203	16	34	54	890	250	228	54	98	209	51	26
1940	111	166	12	26	41	752	189	205	43	74	210	49	17
1939	106	165	12	25	36	631	159	148	40	51	196	44	22
1938	86	145	13	23	27	460	74	110	31	42	178	41	18
1937	97	152	13	24	44	756	208	202	52	72	168	56	21
1936	90	147	11	23	35	516	132	112	36	49	153	49	12
1935	62	91	11	22	29	365	83	63	25	36	126	33	7
1934	61	102	10	23	29	277	66	39	22	31	108	21	7
1933	53	84	8	22	30	205	64	29	19	26	65	8	4

See footnotes at end of chart.

Series M 13-37. Value of Mineral Products, in Current Dollars: 1880 to 1990—Cont'd.
(In millions of dollars)

	Nonmetals (except fuels)–Cont'd.						Metals						
Year	Sand and gravel [5]	Stone [5] (incl. slate)	Phosphate rock	Salt	Sulphur	Total [1]	Iron ore [1]	Copper	Lead	Zinc	Gold	Silver	Molybdenum
	25	26	27	28	29	30	31	32	33	34	35	36	37
1932	58	92	6	20	20	128	13	34	15	12	51	7	1
1931	86	141	9	22	25	287	74	95	29	22	50	9	2
1930	115	187	14	25	36	507	146	181	57	47	47	20	2
1929	133	214	13	27	44	802	197	353	85	81	46	33	2
1928	119	208	12	27	38	655	156	263	73	72	46	34	2
1927	116	210	11	25	38	622	151	221	84	74	45	34	2
1926	111	201	11	25	37	721	174	244	109	92	48	39	1
1925	108	187	12	26	29	715	161	238	114	84	50	46	1
1924	97	174	10	26	25	682	151	214	91	67	52	44	(Z)
1923	91	172	12	28	26	778	241	211	76	69	52	60	(Z)
1922	65	131	10	27	22	524	158	128	52	40	49	56	(NA)
1921	56	114	12	25	17	344	90	65	36	20	50	53	(NA)
1920	66	142	25	30	30	866	285	222	76	73	51	61	(Z)
1919	46	103	12	27	10	744	197	239	45	66	60	64	(Z)
1918	38	88	8	27	28	1,179	244	471	77	90	69	66	1
1917	35	88	8	20	24	1,228	238	515	94	119	84	59	(Z)
1916	30	84	6	14	12	1,107	182	474	76	151	93	49	(Z)
1915	23	80	5	12	5	677	101	243	48	114	101	37	(Z)
1914	24	83	10	10	6	446	72	153	40	35	95	40	(Z)
1913	24	90	12	10	6	538	131	190	36	38	89	40	——
1912	23	84	12	9	5	537	107	205	35	45	93	39	——
1911	21	83	12	8	5	432	87	137	35	31	97	33	——
1910	21	83	11	8	5	470	141	137	33	27	96	31	——
1909	18	77	11	8	5	439	110	142	30	25	100	28	——
1908	13	72	11	8	4	376	82	124	26	18	95	28	——
1907	14	77	11	8	5	501	132	174	37	26	90	37	——
1906	13	72	9	7	3	477	101	177	38	24	94	38	——
1905	11	69	7	6	3	392	75	139	29	24	88	34	——
1904	6	64	7	6	1	309	43	104	26	19	80	33	——
1903	1	64	5	5	1	309	66	96	24	17	74	29	——
1902	1	60	5	6	1	295	65	80	22	15	80	29	——
1901	——	52	5	7	1	299	49	101	22	12	79	33	——
1900	——	41	5	7	(Z)	319	67	101	23	11	79	36	——
1899	——	39	5	7	(Z)	272	35	97	18	15	71	33	——
1898	——	32	3	6	(Z)	213	22	65	15	11	64	32	——
1897	——	30	3	5	(Z)	193	19	59	14	8	57	32	——
1896	——	27	3	4	(Z)	185	23	50	11	6	53	40	——
1895	——	29	4	4	(Z)	161	18	41	10	6	47	36	——
1894	——	30	3	5	(Z)	136	14	34	10	5	40	31	——
1893	——	36	4	4	(Z)	158	19	36	12	6	36	47	——
1892	——	52	3	6	(Z)	186	33	40	14	8	33	56	——
1891	——	50	4	5	(Z)	184	32	36	15	8	33	58	——
1890	——	50	3	5	(Z)	187	35	41	13	7	33	57	——
1889	——	46	3	4	(Z)	164	33	31	12	6	33	47	——
1888	——	29	2	4	(Z)	164	29	38	13	5	33	43	——
1887	——	28	2	4	(Z)	153	34	25	13	5	33	41	——
1886	——	22	2	5	(Z)	138	28	18	12	4	35	39	——
1885	——	21	4	5	(Z)	129	19	18	10	3	32	43	——
1884	——	21	2	4	(Z)	130	21	19	10	3	31	42	——
1883	——	22	2	4	(Z)	136	26	19	12	3	30	40	——
1882	——	23	2	4	(Z)	144	31	17	13	4	32	41	——
1881	——	24	2	4	(Z)	130	24	13	11	3	35	38	——
1880	——	22	1	5	(Z)	125	23	13	10	3	36	35	——

NA Not available.
Z Less than $500,000.
[1] Includes additional mineral products not shown separately; therefore, components frequently will not add to group totals.
[2] Excludes natural and slag cement.
[3] Value of clays used in cement is included here, but excluded from total nonmetals (series M 20) to avoid duplication.
[4] Not available separately; included with value of stone (series M 26).
[5] Beginning 1954, sand and sandstone (ground) included in series M 25 (sand and gravel) and M 26 (stone), respectively.
[6] Includes value of stone used for cement or lime, excluded from total nonmetals (series M 20) to avoid duplication.

Series M 76-92. Production and Calculated Consumption of Mineral Energy Fuels, Electricity from Water Power and Fuel Wood, in B.t.u.s: 1800 to 1990

(In trillions of British thermal units. A British thermal unit (B.t.u.) is the quantity of heat required to raise the temperature of one pound of water 1° F. at or near its point of maximum density)

	Production				Electricity from water power at prevailing central station equivalent	Calculated consumption				Electricity from water power at prevailing central station equivalent
	Mineral fuels						Mineral fuels			
Year	Total	Bituminous coal	Crude petroleum	Natural gas, wet		Total	Bituminous coal	Crude petroleum	Natural gas, dry	
	76	77	79	80	81	83	84	86	88	90
1990	67,600	22,600	15,500	18,100	2,900	81,400	19,000	33,600	19,400	2,900
1989	66,100	21,300	16,100	17,800	2,800	81,300	18,900	34,200	19,400	2,900
1988	66,000	20,700	17,300	17,500	2,300	80,200	18,800	34,200	18,600	2,600
1987	64,800	20,100	17,700	17,100	2,600	76,800	18,000	32,900	17,700	3,100
1986	64,200	19,500	18,400	16,500	3,000	74,200	17,300	32,200	16,700	3,400
1985	64,800	19,300	19,000	16,900	2,900	73,900	17,500	30,900	17,800	3,400
1984	65,800	19,700	18,900	17,900	3,300	74,100	17,100	31,100	18,500	3,800
1983	61,200	17,300	18,400	16,500	3,500	70,500	15,900	30,100	17,400	3,900
1982	63,900	18,600	18,300	18,300	3,300	70,800	15,300	30,200	18,500	3,600
1981	64,400	18,400	18,200	19,700	2,700	74,000	16,000	31,900	19,900	3,100
1980	64,800	18,600	18,200	19,900	2,900	76,000	15,400	34,200	20,400	3,100
1979	63,900	17,700	18,100	20,100	3,000	79,000	15,100	37,100	20,700	3,200
1978	61,200	15,000	18,400	19,500	3,000	78,200	13,900	38,000	20,000	3,200
1977	60,300	15,900	17,500	19,600	2,300	76,400	14,000	37,200	19,900	2,500
1976	66,100	15,900	17,300	19,500	3,000	74,500	13,700	35,200	20,400	3,100
1975	59,900	15,000	17,700	19,600	3,200	70,500	12,700	32,700	19,900	3,200
1974	61,200	14,500	18,600	21,200	3,200	72,800	12,900	33,500	21,700	3,300
1973	62,100	14,000	19,500	22,200	2,900	74,300	13,000	34,800	22,500	3,000
1972	62,800	14,500	20,000	22,200	2,900	71,600	12,500	33,000	22,700	2,900
1971	61,808	13,933	19,559	24,871	3,224	69,010	12,375	28,049	25,177	3,224
1970	59,174	15,001	19,772	24,154	2,630	64,565	12,712	22,367	22,029	2,650
1969	55,947	13,957	18,886	22,838	2,648	62,174	12,509	21,796	21,020	2,659
1968	54,096	13,664	18,593	21,548	2,349	59,291	12,401	21,091	19,580	2,342
1967	52,402	13,904	18,100	20,087	2,347	55,841	11,982	20,208	18,250	2,344
1966	49,745	13,507	16,925	18,984	2,062	54,282	12,205	19,315	17,393	2,073
1965	46,977	13,017	15,930	17,652	2,059	51,247	11,580	18,506	16,098	2,058
1964	45,683	12,418	15,691	17,138	1,886	49,298	10,899	18,194	15,648	1,907
1963	44,188	11,712	15,741	16,271	1,768	47,507	10,353	18,174	14,843	1,767
1962	42,071	10,782	15,495	15,365	1,816	45,577	9,826	17,822	14,121	1,821
1961	40,627	10,308	15,185	14,691	1,656	43,621	9,502	17,348	13,228	1,680
1960	39,939	10,662	14,664	14,135	1,608	42,906	9,693	16,861	12,699	1,657
1959	39,128	10,581	14,662	13,361	1,551	41,547	9,332	16,686	11,990	1,591
1958	37,599	10,663	14,154	12,244	1,592	40,058	9,366	16,250	10,995	1,636
1957	40,675	12,800	15,346	11,885	1,422	40,154	10,640	16,960	10,416	1,551
1956	40,343	13,013	15,344	11,252	1,435	40,213	11,142	16,994	9,834	1,487
1955	37,722	12,080	14,445	10,532	1,360	38,296	10,941	15,956	9,232	1,407
1954	33,916	10,262	13,427	9,488	1,360	34,875	9,512	14,830	8,548	1,388
1953	35,554	11,981	13,671	9,116	1,413	36,147	11,182	14,912	8,156	1,439
1952	35,249	12,231	13,282	8,705	1,466	34,962	10,971	14,248	7,760	1,496
1951	36,209	13,982	13,037	8,106	1,424	35,321	12,285	13,867	7,248	1,454
1950	32,937	13,527	11,449	6,841	1,415	32,552	11,900	12,304	6,150	1,440
1949	29,151	11,472	10,683	5,911	1,425	30,039	11,673	11,402	5,289	1,449
1948	34,490	15,707	11,717	5,615	1,369	32,487	13,622	12,085	5,033	1,393
1947	33,758	16,522	10,771	5,012	1,296	31,709	14,600	11,065	4,518	1,326
1946	30,133	13,989	10,057	4,550	1,406	29,048	13,110	10,270	4,089	1,446
1945	30,891	15,134	9,939	4,423	1,442	30,055	14,661	10,199	3,973	1,486
1944	31,759	16,233	9,732	4,176	1,344	30,434	15,447	9,923	3,775	1,387
1943	29,575	15,463	8,733	3,839	1,304	29,095	15,557	8,538	3,481	1,347
1942	28,278	15,267	8,043	3,436	1,136	26,720	14,149	7,987	3,102	1,177
1941	26,198	13,471	8,133	3,162	934	25,650	12,893	8,343	2,851	975

See footnote at end of chart.

Series M 76-92. Production and Calculated Consumption of Mineral Energy Fuels, Electricity from Water Power and Fuel Wood, in B.t.u.s: 1800 to 1990

(In trillions of British thermal units. A British thermal unit (B.t.u.) is the quantity of heat required to raise the temperature of one pound of water 1° F. at or near its point of maximum density)

	Production					Calculated consumption				
	Mineral fuels				Electricity from water power at prevailing central station equivalent		Mineral fuels			Electricity from water power at prevailing central station equivalent
Year	Total	Bituminous coal	Crude petroleum	Natural gas, wet		Total	Bituminous coal	Crude petroleum	Natural gas, dry	
	76	77	79	80	81	83	84	86	88	90
1940	24,208	12,072	7,849	2,979	880	22,991	11,290	7,662	2,726	917
1939	21,753	10,345	7,337	2,763	838	20,717	9,854	7,327	2,539	872
1938	19,911	9,132	7,043	2,565	866	18,981	8,811	6,921	2,348	899
1937	23,093	11,673	7,419	2,684	871	21,846	11,286	7,004	2,468	905
1936	21,679	11,504	6,378	2,411	812	20,577	10,697	6,426	2,221	841
1935	18,997	9,756	5,780	2,136	806	18,276	9,336	5,799	1,974	831
1934	18,104	9,415	5,267	1,970	698	17,216	9,008	5,136	1,819	721
1933	16,985	8,741	5,253	1,733	711	16,171	8,323	5,143	1,600	729
1932	15,663	8,114	4,554	1,729	713	15,666	8,041	4,830	1,594	726
1931	18,331	10,011	4,936	1,869	668	18,107	9,743	5,304	1,715	692
1930	21,367	12,249	5,208	2,148	752	21,503	11,921	6,148	1,969	785
1929	28,852	14,017	5,842	2,118	816	22,909	13,612	5,894	1,942	847
1928	21,997	13,120	5,229	1,734	854	21,491	13,069	5,474	1,588	890
1927	22,424	13,565	5,227	1,598	776	21,013	13,095	5,027	1,465	815
1926	23,088	15,020	4,471	1,452	728	21,730	13,954	4,876	1,335	765
1925	20,939	13,625	4,430	1,314	668	20,198	13,079	4,641	1,212	701
1924	20,309	12,672	4,141	1,263	648	19,768	12,681	4,228	1,170	685
1923	22,524	14,792	4,248	1,113	685	20,958	13,598	4,419	1,032	727
1922	16,529	11,063	3,234	843	643	16,540	11,185	3,390	785	675
1921	16,666	10,897	2,739	732	620	15,754	10,266	3,016	682	656
1920	20,627	14,899	2,569	883	738	19,007	13,325	3,027	827	775
1919	17,441	12,206	2,195	802	718	16,792	11,688	¹ 2,159	793	766
1918	20,529	15,180	2,064	775	701	19,686	14,588	1,911	771	750
1917	19,787	14,457	1,945	855	700	18,842	13,835	1,755	850	755
1916	17,944	13,166	1,744	810	681	17,052	12,631	1,497	807	729
1915	16,163	11,597	1,630	676	659	15,385	11,134	1,411	673	691
1914	15,559	11,075	1,541	636	636	14,858	10,703	1,320	632	676
1913	16,927	12,535	1,441	626	609	16,074	12,034	1,210	620	645
1912	15,833	11,793	1,293	604	585	15,093	11,402	1,058	594	615
1911	14,763	10,635	1,279	551	565	14,027	10,245	1,040	544	597
1910	14,836	10,928	1,215	547	539	14,261	10,654	1,007	540	539
1909	13,587	9,949	1,062	517	513	13,018	9,685	844	511	513
1908	12,295	8,713	1,035	432	476	11,762	8,478	820	427	476
1907	13,917	10,343	963	437	441	13,390	10,079	781	432	441
1906	11,946	8,983	734	418	414	11,507	8,793	555	411	414
1905	11,386	8,255	781	377	386	10,983	8,091	610	372	386
1904	10,171	7,301	679	333	354	9,816	7,155	534	330	354
1903	10,205	7,408	583	319	321	9,924	7,315	449	317	321
1902	8,685	6,818	515	301	289	8,426	6,733	364	299	289
1901	8,316	5,917	402	283	264	7,996	5,808	250	281	264
1900	7,643	5,563	369	254	250	7,322	5,431	229	252	250
1895	5,467	3,540	307	147	—	5,265	3,511	168	147	90
1890	4,619	2,916	266	257	—	4,475	2,903	156	257	22
1885	3,063	1,880	127	82	—	2,962	1,883	40	82	—
1880	2,210	1,330	152	—	—	2,150	1,337	96	—	—
1875	1,494	856	51	—	—	1,451	862	11	—	—
1870	1,074	536	31	—	—	1,059	545	11	—	—
1865	645	324	14	—	—	642	358	10	—	—
1860	519	237	3	—	—	521	243	3	—	—
1855	417	198	—	—	—	421	205	—	—	—

See footnote at end of chart.

Series M 76-92. Production and Calculated Consumption of Mineral Energy Fuels, Electricity from Water Power and Fuel Wood, in B.t.u.s: 1800 to 1990

(In trillions of British thermal units. A British thermal unit (B.t.u.) is the quantity of heat required to raise the temperature of one pound of water 1° F. at or near its point of maximum density)

		Production Mineral fuels				Calculated consumption Mineral fuels				
Year	Total	Bituminous coal	Crude petroleum	Natural gas, wet	Electricity from water power at prevailing central station equivalent	Total	Bituminous coal	Crude petroleum	Natural gas, dry	Electricity from water power at prevailing station e...
	76	77	79	80	81	83	84	86	88	90
1850	216	106	—	—	—	219	110	—	—	—
1845	122	55	—	—	—	—	—	—	—	—
1840	64	35	—	—	—	—	—	—	—	—
1835	47	28	—	—	—	—	—	—	—	—
1830	23	17	—	—	—	—	—	—	—	—
1825	12	11	—	—	—	—	—	—	—	—
1820	9	9	—	—	—	—	—	—	—	—
1815	7	7	—	—	—	—	—	—	—	—
1810	5	5	—	—	—	—	—	—	—	—
1805	4	4	—	—	—	—	—	—	—	—
1800	3	3	—	—	—	—	—	—	—	—

[1] 1919 and earlier, includes the net imports of petroleum.

Series M 138-142. Crude Petroleum—Production, Value, Foreign Trade and Proved Reserves: 1859 to 1990

(In thousands of 42-gallon barrels, except as indicated)

Year	Production (138)	Average value at well per bbl. (139)	Estimated proved reserves, Dec. 31 (142)
1990	2,685,000	$20.03	26,300,000
1989	2,785,000	15.86	26,500,000
1988	2,979,000	12.58	26,800,000
1987	3,047,000	15.40	27,300,000
1986	3,168,000	12.51	26,900,000
1985	3,275,000	24.09	28,400,000
1984	3,250,000	25.88	28,400,000
1983	3,171,000	26.19	27,735,000
1982	3,157,000	28.52	27,858,000
1981	3,129,000	31.77	29,426,000
1980	3,146,000	21.59	29,800,000
1979	3,121,000	12.64	29,810,000
1978	3,178,000	9.00	27,804,000
1977	3,009,000	8.57	29,486,000
1976	2,976,000	8.19	30,942,000
1975	3,057,000	7.67	32,700,000
1974	3,203,000	6.87	34,250,000
1973	3,361,000	3.89	35,300,000
1972	3,455,000	3.39	36,339,000
1971	3,454,000	3.39	38,063,000
1970	3,517,450	3.18	39,001,000
1969	3,371,751	3.09	29,632,000
1968	3,329,042	2.94	30,707,000
1967	3,216,715	2.92	31,377,000
1966	3,027,763	2.88	31,452,000
1965	2,848,514	2.86	31,352,000
1964	2,786,822	2.88	30,991,000
1963	2,752,723	2.89	30,970,000
1962	2,676,189	2.90	31,389,000
1961	2,621,758	2.89	31,759,000
1960	2,574,933	2.88	31,613,000
1959	2,574,590	2.90	31,719,000
1958	2,448,937	3.01	30,536,000
1957	2,616,901	3.09	30,300,000
1956	2,617,283	2.79	30,434,649
1955	2,484,428	2.77	30,012,170
1954	2,314,988	2.77	29,560,746
1953	2,357,082	2.68	28,944,828
1952	2,289,836	2.53	27,960,554
1951	2,247,711	2.53	27,468,031
1950	1,973,574	2.51	25,268,398
1949	1,841,940	2.54	24,649,489
1948	2,020,185	2.60	23,280,444
1947	1,856,987	1.93	21,487,685
1946	1,733,939	1.41	20,873,560

Year	Production (138)	Average value at well per bbl. (139)	Estimated proved reserves, Dec. 31 (142)
1945	1,713,655	$1.22	20,826,813
1944	1,677,904	1.21	20,453,231
1943	1,505,613	1.20	20,064,152
1942	1,386,645	1.19	20,082,793
1941	1,402,228	1.14	19,559,296
1940	1,353,214	1.02	19,024,515
1939	1,264,962	1.02	18,483,012
1938	1,214,355	1.13	17,348,146
1937	1,279,160	1.18	15,507,268
1936	1,099,687	1.09	13,063,400
1935	996,596	.97	12,400,000
1934	908,065	1.00	12,177,000
1933	905,656	.67	12,000,000
1932	785,159	.87	12,300,000
1931	851,081	.65	13,000,000
1930	898,011	1.19	13,600,000
1929	1,007,323	1.27	13,200,000
1928	901,474	1.17	11,000,000
1927	901,129	1.30	10,500,000
1926	770,874	1.88	8,800,000
1925	763,743	1.68	8,500,000
1924	713,940	1.43	7,500,000
1923	732,407	1.34	7,600,000
1922	557,531	1.61	7,600,000
1921	472,183	1.73	7,800,000
1920	442,929	3.07	7,200,000
1919	378,367	2.01	6,700,000
1918	355,928	1.98	6,200,000
1917	335,316	1.56	5,900,000
1916	300,767	1.10	5,900,000
1915	281,104	.64	5,500,000
1914	265,763	.81	5,400,000
1913	248,446	.95	5,500,000
1912	222,935	.74	5,400,000
1911	220,449	.61	5,000,000
1910	209,557	.61	4,500,000
1909	183,171	.70	4,200,000
1908	178,527	.72	4,000,000
1907	166,095	.72	3,900,000
1906	126,494	.73	3,800,000
1905	134,717	.62	3,800,000
1904	117,081	.86	3,600,000
1903	100,461	.94	3,400,000
1902	88,767	.80	3,200,000

Year	Production (138)	Average value at well per bbl. (139)	Estimated proved reserves, Dec. 31 (142)
1901	69,389	$.96	3,000,000
1900	63,621	1.19	2,900,000
1899	57,071	1.13	2,500,000
1898	55,364	.80	—
1897	60,476	.68	—
1896	60,960	.96	
1895	52,892	1.09	—
1894	49,344	.72	—
1893	48,431	.60	—
1892	50,515	.51	—
1891	54,293	.56	—
1890	45,824	.77	—
1889	35,164	.77	—
1888	27,612	.65	—
1887	28,283	.67	—
1886	28,065	.71	—
1885	21,859	.88	—
1884	24,218	.85	—
1883	23,450	1.10	—
1882	30,350	.78	—
1881	27,661	.92	—
1880	26,286	.94	—
1879	19,914	.86	—
1878	15,397	1.17	—
1877	13,350	2.38	—
1876	9,133	2.52	—
1875	12,163	1.35	—
1874	10,927	1.17	—
1873	9,894	1.83	—
1872	6,293	3.64	—
1871	5,205	4.34	—
1870	5,261	3.86	—
1869	4,215	5.64	—
1868	3,646	3.62	—
1867	3,347	2.41	—
1866	3,598	3.74	—
1865	2,498	6.59	—
1864	2,116	8.06	—
1863	2,611	3.15	—
1862	3,057	1.05	—
1861	2,114	.49	—
1860	500	9.59	—
1859	2	16.00	—

CONSTRUCTION AND HOUSING

CONSTRUCTION AND HOUSING

Highlights

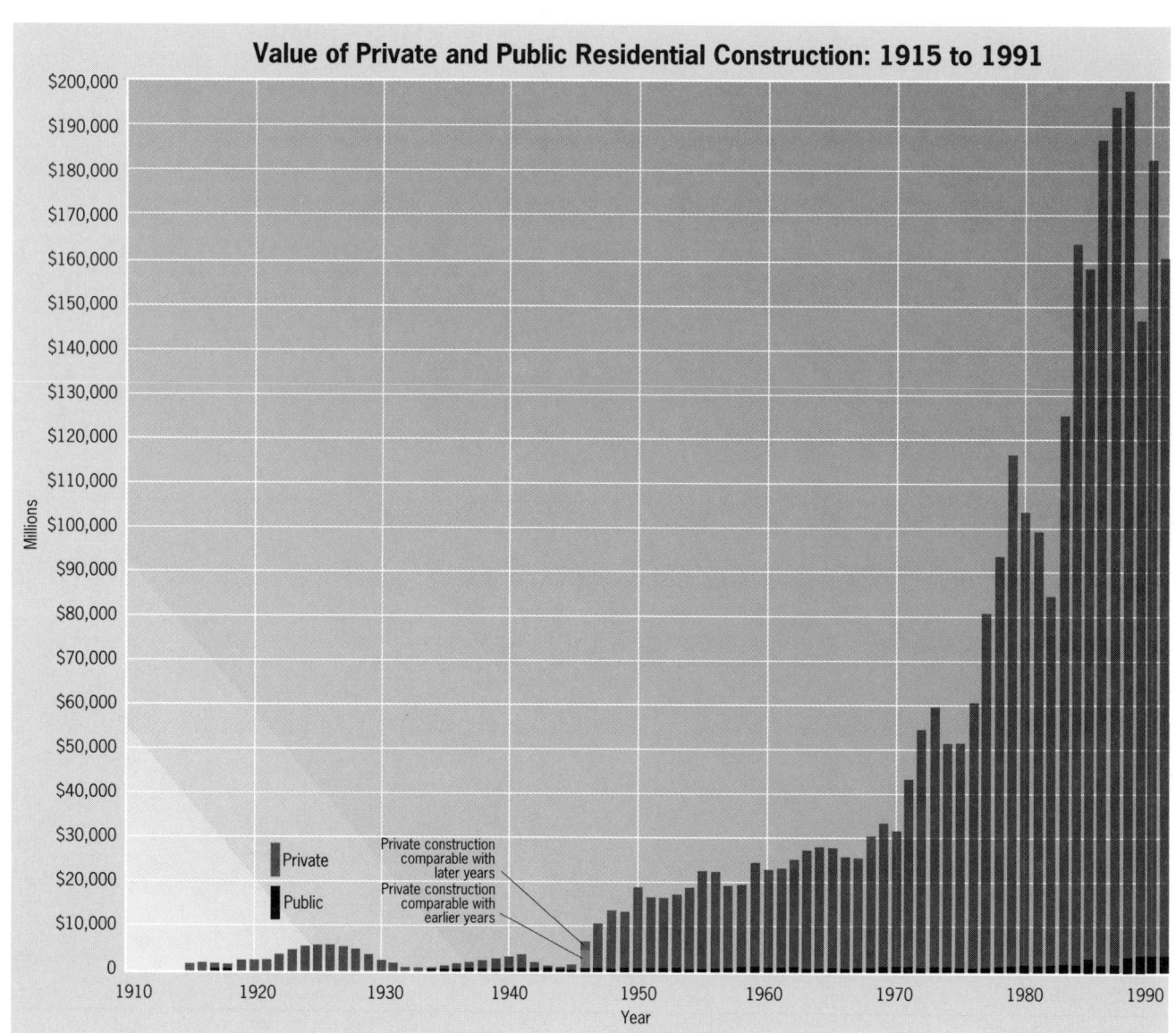

Value of Private and Public Residential Construction: 1915 to 1991

Legend:
- Private
- Public
- Private construction comparable with later years
- Private construction comparable with earlier years

Y-axis (Millions): $200,000 / $190,000 / $180,000 / $170,000 / $160,000 / $150,000 / $140,000 / $130,000 / $120,000 / $110,000 / $100,000 / $90,000 / $80,000 / $70,000 / $60,000 / $50,000 / $40,000 / $30,000 / $20,000 / $10,000 / 0

X-axis (Year): 1910 / 1920 / 1930 / 1940 / 1950 / 1960 / 1970 / 1980 / 1990

1 Housing and construction statistics were collected and published by the Department of Labor until 1959 when the Department of Commerce took over that responsibility. The Bureau of the Census issues a variety of publications providing data in these fields, including *Current Construction Reports, Housing Starts and Housing Completions, New One Family Houses Sold and for Sale, Price Indexes* *of New One-Family Houses Sold, Housing Units Authorized by Building Permits, Expenditures for Residential Upkeep and Improvements, Value of New Construction Put in Place,* and *Current Housing Reports*. Other sources include F.W. Dodge division of McGraw-Hill, National Association of Home Builders, and National Association of Realtors. Censuses of the construction industry were first conducted by the Bureau of the Census for 1929, 1935, and 1939; beginning in 1967, a census has been taken every five years, in years ending in 2 and 7.

2 From 1850 to 1930, the Bureau of the Census collected some housing data as part of its censuses of population and agriculture. Beginning in 1940, separate censuses of housing have been taken at 10-year intervals. Beginning in 1970, information on structural characteristics of housing have been included in the censuses.

3 In 1987, there were 544,200 construction establishments with 5.054 million workers and a payroll of $111.067 billion. The total value of construction work was $499.982 billion, of which the value added was $230.174 billion.

4 In 1990, residential buildings accounted for 39.7% of all new construction, private nonresidential buildings for 23.8%, and public buildings for 26.9%.

5 Condominiums are losing popularity. Only 60,000 condos were built in 1991 compared to 291,000 in 1984.

6 In 1990, 19% of new privately owned one-family homes had no mortgage at all.

7 The average floor area of a new one-family home is 2,075 square feet; 48% have one floor, 47% have two or more, and 5% are split level; 27% have four or more bedrooms and 14% two or fewer; 60% are heated with gas, 32% with electricity, and 4% with oil; 33.9% have central air conditioning; 63% have one or more fireplaces; and 81% have garages.

8 The nationwide median sale price of a one-family home rose from $23,400 in 1970 to $120,000 in 1990. By region, it rose from $30,300 to $155,400 in the Northeast, from $24,400 to $110,000 in the Midwest, from $29,300 to $100,000 in the South, and from $24,000 to $142,300 in the West.

9 In 1991, the most expensive metropolitan areas for one-family homes were Honolulu ($353,800), San Francisco ($256,600), Anaheim-Santa Ana ($239,700), Los Angeles-Long Beach ($214,900), and New York-Northern New Jersey-Long Island ($173,500). The least expensive metro areas were Oklahoma City ($57,000), San Antonio ($64,900), Tulsa and Louisville ($65,400), Omaha ($66,500), Des Moines ($68,200), and Baton Rouge ($69,400).

10 The median rent nationwide in 1990 was $374. It was below average in Midwest and South ($319 and $324 respectively), and higher than average in the Northeast and West ($432 and $473 respectively); 4.1% of all apartments had a monthly rent of $1,000 or more.

11 Between 1980 and 1990, the median value of homes fell in 30 states. The highest increases among the other 20 states were in Massachusetts (111.7%), New York (81.8%), Rhode Island (79.7%), and Connecticut (70.6%).

12 In 1990, only 75.1% of homes had access to public sewers and 84.7% to public water supply.

13 Americans spent $106.773 billion on home improvements and maintenance and repairs in 1990, compared to $14.770 billion in 1970.

14 In 1990, twenty-one major U.S. cities had a combined office space supply of 2,236 billion sq. feet of which 447.1 million sq. feet are available for lease. The cities with the highest rates of vacancy for existing office space were: New Orleans (26.9%), Dallas (24.8%), Houston (24%), Denver (23.7%), San Diego (22.7%), and St. Louis (21.6%).

15 In 1990, 41.9% of all home buyers were first-time buyers. Their average monthly mortgage payment was $1,127, or 33.8% of their income.

Series N 1-29. Value of New Private and Public Construction Put in Place: 1915 to 1991

(In millions of dollars)

| | | | | | Private | | | |
| | | | Residential buildings (including farm) | | | Nonresidential buildings (excluding farm)[4] | | |
Year	Total new construction	Total[1]	Total[2]	New housing units[2]	Additions and alterations[3]	Total[2]	Industrial	Total public utilities[2][5]
	1	2	3	4	5	7	8	12
1991	404,692	295,736	160,961	110,816	—	96,763	21,709	—
1990	446,434	337,777	182,856	127,987	54,869	117,971	23,848	30,953
1989	443,721	345,417	196,551	139,202	57,349	113,988	20,410	29,881
1988	432,223	337,441	198,101	138,947	59,154	106,994	16,452	27,949
1987	397,720	320,106	194,656	139,915	54,741	91,994	13,707	28,730
1986	387,042	315,313	187,148	133,192	53,956	91,171	13,747	32,648
1985	377,366	299,543	158,474	114,662	43,812	103,455	17,116	32,692
1984	328,641	270,977	153,849	113,826	40,023	81,147	13,745	30,915
1983	281,266	227,494	125,521	94,649	30,872	65,675	12,861	31,579
1982	246,568	192,855	84,676	57,001	27,675	69,355	17,343	33,864
1981	260,160	203,611	99,241	69,424	29,817	64,695	17,030	33,795
1980	252,753	194,285	100,381	69,629	30,752	55,431	13,837	31,949
1979	252,411	200,720	116,444	89,272	27,172	49,505	14,950	27,732
1978	205,457	159,556	93,424	75,808	16,349	36,293	10,994	23,302
1977	173,975	135,801	80,956	65,749	14,209	28,695	7,712	20,272
1976	151,054	111,931	60,520	47,277	12,308	26,091	7,183	20,301
1975	144,311	102,610	51,581	36,317	15,264	27,545	8,018	18,684
1974	138,501	100,166	50,376	40,644	8,045	29,637	7,902	16,624
1973	137,917	105,412	59,727	50,087	7,274	27,584	6,243	15,185
1972	124,077	93,893	54,288	44,879	7,420	24,036	4,676	13,196
1971	109,950	80,079	43,267	35,066	6,807	22,749	5,423	11,783
1970	94,855	66,759	31,864	24,272	6,234	21,417	6,538	11,020
1969	93,917	65,953	33,200	25,941	5,882	21,155	6,783	9,535
1968	87,093	59,488	30,565	24,030	5,297	18,164	6,021	8,969
1967	78,082	52,546	25,568	18,985	5,317	17,589	(NA)	7,603
1966	76,414	52,407	25,715	19,352	4,941	18,279	(NA)	6,803
1965	73,747	51,685	27,934	21,721	4,736	16,509	(NA)	5,788
1964	67,675	47,292	28,010	21,786	(NA)	12,955	3,565	5,031
1963	64,812	45,455	27,874	21,735	4,798	11,646	2,906	4,667
1962	60,205	42,336	25,150	19,443	4,484	11,617	2,842	4,330
1961	56,445	39,297	23,107	17,074	4,973	10,734	2,780	4,335
1960	54,738	38,875	22,975	17,279	4,831	10,149	2,851	4,621
1959*	55,392	39,322	[6] 24,251	[6] 19,233	4,253	8,859	2,106	4,521
1958	50,047	34,590	[6] 19,789	[6] 15,445	3,711	8,675	2,382	4,688
1957	49,139	35,080	19,543	15,273	3,769	9,556	3,557	4,908
1956	47,601	34,869	20,707	16,672	3,588	8,818	3,084	4,361
1955	46,519	34,804	22,409	18,774	3,296	7,611	2,399	3,770
1954	41,380	29,668	18,759	15,503	2,960	6,250	2,030	3,685
1953	39,136	27,894	17,213	14,030	2,916	5,680	2,229	3,973
1952	36,828	26,049	16,468	13,516	2,767	5,014	2,320	3,533
1951	35,435	26,180	16,546	13,872	2,484	5,279	2,117	3,357
1950	33,575	26,709	18,768	16,193	2,400	3,904	1,062	3,045
1949	26,722	20,453	13,111	10,726	2,200	3,383	972	2,994
1948	26,078	21,374	13,830	11,208	2,467	3,765	1,397	2,776
1947	20,041	16,422	10,404	8,319	1,960	3,243	1,702	2,126
1946 [7]	14,308	12,077	6,656	5,204	1,307	3,362	1,689	1,255
1946 [8]	12,737	10,375	4,752	3,300	1,307	3,341	1,689	1,374
1945	5,809	3,411	1,376	820	516	1,020	642	827
1944	5,259	2,186	923	678	220	351	208	725
1943	8,301	1,979	1,006	831	160	233	156	570
1942	14,075	3,415	1,850	1,575	225	635	346	786
1941	11,957	6,206	3,692	3,222	375	1,482	801	872

See footnotes at end of chart.

Series N 1-29. Value of New Private and Public Construction Put in Place: 1915 to 1991—Cont'd.

(In millions of dollars)

Year	Total new construction	Total [1]	Private Residential buildings (including farm)			Private Nonresidential buildings (excluding farm) [4]		Total public utilities [2][5]
			Total [2]	New housing units [2]	Additions and alterations [3]	Total [2]	Industrial	
	1	2	3	4	5	7	8	12
1940	8,682	5,054	3,130	2,705	335	1,025	442	771
1939	8,198	4,389	2,786	2,376	320	786	254	683
1938	6,980	3,560	2,069	1,699	295	764	232	605
1937	6,999	3,903	1,975	1,575	320	1,085	492	705
1936	6,497	2,981	1,641	1,286	295	713	266	518
1935	4,232	1,999	1,071	771	250	472	158	363
1934	3,720	1,509	661	416	200	456	191	326
1933	2,879	1,231	499	319	145	406	176	261
1932	3,538	1,676	654	509	105	502	74	467
1931	6,427	3,768	1,624	1,379	175	1,099	221	946
1930	8,741	5,883	2,182	1,677	305	2,003	532	1,527
1929	10,793	8,307	3,772	3,187	340	2,694	949	1,578
1928	11,641	9,156	4,926	4,355	315	2,573	802	1,372
1927	12,034	9,625	5,320	4,700	290	2,534	696	1,450
1926	12,082	9,938	5,737	5,057	270	2,513	727	1,415
1925	11,439	9,301	5,656	5,051	250	2,060	513	1,302
1924	10,407	8,506	5,193	4,708	230	1,675	460	1,356
1923	9,332	7,710	4,542	4,102	210	1,697	549	1,191
1922	7,647	5,963	3,479	3,074	200	1,457	467	787
1921	6,004	4,440	2,203	1,893	185	1,434	574	604
1920	6,749	5,397	2,281	1,976	175	1,964	1,099	771
1919	6,296	4,320	2,123	1,918	130	1,082	621	673
1918	5,118	2,880	1,118	963	110	731	449	697
1917	4,569	3,290	1,389	1,199	125	800	364	788
1916	3,849	3,141	1,529	1,324	145	716	262	658
1915	3,262	2,543	1,329	1,149	140	478	197	549

See footnotes at end of chart.

Series N 1-29. Value of New Private and Public Construction Put in Place: 1915 to 1991—Cont'd.

(In millions of dollars)

| Year | Total [1] | Residential | Public Nonresidential buildings | | | | | |
| | | | Industrial | Educational | Military facilities | Highways, roads and streets | Sewer and water systems | Conservation and development |
	19	20	22	23	25	26	27	28
1991	109,156	3,544	1,828	23,247	1,849	29,041	15,196	5,347
1990	108,657	3,733	1,433	20,566	2,732	30,593	15,376	4,718
1989	98,305	3,621	1,300	17,012	3,520	28,174	13,404	4,989
1988	94,782	3,276	1,413	14,397	3,579	29,228	12,818	4,739
1987	77,614	1,519	1,457	8,838	4,324	25,340	12,437	5,162
1986	71,729	1,456	1,657	8,440	3,867	22,970	11,475	4,646
1985	77,823	2,893	1,968	9,329	3,235	23,741	9,540	5,144
1984	53,772	1,636	1,828	5,557	2,839	18,771	8,862	4,654
1983	53,713	1,700	1,809	5,374	2,544	17,199	7,343	4,820
1982	56,549	1,658	1,632	5,927	2,205	16,164	8,431	5,027
1981	58,468	1,722	1,655	6,737	1,964	16,799	8,939	5,300
1980	58,468	1,648	1,441	8,050	1,880	17,225	10,437	5,090
1979	51,690	1,211	1,112	6,903	1,647	14,895	9,788	4,587
1978	45,902	1,053	1,184	6,264	1,502	10,712	9,426	4,457
1977	38,174	908	1,070	5,459	1,429	9,380	7,184	3,862
1976	39,123	720	905	6,342	1,630	9,743	6,972	3,742
1975	41,702	754	687	7,760	1,389	11,902	6,566	3,257
1974	38,334	1,006	766	7,310	1,185	12,065	4,062	2,741
1973	32,505	941	606	6,647	1,166	10,505	2,022	2,313
1972	30,184	875	534	5,720	1,087	10,420	2,778	2,172
1971	29,871	1,136	572	5,564	901	10,658	2,825	2,095
1970	28,096	1,107	499	5,619	718	9,981	2,638	1,908
1969	27,964	1,047	518	5,868	879	9,250	2,680	1,783
1968	27,605	746	519	6,061	808	9,320	3,065	1,973
1967	25,536	709	408	5,988	695	8,591	2,328	2,124
1966	24,007	655	369	5,333	727	8,405	2,366	2,194
1965	22,062	603	368	4,284	830	7,550	2,641	2,019
1964	20,383	567	403	3,970	910	7,133	2,281	1,750
1963	19,357	531	440	3,477	1,179	7,084	1,829	1,694
1962	17,869	938	422	2,984	1,266	6,365	1,754	1,523
1961	17,148	842	472	3,052	1,371	5,854	1,581	1,384
1960	15,863	716	407	2,818	1,366	5,437	1,487	1,175
1959*	16,070	962	368	2,656	1,465	5,761	1,467	1,121
1958	15,457	846	408	2,875	1,402	5,545	1,387	1,019
1957	14,059	506	473	2,825	1,287	4,934	1,344	971
1956	12,732	292	453	2,556	1,360	4,415	1,275	826
1955	11,715	266	721	2,442	1,287	3,852	1,085	701
1954	11,712	336	1,506	2,134	1,003	3,714	982	773
1953	11,242	556	1,771	1,714	1,290	3,021	883	892
1952	10,779	654	1,684	1,619	1,387	2,677	790	900
1951	9,255	595	974	1,513	887	2,355	775	912
1950	6,866	345	224	1,133	177	2,134	659	942
1949	6,269	359	177	934	137	2,015	619	852
1948	4,704	156	196	618	158	1,661	535	670
1947	3,319	200	96	287	204	1,344	351	424
1946 [7]	2,231	374	113	101	188	764	194	260
1946 [8]	2,362	374	113	101	188	895	194	260
1945	2,398	80	755	59	690	398	97	130
1944	3,073	211	1,230	41	837	362	79	163
1943	6,322	739	1,870	63	2,550	446	107	285
1942	10,660	545	3,437	128	5,016	734	169	357
1941	5,751	430	1,280	158	1,620	1,066	252	500

See footnotes at end of chart.

Series N 1-29.   Value of New Private and Public Construction Put in Place: 1915 to 1991—Cont'd.

(In millions of dollars)

| Year | Total [1] | Residential | Public Nonresidential buildings | | | Highways, roads and streets | Sewer and water systems | Conservation and development |
| | | | Industrial | Educational | Military facilities | | | |
19	20	22	23	25	26	27	28
1940	3,628	200	164	156	385	1,302	338	528
1939	3,809	65	23	468	125	1,381	371	570
1938	3,420	35	12	311	62	1,421	355	551
1937	3,096	93	2	253	37	1,226	311	605
1936	3,516	61	4	366	29	1,362	342	658
1935	2,233	9	2	153	37	845	175	700
1934	2,211	1	11	148	47	1,000	173	518
1933	1,648	——	2	52	36	847	95	359
1932	1,862	——	(1)	130	34	958	156	150
1931	2,659	——	(1)	285	40	1,355	270	156
1930	2,858	——	(1)	364	29	1,516	343	137
1929	2,486	——	(1)	389	19	1,266	253	115
1928	2,485	——	(1)	378	15	1,289	300	72
1927	2,409	——	(1)	367	12	1,222	312	63
1926	2,144	——	(1)	399	11	1,067	285	61
1925	2,138	——	(1)	400	8	1,082	278	73
1924	1,901	——	(1)	353	9	987	263	79
1923	1,622	——	(1)	346	16	805	203	65
1922	1,684	——	(1)	342	25	876	201	48
1921	1,564	——	(1)	274	49	853	178	52
1920	1,352	——	(1)	190	161	656	153	55
1919	1,976	14	(1)	——	1,089	429	124	39
1918	2,238	28	(1)	——	1,555	296	94	29
1917	1,279	——	(1)	——	608	320	91	27
1916	708	——	(1)	——	21	314	95	28
1915	719	——	(1)	——	17	302	106	36

* Denotes first year for which figures include Alaska and Hawaii, except that the nonfarm component of series N 4 should be interpreted as including estimates for Alaska and Hawaii beginning 1946.

NA Not available.

[1] Public industrial and commercial building not segregable from private construction, 1915-1932; amount believed negligible.

[2] Beginning 1946, figures not entirely comparable with those for earlier years.

[3] Prior to 1960, excludes farm housing.

[4] Exclude building by privately-owned public utilities. Beginning 1968, figures not comparable with earlier years because of revision in survey.

[5] Prior to 1959, includes local transit; thereafter, local transit included in "All other private."

[6] Excludes farms.

[7] Comparable with later years.

[8] Comparable with earlier years. Source: U.S. Department of Commerce and U.S. Department of Labor, *Construction Volume and Costs, 1915-1956*, a statistical supplement to *Construction Review*, pp. 2-9.

Series N 78-89. Value of Construction Contracts Awarded (Dodge), by Class of Construction: 1901 to 1991

(In millions of dollars. Includes new structures and alteration to existing structures. Figures for 1901-1909 are for New England states only; 1910-192 for 27 states except as noted; 1923-1924, for 36 states; 1925-1955, for 37 states; 1956-1969, for 48 states; thereafter, for 50 states.)

Year	Total	Nonresidential buildings Total	Commercial	Industrial	Educational and science	Hospital	Public buildings	Religious	Social and recreational	Miscellaneous	Residential buildings	Non-building construct
	78	79	80	81	82	83	84	85	86	87	88	89
1991	228,600	85,000	32,700	7,800	18,900	9,400	6,000	2,400	4,900	2,900	94,300	49,200
1990	246,400	95,600	45,100	8,400	16,600	9,200	5,700	2,200	5,300	3,100	101,000	49,800
1989	271,300	106,100	53,600	12,700	15,900	8,800	5,200	2,000	5,000	2,800	116,200	49,000
1988	262,200	97,900	51,600	9,500	14,100	8,200	4,400	2,200	4,700	3,200	116,200	48,100
1987	259,000	98,800	53,700	8,600	13,200	9,000	4,700	2,100	4,300	3,200	114,100	46,100
1986	249,300	91,600	52,400	7,300	11,700	7,900	3,200	2,100	4,200	2,800	115,600	42,100
1985	235,800	92,300	54,600	8,100	10,000	7,800	3,100	2,000	4,000	2,500	102,100	41,400
1984	214,300	82,100	48,200	7,900	8,500	7,400	2,700	1,700	3,300	2,400	95,300	36,900
1983	194,100	67,900	38,300	5,400	7,100	8,500	2,100	1,500	2,900	2,100	88,400	37,800
1982	157,100	64,600	32,300	9,600	6,800	8,000	1,900	1,200	2,800	2,000	55,000	37,500
1981	157,300	65,500	35,200	9,300	6,600	6,400	1,400	1,200	3,400	2,000	56,300	35,400
1980	151,800	56,900	27,700	9,200	7,400	5,400	1,600	1,200	2,700	1,700	60,400	34,500
1979	168,400	50,200	24,400	7,600	6,300	4,800	1,600	1,300	4,100	(3)	74,600	43,700
1978	159,900	45,000	20,600	9,200	5,700	3,800	1,500	1,200	3,000	(3)	74,900	39,900
1977	139,700	35,100	13,600	5,400	5,200	4,500	2,300	1,000	3,300	(3)	62,000	42,600
1976	110,100	30,000	10,200	4,500	4,900	4,500	2,100	900	3,000	(3)	44,200	35,900
1975	92,700	31,600	9,200	6,800	5,900	3,700	2,100	800	3,100	(3)	31,300	29,800
1974	93,700	33,200	11,800	5,600	6,300	3,800	2,100	800	2,800	(3)	33,600	27,000
1973	99,300	31,400	12,800	4,800	5,100	3,300	2,000	700	2,700	(3)	45,700	22,100
1972	88,885	—	11,369	3,005	4,760	3,516	1,490	640	1,237	1,003	42,882	18,983
1971	80,188	—	9,610	2,619	5,649	3,188	1,493	603	1,296	1,131	34,714	19,883
1970	68,294	24,455	9,056	3,664	5,253	2,811	1,007	575	1,137	952	24,837	19,001
1969	68,294	25,949	9,786	3,915	5,543	2,817	1,154	674	1,116	944	25,633	16,710
1968	61,732	22,513	7,645	3,768	5,347	2,114	1,112	778	954	795	24,838	14,382
1967	54,514	20,139	6,080	3,701	5,216	1,873	959	793	834	683	21,155	13,220
1966	50,150	19,393	5,835	3,623	4,939	1,721	939	825	855	656	17,827	12,930
1965	49,272	17,219	5,457	3,064	4,164	1,515	842	783	800	596	21,248	10,805
1964	47,330	15,522	4,572	2,970	3,554	1,625	789	814	599	598	20,565	11,244
1963	45,546	14,377	4,445	2,274	3,314	1,485	964	755	648	493	20,502	10,667
1962	41,303	13,010	4,216	2,086	3,060	1,079	677	811	704	377	18,039	10,255
1961	37,135	12,115	3,797	1,814	3,015	985	671	805	623	403	16,123	8,897
1960	36,318	12,240	3,725	2,114	3,005	832	679	789	631	464	15,105	8,973
1959	36,269	11,387	3,496	1,880	2,666	865	605	799	601	474	17,150	7,732
1958	35,090	10,948	3,197	1,400	2,907	879	655	746	500	664	14,696	9,446
1957	32,173	11,293	3,267	2,168	2,936	870	470	699	429	455	13,039	7,841
1956	31,612	11,208	3,140	2,381	2,883	678	428	681	422	595	12,862	7,542
1955	24,632	8,497	2,359	1,878	2,134	475	301	551	270	530	11,072	5,063
1954	20,596	7,110	1,816	1,274	2,063	519	249	486	252	452	9,344	4,142
1953	18,804	6,956	1,489	2,051	1,720	434	203	385	222	452	7,840	4,008
1952	18,070	6,695	979	2,558	1,472	444	233	318	153	538	7,963	3,412
1951	17,151	6,823	915	2,883	1,335	581	158	299	136	515	7,605	2,723
1950	16,592	5,182	1,209	1,142	1,180	655	124	336	261	274	8,832	2,578
1949	11,826	3,644	885	559	824	555	119	276	222	204	5,706	2,476
1948	11,121	3,666	975	840	725	405	84	245	232	161	5,299	2,155
1947	9,175	2,716	785	941	392	192	73	118	122	92	4,569	1,890
1946	7,490	2,716	773	1,317	221	131	25	68	93	88	3,142	1,631
1945	3,299	1,850	346	1,027	100	113	16	35	60	153	563	885
1944	1,994	899	81	473	69	59	12	12	33	161	348	746
1943	3,274	1,424	121	766	62	111	25	7	58	274	868	982
1942	8,255	3,897	302	2,228	148	185	102	24	101	808	1,818	2,541
1941	6,007	2,316	471	1,182	141	89	89	53	78	214	1,954	1,738

See footnotes at end of chart.

Series N 78-89. Value of Construction Contracts Awarded (Dodge), by Class of Construction: 1901 to 1991—Cont'd.

millions of dollars. Includes new structures and alteration to existing structures. Figures for 1901-1909 are for New England states only; 1910-22, for 27 states except as noted; 1923-1924, for 36 states; 1925-1955, for 37 states; 1956-1969, for 48 states; thereafter, for 50 states.)

| Year | Total | Nonresidential buildings | | | | | | | | | Residential buildings | Non-building construction |
| | | Total | Commercial | Industrial | Educational and science | Hospital | Public buildings | Religious | Social and recreational | Miscellaneous | | |
	78	79	80	81	82	83	84	85	86	87	88	89
1940	4,004	1,295	318	442	147	94	80	46	63	104	1,597	1,112
1939	3,551	966	247	175	201	83	110	38	82	29	1,334	1,251
1938	3,197	1,072	216	121	334	116	114	36	108	28	986	1,139
1937	2,913	1,156	297	314	223	82	105	37	84	15	905	852
1936	2,675	960	249	198	219	74	102	28	75	14	802	914
1935	1,845	681	165	109	168	47	98	24	55	16	479	685
1934	1,543	551	151	116	112	37	56	18	46	15	249	743
1933	1,256	417	99	128	39	37	51	18	27	19	249	589
1932	1,351	488	123	44	81	48	118	27	34	13	280	583
1931	3,093	1,141	311	116	223	121	181	53	99	36	811	1,141
1930	4,523	1,822	616	257	366	163	140	93	117	71	1,101	1,599
1929	5,751	2,425	929	546	370	152	121	106	147	55	1,916	1,410
1928	6,628	2,438	885	509	390	165	76	128	219	67	2,788	1,402
1927	6,303	2,439	933	376	369	163	80	157	261	102	2,573	1,291
1926	6,381	2,418	921	471	373	133	67	149	252	52	2,671	1,292
1925	6,006	2,202	872	327	419	111	55	153	253	12	2,748	1,057

| Year | Total | Nonresidential buildings | | | | Residential buildings | Non-building construction | Year | Total | Year | Total |
| | | Total ¹ | Commercial | Industrial | Public and institutional | | | | | | |
	78	79	80	81	83-87	88	89		78		78
1924	4,479	1,583	591	233	721	2,052	844	1914	775	1905	107
1923	3,992	1,456	518	313	601	1,736	801	1913	917	1904	97
1922	3,344	1,395	496	278	599	1,340	609	1912	923	1903	104
1921	2,355	998	332	153	461	879	479	1911	828	1902	119
										1901	120
1920 ²	2,564	1,394	444	555	345	570	600	1910	859		
1919 ²	2,590	1,213	406	498	266	849	517	1909	166		
1918	1,767	—	—	—	—	305	—	1908	112		
1917	1,691	—	—	—	—	355	—	1907	129		
1916	1,413	—	—	—	—	483	—	1906	125		
1915	978	—	—	—	—	418	—				

¹ Includes theaters, not shown separately.
² 25 states only. Totals for 27 states are 1919, 2,699; 1920, 2,635.
³ From 1973-1979, included in series N 26.

Series N 170.   Mobile Home Shipments: 1947 to 1991

Year	170 Mobile home shipments	Year	170 Mobile home shipments	Year	170 Mobile home shipments	Year	170 Mobile home shipments
1991	174,000	1979	279,900	1968	317,950	1957	119,300
1990	195,400	1978	279,900	1967	240,360	1956	124,330
1989	202,800	1977	275,700	1966	217,300		
1988	224,300	1976	249,600			1955	111,900
1987	239,200			1965	216,470	1954	76,000
1986	256,100	1975	229,300	1964	191,320	1953	76,900
		1974	332,000	1963	150,840	1952	83,000
1985	283,400	1973	580,000	1962	118,000	1951	67,300
1984	287,900	1972	576,000	1961	90,200		
1983	278,100	1971	497,000			1950	63,100
1982	234,100			1960	103,700	1949	46,200
1981	229,200	1970	401,190	1959	120,500	1948	85,500
		1969	412,690	1958	102,000	1947	60,000
1980	233,700						

Series N 186-191.   Low-Rent Public Housing Units, by Progress Stage, and War and Defense Housing and Veterans' Housing Units Available for Occupancy: 1941 to 1988

(Low-rent public housing units cover those units subsidized by U.S. Department of Housing and Urban Development under annual contributions contracts, including new, conventional and turnkey units and existing housing either acquired or leased. Includes Puerto Rico and Virgin Islands)

Year	186 Total low-rent public housing (1,000) [1]	Year	186 Total low-rent public housing (1,000) [1]	Year	186 Total low-rent public housing (1,000) [1]	Year	186 Total low-rent public housing (1,000) [1]
1988	1,448.8	1976	1,305.4	1964	714.3	1952	436.8
1987	1,443.0			1963	682.3	1951	404.8
1986	1,365.1	1975	1,316.7	1962	646.6		
		1974	1,314.0	1961	624.1	1950 [2]	302.1
1985	1,378.0	1973	1,323.6			1949	204.9
1984	1,524.9	1972	1,260.2	1960	593.3	1948	193.8
1983	1,483.3	1971	1,175.9	1959	585.2	1947	192.0
1982	1,432.2			1958	557.2	1946	—
1981	1,404.0	1970	1,155.3	1957	534.6		
		1969	1,034.7	1956	533.6	1945	—
1980	1,321.1	1968	923.7			1944	—
1979	1,332.9	1967	850.2	1955 [2]	489.7	1943	—
1978	1,224.8	1966	778.2	1954	455.7	1942	—
1977	1,308.8	1965	735.7	1953	455.2	1941	—

[1] As of December 31.
[2] Excludes units which have been sold to mutual housing associations, limited dividend corporations (PWA), and homestead associations on which HUD has mortgages for collection.

Series N 200-215. Value of Gross and Net Stocks of Residential Structures in Current Dollars: 1925 to 1991

(In billions of constant 1970 dollars)

Year	Gross stocks of residential structures	Private nonfarm		Farm	Private non-housekeeping	Mobile homes	Year	Gross stocks of residential structures	Private nonfarm		Farm	Private non-housekeeping	Mobile homes
	Total, all types	1-4 unit	5 or more unit					Total, all types	1-4 unit	5 or more unit			
	200	201	202	205	206	207		200	201	202	205	206	207
1991	7,869	6,345	974	167	32	129	1957	618.4	517.7	40.1	37.0	10.5	2.3
1990	7,543	6,075	933	163	32	124	1956	593.7	496.0	39.0	36.4	10.2	1.9
1989	7,152	5,744	916	164	32	103							
1988	6,662	5,337	854	159	30	101	1955	556.7	463.4	37.4	35.0	9.8	1.5
1987	6,376	5,100	819	159	30	94	1954	517.1	427.7	35.7	34.0	9.5	1.3
1986	5,817	4,643	743	153	28	93	1953	498.8	410.5	35.1	34.0	9.5	1.2
							1952	486.8	398.1	35.0	34.0	9.7	1.0
1985	5,706	4,566	701	150	27	104	1951	465.0	378.6	34.0	33.8	9.6	.8
1984	4,815	3,764	655	134	26	88							
1983	4,522	3,534	606	131	25	86	1950	428.4	347.8	32.1	32.2	9.3	.7
1982	4,292	3,353	569	129	25	82	1949	386.2	312.0	29.6	29.4	8.9	.6
1981	4,211	3,294	554	130	25	78	1948	369.3	297.8	28.5	28.5	8.8	.5
							1947	342.6	274.4	26.8	27.5	8.6	.3
1980	4,380	3,502	522	136	24	79	1946	286.7	228.8	22.9	23.3	7.5	.1
1979	3,494	2,735	452	114	22	66							
1978	3,135	2,455	402	106	20	57	1945	243.4	194.8	19.9	18.9	6.5	(Z)
1977	2,627	2,052	336	91	18	49	1944	226.2	181.3	18.5	17.2	6.2	—
1976	2,274	1,771	292	82	16	42	1943	211.5	168.2	17.2	16.8	5.8	—
							1942	195.1	155.4	15.8	15.8	5.5	—
1975	2,017	1,567	259	75	14	37	1941	179.3	144.3	14.7	14.2	5.1	—
1974	1,862	1,446	239	71	14	34							
1973	1,801	1,429	199	60	42	30	1940	162.9	131.3	13.5	12.9	4.7	—
1972	1,573	1,261	163	55	35	24	1939	151.4	121.7	12.6	12.3	4.5	—
1971	1,395	1,127	135	51	31	19	1938	146.4	117.5	12.1	12.3	4.3	—
							1937	142.3	114.0	11.8	12.1	4.2	—
1970	1,284.7	1,050.2	111.1	50.5	27.9	16.0	1936	132.2	105.9	10.9	11.3	4.0	—
1969	1,197.3	983.4	100.3	47.7	25.6	13.4							
1968	1,094.4	903.3	88.4	44.3	23.4	10.9	1935	121.8	97.5	10.0	10.6	3.7	—
1967	1,010.6	836.5	79.0	42.6	21.2	9.1	1934	119.3	95.4	9.8	10.5	3.6	—
1966	941.8	782.1	72.5	39.5	19.4	7.9	1933	114.2	91.2	9.4	10.2	3.4	—
							1932	109.1	86.9	9.0	9.9	3.3	—
1965	888.9	739.8	67.0	39.5	16.7	6.9	1931	122.2	97.1	10.1	11.3	3.7	—
1964	848.0	707.2	62.2	38.4	16.3	5.9							
1963	807.5	675.1	57.2	38.3	14.9	5.0	1930	140.5	111.6	11.5	13.2	4.2	—
1962	765.7	641.3	52.2	38.0	13.6	4.4	1929	147.4	117.1	12.0	14.0	4.3	—
1961	731.6	614.1	48.2	37.9	12.6	3.9	1928	143.6	113.8	11.3	14.4	4.1	—
							1927	136.3	108.1	10.1	14.4	3.7	—
1960	713.5	600.8	45.6	37.7	11.9	3.6	1926	131.6	105.3	8.2	14.6	3.5	—
1959	689.0	579.8	43.9	37.6	11.4	3.2	1925	127.8	101.7	8.2	14.8	3.1	—
1958	645.1	540.9	41.6	37.2	10.8	2.7							

Z Less than $0.05 billion.

Series N 216-231.   Mean Age of Stocks of Residential Structures: 1925 to 1991

(In years)

Year	Gross stocks of residential structures						Year	Gross stocks of residential structures					
	Total, all types	Private nonfarm		Farm	Private non-housekeeping	Mobile homes		Total, all types	Private nonfarm		Farm	Private non-housekeeping	Mobile homes
		1-4 unit	5 or more unit						1-4 unit	5 or more unit			
	216	217	218	221	222	223		216	217	218	221	222	223
1991	23.8	24.3	20.3	42.9	23.9	11.0	1957	29.4	28.4	29.5	47.3	20.7	3.4
1990	23.6	24.2	19.8	43.2	23.6	10.7	1956	29.6	28.6	29.3	47.0	21.2	3.5
1989	23.7	24.3	19.1	43.6	23.4	8.7							
1988	23.7	24.4	18.8	43.5	23.1	8.5	1955	30.0	29.0	29.0	46.8	21.6	3.8
1987	23.7	24.5	18.6	43.2	22.7	8.4	1954	30.5	29.6	28.6	46.6	21.8	4.0
1986	23.8	24.7	18.4	43.1	22.3	8.3	1953	30.9	30.1	28.2	46.4	21.9	3.8
							1952	31.3	30.6	27.8	46.3	21.8	3.6
1985	23.7	24.3	18.7	43.4	22.0	9.2	1951	31.6	31.0	27.4	46.2	21.6	3.3
1984	24.9	26.3	18.1	46.0	21.6	7.9							
1983	25.0	26.3	18.1	45.8	21.0	7.8	1950	32.1	31.5	27.0	46.2	21.3	2.8
1982	25.0	26.3	17.9	45.5	20.4	7.7	1949	32.8	32.4	27.0	46.2	21.1	2.3
1981	24.8	26.1	17.6	45.5	19.9	7.4	1948	33.2	32.9	27.0	46.3	20.8	1.6
							1947	33.7	33.5	26.9	46.5	20.4	1.2
1980	23.2	23.9	17.8	42.8	19.3	7.7	1946	34.1	33.9	26.6	46.5	20.0	.8
1979	24.6	25.9	17.1	45.4	18.7	6.7							
1978	24.6	25.9	16.9	45.6	18.1	6.4	1945	34.2	34.1	26.1	46.4	19.7	.5
1977	24.7	26.1	16.7	45.8	17.5	6.2	1944	33.6	33.5	25.3	45.6	19.1	—
1976	24.9	26.3	16.4	46.0	17.0	5.8	1943	33.0	32.9	24.5	44.8	18.4	—
							1942	32.5	32.2	23.7	44.1	17.7	—
1975	24.9	26.4	16.0	46.0	16.5	5.4	1941	32.1	31.8	23.0	43.5	17.2	—
1974	24.8	26.3	15.6	46.0	16.1	4.9							
1973	26.8	27.2	15.9	49.8	11.5	4.1	1940	32.0	31.7	22.4	43.0	16.7	—
1972	26.8	27.3	16.9	49.6	11.6	4.1	1939	31.9	31.6	21.9	42.4	16.3	—
1971	27.1	27.4	18.1	49.4	11.6	4.2	1938	31.6	31.4	21.4	42.0	15.8	—
							1937	31.3	31.0	20.8	41.6	15.4	—
1970	27.6	27.7	19.7	49.0	11.5	4.2	1936	30.9	30.6	20.2	41.2	14.9	—
1969	27.6	27.5	20.4	49.1	11.5	4.2							
1968	27.6	27.4	21.3	49.1	11.6	4.3	1935	30.4	30.2	19.5	40.8	14.3	—
1967	27.7	27.4	22.0	49.0	11.9	4.4	1934	29.9	29.6	18.7	40.3	13.7	—
1966	27.7	27.3	22.4	49.0	12.2	4.3	1933	29.2	28.9	17.9	39.7	13.0	—
							1932	28.5	28.2	17.0	39.0	12.4	—
1965	27.7	27.2	23.1	48.8	12.8	4.2	1931	27.8	27.5	16.1	38.4	11.7	—
1964	27.9	27.3	24.0	48.7	13.6	4.1							
1963	28.1	27.4	25.3	48.5	14.6	4.1	1930	27.3	27.0	15.4	37.8	11.0	—
1962	28.3	27.5	26.8	48.3	15.9	4.1	1929	26.8	26.5	14.8	37.4	10.7	—
1961	28.5	27.6	27.9	48.2	16.9	3.9	1928	26.6	26.2	14.7	37.0	10.4	—
							1927	26.6	26.2	15.0	36.6	10.3	—
1960	28.7	27.7	28.8	48.0	18.0	3.6	1926	26.8	26.3	15.8	36.3	10.4	—
1959	28.9	27.8	29.2	47.8	19.0	3.4	1925	27.0	26.4	16.7	35.9	10.8	—
1958	29.2	28.2	29.5	47.5	19.9	3.4							

Series N 238-245.   Occupied Housing Units and Tenure of Homes: 1890 to 1990

Year [1]	Total occupied housing units (1,000)	Tenure of homes			Year [1]	Total occupied housing units (1,000)	Tenure of homes		
		Owner occupied		Number of renter occupied (1,000)			Owner occupied		Number of renter occupied (1,000)
		Number (1,000)	Percent				Number (1,000)	Percent	
	238	**242**	**243**	**244**		**238**	**242**	**243**	**244**
1990	91,947	59,025	64.2	32,923	1973	69,337	41,653	64.4	24,684
1987	90,888	58,164	64.0	32,724	1970 [2]	63,450	39,885	62.9	23,565
1985	88,425	56,145	63.5	32,280					
1983	84,638	54,742	64.7	29,914	1960*	53,024	32,796	61.9	20,227
1981	83,175	54,342	65.3	28,833	1956 [3]	49,874	30,121	60.4	19,753
					1950	42,826	23,560	55.0	19,266
1980	80,390	51,795	64.4	28,595	1945 [3]	37,600	20,009	53.2	17,591
1979	78,572	51,411	65.4	27,160	1940	34,855	15,196	43.6	19,659
1978	77,167	50,283	59.4	26,884					
1977	75,280	48,765	59.2	26,515	1930	29,905	14,002	47.8	15,320
1976	74,005	47,904	64.7	26,101	1920	24,353	10,867	45.6	12,944
					1910	20,256	9,084	45.9	10,698
1975	72,523	46,867	64.6	25,656	1900	15,964	7,205	46.7	8,224
1974	62,562	42,157	67.4	20,405	1890	12,690	6,066	47.8	6,624

* Denotes first year for which figures include Alaska and Hawaii.
[1] Figures for 1956 are for December 31; figures for 1945 are for November 1; figures for decennial years 1890 to 1970 are for census dates.

[2] Farm-nonfarm breakdown will not add to total; "Total" figures were revised as a result of errors found after the tabulations were completed.
[3] These figures are not comparable with other years; based on sample surveys.

Series N 246-258. Housing Units Vacancy Rates, by Region: 1950 to 1991

(In percent. Annual averages, except as noted.)

Year	Homeowner vacancy rate					Rental vacancy rate				
	United States	Northeast	Midwest	South	West	United States	Northeast	Midwest	South	West
	249	250	251	252	253	254	255	256	257	258
1991	1.7	1.5	1.3	2.2	1.7	7.4	6.9	6.7	8.9	6.5
1990	1.7	1.6	1.3	2.1	1.8	7.2	6.1	6.4	8.8	6.6
1989	1.8	1.5	1.4	2.2	1.6	7.4	4.7	6.8	9.7	7.1
1988	1.6	1.6	1.2	1.9	1.6	7.7	4.8	6.9	10.1	7.7
1987	1.7	1.2	1.4	2.0	1.8	7.7	4.1	6.8	10.9	7.3
1986	1.6	1.0	1.5	2.1	1.6	7.3	3.9	6.9	10.1	7.1
1985	1.7	1.0	1.6	2.1	2.1	6.5	3.5	5.9	9.1	6.2
1984	1.7	.8	1.6	2.0	2.0	5.9	3.7	5.9	7.9	5.2
1983	1.5	1.0	1.5	1.8	1.8	5.9	4.0	6.1	6.9	5.2
1982	1.5	1.0	1.6	1.6	1.9	5.3	3.7	6.3	5.8	5.4
1981	1.4	1.1	1.4	1.3	1.7	5.0	3.7	5.9	5.4	5.1
1980	1.4	1.1	1.6	1.3	1.6	5.4	4.2	6.0	6.0	5.2
1979	1.1	.9	1.1	1.1	1.3	5.0	4.0	5.1	5.8	4.9
1978	1.0	.8	1.0	1.3	1.0	5.0	4.8	4.8	5.5	4.8
1977	1.2	.9	.9	1.7	0.9	5.2	5.1	5.1	5.7	5.0
1976	1.2	1.0	1.0	1.6	1.2	5.6	4.7	5.6	6.4	5.4
1975	1.2	1.0	1.0	1.5	1.5	6.0	4.1	5.7	7.7	6.2
1974	1.2	.8	1.0	1.5	1.5	6.2	4.2	6.1	8.0	6.2
1973	1.0	.7	.9	1.2	1.2	5.8	3.9	5.9	7.1	6.3
1972	1.0	.8	1.0	1.2	1.1	5.6	3.3	6.1	7.0	6.0
1971	1.0	1.0	1.2	2.0	1.9	5.4	3.0	5.7	7.3	5.7
1970	1.0	.8	1.0	1.2	1.1	5.3	2.7	5.8	7.2	5.6
1969	1.0	.8	.9	1.2	1.2	5.5	3.0	5.7	7.2	6.1
1968	1.1	.8	1.0	1.4	1.3	5.9	3.7	5.4	7.5	7.1
1967	1.3	.7	1.0	1.7	2.0	6.8	4.8	5.7	8.0	8.9
1966	1.4	.9	1.0	1.8	2.1	7.7	5.3	6.5	8.5	10.9
1965	1.5	1.0	1.2	2.0	1.9	8.3	5.6	7.2	9.0	11.9
1964	1.5	1.1	1.3	1.9	1.8	8.3	5.2	7.9	9.1	11.0
1963	1.5	1.0	1.4	1.9	1.9	8.3	5.1	8.7	9.2	10.2
1962	1.4	1.1	1.2	1.7	1.6	8.1	4.7	9.0	9.9	9.5
1961	1.4	1.1	1.2	1.7	1.3	8.7	4.9	9.3	10.4	10.7
1960*	1.3	1.0	1.2	1.6	1.4	8.1	4.9	8.3	9.5	11.0
1959	1.2	1.0	1.1	1.2	1.4	7.0	3.9	7.1	9.4	8.5
1958	1.2	1.0	1.4	1.0	1.2	6.5	3.8	7.3	7.9	7.5
1957	1.0	.7	.9	.9	1.3	5.6	3.4	5.4	6.7	7.4
1956	1.0	.9	.8	1.0	1.4	6.1	3.1	5.6	8.1	8.7
1950 [1]	.9	—	—	—	—	—	—	—	—	—

* Denotes first year for which figures include Alaska and Hawaii.   [1] As of April.

Series N 273-277.   Residential Nonfarm Mortgage Debt Outstanding, by Type of Property and Government-Underwritten Debt: 1925 to 1990

(In billions of dollars. As of December 31. FHA=Federal Housing Administration; VA=Veterans Administration)

Year	Total 1- to 4-family structures	Total 5-or-more unit structures	Year	Total 1- to 4-family structures	Total 5-or-more unit structures	Year	Total 1- to 4-family structures	Total 5-or-more unit structures	Year	Total 1- to 4-family structures	Total 5-or-more unit structures
	273	276		273	276		273	276		273	276
1990	2,710	307	1973	417	93	1956	99.0	14.9	1940	17.4	5.7
1989	2,430	303	1972	346	76	1955	88.2	14.3	1939	16.3	5.6
1988	2,201	291	1971	308	67	1954	75.7	13.5	1938	15.8	4.4
1987	1,963	279				1953	66.1	12.9	1937	15.5	4.5
1986	1,724	257	1970	280.2	58.0	1952	58.5	12.3	1936	15.4	4.6
			1969	266.8	52.2	1951	51.7	11.5			
1985	1,501	214	1968	251.2	47.3				1935	15.4	4.8
1984	1,334	185	1967	236.1	43.9				1934	15.6	5.1
1983	1,198	161	1966	223.6	40.3	1950	45.2	10.1	1933	15.4	5.7
1982	1,080	146				1949	37.6	8.6	1932	16.7	6.0
1981	1,065	136	1965	212.9	37.2	1948	33.3	7.5	1931	18.1	6.2
			1964	197.6	33.6	1947	28.2	6.6			
1980	965	142	1963	182.2	29.0	1946	23.0	6.1	1930	18.9	6.5
1979	891	128	1962	166.5	25.8				1929	18.9	6.0
1978	771	121	1961	153.1	23.0	1945	18.6	5.7	1928	17.9	5.4
1977	658	112				1944	17.9	5.6	1927	16.4	5.0
1976	561	105	1960	141.3	20.3	1943	17.8	5.8	1926	14.8	4.6
			1959	130.9	18.7	1942	18.2	5.8	1925	13.0	4.2
1975	495	101	1958	117.7	16.8	1941	18.4	5.9			
1974	450	100	1957	107.6	15.3						

MANUFACTURES

MANUFACTURES
Highlights

1 Manufacturing is defined as the mechanical or chemical transformation of inorganic or organic substances into new products or the assembly of component parts of products. Manufacturing activities are classified in the *Standard Industrial Classification (SIC) Manual* published by the Office of Management and Budget. First issued in 1939, it was revised in 1945, 1957, 1972, and 1987.

2 The basic source of data on manufactures has been the Census of Manufactures conducted by the Bureau of the Census, beginning in 1809. A census was taken at 10-year intervals thereafter to 1899 (with the exception of 1829), at five-year intervals from 1904 to 1919, and biennially from 1921 to 1939. It was suspended during World War II but resumed in 1947. Legislation enacted in 1948 provided for a Census of Manufactures every five years with annual sample surveys for interim years. The Annual Survey of Manufactures (ASM) is based on a sample of 55,000 establishments out of an approximate total of 200,000. The scope of the censuses has varied from one census to another. From 1849 to 1899, the minimum size limit of factories was output valued at $500 or more. It was raised to $5,000 or more for 1929 to 1937. Beginning in 1947, the criterion was employment of one or more persons at any time during the census year. However, these changes have not appreciably affected the historical comparability of the census figures except for the data on the number of establishments. There have also been numerous changes in the definition of manufacturing industries. When the changes result in the omission of an entire industry, the adjustments are generally carried back through the previous censuses. Furthermore, the treatment of non-production workers has not been consistent over the years. Personnel in manufacturing industries engaged in distribution and construction have been reported separately since 1939, but not before. Officers of corporations are included as employees, but not proprietors and partners of unincorporated firms, for whom no data have been collected since 1963. Another difference concerns value added in manufacturing. The standard formula for calculating value added by manufacture since 1958 differs from the one used for 1954 and previous years. Prior to 1958, value added by an establishment was calculated by subtracting the cost of materials, supplies, containers, fuels, electrical energy, and contract work from the value of shipments.

This was known as unadjusted value added. Beginning in 1958, the formula was changed to adjusted value added which includes two elements: (1) value added by merchandising, (the difference between the sales value and the cost of merchandise sold without further manufacture, processing and assembly); and (2) an adjustment in the net change in finished goods and work-in-process inventories between the beginning and the end of the year. This concept should not be confused with the National Income Originating in Manufacturing which is obtained by subtracting from the value of shipments not only the cost of materials, but also other costs such as depreciation charges, state and local taxes, allowances for bad debts, and purchases of services from nonmanufacturing enterprises (engineering and management consultants, advertising, telephone, insurance, royalties, patent fees, etc.). It is therefore a net concept of value added in manufacturing and generally exceeds the latter by about a third. The value added by manufacturing exceeded $1.4 trillion in 1990.

3 In 1989, manufacturing contributed slightly less than $1 trillion to the GNP with durable goods contributing $540.995 billion and nondurable goods $425.002 billion. The largest manufacturing sectors were chemicals ($98.763 billion), machinery other than electrical ($97.3 billion), electric and electronic equipment ($96.894 billion), food ($81.458 billion), printing and publishing ($68.236 billion), and fabricated metal products ($68.029 billion).

4 Of the 369,000 manufacturing establishments in 1987, 288,000 were single unit companies and 80,900 multiunit companies; 126,000 had 20 or more employees and 2,000 had 1,000 or more employees. By form of organization, 277,400 were corporations, 35,400 were individual proprietor-ships, and 13,200 were partnerships. The value added by manufacture in 1990 was $1.326 trillion, or 109,600 per production worker, $54.57 per production worker hour, and $4.88 per each dollar of workers' wages. Value of shipments in 1990 was $2.874 trillion or $237.5 per production worker. In 1990, new capital expenditures totaled $102 billion. By region, the North Central region had the highest share of value added with 29.8%, followed by the South (29.5%), the Northeast (23.7%), and the West (17%).

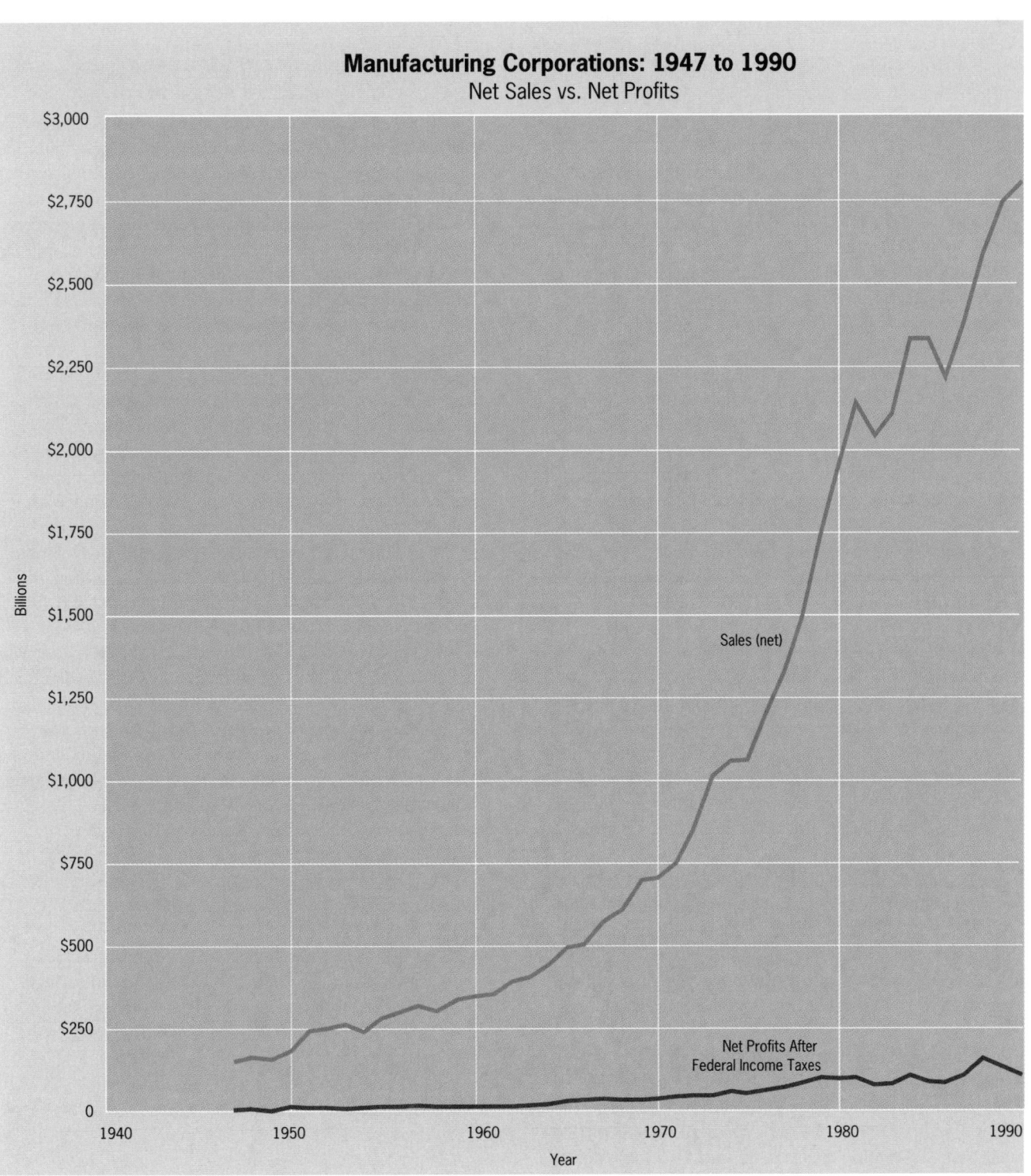

Manufacturing Corporations: 1947 to 1990
Net Sales vs. Net Profits

Sales (net)

Net Profits After
Federal Income Taxes

Billions

Year

5 In 1990, manufacturing corporations with assets over $250,000 had net sales of $2.811 trillion, net profits before taxes of $160 billion, and net profits after taxes of $112 billion. They retained $49 billion and issued $62 billion in dividends.

6 The U.S. share of world manufacturing exports fluctuated in the 1980s. From 16.8% in 1980, it dipped to 13.9% in 1987, rose to 17.1% in 1989 and then fell to 16.3% in 1990. The U.S. share is highest in machinery (20.2%) and lowest in basic manufactures (9.3%). Export-related shipments constitute 15.3% of all shipments and account for 14.7% of all employment.

7 Foreign direct investment in U.S. manufacturing totaled $159.998 billion in 1990. Highest foreign invest-ment participation was in the chemicals sector ($41.678 billion), followed by the machinery sector ($29.677 billion), food products sector ($22.875 billion), and primary and fabricated metals sector ($17.596 billion). The United Kingdom accounted for the largest share of investment ($52.955 billion), followed by the Netherlands ($24.446 billion), Germany ($15.216 billion), and Japan ($15.169 billion).

8 In 1989, the United States had 231 beer breweries producing 198 billion barrels (each of 31 gallons) worth $14.321 billion. Per capita beer consumption in 1987 was 23.7 gallons. In the same year, 119 distilled spirits produc-ers produced 75 million gallons of whiskey, or 1.6 gallons per capita. The production of still wines in 1987 was 677 million gallons (or 2.2 gallons per capita), and production of effervescent wines in 1989 was 30.9 million gallons.

9 The success of anti-cigarette campaigns was reflected in the decline in the per capita consumption of cigarettes from 4,000 in 1970 to 2,800 in 1990. However, total sales of cigarettes rose from 583 billion in 1970 to 710 billion in 1990. Cigars have become less popular. Only 1.9 billion were sold in 1990 compared to 8.4 billion in 1970.

10 The U.S. share of world raw steel production dropped sharply from 20.1% in 1970 to 11.6% in 1990. Compared to a production of 131.5 million tons in 1970, the United States produced only 98.9 million tons in 1990; imported 17.2 million tons; and exported 4.3 million tons.

11 In 1988, 47.2% of manufacturers used computer-aided design (CAD) or computer-aided engineering in fabrication and assembly operations, 55% used numeri-cally controlled machines, 38.7% used programmable controllers, and 32.1% used computer control on factory floor, 25.2% used automated sensor-based inspection or testing, and 5.7% used automated material handling.

12 In the mid-1980s, many predicted that robots were likely to revolutionize the workplace; however, by 1989, robots had lost much of their appeal to manufacturers. Production dropped from 5,466 units in 1985 to 2,217 in 1989 and the value of shipments from $275.7 million to $150.6 million.

13 The computer industry has displaced steel as the bellwether of U.S. industry, with revenues topping $50 billion in 1991. However, the industry is undergoing major structural changes. Mainframes and midrange computers declined both in unit shipments and sales revenues while personal computers and workstations gained enormously. In 1991, 3,800 mainframes and 340,800 midrange comput-ers were sold for $11.739 billion and $10.925 billion respectively compared to 6,100 mainframes and 396,400 midrange computers for $14.055 billion and $13.485 billion respectively in 1987. In 1991, 221,200 workstations were sold for $3.755 billion compared to 61,200 units for $1.391 billion in 1987. The growth of personal computers has been more dramatic. In 1991, 9.5 million units were sold for $27.7 billion compared to 1.11 million units for $3.143 billion in 1981. A total of 45.08 million computers are in use—22.38 million in homes, 20.33 million in workplaces, and 2.36 million in schools and colleges. Computer-related equipment also is in widespread use. It includes 27.3 million impact printers, 10.91 million modems, and 3.42 million nonimpact printers.

14 In 1989, the three fastest selling consumer elec-tronic products were all in the field of communications: telephone answering equipment (12.1 million), fac-simile machines (1.4 million), and cellular telephones (1.08 million).

Series P 1-12.   Manufactures Summary: 1849 to 1990

Year	Establishments Total	With 20 or more employees	Production workers engaged in manufacturing (1,000) [1]	Man-hours, production workers (mil.)	Total payroll (mil. dol.)	Value added by manufacture [2]	Capital expenditures; new (mil. dol.)	End-of-year inventories (mil. dol.)
	1	2	5	6	7	10	11	12
FACTORIES. EXCLUDING HAND AND NEIGHBORHOOD INDUSTRIES								
1990	—	—	12,100	24,300	532,000	1,326,000	102,000	393,000
1989	—	—	12,300	24,700	519,000	1,308,000	97,200	381,000
1988	—	—	12,400	24,800	503,000	1,262,000	80,600	362,000
1987	369,000	126,000	12,200	24,300	476,000	1,166,000	78,600	333,000
1986	—	—	11,800	23,200	451,000	1,035,000	76,400	311,000
1985	—	—	12,200	23,700	443,000	1,000,000	83,100	322,000
1984	—	—	12,600	24,600	429,000	984,000	75,300	330,000
1983	—	—	12,200	23,600	395,000	882,000	61,900	308,000
1982	358,000	123,000	12,400	23,500	380,000	824,000	75,000	307,000
1981	—	—	13,500	26,200	379,000	838,000	78,600	279,000
1980	—	—	13,900	26,700	350,000	774,000	70,100	262,000
1979	—	—	14,500	28,300	329,000	748,000	61,500	239,000
1978	—	—	14,200	27,700	299,000	657,000	55,200	209,000
1977	360,000	119,000	13,700	26,700	264,000	585,000	47,500	188,000
1976	—	—	13,100	25,400	233,000	511,000	40,700	170,000
1975	—	—	12,600	24,100	210,000	442,000	37,300	158,000
1973	—	—	14,200	28,100	193,000	404,000	27,000	125,000
1972	321,000	114,000	13,500	26,700	174,000	354,000	24,100	108,000
1971	—	—	12,900	25,300	156,000	314,000	20,900	102,000
1970	—	—	13,258	26,669	141,886	300,228	22,164	101,285
1969	—	—	14,358	28,600	142,645	304,441	22,291	98,206
1968	—	—	14,041	28,157	132,568	285,059	20,613	90,505
1967	305,680	107,138	13,955	27,838	123,481	261,984	21,503	84,406
1966	—	—	13,827	28,103	117,157	250,880	20,236	77,721
1965	—	—	13,076	26,568	106,643	226,940	16,615	68,009
1964	—	—	12,403	25,246	98,685	206,194	13,294	63,211
1963	306,617	99,352	12,232	24,509	93,283	192,083	11,370	59,913
1962	—	—	12,127	24,270	89,819	179,071	10,436	58,067
1961	—	—	11,779	23,289	83,677	164,281	9,780	54,744
1960	—	—	12,210	24,174	83,673	163,999	10,098	53,560
1959	—	—	12,273	24,444	81,204	161,536	9,140	52,552
1958	299,017	95,278	11,681	22,679	73,875	141,541	9,544	49,947
1957	—	—	12,839	25,208	76,315	147,838	12,144	—
1956	—	—	13,131	26,089	74,015	144,909	11,233	—
1955	—	—	12,954	25,898	69,097	135,023	8,233	—
1954	286,814	90,470	12,372	24,334	62,963	117,032	8,201	40,341
1953	285,000	—	13,501	27,066	66,493	121,659	8,048	—
1952	267,000	—	12,706	25,618	59,598	109,162	7,883	—
1951	262,000	—	12,509	25,264	54,742	102,086	7,782	—
1950	260,000	—	11,779	23,717	46,643	89,750	5,041	—
1949	—	—	11,016	21,770	41,482	75,367	5,067	—
1947	240,807	—	11,918	24,317	39,696	74,291	5,998	26,129
1939 [3]	173,802	—	7,808	—	[4] 12,706	24,487	—	9,632
1937	166,794	—	8,569	—	12,830	25,174	—	9,863
1935	167,916	—	7,204	—	9,565	18,553	—	—
1933	139,325	—	5,788	—	[5] 6,238	14,008	—	—
1931	171,450	—	6,163	—	—	18,601	—	—
1929	206,663	—	8,370	—	14,284	30,591	—	—
1927	187,629	—	7,848	—	13,123	26,325	—	—
1925	183,877	—	7,871	—	12,958	25,668	—	—
1923	192,096	—	8,194	—	12,997	24,570	—	—
1921	192,059	—	6,476	—	9,870	17,253	—	—

See footnotes at end of chart.

Series P 1-12.   Manufactures Summary: 1849 to 1990—Cont'd..

Year	Establishments Total	With 20 or more employees	Production workers engaged in manufacturing (1,000) [1]	Manhours, production workers (mil.)	Total payroll (mil. dol.)	Value added by manufacture [2]	Capital expenditures, new (mil. dol.)	End-of-year inventories (mil. dol.)
	1	2	5	6	7	10	11	12
1919	270,231	—	8,465	—	12,427	23,842	—	—
1914	268,436	—	6,602	—	5,016	9,386	—	—
1909	264,810	—	6,262	—	4,106	8,160	—	—
1904	213,444	—	5,182	—	2,991	6,019	—	—
1899	204,754	—	4,502	—	2,259	4,647	—	—
FACTORIES AND HAND AND NEIGHBORHOOD INDUSTRIES								
1899	509,490	—	5,098	—	2,596	5,475	—	—
1889	353,864	—	4,129	—	2,209	4,102	—	—
1879	253,852	—	2,733	—	—	1,973	—	—
1869	252,148	—	2,054	—	—	1,395	—	—
1859	140,433	—	1,311	—	—	854	—	—
1849	123,025	—	957	—	—	464	—	—

[1] The Bureau of Labor Statistics annual averages for employment in manufacturing indicates 1943 as the year of maximum employment, with 15,147,000 production workers.

[2] For 1849-1933, cost of contract work was not subtracted from value of products in calculating value added by manufacture. For 1935-1953, value added by manufacture represents unadjusted value added; beginning 1954, it represents adjusted value.

[3] Except as noted, figures have been revised by retabulation of returns to exclude data for establishments classified as manufacturing in 1939 but as nonmanufacturing beginning 1947. Value added by manufacture in 1939, prior to revision and on a basis comparable with prior years, was $24.7 billion.

[4] Figures revised on basis of estimates rather than by retabulation of 1939 reports. Estimates made as follows: For nonproduction employees, by multiplying the retabulated figure for number of production workers by the ratio of all employees to production workers computed from unrevised 1939 data; for salaries and wages, by multiplying the retabulated wage figure by the ratio for salaries and wages also derived from the unrevised 1939 data.

[5] Excludes data for salaried officers of corporations and their salaries; therefore, not strictly comparable with figures for other years.

Series P 74-92.   Value of Manufactures' Shipments, Inventories and Orders: 1947 to 1991

(In billions of dollars, except ratios. As of December 31, except shipments are for calendar year)

Year	Total shipments	Inventories Total	Inventories Ratio of inventories to sales [1]	Total new orders	Total unfilled orders	Year	Total shipments	Inventories Total	Inventories Ratio of inventories to sales [1]	Total new orders	Total unfilled orders
	74	77	80	87	90		74	77	80	87	90
1991	2,864	369	1.57	2,847	508	1968	603.4	90.5	1.76	606.1	85.4
1990	2,917	382	1.60	2,924	524	1967	557.4	84.4	1.77	561.2	83.9
1989	2,840	377	1.62	2,889	518	1966	538.4	77.7	1.73	550.9	79.8
1988	2,682	361	1.64	2,724	469						
1987	2,475	333	1.64	2,513	427	1965	492.0	68.0	1.66	502.0	67.2
1986	2,336	318	1.66	2,342	390	1964	448.0	63.0	1.69	455.4	58.0
						1963	420.4	60.0	1.71	424.0	50.2
1985	2,334	330	1.72	2,348	384	1962	397.4	58.0	1.75	396.1	47.0
1984	2,288	334	1.78	2,315	370	1961	371.0	55.0	1.77	373.0	48.0
1983	2,071	308	1.80	2,105	343						
1982	1,960	307	1.91	1,947	309	1960*	370.0	54.0	1.74	361.4	46.0
1981	2,018	280	1.74	2,015	323	1959	363.0	52.5	1.74	368.1	54.1
						1958	327.4	50.0	1.83	323.0	49.0
1980	1,853	262	1.61	1,876	326	1957	345.0	52.0	1.81	330.2	53.3
1979	1,727	239	1.61	1,771	303	1956	333.0	51.0	1.83	341.0	67.5
1978	1,523	209	1.55	1,580	259						
1977	1,358	188	1.58	1,381	202	1955	318.0	45.2	1.71	329.1	60.0
1976	1,186	175	1.66	1,194	180	1954	280.2	42.0	1.80	267.8	48.2
						1953	298.0	44.2	1.79	282.4	60.3
1975	1,039	160	1.77	1,023	171	1952	271.0	42.0	1.84	278.4	75.5
1974	1,018	158	1.86	1,047	187	1951	260.4	39.2	1.80	287.0	67.0
1973	875	124	1.63	913	158						
1972	756	108	1.58	770	120	1950	223.4	32.0	1.70	241.3	41.2
1971	671	102	1.76	672	107	1949	193.1	26.5	1.65	187.4	24.0
						1948	217.3	29.0	1.59	212.3	31.0
1970	630.7	101.4	1.90	620.0	73.8	1947	186.0	26.1	1.69	183.1	34.3
1969	642.7	96.6	1.76	643.7	84.5						

*Denotes first year for which figures include Alaska and Hawaii.

[1] Ratios of average inventories to average monthly sales.

Series P 93-106. Manufacturing Corporations—Sales, Profits and Stockholders' Equity: 1947 to 1990

(In billions of dollars)

| Year | All manufacturing corporations Net profits | | | | | Year | All manufacturing corporations Net profits | | | | |
	Sales (net)	Before federal income taxes	After federal income taxes	Cash dividends	Retained earnings		Sales (net)	Before federal income taxes	After federal income taxes	Cash dividends	Retained earnings
	93	94	95	97	98		93	94	95	97	98
1990	2,811	160	112	62	49	1968	631.9	55.4	32.1	14.2	17.9
1989	2,745	189	136	65	71	1967	575.4	47.8	29.0	13.3	15.7
1988	2,596	216	155	57	98	1966	554.2	51.8	30.9	13.0	18.0
1987	2,378	173	116	50	66						
1986	2,221	129	83	46	37	1965	492.2	46.5	27.5	12.0	15.5
						1964	443.1	39.6	23.2	10.8	12.4
1985	2,331	137	88	46	42	1963	412.7	34.9	19.5	9.9	9.6
1984	2,335	166	108	45	63	1962	389.9	31.9	17.7	9.3	8.4
1983	2,114	133	86	42	44	1961	356.4	27.5	15.3	8.6	6.8
1982	2,039	108	71	41	30						
1981	2,145	158	101	40	61	1960	345.7	27.5	15.2	8.3	6.9
						1959	338.0	29.7	16.3	7.9	8.4
1980	1,897	145	92	36	58	1958	305.3	22.7	12.7	7.4	5.3
1979	1,742	154	99	32	66	1957	320.0	28.2	15.4	7.6	7.9
1978	1,496	133	81	29	52	1956	307.3	29.8	16.2	7.4	8.8
1977	1,328	115	70	27	44						
1976	1,203	105	65	23	42	1955	278.4	28.6	15.1	6.8	8.3
						1954	248.5	20.9	11.2	5.9	5.3
1975	1,065	80	49	20	29	1953	265.9	24.4	11.3	5.6	5.7
1974	1,061	97	59	19	39	1952	250.2	22.9	10.7	5.5	5.2
1973	1,017	81	48	18	30	1951	245.0	27.4	11.9	5.5	6.3
1972	850	63	36	16	20						
1971	751	53	31	15	16	1950	181.9	23.2	12.9	5.7	7.2
						1949	154.9	14.4	9.0	4.5	4.5
1970	708.8	48.1	28.6	15.1	13.5	1948	165.6	18.4	11.5	4.3	7.2
1969 [1]	694.6	58.1	33.2	15.1	18.2	1947	150.7	16.6	10.1	3.7	6.4

[1] Beginning 1969, includes newspapers.

Series P 107-122. Capital in Manufacturing Industries: 1863 to 1989

(In billions of dollars)

Year	107	113	119	Year	107	113	119	Year	107	113	119
1989	104.0	88.6	957.2	1967	21.7	13.6	91.3	1945	2.9	2.0	31.7
1988	88.9	84.7	906.9	1966	20.4	12.4	85.4	1944	1.7	1.9	29.9
1987	78.8	81.7	872.1					1943	1.4	1.9	30.5
1986	76.9	78.4	845.8	1965	16.7	11.3	79.0	1942	1.7	1.9	31.9
				1964	13.4	10.6	74.5	1941	2.6	1.7	32.7
1985	83.7	74.2	811.7	1963	11.5	10.2	72.2				
1984	76.4	71.7	789.0	1962	10.6	9.9	71.2	1940	1.9	1.6	30.7
1983	64.4	69.4	764.7	1961	9.9	9.6	70.7	1939	1.3	1.5	29.8
1982	72.8	71.4	665.0					1938	1.1	1.6	30.1
1981	82.3	65.7	636.4	1960*	10.3	9.4	70.6	1937	1.8	1.5	31.0
				1959	9.0	9.1	70.1	1936	1.3	1.4	30.1
1980	75.3	58.1	633.9	1958	9.7	8.8	70.9				
1979	67.3	49.8	498.3	1957	12.3	8.3	70.8	1935	.9	1.4	30.2
1978	57.7	43.5	437.8	1956	11.4	7.4	67.8	1934	.8	1.4	31.4
1977	51.2	38.5	387.3					1933	.6	1.3	33.0
1976	43.4	34.5	343.9	1955	8.6	6.5	64.5	1932	.4	1.3	34.9
				1954	8.5	6.1	62.8	1931	.9	1.5	37.8
1975	39.8	31.6	319.3	1953	8.4	5.8	61.0				
1974	38.3	26.5	292.7	1952	8.0	5.4	58.9	1930	1.7	1.6	39.6
1973	29.0	23.0	236.1	1951	8.0	5.0	56.8	1929	2.7	1.7	39.6
1972	23.0	21.1	127.7					1928	2.3	1.7	37.2
1971	21.2	19.8	126.0	1950	5.6	4.3	53.9	1927	2.1	1.6	35.5
				1949	5.6	3.9	52.8	1926	2.2	1.6	34.4
1970	22.4	18.2	101.5	1948	6.8	3.6	50.9				
1969	22.5	16.4	99.2	1947	6.7	3.0	45.9	1925	1.8	1.5	32.7
1968	20.9	14.9	95.2	1946	5.2	2.4	38.7				

Year	107	Year	107	Year	107	Year	107
1924	1.6	1908	.5	1892	.3	1877	.1
1923	1.8	1907	.7	1891	.3	1876	.1
1922	1.4	1906	.7				
1921	1.4			1890	.3	1875	(Z)
		1905	.5	1889	.2	1874	.1
1920	2.4	1904	.5	1888	.2	1873	.1
1919	1.6	1903	.6	1887	.2	1872	.1
1918	1.4	1902	.6	1886	.1	1871	.1
1917	1.3	1901	.4				
1916	1.0			1885	.1	1870	.1
		1900	.4	1884	.1	1869	.1
1915	.6	1899	.3	1883	.1	1868	(Z)
1914	.6	1898	.3	1882	.2	1867	(Z)
1931	.9	1897	.3	1881	.2	1866	(Z)
1912	.9	1896	.4				
1911	.7			1880	.1	1865	(Z)
		1895	.3	1879	.1	1864	(Z)
1910	.7	1894	.3	1878	.1	1863	(Z)
1909	.7	1893	.3				

* Denotes first year for which figures include Alaska and Hawaii.   Z Less than $50 million.

TRANSPORTATION

SECTION Q
TRANSPORTATION
Highlights

1 The first transportation agency in the United States, the Office of Road Inquiry, was created in 1894, "to make inquiries in regard to the systems of road management throughout the United States, to make investigations in regard to the best methods of roadmaking, to prepare publications on this subject suitable for distribution." It was succeeded by the Office of Public Roads and Rural Engineering in 1916 and by the Bureau of Public Roads in 1918 (called Public Roads Administration between 1939 and 1949). The Bureau was transferred to the Department of Transportation in 1966 and its functions assigned to the Federal Highway Administration. The first survey of highway mileage, revenues, and expenditures was made in 1904, and followed by others in 1909 and 1914.

2 In 1912, Congress authorized $500,000 for an experimental program of rural post-road construction. However, it was not until the Federal-Aid Road Act of 1916 that the Federal-State Highway Program was established on an ongoing basis. In 1921, Congress authorized designation of a system of principal interstate and intercounty roads, limited to 7% of the rural mileage then existing. The Federal-Aid Highway Act of 1944 specifically authorized the use of funds for highways in urban areas. In addition, the Act provided for the designation of a Federal-Aid secondary system and a national system of interstate highways. Under President Eisenhower, the Federal-Aid Highway Act of 1956 established the goal of a 41,000 mile interstate system, which forms the basis of the U.S. road transportation system today.

3 The principal sources of highway and motor transport data are the *Highway Statistics* of the Federal Highway Administration, the *Transport Statistics of the United States* published by the Interstate Commerce Commission, various surveys and censuses conducted by the U.S. Bureau of the Census, *Factbook* of the U.S. National Highway Traffic Safety Administration, *Motor Vehicle Facts and Figures* published by the Motor Vehicle Manufacturers Association, *Accident Facts* published by the National Safety Council, and *Transportation in America* published by the Eno Foundation for Transportation.

4 The first Federal highway was the Great National Pike, also known as the Cumberland Road, built in sections from 1806 to 1840 between Cumberland, Maryland and Vandalia, Illinois. The total construction cost was $6.821 million.

5 The first hardsurfaced road in what is now the United States was built by the Dutch in 1663. It ran for 100 miles from the Pahaquarry Mines in New Jersey to Kingston, New York. The first toll road was the Little River Turnpike built in 1785 from Alexandria, Virginia, to Snicker's Gap, a pass through the Blue Ridge Mountains leading to the Shenandoah Valley.

6 Total transportation outlays reached $954.3 billion in 1990, of which automobiles accounted for $510.8 billion, for hire transportation for $100.9 billion, and freight for $349.7 billion.

7 In 1990, 80.8% of passengers traveled by car and 17.4% by air; 37.5% of freight was carried by rail and 25% by trucks.

8 Air carriers remained the safest means of transportation, with only 144 accidents and 83 fatalities in 1990. Motor vehicles were the most unsafe means of transportation, with 11.5 million accidents, 44,500 deaths, and 1.7 million injuries. Railroads accounted for 2,879 accidents, 599 deaths, and 22,736 injuries. However, automobile accidents, injuries, and fatalities have declined significantly since 1970 when there were 16 million, 2 million, and 52,600 respectively.

9 In 1990, 59% of urban and rural Interstate roads were rated as excellent with few, if any, visible signs of surface wear; 35% as somewhat inferior with some signs of cracking, patching, and rutting; and 6% as poor with extensive wear. The relative percentages for urban arterial roads were 42%, 54%, and 4% and for rural arterial roads 48%, 49%, and 3%.

10 A total of 123.3 million cars were in use in the United States in 1990; of these, 26% were under three years old while 25.1% were over 12 years old. Americans are keeping their cars longer, the average age rose from 6.6 years in 1980 to 7.8 years in 1990. An average of 8.5 million cars are retired from use each year. A total of 56 million trucks were in use, of which 15.5% were 12 years and older. The average age of a truck rose from 7.1 years in 1980 to 8 years in 1990. Sales of passenger cars in 1990 of 9.3 million were the lowest since 1984, when 10.390 million

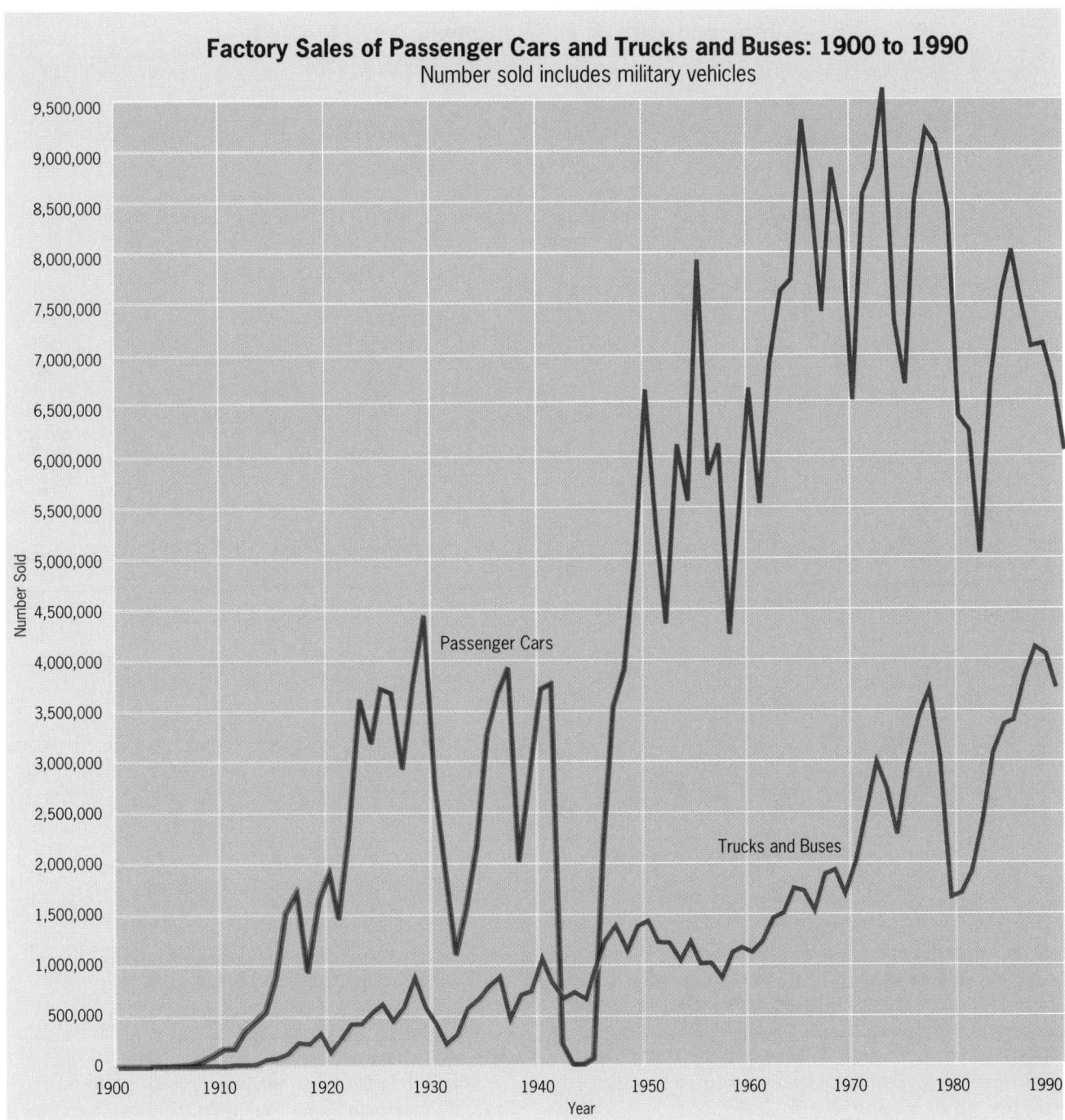

Factory Sales of Passenger Cars and Trucks and Buses: 1900 to 1990
Number sold includes military vehicles

were sold. Of total sales, domestic cars accounted for 6.897 million and imported cars for 2.403 million. Of the 3.945 million cars imported in 1990, 1.868 million were from Japan and 245,000 from Germany. The import value of new passenger cars rose from $16.675 billion in 1980 to $45.716 billion in 1990, making this the largest item in U.S. trade deficit. Sales of motorcycles likewise dropped from a high of 1.305 million in 1984 to 462,000 in 1990.

11 Generally, the most heavily traveled roads are in the smaller states; however, California is an exception. In 1990, vehicle miles of travel per mile of road were 1,976 in Hawaii, 1,717 in New Jersey, 1,583 in California, 1,406 in

Maryland, 1,352 in Massachusetts, 1,315 in Connecticut, 1,148 in Rhode Island, and 1,018 in Florida. The state with the lowest vehicle miles of travel per mile of road was North Dakota, where the relative figure was 68.

12 Personal consumption expenditures on automobiles were $132.4 billion in 1990; $35.8 billion of this was spent on used (or pre-owned) automobiles.

13 Of the 4.261 million trucks sold in 1990, 2.866 million were under 6,000 lbs. Sales of minivans peaked at 110,000 in 1986, then declined to 83,000 in 1990. Sales of compact pickups remained strong at 774,000 in 1990, but also showed signs of weakening.

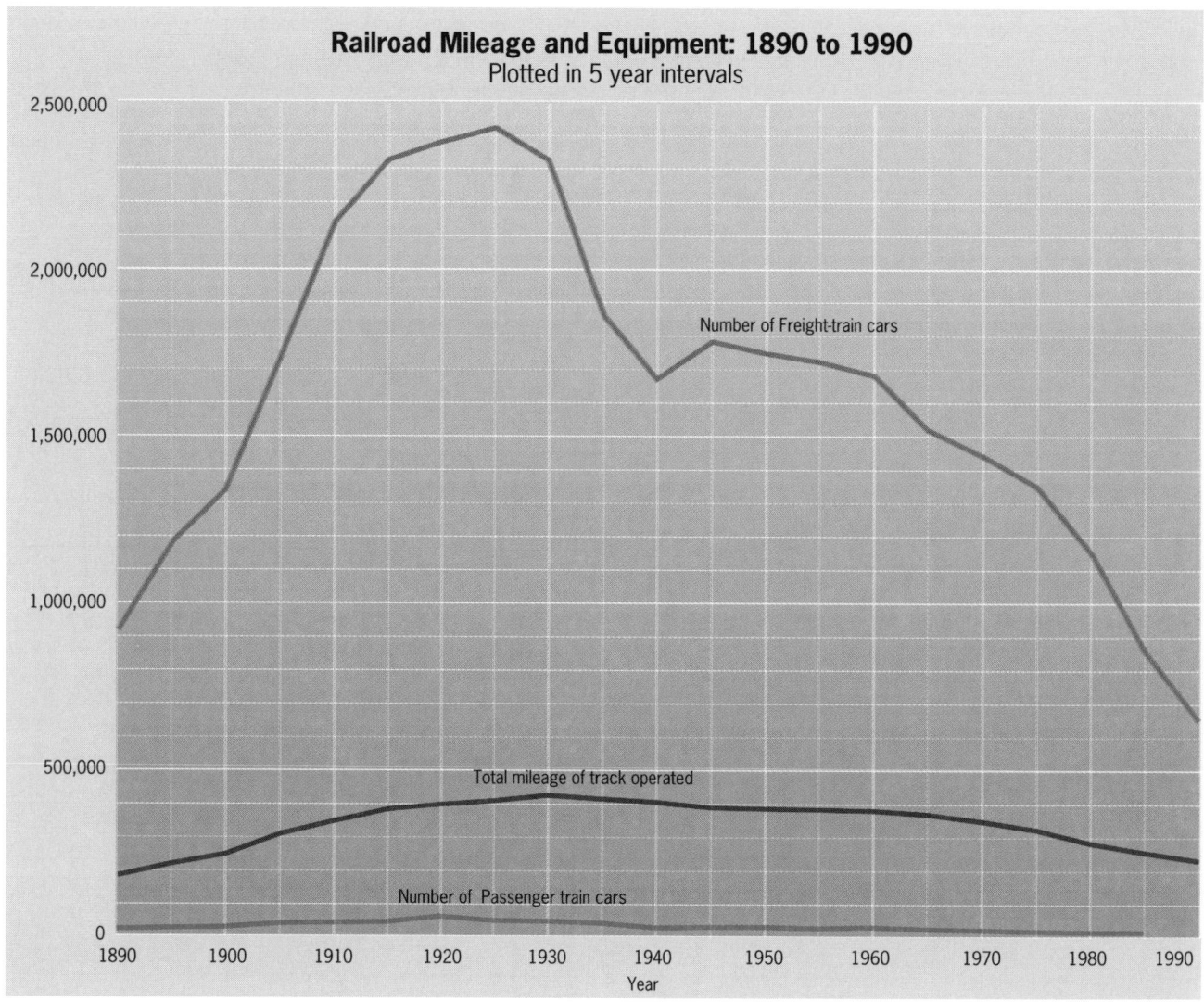

Railroad Mileage and Equipment: 1890 to 1990
Plotted in 5 year intervals

Number of Freight-train cars

Total mileage of track operated

Number of Passenger train cars

Year

14 Recreational vehicles (RV's) also have suffered a decline in popularity since 1970, with their sales plunging from 427,300 in 1988 to 354,500 in 1990. The only type of RV which has done well is the motorized home, of which 226,500 units were sold in 1990 compared to 30,300 in 1970. Excluding motorized homes, sales of RV's were 128,000 in 1990 compared to 350,300 in 1970.

15 A total of 11.5 million motor vehicle accidents were reported on the road in 1990. The economic loss resulting from these accidents, including wage loss, legal, medical and funeral expenses, and property damage, was $95.9 billion. Traffic death rates, however, have fallen on all fronts. Per 100,000 registered vehicles, they fell from 47.3 in 1970 to 23.6 in 1989; per 100 million vehicle miles, they fell from 4.7 in 1970 to 2.2 in 1989; and per 100,000 licensed drivers, they fell from 47.2 in 1970 to 27.6 in 1989.

16 Of the 59,193 fatal motor vehicle accidents reported in 1990, 33,972 involved passenger cars (including 7,198 compacts and 6,959 intermediates); 15,601 involved light

trucks; 4,761 involved medium and heavy trucks; 3,270 involved motorcycles; and 288 involved buses.

17 Interstates and urban roads are safer than rural roads. In 1990, the fatal accident rate per 100 million vehicles miles was 1.36 for urban roads and 0.88 for interstates, but 2.57 for rural roads. Arterial rural highways and local rural highways had the highest accident rates at 5.21 and 4.08 respectively.

18 In the decade between 1980 and 1989, there were 1,742 motor vehicle safety defect recall campaigns by automobile manufacturers, in which 58,635 million vehicles were recalled.

19 In 1986, 1.782 million drivers were arrested for drunken driving compared to 946,000 in 1970. The arrest rate per 100,000 drivers rose from 729 to 1,130. The arrest rate was highest (2,075) among 18 to 24 year olds but remained high for other below 40 groups as well. Of drinking drivers involved in fatal accidents, 25 to 30 year olds constituted almost one-third.

21 The cost per mile of owning and operating an automobile rose from 18.31 cents in 1975 to 41 cents in 1990. Among fixed costs, automobile insurance per car rose from $383 to $675 over the same period.

22 The average consumer expenditures on a new car rose from $3,542 in 1970 to $16,012 in 1990. In 1970, the cost of a new car averaged 18.7 weeks of the median family income, while in 1990 the relative cost equalled 24.5 weeks of the median family income.

23 Environmental regulations and technology have combined to reduce substantially the average fuel consumption of a car and increase the average miles per gallon. Average annual fuel consumption dropped from 760 gallons in 1970 to 505 gallons per car in 1990 and from 2,172 gallons to 1,436 gallons per bus in the same period. The average miles per gallon rose from 13.52 to 21 for cars and from 7.85 to 10.62 for trucks. The average annual mileage remained steady for cars, increasing slightly from 10,000 in 1970 to 10,300 in 1990. Speed regulations have helped to curb speeding on the highways. In 1970, 87% of drivers exceeded 55 miles per hour, 69% exceeded 60 miles per hour, and 44% exceeded 65 miles per hour. In 1990, the relative percentages had fallen to 78%, 50%, and 23%.

24 The number of mass transit systems grew from 1,044 in 1980 to 5,073 in 1990. Of these, 2,686 were motor bus systems and 1,580 publicly owned systems. In 1990, they operated 93,752 passenger vehicles, including 59,753 buses, and carried a total of 8.873 billion passengers. Overall, mass transit had a deficit of $2.358 billion with revenues of $15.982 billion and expenditures of $18.340 billion.

25 Intercity bus lines suffer the same problems as urban transit. Although the number of intercity bus line operators grew from 1,000 in 1970 to 3,550 in 1990, they had fewer buses (18,400 in 1990 compared to 22,000 in 1970), served fewer miles of highway (249,000 miles in 1990 compared to 267,000 in 1970), had fewer employees (39,000 in 1990 compared to 50,000 in 1970), and fewer passengers (333,000 in 1990 compared to 401,000 in 1970). The number of Class I intercity motor carriers of passengers declined from 77 in 1975 to 21 in 1990. In 1990, they carried 43 million passengers compared to 147 million in 1975. Their operations were in the red in 1990, with a reported loss after taxes of $180 million.

26 Of the 259,000 trucks operated by trucking services in 1990, 107,000 were specialty freight carriers and 152,000 general freight carriers. Together, they had operating revenues of $120.19 billion, of which intercity trucking accounted for $88.713 billion. Of the 636 intercity motor carriers of property, 191 were common carriers of general freight, 322 common carriers of other than general freight, 87 contract carriers and 36 carriers of household goods. Of the 44.572 million trucks on the road, 39.686 million were pickups and panels and 29.292 million were used for personal transportation only.

27 Railroad companies reporting to the Interstate Commerce Commission (ICC) are divided into four groups: (1) Regular line-haul, (2) switching and terminal, (3) private (or circular, because they reported on brief circulars), and (4) unofficial. Data on the last three groups are excluded from official statistics. Beginning in 1911, the ICC also divided regular line-haul railroads into Class I, II, and III. Initially, Class I had revenues over $1 million, Class II between $100,000 and $1 million, and Class III under $100,000. In 1978, the categories were redefined with the thresholds for Classes I, II, and III raised to $50 million, $10 to $50 million, and below $10 million respectively. In 1982, the ICC adopted a procedure to adjust the threshold for inflation on the basis of 1978 dollars. On this basis, the number of Class I railroads declined from 71 in 1970 to 14 in 1990, trackage owned from 336,000 miles to 239,000 miles, the number of locomotives from 27,077 to 18,835, the number of passenger train cars from 11,177 to 2,332 (in 1988), and the number of freight cars from 1,424,000 to 659,000.

28 The principal source of information on railways prior to 1890 is *Poor's Manual of Railroads*. Current data are contained in *Railway Age* and *Yearbook of Railroad Facts*, published by the Association of American Railroads.

29 The first interstate railroad was the Petersburg Railroad, chartered by a special act of the General Assembly of Virginia in 1830 and by a special act of the North Carolina Legislature in 1831. It ran for 59 miles along the north bank of the Roanoke River from Petersburg, Virginia, to Blakeley, North Carolina. The first railroad for the commercial transportation of passengers and freight was the Baltimore and Ohio Railroad Company, incorporated in 1827.

30 AMTRAK carried 22.383 million passengers in 1990 and earned $941.9 million in revenues.

31 Railroad freight remained the cheapest form of freight transportation at 2.7 cents per mile in 1990. Railroads carried 2.024 billion tons of freight and earned $24.471 billion, or 2.657 cents per ton-mile. The principal commodities transported by rail are coal, metallic ores, chemicals, grain, motor vehicles, paper and pulp, forest products, metals and products, crushed stone, gravel and sand, waste and scrap, and petroleum.

32 In 1990, there were 168,000 miles of petroleum pipelines and 194,100 miles of natural gas pipelines, which delivered 11.378 billion barrels of petroleum and petroleum products and 5.6 trillion cubic feet of natural gas respectively.

33 Historical statistics on merchant shipping are found in a variety of sources. They include *Merchant Marine Statistics*, 1924-1965; Congressional documents, such as *Decadence of American Shipping and Compulsory Pilotage*, 1789-1882; publications of the Maritime Commission, especially *Ocean-Going Merchant Fleets of Principal Maritime Nations*; and the censuses of water transportation

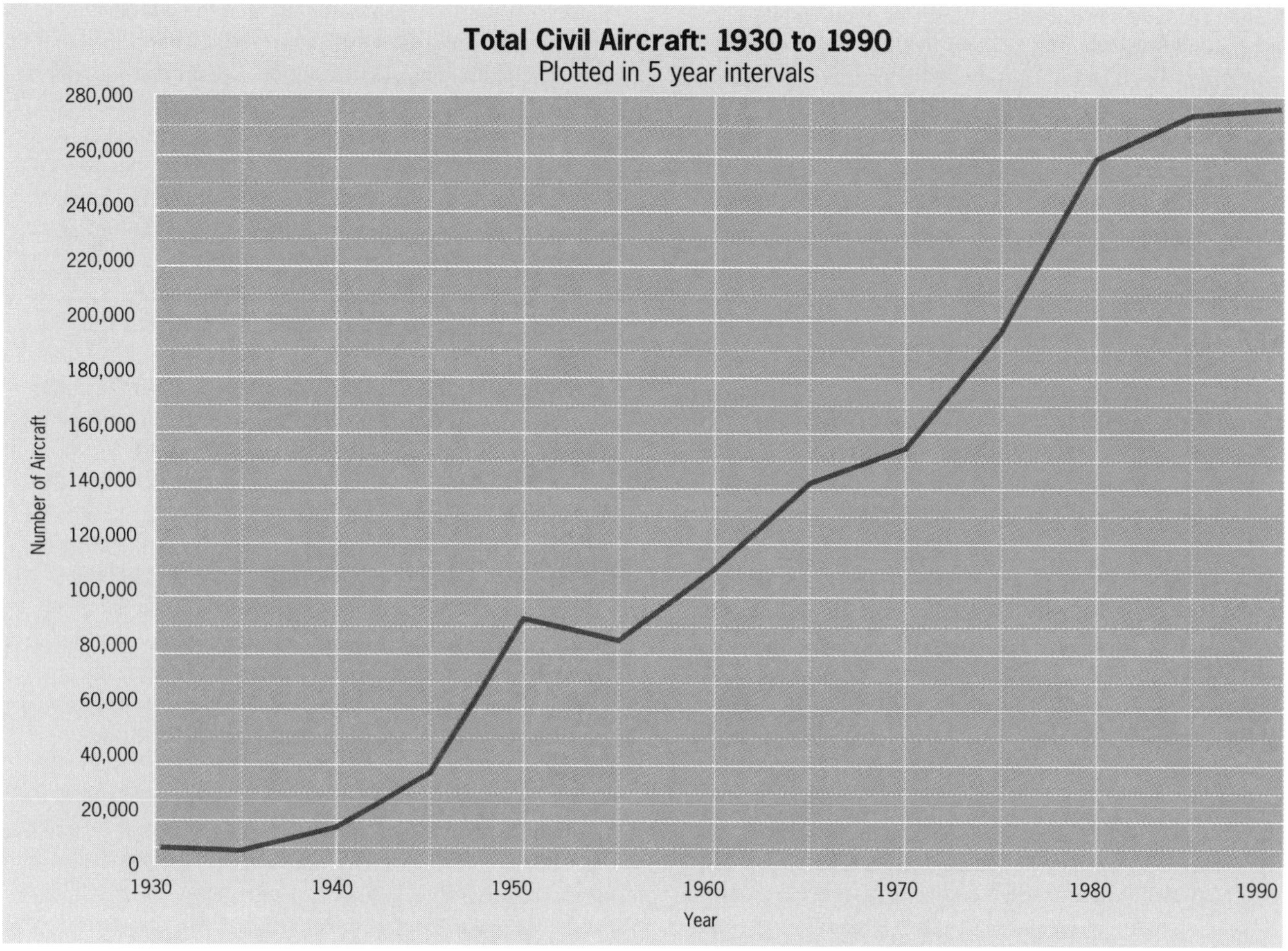

Total Civil Aircraft: 1930 to 1990
Plotted in 5 year intervals
280,000
260,000
240,000
220,000
200,000
180,000
160,000
140,000
120,000
100,000
80,000
60,000
40,000
20,000
0
Number of Aircraft
1930
1940
1950
1960
1970
1980
1990
Year

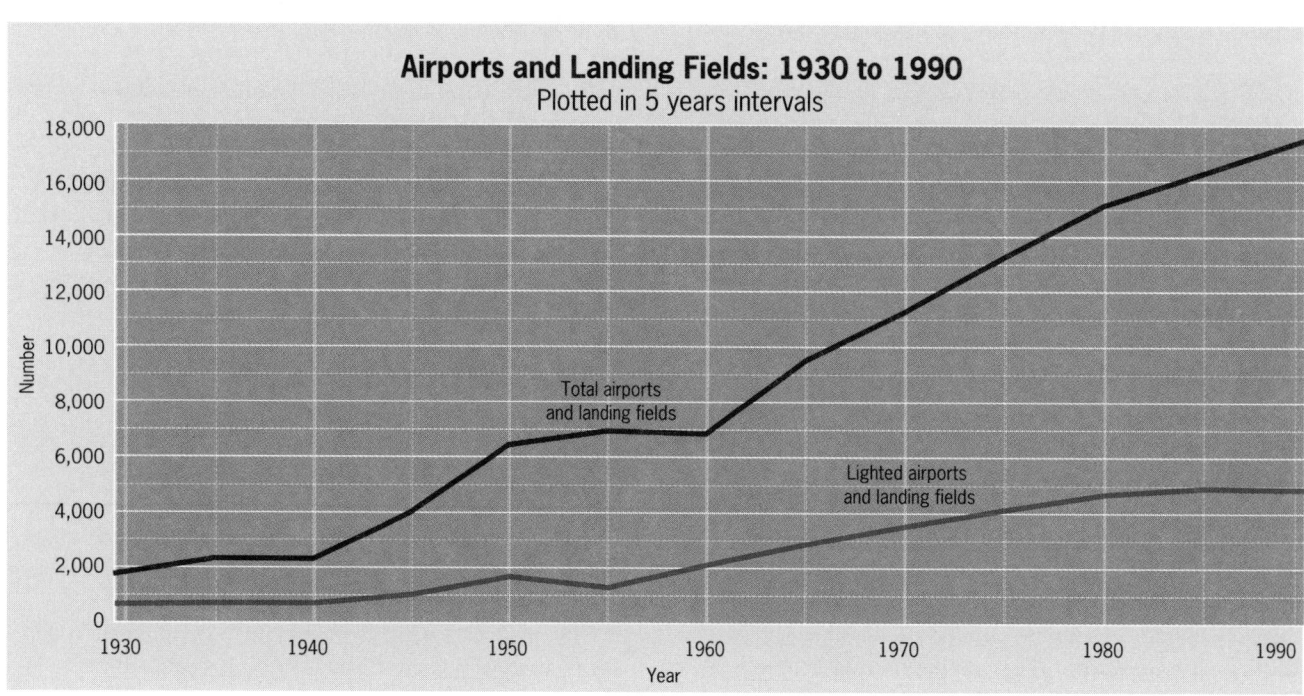

Airports and Landing Fields: 1930 to 1990
Plotted in 5 years intervals
18,000
16,000
14,000
12,000
10,000
8,000
6,000
4,000
2,000
0
Number
Total airports
and landing fields
Lighted airports
and landing fields
1930
1940
1950
1960
1970
1980
1990
Year

conducted by the Bureau of the Census and its predecessors. The first census for 1880 was limited to steam vessels, but those of 1889 and 1906 included all vessels (excluding fishing vessels), and those of 1916 and 1926 provided data for all vessels over 5 tons. Changes in maritime law on admeasurement (a determination or comparison of measurements) of gross tonnage have also affected the data. Gross tonnage is a measurement of space, not weight, in which 100 cubic feet (95 cubic feet before 1865) equals one ton. Also, an Act of 1874 excluded canalboat and unrigged tonnage from the totals. Other measurements used over the years included duty tonnage (tonnage on which duties were collected), district tonnage (reported by district collectors of customs), registered tonnage, and net tonnage.

34 The United States has five major waterways systems: Atlantic Coast, Gulf Coast, Pacific Coast, Mississippi River, and Great Lakes. The total freight carried on these five systems in 1989 was 448.7 billion ton-miles. The Mississippi accounted for 268.1 billion ton-miles, or more than one-half.

35 The output of U.S. shipyards has been falling since 1970, making shipbuilding an industry on the verge of extinction. In 1988, only four merchant vessels, three cargo vessels, and one tanker (with a combined gross tonnage of 206,000) were produced by domestic shipyards. Currently, the United States has only six active passenger ships under its flag. It still has a strong tanker fleet of 233 tankers with a deadweight tonnage of 15.649 million. The U.S. share of world merchant fleet gross tonnage was 5.03% in 1990, compared to 19.14% in 1960.

36 Only scattered data on air transportation are available for the years before 1926. Regular collection of national statistics began with the establishment in that year of an Aeronautics Branch in the Department of Commerce. In 1934, it became the Bureau of Air Commerce. The Civil Aeronautics Act of 1938 created the Civil Aeronautics Authority, reorganized in 1940 into two separate entities: The Civil Aeronautics Board and Civil Aeronautics Administration. In 1958, the latter's functions were transferred to the Federal Aviation Agency, which in turn was made a part of the Department of Transportation and renamed the Federal Aviation Administration (FAA). The FAA's annual *Statistical Handbook of Civil Aviation* is the principal source of data in this field. Air transportation data are also presented annually in *Air Transport Facts and Figures,* published by the Air Transport Association of America.

37 After the Airline Deregulation Act of 1978, the number of domestic air operators grew from 35 to 60. Also, the distinction between domestic and international operators became blurred. Operating revenues soared to $57.991 billion in 1990 from $7.131 billion in 1970, as did expenses to $59.004 billion from $7.128 billion in 1970. This left the industry with a deficit of $1.012 billion.

38 In 1989, 3,190 aircraft were in operation and the mean age of the aircraft was 12 years. Of these, 2,008 aircraft were Boeing, 76 Airbus, 111 Lockheed, and 995 McDonnell-Douglas.

39 Between 1970 and 1990, there were 538 air accidents worldwide, causing 15,828 fatalities. In 1990, there were 46 hijacking incidents; four of which involved U.S. aircraft. In the same year, there were 448 bomb threats in U.S. airports.

40 In 1990, the U.S. airports with the greatest number of passenger enplanings were Chicago (O'Hare—25,636), Dallas/Fort Worth (22,899), Atlanta (22,666), Los Angeles (18,438), San Francisco (13,475), Denver (11,962), Phoenix (10,727), New York (La Guardia—10,725), Detroit (9,903), and Newark (9,854).

41 The percentage of on-time arrivals and departures in U.S. airports has continued to rise. Nationally, it was 85.2% for arrivals and 90.2% for departures in the third quarter of 1991.

42 Consumer complaints against U.S. airlines have been dropping steadily since 1966. In 1991, 6,126 complaints were registered compared to 10,802 in 1966. The most common sources of complaints were flight problems, followed by baggage, refunds, customer service, ticketing/ boarding, fares, oversales, advertising, smoking, tours, and credit.

43 The number of heliports grew from 790 in 1970 to 4,085 in 1990, and the number of private airports from 7,001 in 1970 to 12,412 in 1990. There were 366,600 miles of federal airways in operation, in which 275,900 active aircraft flew. In addition, the sky was crowded with 7,000 balloons, blimps, and gliders.

44 Until recently, aviation was a male-dominated field and there were few woman pilots. The percentage of woman pilots, however, is growing. In 1990, 5.8% of pilots were women, compared to 4% in 1970.

Series Q 1-11. Volume of Domestic Intercity Passenger Traffic, by Type of Transport: 1950 to 1990

(In billions of passenger miles, except percent. Airways, prior to 1959, and other types of transportation, prior to 1960, exclude Alaska and Hawaii. A passenger-mile is the movement of one passenger for the distance of one mile. Comprises public and private traffic, both revenue and nonrevenue)

Year	Total traffic, volume	Private automobiles, volume	Airways[1], volume	Buses[2], volume	Railroads[3], volume	Year	Total traffic, volume	Private automobiles, volume	Airways[1], volume	Buses[2], volume	Railroads[3], volume
	1	2	4	6	8		1	2	4	6	8
1990	2,054	1,660	358	23	13	1970	1,185	1,026	119	25	11
1989	2,012	1,627	347	24	13	1969	1,138	977	120	25	12
1988	1,968	1,586	346	23	13	1968	1,079	936	101	25	13
1987	1,897	1,521	341	23	12	1967	1,021	890	87	25	15
1986	1,808	1,452	320	24	12	1966	971	856	69	25	17
1985	1,744	1,418	291	24	11	1965	920	818	58	24	18
1984	1,739	1,437	263	27	12	1964	896	802	49	23	18
1983	1,647	1,364	245	27	11	1963	853	766	43	23	19
1982	1,609	1,344	227	27	11	1962	818	736	37	22	20
1981	1,574	1,319	216	27	12	1961	791	714	35	20	21
1980	1,557	1,300	219	27	11	1960	784	706	34	19	22
1979	1,590	1,322	228	28	12	1959	765	687	33	20	22
1978	1,602	1,362	203	26	11	1958	760	685	29	21	24
1977	1,529	1,316	177	26	10	1957	748	670	28	21	26
1976	1,460	1,260	164	25	11	1956	751	670	26	25	29
1975	1,354	1,171	148	25	10	1955	716	637	23	25	29
1974	1,331	1,143	146	28	10	1954	673	597	20	26	29
1973	1,341	1,163	143	26	9	1953	655	576	17	28	32
1972	1,300	1,129	133	26	9	1952	575	496	15	29	35
1971	1,230	1,071	120	26	9	1951	535	458	13	27	35
						1950	508	438	10	26	32

[1] Includes domestic commercial revenue service and private, pleasure and business flying.
[2] Excludes school buses.
[3] Includes electric railways.

Series Q 12-22. Volume of Domestic Intercity Freight Traffic, by Type of Transport: 1939 to 1990

(In billions of ton-miles. Motor vehicles and airways, prior to 1959, and other types of transportation, prior to 1960, exclude Alaska and Hawaii, except as noted. A ton-mile is the movement of one ton (2,000 pounds) of freight for the distance of one mile. Comprises public and private traffic, both revenue and nonrevenue)

Year	Total traffic, volume	Rail-roads [1], volume	Motor vehicles, volume	Inland water-ways [2], volume	Oil pipelines, volume	Airways [3], volume	Year	Total traffic, volume	Rail-roads [1], volume	Motor vehicles, volume	Inland water-ways [2], volume	Oil pipelines, volume	Airways [3], volume
	12	13	15	17	19	21		12	13	15	17	19	21
1990	2,855	1,071	735	462	577	11.0	1964	1,556	679	356	250	269	1.5
1989	2,807	1,048	716	449	584	10.0	1963	1,469	644	336	234	253	1.3
1988	2,793	1,034	704	434	612	9.3	1962	1,387	616	309	223	238	1.3
1987	2,640	972	661	411	587	8.7	1961	1,326	586	296	210	233	.9
1986	2,494	889	627	393	578	7.3							
							1960	1,330	595	285	220	229	.8
1985	2,458	895	610	382	564	7.0	1959	1,303	599	279	197	227	.7
1984	2,497	935	605	382	568	6.6	1958	1,231	575	256	189	211	.6
1983	2,337	841	575	359	556	5.9	1957	1,354	645	254	232	223	.6
1982	2,252	810	520	351	566	5.1	1956	1,376	677	249	220	230	.6
1981	2,430	924	527	410	564	5.0							
							1955	1,298	655	223	217	203	.6
1980	2,487	932	555	407	588	5.0	1954	1,144	578	213	174	179	.4
1979	2,573	927	608	425	608	4.8	1953	1,232	643	217	4 202	170	.4
1978	2,467	868	599	409	586	4.8	1952	1,172	651	195	168	158	.4
1977	2,307	834	555	368	546	4.2	1951	1,209	686	188	4 182	152	.4
1976	2,202	800	510	373	515	3.9							
							1950	1,094	628	173	163	129	.3
1975	2,066	759	454	342	507	4.0	1949	947	567	125	139	115	.2
1974	2,213	860	495	348	506	3.9	1948	1,086	689	115	4 162	120	.2
1973	2,232	858	505	358	507	4.0	1947	1,060	707	102	147	105	.2
1972	2,071	783	470	339	476	3.7	1946	944	643	82	124	96	.1
1971	1,953	746	445	315	444	3.5							
							1945	1,072	736	67	143	127	.1
1970	1,936	771	412	319	431	3.3	1944	1,136	795	58	150	133	.1
1969	1,895	774	404	303	411	3.2	1943	1,076	780	57	142	98	.1
1968	1,839	757	396	291	391	2.9	1942	973	689	60	149	75	(Z)
1967	1,776	742	389	281	361	2.6	1941	811	521	81	140	68	(Z)
1966	1,759	762	381	281	333	2.3	1940	651	412	62	118	59	(Z)
							1939	575	370	53	96	56	(Z)
1965	1,651	721	359	262	306	1.9							

Z Less than 50 million ton-miles.
[1] Includes electric railways, express and mail.
[2] Includes Great Lakes. Includes Alaska for all years and Hawaii beginning 1959.

[3] Domestic revenue service only. Includes express, mail and excess baggage.
[4] Part of this increase resulted from coverage of waterways previously existing but not covered.

Series Q 50-63. Mileage of Rural Roads and Municipal Streets: 1921 to 1990

Year	Total mileage		Year	Total mileage		Year	Total mileage		Year	Total mileage	
	Total	Rural roads		Total	Rural roads		Total	Rural roads		Total	Rural roads
	50	51		50	51		50	51		50	51
	1,000 miles	1,000 miles		1,000 miles	1,000 miles		1,000 miles	1,000 miles		1,000 miles	1,000 miles
1990	3,380	3,123	1973	3,807	3,176	1955	3,418	2,954	1937	3,245	2,894
1989	3,877	3,123	1972	3,787	3,173	1954	3,395	2,941	1936	3,267	2,920
1988	3,871	3,132	1971	3,759	3,166	1953	3,366	2,925			
1987	3,874	3,164				1952	3,343	2,925	1935	3,310	3,032
1986	3,880	3,178	1970	3,730	3,169	1951	3,326	2,925	1934	3,309	3,034
			1969	3,710	3,162				1933	3,286	3,029
1985	3,862	3,171	1968	3,684	3,152	1950	3,313	2,922	1932	3,296	3,040
1984	3,892	3,218	1967	3,705	3,184	1949	3,322	2,934	1931	3,291	3,036
1983	3,880	3,217	1966	3,698	3,188	1948	3,323	2,929			
1982	3,866	3,226				1947	3,326	2,933	1930	3,259	3,009
1981	3,853	3,221	1965	3,690	3,009	1946	3,316	2,934	1929	3,272	3,024
			1964	3,644	3,003				1928	3,262	3,016
1980	3,955	3,331	1963	3,620	3,002	1945	3,319	2,939	1927	3,257	3,013
1979	3,918	3,224	1962	3,600	3,005	1944	3,311	2,932	1926	3,242	3,000
1978	3,885	3,190	1961	3,573	2,995	1943	3,311	2,930			
1977	3,867	3,180				1942	3,309	2,925	1925	3,246	3,006
1976	3,857	3,209	1960	3,546	2,989	1941	3,309	2,926	1924	3,243	3,004
			1959*	3,511	2,974				1923	3,233	2,996
1975	3,838	3,199	1958	3,479	2,959	1940	3,287	2,920	1922	3,196	2,960
1974	3,816	3,178	1957	3,453	2,952	1939	3,274	2,913	1921	3,160	2,925
			1956	3,430	2,945	1938	3,257	2,898			

* Denotes first year for which figures include Alaska and Hawaii.

Series Q 69-81. Class I Intercity Motor Carriers of Passengers and Property: 1939 to 1990
(Carriers subject to ICC regulations)

	Carriers of passengers							Carriers of passengers					
Year	Carriers reporting [1]	Operating revenue	Expenses	Net income after income taxes	Vehicles in service [2]	Vehicle miles, passenger [3]	Year	Carriers reporting [1]	Operating revenue	Expenses	Net income after income taxes	Vehicles in service [2]	Vehicle miles, passenger [3]
	69	70	71	72	73	74		69	70	71	72	73	74
		Mil. dol.	Mil. dol.	Mil. dol.		Millions			Mil. dol.	Mil. dol.	Mil. dol.	Millions	
1990	21	943	1,015	-180	(NA)	(NA)	1965	156	607	514	52	13,287	947
1989	20	1,205	1,133	12	(NA)	(NA)	1964	161	655	570	52	16,157	1,056
1988	21	1,122	1,059	(NA)	(NA)	(NA)	1963	148	610	529	48	[4] 13,608	1,009
1987	32	1,079	1,081	-21	(NA)	(NA)	1962	151	589	511	43	[4] 13,873	998
1986	29	1,117	1,082	36	8,300	495	1961	144	485	423	31	[4] 11,036	865
1985	43	1,233	1,168	53	8,400	567	1960*	143	463	405	28	12,680	843
1984	43	1,255	1,254	43	7,000	585	1959	143	439	380	29	[4] 10,763	810
1983	45	1,276	1,283	26	7,300	591	1958	136	410	366	20	[4] 10,791	816
1982	50	1,447	1,416	37	8,100	717	1957	144	407	371	20	[4] 11,301	867
1981	45	1,453	1,381	61	8,400	732	1956	145	377	343	17	[4] 11,032	859
1980	48	1,397	1,318	90	8,600	781	1955	146	362	331	16	13,127	859
1979	45	1,200	1,143	57	8,200	754	1954	155	363	331	15	[4] 12,314	887
1978	43	1,021	983	41	8,500	726	1953	161	395	354	18	[4] 12,940	972
1977	42	969	924	40	8,300	754	1952	160	395	348	22	[4] 13,106	975
1976	78	975	937	32	(NA)	(NA)	1951	166	393	345	25	[4] 13,431	1,011
1975	77	942	880	56	9,700	835	1950	172	351	315	19	14,566	959
1974	81	933	859	61	13,800	886	1949	262	380	346	20	[4] 14,863	1,066
1973	75	815	738	58	12,794	850	1948	260	401	351	31	[4] 15,290	1,130
1972	74	775	690	59	12,122	845	1947	253	367	313	33	[4] 14,149	1,056
1971	71	758	664	65	12,896	856	1946	254	381	299	50	[4] 13,168	1,043
1970	71	722	639	52	13,282	871	1945	231	378	265	32	[4] 12,865	931
1969	70	677	594	56	12,992	869	1944	194	375	245	36	[4] 12,019	905
1968	173	695	613	61	15,398	977	1943	157	344	214	37	[4] 11,000	832
1967	177	670	591	52	15,406	997	1942	136	251	164	24	[4] 9,677	702
1966	166	644	550	54	14,298	988	1941	132	149	120	20	[4] 7,891	556
							1940	135	115	98	15	[4] 6,678	482
							1939	149	113	95	20	[4] 6,408	466

NA Not available
* Denotes first year for which figures include Alaska and Hawaii.
[1] Excludes carriers subject to ICC jurisdiction engaged preponderantly in local or suburban service and carriers engaged in transpsortation of both property and passengers.

[2] Regular route intercity and local.
[3] Vehicles owned, leased and operated under "purchase transportation" arrangements, operated in all revenue service.
[4] Excludes intercity service.

Series Q 136-147. Public Highway Debt—Long-Term Highway Obligations of State and Local Governments: 1945 to 1991

(In millions of dollars. State data are for calendar years; local data are for varying fiscal years. Excludes duplicated and interunit obligations, except as noted. Municipal obligations include data for all municipalities and other political subdivisions urban in character)

Year	Debt issued				Debt redeemed				Total debt outstanding
	Total [1]	State	County and local rural	Municipal	Total [2]	State	County and local rural	Municipal	
	136	137	138	139	140	141	142	143	144
1991	5,418	3,198	800	1,420	3,478	2,070	375	1,033	43,767
1990	5,413	3,233	580	1,600	3,302	1,602	750	950	41,827
1989	5,268	3,096	650	1,522	3,606	2,063	618	925	39,716
1988	4,261	2,384	567	1,310	2,735	1,396	353	986	38,091
1987	3,802	1,927	451	1,424	2,685	1,625	349	711	36,565
1986	6,296	3,946	1,200	1,150	3,132	1,875	432	825	34,465
1985	6,074	3,404	1,387	1,283	2,737	1,580	378	779	31,301
1984	3,151	1,715	524	912	2,411	1,507	216	688	27,964
1983	2,566	1,072	475	1,019	2,172	1,191	303	678	27,224
1982	3,155	1,555	350	1,250	1,831	1,146	185	500	27,285
1981	2,574	965	305	1,204	2,464	1,579	201	684	25,961
1980	2,094	1,128	276	690	1,706	1,022	209	475	25,851
1979	1,904	941	279	684	1,751	960	177	614	25,463
1978	1,883	942	238	703	1,593	934	170	469	25,327
1977	2,230	1,183	339	708	1,648	960	178	510	25,037
1976	2,224	1,402	198	564	1,567	920	172	475	24,455
1975	2,239	1,412	222	605	1,492	908	166	418	23,801
1974	1,657	846	230	581	1,445	887	163	395	23,016
1973	2,066	1,216	250	600	1,367	883	140	344	22,963
1972	2,459	1,672	241	546	1,270	783	148	339	22,264
1971	3,341	2,649	196	496	1,281	815	145	321	21,068
1970	1,886	1,305	174	407	1,252	782	152	318	19,107
1969	2,022	1,351	241	430	1,122	705	137	280	18,572
1968	1,991	1,377	241	373	1,071	657	136	278	17,672
1967	1,633	1,012	194	427	965	540	136	289	16,749
1966	1,680	1,156	158	366	915	519	126	270	16,080
1965	1,070	586	169	315	855	459	123	273	15,316
1964	1,097	634	156	307	752	381	116	255	15,114
1963	981	458	114	409	732	382	114	236	14,773
1962	1,535	1,017	184	334	679	340	110	229	14,537
1961	1,272	718	153	401	665	330	117	218	13,718
1960	1,206	680	190	336	616	300	96	220	13,166
1959*	1,158	669	153	336	610	308	92	210	12,576
1958	1,352	913	140	299	543	252	94	197	12,278
1957	1,200	702	123	375	535	253	92	190	11,422
1956	1,439	1,067	105	267	438	190	97	151	10,659
1955	1,174	646	205	323	421	191	89	141	9,658
1954	2,684	2,317	94	273	433	168	109	156	8,905
1953	1,353	1,038	119	196	344	139	86	119	6,654
1952	1,102	797	100	205	339	157	78	104	5,645
1951	790	535	79	176	349	156	82	111	4,883
1950	652	400	90	162	322	143	83	96	4,436
1949	533	254	98	181	[3] 261	106	81	84	[3] 4,077
1948	476	270	83	123	[3] 266	117	79	78	[3] 3,797
1947	608	80	107	122	[3] 258	115	78	75	[3] 3,589
1946	[3] 161	55	49	62	[3] 261	124	78	72	[3] 3,538
1945	[3] 49	11	22	20	[3] 258	115	87	78	[3] 3,640

* Denotes first year for which figures include Alaska and Hawaii.
[1] Excludes refunding issues.
[2] Excludes redemptions by refunding.
[3] Duplicated and interunit obligations have been excluded from totals only.

Series Q 148-162. Motor Vehicle Factory Sales and Registrations and Motor Fuel Usage: 1900 to 1990

(Number sold includes sales of military vehicles)

Year	Motor-vehicle factory sales			Motor-vehicle registrations		Motor-fuel usage	Year	Motor-vehicle factory sales			Motor-vehicle registrations		Motor-fuel usage
	Number of passenger cars	Number of motor trucks and buses [1]	Total	Automobiles	Total	Passenger vehicles		Number of passenger cars	Number of motor trucks and buses [1]	Total	Automobiles	Total	Passenger vehicles
	148	150	152	153	156	159		148	150	152	153	156	159
	1,000	1,000	1,000	1,000	Mil. gal.	Mil. gal.		1,000	1,000	1,000	1,000	Mil. gal.	Mil. gal.
1990	6,050	3,719	144,000	45,000	131,600	72,400	1945	69.5	655.6	31,035.4	25,796.9	22,046	14,023
1989	6,807	4,062	143,000	44,000	131,800	72,700	1944	.6	737.5	30,479.3	25,566.4	19,292	11,805
1988	7,105	4,121	141,000	43,000	130,100	71,900	1943	.1	699.6	30,888.1	36,009.0	18,642	11,424
1987	7,085	3,821	137,000	42,000	127,500	70,600	1942	222.8	818.6	33,003.6	27,972.8	22,438	[2] 14,974
1986	7,516	3,393	135,000	41,000	125,200	71,400	1941	3,779.6	1,060.8	34,894.1	29,624.2	26,429	18,502
1985	8,002	3,357	132,000	40,000	121,300	69,300	1940	3,717.3	754.9	32,453.2	27,465.8	24,038	16,759
1984	7,621	3,075	128,000	38,000	118,700	68,700	1939	2,888.5	700.3	31,009.9	26,226.3	22,571	15,826
1983	6,739	2,414	126,000	37,000	116,100	69,900	1938	2,019.5	488.8	29,813.7	25.250.4	21,311	15,069
1982	5,049	1,906	124,000	36,000	113,400	70,100	1937	3,929.2	891.0	30,058.8	25,467.2	21,115	15,018
1981	6,255	1,701	123,000	35,000	114,500	71,000	1936	3,679.2	782.2	28,506.8	24,182.6	19,561	14,026
1980	6,400	1,667	122,000	34,000	115,000	71,900	1935	3,273,8	697.3	26,546.1	22,257.8	17,637	—
1979	8,419	3,037	118,000	33,000	122,100	80,200	1934	2,160.8	576.2	25,261.7	21,544.7	16,557	—
1978	9,165	3,706	117,000	32,000	125,100	83,800	1933	1,560.5	329.2	24,159.2	20,657.2	15,367	—
1977	9,201	3,441	112,000	30,000	119,600	80,700	1932	1,103.5	228.3	24,391.0	20,901.4	15,427	—
1976	8,500	2,979	110,000	28,000	115,700	78,800	1931	1,948.1	432.2	26,093.9	22,396.2	16,621	—
1975	6,713	2,272	107,000	26,000	109,000	76,400	1930	2,787.4	575.3	26,749.8	23,034.7	15,777	—
1974	7,331	2,727	129,900	104,800	106,300	74,200	1929	4,455.1	881.9	26,704.8	23,120.8	15,051	—
1973	9,658	2,980	125,700	102,000	110,500	78,000	1928	3,775.4	583.3	24,688.6	21,362.2	13,090	—
1972	8,824	2,447	118,800	97,100	105,100	73,500	1927	2,936.5	464.7	23,303.4	20,193.3	11,936	—
1971	8,585	2,053	113,000	92,700	97,600	69,500	1926	3,692.3	608.6	22,200.1	19,267.9	10,552	—
1970	6,546.8	1,692.4	108,407.3	89,279.8	96,331	66,728	1925	3,735.1	530.6	20,068.5	17,481.0	9,143	—
1969	8,223.7	1,923.1	105,096.6	86,861.3	92,240	63,395	1924	3,185.8	416.6	17,612.9	15,436.0	7,809	—
1968	8,822.1	1,896.0	100,884.7	83,591.6	87,154	59,456	1923	3,624.7	409.2	15,102.1	13,253.0	6,313	—
1967	7,436.7	1,539.4	96,930.9	80,414.1	81,911	56,020	1922	2,274.1	269.9	12,273.5	10,704.0	5,014	—
1966	8,598.3	1,731.0	93,962.0	78,122.9	78,979	54,208	1921	1,468.0	148.0	10,493.6	9,212.1	4,064	—
1965	9,305.5	1,751.8	90,357.6	75,257.5	75,312	51,169	1920	1,905.5	321.7	9,239.1	8,131.5	3,448	—
1964	7,751.8	1,540.4	86,301.2	71,982.7	72,097	48,431	1919	1,651.6	224.7	7,576.8	6,679.1	2,747	—
1963	7,637.7	1,462.7	82,713.7	69,055.4	68,760	46,084	1918	943.4	227.2	6,160.4	5,554.9	—	—
1962	6,933.2	1,240.1	79,173.3	66,108.2	66,101	44,608	1917	1,745.7	128.1	5,118.5	4,727.4	—	—
1961	5,542.7	1,133.8	75,958.2	63,417.3	64,534	42,863	1916	1,525.5	92.1	3,617.9	3,367.8	—	—
1960	6,674.7	1,194.4	73,868.6	61,682.3	63,210	41,996	1915	895.9	74.0	2,490.9	2,332.4	—	—
1959*	5,591.2	1,137.3	71,354.4	59,453.9	61,715	40,879	1914	548.1	24.9	1,763.0	1,664.0	—	—
1958	4,257.8	877.2	68,296.5	56,890.5	58,589	38,904	1913	461.5	23.5	1,258.0	1,190.3	—	—
1957	6,113.3	1,107.1	67,124.9	55,917.8	56,954	37,594	1912	356.0	22.0	944.0	901.5	—	—
1956	5,816.1	1,104.4	65,148.2	54,210.9	55,149	36,128	1911	199.3	10.6	639.5	618.7	—	—
1955	7,920.1	1,249.1	62,688.7	52,144.7	52,565	34,319	1910	181.0	6.0	468.5	548.3	—	—
1954	5,558.8	1,042.1	58,505.3	48,468.4	49,118	31,670	1909	123.9	3.2	312.0	305.9	—	—
1953	6,116.9	1,206.2	56,217.4	46.429,2	47,381	30,384	1908	63.5	1.5	198.4	194.4	—	—
1952	4,320.7	1,218.1	53,262.4	43,823.0	45,037	28,735	1907	43.0	1.0	143.2	140.3	—	—
1951	5,338.4	1,426.8	51,912.7	42,688.3	42,473	26,910	1906	33.2	.8	108.1	105.9	—	—
1950	6,665.8	1,337.1	49,161.6	40,339.0	39,860	25,037	1905	24.2	.7	78.8	77.4	—	—
1949	5,119.4	1,134.1	44,690.2	36,457.9	36,440	23,645	1904	22.1	.7	55.2	54.5	—	—
1948	3,909.2	1,376.2	41,085.5	33,355.2	34,329	22,149	1903	11.2	—	32.9	32.9	—	—
1947	3,558.1	1,239.4	37,841.4	30,849.3	31,680	20,864	1902	9.0	—	23.0	23.0	—	—
1946	2,148.6	940.9	34,373.0	28,217.0	28,876	19,502	1901	7.0	—	14.8	14.8	—	—
							1900	4.1	—	8.0	8.0	—	—

* Denotes first year for which figures include Alaska and Hawaii.
[1] A substantial portion of the number of trucks and buses consists of chassis only, without bodies.
[2] Beginning 1942, includes travel by military vehicles.

Series Q 199-207. Miles of Travel by Motor Vehicles: 1921 to 1990
(In million vehicle-miles)

Year	Total travel, all motor vehicles	Passenger vehicles[1], urban travel	Trucks and combinations, urban travel	Passenger vehicles[1] (Avg miles per vehicle)	Trucks and combinations (Avg miles per vehicle)	Year	Total travel, all motor vehicles	Passenger vehicles[1], urban travel	Trucks and combinations, urban travel	Passenger vehicles[1] (Avg miles per vehicle)	Trucks and combinations (Avg miles per vehicle)
	199	202	204	206	207		199	202	204	206	207
1990	2,148,000	1,530,700	617,000	10,300	13,900	1955	605,646	235,384	39,721	9,400	10,697
1989	2,096,000	1,493,700	603,000	10,100	13,800	1954	561,963	210,671	36,880	9,354	10,883
1988	2,025,000	1,444,500	581,000	9,900	13,600	1953	544,433	199,754	36,304	9,417	10,927
1987	1,921,000	1,370,300	551,000	9,600	13,400	1952	513,581	189,987	34,131	9,442	10,940
1986	1,834,000	1,316,100	519,000	9,300	13,000	1951	491,093	188,670	34,001	9,208	10,790
1985	1,774,000	1,274,900	500,000	9,200	12,700	1950	458,246	184,476	33,772	9,078	10,776
1984	1,720,000	1,238,600	482,000	9,200	12,800	1949	424,461	175,686	29,678	9,468	9,915
1983	1,653,000	1,212,200	441,000	9,100	12,000	1948	397,957	170,331	28,751	9,648	10,030
1982	1,592,000	1,155,600	437,000	8,900	12,400	1947	370,894	158,770	25,318	9,814	9,955
1981	1,556,000	1,131,500	425,000	8,700	12,300	1946	340,880	148,497	21,552	10,033	9,630
1980	1,527,000	1,128,100	399,000	8,900	11,400	1945	250,173	111,401	18,760	7,870	9,270
1979	1,529,000	1,169,100	360,000	9,300	10,800	1944	212,713	93,679	17,071	6,647	8,998
1978	1,548,000	1,200,100	348,000	9,800	11,000	1943	208,192	91,942	17,048	6,366	9,034
1977	1,477,000	1,146,900	330,000	9,600	11,100	1942	268,224	119,653	18,582	7,910	9,616
1976	1,412,000	1,103,800	308,000	9,500	11,100	1941	333,612	143,101	20,490	9,663	10,750
1975	1,330,000	1,056,100	275,000	9,400	10,600	1940	302,188	130,269	19,724	9,129	10,626
1974	1,286,000	1,018,100	268,000	9,200	10,900	1939	285,402	122,805	19,448	9,025	10,504
1973	1,309,000	1,042,000	267,000	9,800	11,500	1938	271,177	117,537	18,727	8,923	10,383
1972	1,268,000	1,009,100	260,000	10,000	12,200	1937	270,110	118,216	19,856	8,819	10,264
1971	1,186,300	959,300	237,000	9,938	11,465	1936	252,128	110,419	19,031	8,675	10,098
1970	1,120,705	496,767	80,606	9,798	11,450	1935	228,568	—	—	—	—
1969	1,070,575	468,275	76,272	9,650	11,565	1934	215,563	—	—	—	—
1968	1,015,649	440,936	72,353	9,507	11,571	1933	200,642	—	—	—	—
1967	961,553	417,209	68,284	9,420	11,268	1932	200,517	—	—	—	—
1966	930,497	402,573	67,204	9,407	11,207	1931	216,151	—	—	—	—
1965	887,640	358,796	65,057	9,278	11,737	1930	206,320	—	—	—	—
1964	846,500	342,755	62,331	9,311	11,723	1929	197,720	—	—	—	—
1963	805,423	327,079	58,343	9,265	11,644	1928	172,856	—	—	—	—
1962	766,852	318,937	49,152	9,467	10,406	1927	158,453	—	—	—	—
1961	737,535	294,191	45,442	9,492	10,461	1926	140,735	—	—	—	—
1960	718,845	286,898	44,687	9,474	10,583	1925	122,346	—	—	—	—
1959 *	700,478	279,931	43,859	9,559	10,552	1924	104,838	—	—	—	—
1958	664,653	265,729	41,340	9,524	10,348	1923	84,995	—	—	—	—
1957	647,004	256,563	40,136	9,425	10,328	1922	67,697	—	—	—	—
1956	631,161	246,961	40,239	9,389	10,813	1921	55,027	—	—	—	—

* Denotes first year for which figures include Alaska and Hawaii.

[1] Passenger cars, buses and taxicabs.

Series Q 208-223. Motor Vehicle Deaths and Death Rates, by Age: 1913 to 1990

(Rates are deaths per 100,000 population)

Year	All ages Number 208	All ages Rate [1] 209	Year	All ages Number 208	All ages Rate [1] 209	Year	All ages Number 208	All ages Rate [1] 209
1990	46,300	(NA)	1970	54,633	25.3	1952	37,794	25.0
1989	47,100	18.4	1969	55,791	27.6	1951	36,996	24.6
1988	49,100	19.2	1968	55,200	28.8			
1987	48,300	19.1	1967	52,924	27.8	1950	34,763	23.3
1986	47,900	19.1	1966	53,041	28.3	1949	31,701	21.5
						1948	32,259	22.3
1985	45,900	18.4	1965	49,163	26.5	1947	32,697	23.0
1984	46,200	18.7	1964	47,700	26.1	1946	33,411	24.0
1983	44,600	18.2	1963	43,564	24.3			
1982	46,000	19.0	1962	40,804	23.1	1945	28,076	21.4
1981	51,400	21.5	1961	38,091	22.0	1944	24,282	18.3
						1943	23,823	17.7
1980	53,200	22.6	1960	38,137	22.4	1938-1942 avg.	33,549	25.5
1979	53,500	22.8	1959	37,910	22.7	1933-1937 avg.	36,313	29.3
1978	52,400	22.7	1958	36,981	22.5			
1977	49,500	22.1	1957	38,702	24.1	1928-1932 avg.	30,900	26.4
1976	47,000	21.2	1956	39,628	25.1	1923-1927 avg.	21,700	19.6
						1918-1922 avg.	12,500	12.3
1975	45,900	20.7	1955	38,426	24.6	1913-1917 avg.	6,700	7.0
1974	46,400	21.4	1954	35,586	23.0			
1973	55,500	25.8	1953	37,955	24.9			
1972	56,300	26.2						
1971	54,000	26.5						

NA Not available.

[1] Based on populations standardized for age (base 1940) to remove influence of changes in age
distribution that occurred between 1913 and 1969.

Series Q 224-232. Motor Vehicle Accidents—Number and Deaths, by Type of Accident: 1913 to 1990

Year	Total motor vehicle accidents (1,000)	Total	Non-collision accidents	With other motor vehicles	With pedestrians	With fixed objects	Per 10,000 motor vehicles	Per 100 million vehicle miles
				Collision accidents	Traffic deaths [1]		Traffic death rates	
	224	225	226	227	228	229	231	232
1990	11,500	46,300	4,900	19,400	7,400	12,900	(NA)	(NA)
1989	12,800	47,100	5,000	20,000	7,600	12,600	2.3	2.2
1988	20,600	49,100	5,300	20,900	7,700	13,400	2.5	2.3
1987	20,800	48,300	5,200	20,700	7,500	13,200	2.5	2.4
1986	17,700	47,900	13,100	20,800	8,900	3,300	2.5	2.5
1985	19,300	45,900	12,600	19,900	8,500	3,200	2.4	2.5
1984	18,800	46,200	12,600	20,300	8,600	3,000	2.8	2.6
1983	18,300	44,600	12,200	19,200	8,200	3,100	2.7	2.6
1982	18,100	46,000	12,600	19,800	8,400	3,200	2.9	2.8
1981	18,000	51,400	14,200	22,200	9,400	3,600	3.4	3.2
1980	17,900	53,200	14,700	23,000	9,700	3,700	3.5	3.3
1979	18,100	53,500	15,200	22,200	9,700	3,500	3.5	3.3
1978	18,300	52,400	14,500	22,400	9,600	3,600	3.5	3.3
1977	17,600	49,500	13,700	20,200	9,100	3,400	3.4	3.3
1976	16,800	47,000	13,000	20,100	8,600	3,200	3.4	3.3
1975	16,500	45,900	12,700	19,500	8,400	3,100	3.4	3.4
1974	15,600	46,400	12,800	19,700	8,500	3,100	3.6	3.5
1973	16,600	55,500	15,600	23,600	10,200	3,800	4.4	4.1
1972	17,000	56,300	15,800	23,900	10,300	3,900	4.4	4.3
1971	16,400	54,000	13,700	23,300	10,600	7,100	4.8	4.7
1970	16,000	54,633	[2] 15,400	23,200	9,900	[2] 3,800	4.9	4.9
1969	15,500	55,791	15,700	23,700	10,100	3,900	5.2	5.2
1968	14,600	54,862	17,400	22,400	9,900	2,700	5.3	5.4
1967	13,700	52,924	16,700	22,000	9,400	2,350	5.4	5.5
1966	13,600	53,041	16,300	22,200	9,400	2,500	5.5	5.7
1965	13,200	49,163	14,900	20,800	8,900	2,200	5.4	5.5
1964	12,300	47,700	14,600	19,600	9,000	2,100	5.5	5.6
1963	11,500	43,564	13,800	17,600	8,200	1,900	5.2	5.4
1962	11,000	40,804	12,900	16,400	7,900	1,750	5.1	5.3
1961	10,400	38,091	12,200	14,700	7,650	1,700	5.0	5.2
1960	10,400	38,137	11,900	14,800	7,850	1,700	5.1	5.3
1959*	10,200	37,910	11,800	14,900	7,850	1,600	5.3	5.4
1958	10,000	36,981	11,600	14,200	7,650	1,650	5.4	5.6
1957	10,200	38,702	11,800	15,400	7,850	1,700	5.7	6.0
1956	10,300	39,628	13,000	15,200	7,900	1,600	6.1	6.3
1955	9,900	38,426	12,100	14,500	8,200	1,600	6.1	6.3
1954	9,550	35,586	11,500	12,800	8,000	1,500	6.1	6.3
1953	9,900	37,955	12,200	13,400	8,750	1,500	6.7	7.0
1952	9,500	37,794	11,900	13,500	8,900	1,450	7.1	7.4
1951	9,400	36,996	11,200	13,100	9,150	1,400	7.1	7.5
1950	8,300	34,763	10,600	11,650	9,000	1,300	7.1	7.6
1949	7,600	31,701	9,100	10,500	8,800	1,100	7.1	7.5
1948	8,200	32,259	8,950	10,200	9,950	1,000	7.9	8.1
1947	8,400	32,697	8,800	9,900	10,450	1,000	8.6	8.8
1946	6,150	33,411	8,900	9,400	11,600	950	9.7	9.8
1945	5,500	28,076	6,600	7,150	11,000	800	9.1	11.2
1944	4,800	24,282	5,600	5,700	9,900	700	8.0	11.4
1943	4,400	23,823	5,690	5,300	9,900	700	7.7	11.4
1942	5,200	28,309	6,740	7,300	10,650	850	8.6	10.6
1941	7,000	39,969	9,450	12,500	13,550	1,350	11.5	12.0

See footnotes at end of chart.

Series Q 224-232. Motor Vehicle Accidents—Number and Deaths, by Type of Accident: 1913 to 1990—Cont'd.

Year	Total motor vehicle accidents (1,000)	Traffic deaths [1]					Traffic death rates	
		Total	Non-collision accidents	Collision accidents			Per 10,000 motor vehicles	Per 100 million vehicle miles
				With other motor vehicles	With pedestrians	With fixed objects		
	224	**225**	**226**	**227**	**228**	**229**	**231**	**232**
1940	6,100	34,501	7,800	10,100	12,700	1,100	10.6	11.4
1939	5,700	32,386	7,900	8,700	12,400	1,000	10.4	11.4
1938	5,800	32,582	7,350	8,900	12,850	940	10.9	12.0
1937	7,000	39,643	9,690	10,320	15,500	1,160	13.2	14.7
1936	—	38,089	9,410	9,500	15,250	1,060	13.4	15.1
1935	—	36,369	9,720	8,750	14,350	1,010	13.7	15.9
1934	—	36,101	9,820	8,110	14,480	1,040	14.3	16.8
1933	—	31,363	8,680	6,470	12,840	900	13.0	15.6
1932	—	29,500	7,000	6,070	11,490	800	12.2	16.1
1931	—	33,700	7,850	6,820	13,370	870	13.0	17.0
1930	—	32,900	8,730	5,880	12,900	720	12.4	17.4
1929	—	31,200	8,430	5,400	12,250	620	11.8	17.3
1928	—	28,000	7,360	4,310	11,420	540	11.4	17.4
1927	—	25,800	7,280	3,430	10,820	500	11.2	17.7
1926	—	23,400	—	—	—	—	10.6	18.0
1925	—	21,900	—	—	—	—	11.0	17.9
1924	—	19,400	—	—	—	—	11.0	—
1923	—	18,400	—	—	—	—	12.2	—
1922	—	15,300	—	—	—	—	—	—
1921	—	13,900	—	—	—	—	—	—
1920	—	12,500	—	—	—	—	—	—
1919	—	11,200	—	—	—	—	—	—
1918	—	10,700	—	—	—	—	—	—
1917	—	10,200	—	—	—	—	—	—
1916	—	8,200	—	—	—	—	—	—
1915	—	6,600	—	—	—	—	—	—
1914	—	4,700	—	—	—	—	—	—
1913	—	4,200	—	—	—	—	—	—

NA Not available.

[1] Totals may not quite equal sums of various types because totals for most types are estimated, and these have been rounded.

[2] Data based on improved reporting procedure; therefore not entirely comparable with other years.

Series Q 235-250.   Public Transit Mileage, Equipment, Passengers and Passenger Revenue: 1922 to 1990

Year	Railway cars	Trolley coaches	Motor buses	Total revenue and nonrevenue passenger (millions)	Passenger revenue (mil. dol.)	Employees (1,000)	Employee payroll (mil. dol.)
	238	239	240	241	246	247	248
1990	10,419	832	59,753	8,873	5,858	276	7,325
1989	10,506	725	58,919	8,931	5,420	272	6,898
1988	10,539	710	62,572	8,666	5,225	276	6,675
1987	10,168	671	63,017	8,735	5,114	277	6,324
1986	10,386	680	66,218	8,777	5,113	278	6,119
1985	9,326	676	64,285	8,636	4,575	270	5,843
1984	9,083	664	67,294	8,829	4,448	263	5,488
1983	9,943	686	62,093	7,889	3,172	195	3,921
1982	9,867	763	62,114	7,741	3,077	194	3,731
1981	9,801	751	60,393	7,964	2,701	193	3,494
1980	9,641	823	59,411	8,567	2,557	187	3,281
1979	9,522	725	54,490	8,130	2,436	178	3,025
1978	9,567	593	52,866	7,616	2,271	165	2,741
1977	9,639	645	51,968	7,286	2,280	163	2,547
1976	9,714	685	52,382	7,081	2,161	163	2,404
1975	9,608	703	50,811	6,972	1,861	160	2,236
1974	9,403	718	48,700	6,935	1,940	153	1,967
1973	9,387	794	48,286	6,660	1,798	141	1,624
1972	9,423	1,030	49,075	6,567	1,729	138	1,455
1971	9,325	1,037	49,150	6,847	1,741	139	1,393
1970	10,600	1,050	49,700	7,332	1,639.1	138	1,274
1969	10,665	1,082	49,600	7,803	1,554.7	141	1,184
1968	10,745	1,185	50,000	8,019	1,470.2	144	1,110
1967	10,645	1,244	50,180	8,172	1,457.4	146	1,055
1966	10,680	1,326	50,130	8,083	1,385.4	144	995
1965	10,664	1,453	49,600	8,253	1,340.1	145	964
1964	10,614	1,865	49,200	8,328	1,326.0	145	917
1963	10,634	2,155	49,400	8,400	1,316.3	147	892
1962	11,084	3,161	48,800	8,695	1,330.2	149	878
1961	11,419	3,593	49,000	8,883	1,320.9	152	856
1960	11,866	3,826	49,600	9,395	1,334.9	156	857
1959*	11,983	4,297	49,500	9,557	1,308.0	159	832
1958	12,201	4,848	50,100	9,732	1,282.2	165	831
1957	12,759	5,412	50,800	10,389	1,319.8	177	840
1956	13,225	5,748	51,400	10,941	1,351.1	186	852
1955	14,532	6,157	52,400	11,529	1,358.9	198	864
1954	15,600	6,598	54,000	12,392	1,410.0	211	895
1953	17,234	6,941	54,700	13,902	1,448.6	220	913
1952	19,176	7,180	55,980	15,119	1,438.1	227	903
1951	20,604	7,071	57,660	16,125	1,411.6	232	872
1950	22,986	6,504	56,820	17,246	1,386.8	240	835
1949	24,728	6,366	57,035	19,008	1,419.7	253	841
1948	26,280	5,687	58,540	21,368	1,416.8	261	829
1947	30,158	4,707	56,917	22,540	1,324.2	266	790
1946	33,479	3,916	52,450	23,372	1,331.5	261	713
1945	36,377	3,711	49,670	23,254	1,313.7	242	632
1944	37,199	3,561	48,400	23,017	1,296.9	242	599
1943	37,505	3,501	47,100	22,000	1,235.6	239	554
1942	37,508	3,385	46,000	18,000	979.1	219	462
1941	37,670	3,029	39,300	14,085	758.8	205	386
1940	37,662	2,802	35,000	13,098	701.5	203	360
1939	40,372	2,184	32,600	12,837	681.5	202	352
1938	42,605	2,032	28,500	12,645	662.9	202	344
1937	45,312	1,655	27,500	13,246	689.7	209	348

See footnote at end of chart.

Series Q 235-250. Public Transit Mileage, Equipment, Passengers and Passenger Revenue: 1922 to 1990—Cont'd.

Year	Railway cars	Trolley coaches	Motor buses	Total revenue and nonrevenue passenger (millions)	Passenger revenue (mil. dol.)	Employees (1,000)	Employee payroll (mil. dol.)
	238	239	240	241	246	247	248
1936	48,103	1,136	23,900	13,146	685.5	206	328
1935	50,466	578	23,800	12,226	642.3	204	311
1934	54,118	441	18,700	12,038	—	204	303
1933	58,124	310	17,200	11,327	—	201	287
1932	—	—	—	12,025	—	—	—
1931	—	—	—	13,924	—	—	—
1930	—	—	—	15,567	—	—	—
1929	—	—	—	16,985	—	—	—
1928	—	—	—	16,989	—	—	—
1927	—	—	—	17,201	—	—	—
1926	—	—	—	17,234	—	—	—
1925	—	—	—	16,651	—	—	—
1924	—	—	—	16,301	—	—	—
1923	—	—	—	16,311	—	—	—
1922	—	—	—	15,735	—	—	—

* Denotes first year for which figures include Alaska and Hawaii.

Series Q 251-263.   Oil Pipelines Operated and Oil Originated: 1921 to 1990

Year	Miles of line operated	Total oil delivered out of system	Investment in carrier property	Net income	Year	Miles of line operated	Total oil delivered out of system	Investment in carrier property	Net income
	251	254	258	263		251	254	258	263
		Mil. bbl.	Mil. dol.	Mil. dol.			Mil. bbl.	Mil. dol.	Mil. dol.
1990	168,000	11,378	25,828	2,340	1955	140,374	4,039	2,586	153
1989	169,000	11,281	24,638	2,227	1954	138,962	3,705	2,501	124
1988	171,000	11,484	24,332	2,505	1953	133,900	3,627	2,312	109
1987	168,000	11,194	21,353	2,475	1952	132,715	3,359	2,064	97
1986	170,000	11,002	22,384	2,051	1951	131,457	3,201	1,822	82
1985	171,000	10,745	21,605	2,431	1950	128,589	2,740	1,656	81
1984	174,000	10,224	19,397	2,545	1949	124,984	2,448	1,498	58
1983	168,000	10,310	22,255	2,353	1948	124,092	2,697	1,381	57
1982	173,000	10,181	21,942	2,162	1947	119,298	2,474	1,225	53
1981	172,800	10,223	21,250	2,031	1946	116,544	2,260	1,106	56
1980	173,000	10,600	19,752	1,912	1945	113,351	2,365	1,043	66
1979	169,800	11,140	18,990	1,648	1944	111,615	2,389	1,001	66
1978	161,600	10,768	17,654	1,696	1943	108,783	2,077	965	61
1977	154,500	10,019	16,736	478	1942	106,485	1,764	919	57
1976	169,900	9,742	13,684	595	1941	105,435	1,642	885	79
1975	171,000	9,391	10,740	456	1940	100,156	1,407	842	80
1974	169,000	9,132	8,038	330	1939	98,681	—	830	81
1973	170,100	9,416	7,000	408	1938	95,938	—	808	93
1972	172,100	8,847	6,749	415	1937	96,612	—	803	103
1971	175,000	8,183	6,305	314	1936	93,926	—	774	92
1970	175,735	8,147	5,786	312	1935	92,037	—	763	78
1969	170,824	7,745	5,379	273	1934	93,070	—	758	84
1968	169,307	7,269	5,139	262	1933	93,724	—	766	106
1967	165,478	6,800	4,745	[1] 261	1932	92,782	—	764	112
1966	163,155	6,238	4,433	236	1931	93,090	—	845	121
1965	161,412	5,864	4,178	218	1930	88,728	—	773	124
1964	159,583	5,565	4,040	210	1929	85,796	—	741	142
1963	156,812	5,322	3,915	201	1928	81,676	—	659	117
1962	155,053	5,109	3,518	204	1927	76,070	—	609	93
1961	153,737	4,923	3,407	181	1926	72,846	—	539	80
1960*	151,968	4,783	3,300	169	1925	70,009	—	511	88
1959	149,159	4,659	3,197	183	1924	68,185	—	496	72
1958	144,354	4,317	2,949	162	1923	64,760	—	432	63
1957	145,236	4,472	2,843	159	1922	57,349	—	382	59
1956	142,686	4,458	2,716	178	1921	55,260	—	365	34

* Denotes first year for which figures include Alaska and Hawaii.

[1] After extraordinary and period items.

Series Q 284-312. Railroad Mileage, Equipment and Passenger Traffic and Revenue: 1890 to 1990

(Includes intercorporate duplications. Unless otherwise noted, covers Class I, II and III railroads, except that prior to 1908 includes returns for switching and terminal companies where applicable)

Year ending x	Total mileage of track operated [1]	Total locomotives in service [3]	Passenger-train cars in service, railroad only	Equipment [2] Freight-train cars in service [5] Number	Average capacity [4]
288	295	301	304	305	
Dec. 31					Tons
1990	239,000	18,835	(NA)	659,000	87.5
1989	249,000	19,015	(NA)	682,000	87.8
1988	251,000	19,364	2,332	725,000	86.4
1987	254,000	19,358	2,350	749,000	85.0
1986	256,000	20,790	2,307	799,000	84.1
1985	257,000	22,932	2,502	867,000	83.2
1984	264,000	22,548	2,580	948,000	83.4
1983	270,000	25,838	2,610	1,007,000	82.4
1982	275,000	27,073	3,736	1,039,000	81.6
1981	278,000	27,808	3,945	1,111,000	80.5
1980	290,000	28,094	4,347	1,168,000	78.5
1979	300,000	27,900	2,400	1,148,000	77.7
1978	322,000	27,000	2,400	1,201,000	76.9
1977	321,000	29,700	5,700	1,275,000	75.5
1976	314,000	29,600	5,600	1,309,000	73.8
1975	324,000	28,210	6,471	1,359,000	72.9
1974	354,000	30,110	7,080	1,373,000	71.4
1973	354,000	29,926	7,363	1,387,000	70.5
1972	356,000	29,338	7,763	1,411,000	69.6
1971	359,194	29,185	8,869	1,441,000	68.4
1970	360,330	29,122	11,378	1,453,708	67.1
1969	364,915	29,090	12,630	1,464,194	65.8
1968	366,238	29,448	14,816	1,484,571	64.3
1967	368,030	29,874	17,822	1,510,963	63.4
1966	370,104	30,124	18,974	1,523,741	61.4
1965	370,636	30,061	20,022	1,515,169	59.8
1964	372,300	30,296	21,510	1,517,564	58.2
1963	374,522	30,506	22,616	1,542,456	56.8
1962	376,290	30,701	23,430	1,581,213	56.3
1961	379,415	30,889	24,433	1,635,342	55.7
1960*	*381,745	*31,178	*25,746	*1,690,396	*55.4
1959	383,912	31,539	27,419	1,708,116	55.0
1958	385,264	31,616	28,999	1,755,775	54.8
1957	386,978	32,391	29,564	1,777,557	54.5
1956	389,668	32,593	30,817	1,738,631	54.0
1955	390,965	33,533	32,118	1,723,747	53.7
1954	392,580	35,033	33,035	1,761,386	53.7
1953	393,736	37,251	34,106	1,801,874	53.5
1952	394,631	39,697	34,942	1,783,352	53.2
1951	395,831	42,473	36,326	1,777,878	52.9
1950	396,380	42,951	37,359	1,745,778	52.6
1949	397,232	43,272	38,006	1,778,811	52.4
1948	397,203	44,474	39,406	1,785,067	51.9
1947	397,355	44,344	39,057	1,759,758	51.5
1946	398,037	45,511	38,697	1,768,400	51.3

Year ending x	Total mileage of track operated [1]	Total locomotives in service [3]	Passenger-train cars in service, railroad only	Equipment [4] Freight-train cars in service [5] Number	Average capacity [4]
288	295	301	304	305	
Dec. 31 (cont'd.)					Tons
1945	398,054	46,253	38,633	1,787,073	51.1
1944	398,437	46,305	38,217	1,797,012	50.8
1943	398,730	45,406	38,331	1,784,472	50.7
1942	399,627	44,671	38,446	1,773,735	50.5
1941	403,625	44,375	38,334	1,732,673	50.3
1940	405,975	44,333	38,308	1,684,171	50.0
1939	408,350	45,172	38,977	1,680,519	49.7
1938	411,324	46,544	39,931	1,731,096	49.4
1937	414,572	47,555	40,949	1,776,428	49.2
1936	416,381	48,009	41,390	1,790,043	48.8
1935	419,228	49,541	42,426	1,867,381	48.3
1934	422,401	51,423	44,884	1,973,247	48.0
1933	425,664	54,228	47,677	2,072,632	47.5
1932	428,402	56,732	50,598	2,184,690	47.0
1931	429,823	58,652	52,096	2,245,904	47.0
1930	429,883	60,189	53,584	2,322,267	46.9
1929	429,054	61,257	53,838	2,323,683	46.3
1928	427,750	63,311	54,800	2,346,751	45.8
1927	424,737	65,348	55,729	2,378,800	45.5
1926	421,341	66,847	56,855	2,403,967	45.1
1925	417,954	68,098	56,814	2,414,083	44.8
1924	415,028	69,486	57,451	2,411,627	44.3
1923	412,993	69,414	57,159	2,379,131	43.8
1922	409,359	68,518	56,827	2,352,483	43.1
1921	407,531	69,122	56,950	2,378,510	42.5
1920	403,580	68,942	56,102	2,388,424	42.4
1919	403,891	68,977	56,290	2,426,889	41.9
1918	402,343	67,936	56,611	2,397,943	41.6
1917	400,353	66,070	55,939	2,379,472	41.5
1916	397,014	65,595	55,193	2,329,475	40.9
June 30					
1916	394,944	65,314	54,774	2,343,378	40.5
1915	391,142	66,502	55,810	2,341,567	39.7
1914	387,208	67,012	54,492	2,349,734	39.1
1913	379,508	65,597	52,717	2,298,478	38.3
1912	371,238	63,463	51,583	2,229,163	37.4
1911	362,824	62,463	49,906	2,208,997	36.9
1910	351,767	60,019	47,179	2,148,478	35.9
1909	342,351	58,219	45,664	2,086,835	35.3
1908	333,646	57,698	45,292	2,100,784	34.9
1907	327,975	55,388	43,973	1,991,557	33.8
1906	317,083	51,672	42,262	1,837,914	32.2
1905	306,797	48,357	40,713	1,731,409	30.8
1904	297,073	46,743	39,752	1,692,194	30.1

See footnotes on next page.

Series Q 284-312. Railroad Mileage, Equipment and Passenger Traffic and Revenue: 1890 to 1990—Cont'd.

(Includes intercorporate duplications. Unless otherwise noted, covers Class I, II and III railroads, except that prior to 1908 includes returns for switching and terminal companies where applicable)

| | | | | Equipment [2] | | | | | | Equipment [4] | | |
| | | | | | Freight-train cars in service [5] | | | | | | | Freight-train c[...] in service [5] |
Year ending x	Total mileage of track operated [1]	Total locomotives in service [3]	Passenger-train cars in service, railroad only	Number	Average capacity [4]	Year ending x	Total mileage of track operated [1]	Total locomotives in service [3]	Passenger-train cars in service, railroad only	Number	Average capacity [4]
	288	**295**	**301**	**304**	**305**		**288**	**295**	**301**	**304**	**305**
June 30 (cont'd.)					*Tons*						
1903	283,822	43,871	38,140	1,653,782	29.4	1895	233,276	35,699	33,112	1,196,119	——
1902	274,196	41,225	36,987	1,546,101	——	1894	229,796	35,492	33,018	1,205,169	——
1901	265,352	39,584	35,969	1,464,328	——	1893	221,864	34,788	31,384	1,013,307	——
						1892	211,051	33,136	28,876	966,998	——
1900	258,784	37,663	34,713	1,365,531	——	1891	207,446	32,139	27,949	947,300	——
1899	250,143	36,703	33,850	1,295,510	——	1890	199,876	30,140	26,820	918,491	——
1898	245,334	36,234	33,595	1,248,826	——						
1897	242,013	35,986	33,626	1,221,730	——						
1896	239,140	35,950	33,003	1,221,887	——						

NA Not available.
* Denotes first year for which figures include Alaska and Hawaii.
[1] For railroads reporting track by class. Excludes circular and unofficial figures which cover road, fast track only.
[2] Includes switching and terminal companies.

[3] For 1890-1927, number of locomotives; for 1928-1970, number of units, except for steam locomotives. (A unit is the least number of wheel bases together with superstructure capable of independent propulsion, but not necessarily equipped with an independent control.)
[4] For 1916-1956, represents steam locomotives and freight cars of class I railroads, excluding switching and terminal companies; for 1957-1967, includes all class I locomotives, excluding switching and terminal companies.
[5] Excludes caboose cars.

Series Q 331-345. Railroad Freight Traffic and Revenue: 1912 to 1990

(In tons of 2,000 pounds)

Year ending x	Total revenue freight originated (Class I railroads) in carloads	Year ending x	Total revenue freight originated (Class I railroads) in carloads	Year ending x	Total revenue freight originated (Class I railroads) in carloads	Year ending x	Total revenue freight originated (Class I railroads) in carloads
	332		**332**		**332**		**332**
Dec. 31	*1,000*		*1,000*		*1,000*		*1,000*
1990	1,425,000	1970	1,484,110	1950	1,343,308	1930	1,123,530
1989	1,403,000	1969	1,472,620	1949	1,213,911	1929	1,303,048
1988	1,429,000	1968	1,430,441	1948	1,488,612	1928	1,248,989
1987	1,372,000	1967	1,406,668	1947	1,514,985	1927	1,243,171
1986	1,306,000	1966	1,447,852	1946	1,342,230	1926	1,296,651
1985	1,312,100	1965	1,386,090	1945	1,404,080	1925	1,206,655
1984	1,429,400	1964	1,353,117	1944	1,471,366	1924	1,146,747
1983	1,292,600	1963	1,283,382	1943	1,462,314	1923	1,234,692
1982	1,268,600	1962	1,231,415	1942	1,403,612	1922	980,516
1981	1,453,000	1961	1,191,154	1941	1,209,559	1921	898,191
1980	1,492,400	1960	1,237,575	1940	994,728	1920	[1] 1,202,219
1979	1,502,100	1959	1,228,277	1939	886,794	1919	[1] 1,045,148
1978	1,390,400	1958	1,185,951	1938	757,470	1918	1,209,957
1977	1,394,700	1957	1,374,884	1937	998,398	1917	1,210,247
1976	1,370,000	1956	1,440,937	1936	942,538	1916	[1] 1,150,456
1975	1,395,100	1955	1,389,346	1935	775,588	June 30	
1974	1,530,000	1954	1,217,005	1934	750,951		
1973	1,532,000	1953	1,376,046	1933	684,592	1916	[1] 878,761
1972	1,448,000	1952	1,343,294	1932	630,989	1915	[1] 982,892
1971	1,391,000	1951	1,467,023	1931	871,412	1914	[1] 1,026,817
						1913	[1] 889,999
						1912	[1] 866,398

[1] Includes the following amounts of unassigned carload tonnage (thousands): 1911, 35,199; 1912, 32,266; 1913, 15,617; 1914, 14,671; 1915, 2,268; 1916, 1,367; and 1919, 338.

Series Q 438-448. Merchant Vessels Completed by U.S. Shipyards: 1914 to 1988

(Tons in thousands. Represents self-propelled steel vessels of 2,000 gross tons and over for domestic use. Excludes Alaska and Hawaii.)

| Year | Merchant vessels | | Cargo | | | Tanker | | |
| | Number | Gross tons | Number | Gross tons | Deadweight tons | Number | Gross tons | Deadweight tons |
	438	439	443	444	445	446	447	448
1988	4	153	3	58	63	1	95	209
1987	4	153	3	58	63	1	95	209
1986	5	215	2	66	53	3	149	271
1985	8	172	4	113	97	4	59	92
1984	5	118	X	X	X	5	118	210
1983	13	376	6	228	219	7	148	277
1982	11	337	6	221	219	5	116	226
1981	12	275	2	53	73	10	222	358
1980	10	375	6	105	114	4	270	354
1979	15	1,149	4	53	47	11	1,096	1,901
1978	14	912	2	27	30	12	885	1,392
1977	17	884	2	25	37	15	859	1,585
1976	16	615	4	57	76	12	558	1,176
1975	15	452	3	65	71	12	387	742
1974	20	697	11	314	402	9	383	759
1973	24	734	18	419	450	6	315	653
1972	13	357	7	151	187	6	206	415
1971	14	394	6	151	170	8	243	473
1970	13	342	6	120	134	7	222	427
1969	22	418	14	217	247	8	201	381
1968	21	319	18	256	291	3	63	113
1967	12	143	12	143	150	X	X	X
1966	13	146	12	125	161	1	21	36
1965	13	173	11	121	154	2	52	92
1964	15	213	10	104	123	4	95	166
1963	35	418	23	250	289	6	117	200
1962	27	392	23	265	303	3	113	186
1961	25	369	18	190	224	7	179	298
1960	26	410	15	134	163	11	276	456
1959	30	714	3	40	73	26	668	1,095
1958	30	572	5	48	67	21	463	759
1957	19	297	3	8	6	16	289	457
1956	8	113	2	7	15	6	106	169
1955	9	119	7	84	95	2	35	55
1954	39	585	11	106	159	27	475	764
1953	45	570	22	212	234	22	354	555
1952	31	399	17	170	289	8	127	202
1951	10	148	4	29	43	4	71	116
1950	26	405	3	27	44	23	378	609
1949	33	541	X	X	X	33	541	863
1948	24	159	17	92	159	6	52	88
1947	39	247	28	154	224	3	19	36
1946	83	646	66	487	729	8	82	121
1945	1,041	7,615	807	5,336	7,206	188	1,770	2,787
1944	1,463	11,403	1,175	8,455	11,858	240	2,486	3,955
1943	1,661	12,486	1,410	10,103	14,921	231	2,163	3,420
1942	724	5,393	652	4,679	6,843	61	612	982
1941	95	749	61	423	598	28	268	424
1940	53	445	31	227	335	16	149	238
1939	28	241	14	92	128	11	119	193
1938	24	181	6	39	56	18	142	228
1937	15	122	X	X	X	15	122	192
1936	8	63	X	X	X	8	63	105

See footnote at end of chart.

Series Q 438-448.   Merchant Vessels Completed by U.S. Shipyards:
1914 to 1988—Cont'd.

(Tons in thousands. Represents self-propelled steel vessels of 2,000 gross tons and over for domestic use. Excludes Alaska and Hawaii.)

| Year | Merchant vessels | | Cargo | | | Tanker | | |
	Number	Gross tons	Number	Gross tons	Deadweight tons	Number	Gross tons	Deadweight tons
	438	439	443	444	445	446	447	448
1935	2	19	X	X	X	2	19	30
1934	2	10	2	10	15	X	X	X
1933	4	50	X	X	X	X	X	X
1932	15	145	2	16	22	X	X	X
1931	14	151	X	X	X	5	42	70
1930	18	164	2	16	24	11	97	161
1929	8	65	5	33	49	1	9	15
1928	7	72	X	X	X	4	28	44
1927	19	155	9	73	104	3	30	50
1926	8	54	2	16	26	1	9	15
1925	12	84	9	65	92	X	X	X
1924	12	84	4	34	48	1	7	11
1923	18	117	9	68	110	2	16	23
1922	19	168	10	78	156	6	48	71
1921	183	1,359	57	317	485	104	786	1,158
1920	467	2,396	375	1,758	2,696	80	538	778
1919	723	3,370	679	3,086	4,680	42	273	395
1918	414	1,770	375	1,508	2,283	34	232	339
1917	125	642	92	414	627	32	218	314
1916	74	370	49	201	300	24	163	247
1915	24	128	17	88	131	4	20	30
1914	26	135	17	88	130	8	45	67

X Represents zero.

Series Q 449-458.   Shipbuilding in Private Shipyards—Summary: 1949 to 1991

(Tons in thousands; gross tons for commercial vessels, light displacement tons for naval vessels. Covers steel self-propelled vessels 1,000 tons or more)

Year		Commercial vessels			Naval vessels		
		Under construction Jan. 1	Contracted for	Delivered	Under construction Jan. 1	Contracted for	Delivered
		449	451	453	454	456	458
1991 [1]		3	3	X	89	(NA)	(NA)
1990		X	3	X	98	89	15
1989		X	X	X	105	98	23
1988		X	X	X	83	105	10
1987		6	X	4	79	83	16
1986		7	6	1	85	79	20
1985		10	7	3	100	85	26
1984		10	10	5	111	100	22
1983		21	10	15	105	111	21
1982		35	21	17	93	105	18
1981		49	35	22	91	93	26
1980		69	49	23	99	91	19
1979		70	69	21	102	99	16
1978		60	30	19	91	25	14
1977		72	13	25	88	15	12
1976		79	16	22	76	20	8
1975		96	79	19	63	76	3
1974		97	24	24	56	16	9
1973		88	43	34	57	7	8
1972		59	48	19	64	14	21
1971		49	24	14	82	15	33
1970	Number	49	13	13	108	6	32
	Tons	1,388	580	370	621	132	166
1969	Number	63	8	22	133	6	31
	Tons	1,495	309	416	701	80	159
1968	Number	64	23	24	134	15	16
	Tons	1,211	613	329	686	153	138
1967	Number	48	29	13	147	8	21
	Tons	596	740	162	745	50	109
1966	Number	45	16	13	106	54	13
	Tons	513	244	161	573	246	74
1965	Number	47	16	18	101	23	18
	Tons	550	166	203	537	158	122
1964	Number	45	18	16	83	39	21
	Tons	517	244	223	450	195	108
1963	Number	54	25	34	71	29	17
	Tons	648	291	422	[2] 383	148	81
1962	Number	66	15	27	67	19	15
	Tons	859	174	285	362	99	76
1961	Number	57	34	25	59	24	16
	Tons	789	[2] 438	369	[2] 403	132	173
1960	Number	60	23	25	52	19	12
	Tons	979	270	404	334	115	39
1959	Number	75	19	32	55	13	16
	Tons	1,514	196	717	335	63	64
1958	Number	93	22	31	46	17	8
	Tons	2,156	176	573	281	78	24
1957	Number	84	35	23	55	14	23
	Tons	1,855	751	320	286	100	114
1956	Number	25	68	9	42	22	9
	Tons	312	1,715	126	247	87	49
1955	Number	15	18	8	44	13	14
	Tons	225	196	105	307	93	146
1954	Number	48	7	38	31	26	13
	Tons	672	122	564	212	138	48
1953	Number	92	4	45	45	2	16
	Tons	1,298	19	570	254	16	51

See footnotes at end of chart.

Series Q 449-458. Shipbuilding in Private Shipyards—Summary: 1949 to 1991—Cont'd.

(Tons in thousands; gross tons for commercial vessels, light displacement tons for naval vessels. Covers steel self-propelled vessels 1,000 tons or more)

Year		Commercial vessels			Naval vessels		
		Under construction Jan. 1	Contracted for	Delivered	Under construction Jan. 1	Contracted for	Delivered
		449	451	453	454	456	458
1952	Number	96	27	31	31	18	6
	Tons	1,222	478	397	158	107	14
1951	Number	29	77	10	11	22	1
	Tons	411	987	148	42	170	765
1950	Number	39	16	26	11	X	X
	Tons	636	181	415	42	X	X
1949	Number	71	5	34	21	X	7
	Tons	1,130	72	539	194	X	58

NA Not available.
X Represents zero.

[1] Figures from 1971-1991 include just the total number of vessels built.
[2] Tonnages revised.

Series Q 473-480. Merchant Vessels Launched and Owned—World and United States: 1895 to 1990

(Vessels of 100 gross tons and over. Excludes sailing ships, nonpropelled craft, and all ships built of wood. Figures for 1895 to 1935 represent annual average 5-year span beginning with the year shown; for example, the figure shown for 1895 is the annual average for 1895 to 1899, that for 1900, the annual average for 1900 to 1904, etc.)

	World				United States			
	Launched		Owned		Launched		Owned	
Year	Number	Gross tons (1,000)	Number	Gross tons (1,000)	Number	Gross tons (1,000)	Number	Gross tons (1,000)
	473	474	475	476	477	478	479	480
1990	1,672	15,885	78,336	423,627	16	15	6,348	21,328
1989	1,593	13,236	76,100	410,481	10	4	6,375	20,588
1988	1,575	10,909	75,680	403,406	60	11	6,442	20,832
1987	1,528	12,259	75,240	403,498	29	164	6,427	20,178
1986	1,634	16,845	75,266	404,910	36	223	6,496	19,901
1985	1,964	18,157	76,395	416,269	66	180	6,447	19,518
1984	2,210	18,334	76,068	418,682	73	84	6,441	19,292
1983	2,276	15,911	76,106	422,590	159	381	6,437	19,358
1982	2,312	16,820	75,151	424,742	204	216	6,133	19,111
1981	2,269	16,932	73,864	420,835	223	360	5,869	18,908
1980	2,412	13,101	73,832	419,911	205	555	5,579	18,464
1979	2,466	14,289	71,129	413,021	182	1,352	5,088	17,542
1978	2,618	18,194	69,020	406,002	151	1,033	4,746	16,188
1977	2,796	27,532	67,945	393,678	129	1,012	4,740	15,300
1976	2,723	33,922	63,611	371,612	143	815	4,035	14,810
1975	2,730	34,202	61,501	341,780	127	476	3,801	14,491
1974	2,949	33,541	58,957	310,934	233	733	3,566	14,337
1973	2,999	30,409	57,347	289,532	277	964	3,539	14,818
1972	2,776	26,749	55,251	267,965	292	482	3,305	14,951
1971	2,645	24,860	52,997	246,840	242	482	3,070	16,211
1970	2,700	21,690	50,472	227,138	150	338	2,822	18,423
1969	2,819	19,315	48,246	211,294	174	400	2,972	19,507
1968	2,798	16,908	45,343	193,770	199	441	3,049	19,623
1967	2,778	15,780	42,234	181,709	231	242	3,115	20,286
1966	2,561	14,307	40,822	170,730	191	167	3,140	20,750
1965	2,280	12,216	39,628	159,979	130	270	3,224	21,478
1964	2,147	10,264	38,602	152,584	80	276	3,344	22,380
1963	2,001	8,539	37,310	145,438	78	294	3,506	23,082
1962	1,901	8,375	36,364	139,549	90	449	3,542	23,220
1961	1,990	7,940	35,465	135,477	59	343	3,728	24,184
1960	2,020	8,356	34,056	129,339	60	485	3,845	24,781
1959	1,808	8,746	33,924	124,494	47	597	3,964	25,227
1958	1,936	9,270	32,857	117,578	64	732	4,054	25,526
1957	1,950	8,501	31,421	109,778	54	359	4,116	25,843
1956	1,815	6,670	30,620	104,720	50	169	4,157	26,074
1955	1,437	5,315	29,967	100,069	26	73	4,225	26,343
1954	1,223	5,251	29,766	96,899	46	477	4,404	27,252
1953	1,134	5,095	29,174	92,826	68	528	4,431	27,144
1952	1,065	4,394	28,751	89,636	64	468	4,458	27,139
1951	1,002	3,639	28,374	86,678	58	164	4,484	27,226
1950	990	3,489	27,922	83,996	51	437	4,531	27,404
1949	899	3,126	27,194	81,954	66	633	4,605	27,707
1948	840	2,303	26,479	79,714	49	126	4,807	29,060
1947	741	2,093	(NA)	(NA)	61	163	(NA)	(NA)
1946	655	2,108	(NA)	(NA)	95	501	(NA)	(NA)
1945	1,311	7,189	(NA)	(NA)	880	5,968	(NA)	(NA)
1944	1,690	11,157	(NA)	(NA)	1,237	9,332	(NA)	(NA)
1943	2,067	13,881	(NA)	(NA)	1,620	11,577	(NA)	(NA)
1942	1,285	7,812	(NA)	(NA)	861	5,671	(NA)	(NA)
1941	489	2,487	(NA)	(NA)	184	1,035	(NA)	(NA)

See footnotes at end of chart.

Series Q 473-480. Merchant Vessels Launched and Owned—World and United States: 1895 to 1990—Cont'd.

(Vessels of 100 gross tons and over. Excludes sailing ships, nonpropelled craft, and all ships built of wood. Figures for 1895 to 1935 represent annual average 5-year span beginning with the year shown; for example, the figure shown for 1895 is the annual average for 1895 to 1899, that for 1900, the annual average for 1900 to 1904, etc.)

	World				United States			
	Launched		Owned			Launched		Owned	
Year	Number	Gross tons (1,000)	Number	Gross tons (1,000)	Number	Gross tons (1,000)	Number	Gross tons (1,000)
	473	474	475	476	477	478	479	480
1940	495	1,754	(NA)	(NA)	167	579	(NA)	(NA)
1939	1,040	2,595	31,186	69,440	117	244	3,270	11,874
1935	(1)	(1)	30,979	64,886	(1)	(1)	3,585	12,773
1930	484	1,020	32,713	69,608	25	83	4,105	13,947
1925	873	2,469	32,905	65,638	74	159	4,790	15,314
1920	942	2,582	31,484	57,281	99	315	5,381	15,997
1915	1,637	4,616	30,643	49,246	605	2,217	3,180	5,846
1910	1,426	2,588	29,943	41,884	140	222	3,380	5,018
1905	1,474	2,218	29,574	35,949	206	352	3,457	3,996
1900	1,611	2,354	27,840	28,957	242	347	3,135	2,750
1895	1,205	1,844	30,288	25,086	155	200	3,200	2,165

NA Not available.

[1] 1935 figures have been combined with 1939 figures.

Series Q 487-502. United States Flag Merchant Vessels, Steam and Motor: 1934 to 1990

(Dead-weight tonnage in thousands. As of June 30, except as indicated. Covers ocean-going vessels of 1,000 gross tons and over engaged in foreign and domestic trade, and inactive vessels. Excludes special types and vessels employed on Great Lakes)

Year and type of vessel	All vessels		Active vessels Foreign trade		Active vessels Total domestic trade	
	Number	Tons	Number	Tons	Number	Tons
	487	488	491	492	493	494
1990	635	24,262	131	5,119	158	8,624
Cargo	199	2,456	27	426	2	24
Tanker	233	15,649	23	1,637	121	7,850
1989	661	24,457	164	7,251	158	8,967
Cargo	422	8,726	125	3,883	32	697
Tanker	239	15,731	39	3,368	126	8,270
1988	684	25,677	170	7,356	177	10,339
Cargo	433	8,887	128	3,861	42	875
Tanker	251	16,790	42	3,495	135	9,464
1987	724	25,114	135	4,702	170	9,581
Cargo	470	9,040	97	2,528	40	881
Tanker	254	16,074	38	2,174	130	8,700
1986	738	24,499	156	5,475	168	9,474
Cargo	484	9,106	123	3,468	37	775
Tanker	254	15,393	33	2,007	131	8,699
1985	748	24,439	161	5,448	171	9,168
Cargo	485	8,792	129	3,623	36	659
Tanker	263	15,647	32	1,825	135	8,909
1984	749	23,965	160	5,432	183	9,606
Cargo	477	7,876	122	3,108	41	813
Tanker	272	16,089	38	2,324	142	8,793
1983	819	24,737	184	5,700	204	10,335
Cargo	517	7,991	141	3,281	40	660
Tanker	302	16,746	43	2,419	164	9,675
1982	828	24,108	197	5,141	224	11,308
Cargo	524	7,597	171	3,426	42	651
Tanker	304	16,511	26	1,715	182	10,657
1981	863	24,477	216	5,141	235	10,951
Cargo	550	7,919	184	3,530	40	667
Tanker	313	16,558	32	1,611	195	10,284
1980	863	23,979	227	6,619	257	11,259
Cargo	553	7,872	195	3,826	46	713
Tanker	310	16,107	32	2,793	211	10,546
1979	871	22,997	276	10,109	208	7,629
Cargo	566	7,844	204	3,886	40	597
Tanker	305	15,153	72	6,223	168	7,032
1978	841	21,253	266	8,484	221	7,721
Cargo	552	7,807	204	3,829	46	685
Tanker	289	13,446	62	4,655	175	7,036
1977	841	19,468	281	6,817	214	7,442
Cargo	566	7,850	240	4,336	44	646
Tanker	275	11,618	41	2,481	170	6,796
1976	843	17,989	294	7,770	194	5,136
Cargo	521	7,519	230	4,140	50	731
Tanker	263	10,086	59	3,586	143	4,399
1975	891	17,608	267	6,204	205	5,687
Cargo	612	8,175	228	3,901	49	832
Tanker	279	9,433	39	2,303	156	4,855
1974	965	17,334	305	6,909	202	5,169
Cargo	594	7,981	241	4,082	53	800
Tanker	275	8,739	60	2,793	148	4,362
1973	1,051	17,297	312	6,618	196	4,725
Cargo	658	8,320	237	3,749	59	796
Tanker	273	8,220	71	2,832	135	3,916
1972	1,233	18,412	262	4,683	201	4,881
Cargo	792	9,366	224	3,452	57	751
Tanker	283	8,047	33	1,185	143	4,124
1971	1,478	20,474	321	5,273	236	5,418
Cargo	1,014	11,515	279	3,955	65	829
Tanker	293	7,848	33	1,232	169	4,576
1970	1,780	23,290	386	5,775	245	5,368
Cargo	1,302	14,298	344	4,605	68	837
Tanker	301	7,835	32	1,076	175	4,518
1969	2,013	25,079	447	6,021	199	4,062
Cargo	1,521	16,462	398	5,100	69	823
Tanker	305	7,403	29	734	128	3,228
1968	2,101	25,699	481	6,332	242	4,934
Cargo	1,581	16,993	421	5,180	65	797
Tanker	315	7,363	38	952	176	4,133
1967	2,209	26,560	460	6,037	233	4,654
Cargo	1,670	17,843	400	4,936	66	810
Tanker	317	7,263	36	860	166	3,840
1966	2,292	27,393	494	6,576	248	4,825
Cargo	1,739	18,565	420	5,093	83	1,050
Tanker	328	7,352	48	1,250	164	3,771
1965	2,425	28,755	512	6,877	217	3,953
Cargo	1,840	19,561	440	5,249	92	1,056
Tanker	349	7,636	54	1,475	124	2,892
1964	2,598	30,084	584	7,271	295	5,504
Cargo	1,959	20,612	509	5,971	100	1,137
Tanker	368	7,685	43	1,010	194	4,362
1963	2,691	30,753	587	7,344	299	5,479
Cargo	2,013	21,047	512	5,979	103	1,157
Tanker	388	7,784	45	1,095	195	4,318
1962	2,716	30,954	543	6,616	340	5,951
Cargo	2,018	21,024	482	5,554	115	1,233
Tanker	409	8,006	32	803	223	4,703
1961	2,810	31,525	415	5,066	182	3,107
Cargo	2,086	21,575	365	4,135	64	642
Tanker	424	7,941	33	781	118	2,465
1960	2,934	32,601	558	6,541	372	5,926
Cargo	2,204	22,813	479	5,265	148	1,589
Tanker	425	7,750	45	972	222	4,323
1959	3,047	33,565	533	5,935	375	5,912
Cargo	2,347	24,333	473	5,189	142	1,512
Tanker	412	7,283	24	422	231	4,386
1958	3,047	33,316	551	6,208	356	5,369
Cargo	2,425	25,125	487	5,348	133	1,366
Tanker	384	6,553	28	516	220	3,973
1957	3,032	32,900	721	8,406	399	5,595
Cargo	2,450	25,412	611	6,649	161	1,675
Tanker	352	5,894	72	1,393	325	3,891
1956	3,150	34,052	644	7,538	402	5,639
Cargo	2,511	26,007	524	5,688	149	1,569
Tanker	392	6,363	82	1,489	252	4,061
1955	3,235	35,017	601	6,992	425	5,880
Cargo	2,560	26,539	492	5,383	160	1,650
Tanker	426	6,790	70	1,248	264	4,220

See footnotes at end of chart.

Series Q 487-502.   United States Flag Merchant Vessels, Steam and Motor: 1934 to 1990—Cont'd.

(Dead-weight tonnage in thousands. As of June 30, except as indicated. Covers ocean-going vessels of 1,000 gross tons and over engaged in foreign and domestic trade, and inactive vessels. Excludes special types and vessels employed on Great Lakes)

Year and type of vessel	All vessels		Active vessels				Year and type of vessel	All vessels		Active vessels			
			Foreign trade		Total domestic trade					Foreign trade		Total domestic trade	
	Number	Tons	Number	Tons	Number	Tons		Number	Tons	Number	Tons	Number	Tons
	487	488	491	492	493	494		487	488	491	492	493	494
1954	3,333	35,860	623	7,299	398	5,324	1941	1,168	10,096	471	4,052	663	5,836
Cargo	2,636	26,435	489	5,226	154	1,581	Cargo	716	5,472	358	2,966	333	2,340
Tanker	445	7,730	95	1,713	239	3,719	Tanker	358	4,083	70	739	286	3,331
1953	3,349	36,255	629	7,390	437	5,725							
Cargo	2,630	27,228	461	4,890	167	1,638	1940	1,300	11,019	425	3,749	693	5,893
Tanker	462	6,988	128	2,122	265	4,064	Cargo	790	6,020	291	2,443	350	2,438
							Tanker	370	4,126	68	791	297	3,273
1952	3,350	36,081	782	9,052	395	5,190	1939	1,398	11,699	319	2,804	772	6,499
Cargo	2,629	27,210	582	6,177	135	1,302	Cargo	851	6,364	193	1,619	415	2,921
Tanker	461	6,827	156	2,481	259	3,884	Tanker	384	4,256	48	565	304	3,343
1951	3,386	36,336	988	11,245	426	5,333							
Cargo	2,650	27,376	743	7,892	176	1,721	1938	1,422	11,814	366	3,301	694	5,718
Tanker	470	6,893	199	3,129	245	3,587	Cargo	882	6,557	213	1,808	379	2,629
							Tanker	373	4,149	77	931	266	2,888
1950	3,408	36,526	711	8,353	434	5,474	1937	1,517	12,335	426	3,643	805	6,608
Cargo	2,846	28,927	505	5,367	177	1,708	Cargo	975	7,231	275	2,286	446	3,058
Tanker	479	6,959	161	2,597	251	3,737	Tanker	357	3,900	52	604	299	3,252
1949	3,379	36,228	1,004	11,416	382	4,628							
Cargo	2,799	28,442	813	8,626	156	1,437	1936	1,563	12,323	430	3,714	776	5,958
Tanker	501	7,177	148	2,415	222	3,178	Cargo	1,007	7,405	250	2,087	442	2,961
							Tanker	355	3,637	76	857	267	2,684
1948	3,490	36,774	1,246	13,767	477	5,785	1935	1,637	12,809	434	3,748	709	5,425
Cargo	2,887	28,674	1,023	10,592	198	1,832	Cargo	1,065	7,847	253	2,096	390	2,624
Tanker	526	7,499	182	2,818	272	3,925	Tanker	355	3,615	73	850	251	2,504
1947 [1]	3,696	38,882	1,603	17,238	511	6,413							
Cargo	2,977	29,206	1,434	14,779	194	1,782	1934	1,673	12,986	438	3,753	657	4,993
Tanker	624	8,934	137	2,200	311	4,606	Cargo	1,079	7,946	258	2,168	336	2,194
							Tanker	361	3,652	69	763	248	2,499
1946 [2]	4,852	50,263	1,890	20,592	442	4,807							
Cargo	3,829	36,675	1,607	16,200	226	1,910							
Tanker	906	12,785	268	4,264	206	2,858							

[1] Data as of December 31.

[2] Data as of September 30.

Series Q 506-517. Net Tonnage Capacity of Vessels Entered and Cleared: 1789 to 1990

(In thousands of net tons. For years ending September 20, 1789-1842; June 30, 1843-1918; December 31 thereafter.
Excludes domestic trade. Includes Alaska, Hawaii, Puerto Rico and, beginning 1935, the Virgin Islands)

	Vessels entered							Vessels cleared					
	All ports			Seaports [1]				All ports			Seaports [1]		
Year	Total	U.S. vessels	Foreign vessels	Total	U.S. vessels	Foreign vessels	Total	U.S. vessels	Foreign vessels	Total	U.S. vessels	Foreign vessels
	506	507	508	509	510	511	512	513	514	515	516	517
1990	589,000	41,000	548,000	564,000	40,000	524,000	592,000	43,000	550,000	566,000	41,000	525,000
1989	587,000	44,000	543,000	558,000	42,000	516,000	590,000	45,000	545,000	561,000	44,000	517,000
1988	556,000	47,000	509,000	527,000	46,000	481,000	561,000	49,000	512,000	531,000	47,000	484,000
1987	518,000	48,000	470,000	492,000	47,000	445,000	521,000	49,000	472,000	495,000	48,000	447,000
1986	489,000	49,000	439,000	463,000	48,000	415,000	491,000	51,000	441,000	466,000	49,000	417,000
1985	541,000	53,000	398,000	426,000	52,000	374,000	461,000	55,000	438,000	435,000	53,000	382,000
1984	459,000	53,000	406,000	429,000	51,000	378,000	468,000	54,000	414,000	414,000	51,000	387,000
1983	442,000	62,000	380,000	416,000	60,000	355,000	449,000	62,000	387,000	423,000	60,000	363,000
1982	438,000	59,000	379,000	412,000	57,000	355,000	448,000	60,000	388,000	421,000	58,000	363,000
1981	470,000	56,000	414,000	439,000	54,000	385,000	477,000	56,000	420,000	446,000	54,000	392,000
1980	492,000	52,000	440,000	460,000	50,000	410,000	487,000	54,000	433,000	456,000	51,000	405,000
1979	499,000	45,000	454,000	462,000	42,000	420,000	497,000	48,000	449,000	459,000	44,000	415,000
1978	487,000	37,000	420,000	423,000	34,000	376,000	447,000	34,000	413,000	412,000	31,000	381,000
1977	440,000	34,000	406,000	407,000	31,000	376,000	430,000	34,000	395,000	397,000	31,000	366,000
1976	401,000	33,000	368,000	370,000	31,000	339,000	404,000	34,000	370,000	374,000	32,000	342,000
1975	355,000	32,000	323,000	326,000	30,000	297,000	363,000	34,000	329,000	334,000	31,000	303,000
1974	346,000	36,000	311,000	322,000	32,000	289,000	352,000	37,000	315,000	327,000	33,000	294,000
1973	344,000	33,000	312,000	314,000	31,000	283,000	348,000	35,000	313,000	317,000	33,000	285,000
1972	295,000	25,000	271,000	267,000	23,000	244,000	300,000	27,000	273,000	271,000	25,000	246,000
1971	256,000	24,000	232,000	229,000	22,000	207,000	258,000	24,000	234,000	231,000	23,000	208,000
1970	254,154	26,239	227,915	226,666	24,234	202,431	253,136	26,953	226,183	225,925	24,898	201,027
1969	238,085	26,662	211,423	213,008	25,264	187,741	237,986	27,235	210,758	212,746	25,738	187,013
1968	229,850	30,389	199,465	203,664	27,456	176,210	230,324	31,198	199,126	204,086	28,244	175,839
1967	220,681	30,830	189,848	195,871	26,990	168,848	220,231	30,827	189,404	195,845	27,089	168,756
1966	217,894	31,487	486,407	191,684	28,621	163,063	219,437	32,738	186,699	193,433	29,925	163,507
1965	209,000	34,041	174,960	183,724	30,919	152,806	208,736	34,016	174,721	183,540	31,048	152,492
1964	199,330	34,956	164,373	174,625	30,909	143,715	202,262	35,337	166,924	177,636	31,409	146,225
1963	186,700	33,300	153,400	165,124	29,677	135,447	187,539	34,106	153,433	166,103	30,440	135,663
1962	178,334	33,774	144,560	158,606	29,963	128,644	178,953	34,165	144,788	159,330	30,337	128,993
1961	166,548	31,144	135,404	148,955	28,266	120,688	168,878	31,941	136,936	151,295	29,062	122,233
1960	162,765	30,189	132,575	145,828	26,708	119,119	166,715	31,280	135,434	149,778	27,649	122,127
1959	154,213	26,417	127,796	137,845	21,897	115,947	155,505	26,623	128,883	139,262	22,042	117,221
1958	149,097	26,842	122,255	136,291	23,642	112,648	148,816	26,449	122,366	136,102	23,234	112,778
1957	162,925	35,898	127,027	146,144	31,189	114,956	162,578	35,118	127,460	145,954	30,569	115,385
1956	147,844	36,247	111,598	130,767	31,254	99,514	148,269	36,317	111,952	131,391	31,510	99,881
1955	128,405	34,321	94,084	113,807	30,407	83,400	129,368	34,407	94,961	114,806	30,615	84,192
1954	109,524	33,860	75,664	97,198	30,133	67,065	109,899	33,579	76,321	97,674	29,969	67,706
1953	112,559	39,319	73,240	97,344	34,969	62,375	112,935	39,188	73,747	97,627	34,775	62,852
1952	116,375	45,223	71,152	101,263	40,732	60,532	114,797	43,726	71,071	99,703	39,273	60,429
1951	108,086	44,571	63,515	93,974	40,482	53,192	110,236	46,763	63,472	96,257	43,024	53,233
1950	86,629	35,376	51,251	73,451	31,757	41,693	87,829	36,043	51,778	74,785	32,510	42,269
1949	85,700	41,251	44,451	74,701	37,626	37,076	84,286	39,681	44,604	73,063	36,136	36,927
1948	90,927	47,726	43,199	76,910	43,270	33,640	89,449	45,775	43,667	75,714	41,348	34,358
1947	93,796	53,627	40,170	80,889	49,044	31,844	97,160	54,088	43,072	84,508	49,558	34,949
1946	80,258	53,045	27,213	69,520	49,143	20,378	77,225	49,124	28,101	66,376	45,113	21,263
1945	94,021	61,375	32,646	81,182	56,499	24,682	94,559	61,460	33,099	81,452	56,332	25,120
1944	81,860	48,071	33,789	66,305	42,196	24,109	87,385	53,050	34,335	71,717	46,919	24,798
1943	61,084	29,292	31,792	44,739	24,508	20,231	66,716	33,862	33,034	50,232	28,826	21,406
1942	43,942	13,611	30,331	28,258	10,326	17,932	47,706	16,354	31,352	31,976	13,149	18,827
1941	59,061	20,940	38,121	42,616	16,767	25,849	62,596	21,869	40,726	46,142	17,701	28,441
1940	58,544	19,220	39,324	45,393	15,740	29,652	62,171	20,248	41,923	48,996	16,766	32,230
1939	68,992	17,769	51,223	57,973	14,553	43,421	70,306	18,156	52,150	59,218	14,903	44,316
1938	70,516	19,020	51,496	59,223	15,899	43,324	71,286	18,829	52,456	60,064	15,742	44,322
1937	71,560	19,527	52,033	59,890	16,747	43,233	72,880	19,938	52,942	61,177	17,134	44,043
1936	65,972	20,682	45,290	55,038	17,510	37,528	66,066	20,069	45,997	55,381	16,967	38,414

See footnotes at end of chart.

Series Q 506-517. Net Tonnage Capacity of Vessels Entered and Cleared: 1789 to 1990—Cont'd.

(In thousands of net tons. For years ending September 20, 1789-1842; June 30, 1843-1918; December 31 thereafter. Excludes domestic trade. Includes Alaska, Hawaii, Puerto Rico and, beginning 1935, the Virgin Islands)

| | Vessels entered | | | | | | Vessels cleared | | | | |
| | All ports | | | Seaports [1] | | | All ports | | | Seaports [1] | |
Year	Total	U.S. vessels	Foreign vessels	Total	U.S. vessels	Foreign vessels	Total	U.S. vessels	Foreign vessels	Total	U.S. vessels	Foreign vessels
	506	507	508	509	510	511	512	513	514	515	516	517
1935	64,612	22,372	42,240	54,289	18,893	35,395	64,887	22,126	42,761	54,722	18,651	36,071
1934	63,787	23,192	40,594	53,132	19,186	33,946	63,702	22,799	40,903	53,162	18,901	34,261
1933	60,936	22,488	38,448	51,564	19,051	32,513	61,287	22,434	38,853	52,083	19,093	32,990
1932	64,837	24,278	40,559	55,229	20,643	34,587	64,446	23,865	40,582	54,900	20,204	34,695
1931	72,782	26,907	45,875	60,427	21,499	38,929	73,501	26,854	46,647	61,204	21,417	39,787
1930	81,253	31,866	49,387	66,499	24,620	41,879	81,307	31,560	49,747	66,500	24,154	42,346
1929	82,602	32,241	50,361	66,853	25,208	41,645	82,343	31,927	50,416	67,030	25,045	41,985
1928	80,211	31,285	48,926	62,809	22,991	39,818	80,667	31,734	48,933	63,331	23,180	40,151
1927	74,310	29,289	45,021	58,921	22,001	36,920	75,440	29,793	45,647	59,759	22,078	37,681
1926	76,933	26,890	50,043	63,759	21,091	42,668	79,041	28,532	50,509	65,583	22,234	43,349
1925	69,378	27,947	41,431	55,636	21,148	34,487	70,229	27,808	42,421	57,160	21,394	35,766
1924	68,292	29,628	38,664	54,726	22,462	32,264	68,910	30,092	38,818	55,294	22,896	32,397
1923	66,319	27,725	38,594	52,775	20,984	31,791	66,624	27,932	38,692	53,215	21,305	31,910
1922	65,191	31,738	33,453	51,701	23,633	28,068	64,839	31,759	33,080	51,799	23,755	28,044
1921	62,285	31,185	31,100	49,958	24,402	25,556	62,665	30,181	32,484	50,423	23,432	26,991
1920	64,104	32,119	31,985	51,531	26,225	25,306	67,817	34,053	33,764	54,980	27,875	27,106
1919	46,702	21,933	24,769	36,381	16,224	20,157	51,257	24,992	26,265	40,751	19,133	21,617
1918 [2]	45,456	19,284	26,173	31,101	11,256	19,845	46,014	19,206	26,808	31,869	11,280	20,589
1917	50,472	18,725	31,747	36,521	10,898	25,623	52,077	19,146	32,931	38,094	11,339	26,755
1916	51,550	17,928	33,622	37,744	9,446	28,298	52,423	17,902	34,521	38,946	9,763	29,182
1915	46,710	13,275	33,435	35,032	6,830	28,202	46,885	13,418	33,467	35,458	7,110	28,347
1914	53,389	13,730	39,659	40,052	5,436	34,616	53,183	13,740	39,443	39,743	5,185	34,558
1913	50,639	13,073	37,567	37,973	5,241	32,732	51,152	13,946	37,206	37,566	5,289	32,277
1912	46,158	11,257	34,901	34,659	4,572	30,087	46,417	11,703	34,713	34,706	4,794	29,912
1911	42,675	9,693	32,982	32,457	4,302	28,155	42,437	9,753	32,684	32,299	4,427	27,871
1910	40,236	8,888	31,347	30,917	4,214	26,703	39,706	8,809	30,897	30,510	4,196	26,314
1909	39,058	8,771	30,287	30,243	4,403	25,840	38,196	8,492	29,705	29,604	4,215	25,389
1908	38,539	7,473	30,066	30,444	4,314	26,130	38,282	8,435	29,846	30,198	4,288	25,910
1907	36,622	8,116	28,507	29,248	3,924	25,324	35,990	8,093	27,898	28,499	3,797	24,702
1906	34,155	7,613	26,543	27,401	4,023	23,379	33,784	7,581	26,204	26,970	3,923	23,047
1905	30,983	7,081	23,903	24,793	4,120	20,673	31,158	7,203	23,955	25,020	4,259	20,760
1904	29,952	6,679	23,273	24,111	3,806	20,305	30,016	6,641	23,374	24,192	3,836	20,356
1903	31,094	6,907	24,187	24,698	3,881	20,817	31,316	6,975	24,341	24,823	3,931	20,892
1902	30,654	6,961	23,693	24,361	4,020	20,342	30,444	6,822	23,623	24,242	3,956	20,287
1901	29,768	6,381	23,387	24,791	3,980	20,811	29,820	6,417	23,403	24,889	4,020	20,870
1900	28,163	6,136	22,027	23,534	3,974	19,559	28,281	6,209	22,072	23,618	4,006	19,612
1899	26,111	5,341	20,770	21,963	3,333	18,631	26,266	5,472	20,794	22,177	3,463	18,714
1898	25,579	5,240	20,339	21,700	3,362	18,338	25,748	5,111	20,637	21,892	3,231	18,661
1897	23,760	5,525	18,235	20,003	3,611	16,391	23,709	5,618	18,091	19,878	3,637	16,241
1896	20,989	5,196	15,793	17,453	3,673	13,779	21,415	5,330	16,085	17,819	3,741	14,078
1895	19,295	4,473	14,822	16,725	3,677	13,049	19,751	4,504	15,246	17,024	3,616	13,408
1894	19,990	4,655	15,335	17,025	3,649	13,376	20,272	4,740	15,532	17,306	3,747	13,560
1893	19,582	4,359	15,223	16,679	3,493	13,186	19,761	4,403	15,357	16,825	3,537	13,288
1892	21,013	4,470	16,543	18,180	3,747	14,434	21,161	4,536	16,625	18,258	3,751	14,507
1891	18,204	4,381	13,823	15,394	3,670	11,724	18,261	4,455	13,805	15,411	3,716	11,695
1890	18,107	4,083	14,024	15,366	3,405	11,961	18,149	4,067	14,082	15,429	3,390	12,039
1889	15,952	3,724	12,228	13,312	3,128	10,184	16,343	3,988	12,355	13,672	3,342	10,329
1888	15,393	3,367	12,026	12,956	2,914	10,042	15,669	3,415	12,254	13,252	2,944	10,308
1887	15,816	3,366	12,451	13,532	2,871	10,661	15,753	3,259	12,494	13,511	2,771	10,740
1886	15,136	3,232	11,904	12,230	2,762	9,468	15,328	3,303	12,024	12,413	2,806	9,607
1885	15,305	3,132	12,173	12,287	2,709	9,578	15,515	3,232	12,283	12,496	2,809	9,688
1884	15,069	3,202	11,867	12,085	2,821	9,264	15,205	3,237	11,968	12,206	2,845	9,361
1883	16,382	3,256	13,126	13,361	2,835	10,526	16,541	3,307	13,234	13,565	2,895	10,670
1882	17,601	3,341	14,260	14,656	2,968	11,688	17,757	3,318	14,439	14,846	2,936	11,911
1881	18,319	3,254	15,066	15,631	2,919	12,711	18,470	3,376	15,094	15,794	3,040	12,754

See footnotes at end of chart.

Series Q 506-517.   Net Tonnage Capacity of Vessels Entered and Cleared: 1789 to 1990—Cont'd.

(In thousands of net tons. For years ending September 20, 1789-1842; June 30, 1843-1918; December 31 thereafter.
Excludes domestic trade. Includes Alaska, Hawaii, Puerto Rico and, beginning 1935, the Virgin Islands)

	Vessels entered						Vessels cleared					
	All ports			Seaports [1]			All ports			Seaports [1]		
Year	Total	U.S. vessels	Foreign vessels	Total	U.S. vessels	Foreign vessels	Total	U.S. vessels	Foreign vessels	Total	U.S. vessels	Foreign vessels
	506	507	508	509	510	511	512	513	514	515	516	517
1880	18,011	3,437	14,574	15,251	3,140	12,111	18,043	3,397	14,646	15,296	3,078	12,218
1879	16,193	3,415	12,778	13,768	3,050	10,718	16,075	3,464	12,611	13,617	3,071	10,545
1878	14,464	3,642	10,821	11,531	3,009	8,521	14,808	3,872	10,935	11,844	3,196	8,647
1877	13,455	3,663	9,791	10,406	2,958	7,449	13,442	3,765	9,677	10,389	3,043	7,345
1876	12,511	3,611	8,899	9,716	2,928	6,788	12,655	3,732	8,923	9,839	3,037	6,802
1875	11,693	3,574	8,119	9,143	2,887	6,256	11,897	3,737	8,160	9,341	3,061	6,279
1874	13,092	3,894	9,198	10,010	2,915	7,095	13,189	3,982	9,207	10,058	2,961	7,097
1873	11,696	3,613	8,083	8,395	2,443	5,951	11,822	3,757	8,065	8,515	2,574	5,941
1872	10,806	3,712	7,095	7,770	2,585	5,185	10,734	3,682	7,051	7,739	2,598	5,141
1871	10,009	3,743	6,266	6,994	2,604	4,391	9,898	3,747	6,152	6,918	2,635	4,283
1870	9,156	3,486	5,670	6,270	2,452	3,818	9,169	3,507	5,662	6,362	2,530	3,832
1869	8,750	3,403	5,348	6,032	2,459	3,573	7,754	3,381	4,373	6,114	2,502	3,612
1868	8,046	3,551	4,495	5,572	2,466	3,106	8,279	3,718	4,561	5,811	2,625	3,186
1867	7,774	3,422	4,319	2,533	2,146	3,121	7,885	3,420	4,465	5,501	2,270	3,230
1866	7,782	3,372	4,410	2,008	1,891	3,117	7,822	3,383	4,438	5,161	2,030	3,131
1865	6,161	2,944	3,217	3,827	1,615	2,212	6,620	3,025	3,595	4,161	1,710	2,450
1864	6,538	3,066	3,471	4,167	1,655	2,512	6,832	3,091	3,741	4,279	1,662	2,617
1863	7,255	4,615	2,640	4,205	2,308	1,898	7,511	4,447	3,064	4,343	2,266	2,077
1862	7,363	5,118	2,245	4,191	2,629	1,562	7,339	4,962	2,377	4,205	2,568	1,637
1861	7,241	5,024	2,218	4,559	3,025	1,534	7,151	4,889	2,262	4,410	2,874	1,536
1860	8,275	5,921	2,354	5,000	3,302	1,698	8,790	6,166	2,624	5,257	3,501	1,756
1859	7,806	5,366	2,540	4,913	3,328	1,585	7,916	5,297	2,618	4,867	3,315	1,552
1858	6,605	4,396	2,209	4,338	3,051	1,587	7,803	4,490	3,313	4,436	3,128	1,309
1857	7,186	4,721	2,465	4,843	3,482	1,361	7,071	4,581	2,490	4,882	3,483	1,398
1856	6,872	4,385	2,487	4,464	3,194	1,270	7,000	4,538	2,462	4,695	—	—
1855	5,945	3,861	2,084	4,178	—	—	6,179	4,069	2,110	4,435	—	—
1854	5,884	3,752	2,132	4,343	—	—	6,019	3,911	2,108	4,524	—	—
1853	6,282	4,004	2,278	4,157	—	—	6,066	3,767	2,299	4,289	—	—
1852	5,293	3,236	2,057	3,926	—	—	5,278	3,231	2,048	(NA)	—	—
1851	4,993	3,054	1,939	3,466	—	—	5,130	3,201	1,930	(NA)	—	—
1850	3,749	2,573	1,176	3,013	—	—	4,361	2,633	1,728	3,167	—	—
1849	4,369	2,658	1,711	2,890	—	—	4,429	2,754	1,676	(NA)	—	—
1848	3,799	2,393	7,105	2,503	—	—	3,865	2,461	1,404	(NA)	—	—
1847	3,322	2,101	1,220	2,429	—	—	3,379	2,202	1,177	(NA)	—	—
1846	3,111	2,151	960	2,022	—	—	3,189	2,221	968	(NA)	—	—
1845	2,946	2,035	911	2,011	—	—	2,984	2,054	930	(NA)	—	—
1844	2,894	1,977	917	1,897	—	—	2,918	2,011	907	(NA)	—	—
1843	1,678	1,144	535	(NA)	—	—	1,792	1,268	524	(NA)	—	—
1842	2,243	1,510	733	(NA)	—	—	2,277	1,536	740	(NA)	—	—
1841	2,368	1,632	736	(NA)	—	—	2,371	1,634	737	(NA)	—	—
1840	2,289	1,577	712	1,788	—	—	2,353	1,647	706	1,861	—	—
1839	2,116	1,491	625	—	—	—	2,090	1,478	612	—	—	—
1838	1,895	1,303	592	—	—	—	2,013	1,409	604	—	—	—
1837	2,065	1,300	766	—	—	—	2,023	1,267	756	—	—	—
1836	1,936	1,255	680	—	—	—	1,990	1,316	674	—	—	—
1835	1,994	1,353	641	—	—	—	2,031	1,401	631	—	—	—
1834	1,643	1,075	568	—	—	—	1,712	1,134	578	—	—	—
1833	1,608	1,111	497	—	—	—	1,639	1,142	497	—	—	—
1832	1,343	950	393	—	—	—	1,362	975	388	—	—	—
1831	1,405	923	482	—	—	—	1,244	973	272	—	—	—
1830	1,099	967	132	—	—	—	1,105	972	133	—	—	—
1829	1,004	873	131	—	—	—	1,078	945	133	—	—	—
1828	1,019	868	150	—	—	—	1,048	897	151	—	—	—
1827	1,056	918	138	—	—	—	1,112	981	131	—	—	—
1826	1,048	942	106	—	—	—	1,052	953	99	—	—	—

See footnotes at end of chart.

Series Q 506-517. Net Tonnage Capacity of Vessels Entered and Cleared: 1789 to 1990—Cont'd.

(In thousands of net tons. For years ending September 20, 1789-1842; June 30, 1843-1918; December 31 thereafter.
Excludes domestic trade. Includes Alaska, Hawaii, Puerto Rico and, beginning 1935, the Virgin Islands)

Year	Vessels entered All ports			Vessels cleared All ports			Year	Vessels entered All ports		
	Total	U.S. vessels	Foreign vessels	Total	U.S. vessels	Foreign vessels		Total	U.S. vessels	Foreign vessels
	506	507	508	512	513	514		506	507	508
1825	974	881	93	1,055	960	95	1806	1,135	1,044	91
1824	952	850	102	1,022	919	103				
1823	895	775	119	931	811	120	1805	1,010	922	88
1822	889	788	101	911	814	97	1804	944	822	122
1821	847	765	82	888	805	83	1803	951	787	164
							1802	944	799	146
1820	880	801	79	—	—	—	1801	1,007	849	157
1819	869	784	86	—	—	—				
1818	917	755	161	—	—	—	1800	804	683	121
1817	992	780	212	—	—	—	1799	732	625	108
1816	1,136	877	259	—	—	—	1798	610	522	88
							1797	681	608	73
1815	918	701	217	—	—	—	1796	722	675	47
1814	108	60	48	—	—	—				
1813	351	238	114	—	—	—	1795	637	580	57
1812	715	668	47	—	—	—	1794	609	526	83
1811	981	948	33	—	—	—	1793	611	448	164
							1792	659	415	244
1810	989	909	80	—	—	—	1791	604	364	241
1809	705	605	99	—	—	—				
1808	586	539	48	—	—	—	1790	606	355	251
1807	1,203	1,116	87	—	—	—	1789	234	127	107

NA Not available.

[1] Comprises all ports except northern border ports.

[2] As of June 30; figures (in thousands of tons) for July-Dec. are as follows: Series Q 506, 25,029; series Q 507, 11,006; series Q 508, 14,023; series Q 512, 25,472; series Q 513, 11,223; and series Q 514, 14,249.

Series Q 577-590. Scheduled Air Transportation, Domestic and International: 1926 to 1990

(As of December 31 or for years ending December 31. All data reflect scheduled operations exclusively. Domestic data include intra-Alaska carriers beginning 1941 for series Q 586 and Q 587; 1948 for series Q 582; and 1961 for series Q 581)

Year	Number of operators	Aircraft in service [1]	Persons employed	Revenue miles flown (1,000)	Revenue passengers carried, unduplicated [2] (1,000)	Revenue passenger miles flown (millions)	Ton-miles flown — Express and freight (1,000)	Ton-miles flown — Mail (1,000)	Fuel consumed, gasoline (mil. gal.)	Average available seats	Average speed (m.p.h.)
	577	578	581	582	584	585	586	587	588	589	590
Domestic											
1990	60	4,665	545,000	4,491,000	466,000	457,900	10,600,000	2,004,000	16,252	151.9	408
1989	62	4,477	507,000	4,193,000	454,000	432,700	10,275,000	1,911,000	15,624	152.1	406
1988	66	4,439	481,000	4,141,000	455,000	423,300	9,632,000	1,837,000	15,094	153.1	409
1987	68	4,231	457,000	3,988,000	448,000	404,500	8,260,000	1,758,000	14,461	152.9	413
1986	74	3,799	422,000	3,725,000	419,000	366,500	7,344,000	1,081,000	13,682	153.4	409
1985	86	2,860	355,000	3,320,000	382,000	336,400	6,020,000	1,659,000	12,603	152.5	409
1984	87	2,692	345,000	3,133,000	345,000	305,100	6,566,000	1,618,000	11,470	153.7	414
1983	84	2,618	329,000	2,809,000	319,000	281,800	6,092,000	1,480,000	10,526	154.1	415
1982	98	2,468	330,000	2,699,000	294,000	259,600	5,482,000	1,404,000	10,268	153.0	408
1981	98	2,523	350,000	2,703,000	286,000	248,800	5,686,000	1,374,000	10,810	147.2	403
1980	72	2,505	371,000	2,816,000	297,000	255,200	5,742,000	1,342,000	11,311	143.1	405
1979	52	2,466	341,000	2,791,000	317,000	262,000	5,964,000	1,225,000	11,369	139.9	406
1978	34	2,345	329,000	2,520,000	275,000	226,800	5,818,000	1,181,000	10,534	140.0	409
1977	32	2,234	314,000	2,419,000	240,000	193,200	4,109,000	1,039,000	10,296	136.9	408
1976	32	2,271	303,000	2,320,000	223,000	179,000	3,855,000	1,001,000	9,832	134.1	406
1975	33	2,260	290,000	2,241,000	205,000	162,800	4,796,000	1,109,000	9,507	130.4	403
1974	31	2,244	305,000	2,258,000	208,000	162,900	3,760,000	1,016,000	9,546	127.7	402
1973	33	2,361	312,000	2,448,000	202,000	161,900	3,692,000	1,048,000	10,671	123.8	404
1972	37	2,361	305,000	2,376,000	191,000	152,406	3,354,000	1,049,000	9,985	118.1	404
1971	38	2,389	285,000	2,378,000	173,000	132,687	3,023,000	1,154,000	9,841	115.3	405
1970	33	2,437	242,206	2,013,484	153,408	104,156	1,966,009	705,711	—	110.4	350
1969	33	2,423	255,386	2,000,269	158,405	102,717	1,916,472	801,416	27	109.8	394
1968	38	2,317	244,742	1,715,857	145,774	87,508	1,578,992	564,084	113	100.8	373
1967	39	2,194	223,381	1,462,240	128,479	75,487	1,314,409	405,352	223	94.4	354
1966	40	2,027	196,298	1,178,458	105,789	60,591	1,108,691	291,277	332	91.2	320
1965	40	1,896	169,952	1,088,112	92,073	51,887	943,128	225,992	448	89.2	314
1964	40	1,863	153,243	957,575	79,139	44,141	743,963	189,782	507	86.1	297
1963	40	1,832	143,112	888,793	69,366	38,457	603,725	174,439	554	83.4	287
1962	40	1,831	138,673	827,694	60,738	33,623	554,599	166,801	696	79.4	274
1961	41	1,867	136,987	795,165	56,900	31,062	454,142	150,452	743	72.9	253
1960	42	1,594	133,717	820,756	56,352	30,567	386,933	135,923	922	65.5	235
1959	39	1,596	132,042	841,925	54,955	29,308	344,728	120,308	1,142	58.7	223
1958	39	1,546	119,746	784,200	48,297	25,375	294,018	107,018	1,188	55.8	220
1957	40	1,494	119,333	791,265	48,761	25,379	268,791	100,218	1,165	53.7	215
1956	40	1,347	103,489	694,050	41,738	22,399	247,255	94,523	1,005	52.4	213
1955	42	1,212	95,548	627,336	38,025	19,852	229,966	88,751	912	51.2	208
1954	43	1,175	84,765	556,880	32,343	16,802	189,765	82,768	776	50.1	206
1953	44	1,139	84,651	525,374	28,721	14,794	179,063	74,106	692	46.1	198
1952	46	1,078	79,687	465,477	25,010	12,559	162,047	70,443	588	42.7	191
1951	49	981	72,898	411,878	22,652	10,590	144,790	64,734	(NA)	39.6	185
1950	52	960	61,903	369,826	17,345	8,007	152,223	47,740	418	37.5	180
1949	51	913	59,886	355,501	15,081	6,752	123,603	41,889	375	35.0	179
1948	39	878	60,416	338,217	13,168	5,976	102,360	38,198	332	32.4	172
1947	27	810	58,998	325,054	12,890	6,105	64,637	33,086	294	30.0	168
1946	23	674	69,182	309,889	12,213	5,945	38,590	32,969	236	25.3	160
1945	19	421	50,313	208,969	6,576	3,360	22,175	65,103	135	19.7	155
1944	18	288	31,198	138,732	4,046	2,177	16,974	51,146	90	19.1	156
1943	18	204	29,654	105,355	3,020	1,632	15,618	36,067	65	18.3	—
1942	19	186	26,910	111,341	3,137	1,418	11,896	21,167	69	17.9	—
1941	19	370	19,223	134,406	[3] 3,464	1,385	5,257	13,108	82	17.5	—

See footnotes at end of chart.

Series Q 577-590. Scheduled Air Transportation, Domestic and International: 1926 to 1990—Cont'd.

(As of December 31 or for years ending December 31. All data reflect scheduled operations exclusively. Domestic data include intra-Alaska carriers beginning 1941 for series Q 586 and Q 587; 1948 for series Q 582; and 1961 for series Q 581)

Year	Number of operators	Aircraft in service [1]	Persons employed	Revenue miles flown (1,000)	Revenue passengers carried, unduplicated [2] (1,000)	Revenue passenger-miles flown (millions)	Ton-miles flown		Fuel consumed, gasoline (mil. gal.)	Average available seats	Average speed (m.p.h.)
							Express and freight (1,000)	Mail (1,000)			
	577	**578**	**581**	**582**	**584**	**585**	**586**	**587**	**588**	**589**	**590**
1940	19	369	15,984	110,101	[3] 2,523	1,052	3,476	10,118	66	16.5	—
1939	[4] 18	[4] 276	[4] 10,639	82,925	[3] 1,561	683	2,713	8,611	47	14.7	—
1938	[5] 16	[5] 260	[5] 9,008	68,610	[3] 1,077	480	2,182	7,449	38	13.9	—
1937	22	291	7,586	66,791	[3] 887	412	2,162	6,698	34	12.5	—
1936	24	280	7,079	64,307	—	[6] 439	1,866	5,741	31	10.7	—
1935	26	363	5,945	55,918	—	[6] 316	1,098	4,133	27	10.3	—
1934	24	423	4,201	41,526	—	[6] 190	[7] 597	[8] 2,237	19	8.9	—
1933	25	418	4,369	49,256	—	[6] 175	[7] 423	[9] 2,568	22	7.6	—
1932	32	456	4,020	45,894	—	[6] 127	[7] 290	[9] 2,701	20	6.6	—
1931	39	490	4,314	43,109	—	[6] 107	[7] 221	[9] 3,140	16	—	—
1930	43	497	2,778	32,645	—	[6] 85	[7] 101	—	12	—	—
1929	38	442	1,958	22,729	—	—	[7] 70	—	6	—	—
1928	34	268	[10] 1,496	10,528	—	—	[7] 59	—	2	—	—
1927	18	—	—	5,856	—	—	[7] 13	—	1	—	—
1926	13	—	—	4,318	—	—	[7] 1	—	1	—	—

NA Not available.
[1] Figures for 1961-1970 for domestic airlines are for total aircraft in service, domestic and international.
[2] Duplication has been eliminated where the same passengers were carried on more than one route of an air carrier, but still exists where the same passengers were carried by more than one air carrier.
[3] Computed by CAA from reports of duplicated revenue passengers.
[4] Excludes Marine Airlines.
[5] Excludes Colonial and Marine Airlines.
[6] Includes nonrevenue passenger miles flown.
[7] Excludes Colonial Airlines, Inc., and Hawaiian Airlines, Ltd.
[8] Excludes 224,236 ton-miles flown by U.S. Army.
[9] Excludes Colonial Airlines, Inc.
[10] Includes employees of Pan American Airways.

Series Q 604-623.   Airports, Aircraft, Pilots and Miles Flown: 1927 to 1990
(As of December 31 or for years ending December 31, except as noted. Includes Alaska, Hawaii and outlying areas for all years)

| | Airports and landing fields[1] | | | Certified airplane pilots[3] | | | |
| | Total | Lighted | Total civil aircraft[2] | Total | Airline transport | Commercial | Private |
Year	604	605	606	607	608	609	610
1990	17,490	4,822	275,900	703,000	108,000	149,000	299,000
1989	17,446	4,443	274,800	700,000	102,000	145,000	293,000
1988	17,327	4,890	272,700	694,000	97,000	143,000	300,000
1987	17,015	4,922	275,100	700,000	91,000	144,000	301,000
1986	16,582	4,954	275,700	709,000	87,000	148,000	306,000
1985	16,318	4,941	274,900	710,000	83,000	152,000	311,000
1984	16,075	4,889	271,500	722,000	79,000	155,000	322,000
1983	16,029	4,878	264,900	718,000	75,000	159,000	319,000
1982	15,831	4,844	259,000	733,000	73,000	165,000	322,000
1981	15,476	4,795	261,600	764,000	70,000	169,000	329,000
1980	15,161	4,738	259,400	827,000	70,000	183,000	357,000
1979	14,746	4,631	251,500	815,000	64,000	182,000	343,000
1978	14,574	4,567	236,800	799,000	56,000	186,000	338,000
1977	14,117	4,483	215,300	784,000	50,000	189,000	327,000
1976	13,770	4,362	205,900	744,000	45,000	188,000	309,000
1975	13,251	4,171	196,300	728,000	43,000	189,000	306,000
1974	13,062	3,999	188,000	734,000	41,000	192,000	306,000
1973	12,700	3,880	179,800	715,000	38,000	182,000	299,000
1972	12,405	3,827	170,800	751,000	38,000	196,000	321,000
1971	12,070	3,759	166,800	741,000	36,000	192,000	313,000
1970	11,261	3,554	154,450	732,729	34,430	186,821	303,779
1969	11,050	3,430	190,749	720,028	31,442	176,585	299,491
1968	10,470	3,312	179,285	691,695	28,607	164,458	281,728
1967	10,126	3,149	166,598	617,931	25,817	150,135	253,312
1966	9,673	2,988	155,132	548,757	23,917	131,539	222,427
1965	9,566	2,878	142,078	479,770	22,440	116,665	196,393
1964	9,490	2,773	137,189	431,041	21,572	108,428	175,574
1963	8,814	2,672	129,975	378,700	20,269	96,341	152,209
1962	8,084	2,481	124,273	830,220	23,220	275,495	531,505
1961	7,715	2,299	117,904	804,707	22,042	268,707	513,958
1960	6,881	2,133	111,580	783,232	20,985	262,437	499,810
1959	6,426	1,943	105,309	758,368	19,364	255,377	483,627
1958	6,018	1,809	98,893	731,078	18,303	245,541	467,234
1957	6,412	1,713	93,189	702,519	16,900	237,149	448,470
1956	7,028	1,399	87,531	669,079	15,295	221,096	432,688
1955	6,839	1,247	85,320	643,201	13,700	211,142	418,359
1954	6,977	1,108	92,067	613,695	13,341	201,441	398,913
1953	[4]6,760	[4]1,050	91,102	585,974	12,757	195,363	377,854
1952	6,042	1,858	89,313	581,218	11,357	193,575	376,286
1951	6,237	(NA)	88,545	580,574	10,813	197,900	371,861
1950	6,403	1,670	92,809	(NA)	(NA)	(NA)	(NA)
1949	6,484	1,480	92,622	525,174	9,025	187,769	328,380
1948	6,414	1,521	95,997	[5]491,306	[5]7,762	[5]176,846	[5]306,699
1947	5,759	1,447	94,821	[6]433,241	[6]7,059	[6]181,912	[6]244,270
1946	4,490	1,019	81,002	400,061	7,654	203,251	189,156
1945	4,026	1,007	37,789	296,895	5,815	162,873	128,207
1944	3,427	964	27,919	183,383	3,046	68,449	111,888
1943	2,769	859	27,180	173,206	2,315	63,940	106,951
1942	2,809	700	27,170	166,626	2,177	55,760	108,689
1941	2,484	662	26,013	129,947	1,587	34,578	93,782
1940	2,331	776	17,928	69,829	1,431	18,791	49,607
1939	2,280	735	13,772	33,706	1,197	11,677	20,832
1938	2,374	719	11,159	22,983	1,159	7,839	13,985

See footnotes at end of chart.

Series Q 604-623.   Airports, Aircraft, Pilots and Miles Flown: 1927 to 1990—Cont'd.

(As of December 31 or for years ending December 31, except as noted. Includes Alaska, Hawaii and outlying areas for all years)

| Year | Airports and landing fields[1] | | | Certified airplane pilots[3] | | | |
	Total	Lighted	Total civil aircraft[2]	Total	Airline transport	Commercial	Private
	604	605	606	607	608	609	610
1937	2,299	720	10,836	17,681	1,064	6,411	10,206
1936	2,342	705	9,229	15,952	842	7,288	7,822
1935	2,368	698	9,072	14,805	736	7,362	6,707
1934	2,297	664	8,322	13,949	676	7,484	5,789
1933	2,188	626	9,284	13,960	554	7,635	5,771
1932	2,117	701	10,324	18,594	[7]330	7,967	10,297
1931	2,093	680	10,780	17,739	—	8,513	9,226
1930	1,782	640	9,818	15,280	—	7,847	7,433
1929	1,550	—	9,922	10,430	—	6,165	4,265
1928	1,364	—	5,104	4,887	—	—	—
1927	1,036	—	2,740	1,572	—	—	—

NA Not available

[1] Includes seaplane bases, heliports, and beginning 1954, military fields having joint civil – military use. Prior to 1954, all military fields are included.

[2] 1946–1952 includes gliders. Beginning 1950, active and inactive aircraft.

[3] Beginning 1963, data are for active certified airplane pilots only. Also beginning 1963, total includes student, helicopter, glider, and other pilots, not shown separately.

[4] As of Mar. 1, 1954.

[5] As of May 1, 1949.

[6] As of Apr. 1, 1948.

[7] Airline transport rating became effective May 5, 1932.

Series Q 624-637. Air Transportation Accidents: 1927 to 1990

Year	Domestic scheduled air carriers [1,2]			Year	Domestic scheduled air carriers [1,2]			Year	Domestic scheduled air carriers [1,2]		
	Total accidents	Number of fatal accidents	Total passenger fatalities		Total accidents	Number of fatal accidents	Total passenger fatalities		Total accidents	Number of fatal accidents	Total passenger fatalities
	624	625	626		624	625	626		624	625	626
1990	24	6	39	1968	44	11	258	1947	44	8	199
1989	25	8	131	1967	43	8	226	1946	33	9	75
1988	28	3	285	1966	50	4	59				
1987	32	4	231					1945	40	8	76
1986	21	2	5	1965	55	6	205	1944	30	5	48
				1964	45	6	106	1943	23	2	22
1985	17	4	197	1963	39	4	48	1942	23	5	55
1984	14	1	4	1962	35	5	158	1941	27	4	35
1983	23	4	15	1961	56	5	124				
1982	15	3	233					1940	30	3	35
1981	25	4	4	1960	62	[3] 10	326	1939	28	2	9
				1959	61	9	209	1938	23	5	25
1980	15	—	38	1958	42	4	114	1937	42	5	40
1979	18	5	352	1957	44	4	32	1936	65	8	44
1978	19	4	16	1956	55	4	143				
1977	18	2	75					1935	58	8	15
1976	21	2	36	1955	[4] 45	8	156	1934	71	8	17
				1954	[5] 49	4	16	1933	100	9	8
1975	29	2	122	1953	37	5	86	1932	108	16	19
1974	43	7	460	1952	44	6	46	1931	118	13	25
1973	32	6	217	1951	45	11	142				
1972	43	7	186					1930	88	9	24
1971	39	6	194	1950	39	4	96	1929	124	21	14
				1949	35	8	96	1928	85	11	14
1970	31	1	X	1948	56	5	83	1927	25	4	1
1969	37	7	132								

X Represents zero.

[1] Includes scheduled revenue operators only.
[2] Figures between 1980 and 1990 represent both domestic and international flights.
[3] Includes two midair collisions nonfatal to air carrier occupants.

[4] Excludes sabotage disaster at Longmont, Colo., on Nov. 1, 1955 in which five crew members and 39 passengers were fatally injured.
[5] Includes one ground collision between two air carrier aircrafts, one in scheduled passenger service and one in other revenue operations.

COMMUNICATIONS

SECTION R

COMMUNICATIONS
Highlights

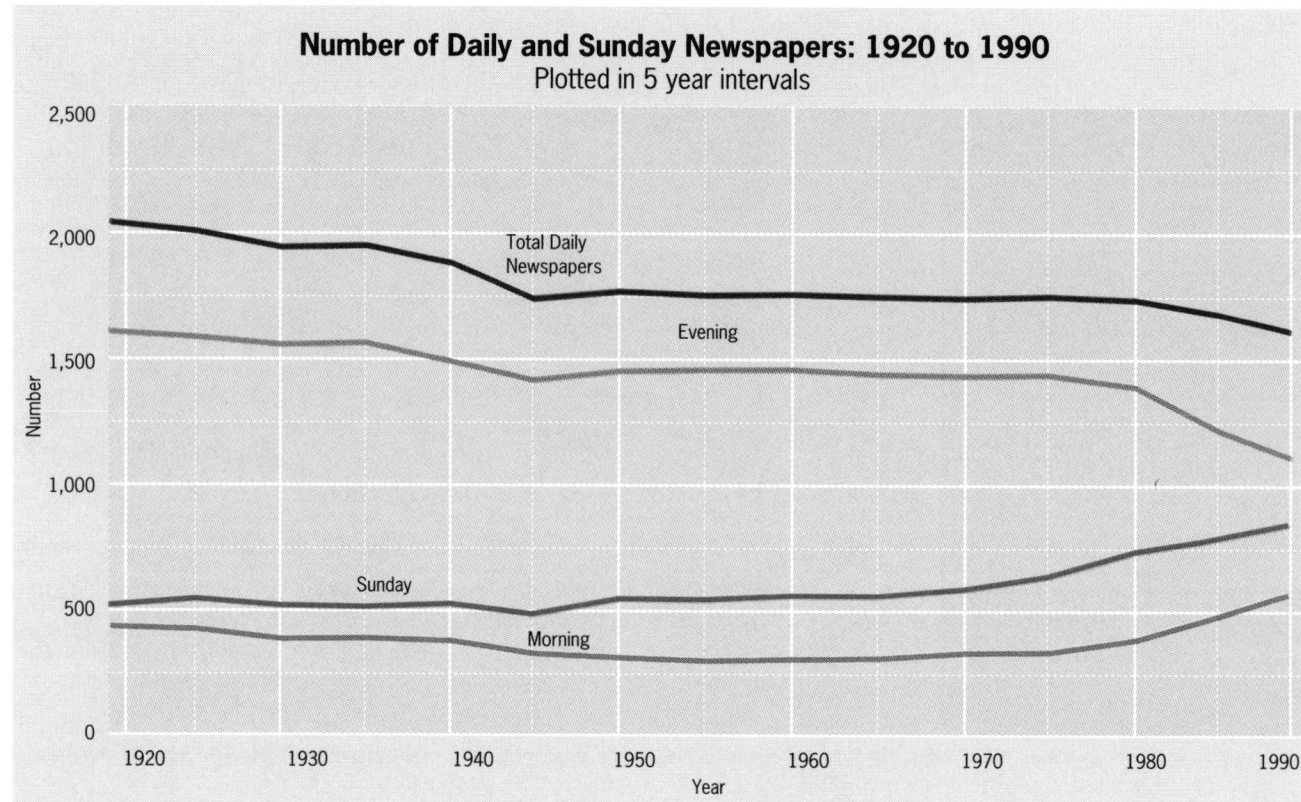

Number of Daily and Sunday Newspapers: 1920 to 1990
Plotted in 5 year intervals

1 Communication systems are regulated primarily by the Federal Communications Commission and also by the Interstate Commerce Commission. The bulk of the regional telephone services is provided by the so-called Baby Bells, and interstate services by the three major telephone companies—AT&T, Sprint, and MCI. Of these three, AT&T is the oldest and the largest. Until the 1980s, AT&T was a behemoth, controlling virtually all local and interstate facilities and services. Through Western Union, it controlled production facilities as well. The number of companies within AT&T (known as American Bell Telephone Company until 1900) varied from time to time. At its peak in 1915-1916, it included 39 companies, but subsequent consolidations reduced it to 25. At the time of its breakup, it included 21 totally owned and controlled regional companies (AT&T owned 100% of the outstanding shares, although these companies operated under their own names), one subsidiary

of one of these regional companies, two companies in which it had substantial minority interests (Cincinnati Bell and Southern New England Telephone Company), Bell Telephone Laboratories, and Western Electric Company.

2 An interesting footnote in the history of U.S. communications is the story of the rise and fall of Western Union Telegraph. Founded in 1851 as the New York and Mississippi Valley Printing and Telegraph Company, it emerged within a few decades as the sole telegraph company in the United States. Western Union developed close contractual ties with the railways, constructing telegraph pole lines along railroad rights-of-way and using railroad stations and personnel for pickup and delivery of telegraph messages. Western Union's most serious rival was the Postal Telegraph, which was acquired in the 1880s by Mackay's Commercial Cable Company (later IT&T). Postal

Telegraph merged with Western Union in 1943, but shortly thereafter telegraph was rendered obsolete by other modern forms of communication.

3 Another 19th century technological breakthrough that has become obsolete is the submarine cable. The first successful cable linking North America with Europe was laid in 1866. The first telegraph rate on cable (presumably from New York to London) was $100 for 10 words! Subsequently, it was reduced—first to $50 and later to $25. By 1868, the rate had fallen to $15.75, and by 1885 to $4.00. In 1916, the New York to London rate was 17 cents per word. Radio was not a significant factor in overseas communications until Radio Corporation of America entered the field as successor to the Marconi Company, which was the first company to utilize and market the invention of wireless.

4 Among all forms of communications, federal control has been most effective in radio and television. In 1912 the Department of Commerce was given authority to license radio equipment, operators, and broadcast stations which began operation in 1921. On February 23, 1927, Congress established the Federal Radio Commission; its powers were transferred to the Federal Communications Commission in 1934.

5 Statistics on radio and television are provided in the annual reports of the FCC as well as its *Statistics of the Communications Industry*. Unlike telephone and telegraph, radio and television are not common carriers (public utilities that are subject to strict government supervision) and therefore are not subject to rate or earnings regulation. Statistics on radio and television broadcasting stations are presented in terms of licensed and authorized stations, the former generally referring to operating stations. FM radio was authorized as a regular service in 1941; in the same year the first commercial station was licensed. Noncommercial FM is a separate service with a specific spectrum allocation. Television was first authorized on a regular commercial basis on July 1, 1941, and two stations in New York were the first to begin operations. Time series broadcasting advertising expenditures were first developed by L. D. H. Weld of McCann-Erickson Advertising Agency and continued after his death in 1946 by Hans Zeisel and others.

6 The first mail service was started in the Colonies in 1673 between New York and Boston, a distance of 260 miles. The trip took two weeks on horseback; much of that time was spent waiting for ferries. Mail was not cheap. At a time when a decent day's wage was 50 cents, a letter from New York to Philadelphia cost $3.50 and from New York to Williamsburg, Virginia, $11.50. The first postage rates were fixed by the Continental Congress in 1782. In the early days the recipient rather than the sender paid the postage. In 1847, postage stamps were introduced and in 1885 compulsory prepayment for all domestic letter mail was established. Postal cards were introduced in 1898. It was not until 1863 that mail was divided into classes. Local rates were often improvised because no one knew for sure how much it cost to transport mail. The first letter rate on the Pony Express (which operated between Missouri and California between 1860 and 1861) was $5 for half oz.; it was later reduced to $2 and then $1. Rates continued to fall well into the 20th century, reaching their lowest in 1928 and 1946 when a first class postage stamp cost only 5 cents. Postage rates have been rising ever since, while telephone rates have done the opposite—in 1915, it cost $20.70 to call New York from San Francisco but only 5 cents to mail a letter; in 1991, it cost $1.35 for the same long-distance call, but 29 cents to mail a letter.

7 A book has never been properly defined, but according to the United Nations Educational, Scientific, and Cultural Organization (UNESCO), it is any printed and bound publication over 49 pages in length that is not a periodical. Book publishing statistics, compiled from a number of sources, are not strictly comparable and may vary depending on what is included as well as excluded. The legal requirement of copyright and deposit of copies with the Library of Congress ensures that the publication of the vast majority of books is documented. The International Standard Book Number (ISBN) system also has the same effect although compliance is voluntary.

8 Since 1970, contrary to popular perceptions, the U.S. Postal Service has become one of the most efficient and productive businesses in the nation. Although the number of post offices declined from 30,754 in 1975 to 28,959 in 1990, the number of pieces of mail handled grew from 89.3 billion to 166.3 billion over that same period, and the pieces of mail per employee from 127 to 206. Operating revenues almost quadrupled from $11.590 billion to $40.074 billion, while compensation and employee benefits grew by 298% from $10.805 billion to $34.214 billion.

9 The United States is fast reaching total saturation in utilization of all media. In 1990, the percentages were 92.8% for television, 56.1% for cable, 84.7% for radio, and 83.9% for newspapers. In the same year, 93.6% of Americans had telephones, 99% had radios, 98.2% had television sets (91% in color), and 71.9% had cable.

10 In 1990, the total operating revenue of telephone companies was $156.003 billion, of which 25.2% came from local calls and 43.8% from long-distance calls. The fastest growing segment of the industry is cellular/radio-telephone, whose income grew 34.3% in 1989-1990 from $2.652 billion to $3.563 billion. Cellular systems numbered 1,252 in 1990 compared to 32 in 1984. Over the same period, the number of subscribers grew from 92,000 to 7.557 million and the number of cell sites from 346 to 7,847. The average monthly bill of a cellular phone subscriber dropped from $96.83 in 1987 to $72.74 in 1991.

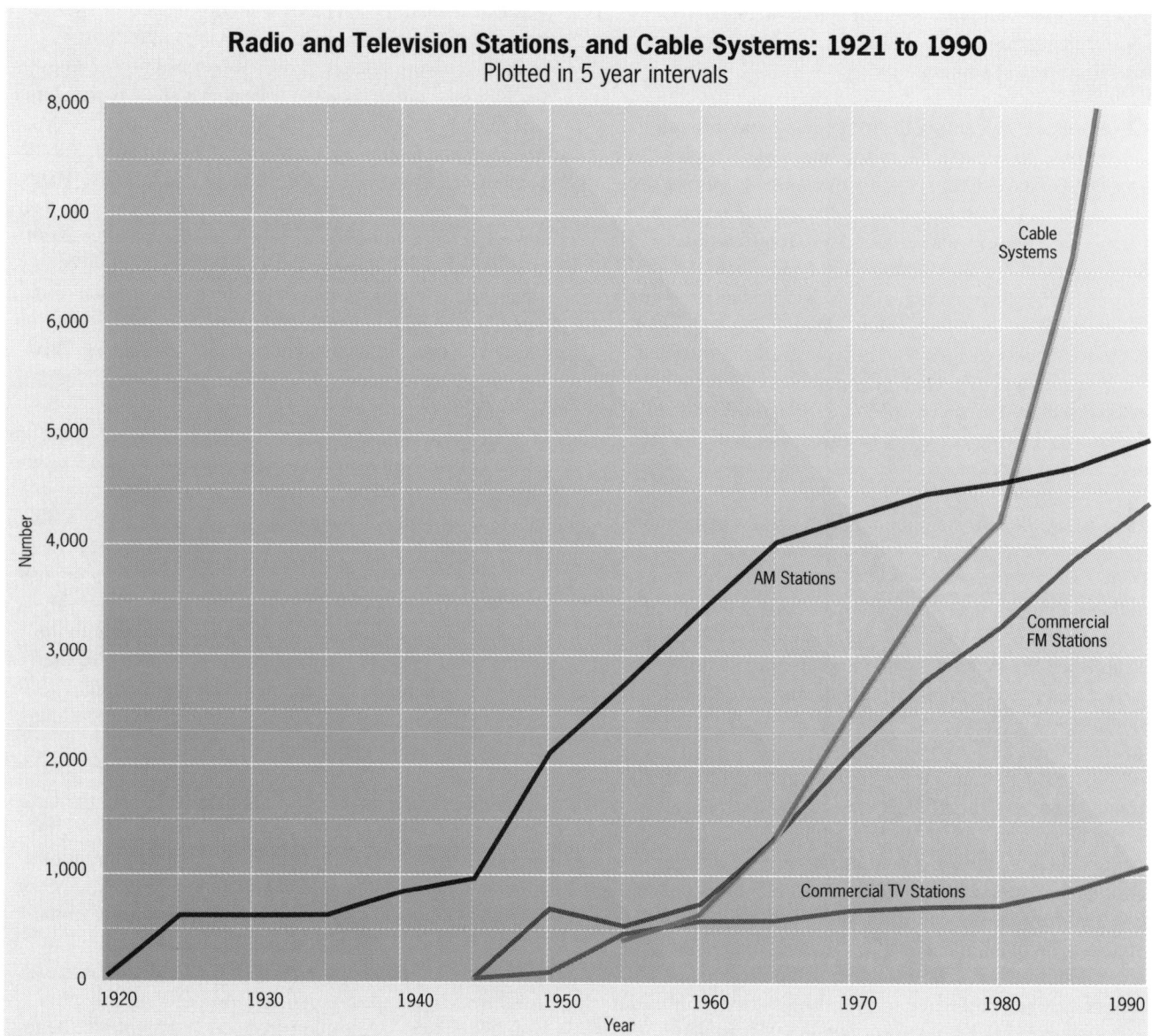

Radio and Television Stations, and Cable Systems: 1921 to 1990
Plotted in 5 year intervals

11 The newspaper industry has experienced little growth, either in numbers or in circulation, since 1970. The total number of daily newspapers declined from 1,748 in 1970 to 1,611 in 1990, while total circulation edged up only slightly from 62.1 million to 62.3 million. Per capita newspaper readership in the United States fell from 0.305 in 1970 to 0.251 in 1991, and currently it is among the lowest in the developed world.

12 Advertising expenditures grew each year from 1950 to 1990, and experienced the first decline only in 1991.

From $5.7 billion in 1950, they reached $126.6 billion in 1991. In 1990, newspapers accounted for 25% of advertising expenditures, television 22%, direct mail 18%, radio 7%, the yellow pages 7%, and magazines 5%.

13 Public television systems are becoming more and more reliant on nonofficial funding. In 1980, they derived 65.8% of their funding from federal and state governments. This percentage had slipped to 46.9% in 1990, but the difference was made up by the rise in the support of private subscribers and corporations from 24.8% to 39.8%.

Series R 93-105.   Radio and Television Stations, Sets Produced and Households With Sets: 1921 to 1991

(Figures as of June 30, except for census figures in italics which are as of April 1)

| Year | Operating broadcast stations [1] | | | Cable television | | Households with x | |
	Standard broadcast (AM)	Frequency modulation (FM), commercial	Television (TV), commercial	Systems	Total subscribers (households) (1,000)	Radio sets (1,000)	Television sets (1,000)
	93	94	96	98	99	104	105
1991	—	—	—	—	—	—	93,000
1990	4,987	4,392	1,092	—	—	94,400	92,000
1989	4,975	4,269	1,061	—	47,800	92,800	90,000
1988	4,932	4,155	1,028	8,500	43,800	91,100	89,000
1987	4,902	4,041	968	7,900	41,000	89,900	87,000
1986	4,863	3,944	919	7,600	37,500	88,100	86,000
1985	4,718	3,875	883	6,644	31,300	87,100	85,000
1984	4,754	3,716	841	6,200	30,000	86,700	84,000
1983	4,733	3,527	813	5,600	25,000	—	83,300
1982	4,668	3,380	777	4,825	21,000	—	81,500
1981	4,634	3,349	756	4,375	18,300	—	79,900
1980	4,589	3,282	734	4,225	15,500	78,600	76,000
1979	4,511	3,036	723	4,150	14,100	—	74,500
1978	4,459	2,922	714	3,875	13,000	—	72,900
1977	4,474	3,007	697	3,832	11,900	—	71,200
1976	—	—	701	3,681	10,800	—	69,600
1975	4,463	2,767	706	3,506	9,800	71,400	69,000
1974	4,305	2,413	694	3,158	8,700	—	—
1973	4,295	2,278	692	2,991	7,300	—	—
1972	4,273	2,229	690	2,841	6,000	—	—
1971	4,250	2,122	688	2,639	5,300	—	—
1970	4,288	2,126	691	2,490	4,500	62,000	59,550
1970	—	—	—	—	—	*[2] 46,108*	*60,594*
1969	4,254	2,018	680	2,260	3,600	60,600	58,250
1968	4,203	1,850	655	2,000	2,800	58,500	56,670
1967	4,135	1,708	626	1,770	2,100	57,500	55,130
1966	4,075	1,515	613	1,570	1,575	57,000	53,850
1965	4,025	1,343	589	1,325	1,275	55,200	52,700
1964	3,976	1,181	582	1,200	1,085	54,000	51,600
1963	3,860	1,120	581	1,000	950	52,300	50,300
1962	3,745	1,012	571	800	850	51,305	48,855
1961	3,602	889	553	700	725	50,695	47,200
1960	3,483	741	579	640	650	50,193	45,750
1960	—	—	—	—	—	*48,504*	*46,312*
1959	3,377	622	566	560	550	* 49,450	* 43,950
1958	3,253	548	556	525	450	48,500	41,924
1957	3,079	530	519	500	350	47,600	38,900
1956	2,896	530	496	450	300	46,800	34,900
1955	2,732	540	458	400	150	45,900	30,700
1954	2,583	553	402	300	65	45,100	26,000
1953	2,458	580	198	150	30	44,800	20,400
1952	2,355	629	108	70	14	42,800	15,300
1951	2,281	649	107	—	—	41,900	10,320
1950	2,144	691	104	—	—	40,700	3,875
1950	—	—	—	—	—	*40,411*	*5,030*
1949	2,066	737	69	—	—	39,300	940
1948	2,034	1,020	108	—	—	37,623	172
1947	1,795	918	66	—	—	35,900	14
1946	1,215	511	30	—	—	33,998	8
1945	955	53	9	—	—	33,100	—
1944	924	52	9	—	—	32,500	—
1943	912	48	8	—	—	30,800	—
1942 [3]	925	42	10	—	—	30,600	—
1941	897	49	2	—	—	29,300	—

See footnotes at end of table.

Series R 93-105.   Radio and Television Stations, Sets Produced and Households With Sets: 1921 to 1991—Cont'd.

(Figures as of June 30, except for census figures in italics which are as of April 1)

Year	Operating broadcast stations (AM)	Households with radio sets (1,000)	Year	Operating broadcast stations (AM)	Households with radio sets (1,000)	Year	Operating broadcast stations (AM)	Households with radio sets (1,000)
	93	104		93	104		93	104
1940	847	28,500	1933	598	19,250	1927	681	6,750
1940	—	*28,048*	1932	604	18,450	1926	528	4,500
1939	778	27,500	1931	612	16,700			
1938	743	26,667				1925	571	2,750
1937	704	24,500	1930	618	13,750	1924	530	1,250
1936	656	22,869	*1930*	—	*12,049*	1923	556	466
			1929	606	10,250	1922	30	60
1935	623	21,456	1928	677	8,000	1921	[4]1	—
1934	593	20,400						

* Denotes first year for which figures include Alaska and Hawaii.
X Represents zero.
[1] Includes Alaska, Hawaii, Puerto Rico, Guam and Virgin Islands for all years. Prior to 1948, the FCC did not keep records on the number of stations on the air. Therefore, data for 1933-1948 are for authorized stations and may include a number that were not actually on the air.

[2] In 1970 census of housing, only battery-operated radios were enumerated.
[3] Authorization of new radio stations and production of radio receivers for commercial use halted from April 1942 until October 1945.
[4] First station to receive regular license as of Sept. 15; other stations in operation experimentally.

Series R 106-122.   Radio Advertising Expenditures, Finances and Employment: 1935 to 1990

Year	Advertising expenditures (mil. dol.)				Year	Advertising expenditures (mil. dol.)			
	Total	Network	National spot	Local		Total	Network	National spot	Local
	106	107	108	109		106	107	108	109
1990	8,726	482	1,635	6,609	1962	736	46	233	457
1989	8,323	476	1,547	6,300	1961	683	43	221	510
1988	7,798	425	1,418	5,955					
1987	7,206	413	1,330	5,463	1960	692	43	222	428
1986	6,949	423	1,348	5,178	1959	656	44	206	406
					1958	619	58	190	372
1985	6,490	365	1,335	4,790	1957	618	64	187	368
1984	5,817	320	1,197	4,300	1956	567	61	161	346
1983	5,210	296	1,038	3,876					
1982	4,670	255	923	3,492	1955	545	84	134	326
1981	4,230	230	879	3,129	1954	559	114	135	309
					1953	611	141	146	324
1980	3,702	183	779	2,740	1952	624	162	142	321
1979	3,310	161	685	2,484	1951	606	180	138	289
1978	3,052	147	620	2,285					
1977	2,634	137	546	1,951	1950	605	196	136	273
1976	2,330	105	518	1,707	1949	571	203	123	245
					1948	562	211	121	230
1975	1,980	83	436	1,461	1947	506	201	106	199
1974	1,837	69	405	1,363	1946	454	200	98	157
1973	1,690	70	380	1,240					
1972	1,555	75	400	1,080	1945	424	198	92	134
1971	1,386	58	387	935	1944	394	192	87	114
					1943	314	157	71	86
1970	1,308	56	371	881	1942	260	129	59	73
1969	1,264	59	368	837	1941	247	125	52	70
1968	1,190	63	360	767					
1967	1,031	64	310	657	1940	216	113	42	60
1966	1,010	64	308	638	1939	184	99	35	50
					1938	167	89	34	44
1965	917	60	275	582	1937	165	89	28	48
1964	846	59	256	531	1936	122	76	23	24
1963	789	56	243	490	1935	113	63	15	35

Series R 123-139.   Television Advertising Expenditures, Finances and Employment: 1949 to 1990

Year	Total	Network	National spot	Local	Year	Total	Network	National spot	Local
	123	**124**	**125**	**126**		**123**	**124**	**125**	**126**
1990	28,405	9,383	7,788	7,856	1968	3,231	1,523	1,131	577
1989	26,891	9,110	7,354	7,812	1967	2,909	1,455	988	466
1988	25,686	9,172	7,147	7,270	1966	2,823	1,393	988	442
1987	23,904	8,500	6,846	6,833					
1986	22,081	8,342	6,570	6,514	1965	2,515	1,237	892	386
					1964	2,289	1,132	806	351
1985	21,022	8,060	6,004	5,714	1963	2,032	1,025	698	309
1984	19,848	8,318	5,488	5,084	1962	1,897	976	629	292
1983	16,759	6,955	4,827	4,345	1961	1,691	887	548	263
1982	14,636	6,144	4,364	3,765					
1981	12,650	5,575	3,730	3,345	1960	1,627	820	527	281
					1959	1,529	776	486	267
1980	11,469	5,130	3,269	2,967	1958	1,387	742	397	248
1979	10,154	4,599	2,873	2,682	1957	1,286	690	352	244
1978	8,955	3,975	2,607	2,373	1956	1,225	643	329	253
1977	7,612	3,466	2,204	1,948					
1976	6,721	2,857	2,154	1,710	1955	1,035	550	260	225
					1954	809	422	207	180
1975	5,263	2,306	1,623	1,334	1953	606	320	146	141
1974	4,851	2,145	1,495	1,211	1952	454	256	94	104
1973	4,460	1,968	1,377	1,115	1951	332	181	70	82
1972	4,091	1,804	1,318	969					
1971	3,520	1,575	1,150	795	1950	171	85	31	55
					1949	58	29	9	19
1970	3,596	1,658	1,234	704					
1969	3,585	1,678	1,253	654					

Series R 140-148. Safety and Special Radio Stations Authorized, by Class: 1913 to 1990

(As of June 30. Includes Alaska, Hawaii, Puerto Rico and outlying area.)

Year	Amateur and disaster services	Aviation services	Industrial services	Land transportation services	Marine services	Public safety services	Year	Amateur and disaster services	Aviation services	Industrial services	Land transportation services	Marine services	Public safety services
	140	141	143	144	145	146		140	141	143	144	145	146
1990	495,700	250,900	864,800	40,100	622,900	234,500	1950	87,967	23,794	6,099	3,495	24,921	7,607
1989	467,300	251,200	873,900	40,400	620,400	228,500	1949	81,675	27,227	4,266	3,588	20,004	5,700
1988	439,100	248,500	875,600	40,100	605,400	221,400	1948	78,434	20,858	2,855	3,122	15,024	4,903
1987	432,600	247,700	871,100	40,000	573,700	212,600	1947	75,000	15,943	1,787	1,692	11,955	4,620
1986	423,700	244,300	864,400	39,800	561,200	207,100	1946	70,000	6,205	702	156	8,676	4,760
1985	415,400	245,700	811,300	37,700	525,300	194,500	1945	60,000	3,793	576	—	—	4,446
1984	413,200	245,300	767,900	35,800	497,500	184,200	1944	60,000	3,445	468	—	6,817	4,144
1983	413,200	245,300	767,900	35,800	497,500	184,200	1943	60,000	3,553	386	—	6,609	3,772
1982	410,600	238,000	649,000	34,400	434,700	166,200	1942	60,000	4,713	356	—	—	3,455
1981	385,200	234,900	605,000	32,500	402,000	158,500	1941	60,000	3,000	306	—	5,822	2,967
1980	389,900	231,600	504,900	28,000	398,300	137,100	1940	56,295	2,099	340	—	4,945	2,334
1979	375,500	227,000	513,900	29,400	371,200	147,000	1939	53,558	1,824	307	—	4,036	1,536
1978	369,300	216,100	426,800	27,500	345,200	136,800	1938	49,911	1,460	232	—	3,516	662
1977	340,900	207,800	357,900	25,400	315,000	127,200	1937	47,444	1,212	221	—	2,422	535
1976	292,800	188,500	277,100	23,000	262,600	105,900	1936	46,850	812	195	—	2,219	403
1975	276,800	184,400	244,600	22,600	250,700	92,600	1935	45,561	678	146	—	2,157	298
1974	273,780	172,466	231,158	21,696	243,276	86,411	1934	46,390	671	129	—	2,195	220
1973	279,505	167,121	195,132	20,753	238,596	75,865	1933	41,555	646	121	—	2,192	152
1972	284,235	161,223	171,387	18,318	238,415	66,209	1932	30,374	579	134	—	2,225	123
1971	286,118	158,328	140,146	16,851	218,527	57,726	1931	22,739	463	130	—	2,392	91
1970	283,461	150,955	222,500	22,262	206,251	72,215	1930	18,994	281	—	—	2,173	20
1969	285,175	143,997	204,266	21,291	186,295	67,730	1929	16,829	131	—	—	—	12
1968	282,525	140,799	185,046	20,016	164,000	63,160	1928	16,928	—	—	—	—	—
1967	279,093	122,568	169,417	18,613	143,612	58,831	1927	16,926	—	—	—	—	—
1966	285,600	105,133	152,315	16,914	137,469	54,839	1926	14,902	—	—	—	1,954	—
1965	280,343	109,897	141,360	15,635	114,075	50,888	1925	15,000	—	—	—	1,901	4
1964	280,818	107,557	124,347	14,815	161,593	47,389	1924	15,540	—	—	—	2,741	3
1963	270,838	106,202	107,796	14,089	143,227	43,168	1923	16,570	—	—	—	—	3
1962	251,659	106,923	93,073	13,278	127,633	38,676	1922	—	—	—	—	—	—
1961	234,681	92,779	77,773	12,075	110,433	36,658	1921	—	—	—	—	—	—
1960	228,206	91,180	64,804	11,452	97,411	32,906	1920	5,719	—	—	—	—	1
1959	205,588	77,682	49,679	10,625	84,947	29,363	1919	—	—	—	—	—	—
1958	187,362	62,684	39,978	10,190	72,514	26,512	1918	—	—	—	—	—	—
1957	165,908	49,699	35,711	9,592	63,844	23,270	1917	—	—	—	—	—	—
1956	154,337	48,745	30,597	8,990	56,915	20,718	1916	—	—	—	—	—	1
1955	142,387	43,855	24,854	7,668	50,714	18,415	1915	—	—	—	—	—	—
1954	124,324	40,154	21,598	6,891	46,299	15,697	1914	—	—	—	—	—	—
1953	111,579	39,315	17,378	5,922	40,357	13,631	1913	1,312	—	—	—	701	—
1952	113,163	32,603	13,680	5,027	35,500	11,143							
1951	90,587	34,061	9,551	4,253	29,544	9,129							

Series R 163-171. Postal Service—Post Offices, Revenues and Expenditures, Postage Stamps, Stamped Envelopes and Postal Cards Issued, and Pieces of Mail Handled: 1789 to 1990

(In thousands, except number of post offices. For years ending June 30. Includes Alaska, Hawaii, Puerto Rico and all outlying areas except the Canal Zone)

Year	Post offices [1]	Revenues [2]	Expenditures [2]	Pieces of matter of all kinds handled	Year	Post offices [1]	Revenues [2]	Expenditures [2]	Pieces of matter of all kinds handled
	163	164	165	169		163	164	165	169
1990	28,959	$40,074,000	$40,490,000	166,300,000	1935	45,686	$630,795	$696,503	22,331,752
1989	29,083	38,920,000	38,370,000	161,600,000	1934	46,506	586,733	630,733	20,625,827
1988	29,203	35,939,000	36,119,000	161,000,000	1933	47,641	587,631	699,887	19,868,456
1987	29,319	32,297,000	32,520,000	153,900,000	1932	48.159	588,172	793,684	24,306,744
1986	29,344	31,021,000	30,716,000	147,400,000	1931	48,733	656,463	802,485	26,544,352
1985	29,557	28,956,000	29,207,000	140,100,000	1930	49,063	705,484	803,667	27,887,823
1984	29,750	26,474,000	26,357,000	131,500,000	1929	49,482	696,948	782,344	27,951,548
1983	29,990	24,699,000	24,083,000	119,400,000	1928	49,944	693,634	725,700	26,837,005
1982	30,155	23,628,000	22,826,000	114,000,000	1927	50,266	683,122	714,577	26,686,556
1981	30,242	20,781,000	21,369,000	110,100,000	1926	50,601	659,820	679,704	25,483,529
1980	30,326	19,106,000	19,412,000	106,300,000	1925	50,957	599,591	639,282	—
1979	30,449	17,999,000	17,529,000	99,800,000	1924	51,266	572,949	587,377	—
1978	30,518	15,841,000	16,220,000	98,900,000	1923	51,613	532,828	556,851	23,054,832
1977	30,521	14,622,000	15,310,000	92,200,000	1922	51,950	484,854	545,644	—
1976	30,521	12,747,000	13,923,000	89,800,000	1921	52,168	463,491	620,994	—
1975	30,754	11,590,000	12,578,000	89,300,000	1920	52,641	437,150	454,323	—
1974	31,000	10,857,000	11,295,000	90,100,000	1919	53,084	[3] 436,239	362,498	—
1973	31,385	9,913,000	9,926,000	89,700,000	1918	54,347	[3] 388,976	324,834	—
1972	31,686	9,347,000	9,522,000	87,200,000	1917	55,414	329,726	319,839	—
1971	31,947	8,751,000	8,955,000	87,000,000	1916	55,935	312,058	306,204	—
1970	32,002	7,701,695	7,867,269	84,881,833	1915	56,380	287,248	298,546	—
1969	32,064	7,025,898	7,168,489	82,004,501	1914	56,810	287,935	283,544	—
1968	32,260	6,423,515	6,543,920	79,516,731	1913	58,020	266,620	262,068	18,567,445
1967	32,626	5,101,982	6,249,027	78,366,572	1912	58,729	246,744	248,525	17,588,659
1966	33,121	4,784,186	5,726,523	75,607,302	1911	59,237	237,880	237,649	16,900,552
1965	33,624	4,483,390	5,275,840	71,873,166	1910	59,580	224,129	229,977	14,850,102
1964	34,040	4,276,123	4,927,825	69,676,477	1909	60,144	203,562	221,004	14,004,577
1963	34,498	3,879,128	4,698,528	67,852,738	1908	60,704	191,479	208,352	13,364,069
1962	34,797	3,557,041	4,331,617	66,493,190	1907	62,658	183,585	190,238	12,255,666
1961	34,955	3,423,059	4,249,414	64,932,859	1906	65,600	167,933	178,450	11,361,091
1960	35,238	3,276,588	3,873,953	63,674,604	1905	68,131	152,827	167,399	10,187,506
1959	35,750	3,035,232	3,640,368	61,247,220	1904	71,131	143,582	152,362	9,502,460
1958	36,308	2,550,221	3,440,810	60,129,911	1903	74,169	134,224	138,784	8,887,467
1957	37,012	2,496,614	3,044,438	59,077,633	1902	75,924	121,848	124,786	8,085,447
1956	37,515	2,419,354	2,883,305	56,441,216	1901	76,945	111,631	115,555	7,424,390
1955	38,316	2,349,477	2,712,150	55,233,564	1900	76,688	102,354	107,740	7,129,990
1954	39,405	2,268,517	2,667,664	52,213,170	1899	75,000	95,021	101,632	6,576,310
1953	40,609	2,091,714	2,742,126	50,948,156	1898	73,570	89,013	98,054	6,214,447
1952	40,919	1,947,316	2,666,860	49,905,875	1897	71,022	82,665	94,077	5,781,002
1951	41,193	1,776,816	2,341,399	46,908,410	1896	70,360	82,499	90,933	5,693,719
1950	41,464	1,677,487	2,222,949	45,063,737	1895	70,064	76,983	87,180	5,134,281
1949	41,607	1,571,851	2,149,322	43,555,108	1894	69,805	75,080	84,994	4,919,090
1948	41,695	1,410,971	1,687,805	40,280,374	1893	68,403	75,897	81,582	5,021,841
1947	41,760	1,299,141	1,504,799	37,427,706	1892	67,119	70,930	76,981	4,776,575
1946	41,751	1,224,572	1,353,654	36,318,158	1891	64,329	65,932	73,060	4,369,900
1945	41,792	1,314,240	1,145,002	37,912,067	1890	62,401	60,882	66,260	4,005,408
1944	42,161	1,112,877	1,068,987	34,930,685	1889	58,999	56,176	62,317	3,860,200
1943	42,654	966,227	952,529	32,818,262	1888	57,376	52,695	56,458	3,576,100
1942	43,358	859,817	873,950	30,117,633	1887	55,157	48,838	53,006	3,495,100
1941	43,739	812,828	836,859	29,235,791	1886	53,614	43,948	51,005	3,747,000
1940	44,024	766,949	807,629	27,749,467	1885	51,252	42,561	50,046	—
1939	44,327	745,955	784,550	26,444,846	1884	48,434	43,326	47,225	—
1938	44,586	728,634	772,308	26,041,979	1883	46,820	45,509	43,283	—
1937	44,877	726,201	772,743	25,801,279	1882	46,231	41,876	40,482	—
1936	45,230	665,343	753,616	23,571,315	1881	44,512	36,785	39,593	—

See footnotes at end of table.

Series R 163-171. Postal Service—Post Offices, Revenues and Expenditures, Postage Stamps, Stamped Envelopes and Postal Cards Issued, and Pieces of Mail Handled: 1789 to 1990—Cont'd.

(In thousands, except number of post offices. For years ending June 30. Includes Alaska, Hawaii, Puerto Rico and all outlying areas except the Canal Zone)

Year	Post offices [1]	Revenues [2]	Expenditures [2]	Year	Post offices [1]	Revenues [2]	Expenditures [2]
	163	164	165		163	164	165
1880	42,989	33,315	36,543	1833	10,127	2,617	2,930
1879	40,588	30,042	33,450	1832	9,205	2,259	2,266
1878	38,253	29,278	34,165	1831	8,686	1,998	1,936
1877	37,345	27,532	33,486				
1876	36,383	28,644	33,263	1830	8,450	1,851	1,933
				1829	8,004	1,707	1,782
1875	35,547	26,791	33,611	1828	7,530	1,660	1,690
1874	34,294	26,471	32,126	1827	7,300	1,525	1,470
1873	33,244	22,997	29,085	1826	6,150	1,448	1,367
1872	31,863	21,915	26,658				
1871	30,345	20,037	24,390	1825	5,677	1,307	1,229
				1824	5,182	1,198	1,188
1870	28,492	18,880	23,999	1823	4,043	1,130	1,157
1869	27,106	17,314	23,698	1822	4,709	1,117	1,168
1868	26,481	16,292	22,731	1821	4,650	1,059	1,165
1867	25,163	15,237	19,235				
1866	29,389	14,387	15,352	1820	4,500	1,112	1,161
				1819	4,000	1,205	1,118
1865	28,882	14,556	13,695	1818	3,618	1,230	1,036
1864	28,878	12,438	12,645	1817	3,459	1,003	917
1863	29,047	11,164	11,314	1816	3,260	962	804
1862	28,875	8,300	11,125				
1861	28,586	8,349	13,607	1815	3,000	1,043	748
				1814	2,670	730	727
1860	28,498	8,518	14,875	1813	2,708	703	631
1859	28,539	7,968	15,754	1812	2,610	649	540
1858	27,977	7,487	12,722	1811	2,403	587	499
1857	26,586	7,354	11,508				
1856	25,565	6,921	10,405	1810	2,300	552	496
				1809	2,012	507	498
1855	24,410	6,642	9,968	1808	1,944	461	463
1854	23,548	6,256	8,577	1807	1,848	479	454
1853	22,320	5,241	7,983	1806	1,710	446	417
1852	20,910	5,185	7,108				
1851	19,796	6,411	6,278	1805	1,558	421	377
				1804	1,405	389	338
1850	18,417	5,500	5,213	1803	1,258	352	322
1849	16,749	4,705	4,479	1802	1,114	327	282
1848	16,159	4,555	4,327	1801	1,025	320	255
1847	15,146	3,880	3,980				
1846	14,601	3,487	4,076	1800	903	281	214
				1799	677	265	188
1845	14,183	4,290	4,321	1798	639	233	179
1844	14,103	4,237	4,299	1797	554	214	150
1843	13,814	4,296	4,375	1796	468	195	132
1842	13,733	4,547	4,628				
1841	13,778	4,408	4,500	1795	453	161	118
				1794	450	129	90
1840	13,468	4,544	4,718	1793	209	105	72
1839	12,780	4,485	4,637	1792	195	67	55
1838	12,519	4,239	4,431	1791	89	46	37
1837	11,767	4,102	3,288				
1836	11,091	3,408	2,842	1790	75	38	32
				1789	75	[4] 8	[4] 8
1835	10,770	2,994	2,757				
1834	10,693	2,824	2,911				

[1] Excludes branches and stations.
[2] Accounting basis changed from cash to accrual basis in 1954; from accrual basis to accrued cost basis in 1963.
[3] For 1918 and 1919, includes $44,500,000 and $71,392,000, respectively, war-tax revenue accruing from increased postage.
[4] For three months only.

Series R 172-187. Postal Service—Revenues, Expenses and Volume of Mail, by Classes of Mail, and Employees: 1926 to 1990

(In millions, except employees in thousands. Includes Alaska, Hawaii, Puerto Rico and all outlying areas except the Canal Zone. Series R 174 also includes airmail from 1971 on)

Year	First-class mail 1,2, pieces 174	Second-class mail, pieces 177	Third-class mail, pieces 180	Fourth-class mail, pieces 183	Post Office employees 187
1990	89,917	10,680	63,725	663	809
1989	85,826	10,523	62,779	626	817
1988	82,381	10,448	81,970	649	824
1987	78,933	10,324	59,734	615	791
1986	76,252	10,588	55,049	602	785
1985	72,517	10,380	52,170	576	744
1984	68,507	9,522	48,249	599	702
1983	64,320	9,220	40,735	568	679
1982	62,271	9,527	36,719	597	675
1981	61,476	9,956	33,607	590	670
1980	60,332	10,221	30,381	633	667
1979	57,976	8,400	27,513	614	663
1978	56,020	8,691	26,330	691	656
1977	53,668	8,673	24,050	762	655
1976	52,459	8,899	22,514	759	679
1975	52,482	9,713	21,867	801	702
1974	52,929	8,838	22,537	859	710
1973	52,291	9,034	22,689	893	701
1972	50,293	9,494	21,908	914	706
1971	51,493	9,604	20,532	968	729
1970	48,640	9,351	19,974	977	741
1969 [3]	46,411	9,206	19,622	1,031	739
1968	43,183	8,907	20,665	1,039	731
1967	41,998	8,711	20,985	1,070	717
1966	40,422	8,634	20,305	1,066	675
1965	38,068	8,600	19,454	1,045	596
1964	36,943	8,559	18,599	1,066	585
1963	35,833	8,227	18,407	1,076	587
1962	35,333	8,090	17,837	1,024	588
1961	34,289	7,966	17,569	978	582
1960	33,235	7,535	17,910	1,016	563
1959	32,274	7,099	16,978	1,038	550
1958	32,218	7,148	15,849	1,170	538

Year	First-class mail 1,2, pieces 174	Second-class mail, pieces 177	Third-class mail, pieces 180	Fourth-class mail, pieces 183	Post Office employees 187
1957	31,561	6,888	15,702	1,184	521
1956	30,078	6,915	14,676	1,173	509
1955	28,713	6,740	15,050	1,136	512
1954	27,085	6,483	13,866	1,195	507
1953	27,257	6,762	12,004	1,245	507
1952	26,502	6,956	11,630	1,257	524
1951	25,578	6,520	10,534	1,235	498
1950	24,500	6,265	10,343	1,179	501
1949	23,206	6,987	9,389	1,209	518
1948	21,948	6,344	8,188	1,143	503
1947	20,665	6,124	6,803	1,067	471
1946	20,059	5,832	6,055	994	487
1945	21,009	5,522	5,446	1,028	436
1944	20,510	4,635	4,409	961	390
1943	(NA)	(NA)	(NA)	(NA)	374
1942	16,972	4,571	5,435	779	360
1941	15,989	4,607	6,075	738	361
1940	15,224	4,577	5,556	712	353
1939	14,657	4,310	5,181	693	349
1938	14,226	4,377	5,272	670	345
1937	13,882	4,529	5,356	685	332
1936	12,731	4,353	4,674	618	324
1935	12,498	4,138	4,030	573	309
1934	11,557	3,956	3,612	531	314
1933	10,878	3,869	3,753	530	322
1932	14,598	4,552	3,641	617	333
1931	15,824	4,857	4,100	766	339
1930	16,901	4,968	4,325	837	340
1929	17,170	4,834	4,341	770	340
1928	16,706	4,678	3,838	752	337
1927	16,284	4,753	4,062	743	332
1926	15,266	4,658	3,962	770	329

NA Not available.
[1] For 1926-1929, domestic airmail included with first class mail.
[2] Includes airmail from 1971.
[3] In fiscal year 1969, the department changed from a fully distributed cost system to an attributable cost system.

Series R 188-190. Postal Rates for First-Class Mail, Letters and Postal Cards: 1861 to 1991

(First-class mail as a mail category not officially established until 1863. Ship and steamboat letters, 1792-1863, carried special rates)

Year of rate change	Letters, nonlocal	Postal cards (cents)	Year of rate change	Letters, nonlocal	Postal cards (cents)	Year of rate change	Letters, nonlocal	Postal cards (cents)
	188	189		188	189		188	189
1991	29¢ per oz.	19	1971	8¢ per oz.	6	1917	3¢ per oz.	2
1988	25¢ per oz.	15	1968-1970	6¢ per oz.	5	1885	2¢ per oz.	1
1985	22¢ per oz.	14	1963	5¢ per oz.	4			
1982 [2]	20¢ per oz.	13	1953, Aug. 1	4¢ per oz.	3	1883	2¢ per $\frac{1}{2}$ oz.	1
1981	18¢ per oz.	12				1872	3¢ per $\frac{1}{2}$ oz.	[3] 1
1978	15¢ per oz.	10	1952	3¢ per oz.	2	1863 [4]	3¢ per $\frac{1}{2}$ oz.	——
			1940	([1])	([1])	1861 [5]	([4])	——
1975	——	9	1932	3¢ per oz.	1			
1974	10¢ per oz.	8	1919	2¢ per oz.	1			

[1] The 1940 rate change provided that the three-cent letter rate was not to apply to first-class matter for local delivery or for delivery within a county with a population of more than 1 million people if it was entirely within a corporate city.

[2] From November 1981.

[3] Government postal cards first authorized in 1872.

[4] A uniform rate regardless of distance, a free city delivery service and a letter unit of $\frac{1}{2}$ ounce instead of the former "single letter" were inaugurated.

[5] Rate between any point in the U.S. east of the Rocky Mountains and any state or territory on the Pacific.

Series R 192-217.   New Books and New Editions Published, by Subject: 1880 to 1991

New Books

Year	Total books published [1]	Agriculture	Art	Biography	Business	Education	Fiction	General works	History	Home Economics	Juvenile	Language
	192	195	196	197	198	199	200	201	202	203	204	205
1991	41,223	468	1,119	1,890	1,298	973	4,199	1,684	2,107	721	4,555	521
1990	46,738	514	1,262	1,957	1,191	1,039	5,764	1,760	2,243	758	5,172	649
1989	53,446	562	1,569	2,193	1,569	1,054	5,941	2,332	2,563	949	5,413	586
1988	55,483	666	1,602	2,250	1,647	1,113	5,564	2,475	3,260	1,057	4,954	628
1987	56,057	652	1,693	2,259	1,462	1,081	6,298	2,620	2,882	1,168	4,642	699
1986	52,637	564	1,697	2,152	1,604	1,029	5,578	2,484	2,471	1,103	4,516	668
1985	50,070	536	1,545	1,953	1,518	1,085	5,105	2,905	2,327	1,228	3,801	632
1984	51,058	507	1,836	2,098	1,696	1,052	5,413	3,021	2,257	1,306	3,128	670
1983	53,280	572	1,896	2,135	1,636	1,059	5,470	2,767	2,296	1,325	3,197	669
1982	46,935	439	1,722	1,752	1,327	1,046	5,419	2,398	2,177	1,099	3,049	576
1981	48,793	474	1,693	1,860	1,342	1,172	5,655	1,743	2,321	1,108	3,102	761
1980	42,377	461	1,691	1,891	1,185	1,011	2,835	1,643	2,220	879	2,659	529
1979	45,182	538	2,021	2,042	1,362	1,121	3,264	1,471	2,160	897	3,052	560
1978	41,216	552	1,483	1,891	1,248	1,063	3,693	1,310	2,016	845	2,909	458
1977	42,780	594	1,795	2,104	1,077	1,194	3,681	1,448	2,022	795	2,918	556
1976	35,141	477	1,369	1,714	843	899	3,458	1,034	1,934	690	2,210	409
1975	39,372	456	1,561	1,968	820	1,038	3,805	1,113	1,823	728	2,292	438
1974	40,846	391	1,525	2,197	925	1,161	3,562	1,191	1,292	828	2,592	441
1973	39,351	382	1,377	2,325	762	1,618	3,688	1,187	1,598	669	2,042	458
1972	38,053	390	1,470	1,986	684	1,292	3,260	1,048	1,629	596	2,526	479
1971	37,692	324	1,246	1,797	700	1,250	3,430	1,012	1,978	477	2,223	536
1970	36,071	200	852	735	658	842	1,998	568	1,010	235	2,472	339
1969	29,579	216	856	718	566	721	1,816	508	1,191	267	1,321	355
1968	30,387	191	930	786	644	917	1,822	521	1,048	245	2,318	387
1967	²28,762	218	844	783	509	871	1,981	426	1,015	203	2,390	382
1966	30,050	212	779	819	478	886	1,699	410	959	219	2,375	459
1965	28,595	214	763	455	437	789	1,615	384	909	241	2,473	385
1964	28,451	209	776	697	411	934	1,703	361	834	188	2,533	414
1963	25,784	219	664	680	396	777	1,859	346	847	205	2,605	334
1962	21,904	215	590	667	308	559	1,787	279	812	156	2,328	226
1961	18,060	194	539	622	286	461	1,645	231	796	143	1,513	248
1960	15,012	121	422	746	240	308	1,642	233	695	155	1,628	—
1959	³14,876	101	354	671	327	368	1,675	326	750	141	1,540	—
1958	13,462	122	409	608	283	276	1,592	213	750	142	1,424	—
1957	13,142	120	304	699	266	254	1,433	360	773	115	1,420	—
1956	12,538	103	283	676	222	229	1,500	305	521	159	1,384	—
1955	12,589	125	305	735	228	231	1,459	315	572	205	1,372	—
1954	11,901	111	285	687	196	223	1,512	339	529	192	1,193	—
1953	12,050	126	265	710	225	201	1,495	360	495	197	1,264	—
1952	11,840	114	267	650	180	238	1,354	336	454	237	1,094	—
1951	11,255	105	272	586	180	229	1,329	329	435	186	982	—
1950	11,022	111	317	538	190	209	1,211	262	456	150	907	—

Year	Total books published [1]	Year	Total books published [1]	Year	Total books published [1]	Year	Total books published [1]	Year	Total books published [1]	Year	Total books published [1]
	192		192		192		192		192		192
1949	10,892	1937	10,912	1925	9,574	1913	12,230	1902	7,833	1891	4,665
1948	9,897	1936	10,436	1924	9,012	1912	10,903	1901	8,141	1890	4,559
1947	9,182			1923	8,863	1911	⁵11,123			1889	4,014
1946	7,735			1922	8,638					1888	4,631
		1935	8,766	1921	8,329	1910	13,470	1900	6,356	1887	4,437
1945	6,548	1934	8,198			1909	10,901	1899	5,321	1886	4,676
1944	6,970	1933	8,092	1920	8,422	1908	9,254	1898	4,886		
1943	8,325	1932	9,035	1919	8,594	1907	9,620	1897	4,928	1885	4,030
1942	9,525	1931	10,307	1918	9,237	1906	7,139	1896	5,703	1884	4,088
1941	11,112			1917	10,060					1883	3,481
		1930	10,027	1916	10,445	1905	8,112	1895	5,469	1882	3,472
1940	11,328	1929	10,187			1904	8,391	1894	4,484	1881	2,991
1939	10,640	1928	10,354	1915	9,734	1903	7,865	1893	5,134	1880	2,076
1938	11,067	1927	10,153	1914	12,010			1892	4,862		
		1926	9,925								

See footnotes at end of table.

Series R 192-217. New Books and New Editions Published, by Subject: 1880 to 1991—Cont'd.

New Books

Year	Law	Literature	Medicine	Music	Philosophy, psychology	Poetry, drama	Religion	Science	Sociology, economics	Sports, recreation	Technology	Travel
	206	207	208	209	210	211	212	213	214	215	216	217
1991	967	1,903	2,710	275	1,611	821	2,059	2,427	5,508	893	2,089	425
1990	896	2,049	3,014	289	1,683	874	2,285	2,742	7,042	973	2,092	495
1989	1,096	2,298	3,447	375	2,058	1,128	2,586	3,288	7,971	1,077	2,690	701
1988	1,343	2,272	3,900	329	1,955	1,270	2,746	3,743	8,247	1,099	2,694	669
1987	1,544	2,358	3,995	352	1,845	1,236	2,850	3,658	8,115	1,263	2,756	629
1986	1,385	2,145	3,445	356	1,689	1,278	2,788	3,360	7,912	1,192	2,698	543
1985	1,349	1,964	3,579	364	1,559	1,166	2,564	3,304	7,441	1,154	2,526	465
1984	1,406	2,006	3,554	387	1,554	1,164	2,482	3,236	7,794	1,299	2,639	551
1983	1,756	1,957	4,002	417	1,578	1,234	2,433	3,620	8,470	1,335	2,994	562
1982	1,451	1,742	3,229	346	1,465	1,049	2,075	3,124	7,449	1,191	2,328	482
1981	1,448	1,777	3,788	398	1,465	1,183	2,278	3,375	7,801	1,264	2,313	472
1980	1,102	1,686	3,292	357	1,429	1,179	2,055	3,109	7,152	971	2,337	504
1979	1,218	1,749	3,257	389	1,377	1,361	2,325	3,156	7,715	1,122	2,391	634
1978	1,065	1,800	2,788	439	1,367	1,297	2,180	2,877	6,465	1,160	1,896	414
1977	948	1,866	2,833	373	1,372	1,437	2,121	3,015	6,814	1,119	2,218	480
1976	698	1,405	2,128	302	1,192	1,307	1,748	2,342	5,960	1,034	1,489	499
1975	915	1,904	2,282	305	1,374	1,501	1,778	2,942	6,590	1,225	1,720	794
1974	1,031	2,285	2,281	273	1,368	1,626	1,851	3,049	6,640	1,132	1,593	1,612
1973	756	2,307	2,002	336	1,406	1,917	1,826	2,714	6,565	1,082	1,347	1,587
1972	716	2,525	1,839	402	1,164	1,484	1,705	2,586	6,415	941	1,425	1,491
1971	661	2,986	1,655	402	1,354	1,494	1,567	2,697	6,095	890	1,309	1,609
1970	355	1,349	1,144	217	843	973	1,315	1,955	3,867	583	930	848
1969	363	1,348	928	227	678	944	1,278	1,999	3,216	585	884	802
1968	432	1,301	1,022	210	669	791	1,511	2,011	3,107	501	1,072	885
1967	392	1,172	935	165	633	739	1,502	1,835	2,761	391	1,051	769
1966	316	1,185	1,007	207	629	728	1,477	2,079	2,632	441	1,091	732
1965	291	1,166	871	183	582	775	1,428	1,850	2,372	474	942	635
1964	256	1,038	876	156	528	681	1,441	1,923	2,445	452	939	747
1963	269	861	752	139	505	578	1,459	1,648	1,932	427	960	595
1962	219	771	688	137	436	505	1,174	1,309	1,603	367	780	532
1961	203	617	595	114	433	517	1,098	1,193	1,289	381	665	455
1960	303	560	388	82	496	404	983	833	651	233	[4] 574	372
1959	245	630	445	93	505	395	984	814	566	204	585	298
1958	245	495	393	89	467	373	941	781	494	201	443	271
1957	252	477	359	73	480	378	883	697	416	195	316	291
1956	221	570	334	88	425	337	810	531	448	160	404	294
1955	240	529	407	85	362	423	747	623	443	175	355	290
1954	226	493	345	69	386	389	774	522	463	201	325	230
1953	196	485	328	58	425	412	725	522	467	194	294	280
1952	236	518	350	71	427	424	715	513	478	168	311	264
1951	223	445	336	80	393	400	636	521	430	151	287	230
1950	228	510	312	88	380	453	626	499	447	153	366	221

NA Not available.

[1] 1880-1919 includes pamphlets; 1920-1928, pamphlets included in total only; thereafter, pamphlets excluded entirely.

[2] Beginning 1967, counting methods were revised; prior years not strictly comparable with subsequent years.

[3] Beginning 1959, data not strictly comparable with previous years because of change in definition of "book."

[4] Prior to 1961, includes military.

[5] Agrees with source; however, figures for components do not add to total shown.

Series R 224-231. Newspapers—Number and Circulation of Daily and Sunday Newspapers: 1920 to 1990

(Circulation in thousands. Figures as of October 1 of each year)

Year	Total		Daily newspapers				Sunday newspapers	
			Morning		Evening			
	Number	Circulation	Number	Circulation	Number	Circulation	Number	Circulation
	224	225	226	227	228	229	230	231
1990	1,611	62,300	559	41,300	1,084	21,000	863	62,600
1989	1,626	62,600	530	40,700	1,125	21,800	847	62,000
1988	1,642	62,700	529	40,400	1,141	22,200	840	61,500
1987	1,645	62,800	511	39,100	1,166	23,700	820	60,100
1986	1,657	62,500	499	37,400	1,188	25,100	802	58,900
1985	1,676	62,800	482	36,400	1,220	26,400	798	58,800
1984	1,688	63,100	458	35,400	1,257	27,700	783	57,500
1983	1,701	62,600	446	33,800	1,284	28,800	772	56,700
1982	1,711	62,500	434	33,200	1,310	29,300	768	56,300
1981	1,731	61,400	408	30,600	1,352	30,900	755	55,200
1980	1,745	62,200	387	29,400	1,388	32,800	736	54,700
1979	1,763	62,200	382	28,600	1,405	33,600	720	54,400
1978	1,756	62,000	355	27,700	1,419	34,300	696	54,000
1977	1,753	61,495	347	26,742	1,424	34,753	668	52,429
1976	1,762	60,977	346	25,858	1,435	35,119	650	51,565
1975	1,756	60,700	339	25,500	1,436	35,200	639	51,100
1974	1,768	61,877	340	26,145	1,449	35,732	641	51,679
1973	1,774	63,147	343	26,524	1,451	36,623	634	51,717
1972	1,761	62,510	337	26,078	1,441	36,432	603	49,339
1971	1,749	62,231	339	26,116	1,425	36,115	590	49,665
1970	[1] 1,748	62,108	334	25,934	1,429	36,174	586	49,217
1969	[1] 1,758	62,060	333	25,812	1,443	36,248	585	49,675
1968	[1] 1,752	62,535	328	25,838	1,443	36,697	578	49,693
1967	[1] 1,749	62,561	327	25,282	1,438	36,279	573	49,224
1966	[1] 1,754	61,397	324	24,806	1,444	36,592	578	49,282
1965	[1] 1,751	60,358	320	24,107	1,444	36,251	562	48,600
1964	[1] 1,763	60,412	323	24,365	1,452	36,048	561	48,383
1963	[1] 1,754	58,905	311	23,459	1,453	35,446	550	46,830
1962	[1] 1,760	59,849	318	24,563	1,451	35,286	558	48,888
1961	[1] 1,761	59,261	312	24,094	1,458	35,167	558	48,216
1960	[1] 1,763	58,882	312	24,029	1,459	34,853	563	47,699
1959	[1] 1,755	58,300	306	23,547	1,455	34,753	564	47,848
1958	[1] 1,751	57,418	307	23,161	1,456	34,258	556	46,955
1957	[1] 1,755	57,805	309	23,171	1,453	34,635	544	47,044
1956	[1] 1,761	57,102	314	22,492	1,454	34,610	546	47,162
1955	[1] 1,760	56,147	316	22,183	1,454	33,964	541	46,448
1954	[1] 1,765	55,072	317	21,705	1,448	33,367	544	46,176
1953	1,785	54,472	327	21,412	1,458	33,060	544	45,949
1952	1,786	53,951	327	21,160	1,459	32,791	545	46,210
1951	1,773	54,018	319	21,223	1,454	32,795	543	46,279
1950	1,772	53,829	322	21,266	1,450	32,563	549	46,582
1949	1,780	52,846	329	21,005	1,451	31,841	546	46,399
1948	1,781	52,285	328	21,082	1,453	31,203	530	46,308
1947	1,769	51,673	328	20,762	1,441	30,911	511	45,151
1946	1,763	50,928	334	20,546	1,429	30,382	497	43,665
1945	1,749	48,384	330	19,240	1,419	29,144	485	39,680
1944	1,744	45,955	338	18,059	1,406	27,896	481	37,946
1943	1,754	44,393	333	17,078	1,421	27,315	467	37,292
1942	1,787	43,375	345	17,111	1,442	26,264	474	35,294
1941	1,857	42,080	377	16,519	1,480	25,561	510	33,436
1940	1,878	41,132	380	16,114	1,498	25,018	525	32,371
1939	1,888	39,671	383	—	1,505	—	524	31,519
1938	1,936	39,572	398	—	1,538	—	523	30,481

See footnote at end of table.

Series R 224-231. Newspapers—Number and Circulation of Daily and Sunday Newspapers: 1920 to 1990—Cont'd.

(Circulation in thousands. Figures as of October 1 of each year)

Year	Total		Daily newspapers		Sunday newspapers	
	Number	Circulation	Number of morning	Number of evening	Number	Circulation
	224	225	226	228	230	231
1937	1,983	41,419	406	1,577	539	30,957
1936	1,989	40,292	405	1,584	520	29,962
1935	1,950	38,156	390	1,560	518	28,147
1934	1,929	36,709	385	1,544	505	26,545
1933	1,911	35,175	378	1,533	506	24,041
1932	1,913	36,408	380	1,533	518	24,860
1931	1,923	38,761	384	1,539	513	25,702
1930	1,942	39,589	388	1,554	521	26,413
1929	1,944	39,426	381	1,563	528	26,880
1928	1,939	37,973	397	1,542	522	25,772
1927	1,949	37,967	411	1,538	526	25,469
1926	2,001	36,002	425	1,576	545	24,435
1925	2,008	33,739	427	1,581	548	23,355
1924	2,014	32,999	429	1,585	539	22,220
1923	2,036	31,454	426	1,610	547	21,463
1922	2,033	29,780	426	1,607	546	19,713
1921	2,028	28,424	427	1,601	545	19,041
1920	2,042	27,791	437	1,605	522	17,084

[1] Total is adjusted to account for "all-day" papers listed in both morning and evening figures. Circulations are divided between morning and evening totals.

Series R 232-243.   Newspapers and Periodicals: 1935 to 1992
(Data refer to year of compilation of the Directory, i.e., generally to year preceding year shown)

| Year | Newspapers | | | | Periodicals | | | | | |
	Total	Semi-weekly	Weekly	Daily	Total	Weekly	Semi-monthly	Monthly	Bi-monthly	Quarterly
	232	233	234	235	237	238	239	240	241	242
1992	11,339	562	8,293	1,755	11,143	466	371	4,326	2,143	3,024
1991	11,689	574	8,546	1,781	11,239	511	412	4,340	2,116	2,861
1990	11,471	579	8,420	1,788	11,092	553	435	4,239	2,087	2,758
1989	10,457	567	7,622	1,773	11,556	828	622	4,445	1,880	2,513
1988	10,088	555	7,438	1,745	11,229	880	619	4,192	1,558	2,245
1987	9,031	510	6,750	1,646	11,593	1,400	858	4,031	1,402	1,984
1986	9,144	495	6,857	1,651	11,328	1,383	789	4,066	1,387	1,895
1985	9,134	517	6,811	1,701	11,090	1,367	801	4,088	1,361	1,759
1984	9,151	525	6,798	1,711	10,809	1,376	658	4,096	1,348	1,711
1983	9,205	508	6,855	1,735	10,952	1,626	724	4,108	1,307	1,627
1982	9,183	498	6,806	1,740	10,688	1,672	689	4,078	1,237	1,554
1981	9,676	508	7,238	1,747	10,873	1,921	667	4,199	1,193	1,484
1980	9,620	537	7,159	1,744	10,236	1,716	645	3,985	1,114	1,444
1979	9,827	543	7,357	1,744	9,719	1,764	594	3,850	1,045	1,261
1978	10,538	569	7,980	1,783	9,582	1,827	541	3,846	1,031	1,172
1977	11,089	550	8,506	1,811	9,732	1,882	548	4,019	1,043	1,149
1976	11,298	511	8,735	1,813	9,872	1,915	557	4,144	1,058	1,161
1975	11,400	506	8,824	1,819	9,657	1,918	537	4,087	1,009	1,093
1974	11,296	523	8,711	1,806	9,755	2,027	529	4,123	942	1,164
1973	11,324	459	8,804	1,792	9,630	2,022	506	4,107	925	1,148
1972	11,299	398	8,682	1,809	9,062	1,606	493	4,093	852	1,106
1971	11,350	412	8,888	1,818	9,657	1,873	544	4,277	1,005	1,124
1970	11,383	423	8,903	1,838	9,573	1,856	589	4,314	957	1,108
1969	11,336	413	8,855	1,833	9,434	1,787	587	4,353	899	1,084
1968	11,293	387	8,858	1,833	9,400	1,796	606	4,331	899	1,078
1967	11,307	366	8,915	2,026	9,238	1,808	573	¹ 4,296	859	1,051
1966	12,365	382	9,785	1,972	10,002	1,884	335	4,796	912	1,119
1965	11,383	357	8,989	1,843	8,990	1,716	550	¹ 4,195	876	1,030
1964	12,332	390	9,761	1,963	9,798	1,724	334	4,847	910	1,065
1963	12,295	391	9,739	1,974	9,643	1,792	313	4,744	858	1,025
1962	12,293	376	9,774	1,970	9,483	1,740	305	4,705	826	1,030
1961	12,285	361	9,783	1,968	9,275	1,656	301	4,634	801	998
1960 *	11,315	324	8,979	1,854	8,422	1,580	527	¹ 4,113	743	895
1959	12,294	359	9,812	1,977	9,004	1,592	302	4,577	712	950
1958	12,207	332	9,768	1,969	8,927	1,705	292	4,490	676	914
1957	12,299	354	9,854	1,946	8,722	1,681	288	4,457	639	842
1956	12,256	338	9,813	1,963	8,718	1,748	283	4,450	614	831
1955	11,415	324	9,126	1,860	7,648	1,602	503	¹ 3,782	608	674
1954	12,398	328	9,960	1,999	8,092	1,584	260	4,218	604	695
1953	12,645	346	10,173	2,009	7,792	1,494	242	4,115	598	673
1952	12,833	341	10,381	1,998	7,711	1,485	246	4,118	558	665
1951	13,009	362	10,514	2,018	7,635	1,491	239	4,132	517	633
1950	12,115	337	9,794	1,894	6,960	1,443	416	¹ 3,694	436	604
1949	12,814	326	10,386	2,014	7,570	1,537	244	4,073	458	635
1948	12,900	301	10,511	2,001	7,346	1,498	262	3,970	412	576
1947	12,877	284	10,523	2,003	7,083	1,394	272	3,805	401	609
1946	12,804	286	10,424	2,020	6,693	1,331	253	3,595	345	595
1945	12,791	283	10,430	2,004	6,569	1,359	246	3,503	309	578
1944	12,889	308	10,504	2,006	6,672	1,456	226	3,500	285	588
1943	13,456	356	10,967	2,043	7,040	1,489	215	3,826	274	596
1942	14,100	408	11,474	2,131	7,374	1,609	248	3,983	288	601
1941	14,284	397	11,617	2,153	7,141	1,449	222	3,966	277	595
1940	13,314	368	10,860	2,086	6,432	1,399	427	¹ 3,466	241	538
1939	14,213	380	11,516	2,216	6,846	1,408	213	3,821	250	563
1938	14,112	383	11,421	2,242	6,412	1,220	202	3,663	219	530
1937	14,336	401	11,592	2,272	6,320	1,251	253	3,512	203	530
1936	13,928	368	11,288	2,189	6,670	1,546	216	3,622	197	497
1935	14,091	369	11,438	2,197	6,546	1,484	203	3,608	196	493

* Denotes first year for which figures include Alaska and Hawaii.   ¹ Includes fortnightly.

SECTION S

ENERGY

Highlights

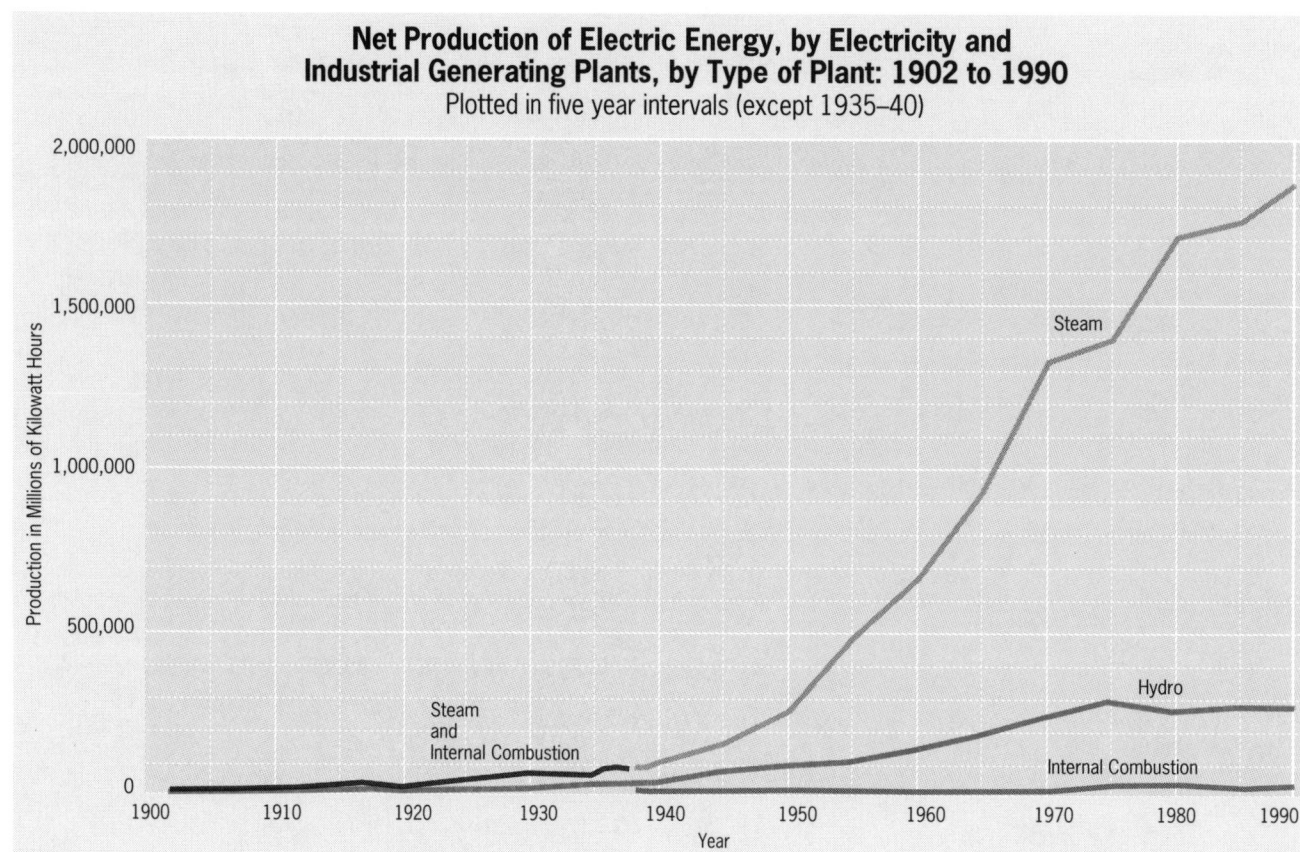

Net Production of Electric Energy, by Electricity and Industrial Generating Plants, by Type of Plant: 1902 to 1990
Plotted in five year intervals (except 1935–40)

1 Data on the production of electric energy have been available since the beginning of the first commercial production in 1882, but because of changing bases of measurement and variations in coverage, the information is difficult to evaluate for the years before 1920. The Bureau of the Census conducted censuses of the light and power industries at five-year intervals from 1902 to 1937. The *Electrical World* (McGraw-Hill) and the National Electric Light Association also published considerable data on this early period. Early data on capacity have to be converted from horsepower (hp) to kilowatts (kW) to be comparable. Data on generation also were often reported without allowance for kWhs used in generation, and end uses were reported by appliances (such as lamps) rather than as kWh. These variations in measurements, classification, and coverage often resulted in differences as high

as 25%. Generators in mobile equipment, such as ships, railroads, and barges, are also unaccounted for in the totals.

2 The principal sources of data on energy are the Energy Information Administration, the Edison Electric Institute, and the American Gas Association. Among the EIA annuals are *Annual Energy Review, Electric Power Annual, Natural Gas Annual, Petroleum Supply Annual, State Energy Data Report, State Energy Price and Expenditure Report, Financial Statistics of Selected Electric Utilities, Performance Profiles of Major Energy Producers, Annual Energy Outlook,* and *International Energy Annual.* The Edison Electric Institute produces the *Statistical Yearbook of Electric Utility Industry* and the *Year End Summary of the Electric Power Situation in the*

United States while the American Gas Association publishes *Gas Facts*.

3 Energy data were presented formerly in widely varying units, but increasingly are being converted to a common thermal unit, the BTU (British Thermal Unit). A BTU is the amount of energy required to raise the temperature of 1 pound of water 1 degree Fahrenheit at or near 39.2 degrees F. The conversion factors are as follows:

	Production	Consumption
Petroleum (barrel)	5,800 mil. BTU	5,449 mil. BTU
Coal (short ton)	211.827 mil. BTU	21.344 mil. BTU
Natural Gas (cu. ft.)	1,031	1,031
Nuclear Power (kWh)	10,724	10,724
Geothermal Power (kWh)	21,096	21,096

4 In 1990, the share of petroleum in total energy production and consumption reached its lowest point since 1960. Petroleum accounted for 22.9% of production and 41.3% of consumption, down from 36% and 45.5% respectively in 1970. During the same period, the share of natural gas also shrank from 34% to 29.9% of production and from 28.3% to 23.8% of consumption. The share of coal grew from 26.1% to 33.5% of production and from 22.5% to 23.4% of consumption. The total production and consumption of nuclear energy have shown slower growth curves, reaching 6.2 quadrillion BTUs in 1990. Other alternative forms of energy, once touted as the wave of the future, have not made much impact on the energy picture. Per capita, Americans produced 272 million BTUs and consumed 327 million BTUs. The energy consumption per dollar of GNP was 19,600 BTUs compared to 27,500 BTUs in 1970. In 1989, energy expenditure per capita was $1,759. Per capita expenditure was highest in Alaska at $3,362 and lowest in New York at $1,404.

5 By end-use sectors (the ultimate consumers of a finished product), the shares of primary energy consumption by residential and commercial users and industrial users were lower in 1990 than in 1960, while the shares of transportation and electricity generation were considerably higher. The share of residential and commercial users fell from 20% to 12.2% and that of industrial users from 37.1% to 24.4%. The share of transportation grew from 24.1% to 27% and that of electricity generation from 18.7% to 36.3%. Much of electricity generation has shifted from oil to coal.

6 In 1990, the average single-family detached home consumed 115 million BTUs at an annual cost of $1,226. Both the consumption and the cost rise in proportion to the age of the house. Houses built before 1939 consume 120 million BTUs, while those built after 1980 consume only 71 million BTUs.

7 Electricity was the most expensive form of residential energy in 1990, costing $20.70 per million BTUs, compared to $5.05 for natural gas and $6.10 for fuel or kerosene. Among fossil fuels, bituminous coal was the cheapest at $1.08 per million BTUs, compared to crude oil which was $3.45 per million BTUs. Natural gas at $1.55 per million BTUs was cheaper than anthracite coal, which cost $1.84 per million BTUs.

8 The U.S. share of world energy consumption, a profligate 37.1% in 1960, dropped to a more tolerable level of 24.5% in 1988. The European share also dropped during the same period from 26.5% to 21.9%. The two regions that now consume more than they did in 1960 are Asia and Russia/Commonwealth of Independent States (CIS). The share of Asia has risen from 13.1% to 22.6% and that of Russia/CIS from 15.2% to 19.5%.

9 The United States has had a negative trade balance in both natural gas and crude oil since 1970. The deficit in 1990 was 1,410 trillion BTUs in natural gas and 12,429 trillion BTUs in crude oil. Between 1970 and 1990, the deficit grew 182% in natural gas and 446% in crude oil.

10 Crude oil imports into the United States in 1990 were 2.151 billion barrels, each barrel being 42 gallons. The major suppliers were (in million barrels) Canada (235), Mexico (251), Nigeria (286), Saudi Arabia (436), and Venezuela (243). Domestic production of crude oil declined 9.2 million barrels per day in 1973 to 7.4 million barrels per day in 1991.

11 The Strategic Petroleum Reserve grew from 7.6 million barrels in 1977 to 585.69 million barrels in 1990, equivalent to 83 days of crude oil imports.

12 The 42 largest petroleum companies had a net income in 1990 of $26.8 billion. They claimed $40.5 billion as depreciation, and paid out $16.5 billion as dividends.

13 Total electric utility sales (covering Class A and B companies) in 1990 was 2,705 billion kWh of which 922 billion kWh were sold to residential customers, 753 billion kWh to commercial customers, and 938 billion kWh to industrial customers. The average price per kWh rose from 1.7 cents in 1970 to 6.6 cents in 1990. Investor owned private companies produced 78.5% of the total output.

14 By source of energy, coal accounted for 55.9% of net electricity generation, hydro power for 10%, and nuclear energy for 20.6% in 1990. Of the 10,296 generating units, 3,479 were hydro, 2,354 were steam conventional, 1,460 were gas turbine, 2,847 were internal combustion, and 111 were nuclear. Of the 111 nuclear plants, 28 were in the Northeast, 31 in the Midwest, 42 in the South, and 10 in the West. Illinois, with 13 nuclear plants, had the largest nuclear production among all states. In 1990, the United States accounted for a little less than one-third of the 362 nuclear plants worldwide. In

1990, the United States produced 8.9 million pounds of uranium concentrate and imported 23.7 million pounds.

15 Solar collectors have yet to realize their potential as cheap energy producers. The number of solar collector manufacturers dropped from a high of 349 in 1979 to 44 in 1989. Total shipments fell from 20,133,000 sq. ft. in 1981 to 11,482,000 sq. ft. in 1989. Commercial and industrial sales have tapered off faster than residential sales.

16 Wood energy consumption has remained fairly steady since 1980, rising only slightly from 2,483 trillion BTUs in 1980 to 2,487 trillion BTUs in 1989. Its share of total energy consumption, however, dropped from 3.3% to 3.1%. The South accounts for over one-half of all wood energy consumption. Five million households burn wood as the main heating fuel, for a total of 23.5 million cords.

17 In 1990, 54.293 million customers used 9,840 trillion BTUs of natural gas. The gas industry had total revenues of $45.174 billion, of which $25.014 billion came from residential customers.

Series S 1-14.   Total Horsepower of All Prime Movers: 1849 to 1990

(In thousands)

								Nonautomotive Inanimate		
Year	Total	Automotive[1]	Total	Factories[2]	Mines	Railroad[3]	Merchant ship powered	Farms[4]	Electric generating Plants	Aircraft
	1	**2**	**3**	**6**	**7**	**8**	**9**	**11**	**13**	**14**
1990	34,919,000	33,062,000	1,857,000	66,000	47,000	50,000	28,000	356,000	1,043,000	267,000
1989	34,579,000	32,790,000	1,789,000	65,000	47,000	50,000	28,000	356,000	976,000	267,000
1988	34,200,000	32,415,000	1,785,000	65,000	47,000	53,000	28,000	356,000	969,000	267,000
1987	33,266,000	31,488,000	1,778,000	65,000	47,000	53,000	29,000	357,000	958,000	269,000
1986	32,660,000	30,893,000	1,767,000	65,000	47,000	56,000	29,000	358,000	942,000	270,000
1985	32,529,000	30,792,000	1,737,000	65,000	47,000	58,000	29,000	358,000	912,000	268,000
1984	31,819,000	30,117,000	1,702,000	65,000	47,000	61,000	30,000	359,000	886,000	254,000
1983	31,337,000	29,662,000	1,675,000	64,000	47,000	62,000	29,000	356,000	877,000	240,000
1982	30,495,000	28,852,000	1,643,000	64,000	48,000	64,000	29,000	352,000	854,000	232,000
1981	29,507,000	27,909,000	1,598,000	64,000	48,000	65,000	29,000	345,000	835,000	212,000
1980	28,922,000	27,362,000	1,564,000	64,000	48,000	63,000	28,000	345,000	806,000	210,000
1979	28,162,000	26,617,000	1,545,000	63,000	48,000	62,000	26,000	342,000	803,000	201,000
1978	27,379,000	25,892,000	1,487,000	63,000	48,000	64,000	25,000	335,000	754,000	198,000
1977	26,469,000	25,025,000	1,444,000	62,000	47,000	62,000	23,000	328,000	728,000	194,000
1976	25,507,000	24,339,000	1,393,000	61,000	47,000	64,000	22,000	324,000	692,000	184,000
1975	25,100,000	23,752,000	1,348,000	60,000	47,000	62,000	22,000	318,000	654,000	185,000
1974	24,516,000	23,224,000	1,292,000	59,000	46,000	61,000	21,000	315,000	605,000	185,000
1973	24,262,000	23,029,000	1,233,000	58,000	46,000	57,000	20,000	308,000	562,000	182,000
1972	22,913,000	21,736,000	1,175,000	57,000	46,000	57,000	21,000	305,000	508,000	181,000
1971	21,862,000	20,732,000	1,130,000	56,000	45,000	56,000	21,000	300,000	473,000	179,000
1970	20,408,000	19,325,000	1,083,000	54,000	45,000	54,000	22,000	[6]288,500	435,000	183,000
1969	19,115,000	18,075,000	1,040,250	53,000	44,000	53,000	19,000	[6]302,000	404,000	165,000
1968	17,912,144	16,937,725	974,419	52,000	43,400	57,607	20,413	290,600	371,756	137,158
1967	17,050,693	16,152,371	898,322	51,000	42,500	49,067	21,493	273,606	342,918	116,093
1966	15,959,175	15,101,836	857,339	49,700	41,200	47,098	22,622	274,227	323,800	96,864
1965	15,096,332	14,306,300	790,023	48,400	40,300	43,838	24,015	269,822	307,025	54,600
1964	14,272,244	13,512,653	759,591	47,000	39,327	46,548	23,175	258,451	287,111	55,154
1963	13,413,072	12,713,712	699,360	45,770	37,000	46,390	23,890	217,928	273,085	52,758
1962	12,586,417	11,930,000	656,417	44,600	[2]36,300	46,694	22,867	204,740	249,059	49,516
1961	11,611,311	10,972,210	639,101	43,250	[2]35,400	47,453	23.046	205,463	235,746	46,000
1960	11,007,889	10,366,880	641,009	42,000	34,700	46,856	23,890	237,020	217,173	36,534
1955	7,158,229	6,632,121	526,108	35,579	[7]30,768	60,304	[8]24,155	[7]207,742	137,576	[8]25,779
1952	5,736,886	5,361,386	375,500	35,045	9,523	101,690	23,207	73,590	103,453	22,941
1950	4,754,038	4,403,617	350,421	32,921	8,500	110,969	[8]23,423	57,533	87,965	[8]22,000
1940	2,773,316	2,511,312	262,004	21,768	7,332	92,361	[8]9,408	57,472	53,542	7,455
1939	—	2,400,000	—	21,239	7,149	90,500	10,000	40,750	52,115	6,000
1930	1,663,944	1,426,568	237,376	19,519	5,620	109,743	9,115	28,610	43,427	3,382
1929	—	1,424,980	—	19,328	5,450	111,881	9,017	27,261	40,014	3,091
1920	453,450	280,900	172,550	19,422	5,146	80,182	6,508	21,443	17,050	—
1919	—	230,432	—	19,432	5,112	76,660	6,229	20,796	15,250	—
1910	138,810	24,686	114,124	16,697	4,473	51,308	3,098	10,460	6,228	—
1909	—	7,714	—	16,393	4,401	48,491	2,750	9,311	5,225	—
1900	63,952	100	63,852	10,309	2,919	24,501	1,663	4,009	1,350	—
1899	—	32	—	9,633	2,754	21,835	1,542	3,420	1,200	—
1890	44,086	—	44,086	6,308	1,445	16,980	1,124	1,452	447	—
1889	—	—	—	5,939	1,300	16,440	1,078	1,233	120	—
1880	26,314	—	26,314	3,664	715	8,592	741	668	—	—
1879	—	—	—	3,411	650	7,720	703	605	—	—
1870	16,931	—	16,931	2,453	380	4,462	632	—	—	—
1869	—	—	—	2,346	350	4,100	624	—	—	—
1860	13,763	—	13,463	1,675	170	2,156	515	—	—	—
1859	—	—	—	1,600	150	1,940	503	—	—	—
1850	8,495	—	8,495	1,150	60	586	325	—	—	—
1849	—	—	—	1,100	50	435	305	—	—	—

* Denotes first year for which figures include Alaska and Hawaii.
[1] Includes passenger cars, trucks, buses and motocycles.
[2] Excludes electric motos.
[3] Beginning 1965, not strictly comparable with earlier years.
[4] Excludes horses and other work animals.
[5] includes private planes and commercial airlines.
[6] Includes windmills.
[7] Beginning 1955, not strictly comparable with earlier years.
[8] Includes Alaska and Hawaii.

Series S 32-43. Net Production of Electric Energy, by Electric Utility and Industrial Generating Plants, by Type of Plant: 1902 to 1990

(In millions of kilowatt hours)

| Year | Total utility and industrial | | | | Year | Total utility and industrial | | | |
	Total	Hydro	Steam	Internal combustion		Total	Hydro	Steam	Internal combustion
	32	33	34	35		32	33	34	35
1990	2,805,000	280,000	1,916,000	22,000	1952	463,055	109,708	344,695	8,652
1989	2,784,000	265,000	1,950,000	29,000	1951	433,358	104,376	321,705	7,277
1988	2,704,000	223,000	1,921,000	22,000					
1987	2,572,000	250,000	1,837,000	18,000	1950	388,674	100,884	281,000	6,790
1986	2,487,000	291,000	1,756,000	15,000	1949	345,066	94,773	244,429	5,864
					1948	336,808	86,992	243,730	6,086
1985	2,470,000	281,000	1,778,000	16,000	1947	307,400	83,066	218,985	5,349
1984	2,416,000	321,000	1,742,000	17,000	1946	269,609	83,150	181,825	4,634
1983	2,310,000	332,000	1,668,000	14,000					
1982	2,241,000	309,000	1,633,000	14,000	1945	271,255	84,747	181,708	4,800
1981	2,295,000	261,000	1,736,000	22,000	1944	279,252	78,905	195,664	4,956
					1943	267,540	79,077	183,952	4,511
1980	2,286,000	276,000	1,726,000	24,000	1942	233,146	69,133	159,725	4,288
1979	2,247,000	280,000	1,680,000	28,000	1941	208,306	55,357	149,157	3,792
1978	2,206,000	280,000	1,613,000	31,000					
1977	2,124,000	220,000	1,619,000	29,000	1940	179,907	51,659	124,941	3,307
1976	2,038,000	284,000	1,534,000	24,000	1939	161,308	47,691	110,635	2,982
					1938	141,955	48,394	93,561	
1975	1,918,000	300,000	1,417,000	22,000	1937	146,476	48,272	98,204	
1974	1,867,000	301,000	1,414,000	32,000	1936	136,006	42,750	93,256	
1973	1,860,000	272,000	1,552,000	30,000					
1972	1,752,000	275,000	1,441,000	29,000	1935	118,935	42,253	76,682	
1971	1,614,000	266,000	1,319,000	22,000	1934	110,404	35,922	74,482	
					1933	102,655	36,730	65,925	
1970	1,639,771	250,699	1,345,252	13,820	1932	99,359	35,998	63,361	
1969	1,552,757	253,468	1,285,448	13,841	1931	109,373	32,106	77,267	
1968	1,436,029	225,874	1,196,587	13,568					
1967	1,317,301	224,978	1,079,508	12,844	1930	114,637	34,874	79,763	
1966	1,249,444	197,938	1,038,645	12,861	1929	116,747	37,038	79,709	
					1928	108,069	37,297	70,772	
1965	1,157,583	196,984	947,890	12,709	1927	101,390	32,924	68,466	
1964	1,083,741	180,301	890,887	12,553	1926	94,222	30,355	63,867	
1963	1,011,417	168,990	830,285	12,142					
1962	946,526	172,086	763,313	11,127	1925	84,666	26,112	58,554	
1961	881,495	155,630	716,161	9,705	1924	75,892	24,138	51,754	
					1923	71,399	23,421	47,978	
1960	844,188	149,515	683,941	10,733	1922	61,204	21,262	39,942	
1959*	797,567	141,500	645,164	10,903	1921	53,125	18,732	34,393	
1958	724,752	143,614	571,037	10,101					
1957	716,356	133,358	571,405	11,593	1920	56,559	20,311	36,248	
1956	684,804	125,237	548,306	11,261	1917	43,429	13,948	29,481	
					1912	24,752	7,387	17,365	
1955	629,010	116,236	502,388	10,386	1907	14,121	4,003	10,118	
1954	544,645	111,640	423,151	9,854	1902	5,969	2,166	3,803	
1953	514,169	109,617	394,726	9,826					

* Denotes first year for which figures include Alaska and Hawaii.

Series S 95-107. Consumption of Fuels by Electric Utilities: 1920 to 1990

Year	Net generation, by fuel					Fuel consumed		
	Total[1]	Coal	Fuel oil	Gas	Nuclear	Coal	Oil	Gas
	95	96	97	98	99	101	102	103
	Millions of kilowatt hours	Millions of kilowatt hours	Millions of kilowatt hours	Millions of kilowatt hours	Millions of kilowatt hours	1,000 short tons	1,000 42-gallon barrels	Millions of cubic feet
1990	2,525,000	1,557,000	117,000	263,000	577,000	772,000	196,000	2,776,000
1989	2,519,000	1,554,000	158,000	267,000	529,000	767,000	267,000	2,787,000
1988	2,481,000	1,541,000	149,000	253,000	527,000	758,000	250,000	2,636,000
1987	2,322,000	1,464,000	118,000	273,000	455,000	718,000	201,000	2,844,000
1986	2,197,000	1,386,000	137,000	249,000	414,000	685,000	232,000	2,602,000
1985	2,189,000	1,402,000	100,000	292,000	384,000	694,000	175,000	3,044,000
1984	2,095,000	1,342,000	120,000	297,000	328,000	664,000	206,000	3,111,000
1983	1,978,000	1,259,000	144,000	274,000	294,000	625,000	247,000	2,911,000
1982	1,932,000	1,192,000	147,000	305,000	283,000	594,000	251,000	3,226,000
1981	2,034,000	1,203,000	206,000	346,000	273,000	597,000	352,000	3,640,000
1980	2,010,000	1,162,000	246,000	346,000	251,000	569,000	421,000	3,682,000
1979	1,968,000	1,076,000	303,000	329,000	255,000	527,000	523,000	3,491,000
1978	1,926,000	977,000	364,000	305,000	276,000	482,000	636,000	3,188,000
1977	1,904,000	985,000	358,000	306,000	251,000	477,000	624,000	3,191,000
1976	1,754,000	945,000	320,000	295,000	191,000	448,000	556,000	3,081,000
1975	1,618,000	853,000	289,000	300,000	173,000	406,000	506,000	3,158,000
1974	1,566,000	830,000	299,000	320,000	114,000	392,000	536,000	3,429,000
1973	1,588,000	849,000	313,000	341,000	83,000	390,000	560,000	3,644,000
1972	1,478,000	773,000	273,000	376,000	54,000	352,000	494,000	3,977,000
1971	1,348,000	—	—	—	—	328,000	396,000	3,993,000
1970	1,284,153	706,102	182,488	372,884	21,797	320,818	335,514	3,931,966
1969	1,191,989	706,110	137,847	333,279	13,928	310,641	251,027	3,487,642
1968	1,106,952	684,905	104,276	304,433	12,528	297,779	188,642	3,147,909
1967	992,847	630,483	89,271	264,806	7,655	274,185	161,278	2,746,352
1966	949,594	613,475	78,926	251,151	5,520	266,477	140,949	2,609,949
1965	861,401	570,926	64,801	221,559	3,657	244,788	115,203	2,321,101
1964	806,917	526,230	56,954	220,038	3,343	225,425	101,141	2,322,896
1963*	751,038	493,927	52,001	201,602	3,212	211,332	93,314	2,144,473
1962	684,031	450,249	46,983	184,301	2,270	193,238	85,768	1,965,974
1961	640,189	421,871	47,120	169,286	1,692	182,121	85,736	1,825,117
1960	607,660	403,067	46,105	157,970	518	176,634	85,340	1,724,762
1959	572,071	378,424	46,840	146,619	188	168,423	88,263	1,628,509
1958	504,662	344,366	40,372	119,759	165	155,724	77,668	1,372,853
1957	501,108	346,386	40,500	114,212	10	160,769	79,693	1,336,141
1956	478,487	338,503	35,947	104,037	—	158,279	72,711	1,239,311
1955	433,786	301,363	37,138	95,285	—	143,759	75,274	1,153,280
1954	364,354	239,146	31,520	93,688	—	118,385	66,745	1,165,498
1953	337,042	218,846	38,404	79,791	—	115,897	82,238	1,034,272
1952	293,640	195,437	29,750	68,453	—	107,071	67,218	910,117
1951	270,531	185,204	28,712	56,616	—	105,768	63,945	763,898
1950	232,813	—	—	—	—	91,871	75,420	628,919
1949	200,965	—	—	—	—	83,963	66,301	550,121
1948	199,796	—	—	—	—	99,586	42,345	478,097
1947	176,983	—	—	—	—	89,531	45,309	373,054
1946	144,555	—	—	—	—	72,197	36,316	306,942

See footnotes at end of table.

Series S 95-107. Consumption of Fuels by Electric Utilities: 1920 to 1990—Cont'd.

| Year | Net generation, by fuel | | | | | Fuel consumed | | |
	Total[1]	Coal	Fuel oil	Gas	Nuclear	Coal	Oil	Gas
	95	96	97	98	99	101	102	103
	Millions of kilowatt hours	Millions of kilowatt hours	Millions of kilowatt hours	Millions of kilowatt hours	Millions of kilowatt hours	1,000 short tons	1,000 42-gallon barrels	Millions of cubic feet
1945	142,331	—	—	—	—	74,725	20,228	326,212
1944	153,868	—	—	—	—	80,084	20,862	358,784
1943	143,785	—	—	—	—	77,301	17,986	301,937
1942	121,585	—	—	—	—	66,257	15,236	235,208
1941	113,272	—	—	—	—	62,668	20,177	201,763
1940	93,963	—	—	—	—	51,474	16,325	180,096
1939	83,628	—	—	—	—	44,539	17,139	188,878
1938	69,255	—	—	—	—	38,394	12,942	165,504
1937	74,502	—	—	—	—	42,929	13,829	169,127
1936	69,823	—	—	—	—	40,085	14,079	154,084
1935	56,688	—	—	—	—	32,715	11,257	124,118
1934	54,418	—	—	—	—	34,414	10,258	127,071
1933	48,170	—	—	—	—	28,543	9,606	101,985
1932	46,422	—	—	—	—	28,056	7,583	107,103
1931	58,014	—	—	—	—	36,115	7,922	138,458
1930	59,583	—	—	—	—	40,278	8,805	119,553
1929	59,154	—	—	—	—	41,827	9,783	112,353
1928	49,622	—	—	—	—	38,042	6,818	77,155
1927	46,660	—	—	—	—	38,199	6,552	62,485
1926	43,472	—	—	—	—	36,842	8,999	52,647
1925	39,443	—	—	—	—	35,615	9,794	45,472
1924	34,963	—	—	—	—	32,790	16,060	47,301
1923	32,088	—	—	—	—	33,636	13,925	29,340
1922	26,561	—	—	—	—	29,193	12,443	24,996
1921	22,343	—	—	—	—	26,604	11,505	21,701
1920	23,495	—	—	—	—	31,640	12,690	22,136

* Denotes first year for which figures include Alaska and Hawaii.

[1] Excludes generations by wood and waste fuels. Beginning 1961, includes limited output by use of wood, waste and geothermal power, as follows, in million kw.-hr: 220 in 1961; 228 in 1962, 296 in 1963, 352 in 1964, 458 in 1965, 522 in 1966, 632 in 1967, 811 in 1968, 935 in 1969, and 882 in 1970.

Series S 160-175. Developed and Underdeveloped Water Power, by Geographic Division: 1920 to 1990
(In thousands of kilowatts. As of December 31)

| Year | Developed water power [1] | | | | | | | |
| | United States | New England | Middle Atlantic | North Central | South Atlantic | South Central | Mountain | Pacific |
	160	161	162	163	164	165	166	167
1990	73,000	1,900	4,900	4,200	6,700	8,600	9,200	37,500
1989	71,800	1,900	4,800	4,200	6,700	8,300	8,900	37,000
1988	71,300	1,900	4,800	4,200	6,600	8,300	8,500	37,100
1987	70,800	1,800	4,700	4,100	6,700	8,200	8,300	36,800
1986	69,600	1,700	4,600	4,100	6,700	8,200	8,200	36,100
1985	68,800	1,700	4,500	4,000	6,500	8,200	8,100	35,800
1984	67,700	1,600	4,300	3,900	6,100	8,000	8,100	35,700
1983	66,800	1,600	4,300	3,900	6,000	8,100	7,900	35,000
1982	65,900	1,500	4,300	4,000	5,900	7,900	7,700	34,600
1981	65,500	1,500	4,300	3,800	6,000	7,900	7,700	34,300
1980	64,400	1,500	4,300	3,700	5,900	7,900	7,400	33,700
1979	63,300	1,500	4,200	3,800	5,900	7,700	7,300	33,000
1978	61,000	1,500	4,200	3,800	5,800	7,600	7,300	30,800
1977	59,200	1,500	4,200	3,800	5,800	7,900	7,100	29,000
1976	58,600	1,500	4,200	3,700	5,800	7,800	7,100	28,500
1975	57,000	1,500	4,200	3,700	5,800	7,800	6,900	27,200
1974	55,400	1,500	4,200	3,700	5,700	7,700	6,700	26,000
1973	54,974	1,490	4,246	3,704	5,467	7,578	6,665	25,824
1972	53,778	1,510	4,252	3,660	5,470	7,386	6,235	25,265
1971	53,404	1,511	4,252	3,670	5,473	7,321	6,219	24,958
1970	51,952	1,473	4,264	3,664	5,265	7,170	6,202	23,914
1969	50,248	1,495	4,231	3,718	5,271	6,951	6,097	22,481
1968	48,741	1,487	4,243	3,665	5,255	6,874	6,095	21,122
1967	45,826	1,491	4,247	3,703	5,349	6,350	6,083	18,425
1966	44,288	1,487	4,246	3,625	5,184	6,298	6,022	17,426
1965	42,948	1,488	4,237	3,460	4,700	6,088	5,551	17,424
1964	41,827	1,491	4,237	3,302	4,635	5,851	5,218	17,093
1963	40,230	1,497	4,218	3,197	4,600	5,419	4,845	16,454
1962	37,835	1,508	4,239	2,942	4,099	5,164	4,773	15,110
1961	36,193	1,518	3,852	2,618	3,795	4,897	4,821	14,694
1960	33,180	1,520	2,472	2,522	3,773	4,695	4,621	13,578
1959	* 31,794	1,513	2,475	2,369	3,788	4,697	4,511	* 12,439
1958	30,089	1,521	2,113	2,376	3,732	4,697	4,157	11,592
1957	27,761	1,528	1,600	2,277	3,732	4,674	3,785	10,165
1956	26,386	1,388	1,479	2,243	3,611	4,524	3,701	9,440
1955	25,742	1,385	1,789	1,905	3,536	4,524	3,706	8,898
1954	24,238	1,335	1,750	1,783	3,423	4,418	3,629	7,901
1953	23,055	1,282	1,704	1,620	3,212	4,371	3,438	7,425
1952	21,416	1,262	1,707	1,564	2,834	4,054	3,181	6,814
1951	19,871	1,254	1,677	1,559	2,785	3,547	2,627	6,421
1950	18,675	1,239	1,678	1,530	2,767	3,195	2,286	5,980
1949	17,662	1,202	1,687	1,469	2,687	2,993	2,202	5,423
1948	16,635	1,192	1,668	1,437	2,662	2,731	2,056	4,888
1947	15,956	1,165	1,662	1,435	2,662	2,618	2,026	4,387
1946	15,828	1,167	1,669	1,434	2,663	2,618	2,008	4,269
1945	14,912	895	1,591	1,300	2,222	2,592	2,002	4,309
1944	14,586	894	1,593	1,303	2,086	2,393	2,003	4,314
1943	13,884	893	1,587	1,314	2,085	2,151	1,924	3,929
1942	12,842	891	1,596	1,294	2,084	1,936	1,784	3,256
1941	11,817	855	1,589	1,280	1,912	1,588	1,692	2,902

See footnotes at end of table.

Series S 160-175.   Developed and Underdeveloped Water Power, by Geographic Division: 1920 to 1990—Cont'd.
(In thousands of kilowatts. As of December 31)

				Developed water power [1]				
Year	United States	New England	Middle Atlantic	North Central	South Atlantic	South Central	Mountain	Pacific
	160	161	162	163	164	165	166	167
1940	11,224	858	1,588	1,219	1,882	1,397	1,612	2,668
1939	11,004	833	1,563	1,204	1,803	1,279	1,581	2,741
1938	10,657	824	1,561	1,204	1,728	1,223	1,381	2,736
1937	10,176	832	1,550	1,147	1,710	1,114	1,160	2,662
1936	10,037	832	1,533	1,111	1,709	1,079	1,152	2,622
1935	9,399	804	1,517	1,071	1,678	924	792	2,613
1934	9,345	767	1,489	1,071	1,680	924	782	2,631
1933	9,334	768	1,489	1,065	1,680	916	791	2,624
1932	9,258	768	1,457	1,058	1,634	954	788	2,599
1931	9,091	762	1,338	1,056	1,635	945	788	2,566
1930	8,585	753	1,290	881	1,603	882	784	2,391
1929	7,831	554	1,218	879	1,351	841	680	2,308
1928	7,702	557	1,205	862	1,346	840	679	2,213
1927	6,802	496	1,151	842	963	700	673	1,977
1926	6,405	474	1,115	835	945	618	592	1,826
1925	5,922	415	1,027	813	878	482	570	1,738
1924	5,024	381	905	741	760	280	544	1,413
1923	4,507	350	766	705	659	248	520	1,259
1922	4,128	337	757	664	534	195	509	1,132
1921	3,902	314	741	632	536	187	494	998
1920	3,704	291	662	629	589	174	487	872

See footnotes at end of table.

Series S 160-175.   Developed and Underdeveloped Water Power, by Geographic Division: 1920 to 1990—Cont'd.

(In thousands of kilowatts. As of December 31)

Year	United States	New England	Middle Atlantic	North Central	South Atlantic	South Central	Mountain	Pacific
	Undeveloped water power [1]							
	168	169	170	171	172	173	174	175
1990	73,900	4,400	5,100	4,800	7,000	7,000	19,400	26,200
1989	75,200	4,500	5,200	4,800	7,100	7,200	19,300	27,100
1988	75,800	4,500	5,800	4,800	7,200	7,300	19,400	26,900
1987	76,100	4,300	5,800	4,900	7,200	7,600	20,000	26,300
1986	74,400	4,300	5,200	4,800	7,300	8,100	19,200	26,100
1985	76,400	4,400	5,400	4,900	7,400	8,100	19,400	26,800
1984	76,400	4,500	5,400	4,900	8,100	8,100	18,200	27,200
1983	77,300	4,600	5,400	4,800	8,400	8,100	18,200	27,800
1982	79,100	4,500	5,400	4,800	8,500	8,200	18,500	29,200
1981	108,700	4,600	5,300	5,400	8,900	7,300	20,600	56,600
1980	129,900	4,700	5,100	5,400	9,600	8,000	34,200	62,900
1979	110,500	3,000	4,400	3,600	8,100	6,700	20,800	63,900
1978	109,900	2,800	4,600	3,900	8,500	6,300	17,800	66,000
1977	102,700	3,300	4,500	3,400	7,000	5,100	17,600	61,800
1976	109,900	3,200	4,100	3,500	7,100	5,500	19,000	67,500
1975	113,700	3,300	4,300	3,500	8,400	5,800	19,600	68,800
1974	118,500	3,200	4,300	7,400	9,300	6,000	21,800	66,400
1973	119,202	3,327	4,301	5,606	9,066	6,625	21,829	68,448
1972	126,078	3,315	4,301	5,647	8,965	6,841	25,518	71,491
1971	125,203	3,318	4,269	5,634	9,059	6,906	26,174	69,843
1970	127,990	3,330	4,455	5,966	9,556	7,089	26,655	70,939
1969	128,900	3,300	4,545	5,892	9,708	7,054	26,923	71,478
1968	129,709	3,302	4,545	5,892	9,716	7,063	26,923	72,268
1967	130,444	3,304	4,514	5,619	9,468	7,008	26,891	73,640
1966	130,640	3,312	4,332	5,312	9,812	7,031	26,822	74,019
1965	124,087	3,240	4,986	5,497	9,977	7,343	26,530	66,514
1964	117,793	3,125	4,950	5,691	10,017	7,549	27,253	59,208
1963*	115,734	3,128	5,179	5,866	9,903	8,023	26,652	56,983
1962	116,100	3,100	5,200	6,800	11,000	8,200	26,900	54,900
1961	112,700	2,800	5,700	9,000	8,900	8,100	24,100	54,100
1960	114,200	2,900	7,600	9,400	8,400	8,500	23,600	53,800
1959	* 114,287	2,858	7,465	9,591	8,388	8,499	23,243	* 54,243
1958	93,783	2,708	7,869	9,323	8,393	7,854	23,141	34,495
1957	90,242	2,728	8,382	8,967	7,645	7,480	21,245	33,795
1956	90,102	2,728	8,012	9,000	7,586	7,721	21,333	33,722
1955	86,895	2,589	8,023	9,335	7,943	7,213	20,668	31,127
1954	82,804	2,990	6,395	9,211	8,058	7,035	20,105	29,010
1953	85,562	3,122	6,449	9,412	8,281	7,464	21,618	29,216
1952	87,992	3,233	3,415	9,480	8,677	7,784	21,895	30,508
1951	86,174	3,239	3,598	8,117	8,255	8,168	22,089	29,708
1950	87,604	3,250	6,572	8,119	8,151	8,304	23,440	29,768
1949	88,070	3,249	6,503	8,192	8,184	8,374	23,426	30,142
1948	(NA)	(NA)	(NA)	(NA)	(NA)	(NA)	(NA)	(NA)
1947	77,130	3,348	5,175	7,309	7,462	7,446	17,755	28,635
1946	—	—	—	—	—	—	—	—

* Denotes first year for which figures include Alaska and Hawaii.
NA Not available.

[1] Nameplate capacity of existing installations only. Includes capacity at electric utility and industrial plants, but excludes pumped storage capacity. Prior to 1946, includes capacity at electric utility plants only.

Series S 190-204. Gas Utility Industry—Customers, Sales, and Revenues, by Type of Service: 1932 to 1990

Year	Customers[1] (1,000)				Sales[2] (mil. therms[3])				Revenues[2] (mil. dol.)			
	Total	Residential	Commercial	Industrial	Total	Residential	Commercial	Industrial	Total	Residential	Commercial	Industrial
	190	191	192	193	195	196	197	198	200	201	202	203
1990	54,293	49,830	4,249	214	98,460	44,710	21,940	30,110	45,174	25,014	10,610	8,997
1989	53,356	48,980	4,161	215	105,510	47,980	23,220	32,430	47,493	26,172	11,074	9,666
1988	52,422	48,133	4,060	220	107,050	46,950	23,060	35,440	46,162	24,828	10,681	10,113
1987	51,576	47,362	3,980	234	105,430	43,850	21,560	38,480	45,492	23,622	10,271	11,069
1986	50,704	46,583	3,892	229	111,250	43,810	22,390	43,380	51,201	24,759	11,274	14,495
1985	49,971	45,929	3,616	226	126,160	45,130	23,380	56,350	63,293	26,864	12,722	23,086
1984	49,325	45,367	3,730	228	131,620	46,280	23,960	59,910	67,496	27,485	13,205	26,094
1983	48,799	44,894	3,676	229	128,580	44,500	22,980	59,700	65,837	26,173	12,659	26,315
1982	48,415	44,552	3,631	232	141,830	47,700	24,710	67,950	63,200	23,700	11,666	27,200
1981	47,947	44,149	3,564	234	153,750	46,100	23,760	82,390	56,110	19,180	9,286	27,124
1980	47,223	43,489	3,498	236	154,130	48,260	24,530	79,570	48,303	17,432	8,183	22,215
1979	46,478	42,821	3,423	234	154,400	50,830	24,860	74,550	38,947	14,833	6,624	16,961
1978	45,789	42,183	3,370	236	147,480	51,070	25,000	68,410	32,150	12,939	5,696	13,065
1977	45,274	41,682	3,371	220	143,410	49,460	24,090	67,110	28,303	11,541	4,980	11,385
1976	44,942	41,338	3,371	233	148,140	50,140	24,230	71,070	23,701	9,941	4,075	9,374
1975	44,555	40,950	3,367	237	148,630	49,910	23,870	68,370	19,101	8,445	3,302	6,745
1974	44,267	40,628	3,392	249	160,000	48,650	22,930	81,530	15,242	6,899	2,539	5,391
1973	43,715	40,119	3,332	209	164,840	49,940	22,830	83,720	12,990	6,247	2,174	4,198
1972	42,955	39,431	3,261	209	170,820	51,440	22,790	87,770	12,465	6,096	2,064	3,943
1971	42,241	38,788	3,199	205	166,800	50,400	21,560	86,430	11,355	5,635	1,829	3,568
1970	41,482	38,097	3,131	199	160,435	49,237	20,066	84,392	10,283	5,207	1,620	3,181
1969	40,854	37,538	3,074	193	153,916	48,204	18,781	81,358	9,480	4,883	1,459	2,919
1968	39,930	36,691	3,004	188	144,724	45,527	17,049	75,951	8,781	4,567	1,315	2,675
1967	39,077	35,915	2,934	181	134,883	43,653	15,776	70,143	8,261	4,383	1,224	2,461
1966	38,228	35,142	2,868	174	128,591	41,754	14,628	66,533	7,870	4,195	1,135	2,335
1965	37,338	34,341	2,790	166	119,803	39,990	13,448	61,465	7,407	4,030	1,054	2,148
1964	36,463	33,551	2,712	159	115,912	38,697	12,735	59,120	7,133	3,895	998	2,049
1963	35,551	32,711	2,640	162	107,663	36,680	11,366	54,381	6,727	3,728	910	1,906
1962	34,683	31,893	2,598	156	102,348	35,369	10,929	51,001	6,445	3,603	874	1,796
1961	33,831	31,118	2,529	147	95,890	33,210	9,881	47,856	5,993	3,377	789	1,658
1960*	33,054	30,418	2,458	141	92,877	31,881	9,198	47,094	5,617	3,177	723	1,563
1959[4]	32,066	29,530	2,364	136	87,917	29,739	8,275	45,631	5,065	2,870	633	1,431
1958	31,242	28,786	2,287	134	80,285	28,125	7,649	40,764	4,568	2,658	571	1,229
1957	30,476	28,101	2,211	132	77,034	25,985	6,989	40,476	4,134	2,379	506	1,150
1956	29,536	27,241	2,141	125	72,541	24,643	6,558	38,687	3,850	2,237	471	1,066
1955	28,479	26,283	2,048	121	66,586	22,387	6,029	35,351	3,450	2,007	424	938
1954	27,528	25,398	1,990	112	61,026	20,031	5,405	33,096	3,049	1,783	378	821
1953	26,705	24,647	1,926	107	56,073	18,033	4,980	30,373	2,716	1,574	339	739
1952	25,850	23,852	1,869	104	52,392	17,348	4,929	27,990	2,466	1,457	321	639
1951	24,953	23,042	1,787	101	48,222	16,205	4,559	35,522	2,228	1,335	294	557
1950	24,001	22,146	1,739	100	42,090	13,839	4,104	22,887	1,948	1,177	266	480
1949	23,035	21,264	1,657	97	35,790	11,827	3,724	18,979	1,689	1,031	238	396
1948	22,245	20,562	1,571	94	33,885	11,153	3,535	17,981	1,579	958	221	377
1947	21,416	19,835	1,474	91	29,882	10,087	3,107	15,792	1,396	862	191	326
1946	20,636	19,157	1,377	87	26,379	8,482	2,630	14,602	1,213	754	161	284
1945	19,977	18,607	1,278	80	25,868	7,749	2,497	14,523	1,153	705	149	281
1944	19,585	18,320	1,177	82	25,120	7,313	2,208	14,635	1,108	667	133	293
1943	19,064	17,838	1,141	77	23,415	7,001	2,083	13,582	1,064	648	128	277
1942	18,734	17,511	1,137	78	20,849	6,679	1,990	11,723	994	623	127	238
1941	18,126	16,904	1,137	78	19,009	5,862	1,650	11,206	914	575	114	220

See footnotes at end of table.

Series S 190-204. Gas Utility Industry—Customers, Sales, and Revenues, by Type of Service: 1932 to 1990—Cont'd.

Year	Customers[1] (1,000)				Sales[2] (mil. therms[3])				Revenues[2] (mil. dol.)			
	Total	Residential	Commercial	Industrial	Total	Residential	Commercial	Industrial	Total	Residential	Commercial	Industrial
	190	191	192	193	195	196	197	198	200	201	202	203
1940	17,600	16,381	1,138	73	17,235	5,823	1,598	9,544	872	573	112	182
1939	17,128	15,926	1,121	73	15,927	5,289	1,469	8,768	814	538	105	156
1938	16,876	15,697	1,094	75	14,682	4,956	1,380	7,941	777	523	101	145
1937	16,605	15,466	1,056	74	15,773	4,987	1,382	9,041	802	528	100	167
1936	16,170	15,026	1,058	77	14,693	4,784	1,369	8,280	770	516	97	151
1935	15,819	14,725	1,014	72	12,924	4,445	1,211	7,221	727	503	91	130
1934	15,512	14,440	990	74	12,063	4,202	1,102	6,699	703	494	87	119
1933	15,195	14,141	978	68	10,531	4,237	1,150	5,114	680	495	88	95
1932	15,532	14,452	999	73	10,441	4,672	1,193	4,534	723	537	93	91

* Denotes first year for which figures include Alaska and Hawaii.
[1] Yearly averages.
[2] Excludes sales for resale.

[3] A therm is equivalent to 100,000 British thermal units. A B.t.u. is the quantity of heat required to raise the temperature of one pound of water 1° F. at or near its point of maximum density.
[4] Includes Hawaii.

DISTRIBUTION AND SERVICES

DISTRIBUTION AND SERVICES
Highlights

1 The *Survey of Current Business,* issued by the Bureau of Economic Analysis, is the principal source of data on domestic trade and services. Financial data relating to this sector appear in the *Statistics of Income,* published by the Internal Revenue Service. Censuses of retail and wholesale trade have been taken at various intervals since 1929. Limited coverage of service industries started in 1933. Beginning with the 1967 census, legislation has provided that a census of each area be conducted every five years, in years ending in 2 or 7. The industries covered in the censuses and surveys are classified in three divisions defined in the *Standard Industrial Classification Manual*: retail trade, wholesale trade, and services. The purview of the censuses has varied over the years to make some of the data incomparable over time. Since 1954, data for nonemployer establishments have been published separately and establishments with no paid employees are excluded from wholesale trade. Since 1977, sales taxes and finance charges have been excluded from sales figures. After 1987, number of establishments was defined as those in business at any time during the year, rather than at the end of the year as before. From 1987 hospitals are included among services, but government operated services are excluded. In 1982 and 1987, data were not collected from educational institutions, nor from services run by labor unions or political organizations. Beginning in 1982, each leased department in a store was classified separately, rather than consolidated with the store as before. Current retail and wholesale trade data appear in the *Monthly Retail Trade Report* and the *Monthly Wholesale Trade Report* respectively.

2 Since 1980, the share of retail and wholesale trade in the GNP has remained stable at 16%. The share of services, on the other hand, jumped from 13.7% in 1980 to 18.7% in 1989, reflecting the strength of this sector in the post-industrial economy. Among services, the largest subsectors were health services ($273.3 billion), business services ($222.9 billion), legal services ($75.2 billion), social services ($56 billion), and hotels and lodging places ($44.5 billion). In 1990, 30.267 million persons were employed in the service sector compared to 24.573 million in the retail and wholesale trade sector. Medical services employed 7.529 million and business services 5.733 million.

3 Retail trade establishments are the most ubiquitous and most visible of all businesses. In 1989, there were 1.495 million in the United States, including 391,500 eating and drinking places, 208,200 automotive dealers and service stations, 183,900 food stores, 147,500 apparel and accessory stores, 104,600 furniture and home furnishing stores, 71,200 building materials and garden supplies stores, 50,600 drug stores, 31,700 liquor stores, 28,800 gift, novelty and souvenir shops, 27,400 jewelry stores, 25,900 florists, 13,400 optical goods stores, 11,500 bookstores, 10,100 department stores, and 6,900 catalog and mail-order houses. Per capita retail sales in 1991 were $7,223. Metro areas accounted for 82.4% of all retail sales. Chains or multiunit stores accounted for 38.7% of retail sales, but in the general merchandise group they accounted for 91.8%. Chain stores accounted for more than half of all retail sales in drug and proprietary goods, shoes, food and groceries, and apparel and accessories.

4 Among metropolitan areas, the highest sales per household (the total purchases of retail goods and services by each household in one year) in 1990 were recorded in St. Cloud, Minnesota, at $36,640; followed by Portland, Maine ($32,650); Honolulu, Hawaii ($31,340); Anchorage, Alaska ($29,963); and Terre Haute, Indiana ($29,663). The lowest household sales were in Cleveland-Akron, Ohio, at $18,006. Among states, the highest household sales were in Hawaii ($31,121), followed by New Hampshire ($28,373), Alaska ($24,533), and Delaware ($24,145). The lowest household sales were in Wyoming ($16,314) and Idaho ($15,591).

5 In 1990, there were 23,813 supermarkets with total sales of $260.1 billion. Conventional supermarkets and superstores each accounted for one-third of sales.

6 In 1991, there were 720,043 eating establishments with sales of $237.7 billion. These included 163,514 restaurants, 37,227 bars and taverns, and 27,158 restaurant and motel restaurants.

7 Shopping centers are uniquely American phenomena. In 1991, there were 37,975 of them, with 4.586 billion sq. ft. of space, and retail sales of $716.9 billion, or $156.32 per sq. ft. There were 364 shopping centers with over

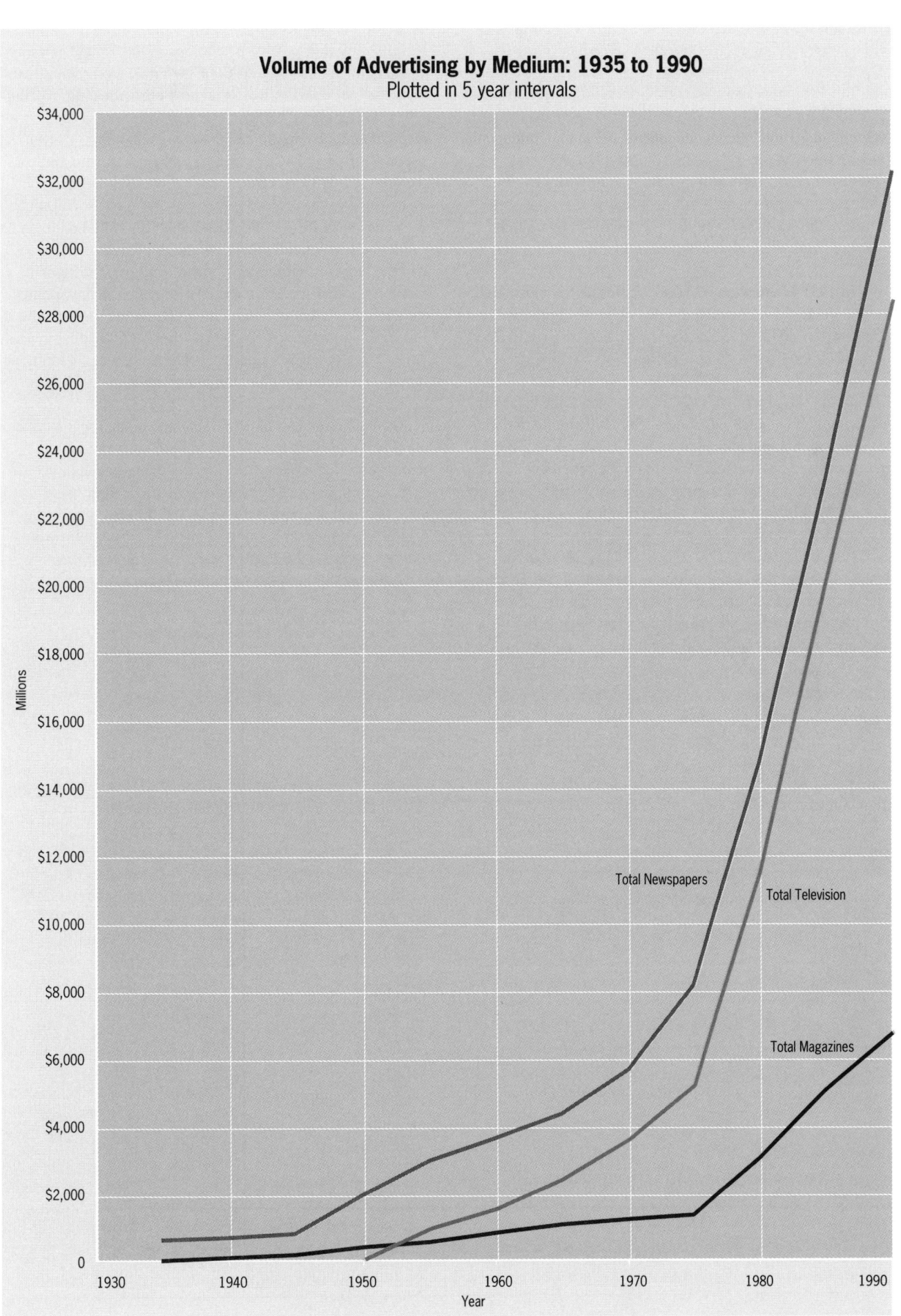

Volume of Advertising by Medium: 1935 to 1990
Plotted in 5 year intervals

Millions

Total Newspapers

Total Television

Total Magazines

Year

1 million sq. ft. of space each, but 64% of shopping centers had less than 100,000 sq. ft. of space.

8 In 1991, there were 543,000 franchised establishments (442,000 franchisee-owned and 101,000 company-owned), with $758 billion in sales. In number of establishments, the most numerous were gasoline stations (111,700) and restaurants (102,100). But in sales, the largest were auto and truck dealers ($362.3 billion), followed by gasoline service stations ($115.1 billion). Franchised restaurants were in third place with $76.5 billion.

9 In 1987, there were 470,000 wholesale trade establishments, of which 222,000 had sales of $1 million or more. Total wholesale trade sales topped $2.525 trillion, divided almost equally between durable and nondurable goods.

10 In 1987, there were 6.254 million service establishments subject to Federal Income Tax and 175,800 service establishments not subject to Federal Income Tax. Total receipts were $868.3 billion and total employment 16.055 million. Among the emerging services are child care which earned $2.8 billion in 1990, and residential care which earned $8.7 billion.

11 The growth of the computer industry is reflected in the number of establishments for computer programming and data processing. In 1989, there were 37,752 such establishments with 721,800 employees.

12 According to the *Encyclopedia of Associations*, there were 22,389 non-profit associations in the United States in 1991, compared to 14,726 in 1980. Trade, commercial, and business associations were the most numerous, numbering 3,911. Other major category groups were health and medical (2,229), public affairs (2,182), cultural (1,884), social welfare (1,742), hobbies (1,499), scientific and technical (1,378), and religious (1,177). The largest association in the United States was the AARP (American Association of Retired Persons) which in 1991 had over 22 million members and whose magazine, *Modern Maturity*, had the largest circulation of any magazine in the world. Among learned societies, the largest were the American Psychological Association with 76,000 members and the Modern Language Association with 30,000 members. The American Council of Learned Societies had 52 constituent societies with a combined membership of 314,925.

13 With growing leisure time, amusement and recreation services have burgeoned in both conventional and unconventional areas—the latter focusing on small groups (e.g., dating services for singles). In 1987, there were 467,000 such services, including 186,900 theatrical producers, bands, and entertainers; 50,600 commercial sports services; 22,300 physical fitness centers; 8,300 bowling centers; and 700 amusement parks.

Series T 15-28. Persons Engaged in Distribution and Selected Service Industries: 1869 to 1990

(In thousands. Data represent man-years of full-time equivalent by persons working for wages or salaries and by active proprietors or unincorporated businesses devoting the major portion of their time to the business)

Year	Wholesale trade	Retail trade [1]	Hotels and other lodging places	Personal services	Miscellaneous business services	Automobile repair, services and garages [1]	Miscellaneous repair services
	15	16	17	18	19	20	21
1990	6,362	18,211	1,865	1,592	5,733	1,289	602
1989	6,436	18,091	1,851	1,618	5,399	1,258	582
1988	6,188	17,553	1,788	1,632	5,075	1,231	569
1987	6,029	17,092	1,684	1,535	4,659	1,177	550
1986	5,838	16,377	1,603	1,528	5,010	1,129	544
1985	5,804	15,943	1,571	1,503	4,650	1,090	555
1984	5,697	15,341	1,461	1,443	4,273	1,022	548
1983	5,409	14,406	1,382	1,379	3,703	927	523
1982	5,409	14,010	1,340	1,334	3,345	909	515
1981	5,522	14,082	1,310	1,337	3,251	865	519
1980	5,396	13,999	1,261	1,330	3,077	838	475
1979	5,284	13,768	1,215	1,251	2,847	781	465
1978	5,017	13,433	1,188	1,220	2,586	730	426
1977	4,785	12,733	1,161	1,193	2,317	674	412
1976	4,647	12,153	1,100	1,167	2,144	635	390
1975	4,521	11,979	1,117	1,182	2,054	638	399
1974	4,292	11,991	1,145	1,200	1,970	590	386
1973	4,172	11,799	1,099	1,242	1,864	582	348
1972	3,956	11,377	1,058	1,255	1,703	561	336
1971	3,886	11,667	817	1,395	1,635	545	335
1970	3,838	11,386	799	1,452	1,627	512	324
1969	3,767	11,157	793	1,468	1,573	500	312
1968	3,647	10,730	760	1,485	1,442	492	306
1967	3,561	10,374	732	1,488	1,353	483	295
1966	3,487	10,118	722	1,482	1,255	465	304
1965	3,358	9,813	704	1,424	1,144	456	300
1964	3,252	9,483	683	1,394	1,056	446	294
1963	3,180	9,179	662	1,360	982	426	287
1962	3,141	9,132	652	1,333	928	407	279
1961	3,100	9,077	641	1,311	860	394	279
1960*	3,090	9,209	639	1,289	810	388	265
1959	3,018	9,041	624	1,250	754	359	259
1958	2,966	8,902	612	1,258	678	350	265
1957	2,976	9,002	625	1,280	654	333	268
1956	2,953	8,955	621	1,248	609	322	259
1955	2,842	8,750	618	1,223	549	310	249
1954	2,795	8,541	641	1,218	500	302	240
1953	2,820	8,660	656	1,223	486	305	255
1952	2,793	8,605	638	1,230	455	308	264
1951	2,740	8,505	625	1,232	425	306	254
1950	2,605	8,178	605	1,217	395	310	232
1949	2,591	8,071	611	1,218	382	325	235
1948 [2]	2,664	8,087	636	1,241	385	340	253
1948 [3]	2,712	8,597	640	1,241	486	—	504
1947	2,625	8,376	636	1,243	455	—	535
1946	2,419	7,973	632	1,210	418	—	504
1945	2,052	6,862	584	1,073	343	—	399
1944	1,936	6,598	584	1,053	320	—	394
1943	1,912	6,648	573	1,090	305	—	378
1942	2,041	6,916	561	1,115	310	—	328
1941	2,136	7,126	557	1,095	314	—	320
1940	2,015	6,768	538	1,050	296	—	293
1939	1,942	6,440	526	996	290	—	300
1938	1,857	6,218	522	1,008	276	—	314
1937	1,857	6,305	520	1,034	269	—	311
1936	1,690	5,949	494	994	265	—	311
1935	1,572	5,608	469	950	233	—	311

See footnotes at end of table.

Series T 15-28. Persons Engaged in Distribution and Selected Service Industries: 1869 to 1990–Cont'd.

(In thousands. Data represent man-years of full-time equivalent by persons working for wages or salaries and by active proprietors or unincorporated businesses devoting the major portion of their time to the business)

Year	Wholesale trade	Retail trade [1]	Hotels and other lodging places	Personal services	Miscellaneous business services	Miscellaneous repair services
	15	16	17	18	19	21
1934	1,530	5,431	453	910	231	309
1933	1,393	5,038	403	860	204	312
1932	1,395	5,058	417	886	198	315
1931	1,533	5,507	465	941	192	299
1930	1,685	5,839	504	996	207	281
1929	1,744	6,077	518	1,008	209	264
1919	1,233	3,977	—	—	—	—
1909	1,034	3,177	—	—	—	—
1899	783	2,218	—	—	—	—
1889	397	1,775	—	—	—	—
1879	250	1,087	—	—	—	—
1869	169	716	—	—	—	—

See footnotes at end of table.

Series T 15-28. Persons Engaged in Distribution and Selected Service Industries: 1869 to 1990—Cont'd.

(In thousands. Data represent man-years of full-time equivalent by persons working for wages or salaries and by active proprietors or unincorporated businesses devoting the major portion of their time to the business)

Year	Motion pictures	Amusement and recreation, except motion pictures	Medical and other health services	Legal services	Educational services	Miscellaneous professional services	Nonprofit membership organizations
	22	23	24	25	26	27	28
1990	456	1,029	7,529	1,141	1,623	—	3,538
1989	437	977	7,194	1,169	1,600	1,960	3,289
1988	395	895	6,848	1,132	1,549	1,830	3,213
1987	327	835	6,708	1,080	1,515	1,744	3,107
1986	295	764	6,356	952	1,480	1,671	2,915
1985	283	751	6,142	921	1,470	1,633	2,725
1984	280	747	5,972	883	1,414	1,541	2,607
1983	274	717	5,821	830	1,360	1,447	2,540
1982	266	702	5,677	786	1,311	1,435	2,470
1981	268	695	5,461	732	1,277	1,402	2,382
1980	249	683	5,218	690	1,241	1,348	2,361
1979	247	629	4,864	612	1,239	1,202	2,108
1978	238	604	4,616	575	1,200	1,112	2,019
1977	231	569	4,493	541	1,204	1,008	1,924
1976	217	541	4,219	498	1,185	936	1,898
1975	217	520	4,114	501	1,151	939	1,856
1974	206	509	3,793	448	1,139	1,013	1,681
1973	207	484	3,542	422	1,123	950	1,662
1972	192	455	3,339	399	1,115	869	1,655
1971	191	554	3,505	418	1,269	870	1,400
1970	191	523	3,359	405	1,271	850	1,387
1969	193	505	3,176	383	1,247	814	1,358
1968	186	488	2,996	371	1,210	745	1,318
1967	185	469	2,813	368	1,162	698	1,273
1966	179	448	2,654	363	1,093	662	1,218
1965	173	433	2,479	346	1,036	617	1,175
1964	169	426	2,350	338	989	590	1,128
1963	168	414	2,239	327	947	565	1,103
1962	170	401	2,128	327	902	545	1,082
1961	177	384	2,041	314	861	518	1,042
1960	179	370	1,968	310	823	503	1,028
1959	185	348	1,895	298	779	489	983
1958	188	331	1,807	277	743	468	948
1957	203	320	1,719	266	703	482	911
1956	213	316	1,642	262	658	456	885
1955	216	307	1,558	257	625	404	843
1954	218	296	1,484	254	588	383	801
1953	221	297	1,417	251	564	378	780
1952	228	291	1,355	246	543	354	750
1951	233	294	1,307	243	530	314	738
1950	234	296	1,239	235	519	273	713
1949	235	296	1,170	228	502	271	697
1948[2]	234	298	1,132	217	482	275	649
1948[3]	234	299	1,131	217	421	160	554
1947	237	284	1,071	212	387	144	599
1946	236	275	983	210	364	131	572
1945	222	232	892	195	343	112	493
1944	221	232	895	200	344	104	479
1943	211	234	894	211	340	110	455
1942	200	255	878	228	335	129	448
1941	191	256	861	245	329	103	427

See footnotes at end of table.

Series T 15-28. Persons Engaged in Distribution and Selected Service Industries: 1869 to 1990–Cont'd.

(In thousands. Data represent man-years of full-time equivalent by persons working for wages or salaries and by active proprietors or unincorporated businesses devoting the major portion of their time to the business)

Year	Motion pictures	Amusement and recreation, except motion pictures	Medical and other health services	Legal services	Educational services	Miscellaneous professional services	Nonprofit membership organizations
	22	23	24	25	26	27	28
1940	181	240	841	244	324	91	390
1939	179	223	813	242	318	86	328
1938	178	212	807	236	312	82	331
1937	184	230	785	230	304	80	332
1936	171	212	750	225	297	78	342
1935	155	197	711	223	293	74	338
1934	141	193	695	216	287	72	339
1933	124	180	679	217	286	69	225
1932	128	200	691	214	289	69	341
1931	147	248	725	212	292	77	354
1930	153	277	749	202	291	85	358
1929	153	295	750	194	287	83	351

* Denotes first year for which figures include Alaska and Hawaii.
[1] For 1948 and prior year, "Automobile repair, services and garages" included with "Retail trade."

[2] Comparable with later years.
[3] Comparable with earlier years.

Series T 79-196.   Retail Establishments, Sales and Persons, by Kind of Business: 1929 to 1987

Year	All establishments			Establishments with payroll		
	Number	Amount (mil. dol.)	Per capita	Number	Payroll, entire year, amount (mil. dol.)	Paid employees, workweek ended nearest Nov. 15
	Sales					
	79	80	81	82	84	87
1987	1,992,000	1,540,000	6,328	1,504,000	177,500	17,780,000
1982	1,573,000	1,066,000	4,599	1,324,000	123,600	14,468,000
1977	1,567,000	723,000	3,291	1,304,000	85,900	13,040,000
1972	1,665,000	457,000	2,186	1,265,000	55,400	11,211,000
1967	1,763,324	310,214	1,557	1,191,546	36,175	[1] 9,380,616
1963 *	1,707,931	244,202	1,294	1,206,087	27,632	8,410,199
1958	1,788,325	199,646	1,152	1,180,641	21,589	7,911,081
1954	1,721,650	269,968	1,054	1,124,040	18,199	7,124,331
1948 [2]	1,688,479	128,849	882	1,118,692	(NA)	(NA)
1948 [3]	1,769,540	130,521	866	1,100,223	13,568	6,918,061
1939	1,770,355	42,042	321	1,017,062	4,529	4,821,806
1935	1,587,718	32,791	258	——	3,568	[4] 3,898,258
1933	1,526,119	25,037	199	——	2,910	[4] 2,703,325
1929	1,476,365	48,330	396	——	5,044	[4] 4,286,516

NA Not available.
* Denotes first year for which figures include Alaska and Hawaii.
[1] For 1967, paid employees for week including March 12.
[2] Comparable with later years.
[3] Comparable with earlier years.
[4] Average annual number of full-time and part-time for year; comparable figure for 1939 is 4,600,217.

Series T 245-271.   Retail Store Sales, by Kind of Business: 1929 to 1991
(In millions of dollars. Includes nonstores)

| | | | | | Durable goods stores | | | | Nondurable goods stores | |
| | | | | | Furniture and appliance group | | Lumber, building, hardware group | | | Apparel group |
Year	All stores	Total sales [1]	Passenger car, other automotive dealers	Furniture, home furnishings stores	Household appliance, T.V., radio stores	Lumber, building, materials dealers [2]	Hardware stores	Total sales [1]	Total	Shoe stores
	245	246	247	250	251	252	253	255	256	260
1991	1,821,500	644,800	374,500	48,900	32,300	68,000	13,100	1,176,700	95,600	17,600
1990	1,807,200	654,800	382,000	51,600	33,000	66,800	13,300	1,152,500	94,700	17,900
1989	1,741,700	652,200	383,600	51,100	32,400	67,000	12,600	1,089,600	91,400	17,200
1988	1,651,400	627,400	371,600	47,500	30,500	66,600	11,900	1,024,000	84,900	15,400
1987	1,542,100	576,600	342,900	44,500	27,100	61,300	11,000	965,500	79,300	14,600
1986	1,450,300	541,500	326,300	43,000	27,000	56,500	10,700	908,900	75,600	13,900
1985	1,375,700	498,800	303,300	38,300	25,100	50,800	10,500	876,900	70,200	13,100
1984	1,297,000	464,300	277,000	35,100	24,000	49,800	9,500	832,700	66,900	10,300
1983	1,174,300	396,500	232,800	31,000	19,700	42,400	9,000	777,800	60,300	9,800
1982	1,072,100	336,700	193,200	27,000	15,700	35,200	8,700	735,400	55,300	9,100
1981	1,041,300	325,100	182,400	27,400	15,300	35,700	8,400	716,300	53,000	9,500
1980	957,400	299,200	164,100	26,300	14,000	35,000	8,300	658,100	49,300	10,500
1979	899,100	306,400	178,600	25,600	12,700	36,300	7,900	592,800	44,600	7,800
1978	806,800	280,400	167,900	22,500	10,700	31,900	6,600	526,400	41,100	6,600
1977	725,200	248,700	150,000	20,300	10,000	27,100	6,100	476,500	35,600	5,700
1976	657,400	217,800	129,800	18,000	9,200	22,500	5,500	439,600	33,700	5,000
1975	588,100	183,000	106,600	16,200	8,300	18,000	5,100	405,200	31,300	4,600
1974	541,000	169,400	96,500	16,300	7,600	17,800	4,500	371,600	28,900	4,400
1973	509,500	172,900	103,300	15,200	7,400	17,200	4,100	336,600	27,700	4,500
1972	449,100	148,400	88,500	13,700	6,800	15,000	3,900	300,700	24,100	4,000
1971	408,900	131,800	72,500	11,000	6,200	13,700	3,600	277,000	20,800	3,500
1970	375,527	114,288	59,388	10,483	6,073	11,995	3,351	261,239	19,810	3,501
1969	362,935	115,517	63,091	10,523	5,693	11,630	3,367	247,418	19,866	3,618
1968	339,324	110,245	60,660	10,227	5,235	10,984	(NA)	229,079	19,265	3,196
1967	313,809	100,173	53,966	(NA)	(NA)	9,781	2,894	213,636	18,123	(NA)
1966	303,956	98,301	54,144	(NA)	(NA)	9,769	2,804	205,655	17,291	(NA)
1965	284,128	94,186	53,484	(NA)	(NA)	9,731	2,657	189,841	15,765	(NA)
1964	261,870	84,593	46,029	(NA)	(NA)	9,089	2,505	177,277	15,295	(NA)
1963	246,666	79,927	43,609	(NA)	(NA)	9,139	2,399	166,739	14,233	(NA)
1962	235,563	74,894	40,472	(NA)	(NA)	9,017	2,401	160,669	14,164	(NA)
1961 [3]	218,992	67,302	34,695	(NA)	(NA)	8,697	2,358	151,690	13,614	(NA)
1961 [4]	218,811	66,968	34,523	(NA)	(NA)	8,316	2,495	151,843	13,601	(NA)
1960*	219,529	70,560	37,038	(NA)	(NA)	8,567	2,655	148,969	13,631	2,437
1959	215,413	71,608	36,901	(NA)	(NA)	9,086	2,737	143,805	13,239	2,330
1958	200,353	63,409	31,577	6,636	3,688	8,154	2,653	136,944	12,559	2,222
1957	200,002	68,352	36,298	6,601	3,983	7,950	2,737	131,650	12,277	2,091
1956	189,729	65,810	34,050	6,568	4,099	8,312	2,893	123,919	11,610	2,068
1955	183,851	66,978	36,267	6,116	3,939	8,242	2,788	116,873	10,971	2,009
1954	169,135	58,173	29,962	5,291	3,788	7,433	2,702	110,962	10,147	1,809
1953	169,094	60,371	31,489	5,136	3,989	7,715	2,706	108,723	10,256	1,736
1952	162,353	55,270	26,393	5,255	3,671	7,572	2,628	107,083	10,633	1,693
1951	156,548	54,479	26,282	5,095	3,509	7,470	2,738	102,069	10,209	1,684
1950	147,213	54,275	27,405	4,997	3,798	7,155	2,526	92,938	9,485	1,556
1949	133,783	44,983	22,211	4,284	2,956	5,648	2,248	88,800	9,493	1,498
1948	133,619	42,888	19,212	4,503	2,853	6,007	2,398	90,731	9,971	1,510
1947	122,406	37,542	16,198	4,167	2,593	5,204	2,171	84,864	9,467	1,487
1946 [3]	104,802	28,231	10,912	3,366	1,766	3,935	1,836	76,571	9,054	1,417
1946 [4]	102,488	27,570	10,647	3,264	1,575	4,106	1,911	74,918	8,880	1,377

See footnotes at end of table.

Series T 245-271. Retail Store Sales, by Kind of Business: 1929 to 1991—Cont'd.

(In millions of dollars. Includes nonstores)

| | | | | Durable goods stores | | | | | Nondurable goods stores | | |
| | | | | | Furniture and appliance group | | Lumber, building, hardware group | | | Apparel group | |
Year	All stores	Total sales [1]	Passenger car, other automotive dealers	Furniture, home furnishings stores	Household appliance, T.V., radio	Lumber, building, materials dealers [2]	Hardware stores	Total sales [1]	Total	Shoe stores
	245	246	247	250	251	252	253	255	256	260
1945	78,034	16,026	5,000	2,101	639	2,502	1,237	62,008	7,689	1,140
1944	70,208	13,952	4,420	1,848	462	2,102	1,030	56,266	6,704	1,001
1943	63,235	12,221	3,768	1,692	415	2,024	903	51,014	6,158	969
1942	57,212	12,320	6,404	1,776	594	2,332	973	44,892	5,089	914
1941	55,274	17,213	8,185	1,780	796	2,442	905	38,061	4,137	726
1940	46,375	13,576	6,429	1,386	625	2,023	712	32,799	3,451	632
1939	42,042	11,312	5,025	1,200	533	1,761	629	30,730	3,259	617
1938	38,053	9,475	3,909	1,014	476	1,530	563	28,578	2,998	591
1937	42,150	12,048	5,568	1,254	592	1,739	651	30,102	3,323	636
1936	38,339	10,751	5,102	1,082	533	1,463	576	27,588	3,102	586
1935	32,791	8,321	3,863	852	438	1,105	467	24,470	2,656	511
1933	24,517	5,384	2,142	646	313	854	311	19,133	1,930	425
1929	48,459	15,610	6,432	1,813	942	2,621	706	32,849	4,241	807

See footnotes at end of table.

Series T 245-271. Retail Store Sales, by Kind of Business: 1929 to 1991—Cont'd.
(In millions of dollars. Includes nonstores)

Nondurable goods stores - Cont'd.

General merchandise groups

Year	Drug and proprietary stores	Eating and drinking places	Grocery stores	Gasoline service stations	Total [1][6]	Department stores, excl. mail order	Mail order (catalog sales)[7]	Variety stores	Other general merchandise	Liquor stores
	261	262	264	265	266	267	268	269	270	271
1991	74,900	189,500	346,300	128,500	217,600	177,300	4,500	7,100	33,200	21,400
1990	68,600	182,000	388,700	131,700	211,900	170,700	4,700	7,300	33,900	20,800
1989	62,500	173,900	324,000	117,800	204,400	164,400	4,700	7,400	32,700	20,000
1988	57,400	166,900	307,200	107,900	191,800	155,100	4,400	7,200	29,500	19,600
1987	54,100	153,500	291,000	104,800	182,000	147,200	4,100	7,100	27,700	19,800
1986	50,500	139,400	280,800	102,100	169,200	137,800	4,300	7,400	24,000	19,900
1985	47,000	127,900	269,500	113,300	158,600	129,800	4,700	8,500	20,300	19,500
1984	44,200	124,100	252,900	101,000	153,600	129,300	4,700	9,100	15,300	19,500
1983	40,100	114,700	239,100	98,900	139,400	116,600	4,400	8,600	14,200	19,000
1982	36,200	104,400	230,100	97,100	128,700	107,200	4,400	8,300	13,200	18,100
1981	33,700	98,000	220,100	102,800	125,400	103,500	4,400	8,300	13,500	17,600
1980	31,000	90,100	205,600	94,100	108,700	88,300	4,300	7,800	12,600	16,900
1979	28,200	82,000	184,900	73,300	109,300	89,200	4,200	7,900	12,200	15,100
1978	25,400	71,700	163,800	59,700	103,200	84,400	4,000	7,300	11,500	13,600
1977	23,200	63,300	147,800	56,500	90,700	73,600	6,800	7,100	—	13,000
1976	21,600	57,200	138,200	52,000	81,800	65,700	6,100	7,200	—	12,400
1975	19,900	51,100	129,200	47,500	78,400	62,100	5,600	8,000	—	11,800
1974	18,400	44,700	117,200	43,000	71,200	55,400	5,400	7,700	—	11,000
1973	17,000	40,400	103,500	37,000	67,400	52,600	5,000	7,400	—	10,200
1972	15,300	36,200	91,700	33,400	60,900	47,300	4,300	7,200	—	9,700
1971	13,700	31,100	82,800	29,200	68,100	42,000	4,300	7,000	—	9,200
1970	13,366	29,689	79,756	27,994	61,320	37,295	3,853	6,959	—	7,980
1969	12,224	26,970	77,942	25,909	57,606	35,659	3,538	6,426	—	7,384
1968	11,458	25,285	67,925	24,526	54,493	33,323	3,256	6,152	—	6,969
1967	10,721	23,473	(NA)	22,739	49,820	29,589	(NA)	(NA)	—	6,409
1966	9,988	22,098	(NA)	21,792	46,961	27,868	(NA)	(NA)	—	6,081
1965	9,186	20,201	(NA)	20,611	42,299	25,014	(NA)	(NA)	—	5,674
1964	8,476	18,462	(NA)	19,196	38,289	22,224	(NA)	(NA)	—	5,410
1963	8,068	17,194	(NA)	18,319	34,232	(NA)	(NA)	(NA)	—	5,138
1962	7,917	16,434	(NA)	17,644	32,537	(NA)	(NA)	(NA)	—	4,892
1961[3]	7,629	15,549	(NA)	17,007	29,874	(NA)	(NA)	(NA)	—	4,433
1961[4]	7,752	16,488	50,369	17,959	25,059	(NA)	(NA)	(NA)	—	4,927
1960*	7,538	16,146	48,610	17,588	24,085	(NA)	(NA)	(NA)	—	4,893
1959	7,150	15,618	46,132	16,793	23,420	(NA)	(NA)	(NA)	(5)	4,743
1958	6,600	14,792	44,547	15,757	21,667	12,563	1,536	3,609	3,943	4,439
1957	6,325	14,787	42,444	15,070	21,157	(NA)	1,477	3,523	4,254	4,212
1956	5,775	14,317	39,180	13,738	20,762	11,327	1,407	3,423	4,605	3,944
1955	5,232	13,662	36,919	12,411	20,100	10,882	1,331	3,295	4,592	3,546
1954	4,940	13,127	34,993	11,443	18,857	10,272	1,222	3,027	4,336	3,415
1953	4,790	13,003	33,623	10,536	19,006	10,370	1,327	3,095	4,214	3,325
1952	4,717	12,688	32,238	9,976	18,694	10,277	1,339	2,996	4,082	3,165
1951	4,547	12,207	30,346	9,151	18,202	10,095	1,309	2,859	3,939	3,975
1950	4,205	11,158	26,886	8,240	17,275	9,649	1,258	2,632	3,736	2,669
1949	4,074	10,994	25,248	7,590	16,339	9,083	1,178	2,555	3,523	2,598
1948	4,050	11,218	25,215	7,077	17,170	9,579	1,328	2,556	3,707	2,711
1947	3,904	11,183	22,907	5,979	16,088	9,108	1,194	2,363	3,123	2,782
1946[3]	3,759	11,152	18,980	4,922	14,755	8,431	976	2,197	3,151	2,823
1946[4]	3,723	10,619	18,640	4,511	14,724	9,183		2,158	3,383	2,688

See footnotes at end of table.

Series T 245-271.   Retail Store Sales, by Kind of Business: 1929 to 1991—Cont'd.

(In millions of dollars. Includes nonstores)

Year	Drug and proprietary stores	Eating and drinking places	Grocery stores	Gasoline service stations	Total [1] [6]	General merchandise groups				
						Department stores, excl. mail order	Mail order, (catalog sales) [7]	Variety stores	Other general merchandise	Liquor stores
	261	262	264	265	266	267	268	269	270	271
1945	3,155	9,575	14,593	3,284	11,802	7,092		1,845	2,865	2,288
1944	2,924	8,305	13,665	2,812	11,076	6,488		1,774	2,814	1,926
1943	2,628	7,216	12,481	2,628	10,162	5,889		1,642	2,631	1,557
1942	2,213	5,699	11,368	3,089	9,204	5,389		1,536	2,279	1,212
1941	1,847	4,570	9,312	3,466	7,973	4,862		1,320	1,791	854
1940	1,636	3,787	8,169	2,970	6,859	4,128		1,153	1,578	681
1939	1,563	3,529	7,722	2,822	6,475	3,872		1,080	1,523	586
1938	1,474	3,188	7,187	2,696	6,145	(NA)	(NA)	1,015	1,536	539
1937	1,527	3,293	7,266	2,641	6,673	(NA)	(NA)	1,025	1,755	558
1936	1,409	2,748	6,850	2,318	6,366	(NA)	(NA)	967	1,731	475
1935	1,233	2,395	6,352	1,968	5,730	2,833	386	873	1,638	328
1933	1,066	1,434	5,004	1,532	4,982	(NA)	(NA)	756	1,766	17
1929	1,690	2,132	7,353	[8] 1,787	9,015	3,903	447	904	3,761	—

* Denotes first year for which figures include Alaska and Hawaii.
NA Not available.
[1] Totals include subclasses not shown separately.
[2] Includes lumber yards; building materials dealers; and paint, plumbing and electrical stores.
[3] Comparable with later years.
[4] Comparable with earlier years.

[5] No longer available separately; included in total for group.
[6] Includes nonstores, i.e., establishments selling merchandise primarily through coin-operated vending machines, house-to-house canvass and mail orders.
[7] Includes sales made by mail order catalog desks located within department stores of mail order firms.
[8] Excludes garages primarily selling gasoline and oil.

Series T 274-371.   Wholesale Establishments, Sales, Operating Expenses and Persons Engaged, by Kind of Business: 1929 to 1987

(Sales, inventories and payroll in millions of dollars; paid employees and active proprietors in thousands)

| Year | All wholesale establishments [1] | | | | Merchant wholesalers [2] | | | |
	Number	Sales	Payroll, entire year	Paid employees, work week ended nearest Nov. 15	Number	Sales	Operating expenses (percent)	Inventories, end of year
	274	**275**	**277**	**278**	**280**	**281**	**282**	**283**
1987	466,700	2,523,688	133,153	5,581	388,100	1,477,132	100,210	4,461
1982	435,100	1,997,895	95,209	4,985	353,100	1,159,334	69,936	3,918
1977	382,800	1,258,400	58,290	4,397	307,300	676,058	42,067	3,368
1972	369,800	695,224	36,893	4,026	290,000	353,919	25,916	3,023
1967	311,464	459,476	23,922	[3] 3,519	212,993	206,055	13.5	21,463
1963 *	308,177	358,386	18,101	3,089	208,997	157,392	13.5	14,992
1958	285,996	284,977	13,199	2,791	190,492	122,060	13.4	11,253
1954	250,322	233,976	10,868	2,555	163,157	100,103	13.0	9,492
1948 [4]	216,099	180,577	7,734	2,305	129,117	76,533	11.5	7,056
1948 [5]	243,366	188,689	7,991	2,383	146,518	79,767	11.6	7,207
1939 [6]	190,379	53,766	2,511	[7] 1,553	100,961	22,538	13.1	2,621
1935	176,756	42,803	2,022	[7] 1,261	88,931	17,662	7.6	2,068
1933 [6]	163,583	30,010	1,659	[7] 1,188	82,844	12,960	15.0	1,971
1929 [6]	163,830	65,378	2,922	[7] 1,550	79,840	29,556	11.7	3,383

* Denotes first year for which figures include Alaska and Hawaii.
[1] Beginning 1954, excludes ready-mixed concrete distributors, no longer part of wholesale trade but included in selected service trade.
[2] Includes subclasses not shown separately.
[3] For workweek ended nearest March 12.

[4] Comparable with later years.
[5] Comparable with earlier years.
[6] Data for series T 274-279 for 1939, 1933, and 1929 are revised; revised data for other series for these years not available.
[7] Average annual number of full-time and part-time employees.

Series T 391-443.   Selected Service Establishments and Receipts: 1933 to 1987

(Receipts and payroll in millions of dollars; paid employees and active proprietors in thousands)

Year	Number of establishments	Receipts, all establishments	Payroll, entire year	Paid employees, work week ended nearest Nov. 15	Year	Number of establishments	Receipts, all establishments	Payroll, entire year	Paid employees, work week ended nearest Nov. 15
	391	**393**	**398**	**400**		**391**	**393**	**398**	**400**
1987	1,626,000	772,194	289,807	15,688	1954	785,589	23,508	6,534	2,362
1982	1,261,700	426,982	158,625	11,106	1948 [2]	617,002	13,230	(NA)	(NA)
1977	725,000	164,200	56,055	6,337	1948 [3]	665,475	13,296	4,164	2,100
1972	569,928	84,754	27,002	4,671					
1967	1,187,814	60,542	17,524	[1] 3,841	1939 [2]	656,482	4,872	1,384	1,497
					1939 [3]	646,028	3,420	1,070	[4] 1,102
1963 *	1,061,673	44,586	12,192	3,262	1935	631,309	3,001	(NA)	(NA)
1958	975,250	32,376	9,006	2,889	1933	502,416	2,761	702	[4] 657

NA Not available.
* Denotes first year for which figures include Alaska and Hawaii.
[1] Paid employees for week including March 12.

[2] Comparable with later years.
[3] Comparable with earlier years.
[4] Average annual number of full-time and part-time employees.

Series T 444-471.   Volume of Advertising, by Medium: 1935 to 1990
(In millions of dollars)

Year	Total	National	Local	Newspapers Total	National	Local	Magazines Total	Weeklies
	444	445	446	447	448	449	450	451
1990	128,640	72,780	72,780	32,281	3,867	28,414	6,803	2,864
1989	123,390	68,990	54,940	32,368	3,720	28,648	6,716	2,813
1988	118,050	65,610	52,440	31,197	3,586	27,611	6,072	2,646
1987	109,650	60,625	49,025	29,412	3,494	25,918	5,607	2,445
1986	102,140	56,850	45,290	26,990	3,376	23,614	5,317	2,327
1985	94,750	53,355	41,395	25,170	3,352	21,818	5,155	2,297
1984	87,820	49,690	38,130	23,522	3,081	20,441	4,932	2,224
1983	75,850	42,525	33,325	20,582	2,734	17,848	4,233	1,917
1982	66,580	37,785	28,795	17,694	2,452	15,242	3,710	1,659
1981	60,430	33,890	26,540	16,528	2,259	14,269	3,533	1,598
1980	53,550	29,815	23,735	14,794	1,963	12,831	3,149	1,418
1979	48,780	26,695	22,085	13,863	1,770	12,093	2,932	1,327
1978	43,330	23,720	19,610	12,214	1,541	10,673	2,597	1,158
1977	38,120	21,055	17,056	11,132	1,677	9,455	2,162	903
1976	33,720	18,585	15,135	9,910	1,502	8,408	1,789	748
1975	27,900	15,200	12,700	8,234	1,109	7,125	1,465	612
1974	26,780	14,755	12,025	8,001	1,194	6,807	1,504	630
1973	25,080	13,755	11,325	7,595	1,111	6,484	1,448	583
1972	23,130	12,940	10,190	7,008	1,103	5,905	1,440	610
1971	20,500	11,720	8,780	6,215	1,125	5,090	1,405	630
1970	19,600	11,485	8,115	5,745	1,014	4,731	1,323	617
1969	19,482	11,518	7,964	5,753	1,059	4,694	1,376	662
1968	18,127	10,883	7,244	5,265	990	4,275	1,318	657
1967	16,866	10,250	6,616	4,942	936	4,006	1,280	651
1966	16,670	10,213	6,457	4,896	975	3,920	1,291	658
1965	15,255	9,398	5,857	4,457	869	3,587	1,199	610
1964	14,155	8,745	5,410	4,148	848	3,300	1,108	583
1963	13,107	8,148	4,959	3,904	765	3,039	1,034	540
1962	12,381	7,683	4,698	3,681	782	2,900	973	519
1961	11,845	7,270	4,575	3,623	802	2,821	924	508
1960	11,932	7,296	4,636	3,703	836	2,867	941	525
1959	11,255	6,835	4,420	3,546	826	2,720	866	478
1958	10,302	6,331	3,971	3,193	769	2,424	767	425
1957	10,311	6,253	4,057	3,283	810	2,474	814	451
1956	9,905	5,926	3,979	3,236	789	2,447	795	440
1955	9,194	5,407	3,788	3,088	743	2,345	729	396
1954	8,164	4,812	3,352	2,695	635	2,060	668	363
1953	7,755	4,521	3,235	2,645	643	2,002	667	351
1952	7,156	4,096	3,060	2,473	562	1,910	616	325
1951	6,426	3,701	2,725	2,258	549	1,709	574	297
1950	5,710	3,257	2,453	2,076	533	1,542	515	261
1949	5,202	2,965	2,237	1,916	476	1,440	493	245
1948	4,864	2,776	2,088	1,750	394	1,356	513	258
1947	4,260	2,487	1,772	1,475	336	1,139	493	246
1946	3,364	1,963	1,401	1,158	248	911	427	202
1945	2,875	1,775	1,099	921	211	710	365	188
1944	2,724	1,669	1,054	888	197	691	324	173
1943	2,496	1,452	1,045	900	182	718	275	154
1942	2,156	1,212	944	798	144	654	199	107
1941	2,236	1,259	977	844	165	680	214	117
1940	2,088	1,163	925	815	163	652	198	104
1939	1,980	1,086	895	793	153	640	180	88
1938	1,004	1,031	873	782	150	632	169	75
1937	2,072	1,103	969	873	173	700	193	83
1936	1,902	1,003	899	844	171	673	162	67
1935	1,690	859	831	762	152	610	136	54

Series T 444-471.   Volume of Advertising, by Medium: 1935 to 1990—Cont'd.

(In millions of dollars)

Year	Magazines - Cont'd. Women's	Monthlies	Farm, national	Television Total	Network	Spot	Local
	452	453	454	455	456	457	458
1990	1,713	2,226	215	28,405	9,383	7,758	7,856
1989	1,710	2,193	212	26,841	9,110	7,354	7,612
1988	1,504	1,922	196	25,686	9,172	7,147	7,270
1987	1,417	1,745	196	23,904	8,500	6,846	6,833
1986	1,376	1,614	192	22,881	8,342	6,570	6,514
1985	1,294	1,564	186	21,022	8,060	6,004	5,714
1984	1,209	1,499	181	19,848	8,318	5,488	5,084
1983	1,056	1,260	163	16,759	6,955	4,827	4,345
1982	904	1,147	148	14,636	6,144	4,364	3,765
1981	853	1,082	146	12,650	5,575	3,730	3,345
1980	782	949	130	11,469	5,130	3,269	2,967
1979	730	875	120	10,154	4,599	2,873	2,682
1978	672	767	104	8,955	3,925	2,607	2,373
1977	565	694	90	7,612	3,460	2,204	1,948
1976	457	584	86	6,721	2,857	2,154	1,710
1975	368	485	74	5,263	2,306	1,623	1,334
1974	372	502	72	4,851	2,145	1,495	1,211
1973	362	503	65	4,460	1,968	1,377	1,115
1972	368	462	59	4,091	1,804	1,318	969
1971	340	406	29	3,520	1,575	1,150	795
1970	301	374	31	3,665	1,712	1,247	706
1969	308	374	32	3,585	1,678	1,253	654
1968	284	342	35	3,231	1,523	1,131	577
1967	282	312	35	2,889	1,455	968	466
1966	280	316	37	2,823	1,393	988	442
1965	269	282	37	2,515	1,237	892	386
1964	231	260	34	2,289	1,132	806	351
1963	218	244	32	3,032	1,025	698	309
1962	200	223	31	1,897	976	629	292
1961	187	200	29	1,691	887	548	256
1960	184	200	32	1,590	783	527	281
1959	168	185	35	1,494	740	486	267
1958	151	158	33	1,354	709	397	248
1957	164	161	38	1,265	670	352	244
1956	166	153	37	1,207	625	329	253
1955	161	133	39	1,025	540	260	225
1954	152	114	39	809	422	207	180
1953	158	118	41	606	320	146	141
1952	149	101	41	454	256	94	104
1951	144	95	38	332	181	70	82
1950	129	88	37	171	85	31	55
1949	129	84	35	58	29	9	19
1948	133	87	35	—	—	—	—
1947	133	85	29	—	—	—	—
1946	127	76	22	—	—	—	—
1945	97	59	20	—	—	—	—
1944	82	51	18	—	—	—	—
1943	65	39	16	—	—	—	—
1942	51	28	12	—	—	—	—
1941	52	32	12	—	—	—	—
1940	49	34	12	—	—	—	—
1939	48	32	11	—	—	—	—
1938	52	31	11	—	—	—	—
1937	60	38	12	—	—	—	—
1936	57	30	8	—	—	—	—
1935	52	25	6	—	—	—	—

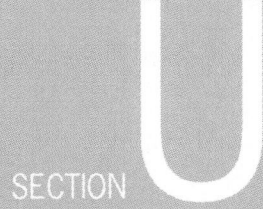

SECTION U

INTERNATIONAL TRANSACTIONS AND FOREIGN COMMERCE

INTERNATIONAL TRANSACTIONS AND FOREIGN COMMERCE

Highlights

1 The first edition of the *Statistical Abstract of the United States*, published in 1879, was almost wholly devoted to foreign trade and shipping. Data on imports of gold, silver coins, and bullion took up 11 of its 154 pages, and nearly 100 pages were devoted to imports and exports. The section on exports showed that the major U.S. exports were raw cotton and wheat, which together accounted for 38% of all exports. In the early years of the republic, international trade and transactions loomed large in public economy and received considerable attention from statisticians, because at that time the United States was more heavily dependent on foreign markets than it has been in the 20th century. Records of foreign trade have been kept by the Treasury Department beginning in August 1, 1789 (in a more or less complete fashion), although they do not show the value of commerce with each country. However, Edward Ely, author of *International Trade Statistics*, observes that the United States may be said to have an adequate set of import and export statistics only since about 1821. No information was compiled on the amounts of articles that were imported free of duty or on imports subject to specific rates of duty. The total dollar value of imports from 1795 to 1801 was apparently estimated at the time by the Secretary of the Treasury, and the figures for 1790 to 1794 and from 1802 to 1820 were apparently estimated many years later. The adequacy of these early records, of course, depends on the use made of them. Some of the earliest records were not published officially, and scholars have had to rely on other sources, particularly, *A View of the United States of America* by Tench Coxe, *A Statistical Manual of the United States of America* by Samuel Blodgett, Jr., *A Statistical View of Commerce of the United States of America* by Timothy Pitkin, and *History of Domestic and Foreign Commerce of the United States* by Emory Johnson.

2 Foreign trade data are subject to a variety of special statistical problems. The record of gold movements, in particular, has been subject to considerable error because of smuggling. The Civil War introduced two special difficulties. Since the ports of the Southern States stopped furnishing reports to the Treasury in 1861, exports of cotton are based on estimates derived from records of recipient countries. A second difficulty was introduced in 1862 when the United States abandoned its specie backing for its money. The dollar fluctuated against foreign currencies and gold with each

reverse or success of the Northern forces. While imports and reexports continued to be valued in specie (dollars of a fixed parity to gold), domestic exports were recorded in mixed values from 1862 until the resumption of specie payment in 1879. A third problem affecting the comparability of trade statistics arose between 1934 and 1953 when the foreign exchange value of the dollar was allowed to depreciate as a result of the restriction placed on gold shipments to foreign countries. World War II introduced such complications as Lend-Lease, surplus property disposal after the war, and economic and military aid.

3 In 1820, Congress established the Division of Commerce and Navigation in the Register of the Treasury. Collectors of customs were required to compile and transmit annual reports to that office on trade and navigation with foreign countries. Beginning in 1821, these reports were consolidated and published annually in *Commerce and Navigation of the United States*. In 1866, Congress established the Bureau of Statistics and charged it with the collection of data on all articles imported, exported, and reexported classified by countries of destination. Since 1866, monthly trade statistics have been published in addition to annual data.

4 Balance of International Payments data for the period from 1790 to 1918 are derived basically from private authors. They illustrate U.S. foreign relations, territorial expansion, immigration, and the cost of wars and the Civil War. For example, $600,000 was paid between 1794 and 1796 to the Barbary pirates; $11.2 million was paid to France in 1803 for the Louisiana Purchase; $15 million was paid to Mexico between 1849 and 1852 for the territory now constituting the states of Arizona, New Mexico, California, Nevada, Utah, and Colorado; $10 million to Mexico between 1854 and 1856 for the Gadsden Purchase; $7.2 million to Russia in 1869 for Alaska; and $20 million to Spain in 1898 for the Philippines, Guam, and Puerto Rico. Similarly, the United States received $5.5 million from France in 1836-38 as indemnity for losses during the Napoleonic Wars, as well as $15.5 million from Great Britain for losses suffered from British privateers during the Civil War. After World War II, the United States became a grantor, providing extensive grants and credits to its allies in the Cold War. Data for foreign aid programs are presented by the Agency for International Development (AID).

Value of Exports and Imports: 1790 to 1990
Plotted in 5 year intervals

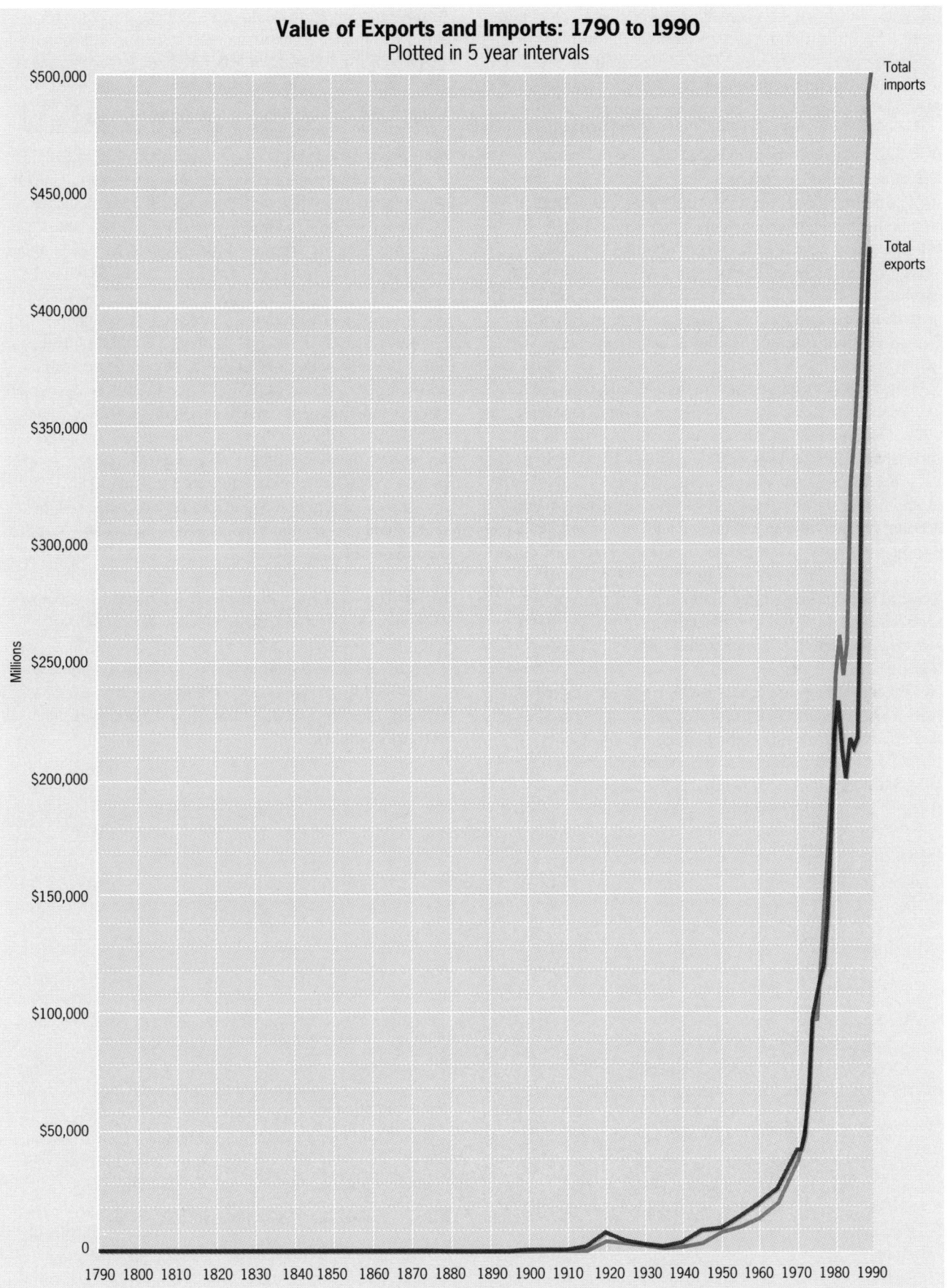

Millions

Total imports

Total exports

Year

5 Exports and imports constitute the backbone of foreign trade. The Bureau of the Census compiles export data primarily from the Shippers' Export Declarations that are required to be filed with customs officials for shipments leaving the United States. Import data are compiled from various required customs forms as well. The data suffer from serious underreporting because of the exclusion of low valued shipments exported and imported. For exports the minimum is $2,500 and for imports $1,250. Data for shipments below these limits are estimated and such estimates may have a wide margin of error. Low value shipments are believed to represent less than 2.5% of U.S. exports and 4% of U.S. imports. Since 1982, import prices have been based on customs values and export prices on f.a.s. (free alongside ship) values at the U.S. port of export.

6 Since 1983, foreign assets in the United States have exceeded U.S. assets abroad by a considerable margin. In 1990, U.S. assets abroad amounted to $1.764 trillion and foreign assets in the United States, $2.176 trillion. Similarly, the United States runs a deficit on current accounts in international transactions. In 1991, a negative current account balance of $23.924 billion with Japan and $15.218 billion with other Asian and African countries wiped out a positive account balance with Europe and Canada of $23.262 billion. The United States runs a surplus on net services and travel and transportation receipts, but has a substantial shortfall in merchandise trade.

7 Foreign direct investment in the United States rose from $83 billion in 1980 to $403.7 billion in 1990. The largest investor was the United Kingdom with $108 billion, followed by Japan ($83.4 billion), the Netherlands ($64.3 billion), and West Germany ($27.7 billion).

Manufacturing accounted for $159.9 billion, trade for $61.9 billion, finance and insurance for $58.4 billion, and petroleum for $38 billion. Foreign direct investment was concentrated in a few states, notably California ($61 billion) and New York ($31.9 billion).

8 Of the total 1990 U.S. foreign investment of $421.4 billion, developing countries accounted for only 25%. Of the investment in developing countries, Latin America accounted for 68%. Of the investment in developed countries, Canada accounted for 22%, the United Kingdom for 21%, Germany for 9%, and Japan for 6.7%.

9 From 1946 to 1990, the United States extended $374.076 billion in foreign grants and credits. Of this total, $269.375 billion were extended to developing countries under assistance programs and $14.846 billion represented famine and emergency relief. In 1990, the United States forgave $7.2 billion in foreign debt owed by severely underdeveloped countries. Political considerations have played a major role in determining the size of U.S. assistance. Among the countries that have received the most aid are Israel, Pakistan, South Korea, South Vietnam, Turkey, and Egypt.

10 The 10 states with the largest exports by value in 1990 were California ($50.4 billion), Texas ($40.079 billion), Washington ($27.053 billion), New York ($23.261 billion), Michigan ($20.236 billion), Louisiana ($15.456 billion), Ohio ($14.855 billion), Illinois ($14.025 billion), Florida ($13.257 billion), and Massachusetts ($10.018 billion).

Series U 1-25. Balance of International Payments: 1790 to 1991

(In millions of dollars. For fiscal years, 1790-1900; thereafter, calendar years)

| | Exports of goods and services [1] | | | | Imports of goods and services | | | |
| | Total | Merchandise, adjusted [2] | Travel | Income on government investments abroad | Total | Merchandise, adjusted | Direct military expenditures | Income on foreign investments in U.S. [3] |
Year	1	2	4	6	8	9	12	13
1991	676,498	416,517	45,551	7,541	704,842	490,103	15,709	105,943
1990	652,936	389,550	40,579	9,945	722,730	497,665	17,119	118,146
1989	606,593	361,451	35,173	5,640	697,407	477,368	14,595	125,963
1988	533,441	320,337	28,935	6,703	644,735	447,323	15,127	105,317
1987	431,890	250,266	23,366	5,311	577,418	409,766	14,803	82,908
1986	384,135	223,367	20,273	6,413	513,519	368,425	13,503	70,013
1985	366,049	215,935	17,663	5,499	472,908	338,083	12,795	66,115
1984	379,318	219,900	17,050	5,227	465,703	332,422	12,116	69,542
1983	343,877	201,820	10,947	4,832	374,065	268,900	12,687	54,549
1982	356,060	211,198	12,393	4,118	352,154	247,642	12,460	57,097
1981	372,892	236,254	12,913	3,685	361,813	264,143	11,288	52,908
1980	343,241	224,269	10,588	2,562	333,774	249,750	10,851	42,532
1979	286,772	184,473	——	2,292	281,677	211,819	8,584	32,914
1978	220,137	142,054	——	1,843	229,880	175,813	7,352	21,680
1977	184,337	120,816	——	1,625	193,788	151,689	5,823	14,217
1976	171,630	114,745	——	1,332	162,248	124,051	4,895	13,311
1975	155,729	107,088	——	1,112	132,836	98,041	4,795	12,564
1974	146,666	98,306	——	1,074	137,357	103,649	5,032	12,084
1973	110,241	71,410	——	936	99,219	70,499	4,629	9,655
1972	77,495	49,381	——	866	79,435	55,197	4,784	6,572
1971	65,449	42,754	——	——	65,619	45,476	4,819	4,809
1970	62,870	41,963	2,319	909	59,307	39,799	4,852	5,167
1969	55,502	36,417	2,058	932	53,591	35,796	4,856	4,564
1968	50,603	33,576	1,775	765	48,178	32,964	4,535	3,013
1967	46,177	30,638	1,646	638	41,041	26,821	4,378	2,453
1966	43,277	29,287	1,590	593	38,108	25,463	3,764	2,206
1965	39,408	26,438	1,380	509	32,310	21,496	2,952	1,797
1964	37,281	25,478	1,207	456	28,715	18,647	2,880	1,524
1963	32,603	22,252	1,015	498	26,646	17,011	2,961	1,386
1962	30,507	20,779	957	471	25,382	16,218	3,105	1,167
1961	28,772	20,107	947	381	23,173	14,519	2,998	1,050
1960	27,490	19,650	919	348	23,383	14,744	3,087	1,098
1959	23,652	16,458	902	349	23,342	15,310	3,107	860
1958	23,217	16,414	825	307	20,861	12,952	3,435	703
1957	26,653	19,562	785	205	20,752	13,291	3,216	675
1956	23,772	17,556	705	194	19,627	12,803	2,949	606
1955	19,945	14,424	654	274	17,795	11,527	2,901	520
1954	17,889	12,929	595	272	15,930	10,353	2,642	443
1953	17,078	12,412	574	252	16,546	10,975	2,615	483
1952	18,122	13,449	550	204	15,766	10,838	2,054	445
1951	18,864	14,243	473	198	15,047	11,176	1,270	434
1950	13,893	10,203	419	109	12,001	9,081	576	379
1949	15,834	12,213	392	98	9,616	6,874	621	342
1948	16,861	13,265	334	102	10,343	7,557	799	291
1947	19,819	16,097	364	66	8,202	5,973	455	256
1946	14,792	11,764	271	21	6,985	5,067	493	222
1945	16,273	12,473	162	17	10,232	5,245	2,434	231
1944	21,438	16,969	117	17	8,986	5,043	1,982	161
1943	19,134	15,115	84	12	8,096	4,599	1,763	155
1942	11,769	9,187	82	18	5,356	3,499	953	158
1941	6,896	5,343	70	9	4,486	3,416	162	187
1940	5,355	4,124	95	3	3,636	2,698	61	210
1939	4,432	3,347	135	2	3,366	2,409	46	230
1938	4,336	3,243	130	2	3,045	2,173	41	200
1937	4,553	3,451	135	1	4,256	3,181	41	295
1936	3,539	2,590	117	2	2,424	2,546	38	270
1935	3,265	2,404	101	——	3,137	2,462	41	155
1934	2,975	2,238	81	——	2,374	1,763	34	135

See footnotes at end of table.

Series U 1-25. Balance of International Payments: 1790 to 1991—Cont'd.

(In millions of dollars. For fiscal years, 1790-1900; thereafter, calendar years)

| | | Exports of goods and services [1] | | | Imports of goods and services | | | |
	Year	Total	Merchandise, adjusted [2]	Travel	Income on government investments abroad	Total	Merchandise, adjusted	Direct military expenditures	Income on foreign investments in U.S. [3]
		1	**2**	**4**	**6**	**8**	**9**	**12**	**13**
1933	2,402	1,736	66	20	2,044	1,510	41	115
1932	2,474	1,667	65	67	2,067	1,343	47	135
1931	3,641	2,494	94	92	3,125	2,120	48	220
1930	5,448	3,929	129	164	4,416	3,104	49	295
1929	7,034	5,347	139	157	5,886	4,463	50	330
1928	6,842	5,249	121	158	5,465	4,159	44	275
1927	6,456	4,982	114	160	5,383	4,240	38	240
1926	6,381	4,922	110	160	5,555	4,500	43	200
1925	6,348	5,011	83	160	5,261	4,291	39	170
1924	5,911	4,741	77	160	4,560	3,684	36	140
1923	5,494	4,266	71	164	4,652	3,866	33	130
1922	4,954	3,929	61	126	3,957	3,184	42	105
1921	5,505	4,586	76	40	3,383	2,572	65	105
1920	10,264	8,481	67	8	6,741	5,384	123	120
1919	10,776	8,891	56	175	5,908	3,995	757	130
1918	7,272	6,432	44	—	4,814	3,103	1,018	100
1917	7,072	6,398	34	—	3,597	3,006	—	100
1916	6,029	5,560	22	—	2,927	2,423	—	118
1915	3,948	3,686	24	—	2,200	1,813	—	136
1914	2,445	2,230	39	—	2,389	1,815	—	200
1913	2,816	2,600	50	—	2,442	1,829	—	210
1912	2,738	2,532	49	—	2,481	1,866	—	197
1911	2,405	2,228	41	—	2,131	1,576	—	190
1910	2,160	1,995	38	—	2,114	1,609	—	172
1909	2,013	1,857	41	—	1,987	1,522	—	164
1908	2,022	1,880	39	—	1,595	1,159	—	160
1907	2,192	2,021	35	—	1,896	1,469	—	153
1906	2,052	1,921	27	—	1,756	1,365	—	148
1905	1,859	1,751	18	—	1,561	1,215	—	145
1904	1,657	1,563	13	—	1,378	1,062	—	141
1903	1,663	1,575	9	—	1,323	1,019	—	139
1902	1,550	1,473	9	—	1,292	996	—	137
1901	1,651	1,585	8	—	1,213	912	—	135
1900 [4]	1,686	1,623	8	—	1,179	869	—	137
1900 [5]	1,578	1,534	19	—	1,149	894	—	144
1899	1,400	1,363	17	—	973	735	—	124
1898	1,340	1,301	16	—	896	653	—	133
1897	1,173	1,136	15	—	1,041	803	—	127
1896	1,082	1,048	15	—	1,048	816	—	122
1895	888	855	14	—	1,015	774	—	126
1894	981	943	20	—	883	692	—	113
1893	1,021	974	26	—	1,140	898	—	139
1892	1,122	1,084	14	—	1,142	888	—	143
1891	1,035	997	13	—	1,124	875	—	134
1890	960	921	15	—	1,109	866	—	125
1889	880	841	14	—	1,046	817	—	118
1888	786	750	14	—	1,013	791	—	107
1887	810	774	14	—	967	759	—	98
1886	817	781	15	—	894	698	—	93
1885	830	792	17	—	818	635	—	86
1884	862	822	15	—	921	730	—	90
1883	915	875	13	—	927	748	—	89
1882	859	824	7	—	915	747	—	84
1881	971	936	6	—	834	672	—	88
1880	963	929	7	—	848	694	—	79
1879	813	784	5	—	612	469	—	78

See footnotes at end of table.

Series U 1-25. Balance of International Payments: 1790 to 1991—Cont'd.

(In millions of dollars. For fiscal years, 1790-1900; thereafter, calendar years)

Year	Exports of goods and services [1]			Imports of goods and services		
	Total	Merchandise, adjusted [2]	Travel	Total	Merchandise, adjusted	Income on foreign investments in U.S. [3]
	1	2	4	8	9	13
1878	813	780	4	595	462	76
1877	716	687	3	614	475	86
1876	654	620	4	634	478	96
1875	623	590	3	722	556	99
1874	707	669	3	767	593	102
1873	675	631	2	856	683	99
1872	578	539	4	824	662	86
1871	603	564	6	704	557	84
1870	507	473	3	608	475	80
1869	395	365	2	567	450	69
1868	428	395	2	505	382	67
1867	401	369	1	550	430	58
1866	481	446	1	572	459	51
1865	279	261	—	343	256	45
1864	304	288	—	418	339	34
1863	313	287	1	328	260	31
1862	272	248	1	272	211	30
1861	303	261	1	406	344	24
1860	438	401	2	438	376	25
1859	384	358	1	416	352	23
1858	350	326	2	334	293	15
1857	385	366	2	416	375	15
1856	359	329	2	378	327	23
1855	303	279	2	325	272	22
1854	314	281	4	377	316	20
1853	258	231	4	333	279	16
1852	232	211	4	265	221	15
1851	251	219	4	271	225	13
1850	166	153	4	210	185	12
1849	166	146	3	173	154	12
1848	174	155	2	188	161	12
1847	181	160	2	178	151	9
1846	133	114	2	143	126	9
1845	135	115	1	138	120	9
1844	126	112	1	126	111	7
1843	101	85	1	81	66	7
1842	119	105	1	119	102	8
1841	136	122	1	148	130	8
1840	160	133	1	134	109	12
1839	135	121	1	188	165	14
1838	128	109	1	135	116	10
1837	133	118	2	161	144	9
1836	141	129	2	209	194	9
1835	132	122	1	166	153	7
1834	116	105	1	140	129	6
1833	101	90	1	119	110	5
1832	101	88	1	112	103	5
1831	97	82	1	112	103	4
1830	86	74	1	79	71	5
1829	83	73	—	83	75	5
1828	84	73	1	97	89	4
1827	98	83	—	90	80	5
1826	91	78	—	95	85	5
1825	112	100	—	106	96	5
1824	90	77	—	90	81	5
1823	89	75	—	87	78	5
1822	83	73	—	92	83	5

See footnotes at end of table.

Series U 1-25. Balance of International Payments: 1790 to 1991—Cont'd.

(In millions of dollars. For fiscal years, 1790-1900; thereafter, calendar years)

| Year | Exports of goods and services [1] | | Imports of goods and services | | |
| | Total | Merchandise, adjusted [2] | Total | Merchandise, adjusted | Income on foreign investments in U.S. [3] |
	1	2	8	9	13
1821	76	66	72	63	5
1820	84	70	84	75	5
1819	91	72	105	94	6
1818	116	95	141	128	6
1817	103	89	113	102	7
1816	105	84	163	151	5
1815	81	55	96	85	4
1814	11	8	20	16	3
1813	45	32	30	22	4
1812	75	39	96	83	3
1811	114	63	78	61	5
1810	117	68	110	91	6
1809	88	55	76	61	6
1808	55	26	71	58	5
1807	162	109	167	146	5
1806	148	105	155	137	4
1805	134	97	144	128	4
1804	114	81	102	87	5
1803	88	59	80	67	4
1802	98	75	91	78	5
1801	134	95	132	114	5
1800	107	74	108	93	5
1799	111	80	96	81	6
1798	83	62	84	72	6
1797	79	57	90	77	5
1796	94	67	97	84	5
1795	72	48	85	73	4
1794	55	36	46	36	5
1793	43	28	42	33	5
1792	32	23	40	33	4
1791	29	21	37	31	4
1790	29	21	30	24	4

[1] Prior to 1946, includes transfers of goods and services under U.S. military grant programs.
[2] Includes receipts from military cash and credit transactions, the major portion of which is merchandise.

[3] Net for 1790-1900.
[4] Comparable with later years.
[5] Comparable with earlier years.

Series U 26-39. International Investment Position of the United States: 1843 to 1990

(In billions of dollars)

Year	U.S. investments abroad			Total foreign investments in U.S.	Year	U.S. investments abroad			Total foreign investments in U.S.
	Total [1]	Total private	U.S. government			Total [1]	Total private	U.S. government	
	26	27	32	33		26	27	32	33
1990	1,764.0	1,508.1	81.2	2,176.2	1960	85.6	49.3	36.3	40.9
1989	1,672.5	1,253.5	84.3	2,076.2	1959	82.2	44.8	37.4	39.1
1988	1,533.6	1,132.2	85.5	1,796.7	1958	79.2	41.1	38.1	34.4
1987	1,463.4	1,041.5	88.5	1,553.9	1957	76.4	36.9	39.5	30.7
1986	1,319.0	935.2	89.5	1,347.2	1956	70.8	33.4	37.4	30.5
1985	1,173.8	818.8	87.6	1,066.9	1955	65.1	29.1	35.9	27.8
1984	1,104.6	795.1	84.6	886.4	1954	62.4	26.6	35.8	25.0
1983	893.8	780.8	79.2	787.6	1953	60.2	23.8	36.4	21.9
1982	839.0	730.7	74.3	692,0	1952	59.1	22.7	36.4	20.8
1981	719.6	621.2	68.4	579.0	1951	56.4	20.8	35.6	18.7
1980	606.9	516.6	63.5	500.8	1950	54.4	19.0	35.4	17.6
1979	510.6	433.2	58.4	416.1	1949	53.9	16.9	37.0	14.8
1978	447.8	375.0	54.2	371.7	1948	52.5	16.3	36.2	14.4
1977	379.1	310.2	49.5	306.4	1947	48.3	14.9	33.4	13.8
1976	347.2	282.4	46.0	263.6	1946	39.4	13.5	25.9	15.2
1975	295.1	237.1	41.8	220.9	1945	36.9	14.7	22.2	17.0
1974	255.7	201.5	38.3	197.0	1940	34.3	12.2	22.1	13.5
1973	226.1	165.3	38.8	163.1	1935	23.6	13.5	10.1	6.4
1972	200.6	145.7	36.1	149.4	1931	20.1	15.9	4.2	3.8
1971	180.8	130.5	34.2	123.1	1930	21.5	17.2	4.3	8.4
1970	166.9	120.2	46.7	97.7	1927	17.9	13.8	4.1	6.6
1969	158.1	110.4	47.7	90.8	1924	15.1	10.9	4.2	3.9
1968	146.8	102.5	44.3	81.2	1919	9.7	7.0	2.7	3.3
1967	134.7	93.6	41.1	69.7	1914 (June 30)	5.0	3.5	1.5	7.2
1966	125.2	86.4	38.8	60.4	1908	2.5	2.5	—	6.4
1965	120.4	81.5	38.8	58.8	1897	.7	.7	—	3.4
1964	114.7	75.9	38.8	56.9	1869	.1	.1	—	1.5
1963	103.9	66.6	37.4	51.5	1843	(Z)	—	—	.2
1962	96.5	60.1	36.4	46.3					
1961	92.0	55.6	36.4	46.0					

Z Less than 50 million.

[1] Beginning 1914, includes U.S. monetary gold stock.

Series U 41-46.   Value of Direct Investment in Foreign Countries, by Area: 1929 to 1990

(In millions of dollars)

Year	Total, all areas	Canada	Latin American Republics	Western Europe [1]	Year	Total, all areas	Canada	Latin American Republics	Western Europe [1]
	41	42	43	44		41	42	43	44
1990	421,494	68,431	72,467	204,204	1968	64,983	19,535	11,033	19,407
1989	370,091	65,548	62,727	175,213	1967	59,491	18,102	10,270	17,926
1988	335,893	62,656	53,506	157,077	1966	54,799	17,017	9,876	16,234
1987	314,307	57,783	47,551	150,439					
1986	259,582	49,994	34,790	122,165	1965	49,474	15,318	9,441	13,985
					1964	44,480	13,855	8,742	12,129
1985	230,250	46,909	28,261	105,171	1963	40,736	13,044	8,712	10,340
1984	211,480	46,730	24,627	91,589	1962	37,276	12,133	8,474	8,930
1983	207,203	44,339	24,133	92,178	1961	34,717	11,602	8,286	7,742
1982	221,343	44,509	31,175	99,877					
1981	226,359	45,129	30,020	101,514	1960	31,865	11,197	7,481	6,691
					1959	29,827	10,310	8,120	5,323
1980	215,375	45,119	38,761	96,287	1958	27,409	9,470	7,773	4,573
1979	187,658	40,662	22,792	85,056	1957	25,394	8,769	7,434	4,151
1978	167,804	37,071	21,467	69,553	1956	22,505	7,795	6,844	3,561
1977	149,848	35,200	18,882	60,930					
1976	136,809	33,838	17,125	55,139	1955	19,395	6,761	6,031	3,002
					1954	17,631	6,043	5,741	2,643
1975	124,050	31,038	16,394	49,305	1953	16,253	5,349	5,589	2,375
1974	118,819	28,404	14,597	44,782	1952	14,721	4,641	5,355	2,153
1973	103,675	25,541	13,527	38,255	1951	12,979	3,969	4,818	1,989
1972	94,337	25,771	13,667	30,817					
1971	86,198	24,105	12,982	27,740	1950	11,788	3,579	4,445	1,733
					1940	7,000	2,103	2,771	1,420
1970	78,178	22,790	12,252	24,516	1936	6,691	1,952	2,847	1,245
1969	71,016	21,127	11,694	21,650	1929	7,528	2,010	3,519	1,353

[1] Western Europe includes Eastern Europe for 1929, 1936, and 1940 but excludes Turkey for 1936 and 1940.

Series U 47-74.   Value of Foreign Direct Investment in the United States, by Area and Industry: 1937 to 1990

(In millions of dollars. Book value at year end. Covers U.S. business enterprises, including real estate investments, in which there was a foreign interest or ownership of 25 percent or more)

	All areas				Canada			
Year	Total [1]	Petroleum	Manufacturing	Finance and insurance	Total [1]	Petroleum	Manufacturing	Finance and insurance
	47	48	49	50	51	52	53	54
1990	403,735	38,004	159,998	58,437	27,733	1,417	9,327	7,325
1989	373,763	37,201	151,820	58,215	28,686	1,233	9,934	7,227
1988	314,754	36,006	122,582	44,010	26,566	1,181	9,730	5,769
1987	263,394	37,815	93,865	39,455	24,684	1,088	8,085	5,797
1986	220,414	29,094	71,963	34,978	20,318	1,432	6,108	4,283
1985	184,615	28,270	59,584	27,429	17,131	1,589	4,607	4,008
1984	164,583	25,400	51,802	24,881	15,286	1,544	4,115	3,245
1983	137,061	18,209	47,665	10,934	11,434	1,391	3,313	1,061
1982	124,677	17,660	44,065	17,933	11,708	1,550	3,500	1,801
1981	90,421	18,005	29,976	12,574	9,883	1,387	3,519	818
1980	83,046	12,200	32,993	12,027	12,162	1,817	5,227	1,612
1979	54,462	9,906	20,876	7,575	7,154	943	3,615	505
1978	42,471	7,762	17,202	5,231	6,180	723	3,213	397
1977	34,595	6,573	14,030	4,544	5,650	710	3,077	367
1976	30,770	5,921	12,620	2,943	5,907	676	3,386	422
1975	27,662	6,213	11,386	3,152	5,352	596	3,061	341
1974	22,421	5,979	10,685	2,864	4,930	468	2,966	342
1973	18,284	4,649	8,559	2,854	4,044	296	2,430	320
1972	14,868	3,272	7,262	2,911	3,466	243	2,201	353
1971	13,914	3,139	6,722	2,553	3,335	207	2,013	330
1970	13,270	2,992	6,140	2,256	3,117	190	1,836	324
1969	11,818	2,493	5,344	2,189	2,834	132	1,644	352
1968	10,815	2,261	4,475	2,305	2,659	100	1,413	376
1967	9,923	1,885	4,181	2,193	2,575	99	1,397	354
1966	9,054	1,740	3,789	2,072	2,439	98	1,342	386
1965	8,797	1,710	3,478	2,169	2,388	208	1,219	370
1964	8,363	1,621	3,213	2,181	2,284	205	1,129	382
1963	7,944	1,513	3,018	2,045	2,183	213	1,063	337
1962	7,612	1,419	2,885	1,943	2,064	212	1,015	269
1961	7,392	1,325	2,754	2,025	1,989	194	975	274
1960	6,910	1,238	2,611	1,810	1,934	203	932	246
1959	6,604	1,184	2,471	1,734	1,896	207	907	227
1958	6,115	1,099	2,232	1,660	1,835	214	863	222
1957	5,710	1,043	2,083	1,496	1,773	211	816	208
1956	5,459	937	1,940	1,534	1,690	200	775	196
1955	5,076	853	1,759	1,499	1,542	196	711	179
1954	4,633	776	1,582	1,371	1,427	192	651	168
1953	4,251	706	1,451	1,219	1,350	168	611	162
1952	3,945	552	1,377	1,170	1,218	90	592	149
1951	3,658	466	1,274	1,105	1,119	62	525	150
1950	3,391	405	1,138	1,065	1,029	56	468	153
1941	2,312	222	714	521	530	—	—	—
1937	1,882	283	729	412	463	—	—	—

See footnote at end of table.

Series U 47-74. Value of Foreign Direct Investment in the United States, by Area and Industry: 1937 to 1990—Cont'd.

(In millions of dollars. Book value at year end. Covers U.S. business enterprises, including real estate investments, in which there was a foreign interest or ownership of 25 percent or more)

| | | | | | Europe | | | |
| | | | | | | | United Kingdom | |
Year	Total [1]	Petroleum	Manufacturing	Finance and insurance	Total [1]	Petroleum	Manufacturing	Finance and insurance
	55	56	57	58	59	60	61	62
1990	256,496	31,197	125,568	30,329	108,055	15,310	52,955	13,139
1989	242,961	32,476	120,132	31,609	105,511	16,545	51,798	11,859
1988	208,942	33,499	95,641	27,121	95,698	19,522	41,708	11,256
1987	181,006	35,700	74,300	26,336	75,519	17,950	30,372	9,801
1986	144,181	26,139	56,016	21,787	55,935	11,758	16,500	10,163
1985	121,413	25,636	45,841	17,022	43,555	12,155	11,687	6,483
1984	108,211	23,142	39,083	15,945	38,387	10,991	9,179	5,485
1983	92,936	16,326	36,866	8,450	32,152	5,955	9,221	3,777
1982	83,193	15,071	33,032	12,601	28,447	5,444	8,504	5,661
1981	60,510	14,937	21,995	8,841	15,576	-165	6,109	4,330
1980	54,688	10,137	21,953	8,673	14,105	-257	6,159	3,350
1979	37,403	8,010	13,952	5,529	9,796	199	3,547	2,432
1978	29,180	6,569	11,717	3,575	7,638	492	3,014	1,596
1977	23,754	5,523	9,267	3,076	6,397	486	2,305	1,425
1976	20,162	4,999	7,426	2,637	5,802	602	1,963	1,211
1975	18,584	5,478	6,673	2,088	6,331	—	1,833	932
1974	14,627	3,871	7,143	2,181	6,188	1,650	2,476	1,363
1973	12,504	3,438	5,828	2,261	5,649	1,377	2,250	1,506
1972	11,087	3,011	4,836	2,335	4,987	1,297	1,719	1,567
1971	10,336	2,893	4,455	2,047	4,853	1,270	1,615	1,326
1970	9,554	2,777	4,091	1,805	4,127	1,220	1,391	1,141
1969	8,510	2,322	3,530	1,766	3,496	829	1,176	1,143
1968	7,750	2,146	2,941	1,855	3,409	749	1,076	1,239
1967	7,005	1,772	2,669	1,758	3,156	612	1,009	1,189
1966	6,273	1,620	2,335	1,611	2,864	558	906	1,075
1965	6,076	1,481	2,167	1,724	2,852	511	839	1,176
1964	5,819	1,404	2,005	1,723	2,796	498	812	1,154
1963	5,491	1,306	1,881	1,640	2,665	480	779	1,085
1962	5,245	1,203	1,797	1,611	2,474	416	762	1,023
1961	5,129	1,125	1,708	1,690	2,484	381	750	1,091
1960	4,707	1,028	1,611	1,504	2,248	339	722	953
1959	4,452	972	1,501	1,451	2,167	316	698	927
1958	4,070	885	1,332	1,384	2,024	283	640	889
1957	3,753	832	1,248	1,238	1,881	271	611	794
1956	3,598	737	1,155	1,289	1,833	227	566	841
1955	3,369	657	1,040	1,272	1,749	204	510	836
1954	3,049	584	925	1,158	1,590	180	460	751
1953	2,751	538	836	1,014	1,422	163	419	647
1952	2,575	462	782	977	1,345	137	395	626
1951	2,410	404	747	912	1,273	118	388	583
1950	2,228	349	669	870	1,168	95	337	554
1941	1,569	—	—	—	712	—	—	—
1937	1,337	—	—	—	833	—	—	—

[1] Includes industries not shown separately: Mining and smelting, transportation and utilities, trade and miscellaneous.

Series U 187-200. Value of Exports and Imports: 1790 to 1990

(In millions of dollars. For years ending September 30, 1790-1842; June 30, 1843-1915, thereafter, calendar years)

Year	Merchandise[1] — Exports and re-exports — Total (190)	Exports of U.S. merchandise (191)	Total general imports (193)	Excess of exports (+) or imports (-) (196)	Year	Merchandise[1] — Exports and re-exports — Total (190)	Exports of U.S. merchandise (191)	Total general imports (193)	Excess of exports (+) or imports (-) (196)
1991	421,900	400,900	488,100	-66,200	1938	3,094	3,057	1,960	+1,134
1990	393,600	375,100	495,300	-101,700	1937	3,349	3,299	3,084	+265
1989	363,800	349,400	473,400	-109,600	1936	2,456	2,419	2,423	+33
1988	322,400	310,000	441,000	-118,600					
1987	254,100	243,900	406,200	-152,100	1935	2,283	2,243	2,047	+235
1986	217,300	206,400	370,000	-152,700	1934	2,133	2,100	1,655	+478
					1933	1,675	1,647	1,450	+225
1985	213,100	206,900	345,300	-132,100	1932	1,611	1,576	1,323	+288
1984	217,900	212,100	325,700	-107,900	1931	2,424	2,378	2,091	+334
1983	200,500	196,000	258,000	-57,500					
1982	212,300	207,100	244,000	-31,800	1930	3,843	3,781	3,061	+782
1981	233,700	228,900	261,000	-27,300	1929	5,241	5,157	4,399	+842
					1928	5,128	5,030	4,091	+1,037
1980	220,600	216,500	244,900	-24,200	1927	4,865	4,759	4,185	+681
1979	181,900	178,600	209,500	-27,600	1926	4,809	4,712	4,431	+378
1978	143,700	141,000	174,800	-31,100					
1977	121,200	118,900	150,400	-29,200	1925	4,910	4,819	4,227	+683
1976	115,200	113,500	123,500	-8,300	1924	4,591	4,498	3,610	+981
					1923	4,167	4,091	3,792	+375
1975	107,700	106,100	98,500	+9,100	1922	3,832	3,765	3,113	+719
1974	98,100	96,500	102,600	-4,500	1921	4,485	4,379	2,509	+1,976
1973	70,800	69,700	69,500	+1,300					
1972	49,200	48,400	55,600	-6,400	1920	8,228	8,080	5,278	+2,950
1971	43,500	42,900	45,600	-2,000	1919	7,920	7,750	3,904	+4,016
					1918	6,149	6,048	3,031	+3,118
1970	43,224	42,590	39,952	+3,272	1917	6,234	6,170	2,952	+3,281
1969	38,006	37,462	36,043	+1,964	1916	5,483	5,423	2,392	+3,091
1968	34,636	34,199	33,226	+1,410					
1967	31,526	31,142	26,812	+4,714	1915[4]	2,769	2,716	1,674	+1,094
1966	30,320	29,884	25,542	+4,777	1914	2,365	2,330	1,894	+471
					1913	2,466	2,429	1,813	+653
1965	27,470	27,127	21,364	+6,105	1912	2,204	2,170	1,653	+551
1964	26,508	26,156	18,684	+7,824	1911	2,049	2,014	1,527	+522
1963	23,347	23,062	17,138	+6,209					
1962	21,700	21,431	16,380	+5,320	1910	1,745	1,710	1,557	+188
1961	20,999	20,755	14,714	+6,286	1909	1,663	1,638	1,312	+351
					1908	1,861	1,835	1,194	+666
1960	20,575	20,375	14,654	+5,922	1907	1,881	1,854	1,434	+446
1959	17,634	17,451	15,207	+2,427	1906	1,744	1,718	1,227	+517
1958	17,910	17,745	12,792	+5,118					
1957	20,850	20,671	12,982	+7,868	1905	1,519	1,492	1,118	+401
1956	19,090	18,940	12,615	+6,475	1904	1,461	1,435	991	+470
					1903	1,420	1,392	1,026	+394
1955	15,547	15,419	11,384	+4,163	1902	1,382	1,355	903	+478
1954	15,110	14,981	10,215	+4,894	1901	1,488	1,460	823	+665
1953	15,774	15,652	10,873	+4,900					
1952	15,201	15,049	10,717	+4,483	1900	1,394	1,371	850	+545
1951	15,032	14,879	10,967	+4,065	1899	1,227	1,204	697	+530
					1898	1,231	1,210	616	+615
1950	10,275	10,142	8,852	+1,423	1897	1,051	1,032	765	+286
1949	12,051	11,936	6,622	+5,429	1896	883	863	780	+103
1948	12,653	12,532	7,124	+5,529					
1947	[2] 14,430	14,252	5,756	+8,673	1895	808	793	732	+76
1946	[2] 9,738	9,500	4,942	+4,796	1894	892	869	655	+237
					1893	848	831	866	-19
1945	[2] 9,806	9,585	[3] 4,159	+5,646	1892	1,030	1,016	827	+203
1944	[2] 14,259	14,162	[3] 3,929	+10,330	1891	884	872	845	+40
1943	12,965	12,842	3,381	+9,583					
1942	8,079	8,003	[3] 2,756	+5,323	1890	858	845	789	+69
1941	5,147	5,020	3,345	+1,802	1889	742	730	745	-3
					1888	696	684	724	-28
1940	4,021	3,934	2,625	+1,396	1887	716	703	692	+24
1939	3,177	3,123	2,318	+859	1886	680	666	635	+44

See footnotes at end of table.

Series U 187-200. Value of Exports and Imports: 1790 to 1990—Cont'd.

(In millions of dollars. For years ending September 30, 1790-1842; June 30, 1843-1915, thereafter, calendar years)

Year	Merchandise[1] Total (190)	Exports of U.S. merchandise (191)	Total general imports (193)	Excess of exports (+) or imports (-) (196)	Year	Merchandise[1] Total (190)	Exports of U.S. merchandise (191)	Total general imports (193)	Excess of exports (+) or imports (-) (196)
1885	742	727	578	+165	1837	111	94	130	-19
1884	741	725	668	+73	1836	124	107	177	-52
1883	824	804	723	+101					
1882	751	733	725	+26	1835	115	100	137	-22
1881	902	884	643	+260	1834	102	81	109	-6
					1833	88	70	101	-14
1880	836	824	668	+168	1832	82	62	95	-14
1879	710	698	446	+265	1831	72	59	96	-24
1878	695	681	437	+258					
1877	602	590	451	+151	1830	72	59	63	+9
1876	540	526	461	+80	1829	67	55	67	(Z)
					1828	64	50	81	-17
1875	513	499	533	-20	1827	74	58	71	+3
1874	596	569	567	+19	1826	73	52	78	-5
1873	522	505	642	-120					
1872	444	428	627	-182	1825	91	67	90	+1
1871	443	428	520	-77	1824	69	51	72	-3
					1823	68	47	72	-4
1870	393	377	436	-43	1822	61	50	80	-19
1869	286	275	418	-131	1821	55	41	55	(Z)
1868	282	269	357	-75					
1867	295	290	396	-101	1820	70	52	74	-5
1866	349	338	435	-86	1819	70	51	87	-17
					1818	93	74	122	-28
1865	166	137	239	-73	1817	88	68	99	-12
1864	159	144	316	-158	1816	82	65	147	-65
1863	204	186	243	-39					
1862	191	180	189	+1	1815	53	46	113	-60
1861	220	205	289	-70	1814	7	7	13	-6
					1813	28	25	22	+6
1860	334	316	354	-20	1812	39	30	77	-39
1859	293	278	331	-38	1811	61	45	53	+8
1858	272	251	263	+9					
1857	294	279	348	-55	1810	67	42	85	-19
1856	281	166	310	-29	1809	52	31	59	-7
					1808	22	9	57	-35
1855	219	193	258	-39	1807	108	49	139	-30
1854	237	215	298	-61	1806	102	41	129	-28
1853	203	190	264	-60					
1852	167	155	207	-40	1805	96	42	121	-25
1851	189	179	211	-22	1804	78	41	85	-7
					1803	56	42	65	-9
1850	144	135	174	-29	1802	72	36	76	-4
1849	140	132	141	-1	1801	93	46	111	-18
1848	138	130	149	-10					
1847	157	151	122	+34	1800	71	32	91	-20
1846	110	102	118	-8	1799	79	33	79	(Z)
					1798	61	28	69	-7
1845	106	98	113	-7	1797	51	24	75	-24
1844	106	100	103	+3	1796	59	32	81	-23
1843[5]	83	78	42	+40					
1842	100	92	96	+4	1795	48	40	70	-22
1841	112	104	123	-11	1794	33	27	35	-2
					1793	26	24	31	-5
1840	124	112	98	+25	1792	21	19	32	-11
1839	112	102	156	-44	1791	19	19	29	-10
1838	105	96	96	+9	1790	20	—	23	-3

Z Less than $500,000 or less than -$500,000.
[1] Includes gold and silver prior to 1821. Beginning 1961, includes exports and imports of uranium, thorium and related products; beginning 1968, includes silver ore and bullion.
[2] Figures which include estimates of civilian supplies shipped to occupied areas through U.S. Armed Forces and other relief agencies are as follows (in millions of dollars); 1944, 14,414; 1945, 10,560; 1946,10,184; 1947, 15,338.
[3] Does not add due to revisions not carried to detail.
[4] Figures for six-month period July 1, 1915-Dec. 31, 1915, are as follows: Series U 190, 1,853; series U 191, 1,820; series U 193, 913; series U 196, 940.
[5] Period beginning Oct. 1, 1842, and ending June 30, 1843.

Series U 317-334. Value of Exports (Including Re-exports) of U.S. Merchandise, by Country of Destination: 1790 to 1991

(In millions of dollars. Figures shown here are mixed values for 1862-1879. For years ending September 30, 1790-1842; June 30, 1843-1915; thereafter, calendar years. Beginning 1961, includes uranium, thorium and related products. Beginning 1869, includes silver ores, base bullion and refined bullion)

	America			Europe			
Year	Canada [1]	Mexico	Brazil	United Kingdom	France	Germany [2]	Japan [3]
	319	321	322	325	326	327	331
1991	85,103	33,276	6,154	22,064	15,365	21,317	48,147
1990	83,674	28,279	5,048	23,490	13,665	18,760	48,580
1989	78,809	24,982	4,804	20,837	11,579	16,956	44,494
1988	69,233	20,643	4,289	18,404	10,133	14,331	37,732
1987	59,814	14,582	4,040	14,114	7,943	11,748	28,249
1986	45,333	12,392	3,885	11,418	7,216	10,561	26,882
1985	47,251	13,635	3,140	11,273	6,096	9,050	22,631
1984	46,524	11,992	2,640	12,210	6,037	9,084	23,575
1983	38,244	9,082	2,557	10,621	5,961	8,737	21,894
1982	33,720	11,817	3,423	10,645	7,110	9,291	20,966
1981	39,564	17,789	3,798	12,439	7,341	10,227	21,823
1980	35,395	15,145	4,343	12,694	7,485	10,960	20,790
1979	33,096	9,847	3,442	10,635	5,587	8,478	17,581
1978	28,374	6,680	2,981	7,116	4,166	6,957	12,885
1977	25,768	4,822	2,490	5,951	3,503	5,989	10,529
1976	24,106	4,990	2,809	4,801	3,446	5,731	10,145
1975	21,744	5,141	3,056	4,527	3,031	5,194	9,563
1974	19,936	4,855	3,088	4,574	2,942	4,985	10,679
1973	15,104	2,937	1,916	3,564	2,263	3,756	8,313
1972	12,415	1,982	1,243	2,658	1,609	2,808	4,963
1971	10,365	1,620	966	2,369	1,373	2,831	4,055
1970	9,079	1,704	840	2,536	1,483	2,741	4,652
1969	9,137	1,450	672	2,335	1,195	2,142	3,490
1968	8,072	1,378	705	2,289	1,095	1,709	2,954
1967	7,165	1,222	547	1,960	1,025	1,706	2,695
1966	6,661	1,180	575	1,737	1,007	1,674	2,364
1965	5,642	1,104	341	1,615	971	1,649	2,080
1964	4,915	1,107	402	1,532	990	1,606	2,009
1963	4,251	873	405	1,213	813	1,582	1,844
1962	4,045	821	449	1,128	735	1,581	1,574
1961	3,826	828	545	1,206	704	1,343	1,837
1960	3,810	831	464	1,487	699	1,272	1,447
1959	3,825	755	435	1,097	483	878	1,079
1958	3,539	904	567	905	570	887	987
1957	4,041	917	512	1,162	708	1,330	1,319
1956	4,149	860	326	982	829	943	998
1955	3,404	719	273	1,006	536	617	683
1954	2,966	649	507	808	783	505	693
1953	3,197	663	379	826	1,236	363	686
1952	3,003	683	597	787	1,013	450	633
1951	2,693	730	739	1,000	843	523	601
1950	2,039	526	365	548	475	441	418
1949	1,959	468	383	700	497	822	468
1948	1,944	522	497	644	591	863	325
1947	2,114	630	643	1,103	817	128	60
1946	1,442	505	356	855	709	83	102
1945	1,178	307	219	2,193	472	2	1
1944	1,441	264	218	5,243	18	(Z)	—
1943	1,444	187	156	4,505	—	—	2
1942	1,334	148	105	2,529	1	—	—
1941	994	159	148	1,637	2	(Z)	60
1940	713	97	111	1,011	252	(Z)	227
1939	489	83	80	505	182	46	232

See footnotes at end of table.

Series U 317-334. Value of Exports (Including Re-exports) of U.S. Merchandise, by Country of Destination: 1790 to 1991—Cont'd.

(In millions of dollars. Figures shown here are mixed values for 1862-1879. For years ending September 30, 1790-1842; June 30, 1843-1915; thereafter, calendar years. Beginning 1961, includes uranium, thorium and related products. Beginning 1869, includes silver ores, base bullion and refined bullion)

	America			Europe			
Year	Canada [1]	Mexico	Brazil	United Kingdom	France	Germany [2]	Japan [3]
	319	321	322	325	326	327	331
1938	468	62	62	521	134	107	240
1937	509	109	69	536	165	126	289
1936	384	76	49	440	129	102	204
1935	323	66	44	433	117	92	203
1934	302	55	40	383	116	109	210
1933	211	38	30	312	122	140	143
1932	241	32	29	288	112	134	135
1931	396	52	29	456	122	166	156
1930	689	116	54	678	224	278	165
1929	948	134	109	848	266	410	259
1928	915	116	100	847	241	467	288
1927	837	109	89	840	229	482	258
1926	739	135	95	973	264	364	261
1925	649	145	87	1,034	280	470	230
1924	624	135	65	983	282	440	253
1923	652	120	46	882	272	317	267
1922	577	110	43	856	267	316	222
1921	594	222	58	942	225	372	238
1920	972	208	157	1,825	676	311	378
1919	734	131	115	2,279	893	93	366
1918	887	98	57	2,061	931	—	274
1917	829	111	66	2,009	341	(Z)	186
1916	605	54	48	1,887	861	2	109
1915	301	34	26	912	369	29	41
1914	345	39	30	594	106	345	51
1913	415	54	43	597	146	332	58
1912	329	53	35	564	135	307	53
1911	270	61	27	577	135	287	37
1910	216	58	23	506	118	250	22
1909	163	50	18	515	109	235	27
1908	167	56	19	581	116	277	41
1907	183	66	19	608	114	257	39
1906	157	58	15	583	98	235	38
1905	141	46	11	523	76	194	52
1904	131	46	11	537	84	215	25
1903	123	42	11	524	77	194	21
1902	110	40	10	549	72	173	21
1901	106	36	12	631	79	192	19
1900	95	35	12	534	83	187	29
1899	88	25	12	512	61	156	17
1898	84	21	13	541	95	155	20
1897	65	23	12	483	58	125	13
1896	60	19	14	406	47	98	8
1895	53	15	15	387	45	92	5
1894	57	13	14	431	55	92	4
1893	47	20	12	421	47	84	3
1892	43	14	14	499	99	106	3
1891	38	15	14	445	61	93	5
1890	40	13	12	448	50	86	5
1889	41	11	9	383	46	68	5
1888	36	10	7	362	39	56	4
1887	35	8	8	366	57	59	3
1886	33	8	7	348	42	62	3

See footnotes at end of table.

Series U 317-334. Value of Exports (Including Re-exports) of U.S. Merchandise, by Country of Destination: 1790 to 1991—Cont'd.

(In millions of dollars. Figures shown here are mixed values for 1862-1879. For years ending September 30, 1790-1842; June 30, 1843-1915; thereafter, calendar years. Beginning 1961, includes uranium, thorium and related products. Beginning 1869, includes silver ores, base bullion and refined bullion)

	America			Europe			
Year	Canada [1]	Mexico	Brazil	United Kingdom	France	Germany [2]	Japan [3]
	319	321	322	325	326	327	331
1885	38	8	7	398	47	62	3
1884	44	13	9	386	51	61	3
1883	44	17	9	425	59	66	3
1882	37	15	9	408	50	54	3
1881	38	11	9	481	94	70	1
1880	29	8	9	454	100	57	3
1879	30	7	8	349	90	57	3
1878	37	7	9	387	55	55	2
1877	37	6	8	346	45	58	1
1876	33	6	7	336	40	51	1
1875	35	6	8	317	34	50	2
1874	42	6	8	345	43	63	1
1873	33	6	7	317	34	62	1
1872	29	6	6	265	31	41	1
1871	32	8	6	273	27	35	1
1870	25	6	6	248	46	42	1
1869	23	5	6	185	33	38	1
1868	24	6	6	198	26	31	1
1867	21	5	5	225	34	22	1
1866	24	5	6	288	51	22	1
1865	29	16	6	103	11	20	(Z)
1864	27	9	5	97	13	13	(Z)
1863	28	9	5	128	14	14	(Z)
1862	21	2	4	86	20	10	(Z)
1861	23	2	5	108	15	11	(Z)
1860	23	5	6	169	39	15	(Z)
1859	28	3	6	133	30	15	(Z)
1858	24	3	5	129	28	12	(Z)
1857	24	4	5	135	32	15	(Z)
1856	29	4	5	128	35	13	——
1855	28	3	4	92	29	9	(Z)
1854	24	3	4	117	25	9	——
1853	12	4	4	103	22	7	——
1852	10	2	3	81	19	6	——
1851	12	2	3	101	21	6	——
1850	10	2	3	71	18	5	——
1849	8	2	3	78	13	3	——
1848	8	4	3	67	15	4	——
1847	7	1	3	87	19	5	——
1846	7	2	3	46	14	5	——
1845	6	1	3	45	12	6	——
1844	6	2	3	49	13	4	——
1843 [4]	3	1	2	41	12	4	——
1842	6	2	3	40	17	5	——
1841	6	2	3	47	18	5	——
1840	6	3	2	55	20	4	——
1839	4	3	2	57	18	3	——
1838	2	2	2	52	15	3	——
1837	3	4	2	52	19	4	——
1836	3	6	2	58	21	4	——
1835	3	9	2	52	19	4	——
1834	3	5	2	44	15	5	——
1833	4	5	3	32	14	3	——

See footnotes at end of table.

Series U 317-334. Value of Exports (Including Re-exports) of U.S. Merchandise, by Country of Destination: 1790 to 1991—Cont'd.

(In millions of dollars. Figures shown here are mixed values for 1862-1879. For years ending September 30, 1790-1842; June 30, 1843-1915; thereafter, calendar years. Beginning 1961, includes uranium, thorium and related products. Beginning 1869, includes silver ores, base bullion and refined bullion)

| | America | | | Europe | | | |
	Canada [1]	Mexico	Brazil	United Kingdom	France	Germany [2]	Japan [3]
Year	319	321	322	325	326	327	331
1832	3	3	2	29	12	4	—
1831	3	6	2	31	6	3	—
1830	3	5	2	26	11	2	—
1829	2	2	2	24	10	3	—
1828	2	3	2	20	9	3	—
1827	2	4	2	26	11	3	—
1826	2	6	2	21	11	2	—
1825	3	6	2	37	10	3	—
1824	2	—	2	21	10	2	—
1823	2	—	1	22	9	3	—
1822	2	—	1	24	6	3	—
1821	2	—	1	19	6	2	—
1820	—	—	—	24	8	3	—
1819	—	—	—	24	9	4	—
1818	—	—	—	38	12	3	—
1817	—	—	—	33	9	3	—
1816	—	—	—	30	10	4	—
1815	—	—	—	18	7	2	—
1814	—	—	—	—	(Z)	—	—
1813	—	—	—	—	4	(Z)	—
1812	—	—	—	6	3	—	—
1811	—	—	—	14	2	(Z)	—
1810	—	—	—	12	(Z)	2	—
1809	—	—	—	6	—	2	—
1808	—	—	—	3	3	(Z)	—
1807	—	—	—	23	13	3	—
1806	—	—	—	16	11	6	—
1805	—	—	—	15	13	4	—
1804	—	—	—	13	9	6	—
1803	—	—	—	18	4	4	—
1802	—	—	—	16	8	6	—
1801	—	—	—	31	4	11	—
1800	—	—	—	19	(Z)	8	—
1799	—	—	—	19	—	18	—
1798	—	—	—	12	1	15	—
1797	—	—	—	6	4	10	—
1796	—	—	—	17	3	10	—
1795	—	—	—	6	8	10	—
1794	—	—	—	6	1	5	—
1793	—	—	—	6	2	2	—
1792	—	—	—	5	2	1	—
1791	—	—	—	6	1	(Z)	—
1790	—	—	—	7	1	(Z)	—

Z Less than $500,000.

[1] Prior to 1873, data are for trade with British North American Provinces which is a somewhat larger area than the Dominion of Canada. In the year ending June 30, 1873, the U.S. traded with British North American Provinces the following amounts: exports, $34.6 million and imports, $37.6 million. Beginning 1950, includes Newfoundland and Labrador.

[2] Prior to January 1952, East and West Germany; thereafter, only West Germany.
[3] Beginning 1954, excludes Ryukyu Islands. No records available prior to 1855.
[4] For nine months.

Series U 335-352. Value of General Imports, by Country of Origin: 1821 to 1991

(In millions of dollars. Totals shown here in mixed values. For years ending September 30, 1790-1842; June 30, 1843-1915; thereafter, calendar years. Beginning 1961, includes uranium, thorium and related products)

| Year | America | | | Europe | | | |
	Canada [1]	Mexico	Brazil	United Kingdom	France	Germany [2]	Japan [3]
	337	339	340	343	344	345	349
1991	91,141	31,194	6,727	18,520	13,372	26,229	91,583
1990	91,380	30,157	7,898	20,188	13,153	28,162	89,684
1989	87,953	27,162	8,410	18,319	13,014	24,971	93,553
1988	80,921	23,277	9,324	18,042	12,228	26,503	89,802
1987	71,085	20,271	7,865	17,341	10,730	27,069	84,575
1986	68,253	17,302	6,813	15,396	10,129	25,124	81,911
1985	69,006	19,132	7,526	14,937	9,482	20,239	68,783
1984	66,478	18,020	7,621	14,492	8,113	16,996	57,135
1983	52,130	16,776	4,946	12,470	6,025	12,695	41,183
1982	46,477	15,566	4,285	13,095	5,545	11,975	37,744
1981	46,414	13,765	4,475	12,835	5,851	11,379	37,612
1980	41,459	12,580	3,715	9,842	5,265	11,693	30,714
1979	38,046	8,800	3,118	8,028	4,768	10,995	26,248
1978	33,525	6,094	2,826	6,514	4,051	9,962	21,458
1977	29,599	4,694	2,241	5,141	3,032	7,238	18,550
1976	26,237	3,598	1,737	4,254	2,509	5,592	15,504
1975	22,151	3,066	1,467	3,773	2,164	5,410	11,425
1974	22,286	3,386	1,705	4,023	2,305	6,429	12,456
1973	17,715	2,306	1,189	3,657	1,732	5,345	9,676
1972	14,907	1,632	942	2,987	1,369	4,250	9,064
1971	12,692	1,262	762	2,499	1,088	3,651	7,259
1970	11,092	1,209	670	2,194	942	3,127	5,875
1969	10,384	1,029	617	2,120	842	2,603	4,888
1968	9,005	910	670	2,058	842	2,721	4,054
1967	7,107	749	559	1,710	690	1,955	2,999
1966	6,125	750	600	1,786	698	1,976	2,963
1965	4,833	638	512	1,405	625	1,341	2,414
1964	4,239	643	535	1,143	495	1,171	1,768
1963	3,829	594	562	1,079	431	1,003	1,498
1962	3,660	578	541	1,005	428	962	1,358
1961	3,270	538	562	898	485	856	1,055
1960	2,901	443	570	993	396	897	1,149
1959	3,042	435	628	1,137	462	920	1,029
1958	2,674	454	565	864	308	629	666
1957	2,907	430	700	766	256	607	601
1956	2,894	401	745	726	236	494	558
1955	2,653	397	633	616	202	366	432
1954	2,377	328	682	501	157	278	279
1953	2,462	355	768	543	186	277	262
1952	2,386	410	808	485	167	212	229
1951	2,275	326	911	466	263	233	205
1950	1,960	315	715	335	132	104	182
1949	1,551	243	552	228	61	45	82
1948	1,593	246	514	290	73	32	63
1947	1,127	247	446	205	47	6	35
1946	883	232	408	158	63	3	81
1945	1,125	231	311	90	13	1	(Z)
1944	1,260	204	293	84	(Z)	(Z)	(Z)
1943	1,024	192	228	105	(Z)	(Z)	(Z)
1942	717	124	165	134	1	(Z)	(Z)
1941	554	98	184	136	5	3	78
1940	424	76	105	155	37	5	158
1939	340	56	107	149	62	52	161

See footnotes at end of table.

Series U 335-352.   Value of General Imports, by Country of Origin: 1821 to 1991—Cont'd.

(In millions of dollars. Totals shown here in mixed values. For years ending September 30, 1790-1842; June 30, 1843-1915; thereafter, calendar years. Beginning 1961, includes uranium, thorium and related products)

	America			Europe			
Year	Canada [1]	Mexico	Brazil	United Kingdom	France	Germany [2]	Japan [3]
	337	339	340	343	344	345	349
1938	260	49	98	118	54	65	127
1937	398	60	121	203	76	92	204
1936	376	49	102	200	65	80	172
1935	286	42	100	155	58	78	153
1934	232	36	91	115	61	69	119
1933	185	31	83	111	50	78	128
1932	174	37	82	75	45	74	134
1931	266	48	110	135	79	127	206
1930	402	80	131	210	114	177	279
1929	503	118	208	330	171	255	432
1928	489	125	221	349	159	222	384
1927	475	138	203	358	168	201	402
1926	476	169	235	383	152	198	401
1925	454	179	222	413	157	164	384
1924	399	167	179	366	148	139	340
1923	416	140	143	404	150	161	347
1922	364	132	120	357	143	117	354
1921	335	119	96	239	142	80	251
1920	612	179	228	514	166	89	415
1919	495	149	234	309	124	11	410
1918	452	159	98	149	60	(Z)	302
1917	414	130	145	280	99	(Z)	254
1916	237	105	132	305	109	6	182
1915	160	78	99	256	77	91	99
1914	161	93	101	294	141	190	107
1913	121	78	120	296	137	189	92
1912	109	66	124	273	125	171	81
1911	101	57	101	261	115	163	79
1910	95	59	108	271	132	169	66
1909	79	48	98	209	108	144	70
1908	75	47	75	190	102	143	68
1907	73	57	98	246	128	162	69
1906	68	51	80	210	108	135	53
1905	62	46	100	176	90	118	52
1904	52	44	76	166	81	109	47
1903	55	41	67	190	90	120	44
1902	48	40	79	166	83	102	38
1901	42	29	71	143	75	100	29
1900	39	29	58	160	73	97	33
1899	31	23	58	118	62	84	27
1898	32	19	62	109	53	70	25
1897	40	19	69	168	68	111	24
1896	41	17	71	170	66	94	26
1895	37	16	79	159	62	81	24
1894	31	29	79	107	48	69	19
1893	38	34	76	183	76	96	27
1892	35	28	119	156	69	83	24
1891	39	27	83	195	77	97	19
1890	39	23	59	186	78	99	21
1889	43	21	60	178	70	82	17
1888	43	17	54	178	71	78	19
1887	38	15	53	165	68	81	17
1886	37	11	42	154	63	69	15

See footnotes at end of table.

Series U 335-352.   Value of General Imports, by Country of Origin: 1821 to 1991—Cont'd.

(In millions of dollars. Totals shown here in mixed values. For years ending September 30, 1790-1842; June 30, 1843-1915; thereafter, calendar years. Beginning 1961, includes uranium, thorium and related products)

	America			Europe			
Year	Canada [1]	Mexico	Brazil	United Kingdom	France	Germany [2]	Japan [3]
	337	339	340	343	344	345	349
1885	37	9	45	137	57	63	12
1884	38	9	50	163	71	65	11
1883	44	8	44	189	98	57	15
1882	51	8	49	196	89	56	14
1881	38	8	53	174	70	53	14
1880	33	7	52	211	69	52	15
1879	26	5	39	109	51	36	10
1878	25	5	43	107	43	35	7
1877	24	5	43	114	48	33	14
1876	29	5	45	123	51	35	15
1875	28	5	42	155	60	40	8
1874	34	4	44	180	52	44	6
1873	37	4	39	237	34	61	8
1872	36	4	30	249	43	46	7
1871	33	3	31	221	28	25	5
1870	36	3	25	152	43	27	3
1869	29	2	25	159	30	25	3
1868	26	2	24	132	25	22	2
1867	25	1	19	172	29	27	3
1866	49	2	17	202	23	26	2
1865	33	6	10	85	7	10	(Z)
1864	30	6	14	142	11	14	(Z)
1863	17	3	11	113	11	13	(Z)
1862	19	1	13	75	8	14	(Z)
1861	23	1	18	105	32	15	(Z)
1860	24	2	21	138	43	19	(Z)
1859	19	1	22	126	41	18	(Z)
1858	16	1	17	89	33	14	(Z)
1857	22	1	21	127	46	15	(Z)
1856	21	1	19	122	49	15	(Z)
1855	15	1	15	106	32	13	(Z)
1854	9	1	14	146	36	17	—
1853	7	1	15	130	33	14	—
1852	5	1	12	89	25	8	—
1851	5	1	12	93	31	10	—
1850	5	1	9	75	27	9	—
1849	2	1	8	58	24	8	—
1848	3	1	8	60	28	6	—
1847	1	(Z)	7	48	24	4	—
1846	1	1	7	45	24	3	—
1845	1	1	6	45	21	3	—
1844	1	1	7	41	17	2	—
1843 [4]	(Z)	1	4	12	5	1	—
1842	1	1	6	34	17	2	—
1841	1	1	6	46	24	2	—
1840	1	1	5	33	16	3	—
1839	2	1	5	65	32	5	—
1838	1	1	3	36	16	3	—
1837	2	1	5	45	21	6	—
1836	2	1	7	76	32	5	—
1835	1	1	6	60	22	4	—
1834	1	1	5	41	15	3	—

See footnotes at end of table.

Series U 335-352.   Value of General Imports, by Country of Origin: 1821 to 1991—Cont'd.

(In millions of dollars. Totals shown here in mixed values. For years ending September 30, 1790-1842; June 30, 1843-1915; thereafter, calendar years. Beginning 1961, includes uranium, thorium and related products)

| | America | | | Europe | | | |
| | Canada [1] | Mexico | Brazil | United Kingdom | France | Germany [2] | Japan [3] |
Year	337	339	340	343	344	345	349
1833	1	1	5	38	13	2	—
1832	1	1	4	37	12	3	—
1831	1	1	2	44	14	4	—
1830	(Z)	1	2	24	8	2	—
1829	(Z)	1	2	25	9	2	—
1828	(Z)	1	3	33	9	3	—
1827	(Z)	1	2	30	8	2	—
1826	(Z)	1	2	26	8	3	—
1825	(Z)	1	2	37	11	3	—
1824	(Z)	—	2	28	7	2	—
1823	(Z)	—	1	28	6	2	—
1822	(Z)	—	1	35	6	2	—
1821	(Z)	—	1	24	4	1	—

Z Less than $500,000.

[1] Prior to 1873, data are for trade with British North American Provinces which is a somewhat larger area than the Dominion of Canada. In the year ending June 30, 1873, the U.S. traded with British North American Provinces the following amounts: exports, $34.6 million and imports, $37.6 million. Beginning 1947, includes Newfoundland and Labrador.

[2] Prior to January 1952, East and West Germany; thereafter, only West Germany.
[3] Beginning 1954, excludes Ryukyu Islands. No records available prior to 1855.
[4] For nine months.

SECTION V

BUSINESS ENTERPRISE

Highlights

1 As President Calvin Coolidge said, "The business of America is business." This business is conducted by over 14 million firms, but data on the total number and size distribution of firms must be used with caution. There has never been a satisfactory definition of a firm and the boundary between self-employment and a firm is tenuous at best. In addition, there are problems with inactive or partly active firms and seasonal firms. This problem is compounded when an effort is made to group firms into industrial categories whose boundaries are arbitrary and too tidy for real life. There are activities that defy known categories. Because small firms predominate the business landscape, and because many small firms are on the boundary line, a slight difference in method may generate considerable change in the total. If, however, the focus is on activity and output rather than number, then the unequal size distribution of firms becomes a statistical advantage because it permits a more efficient sample design at lower cost. Similarly, mergers and acquisitions, changes in public taste, and cyclical economic fluctuations all help to distort the structural profile of American business in ways of which statisticians may not be conscious.

2 The principal sources of business data include official and nonofficial ones. Official sources include the *Survey of Current Business* published by the Bureau of Economic Analysis and the *Statistics of Income* produced by the Internal Revenue Service. Unofficial sources include publications of Dun & Bradstreet, including *Business Failure Record*.

3 Business firms are conventionally divided into the categories of corporation, partnership, and proprietorship. Of the total of 18.896 million business firms in 1990, proprietorships were the most numerous (13 million), partnerships the least numerous (1.654 million), and corporations in the middle (3.5 million). However, in terms of receipts, corporations accounted for 90%, proprietorships for 6%, and partnerships for 4%.

4 The dependence of U.S. corporations on external funds has been falling steadily since 1970. In 1970, 37.8% of corporate funds were obtained externally, the percentage declined to 17.2% in 1991.

5 Corporate officers received $203 billion in compensation in 1988, compared to $109 billion in 1980. This represented 2.06% of all business receipts.

6 In 1987, there were 4,114,800 firms owned by women in the United States, representing 30% of all firms in number. These firms had total sales and receipts of $98.292 billion, representing 17% of the total receipts of all firms. The percentage of women-owned firms was highest in social services (83%), apparel (55%), personal services (53%), apparel accessory stores (47%), real estate (46%), and business services (38%).

7 In 1987, there were 424,165 Black-owned businesses, 422,373 Hispanic-owned businesses, 21,380 American Indian-owned businesses, and 355,331 Asian and Pacific Islander-owned businesses in the United States. However, there were wide variations in the size and profitability of these businesses. Average sales and receipts were $46,592 for a Black-owned firm, $58,554 for a Hispanic-owned firm, $42,610 for an American Indian-owned firm, and $93,220 for an Asian and Pacific Islander-owned firm.

8 In 1991, there were 628,580 new business incorporations in the United States and 60,432 business failures. The index of net business formations in 1991 (with 1967=100) was 115.4. Despite the recession, the failure rate per 10,000 concerns declined to 75 in 1990 compared to 120 in 1986.

9 In 1991, there were 880,400 business bankruptcies, compared to 360,300 in 1980. Of these, 124,200 were in California.

10 Of the 163,775 Federal contracts awarded in 1990, the share of small minority-owned firms was 4%.

11 The 1980s was the decade of mergers and leveraged buyouts. Between 1980 and 1990, there were 31,673 mergers valued at $1.408 trillion. Of the mergers, 2,386 were leveraged buyouts, valued at $254.536 billion.

12 Employee Stock Ownership Plans (ESOP) multiplied almost six times between 1970 and 1990. In 1990, there were 9,870 ESOPs involving 11.2 million workers.

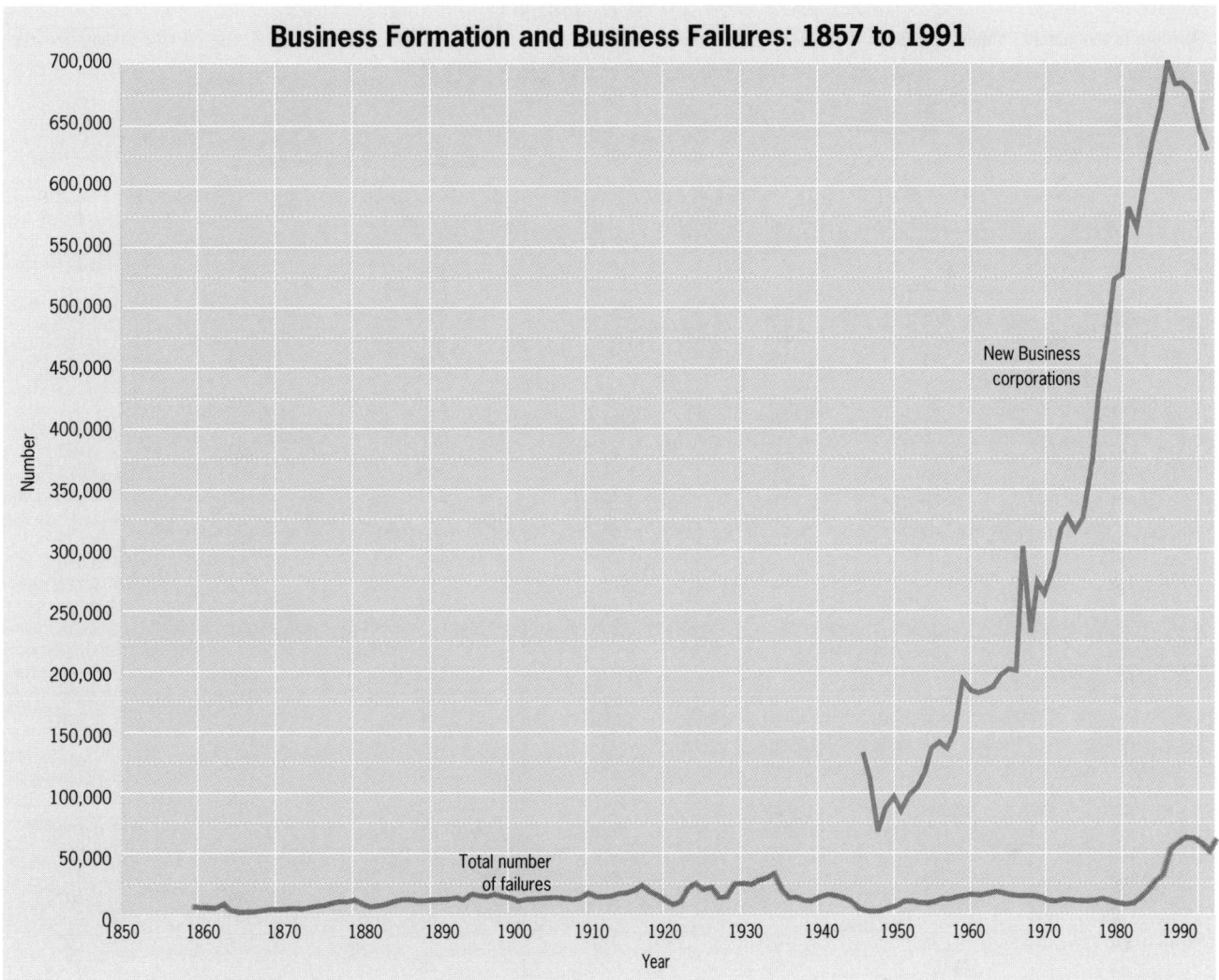

Business Formation and Business Failures: 1857 to 1991

New Business corporations

Total number of failures

Number

Year

13 The vitality of American industry is reflected by the introduction of new consumer products to meet new needs or to utilize new technology. Between 1980 and 1990, 60,151 new products were placed on the market—30,217 were food items, 15,278 were health and beauty products, 6,222 were beverages, 4,479 were household products, 2,354 were miscellaneous, and 1,601 were pet products.

14 In 1992, business expenditures for new plants and equipment, a key indicator of business growth, were $558.6 billion. Manufacturing accounted for $184.1 billion.

15 Corporations with assets over $1 billion accounted for only 0.05% of all corporations in number; yet, they accounted for 71.2% of corporate assets and 73.2% of net profits. In 1991, the top 500 corporations had sales of $2.263 trillion, assets of $2.458 trillion, and profits of $55 billion. All manufacturing corporations earned 4 cents on each dollar of sales, had a ratio of profits to stockholders' equity of 10.7%, and a ratio of stockholders' equity to debt of 1.3.

16 Corporate spending on philanthropy is meager. As a percentage of worldwide pretax income, manufacturing corporations spent only 0.9% on philanthropy in 1990.

Series V 1-12. Proprietorships, Partnerships and Corporations—Number, Receipts and Profit: 1939 to 1988

(Number in thousands; money figures in billions of dollars. Based on sample of unaudited tax returns filed for accounting periods ending between July 1 of year shown and June 30 of following year)

| Year | Proprietorships | | Partnerships | | Corporations | |
	Number	Business receipts	Number	Total receipts	Number	Total receipts
	4	5	7	8	10	11
1988	13,679	672	1,654	464	3,563	9,804
1987	13,091	611	1,648	411	3,612	9,186
1986	12,394	559	1,703	379	3,429	8,282
1985	11,929	540	1,714	349	3,277	8,050
1984	11,262	516	1,644	375	3,171	7,861
1983	10,704	465	1,542	291	2,999	7,135
1982	10,106	434	1,514	297	2,926	7,024
1981	9,585	427	1,461	272	2,812	7,026
1980	8,932	411	1,380	286	2,711	6,172
1979	—	—	1,300	258	2,557	5,599
1978	—	—	1,234	219	2,377	4,715
1977	—	—	1,153	177	2,242	4,128
1976	—	—	1,096	160	2,082	3,635
1975	7,221	274	1,073	147	2,024	3,199
1974	—	—	1,062	139	1,966	3,090
1973	—	—	1,039	124	1,905	2,558
1972	—	—	992	104	1,813	2,171
1971	—	—	959	100	1,733	1,906
1970	9,399	238	936	93	1,665	1,751
1969	9,429	234	920	87	1,659	1,680
1968	9,212	222	918	83	1,542	1,508
1967	9,126	211	906	80	1,534	1,375
1966	9,087	207	923	80	1,469	1,307
1965	9,078	199	914	75	1,424	1,195
1964	9,193	189	922	75	1,374	1,087
1963	9,136	182	924	73	1,323	1,009
1962	9,193	178	932	74	1,268	949
1961	9,242	171	939	75	1,190	873
1960	9,090	171	941	74	1,141	849
1959	9,142	176	949	78	1,074	817
1958	8,800	163	954	78	990	735
1957	8,738	163	971	82	940	720
1956	8,973	(NA)	(NA)	(NA)	886	680
1955	8,239	139	(NA)	(NA)	807	642
1954	7,786	(NA)	(NA)	(NA)	723	555
1953	7,715	144	959	79	698	558
1952	6,873	(NA)	(NA)	(NA)	672	531
1951	7,340	132	(NA)	(NA)	652	517
1950	6,865	(NA)	(NA)	(NA)	629	458
1949	6,901	110	(NA)	(NA)	615	393
1948	7,208	(NA)	(NA)	(NA)	594	411
1947	6,624	101	889	60	552	368
1946	6,944	(NA)	(NA)	(NA)	491	289
1945	5,689	79	627	47	421	255
1944	6,134	66	(NA)	(NA)	412	262
1943	5,121	58	(NA)	(NA)	421	250
1942	(NA)	(NA)	(NA)	(NA)	443	218
1941	3,169	38	(NA)	(NA)	469	190
1940	2,018	31	(NA)	(NA)	473	148
1939	1,052	24	271	13	470	133

NA Not available.

Series V 20-30. Business Formation and Business Failures: 1857 to 1991

Year	Total concerns in business (1,000)	New business corporations (number)	Business failure rate [2]	Total number of failures	Total current liabilities (mil. dol.)	Year	Total concerns in business (1,000)	Business failure rate [2]	Total number of failures	Total current liabilities (mil. dol.)
	20	**21**	**23**	**24**	**27**		**20**	**23**	**24**	**27**
1991	8,218	629,000	—	—	—	1935	1,983	62	12,244	311
1990	8,039	647,000	75	60,432	64,044	1934	1,974	61	12,091	334
1989	7,694	677,000	65	50,361	44,261	1933 [3]	1,961	100	19,859	458
1988	5,804	685,000	98	57,098	39,126	1932	2,077	154	31,822	928
1987	6,004	685,000	102	61,111	34,724	1931	1,215	133	28,285	736
1986	5,119	702,000	120	61,616	44,724					
						1930	2,183	122	26,355	668
1985	4,990	663,000	115	57,078	36,937	1929	2,213	104	22,909	483
1984	4,885	635,000	107	52,078	29,269	1928	2,199	109	23,842	490
1983	2,851	602,000	110	31,334	16,073	1927	2,172	106	23,146	520
1982	2,806	566,000	68	24,908	15,611	1926	2,158	101	12,773	409
1981	2,745	581,000	61	16,794	6,955					
						1925	2,113	100	12,214	444
1980	2,780	532,000	42	11,742	4,635	1924	2,047	100	20,615	543
1979	2,708	525,000	28	7,564	2,667	1923	1,996	93	18,718	539
1978	2,786	478,000	24	6,619	2,656	1922	1,983	120	23,676	624
1977	2,793	438,000	28	7,919	3,095	1921	1,927	102	19,652	627
1976	2,782	376,000	35	9,628	3,011					
						1920	1,821	48	8,881	295
1975	2,679	326,000	43	11,432	4,380	1919	1,711	37	6,451	113
1974	2,591	319,000	38	9,915	3,053	1918	1,708	59	9,982	163
1973	2,567	329,000	36	9,345	2,299	1917	1,733	80	13,855	182
1972	2,490	317,000	38	9,566	2,000	1916	1,708	100	16,993	196
1971	2,466	288,000	42	10,326	1,917					
						1915	1,675	133	22,156	302
1970	2,442	264,209	44	10,748	1,888	1914	1,655	118	18,280	358
1969	2,444	274,267	37	9,154	1,142	1913	1,617	98	16,037	273
1968	2,481	233,635	39	9,636	941	1912	1,564	100	15,452	203
1967	2,519	306,569	49	12,364	1,265	1911	1,525	88	13,441	191
1966	2,520	200,010	52	13,061	1,386					
						1910	1,515	84	12,652	202
1965	2,527	203,897	53	13,514	1,322	1909	1,486	87	12,924	154
1964	2,524	197,724	53	13,501	1,329	1908	1,448	108	15,690	222
1963	2,544	186,404	56	14,374	1,353	1907	1,418	83	11,725	197
1962	2,589	182,057	61	15,872	1,214	1906	1,393	77	10,682	119
1961	2,641	181,535	64	17,075	1,090					
						1905	1,357	85	11,520	103
1960	2,708	182,713	57	15,445	939	1904	1,320	92	12,199	144
1959	2,708	193,067	52	14,053	693	1903	1,281	94	12,069	155
1958	2,675	150,781	56	14,964	728	1902	1,253	93	11,615	117
1957	2,652	137,112	52	13,739	615	1901	1,219	90	11,002	113
1956	2,629	141,163	48	12,686	563					
						1900	1,174	92	10,774	138
1955	2,633	139,915	42	10,969	449	1899	1,148	82	9,337	91
1954	2,632	117,411	42	11,086	463	1898	1,106	111	12,186	131
1953	2,997	102,706	33	8,862	394	1897	1,059	125	13,351	154
1952	2,637	92,946	29	7,611	283	1896	1,152	133	15,088	226
1951	2,608	83,778	31	8,058	260					
						1895	1,209	112	13,197	173
1950	2,687	93,092	34	9,162	248	1894	1,114	123	13,885	173
1949	2,679	85,640	34	9,246	308	1893	1,193	130	15,242	347
1948	2,550	69,649	20	5,250	235	1892	1,173	89	10,344	114
1947	2,405	112,897	14	3,474	205	1891	1,143	107	12,273	190
1946	2,142	132,916	5	1,129	67					
						1890	1,111	99	10,907	190
1945	1,909	—	4	809	30	1889	1,051	103	10,882	149
1944	1,855	—	7	1,222	32	1888	1,047	103	10,679	124
1943	2,023	—	16	3,221	45	1887	994	97	9,634	168
1942	2,152	—	45	9,405	101	1886	970	101	9,834	115
1941	2,171	—	55	11,848	136					
						1885	920	116	10,637	134
1940	2,156	—	63	13,619	167	1884	905	121	10,638	226
1939 [3]	2,116	—	70	14,768	183	1883	864	106	9,184	173
1938	2,102	—	61	12,836	247	1882	822	82	6,738	102
1937	2,057	—	46	9,490	183	1881	782	71	5,582	81
1936	2,010	—	48	9,607	203					

See footnotes at end of chart.

Series V 20-30.　Business Formation and Business Failures: 1857 to 1991—Cont'd.

Year	Business failures [1]				Year	Business failures [1]			
	Total concerns in business (1000)	Business failure rate [2]	Total number of failures	Total current liabilities (mil. dol.)		Total concerns in business (1,000)	Business failure rate [2]	Total number of failures	Total current liabilities (mil. dol.)
	20	23	24	27		20	23	24	27
1880	747	63	4,735	66	1868	(NA)	(NA)	2,608	64
1879	702	95	6,658	98	1867	(NA)	(NA)	2,780	97
1878	661	158	10,478	234	1866	(NA)	(NA)	1,505	54
1877	637	139	8,872	191					
1876	639	142	9,092	191	1865	(NA)	(NA)	530	18
					1864	(NA)	(NA)	520	9
1875	603	128	7,740	201	1863	(NA)	(NA)	495	8
1874	559	104	5,830	155	1862	(NA)	(NA)	1,652	23
1873	494	105	5,183	229	1861	(NA)	(NA)	6,993	207
1872	500	81	4,069	121					
1871	457	64	2,915	85	1860	(NA)	(NA)	3,676	80
					1859	230	170	3,913	64
1870	427	83	3,546	88	1858	(NA)	(NA)	4,225	96
1869	(NA)	(NA)	2,799	75	1857	204	242	4,932	292

NA Not available.

[1] Commercial and industrial failures only. Excludes failures of banks and railroads and, beginning 1933, of real estate, insurance, holding and financial companies, steamship lines, travel agencies, etc.

[2] Failure rate per 10,000 listed enterprises.

[3] Series revised; not strictly comparable with earlier data.

Series V 38-40. Recorded Mergers in Manufacturing and Mining: 1895 to 1990

(Merger values in millions of dollars)

Year	Recorded mergers (FTC) 38	Value of recorded mergers (Eis) 40	Year	Recorded mergers (FTC) 38	Value of recorded mergers (Eis) 40	Year	Recorded mergers (FTC) 38	Value of recorded mergers (Nelson) 40	Year	Recorded mergers (FTC) 38	Value of recorded mergers (Nelson) 40
1990	4,168	172,319	1965	1,008	—	1941	111	—	1918	—	254
1989	4,167	254,020	1964	854	—				1917	—	679
1988	4,233	240,177	1963	861	—	1940	140	—	1916	—	470
1987	4,024	177,900	1962	853	—	1939	87	—			
1986	4,463	205,958	1961	954	—	1938	110	—	1915	—	158
						1937	124	—	1914	—	160
1985	3,489	145,978	1960	844	—	1936	126	—	1913	—	176
1984	2,543	126,140	1959	835	—				1912	—	322
1983	2,533	52,208	1958	589	—	1935	130	—	1911	—	210
1982	2,346	—	1957	585	—	1934	101	—			
1981	2,395	—	1956	673	—	1933	120	—	1910	—	257
						1932	203	—	1909	—	89
1980	1,889	32,830	1955	683	—	1931	464	—	1908	—	188
1979	1,214	—	1954	387	—				1907	—	185
1978	1,279	—	1953	295	—	1930	799	1,757	1906	—	378
1977	1,182	—	1952	288	—	1929	1,245	1,993			
1976	1,081	—	1951	235	—	1928	1,058	1,653	1905	—	243
						1927	870	727	1904	—	110
1975	—	—	1950	219	—	1926	856	1,135	1903	—	298
1974	1,276	—	1949	126	—				1902	—	911
1973	1,919	—	1948	223	—	1925	554	721	1901	—	2,053
1972	2,113	—	1947	404	—	1924	368	466			
1971	1,011	—	1946	419	—	1923	311	1,171	1900	—	442
						1922	309	502	1899	—	2,263
1970	1,351	—	1945	333	—	1921	487	430	1898	—	651
1969	2,307	—	1944	324	—				1897	—	120
1968	2,407	—	1943	213	—	1920	760	809	1896	—	25
1967	1,496	—	1942	118	—	1919	438	777	1895	—	41
1966	995	—									

Series V 108-140.   Corporate Asset, Liability, Income, Deduction, Tax and Profit Items and Dividends Paid for All Industries: 1926 to 1988

(In millions of dollars, except number of tax returns)

Year	Number of corporate tax returns	Total assets	Total liabilities	Total receipts	Total compiled deductions	Total receipts less total deductions
	108	109	117	129	132	136
1988	3,563,000	16,568,000	16,568,000	10,265,000	9,853,000	413,000
1987	3,612,000	15,311,000	15,311,000	9,582,000	9,244,000	328,000
1986	3,429,000	14,163,000	14,163,000	8,669,000	8,395,000	270,000
1985	3,277,000	12,773,000	12,773,000	8,398,000	8,158,000	240,000
1984	3,171,000	11,107,000	11,107,000	7,861,000	7,629,000	233,000
1983	2,999,000	10,201,000	10,201,000	7,135,000	6,945,000	188,000
1982	2,926,000	9,358,000	9,358,000	7,024,000	6,869,000	154,000
1981	2,812,000	8,547,000	8,547,000	7,026,000	6,814,000	214,000
1980	2,711,000	7,617,000	7,617,000	6,361,000	6,125,000	235,900
1979	2,557,000	6,835,000	6,835,000	5,598,700	5,315,700	283,000
1978	2,377,000	6,014,000	6,014,000	4,714,600	4,467,000	247,400
1977	2,242,000	5,326,000	5,326,000	4,128,300	3,908,900	219,500
1976	2,082,000	4,721,000	4,721,000	3,635,500	3,448,900	186,600
1975	2,024,000	4,287,000	4,287,000	3,198,600	3,052,700	146,000
1974	1,966,000	4,016,000	4,016,000	3,089,700	2,941,500	148,200
1973	1,905,000	3,649,000	3,649,000	2,557,700	2,435,000	122,600
1972	1,813,000	3,257,000	3,257,000	2,171,200	2,071,700	99,500
1971	1,733,300	2,889,000	2,889,000	1,906,000	1,824,000	81,900
1970	1,665,477	2,634,707	2,634,707	1,750,728	1,682,779	67,949
1969	1,658,820	2,445,328	2,445,628	1,680,482	1,598,348	82,135
1968	1,541,670	2,215,625	2,215,625	1,507,786	1,420,309	87,477
1967	1,534,360	2,010,443	2,010,443	1,374,599	1,295,348	79,520
1966	1,468,725	1,844,775	1,844,775	1,306,518	1,225,225	81,293
1965	1,423,980	1,723,524	1,723,524	1,194,601	1,119,860	74,742
1964	1,373,517	1,585,619	1,585,619	1,086,739	1,023,680	63,059
1963	1,323,187	1,481,236	1,481,236	1,008,743	953,006	55,737
1962	1,268,042	1,388,127	1,388,127	949,305	898,463	50,842
1961	1,190,286	1,289,516	1,289,516	873,178	826,144	47,034
1960	1,140,574	1,206,662	1,206,662	849,132	804,633	44,499
1959	1,074,120	1,136,668	1,136,668	816,800	769,145	47,655
1958	990,381	1,064,481	1,064,481	735,338	696,114	39,224
1957	940,147	996,400	996,400	720,414	675,340	45,073
1956	827,916	948,951	948,951	673,493	626,309	47,184
1955	746,962	888,621	888,621	634,508	586,907	47,601
1954	667,856	805,300	805,300	547,001	510,515	36,486
1953	640,073	761,877	[1] 761,877	551,984	512,402	39,582
1952	615,698	721,864	721,864	525,011	486,504	38,507
1951	596,385	647,524	647,524	511,849	468,354	43,495
1950	569,961	598,369	598,369	452,523	409,988	42,535
1949	554,573	543,562	543,562	387,636	359,505	28,130
1948	536,833	525,136	525,136	405,430	371,182	34,248
1947	496,821	494,615	494,625	361,521	330,314	31,207
1946	440,750	454,705	454,705	283,917	258,893	25,025
1945	374,950	441,461	441,461	252,636	231,417	21,220
1944	363,056	418,324	418,324	258,880	232,426	26,454
1943	366,870	389,524	389,524	245,796	217,863	27,933
1942	383,534	360,018	360,018	213,777	190,497	23,280
1941	407,053	340,452	340,452	186,137	169,546	16,592
1940	413,716	320,478	320,478	145,427	135,955	9,472
1939	412,759	306,801	306,801	130,365	123,129	7,236
1938	411,941	300,022	300,022	117,596	113,452	4,144
1937	416,902	303,357	303,357	138,907	131,130	7,777
1936	415,654	303,180	303,180	126,269	118,651	7,618

See footnotes at end of chart.

Series V 108-140.   Corporate Asset, Liability, Income, Deduction, Tax and Profit Items and Dividends Paid for All Industries: 1926 to 1988—Cont'd.

(In millions of dollars, except number of tax returns)

Year	Number of corporate tax returns	Total assets	Total liabilities	Total receipts	Total compiled deductions	Total receipts less total deductions
	108	109	117	129	132	136
1935	415,205	303,150	303,150	112,098	106,599	5,500
1934	410,626	301,307	301,307	99,095	96,058	3,037
1933	388,564	268,206	268,206	82,148	82,787	³639
1932	392,021	280,083	280,083	79,701	83,211	³3,511
1931	381,088	296,497	296,497	105,238	105,725	³487
1930	403,173	334,002	334,002	(²)	(²)	(²)
1929	398,815	335,775	335,778	(²)	(²)	(²)
1928	384,548	307,218	307,218	(²)	(²)	(²)
1927	379,156	287,542	287,542	(²)	(²)	(²)
1926	359,449	262,179	262,179	(²)	(²)	(²)

NA Not available.
¹ Includes deficit of $7,655 million.

² Not available separately for returns with balance sheets.
³ Loss.

PRODUCTIVITY AND TECHNOLOGICAL DEVELOPMENT

SECTION W

PRODUCTIVITY AND TECHNOLOGICAL DEVELOPMENT

Highlights

1 Productivity is the ratio of output to input expressed in a number of ways; the most common is that of output per unit of labor. Work in the field of productivity is carried on by many organizations, particularly the Bureau of Labor Statistics and the National Bureau of Economic Research. Labor productivity also reflects the state of the technology, availability of capital and physical resources, efficiency of management, quality of training, and other factors. Productivity may be affected by the specific year chosen as the weight base, since items which increase most in volume output are those with price declines or lower price increases. Productivity series also suffer from certain statistical limitations since they do not measure the quality of output.

2 Copyright, or that body of exclusive rights granted to authors by law, is the oldest of such protective statutes for intellectual property. The first copyright law of 1790 applied only to maps, charts, and books. Amendments extended the protection to prints (1802); musical compositions (1831); dramatic compositions (1856); photographs (1865); paintings, drawings, sculpture, and models or designs for works of fine arts (1870); performed music (1897); motion pictures and photoplays (1912); performance rights in nondramatic literary works (1952); and electronic books (1978). The original term of copyright was 15 years, with the privilege of renewal for another 14. In 1831, the first term was increased to 28 years, and in 1909 the second term was also increased to 28 years. Before 1891, only citizens or residents of the United States could obtain copyrights; the Act of 1891 extended the privilege to citizens of other countries with which the United States had reciprocal copyright agreements, as well as countries which adhered to international copyright conventions (such as the Universal Copyright Convention of 1952) to which the United States was also a party.

3 A patent is a grant by the government to an inventor and his or her heirs or assigns of the right to exclude others from making, using, or selling the invention without proper authorization. Patents may be obtained for any new and "useful" machine, composition of matter, or process, subject to the requirements of law. Since 1946, inventions useful solely in the utilization of fissionable materials have been unpatentable. Patents have been issued by the Federal

government since April 10, 1790. The first body in charge of issuing patents (known as the Patent Board, or the Patent Commission, or the Commission for the Promotion of Useful Arts) had three members: Thomas Jefferson, Henry Knox, and Edmund Randolph. The responsibility for administering patent laws was vested in the Department of State. The first U.S. patent was issued to Samuel Hopkins of Vermont on July 31, 1790, for a process for making potash and pearl ashes. The patent bore the signatures of George Washington, Thomas Jefferson, and Edmund Randolph. Only three patents were issued in the first year. In 1833, the head of the Patent Office recommended to President Andrew Jackson that his office be abolished because "everything that could possibly be invented has already been invented" (From H.W. Wilson's *Famous First Facts*). From 1790-1861, the term of a patent was 14 years. After 1861, it could be extended for an additional seven years. Since 1861, the term of a patent on an invention has been fixed at 17 years with extensions possible only by a special act of Congress. Patents are numbered serially, beginning with the first patent issued after the Act of July 4, 1836.

4 The Federal Trademark Law of 1870 was based on the patent and copyright clause of the Constitution, instead of the interstate and foreign commerce clause, and was found unconstitutional in 1879. The Trademark Law of 1881 was limited to marks used in foreign commerce, but it was extended to interstate commerce by the Act of 1905. The Act of 1920 permitted the registration of a secondary class of marks not previously registrable. It was superseded by the Act of 1946, which granted registrations for a term of 20 years with a possible renewal for successive 20-year terms.

5 National estimates of funds for research and development (R&D) for the four major sectors of the economy have been made by the National Science Foundation since 1953. The data cover basic and applied research as well as development; the last includes processes, materials, methods, and prototypes. The federal budget provides data on expenditures and/or obligations for research and development on an agency basis.

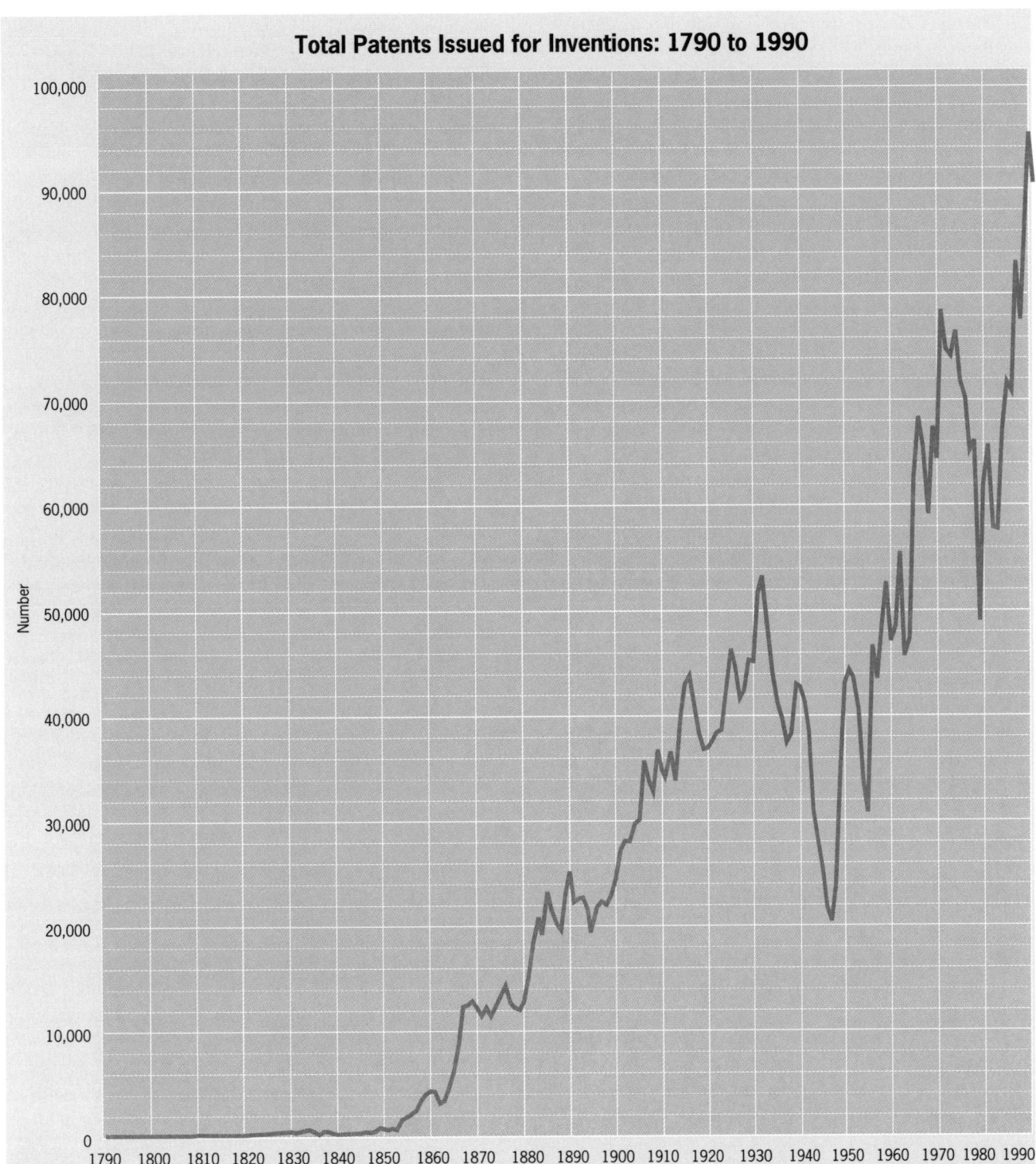

Total Patents Issued for Inventions: 1790 to 1990

6 The top 15 universities receiving federal research and development funds in 1989 were: Johns Hopkins ($411.8 million), Stanford ($239.8 million), MIT ($207.1 million), University of Washington ($203.6 million), University of California-Los Angeles ($170.8 million), University of Michigan ($167.8 million), University of California-San Diego ($166.6 million), University of California-San Francisco ($159.0 million), University of Wisconsin-Madison ($150.4 million), Columbia University ($150.2 million), Yale ($146.2 million), Harvard ($141.7 million), Cornell ($139.9 million), University of Pennsylvania ($132.8 million), and University of California-Berkeley ($131.0 million).

7 In national research and development expenditures as a percentage of the 1990 GNP, the United States ranked below Japan and Germany but slightly above France and the United Kingdom. Japan was the leader with 3% followed by Germany (2.9%), the United States (2.7%), France (2.3%), and the United Kingdom (2.0%). However, in aggregate R&D expenditures, the United States led the world with $110.5 billion. Defense expenditures accounted for $43.2 billion; the falling curve of military-oriented research may significantly change the pattern of research and development in the United States.

8 Foreign graduates constitute over one-fourth of all science and engineering students in doctorate granting institutions of higher education. In certain fields, their

percentage is much higher: engineering (36.0%), physical sciences (36.9%), mathematical sciences (35.2%), and computer sciences (33.1%). In doctorates conferred, the share of foreign students was 21.9%. Asian-Americans received 4.3% of doctorates, while Blacks received 4.2%.

9 The United States has a commanding lead in the number of Nobel laureates. Between 1901 and 1990, Americans received 162 Nobel Prizes (out of a total of 406 awarded) — 115 in chemistry, 69 in physiology and medicine, and 57 in physics. However, a number of these Nobel laureates were naturalized U.S. citizens, and some of them had fled their native lands as refugees.

10 Between 1965 (when the Federal Space Program was fully under way) and 1991, the total expenditures by NASA and the Department of Defense were $328.7 billion, of which NASA's share was 39.5%.

11 In constant 1982 dollars, the Space Shuttle Program cost $46.6 billion between 1973 and 1991, although total costs are likely to be much higher. This program launched 53 space shuttles, of which 14 were named Discovery, 13 Columbia, 12 Atlantis, 10 Challenger, and two Endeavor. These flights remained in space for a total of 318 days.

Series W 82-95. Copyright Registrations, by Type: 1870 to 1991

Year	Total copyright registrations [1]	Total books and pamphlets [2]	Periodicals	Musical compositions	Renewals, all classes [3]	Year	Total copyright registrations [1]	Total books and pamphlets [2]	Periodicals	Musical compositions	Renewals, all classes [3]
	82	83	85	88	95		82	83	85	88	95
1991	663,700	193,800	109,200	191,200	52,300	1933	137,424	40,694	35,464	26,846	6,411
1990	643,500	179,700	111,500	185,300	51,800	1932	151,735	46,576	39,177	29,264	5,888
1989	618,300	153,800	133,900	197,200	38,600	1931	164,642	46,855	42,415	31,488	5,998
1988	565,300	158,100	114,000	159,500	43,800						
1987	582,200	153,900	131,000	161,600	45,500	1930	172,792	47,248	43,939	32,129	5,937
1986	561,000	148,200	130,000	—	45,300	1929	161,959	44,040	44,161	27,023	4,948
						1928	193,914	50,095	47,364	26,897	5,447
1985	539,800	154,500	120,000	147,900	43,800	1927	184,000	47,801	41,475	25,282	4,686
1984	502,700	147,200	113,600	—	37,300	1926	177,635	73,455	41,169	25,484	4,029
1983	488,200	135,300	106,100	127,800	39,100						
1982	468,100	116,300	112,400	125,400	36,300	1925	165,848	65,670	40,880	25,548	3,309
1981	471,100	119,000	118,500	125,000	34,200	1924	162,694	61,982	39,806	26,734	3,433
						1923	148,946	55,561	37,104	24,900	2,689
1980	464,700	119,200	117,900	120,200	33,000	1922	138,633	46,307	35,471	27,381	2,726
1979	429,000	122,800	109,600	108,300	27,000	1921	135,280	41,245	34,074	31,054	2,206
1978	415,700	112,900	110,900	114,800	21,200						
1977	452,700	122,100	106,500	131,200	31,000	1920	126,562	39,090	28,935	29,151	2,112
1976	411,000	113,200	96,000	118,500	27,700	1919	113,003	37,710	25,083	26,209	1,906
						1918	106,728	33,617	25,822	21,849	1,857
1975	401,300	111,900	95,100	114,800	28,200	1917	111,438	33,552	26,467	20,115	1,992
1974	372,800	104,800	92,200	104,500	25,500	1916	115,967	32,897	26,553	20,644	1,628
1973	353,600	104,500	88,600	95,300	23,100						
1972	344,600	103,200	84,700	97,500	23,200	1915	115,193	31,926	24,938	21,406	1,326
1971	329,696	96,124	84,491	95,202	20,835	1914	123,154	31,891	24,134	28,493	1,231
						1913	119,495	29,572	23,002	26,292	1,065
1970	316,466	88,432	83,862	88,949	23,316	1912	120,931	29,286	22,580	26,777	1,349
1969	301,258	83,603	80,706	83,608	25,667	1911	115,198	26,970	23,393	25,525	928
1968	303,451	85,189	81,773	80,479	25,774						
1967	294,406	80,910	81,647	79,291	23,499	1910	109,074	24,740	21,608	24,345	1,007
1966	286,866	77,300	77,963	76,805	25,464	1909	120,131	32,533	21,195	26,306	—
						1908	119,742	30,191	22,409	28,427	—
1965	293,617	76,098	78,307	80,881	23,520	1907	123,829	30,879	23,078	31,401	—
1964	278,987	71,618	74,611	75,256	22,574	1906	117,704	29,261	23,163	26,435	—
1963	264,845	68,445	69,682	72,583	20,164						
1962	254,776	66,571	67,523	67,612	19,274	1905	113,374	29,860	22,591	24,595	—
1961	247,014	62,415	66,251	65,500	18,194	1904	103,130	27,824	21,496	23,110	—
						1903	97,979	27,466	22,625	21,161	—
1960	243,926	60,034	64,204	65,558	21,393	1902	92,978	24,272	21,071	19,706	—
1959	241,735	55,967	62,246	70,707	21,533	1901	92,351	—	(NA)	(NA)	—
1958	238,935	57,242	60,691	66,515	22,593						
1957	225,807	53,503	59,724	59,614	21,473	1900	94,798	—	(NA)	(NA)	—
1956	224,908	53,942	58,576	58,330	20,926	1899	80,968	—	(NA)	(NA)	—
						1898	75,545	—	(NA)	(NA)	—
1955	224,732	54,414	59,448	57,527	19,519	1897	75,000	—	(NA)	(NA)	—
1954	222,665	51,763	60,667	58,213	18,508	1896	72,470	—	12,892	20,951	
1953	218,506	49,059	59,371	59,302	17,101						
1952	203,705	46,083	56,509	51,538	16,690	1895	67,572	—	12,155	18,563	—
1951	200,354	47,125	55,129	48,319	16,372	1894	62,762	—	12,149	18,460	—
						1893	58,956	—	11,094	16,273	—
1950	210,564	50,456	55,436	52,309	14,531	1892	54,735	—	10,327	14,649	—
1949	201,190	47,422	54,163	48,210	13,675	1891	48,908	—	9,477	11,688	—
1948	238,121	48,811	59,699	72,339	15,816						
1947	230,215	49,525	58,340	68,709	13,201	1890	42,794	—	8,164	9,132	—
1946	202,144	42,356	48,289	63,367	12,516	1889	40,985	—	7,646	8,958	—
						1888	38,225	—	7,086	8,066	—
1945	178,848	35,688	45,763	57,835	11,367	1887	35,083	—	6,708	7,744	—
1944	169,269	35,952	44,364	52,087	10,247	1886	31,241	—	6,089	7,514	—
1943	160,795	36,889	42,995	48,348	9,650						
1942	182,232	45,157	45,145	50,023	11,488	1885	28,411	—	6,060	6,808	—
1941	180,647	46,040	42,207	49,135	10,342	1884	26,893	—	5,570	6,241	—
						1883	25,274	—	5,489	6,280	—
1940	176,997	50,125	40,173	37,975	10,207	1882	22,918	—	4,612	6,143	—
1939	173,135	49,901	38,307	40,961	10,177	1881	21,075	—	4,339	5,578	—
1938	166,248	49,156	39,249	35,334	9,940						
1937	154,424	45,504	38,053	31,821	8,589	1880	20,686	—	4,369	5,628	—
1936	156,962	47,667	38,418	33,250	8,180	1879	18,125	—	3,608	4,688	—
						1878	15,798	—	3,242	3,772	—
1935	142,031	43,134	36,351	27,459	6,661	1877	15,758	—	—	—	—
1934	139,047	40,658	35,819	27,001	6,989	1876	14,882				

See footnotes at end of chart.

Series W 82-95.   Copyright Registrations, by Type: 1870 to 1991—Cont'd.

Year	Total copyright registrations [1]
	82
1875	15,927
1874	16,283
1873	15,352
1872	14,164
1871	12,688
1870 [4]	5,600

NA Not available.

[1] Prior to 1941, commercial prints and labels not included in total; jurisdiction moved to copyright office in 1940.

[2] Prior to 1927, contributions to periodicals included with books and pamplets.

[3] Prior to 1941, excludes renewals of commercial prints and labels.

[4] July-December.

Series W 96-106. Patent Applications Filed and Patents Issued, by Type and Patentee: 1790 to 1990

	Patent applications filed			Patents issued		Inventions					
						Corporations					
Year	Inventions	Designs	Botanical plants	Total [1]	Individuals	U.S.	Foreign	U.S. government [2]	Designs	Botanical plants	To residents of foreign countries
	96	97	98	99	100	101	102	103	104	105	106
1990	164,500	11,300	400	90,400	17,300	36,100	36,000	1,000	8,000	300	46,200
1989	152,800	12,600	400	95,500	17,900	38,700	38,000	900	6,100	600	47,900
1988	139,800	11,300	400	77,900	14,300	31,400	31,400	700	5,700	400	39,700
1987	127,900	11,200	400	83,000	15,300	33,800	32,900	1,000	6,000	200	41,700
1986	122,400	9,900	300	70,900	13,300	29,600	27,000	1,000	5,500	200	34,900
1985	117,000	9,600	200	71,700	12,900	31,300	26,400	1,100	5,100	200	33,900
1984	111,300	8,700	300	67,200	12,300	30,100	23,600	1,200	4,900	200	30,500
1983	103,700	8,100	300	56,900	10,500	25,700	19,600	1,000	4,600	200	25,400
1982	109,600	8,200	200	57,900	11,900	25,800	19,200	1,000	4,900	200	25,600
1981	106,400	7,400	200	65,800	14,100	29,500	21,000	1,100	4,700	200	26,500
1980	104,300	7,800	200	61,800	13,300	29,400	18,200	1,000	3,900	100	25,400
1979	100,500	7,500	200	48,900	9,300	23,800	14,800	900	3,100	100	18,200
1978	100,900	7,500	200	66,100	14,300	31,300	19,300	1,200	3,900	200	25,100
1977	100,900	7,300	200	65,300	14,000	31,500	18,200	1,500	3,900	200	23,900
1976	102,300	7,100	200	70,200	14,100	34,400	19,900	1,800	4,600	200	26,100
1975	101,014	6,292	150	71,994	17,192	34,577	18,344	1,881	4,282	150	25,391
1974	102,206	4,780	130	76,275	18,083	37,807	18,686	1,699	4,303	261	25,632
1973	103,695	5,425	118	74,139	16,929	38,615	16,513	2,082	4,033	132	22,638
1972	98,928	5,867	135	74,808	17,729	38,890	16,414	1,775	2,901	199	23,293
1971	104,566	6,211	155	78,316	17,299	43,022	16,048	1,947	3,156	71	22,850
1970	102,868	5,996	188	64,427	13,511	36,896	12,294	1,726	3,214	52	17,872
1969	98,386	5,496	111	67,557	14,772	38,847	12,188	1,750	3,335	103	17,573
1968	93,136	5,171	95	59,102	13,555	34,886	9,172	1,489	3,352	72	13,722
1967	87,872	4,744	103	65,652	15,647	38,353	9,895	1,757	3,165	85	14,711
1966	88,293	4,853	104	68,406	16,018	41,634	9,222	1,532	3,188	114	14,008
1965	94,632	5,413	105	62,857	16,063	37,158	8,096	1,540	3,424	120	12,782
1964	87,597	5,259	120	47,376	12,504	27,836	5,854	1,182	2,686	128	9,168
1963	85,724	4,968	145	45,679	12,525	26,632	5,501	1,021	2,965	129	8,736
1962	85,029	4,897	151	55,691	15,470	32,560	6,380	1,281	2,300	91	10,255
1961	83,100	4,714	107	48,368	13,383	28,351	5,161	1,473	2,487	108	8,384
1960	79,590	4,525	131	47,170	13,069	28,187	4,670	1,244	2,543	116	7,850
1959	78,594	4,879	114	52,408	16,017	29,888	5,081	1,422	2,768	101	8,340
1958	77,495	4,923	134	48,330	15,706	27,116	4,230	1,278	2,374	120	7,395
1957	74,197	4,714	101	42,744	15,154	23,255	3,372	963	2,362	129	6,282
1956	74,906	4,824	104	46,817	16,643	25,502	3,690	982	2,977	101	6,646
1955	77,188	5,764	118	30,432	11,914	16,084	1,744	689	2,713	103	4,065
1954	77,185	5,465	95	33,809	12,531	18,319	2,301	658	2,536	101	4,433
1953	72,284	5,450	99	40,468	16,284	21,230	2,294	658	2,713	78	4,331
1952	64,554	4,993	84	43,616	18,538	22,340	2,035	695	2,959	101	5,635
1951	60,438	4,279	71	44,326	19,192	22,305	2,163	659	4,163	58	4,888
1950	67,264	6,739	105	43,040	18,960	21,782	1,660	622	4,718	89	4,408
1949	67,592	6,998	70	35,131	14,957	18,536	1,127	485	4,450	93	3,105
1948	68,740	7,048	59	23,963	9,812	13,124	628	652	3,968	44	1,984
1947	75,443	7,644	92	20,139	7,784	11,448	669	155	2,102	52	1,617
1946	81,056	10,698	72	21,803	7,444	13,486	585	147	2,778	56	1,656
1945	67,846	8,066	52	25,695	8,981	15,665	580	87	3,524	17	2,112
1944	54,190	5,063	42	28,053	9,636	16,769	645	106	2,914	38	2,564
1943	45,493	2,986	41	31,054	11,654	18,022	524	48	2,228	47	2,625
1942	45,549	4,218	60	38,449	14,534	22,019	1,286	62	3,728	65	3,943
1941	52,339	7,203	67	41,109	16,322	22,632	2,112	43	6,486	62	5,311
1940	60,863	8,530	91	42,238	17,627	22,165	2,406	40	6,145	85	6,148
1939	64,093	7,137	76	43,073	18,583	21,800	2,640	50	5,592	45	6,338
1938	66,874	8,084	48	38,061	16,304	19,635	2,063	59	5,026	41	5,776
1937	65,324	7,207	45	37,683	15,995	19,831	1,824	33	5,136	55	5,638
1936	62,599	6,478	66	39,782	16,639	21,207	1,903	33	4,556	49	5,734

See footnotes at end of table.

Series W 96-106. Patent Applications Filed and Patents Issued, by Type and Patentee: 1790 to 1990—Cont'd.

Year	Patent applications filed			Total [1]	Patents issued						
	Inventions	Designs	Botanical plants		Individuals	Inventions Corporations		U.S. government [2]	Designs	Botanical plants	To residents of foreign countries
						U.S.	Foreign				
	96	**97**	**98**	**99**	**100**	**101**	**102**	**103**	**104**	**105**	**106**
1935	58,117	5,728	72	40,618	17,757	20,821	2,018	22	3,864	45	5,980
1934	56,643	4,399	28	44,420	19,731	22,529	2,131	29	2,919	32	6,489
1933	56,558	3,600	27	48,774	22,713	23,667	2,343	51	2,411	33	7,170
1932	67,006	4,345	46	53,458	26,274	24,822	2,325	37	2,942	46	7,376
1931	79,740	4,190	37	51,756	26,618	23,149	1,961	28	2,438	5	6,897
1930	89,554	4,182	16	45,226	23,726	19,700	1,800	—	2,710	—	6,085
1929	89,752	4,520	—	45,267	25,367	18,500	1,400	—	2,905	—	5,921
1928	87,603	4,761	—	42,357	23,357	17,800	1,200	—	3,182	—	5,218
1927	87,219	4,473	—	41,717	25,417	15,100	1,200	—	2,387	—	4,918
1926	81,365	4,343	—	44,733	28,633	15,200	900	—	2,897	—	5,103
1925	80,208	4,082	—	46,432	30,332	14,800	1,300	—	2,819	—	5,347
1924	87,987	3,635	—	42,574	29,174	12,400	1,000	—	2,670	—	4,723
1923	76,783	3,550	—	38,616	27,016	10,800	800	—	1,927	—	4,133
1922	83,962	4,763	—	38,369	27,369	10,300	700	—	1,609	—	4,455
1921	87,467	5,596	—	37,798	27,098	9,860	840	—	3,265	—	3,963
1920	81,915	4,660	—	37,060	—	—	—	—	2,481	—	3,762
1919	76,710	3,627	—	36,797	—	—	—	—	1,521	—	3,687
1918	57,347	2,234	—	38,452	—	—	—	—	1,206	—	2,883
1917	67,590	3,545	—	40,935	—	—	—	—	1,505	—	3,209
1916	68,075	2,684	—	43,892	31,742	11,540	610	—	1,745	—	3,767
1915	67,138	2,734	—	43,118	—	—	—	—	1,538	—	4,334
1914	67,774	2,454	—	39,892	—	—	—	—	1,711	—	4,595
1913	68,117	2,060	—	33,917	—	—	—	—	1,677	—	4,212
1912	68,968	1,850	—	36,198	—	—	—	—	1,341	—	4,498
1911	67,370	1,534	—	32,856	24,756	7,580	520	—	1,004	—	4,058
1910	63,293	1,155	—	35,141	—	—	—	—	636	—	3,719
1909	64,408	1,234	—	36,561	—	—	—	—	679	—	3,812
1908	60,142	1,131	—	32,735	—	—	—	—	755	—	3,338
1907	57,679	896	—	35,859	—	—	—	—	589	—	3,866
1906	55,471	806	—	31,170	24,750	6,040	380	—	620	—	3,471
1905	54,034	781	—	29,775	—	—	—	—	486	—	3,292
1904	51,168	818	—	30,258	—	—	—	—	553	—	3,285
1903	49,289	770	—	31,029	—	—	—	—	536	—	3,763
1902	48,320	1,170	—	27,119	—	—	—	—	639	—	3,499
1901	43,973	2,361	—	25,546	20,896	4,370	280	—	1,729	—	3,402
1900	39,673	2,225	—	24,644	—	—	—	—	1,754	—	3,483
1899	38,937	2,400	—	23,278	—	—	—	—	2,137	—	2,311
1898	33,915	1,843	—	20,377	—	—	—	—	1,799	—	2,752
1897	45,661	2,150	—	22,067	—	—	—	—	1,620	—	2,221
1896	42,077	1,828	—	21,822	—	—	—	—	1,441	—	2,027
1895	39,145	1,463	—	20,856	—	—	—	—	1,108	—	2,049
1894	36,987	1,357	—	19,855	—	—	—	—	927	—	2,166
1893	37,293	1,060	—	22,750	—	—	—	—	899	—	2,473
1892	29,514	1,130	—	22,647	—	—	—	—	816	—	2,051
1891	39,418	1,025	—	22,312	—	—	—	—	835	—	1,928
1890	39,884	1,046	—	25,313	—	—	—	—	886	—	2,105
1889	39,607	857	—	23,324	—	—	—	—	723	—	2,003
1888	34,713	971	—	19,551	—	—	—	—	832	—	1,536
1887	37,420	1,041	—	20,403	—	—	—	—	948	—	1,466
1886	35,161	645	—	21,767	—	—	—	—	594	—	1,489
1885	34,697	862	—	23,285	—	—	—	—	769	—	1,549
1884	34,192	1,230	—	19,118	—	—	—	—	1,150	—	1,284
1883	33,073	1,238	—	21,162	—	—	—	—	1,017	—	1,259
1882	30,270	948	—	18,091	—	—	—	—	858	—	1,135
1881	24,878	678	—	15,500	—	—	—	—	565	—	995
1880	21,761	634	—	12,903	—	—	—	—	514	—	786
1879	20,059	—	—	12,125	—	—	—	—	591	—	648

See footnotes at end of table.

Series W 96-106.   Patent Applications Filed and Patents Issued, by Type and Patentee: 1790 to 1990—Cont'd.

Year	Inventions; patent applications filed [3]	Patents issued			Year	Inventions; patent applications filed [3]	Patents issued		
		Inventions	Designs	To residents of foreign countries			Inventions	Designs	To residents of foreign countries
	96	99	104	106		96	99	104	106
1878	20,260	12,345	590	581	1857	4,771	2,674	113	45
1877	20,308	12,920	699	590	1856	4,960	2,302	107	31
1876	21,425	14,169	802	787					
					1855	4,435	1,881	70	41
1875	21,638	13,291	915	563	1854	3,328	1,755	57	35
1874	21,602	12,230	886	547	1853	2,673	844	86	26
1873	20,414	11,616	747	493	1852	2,639	885	109	20
1872	18,246	12,180	884	581	1851	2,258	752	90	17
1871	19,472	11,659	903	522					
					1850	2,193	883	83	20
1870	19,171	12,137	737	644	1849	1,955	984	49	17
1869	19,271	12,931	506	377	1848	1,628	583	46	14
1868	20,420	12,526	445	337	1847	1,531	495	60	21
1867	21,276	12,277	325	275	1846	1,272	566	59	19
1866	15,269	8,863	294	244					
					1845	1,246	473	17	12
1865	10,664	6,088	221	181	1844	1,045	478	12	20
1864	6,932	4,630	139	181	1843	819	493	14	8
1863	6,014	3,773	176	125	1842	761	488	1	11
1862	5,038	3,214	195	80	1841	847	490	—	21
1861	4,643	3,020	142	83					
					1840	765	458	—	19
1860	7,653	4,357	183	49	1839	[4] 800	404	—	10
1859	6,225	4,160	107	47	1838	[4] 900	514	—	17
1858	5,364	3,455	102	28	1837	[4] 650	426	—	7
					1836	[4][5] 400	[5] 103	—	8
					1836	—	[6] 509	—	—

Year	Patents issued for inventions	Year	Patents issued for inventions	Year	Patents issued for inventions
	99		99		99
1835	752	1820	155	1805	57
1834	630	1819	156	1804	84
1833	586	1818	222	1803	97
1832	474	1817	174	1802	65
1831	573	1816	206	1801	44
				1800	41
1830	544	1815	173	1799	44
1829	447	1814	210	1798	28
1828	368	1813	181	1797	51
1827	331	1812	238	1796	44
1826	323	1811	215		
				1795	12
1825	304	1810	223	1794	22
1824	228	1809	203	1793	20
1823	173	1808	158	1792	11
1822	200	1807	99	1791	33
1821	168	1806	63	1790	3

[1] Since 1942, includes patents issued to Alien Property Custodian, not shown separately.
[2] Excludes patents issued to Alien Property Custodian.
[3] Applications for reissue included with inventions, 1836-1876; design applications included with inventions, 1836-1879.

[4] Estimate.
[5] From July 4 to end of year.
[6] To July 4.

Series W 107-108. Trademarks Registered and Renewed: 1870 to 1990

Year	Registered 107	Renewed 108	Year	Registered 107	Renewed 108	Year	Registered 107	Renewed 108	Year	Registered 107
1990	53,600	7,200	1960	18,434	3,933	1930	13,246	1,661	1900	1,721
1989	55,300	7,800	1959	18,709	3,272	1929	14,514	1,750	1899	1,649
1988	47,400	6,900	1958	15,351	3,070	1928	14,133	2,049	1898	1,238
1987	47,300	4,100	1957	17,480	3,488	1927	14,579	3,063	1897	1,671
1986	46,700	5,100	1956	20,753	3,756	1926	14,955	4,273	1896	1,813
1985	65,800	5,900	1955	18,207	4,268	1925	13,815	2,278	1895	1,829
1984	48,600	5,400	1954	15,946	3,491	1924	15,727	227	1894	1,806
1983	40,500	6,200	1953	15,610	3,103	1923	14,834	251	1893	1,677
1982	42,400	6,000	1952	16,172	3,419	1922	12,793	254	1892	1,737
1981	42,700	5,900	1951	17,376	3,350	1921	11,363	117	1891	1,762
1980	18,900	5,900	1950	16,817	3,564	1920	10,268	73	1890	1,415
1979	20,500	5,400	1949	15,968	3,788	1919	4,208	64	1889	1,229
1978	29,600	5,500	1948	11,472	5,056	1918	4,061	38	1888	1,059
1977	25,900	6,100	1947	8,976	6,139	1917	5,339	52	1887	1,133
1976	26,300	6,800	1946	8,106	5,725	1916	6,791	55	1886	1,029
1975	30,931	6,132	1945	7,490	4,210	1915	6,262	57	1885	1,067
1974	28,099	5,513	1944	6,025	4,052	1914	6,817	48	1884	1,021
1973	26,112	5,397	1943	5,595	3,835	1913	5,065	—	1883	902
1972	23,252	5,637	1942	6,795	2,894	1912	5,020	—	1882	947
1971	21,019	6,213	1941	8,530	2,765	1911	4,205	—	1881	834
1970	21,745	6,076	1940	9,974	2,547	1910	4,239	—	1880	349
1969	20,613	6,176	1939	10,521	1,398	1909	4,184	—	1879	872
1968	21,528	4,646	1938	10,204	1,051	1908	5,191	—	1878	1,455
1967	20,036	3,801	1937	11,242	1,524	1907	7,878	—	1877	1,216
1966	20,259	3,585	1936	10,722	1,888	1906	10,568	—	1876	959
1965	18,501	3,165	1935	10,886	1,874	1905	4,490	—	1875	1,138
1964	20,087	2,702	1934	11,362	2,445	1904	2,158	—	1874	559
1963	19,740	2,655	1933	9,130	1,671	1903	2,186	—	1873	492
1962	17,023	2,809	1932	9,603	1,587	1902	2,006	—	1872	491
1961	16,595	3,358	1931	11,400	1,643	1901	1,928	—	1871	486
									1870	121

Series W 109-125. Funds Expended for Performance of Research and Development and Basic Research, by Sector and Major Function: 1953 to 1990

(Basic research, applied research, and development; amounts in millions of dollars)

| | | | | By performance sector | | | | | | | | |
| | | | | Industry | | Universities and colleges | | | | | Other nonprofit institutions | | |
Year	Total funds	Percent federal as source	Federal government — Federal funds	Federal funds	Industry funds	Federal funds	Industry funds	Universities and colleges funds [1]	Other nonprofit institutions funds [1]	FFRDC's [2]	Federal funds	Industry funds	Other funds [3]
	109	110	111	112	113	114	115	116	117	118	119	120	121
1990	145,450	44.0	16,100	31,200	73,000	9,250	1,100	4,450	1,200	4,800	2,850	600	1,100
1989	140,486	44.6	15,121	31,366	70,233	8,972	984	3,948	1,083	4,729	2,500	550	1,000
1988	133,741	46.0	14,281	32,306	65,583	8,181	870	3,473	941	4,531	2,200	500	875
1987	125,352	46.2	13,413	30,752	61,403	7,333	789	3,200	831	4,206	2,200	450	775
1986	119,529	45.4	13,535	27,891	59,932	6,702	699	2,790	735	3,895	2,250	425	675
1985	113,818	45.8	12,945	27,196	57,043	6,056	559	2,376	695	3,523	2,400	375	650
1984	101,139	45.1	11,572	23,396	51,404	5,423	475	2,104	615	3,150	2,100	325	570
1983	89,139	45.8	10,582	20,680	44,588	4,983	388	1,929	577	2,737	1,850	275	550
1982	80,317	46.1	9,141	19,059	39,952	4,749	326	1,683	503	2,479	1,625	250	550
1981	71,912	46.4	8,425	16,382	35,476	4,559	288	1,523	448	2,486	1,550	225	550
1980	62,610	47.1	7,632	14,029	30,476	4,104	236	1,334	403	2,246	1,450	200	500
1979	54,933	48.8	7,417	12,518	25,708	3,595	193	1,200	373	1,935	1,350	180	464
1978	48,129	49.6	6,811	11,189	22,115	3,059	170	1,037	359	1,717	1,100	165	407
1977	42,783	50.5	6,012	10,485	19,340	2,726	139	888	314	1,384	987	150	358
1976	38,581	50.6	5,710	9,285	17,392	2,501	123	815	285	1,147	925	120	278
1975	35,196	51.6	5,397	8,605	15,559	2,291	113	743	258	987	875	115	253
1974	32,677	51.2	4,815	8,199	14,617	2,032	96	671	218	865	822	111	231
1973	30,581	53.3	4,619	8,131	13,068	2,041	86	613	200	817	690	105	211
1972	28,296	55.5	4,482	8,010	11,512	1,839	75	576	186	764	653	101	198
1971	27,336	54.9	4,156	7,685	10,647	1,724	70	1,099	177	716	732	100	230
1970	26,545	55.6	3,853	7,779	10,283	1,648	61	961	166	737	748	90	220
1969	26,169	57.0	3,501	8,451	9,867	1,595	60	895	145	725	640	81	209
1968	25,119	59.5	3,493	8,560	8,869	1,572	55	841	131	719	608	73	198
1967	23,613	61.1	3,396	8,365	8,020	1,409	48	753	119	673	577	66	187
1966	22,264	62.8	3,220	8,332	7,216	1,262	42	673	108	630	546	59	176
1965	20,439	63.8	3,093	7,740	6,445	1,073	41	615	93	629	498	53	159
1964	19,214	65.3	2,838	7,720	5,792	916	41	555	83	629	450	47	143
1963	17,371	64.6	2,279	7,270	5,360	760	41	485	73	530	380	48	145
1962	15,665	63.4	2,098	6,435	5,029	613	40	424	66	470	310	45	135
1961	14,552	63.7	1,874	6,240	4,668	500	40	371	58	410	240	41	110
1960	13,730	63.7	1,726	6,081	4,428	405	40	328	52	360	180	40	90
1959	12,540	64.3	1,640	5,635	3,983	306	39	290	47	338	140	35	87
1958	10,870	62.5	1,374	4,759	3,630	254	39	257	42	293	111	31	80
1957	9,912	61.7	1,220	4,335	3,396	229	34	230	38	240	95	30	65
1956	8,483	57.3	1,040	3,328	3,277	213	29	204	34	194	84	30	50
1955	6,279	55.9	905	2,180	2,460	169	25	185	30	180	75	28	42
1954	5,738	54.7	1,020	1,750	2,320	160	22	167	28	141	67	25	38
1953 [4]	5,207	53.0	1,010	1,430	2,200	138	19	151	26	121	60	20	32

[1] Includes state and local government funds received by these institutions and used for research and development.
[2] Federally Funded Research and Development Centers administered by individual universities and colleges and by university consortia.
[3] Includes estimates for independent nonprofit hospitals and voluntary health agencies.
[4] Calendar year data for industry and nonprofit institutions combined with federal and university data for fiscal year 1953 (July 1952-June 1953).

FINANCIAL MARKETS AND INSTITUTIONS
Highlights

1 Financial markets and institutions not only influence but also drive the U.S. economy. Financial data summarize the types of claims, liabilities, and assets, and also illustrate how lending and borrowing are related to income and expenditure flows. They are derived from banking statistics, Treasury accounts, Census data, tax returns, balance of payments, and security market reports. The data present a picture of the distribution of wealth ownership and of the major components of national wealth. Financial data also provide information on the structure of debt—who owes what to whom—which has a bearing on corporate and private spending decisions. Other types of data cover saving, investment, money supplies, U.S. government securities, bonds and mortgages, and corporate equities.

2 Money supply, broadly defined, includes both bank deposits and currency. Prior to 1934, gold was also a part of means of payment, but in January of that year it was withdrawn from circulation. Until 1971, gold served as a means of settlement of international accounts and until 1968 as domestic reserve money. At present, gold is held solely by the Treasury Department. Private gold holdings are forbidden except in limited amounts for licensed purposes. U.S. residents may purchase, hold, or sell foreign and domestic gold coins minted before April 5, 1933 but those minted after that date may be held only by collectors. From 1873 to 1907, gold coins in circulation in the United States were included in the estimates of the Annual Report of the Director of the Mint. In 1934, gold coins worth $287 million were still in circulation, but they disappeared from circulation immediately after the U.S. dollar was taken off the gold standard. Following the enactment of the Old Series Currency Adjustment Act of 1961, both gold and silver certificates were retired.

3 The chief money market in the country is New York City. The New York money market comprises a number of markets with differences in rates corresponding to differences in the supply of funds relative to demand. These markets are called "open" markets since transactions on them are usually made on an impersonal basis with the borrower and lender dealing through agents; as opposed to a "customer" market where borrower and lender deal directly with each other and transactions are often made on a personal basis.

4 Although investment companies date back to the 19th century, they became popular only after the rise of mutual funds. A mutual fund is a company which combines the funds of many investors whose investment goals are similar, and which invests those funds in a wide variety of securities. Different mutual funds have different investment objectives, management policies, and degrees of risk. Some emphasize capital growth; others current income; still others are highly speculative. Mutual funds are technically known as open-end investment companies, because they are always ready to redeem outstanding shares at the request of the investor. They are regulated by both Federal and state governments. The major Federal statutes governing them are the Securities Act of 1933, the Securities Exchange Act of 1934, and the Investment Company Act of 1940.

5 The banking system of the United States has evolved over two centuries. Banks are in part under state governments and part under the Federal government. Supervision and regulation of banks are the primary responsibility of the chartering authorities—the Comptroller of the Currency in the case of national banks organized under the Federal Law of 1863, and state officials in the case of state banks. Two other Federal entities with additional supervisory authority have been superimposed on the banking system: the Federal Reserve System, established in 1914 to exercise central banking functions; and the Federal Deposit Insurance Corporation, created in 1933 to insure bank deposits. The Federal Reserve System includes all national banks and such state banks which choose to join voluntarily. Insurance of bank deposits is obligatory for all banks belonging to the Federal Reserve System and optional for others. Prior to the National Banking Act of 1863, the only official banking statistics were compiled by the Treasury Department based on reports submitted by the banks voluntarily. No data on state banks were included in these reports, but the Act of 1873 authorized the Comptroller to obtain data about non-national banks from state authorities. Although coverage was improved, it was far from complete because many banks operated outside the state system, and some states had no departments to collect the information. Efforts to promote uniformity in bank statistics culminated in 1947 when a standardized balance-sheet report form was approved and

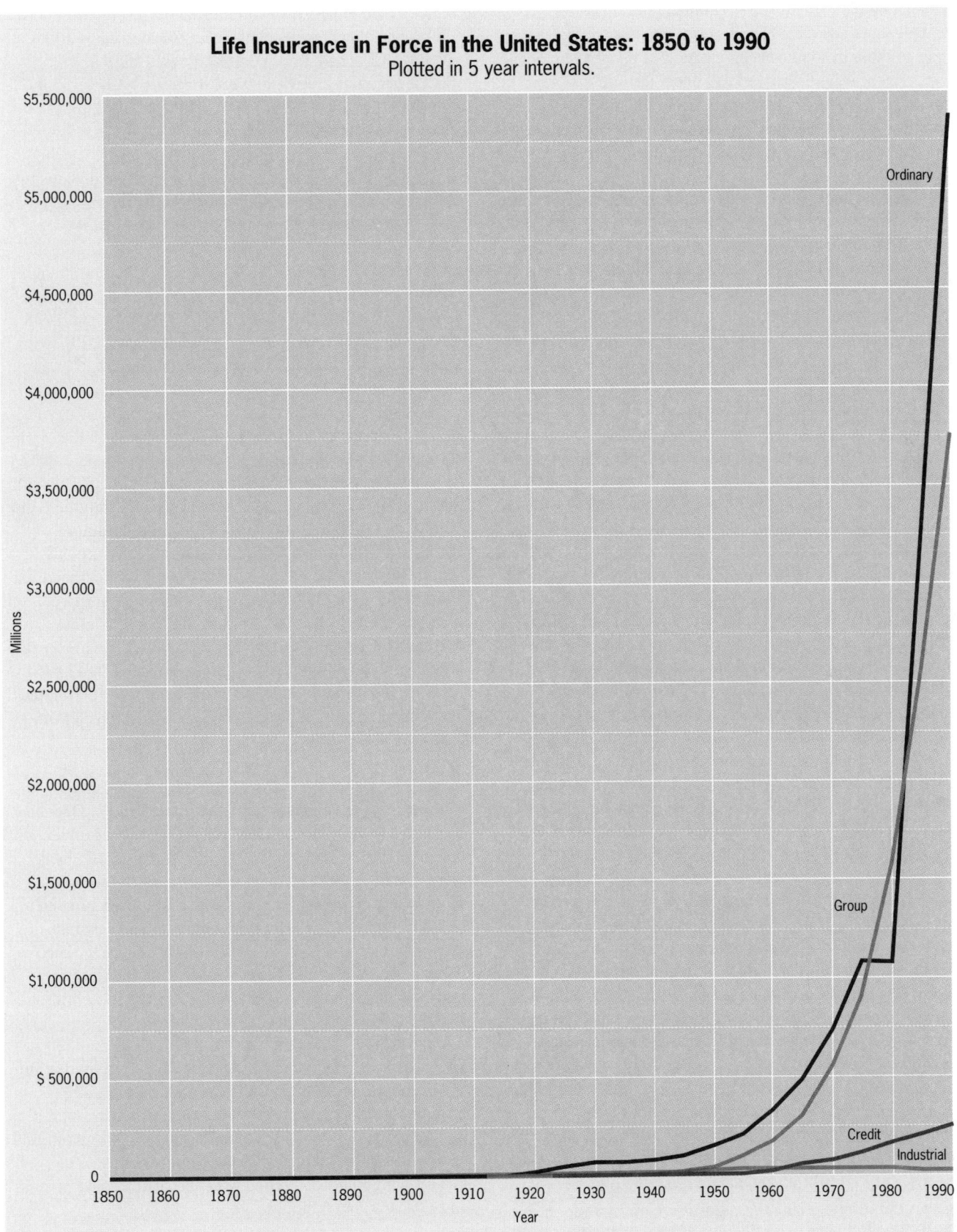

Life Insurance in Force in the United States: 1850 to 1990
Plotted in 5 year intervals.

adopted by the Federal and state banking agencies. To provide more adequate historical banking statistics comparable to those available beginning 1947, a revised retrospective series was published in 1959 under the title *All-Bank Statistics, 1896-1955.* This series covered number of banks, principal assets and liabilities for major classes of banks, and data for individual states and outlying territories.

6 The first bank chartered by Congress was the Bank of North America in Philadelphia founded in 1781. The Bank of the United States was sponsored by the Federalist Party and chartered in 1791 in Philadelphia. Secretary of the Treasury Alexander Hamilton used it as a fiscal agent—a depository bank for government funds. Its charter expired in 1811 and was not renewed by Congress. The Second Bank of the United States was authorized in 1816 and opened in 1817. Its 20-year charter was not renewed either. It failed in 1841 and was liquidated in 1856.

7 There are three sources of primary data about life insurance: Reports of the state insurance departments; commercial publishers, such as A. M. Best Company; and trade associations, such as the American Life Insurance Association.

8 The first life insurance company was the Corporation for the Relief of Poor and Distressed Presbyterian Ministers and of the Poor and Distressed Widows and Children of Presbyterian Ministers, incorporated in 1759 in Philadelphia. The first health insurance company was the Massachusetts Health Insurance Company of Boston, founded in 1847. The first accident insurance company was Travelers Insurance Company of Hartford, chartered in 1863. It issued the first automobile insurance policy in 1898 to Dr. Truman J. Martin of Buffalo—the one-year premium was $11.25. The first fire insurance company to receive a charter was the Philadelphia Contributionship for the Insurance of Houses from Loss by Fire in 1868.

9 Savings institutions are primarily involved in credit extension in the form of mortgage loans. Statistics on savings institutions are collected by the U.S. Office of Thrift Supervision. The Financial Institutions Reform, Recovery, and Enforcement Act of 1989 authorized the establishment of the Resolution Trust Corporation (RTC), which is responsible for the disposal of assets from failed savings institutions.

10 The FIRE (Finance, Insurance, Real Estate) sector contributed 17% to the GNP in 1989. Of the total share of $896.7 billion, real estate contributed $607.1 billion, banking $119.4 billion, and insurance $60.4 billion.

11 In 1989, 72.7% of all households carried some debt, compared to 69.6% in 1989. Of these, 39.9% carried credit cards, 38.7% carried home mortgages, and 35.1% carried car loans. The median debt in 1989 was $15,200, compared to $13,400 in 1983.

12 In 1989, 87.5% of families had assets of some sort; 75.4% had checking accounts, 43.5% had savings accounts, 33.3% had retirement accounts, 22.2% had money market accounts, 19.6% had certificates of deposits, 19% had stocks, and 4.4% had bonds. The median value of financial assets was $10,400.

13 The FIRE sector employed 7.23 million persons in 1990, compared to 6.9 million in 1987. Banks employed 2.161 million, real estate 1.603 million, and insurance 1.462 million.

14 Of the total 66,945 banking offices in the United States in 1990, 63,130 were commercial banks and 3,785 are savings banks. Of the commercial banks, 38,201 were members of the Federal Reserve System and 31,279 were national banks.

15 Over the past 20 years, U.S. banks have lost their former preeminence in the world banking system and have been overtaken by Japanese and German banks. Of the largest 500 banks in the world in 1990, only 96 were American compared to 185 in 1970. In the number of banks, the U.S. share was reduced from 37% to 19% during this period. At the same time Japan increased its share from 14% to 21%, with its number of banks growing from 71 to 106. Among the top 10, Japan is dominant. Germany also slightly increased its presence with 39 banks among the top 500 compared to 37 banks in 1970. Total bank deposits worldwide were estimated at $15.854 trillion of which the U.S. share was 8% and Japanese share 37%.

16 The 1980s represented both the best and the worst of times for U.S. commercial banks. The Federal Deposit Insurance Corporation (FDIC) identified 1,069 problem banks in 1991, compared to 217 in 1980; also, 127 banks were closed in 1991 compared to 11 in 1980. Net income of all banks grew only slightly from $14 billion in 1980 to $18.6 billion in 1991. The percentage of banks losing money grew from 3.7% in 1980 to 10.8% in 1991. The value of nonperforming assets (assets which do not earn interest) rose from $49.5 billion in 1984 to $102.5 billion in 1991.

17 In 1990, there were 288 foreign banks operating in the United States, with 718 offices and assets of $754.7 billion. The most numerous were Japanese banks, which numbered 45 with 137 offices and assets of $408.9 billion (more than half the total assets of foreign banks.) The United Kingdom was second with 11 banks and 42 offices, and assets of $46.6 billion.

18 In 1991, U.S. bank loans overseas amounted to $87.912 billion. Japan was the largest borrower with $16.082 billion, followed by the United Kingdom with $15.688 billion.

19 The number of Federal credit unions declined from 12,977 in 1970 to 8,511 in 1990, and the number of state credit unions from 4,910 in 1980 to 4,349 in 1990. However, membership in the Federal credit unions grew from 11.966 million in 1970 to 36.241 million in 1990, and assets from $8.861 billion to $130.073 billion. Growth of state credit unions was more modest: membership grew from 12.338 million in 1980 to 19.454 million in 1990, and assets from $20.870 billion to $68.133 billion.

20 The nation's 3,500 savings institutions were the hardest hit by the recession at the turn of the decade. In 1989 and 1990 alone, 531 savings institutions were transferred to the Resolution Trust Corporation (RTC) and 605 savings institutions were approved for merger by the U.S. Office of Thrift Supervision. In 1990, they had net losses after taxes of $8.6 billion and their return on assets had deteriorated to -1.08% from 0.57% in 1970. Delinquent mortgage loans cost these institutions $36.3 billion in 1990, when 52,800 mortgage loans were foreclosed.

21 Outstanding mortgage debt reached $3.858 trillion in 1990, compared to $474 billion in 1970. Nonfarm residences accounted for $3.017 trillion. In 1991, the mortgage delinquency rate was 5.02%; lowest in the Pacific region (3.45%), and highest in East South Central region (6.7%).

22 The number of credit card holders is expected to reach 124.8 million in 2000, compared to 86 million in 1980. By 2000, the number of cards is expected to reach 1.319 billion, or over 10 cards per person, and credit card spending $882 billion.

23 Conventional home mortgages reached their lowest interest rates in over 20 years in 1993. The highest recorded rate was 16.55% in 1981, when the Federal Reserve Bank discount rate was 14%.

24 The daily volume of trading on the New York Stock Exchange is 45.599 billion shares (of which 45.266 billion are round lots) with a value of $1.533 trillion. In 1991, 4,094 companies were listed on NASDAQ (National Association of Securities Dealers Automated Questions). The volume of shares traded was 41.311 billion and their value $693.9 billion.

25 In 1990, 3,122 mutual funds were in operation. Of these, 508 were money market funds, 1,133 equity funds, 777 income and bond funds, and 704 municipal bond funds. Together they had assets of $1.069 trillion and serviced 81.8 million shareholder accounts.

26 In 1989, health insurance premiums totaled $108 billion, compared to $11.5 billion in 1970. Of these, group policies accounted for $96.1 billion, and individual and family policies for $11.8 billion.

27 Property and casualty insurance premiums in 1990 totaled $217.8 billion, of which auto insurance accounted for $95.4 billion. Operating earnings (after taxes) for insurers were $8.5 billion.

28 In 1990, there were 2,200 life insurance companies in the United States with sales of $2.024 trillion; 389 million life insurance policies were in force with a value of $9.393 trillion. The average size of a life insurance policy in force was $37,910 and the average amount per household $98,400.

Series X 114-147.   Financial Assets and Liabilities of Households, Personal Trusts, and Nonprofit Organizations: 1945 to 1991

(In billions of dollars)

						Financial assets						
						Deposits and credit market instruments						
						Credit market instruments						
							U.S. government securities					
Year	Total	Total	Demand deposits and currency	Total savings accounts	Total	Total	Agency issues	Savings bonds	Commercial paper	Corporate and foreign bonds	Mortgages	Total corporate equities
	114	115	116	117	120	121	124	125	127	128	129	130
1991	15,190	5,371	583	2,297	1,995	838	334	138	177	178	248	2,334
1990	13,969	5,339	516	2,227	2,004	822	330	126	212	195	226	2,008
1989	13,806	5,002	497	2,226	1,738	739	308	118	195	65	213	2,205
1988	12,222	4,584	479	2,137	1,517	622	212	110	196	52	182	1,877
1987	11,235	4,179	480	2,005	1,297	492	136	101	151	91	165	1,751
1986	11,063	3,945	507	1,946	1,086	552	66	93	60	96	147	1,845
1985	9,707	3,546	381	1,830	1,027	448	91	80	129	19	127	1,700
1984	9,118	3,353	368	1,686	917	495	52	75	30	48	151	1,321
1983	6,057.4	2,916.9	355.7	1,537.6	739.4	328	59.5	71.5	7.9	45.8	183.8	1,466.2
1982	5,377.3	2,645.6	315.9	1,323.8	662.3	277.3	51.1	68.3	14.7	45.7	191.7	1,274.8
1981	4,826.3	2,433.9	299.4	1,187.1	603.7	264.8	56.5	68.2	16.5	50.4	171.2	1,134.3
1980	6,350.0	2,101.0	260.0	1,141.0	523.0	241.0	47.0	73.0	43.0	31.0	107.0	1,111.0
1979	3,827.1	2,007.1	228.4	1,181.1	552.5	243.0	53.6	79.9	40.6	71.6	123.0	906.9
1978	3,374.3	1,795.9	218.9	1,103.9	473.1	172.9	33.3	80.7	—	63.2	106.0	791.9
1977	2,920.6	1,570.0	192.0	992.4	385.6	146.8	29.8	76.8	—	65.3	91.4	634.6
1976	2,788.1	1,424.2	174.8	884.2	365.1	141.2	24.4	72.0	—	65.2	79.8	708.9
1975	2,558.9	1,294.8	170.4	719.6	354.7	138.7	12.5	67.4	10.9	60.9	76.2	646.9
1974	2,183.2	1,147.2	173.9	694.7	278.5	118.2	30.5	62.9	5.3	53.8	38.9	525.2
1973	2,302.3	1,062.2	170.2	635.6	256.4	105.3	21.1	50.8	5.7	56.8	38.1	744.4
1972	—	—	—	—	—	—	—	—	—	—	—	—
1971	2,081.3	353.6	135.1	471.4	218.5	89.0	—	53.9	—	47.5	43.8	—
1970	1,944.3	785.0	126.5	422.4	236.1	100.4	17.4	51.4	6.1	39.8	42.5	763.1
1969	1,867.6	723.9	120.4	377.8	225.7	104.8	14.8	51.1	7.9	27.4	40.2	775.5
1968	1,907.1	681.4	116.7	371.8	192.9	92.7	10.5	51.5	1.9	21.7	38.4	874.4
1967	1,703.4	625.6	104.1	341.5	180.0	88.2	9.0	51.1	(Z)	16.8	36.6	754.6
1966	1,468.7	579.6	92.9	306.8	179.9	89.0	7.9	50.2	2.3	12.8	35.7	595.5
1965	1,485.8	540.6	90.3	287.5	162.8	80.7	4.0	49.6	.1	11.3	34.3	667.0
1964	1,344.7	500.7	82.5	259.5	158.7	79.0	3.8	49.0	(Z)	10.0	35.1	588.7
1963	1,214.4	464.1	77.9	232.1	154.0	77.0	3.3	48.0	.1	9.5	34.8	514.9
1962	1,085.3	430.1	74.1	207.5	148.5	73.0	2.9	46.9	.1	9.7	34.5	437.8
1961	1,112.1	403.3	72.5	181.8	149.0	72.7	2.6	46.4	.2	10.3	33.5	501.6
1960	967.9	381.5	70.2	165.3	146.0	73.5	2.7	45.6	.1	9.8	31.8	396.1
1959	944.6	364.0	69.9	153.8	140.3	73.3	3.0	45.9	.3	9.4	29.9	402.7
1958	878.4	340.0	68.0	142.1	130.0	67.8	1.5	47.7	.3	9.5	28.1	374.0
1957	740.9	322.2	65.6	128.0	128.6	70.7	1.9	48.2	.1	8.5	25.8	267.7
1956	753.6	306.3	66.9	115.9	123.5	70.4	1.2	50.1	.1	7.4	23.9	305.4
1955	707.8	289.2	65.3	106.3	117.6	69.2	.9	50.2	.1	6.6	22.4	286.7
1954	627.4	271.5	64.5	97.5	109.4	66.6	.3	50.0	.1	5.5	21.2	235.0
1953	533.8	259.0	62.9	88.3	107.8	68.6	.4	49.4	.1	5.6	20.0	162.4
1952	520.6	246.4	61.8	80.0	104.6	68.3	.3	49.2	(Z)	5.7	19.0	170.4
1951	486.4	234.6	59.7	72.2	102.7	68.1	.2	49.1	.1	6.0	18.3	156.4
1950	447.5	225.1	56.5	67.3	101.3	69.1	.2	49.6	(Z)	4.9	17.4	133.7
1949	413.1	222.4	54.3	64.8	103.3	69.6	.1	49.3	(Z)	7.5	16.7	109.5
1948	394.7	219.4	56.2	62.1	101.0	68.6	.2	47.8	(Z)	7.7	15.9	100.2
1947	388.6	217.8	58.9	59.9	99.1	68.2	.1	46.2	.1	8.1	14.8	101.3
1946	380.5	213.4	60.3	56.4	96.7	67.1	(Z)	44.2	.1	8.7	13.5	103.5
1945	372.8	203.7	56.4	50.1	97.2	68.3	-.1	42.9	(Z)	9.6	12.0	111.6

See footnote at end of chart.

Series X 114-147.   Financial Assets and Liabilities of Households, Personal Trusts, and Nonprofit Organizations: 1945 to 1991—Cont'd.

(In billions of dollars)

	Financial assets					Liabilities						
							Credit market instruments					
Year	Life insurance reserves	Pension fund reserves	Security credit	Miscellaneous	Total	Total	Home mortgages	Installment consumer credit	Other consumer credit	Bank loans	Security credit	Trade credit
	133	134	135	136	137	138	139	141	142	143	145	146
1991	409	3,473	74	227	4,190	4,061	2,998	744	49	54	50	61
1990	377	2,963	62	217	4,008	3,898	2,848	748	61	43	39	55
1989	352	2,848	53	202	3,609	3,502	2,473	731	64	52	43	49
1988	326	2,451	41	188	3,292	3,189	2,228	675	69	40	44	44
1987	300	2,182	39	171	2,972	2,875	1,970	620	74	42	42	40
1986	274	2,054	39	166	2,739	2,635	1,693	586	137	52	60	31
1985	257	1,795	35	133	2,395	2,296	1,484	527	75	44	51	34
1984	246	1,513	18	117	2,150	2,074	1,344	453	109	37	35	26
1983	240.8	1,321.7	19.3	92.5	1,975.7	1,887.5	1,239.0	396.1	96.9	38.4	48.1	24.0
1982	232.8	1,122.7	16.0	85.3	1,778.7	1,712.1	1,133.3	355.8	85.9	34.4	28.8	22.2
1981	225.6	941.2	12.7	78.5	1,679.3	1,619.2	1,084.8	335.7	80.7	31.2	25.6	19.8
1980	216.0	916.0	16.0	74.0	1,485.0	1,430.0	974.0	302.0	53.0	30.0	25.0	17.0
1979	210.7	622.1	11.3	40.6	1,375.8	1,326.9	875.9	311.3	70.9	23.2	22.9	14.6
1978	188.6	530.1	8.8	59.0	1,209.7	1,164.3	762.3	275.6	64.3	22.7	22.2	9.1
1977	180.8	477.7	7.1	50.3	1,026.1	985.5	653.9	216.6	43.3	36.2	20.5	11.8
1976	172.1	431.8	6.3	44.9	890.4	854.5	566.1	185.5	38.7	30.9	17.2	10.5
1975	166.5	405.6	4.5	40.6	808.0	778.8	507.7	172.3	50.9	13.7	12.1	9.4
1974	157.5	313.7	4.6	35.1	702.2	677.4	411.2	156.1	34.0	21.2	10.7	7.3
1973	150.3	307.8	4.8	32.8	661.1	634.8	379.0	147.4	33.0	24.7	13.1	6.8
1972	—	—	—	—	—	—	—	—	—	—		—
1971	134.8	256.2	—	—	523.8	500.4	316.4	137.2	—	24.4	17.9	
1970	130.3	237.4	2.2	26.3	483.6	463.2	273.1	101.2	25.6	21.9	10.0	5.3
1969	125.0	216.8	2.6	23.8	461.9	440.6	260.4	98.2	24.3	20.4	11.9	4.7
1968	120.0	206.2	3.5	21.6	430.8	407.9	244.1	89.9	23.3	17.5	14.4	4.2
1967	115.4	185.2	2.7	19.8	395.8	375.8	229.4	80.9	21.2	14.4	12.3	3.7
1966	110.6	163.2	1.6	18.2	372.2	356.2	219.0	77.5	20.0	12.2	9.0	3.3
1965	105.9	153.7	1.7	17.0	349.4	333.8	206.4	71.3	19.0	11.9	9.2	3.0
1964	101.1	137.3	1.2	15.7	319.3	305.1	191.1	62.7	17.6	10.5	8.4	2.8
1963	96.6	122.8	1.2	14.8	291.2	277.2	175.1	55.5	16.3	9.1	8.6	2.5
1962	92.4	109.5	1.2	14.3	264.1	252.4	160.4	48.7	15.1	8.6	6.6	2.4
1961	88.6	103.5	1.2	13.8	243.1	231.6	147.7	43.9	14.1	8.1	6.7	2.2
1960	85.2	90.7	1.1	13.3	226.2	216.3	136.8	43.0	13.2	7.2	5.4	2.1
1959	82.0	82.1	1.0	12.8	208.4	198.6	126.0	39.2	12.3	6.7	5.5	2.1
1958	78.5	72.4	1.2	12.3	186.4	177.2	113.4	33.6	11.5	5.7	5.5	1.8
1957	75.5	62.6	.9	12.0	174.0	166.1	104.6	33.9	11.1	5.0	4.4	1.6
1956	72.7	56.6	.9	11.7	161.2	153.2	95.8	31.7	10.6	4.8	4.8	1.5
1955	69.3	50.4	.9	11.4	144.8	137.1	84.6	28.9	9.9	4.4	4.8	1.4
1954	66.3	42.6	1.0	10.9	124.1	117.4	72.4	23.6	8.9	4.1	4.1	1.3
1953	63.6	37.4	.7	10.6	111.8	106.3	63.8	23.0	8.4	3.7	3.0	1.2
1952	60.7	32.4	.7	10.0	98.7	93.8	56.1	19.4	8.1	3.5	2.6	1.1
1951	57.8	27.5	.8	9.3	87.1	82.7	49.7	15.3	7.4	4.3	2.4	.9
1950	55.0	24.0	.9	8.7	77.4	73.0	42.6	14.7	6.8	3.8	2.5	.9
1949	52.1	20.1	.6	8.4	63.2	59.7	35.2	11.6	5.8	2.7	1.8	.8
1948	49.4	17.2	.6	8.0	54.9	51.8	31.1	9.0	5.5	2.5	1.5	.7
1947	46.5	14.8	.6	7.6	46.3	43.1	26.1	6.7	4.9	2.3	1.8	.7
1946	43.4	12.5	.7	7.1	38.7	35.2	21.8	4.2	4.2	2.3	2.2	.6
1945	39.6	11.0	.6	6.3	34.1	28.1	18.0	2.5	3.2	1.8	4.9	.5

Z Less than $50 million or less than -$50 million.

Series X 410-419. Money Stock—Currency, Deposits, Bank Vault Cash and Gold: 1867 to 1991

(In billions of dollars. Annual averages)

Year	Currency held by the public	Demand deposits adjusted, commercial banks	M₁ Money supply (currency plus demand deposits)	M₂ Money supply (M₁ plus time deposits)	Year	Currency held by the public	Demand deposits adjusted, commercial banks	M₁ Money supply (currency plus demand deposits)	M₂ Money supply (M₁ plus time deposits)
	410	412	414	415		410	412	414	415
1991	267	289	898	3,439	1935	4.80	21.08	25.88	39.07
1990	247	277	826	3,339	1934	4.63	17.23	21.86	34.36
1989	223	279	794	3,227	1933	5.09	14.82	19.91	32.22
1988	212	287	787	3,071	1932	4.92	16.19	21.11	36.05
1987	197	287	750	2,911	1931	4.16	19.98	24.14	42.69
1986	181	302	725	2,811					
					1930	3.73	22.03	25.76	45.73
1985	168	267	620	2,569	1929	3.90	22.74	26.64	46.60
1984	156	244	552	2,374	1928	3.89	22.49	26.38	46.42
1983	146	238	521	2,186	1927	3.98	22.12	26.10	44.73
1982	133	234	475	1,952	1926	4.00	22.18	26.18	43.68
1981	123	231	437	1,794					
					1925	3.96	21.70	25.66	42.05
1980	115	261	409	1,629	1924	3.96	19.71	23.67	38.58
1979	106	253	391	1,525	1923	3.96	18.97	22.93	36.60
1978	97	254	364	1,404	1922	3.69	17.98	21.67	33.72
1977	89	240	336	1,296	1921	4.04	17.47	21.51	32.85
1976	81	224	311	1,169					
					1920	4.48	19.25	23.73	34.80
1975	74	214	292	1,024	1919	4.02	17.77	21.79	31.01
1974	68	207	278	908	1918	2.76	16.20	18.96	26.73
1973	62	203	266	860	1917	2.17	14.91	17.08	24.37
1972	57	199	256	822	1916	2.17	12.53	14.70	20.85
1971	53	183	235	727					
					1915	1.93	10.55	12.48	17.59
1970	47.69	162.30	209.98	401.29	1914	1.91	—	—	16.39
1969	44.82	156.94	201.77	385.17	1913	1.89	—	—	15.73
1968	41.97	148.47	190.41	361.60	1912	1.82	—	—	15.13
1967	39.37	138.38	177.77	331.78	1911	1.76	—	—	14.12
1966	37.48	133.58	171.05	308.02					
					1910	1.74	—	—	13.34
1965	35.26	128.54	163.79	285.89	1909	1.71	—	—	12.68
1964	33.49	123.74	157.22	264.73	1908	1.76	—	—	11.44
1963	31.55	119.74	151.28	249.15	1907	1.72	—	—	11.30
1962	30.09	116.91	147.00	233.92	1906	1.63	—	—	11.08
1961	29.10	114.82	143.93	221.24					
					1905	1.50	—	—	10.24
1960	28.99	112.62	141.59	210.67	1904	1.44	—	—	9.24
1959	28.90	114.38	143.27	210.09	1903	1.42	—	—	8.68
1958	28.37	109.98	138.35	201.12	1902	1.34	—	—	8.17
1957	28.26	108.48	136.75	191.82	1901	1.27	—	—	7.48
1956	27.98	108.05	136.02	186.87					
					1900	1.21	—	—	6.60
1955	27.63	106.79	134.44	183.69	1899	1.10	—	—	6.09
1954	27.52	102.75	130.27	177.16	1898	1.00	—	—	5.26
1953	27.78	100.64	128.34	171.19	1897	.92	—	—	4.64
1952	26.70	98.52	125.22	164.92	1896	.89	—	—	4.35
1951	25.53	93.67	119.23	156.45					
					1895	.91	—	—	4.43
1950	25.05	89.08	114.14	150.81	1894	.93	—	—	4.28
1949	25.50	85.67	111.16	147.46	1893	1.00	—	—	4.26
1948	26.07	86.24	112.31	148.11	1892	.96	—	—	4.43
1947	26.58	85.22	111.79	146.00	1891	.96	—	—	4.08
1946	28.48	79.98	103.46	138.73					
					1890	.93	—	—	3.92
1945	25.33	73.91	99.23	126.63	1889	.87	—	—	3.60
1944	21.22	64.12	85.34	106.82	1888	.85	—	—	3.40
1943	16.35	55.89	72.24	89.91	1887	.83	—	—	3.31
1942	11.54	43.82	55.36	71.16	1886	.78	—	—	3.10
1941	8.40	38.12	46.52	62.51					
					1885	.80	—	—	2.87
1940	6.76	32.89	39.65	55.20	1884	.84	—	—	2.80
1939	6.04	28.11	34.15	49.27	1883	.87	—	—	2.80
1938	5.55	24.97	30.52	45.51	1882	.84	—	—	2.63
1937	5.59	25.32	30.91	45.68	1881	.78	—	—	2.44
1936	5.23	24.32	29.55	43.48					

Series X 410-419. Money Stock—Currency, Deposits, Bank Vault Cash and Gold: 1867 to 1991—Cont'd.

(In billions of dollars. Annual averages)

Year	Currency held by the public	M_2, Money supply (M_1 plus time deposits)
	410	415
1880	.67	2.03
1879	.58	1.66
1878	.54	1.58
1877	.54	1.65
1876	.53	1.68
1875	.54	1.72
1874	.54	1.65
1873	.56	1.62
1872	.55	1.61
1871	.54	1.50
1870	.54	1.35
1869	.55	1.28
1868	.54	1.27
1867	.58	1.28

Series X 444-455.   Money Market Rates: 1890 to 1992

(Percent per annum. Open market rates in New York City)

Year	Prime commercial paper, 4 to 6 months [1]	Finance company paper, placed directly, 3 to 6 months [2]	Prime bankers' acceptances, 90 days [1]	U.S. government securities [3], 3-month bills [4], rate on new issues	Federal Reserve Bank of New York discount rate Low	High
	445	**446**	**449**	**450**	**454**	**455**
1992	—	—	—	—	3.50	—
1991	8.46	5.71	5.70	5.38	3.50	6.00
1990	10.01	7.87	7.93	7.50	6.50	6.50
1989	10.87	8.72	8.87	8.11	7.00	7.00
1988	9.32	7.38	7.56	6.67	6.50	6.50
1987	8.21	6.54	6.75	5.78	6.00	6.00
1986	8.33	6.38	6.38	5.97	5.50	7.00
1985	9.93	7.77	7.91	7.47	7.50	7.50
1984	12.04	9.73	10.17	9.54	8.50	9.0
1983	10.79	8.70	8.91	8.62	—	—
1982	14.85	11.23	11.89	10.60	8.50	11.50
1981	18.87	14.08	15.34	14.04	12.00	14.00
1980	15.26	11.49	12.67	11.39	10.00	13.00
1979	12.67	10.47	11.04	10.07	10.50	12.00
1978	9.06	7.80	8.11	7.19	10.00	12.00
1977	6.83	5.49	5.60	5.27	7.00	9.50
1976	6.84	5.20	5.19	4.97	5.75	6.00
1975	7.86	6.15	6.29	5.77	6.25	7.25
1974	10.81	8.65	9.89	7.83	7.75	8.00
1973	8.15	7.40	8.08	7.03	5.00	8.50
1972	4.69	4.52	4.47	4.07	—	—
1971	5.11	4.91	4.85	4.33	4.25	5.25
1970	7.72	7.23	7.31	6.458	5.50	6.00
1969	7.83	7.16	7.61	6.677	5.50	6.00
1968	5.90	5.69	5.75	5.339	4.50	5.50
1967	5.10	4.89	4.75	4.321	4.00	4.50
1966	5.55	5.42	5.36	4.881	4.50	4.50
1965	4.38	4.27	4.22	3.954	4.00	4.50
1964	3.97	3.83	3.77	3.549	3.50	4.00
1963	3.55	3.40	3.36	3.157	3.00	3.50
1962	3.26	3.07	3.01	2.778	3.00	3.00
1961	2.97	2.68	2.81	2.378	3.00	3.00
1960	3.85	3.54	3.51	2.928	3.00	4.00
1959	3.97	3.82	3.49	3.405	2.50	4.00
1958	2.46	2.12	2.04	1.839	1.75	3.00
1957	3.81	3.55	3.45	3.267	3.00	3.50
1956	3.31	3.06	2.64	2.658	2.50	3.00
1955	2.18	1.97	1.71	1.753	1.50	2.50
1954	1.58	1.42	1.35	.953	1.50	2.00
1953	2.52	2.33	1.87	1.931	1.75	2.00
1952	2.33	2.16	1.75	1.766	1.75	1.75
1951	2.16	1.87	1.60	1.552	1.75	1.75
1950	1.45	1.41	1.15	1.218	1.50	1.75
1949	1.49	1.46	1.13	1.102	1.50	1.50
1948	1.44	1.34	1.11	1.040	1.00	1.50
1947	1.03	.94	.87	.594	1.00	1.00
1946	.81	—	.61	.375	[5] .50	1.00
1945	.75	—	.44	.375	[5] .50	1.00
1944	.73	—	.44	.375	[5] .50	1.00
1943	.69	—	.44	.373	[5] .50	1.00
1942	.66	—	.44	.326	[5] .50	1.00

Year	Prime commercial paper, 4 to 6 months [1]	Prime bankers' acceptances, 90 days [1]	U.S. government securities [3], 3-month bills [4], rate on new issues	Federal Reserve Bank of New York discount rate Low	High
	445	**449**	**450**	**454**	**455**
1941	.53	.44	.103	1.00	1.00
1940	.56	.44	.014	1.00	1.00
1939	.59	.44	.023	1.00	1.00
1938	.81	.44	.053	1.00	1.00
1937	.94	.43	.447	1.00	1.50
1936	.75	.15	.143	1.50	1.50
1935	.75	.13	.137	1.50	1.50
1934	1.02	.25	.256	1.50	2.00
1933	1.73	.63	.252	2.00	3.50
1932	2.73	1.28	.879	2.50	3.50
1931	2.64	1.57	1.402	1.50	3.50
1930	3.59	2.48	—	2.00	4.50
1929	5.85	5.03	—	4.50	6.00
1928	4.85	4.09	—	3.50	5.00
1927	4.11	3.45	—	3.50	4.00
1926	4.34	3.59	—	3.50	4.00
1925	4.02	3.29	—	3.00	3.50
1924	3.98	2.98	—	3.00	4.50
1923	5.07	4.09	—	4.00	4.50
1922	4.52	3.51	—	4.00	4.50
1921	6.62	5.28	—	4.50	7.00
1920	7.50	6.06	—	4.75	7.00
1919	5.37	4.37	—	4.00	4.75
1918	6.02	4.19	—	3.50	4.00
1917	5.07	—	—	3.00	3.50
1916	3.84	—	—	3.00	4.00
1915	4.01	—	—	4.00	5.00
1914	5.47	—	—	5.00	6.00
1913	6.20	—	—	—	—
1912	5.41	—	—	—	—
1911	4.75	—	—	—	—
1910	5.72	—	—	—	—
1909	[6] 4.67	—	—	—	—
1908	[6] 5.00	—	—	—	—
1907	[6] 6.66	—	—	—	—
1906	6.25	—	—	—	—
1905	5.18	—	—	—	—
1904	5.14	—	—	—	—
1903	6.16	—	—	—	—
1902	5.81	—	—	—	—
1901	5.40	—	—	—	—
1900	5.71	—	—	—	—
1899	5.50	—	—	—	—
1898	5.34	—	—	—	—
1897	4.72	—	—	—	—
1896	7.02	—	—	—	—
1895	5.80	—	—	—	—
1894	5.22	—	—	—	—
1893	7.64	—	—	—	—
1892	5.40	—	—	—	—
1891	6.48	—	—	—	—
1890	6.91	—	—	—	—

[1] Averages of weekly prevailing rates through 1934; averages of the most representative daily offering rates quoted by dealers thereafter.
[2] Averages of the most representative daily offering rates published by finance companies, for varying maturities in the 90-170 day range.
[3] Yields are averages computed from daily closing bid prices.
[4] Bills quoted on bank discount rate basis.
[5] Preferential rate on advances secured by government securities.
[6] Includes one or more interpolated items.

Series X 474-486. Bond and Stock Yields: 1900 to 1991

(Percent per annum)

Year	Bonds U.S. government	Bonds Municipal high grade	Bonds Corporate Aaa (Moody's)	Preferred stocks	Common stocks, Moody's composite
	474	475	477	478	483
1991	8.16	6.89	8.77	8.17	9.23
1990	8.74	7.25	9.32	8.96	9.77
1989	8.58	7.24	9.26	9.04	9.66
1988	8.98	7.74	9.71	9.23	10.18
1987	8.64	7.73	9.38	8.37	9.91
1986	8.14	7.38	9.02	8.76	9.71
1985	10.75	9.18	11.37	10.49	12.05
1984	11.99	10.15	12.71	11.59	13.49
1983	10.84	9.47	12.04	11.02	12.78
1982	12.23	11.57	13.79	12.53	14.94
1981	12.87	11.23	14.17	12.36	15.06
1980	10.81	8.51	11.94	10.60	12.75
1979	8.74	6.39	9.63	9.11	10.12
1978	7.89	5.90	8.73	8.25	9.07
1977	7.06	5.56	8.02	7.61	8.43
1976	6.78	6.49	8.43	7.98	9.01
1975	6.98	6.89	8.83	8.36	9.57
1974	6.98	6.09	8.57	8.24	9.03
1973	6.30	5.18	7.44	7.23	7.80
1972	5.63	5.27	7.01	6.89	7.63
1971	5.74	5.70	7.12	6.75	7.94
1970	6.59	6.51	8.04	7.22	3.97
1969	6.10	5.81	7.03	6.41	3.42
1968	5.25	4.51	6.18	5.78	3.22
1967	4.85	3.98	5.51	5.34	3.35
1966	4.66	3.82	5.13	4.97	3.57
1965	4.21	3.27	4.49	4.33	3.06
1964	4.15	3.22	4.40	4.32	3.00
1963	4.00	3.23	4.26	4.30	3.17
1962	3.95	3.18	4.33	4.50	3.37
1961	3.90	3.46	4.35	4.66	3.07
1960	4.01	3.73	4.41	4.75	3.60
1959	4.07	3.95	4.38	4.69	3.31
1958	3.43	3.56	3.79	4.54	4.01
1957	3.47	3.60	3.89	4.63	4.33
1956	3.08	2.93	3.36	4.25	4.07
1955	2.84	2.53	3.06	4.01	4.05
1954	2.55	2.37	2.90	4.02	4.75
1953	2.94	2.72	3.20	4.27	5.49
1952	2.68	2.19	2.96	4.13	5.49
1951	2.57	2.00	2.86	4.11	6.11
1950	2.32	1.98	2.62	3.85	6.28
1949	2.31	2.21	2.66	3.97	6.62
1948	2.44	2.40	2.82	4.15	5.77
1947	2.25	2.01	2.61	3.79	5.12
1946	2.19	1.64	2.53	3.53	3.93
1945	2.37	1.67	2.62	3.70	4.17
1944	2.48	1.86	2.72	3.99	4.83
1943	2.47	2.06	2.73	4.06	4.89
1942	2.46	2.36	2.83	4.31	6.64
1941	2.05	2.10	2.77	4.08	6.23
1940	2.26	2.50	2.84	4.14	5.26
1939	2.41	2.76	3.01	4.19	4.14
1938	2.61	2.91	3.19	4.34	4.30
1937	2.74	3.10	3.26	4.45	4.63
1936	2.69	3.07	3.24	4.33	3.50
1935	2.79	3.40	3.60	4.63	4.01
1934	3.12	4.03	4.00	5.29	4.07
1933	3.31	4.71	4.49	5.75	4.22
1932	3.68	4.65	5.01	6.13	7.13
1931	3.34	4.01	4.58	5.04	5.93
1930	3.29	4.07	4.55	4.95	4.45
1929	3.60	4.27	4.73	5.12	3.36
1928	3.33	4.05	4.55	5.12	—
1927	3.34	3.98	4.57	5.51	—
1926	3.68	4.08	4.73	5.78	—
1925	3.86	4.09	4.88	5.90	—
1924	4.06	4.20	5.00	6.08	—
1923	4.36	4.25	5.12	6.12	—
1922	4.30	4.23	5.10	6.14	—
1921	5.09	5.09	5.97	6.80	—
1920	5.32	4.98	6.12	6.79	—
1919	4.73	4.46	5.49	6.31	—
1918	—	4.50	—	6.70	—
1917	—	4.20	—	6.42	—
1916	—	3.94	—	6.19	—
1915	—	4.16	—	6.48	—
1914	—	4.12	—	6.49	—
1913	—	4.22	—	6.57	—
1912	—	4.02	—	6.27	—
1911	—	3.98	—	6.28	—
1910	—	3.97	—	6.30	—
1909	—	3.78	—	—	—
1908	—	3.93	—	—	—
1907	—	3.86	—	—	—
1906	—	3.57	—	—	—
1905	—	3.40	—	—	—
1904	—	3.45	—	—	—
1903	—	3.38	—	—	—
1902	—	3.20	—	—	—
1901	—	3.13	—	—	—
1900	—	3.12	—	—	—

Series X 517-530. Market Value and Volume of Sales of Stocks and Bonds on Registered Securities Exchanges: 1935 to 1990

(In millions)

Year	All exchanges Market value, all sales	Shares of stocks	New York Stock Exchange Market value, all sales	Shares of stocks	Year	All exchanges Market value, all sales	Shares of stocks	New York Stock Exchange Market value, all sales	Shares of stocks
	517	519	524	526		517	519	524	526
1990	$1,751,000	53,338	$1,394,000	43,829	1962	56,564	1,664	49,019	1,187
1989	2,010,000	54,239	1,581,000	44,140	1961	66,068	2,010	54,785	1,292
1988	1,702,000	52,533	1,380,000	44,018					
1987	2,492,000	63,771	1,987,000	50,038	1960	46,901	1,389	39,552	958
1986	1,868,000	48,338	1,453,000	39,258	1959	53,877	1,605	45,368	1,039
					1958	39,962	1,400	34,351	999
1985	1,260,000	37,046	1,024,000	30,222	1957	33,360	1,292	28,686	914
1984	1,004,000	30,456	815,000	25,150	1956	36,360	1,182	31,064	784
1983	1,023,000	30,146	816,000	24,253					
1982	658,000	22,423	514,000	18,203	1955	39,261	1,212	34,038	820
1981	533,000	15,910	416,000	12,843	1954	29,156	1,053	25,267	749
					1953	17,488	716	15,010	520
1980	522,000	15,480	398,000	12,390	1952	18,179	732	15,531	522
1979	323,000	10,850	252,000	8,675	1951	22,127	863	19,013	643
1978	269,000	9,483	211,000	7,617					
1977	198,000	7,023	157,000	5,613	1950	22,840	857	19,735	655
1976	207,000	7,036	165,000	5,649	1949	11,443	516	9,674	380
					1948	13,749	570	11,731	413
1975	167,000	6,231	143,000	5,051	1947	12,541	512	10,617	358
1974	125,000	4,846	106,000	3,822	1946	20,001	802	16,675	531
1973	187,000	5,732	155,000	4,337					
1972	215,000	6,310	169,000	4,496	1945	18,112	744	15,190	496
1971	195,000	5,916	155,000	4,265	1944	11,780	464	10,089	342
					1943	10,986	485	9,457	362
1970	136,465	4,539	107,649	3,213	1942	5,570	220	4,796	169
1969	180,877	4,963	133,173	3,174	1941	7,603	310	6,408	230
1968	202,772	5,312	149,395	3,299					
1967	168,258	4,504	160,791	2,886	1940	9,726	372	8,223	283
1966	127,914	3,188	102,754	2,205	1939	13,347	467	11,488	366
					1938	13,927	542	12,306	424
1965	93,325	2,587	76,878	1,809	1937	23,709	837	20,769	614
1964	75,328	2,045	63,284	1,482	1936	27,283	956	23,323	702
1963	66,157	1,838	56,564	1,351	1935 [1]	19,115	662	16,138	499

[1] Stock and bond sales for New York Stock Exchange and New York Curb Exchange, January to March, exclude stopped sales; stock sales for these exchanges also exclude odd-lot sales.

Series X 536-539.   Net Assets, Sales and Redemptions of Mutual Funds: 1940 to 1990

(In thousands of dollars)

Year	Number of funds	Net assets	Sales	Redemptions	Year	Number of funds	Net assets	Sales	Redemptions
	536	537	538	539		536	537	538	539
1990	3,122	1,069,000,000	1,566,000,000	1,471,000,000	1964	160	29,116,254	958,489	411,053
1989	2,918	982,000,000	1,445,000,000	1,327,000,000	1963	165	25,214,436	648,609	387,643
1988	2,718	810,000,000	1,177,000,000	1,167,000,000	1962	169	21,270,735	510,870	285,579
1987	2,323	770,000,000	1,252,000,000	1,179,000,000	1961	170	22,788,812	813,127	263,335
1986	1,843	716,000,000	1,206,000,000	1,016,000,000					
					1960	161	17,025,684	481,318	192,556
1985	1,531	496,000,000	954,000,000	665,000,000	1959	155	15,817,962	541,087	171,650
1984	1,246	371,000,000	680,000,000	607,000,000	1958	151	13,242,388	482,429	174,773
1983	1,026	293,000,000	548,000,000	566,000,000	1957	143	8,714,143	331,580	95,759
1982	857	282,900,000	547,800,000	565,800,000	1956	135	9,046,431	342,606	90,661
1981	669	241,400,000	472,200,000	362,600,000					
					1955	125	7,837,524	290,417	92,501
1980	564	135,000,000	248,000,000	217,000,000	1954	115	6,109,390	270,594	98,709
1979	524	94,500,000	119,300,000	86,800,000	1953	110	4,146,061	160,368	56,835
1978	505	55,800,000	37,200,000	31,500,000	1952	110	3,931,407	214,401	49,255
1977	477	48,500,000	17,100,000	16,700,000	1951	103	3,129,629	194,039	62,150
1976	452	51,000,000	13,700,000	16,400,000					
					1950	98	2,530,563	135,372	82,766
1975	426	45,800,000	10,100,000	9,600,000	1949	91	1,973,547	125,850	40,650
1974	431	35,800,000	5,300,000	3,900,000	1948	87	1,505,762	75,284	34,384
1973	421	46,500,000	4,400,000	5,700,000	1947	80	1,409,165	67,276	28,295
1972	410	59,800,000	4,900,000	6,600,000	1946	74	1,311,108	82,929	31,958
1970	356	47,618,100	1,230,408	765,375	1945	73	1,284,185	92,671	29,692
1969	269	48,290,733	1,503,002	846,722	1944	68	882,191	52,957	16,919
1968	240	52,677,188	1,994,117	1,027,517	1943	68	653,653	116,062	51,221
1967	204	44,701,302	1,377,668	743,027	1942	68	486,850	73,140	25,440
1966	182	34,829,353	924,435	426,847	1941	68	401,611	53,312	45,024
1965	170	35,220,243	1,228,170	512,187	1940	——	447,959	—	—

Series X 551-560. Short- and Intermediate-Term Consumer Credit, by Major Types: 1919 to 1991

(In millions of dollars. Estimated credit as of end of year)

Year	Total credit outstanding	Installment credit outstanding		Total noninstallment credit outstanding	Year	Total credit outstanding	Installment credit outstanding		Total noninstallment credit outstanding
		Total	Automobile paper				Total	Automobile paper	
	551	552	553	557		551	552	553	557
1991	777,300	729,400	267,900	47,900	1955	38,830	28,906	13,460	9,924
1990	794,400	735,100	284,600	59,300	1954	32,464	23,568	9,809	8,896
1989	781,200	718,900	290,700	62,300	1953	31,393	23,005	9,835	8,388
1988	731,200	664,000	284,200	67,100	1952	27,520	19,403	7,733	8,117
1987	681,900	610,500	265,900	71,400	1951	22,712	15,294	5,972	7,418
1986	649,100	573,000	247,400	76,100					
					1950	21,471	14,703	6,074	6,768
1985	592,100	518,300	210,200	73,800	1949	17,364	11,590	4,555	5,774
1984	511,300	442,600	173,600	68,700	1948	14,447	8,996	3,018	5,451
1983	431,200	369,000	143,600	62,200	1947	11,598	6,695	1,924	4,903
1982	383,100	325,800	125,900	57,300	1946	8,384	4,172	981	4,212
1981	366,900	311,300	119,000	55,600					
					1945	5,665	2,462	455	3,203
1980	350,300	298,200	112,000	52,100	1944	5,111	2,176	397	2,935
1979	383,300	312,000	116,400	71,300	1943	4,901	2,136	355	2,765
1978	337,900	273,600	101,600	64,300	1942	5,983	3,166	742	2,817
1977	289,200	230,600	82,900	58,600	1941	9,172	6,085	2,458	3,087
1976	248,900	193,500	67,700	55,400					
					1940	8,338	5,514	2,071	2,824
1975	223,100	172,000	57,200	51,100	1939	7,222	4,503	1,497	2,719
1974	213,400	164,600	54,300	48,800	1938	6,370	3,686	1,099	2,684
1973	203,100	155,100	53,800	48,000	1937	6,948	4,118	1,494	2,830
1972	177,700	133,200	47,900	44,500	1936	6,375	3,747	1,372	2,628
1971	138,400	111,300	38,700	27,100					
					1935	5,190	2,817	992	2,373
1970	126,802	101,161	35,490	25,641	1934	4,218	1,999	614	2,219
1969	122,469	98,169	36,602	24,300	1933	3,885	1,723	493	2,162
1968	113,191	89,890	34,130	23,301	1932	4,026	1,672	356	2,354
1967	102,132	80,926	30,724	21,206	1931	5,315	2,463	684	2,852
1966	97,543	77,539	30,556	20,004					
					1930	6,351	3,022	986	3,329
1965	90,314	71,324	28,619	18,990	1929	7,116	3,524	1,384	3,592
1964	80,268	62,692	24,934	17,576	1928	6,258	2,935	1,134	3,323
1963	71,739	55,486	22,254	16,253	1927	5,344	2,319	765	3,025
1962	63,821	48,720	19,381	15,101	1926	5,227	2,363	977	2,864
1961	57,982	43,891	17,135	14,091					
					1925	4,715	2,115	914	2,600
1960	56,141	42,968	17,658	13,173	1924	4,025	1,646	670	2,379
1959	51,544	39,247	16,420	12,297	1923	3,652	1,368	526	2,284
1958	45,129	33,642	14,152	11,487	1922	3,166	1,047	295	2,119
1957	44,971	33,868	15,340	11,103	1921	2,966	919	317	2,047
1956	42,334	31,720	14,420	10,614					
					1920	2,964	969	376	1,995
					1919	2,642	800	304	1,842

Series X 716-724.   Number of Banking Offices, by Deposit Insurance Status: 1900 to 1990

Year [1]	All banking offices	Total	Commercial bank offices [2]					Mutual savings bank offices [2] [4]	
			Member banks [2] [3]			Nonmember banks			
			National	State [4] [5]	Insured	Non-insured	Total	Insured [5]	
	716	**717**	**718**	**719**	**720**	**721**	**722**	**723**	
1990	66,945	69,160	31,279	6,922	24,959	—	3,785	3,785	
1989	64,570	60,796	30,019	6,736	24,041	—	3,774	3,774	
1988	63,960	60,200	29,270	6,493	24,437	—	3,760	3,760	
1987	62,914	59,423	28,744	6,452	24,227	—	3,491	3,491	
1986	61,897	58,565	28,218	6,324	24,023	—	3,332	3,332	
1985	60,890	57,764	27,844	6,010	23,910	—	3,126	3,126	
1984	60,067	57,010	27,037	5,772	23,535	666	3,057	2,728	
1983	59,050	55,960	26,080	5,866	23,380	634	3,090	2,760	
1982	57,913	54,829	24,867	6,054	23,314	594	3,084	2,733	
1981	59,348	55,749	25,221	6,193	23,788	547	3,599	3,217	
1980	57,232	53,649	24,217	5,768	23,186	478	3,583	3,066	
1979	54,926	51,588	23,307	5,856	21,993	432	3,338	2,840	
1978	52,608	49,602	22,731	5,725	20,730	416	3,006	2,517	
1977	50,645	47,914	22,294	5,610	19,619	391	2,781	2,302	
1976	48,653	46,100	21,459	5,695	18,578	368	2,553	2,125	
1975	47,239	44,917	21,073	5,453	18,043	348	2,322	1,897	
1974	45,011	42,890	20,437	5,281	16,884	288	2,121	1,706	
1973	42,593	40,620	19,567	5,127	15,673	253	1,973	1,562	
1972	40,377	35,538	18,571	5,073	14,643	251	1,839	1,437	
1971	38,588	36,903	17,871	4,947	13,864	221	1,685	1,310	
1970	36,910	35,330	17,142	4,798	13,159	231	1,580	1,222	
1969	35,340	33,858	16,384	4,683	12,546	245	1,482	1,137	
1968	34,100	32,691	15,700	4,827	11,919	245	1,409	1,072	
1967	32,983	31,652	14,940	4,983	11,470	259	1,331	1,001	
1966	31,934	30,673	14,404	4,867	11,103	299	1,261	944	
1965	30,776	29,556	13,776	4,738	10,723	319	1,220	911	
1964	29,549	28,370	12,937	4,751	10,356	326	1,179	876	
1963	28,197	27,064	12,032	4,684	10,012	336	1,133	832	
1962	26,865	25,768	11,140	4,549	9,718	361	1,097	797	
1961	25,839	24,782	10,554	4,453	9,407	368	1,057	757	
1960	24,954	23,954	10,036	4,265	9,253	400	1,000	706	
1959	* 24,094	* 23,130	* 9,514	4,206	* 9,001	* 409	964	586	
1958	23,305	22,361	9,109	4,120	8,693	439	944	546	
1957	22,699	21,772	8,795	3,969	8,545	463	927	535	
1956	22,123	21,230	8,459	3,884	8,405	482	893	480	
1955	21,494	20,638	8,055	3,785	8,263	535	856	454	
1954	20,982	20,147	7,844	3,598	8,132	573	835	439	
1953	20,608	19,810	7,602	3,536	8,062	610	798	411	
1952	20,288	19,513	7,465	3,436	7,947	665	775	383	
1951	20,003	19,244	7,309	3,365	7,879	691	759	367	
1950	19,709	18,966	7,188	3,271	7,766	741	742	346	
1949	19,465	18,735	7,060	3,216	7,679	780	730	333	
1948	19,234	18,520	6,956	3,156	7,582	826	714	325	
1947 [6]	19,046	18,342	6,875	3,096	7,521	850	704	318	
1946	18,863	18,165	6,794	3,022	7,464	885	698	306	
1945	18,781	18,096	6,831	2,963	7,397	905	685	293	
1944	18,741	18,058	6,840	2,866	7,430	922	683	291	
1943	18,646	17,965	6,782	2,744	7,487	952	681	279	
1942	18,562	17,878	6,675	2,619	7,602	982	683	91	
1941	18,524	17,841	6,682	2,514	7,742	903	683	84	
1940	18,561	17,875	6,683	2,344	7,892	956	686	84	
1939	18,663	17,980	6,705	2,177	8,099	999	683	75	
1938	18,774	18,084	6,723	2,106	8,226	1,029	690	64	

See footnotes at end of table.

Series X 716-724. Number of Banking Offices, by Deposit Insurance Status: 1900 to 1990—Cont'd.

Year [1]	All banking offices	Commercial bank offices [2]					Mutual savings bank offices [2][4]	
		Total	Member banks [2][3]		Nonmember banks		Total	
			National	State [4][5]	Insured	Non-insured		Insured [5]
	716	**717**	**718**	**719**	**720**	**721**	**722**	**723**
1937	18,927	18,236	6,745	2,075	8,342	1,074	691	67
1936	19,066	18,373	6,723	2,032	8,440	1,178	693	67
1935	19,153	18,455	6,715	1,953	8,562	1,225	698	67
1934	19,196	18,491	6,705	1,961	[7] 9,825		705	(7)
1933	17,940	17,236	6,275	1,817	[7] 9,144		704	(7)
1932	—	20,997	7,231		13,766		—	—
1931	—	22,842	7,478		15,364		—	—
1930	—	25,694	8,075		17,619		—	—
1929	—	27,379	8,398		18,981		—	—
1928	—	28,106	8,563		19,543		—	—
1927	—	28,714	8,482		20,232		—	—
1926	—	29,454	8,327		21,127		—	—
1925	—	30,163	8,366		21,797		—	—
1924	—	30,482	8,299		22,183		—	—
1923	—	30,931	8,383		22,548		—	—
1922	—	31,259	8,384		22,875		—	—
1921	—	31,243	8,222		23,021		—	—
1920	—	30,368	8,088		22,280		—	—
1915	—	26,660	7,624		19,036		—	—
1910	—	22,034	7,150		14,884		—	—
1905	—	15,032	5,669		9,363		—	—
1900	—	8,857	3,736		5,121		—	—

* Denotes first year for which figures include Alaska and Hawaii.
[1] For 1925, 1926 and 1932-70, figures are as of December; for earlier years they are as of different dates for banks and branches: for banks, 1927-1931 and 1923-1924, as of December; for 1915-1922, as of June; for branches, 1924 and 1927-1931, as of June; prior to 1924, not for any uniform month.
[2] Comparability of figures for classes of banks is affected somewhat by changes in Federal Reserve membership, deposit insurance status and reserve classifications of cities and individual banks, and by mergers, etc.

[3] Federal deposit insurance is compulsory for member banks of the Federal Reserve System.
[4] None in Alaska and Hawaii.
[5] Member commercial banks exclude, and mutual savings banks include, mutual savings banks which are members of the Federal Reserve System as follows: 3, 1941-1959, 2 in 1960 and 1 in 1961-1970.
[6] In 1947, the series was revised.
[7] Federal insurance of bank deposits did not become effective until Jan. 1, 1934, and the number of nonmember banking offices by insurance status is not available prior to 1935.

Series X 741-755. Bank Suspensions—Number and Deposits of Suspended Banks: 1864 to 1991

Year [1]	Total number of suspensions 741	Total deposits of suspended banks [2] (mil. dol.) 748	Year [1]	Total number of suspensions 741	Total deposits of suspended banks [2] (mil. dol.) 748	Year [1]	Total number of suspensions 741	Year [1]	Total number of suspensions 741
1991	127	(NA)	1963	2	23	1915	152	1887	25
1990	169	14,489	1962	3	4	1914	151	1886	20
1989	207	24,097	1961	9	10	1913	105		
1988	221	37,215				1912	80		
1987	203	8,568	1960	2	8	1911	87	1885	46
1986	145	6,597	1959	3	3			1884	63
			1956-1960	20	45	1910	63	1883	33
1985	120	8,059	1951-1955	23	70	1909	79	1882	22
1984	80	29,883	1947-1950	23	33	1908	155	1881	11
1983	48	5,442				1907	91		
1982	42	9,908	1941-1946	49	[3] 59	1906	53	1880	18
1981	10	3,826	1934-1940	[4] 448	[5] 477			1879	37
			1933 [6]	4,004	3,601	1905	80	1878	140
1980	10	5,216	1932	1,456	725	1904	128	1877	99
1979	10	110	1931	2,294	1,691	1903	52	1876	59
1978	7	854				1902	54		
1977	6	205	1930	1,352	869	1901	69	1875	28
1976	17	865	1929	659	231			1874	57
			1928	499	143	1900	36	1873	41
1975	14	340	1927	669	199	1899	36	1872	19
1974	4	1,575	1926	976	260	1898	67	1871	10
1973	3	21				1897	145		
1972	2	57	1925	618	168	1896	155	1870	3
1971	3	5	1924	775	210			1869	7
			1923	646	150	1895	124	1868	14
1970	7	53	1922	367	93	1894	89	1867	8
1969	9	40	1921	505	172	1893	496	1866	7
1968	3	23				1892	83		
1967	4	11	1920	168	——	1891	62	1865	6
1966	8	106	1919	63	——			1864	2
			1918	47	——	1890	37		
1965	9	45	1917	49	——	1889	18		
1964	8	24	1916	52	——	1888	33		

NA Not available.

[1] For 1864-1891, all series except mutual savings banks are for year ending June 30; for mutual saving banks the date is not specified in the source. For 1892-1920, for all banks other than private, figures are for calendar year; for private banks, figures vary in ending date of reporting year as follows: 1892, June 30; 1893 (14 months), Aug. 31; 1894-1899, Aug. 31; 1900-1919, June 30; and 1920 (18 months), Dec. 31. For 1921-1970, all series are for calendar years.

[2] Excludes deposits for seven noninsured banks, for which data were unavailable.

[3] Excludes deposits for one foreign-owned bank closed in 1941 by order of the federal government, requiring disbursements by the corporation.

[4] Excludes one noninsured bank placed in receivership in 1934 with no deposits at time of closing.

[5] Excludes deposits for two cases requiring disbursements by the corporation; one bank in voluntary liquidation in 1937, one noninsured bank in 1938 with insured deposits at date of suspensions, its insurance status having been terminated prior to suspension.

[6] Figures not wholly comparable with earlier years.

Series X 834-844. Selected Assets and Liabilities of Savings and Loan Associations: 1900 to 1989

(Includes Alaska, Guam, Hawaii, Puerto Rico and Virgin Islands)

Year	Number of associations	Total assets (mil. dol.) [1]	Year	Number of associations	Total assets (mil. dol.) [1]	Year	Number of associations	Total assets (mil. dol.) [1]	Year	Number of associations	Total assets (mil. dol.) [1]
	834	835		834	835		834	835		834	835
1989	2,271	756,000	1967	6,036	143,534	1945	6,149	8,747	1922	10,009	3,343
1988	2,554	933,000	1966	6,112	133,933	1944	6,279	7,458	1921	9,255	2,891
1987	2,886	974,000				1943	6,498	6,604			
1986	3,084	962,000	1965	6,185	129,580	1942	6,941	6,150	1920	8,633	2,520
			1964	6,222	119,355	1941	7,211	6,049	1919	7,788	2,127
1985	3,233	948,000	1963	6,248	107,559				1918	7,484	1,898
1984	3,362	902,000	1962	6,289	93,605	1940	7,521	5,733	1917	7,269	1,769
1983	3,502	773,400	1961	6,246	82,135	1939	8,006	5,597	1916	7,072	1,599
1982	3,825	707,600				1938	8,762	5,632			
1981	4,292	664,200	1960	6,320	71,476	1937	9,225	5,682	1915	6,806	1,484
			1959	6,223	63,530	1936	10,042	5,772	1914	6,616	1,358
1980	4,613	630,000	1958	6,207	55,139				1913	6,429	1,248
1979	4,684	579,000	1957	6,169	48,138	1935	10,266	5,875	1912	6,273	1,138
1978	4,725	523,600	1956	6,136	42,875	1934	10,744	6,406	1911	6,099	1,031
1977	4,761	459,200				1933	10,596	7,018			
1976	4,821	391,900	1955	6,071	37,656	1932	10,915	7,737	1910	5,869	932
			1954	6,037	31,633	1931	11,442	8,417	1909	5,713	856
1975	4,931	338,200	1953	6,012	26,733				1908	5,599	784
1974	5,086	295,500	1952	6,004	22,660	1930	11,777	8,829	1907	5,424	732
1973	5,200	271,900	1951	5,995	19,222	1929	12,342	8,695	1906	5,316	673
1972	5,300	243,100				1928	12,666	8,016			
1971	5,500	206,000	1950	5,992	16,893	1927	12,804	7,179	1905	5,264	629
			1949	5,983	14,622	1926	12,626	6,334	1904	5,265	600
1970	5,699	176,183	1948	6,011	13,028				1903	5,308	580
1969	5,835	162,149	1947	6,045	11,687	1925	12,403	5,509	1902	5,299	577
1968	5,947	152,890	1946	6,093	10,202	1924	11,844	4,766	1901	5,302	565
						1923	10,744	3,943	1900	5,356	571

[1] Includes assets not shown separately.

Series X 864-878. Federal and State-Chartered Credit Unions—Number, Members, Savings, Loans and Total Assets: 1925 to 1990

(As of end of year)

Year	Operating credit unions		Number of members (1,000's)		Members' savings (mil. dol.)		Outstanding loans (mil. dol.)		Total assets (mil. dol.)	
	Federal	State[1]	Federal	State[1]	Federal[2]	State[3]	Federal	State[1]	Federal[2]	State[1]
	865	**866**	**868**	**869**	**871**	**872**	**874**	**875**	**877**	**878**
1990	8,511	4,349	36,241	19,454	117,892	62,082	83,029	44,102	130,073	68,133
1989	8,821	4,550	35,612	18,858	109,653	57,658	80,272	42,373	120,666	63,175
1988	9,118	4,760	34,438	18,519	104,431	55,217	73,766	39,977	114,565	60,740
1987	9,401	4,934	32,067	17,999	96,346	52,083	64,104	35,436	105,190	56,972
1986	9,758	4,935	31,041	17,636	87,954	48,097	55,305	30,834	95,484	52,244
1985	10,125	4,920	29,579	15,689	71,616	37,917	48,241	26,168	78,188	41,525
1984	10,548	4,645	28,170	15,205	57,927	26,327	42,132	19,951	63,657	29,188
1983	10,962	4,915	28,798	14,278	49,889	24,850	33,201	17,215	54,482	27,479
1982	11,426	8,464	26,105	20,393	41,352	33,236	28,192	23,454	45,494	36,886
1981	11,951	8,746	25,449	19,620	35,248	28,971	27,238	23,156	39,181	32,596
1980	12,440	9,025	24,519	19,235	36,263	29,480	26,350	22,633	40,092	33,143
1979	12,738	9,274	24,790	18,409	31,831	25,628	25,547	23,677	36,468	29,524
1978	12,759	9,443	23,259	17,461	29,803	23,715	27,687	23,715	34,760	27,588
1977	12,750	9,580	20,427	16,375	25,576	21,120	22,718	19,389	29,688	24,500
1976	12,757	9,775	18,624	15,129	21,130	17,968	18,311	15,999	24,396	20,640
1975	12,737	9,871	17,066	14,196	17,530	15,522	14,869	13,300	20,209	17,804
1974	12,748	10,105	15,870	13,581	14,371	13,148	12,730	11,702	16,715	15,233
1973	12,688	10,191	14,666	12,886	12,598	11,914	11,109	10,650	14,569	13,806
1972	12,708	10,354	13,572	12,118	10,956	10,622	9,424	9,239	12,514	12,275
1971	12,717	10,536	12,702	11,382	9,191	9,167	8,071	8,081	10,553	10,569
1970	12,977	10,679	11,966	10,853	7,629	7,894	6,969	7,137	8,861	9,089
1969	12,921	10,838	11,302	10,326	6,713	7,027	6,329	6,630	7,794	8,124
1968	12,584	10,794	10,509	9,720	5,986	6,326	5,398	5,895	6,902	7,310
1967	12,210	10,787	9,874	9,189	5,421	5,682	4,677	5,204	6,208	6,568
1966	11,941	10,644	9,272	8,651	4,944	5,127	4,324	4,769	5,669	5,938
1965	11,543	10,521	8,641	8,115	4,538	4,682	3,865	4,233	5,166	5,385
1964	11,278	10,452	8,092	7,530	4,017	4,208	3,349	3,699	4,559	4,800
1963	10,955	10,346	7,500	7,080	3,453	3,711	2,911	3,260	3,917	4,213
1962	10,632	10,337	7,008	6,745	3,020	3,311	2,561	2,917	3,430	3,758
1961	10,271	10,296	6,543	6,336	2,673	2,966	2,245	2,607	3,028	3,354
1960	9,905	10,151	6,087	5,971	2,344	2,637	2,021	2,381	2,670	2,989
1959	9,447	9,961	5,643	5,677	2,075	2,366	1,667	2,051	2,353	2,676
1958	9,030	9,740	5,210	5,329	1,812	2,057	1,380	1,698	2,035	2,312
1957	8,735	9,314	4,898	4,964	1,589	1,792	1,257	1,521	1,789	2,021
1956	8,350	8,763	4,502	4,549	1,366	1,548	1,049	1,277	1,529	1,742
1955	7,806	8,258	4,032	4,121	1,135	1,312	863	1,071	1,267	1,476
1954	7,227	7,713	3,599	3,757	931	1,109	682	870	1,033	1,237
1953	6,578	6,986	3,255	3,380	768	923	574	734	854	1,041
1952	5,925	6,324	2,853	3,035	597	758	415	570	662	854
1951	5,398	5,886	2,464	2,732	457	622	300	447	505	694
1950	4,984	5,587	2,127	2,483	362	522	264	416	406	900
1949	4,495	5,402	1,820	2,271	285	445	186	329	316	511
1948	4,058	5,271	1,628	2,121	235	395	138	261	258	443
1947	3,845	5,097	1,446	1,894	192	341	91	189	210	381
1946	3,761	4,954	1,302	1,718	160	291	57	131	173	322
1945	3,757	4,858	1,217	1,626	141	243	35	91	153	282
1944	3,815	4,907	1,306	1,630	134	221	34	87	144	254
1943	3,938	5,124	1,312	1,721	117	206	35	87	127	228
1942	4,145	5,400	1,357	1,797	110	193	43	106	120	221
1941	4,228	5,506	1,409	1,908	97	190	69	151	106	217
1940	3,756	5,175	1,128	1,700	66	157	56	135	73	181
1939	3,182	4,677	851	1,459	43	126	38	111	48	146

See footnotes at end of table.

Series X 864–878. Federal and State-Chartered Credit Unions—Number, Members, Savings, Loans and Total Assets: 1925 to 1990—Cont'd.

(As of end of year)

| Year | Operating credit unions | | Number of members (1,000's) | | Members' savings (mil. dol.) | | Outstanding loans (mil. dol.) | | Total assets (mil. dol.) | |
	Federal	State[1]	Federal	State[1]	Federal[2]	State[3]	Federal	State[1]	Federal[2]	State[1]
	865	866	868	869	871	872	874	875	877	878
1938	2,760	3,977	632	1,237	27	100	24	84	30	118
1937	2,313	3,128	484	1,056	18	80	16	62	19	97
1936	1,751	2,734	310	854	9	59	7	52	9	74
1935	772	2,122	119	523	2	36	2	34	2	48
1934	39	2,028	3	427	(Z)	28	(Z)	28	(Z)	40
1933	—	1,772	—	360	—	23	—	26	—	35
1932	—	1,472	—	301	—	22	—	25	—	31
1931	—	1,244	—	286	—	—	—	—	—	34
1929	—	868	—	265	—	—	—	—	—	—
1925	—	176	—	108	—	—	—	—	—	—

Z Less than $500,000.
[1] Reports not received from all operating credit unions.
[2] Data for 1935-1944, partly estimated.
[3] Includes members' deposits.

Series X 879-889. Life Insurance Companies and Life Insurance in Force in the United States, by Type: 1815 to 1990

(As of December 31)

Year	Policies (mil.)	Total	Ordinary	Group [1]	Industrial [2]	Credit [3]	Ordinary	Group
			Life insurance in force — Value (mil. dol.)				Average size policy in force (dol.)	
	880	882	883	884	885	886	887	888
1990	389	9,393,000	5,367,000	3,754,000	24,000	248,000	37,910	26,630
1989	394	8,694,000	4,940,000	3,469,000	24,000	260,000	34,410	24,510
1988	391	8,020,000	4,512,000	3,232,000	26,000	251,000	31,390	23,410
1987	395	7,452,000	4,139,000	3,043,000	27,000	243,000	28,510	22,380
1986	391	6,720,000	3,658,000	2,801,000	27,000	234,000	25,540	20,720
1985	386	6,053,000	3,247,000	2,562,000	28,000	216,000	22,780	19,720
1984	385	5,500,000	2,888,000	2,392,000	30,000	190,000	19,970	18,780
1983	387	4,966,000	2,544,000	2,220,000	31,000	171,000	17,380	17,530
1982	389	4,477,000	2,217,000	2,066,000	33,000	161,000	15,140	16,630
1981	400	4,064,000	1,978,000	1,889,000	35,000	162,000	13,310	15,400
1980	402	3,541,000	1,761,000	1,579,000	38,000	165,000	11,920	13,410
1979	407	3,222,000	1,586,000	1,419,000	37,800	179,300	10,890	12,350
1978	401	2,870,000	1,425,000	1,244,000	38,100	163,100	10,010	11,260
1977	390	2,583,000	1,289,000	1,115,000	39,000	139,400	9,240	10,550
1976	382	2,343,000	1,178,000	1,003,000	39,200	123,600	8,610	10,010
1975	380	2,140,000	1,083,000	905,000	39,400	112,000	8,090	9,360
1974	380	1,985,000	1,009,000	827,000	39,400	109,600	7,690	8,840
1973	369	1,778,000	928,000	708,000	40,600	101,200	7,230	8,010
1972	365	1,628,000	849,000	631,000	40,000	108,800	6,790	7,730
1971	357	1,503,000	788,000	581,000	39,200	95,000	6,440	7,170
1970	355	1,402,123	734,730	551,357	38,644	77,392	6,105	6,905
1969	351	1,284,529	682,453	488,864	38,614	74,598	5,773	6,473
1968	346	1,183,354	633,392	442,778	38,827	68,357	5,453	6,074
1967	336	1,079,821	584,570	394,501	39,215	61,535	5,150	5,733
1966	331	984,689	541,022	345,945	39,663	58,059	4,938	5,356
1965	320	900,554	499,638	308,078	39,818	53,020	4,662	5,056
1964	308	797,808	457,868	253,620	39,833	46,487	4,382	4,637
1963	299	730,623	420,808	229,477	39,672	40,666	4,136	4,494
1962	290	675,977	391,048	209,950	39,638	35,341	3,932	4,323
1961	286	629,493	366,141	192,794	39,451	31,107	3,766	4,167
1960 *	282	586,448	341,881	175,903	39,563	29,101	3,597	4,034
1959	275	542,128	317,158	160,163	39,809	24,998	3,424	3,875
1958	267	493,561	288,607	144,772	39,646	20,536	3,227	3,736
1957	266	458,359	264,949	133,905	40,139	19,366	3,041	3,580
1956	261	412,630	238,348	117,399	40,109	16,774	2,853	3,361
1955	251	372,332	216,812	101,345	39,682	14,493	2,721	3,202
1954	237	333,719	198,599	86,410	38,664	10,046	2,619	3,018
1953	229	304,259	185,007	72,913	37,781	8,558	2,530	2,755
1952	219	276,591	170,875	62,913	36,448	6,355	2,452	2,667
1951	210	253,140	159,109	54,398	34,870	4,763	2,378	2,535
1950	202	234,168	149,116	47,793	33,415	3,844	2,319	2,478
1949	194	213,672	138,862	40,207	32,087	2,516	2,264	2,330
1948	187	201,208	131,158	37,068	31,253	1,729	2,240	2,280
1947	182	186,035	122,393	32,026	30,406	1,210	2,200	2,050
1946	173	170,066	112,818	27,206	29,313	729	2,150	2,060
1945	163	151,762	101,550	22,172	27,675	365	2,100	1,930
1944	159	145,771	95,085	23,922	26,474	290	2,080	1,860
1943	151	137,158	89,596	22,413	24,874	275	2,080	1,760
1942	144	127,721	85,139	19,316	22,911	355	2,090	1,740
1941	140	122,178	82,525	17,359	21,825	469	2,100	1,710
1940	134	115,530	79,346	14,938	20,866	380	2,130	1,700
1939	131	111,569	77,121	13,641	20,500	307	2,130	1,790

See footnotes at end of table.

Series X 879-889. Life Insurance Companies and Life Insurance in Force in the United States, by Type: 1815 to 1990—Cont'd.

(As of December 31)

Year	Policies (mil.)	Life insurance in force — Value (mil. dol.)					Average size policy force (dol.)	
		Total	Ordinary	Group [1]	Industrial [2]	Credit [3]	Ordinary	Group
	880	882	883	884	885	886	887	888
1938	129	108,927	75,772	12,503	20,396	256	2,150	1,890
1937	128	107,794	74,836	12,638	20,104	216	2,180	1,710
1936	124	102,653	72,361	11,291	18,863	138	2,160	1,670
1935	121	98,464	70,684	10,208	17,471	101	2,160	1,590
1934	117	96,677	70,094	9,472	17,036	75	2,210	1,710
1933	115	96,246	70,872	8,681	16,630	63	2,260	1,780
1932	116	101,559	75,898	8,923	16,669	69	2,380	1,860
1931	124	106,970	79,514	9,736	17,635	85	2,420	1,730
1930	124	106,413	78,576	8,901	17,963	73	2,460	1,700
1929	123	102,086	75,686	8,994	17,349	57	2,470	1,590
1928	116	92,590	68,430	7,889	16,231	40	2,410	1,580
1927	110	84,775	63,334	6,333	15,078	30	2,400	1,450
1926	104	77,642	58,453	5,362	13,803	24	2,350	1,400
1925	97	69,475	52,892	4,247	12,318	18	2,270	1,340
1924	90	61,327	47,283	3,127	10,905	12	2,200	1,280
1923	83	55,097	43,077	2,393	9,618	9	2,160	1,180
1922	76	48,342	38,053	1,795	8,486	8	2,090	1,150
1921	70	43,944	34,777	1,527	7,633	7	2,040	1,070
1920	65	40,540	32,018	1,570	6,948	4	1,990	960
1919	60	32,971	25,783	1,092	6,092	4	1,860	920
1918	53	27,924	21,818	630	5,474	2	1,840	840
1917	49	25,243	19,868	349	5,026	(3)	1,830	780
1916	45	22,853	18,081	155	4,617	—	1,800	780
1915	41	21,029	16,650	100	4,279	—	1,800	830
1914	39	19,737	15,661	65	4,011	—	1,810	970
1913	37	18,683	14,827	31	3,825	—	1,810	910
1912	34	17,301	13,709	13	3,579	—	1,800	1,080
1911	31	16,125	12,772	(Z)	3,353	—	1,790	—
1910	29	14,908	11,783	—	3,125	—	1,830	—
1909	27	13,878	10,960	—	2,918	—	1,830	—
1908	25	13,085	10,450	—	2,635	—	1,850	—
1907	24	12,639	10,103	—	2,536	—	1,860	—
1906	23	12,285	9,871	—	2,414	—	1,870	—
1905	22	11,863	9,585	—	2,278	—	1,880	—
1904	20	11,165	9,059	—	2,106	—	1,930	—
1903	19	10,217	8,264	—	1,953	—	1,970	—
1902	17	9,369	7,594	—	1,775	—	2,020	—
1901	16	8,369	6,766	—	1,603	—	2,040	—
1900	14	7,573	6,124	—	1,449	—	2,160	—
1899	12	6,822	5,547	—	1,275	—	2,210	—
1898	11	6,053	4,952	—	1,101	—	2,310	—
1897	10	5,555	4,563	—	992	—	2,340	—
1896	9	5,207	4,323	—	884	—	2,420	—
1895	9	4,988	4,170	—	818	—	2,440	—
1894	—	4,847	4,048	—	799	—	—	—
1893	—	4,609	3,948	—	661	—	—	—
1892	—	4,267	3,685	—	582	—	—	—
1891	—	3,868	3,388	—	481	—	—	—
1890	—	3,522.2	3,094.7	—	427.5	—	—	—
1889	—	3,122.6	2,758.1	—	364.5	—	—	—
1888	—	2,742.0	2,437.8	—	304.2	—	—	—
1887	—	2,456.3	2,201.8	—	254.5	—	—	—
1886	—	2,096.9	1,899.1	—	197.8	—	—	—

See footnotes at end of table.

Series X 879-889. Life Insurance Companies and Life Insurance in Force in the United States, by Type: 1815 to 1990—Cont'd.

(As of December 31)

Year	Value of life insurance in force (mil. dol.)			Year	Value of life insurance in force (mil. dol.)	
	Total	Ordinary	Industrial[2]		Total	Ordinary
	882	**883**	**885**		**882**	**883**
1885	2,007.1	1,861.3	145.8	1850	97.1	97.1
1884	1,995.9	1,884.8	111.1	1849	(NA)	(NA)
1883	1,872.1	1,784.9	87.2	1848	(NA)	(NA)
1882	1,720.8	1,664.6	56.2	1847	(NA)	(NA)
1881	1,606.5	1,573.0	33.5	1846	(NA)	(NA)
1880	1,522.7	1,502.2	20.5	1845	14.5	14.5
1879	1,474.9	1,469.5	5.4	1844	(NA)	(NA)
1878	1,519.7	1,517.7	2.0	1843	(NA)	(NA)
1877	1,512.1	1,511.1	1.0	1842	(NA)	(NA)
1876	1,690.6	1,690.2	.4	1841	(NA)	(NA)
1875	1,873.9	1,873.9	—	1840	4.7	4.7
1874	1,947.6	1,947.6	—	1839	(NA)	(NA)
1873	2,040.8	2,040.8	—	1838	(NA)	(NA)
1872	2,079.2	2,079.2	—	1837	(NA)	(NA)
1871	2,083.0	2,083.0	—	1836	(NA)	(NA)
1870	2,006.1	2,006.1	—	1835	2.8	2.8
1869	1,824.8	1,824.8	—	1834	(NA)	(NA)
1868	1,534.6	1,534.6	—	1833	(NA)	(NA)
1867	1,168.0	1,168.0	—	1832	(NA)	(NA)
1866	874.2	874,2	—	1831	(NA)	(NA)
1865	589.9	589.9	—	1830	.6	.6
1864	404.3	404.3	—	1829	(NA)	(NA)
1863	276.1	276,1	—	1828	(NA)	(NA)
1862	191.8	191.8	—	1827	(NA)	(NA)
1861	173.3	173.3	—	1826	(NA)	(NA)
1860	173.3	173.3	—	1825	.2	.2
1859	151.7	151.7	—	1824	(NA)	(NA)
1858	130.5	130.5	—	1823	(NA)	(NA)
1857	120.6	120.6	—	1822	(NA)	(NA)
1856	106.5	106.5	—	1821	(NA)	(NA)
1855	106.0	106.0	—	1820	.1	.1
1854	94.0	94.0	—	1819	(NA)	(NA)
1853	(NA)	(NA)	—	1818	(NA)	(NA)
1852	(NA)	(NA)	—	1817	(NA)	(NA)
1851	(NA)	(NA)	—	1816	(NA)	(NA)
				1815	(Z)	(Z)

* Denotes first year for which figures include Alaska and Hawaii.
NA Not available.
Z Less than $50,000 or less than $500,000.

[1] Initial year 1911.
[2] First weekly premium policy issued 1873; industrial agency system introduced 1875.
[3] Initial year 1917.

Series X 957-962. Subscription or Premium Income and Benefit Expenditures of Private Health Insurance: 1948 to 1989

(In millions of dollars, except percent)

Year	Subscription or premium income 957	Total benefit expenditures 958	Year	Subscription or premium income 957	Total benefit expenditures 958	Year	Subscription or premium income 957	Total benefit expenditures 958
1989	108,000	89,400	1975	20,800	16,500	1961	6,673	5,965
1988	98,200	83,000	1974	17,900	13,600	1960	5,841	4,996
1987	84,100	72,500	1973	16,100	11,900	1959	5,139	4,399
1986	75,500	64,300	1972	14,800	10,600	1958	4,498	3,877
			1971	12,777	9,497	1957	4,144	3,474
1985	75,200	60,000				1956	3,624	3,015
1984	70,400	56,000	1970	17,185	15,744			
1983	63,200	51,700	1969	14,658	13,069	1955	3,150	2,536
1982	58,300	49,200	1968	12,861	11,310	1954	2,756	2,179
1981	49,000	41,600	1967	11,105	9,545	1953	2,405	1,919
			1966	10,564	9,142	1952	1,993	1,604
1980	43,700	37,000				1951	1,660	1,353
1979	35,800	29,600	1965	10,001	8,729			
1978	32,700	26,400	1964	8,984	7,832	1950	1,292	992
1977	28,700	22,100	1963	8,054	6,980	1949	1,015	767
1976	24,500	20,200	1962	7,411	6,344	1948	862	606

GOVERNMENT
Highlights

1 Although the United States was founded as a democracy, it took over 200 years for its electoral mechanisms to evolve from a highly elite, nondemocratic format to their present state. For the first 100 or so years, each state determined for itself who its voters were and how they should be enrolled and permitted to vote. Over the years, Constitutional amendments, Congressional legislation, and judicial decisions applied certain constraints to the states' discretion in specified areas of legal procedure pertaining to elections. In the South, for example, fraudulent stuffing of boxes, suppression of returns, and other irregularities were fairly common after the Civil War and well into the 20th century; as late as the 1940s Lyndon Johnson's victory in his Senate race was attributed to such practices. Originally, only free White males were enfranchised. Women were universally enfranchised in 1920, but a number of states gave women suffrage earlier: Wyoming, as a territory, in 1869; Colorado in 1893; Utah in 1896; Idaho in 1897; Washington and California in 1911; Oregon, Arizona, and Kansas in 1913; Montana and Nevada in 1914; Illinois in 1916; and Michigan and New York in 1918. Blacks were enfranchised in 1870 by the 15th Amendment but were hobbled in the South by a number of procedural and technical restrictions designed to keep them away from the ballot box. In the 1960s, the Civil Rights Act made such restrictions unconstitutional. Until 1928, citizenship was not a requirement for voting and aliens voted freely in many states. Because of the difficulty in estimating the number of foreign-born males in the population, the electoral data for years before and after 1928 are not strictly comparable.

2 Article II, Section I of the U.S. Constitution lays down the method for the election of the President of the United States—the establishment of an electoral college in each state. The method of casting the electoral votes was modified in 1804 by the adoption of the 12th Amendment to the Constitution. With a few exceptions, presidential electors have been chosen by direct popular vote since 1828, although state legislatures still have the right to choose the electors. On four occasions in U.S. history, the entire electoral vote of a state remained uncast for technical reasons.

3 The number of members in the House of Representatives is fixed by Congress at the time of each apportion-ment and is based on the population of each state as shown in the decennial censuses. No change in total House membership has been made since 1912, except to allot one representative each to Hawaii and Alaska when they attained statehood. Membership was increased to 437 in 1960, but reverted to 435 after 1962. Prior to the passage of the 14th Amendment, Indians were excluded from the Census and only three out of five slaves were included. Prior to 1850, apportionment ratios were chosen arbitrarily; from 1850 to 1900 by dividing the total population by a predetermined number of Representatives; and from 1910 on by dividing the eligible population by a fixed number of Representatives.

4 In any given place, an American lives under at least five governments: Federal, state, county, township, and school district. In addition, there are many offshoots such as single-function and multiple-function districts, authorities, commissions, and boards with varying degrees of autonomy and budgetary powers. When William Anderson's monograph, *The Units of Government in the United States,* was published in 1934 there were 175,418 governments in the country. It declined to 155,116 in 1942, and to 83,237 by 1987. This was mainly a result of mergers or eliminations of school districts; they shrunk in number from 108,579 in 1942 to 14,721 in 1987. Complete censuses of government covering structure, personnel, expenditures, revenues, and debt were conducted in 1932, 1942, and 1957 and at five-year intervals thereafter. Earlier censuses were held decennially from 1850 to 1890 and for 1902, 1912, and 1922, but were much narrower in scope. These censuses differ not only in scope but also in basic concepts and classifications, thus affecting their comparability. Statistics on government employment and payroll have been published by the Bureau of Labor Statistics since 1955; from 1940 to 1955 they were published by the Bureau of the Census. Data for municipalities are for city, borough, village, and—except in New England, New York and Wisconsin—town governments. Data for school districts are restricted to independent districts and do not include school systems operated by state, city, county or township governments.

5 The first Federal budget of 1789-91 showed net revenues of $4.399 million, of which all but $20,000 were

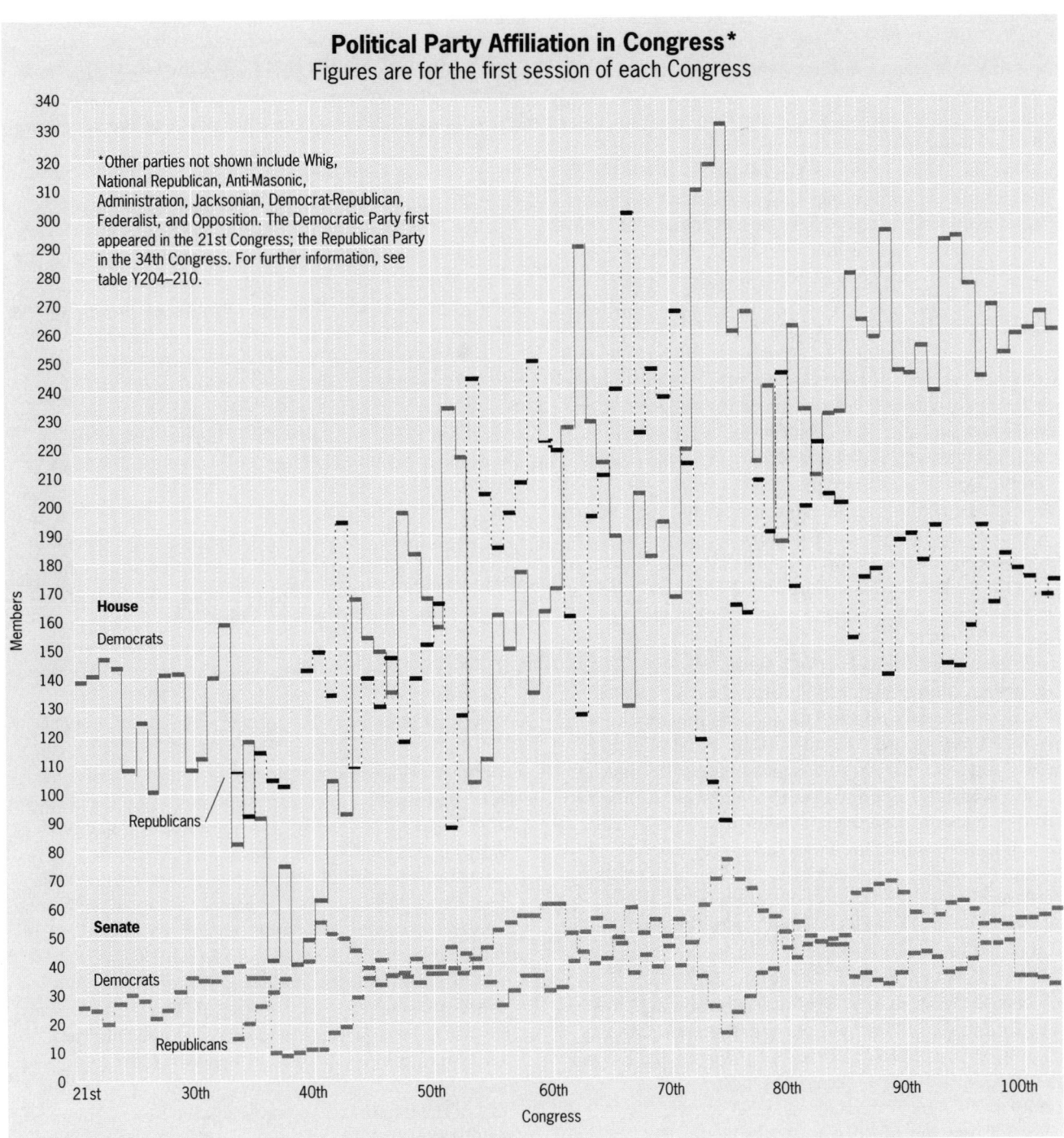

Political Party Affiliation in Congress*
Figures are for the first session of each Congress

*Other parties not shown include Whig, National Republican, Anti-Masonic, Administration, Jacksonian, Democrat-Republican, Federalist, and Opposition. The Democratic Party first appeared in the 21st Congress; the Republican Party in the 34th Congress. For further information, see table Y204–210.

Members

House
Democrats
Republicans

Senate
Democrats
Republicans

Congress

derived from customs duties. The budget remained under $100 million until 1863 when under the financial strains of the Civil War it rose to $112 million in 1863. It crossed the $1 billion mark in 1917, again during wartime; the $100 billion mark in 1963, as the Vietnam War was escalating; and the $1 trillion mark in 1990. As a percentage of GNP, it inched up from 16% in 1950 to 25.2% in 1992. The last year in which it showed a surplus was in 1960, when a modest surplus of $510 million was recorded in the penultimate budget of President Eisenhower. The Unified Federal Budget concept was introduced in 1968 to incorporate

reforms recommended by the Presidential Commission on Budget Concepts. Under the Unified Budget, trust funds were included in the Federal Budget in order to show the total impact of government spending on the economy.

6 When income tax was first introduced in 1913, the effective rate was 0.4% for a family in the $5,000 annual earnings range and only 6% for a family earning over $1 million (in 1912 dollars). The total number of returns in 1913 was 357,598. Before the introduction of income tax, 54% of internal revenue collections was from alcohol and 20% from tobacco.

7 In 1816, the total number of Federal employees was 4,837, of whom 535 worked in Washington D.C. Under George Washington, the entire White House staff consisted of two people.

8 For a number of years there were two categories of public debt: Public Debt and debt subject to the debt limit. The Public Debt is that which originates from the Treasury Department, but it excludes debt incurred by public agencies, such as the Tennessee Valley Authority. Gross Public Debt is a new concept which includes both public and agency debt. About three-fourths of the gross debt is owed to the public and the rest is a paper debt consisting of surpluses of trust funds invested by the government in public debt securities. Interest payments on this part of the debt are paid from one account within the budget to another account also within the budget, and therefore do not affect the budget surplus or deficit. Since the Federal Reserve System is an independent body outside the Federal budget, the U.S. government pays the Fed interest on money borrowed from it for budgetary purposes. Debt held by the system is shown as debt held by the public, and interest paid to the system affects budget surplus or deficit. In years of heavy borrowing, the government has to pay billions of dollars in interest, thus adding to the deficit, and vice versa. However, since 1947, the Federal Reserve has made annual payments to the Treasury from its surplus, which in turn arises primarily as a result of interest payments made by the Treasury. The public debt in 1791 was $75.463 million, or $19.21 per capita. By the time of the Civil War, it had been reduced to $2.85 per capita. The Civil War and the half century following saw an expansion in public debt, but it came down to the very low level of $11.99 per capita by the start of World War I. Thereafter it rose steadily, crossing the $1,000 per capita mark in 1944. In 1992, with a gross public debt of $4.077 trillion, per capita debt stood at $16,140.

9 The Department of War (now Department of Defense) was established in 1789. The Navy started functioning in 1794 and a separate Navy Department was authorized and organized in 1798. The Department of the Air Force was set up in 1947 under the National Security Act. The Marine Corps was founded in 1775, disbanded in 1783, and reactivated in 1794. In 1794, under George Washington, the defense force of the new republic consisted of an army of 3,813 persons (including 235 officers) and a navy of 1,856 persons (including 150 officers). The total military budget was $2.639 million for the army and $61,000 for the navy.

10 The power of incumbency in Congress is illustrated by the fact that 96.1% of incumbent representatives and 96.9% of incumbent senators were reelected in 1990.

11 Since 1970, Blacks, women, and Hispanics have been increasing their political and legislative power. The 102nd Congress (1991) contained 28 females, 25 Blacks,

and 11 Hispanics compared to 18 females, 16 Blacks, and five Hispanics in the 95th Congress (1977). The number of Black elected officials grew from 1,479 in 1970 to 7,445 in 1991. The most significant expansion of Black presence in politics has been in state legislatures, where there were 476 Blacks in 1990, compared to 179 in 1970; and in city and county governments where there were 4,493 Blacks in 1990, compared to 719 in 1970. The number of Hispanic public officials grew from 3,063 in 1984 to 4,004 in 1990. There were 134 Hispanic legislators and executives at the state level in 1990, and 1,819 Hispanic county and municipal officials. Women occupied 60 statewide elective executive offices and 1,375 seats in state legislatures. There were also 14,672 female mayors and municipal council members.

12 In 1990, the state with the highest percentage of registered voters was Maine (94%), and the lowest was South Carolina (52%).

13 In 1990, there were 4,094 political action committees: 1,738 were corporate; 338 labor; and 742 trade, membership, and health organizations. Their contributions to Congressional campaigns totaled $108.5 million, of which $72.2 million went to Democrats, $36.2 million to Republicans, $87.5 million to incumbents and $7.3 million to challengers. Incumbents also received 64% of all Congressional campaign money.

14 The United States has one of the lowest rates of voter participation in elections and one of the highest rates of political apathy among all democracies (as measured by voter turnout for elections, number of citizens running for office, membership in political parties, etc.). Generally, presidential election years draw more voters to the polling booths than mid-term election years. Even so, only 50.1% of eligible voters turned out to vote in 1988. The highest percentage of voting age population participating in a presidential election was 62.8% in 1960. In Congressional elections, the percentage is much lower, reaching only 33.1% in 1990.

15 The number of measures enacted by Congress has declined since 1972, primarily because many private bills are being bundled together as omnibus bills. Nevertheless, both representatives and senators are working more than they used to—working a fewer number of days in each session, but a greater number of hours per day. On an average, a representative spent 6.0 hours and a senator 8.2 hours each day at work during a session.

16 Alaska, Florida, Nevada, South Dakota, Texas, Washington, and Wyoming are the seven states that still do not have personal income taxes. Illinois, Indiana, Massachusetts, Michigan, and Pennsylvania have flat rates while Colorado, Rhode Island, and Vermont have taxes calculated as a percentage of Federal tax liability.

Public Debt of the Federal Government: 1853 to 1991
Plotted in 5 year intervals (except 1940–1945)

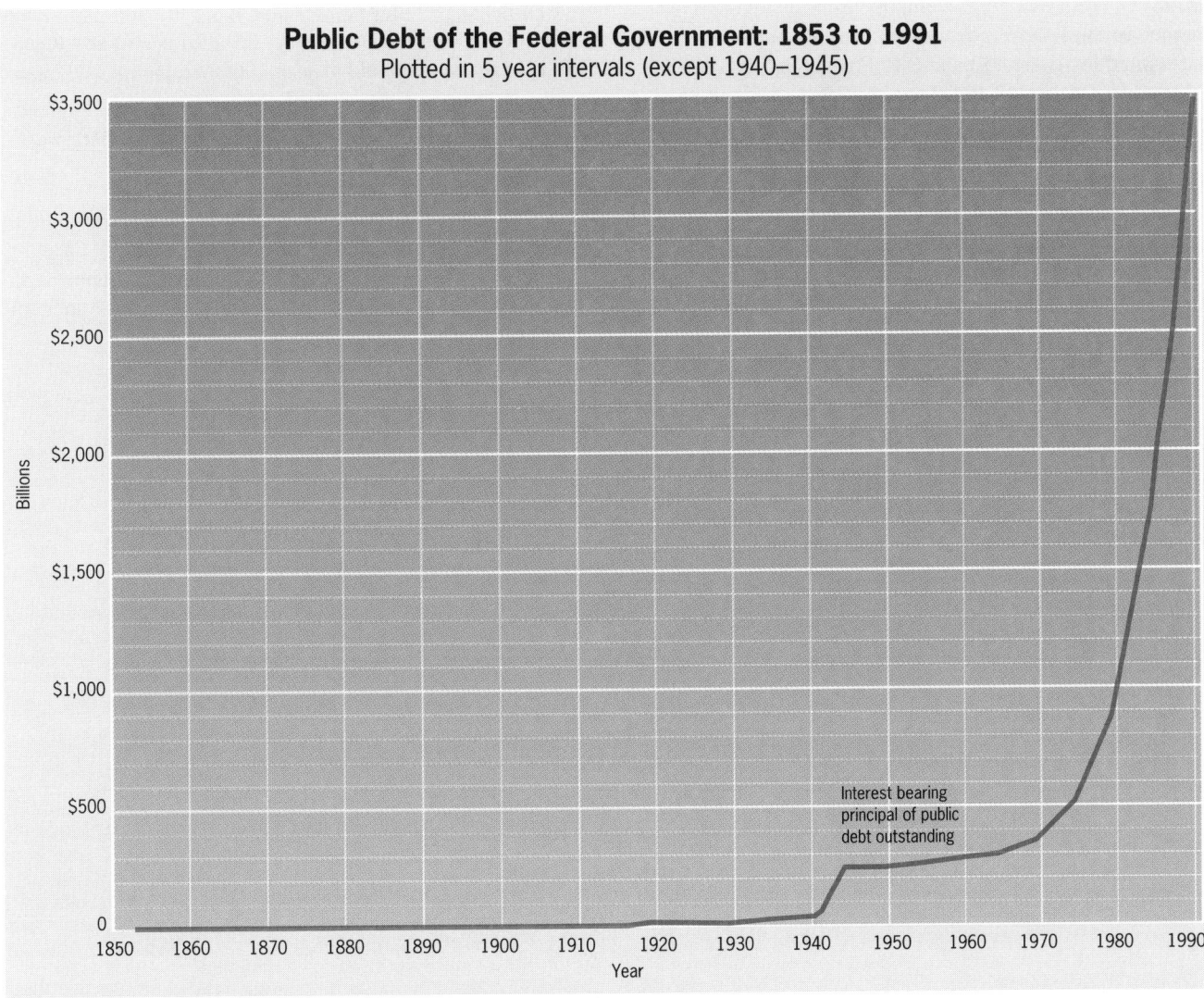

Billions

Interest bearing
principal of public
debt outstanding

Year

17 Of the 3,042 counties, 167 have populations of more than 250,000 and 698 fewer than 5,000. Of the 19,200 municipalities, 61 have more than 250,000 inhabitants and 9,369 fewer than 1,000. Of the 16,691 townships, four have more than 250,000 inhabitants and 9,143 fewer than 1,000.

18 Of the largest cities in the nation, Washington D.C. has the highest tax incidence per capita at $3,744, followed by New York City with $2,063. Mesa, Arizona has the lowest tax incidence per capita at $253.

19 State and local governments collected $152.1 billion in property taxes in 1990. In effective tax rates per $100, the 10 cities with the highest tax rates were Detroit, Michigan (4.40); Milwaukee, Wisconsin (3.78); Portland, Oregon (3.32); Des Moines, Iowa (3.10); Newark, New Jersey (2.96); Philadelphia, Pennsylvania (2.64); Omaha, Nebraska (2.63); Providence, Rhode Island (2.55); Baltimore, Maryland (2.46); and Manchester, New Hampshire (2.36). The five cities with the lowest rates were Honolulu,

Hawaii (0.48); Charleston, South Carolina (0.61); Los Angeles, California (0.63); Birmingham, Alabama (0.70); Casper, Wyoming (0.71); and New York City, New York (0.79).

20 Income from lotteries in 1990 was $53.9 billion, of which $39.8 billion was converted into revenues. Only 10 states do not have lotteries: Alabama, Alaska, Arkansas, Louisiana, Nebraska, Nevada, New Mexico, North Dakota, Oklahoma, and South Carolina.

21 Of the 18.369 million public employees in 1990, 3.105 million were in the Federal government, 4.503 million in state governments, and 10.760 million in local governments. There are wide variations among cities in the number of employees per 10,000 population—ranging from 776 for Washington D.C.; 537 for New York City, New York; and 397 for Buffalo, New York to 66 for San Jose, California; 69 for Arlington, Texas; 71 for Santa Ana, California; 77 for Omaha, Nebraska; and 83 for Mesa, Arizona.

22 Of the 3.067 million employees in the Executive branch of the Federal government in 1990, Defense accounted for 1,034,152, the U.S. Postal Service 816,886, Veteran's Affairs 248,174, Treasury 158,655, Health and Human Services 123,959, Agriculture 122,594, and independent agencies 999,894.

23 Despite the end of the Cold War, defense outlays are still climbing, reaching an all-time high of $341.1 billion in 1992 after modest declines in 1991 (8.7%) and 1990 (1.4%) However, as a percentage of GNP, defense accounts for less of the GNP today (5.2%) than it did in 1968 (9.6%). Its share of the total Federal outlays (20.8%) is also less than at the height of the Cold War in 1960 (52.2%).

24 In 1989, the worldwide military budget was $1.035 trillion, of which the U.S. share was 29.4%.

25 In 1990, the United States was the world's second largest arms exporter, next to the Soviet Union. Of the world total in arms trade of $45.43 billion, the Soviet Union accounted for $19.6 billion and the United States for $11.2 billion.

Series Y 79-83.   Electoral and Popular Vote Cast for President, by Political Party: 1789 to 1992

(Excludes unpledged tickets and minor candidates polling under 10,000 votes. Various party labels may have been used by a candidate in different states; the more important of these are listed below)

Year	No. of states	Presidential candidate	Political party	Electoral	Popular
	79	80	81	82	83
1992	50	Bill Clinton	Democratic	370	43,682,000
		George Bush	Republican	168	38,117,000
		H. Ross Perot	Independent	X	19,217,000
1988	50	George Bush	Republican	426	48,886,000
		Michael Dukakis	Democratic	111	41,809,000
1984	50	Ronald Reagan	Republican	525	54,455,000
		Walter Mondale	Democratic	13	37,577,000
1980	50	Ronald Reagan	Republican	489	43,904,000
		Jimmy Carter	Democratic	49	35,484,000
1976	50	Jimmy Carter	Democratic	297	40,831,000
		Gerald Ford	Republican	240	39,148,000
1972	50	Richard Nixon	Republican	520	47,170,000
		George McGovern	Democratic	17	29,170,000
1968	50	Richard M. Nixon	Republican	301	31,785,480
		Hubert H. Humphrey	Democratic	191	31,275,166
		George C. Wallace	American Independent	46	9,906,473
		Henning A. Blomen	Socialist Labor	X	52,588
		Dick Gregory	(1)	X	47,133
		Fred Halstead	Socialist Workers	X	41,388
		Eldridge Cleaver	Peace and Freedom	X	36,563
		Eugene J. McCarthy	(2)	X	25,552
		E. Harold Munn	Prohibition	X	15,123
1964	50	Lyndon B. Johnson	Democratic	486	43,129,566
		Barry M. Goldwater	Republican	52	27,178,188
		Eric Hass	Socialist Labor	X	45,219
		Clifton DeBerry	Socialist Workers	X	32,720
		E. Harold Munn	Prohibition	X	23,267
1960	50	John F. Kennedy	Democratic	[3] 303	34,226,731
		Richard M. Nixon	Republican	219	34,108,157
		Eric Hass	Socialist Labor	X	47,522
		Rutherford L. Decker	Prohibition	X	46,203
		Orval E. Faubus	National States' Rights	X	44,977
		Farrell Dobbs	Socialist Workers	X	40,165
		Charles L. Sullivan	Constitution	X	18,162
1956	48	Dwight D. Eisenhower	Republican	457	35,590,472
		Adlai E. Stevenson	Democratic	[4] 73	26,022,752
		T. Coleman Andrews	States' Rights	X	111,178
		Eric Hass	Socialist Labor	X	44,450
		Enoch A. Holtwick	Prohibition	X	41,937
1952	48	Dwight D. Eisenhower	Republican	442	33,936,234
		Adlai E. Stevenson	Democratic	89	27,314,992
		Vincent Hallinan	Progressive	X	140,023
		Stuart Hamblen	Prohibition	X	72,949
		Eric Hass	Socialist Labor	X	30,267
		Darlington Hoopes	Socialist	X	20,203
		Douglas A. MacArthur	Constitution	X	17,205
		Farrell Dobbs	Socialist Workers	X	10,312
1948	48	Harry S. Truman	Democratic	303	24,179,345
		Thomas E. Dewey	Republican	189	21,991,291
		Strom Thurmond	States' Rights	39	1,176,125
		Henry Wallace	Progressive	X	1,157,326
		Norman Thomas	Socialist	X	139,572
		Claude A. Watson	Prohibition	X	103,900
		Edward A. Teichert	Socialist Labor	X	29,241
		Farrell Dobbs	Socialist Workers	X	13,614

See footnotes at end of table.

Series Y 79-83. Electoral and Popular Vote Cast for President, by Political Party: 1789 to 1992—Cont'd.

(Excludes unpledged tickets and minor candidates polling under 10,000 votes. Various party labels may have been used by a candidate in different states; the more important of these are listed below)

Year	No. of states	Presidential candidate	Political party	Vote cast Electoral	Vote cast Popular
79	**80**	**81**	**82**	**83**	
1944	48	Franklin D. Roosevelt	Democratic	432	25,606,585
		Thomas E. Dewey	Republican	99	22,014,745
		Norman Thomas	Socialist	X	80,518
		Claude A. Watson	Prohibition	X	74,758
		Edward A. Teichert	Socialist Labor	X	45,336
1940	48	Franklin D. Roosevelt	Democratic	449	27,307,819
		Wendell L. Willkie	Republican	82	22,321,018
		Norman Thomas	Socialist	X	99,557
		Roger Q. Babson	Prohibition	X	57,812
		Earl Browder	Communist	X	46,251
		John W. Aiken	Socialist Labor	X	14,892
1936	48	Franklin D. Roosevelt	Democratic	523	27,752,869
		Alfred M. Landon	Republican	8	16,674,665
		William Lemke	Union	X	882,479
		Norman Thomas	Socialist	X	187,720
		Earl Browder	Communist	X	80,159
		D. Leigh Colvin	Prohibition	X	37,847
		John W. Aiken	Socialist Labor	X	12,777
1932	48	Franklin D. Roosevelt	Democratic	472	22,809,638
		Herbert C. Hoover	Republican	59	15,758,901
		Norman Thomas	Socialist	X	881,951
		William Z. Foster	Communist	X	102,785
		William D. Upshaw	Prohibition	X	81,869
		Verne L. Reynolds	Socialist Labor	X	33,276
		William H. Harvey	Liberty	X	53,425
1928	48	Herbert C. Hoover	Republican	444	21,391,993
		Alfred E. Smith	Democratic	87	15,016,169
		Norman Thomas	Socialist	X	267,835
		Verne L. Reynolds	Socialist Labor	X	21,603
		William Z. Foster	Workers	X	21,181
		William F. Varney	Prohibition	X	20,106
1924	48	Calvin Coolidge	Republican	382	15,718,211
		John W. Davis	Democratic	136	8,385,283
		Robert M. LaFollette	Progressive	13	4,831,289
		Herman P. Faris	Prohibition	X	57,520
		Frank T. Johns	Socialist Labor	X	36,428
		William Z. Foster	Workers	X	36,386
		Gilbert O. Nations	American	X	23,967
1920	48	Warren G. Harding	Republican	404	16,143,407
		James M. Cox	Democratic	127	9,130,328
		Eugene V. Debs	Socialist	X	919,799
		P.P. Christensen	Farmer-Labor	X	265,411
		Aaron S. Watkins	Prohibition	X	189,408
		James E. Ferguson	American	X	48,000
		W.W. Cox	Socialist Labor	X	31,715
1916	48	Woodrow Wilson	Democratic	277	9,127,695
		Charles E. Hughes	Republican	254	8,533,507
		A.L. Benson	Socialist	X	585,113
		J. Frank Hanly	Prohibition	X	220,506
		Arthur E. Reimer	Socialist Labor	X	13,403
1912	48	Woodrow Wilson	Democratic	435	6,296,547
		Theodore Roosevelt	Progressive	88	4,118,571
		William H. Taft	Republican	8	3,486,720
		Eugene V. Debs	Socialist	X	900,672
		Eugene W. Chafin	Prohibition	X	206,275
		Arthur E. Reimer	Socialist Labor	X	28,750

See footnotes at end of table.

Series Y 79-83. Electoral and Popular Vote Cast for President, by Political Party: 1789 to 1992—Cont'd.

(Excludes unpledged tickets and minor candidates polling under 10,000 votes. Various party labels may have been used by a candidate in different states; the more important of these are listed below)

Year	No. of states	Presidential candidate	Political party	Vote cast Electoral	Vote cast Popular
	79	80	81	82	83
1908	46	William H. Taft	Republican	321	7,675,320
		William J. Bryan	Democratic	162	6,412,294
		Eugene V. Debs	Socialist	X	420,793
		Eugene W. Chafin	Prohibition	X	253,840
		Thomas L Hisgen	Independence	X	82,872
		Thomas E. Watson	People's	X	29,100
		August Gillhaus	Socialist Labor	X	14,021
1904	45	Theodore Roosevelt	Republican	336	7,628,461
		Alton B. Parker	Democratic	140	5,084,223
		Eugene V. Debs	Socialist	X	402,283
		Silas C. Swallow	Prohibition	X	258,536
		Thomas E. Watson	People's	X	117,183
		Charles H. Corregan	Socialist Labor	X	31,249
1900	45	William McKinley	Republican	292	7,218,491
		William J. Bryan	Democratic [5]	155	6,356,734
		John C. Wooley	Prohibition	X	208,914
		Eugene V. Debs	Socialist	X	87,814
		Wharton Barker	People's	X	50,373
		Joseph F. Malloney	Socialist Labor	X	39,739
1896	45	William McKinley	Republican	271	7,102,246
		William J. Bryan	Democratic [5]	176	6,492,559
		John M. Palmer	National Democratic	X	133,148
		Joshua Levering	Prohibition	X	132,007
		Charles H. Matchett	Socialist Labor	X	36,274
		Charles E. Bentley	Nationalist	X	13,969
1892	44	Grover Cleveland	Democratic	277	5,555,426
		Benjamin Harrison	Republican	145	5,182,690
		James B. Weaver	People's	22	1,029,846
		John Bidwell	Prohibition	X	264,133
		Simon Wing	Socialist Labor	X	21,164
1888	38	Benjamin Harrison	Republican	233	5,447,129
		Grover Cleveland	Democratic	168	5,537,857
		Clinton B. Fisk	Prohibition	X	249,506
		Anson J. Streeter	Union Labor	X	146,935
1884	38	Grover Cleveland	Democratic	219	4,879,507
		James G. Blaine	Republican	182	4,850,293
		Benjamin F. Butler	Greenback-Labor	X	175,370
		John P. St. John	Prohibition	X	150,369
1880	38	James A. Garfield	Republican	214	4,453,295
		Winfield S. Hancock	Democratic	155	4,414,082
		James B. Weaver	Greenback-Labor	X	308,578
		Neal Dow	Prohibition	X	10,305
1876	38	Rutherford B. Hayes	Republican	185	4,036,572
		Samuel J. Tilden	Democratic	184	4,284,020
		Peter Cooper	Greenback	X	81,737
1872	37	Ulysses S. Grant	Republican	286	3,596,745
		Horace Greeley	Democratic	(6)	2,843,446
		Charles O'Connor	Straight Democratic	X	29,489
		Thomas A. Hendricks	Independent Democratic	42	—
		B. Gratz Brown	Democratic	18	—
		Charles J. Jenkins	Democratic	2	—
		David Davis	Democratic	1	—
		(Not voted)		7	—

See footnotes at end of table.

Series Y 79-83. Electoral and Popular Vote Cast for President, by Political Party: 1789 to 1992—Cont'd.

(Excludes unpledged tickets and minor candidates polling under 10,000 votes. Various party labels may have been used by a candidate in different states; the more important of these are listed below)

Year	No. of states	Presidential candidate	Political party	Vote cast Electoral	Vote cast Popular
	79	80	81	82	83
1868	37	Ulysses S. Grant	Republican	214	3,013,421
		Horatio Seymour	Democratic	80	2,706,829
		(Not voted)		23	—
1864	36	Abraham Lincoln	Republican	212	2,206,938
		George B. McClellan	Democratic	21	1,803,787
		(Not voted)		81	—
1860	33	Abraham Lincoln	Republican	180	1,865,593
		J.C. Breckinridge	Democratic (S)	72	848,356
		Stephen A. Douglas	Democratic	12	1,382,713
		John Bell	Constitutional Union	39	592,906
1856	31	James Buchanan	Democratic	174	1,832,955
		John C. Fremont	Republican	114	1,339,932
		Millard Fillmore	American	8	871,731
1852	31	Franklin Pierce	Democratic	254	1,601,117
		Winfield Scott	Whig	42	1,385,453
		John P. Hale	Free Soil	X	155,825
1848	30	Zachary Taylor	Whig	163	1,360,967
		Lewis Cass	Democratic	127	1,222,342
		Martin Van Buren	Free Soil	X	291,263
1844	26	James K. Polk	Democratic	170	1,338,464
		Henry Clay	Whig	105	1,300,097
		James G. Birney	Liberty	X	62,300
1840	26	William H. Harrison	Whig	234	1,274,624
		Martin Van Buren	Democratic	60	1,127,781
1836	26	Martin Van Buren	Democratic	170	765,483
		William H. Harrison	Whig	73	
		Hugh L. White	Whig	26	[7] 739,795
		Daniel Webster	Whig	14	
		W.P. Mangum	Anti-Jackson	11	—
1832	24	Andrew Jackson	Democratic	219	687,502
		Henry Clay	National Republican	49	530,189
		William Wirt	Anti-Masonic	7	—
		John Floyd	Nullifiers	11	—
		(Not voted)		2	—
1828	24	Andrew Jackson	Democratic	178	647,286
		John Q. Adams	National Republican	83	508,064
1824	24	John Q. Adams	No distinct party	[8] 84	108,740
		Andrew Jackson	designations	[8] 99	153,544
		Henry Clay		37	47,136
		W.H. Crawford		41	46,618
1820	24	James Monroe	Republican	231	—
		John Q. Adams	Independent-Republican	1	—
		(Not voted)		3	—
1816	19	James Monroe	Republican	183	—
		Rufus King	Federalist	34	—
		(Not voted)		4	—
1812	18	James Madison	Democratic-Republican	128	—
		DeWitt Clinton	Fusion	89	—
		(Not voted)		1	—

See footnotes at end of table.

Series Y 79-83.   Electoral and Popular Vote Cast for President, by Political Party: 1789 to 1992—Cont'd.

(Excludes unpledged tickets and minor candidates polling under 10,000 votes. Various party labels may have been used by a candidate in different states; the more important of these are listed below)

Year	No. of states	Presidential candidate	Political party	Vote cast, Electoral
	79	80	81	82
1808	17	James Madison	Democratic-Republican	122
		C.C. Pinckney	Federalist	47
		George Clinton	Independent-	6
		(Not voted)	Republican	1
1804	17	Thomas Jefferson	Democratic-Republican	162
		C.C. Pinckney	Federalist	14
1800 [9]	16	Thomas Jefferson	Democratic-Republican	73
		Aaron Burr	Democratic-Republican	73
		John Adams	Federalist	65
		C.C. Pinckney	Federalist	64
		John Jay	Federalist	1
1796 [9]	16	John Adams	Federalist	71
		Thomas Jefferson	Democratic-Republican	68
		Thomas Pinckney	Federalist	59
		Aaron Burr	Anti-Federalist	30
		Samuel Adams	Democratic-Republican	15
		Oliver Ellsworth	Federalist	11
		George Clinton	Democratic-Republican	7
		John Jay	Independent-Federalist	5
		James Iredell	Federalist	3
		George Washington	Federalist	2
		John Henry	Independent	2
		S. Johnston	Independent-Federalist	2
		C.C. Pinckney	Independent-Federalist	1
1792 [9]	15	George Washington	Federalist	132
		John Adams	Federalist	77
		George Clinton	Democratic-Republican	50
		Thomas Jefferson	——	4
		Aaron Burr	——	1
1789 [9]	10	George Washington	——	69
		John Adams	——	34
		John Jay	——	9
		R.H. Harrison	——	6
		John Rutledge	——	6
		John Hancock	——	4
		George Clinton	——	3
		Samuel Huntington	——	2
		John Milton	——	2
		James Armstrong	——	1
		Benjamin Lincoln	——	1
		Edward Telfair	——	1
		(Not voted)		12

X Represents zero.
[1] Total vote for Gregory includes write-in votes as well as votes for the Freedom and Peace Party, the Peace Freedom Alternative, the Peace and Freedom Party and the New Party.
[2] Total vote for McCarthy includes write-in votes as well as votes for the Alternative in November Party and the New Party.
[3] Six Democratic electors in Alabama, all eight unpledged Democratic electors in Mississippi and one Republican elector in Oklahoma voted for Senator Harry F. Byrd.
[4] One Democratic elector in Alabama voted for Walter Jones.
[5] Includes a variety of joint tickets with People's Party electors committed to Bryan.

[6] Greeley died shortly after the election and presidential electors supporting him cast their votes as indicated, including three for Greeley, which were not counted.
[7] Whig tickets were pledged to various candidates in various states.
[8] No candidate having a majority in the electoral college, the election was decided in the House of Representatives.
[9] Prior to the election of 1804, each elector voted for two candidates for president; the one receiving the highest number of votes, if a majority, was declared elected president, the next highest, vice president. This provision was modified by adoption of the 12th amendment, which was declared ratified by the legislatures of three-fourths of the states in a proclamation of the Secretary of State, Sept. 25, 1804.

Series Y 135-186.   Popular Vote Cast for President, by State and Political Party: 1836 to 1992

(In thousands. Rep.-Republican; Dem.-Democratic; Ind.-Independent. Vote listed is normally that of the highest candidate for presidential elector for each party. Democratic vote in 1896 and 1900 includes a variety of joint elector tickets with the People's Party, and party totals generally include votes cast for the presidential candidate under other designations than that of the party itself)

Series No.	State	1992 Rep.	1992 Dem.	1992 Ind.	1992 Total	1988 Rep.	1988 Dem.	1988 Total	1984 Rep.	1984 Dem.
135	**United States**	**38,117**	**43,682**	**19,217**	**91,595**	**48,886**	**41,809**	**92,653**	**54,455**	**37,577**
136	Alabama	797	686	180	1,378	816	550	1,442	873	552
137	Alaska	73	57	50	200	119	73	208	138	62
138	Arizona	543	521	339	1,172	703	454	1,026	681	334
139	Arkansas	331	495	97	828	467	349	884	535	339
140	California	3,338	4,812	2,144	9,887	5,055	4,702	9,505	5,467	3,923
141	Colorado	557	625	362	1,372	728	621	1,295	822	455
142	Connecticut	574	681	348	1,443	750	677	1,467	891	570
143	Delaware	102	125	59	250	140	109	255	152	102
144	District of Columbia	—	—	—	—	—	—	—	—	—
145	Florida	2,131	2,051	1,040	4,302	2,619	1,657	4,180	2,730	1,449
146	Georgia	985	1,002	366	1,810	1,081	715	1,776	1,069	707
147	Hawaii	136	178	52	354	159	192	336	185	147
148	Idaho	201	136	129	409	254	147	411	298	109
149	Illinois	1,717	2,378	832	4,559	2,311	2,216	4,819	2,707	2,086
150	Indiana	978	839	451	2,169	1,298	861	2,233	1,377	841
151	Iowa	503	583	251	1,226	545	671	1,320	703	606
152	Kansas	443	386	312	993	554	423	1,022	677	333
153	Kentucky	617	661	203	1,323	734	580	1,369	822	540
154	Louisiana	729	815	210	1,628	884	717	1,707	1,037	652
155	Maine	207	261	205	555	307	244	553	337	215
156	Maryland	671	941	271	1,714	876	826	1,676	880	788
157	Massachusetts	803	1,315	630	2,633	1,195	1,401	2,559	1,311	1,240
158	Michigan	1,585	1,854	819	3,669	1,965	1,676	3,802	2,252	1,530
159	Minnesota	734	994	549	2,007	962	1,109	2,084	1,033	1,036
160	Mississippi	478	391	83	932	558	364	941	852	352
161	Missouri	810	1,051	517	2,094	1,085	1,002	2,123	1,274	849
162	Montana	143	153	106	366	190	169	384	232	147
163	Nebraska	338	214	171	661	398	259	652	460	188
164	Nevada	171	185	129	350	206	133	287	189	92
165	New Hampshire	199	207	120	451	282	164	389	267	120
166	New Jersey	1,303	1,361	504	3,100	1,743	1,320	3,218	1,934	1,261
167	New Mexico	209	255	90	521	270	244	514	307	202
168	New York	2,240	3,244	1,028	6,486	3,082	3,348	6,807	3,665	3,120
169	North Carolina	1,122	1,103	353	2,134	1,237	890	2,175	1,346	824
170	North Dakota	133	97	69	297	167	128	309	200	104
171	Ohio	1,876	1,964	1,024	4,394	2,417	1,940	4,548	2,679	1,825
172	Oklahoma	592	473	319	1,171	678	483	1,256	862	385
173	Oregon	393	524	307	1,202	560	616	1,227	686	536
174	Pennsylvania	1,777	2,223	895	4,536	2,300	2,195	4,845	2,584	2,228
175	Rhode Island	121	198	94	405	178	225	410	212	197
176	South Carolina	572	475	137	986	606	371	969	616	344
177	South Dakota	136	124	73	313	165	146	318	200	116
178	Tennessee	840	933	199	1636	947	680	1,712	990	712
179	Texas	2,460	2,278	1,349	5,427	3,037	2,353	5,398	3,433	1,949
180	Utah	320	182	202	647	428	207	630	469	155
181	Vermont	85	125	61	243	124	116	235	136	96
182	Virginia	1,146	1,033	344	2,192	1,309	860	2,147	1,337	796
183	Washington	609	855	470	1,865	904	934	1,884	1,052	807
184	West Virginia	236	324	105	653	341	310	736	405	328
185	Wisconsin	926	1,035	542	2,192	1,047	1,127	2,212	1,199	996
186	Wyoming	79	67	51	177	107	67	189	133	53

See footnotes at end of table.

Series Y 135-186. Popular Vote Cast for President, by State and Political Party: 1836 to 1992—Cont'd.

(In thousands. Rep.-Republican; Dem.-Democratic; Ind.-Independent. Vote listed is normally that of the highest candidate for presidential elector for each party. Democratic vote in 1896 and 1900 includes a variety of joint elector tickets with the People's Party, and party totals generally include votes cast for the presidential candidate under other designations than that of the party itself)

Series No.	State	1980 Total	1980 Rep.	1980 Dem.	1976 Total	1976 Rep.	1976 Dem.	1972 Total	1972 Rep.	1972 Dem.
135	**United States**	**86,515**	**43,904**	**35,484**	**81,556**	**39,148**	**40,831**	**77,719**	**47,170**	**29,170**
136	Alabama	1342	654	637	1,183	504	659	1,006	729	257
137	Alaska	158	86	42	124	72	44	95	55	33
138	Arizona	874	530	247	743	419	296	623	403	109
139	Arkansas	838	403	398	768	268	499	651	449	200
140	California	8,587	4,525	3,084	7,867	3,882	3,742	8,368	4,602	3,476
141	Colorado	1,184	652	368	1,082	584	460	954	597	330
142	Connecticut	1,406	677	542	1,382	719	648	1,384	811	555
143	Delaware	236	111	106	236	110	123	236	140	92
144	District of Columbia	——	——	——	——	——	——	——	——	——
145	Florida	3,687	2,047	1,419	3,151	1,470	1,636	2,583	1,858	718
146	Georgia	1,597	654	891	1,467	484	979	1,175	881	290
147	Hawaii	303	130	136	291	140	147	270	169	101
148	Idaho	437	291	110	344	204	127	310	199	81
149	Illinois	4,750	1,981	2,358	4,719	2,364	2,271	4,723	2,788	1,913
150	Indiana	2,242	1,256	844	2,220	1,184	1,015	2,126	1,405	709
151	Iowa	1,318	676	509	1,279	633	620	1,226	706	496
152	Kansas	980	567	326	958	503	430	916	620	270
153	Kentucky	1,295	635	616	1,167	532	616	1,067	676	371
154	Louisiana	1,549	793	708	1,278	587	661	1,051	687	298
155	Maine	523	239	221	483	236	232	417	256	161
156	Maryland	1,540	681	726	1,440	673	760	1,354	829	506
157	Massachusetts	2,524	1,058	1,054	2,548	1,030	1,429	2,459	1,112	1,333
158	Michigan	3,910	1,915	1,662	3,654	1,894	1,697	3,490	1,962	1,459
159	Minnesota	2,052	873	954	1,950	819	1,070	1,742	898	802
160	Mississippi	893	441	429	769	367	381	646	505	127
161	Missouri	2,100	1,074	931	1,954	927	998	1,856	1,154	697
162	Montana	364	207	118	329	174	149	318	184	120
163	Nebraska	641	420	167	608	360	234	576	406	170
164	Nevada	248	155	67	202	101	92	182	116	66
165	New Hampshire	384	222	109	340	186	148	334	214	116
166	New Jersey	2,976	1,547	1,147	3,014	1,510	1,445	2,997	1,846	1,102
167	New Mexico	457	251	168	418	211	201	386	236	141
168	New York	6,202	2,894	2,728	6,534	3,101	3,390	7,166	4,193	2,951
169	North Carolina	1,856	915	876	1,679	742	927	1,519	1,055	439
170	North Dakota	302	194	79	297	153	136	281	174	100
171	Ohio	4,284	2,207	1,752	4,112	2,001	2,012	4,095	2,442	1,559
172	Oklahoma	1,150	696	402	1,092	546	532	1,030	759	247
173	Oregon	1,182	571	457	1,030	492	490	928	487	393
174	Pennsylvania	4,562	2,262	1,938	4,621	2,206	2,329	4,592	2,715	1,797
175	Rhode Island	416	155	198	411	181	228	416	220	195
176	South Carolina	894	442	430	803	346	451	674	477	187
177	South Dakota	328	198	104	301	152	147	307	166	140
178	Tennessee	1,618	788	783	1,476	634	826	1,201	813	357
179	Texas	4,542	2,511	1,881	4,072	1,953	2,082	3,471	2,299	1,154
180	Utah	604	440	124	541	338	182	478	324	126
181	Vermont	213	95	82	188	102	81	187	117	68
182	Virginia	1,866	990	752	1,697	837	814	1,457	988	439
183	Washington	1,742	865	650	1,556	778	717	1,471	837	568
184	West Virginia	738	334	367	751	315	436	762	485	277
185	Wisconsin	2,273	1,089	982	2,104	1,005	1,040	1,853	989	810
186	Wyoming	177	111	49	156	93	62	146	100	44

See footnotes at end of table.

Series Y 135-186.   Popular Vote Cast for President, by State and Political Party: 1836 to 1992—Cont'd.

(In thousands. Rep.-Republican; Dem.-Democratic; Ind.-Independent. Vote listed is normally that of the highest candidate for presidential elector for each party. Democratic vote in 1896 and 1900 includes a variety of joint elector tickets with the People's Party, and party totals generally include votes cast for the presidential candidate under other designations than that of the party itself)

Series No.	State	1968			1964			1960		
		Total	Rep.	Dem.	Total	Rep.	Dem.	Total	Rep.	Dem.
135	**United States**	**73,212**	**31,785**	**31,275**	**70,645**	**27,178**	**43,130**	**68,838**	**34,108**	**34,277**
136	Alabama	1,050	147	197	690	479	—	570	238	324
137	Alaska	83	38	35	67	23	44	61	31	30
138	Arizona	487	267	171	481	243	238	398	221	177
139	Arkansas	620	191	188	560	243	314	429	185	215
140	California	7,252	3,468	3,244	7,058	2,879	4,172	6,507	3,260	3,224
141	Colorado	811	409	335	777	297	476	736	402	331
142	Connecticut	1,256	557	622	1,219	391	826	1,223	566	657
143	Delaware	214	97	89	201	78	123	197	96	100
144	District of Columbia	171	31	140	199	29	170	—	—	—
145	Florida	2,188	887	677	1,854	906	949	1,544	795	749
146	Georgia	1,250	380	334	1,139	617	523	733	274	459
147	Hawaii	236	91	141	207	44	163	185	92	92
148	Idaho	291	165	89	292	144	149	300	162	139
149	Illinois	4,620	2,175	2,040	4,703	1,906	2,797	4,757	2,369	2,378
150	Indiana	2,124	1,068	807	2,092	911	1,171	2,135	1,175	952
151	Iowa	1,168	619	477	1,185	449	733	1,274	722	551
152	Kansas	873	479	303	858	387	464	929	561	363
153	Kentucky	1,056	462	398	1,046	373	670	1,124	603	522
154	Louisiana	1,097	258	310	896	509	387	808	231	407
155	Maine	393	169	217	381	119	262	422	241	181
156	Maryland	1,235	518	538	1,116	385	731	1,055	490	566
157	Massachusetts	2,332	767	1,469	2,345	550	1,786	2,469	977	1,487
158	Michigan	3,306	1,371	1,593	3,203	1,060	2,137	3,318	1,620	1,687
159	Minnesota	1,589	659	858	1,554	560	991	1,542	758	780
160	Mississippi	655	89	151	409	357	53	298	74	108
161	Missouri	1,810	812	791	1,818	654	1,164	1,934	962	972
162	Montana	274	139	114	279	113	164	278	142	135
163	Nebraska	537	321	171	584	277	307	613	381	233
164	Nevada	154	73	61	135	56	79	107	52	55
165	New Hampshire	297	155	131	288	104	184	296	158	138
166	New Jersey	2,875	1,325	1,264	2,848	964	1,868	2,773	1,363	1,385
167	New Mexico	327	170	130	329	133	194	311	154	156
168	New York	6,792	3,008	3,378	7,166	2,244	4,913	7,291	3,446	3,830
169	North Carolina	1,587	627	464	1,425	625	800	1,369	655	713
170	North Dakota	248	139	95	258	108	150	278	154	124
171	Ohio	3,960	1,791	1,701	3,969	1,471	2,498	4,162	2,218	1,944
172	Oklahoma	943	450	302	932	413	520	903	533	370
173	Oregon	820	408	359	786	283	501	776	408	367
174	Pennsylvania	4,748	2,090	2,259	4,823	1,674	3,131	5,007	2,440	2,556
175	Rhode Island	385	122	247	390	75	315	406	148	258
176	South Carolina	667	254	197	525	309	216	387	189	198
177	South Dakota	281	150	118	293	130	163	306	178	128
178	Tennessee	1,249	473	351	1,144	509	635	1,052	557	481
179	Texas	3,079	1,228	1,267	2,627	959	1,663	2,311	1,121	1,168
180	Utah	423	239	157	401	182	220	375	205	169
181	Vermont	161	85	70	163	55	108	167	98	69
182	Virginia	1,361	590	442	1,042	481	558	771	405	362
183	Washington	1,304	589	616	1,259	470	780	1,242	629	599
184	West Virginia	754	308	374	792	254	538	838	396	442
185	Wisconsin	1,692	810	749	1,692	638	1,050	1,729	895	831
186	Wyoming	127	71	45	143	62	81	141	77	63

See footnotes at end of table.

Series Y 135-186. Popular Vote Cast for President, by State and Political Party: 1836 to 1992—Cont'd.

(In thousands. Rep.-Republican; Dem.-Democratic; Ind.-Independent. Vote listed is normally that of the highest candidate for presidential elector for each party. Democratic vote in 1896 and 1900 includes a variety of joint elector tickets with the People's Party, and party totals generally include votes cast for the presidential candidate under other designations than that of the party itself)

Series No.	State	1956			1952			1948		
		Total	Rep.	Dem.	Total	Rep.	Dem.	Total	Rep.	Dem.
135	**United States**	**62,034**	**35,590**	**26,023**	**61,551**	**33,936**	**27,315**	**48,794**	**21,991**	**24,179**
136	Alabama	497	196	281	426	149	275	215	41	X
138	Arizona	290	177	113	261	152	109	177	78	95
139	Arkansas	407	186	213	405	177	226	242	51	150
140	California	5,466	3,028	2,420	5,142	2,897	2,198	4,022	1,895	1,913
141	Colorado	657	394	258	630	380	246	515	240	267
142	Connecticut	1,117	712	405	1,097	611	482	884	438	423
143	Delaware	178	98	79	174	90	83	139	70	68
145	Florida	1,126	644	480	989	544	445	578	194	282
146	Georgia	670	223	445	656	199	457	419	77	255
148	Idaho	273	167	106	276	181	95	215	102	107
149	Illinois	4,407	2,623	1,776	4,481	2,457	2,014	3,984	1,961	1,995
150	Indiana	1,975	1,183	784	1,955	1,136	802	1,656	821	808
151	Iowa	1,235	729	502	1,269	809	452	1,038	494	522
152	Kansas	866	567	296	896	616	273	789	423	352
153	Kentucky	1,054	572	476	993	495	496	823	341	467
154	Louisiana	618	329	244	652	307	345	416	73	136
155	Maine	352	249	102	352	232	119	265	150	112
156	Maryland	933	560	373	902	499	395	597	295	287
157	Massachusetts	2,349	1,393	948	2,383	1,292	1,084	2,107	909	1,152
158	Michigan	3,080	1,714	1,360	2,799	1,552	1,231	2,110	1,039	1,003
159	Minnesota	1,340	719	618	1,379	763	608	1,212	484	693
160	Mississippi	248	61	144	286	113	173	192	5	19
161	Missouri	1,833	914	918	1,892	959	930	1,579	655	917
162	Montana	271	155	116	265	157	106	224	97	119
163	Nebraska	577	378	199	610	422	188	489	265	224
164	Nevada	97	56	41	82	51	32	62	29	31
165	New Hampshire	267	177	90	273	166	107	231	121	108
166	New Jersey	2,484	1,607	850	2,419	1,374	1,016	1,950	981	895
167	New Mexico	254	147	106	239	132	106	187	80	105
168	New York	7,096	4,346	2,748	7,128	3,953	3,105	6,177	2,841	2,780
169	North Carolina	1,166	575	591	1,211	558	653	791	259	459
170	North Dakota	254	157	97	270	192	77	221	115	96
171	Ohio	3,702	2,263	1,440	3,701	2,100	1,600	2,936	1,446	1,453
172	Oklahoma	859	474	386	949	518	431	722	269	453
173	Oregon	736	406	329	695	421	271	524	261	243
174	Pennsylvania	4,577	2,585	1,982	4,581	2,416	2,146	3,735	1,902	1,752
175	Rhode Island	388	226	162	414	211	203	328	136	189
176	South Carolina	301	76	136	341	168	173	143	5	34
177	South Dakota	294	172	122	294	204	90	250	130	118
178	Tennessee	939	462	457	893	446	444	550	203	270
179	Texas	1,955	1,081	860	2,076	1,103	969	1,250	303	824
180	Utah	334	216	118	330	194	135	276	124	149
181	Vermont	153	110	43	154	110	43	123	76	46
182	Virginia	698	386	268	620	349	269	419	172	201
183	Washington	1,151	620	523	1,103	599	493	905	386	476
184	West Virginia	831	449	382	874	420	454	749	316	429
185	Wisconsin	1,551	955	587	1,607	980	622	1,277	591	647
186	Wyoming	124	75	50	129	81	48	101	48	52

See footnotes at end of table.

Series Y 135-186. Popular Vote Cast for President, by State and Political Party: 1836 to 1992—Cont'd.

(In thousands. Rep.-Republican; Dem.-Democratic; Ind.-Independent. Vote listed is normally that of the highest candidate for presidential elector for each party. Democratic vote in 1896 and 1900 includes a variety of joint elector tickets with the People's Party, and party totals generally include votes cast for the presidential candidate under other designations than that of the party itself)

Series No.	State	1944 Total	1944 Rep.	1944 Dem.	1940 Total	1940 Rep.	1940 Dem.	1936 Total	1936 Rep.	1936 Dem.
135	**United States**	**47,969**	**22,015**	**25,607**	**49,891**	**22,321**	**27,308**	**45,643**	**16,675**	**27,753**
136	Alabama	245	45	199	294	42	251	276	35	238
138	Arizona	138	56	81	150	54	95	124	33	87
139	Arkansas	213	64	149	200	42	157	179	32	147
140	California	3,521	1,513	1,989	3,269	1,351	1,878	2,638	836	1,767
141	Colorado	505	269	234	549	280	266	489	181	295
142	Connecticut	832	391	435	782	361	418	691	279	382
143	Delaware	125	57	68	136	61	75	128	54	70
145	Florida	483	143	339	485	126	359	327	78	249
146	Georgia	328	57	268	313	24	265	293	37	255
148	Idaho	208	100	107	235	107	128	200	66	126
149	Illinois	4,036	1,939	2,079	4,218	2,047	2,150	3,957	1,570	2,283
150	Indiana	1,672	876	781	1,783	899	874	1,651	692	935
151	Iowa	1,053	547	500	1,215	632	579	1,143	488	622
152	Kansas	734	442	287	860	489	365	859	394	462
153	Kentucky	868	392	473	968	410	557	923	370	539
154	Louisiana	349	68	282	372	52	320	330	37	293
155	Maine	296	155	141	321	164	156	304	169	126
156	Maryland	608	293	315	660	270	385	625	231	390
157	Massachusetts	1,961	921	1,035	2,027	940	1,077	1,840	769	943
158	Michigan	2,205	1,084	1,107	2,086	1,040	1,033	1,805	700	1,017
159	Minnesota	1,126	527	590	1,251	596	644	1,130	350	699
160	Mississippi	180	12	169	176	7	168	162	4	157
161	Missouri	1,572	761	807	1,834	871	958	1,829	698	1,111
162	Montana	207	93	113	248	100	146	231	64	160
163	Nebraska	563	330	233	616	352	264	608	248	347
164	Nevada	54	25	30	53	21	32	44	12	32
165	New Hampshire	230	110	120	235	110	125	218	105	108
166	New Jersey	1,964	961	988	1,974	945	1,016	1,819	719	1,084
167	New Mexico	152	71	81	183	79	104	169	62	106
168	New York	6,317	2,988	3,304	6,302	3,027	3,252	5,596	2,181	3,293
169	North Carolina	791	263	527	823	214	609	839	223	616
170	North Dakota	220	119	100	281	155	124	274	73	163
171	Ohio	3,153	1,582	1,571	3,320	1,587	1,733	3,012	1,128	1,747
172	Oklahoma	722	319	401	826	349	474	750	245	501
173	Oregon	480	225	249	481	220	258	414	123	267
174	Pennsylvania	3,795	1,835	1,940	4,078	1,890	2,171	4,138	1,690	2,354
175	Rhode Island	299	123	175	321	139	182	310	125	164
176	South Carolina	103	5	91	100	2	95	115	2	114
177	South Dakota	232	135	97	308	177	131	296	126	160
178	Tennessee	511	200	309	523	169	352	477	147	328
179	Texas	1,144	192	816	1,117	212	905	850	103	742
180	Utah	248	98	150	248	93	154	217	65	150
181	Vermont	125	72	54	143	78	64	144	81	62
182	Virginia	388	145	242	347	109	236	335	98	235
183	Washington	856	362	487	794	322	462	692	207	460
184	West Virginia	716	323	393	868	372	496	830	325	503
185	Wisconsin	1,339	675	650	1,403	679	705	1,259	381	803
186	Wyoming	101	52	49	112	53	59	103	39	63

See footnotes at end of table.

Series Y 135-186. Popular Vote Cast for President, by State and Political Party: 1836 to 1992—Cont'd.

(In thousands. Rep.-Republican; Dem.-Democratic; Ind.-Independent. Vote listed is normally that of the highest candidate for presidential elector for each party. Democratic vote in 1896 and 1900 includes a variety of joint elector tickets with the People's Party, and party totals generally include votes cast for the presidential candidate under other designations than that of the party itself)

Series No.	State	1932 Total	1932 Rep.	1932 Dem.	1928 Total	1928 Rep.	1928 Dem.	1924 Total	1924 Rep.	1924 Dem.
135	**United States**	**39,732**	**15,759**	**22,810**	**36,812**	**21,392**	**15,016**	**29,086**	**15,718**	**8,385**
136	Alabama	242	35	205	249	121	128	165	43	113
138	Arizona	118	36	79	91	53	39	74	31	26
139	Arkansas	219	27	190	202	78	123	139	41	85
140	California	2,266	848	1,324	1,797	1,162	614	1,282	733	106
141	Colorado	457	190	251	392	254	133	342	195	75
142	Connecticut	594	288	282	553	297	252	400	246	110
143	Delaware	113	57	54	105	69	35	90	52	33
145	Florida	275	69	206	254	144	102	109	31	62
146	Georgia	256	20	234	231	65	130	166	30	123
148	Idaho	187	71	109	154	100	53	148	70	24
149	Illinois	3,408	1,433	1,882	3,107	1,769	1,313	2,470	1,453	577
150	Indiana	1,575	677	862	1,421	848	563	1,272	703	492
151	Iowa	1,037	414	598	1,010	624	379	972	537	160
152	Kansas	790	348	423	713	514	193	662	408	156
153	Kentucky	983	395	581	941	558	381	814	397	376
154	Louisiana	269	19	249	216	51	165	122	25	93
155	Maine	298	167	129	262	180	81	192	138	42
156	Maryland	511	184	314	528	301	224	359	162	148
157	Massachusetts	1,580	737	800	1,578	776	793	1,130	703	281
158	Michigan	1,665	740	872	1,372	965	397	1,160	875	152
159	Minnesota	1,003	364	601	971	561	396	822	421	56
160	Mississippi	146	5	140	152	26	125	112	8	100
161	Missouri	1,610	565	1,025	1,501	834	663	1,310	648	575
162	Montana	216	75	127	194	113	79	174	74	34
163	Nebraska	570	201	359	547	346	198	464	219	137
164	Nevada	41	13	29	32	18	14	27	11	6
165	New Hampshire	206	104	101	197	115	81	165	99	57
166	New Jersey	1,630	775	806	1,548	925	616	1,086	675	298
167	New Mexico	151	54	95	118	70	48	114	55	49
168	New York	4,689	1,938	2,535	4,406	2,193	2,090	3,264	1,820	951
169	North Carolina	712	208	498	635	349	286	482	191	284
170	North Dakota	256	72	178	240	131	107	199	95	14
171	Ohio	2,610	1,228	1,302	2,508	1,628	864	2,016	1,176	478
172	Oklahoma	705	188	516	618	394	219	528	226	256
173	Oregon	369	136	214	320	205	109	279	143	68
174	Pennsylvania	2,859	1,454	1,296	3,160	2,055	1,077	2,145	1,401	409
175	Rhode Island	266	115	147	237	118	119	210	125	77
176	South Carolina	104	2	102	69	3	63	51	1	49
177	South Dakota	288	99	184	262	3,158	103	204	101	27
178	Tennessee	390	127	259	353	195	157	301	131	159
179	Texas	856	98	753	708	367	340	656	130	483
180	Utah	207	85	117	177	95	81	157	77	47
181	Vermont	137	79	56	135	90	44	103	80	16
182	Virginia	298	91	204	305	165	140	224	73	140
183	Washington	615	209	353	501	336	157	422	220	43
184	West Virginia	744	331	405	643	376	264	584	289	257
185	Wisconsin	1,115	348	707	1,017	544	450	841	321	68
186	Wyoming	97	40	54	83	53	29	80	42	13

See footnotes at end of table.

Series Y 135-186.   Popular Vote Cast for President, by State and Political Party: 1836 to 1992—Cont'd.

(In thousands. Rep.-Republican; Dem.-Democratic; Ind.-Independent. Vote listed is normally that of the highest candidate for presidential elector for each party. Democratic vote in 1896 and 1900 includes a variety of joint elector tickets with the People's Party, and party totals generally include votes cast for the presidential candidate under other designations than that of the party itself)

Series No.	State	1920 Total	1920 Rep.	1920 Dem.	1916 Total	1916 Rep.	1916 Dem.	1912 Total	1912 Rep.	1912 Dem.
135	**United States**	**26,748**	**16,143**	**9,130**	**18,531**	**8,534**	**9,128**	**15,037**	**3,487**	**6,297**
136	Alabama	234	75	156	131	29	99	118	10	82
138	Arizona	67	37	30	58	21	33	23	3	10
139	Arkansas	183	72	106	168	47	112	124	24	69
140	California	943	625	229	1,000	463	466	678	4	283
141	Colorado	292	173	105	294	102	179	266	58	114
142	Connecticut	366	229	121	214	107	100	190	68	75
143	Delaware	95	53	40	52	26	25	49	16	23
145	Florida	145	45	91	81	15	56	52	4	36
146	Georgia	149	43	106	160	11	128	121	6	94
148	Idaho	136	89	47	135	55	70	106	33	34
149	Illinois	2,095	1,420	534	2,193	1,153	950	1,146	254	405
150	Indiana	1,263	696	511	719	341	334	654	151	282
151	Iowa	895	635	228	515	279	221	492	120	185
152	Kansas	570	369	185	628	276	314	365	75	144
153	Kentucky	919	452	456	520	242	270	453	116	219
154	Louisiana	126	39	88	93	6	80	79	4	60
155	Maine	198	136	59	136	70	64	130	27	51
156	Maryland	428	236	181	262	117	138	232	55	113
157	Massachusetts	994	681	277	532	269	248	489	156	174
158	Michigan	1,038	756	231	647	338	284	548	151	150
159	Minnesota	736	519	143	387	180	179	334	64	106
160	Mississippi	82	12	69	86	4	80	64	2	57
161	Missouri	1,332	727	575	787	369	398	699	208	331
162	Montana	179	109	57	178	67	101	80	19	28
163	Nebraska	383	248	120	287	118	159	249	54	109
164	Nevada	27	15	10	33	12	18	20	3	8
165	New Hampshire	159	958	63	89	44	44	88	33	35
166	New Jersey	904	611	257	494	269	211	434	89	179
167	New Mexico	106	58	47	67	31	34	49	18	20
168	New York	2,899	1,871	781	1,706	869	759	1,588	455	656
169	North Carolina	538	233	305	290	121	168	244	29	144
170	North Dakota	204	160	37	115	53	55	86	23	30
171	Ohio	2,021	1,182	780	1,164	514	604	1,037	278	425
172	Oklahoma	489	248	218	292	97	148	253	91	119
173	Oregon	239	144	80	262	127	120	137	35	47
174	Pennsylvania	1,853	1,218	504	1,297	704	522	1,218	273	396
175	Rhode Island	168	107	55	88	45	40	78	28	30
176	South Carolina	67	2	34	64	2	62	50	1	48
177	South Dakota	182	111	36	129	64	59	117	X	49
178	Tennessee	428	219	207	273	117	153	253	60	133
179	Texas	486	115	288	373	65	287	302	29	220
180	Utah	146	82	57	143	54	84	112	42	37
181	Vermont	90	68	21	64	40	23	63	23	15
182	Virginia	231	87	142	154	49	103	137	23	90
183	Washington	399	223	84	381	167	183	322	70	87
184	West Virginia	510	282	221	290	143	140	264	57	113
185	Wisconsin	701	499	113	447	221	192	400	131	164
186	Wyoming	55	35	17	52	22	28	42	15	15

See footnotes at end of table.

Series Y 135-186.   Popular Vote Cast for President, by State and Political Party: 1836 to 1992—Cont'd.

(In thousands. Rep.-Republican; Dem.-Democratic; Ind.-Independent. Vote listed is normally that of the highest candidate for presidential elector for each party. Democratic vote in 1896 and 1900 includes a variety of joint elector tickets with the People's Party, and party totals generally include votes cast for the presidential candidate under other designations than that of the party itself)

Series No.	State	1908			1904			1900		
		Total	Rep.	Dem.	Total	Rep.	Dem.	Total	Rep.	Dem.
135	**United States**	**14,884**	**7,675**	**6,412**	**13,521**	**7,628**	**5,084**	**13,968**	**7,218**	**6,357**
136	Alabama	105	26	74	109	22	80	160	56	97
139	Arkansas	152	57	88	117	48	64	128	45	81
140	California	387	214	127	332	205	89	303	165	125
141	Colorado	264	124	127	244	135	100	221	93	123
142	Connecticut	190	113	68	191	111	73	180	103	74
143	Delaware	48	25	22	44	24	19	42	23	19
145	Florida	49	11	31	39	8	27	40	7	28
146	Georgia	132	41	72	130	24	84	121	34	81
148	Idaho	98	53	36	73	48	18	58	27	29
149	Illinois	1,155	630	451	1,076	633	238	1,132	598	503
150	Indiana	721	319	338	682	369	274	663	335	310
151	Iowa	495	275	201	486	308	149	530	308	209
152	Kansas	376	197	161	329	213	86	352	186	131
153	Kentucky	490	235	244	436	205	217	468	227	235
154	Louisiana	76	9	64	54	5	48	68	14	54
155	Maine	106	67	35	97	65	28	108	66	38
156	Maryland	239	117	116	224	109	109	264	136	122
157	Massachusetts	457	266	156	445	258	166	415	239	157
158	Michigan	538	333	175	520	362	134	544	316	211
159	Minnesota	330	196	109	293	217	55	316	190	113
160	Mississippi	67	4	60	59	3	53	58	6	51
161	Missouri	716	347	347	644	321	296	684	314	352
162	Montana	69	32	29	64	35	22	64	25	37
163	Nebraska	267	127	131	226	139	53	241	122	114
164	Nevada	25	11	11	12	7	4	10	4	6
165	New Hampshire	90	53	34	90	54	34	92	55	35
166	New Jersey	467	265	183	432	245	165	401	222	165
168	New York	1,638	870	667	1,618	860	684	1,548	822	678
169	North Carolina	252	115	137	208	82	124	292	133	158
170	North Dakota	95	58	33	70	53	14	58	36	21
171	Ohio	1,122	572	503	1,004	600	345	1,040	544	475
172	Oklahoma	256	107	127	—	—	—	—	—	—
173	Oregon	111	63	38	90	60	17	84	47	33
174	Pennsylvania	1,265	746	447	1,237	841	338	1,173	713	424
175	Rhode Island	72	44	25	69	42	25	57	34	20
176	South Carolina	66	4	62	56	3	53	51	4	47
177	South Dakota	115	68	40	101	72	22	96	55	40
178	Tennessee	257	118	136	243	105	132	274	123	145
179	Texas	298	69	218	233	51	167	422	131	268
180	Utah	109	61	43	102	62	33	93	47	45
181	Vermont	53	40	11	52	40	10	56	13	13
182	Virginia	137	53	83	131	48	81	264	116	156
183	Washington	184	106	58	145	102	28	108	57	45
184	West Virginia	258	138	111	240	133	101	221	120	99
185	Wisconsin	454	248	167	443	280	124	442	266	159
186	Wyoming	36	21	15	31	20	9	25	14	10

See footnotes at end of table.

Series Y 135-186. Popular Vote Cast for President, by State and Political Party: 1836 to 1992—Cont'd.

(In thousands. Rep.-Republican; Dem.-Democratic; Ind.-Independent. Vote listed is normally that of the highest candidate for presidential elector for each party. Democratic vote in 1896 and 1900 includes a variety of joint elector tickets with the People's Party, and party totals generally include votes cast for the presidential candidate under other designations than that of the party itself)

Series No.	State	1896			1892			1888		
		Total	Rep.	Dem.	Total	Rep.	Dem.	Total	Rep.	Dem.
135	**United States**	13,907	7,102	6,493	12,061	5,183	5,555	11,383	5,447	5,538
136	Alabama	195	56	130	233	9	138	175	57	117
139	Arkansas	140	38	101	148	47	88	157	60	86
140	California	299	147	123	270	118	118	250	125	118
141	Colorado	187	26	159	96	39	X	91	50	37
142	Connecticut	174	110	57	165	77	82	154	75	75
143	Delaware	32	17	13	37	18	19	30	13	16
145	Florida	46	11	31	35	—	30	67	27	40
146	Georgia	156	59	93	221	48	129	142	40	100
148	Idaho	30	6	23	19	9	—	—	—	—
149	Illinois	1,088	607	465	874	399	426	748	370	348
150	Indiana	637	324	306	552	254	263	537	263	261
151	Iowa	521	289	224	443	220	196	404	212	180
152	Kansas	336	159	172	325	157	—	331	183	103
153	Kentucky	446	218	218	341	136	148	344	155	184
154	Louisiana	101	22	77	114	26	88	116	31	85
155	Maine	118	80	35	116	63	48	128	74	50
156	Maryland	251	137	105	213	93	114	211	100	106
157	Massachusetts	402	279	106	391	203	177	345	184	152
158	Michigan	546	293	237	467	223	202	475	236	213
159	Minnesota	342	194	140	268	123	101	262	143	104
160	Mississippi	70	5	63	53	1	41	115	29	85
161	Missouri	674	305	364	542	228	268	521	236	262
162	Montana	53	10	42	44	19	18	—	—	—
163	Nebraska	223	103	115	200	87	24	203	108	80
164	Nevada	10	2	8	11	3	1	12	7	5
165	New Hampshire	84	57	21	89	46	42	91	46	43
166	New Jersey	371	221	134	336	156	171	304	144	152
168	New York	1,424	820	551	1,337	609	655	1,320	650	363
169	North Carolina	330	154	175	278	101	133	286	135	148
170	North Dakota	47	26	21	36	18	—	—	—	—
171	Ohio	1,014	526	477	851	405	405	839	416	395
173	Oregon	97	49	45	78	35	14	62	33	27
174	Pennsylvania	1,194	728	427	1,003	516	452	998	526	447
175	Rhode Island	55	37	14	53	27	24	41	22	18
176	South Carolina	66	7	59	71	13	55	80	14	66
177	South Dakota	83	41	41	71	35	9	—	—	—
178	Tennessee	318	149	164	266	101	136	304	139	159
179	Texas	539	163	369	423	75	240	364	94	236
180	Utah	78	13	65	—	—	—	—	—	—
181	Vermont	64	51	10	56	38	16	63	45	17
182	Virginia	295	135	155	292	113	164	304	150	152
183	Washington	94	39	52	88	37	30	—	—	—
184	West Virginia	202	105	94	171	80	84	159	78	79
185	Wisconsin	447	268	166	371	171	177	355	177	155
186	Wyoming	21	10	10	17	8	—	—	—	—

See footnotes at end of table.

Series Y 135-186. Popular Vote Cast for President, by State and Political Party: 1836 to 1992—Cont'd.

(In thousands. Rep.-Republican; Dem.-Democratic; Ind.-Independent. Vote listed is normally that of the highest candidate for presidential elector for each party. Democratic vote in 1896 and 1900 includes a variety of joint elector tickets with the People's Party, and party totals generally include votes cast for the presidential candidate under other designations than that of the party itself)

Series No.	State	1884			1880			1876		
		Total	Rep.	Dem.	Total	Rep.	Dem.	Total	Rep.	Dem.
135	**United States**	10,053	4,850	4,880	9,217	4,453	4,414	8,422	4,037	4,284
136	Alabama	154	59	93	152	56	91	172	69	103
139	Arkansas	126	51	73	109	42	61	97	39	58
140	California	197	102	89	164	80	80	156	79	76
141	Colorado	64	36	28	54	28	25	—	—	—
142	Connecticut	137	66	67	133	67	64	122	59	62
143	Delaware	30	13	17	29	14	15	24	11	13
145	Florida	60	28	32	52	24	28	48	24	24
146	Georgia	143	48	94	157	54	103	181	51	130
149	Illinois	673	337	312	622	318	277	553	277	259
150	Indiana	495	239	245	471	232	226	430	107	214
151	Iowa	377	197	178	323	184	106	295	174	112
152	Kansas	266	154	90	201	122	60	124	78	38
153	Kentucky	276	118	153	267	106	149	260	97	160
154	Louisiana	109	46	63	103	38	65	146	75	71
155	Maine	130	72	52	144	74	65	116	66	50
156	Maryland	186	86	97	173	79	94	164	72	92
157	Massachusetts	303	147	122	283	165	112	259	150	109
158	Michigan	403	193	150	353	185	132	317	167	141
159	Minnesota	190	112	70	151	94	53	124	73	49
160	Mississippi	121	44	78	116	34	76	165	53	112
161	Missouri	441	203	236	397	154	209	351	145	202
163	Nebraska	134	77	54	87	55	29	58	32	17
164	Nevada	13	7	6	18	9	10	20	10	9
165	New Hampshire	84	43	39	86	45	41	80	42	39
166	New Jersey	261	123	128	246	121	123	220	104	116
168	New York	1,167	562	563	1,104	556	535	1,016	490	522
169	North Carolina	268	125	143	241	116	125	234	108	125
171	Ohio	785	400	368	725	375	341	659	331	323
173	Oregon	53	27	25	41	21	20	30	15	14
174	Pennsylvania	900	473	395	875	445	107	755	385	362
175	Rhode Island	33	19	12	29	18	11	26	16	11
176	South Carolina	93	22	70	171	58	112	183	92	91
178	Tennessee	259	124	134	243	108	130	223	90	133
179	Texas	326	93	226	241	57	156	151	45	106
181	Vermont	59	40	17	65	46	18	65	44	20
182	Virginia	285	139	145	212	84	97	237	96	141
184	West Virginia	132	63	67	113	46	57	100	42	57
185	Wisconsin	320	161	146	266	144	114	257	130	124

See footnotes at end of table.

Series Y 135-186.   Popular Vote Cast for President, by State and Political Party: 1836 to 1992—Cont'd.

(In thousands. Rep.-Republican; Dem.-Democratic; Ind.-Independent. Vote listed is normally that of the highest candidate for presidential elector for each party. Democratic vote in 1896 and 1900 includes a variety of joint elector tickets with the People's Party, and party totals generally include votes cast for the presidential candidate under other designations than that of the party itself)

Series No.	State	1872 Total	Rep.	Dem.	1868 Total	Rep.	Dem.	1864 Total	Rep.	Dem.
135	**United States**	6,460	3,597	2,843	5,720	3,013	2,707	4,011	2,207	1,804
136	Alabama	170	90	79	149	76	72	—	—	—
139	Arkansas	79	41	38	41	22	19	—	—	—
140	California	96	54	41	109	55	54	106	62	44
142	Connecticut	96	50	46	99	51	48	87	45	42
143	Delaware	22	11	10	19	8	11	17	8	9
145	Florida	33	18	15	—	—	—	—	—	—
146	Georgia	143	63	76	160	57	103	—	—	—
149	Illinois	430	242	185	448	250	198	348	190	159
150	Indiana	350	186	164	344	177	167	280	150	130
151	Iowa	205	132	71	194	120	74	135	86	48
152	Kansas	100	67	33	44	30	14	21	17	4
153	Kentucky	189	89	100	155	39	116	90	27	63
154	Louisiana	129	72	57	114	33	80	—	—	—
155	Maine	91	61	29	113	70	42	109	64	45
156	Maryland	135	67	68	93	30	62	70	37	32
157	Massachusetts	199	133	65	196	136	59	175	127	49
158	Michigan	222	139	79	226	129	97	160	89	72
159	Minnesota	91	56	35	72	44	28	42	25	17
160	Mississippi	129	82	47	—	—	—	—	—	—
161	Missouri	271	119	151	152	87	66	104	73	31
163	Nebraska	25	17	8	15	10	6	—	—	—
164	Nevada	15	8	6	12	6	5	16	10	7
165	New Hampshire	69	37	31	68	38	31	69	36	33
166	New Jersey	168	92	77	163	80	83	129	34	68
168	New York	830	441	387	850	420	430	731	369	362
169	North Carolina	165	95	70	181	97	85	—	—	—
171	Ohio	529	282	244	519	280	239	471	266	206
173	Oregon	20	12	8	22	11	11	18	10	8
174	Pennsylvania	562	349	213	656	342	314	574	296	277
175	Rhode Island	19	14	5	20	13	6	23	14	9
176	South Carolina	95	72	23	108	62	45	—	—	—
178	Tennessee	181	86	95	82	57	25	—	—	—
179	Texas	116	48	68	—	—	—	—	—	—
181	Vermont	52	41	11	56	44	12	56	42	13
182	Virginia	185	93	92	—	—	—	—	—	—
184	West Virginia	62	32	30	49	29	20	34	23	10
185	Wisconsin	192	105	86	194	109	85	145	80	63

See footnotes at end of table.

Series Y 135-186. Popular Vote Cast for President, by State and Political Party: 1836 to 1992—Cont'd.

(In thousands. Rep.-Republican; Dem.-Democratic; Ind.-Independent. Vote listed is normally that of the highest candidate for presidential elector for each party. Democratic vote in 1896 and 1900 includes a variety of joint elector tickets with the People's Party, and party totals generally include votes cast for the presidential candidate under other designations than that of the party itself)

Series No.	State	1860			1856			1852		
		Total	Rep.	Dem.	Total	Rep.	Dem.	Total	Whig	Dem.
135	**United States**	**4,690**	**1,866**	**1,383**	**4,045**	**1,340**	**1,833**	**3,162**	**1,385**	**1,601**
136	Alabama	90	—	14	75	—	47	44	15	27
139	Arkansas	54	—	5	33	—	22	20	7	12
140	California	120	39	38	110	21	53	77	36	41
142	Connecticut	80	43	17	81	43	35	67	30	33
143	Delaware	16	4	1	14	—	8	13	6	6
145	Florida	13	—	—	11	—	6	7	3	4
146	Georgia	107	—	12	99	—	57	62	17	35
149	Illinois	337	171	158	239	96	106	155	65	80
150	Indiana	272	139	116	235	94	119	184	81	95
151	Iowa	128	70	55	90	44	36	35	16	18
153	Kentucky	146	1	26	133	—	70	111	57	54
154	Louisiana	51	—	8	43	—	22	36	17	19
155	Maine	101	63	30	110	67	39	82	33	42
156	Maryland	93	2	6	87	—	39	75	35	40
157	Massachusetts	169	107	34	167	108	39	125	53	45
158	Michigan	155	88	65	126	72	52	83	34	42
159	Minnesota	35	22	12	—	—	—	—	—	—
160	Mississippi	69	—	4	59	—	34	45	18	27
161	Missouri	165	17	59	106	—	58	69	30	39
165	New Hampshire	66	38	26	70	37	32	51	15	29
166	New Jersey	121	58	63	100	28	47	84	39	44
168	New York	677	363	314	597	276	196	525	235	263
169	North Carolina	96	—	3	85	—	48	79	39	40
171	Ohio	443	232	187	386	187	171	353	153	169
173	Oregon	14	5	3	—	—	—	—	—	—
174	Pennsylvania	476	268	17	460	148	231	386	179	199
175	Rhode Island	20	12	8	20	11	7	17	8	9
178	Tennessee	144	—	11	140	—	74	115	59	57
179	Texas	63	34	—	48	—	32	20	5	15
181	Vermont	45	2	9	51	40	11	44	22	13
182	Virginia	167	2	16	150	—	90	133	59	74
185	Wisconsin	152	86	65	120	66	53	62	21	32
186	Wyoming	—	—	—	—	—	—	—	—	—

See footnotes at end of table.

Series Y 135-186. Popular Vote Cast for President, by State and Political Party: 1836 to 1992—Cont'd.

(In thousands. Rep.-Republican; Dem.-Democratic; Ind.-Independent. Vote listed is normally that of the highest candidate for presidential elector for each party. Democratic vote in 1896 and 1900 includes a variety of joint elector tickets with the People's Party, and party totals generally include votes cast for the presidential candidate under other designations than that of the party itself)

Series No.	State	1848 Total	1848 Whig	1848 Dem.	1844 Total	1844 Whig	1844 Dem.	1840 Total	1840 Whig	1840 Dem.
135	**United States**	2,879	1,361	1,222	2,701	1,300	1,338	2,412	1,275	1,128
136	Alabama	62	30	31	63	26	37	63	29	34
139	Arkansas	17	8	9	15	6	10	12	5	7
142	Connecticut	62	30	27	65	33	30	57	32	25
143	Delaware	12	6	6	12	6	6	11	6	5
145	Florida	7	4	3	—	—	—	—	—	—
146	Georgia	92	48	45	86	42	44	72	40	32
149	Illinois	125	53	56	108	46	59	93	46	47
150	Indiana	153	70	75	140	68	70	117	65	52
151	Iowa	22	10	11	—	—	—	—	—	—
153	Kentucky	115	67	49	113	61	52	91	59	33
154	Louisiana	34	18	15	27	13	14	19	11	8
155	Maine	87	35	40	85	34	46	93	47	46
156	Maryland	72	38	34	69	36	33	62	34	29
157	Massachusetts	134	61	35	130	68	52	126	73	52
158	Michigan	65	24	31	56	24	28	44	23	21
160	Mississippi	52	26	27	46	20	26	37	20	17
161	Missouri	73	33	40	73	31	41	53	23	30
165	New Hampshire	50	15	28	49	18	27	59	26	33
166	New Jersey	78	40	37	76	38	37	64	33	31
168	New York	456	219	114	486	232	238	442	226	213
169	North Carolina	80	44	36	82	43	39	79	46	34
171	Ohio	329	139	155	312	155	149	273	148	124
174	Pennsylvania	369	185	173	331	160	167	288	144	144
175	Rhode Island	11	7	4	12	7	5	9	5	3
178	Tennessee	122	64	58	120	60	60	108	60	48
179	Texas	17	5	12	—	—	—	—	—	—
181	Vermont	48	23	11	49	27	18	51	32	18
182	Virginia	92	45	47	96	45	51	86	43	44
185	Wisconsin	39	14	15	—	—	—	—	—	—

See footnotes at end of table.

Series No.	State	1836 Total	1836 Whig	1836 Dem.	Series No.	State	1836 Total	1836 Whig	1836 Dem.
135	**United States**	1,505	740	765	160	Mississippi	20	10	10
136	Alabama	37	17	21	161	Missouri	18	7	11
139	Arkansas	4	1	2	165	New Hampshire	25	6	19
142	Connecticut	38	19	19	166	New Jersey	52	26	26
143	Delaware	9	5	4	168	New York	306	139	167
146	Georgia	47	24	23	169	North Carolina	50	24	27
149	Illinois	33	15	18	171	Ohio	203	106	97
150	Indiana	74	41	32	174	Pennsylvania	179	87	91
153	Kentucky	69	37	33	175	Rhode Island	6	3	3
154	Louisiana	7	4	4	178	Tennessee	62	36	26
155	Maine	38	15	23	181	Vermont	35	21	14
156	Maryland	48	26	22	182	Virginia	54	23	30
157	Massachusetts	78	42	35					
158	Michigan	12	6	7					

X Represents zero.

Series Y 189-198. Congressional Bills, Acts and Resolutions: 1789 to 1989

(Excludes simple and concurrent resolutions)

Period of session	Congress	Measures introduced			Measures passed		
		Total	Bills	Joint resolutions	Total	Total public	Total private
		189	**190**	**191**	**192**	**193**	**196**
1989-1990	101	6,664	5,977	687	666	650	16
1987-1988	100	9,588	8,515	1,073	761	713	48
1985-1986	99	9,885	8,697	1,188	483	466	17
1983-1984	98	11,156	10,134	1,022	677	623	54
1981-1982	97	11,490	10,582	908	529	473	56
1979-1980	96	12,583	11,722	861	736	613	123
1977-1978	95	19,387	18,045	1,342	803	633	170
1975-1976	94	21,096	19,762	1,334	729	588	141
1973-1974	93	23,296	21,950	1,446	774	651	123
1971-1972	92	22,969	21,363	1,606	768	607	161
Jan. 1969-Jan. 1971	91	26,303	24,631	1,672	941	695	246
Jan. 1967-Oct. 1968	90	26,460	24,786	1,674	1,002	640	362
Jan. 1965-Oct. 1966	89	24,003	22,483	1,520	1,283	810	473
Jan. 1963-Oct. 1964	88	17,480	16,079	1,401	1,026	666	360
Jan. 1961-Oct. 1962	87	18,376	17,230	1,146	1,569	885	684
Jan. 1959-Sept. 1960	86	18,261	17,230	1,031	1,292	800	492
Jan. 1957-Aug. 1958	85	19,112	18,205	907	1,720	936	784
Jan. 1955-July 1956	84	17,687	16,782	905	1,921	1,028	893
Jan. 1953-Dec. 1954	83	14,952	14,181	771	1,783	781	1,002
Jan. 1951-July 1952	82	12,730	12,062	668	1,617	594	1,023
Jan. 1949-Jan. 1951	81	14,988	14,219	769	2,024	921	1,103
Jan. 1947-Dec. 1948	80	10,797	10,108	689	1,363	906	457
Jan. 1945-Aug. 1946	79	10,330	9,748	582	1,625	733	892
Jan. 1943-Dec. 1944	78	8,334	7,845	489	1,157	568	589
Jan. 1941-Dec. 1942	77	11,334	10,793	541	1,485	850	635
Jan. 1939-Jan. 1941	76	16,105	15,174	931	1,662	1,005	657
Jan. 1937-June 1938	75	16,156	15,120	1,036	1,759	919	840
Jan. 1935-June 1936	74	18,754	17,819	935	1,724	987	737
March 1933-June 1934	73	14,370	13,774	596	975	539	436
Dec. 1931-March 1933	72	21,382	20,501	881	843	516	327
April 1929-March 1931	71	24,453	23,652	801	1,522	1,009	513
Dec. 1927-March 1929	70	23,897	23,238	659	1,722	1,145	577
Dec. 1925-March 1927	69	23,799	23,250	549	1,423	879	544
Dec. 1923-March 1925	68	17,462	16,884	578	996	707	289
April 1921-March 1923	67	19,889	19,133	756	930	654	276
May 1919-March 1921	66	21,967	21,222	745	594	470	124
May 1917-Dec. 1919	65	22,594	21,919	675	453	405	48
Dec. 1915-March 1917	64	30,052	29,438	614	684	458	226
March 1913-March 1915	63	30,053	29,367	686	700	417	283
April 1911-March 1913	62	38,032	37,459	573	716	530	186
March 1909-March 1911	61	44,363	43,921	442	884	595	289
Dec. 1907-March 1909	60	38,388	37,981	407	646	411	235
March 1905-March 1907	59	34,879	34,524	355	7,024	775	6,249
March 1903-March 1905	58	26,851	26,504	347	4,041	575	3,466
March 1901-March 1903	57	25,460	25,007	453	2,790	480	2,310
Dec. 1899-March 1901	56	20,893	20,409	484	1,942	443	1,499
March 1897-March 1899	55	18,463	17,817	646	1,437	552	885
Dec. 1895-March 1897	54	14,585	14,114	471	948	434	514
March 1893-March 1895	53	12,226	11,796	430	711	463	248
Dec. 1891-March 1893	52	14,893	14,518	375	722	398	324
March 1889-March 1891	51	19,630	19,163	467	2,251	611	1,640
Dec. 1887-March 1889	50	17,078	16,664	414	1,824	570	1,254
March 1885-March 1887	49	15,002	14,618	384	1,452	424	1,028
Dec. 1883-March 1885	48	11,443	10,961	482	969	284	685
March 1881-March 1883	47	10,704	10,194	510	761	419	342

Series Y 189-198. Congressional Bills, Acts and Resolutions: 1789 to 1989—Cont'd.

(Excludes simple and concurrent resolutions)

Period of session	Congress	Measures introduced			Measures passed		
		Total	Bills	Joint resolutions	Total	Total public	Total private
		189	190	191	192	193	196
March 1879-March 1881	46	10,067	9,481	586	650	372	278
March 1877-March 1879	45	8,735	8,413	322	746	303	443
March 1875-March 1877	44	6,230	6,001	229	580	278	302
March 1873-March 1875	43	6,434	6,252	182	859	415	444
March 1871-March 1873	42	5,943	5,725	218	1,012	531	481
March 1869-March 1871	41	5,314	4,466	848	769	470	299
April 1867-March 1869	40	3,723	3,003	720	765	354	411
March 1865-March 1867	39	2,348	1,864	484	714	427	287
March 1863-March 1865	38	1,708	1,402	306	515	411	104
March 1861-March 1863	37	1,661	1,370	291	521	428	93
March 1859-March 1861	36	1,746	1,595	151	370	157	213
March 1857-March 1859	35	1,686	1,544	142	312	129	183
Dec. 1855-March 1857	34	1,608	1,515	93	433	157	276
March 1853-March 1855	33	1,660	1,552	108	540	188	352
March 1851-March 1853	32	1,167	1,011	156	306	137	169
March 1849-March 1851	31	1,080	978	102	167	109	58
Dec. 1847-March 1849	30	1,433	1,305	128	446	176	270
March 1845-March 1847	29	1,051	956	95	303	142	161
Dec. 1843-March 1845	28	1,085	979	106	279	142	137
March 1841-March 1843	27	1,210	1,146	64	524	201	323
Dec. 1839-March 1841	26	1,122	1,081	41	147	55	92
March 1837-March 1839	25	1,631	1,566	65	532	150	382
Dec. 1835-March 1837	24	1,107	1,055	52	459	144	315
Dec. 1833-March 1835	23	993	946	47	390	128	262
Dec. 1831-March 1833	22	1,000	976	24	462	191	271
March 1829-March 1831	21	856	842	14	369	152	217
Dec. 1827-March 1829	20	632	612	20	235	134	101
March 1825-March 1827	19	622	609	13	266	153	113
Dec. 1823-March 1825	18	498	481	17	335	141	194
Dec. 1821-March 1823	17	492	492	——	238	136	102
Dec. 1819-March 1821	16	480	480	——	208	117	91
March 1817-March 1819	15	507	507	——	257	156	101
Dec. 1815-March 1817	14	465	465	——	298	173	125
March 1813-March 1815	13	400	400	——	273	185	88
March 1811-March 1813	12	406	406	——	209	170	39
March 1809-March 1811	11	348	348	——	119	94	25
Oct. 1807-March 1809	10	266	266	——	105	88	17
March 1805-March 1807	9	219	219	——	106	90	16
Oct. 1803-March 1805	8	217	217	——	111	93	18
March 1801-March 1803	7	161	161	——	95	80	15
Dec. 1799-March 1801	6	157	157	——	112	100	12
March 1797-March 1799	5	234	234	——	155	137	18
June 1795-March 1797	4	132	132	——	85	75	10
March 1793-March 1795	3	122	122	——	127	103	24
March 1791-March 1793	2	105	105	——	77	65	12
March 1789-March 1791	1	144	144	——	118	108	10

Series Y 199-203. Congressional Bills Vetoed: 1789 to 1992

Period	President	Vetoed bills			Vetoes sustained	Bills passed over veto
		Total	Regular	Pocket		
		199	**200**	**201**	**202**	**203**
1989-1992	Bush	34	29	5	33	1
1981-1989	Reagan	78	39	39	69	9
1977-1981	Carter	31	13	18	29	2
1974-1977	Ford	72	53	19	60	12
1969-1970	Nixon	11	7	4	9	2
1963-1969	L. Johnson	30	16	14	30	—
1961-1963	Kennedy	21	12	9	21	—
1953-1961	Eisenhower	181	73	108	179	2
1945-1953	Truman	250	180	70	238	12
1933-1945	F. Roosevelt	635	372	263	626	9
1929-1933	Hoover	37	21	16	34	3
1923-1929	Coolidge	50	20	30	46	4
1921-1923	Harding	6	5	1	6	—
1913-1921	Wilson	44	33	11	38	6
1909-1913	Taft	39	30	9	38	1
1901-1909	T. Roosevelt	82	42	40	81	1
1897-1901	McKinley	42	6	36	42	—
1893-1897	Cleveland	170	42	128	165	5
1889-1893	B. Harrison	44	19	25	43	1
1885-1889	Cleveland	414	304	110	412	2
1881-1885	Arthur	12	4	8	11	1
1881	Garfield	—	—	—	—	—
1877-1881	Hayes	13	12	1	12	1
1869-1877	Grant	93	45	48	89	4
1868-1869	A. Johnson	29	21	8	14	15
1861-1865	Lincoln	6	2	4	6	—
1857-1861	Buchanan	7	4	3	7	—
1853-1857	Pierce	9	9	—	4	5
1850-1853	Fillmore	—	—	—	—	—
1849-1850	Taylor	—	—	—	—	—
1845-1849	Polk	3	2	1	3	—
1841-1845	Tyler	10	6	4	9	1
1841	W. H. Harrison	—	—	—	—	—
1837-1841	Van Buren	1	—	1	1	—
1829-1837	Jackson	12	5	7	12	—
1825-1829	John Q. Adams	—	—	—	—	—
1817-1825	Monroe	1	1	—	1	—
1809-1817	Madison	7	5	2	7	—
1801-1809	Jefferson	—	—	—	—	—
1797-1801	John Adams	—	—	—	—	—
1789-1797	Washington	2	2	—	2	—

Series Y 204-210. Political Party Affiliation in Congress and the Presidency: 1789 to 1993

(Letter symbols for political parties: Ad="Administration"; AM=Anti-Masonic; C=Coalition; D=Democratic; DR=Democratic-Republican; F=Federalist; J=Jacksonian; NR=National Republican; Op="Opposition"; R=Republican; U=Unionist; W=Whig. Figures are for the beginning of the first session of each Congress)

Year	Congress	House Majority party	House Principal minority party	Senate Majority party	Senate Principal minority party	President
		204	205	207	208	210
1993	103d	D-261	R-173	D-58	R-42	D-Clinton
1991	102d	D-267	R-167	D-56	R-44	R-Bush
1989	101st	D-259	R-174	D-55	R-45	R-Bush
1987	100th	D-258	R-177	D-55	R-45	R-Reagan
1985	99th	D-252	R-182	R-53	D-47	R-Reagan
1983	98th	D-269	R-165	R-54	D-46	R-Reagan
1981	97th	D-243	R-192	R-53	D-46	R-Reagan
1979	96th	D-276	R-157	D-58	R-41	D-Carter
1977	95th	D-292	R-143	D-61	R-38	D-Carter
1975	94th	D-291	R-144	D-60	R-37	R-Ford
1973	93d	D-239	R-192	D-56	R-42	R-Nixon
1971	92d	D-254	R-180	D-54	R-44	R-Nixon
1969-1970	91st	D-245	R-189	D-57	R-43	R-Nixon
1967-1968	90th	D-246	R-187	D-64	R-36	D-L. Johnson
1965-1966	89th	D-295	R-140	D-68	R-32	D-L. Johnson
1963-1964	88th	D-258	R-177	D-67	R-33	D-L. Johnson
						D-Kennedy
1961-1962	87th	D-263	R-174	D-65	R-35	D-Kennedy
1959-1960 [1]	86th	D-283	R-153	D-64	R-34	R-Eisenhower
1957-1958	85th	D-233	R-200	D-49	R-47	R-Eisenhower
1955-1956	84th	D-232	R-203	D-48	R-47	R-Eisenhower
1953-1954	83d	R-221	D-211	R-48	D-47	R-Eisenhower
1951-1952	82d	D-234	R-199	D-49	R-47	D-Truman
1949-1950	81st	D-263	R-171	D-54	R-42	D-Truman
1947-1948	80th	R-245	D-188	R-51	D-45	D-Truman
1945-1946	79th	D-242	R-190	D-56	R-38	D-Truman
1943-1944	78th	D-218	R-208	D-58	R-37	D-F. Roosevelt
1941-1942	77th	D-268	R-162	D-66	R-28	D-F. Roosevelt
1939-1940	76th	D-261	R-164	D-69	R-23	D-F. Roosevelt
1937-1938	75th	D-331	R-89	D-76	R-16	D-F. Roosevelt
1935-1936	74th	D-319	R-103	D-69	R-25	D-F. Roosevelt
1933-1934	73d	D-310	R-117	D-60	R-35	D-F. Roosevelt
1931-1933	72d	D-220	R-214	R-48	D-47	R-Hoover
1929-1931	71st	R-267	D-167	R-56	D-39	R-Hoover
1927-1929	70th	R-237	D-195	R-49	D-46	R-Coolidge
1925-1927	69th	R-247	D-183	R-56	D-39	R-Coolidge
1923-1925	68th	R-225	D-205	R-51	D-43	R-Coolidge
1921-1923	67th	R-301	D-131	R-59	D-37	R-Harding
1919-1921	66th	R-240	D-190	R-49	D-47	D-Wilson
1917-1919	65th	D-216	R-210	D-53	R-42	D-Wilson
1915-1917	64th	D-230	R-196	D-56	R-40	D-Wilson
1913-1915	63d	D-291	R-127	D-51	R-44	D-Wilson
1911-1913	62d	D-228	R-161	R-51	D-41	R-Taft
1909-1911	61st	R-219	D-172	R-61	D-32	R-Taft
1907-1909	60th	R-222	D-164	R-61	D-31	R-T. Roosevelt
1905-1907	59th	R-250	D-136	R-57	D-33	R-T. Roosevelt
1903-1905	58th	R-208	D-178	R-57	D-33	R-T. Roosevelt
1901-1903	57th	R-197	D-151	R-55	D-31	R-T. Roosevelt
						R-McKinley
1899-1901	56th	R-185	D-163	R-53	D-26	R-McKinley
1897-1899	55th	R-204	D-113	R-47	D-34	R-McKinley
1895-1897	54th	R-244	D-105	R-43	D-39	D-Cleveland
1893-1895	53d	D-218	R-127	D-44	R-38	D-Cleveland
1891-1893	52d	D-235	R-88	R-47	D-39	R-B. Harrison
1889-1891	51st	R-166	D-159	R-39	D-37	R-B. Harrison

See footnotes at end of table.

Series Y 204-210.   Political Party Affiliation in Congress and the Presidency: 1789 to 1993—Cont'd.

(Letter symbols for political parties: Ad="Administration"; AM=Anti-Masonic; C=Coalition; D=Democratic; DR=Democratic-Republican; F=Federalist; J=Jacksonian; NR=National Republican; Op="Opposition"; R=Republican; U=Unionist; W=Whig. Figures are for the beginning of the first session of each Congress)

Year	Congress	House Majority party	House Principal minority party	Senate Majority party	Senate Principal minority party	President
		204	205	207	208	210
1887-1889	50th	D-169	R-152	R-39	D-37	D-Cleveland
1885-1887	49th	D-183	R-140	R-43	D-34	D-Cleveland
1883-1885	48th	D-197	R-118	R-38	D-36	R-Arthur
1881-1883	47th	R-147	D-135	R-37	D-37	R-Arthur
						R-Garfield
1879-1881	46th	D-149	R-130	D-42	R-33	R-Hayes
1877-1879	45th	D-153	R-140	R-39	D-36	R-Hayes
1875-1877	44th	D-169	R-109	R-45	D-29	R-Grant
1873-1875	43d	R-194	D-92	R-49	D-19	R-Grant
1871-1873	42d	R-134	D-104	R-52	D-17	R-Grant
1869-1871	41st	D-149	D-63	R-56	D-11	R-Grant
1867-1869	40th	R-143	D-49	R-42	D-11	R-A. Johnson
1865-1867	39th	U-149	D-42	U-42	D-10	R-A. Johnson
						R-Lincoln
1863-1865	38th	R-102	D-75	R-36	D-9	R-Lincoln
1861-1863	37th	R-105	D-43	R-31	D-10	R-Lincoln
1859-1861	36th	R-114	D-92	D-36	R-26	D-Buchanan
1857-1859	35th	D-118	R-92	D-36	R-20	D-Buchanan
1855-1857	34th	R-108	D-83	D-40	R-15	D-Pierce
1853-1855	33d	D-159	W-71	D-38	W-22	D-Pierce
1851-1853	32d	D-140	W-88	D-35	W-24	W-Fillmore
1849-1851	31st	D-112	W-109	D-35	W-25	W-Fillmore
						W-Taylor
1847-1849	30th	W-115	D-108	D-36	W-21	D-Polk
1845-1847	29th	D-143	W-77	D-31	W-25	D-Polk
1843-1845	28th	D-142	W-79	W-28	D-25	W-Tyler
1841-1843	27th	W-133	D-102	W-28	D-22	W-Tyler
						W-W. H. Harrison
1839-1841	26th	D-124	W-118	D-28	W-22	D-Van Buren
1837-1839	25th	D-108	W-107	D-30	W-18	D-Van Buren
1835-1837	24th	D-145	W-98	D-27	W-25	D-Jackson
1833-1835	23d	D-147	AM-53	D-20	NR-20	D-Jackson
1831-1833	22d	D-141	NR-58	D-25	NR-21	D-Jackson
1829-1831	21st	D-139	NR-74	D-26	NR-22	D-Jackson
1827-1829	20th	J-119	Ad-94	J-28	Ad-20	C-J. Q. Adams
1825-1827	19th	Ad-105	J-97	Ad-26	J-20	C-J. Q. Adams
1823-1825	18th	DR-187	F-26	DR-44	F-4	DR-Monroe
1821-1823	17th	DR-158	F-25	DR-44	F-4	DR-Monroe
1819-1821	16th	DR-156	F-27	DR-35	F-7	DR-Monroe
1817-1819	15th	DR-141	F-42	DR-34	F-10	DR-Monroe
1815-1817	14th	DR-117	F-65	DR-25	F-11	DR-Madison
1813-1815	13d	DR-112	F-68	DR-27	F-9	DR-Madison
1811-1813	12d	DR-108	F-36	DR-30	F-6	DR-Madison
1809-1811	11th	DR-94	F-48	DR-28	F-6	DR-Madison
1807-1809	10th	DR-118	F-24	DR-28	F-6	DR-Jefferson
1805-1807	9th	DR-116	F-25	DR-27	F-7	DR-Jefferson
1803-1805	8th	DR-102	F-39	DR-25	F-9	DR-Jefferson
1801-1803	7th	DR-69	F-36	DR-18	F-13	DR-Jefferson
1799-1801	6th	F-64	DR-42	F-19	DR-13	F-John Adams
1797-1799	5th	F-58	DR-48	F-20	DR-12	F-John Adams
1795-1797	4th	F-54	DR-52	F-19	DR-13	F-Washington
1793-1795	3d	DR-57	F-48	F-17	DR-13	F-Washington
1791-1793	2d	F-37	DR-33	F-16	DR-13	F-Washington
1789-1791	1st	Ad-38	Op-26	Ad-17	Op-9	F-Washington

[1] Excludes Hawaii; two senators (1-R, 1-D) and one representative (D) seated August 1959.

Series Y 272-289.   Public Employees, by Type of Government: 1940 to 1990

(In thousands. As of October 31 except as noted)

Year	All governments	Federal [1] (civilian)	Total state and local	Total state	Total local	Local [2] Total municipalities	Total counties	School districts
	272	273	274	277	280	283	285	287
1990	18,369	3,105	15,263	4,503	10,760	2,642	2,167	4,950
1989	17,879	3,114	14,765	4,365	10,400	2,569	2,085	4,774
1988	17,588	3,112	14,476	4,236	10,240	2,570	2,024	4,679
1987	17,212	3,091	14,121	4,116	10,005	2,493	1,963	4,627
1986	16,933	3,019	13,913	4,068	9,846	2,494	1,926	4,502
1985	16,690	3,021	13,669	3,984	9,685	2,467	1,891	4,416
1984	16,436	2,942	13,494	3,898	9,595	2,434	1,872	4,387
1983	16,034	2,875	13,159	3,816	9,344	2,424	1,811	4,211
1982	15,918	2,848	13,071	3,747	9,324	2,460	1,804	4,182
1981	15,968	2,865	13,103	3,726	9,377	2,469	1,808	4,222
1980	16,213	2,898	13,315	3,753	9,562	2,561	1,853	4,270
1979	15,971	2,869	13,102	3,699	9,403	2,553	1,804	4,200
1978	15,628	2,885	12,743	3,539	9,204	2,509	1,768	4,113
1977	15,459	2,848	12,611	3,491	9,120	2,469	1,761	4,127
1976	15,012	2,843	12,169	3,343	8,826	2,107	1,448	3,272
1975	14,973	2,890	12,084	3,271	8,813	2,506	1,563	3,969
1974	14,628	2,874	11,754	3,155	8,599	2,127	1,343	3,183
1973	14,139	2,786	11,353	3,013	8,339	2,109	1,318	3,074
1972	14,759	2,795	10,964	2,957	8,007	2,029	1,242	2,981
1971	13,316	2,872	10,444	2,832	7,612	1,960	1,153	2,865
1970	13,028	2,881	10,147	2,755	7,392	2,244	1,229	3,316
1969	12,685	2,969	9,716	2,614	7,102	2,165	1,163	3,176
1968	12,342	2,984	9,358	2,495	6,864	2,112	1,151	3,028
1967	11,867	2,993	8,874	2,335	6,539	1,993	1,077	2,919
1966	11,388	2,861	8,527	2,211	6,316	1,971	1,043	2,850
1965	10,589	2,588	8,001	2,028	5,973	1,884	979	2,598
1964	10,064	2,528	7,536	1,873	5,663	1,817	936	2,436
1963	9,736	2,548	7,188	1,775	5,413	1,782	875	2,300
1962	9,388	2,539	6,849	1,680	5,169	1,696	862	2,161
1961	9,100	2,484	6,616	1,625	4,992	1,734	821	2,049
1960	8,808	2,421	6,387	1,527	4,860	1,692	788	1,921
1959 *	8,487	2,399	6,088	1,454	4,634	1,636	767	1,820
1958	8,297	2,405	5,892	1,408	4,484	1,594	738	1,752
1957 [3]	8,047	2,439	5,608	1,300	4,307	1,539	726	1,651
1956	7,685	2,410	5,275	1,268	4,007	1,485	674	1,533
1955	7,432	2,378	5,054	1,199	3,855	1,436	648	1,455
1954	7,232	2,373	4,859	1,149	3,710	1,420	628	1,365
1953	7,048	2,385	4,663	1,082	3,580	1,382	597	1,293
1952	7,105	2,583	4,522	1,060	3,461	1,341	573	1,234
1951	6,802	2,515	4,287	1,070	3,218	1,297	505	1,136
1950	6,402	2,117	4,285	1,057	3,228	1,311	500	1,102
1949	6,203	2,047	4,156	1,037	3,119	1,281	476	1,056
1948	6,042	2,076	3,966	963	3,002	1,249	469	986
1947	5,791	2,002	3,789	909	2,880	1,202	434	962
1946	6,001	2,434	3,567	804	2,762	1,155	417	934
1945	6,556	3,375	3,181	——	——	——	——	——
1944	6,537	3,365	3,172	——	——	——	——	——
1943	6,358	3,166	3,192	——	——	——	——	——
1942	5,915	2,664	3,251	——	——	——	——	——
1941	4,970	1,598	3,372	——	——	——	——	——
1940	4,474	1,128	3,346	——	——	——	——	——

* Denotes first year for which figures include Alaska and Hawaii.
[1] Includes federal civilian employees outside continental United States. Prior to 1953, figures as of September 30.

[2] Local government data, except for 1067, 1962 and 1957, are subject to sampling variation.
[3] As of April 30.

Series Y 335-338.   Summary of Federal Government Finances — Administrative Budget: 1789 to 1939

(In thousands of dollars. For 1789-1842, years ending December 31; 1844-1939, June 30; 1843 figures are for January 1-June 30)

Year	Budget receipts [1]	Budget expenditures [2]	Surplus or deficit [3] (−)	Total public debt [4]	Year	Budget receipts [1]	Budget expenditures [2]	Surplus or deficit [3] (−)	Total public debt [4]
	335	336	337	338		335	336	337	338
1939	4,979,066	8,841,224	-3,862,158	40,439,532	1885	323,691	260,227	63,464	1,578,551
1938	5,588,012	6,764,628	-1,176,617	37,164,740	1884	348,520	244,126	104,394	1,625,307
1937	4,955,613	7,733,033	-2,777,421	36,424,614	1883	398,288	265,408	132,879	1,721,959
1936	3,997,059	8,421,608	-4,424,549	33,778,543	1882	403,525	257,981	145,544	1,856,916
					1881	360,782	260,713	100,069	2,019,286
1935	3,705,956	6,497,008	-2,791,052	28,700,893					
1934	3,014,970	6,644,602	-3,629,632	27,053,141	1880	333,527	267,643	65,884	2,090,909
1933	1,996,844	4,958,496	-2,601,652	22,538,673	1879	273,827	266,948	6,879	2,298,913
1932	1,923,892	4,659,182	-2,735,290	19,487,002	1878	257,764	236,964	20,800	2,159,418
1931	3,115,557	3,577,434	-461,877	16,801,281	1877	281,406	241,334	40,072	2,107,760
					1876	294,096	265,101	28,995	2,130,846
1930	4,057,884	3,320,211	737,673	16,185,310					
1929	3,861,589	3,127,199	734,391	16,931,088	1875	288,000	274,623	13,377	2,156,277
1928	3,900,329	2,961,245	939,083	17,604,293	1874	304,979	302,634	2,345	2,159,933
1927	4,012,794	2,857,429	1,155,365	18,511,907	1873	333,738	290,345	43,393	2,151,210
1926	3,795,108	2,929,964	865,144	19,643,216	1872	374,107	277,518	96,589	2,209,991
					1871	383,324	292,177	91,147	2,322,052
1925	3,640,805	2,923,762	717,043	20,516,194					
1924	3,871,214	2,907,847	963,367	21,250,813	1870	411,255	309,654	101,602	2,436,453
1923	3,852,795	3,140,287	712,508	22,349,707	1869	370,944	322,865	48,078	2,545,111
1922	4,025,901	3,289,404	736,496	22,963,382	1868	405,638	377,640	28,298	2,583,446
1921	5,570,790	5,061,785	509,005	23,977,451	1867	490,634	357,543	133,091	2,650,168
					1866	558,033	520,809	37,223	2,755,764
1920	6,648,898	6,357,677	291,222	24,299,321					
1919	5,130,042	18,492,665	-13,362,623	25,484,506	1865	333,715	1,297,555	-963,841	2,677,929
1918	3,645,240	12,677,359	-9,032,120	12,455,225	1864	264,627	865,323	-600,696	1,815,831
1917	1,100,500	1,953,857	-853,357	2,975,619	1863	112,697	714,741	-602,043	1,119,774
1916	761,445	712,967	48,478	1,225,146	1862	51,987	474,762	-422,774	524,178
					1861	41,510	66,547	-25,037	90,582
1915	683,417	746,093	-62,676	1,191,264					
1914	725,117	725,525	-408	1,188,235	1860	56,065	63,131	-7,066	64,844
1913	714,463	714,864	-401	1,193,048	1859	53,486	69,071	-15,585	58,498
1912	692,609	689,881	2,728	1,193,839	1858	46,655	74,185	-27,530	44,913
1911	701,833	691,202	10,631	1,153,985	1857	68,965	67,796	1,170	28,701
					1856	74,057	69,571	4,486	31,974
1910	675,512	693,617	-18,105	1,146,940					
1909	604,320	693,744	-89,423	1,148,315	1855	65,351	59,743	5,608	35,588
1908	601,862	659,196	-57,334	1,177,690	1854	73,800	58,045	15,755	42,244
1907	665,860	579,129	86,732	1,147,178	1853	61,587	48,184	13,403	59,805
1906	594,984	570,202	24,782	1,142,523	1852	49,847	44,195	5,652	66,199
					1851	52,559	47,709	4,850	68,305
1905	544,275	567,279	-23,004	1,132,357					
1904	541,087	583,660	-42,573	1,136,259	1850	43,603	39,543	4,060	63,453
1903	561,881	517,006	44,875	1,159,406	1849	31,208	45,052	-13,844	63,062
1902	562,478	485,234	77,244	1,178,031	1848	35,736	45,377	-9,641	47,045
1901	587,685	524,617	63,068	1,221,572	1847	26,496	57,281	-30,786	38,827
					1846	29,700	27,767	1,933	15,550
1900	567,241	520,861	46,380	1,263,417					
1899	515,961	605,072	-89,112	1,436,701	1845	29,970	22,937	7,033	15,925
1898	405,321	443,369	-38,047	1,232,743	1844	29,321	22,338	6,984	23,462
1897	347,722	365,774	-18,052	1,226,794	1843	8,303	11,858	-3,555	32,743
1896	338,142	352,179	-14,037	1,222,729	1842	19,976	25,206	-5,230	20,201
					1841	16,860	26,522	-9,706	13,594
1895	324,729	356,195	-31,466	1,096,913					
1894	306,355	367,525	-61,170	1,016,898	1840	19,480	24,318	-4,837	5,351
1893	385,820	383,478	2,342	961,432	1839	31,483	26,899	4,584	3,573
1892	354,938	345,023	9,914	968,219	1838	26,303	33,865	-7,562	10,434
1891	392,612	365,774	26,839	1,005,807	1837	24,954	37,243	-12,289	3,308
					1836	50,827	30,868	-19,959	337
1890	403,081	318,041	85,040	1,122,397	1835	35,430	17,573	17,857	38
1889	387,050	299,289	87,761	1,249,471	1834	21,792	18,628	3,164	38
1888	379,266	267,925	111,341	1,384,632	1833	33,948	23,018	10,931	4,760
1887	371,403	267,932	103,471	1,465,485	1832	31,866	17,289	14,577	7,012
1886	336,440	242,483	93,957	1,555,660	1831	28,527	15,248	13,279	24,322

See footnotes at end of table.

Series Y 335-338. Summary of Federal Government Finances—Administrative Budget: 1789 to 1939—Cont'd.

(In thousands of dollars. For years ending June 30. Data for 1929-1953 are consolidated cash statement figures; for 1954-1970, unified budget figures. For 1789-1842, years ending December 31; 1844-1939, June 30; 1843 figures are for January 1-June 30)

Year	Budget receipts [1]	Budget expenditures [2]	Surplus or deficit [3] (—)	Total public debt [4]	Year	Budget receipts [1]	Budget expenditures [2]	Surplus or deficit [3] (—)	Total public debt [4]
	335	336	337	338		335	336	337	338
1830	24,844	15,143	9,701	39,123	1810	9,384	8,157	1,228	48,006
1829	24,828	15,203	9,624	48,565	1809	7,773	10,281	-2,507	53,173
1828	24,764	16,395	8,369	58,421	1808	17,061	9,932	7,128	57,023
1827	22,966	16,139	6,827	67,475	1807	16,398	8,354	8,044	65,196
1826	25,260	17,036	8,225	73,987	1806	15,560	9,804	5,756	69,218
1825	21,841	15,857	5,984	81,054	1805	13,561	10,506	3,054	75,723
1824	19,381	20,327	-945	83,788	1804	11,826	8,719	3,107	82,312
1823	20,541	14,707	5,834	90,270	1803	11,064	7,852	3,212	86,427
1822	20,232	15,000	5,232	90,876	1802	14,996	7,862	7,134	77,055
1821	14,573	15,811	-1,237	93,547	1801	12,935	9,395	3,541	80,713
1820	17,881	18,261	-380	89,987	1800	10,849	10,786	63	83,038
1819	24,603	21,464	3,140	91,016	1799	7,547	9,666	-2,120	82,976
1818	21,585	19,825	1,760	95,530	1798	7,900	7,677	224	78,409
1817	33,099	21,844	11,255	103,467	1797	5,689	6,134	2,555	79,229
1816	47,678	30,587	17,091	123,492	1796	8,378	5,727	2,651	82,064
1815	15,729	32,709	-16,979	127,335	1795	6,115	7,540	-1,425	83,762
1814	11,182	34,721	-23,539	99,834	1794	5,432	6,991	-1,559	80,748
1813	14,340	31,682	-17,341	81,488	1793	4,653	4,482	171	78,427
1812	9,801	20,281	-10,480	55,963	1792	3,670	5,080	-1,410	80,359
1811	14,424	8,058	6,365	45,210	1789-1791	4,419	4,269	150	77,228

[1] Excludes receipts from borrowing. Prior to 1913, total receipts; thereafter, net receipts.
[2] Excludes debt repayment. Prior to 1913, total expenditures; thereafter, net expenditures.
[3] Receipts compared with expenditures.
[4] As of end of period.

Series Y 339-342.   Summary of Federal Government Finances: 1940 to 1992

(For years ending June 30. Data for 1940-1953 are consolidated cash statement figures; for 1954-1992, unified budget figures.)

Year	Receipts	Outlays	Surplus or deficit (−)	Total gross Federal debt	Year	Receipts	Outlays	Surplus or deficit (−)	Total gross Federal debt
	339	340	341	342		339	340	341	342
1992	1,075,706,000	1,475,439,000	-399,733,000	4,077,510,000	1965	116,800,000	118,400,000	-1,600,000	323,200,000
1991	1,054,264,000	1,323,011,000	-268,746,000	3,598,993,000	1964	112,700,000	118,600,000	-5,900,000	316,800,000
1990	1,031,308,000	1,251,778,000	-220,470,000	3,206,347,000	1963	106,600,000	111,300,000	-4,800,000	310,800,000
1989	990,691,000	1,144,169,000	-206,132,000	2,867,538,000	1962	99,700,000	106,800,000	-7,100,000	303,300,000
1988	908,954,000	1,064,140,000	-193,897,000	2,600,760,000	1961	94,400,000	97,800,000	-3,400,000	292,900,000
1987	854,143,000	1,003,911,000	-169,257,000	2,345,578,000					
1986	769,091,000	990,336,000	-237,898,000	2,120,082,000	1960	92,500,000	92,200,000	300,000	290,900,000
					1959	79,200,000	92,100,000	-12,900,000	287,800,000
1985	734,057,000	946,391,000	-221,623,000	1,816,974,000	1958	79,600,000	82,600,000	-2,900,000	279,700,000
1984	666,457,000	851,846,000	-185,586,000	1,564,110,000	1957	80,000,000	76,700,000	3,200,000	272,400,000
1983	600,562,000	808,380,000	-207,977,000	1,371,164,000	1956	74,500,000	70,500,000	4,100,000	272,800,000
1982	617,766,000	745,755,000	-120,003,000	1,136,798,000					
1981	599,272,000	678,249,000	-73,916,000	994,298,000	1955	65,500,000	68,500,000	-3,000,000	274,400,000
					1954	69,700,000	70,900,000	-1,200,000	270,800,000
1980	517,112,000	590,920,000	-72,689,000	908,503,000	1953	71,500,000	76,800,000	-5,300,000	266,000,000
1979	463,302,000	530,464,000	-38,178,000	828,923,000	1952	68,000,000	68,000,000	(Z)	259,100,000
1978	399,561,000	458,729,000	-54,902,000	776,602,000	1951	53,400,000	45,800,000	7,600,000	255,300,000
1977	355,559,000	409,203,000	-49,745,000	706,398,000					
1976	298,060,000	371,779,000	-70,499,000	628,970,000	1950	40,900,000	43,100,000	-2,200,000	256,900,000
					1949	41,600,000	40,600,000	1,000,000	252,600,000
1975	279,090,000	332,332,000	-55,260,000	541,925,000	1948	45,400,000	36,500,000	8,900,000	252,000,000
1974	263,224,000	269,359,000	-7,971,000	483,893,000	1947	43,500,000	36,900,000	6,600,000	257,100,000
1973	230,799,000	245,707,000	-15,403,000	466,291,000	1946	43,500,000	61,700,000	-18,200,000	271,000,000
1972	207,309,000	230,681,000	-26,423,000	435,936,000					
1971	187,139,000	210,172,000	-26,052,000	408,176,000	1945	50,200,000	95,200,000	-45,000,000	260,100,000
					1944	47,800,000	94,000,000	-46,100,000	204,100,000
1970	193,700,000	196,600,000	-2,800,000	382,600,000	1943	25,100,000	78,900,000	-53,800,000	142,600,000
1969	187,800,000	184,500,000	3,200,000	367,100,000	1942	15,100,000	34,500,000	-19,400,000	79,200,000
1968	153,700,000	178,800,000	-25,200,000	369,800,000	1941	9,200,000	14,000,000	-4,800,000	57,500,000
1967	149,600,000	158,300,000	-8,700,000	341,300,000					
1966	130,900,000	134,700,000	-3,800,000	329,500,000	1940	6,900,000	9,600,000	-2,700,000	50,700,000

Z Less than $50 million.

Series Y 393-401. Individual Income Tax Returns: 1944 to 1989

(In thousands of dollars, except number of returns)

Income Year	Total number of returns	Taxable income	Returns with adjusted gross income, Income tax (after credits)	Income Year	Total number of returns	Taxable income	Returns with adjusted gross income, Income tax (after credits)
	393	398	399		393	398	399
1989	112,136,000	2,173,346,000	432,940,000	1965	67,596,300	255,082,124	49,529,695
1988	109,708,000	2,069,967,000	412,870,000	1964	65,375,601	229,875,078	47,152,855
1987	106,996,000	1,850,597,000	369,203,000	1963	63,943,236	209,090,323	48,203,580
1986	103,045,000	1,947,025,000	367,287,000	1962	62,712,386	195,320,479	44,902,840
				1961	61,499,420	181,779,732	42,225,498
1985	101,660,000	1,820,741,000	325,710,000				
1984	99,400,000	1,701,400,000	301,900,000	1960	61,027,931	171,627,771	39,464,156
1983	96,300,000	1,544,900,000	274,200,000	1959	60,271,297	166,540,616	38,645,299
1982	95,300,000	1,473,300,000	277,600,000	1958	59,085,182	149,337,414	34,335,652
1981	95,400,000	1,410,900,000	284,100,000	1957	59,825,121	149,363,077	34,393,639
				1956	59,197,004	141,532,061	32,732,132
1980	93,902,000	1,279,985,000	250,341,000				
1979	92,700,000	1,157,200,000	213,300,000	1955	58,250,188	128,020,111	29,613,722
1978	89,800,000	1,062,200,000	186,700,000	1954	56,747,008	115,331,301	26,665,753
1977	86,600,000	939,000,000	158,500,000	1953	57,838,184	—	29,430,659
1976	84,700,000	674,900,000	140,800,000	1952	56,528,817	—	27,802,831
				1951	55,447,009	—	24,227,780
1975	82,200,000	595,500,000	124,500,000				
1974	83,300,000	573,600,000	123,500,000	1950	53,060,098	—	18,374,922
1973	80,700,000	511,900,000	107,900,000	1949	51,814,124	—	14,538,141
1972	77,570,000	444,600,000	93,354,000	1948	52,072,006	—	15,441,529
1971	74,573,000	413,400,000	85,253,000	1947	55,099,008	—	18,076,281
				1946	52,816,547	—	16,075,913
1970	74,279,831	400,859,064	83,909,314	1945	49,932,783	—	17,050,378
1969	75,834,388	388,153,971	86,568,215	1944	47,111,495	—	16,216,401
1968	73,728,708	352,799,662	76,637,902				
1967	71,651,909	315,108,212	62,919,958				
1966	70,160,425	286,296,994	56,087,084				

Series Y 402-411. Individual Income Tax Returns: 1913 to 1943

Income Year	Total number of returns with net income [1]	Income Year	Total number of returns with net income [1]	Income Year	Total number of returns with net income [1]
	402		402		402
1943	43,506,553	1932	3,877,430	1922	6,787,481
1942	36,456,110	1931	3,225,924	1921	6,662,176
1941	26,770,089				
		1930	3,707,509	1920	7,259,944
1940	14,598,074	1929	4,044,327	1919	5,332,760
1939	7,570,320	1928	4,070,851	1918	4,425,114
1938	6,150,776	1927	4,101,547	1917	3,472,890
1937	6,301,833	1926	4,138,092	1916	437,036
1936	5,413,499				
		1925	4,171,051	1915	336,652
1935	4,575,012	1924	7,369,788	1914	357,515
1934	4,094,420	1923	7,698,321	1913 [2]	357,598
1933	3,723,558				

[1] Includes fiduciary returns with net income filed on Form 1040, 1913-1936. [2] Data pertain to last 10 months of year.

Series Y 493-504. Public Debt of the Federal Government: 1853 to 1991
(As of June 30)

Year	Interest-bearing principal of public debt outstanding [1]	U.S. savings bonds	Composition of interest-bearing debt Treasury bills [2]	Composition of interest-bearing debt Notes [3]	Year	Interest-bearing principal of public debt outstanding [1]	Composition of interest-bearing debt Treasury bills [2]	Composition of interest-bearing debt Notes [3]
	497	500	502	503		497	502	503
	1,000 dollars	Million dollars	Million dollars	Million dollars		1,000 dollars	Million dollars	Million dollars
1991	3,663,000,000	134,000	565,000	1,388,000	1935	27,645,241	2,053	10,023
1990	3,211,000,000	122,000	482,000	1,218,000	1934	26,480,488	2,921	6,653
1989	2,836,000,000	114,000	407,000	1,133,000	1933	22,157,643	3,063	4,548
1988	2,600,000,000	106,000	398,000	1,090,000	1932	19,161,274	3,341	1,261
1987	2,348,000,000	97,000	378,300	1,005,100	1931	16,519,589	2,246	452
1986	2,123,000,000	85,600	410,700	896,900				
					1930	15,921,892	1,420	1,626
1985	1,821,000,000	77,000	384,000	776,000	1929	16,638,941	1,640	2,267
1984	1,560,000,000	72,800	356,800	661,700	1928	17,317,694	1,252	2,582
1983	1,376,000,000	70,000	340,700	557,500	1927	18,252,665	686	1,986
1982	1,141,000,000	67,300	277,900	442,900	1926	19,383,771	453	1,799
1981	996,000,000	68,000	223,400	363,600				
					1925	20,210,907	533	2,740
1980	906,000,000	73,000	200,000	311,000	1924	20,981,242	808	4,148
1979	819,000,000	80,400	161,400	274,200	1923	22,007,044	1,031	4,441
1978	767,000,000	79,800	160,900	267,900	1922	22,710,338	1,829	4,916
1977	698,000,000	75,400	156,100	241,700	1921	23,738,900	2,700	4,920
1976	619,000,000	69,700	161,200	191,800				
					1920	24,062,500	2,769	5,075
1975	532,000,000	65,000	129,000	150,000	1919	25,236,947	3,625	4,422
1974	473,000,000	61,900	105,000	128,400	1918	12,197,508	1,706	369
1973	456,000,000	59,400	100,100	117,800	1917	2,712,549	273	27
1972	425,400,000	56,000	94,600	113,400	1916	971,563	—	4
1971	396,300,000	53,000	86,700	104,800				
					1915	969,759	—	—
1970	369,025,522	51,281	78,050	97,821	1914	967,953	—	—
1969	351,729,445	51,711	69,039	82,761	1913	965,707	—	—
1968	344,400,507	51,712	65,580	73,793	1912	963,777	—	—
1967	322,285,952	51,213	64,899	49,774	1911	915,353	—	—
1966	315,431,055	50,537	57,348	50,987				
					1910	913,317	—	—
1965	313,112,817	50,043	54,537	52,699	1909	913,317	—	—
1964	307,356,562	49,299	51,028	67,436	1908	897,504	14	—
1963	301,953,731	48,314	69,891	52,328	1907	894,834	(Z)	—
1962	294,442,001	47,607	56,518	65,464	1906	895,159	(Z)	—
1961	285,671,609	47,514	50,062	56,257				
					1905	895,158	(Z)	—
1960	283,241,183	47,544	51,065	51,483	1904	895,157	(Z)	—
1959	281,833,362	50,503	65,860	27,314	1903	914,541	(Z)	—
1958	274,697,560	51,984	55,326	20,416	1902	931,070	(Z)	—
1957	268,485,563	54,622	43,893	30,973	1901	987,141	(Z)	—
1956	269,883,068	57,497	37,111	35,952				
					1900	1,023,479	(Z)	—
1955	271,741,538	58,365	33,350	42,642	1899	1,046,049	(Z)	—
1954	268,909,767	58,061	37,920	37,039	1898	847,367	(Z)	—
1953	263,946,018	57,886	35,561	34,878	1897	847,365	(Z)	—
1952	256,862,861	57,685	45,642	25,575	1896	847,364	(Z)	—
1951	252,851,765	57,572	23,123	43,624				
					1895	716,202	(Z)	—
1950	255,209,353	57,536	31,951	28,876	1894	635,042	(Z)	—
1949	250,761,637	56,260	40,964	8,456	1893	585,037	(Z)	—
1948	250,063,348	53,274	36,345	15,769	1892	585,029	(Z)	—
1947	255,113,412	51,367	41,071	13,702	1891	610,529	(Z)	—
1946	268,110,842	49,035	51,843	24,972				
					1890	711,313	(Z)	—
1945	256,356,616	45,586	51,177	33,633	1889	815,854	(Z)	—
1944	199,543,355	34,606	43,557	26,962	1888	936,523	(Z)	—
1943	135,380,306	21,256	28,425	16,663	1887	1,007,692	(Z)	—
1942	71,968,418	10,188	5,604	9,703	1886	1,132,014	(Z)	—
1941	48,387,400	4,314	1,603	5,698				
					1885	1,182,151	(Z)	—
1940	42,376,496	2,905	1,302	6,383	1884	1,212,564	(Z)	—
1939	39,885,970	1,868	1,308	7,243	1883	1,324,229	(Z)	—
1938	36,575,926	1,238	1,154	9,147	1882	1,449,810	1	—
1937	35,800,109	800	2,303	10,617	1881	1,625,568	1	—
1936	32,988,790	316	2,354	11,381				

See footnotes at end of table.

Series Y 493-504.   Public Debt of the Federal Government: 1853 to 1991—Cont'd.

(As of June 30)

Year	Interest-bearing principal of public debt outstanding [1]	Year	Interest-bearing principal of public debt outstanding [1]	Year	Interest-bearing principal of public debt outstanding [1]
	497		**497**		**497**
	1,000 dollars		1,000 dollars		1,000 dollars
1880	1,709,993	1870	2,035,881	1860	64,683
1879	1,887,716	1869	2,151,495	1859	58,333
1878	1,780,736	1868	2,191,326	1858	44,743
1877	1,697,889	1867	2,238,955	1857	28,503
1876	1,696,685	1866	2,322,116	1856	31,805
1875	1,708,676	1865	2,217,709	1855	35,418
1874	1,724,931	1864	1,360,027	1854	42,045
1873	1,696,484	1863	707,834	1853	59,642
1872	1,800,794	1862	365,356		
1871	1,920,697	1861	90,423		

Z Less than $500,000.

[1] Exclusive of bonds issued to Pacific Railways (provision was made by law to secure the Treasury against both principal and interest) and the Navy pension fund (which was not a debt, the principal being the property of the United States). The Statement of the Public Debt included the railroad bonds from issuance and the Navy fund from Sept. 1, 1896, until the statement of June 30, 1890.

[2] Includes certificates of indebtedness. Also includes refunding certificates of deposit, 1880-1907, inclusive.

[3] Includes old Treasury (War) savings securities from 1918 through 1929.

Series Y 533-566.   Federal, State and Local Government Expenditure, by Function: 1902 to 1990

(In millions of dollars)

General expenditure

Year	Total expenditure [1]	Total	Total education	Highways	Total public welfare	Hospitals [2]	Police	Local fire protection
	533	534	538	542	543	547	549	550
1990	2,218,793	1,686,774	305,552	61,913	140,734	92,487	35,921	13,186
1988	1,920,413	1,461,857	256,960	55,998	115,125	78,789	30,934	11,753
1987	1,810,006	1,374,297	240,686	52,822	106,277	72,488	28,720	10,910
1986	1,696,208	1,284,261	224,400	49,936	99,665	68,706	26,228	9,587
1985	1,580,997	1,192,375	205,894	45,856	94,811	63,698	24,386	8,917
1984	1,428,100	1,068,400	188,600	40,300	88,400	59,300	21,400	8,200
1983	1,350,900	1,002,400	176,600	37,200	83,900	56,400	20,300	7,600
1982	1,233,500	917,500	165,800	35,100	78,800	53,300	18,500	7,000
1981	1,109,800	827,900	158,000	34,900	74,600	47,300	16,900	6,300
1980	958,700	723,100	143,800	33,700	64,800	43,300	15,200	5,700
1979	832,400	630,700	129,400	29,000	59,100	37,100	13,900	5,100
1978	745,400	564,300	118,800	24,900	54,200	33,000	12,900	4,800
1977	682,500	514,200	110,600	23,300	49,400	30,600	11,800	4,400
1976	625,100	476,100	106,300	24,200	45,100	27,500	10,700	3,900
1975	560,100	433,600	95,000	22,800	39,400	24,900	9,600	3,500
1974	478,300	377,200	81,700	20,200	31,000	21,700	8,300	3,000
1973	436,900	348,500	74,900	18,900	27,000	18,700	7,800	2,800
1972	397,400	321,400	70,000	19,400	23,600	17,000	6,500	2,600
1971	369,400	301,100	64,000	18,400	20,400	14,800	5,700	2,300
1970	332,985	275,017	55,771	16,746	17,517	9,693	4,903	2,024
1969	308,344	255,924	50,377	15,738	14,730	8,593	4,242	1,793
1968	282,645	236,348	43,614	14,654	11,245	7,801	3,700	1,623
1967	257,800	216,888	40,214	14,033	9,592	6,951	3,331	1,499
1966	224,813	189,406	34,837	12,895	6,965	6,297	3,033	1,376
1965	205,550	173,613	29,613	12,348	6,420	5,865	2,792	1,306
1964	196,431	166,088	27,342	11,828	5,880	5,461	2,586	1,222
1963	184,996	156,002	24,480	11,315	5,538	5,106	2,446	1,161
1962	176,240	149,159	22,814	10,508	5,147	4,791	2,326	1,124
1961	164,875	139,161	21,214	9,995	4,779	4,549	2,210	1,087
1960 *	151,288	128,600	19,404	9,565	4,462	4,213	2,030	995
1959 [2]	145,748	124,217	18,119	9,726	4,193	4,074	1,880	914
1958	134,931	115,714	16,836	8,702	3,866	3,805	1,769	873
1957	125,463	109,765	15,098	7,931	3,534	3,416	1,623	810
1956	115,796	102,156	14,160	7,035	3,184	3,068	1,486	737
1955	110,717	97,828	12,710	6,520	3,210	2,721	1,358	694
1954	111,332	100,365	11,196	5,586	3,103	2,676	1,254	653
1953	110,054	100,733	10,117	5,053	2,956	2,548	1,160	598
1952	99,847	91,291	9,598	4,714	2,830	2,460	1,080	586
1950	70,334	60,701	9,647	3,872	2,964	2,050	864	488
1948	55,081	50,088	7,721	3,071	2,144	1,398	724	406
1946	79,707	75,582	3,711	1,680	1,435	762	549	294
1944	109,947	107,823	2,805	1,215	1,150	568	497	251
1942	45,576	43,483	2,696	1,765	1,285	517	444	236
1940	20,417	18,125	2,827	2,177	1,314	537	386	235
1938	17,675	16,273	2,653	2,150	1,233	496	378	231
1936	16,758	15,835	2,365	1,945	997	461	331	205
1934	12,807	12,086	2,005	1,829	979	416	306	189
1932	12,437	11,748	2,325	1,766	445	462	349	210
1927	11,220	10,590	2,243	1,819	161	347	290	203
1922	9,297	8,854	1,713	1,296	128	287	204	158
1913	3,215	3,022	582	419	57	80	92	76
1902	1,660	1,578	258	175	41	45	50	40

See footnotes at end of table.

Series Y 533-566. Federal, State and Local Government Expenditure, by Function: 1902 to 1990—Cont'd.

(In millions of dollars)

General expenditure–Cont'd.

Year	Local sanitation	Total natural resources	Housing and urban renewal	Financial administration and general control	Interest on general debt [4]	Utility and liquor stores expenditure	Total insurance trust expenditure
	551	**552**	**555**	**557**	**558**	**561**	**562**
1990	28,453	96,922	32,430	57,546	237,691	77,801	454,218
1988	23,679	103,789	25,212	48,111	202,437	70,051	388,505
1987	21,323	105,282	21,304	44,125	187,971	68,440	367,269
1986	19,142	79,313	19,210	40,422	181,231	65,297	346,651
1985	17,398	71,152	18,592	37,200	172,708	59,798	328,824
1984	16,200	65,300	17,600	30,100	137,900	55,100	304,700
1983	15,600	54,800	18,500	27,900	132,900	52,800	297,400
1982	14,900	45,500	16,500	24,900	122,000	48,400	267,400
1981	14,900	43,600	13,900	22,500	97,600	43,000	238,900
1980	13,200	35,200	12,100	20,700	76,000	36,200	199,400
1979	11,800	30,300	8,000	18,700	61,800	30,800	170,900
1978	9,900	26,300	6,000	16,700	51,300	26,300	154,800
1977	9,400	22,400	5,600	14,800	44,500	24,200	144,100
1976	8,200	19,400	5,400	13,400	39,600	19,500	129,400
1975	7,500	18,100	5,900	11,900	33,800	17,300	109,200
1974	6,000	17,400	5,900	10,000	30,100	14,400	86,700
1973	5,300	16,700	6,900	4,600	25,100	13,000	75,300
1972	4,700	14,200	5,400	4,000	23,100	11,400	64,600
1971	4,100	13,700	4,500	3,600	21,700	10,300	58,000
1970	3,413	11,469	3,189	6,370	18,411	9,447	48,521
1969	2,969	10,024	2,505	5,563	16,992	8,820	43,600
1968	2,707	9,200	2,841	4,966	14,873	8,170	38,127
1967	2,523	10,145	2,413	4,537	13,406	7,350	33,561
1966	2,571	10,301	2,415	4,105	12,478	7,282	28,126
1965	2,360	10,990	2,198	3,842	11,430	7,058	24,880
1964	2,267	10,042	2,037	3,583	10,649	6,184	24,161
1963	1,996	9,511	1,688	3,362	9,846	5,736	23,260
1962	1,958	10,468	1,701	3,187	9,173	5,453	21,628
1961	1,774	9,756	1,320	3,025	9,309	5,523	20,191
1960 *	1,727	7,087	1,142	2,859	9,332	5,088	17,596
1959 [3]	1,609	7,966	838	2,750	6,959	4,901	16,631
1958	1,505	6,160	801	2,536	7,360	4,693	14,524
1957	1,443	6,137	624	2,405	6,603	4,429	11,269
1956	1,326	6,630	562	2,235	6,297	4,065	9,576
1955	1,142	6,338	611	2,060	5,684	3,886	9,002
1954	1,058	6,377	742	1,997	5,515	3,482	7,484
1953	908	4,816	768	1,866	5,477	3,316	6,006
1952	992	3,252	875	1,801	4,814	3,067	5,489
1950	834	5,005	573	1,555	4,862	2,739	6,894
1948	670	2,223	245	1,325	4,722	2,379	2,614
1946	370	3,111	221	1,163	4,286	1,733	2,392
1944	245	2,731	574	1,087	2,650	1,281	842
1942	229	2,468	622	828	1,591	1,106	986
1940	207	2,730	267	739	1,552	1,324	968
1938	226	2,089	109	725	1,513	848	554
1936	204	2,158	71	662	1,455	701	222
1934	177	1,241	3	533	1,473	528	193
1932	223	326	X	601	1,323	518	171
1927	312	206	1	526	1,348	491	139
1922	189	140	1	439	1,370	359	84
1913	97	44	——	256	170	186	7
1902	51	17	——	175	97	82	——

* Denotes first year for which figures include Alaska and Hawaii.
X Represents zero.
[1] To avoid duplication, transactions between governments are excluded.

[2] From 1971 to 1990, combines hospitals (547) and health (548).
[3] Includes Alaska.
[4] Excludes interest on federal securities held by federal agencies and funds.

Series Y 652-670. State and Local Government Revenue, by Source: 1902 to 1990

(In millions of dollars)

Revenue from state and local sources—General revenue

Taxes

Year	Total revenue from all sources	Total general revenue	Total	Individual income	Corporation income	Sales and gross receipts	Property	Charges and miscellaneous
	652	656	657	658	659	660	661	663
1990	2,047,000	1,493,000	1,134,000	573,000	117,000	232,000	156,000	359,000
1989	1,917,000	1,400,000	1,085,000	543,000	129,000	219,000	143,000	316,000
1988	1,776,000	1,299,000	998,000	490,000	118,000	209,000	132,000	301,000
1987	1,678,000	1,236,000	945,000	476,000	107,000	193,000	121,000	291,000
1986	1,516,000	1,107,000	845,000	423,000	83,000	182,000	112,000	262,000
1985	1,419,000	1,050,000	804,000	401,000	80,000	176,000	104,000	246,000
1984	1,307,000	975,000	735,000	361,000	74,000	127,000	96,000	240,000
1983	1,181,300	878,400	665,600	344,100	51,300	144,700	89,100	213,000
1982	1,146,300	866,400	671,500	348,800	64,200	139,300	82,100	194,900
1981	1,075,400	820,800	650,200	332,000	75,300	134,500	75,000	170,600
1980	932,000	717,000	574,000	286,000	78,000	112,000	68,000	142,000
1979	829,400	640,500	524,400	245,800	77,800	101,000	64,900	116,100
1978	731,700	565,600	468,200	214,200	70,700	93,000	66,400	97,400
1977	657,500	506,300	419,800	186,000	64,100	83,800	62,500	86,500
1976	571,200	483,300	358,200	156,200	48,700	76,300	57,000	80,100
1975	519,300	402,900	331,400	143,800	47,300	70,900	51,500	71,400
1974	484,000	383,100	314,800	138,400	44,600	66,600	47,700	68,300
1973	432,100	344,400	286,200	121,200	41,600	61,800	45,300	58,300
1972	381,849	307,220	262,534	109,974	36,582	57,589	42,133	44,688
1971	342,489	275,669	232,252	98,130	30,209	52,660	37,852	43,417
1970	150,106	108,898	86,795	10,812	3,738	30,322	34,054	22,103
1969	132,153	95,397	76,712	8,908	3,180	26,519	30,673	18,686
1968	117,581	84,083	67,572	7,308	2,518	22,911	27,747	16,511
1967	106,581	75,827	61,000	5,826	2,227	20,530	26,047	14,827
1966	97,619	69,822	56,647	4,760	2,038	19,085	24,670	13,175
1965	87,777	62,971	51,243	4,090	1,929	17,118	22,583	11,729
1964	81,455	58,440	47,785	3,791	1,695	15,762	21,241	10,655
1963	74,408	53,606	44,014	3,267	1,505	14,446	19,833	9,593
1962	69,492	50,381	41,554	3,037	1,308	13,494	19,054	8,827
1961	64,531	46,907	38,861	2,613	1,266	12,463	18,002	8,045
1960 *	60,277	43,530	36,117	2,463	1,180	11,849	16,405	7,414
1959 [1]	53,972	38,929	32,379	1,994	1,001	10,437	14,983	6,550
1958	49,262	36,354	30,380	1,759	1,018	9,829	14,047	5,974
1957	45,929	34,320	28,817	1,754	984	9,467	12,864	5,503
1956	41,692	31,332	26,368	1,538	890	8,691	11,749	4,964
1955	37,619	27,942	23,483	1,237	744	7,643	10,735	4,459
1954	35,386	26,046	22,067	1,127	778	7,276	9,967	3,979
1953	33,411	24,437	20,908	1,065	817	6,927	9,375	3,529
1952	31,013	22,615	19,323	998	846	6,357	8,652	3,292
1950	25,639	18,425	15,914	788	593	5,154	7,349	2,511
1948	21,613	15,389	13,342	543	592	4,442	6,126	2,047
1946	15,983	11,501	10,094	422	447	2,986	4,986	1,407
1944	14,333	9,954	8,774	342	451	2,289	4,604	1,180
1942	13,148	9,560	8,528	276	272	2,351	4,537	1,031
1940	11,749	8,664	7,810	224	156	1,982	4,430	854
1938	11,058	8,428	7,605	218	165	1,794	4,440	823
1936	9,360	7,447	6,701	153	113	1,484	4,093	746
1934	8,430	6,662	5,912	80	49	1,008	4,076	750
1932	7,887	7,035	6,164	74	79	752	4,487	871
1927	7,383	7,155	6,087	70	92	470	4,730	1,068
1922	5,169	4,673	4,016	43	58	154	3,321	657
1913	2,030	1,900	1,609	—	—	58	1,332	291
1902	1,048	979	860	—	—	28	706	119

* Denotes first year for which figures include Alaska and Hawaii.   [1] Includes Alaska.

Series Y 736-782. State Government Expenditure, by Character and Object, by Function and State Government: 1902 to 1990

(In millions of dollars)

	Direct expenditure by character and object								Direct expenditure by function	
			Capital outlay						General expenditure	
Year	Total	Current operation	Total	Construction	Assistance and subsidies	Interest on debt	Insurance benefits and repayments	Outstanding debt at end of fiscal year	Total education	Highways
	738	739	740	741	743	744	745	747	759	763
1990	972,662	700,131	123,069	89,114	27,227	58,914	63,321	860,584	288,148	61,057
1988	824,507	591,247	104,314	78,592	23,928	52,803	52,216	755,034	242,683	55,621
1987	772,863	550,061	98,276	73,616	23,610	50,101	50,815	718,657	226,658	52,199
1986	715,324	511,378	90,449	67,968	22,588	44,370	46,538	658,875	210,819	49,368
1985	656,188	472,543	79,930	60,685	20,707	38,817	44,191	571,351	192,686	45,022
1984	598,945	433,653	70,651	53,833	19,694	34,439	40,508	506,330	176,108	39,419
1983	565,146	401,967	67,981	53,266	18,684	29,178	47,335	454,501	163,876	36,655
1982	523,023	375,057	66,802	53,668	17,335	24,321	39,508	404,579	154,282	34,520
1981	485,174	343,623	67,596	54,950	16,861	20,511	36,583	363,892	145,784	34,603
1980	432,328	307,811	62,894	51,492	15,222	17,604	28,797	335,603	133,211	33,311
1979	380,374	274,167	53,196	43,326	14,044	15,463	23,504	304,103	119,448	28,440
1978	345,313	249,222	44,769	36,199	13,753	14,044	23,525	284,330	110,758	24,609
1977	323,168	225,650	45,154	36,334	13,077	13,137	26,149	259,658	102,780	23,058
1976	304,229	204,387	46,531	38,299	12,494	11,681	27,954	240,532	97,216	23,907
1975	268,241	180,976	44,824	36,356	11,146	10,087	21,209	219,926	87,858	22,528
1974	225,691	154,810	38,084	30,542	11,290	8,840	12,667	206,616	75,833	19,946
1973	205,336	138,974	35,272	28,251	12,187	7,828	11,074	188,485	69,714	18,615
1972	188,825	125,630	34,237	28,107	11,527	6,893	10,358	174,502	64,886	19,010
1971	170,766	111,829	33,137	26,970	10,104	5,904	9,793	158,827	59,413	18,095
1970	56,163	30,971	13,295	11,185	4,387	1,499	6,010	42,008	13,780	11,044
1969	49,448	27,052	12,701	10,610	3,509	1,275	4,911	39,553	12,304	10,414
1968	44,304	23,379	12,210	10,053	2,960	1,128	4,626	35,666	10,957	9,819
1967	39,704	20,201	11,544	9,550	2,665	1,026	4,268	32,472	9,384	9,423
1966	34,195	16,855	10,193	8,287	2,301	894	3,952	29,564	7,572	8,624
1965	31,465	14,930	9,307	7,600	2,236	822	4,170	27,034	6,181	8,214
1964	29,616	13,492	8,820	7,263	2,175	765	4,364	25,041	5,465	7,850
1963	27,698	12,449	8,110	6,717	2,112	721	4,306	23,176	4,718	7,425
1962	25,495	11,290	7,214	5,960	2,118	635	4,238	22,023	4,270	6,635
1961	24,578	10,384	6,865	5,699	2,044	584	4,701	19,993	3,792	6,230
1960 *	22,152	9,534	6,607	5,509	2,015	536	3,461	18,543	3,396	6,070
1959 [1]	22,436	8,775	7,059	5,937	1,891	453	4,259	16,930	3,093	6,414
1958	19,991	8,161	5,946	5,022	1,813	396	3,675	15,394	2,728	5,507
1957	16,796	7,330	5,163	4,318	1,639	351	2,313	13,738	2,342	4,875
1956	15,148	6,758	4,564	3,872	1,531	311	1,984	12,890	2,138	4,367
1955	14,371	6,234	3,992	3,404	1,482	251	2,411	11,198	1,905	3,899
1954	13,008	5,886	3,347	2,831	1,486	193	2,096	9,600	1,715	3,254
1953	11,466	5,540	2,847	2,472	1,501	162	1,416	7,824	1,634	2,781
1952	10,790	5,173	2,658	2,323	1,402	144	1,413	6,874	1,494	2,556
1950	10,864	4,450	2,237	1,966	1,891	109	2,177	5,285	1,358	2,058
1948	7,897	3,837	1,456	1,268	1,499	86	1,020	3,676	1,081	1,510
1946	4,974	2,701	368	292	663	84	1,158	2,353	518	613
1944	3,319	2,134	330	288	527	101	226	2,776	489	540
1942	3,563	1,827	642	560	466	122	505	3,257	391	790
1940	3,555	1,570	737	643	517	130	601	3,590	375	793
1938	3,082	1,503	701	612	448	128	302	3,343	347	815
1936	2,445	1,192	634	553	416	124	79	3,413	297	754
1934	2,143	985	619	540	356	119	64	2,248	228	738
1932	2,028	982	786	686	83	114	63	2,832	278	843
1927	1,451	762	492	430	43	83	71	1,971	218	514
1922	1,085	562	302	263	122	45	54	1,131	164	303
1913	297	218	48	42	17	14	—	379	55	26
1902	136	114	2	2	10	10	—	230	17	4

See footnotes at end of table.

Series Y 736-782. State Government Expenditure, by Character and Object, by Function and State Government: 1902 to 1990—Cont'd.

(In millions of dollars)

					Direct expenditure by function—Cont'd.				
					General expenditure—Cont'd.				
Year	Total public welfare	Hospitals	Health	Police	Natural resources	Financial administration and general control	Interest on general debt	Liquor stores expenditure	Total insurance trust expenditure
	764	768	769	770	771	773	774	778	779
1990	107,287	50,412	24,223	30,577	12,330	16,217	49,739	77,801	63,321
1988	86,469	43,452	18,488	26,277	10,238	13,589	44,318	70,052	52,216
1987	80,090	40,108	16,864	24,684	9,738	12,841	41,816	68,440	50,815
1986	73,785	37,958	15,550	22,685	9,074	11,897	37,064	65,297	46,538
1985	69,577	36,000	13,711	20,956	8,357	10,448	32,427	59,800	44,191
1984	64,709	34,142	12,277	19,262	7,421	9,502	28,696	55,062	40,508
1983	59,157	32,452	11,546	17,958	7,082	8,789	24,136	52,812	47,335
1982	56,216	30,245	10,636	16,511	6,567	8,106	20,160	48,412	39,508
1981	52,248	26,330	9,771	14,947	6,175	7,230	17,131	43,016	36,583
1980	45,552	23,787	8,387	13,494	5,509	6,719	14,747	36,191	28,797
1979	40,418	21,039	7,179	12,207	4,706	6,071	12,987	30,846	23,504
1978	37,679	18,648	6,303	11,306	4,225	5,292	11,983	26,277	23,526
1977	34,529	17,542	5,497	10,445	4,049	4,489	11,234	24,191	26,149
1976	32,604	15,726	4,960	9,531	4,662	3,960	10,269	19,542	27,954
1975	27,181	14,432	4,414	8,526	4,223	3,594	8,782	17,285	21,209
1974	24,745	12,493	3,452	7,289	3,661	3,165	7,666	14,406	12,667
1973	23,582	11,112	2,732	6,710	3,278	2,811	6,785	13,035	11,074
1972	21,070	10,293	2,574	5,976	3,110	2,480	5,963	11,414	10,538
1971	18,226	9,086	2,119	5,228	3,082	2,271	5,089	10,300	9,793
1970	8,203	4,002	786	688	2,158	1,720	1,499	1,404	6,010
1969	6,464	3,582	676	585	2,035	1,496	1,275	1,293	4,911
1968	5,122	3,233	599	516	1,954	1,310	1,128	1,233	4,626
1967	4,291	2,857	501	441	1,801	1,175	1,026	1,187	4,268
1966	3,138	2,533	433	385	1,532	1,024	894	1,081	3,952
1965	2,998	2,317	384	348	1,343	948	822	1,022	4,170
1964	2,796	2,127	337	315	1,185	871	765	977	4,364
1963	2,712	2,006	324	297	1,097	830	721	900	4,306
1962	2,509	1,878	283	276	973	763	635	882	4,238
1961	2,311	1,799	260	261	906	726	584	873	4,701
1960 *	2,221	1,664	232	245	842	654	536	907	3,461
1959 [1]	2,124	1,627	223	228	813	619	453	860	4,259
1958	1,944	1,549	211	214	753	569	396	869	3,675
1957	1,826	1,373	198	179	688	531	351	836	2,313
1956	1,603	1,268	202	159	670	477	311	845	1,984
1955	1,600	1,145	193	139	597	447	251	770	2,411
1954	1,548	1,089	187	130	563	419	193	803	2,096
1953	1,534	1,014	170	119	531	399	162	757	1,416
1952	1,410	968	164	106	539	361	144	723	1,413
1950	1,566	788	159	85	468	317	109	654	2,177
1948	962	533	130	65	344	266	86	691	1,020
1946	680	308	116	45	207	192	84	663	1,158
1944	577	253	78	41	164	162	101	426	226
1942	523	235	64	40	159	164	122	288	505
1940	527	236	64	34	144	151	130	224	601
1938	453	209	59	30	128	146	128	204	302
1936	422	180	41	19	93	130	124	143	97
1934	363	167	36	15	85	108	119	70	64
1932	74	181	34	15	119	114	114	—	63
1927	40	146	24	7	94	96	83	—	71
1922	38	105	20	4	61	69	45	—	54
1913	16	47	6	1	14	38	14	—	—
1902	10	28	4	—	9	23	10	2	—

* Denotes first year for which figures include Alaska and Hawaii.

[1] Includes Alaska.

Series Y 856-903. Selected Characteristics of the Armed Forces, by War

(For Revolutionary War, number of personnel serving not known, but estimates range from 184,000 to 250,000; for War of 1812, 286,730 served; for Mexican War, 78,718 served. Dates of the major conflicts may differ from those specified in various laws providing benefits for veterans. See *Historical Statistics, Colonial Times to 1970*, series Y 856-903)

Series No.	Item	Unit	Civil War [1]	Spanish-American War	World War I	World War II	Korean conflict	Vietnam conflict
856	Personnel serving [2]	1,000	2,213	307	4,735	[3] 16,113	[4] 5,720	[5] 8,744
866	Average duration of service	Months	20	8	12	33	19	23
869	Service abroad: Personnel serving	Percent	(NA)	[6] 29	53	73	[7] 56	(NA)
870	Average duration [8]	Months	(NA)	1.5	6	16	13	(NA)
880	Casualties: [9] Battle deaths [2]	1,000	140	(Z)	53	292	34	[10] 47
882	Wounds not mortal [2]	1,000	282	2	204	671	103	[10] 153
862	Draftees: Classified	1,000	777	(X)	24,234	36,677	9,123	[5] 75,717
863	Examined	1,000	522	(X)	3,764	17,955	3,685	[5] 8,611
864	Rejected	1,000	160	(X)	803	6,420	1,189	[5] 3,880
865	Inducted	1,000	46	(X)	2,820	10,022	1,560	[5] 1,759

NA Not available.
X Not applicable.
Z Fewer than 500.
[1] Union forces only. Estimates of the number serving in Confederate forces range from 600,000 to 1.5 million.
[2] Source U.S. Department of Defense, *Selected Manpower Statistics, FY 1988*, annual.
[3] Covers Dec. 1, 1941 to Dec. 31, 1946.

[4] Covers June 25, 1950 to July 27, 1953.
[5] Covers Aug. 4, 1964 to Jan. 27, 1973.
[6] Army and Marines only.
[7] Excludes Navy. Covers July 1950 through Jan. 1955. Far East area only.
[8] During hostilities only.
[9] For periods covered, see footnotes 3, 4 and 5.
[10] Covers Jan. 1, 1961 to Jan. 27, 1973. Includes known military service personnel who have died from combat-related wounds.

Sources

Unless otherwise indicated, all publications are from the United States Federal Government

A. Population

Census of Population: General Population Characteristics
Current Population Reports
Population Profile of the United States

B. Vital Statistics and Health and Medical Care

Monthly Vital Statistics Report
Vital Statistics of the United States

Abortion Service in the United States. Alan Guttmacher Institute
Annual Medicare Program Statistics Series
Cancer Incidence and Mortality in the United States
Data on Health Resources Utilization
Data on Health Resources: Manpower and Facilities
Dental Statistics Handbook. American Dental Association
Food Consumption: Prices and Expenditures
Healthcare Financing Review
Healthcare Financing Program Statistics
Health United States
Hospital Statistics. American Hospital Association
Mental Health
Mental Health Statistics
Morbidity and Mortality Weekly Report
Physician Characteristics and Distribution in the United States. American Medical Association
Physician's Earnings and Expenses. Medical Economics
Reference Data on the Profile of Medical Practice. American Medical Association
Statistical Bulletin. Metropolitan Life Insurance Company
Statistical Summary. American Nurses Association
Teenage Pregnancy in the United States. Alan Guttmacher Institute
U.S. Medical Licensure Statistics. American Medical Association

C. Migration

Statistical Yearbook of the Immigration and Naturalization Service

D. Labor

Compensation and Working Conditions
Employment and Earnings
Employment, Hours and Earnings, 1909-1990
Employment and Earnings: Characteristics of Families
Employment Benefits in Medium and Large Firms
Employment Benefits in State and Local Governments
Employment Cost Index
Employment in Perspective: Minority Workers
Employment in Perspective: Women in the Labor Force
Employment in the Aerospace Industry
Aerospace Industries Association
Employment Outlook. Bureau of National Affairs
The Employment Situation
Geographic Profile of Employment and Unemployment
Handbook of Labor Statistics
Job Absence and Turnover. Bureau of National Affairs
Key Statistics on Work and Family Issues.
Bureau of National Affairs
Labor Force Statistics Derived from the Current Population Survey
Major Collective Bargaining Settlements
Major Work Stoppages
Monthly Labor Review
Mass Layoffs
Occupational Employment in Selected Non-Manufacturing Industries
Occupational Illnesses and Injuries in the United States by Industry
Occupational Projections and Training Data
Outlook 2000
Permanent Mass Layoffs and Plant Closings
Productivity Measures for Certain Industries
Real Earnings
Revised Seasonally Adjusted Labor Force Statistics
State and Metropolitan Area Employment and Unemployment
Weekly Wage Earnings of Wage and Salary Workers
White Collar Pay
Work Experiences of the Population
Working Woman: A Chartbook
Farm Labor
Unemployment Insurance Claims

E. Price and Price Indexes

Commodity Yearbooks. Commodity Research Bureau
Consumer Price Index: Energy and Food
CPI Detailed Report
Handbook of Labor Statistics
Producer Price Index
Relative Importance of Components in the CPI
U.S. Import and Export Price Indexes

F. National Income and Wealth

Consumer Expenditure Survey
Economic Indicators
Flow of Funds Accounts
National Income and Product Accounts
Statistics of Income Bulletin
Survey of Current Business

G. Consumer Income and Expenditures

Consumer Expenditure Survey
Federal Reserve Bulletin
Individual Income Tax Returns
Local Area Personal Income
Statistics of Income Bulletin
Trends in Family Income, 1970-86
Trends Since 1960 in the Economic Situation of Aged Men and
    Women

H. Social Statistics

American Red Cross Annual
Benefits and Beneficiaries Under Public Employment Retirement
    Systems
Characteristics of Social Security Disability
Insurance Beneficiaries
Compensation Report
Giving USA. American Association of Fundraising Councils.
Employment and Trends
Income of Population 55 and Over
Private Social Welfare Expenditures
Public Social Welfare Expenditures
Quarterly Public Assistance Statistics
Railroad Retirement Board. Monthly Benefit Statistics
Social Security Beneficiaries by State and County
Social Security Bulletin
Social Security Programs in the United States
Supplemental Security Income: State and County Data Annual
Trend Data of Department of Veterans Affairs
Unemployment Insurance Claims
Unemployment Insurance: Financial Data
Worker's Compensation Coverage, Benefits and Costs

Catholic Schools in America. National Catholic Education
    Association (NCEA)
Condition of Education
Digest of Education Statistics
Earned Degrees Conferred
Estimates of School Statistics. National Education Association
Factbook of Higher Education. American Council on Education
Faculty Salaries, Tenure and Benefits
Fall Enrollment in Colleges and Universities
Projections of Education Statistics
Racial, Ethnic and Sex Enrollment Data from Institutions of
    Higher Education
Rankings of the States
Revenues and Expenditures for Public Elementary and Secondary
    Education
States' Profiles: Financing Public Higher Education. Research
    Associates

U.S. Catholic Elementary Schools Staffing and Enrollment.
    NCEA
U.S. Catholic Secondary Schools and their Finances. NCEA
U.S. Catholic Elementary Schools and their Finances. NCEA

American Jewish Yearbook
Churches and Church Membership in the United States. Glenmary
    Research Center
Yearbook of American and Canadian Churches. National Council
    of Churches.

Boating: A Statistical Report. National Marine Manufacturers
    Association
Federal Recreation Fee Report
International Air Travel Statistics
International Travel to the United States
National Parks Statistical Abstract
National Parks Index
Public Land Statistics
Report of the Forest Service
Sporting Goods Market. National Sporting Goods Association
Statistics on Outdoor Recreation. Resources for the Future
Trends in the Golf Industry. National Golf Foundation

Capital Punishment Annual
Census of Jails
Census of State Correctional Facilities
Children in Custody
Crime in the United States
Criminal Victimization in the United States
Drug Abuse and Law Enforcement Statistics
Expenditure and Employment Data for the Criminal Justice
    System
Federal Bureau of Prisons Statistical Report
Federal Court Management Statistics
Federal Judicial Workload Statistics
Federal Offenders and Sentences Imposed
Households Touched by Crime
Law Enforcement Officers Killed and Assaulted
National Crime Survey
National Survey of Courts
Parole in the Untied States
Prisoners in State and Federal Institutions
Sourcebook of Criminal Justice Statistics
State Court Caseload Statistics
Survey of Prison Inmates
Uniform Crime Reports

J. Land, Water, and Climate

Air Quality Data
Climatological Data
Environmental Quality
Environmental Trends
Estimated Use of Water in the United States
General Summary of Tornadoes
Hourly Precipitation Data
Local Climatological Data
National Air Quality and Emissions Trends Report
National Inventory of Land Resources

Radiation Data and Reports
State of the Environment. Conservation Foundation
Storm Data

K. Agriculture

Agricultural Income and Finance
Agricultural Outlook
Agricultural Price Reports
Agricultural Statistics
Crop Production
Crop Values
Economic Indicators of the Farm Sector
Farmline
Fertilizer Use and Price Statistics
Financial Characteristics of U.S. Farms
Food Consumption, Prices and Expenditures
Food Marketing Review
Food Spending in American Households
Foreign Agricultural Trade of the United States
Fruit and Vegetable Reports
Journal of American Agricultural Economics Research
Livestock Production, Disposition and Income
Milk and Dairy Products Reports
Poultry and Egg Reports
Rural Development Perspectives
Stock Reports
U.S. Egg and Poultry Statistical Series
U.S. Rice Distribution Patterns

L. Forestry and Fisheries

Analysis of the Timber Situation in the United States
Aquaculture
Fisheries of the United States
Forest Statistics of the United States
Land Areas of the National Forest System
Marine Recreational Fishery Statistical Survey
Statistical Roundup. National Forest Products Association
U.S. Timber Production, Trade, Consumption and Price Statistics

M. Minerals

Annual Energy Review
Annual Statistical Report. American Iron and Steel Institute
Census of Mineral Industries
Coal Data Annual
Coal Production
Comparative Oil Company Statistics.
    Carl H. Pforzheimer Co.
Domestic Uranium Mining and Milling Industry
Engineering and Mining Journal
Gas Facts. American Gas Association
International Energy Annual
The Iron Age. Chilton Co.
Metal Statistics. American Metal Market
Mineral Commodity Summaries
Mineral Industry Surveys
Minerals Today
Minerals Yearbook
Monthly Energy Review

Natural Gas Annual
Non-Ferrous Metal Data. American Bureau of Metal Statistics
Offshore. Pennwell Publishing
Petroleum Supply Annual
Quarterly Coal Report
Quarterly Review of Drilling Statistics. American Petroleum
    Institute
U.S. Crude Oil, Natural Gas and Natural Gas Liquids Reserves
U.S. Petroleum Statistics
Weekly Oil Trends. Independent Petroleum Association
Wholesale Oil Prices. Independent Petroleum Association

N. Construction and Housing

Census of Housing
Characteristics of Apartments Completed
Construction Potentials. F.W. Dodge
Construction Review
Current Construction Reports
Current Housing Reports: Housing Vacancies
Expenditures for Residential Upkeep and Improvements
Home Sales Monthly. National Association of Realtors
Housing Starts and Housing Completions
Housing Units Authorized by Building Permits
Market Absorption of Apartments
New One-Family Houses Sold and For Sale
Price Index of New One-Family Houses Sold
Residential Alterations and Repairs
Savings and Home Finance Source Book
Survey of Mortgage Lending Activity
Value of New Construction Put in Place

P. Manufactures

Aerospace Facts and Figures. Aerospace Industries Association
Annual Survey of Manufacturers
Annual Statistical Report. American Iron and Steel Institute
Business Statistics
Canned Fruit and Vegetable Pack and Stock
Situation Reports. National Food Processors Association
Commercial Helicopter Shipments
Concentration Ratios in Manufacturing Industries
Cotton Production and Distribution
County Business Patterns
Current Industrial Reports
Electronic Market Data Book. Electronic Industries Association
Exports from Manufacturing Establishments
Frozen Food Pack Statistics. American Frozen Food Institute
Hosiery Statistics. National Association of Hosiery Manufacturers
Industrial Production and Capacity Utilization
Manufacturing Production, Capacity and Utilization in Aerospace
    and Aircraft and Parts. Aerospace Industries Association
Manufacturers Shipments, Inventories and Orders
Motor Vehicle Facts and Figures. Motor Vehicle Manufacturers
    Association
Plant and Equipment Expenditures and Plans
Pollution Abatement, Cost and Expenditures
Quarterly Financial Report for Manufacturing, Mining and Trade
    Corporations
Quarterly Survey of Capital Appropriations Conference Board

Quarterly Survey of Capital Investment and Supply Conditions in Manufacturing

Survey of Current Business

Synthetic Organic Chemicals: U.S. Production and Sales

U.S. Commodity Exports and Imports as Related to Output

U.S. Industrial Outlook

Q. Transportation

Accident Facts

Bus Facts. American Bus Association

Drivers Licenses

Factbook of National Highway Safety

Fatal Accident Reporting System

Highway Statistics

Large Class I Household Goods Carriers: Selected Earnings Data

Large Class I Motor Carriers of Passengers: Selected Earnings Data

Large Class I Motor Carriers of Property: Selected Earnings Data

Motor Vehicle Facts and Figures. Motor Vehicle Manufacturers Association

Transit Fact Book

Transportation in America. ENO Foundation

Transport Statistics in the United States

Truck Inventory

Analysis of Class I Railroads. Association of American Railroads

Cars of Revenue Freight Loaded. Association of American Railroads

Class I Freight Railroads, Selected Earnings Data

Freight Commodity Statistics, Class I Railroads. Association of American Railroads

Yearbook of Railroad Facts

Air Carrier Financial Statistics

Air Carrier Industry Scheduled Service Traffic Statistics

Air Traffic Activity

Air Transport Facts and Figures. Air Transport Association

Airport Activity Statistics of Certified Route Carriers

Aviation Forecasts

Census of U.S. Civil Aircraft

General Aviation Activity and Avionics Survey

Statistical Data Book. General Aviation Manufacturers Association

Statistical Handbook of Aviation

Statistical Report. Regional Airline Association

Summary of Passport Statistics

U.S. Civil Airman Statistics Annual

U.S. International Air Transport Statistics

Annual Summary of Merchant Ships Completed in the World. Lloyd's Register

Annual Report of Shipbuilders Council

The Bulletin. American Bureau of Shipping

Bulk Carriers of the World Fleet

Containerized Cargo Statistics

Foreign Flag Merchant Ships Owned by U.S. Parent Companies

Maritime Manpower Report

Merchant Fleets of the World

Merchant Vessels of the United States

Monthly Bulk Commodities Report. Lake Carriers Association

New Ship Construction

Statistical Tables. Lloyd's Register

Vessel Entrances and Clearances

Waterborne Exports and General Imports

R. Communications

Annual Survey of Communication Services

Book Industry Trends. Book Industry Study Group

Market Guide. Editor & Publisher

Radio Facts Annual. Radio Advertising Bureau

Public Broadcasting: Statistical Brief. Corporation for Public Broadcasting

Statistical Trends in Broadcasting. John Blair

Statistics of Communications Common Carriers

Statistics of Independent Telephone Industry. United States Telephone Association

Television and Cable Factbook. Warren Publishing

U.S. Postal Service Cost and Revenue Analysis

S. Energy

Annual Energy Outlook

Basic Petroleum Data Book. American Petroleum Institute

Coal Distribution

Coal Production

Comparative Oil Company Statistics. Carl H. Pforzheimer Co.

Electric Power Annual

Electric Sales, Revenue and Bills

Energy Conservation Indicators

Financial Statistics of Selected Electric Utilities

Gas Facts. American Gas Association

Gas Statistics. American Gas Association

International Energy Annual

Key Data on Nuclear Energy

Natural Gas Annual

Performance Profiles of Major Energy Producers

Petroleum Supply Annual

Quarterly Coal Report

Residential Energy Consumption Survey

Residential Transportation Energy Consumption Survey

Short-Term Energy Outlook

Solar Collector Manufacturing Activity

Statistics of Interstate Natural Gas Pipeline Companies

Uranium Industry

Weekly Coal Production

T. Distribution and Services

Annual Retail Trade Report

Annual Wholesale Trade Report

Census of Service Industries

Foodservice Numbers: A Statistical Digest. National Restaurant Association

Service Annual Survey

Survey of Current Business

Trends in Hotel Industry. Pannell, Kerr, Forster

U.S. Lodging Industry. Laventhol and Horwath

U. International Transactions

Containerized Cargo Statistics
Exports/Imports of Aerospace Products
Aerospace Industries Association
Foreign Agricultural Trade of the United States
Guide to Foreign Trade Statistics
Highlights of the U.S. Export and Import Trade
Summary of the U.S. Export and Import Merchandise Trade
U.S. Airborne Exports and General Imports
U.S. Commodity Exports and Imports as Related to Output
U.S. Merchandise Trade Exports and Imports for Consumption
U.S. Trade Performance Outlook Annual
U.S. Overseas Loan and Grants
Waterborne Commerce of the United States

V. Business Enterprise

Annual Report of the Small Business Administration
Business Failure Record. Dun and Bradstreet
Business Statistics
Economic Indicators
Economic Road Maps Conference Board
Fortune Directory of the 500 Largest Industrial Corporations
Fortune Directory of the 500 Largest Non-Industrial Corporations
Monthly Business Starts Report. Dun and Bradstreet
Monthly New Business Incorporations. Dun and Bradstreet
Quarterly Financial Report for Manufacturing, Mining, and Trade
    Corporations
Statistics of Income: Corporate Income Tax Returns
Survey of Current Business

W. Productivity and Technological Development

Characteristics of Recent Scientists and Engineers
Commissioner of Patents and Trademarks Annual Report
Comparative Analysis of Information on National and R&D
    Expenditures
Federal Funds for Research and Development
Immigrant Scientists and Engineers: Detailed Statistical Tables
International Science and Technology Data Update
National Patterns of R&D Resources
Planned R&D Expenditures of Major U.S. Firms
Research and Development in Industry: Detailed Statistical Report
Science and Engineering Indicators
Science and Technology Data Book
Science and Engineering Personnel
Science and Technology Resources in U.S. Industry
Scientists, Engineers and Technicians in Manufacturing Industries
Scientists, Engineers and Technicians in Non-Manufacturing
    Industries
Scientists, Engineers and Technicians in Trade and Regulated
    Industries
Women and Minorities in Science and Engineering

X. Financial Markets and Institutions

Annual Report, National Credit Union Administration
Fact Book of National Council of Savings Institutions
Fact Book of New York Stock Exchange
Fact Book of Securities Industry Association
Federal Reserve Bulletin
Flow of Funds Accounts
Insurance Facts. Insurance Information Institute
Life Insurance Fact Book. American Council of Life Insurance
Life Reports: Life Company Financial Data
Mutual Fund Fact Book. Investment Company Institute
Reports of Condition. Comptroller of Currency
Savings Institutions Source Book. U.S. League of Savings
    Institutions
SEC Annual Report
Source Book of Health Insurance Data. Health Insurance
    Association
Statistics of Banking Annual
Trust Assets of Insured Commercial Banks
Yearend Statistics. National Credit Union Administration

Y. Government

Affirmative Employment Statistics
America Votes. Congressional Quarterly
Atlas/Data Abstract for the United States and Selected Areas
Book of the States
Budget of the United States Government
Census of Governments
City Employment
City Government Finances
County Government Employment
County Government Finances
Congressional District Data
Facts and Figures on Government Finance. Tax Foundation
Federal Civilian Workforce Statistics: Employment and Trends
Federal Expenditures by States
Government Finances
Local Government Employment in Major County Areas
Local Government Finances in Major County Areas
Monthly Statement of the Public Debt of the United States
Municipal Year Book
Public Employment
Quarterly Summary of Federal, State and Local Tax Revenue
Selected Manpower Statistics
State Government Finances
Statistics of the Presidential and Congressional Election
United States Government Annual Report

Index

*Note: Page numbers in italics
indicate graphs.*